ENCYCLOPEDIA OF THE HARLEM RENAISSANCE

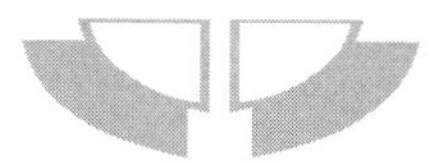

ABERJHANI
AND
SANDRA L. WEST

Foreword by Clement Alexander Price

Facts On File, Inc.

Note on Photos

Many of the illustrations and photographs used in this book are old, historical images. The quality of the prints is not always up to modern standards, as in some cases the originals are from damaged negatives or prints. The content of the illustrations, however, made their inclusion important despite problems in reproduction.

Encyclopedia of the Harlem Renaissance

Facts On File, Inc.
132 West 31st Street
New York NY 10001

Library of Congress Cataloging-in-Publication Data
Aberjhani, 1957 –
Encyclopedia of the Harlem Renaissance / Aberjhani, Sandra L. West; foreword by Clement Alexander Price.
p. cm.
Includes bibliographical references and index.
ISBN 0-8160-4539-9 (acid-free paper)
1. American literature—African American authors—Encyclopedias. 2. Harlem (New York, N.Y.)—Intellectual life—20th century—Encyclopedias. 3. African Americans—Intellectual life—20th century—Encyclopedias. 4. African Americans in literature—Encyclopedias. 5. African American arts—Encyclopedias. 6. Harlem Renaissance—Encyclopedias. I. West,
Sandra L. II. Title.
PS153.N5 A24 2003
810.9′896073′07471009042—dc21 2002152067

Facts On File books are available at special discounts when purchased in bulk quantities for businesses, associations, institutions, or sales promotions. Please call our Special Sales Department in New York at (212) 967-8800 or (800) 322-8755.

You can find Facts On File on the World Wide Web at http://www.factsonfile.com

Text design by Joan M. Toro
Cover design by Cathy Rincon
Maps by Jeremy Eagle

Printed in the United States of America

VB Hermitage 10 9 8 7 6 5 4 3 2

This book is printed on acid-free paper.

I dedicate this book in honor of the memory of the men and women whose brave and troubled lives gave meaning and substance to every page that follows.

And to the people of New York City, whose great and modern adventure continues to inspire the world with their creative visions of culture, history, and human possibility.

—Aberjhani

I dedicate this book to my father, Willie Andrew West, decorated World War II veteran and committed union leader with the A. Philip Randolph Institute and the United Auto Workers (UAW). He was a tireless community activist, an honorable church leader, and a lover of the funky blues, who, in his roaring youth, wore zoot suits and jitterbugged at the Savoy Ballroom in Harlem. He smiled when I told him about this book but died while I was writing it.

—Sandra L. West

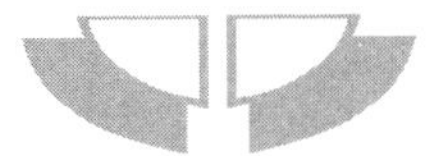

Up from the pain of damning chains
We lift our hearts as family
To forge the future sure and free.
Look upon us all you souls
And see that we are redeemed
Who labored under unrewarding skies
Tilling unfulfilling soil;
Yet will our quest forever be
Sweet liberty.

— Ja A. Jahannes, "Black Voices Rising"

Contents

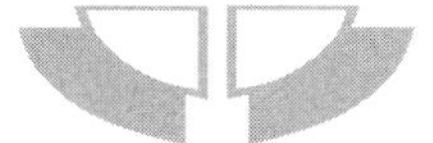

List of Entries

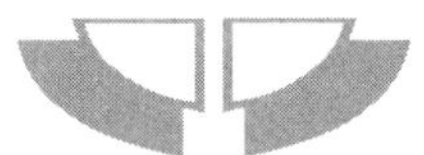

Acknowledgments

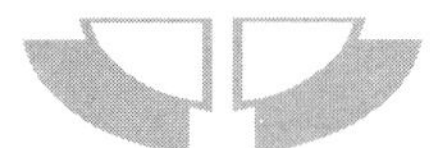

I am deeply grateful to those friends and family members who assisted me in the completion of this project by contributing to my efforts such valuable research materials as books and articles and, most important, by helping me maintain a functional computer. An encyclopedia on the Harlem Renaissance cannot, of course, be written without the extensive use of work by those scholars who have cut a diamond-clear path for a more expanded study of the era and I am very much in their debt.

I am particularly grateful to my fellow writers: Iris Formey Dawson and Vaughnette Goode, who lightened my load by writing two very important articles. And to Dr. Charles Elmore, Dr. Modibo M. Kadalie, Dr. Ja A. Jahannes, and Father Charles Lwanga, whose works helped to provide a final direction for my own.

Knowing the time and energy it took away from many other serious professional and personal concerns, Dr. Clement A. Price's foreword is a blessing for which I can hardly thank him enough.

As heroes come in all shapes, colors, and sizes, I was particularly glad to discover four of mine at Facts On File in the form of editor Nicole Bowen and production assistants Seth Pauley, Laura Shauger, and Jamaal Thompson. Thank you.

And I was delighted to learn that my agent, Stephany Evans, is not so much a kind and wise human being as she is a necessary angelic presence.

I will always be thankful for the critical help provided by my superb research assistant, Amii L. Griffin. Also, it would have been literally impossible for me to complete this encyclopedia without the invaluable assistance of Viola Broadus, who without taking time off often worked for weeks and months on end to help ease my responsibilities as a caregiver by providing quality homecare assistance for my mother, Mrs. Willie Mae Griffin Lloyd, while I went treasure-hunting in the 1920s, 1930s, and 1940s.

And last, but certainly not least, my gratitude to my coauthor, Sandra L. West, who invited me to share her marvelous journey through the wonders and genius of the Harlem Renaissance.

— Aberjhani

Writing *Encyclopedia of the Harlem Renaissance* was a Herculean task, a labor of love, and a conscious act of nationalism. A legion of people assisted.

My coauthor and friend of many seasons, Aberjhani, was a perfect writing partner. David Morgan and Dorothy Marie Rice pointed the book project our way. Stephany Evans of Imprint Library Services and Nicole Bowen of Facts On File, Inc. guided us through a project we trust will be of service for generations to come. My friend and colleague of three decades, Dr. Clement A. Price, wrote a foreword that honors the people of Harlem. Thank you all.

For introducing me to Harlem's genius I thank my aunt, Helen Jackson Foy, and cousins, Carolyn, Moses, and Theodore Foy, all Harlem residents. For formal instruction about the Harlem Renaissance I am grateful to Rutgers University professors George Harriston and Rashidah Ismaili AbuBakr. For unselfish gifts of information about the era that sometimes just showed up in my mailbox I thank Jeannette Drake, Dorothea M. Moore, E. Ethelbert Miller, the late W. W. Law, and Karen E. Johnson.

Johnson is one of two writers I asked to contribute to these pages, along with Mary C. Lewis. They did an outstanding job, and I thank them both.

I am indebted to the staffs of Cabell Library, Virginia Commonwealth University, and Mooreland-Spingarn Research Center, Howard University, and grateful for the resources of William Smith Morton Library at Union Theological Seminary. Also, thanks to Mark Kuls, Free Library of Philadelphia, and Shannon Humphries and Bruce Simon of Richmond Public Library.

For unwavering, unconditional support of this and all my work I thank Marilyn Feitel, Weequahic High School; Roberta Young-Jackson, computer aide; Marita Golden and the Zora Neale Hurston/Richard Wright Foundation, opportunities unparalleled; and my mentors Dean Phillip G. Jones, Dean James Credle, and Dr. Charshee McIntyre, all of Rutgers; Dr. Lisa Knopp, Goucher College; and Gloria Wade-Gayles, Spelman College.

— Sandra L. West

Foreword: RACE, BLACKNESS, AND MODERNISM DURING THE HARLEM RENAISSANCE

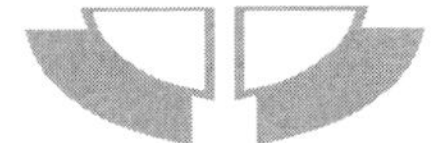

Our interest in the flourishing of black artistic talent, racial chauvinism, and group expressiveness known as the Harlem Renaissance is both durable and understandable. No other period in 20th-century African-American history, with the possible exception of the modern Civil Rights movement, has drawn as much of our attention or encouraged as many exemplary works of scholarship. The years that surround that unique cultural, intellectual, and social phenomenon, which began in earnest on the eve of the 1920s and continued well into the 1930s, also stand out as one of the most important chapters in the overall history of Americans of African ancestry and of American culture generally.

The Harlem Renaissance is singularly important on its own merits, as Sandra L. West and Aberjhani's *Encyclopedia of the Harlem Renaissance* abundantly makes clear. Our contemporary engagement of the life and times of the Harlem Renaissance's women and men, those whose voices still seem fresh and compelling, suggests our affinity to modern American life. We are drawn to the Harlem Renaissance because of the hope for black uplift and interracial interaction and empathy that it embodied and because there is a certain element of romanticism associated with the era's creativity, its seemingly larger-than-life heroes and heroines, and its most brilliantly lit terrain, Harlem, USA. Indeed, for the past generation, the Harlem Renaissance has existed in the nation's historical imagination as an intellectual and cultural fulcrum, suggesting the distance from the end of African slavery in the United States and the advent of more recognizable Americana in which blacks are among the most prominent cultural and political personalities.

This volume, which will be of interest to a cross section of students of American history, culture, and African-American history, provides a detailed accounting of the rich diversity of the Harlem Renaissance as a cultural and social phenomenon. It also illuminates the breadth of individuals and activities that gave the Harlem Renaissance its momentum.

What explains the Harlem Renaissance? And what are its most important legacies? Much of the confidence that characterized the rhetoric, creativity, and activities associated with the Harlem Renaissance was enabled by contemporary changes in the perception of race and culture. Beginning in the late 19th century, new intellectual insights offered by the fields of anthropology, history, and the sciences brought into question the old racial hierarchy upon which rested much of the ill perception of black people and their cultures. By the Armistice ending World War I, in 1918, a significant cohort of scholars, artists, and social reformers had come to believe that race was an invention and that the world's "races" were not distinctly different in terms of their potential and essential worth. Such views figured into the intellectual cadence of the Harlem Renaissance, giving a new generation of black modernists confidence that black culture and those who contributed to it were of value to world civilization.

The Harlem Renaissance also occurred at a time when demographic shifts in the United States and other industrial nations brought new settlers from rural areas into cities. No other city in the country benefited as much from that change as New York, which by the 1920s was the undisputed commercial, artistic, and publishing hub of the United States. From the perspective of African-American history, the so-called Great Migration contributed mightily to the social grandeur of urban America, as blacks from the southern states left the seemingly most backward parts of the nation for the seemingly most progressive. A significant number of those migrants left for New York City, forging, with considerable help from racist real estate interests, Harlem, USA, as both "Negro Capital" and "Negro Ghetto" by the 1920s. In places like Harlem, where blacks were in the majority, it was easier for blacks to forge a modern ethnic group consciousness. They did so through an array of social, religious, civic, and cultural organizations, through public rituals like the parades given by Marcus Garvey's Universal Negro Improvement Association, through newspapers and journals devoted to their interests and to the events by which their progress and frustrations were accounted for, through the ascent of race leaders in civic matters, and in other ways that over time created a formidable black institutional community.

But perhaps the most important cause for the Harlem Renaissance was the aroused self-consciousness of American blacks in the years surrounding World War I. This war, which President Woodrow Wilson envisioned as making the world safe for democracy, heightened awareness of the predicament that blacks faced in the society. And it strengthened the resolve of blacks to bring about meaningful changes in their legal and social status. That black men and women were engaged in the war was important, of course; but more important is that upon returning from the war, to a society at once changed by the international conflict and yet seeking to retreat to a forever-lost past, blacks had actually changed far more than those white Americans who were determined to keep them in their place.

While these transformations were prominently expressed in various ways by the Harlem Renaissance, they did not begin in the 1920s. Rather, during that decade historical forces of long standing gained momentum as New York City emerged as the hub of the publishing industry, as Harlem became the indisputable "Capital of the Black World," and as blacks in other parts of the nation—especially in cities—became more active in public affairs. Seemingly during the 1920s African Americans of talent and sophistication became more noticeable and influential in how the race was perceived and how the race perceived itself. They wrote, painted, composed, argued, marched, and protested on a scale not seen, or accounted for, earlier. In keeping with trends found throughout the society, blacks during the decade took an interest in consumer conceits—style, automobiles, recorded music, film, and fun. The lowly status of most blacks was not forgotten, of course, but that reality increasingly had to share the stage of public perception with images of modern, upwardly mobile Negroes doing their thing, making their mark on the nation and the world. It was a time when black individualism began to overshadow the collective ethos of folk traditions, a time when white Americans had to contend with the complexity of black modern life. Years after the era ended, the Harlem Renaissance would be remembered as the coming of age of urban African Americans.

Normally associated with the cultural expressiveness of articulate Negroes in New York City, the Harlem Renaissance was much more. It was the centerpiece of social, intellectual, and cultural change in black American life. By the time that Harlem emerged as the most important black community in the United States and beyond, the embittered past of slavery had become less of a daily reminder of the ill fortune of being black in America. Racial prejudice, of course, remained the reality that shaped the lives of most blacks, but as the new century took on the quickening pace of modern life, blacks were able to envision themselves, and their predicament, through a more complicated, nuanced lens.

Perhaps the most important of the many legacies of the Harlem Renaissance was that a spirited creativity by blacks survived the end of the period. In the years that followed the 1920s, black writers continued to craft narratives that placed the black experience within an honorable if still troubled context. In fact, the literary marketplace that Harlem Renaissance writers entered and enriched continued as one of the most important arenas for the shaping of ideas about race and inequality in America. As a result, creative and academic writers of the Harlem Renaissance had enduring influence on the gathering sentiments that would, within a generation, take African Americans into the modern Civil Rights movement. Words crafted without apology to white society had political resonance over time, as did the quest for a certain kind of black authenticity in the visual arts and in dance.

Interracialism was another important and lasting outcome of the Harlem Renaissance. Scholars of the period have largely pointed to the exploitative characteristic of the relationship that brought blacks and whites into contact as visual artists and art patrons, as entertainers and party goers, as jazz musicians and consumers of popular culture, and, always, as citizens of seemingly interminably unequal social status. Without much of a precedent for mutually beneficial interracial contact between Americans, with the possible exception of the distant abolitionist movement of the slavery era, the Harlem Renaissance became an arena for awkward cultural exchanges across the color line. For some observers, the interest in black people and their culture by white cosmopolitans grew out of a fascination with the new, the exotic, and their imaginings of blacks as New World primitives. There is, to be sure, considerable evidence of that kind of racial arrogance in the ability of white New Yorkers and other Americans to consume blackness while contributing to the white-over-black social equation. Nonetheless, once modern whites and blacks encountered each other in early 20th-century cities like New York, the traditional racial calculus was to an extent challenged. Over time, as a result of the cross-fertilization of ideals, curiosities about "the others" and, no doubt, friendships along and across the color bar, interracial efforts to reform American society and end blatant forms of racial exclusion became a part of the fabric of the nation's culture.

For white Americans, Harlem and its renaissance of the 1920s was part flirtation with America's alter ego: the Negro, who as the racialized other represented "spiritual and emotional enthusiasm, indulgence, play, passion, and lust," as historian Nathan Huggins observed in 1971. For African Americans, Harlem, and what it symbolized, was something far more complicated. It was, for better or worse, the harbinger of things to come.

Yet, it is important to remember that the modernist sensibilities to which the Harlem Renaissance responded also arose at a time when Harlem, as well as most other urban communities, was troubled by an array of challenges that would mark the 20th-century city experience of blacks as uniquely problematic. The coterie of talented blacks in the arts and culture, business, and intellectual life who helped to recast the image of black Americana was actually part of a larger stream of black urbanites whose lives were challenged by the legacies of slavery, its blunt realities found in the 20th-century, when many other ethnic groups in the nation moved forward. Most blacks during the period lived on the margins of urban America, barred from the best employment, subject to daily racial slights and other manifestations of injustice and the society's obsession with maintaining their social inferiority. They were even barred from places, like Harlem's famous Cotton Club, where aspects of their culture were on stage for the entertainment of whites only.

In retrospect, the Harlem Renaissance was not nearly as inconsistent with the harsh realities and the despair of black urban life as some observers have argued. Rather it was a corollary to the transformation of black life during an era in which the vast majority of African Americans were, unlike their forebears, born free. Notwithstanding the memories of slavery, and in the face of poverty, ignorance, terrorism, and subjugation still deeply woven into their lives, the embittered past of blacks was taken onto a much higher plane of intellectual and artistic consideration during the Harlem Renaissance. The story of African Americans was crafted anew into a poignant commentary on individual and group progress under great pressure, a story that over time became one of the most compelling of American narratives.

Sandra L. West and Aberjhani have compiled an encyclopedia that makes an important contribution to our need to know more about one of modern America's truly significant artistic and cultural movements. It helps us to acknowledge the complexity of African-American life at a time when the nation's culture was taking on a recognizable shape, when race was becoming less of a crushing burden and more of a challenge to progressive people and their ideals, and when cities and their inhabitants symbolized the end of the past and the seductiveness of the new. And it sheds light onto the many personalities, events, cultural products, and social rhythms of the Harlem Renaissance, justly giving the period and its champions the detailed rendering that is needed and deserved.

— Clement Alexander Price
Professor of History
Director, Institute on Ethnicity, Culture, and the Modern Experience
Rutgers University
Newark, New Jersey

Author's Note

In the pages of *Encyclopedia of the Harlem Renaissance,* my coauthor, Sandra L. West, and I have sought to provide meaningful insight into the people, places, and events that became the Harlem Renaissance. That the Harlem Renaissance represents one of those rare moments in history when the greater integrity of the human spirit triumphed brilliantly over the lesser impulses of human bigotry and prejudice remains indelibly evident.

The music, sculpture, paintings, poems, and novels of the era continue to inform the sensibilities of students of human nature in general and African-American culture in particular, just as they continue to stand in their own right as enduring works of art transcending the fertile grounds of history, geography, and race from which they sprung. What is possibly less evident is that the leaders and followers of the Harlem Renaissance were every bit as intent on using black culture to help make the United States a more functional democracy as they were on employing black culture to "vindicate" black people. If the founding fathers and mothers had presented America with a good start in those goals and principles stated so eloquently in the *U.S. Constitution,* the *Declaration of Independence,* and the *Emancipation Proclamation,* then women and men such as IDA BELL WELLS-BARNETT, W. E. B. DU BOIS, FLORENCE MILLS, JAMES WELDON JOHNSON, ALAIN LOCKE, CHARLES SPURGEON JOHNSON, and LANGSTON HUGHES all thought the first half of the 20th century a good time to put such goals and principles into lifesaving practice.

If ever there were a generation of 20th-century African Americans who could have claimed justification for attempting to overthrow the American government, it would have been those black men and women, known then as "Negroes," who lived during the first half of the century. Few of them could have imagined that Supreme Court Justice Harlan, commenting on the *Plessy v. Ferguson* case that legalized segregation in 1896, was describing a document relevant to them when he wrote that, "Our constitution is color-blind, and neither knows nor tolerates classes among citizens." A more apt observation came later from Alain Locke, who, writing in the *NEW NEGRO* anthology, knew that whereas the U.S. Constitution might be "color-blind," those elected to enforce it were often the exact opposite when it came to African Americans. As a result, stated Locke, in the United States, "Democracy itself is obstructed and stagnated to the extent that any of its channels are closed. . . . So the choice is not between one way for the Negro and another way for the rest, but between American institutions frustrated on the one hand and American ideals progressively fulfilled and realized on the other."

In such terms, the idea of "Negroes" as Americans was little more than precisely that: an idea awaiting realization. The social and political acceptance of the phenomenon known as LYNCHING for all intended purposes made it legal for any given white American to kill any given black American at will. Sharecropping as it was practiced in many rural areas of the South was only one step removed from slavery as it had existed in the previous century, and according to some accounts it was actually worse. And those African Americans who vanished as teenagers or young adults through the court system and into the world of prisons and chain gangs did become the equivalent of slaves, whether the charges that condemned them to such a fate had been proved or not.

For African Americans, the reality of apartheid in America, euphemistically referred to as JIM CROW, far outweighed the practice or the promise of democracy. America routinely reaffirmed the nonpersonhood of blacks by denying them the right to vote, the right to equal protection before the law, the rights to equal opportunities for education, economic advancement, housing, and the simple recognition of one's humanity. Yet the bulk of those black organizations that formed during the period more often than not stressed in their eloquent appeals a recognition of their attempts to apply with love and reason the basic tenets of democracy: life, liberty, and the pursuit of happiness. The attainment of such in regard to African Americans, Du Bois indicated in *THE SOULS OF BLACK FOLK* in 1903, would help secure "the ideal of fostering and developing the traits and talents of the Negro, not in opposition to or contempt for other races, but rather in large conformity to the greater ideals of the American Republic, in order that some day on American soil two world-races may give each to each those characteristics both so sadly lack." As it stood at the time, he noted, "there are to-day no truer exponents of the pure human spirit of the Declaration of Independence than the American Negroes. . . ." It was a spirit of perseverance, loyalty, and courage that he would exhort African Americans to exercise time and again over some 24 years as editor of the *CRISIS: A RECORD OF THE DARKER RACES* and as a tireless advocate for human rights worldwide until his death in 1963.

Moreover, it was a pioneering spirit that found its way repeatedly into the charters of the first black Greek-lettered fraternities and sororities, initiated among the fraternities by ALPHA PHI ALPHA in 1906 and among the sororities by ALPHA KAPPA ALPHA in 1908. For the many chapters that followed, the call was always for the development of individual integrity and greater service to humanity. It was answered by the women and men who would staff such institutions as the NATIONAL URBAN LEAGUE, the ASSOCIATION FOR THE STUDY OF NEGRO LIFE, the NATIONAL ASSOCIATION FOR THE ADVANCEMENT OF COLORED PEOPLE, the ABYSSINIAN BAPTIST CHURCH, black-owned newspapers, and black colleges and universities throughout the country.

As Locke put it, writing two decades after Du Bois published *The Souls of Black Folk,* "The Negro question is too often put forward as the Negro question. It is just as much, and even more seriously, the question of democracy. . . ." In both cases, Du Bois had already articulated the answer. What remained to come and what in fact did come in the 1920s, the 1930s, 1940s and even later, was a sizable body of works in different creative disciplines that transformed theory into canonical substance that would stand as both critiques and affirmations of American democracy. Such works were brilliantly rendered by visionaries who happened to be, like LOUIS ARMSTRONG and DUKE ELLINGTON, geniuses as well as musicians; like Charles S. Johnson, editors as well as social scientists; like JACOB ARMSTEAD LAWRENCE, historians as well as artists; like JESSIE REDMOND FAUSET, educators as well as novelists; and like ARTHUR SCHOMBURG, authors of exceptional books as well as collectors of the same.

Certainly with the enslavement of their parents and grandparents fewer than 70 years behind them, the odds of successfully utilizing black culture to better refine the application of democracy in America was against them. Yet the planners and participants in this would-be renaissance moved forward with all the faith and visionary certainty of Betsy Ross stitching the American flag or General William T. Sherman blazing a trail of victory through the Civil War South. Whether the tool in question was a novel, a painting, a song, a scandalous court case, or a thrilling Broadway production, the purpose behind its use was always, on one level or another, the ongoing construction of democracy in the United States. During his tenure as editor of *OPPORTUNITY* Magazine, Charles S. Johnson did not consider himself simply as an editor with a good eye for spotting such gifted individuals as ERIC DERWENT WALROND, E. Franklin Frazier, GWENDOLYN BENNETTA BENNETT, and AARON DOUGLAS. He was very much a social scientist applying the theoretical tools of his trade to make his own contribution to the greater experiment in American possibilities. Having studied at the University of Chicago the use of media as a method to direct and shape social trends, he aggressively applied that knowledge to help his country evolve beyond what he viewed as one stage of race relations moving away from the inevitability of conflict toward the inevitability of integration.

Nor was it solely for the sake of racial equality that the many participants in the Harlem Renaissance hoped to strengthen democracy. Many were just as committed to gaining greater equality for women and to fostering respect for differences in political ideology, religious preferences, sexual orientation, or intellectual aesthetics. Locke, writing in *The Crisis* about that period just before the renaissance, noted that "The leading conception of freedom now was to be oneself and different." It could be argued that such a statement from Locke was prompted more by personal concerns than objective ones, yet it should be remembered that white modernists of the same period did indeed champion individual expressiveness over the more conservative Victorian values of their parents and grandparents.

And while Du Bois may have issued his call for a "Talented Tenth" specifically to help alleviate the political oppression of African Americans, it was his contention that some form of higher education must be available to citizens of the country as a whole in order to alleviate the cultural and spiritual oppression of all Americans. In this way, the United States would realize its potential to become a truly civilized and democratic country. In the words of JEAN TOOMER from his epic poem *Blue Meridian,* the goal was to establish "a new America/ To be spiritualized by each new American." Thus a strategic use of black culture could help generate a more efficient use of American democracy, and democracy more effectively practiced could then produce a genuinely spiritual nation of people.

Whereas it might be erroneous to claim that the literature, art, and music of the Harlem Renaissance revolutionized the practice of democracy in the United States, it would not be an error to point out that the ideas they championed did impact America's understanding, and subsequently its application, of democracy. The absurdities, contradictions, and hypocrisies of the racist mentality that ruled America was publicly dissected time and again to clarify the painful difference between what the country proposed to do in the name of freedom and what it in fact did do under the presumptions of white superiority. Harlem Renaissance writers and artists fashioned a powerful mirror of conscience that forced the United States to confront the reality of its moral and political failures in regard to its citizen "Negroes." By promoting and sharing the experience of black culture the men and women of the Harlem Renaissance set in motion the mechanism that would allow the idea of "Negroes" as Americans to become, in the long decades that followed, the reality of blacks as African Americans. It is my hope that those reading about their many challenging experiences will feel as honored by their integrity and as inspired by their triumphs as we were when writing about them.

— Aberjhani

Introduction: BLACK PHOENIX RISING

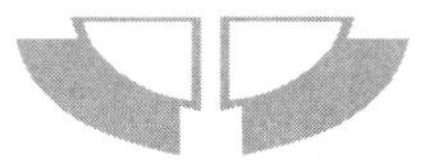

In the decades of the 1920s and 1930s in the section of NEW YORK CITY known as HARLEM, there developed a unique awakening of mind and spirit, of race consciousness and artistic advancement. This declaration of African-American independence became known alternately as the Harlem Renaissance, the Negro Renaissance, or the NEW NEGRO movement. It was an artistic and sociocultural stirring that occurred in the African-American community as a result of the GREAT MIGRATION when the masses of blacks living in the rural South made their way to the urban centers of the North and Midwest. Well-known author and political advocate JAMES WELDON JOHNSON refused to call the era the Harlem Renaissance, preferring instead "the flowering of Negro literature." Whatever its name, during this time in Harlem there was an emergence of new ideas in political thought; numerous groundbreaking artistic developments in theatre, music, literature, and visual arts; and an inauguration of civil rights organizations, unions, and other associations.

Though headquartered in Harlem, many Harlem Renaissance leaders were not Harlem natives. Writer ARNA BONTEMPS was born in Louisiana, folklorist ZORA NEALE HURSTON was from Florida, and poet CLAUDE MCKAY came from Jamaica. Some participants were African Americans, others African or African Caribbean. The influence of these people and what they developed affected places as far away as France and Africa. It also spread inside the United States to CHICAGO; Kansas City; Boston; WASHINGTON, D.C.; the "Harlem of the South," otherwise known as Jackson Ward in RICHMOND, VIRGINIA; and other locations of dense African-American population. These locations experienced capitalistic energy, creative genius, and intellectual vigor stimulated by Harlem's rebirth.

In *Southern Road,* poet STERLING ALLEN BROWN commented on this situation: "The New Negro is not to me a group of writers centered in Harlem during the second half of the twenties. Most of the writers were not Harlemites; much of the best writing was not about Harlem, which was the show-window, the cashier's till, but no more Negro America than New York is America."

Because of the impact of the GREAT MIGRATION on the North, Harlem saw its black population increase dramatically from 14,000 in 1914 to 175,000 by 1925. These migrants took the development of their new community seriously. As such, the NATIONAL ASSOCIATION FOR THE ADVANCEMENT OF COLORED PEOPLE (NAACP) was initiated by Dr. W. E. B. DU BOIS and others, while MARCUS GARVEY activated the UNIVERSAL NEGRO IMPROVEMENT ASSOCIATION (UNIA) with a "Back to Africa" component devised to empower the black American with racial pride and self-sufficiency. Influenced by BOOKER TALIAFERRO WASHINGTON, Garvey's philosophy was similar to that of the founder of Tuskegee University, and like Washington, he was perpetually at odds with Du Bois. Additionally, A. PHILIP RANDOLPH initiated a union for working-class people, the BROTHERHOOD OF SLEEPING CAR PORTERS.

Raised in Florida, Zora Neale Hurston, like many other African Americans during the Harlem Renaissance, moved to New York City in 1925. *(Library of Congress, Prints & Photographs Division [LCUSZ62-62394])*

Though civil rights organizations, unions, and associations were developed during this time, the Harlem Renaissance is known primarily for the literature, music, and visual arts produced by African Americans during the period. In the field of literature, scores of books, literary journals, magazines, and newspapers were dedicated to the uplift of the "New Negro," and to the documentation of the observations of blacks. Du Bois presented new poets, playwrights, novelists, and artists within the pages of *THE CRISIS: A RECORD OF THE DARKER RACES,* published by the NAACP. Sociologist CHARLES SPURGEON JOHNSON of the NATIONAL URBAN LEAGUE and editor of *OPPORTUNITY* magazine organized the legendary CIVIC CLUB DINNER as a "coming out party" to introduce emerging black literary artists such as GWENDOLYN BENNETTA BENNETT and COUNTEE CULLEN.

The publication of books was so considerable that major black periodicals established book review sections. In addition, literary associations or reading group societies—such as the Book Lover's Club at the public library in Harlem and the still operating Just-A-Mere Literary Society in Roselle, New Jersey—flourished. Before 1910, according to the editor and professor of philosophy ALAIN LOCKE, black American fiction numbered approximately 38 titles. These included *Iola Leroy* by Frances E. W. Harper (1892) and *Diane* by Katharine H. Brown (1905). ARTHUR (Arturo) SCHOMBURG's impressive list of early books by African Americans includes Henry Bibb's *Narrative of the Life and Character of H.B., an American Slave, Written By Himself* (1849) and Prince Hall's *A Charge Delivered to the African Lodge* (1797), but no previous period of literary output compared to that of the Harlem Renaissance, when popular books were read by the white and black masses alike. It was also a time when black writers and artists received financial assistance from white and black patrons so that they could write, paint, compose music, and sculpt full-time, when new or experimental forms, including LANGSTON HUGHES's jazz poetry, emerged, and many books by black authors were published, for the first time, by major houses such as Knopf and Harcourt Brace.

JEAN TOOMER's experimental fictional work *Cane* (1923) is generally recognized as the first novel of the Harlem Renaissance. In 1924, Du Bois followed with a collection of essays titled *The Gift of Black Folk,* and JESSIE REDMOND FAUSET's novel of black middle-class life, *There Is Confusion,* was also published. Added to these were Marcus Garvey's *Aims and Objects for a Solution of the Negro Problem Outlined* and WALTER WHITE's *The Fire in the Flint.*

Locke edited in 1925 *The New Negro: Voices of the Harlem Renaissance,* now a "bible" for students of the phenomena called the Harlem Renaissance, illustrated by WINOLD REISS and AARON DOUGLAS. *The New Negro* contains many components: an essay on Negro art by ALBERT COOMBS BARNES, the Negro in literature by WILLIAM STANLEY BEAUMONT BRAITHWAITE, fiction by RUDOLPH FISHER, poetry by salon hostess Georgia Johnson and dramatist ANGELINA EMILY WELD GRIMKE, drama by *Crisis* literary editor Jessie Redmond Fauset, articles on the new musical form JAZZ by historian J. A. Rodgers, and FOLK LITERATURE. And, in an effort to document the spirit of the renaissance for generations to come, other anthologies such as Countee Cullen's *Caroling Dusk* and Charles S. Johnson's *Ebony and Topaz* were also published.

The movement continued to grow and expand in 1928 with CLAUDE MCKAY's novel *HOME TO HARLEM*, which became the first best-selling novel by an African American. Editor, playwright, and novelist WALLACE THURMAN satirized the sometimes overwhelming seriousness of the Harlem Renaissance with his 1932 novel, *Infants of the Spring.* Never before had such an array of literature been written by the African American and published by mainstream publishers.

Notwithstanding books, there was also a proliferation of journalism during this period as well as several decades before and after the years of the Harlem Renaissance. Many Harlem Renaissance writers contributed to or served as editors on these magazines. *Half-Century Magazine* circulated in Chicago from 1916 to 1925. The *Competitor* magazine urged black Philadelphians to racial greatness from 1920 to 1921. *Opportunity* magazine, underwritten by the National Urban League under the editorship of Charles S. Johnson, was a backbone of the Renaissance during the 1920s and 1930s and, along with *The Crisis,* sponsored major literary prizes for black artists and writers. *Color-Line: A Monthly Round-up of the Facts of Negro American Progress and of the Growth of American Democracy* was published in Mt. Vernon, New York, from 1946 to 1947. And DOROTHY WEST, the last survivor of the Harlem Renaissance writers before she died in 1998, edited *Challenge* and *New Challenge* magazines in Boston from 1934 to 1937. Many more became quite famous and others much less so.

Dedicated to pursuing equality for all people, W. E. B. Du Bois cofounded the National Association for the Advancement of Colored People (NAACP). *(Library of Congress, Prints & Photographs Division [LCUSZ62-16767])*

Literature, however, was only one aspect of the Harlem Renaissance. The birth and development of RAGTIME, jazz, and the BLUES were all part of this "flowering," as James Weldon Johnson so eloquently put it, in black America. Propelled by the development of the phonograph, radio, and the works of such musicians as Scott Joplin and EUBIE BLAKE, ragtime by 1920 had become America's preeminent popular music. Influencing the classic, more conservative sounds of European and American folk music, it not only paved the way for the domination of the blues and jazz but remained a principal element of those musical forms.

And the birth of these musical genres in turn spawned a decade of black Broadway musicals, beginning with NOBLE SISSLE's and Eubie Blake's *SHUFFLE ALONG* in 1921. *Shuffle Along* made black musical revue history in 1921 and opened doors for a black theater season that extended an entire decade. Langston Hughes felt that the Harlem Renaissance began with musicals and a dance craze: "*Shuffle Along,* RUNNING

WILD and the *Charleston.* Perhaps some people would say even with *The EMPEROR JONES*, CHARLES GILPIN, and tom-toms at Provincetown. But certainly it was the musical review, *Shuffle Along,* that gave a scintillating send-off to that Negro vogue in Manhattan, which reached its peak just before the crash of 1929 . . ."

Moreover, by the end of the 1930s, the music had given birth to talents and careers that would provide America with an enduring body of treasured musical artistry. BESSIE SMITH, JELLY ROLL MORTON, FATS WALLER, LOUIS ARMSTRONG, DUKE ELLINGTON, BILLIE HOLIDAY, Ella Fitzgerald, LENA HORNE, and CHARLIE PARKER were only some of the creative giants born out of the Harlem Renaissance.

Likewise, it spawned an astounding wealth of visual artistry commanded by individuals like the sculptors AUGUSTA FELLS SAVAGE and Marion Perkins, and the painters HENRY OSSAWA TANNER, ROMARE BEARDEN, and JACOB ARMSTEAD LAWRENCE, all of whose works are now featured in museums, institutions, and private collections around the world. Just as black writers received crucial assistance with the publication of their works from major houses and individual patrons, black visual artists were also able to achieve unprecedented professional success with assistance from the HARMON FOUNDATION, the New York–based organization that hosted the first art exhibit in the United States devoted entirely to art by African Americans.

In short, there were no areas of life in the United States and in many other parts of the world that the Harlem Renaissance did not touch and help to transform. Politics, religion, economics, education, science, and the very structure of social demographics that give America its unique cross-cultural profile all felt and absorbed the vibrations of its impact. They all evolved upon its arrival. It was one of the most colorful and culturally productive eras in African-American history.

— Sandra L. West

A to Z Entries

A

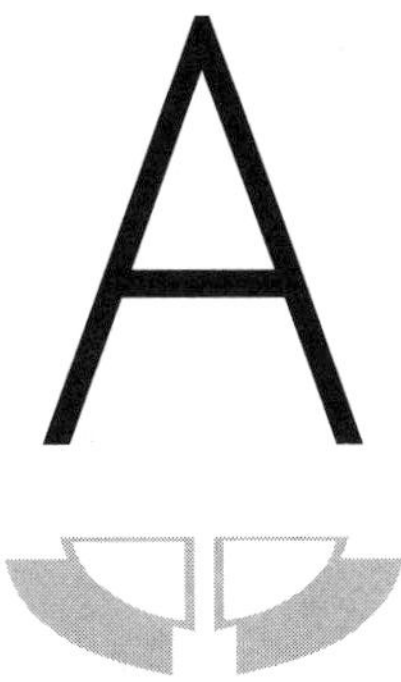

Abbott, Robert (1870–1940) *journalist*
Robert Abbott, the militant editor and publisher of the CHICAGO DEFENDER, was born on November 24, 1870, on Saint Simons Island, Georgia. Both of his parents, Thomas and Flora Butler Abbott, had been born in slavery. After the death of her husband, Flora Butler later married John J. Sengstacke, the son of a German merchant father and a black American slave mother.

Recognizing that his son would have to bear the same racial hardships as his mother had if kept in the United States, Sengstacke's father took him back to Germany, where he was raised by relatives. John J. Sengstacke returned to the United States as a young adult and learned the trade of American journalism by working as a translator of German for the *Savannah Morning News.* He later started his own newspaper, the *Woodville Times,* which he ran with the help of sons Robert and Alexander.

In addition to helping his father out, Robert Abbott also worked in the print shop of another newspaper, the *Savannah Echo.* He attended school in the southeastern town of Savannah, Georgia, until graduating and moving on to Hampton Institute, Virginia. While still at Hampton, he traveled to Chicago for the first time as part of a group of students who sang spirituals. Journalist IDA BELL WELLS-BARNETT and abolitionist Frederick Douglass were in Chicago during the same period. Abbott was fortunate enough to hear the 74-year-old Douglass, two years before his death, deliver at the 1893 Columbian Exposition a scalding address on the injustices of American racism. Three years later, Abbott graduated from Hampton Institute and returned to Chicago to attend Kent Law School, graduating from there in 1899.

Although he had graduated from law school, the color barrier prevented Abbott from finding steady employment as anything but a printer, despite applications for the bar in Chicago, Illinois; Gary, Indiana; and Topeka, Kansas. In 1905, he spent 25¢ to arm himself with pencil and paper, sat down at the kitchen table of his State Street dwelling on the South Side of Chicago, and produced the first edition of the *Chicago Defender,* subtitled "the world's greatest weekly." Abbott printed the handbill-sized four sheets of paper on credit, and at four cents each sold the first 300 copies himself. For the next five years, his landlady, Harriet Plummer Lee, supported the fledgling publisher with meals, living space, and the use of her telephone. She also allowed her daughter to act as his assistant.

As his paper grew, Abbott decided to extend his journalistic reach beyond the events of his adopted South Side Chicago neighborhood and make his paper a forum in which issues pertaining to African Americans on a national and international scale could be addressed openly and boldly. From the prostitution that marred many black urban neighborhoods to the JIM CROW brutalities that destroyed black lives, week after week Abbott's *Chicago Defender* announced the state of black America in bold red headlines and scathing, often satirical, editorials. In a true demonstration of his paper's name, Abbott advised African Americans to be neither accommodating nor gradual in the push for equality but to struggle hard for their rights and fight back when physically attacked. Whereas he had not been allowed to effectively address legal and political issues in the Chicago courtroom, he began to address such issues through his newspaper before the entire country. The more militant Abbott's stance, the more papers he sold until the *Chicago Defender* commanded the largest national circulation of any black publication in the United States. From its beginnings of 300 copies, it soared to more than a quarter million by the end of the 1920s with the bulk of its readership outside the Chicago area.

His call on May 15, 1917, for African Americans to undertake a massive exodus out of the South made the paper one of the most controversial in the country. White southerners were as anxious to keep the *Chicago Defender* out of their communities as black southerners were to obtain it by any means necessary. The impact of Abbott's promise that life in the North was a far sweeter deal than anything the South had to offer African Americans might be measured by the growth of Chicago's black population from an estimated 55,000 in 1915 to 165,000 in 1918. By 1930, that figure reached 240,000.

Abbott's ability to help tilt and more equally balance the country's racial demographics placed him among the most powerful African-American leaders of his time. He was appointed to the Chicago Commission of Race Relations to help the city find solutions to the volatile problems that too often erupted into race riots. Along with JAMES WELDON JOHNSON and 12 other delegates, he presented President Calvin Coolidge in February 1924 with a petition containing 120,000 signatures of American citizens requesting the pardon of 54 black soldiers from the U.S. 24th Infantry imprisoned in Leavenworth, Kansas, for their involvement in the 1917 Houston, Texas, riot.

In 1934, Abbott adopted the Baha'i faith. The religion's advocacy for a world liberated from racial and sexual oppression was a sound spiritual complement to the *Defender's* motto proclamation that, "America's race prejudice must be destroyed." By the time of his death in 1940, his bold journalistic strategies had made him the first African American in publishing to become a millionaire. As such, he was often able to act as a patron to both his extended step-family in Germany and those whom he had left behind in Georgia. His nephew, John Herman Sengstacke, also from Savannah, took over the *Chicago Defender*'s editorship upon his uncle's death February 22, 1940.

Further Reading

Ottley, Roi. *The Lonely Warrior: The Life and Times of Robert S. Abbott.* Chicago: H. Regnery, 1955.

Simmons, Charles A. *African American Press: A History of News Coverage During National Crises, With Special Reference to Four Black Newspapers, 1827–1965.* New York: McFarland and Company, 1997.

— Aberjhani

Abyssinian Baptist Church

During the Harlem Renaissance and GREAT DEPRESSION, the largest, most socially active, influential, and political black congregation in NEW YORK CITY, as well as in the United States, was that of the Abyssinian Baptist Church, led by ADAM CLAYTON POWELL, SR., from 1908 to 1937, and by ADAM CLAYTON POWELL, JR., from 1937 to 1971.

Abyssinian Baptist Church was founded in 1808, on Worth Street in lower Manhattan, an area where black people lived before they migrated uptown to what was then the village of HARLEM. The church was established by African Americans and Ethiopian merchants as an act of protest against racial segregation in the First Baptist Church of New York City. When a new building was needed, the Worth Street building was sold. Services were held at several locations until a new church on Waverly Place in the West Village could be purchased. By 1908, the Waverly building was sold, and a church and apartment house on 40th Street were bought. During the Harlem Renaissance, as in succeeding decades, the black church was one of the most powerful institutions in the African-American community. Throngs of blacks left small,

First established by African Americans and Ethiopian merchants in 1808, the congregation of the Abyssinian Baptist Church grew into one of the most socially and politically influential groups in the United States at the time of the Harlem Renaissance. This photo, ca. 1907, shows the Waverly Street location just before it was sold. *(Library of Congress, Prints & Photographs Division [LC-USZ62-113857])*

communal churches in the U.S. South and Caribbean islands and founded or joined larger houses of worship in the new, industrialized "promised land" of New York City. In urban America, migrants suffered culture shock, northern discrimination in housing and employment, and experienced worship decorum that was alien to them. Urban religious leaders were challenged as never before to creatively pastor the new communicants.

George E. Haynes wrote in "The Church and the Negro Spirit," in March 1925, that there were several specific challenges facing the black church that the migrants found in urban areas such as New York. Some of these included: "to provide adequate buildings to attract and serve the rapidly increasing population, to give fellowship to newcomers fresh from the Southland, to have organization for rendering social service in housing, health, recreational and other needs for the community, and to meet with understanding and wisdom the increasing throng of intelligent people."

Abyssinian Baptist Church had a membership of 1,600 and was indebted for more than $100,000 when Powell, Sr., first joined in 1908. The congregation moved in 1923 to a Neo-Gothic structure at 136–142 West 138th Street in Harlem. The cost of the new structure was $325,000. The church grew in the 1930s to become one of the most prosperous in the United States, with more than 10,000 members, a social and religious education program, and a reputation as a catalyst for change in the African-American community.

In 1937, Powell, Jr., became the church's leader and continued the tradition of social and political progression established by his father.

Church members in 1986 and 1987 formed The Abyssinian Development Corporation (ADC), a not-for-profit organization created to fight drug traffic, unemployment, and other societal ills that continued to diminish the quality of life for residents in the 125th to 139th Street area. The official mission statement of ADC is: to increase the availability of quality housing for people of different income levels; to enhance the delivery of social services, particularly to the homeless and elderly; to foster economic revitalization; to enhance educational and development opportunities for youth; and to build community capacity. ADC in 2003 began building a high school in the former edifice of the Harlem Renaissance nightclub SMALL'S PARADISE. Abyssinian Baptist Church, operating in 2003 from 132 West 138th Street, continued to be a force in the Harlem community. Among other campaigns, in 2003 pastor Reverend Calvin O. Butts III took on the powerful tobacco industry by leading a protest against cigarette billboard advertisements in Harlem.

Further Reading

Anderson, Jervis. *This Was Harlem: A Cultural Portrait, 1900–1950.* New York: Farrar, Straus, & Giroux, 1981.

Dolkhart, Andrew S., and Gretchen S. Sorin. *Touring Historic Harlem: Four Walks in Northern Manhattan.* New York: New York Landmarks Conservancy, 1997.

Gore, Robert L., Jr. *We've Come This Far: The Abyssinian Baptist Church: A Photographic Journal.* New York: Stewart, Tabori & Chang, 2001.

Haynes, George E. "The Church and the Negro Spirit." *Survey Graphic* (March 1925): 695–697, 708–709.

— Sandra L. West

African Blood Brotherhood

The African Blood Brotherhood developed out of the climate of radical politics that enveloped much of HARLEM in response to the riots that swept through the United States during the so-called RED SUMMER OF 1919.

The brotherhood was founded by socialist Cyril V. Briggs, a native of the West Indies who emigrated to NEW YORK CITY in 1905. Briggs worked as a reporter for the New York *AMSTERDAM NEWS* prior to establishing the monthly newspaper the *Crusader* in 1918. In addition to starting the newspaper, Briggs also began a *Crusader* news service that supplied black-owned newspapers throughout the country with information concerning people of African descent all over the world.

Aside from Briggs, the founding members of the African Blood Brotherhood included political activist Lovett Ford-Whiteman, activist and writer Richard B. Moore, political activist Harry Haywood, and writer CLAUDE MCKAY.

The African Blood Brotherhood operated as an underground organization of black men and women. The brotherhood dedicated itself to political and social equality between the races, economic advancement for blacks, greater unity among blacks regardless of their national origins, and active opposition to the Ku Klux Klan. In regard to the latter, particularly when the murder of blacks by LYNCHING was involved, the brotherhood advocated armed self-defense.

The African Blood Brotherhood reportedly grew to include up to 50,000 members comprising some 150 branches internationally. Because it sought to maintain itself as an underground operation, its exact size was debatable.

The *Crusader* served as the official organ of the brotherhood. With editorials by Briggs, it also published the works of McKay, *NEW YORK AGE* founder Thomas T. Fortune, poet and playwright Paul Laurence Dunbar, and celebrated Russian author Maxim Gorky. On a par with the *MESSENGER* and *NEGRO WORLD*, in addition to articles on its political interests, the paper carried pieces on sports, theatre, literary events, and various business developments in Harlem. In 1920, the paper backed A. PHILIP RANDOLPH in his failed election bid for state comptroller of New York.

Despite its generally covert activities, Briggs promoted the African Blood Brotherhood in the pages of the *Crusader* as an organization originally supporting the same goals as MARCUS GARVEY and the UNITED NEGRO IMPROVEMENT ASSOCIATION (UNIA). Like Garvey, Briggs promoted what he called "self-government for the Negro and Africa for Africans" but also proposed emigration for blacks to either South America or the Caribbean. Briggs disagreed with Garvey's official endorsement of capitalism as part of the UNIA's overall economic philosophy, and Garvey criticized Briggs for the lightness of his complexion. In a volley of editorials from late 1921 to early 1922, Briggs accused Garvey of fraud and calculated deception. A number of Briggs's observations were used by federal investigators to help them win the court case that ultimately resulted in Garvey's imprisonment and deportation. Following Garvey's imprisonment, Briggs ceased publication of the *Crusader* but continued operating the Crusader news service.

The African Blood Brotherhood was criticized by its communist supporters for what was termed a failure to win mass support on a scale comparable to that afforded UNIA and the NATIONAL ASSOCIATION FOR THE ADVANCEMENT OF COLORED PEOPLE (NAACP). From 1923 to 1925, the organization slowly dissolved and its members merged first with the newly founded Workers Party then later helped form the American Negro Congress, headed by Lovett Ford-Whiteman. Often criticized for his divided loyalties, Briggs continued to support both BLACK NATIONALISM and COMMUNISM until his death in 1966.

Further Reading

Buhle, Mari Jo, Paul Buhle, and Dan Georgakas. *Encyclopedia of the American Left.* New York: Oxford University Press, 1998.

Maxwell, William J. *New Negro, Old Left: African-American Writing and Communism Between the Wars.* New York: Columbia University Press, 1999.

— Aberjhani

Aiken, Loretta Mary See MABLEY, MOMS.

Ain't Misbehavin' See WALLER, FATS.

Alhambra Ballroom

Featuring a million-dollar ballroom and top bands from all over the United States, the Alhambra Ballroom competed with the SAVOY BALLROOM in HARLEM and the Roseland Ballroom in lower Manhattan in NEW YORK CITY for the position of leading dance hall from the end of the 1920s throughout the 1930s.

Like the Savoy, the Alhambra announced its arrival on Harlem's entertainment scene with a gala battle of musicians featuring five of New York's biggest bands. Because DUKE ELLINGTON had begun headlining at the COTTON CLUB and CHICK WEBB was doing the same at the Savoy, they were absent from the battle royal that took place on September 13, 1929. Battling that evening for the audience's votes at the Alhambra were the Benny Carter Band, the MISSOURIANS, the Zach Whyte Band, the Luis Russell Band, and Johnson's Happy Pals.

Located at SEVENTH AVENUE and 126th Street, the Alhambra Ballroom did not practice JIM CROW segregation in the form of barring black patrons from the club altogether, as was the practice of most of the clubs located in Harlem's JUNGLE ALLEY. It did, however, separate blacks and whites by alternating the nights on which each could be present at the ballroom.

Bands that played the Alhambra Ballroom, such as the well-known Missourians, were among those that established JAZZ as an enduring musical art form and that laid the foundation for the SWING SOUND era of the 1940s.

Further Reading

Jamison, Judith, and Howard Kaplan. *Dancing Spirit: an Autobiography.* New York: Doubleday and Company, 1993.

Waggoner, Susan. *Nightclub Nights: Art, Legend, and Style 1920–1960.* Italy: Rizzoli International Publishers, 2001.

— Aberjhani

Alpha Kappa Alpha Sorority, Inc.

Like African-American men seeking college educations and forming supportive brotherhoods at the beginning of the 1900s, African-American women recognized the advantage of forming an official sisterhood and established the Alpha Kappa Alpha Sorority at HOWARD UNIVERSITY in WASHINGTON, D.C., on January 15, 1908.

Acting on the suggestion of Ethel H. Lyle, eight other young women joined her to create America's first black sorority. In addition to Lyle, the group's founding members were: Beulah E. Burke, Lillie Burke, Margaret F. Holmes, Marjorie Hill, Lucy D. Slowe, Marie W. Taylor, Anna E. Brown, and Lavinia Norman.

The Alphas welcomed their first line of initiates in 1909 and in that same year began cultivating the plant that would become their symbol: the ivy. The plant would become so closely associated with the group that years later the sorority would name its journal the *Ivy Leaf Magazine.*

An internal dispute with undergraduates desiring to change such fundamental aspects of the sorority as its motto and adopted color caused a split that ended with the creation of a new sorority, DELTA SIGMA THETA, in 1912. The division provided outlets for women of diverse interests and outlooks. It also spurred the Alphas' Nellie Quander to head a drive for national organization and the sorority's incorporation.

The Alpha Kappa Alpha Sorority during the 1910s lent its voice to the rising chorus of protests against LYNCHING and worked in partnership with the NATIONAL ASSOCIATION FOR THE ADVANCEMENT OF COLORED PEOPLE (NAACP) to combat the practice of white mobs mutilating and murdering African Americans. They teamed up as well with the Travel Aid Society to assist those African Americans leaving the South and moving north during the GREAT MIGRATION. On their own behalf, and that of all American women, they participated in the women's suffrage movement to secure the right to vote. As the sorority grew and expanded, it encouraged members to do the same by maintaining an organization fund used to help support travel abroad.

Throughout each decade of the 1900s, the Alphas sought ways to integrate the pursuit of academic excellence with service to their community and country. They were particularly active in the Mississippi Delta during the 1930s and 1940s, implementing a health awareness program for blacks generally receiving little, irregular, or no health care. During World War II, they designed a three-part program that allowed them to support the U.S. war effort, a campaign for African Americans' struggle for full citizenship at home, and adjustment to the impact of the war at its conclusion.

In 1958, Marjorie Holmes wrote the first history of the Alphas and it has since been updated through four editions. As with their fraternal counterpart, the sorority has over the years attracted individuals of superlative achievement and distinction. Among them are the singer MARIAN ANDERSON, political leader Yvonne Braithwaite-Burke, astronaut Mae Jamison, and writer Sonia Sanchez.

At the start of the 21st century, the sorority continued to maintain a strong focus on academics combined with community service. It sponsored programs ranging from tutorial services in mathematics and science to outreach programs geared toward providing senior citizens with companionship and interaction with youth. Programs targeting black families explored and proposed survival strategies for the modern era and offered workshops on Kwaanza celebrations. In keeping with its tradition to keep the black community informed regarding health issues, the sorority also hosted workshops on the increasing threat of the virus that causes AIDS.

With corporate offices in CHICAGO, the Alpha Kappa Alpha Sorority, Inc., in 2002 had some 890 chapters.

Further Reading

Bobo, Jacqueline. *Black Women as Cultural Leaders.* New York: Columbia University Press, 1995.

Giddings, Paula. *In Search of Sisterhood: Delta Sigma Theta and the Challenge of the Black Sorority Movement.* New York: William Morrow and Company, 1994.

Ross, Lawrence C., Jr. *The Divine Nine, The History of African American Fraternities and Sororities.* New York: Kensington Books, 2000.

— Aberjhani

Alpha Phi Alpha Fraternity, Inc.

The social alienation and academic challenges faced by African Americans seeking higher education at predominately white schools led seven students at Cornell University in Ithaca, New York, to establish Alpha Phi Alpha, the first black Greek lettered fraternity, on December 4, 1906.

Vertner W. Tandy, Henry A. Callis, Eugene K. Jones, Robert H. Ogle, Charles H. Chapman, Nathaniel A. Murray, and George B. Kelly had already joined forces to support each other as a study group when they elected to formalize their gathering as a new fraternity. They adopted as their guiding principles the aspirations to perform "manly deeds," achieve academic excellence, and practice a genuine love for all humanity. Having established themselves as the first black college fraternity, they went on also to become the first incorporated black fraternity.

In its quiet refusal to follow the accommodationist route spelled out by BOOKER TALIAFERRO WASHINGTON, the fraternity's chosen principles were much in line with the developing ideals of the *NEW NEGRO*, which philosopher and editor ALAIN LOCKE would champion nearly two decades later in the book of the same name. As such, the new organization developed to attract some of the most outstanding talents of the era, including poet COUNTEE CULLEN; sociologist W. E. B. DU BOIS; performing artist PAUL ROBESON; track and field athlete JESSE OWENS; minister and politician ADAM CLAYTON POWELL, JR.; and musician DUKE ELLINGTON.

Moreover, each of Alpha Phi Alpha's founding members, who came to be known as the Seven Jewels, would make significant contributions to African Americans and the United States in general. Particularly outstanding was Tandy, who became New York State's first black licensed architect and who designed Villa Lewaro, MADAME C. J. WALKER's Italianate mansion named after her daughter, A'LELIA WALKER. (The name is taken from first letters of her married name: *Le*lia *Wa*lker *Ro*binson.) A second outstanding founder was Jones, who helped organized the NATIONAL URBAN LEAGUE (NUL) in its early years and later led the organization for 23 years, from 1918 to 1941.

Among the new organization's first major tasks was to expand its operations in 1907 with a second chapter at HOWARD UNIVERSITY in WASHINGTON, D.C. With continued expansion in the 1920s, the fraternity began to put its principles into extended action with such community-targeted drives as its "Go to High School, Go to College Program." The campaign both exemplified a value of the New Negro and helped set the stage for the strategy of "equality through education" that African Americans would employ throughout the 20th century. Fraternity members backed it up with both tutorial programs and financial assistance. The fraternity also challenged disfranchisement with voter registration drives and its politically provocative slogan, "A Voteless People Is a Hopeless People."

Annual conventions and a variety of social functions also became part of Alpha Phi Alpha's developing programs. Members published news of fraternity events as well as essays on the state of black America in a national magazine called the *Sphinx.*

The abundance of African-American Greek-lettered fraternities on college campuses throughout the United States at the start of the 21st century bears favorable witness to the original vision of the Alpha Phi Alpha's Seven Jewels. True to its pledge to embrace all humanity, the fraternity became interracial in 1945 and since its founding has initiated more than 100,000 members. Undergraduate and graduate chapters totaling 700 can be found in the United States, the Caribbean, Asia, Europe, and Africa.

Alpha Phi Alpha in 2002 enjoyed an ongoing partnership with a number of social service and political agencies. The fraternity maintained a particularly strong association with the NATIONAL ASSOCIATION FOR THE ADVANCEMENT OF COLORED PEOPLE (NAACP) and in the 1980s raised a million dollars to benefit the organization. Although the right to vote has long been established, the fraternity still holds drives to encourage registration. It also maintained a strong presence on and off campuses with orientation programs for new college students, workshops on black culture, and mentoring programs for youth. The fraternity's stepshow, featuring coordinated drill presentations, has become a staple of modern college culture.

Among the celebrated Alphas who have made a significant impact on American life in the modern era are Thurgood Marshall, Andrew Young, Maynard Jackson, Lionel Ritchie, and Cornel West.

As of 2002 the Alpha Phi Alpha Fraternity, Inc., was headquartered in CHICAGO.

Further Reading

Bracey, Ernest N. *Prophetic Insight: The Higher Education and Pedagogy of African Americans.* Lanham, Md.: University Press of America, 2001.

Ross, Lawrence C., Jr. *The Divine Nine, the History of African American Fraternities and Sororities.* New York: Kensington Books, 2000.

— Aberjhani

Alston, Charles Henry (1907–1977) *painter*

Charles Henry Alston was a painter, sculptor, and graphic artist whose career spanned the Harlem Renaissance of the 1920s and 1930s and the Black Arts Movement of the 1960s and 1970s. He created murals for a federally directed arts program during the GREAT DEPRESSION and taught art at an eminent HARLEM arts center. Associated with the "Renaissance of the Illustrated Book," the revival of an art form so designated by the American Institute of Graphic Arts in 1926, he cofounded several guilds and organizations to support and nurture African-American artists.

Charles Henry Alston was born on November 28, 1907, in Charlotte, North Carolina. The youngest of five children born to Rev. Primus Priss Alston and Anna Elizabeth Miller Alston, Charles Alston's childhood nickname was "Spinky." Alston's parents were educated, prominent figures in the community. Rev. Alston, an Episcopalian minister born into slavery in Chatham County, North Carolina, attended Saint Augustine's School (now Saint Augustine's College) in Raleigh. He became a deacon in 1883, was ordained a priest in 1892, and served for 30 years as the rector of St. Michaels of All Angels Church in Charlotte. During his lifetime, Rev. Alston was known as "the Booker T. Washington of Charlotte." (BOOKER TALIAFERRO WASHINGTON, an accommodationist on racial issues, founded Tuskegee Institute in Alabama and wrote a celebrated autobiography, *Up From Slavery,* [1901].) Rev. Alston died in 1910 and his widow later married Harry Pierce Bearden, the uncle of artist ROMARE BEARDEN. The family moved to NEW YORK CITY in 1913.

Artistic as a child, Charles Alston was 14 when he won a prize in school for his art. When the family migrated to New York, he began to study illustration. He honed his illustration skills on student publications at De Witt Clinton High School, where he was president of the art club, served as art editor of the school magazine, the *Clinton Magpie,* and was elected to the honorary society, Arista.

His good grades and artistic promise earned him a scholarship to the Yale School of Fine Arts, but he went to Columbia, where, in 1929, he graduated with a bachelor of arts degree. In 1931, funded by an Arthur Wesley Dow Fellowship, he earned a master of arts degree from Teachers College, Columbia University.

Alston's illustrations found their way into magazines, onto book jacket covers, and, eventually, to album covers of records. *The New Yorker, Collier's,* and *American Magazine* purchased his work, and he evolved into a recognized illustrator of book jackets produced by Harlem Renaissance writers. While still in college, he illustrated LANGSTON HUGHES's *Weary Blues.* He also created the cover of *The Conjure-Man Dies: A Harlem Mystery,* the 1932 detective novel by RUDOLPH FISHER. Alston's own painting was influenced by the literature of the era: His "Girl in a Red Dress" is implicative of WALLACE THURMAN's 1929 novel *The Blacker the Berry.*

Armed with several academic degrees, Alston slid easily into the life of an art educator. In 1929, he worked as art director for a summer camp at St. Philips Episcopal Church in Harlem. He then worked as director of a Harlem-based after-school program, Utopia House, where he taught JACOB ARMSTEAD LAWRENCE, a fellow North Carolinian and cousin, who would gain recognition as one of the greatest artists of the 20th century.

In addition to the young and, as yet, uncelebrated painter Lawrence, Alston formed friendships and exchanged correspondences with some of the brightest and most creative minds of the day, including activist PAUL ROBESON, writers JAMES WELDON JOHNSON and his brother JOHN ROSAMOND JOHNSON, LANGSTON HUGHES, CLAUDE MCKAY, NATIONAL ASSOCIATION FOR THE ADVANCEMENT OF COLORED PEOPLE (NAACP) director WALTER WHITE, singer BILLIE HOLIDAY, and fellow visual artists AUGUSTA FELLS SAVAGE and AARON DOUGLAS. In this environment of intellectualism and creativity, Alston produced art and initiated significant community development efforts.

When the GREAT DEPRESSION hit Harlem in the 1930s, Alston found work teaching art at the Harlem Arts Workshop, which was established by sculptor Augusta Savage at the 135th Street Library. The workshop was initially funded by the Carnegie Foundation and continued with funds from the WORKS PROGRESS ADMINISTRATION (WPA). Space at the workshop was soon at a premium, and Savage asked Alston to scour the neighborhood to secure an additional building. Alston found a three-story structure at 306 West 141st Street that was complete with two apartments, dubbed "306" (THREE-O-SIX.) Alston lived in one of the apartments and sculptor Henry Bannarn lived in the other. The acquisition of this building turned yet another page in the legacy of artistic and intellectual history in Harlem.

Creativity thrived, but it was the mid-1930s, and LYNCHING remained an issue. The depression had dealt a serious blow to the economy, and jobs were hard to find. Harlem erupted into a bloody riot in 1935. Alston responded to these events with art: He participated in an exhibition, "Struggle for Negro Rights," to support antilynching legislation. Right after the riots, Alston, Savage, and Douglas formed the Harlem Art Committee. The committee exhibited works of African-American artists at the 137th Street YMCA.

Also in 1935, Alston joined with Savage and ARTHUR SCHOMBURG, African-Caribbean bibliophile for whom the SCHOMBURG CENTER FOR RESEARCH IN BLACK CULTURE is named, and organized the Harlem Artists Guild. One of the main purposes of the guild was to advocate for fair treatment from the WPA in regard to African-American artists. Under the strength of the guild, the HARLEM COMMUNITY ART CENTER was formed in 1937, led by Augusta Savage. Along with fellow artists, Alston fought for the dignity and economic equality of African-American artists, a battle that led to further employment. Under the auspices of the WPA, during the 1930s and even decades later, Alston was hired as painter and site supervisor for a HARLEM HOSPITAL mural, and he shared a mural commission with HALE ASPACIO WOODRUFF.

The Harlem Hospital painting, *Magic and Medicine* (1937), depicted the history of medicine in, it was alleged, a primitive manner. It created a major public controversy. Under Alston's supervision were Harlem photographers Marvin and Morgan Smith, who were twin brothers.

When WPA dollars decreased, in 1938 Alston secured a Rosenwald fellowship to study, sketch, and photograph the rural South for two years. This endeavor resulted in background for his narrative on canvas, *Family Series.* In the 1940s, back in New York, Alston returned to illustration for *Fortune* magazine and, under the leadership of journalist Ted Poston, created war-effort cartoons and posters at the Office of War Information and Public Relations in WASHINGTON, D.C., from 1940 to 1941.

It was World War II, and at the age of 36 Alston was drafted into the all-black 372nd Infantry to create visual training aids. When he returned from military service, he married Dr. Myra Logan, who was an intern when he had worked on the Harlem Hospital mural. He returned to fine art. A two-part mural that he and Woodruff produced at Golden State Mutual Life Insurance Company of Los Angeles in 1948 documented African-American settlers in California. Alston was responsible for the first part of the mural entitled *Exploration and Colonization: 1527–1850.*

An accomplished muralist, during the 1950s, Alston completed a painting for Abraham Lincoln High School in Brooklyn, New York, and one for the American Museum of Natural History in New York City. By the 1950s, Alston had sold an abstract entitled *Painting* to the prestigious Metropolitan Museum of Art. He joined the faculty at the Art Student's League and, an academician who had come full circle, was appointed as a full professor at City College of New York (CCNY) in 1973.

Ever the organizer and community activist, Alston joined a discussion group of black artists in the 1960s, the era of the Black Arts Movement. The group, Spiral, met at 147 Christopher Street in the Greenwich Village area of New York City. Spiral put together an art exhibit in May 1964 but was no longer operative by 1965.

Charles Alston's major exhibitions included shows at The High Museum of Art in Atlanta, Georgia, 1933 to 1934; the HARMON FOUNDATION in New York City, 1933 to 1934; American Negro Exhibition in Chicago in 1940; and the Gallery of Modern Art (a major retrospective of his work) in 1968. One year later Mayor John V. Lindsay appointed Alston as a member of the New York City Arts Commission. In 1971, he received the Thomas B. Clarke Award of the National Academy of Design, and in 1975 he completed mosaic murals for the Bronx County Family and Criminal Court building.

He died at the age of 69 in April of 1977, four months after his wife.

Charles Alston's papers include many newspaper clippings, drawings from his military days, congratulatory letters from U.S. presidents, favorite recipes, and holiday cards from friends. They are collected in the Manuscripts Department of the Library of the University of North Carolina at Chapel Hill.

Further Reading

Bailey, David A., and Paul Gilroy. *Rhapsodies in Black: Art of the Harlem Renaissance.* Berkeley: University of California Press, 1997.

Hotton, Julie, ed. *Charles Alston and the "306" Legacy. Exhibition Catalogue, September 21–December 4, 2000.* New York: Cinque Gallery, 2000.

— Sandra L. West

American Negro Academy (ANA)

Founded in March 1897 by missionary and educator Alexander Crummel, the American Negro Academy was an early literary and intellectual society that contributed to a cultural renaissance in WASHINGTON, D.C. The academy survived into the Harlem Renaissance and influenced the ASSOCIATION FOR THE STUDY OF NEGRO LIFE, a prominent historical and publishing organization founded by historian CARTER GODWIN WOODSON.

Alexander Crummel was born in New York on March 3, 1819. His father was Boston Crummel, a kidnapped African from Sierra Leone's Temene tribe. Among Boston Crummel's friends were dramatist Ira Aldridge and publisher John Brown Russwurm. Russwurm published *Freedom's Journal,* the first black newspaper in the United States, in the Crummel household in 1827. Alexander inherited his father's regal, aristocratic bearing, respect for education, and philosophy on African-American nationalism and self-help.

Alexander Crummel was educated in parochial schools in NEW YORK CITY and Canaan, New Hampshire, the Oneida Institute in New York, and Cambridge University in England. Raised as an Episcopalian, he served as a missionary in West Africa from 1850 to 1870. While in Africa, he was a strong supporter of the BACK-TO-AFRICA MOVEMENT. He later served as rector of St. Philip's Church in New York. In 1873, Crummel returned to Washington. He established St. Luke's Church in 1880 and organized the black Episcopal clergy to fight racism in the church.

Crummel advocated an "educated gentry" for African Americans. All of his academic life he spoke of "the Negro genius" and worked to build an international organization of black scholars, based in the United States, that would confirm and sustain that genius. With support from African-American intellectuals and black scholars in Haiti and England, Crummel organized the American Negro Academy when he was almost 80 years old. His mission was to "promote literature, science, and art; to foster higher education and high culture; and to defend the Negro against racist attacks." Members of ANA called him "the Apostle of Culture."

The original 40 members of Crummel's ANA included poet and novelist Paul Laurence Dunbar, sociologist and Harlem Renaissance intelligentsia leader Dr. W. E. B. DU BOIS; bibliophile ARTHUR SCHOMBURG, for whom the SCHOMBURG CENTER FOR RESEARCH IN BLACK CULTURE in New York is named; and BOOKER TALIAFERRO WASHINGTON, founder of Tuskegee Institute in Alabama and Du Bois's eminent rival. Reportedly the only woman who joined the academy was Dr. ANNA JULIA COOPER.

The first meeting of the brotherhood of scholars and writers convened at Lincoln Memorial Church in Washington, D.C. Meetings were also held at HOWARD UNIVERSITY's chapel in Washington, D.C.

Shortly after establishing the ANA, Crummel died on September 12, 1898, in Point Pleasant, New Jersey. Du Bois, who eulogized Crummel in *THE SOULS OF BLACK FOLK,* inherited the presidency. By 1924, in the middle of the Harlem Renaissance, Schomburg served as ANA president.

ANA members discussed the many concerns of the African American and nurtured African-American genius by publishing books and 22 scholarly papers in pamphlet form that were called "occasional papers." The 22 papers, written between 1897 and 1924, include "A Review of Hoffman's Race

Traits and Tendencies of the American Negro" (1897) by Kelly Miller (born in slavery, Miller later became a dean at Howard University); "The Economic Contribution by the Negro to America" (1915) by Arthur Schomburg; and "The Challenge of the Disfranchised: A Plea for the Enforcement of the 15th Amendment" (1924) by John W. Cromwell.

The intellectual authority of the ANA helped stimulate a Washington, D.C., renaissance that was resplendent with scholars and writers, years before Harlem's 1920s to 1930s cultural revolution.

Further Reading

Bracey, Ernest N. *Prophetic Insight: The Higher Education and Pedagogy of African Americans.* Lanham, Md.: University Press of America, 2001.

Fontenot, Chester, ed. Mary A Morgan, and Sarah Gardner. *W. E. B. Du Bois and Race: Essays Celebrating the Centennial Publication of* The Souls of Black Folk. Macon, Ga.: Mercer University Press, 2001.

— Sandra L. West

American Tennis Association (ATA)

The United States Lawn Tennis Association (USLTA) was formed in 1881, but it was closed to black participation due to the practice of racial discrimination known as JIM CROW. African Americans established the American Tennis Association (ATA) for black players, complete with national competitions, during the Harlem Renaissance era to counter the Jim Crow discrimination of the USLTA.

African Americans began to play tennis in the 1890s at various black colleges. Some of the pioneers in this arena were Emmett J. Scott of Tuskegee Institute in Alabama; Charles Cook of HOWARD UNIVERSITY in WASHINGTON, D.C., and Thomas Jefferson of Lincoln University in Missouri.

While the NATIONAL ASSOCIATION FOR THE ADVANCEMENT OF COLORED PEOPLE fought tennis court discrimination, the ATA held its first national tournament at Druid Hill Park, Baltimore, Maryland, in 1917. The first black national tennis champion was Talley Holmes. He won in 1917, 1918, 1921, and 1925.

Reginald Weir was another star of the ATA circuit. He was captain of the tennis team at the City College of New York in Harlem and won the singles championship in 1931, 1932, 1933, 1937, and 1942.

Attempts were made to derail the early black tennis initiative. However, in the 21st-century two leaders of the tennis world are African-American sisters Venus and Serena Williams. The Williams sisters stand upon the shoulders of Althea Gibson, winner of both the Wimbledon and U.S. championships in 1957 and 1958, and Arthur Ashe, who, among other achievements, in 1968 guided the U.S. Davis Cup team to its first championship in five years.

Further Reading

Ploski, Harry A., and James D. Williams, eds. *Reference Library of Black America, Volume IV.* Detroit: Gale Research Inc., 1990.

Rust, Edna, and Art Rust, Jr. *Art Rust's Illustrated History of the Black Athlete.* New York: Doubleday and Company, Inc., 1985.

— Sandra L. West

Amos 'n' Andy

The extreme popularity of *Amos 'n' Andy,* both as a radio and television show focusing on the lives of its black characters, could not prevent the controversy that ultimately resulted in the show's cancellation from American programming.

The characters of Amos and Andy were first introduced to the American public on a radio program in CHICAGO called *Sam 'n' Henry* in 1928. Although the exaggerated black dialect employed by the characters made many assume the performers were black, they were actually white entertainers Freeman F. Gosden and Charles J. Correll. The creators and owners of the show, Gosden and Correll changed its name to *Amos 'n' Andy,* also in 1928, and switched to national programming with the National Broadcasting Company (NBC). Broadcasting five times a week from 7 to 7:15 p.m., the show became an immediate hit and national phenomenon. Gosden and Correll played each of several parts themselves until later hiring black performers to fill in supporting rolls.

An estimated 25,000 listeners, including Presidents Calvin Coolidge, Harry S. Truman, and Dwight D. Eisenhower during their respective terms, tuned in to laugh at the antics of Amos and Andy on a regular basis. Set in HARLEM, the show focused on the daily lives of the somewhat sensible proprietor of a taxi company, Amos Jones, the not so sensible or clever Andrew Brown, and the endlessly scheming Kingfish. The latter was often in search of ways to make a lot of money with little or no effort and many Americans during the GREAT DEPRESSION found themselves laughing at their own troubles through the unabashedly stereotypical Amos and Andy. However, in the era of the *NEW NEGRO,* when African Americans had declared an all-out assault on such images, at least as much protest as laughter stirred over the show. The *PITTSBURGH COURIER* in 1931 launched a national campaign to have it taken off the air. The newspaper collected almost a million signatures in support of its initiative but failed to have the show canceled. In fact, the exact opposite happened when *Amos 'n' Andy* moved from NBC radio to Columbia Broadcasting System (CBS) radio in 1943 and expanded its 15-minute format to 30 minutes.

CBS television paid Gosden and Correll a record figure of $2.5 million for rights to the show around 1949. Rather than risk any backlash from Gosden and Correll appearing on national television in blackface, CBS conducted a highly publicized two-year search for the black performers needed to successfully make the transition from radio to television. The chosen actors were all show business veterans. Alvin Childress won the more moderate role of Amos. Childress was a native of Meridian, Mississippi, who had earned some acclaim performing in the BLACK UNIT OF THE FEDERAL THEATER PROJECT's production of *Haiti.* Spencer Williams was hired to play the more central part of Andy, a regular target for Kingfish's schemes. Originally from Vidalia, Louisiana, Williams's track record included work in Hollywood as an actor, writer, and director. He directed the films *Go Down Moses* and *The Blood of Jesus.* He also lent his talents as writer and actor to the movies *Harlem Rides Again* and *Harlem on the Prairie.* The role of Kingfish (George Stevens) went to Tim Moore, a native of Rock Island, Illinois. Moore had a mixed background as an athlete and performer, having at different times been a boxer and a vaudeville performer. He went on tour with the hit musical *BLACKBIRDS OF 1928* and performed in the movie *Boy! What a Girl.* Both Moore and Williams came out of retirement to play their respective roles. The only actors to make the transition from the radio show to the television show were Ernestine Wade in the part of Sapphire Stevens, Kingfish's wife, and Amanda Randolph as Ramona Smith, Sapphire's mother.

Amos 'n' Andy debuted on television June 28, 1951. It was the first TV program to feature an all-black cast. Its weekly episodes included such scenarios as Kingfish trying to swindle Andy out of his car by sabotaging Andy's road test or Kingfish attempting to adopt the very adult Andy in order to become eligible for a $2,000 inheritance from his cousin Effies. Seemingly, neither white people—except as occasional authority figures—nor such race-related problems as JIM CROW racism, disfranchisement, or discrimination in housing or hiring existed for the characters in 1951. This was the same year that black feminist leader Mary Church Terrell led a movement to end segregation in Washington, D.C.'s restaurants and the year 3,000 whites rioted in protest of a black family moving into an all-white neighborhood in Cicero, Illinois.

While the television show generated the same kind of popularity as the radio version of *Amos 'n' Andy*, it also generated similar controversy. The NATIONAL ASSOCIATION FOR THE ADVANCEMENT OF COLORED PEOPLE (NAACP) issued a public bulletin charging that the show routinely portrayed African Americans as "inferior, lazy, dumb, and dishonest." Moreover, it considered the television show worse than the radio version because of its more powerful visual impact upon American society in general and children in particular. The NAACP and other organizations maintained a steady protest over a period of two years, calling for the show's cancellation and threatening to boycott its sponsor, Blatz Beer of Milwaukee, Wisconsin.

The show was forced to cease production in 1953. However, the series went into syndication and continued to broadcast reruns. CBS also managed to sell the show to the African nations of Kenya and Nigeria. Afterward, public protest caused cancellation of the show there as well. It remained in syndication in the United States until 1966, the height of the Civil Rights movement, when all broadcasts of the program were ended.

Further Reading

Douglas, Susan J. *Listening In: Radio and the American Imagination, from Amos 'n' Andy and Edward R. Murrow to Wolfman Jack and Howard Stern.* New York: Crown Publishing Company, 2000.

Ely, Melvin Patrick. *Adventures of Amos 'n' Andy: A Social History of an American Phenomenon.* New York: The Free Press, 1992.

— Aberjhani

Amsterdam News

Following the lead of Thomas T. Fortune's *NEW YORK AGE*, James H. Anderson founded the *Amsterdam News* in NEW YORK CITY in 1909. Over the next two decades, the paper achieved circulation rates comparable to those of the *CHICAGO DEFENDER* and the *Baltimore Afro American.*

Like the *Chicago Defender*, the *Amsterdam News* was unrelenting in its commitment to reporting on events from a black perspective and in its militant criticisms of the U.S. government. The paper championed black radicalism as an appropriate and necessary response to white racism in general and the murderous practice of LYNCHING in particular. Its criticisms of the government's failure to correct racist practices in the military during WORLD WAR I made it subject to investigation under the Wartime Espionage Act.

Similarly, when race riots caused the loss of lives and destruction of property in cities across the United States during the RED SUMMER OF 1919, the *Amsterdam News* advocated blacks defending themselves rather than giving up their lives, properties, or civil rights. Editors of the paper also challenged A. PHILIP RANDOLPH's promotion of socialism in the MESSENGER and the call for COMMUNISM as promoted by white American political radicals.

Moreover, the paper was not opposed to rendering critical reviews of works produced by the writers and artists of the *NEW NEGRO* movement in the 1920s. It was particularly critical of LANGSTON HUGHES's *Fine Clothes for the Jew*, when the poetry collection was published in 1927. In addition, journalist Edgar M. Gray regularly reported on economic and social issues impacting upon HARLEM and black Americans nationwide. In at least one article, "The Sleeping Giant—The Harlem Negro," he took the entire community to task for what he considered its political apathy at the time.

The paper also featured the works of many of the era's exceptional writers and political leaders, including W. E. B. DU BOIS, Cyril Briggs, founder of the AFRICAN BLOOD BROTHERHOOD, and political advocate ADAM CLAYTON POWELL, JR.

Now known as the *New York Amsterdam News*, the publication achieved a peak circulation of 100,000 during World War II. Though circulation declined to less than half that number in the latter half of the 1900s, at the end of the 1990s it remained one of the country's largest, oldest, and most influential black-owned newspapers.

Further Reading

Jordan, William G. *Black Newspapers and America's War for Democracy.* Durham: University of North Carolina Press, 2001.

Korn Weibel, Theodore, Jr. *Seeing Red: Federal Campaigns Against Black Militancy, 1919–1925.* Bloomington: Indiana University Press, 1998.

— Aberjhani

New York's *Amsterdam News* was one of the leading radical newspapers of the early 20th century. It operated out of one the buildings pictured here—probably the one on the left. Its offices were located at 2293 Seventh Avenue. *(Library of the Congress, Prints & Photographs Division [HABS, NY,31-NEYO,98-6])*

Anderson, Eddie "Rochester" (Edward Anderson) (1905–1977) *actor*

Best known for his role as a valet on the *Jack Benny Show,* Eddie Anderson was an actor whose exceptional career included vaudeville, radio, movies, and television.

Anderson was born Edward Anderson on September 18, 1905, in Oakland, California. His parents, Ella Mae Anderson and "Big Ed" Anderson, were both vaudeville performers. Eddie Anderson began acting as a child. By the time he was a teenager, he was touring as part of a song and dance act with his older brother Cornelius.

Anderson moved to Los Angeles in the early 1930s and played a number of uncredited bit parts in such movies as *What Price Hollywood* in 1932 and *Showboat* in 1936. A pivotal point in his career came when he was cast as Noah in the movie of Marc Connelly's play *GREEN PASTURES.*

In 1937, Anderson made his debut on the *Jack Benny Radio Show,* which had been on the air since 1932. Playing the role of a Pullman Car Porter, Anderson was slated to perform only a single episode of the show, but the radio audience's response to his character prompted producers to bring him back. He eventually became a regular on the series, playing the role of Rochester Van Jones, a valet who allowed his employer to think he was in charge when more often than not it was Rochester who manipulated various situations to his own advantage. The character became famous both for his cool craftiness and for his raspy and hoarse voice.

Anderson made such a powerful impression in the role of Rochester on radio that he was able to play the character alongside Jack Benny in four movies: *Man About Town* in 1939, the same year he also played Uncle Peter in *Gone With the Wind; Buck Benny Rides Again* in 1940; *Love Thy Neighbor* in 1940; and *The Meanest Man in the World* in 1943.

Building on its success in radio and film, the *Jack Benny Show* debuted as a television series on the Columbia Broadcasting System (CBS) in October 1950 and ran on that network until September 1964. It appeared for its final year on the National Broadcasting Company (NBC) network. The end of the show marked the end of a 27-year partnership between Benny and Anderson.

In addition to his work with Benny, Anderson performed on his own in dozens of films and as a guest on various television shows. His other television appearances included roles on *Bachelor Father* in 1962, *Dick Powell Theater* in 1963, and *Love American Style* in 1969. Among his most significant movies was *Birth of the Blues* in 1941 and *Cabin in the Sky* in 1943. The latter movie brought him widespread critical acclaim for his work in the central role of Little Joe Jackson. Starring with him were ETHEL WATERS and LENA HORNE. His last movie was *It's a Mad, Mad, Mad, Mad World* in 1963.

Anderson died February 28, 1977, in Los Angeles.

Further Reading

Bogle, Donald. *Primetime Blues: African Americans on Network Television.* New York: Farrar, Straus, and Giroux, 2001.

Nachman, Gerald. *Raised on Radio.* New York: Pantheon Books, 1998.

— Aberjhani

Anderson, Garland (1886–1939) *playwright*

Garland Anderson overcame the limitations of a fourth-grade education and his job as a bellhop at the Braeburn Hotel in San Francisco, California, to become the first African-American playwright to stage a full-length drama on Broadway.

Anderson was born in 1886 in Wichita, Kansas, the fourth of 12 children. His father was a janitor who moved his family to Sacramento when he secured a job with the U.S. Post Office. Anderson's mother died before he entered his teens, and he ran away from home at the age of 11.

Traveling through California, the young Anderson survived by performing various odd jobs, at times selling newspapers and later working as a dining car waiter for the railroad. Exposure to the teachings of Christian Science convinced Anderson that his life possessed greater potential than he had tapped up to that point. Founded in 1879 by Mary Baker Eddy, Christian Science was recognized largely as a doctrine geared toward faith healing. Many, however, like Anderson, expanded that belief to include the ability of faith to accomplish anything at all.

Anderson was working in 1922 as a bellhop at the Braeburn Hotel in San Francisco when a customer treated him to a ticket to see Channing Pollock's morality play, *The Fool.* The production inspired Anderson to test his own faith by attempting to write a play that would reflect the spiritual philosophy he had adopted. The result was a three-act drama that he first called *Don't Judge by Appearances,* then later shortened to *APPEARANCES.*

The bellhop-turned-playwright believed in his vision enough that he began to seek backers and supporters. Famed entertainer Al Jolson felt the play impressive enough that he financed a trip to New York for Anderson and provided him with funds sufficient for two months. Anderson stretched his stay into seven months and during that time managed two public readings of his play. The first was held at the Waldorf-Astoria Hotel with RICHARD B. HARRISON reading before some 600 guests. The effort gained Anderson $140. The second reading took place at the Manhattan Opera House. He also managed to place a copy of his play in the hands of President Calvin Coolidge, whom he then informed the press was delighted with it and believed it should have a New York production.

Lester A. Sagar, manager of the Central Theater, agreed to invest half the monies needed for the play. Anderson returned to San Francisco and secured the remaining funds from two patrons, H. S. and Fergus Wilkinson. The new playwright then ingeniously used his return trip to New York as a promotion vehicle for his play. He agreed to carry with him a letter from the mayor of San Francisco to the mayor of New York, in the process garnering publicity for himself and his play. He and his patrons drove two cars from San Francisco to New York with streamers advertising Anderson as the San Francisco bellhop who had become a playwright.

Appearances debuted on October 13, 1925, at Broadway's Frolic Theater. The play embarked on a two-year run that took it to theaters all over the United States, including in San Francisco. It reopened for a second run in New York on April 1, 1929, and had its London debut in March 1930.

The run in London allowed Anderson to shed his former identity completely as he became the first African American inducted into the renowned PEN international writers organization. It was also there that he met Doris Sequirra, the daughter of an English physician, and they married. His wife later displayed her disdain for racial prejudice by publishing a book about her interracial marriage called *Nigger Lover.*

Anderson reportedly continued to write plays but was possibly better known as an ordained minister of Constructive Thinking at the Truth Center. In that role, he wrote an inspirational book entitled *Uncommon Sense.* He also traveled and lectured extensively. He died in 1939.

Further Reading

Hill, Anthony D. *Pages from the Harlem Renaissance: A Chronicle of Performance.* New York: Lang Publishing, 1996.

Johnson, James Weldon. *Black Manhattan.* New York: Da Capo Press, 1991.

— Aberjhani

Anderson, Ivie Marie See ELLINGTON, DUKE.

Anderson, Marian (1897–1993) *opera singer*

Marian Anderson was the first African American to sing a role at the Metropolitan Opera House and became a U.S. State Department goodwill ambassador to Asia. Her rich operatic contralto won the New York Philharmonic voice competition in 1924. Acknowledged for her modesty, humility, and unwavering religious faith, she was often called "The Lady of Philadelphia."

Anderson was born on February 27, 1897, in Philadelphia, Pennsylvania. Her mother was Annie Anderson, a former teacher. Her father, John Anderson, who died when Marion was eight years old, worked in the refrigerator room of the Reading Terminal Market and sold coal and ice to make ends meet. Her sisters were Ethel and Alyce. Ethel's son, James DePriest, became an eminent orchestra conductor. The family lived on Colorado Street and South Martin Street in Philadelphia.

Anderson attended William Penn High School and South Philadelphia High School, where she sang at assemblies and struggled with stenography and bookkeeping. She also attended Union Baptist Church, singing there for the first time when she was eight years old and giving concerts in neighboring churches where she was billed "the baby contralto." She participated in both junior and senior choirs at Union Baptist until becoming an adult. Opera star ROLAND HAYES visited Union Baptist and, quite impressed with her soprano to bass range, invited her to sing with him in cantatas and oratorios. He made it possible for her to participate in concert tours to black colleges and churches outside Philadelphia while she was still a high school student. For these concerts, Anderson was paid $5, if anything at all. The caring, concerned congregation once gave to her a "love offering" of $17.02 with which she purchased a satin and hand-fashioned formal dress that she wore to her earlier recitals at churches, colleges, the YMCA, and the YWCA.

Denied permission to perform at Washington, D.C.'s, Constitution Hall, Marian Anderson instead sang at the Lincoln Memorial before a crowd of 75,000 and became one of America's most celebrated opera singers. She is shown here in 1940. *(Library of Congress, Prints & Photographs Division, Carl Van Vechten Collection, [LC-USZ62-42524])*

She studied violin for a very short time and played simple songs on the piano to accompany herself, but she did not have formal voice instruction until she was a high school junior. Anderson did not have early formal lessons because the Philadelphia music school with which she registered did not take "colored" and because her fatherless family did not think she required lessons since she was already singing quite well and performing in church.

Her initial vocal teacher was Mary Saunders Patterson, who also gave Anderson her first bona fide evening gown. (Several gowns worn by Anderson are in the permanent collection of the Black History Museum and Cultural Center of Virginia in RICHMOND, VIRGINIA.) She then studied with Patterson and Agnes Reifsnyder, whose fees were paid by the Philadelphia Choral Society, an African-American group Anderson sang with when she was a teen. Union Baptist Church paid the $600 required for her vocal studies with Giuseppe Borghetti. Anderson remained under the tutelage and influence of the demanding Borghetti even after she became an accomplished opera singer.

After a disastrous under-capacity Town Hall concert in which Anderson sang "Von Ewiger Liebe" rather badly in German and was written about unkindly in the press, in 1925 she sang "O mio Fernando" from Donizetti's *La Favorita* and captured first place in a vocal competition sponsored by the New York Philharmonic Symphony at Lewisohn Stadium. With this win, Anderson garnered the attention of serious music lovers. The prize was an appearance with the symphony in New York on August 26, 1925, and, although the press was only cordial, her engagement schedule expanded. She intently studied foreign languages, and her performance fee, $5 when she began, increased to $350 and $500 for very special occasions. Because Marian Anderson was the first African American to win vocal competitions in the 1920s, the doors of opera, virtually closed to black performers, opened and never closed again.

In 1929, Anderson won a Julius Rosenwald Fellowship to study in Europe and by 1932 had a successful European career. Conductor Arturo Toscanini described her voice as "a voice that comes once in a hundred years." When she returned to the United States, her recitals, unlike the Town Hall fiasco of years previous, were filled to capacity and critically acclaimed. However, in the midst of her success, she encountered the practice of JIM CROW racism.

In 1939, the Daughters of the American Revolution (DAR) refused her right to perform in Constitution Hall in WASHINGTON, D.C., because she was a black woman. The NATIONAL ASSOCIATION FOR THE ADVANCEMENT OF COLORED PEOPLE (NAACP) expressed outrage over the incident and First Lady ELEANOR ROOSEVELT renounced her DAR membership. Between the efforts of the civil rights organization and the White House, Anderson arranged to perform on Easter Sunday 1939 on the steps of the Lincoln Memorial, where 75,000 people came out to hear her.

By 1955, she became the first African American to appear with the Metropolitan Opera Company in New York, gracing the role of Ulrica in Verdi's *Un Ballo in Maschera.* Because of her natural humility and refinement, Anderson was asked by the State Department to tour Asia as a goodwill ambassador. She subsequently served as delegate to the United Nations, received decorations from governments of many nations, including Liberia and Sweden, and earned several doctorates in music and humane letters.

Marian Anderson died on April 8, 1993, at the age of 96.

Further Reading

Anderson, Marian, *My Lord What a Morning.* Madison: University of Wisconsin Press, 1956.

Keiler, Allan. *Marian Anderson: A Singer's Journey.* New York: Scribner, 2000.

Sims, Janet. *Marian Anderson: An Annotated Bibliography and Discography.* Westport, Conn.: Greenwood, 1981.

— Sandra L. West

Anderson, Sherwood (1876–1941) *novelist*

Together with white author Waldo Frank, the white novelist Sherwood Anderson and black novelist JEAN TOOMER engaged in a friendship and correspondence that influenced discussion on race and literature during the Harlem Renaissance.

Sherwood Anderson was born on September 13, 1876, in Camden, Ohio. After fighting in the Spanish-American War in 1898, Anderson worked in advertising and established his own business, the Anderson Manufacturing Company. Fairly successful, his business specialized in paints and roofing materials. In 1912, however, he abandoned the world of business to join poet Carl Sandburg and others to participate in the CHICAGO Renaissance as a writer.

Anderson's first wife was named Cornelia, and the couple had three children before divorcing in 1914. Although he would marry three more times, he inevitably found the conflict between marriage and his creative impulses too great.

With the 1919 publication of his fourth book, *Winesburg, Ohio,* a collection of interrelated stories and novella, Anderson achieved critical and commercial literary success. The book made him one of the most acclaimed authors of his time and he was influential in launching the careers of both Ernest Hemingway and William Faulkner. Anderson followed *Winesburg, Ohio* with *Poor White* (1920), *Triumph of the Egg* (1921), and *Dark Laughter* (1925). One of Anderson's many admirers was Toomer, who, like Anderson, published a number of stories in *Dial* magazine and also wrote articles for the *CRISIS* and the *Liberator.*

Anderson had limited contact with the Harlem Renaissance outside of his friendship with Toomer, although Dr. ALAIN LOCKE, intelligentsia leader of the era, asked him to contribute to his anthology *THE NEW NEGRO* (1925). Anderson declined but wrote a response to "The Negro in Art: How Shall He Be Portrayed?" for the *Crisis* (1926) at the behest of Harlem Renaissance "midwife" JESSIE REDMOND FAUSET.

The correspondence between Toomer and Anderson began in the early 1920s. In 1921, Toomer went to Georgia to work in a rural school and was introduced to the spirituals and folk songs of sharecroppers. As Toomer had been raised privileged in aristocratic WASHINGTON, D.C., with little exposure to black arts, the music provided him with material for his book in progress, *Cane.* He wrote to Anderson that the experience had touched him "body and soul." In 1922, Toomer planned to publish a black culture magazine and requested Anderson's participation, but Anderson refused. Anderson read Toomer's articles with interest, however. He was also aware that Toomer was writing *Cane,* a book that Toomer admitted was heavily influenced by characterizations in *Winesburg, Ohio* and *Triumph of the Egg.* Anderson wrote to Toomer that his writing was the "first negro work I have seen that strikes me as really new."

Multiracial Toomer did not want to be known, at any costs, as a "negro writer." Anderson referred to him as such while at the same time cautioning him, as did Frank, against falling into such a limiting category. Toomer complained about Anderson's reference to him as a "negro writer" in a letter to Frank: "He limits me to Negro. As an approach, as a constant element (part of a larger whole) of interest Negro is good. But to tie me to one of my parts is to lose me."

When Boni & Liveright published Toomer's *Cane* in 1923, Frank wrote the introduction even though Anderson had offered his services. Though Toomer, Frank, and Anderson were a social trio in New York's Greenwich Village, Anderson did not feel an attachment to the people or doings of the era and in 1926 retired to a farm in Virginia. There Anderson published two rural newspapers and wrote nearly two dozen more books.

Anderson died on March 8, 1941. In 2002 the Sherwood Anderson–Jean Toomer papers were housed at FISK UNIVERSITY in Nashville, Tennessee.

Further Reading

Hutchinson, George. *The Harlem Renaissance in Black and White.* Cambridge and London: The Belknap Press of Harvard University Press, 1995.

Lewis, Levering David. *When Harlem Was in Vogue.* New York: Vintage Books, 1981.

Townsend, Kim. *Sherwood Anderson: A Biography.* Boston: Houghton Mifflin Co., 1987.

— Sandra L. West

Anderson, Cat

See ELLINGTON, DUKE.

Andrews, Regina (Regina Grant, Ursula Trelling)

(1901–1993) *playwright, librarian*

Regina Andrews enjoyed a career as a librarian from the mid-1920s to 1967 while simultaneously writing and helping produce plays in HARLEM.

She was born Regina Grant in CHICAGO on May 21, 1901, to Margaret Simons Anderson and William Grant, a lawyer. She graduated from Hyde Park High School and later attended Wilberforce University in Ohio and the University of Chicago. She obtained a master of library science degree from the Columbia University Library School. In 1926, she married William T. Andrews.

In her work as a librarian, Regina Andrews hosted a series of cultural events that allowed her to showcase the ideas, talents, and work of such figures as MARCUS GARVEY, LANGSTON HUGHES, A. PHILIP RANDOLPH, and many others. Prior to its transformation to the SCHOMBURG CENTER FOR RESEARCH IN BLACK CULTURE, she worked at the 135th Street Branch of the New York Public Library. In 1945 she became the first African-American woman to serve as supervisor at the 115th Street Library.

It was in the basement of the 135th Street Library branch that Andrews helped W. E. B. DU BOIS establish the Harlem Library Little Theater. The basement theater served as home first to Du Bois's KRIGWA PLAYERS in 1925, then to the HARLEM EXPERIMENTAL THEATER Players in 1929. It would also provide the starting point for Langston Hughes's HARLEM SUITCASE THEATER.

Andrews was one of the principal founders of the Harlem Experimental Theater Players, a group that took much of its artistic philosophy from Du Bois's Krigwa Players. Like the latter, the former's goal was to write and produce plays by, for, and about African Americans.

Writing under the pen name Ursula Trelling, Andrews wrote several one-act plays performed by the Harlem Experimental Theater Players. With critical input from Du Bois and inspiration from the stories on LYNCHING written by IDA BELL WELLS-BARNETT, she completed *Climbing Jacob's Ladder* in 1931. Considered one of her strongest, the play depicts a lynching that occurs at the same time that a church service is in progress. Other plays included *The Man Who Passed* and *Underground,* dramatizing the dangers and heroics of the Underground Railroad.

In addition to producing her own works and cofounding different theater groups, Andrews assisted other aspiring dramatists and actors by hosting salons at her home, an apartment located on Harlem's fabled SUGAR HILL. Moreover, she was one of the primary organizers of the CIVIC CLUB DINNER, the March 21, 1924, event that for many marked the official beginning of the Harlem Renaissance.

In addition to her dramatic works, Andrews has authored a number of nonfiction titles, including *Chronology of African Americans in New York, 1621–1966,* which she coauthored with Ethel Ray Nance.

During her career as a librarian, Andrews hosted many programs featuring scholars, statesmen, and artists from all over the world. She enjoyed the opportunity to visit the homelands of some of her guests during her extensive travels throughout Asia, the Middle East, and India. She retired from the New York Public Library in 1969. Andrews died on February 5, 1993.

Further Reading

Hubbard, Dolan, ed. *Recovered Writers/Recovered Texts: Race, Class, and Gender in Black Women's Literature.* Knoxville: University of Tennessee Press, 1997.

Schomburg Center of the New York Public Library. *The Black New Yorkers: The Schomburg Illustrated Chronology.* New York: John Wiley and Sons, 1998.

— Aberjhani

Apollo Theatre

Neither the GREAT DEPRESSION nor competition in the form of first-rate clubs stopped HARLEM's Apollo Theatre from becoming one of the most enduring and famous entertainment centers in the world.

Credited with helping to launch the careers of some of the most famous black entertainers of the 1900s, the Apollo Theatre started out as a small club located above the Harlem Opera House on 125th Street. The owner was Sidney Cohen, who also operated the Roxy and Gaiety Clubs. Along with Frank Schiffman and Leo Brecher, who became business partners, Cohen was one of a few whites who owned all of the major entertainment outlets in HARLEM. Schiffman and Brecher in particular had been instrumental in making such entertainment accessible to African Americans, as both entertainers and audience members, through such locations as the LAFAYETTE THEATER, the LINCOLN THEATRE, and the Harlem Opera House. Amateur Night, an event that would become one of the Apollo's most popular, was still held regularly at the Harlem Opera House when Ella Fitzgerald won it in 1934.

The ever-increasing African-American presence in Harlem was not lost on white businessmen and club operators who often competed for top entertainers, the best locations, and the dollars and pocket change of black audiences. Cohen remained a leading competitor long enough to move the Apollo Theatre from its original location to 253 West 125th Street. Until then, the location was known as Hurtig and Seamon's Burlesque. A music hall and vaudeville house that specialized in risqué entertainment, Hurtig and Seamon's was one of the establishments to come under attack when Mayor FIORELLO HENRY LA GUARDIA campaigned against burlesques in 1933. La Guardia's campaign coupled with the increasing drawing power of Broadway made it wise to take black entertainment seriously. Cohen, accordingly, moved the Apollo into the facility for black patronage. Located for a time in its basement was a club for white patronage, Joe Ward's Swannee Club, where JAZZ great LOUIS ARMSTRONG made his New York debut. Eventually, the basement became a rehearsal space for the top acts that began to play the Apollo.

The new Apollo Theatre opened its doors to the public on January 26, 1934. The featured entertainment was "Jazz a la Carte," with a host of singers and dancers that included the Three Rhythm Kings, Aida Ward, Mabel Scott, and Benny Carter and his orchestra. The theater made 1,700 seats available to its patrons and boasted acoustics superior to its neighborhood competition. A year later, ownership of the theater switched hands when Schiffman acquired it following Cohen's death.

From its beginning, the Apollo maintained a policy of patronage open to blacks and whites, an exception to the general policy of segregation in clubs during the period. Though it specialized in black entertainment, the vogue of whites coming uptown to enjoy such entertainment was still strong in 1934. The number of whites making the trip uptown was reduced following the HARLEM RIOT of 1935 and decreased considerably more after the riot of 1943. In addition to functioning as a performance outlet for black entertainers, during the mid-1930s it was the only major theater to hire blacks as regular employees holding such positions as stage managers, musical directors, light technicians, and sound technicians.

The Apollo Theatre picked up where the Lafayette had left off, with a smorgasbord of entertainment that offered tap-dancing duos, blues singers, jazz musicians, comics, movies, and bona fide play productions. While much of its entertainment might be described as predictable, other parts were not. The gospel music that evolved out of the spirituals would seemingly belong more in the black church than the black club but the Apollo leaned more toward the excellence of a given group's presentation than the genre of music performed. The *NEW YORK AGE* protested that some of its programs were too close to the older styles of vaudeville, with performers still made up in blackface and some of the dancers' routines too sexually suggestive. The theater's immediate success, however, was not something anyone could debate as crowds lined up weekly to see such shows as *Modern Rhythm, Harlem Goes Hollywood, Hill Billy Revue,* and *Ebony Showboat.* Acknowledging the popularity of one of its principal competitors, the Apollo also presented an annual COTTON CLUB Show.

Moreover, Schiffman often maintained he was determined to make the Apollo a true part of the Harlem community rather than simply another business establishment. Opinions divide regarding his sincerity, yet programs such as one headlining a visit from the Scottsboro Boys, nine young black men accused of raping two young white women, clearly involved more than entertainment. Similarly, fund-raising events for the NATIONAL ASSOCIATION FOR THE ADVANCEMENT OF COLORED PEOPLE (NAACP) and the NATIONAL URBAN LEAGUE were held at the theater.

Emcee RALPH COOPER moved his Amateur Night, an event originally held at the Lafayette Theater, to the Apollo in 1935. Amateur Night provided an open invitation for anyone considering becoming a professional performer to test their talents before two audiences. The first was the very live audience within the theater. The second was the audience listening to the program through broadcasts by radio station WMCA and almost two dozen national affiliates. Sarah Vaughan and Pearl Bailey, along with the aforementioned Ella Fitzgerald, were Amateur Night winners who went on to spectacular entertainment careers.

The radio broadcasts from the Apollo played a significant role in the popularization of SWING music and culture in the 1940s. Like the spirituals and jazz before it, swing was a style of music that got its start in black communities and was refined in the works of such Apollo regulars as DUKE ELLINGTON and COUNT BASIE. White musicians looking for the next big thing in American music found it in swing. Bandleaders such as Charlie Barnet, Woody Herman, and Bunny Berrigan all made the sound the focus of their work and helped create a national craze similar to the jazz mania that swept the United States in the 1920s. CHICK WEBB teamed up with Ella Fitzgerald to make his band one of the hottest in the country. Ironically, the increasing popularity of swing would eventually help expand the market for black talent and take some of the Apollo's top acts on the road away from New York. The same would occur when Dizzy Gillespie and CHARLIE PARKER introduced the even more intense sounds of bebop.

The Apollo Theatre maintained an ongoing daily presentation of entertainment starting at 10 A.M. Cartoons, early movies, and newsreels entertained younger and general audiences before giving way in the evening to a chorus line of beautiful dancers and some of the best musicians in the country. Comedians formed an important part of the theater's lineup. BUTTERBEANS AND SUSIE and PIGMEAT MARKHAM were vaudeville veterans who became favorites at the theater. STEPIN FETCHIT was not only among the most famous and successful of the comedians but one of the most controversial due to the stereotypical roles he played in movies and the lavish lifestyle he flaunted offscreen. Timmy Rogers was one of the first comedians at the Apollo, and in the country, to go on record in 1943 in protest against performing in blackface. Insisting that black comedians could and should rely on the quality of their material for laughs, Rogers dressed in a tuxedo to deliver his act. Many older black performers at first resisted the trend to do away with blackface but soon followed Rogers's lead. Moreover, white comedians like Milton Berle and Joey Adams agreed enough with Rogers that they unabashedly sat in the audience studying their acts and, reportedly, sometimes adapting material for their own performances.

A downside to the success of the Apollo Theatre was the criminal interest it attracted. It was commonly understood that gangsters took over the Cotton Club after the previous owner, heavyweight boxing champion JOE LOUIS, sold it. They did not take over the Apollo, but owner Frank Schiffman and his sons, Bobby and Jack, did occasionally pay what they called graft money to criminals who disrupted shows or threatened participants when such money was not paid. The more legitimate owners of surrounding restaurants, record stores, and other shops on West 125th Street simply took advantage of the crowds that attended the Apollo's sold-out shows and used the increased traffic to boost their own sales.

The Apollo Theatre audience gained nearly as much fame as its performers when it became recognized simultaneously as one of the most appreciative and discerningly critical audiences in the world. It became a given that any performer who could please the Apollo audience necessarily had what it took to make it in show business anywhere in the world. Conversely, performers who had already "made it" in the commonly accepted sense of the term sometimes played the Apollo to prove their success was not a fluke or simply to enjoy the audience's response. Johnny Mathis, Eartha Kitt, and JOSEPHINE BAKER were well-established international stars when they played the theater in the 1950s. At the same time, newer talents continued to find their way to the Apollo's increasingly legendary stage. A teenaged Esther Phillips sang the BLUES like someone three times her age when on stage and then reverted to typical adolescent conduct once outside the theater's doors. Leslie Uggams was only nine when she began to sing, dance, and charm her way into the hearts of the Apollo audience.

The 1960s ushered in the era of rhythm and blues, and the Apollo became home both to some of the most successful individual musical acts in entertainment history and to some of the most star-packed revues ever featured at a single location on a single evening. The Motown Revue gave Harlem front-row seats to Detroit's stable of megastars: Smoky Robinson and the Miracles, the Supremes, the Temptations, Martha and the Vandellas, the Four Tops, and others creating the music that would go down in history as the Motown Sound. The genius of Ray Charles, Sam Cooke, Dionne Warwick, and Nancy Wilson was noted and promoted as exactly that: musical genius which crowds lined up nightly to experience.

James Brown created an entertainment revolution at the theater when his performances repeatedly brought in so much money that he requested a percentage of the box office profits as opposed to a single payment amount stipulated by contract. It was a request that proved beneficial to both parties when Brown recorded his landmark 1963 album, *James Brown Live at the Apollo.*

Toward the end of the 1960s and going into the 1970s, the Apollo Theatre's status as the dominant venue for black entertainment began to decline as increased integration made more locations available to black entertainers and audiences. Stars whose careers had taken them beyond the range of money they could make at the Apollo periodically returned to the theater and gave performances out of a sense of loyalty and for the special rapport they shared with the Apollo audience. The theater also began to premiere the growing number of black films produced in the 1970s. It was not enough, however, to keep the theater open, and Bobby Schiffman closed it in January 1976.

In May 1978, the Apollo reopened for a year before problems with taxes caused it to shut down again. Occasional live shows were held until the last one presented by Parliament and Funkadelic in March 1980. However, the Harlem Commonwealth Council and Perry Sutton's Inner City Theatre Group acquired the theater in 1982 and two years later, in February 1984, welcomed a crowd of 1,000 to a modernized version of Amateur Night. Perhaps even more significant, in 1983 the landmark commission declared the Apollo Theatre a national landmark, and in 1992, the Apollo Theatre Foundation was established and the facility was presented as a gift to the Harlem community. The Apollo Theatre remains synonymous with excellence in black entertainment, as its Amateur Night programs featuring novices and professionals are seen weekly on national television.

Further Reading

Cooper, Ralph. *Amateur Night at the Apollo: Ralph Cooper Presents Five Decades of Great Entertainment.* New York: HarperTrade, 1990.

Peretti, Burton W. *The Creation of Jazz: Music, Race, and Culture in Urban America (Music in American Life).* Chicago: University of Illinois Press, 1992.

Peterson, Bernard L. *The African American Theatre Directory, 1816–1960: A Comprehensive Guide to Early Black Theatre Organizations, Companies, Theatres, and Performing Groups.* Westport, Conn.: Greenwood Publishing Group, Inc., 1997.

— Aberjhani

Appearances

Appearances was the first full-length drama by an African American produced on a Broadway stage. It made its debut at the Frolic Theater on October 13, 1925.

Written by GARLAND ANDERSON, a former bellhop turned playwright, the play broke the Broadway color barrier both as a drama written by a black man and because it featured a biracial cast of 11 white actors and three black actors. The African Americans sharing the stage with their white coworkers were Evelyn Mason, Doe Doe Green, and Lionel Monagas.

As JAMES WELDON JOHNSON noted in *Black Manhattan,* the drama behind the production of *Appearances* was as compelling as the play itself. The author had no more than a fourth-grade education and was working as a bellhop at San Francisco's Braeburn Hotel Apartments when he wrote the play. He did so in a daring move to demonstrate for audiences his belief in the teachings of Christian Science while simultaneously creating a vehicle to help promote those same beliefs.

With its focus on a metaphysically inclined black bellhop who is falsely accused of assaulting a white woman, Anderson's play in 1925 was as bold in its political implications as it was in its spiritual overtones. In short, he reversed the social trend of white mobs mindlessly condemning black men to death by LYNCHING and presented a Christ-like black male character in the form of Charles Sanderson who asserted his moral superiority by forgiving the mob even as it was calling for his death. By testifying to nothing but his faith, Sanderson reveals the truth behind various *Appearances:* the white woman screaming rape turns out to be a black woman, a minstrel-like black man is shown to be a champion boxer, and a simple bellhop the author of different people's destinies.

Anderson won support for his play from a number of political and entertainment personalities. Al Jolson sponsored him on his first visit to New York. Lester A. Sagar of the Central Theater agreed to share the cost of producing the play with two of Anderson's San Francisco patrons, H. S. and Fergus Wilkinson. He also managed a visit to President Calvin Coolidge and walked away from the White House with an endorsement of his play that made its way into the newspapers.

Following its opening, *Appearances* ran for two years with productions in Los Angeles, San Francisco, CHICAGO, and Seattle. It played a return engagement in New York on April 1, 1929, at the Hudson Theater and ran for another 24 performances. In 1930, Anderson took the play overseas for its debut in London. There, it made a star out of Doe Doe Green in the apparently stereotypical "coon" role of Rufus George Washington Jones. Despite Lionel Monagas's unambiguous portrayal of the sagacious Carl, it was Green's name that dominated even that of the play's in England.

Louis Armstrong, with trumpet in foreground, was a pioneer of jazz and remains one of the most acclaimed figures in the history of the music. He is shown here in 1937. *(Library of Congress, Prints & Photographs Division [LC-USZ62-118977])*

Further Reading

Baker, Houston A. *Modernism and the Harlem Renaissance.* Chicago: University of Chicago Press, 1990.

Hatch, James V., and Ted Shine. *Black Theatre U.S.A.* New York: The Free Press, 1996.

— Aberjhani

Armstrong, Louis (Daniel Louis Armstrong, Satchmo, Pops) (1901–1971) *jazz musician*

Louis Armstrong was a founding father of JAZZ, also called African-American classical music. With the force of his searing trumpet and hoarse singing voice, he brought world recognition to jazz as an art form and used his status as a celebrity to battle racial segregation.

Daniel Louis Armstrong, grandson of former slaves, was born on August 4, 1901, in the JIM CROW segregated city of NEW ORLEANS, Louisiana, but usually cited his birth as Independence Day, July 4, 1900. His mother, Mary Albert, was a domestic worker and prostitute, and his father, William Armstrong, was a turpentine worker. He had a sister named Lucy. William Armstrong abandoned his family when his son was a small child, and Louis Armstrong was raised by his paternal grandmother, Josephine, in the rough neighborhood of Storyville in New Orleans's Third Ward. Armstrong sang in the church choir while growing up and often visited a section of New Orleans called Brick Row where he listened to musicians play. He and his friends sang in the streets for spare change. He got a job selling coal for the Karnofsky family, rag and coal merchants, who loaned him $5.00 to purchase his first cornet from a pawn shop.

At the age of 12, Armstrong fired off a gun filled with blanks on New Year's Day, January 1, 1913. For this act, he was then placed in a Colored Waif's home, where Peter Davis, a janitor and music teacher, recognized the young boy's talent and encouraged him to play the alto horn, bugle, and cornet. Armstrong became the bandleader at the orphanage, leading the band in street parades. He spent one and a half years in the home, then was released in the custody of his father, who, although remarried, eventually sent Louis back to his mother.

By the time Armstrong was 17 years old, he worked a number of odd jobs, including shoveling coal. He also practiced playing the cornet until he became good enough to play full-time at nightclubs. He learned to read music and played on steamers with Fate Marable's band. He was still 17 when he gained a mentor in KING OLIVER, who was also a cornetist and who was then playing in Kid Ory's Jazz Band. When Oliver left for CHICAGO, Armstrong took his place in the band.

Nicknamed "Satchelmouth" (later shortened to "Satchmo"), Armstrong traveled to Chicago in 1922, where he joined King Oliver's Creole Jazz Band. Armstrong made his recording debut with Oliver, recording *Chimes Blues* in 1923. To add "sweet to sugar," Armstrong was smitten by Oliver's pianist, Lillian Hardin, and married her on February 25, 1924. It was a second marriage for them both. Armstrong had married a prostitute, Daisy, in 1918.

Lil Hardin was born in Memphis, Tennessee, on February 3, 1898. She had attended FISK UNIVERSITY with dreams of becoming a concert pianist but left school and moved to Chicago in 1917. Hardin was a musical innovator who had led her own bands and whose husband performed with her. A doting wife, she wrote material and sang on recordings done by Armstrong's Hot Five, sometimes called Lil's Hot Shots, studied tailoring, and made a tuxedo for him. Some of her compositions are *Struttin' with Some Barbecue,* which she wrote with her husband, and *Just for a Thrill* (which became a hit for Ray Charles in 1959).

Right after his 1924 marriage, Armstrong went to NEW YORK CITY to work with FLETCHER HENDERSON's band at the Roseland Ballroom, and he toured with Henderson until 1925. Armstrong's notoriety grew and he accompanied blues singers BESSIE SMITH and Mamie Smith on their recordings. He returned to Chicago and began recording with his own bands, Hot Five and Hot Seven, on the Okeh label. With his band, he sang for the first time, in an honest but gravelly voice, performing the improvisational scat vocals on *Heebie Jeebies.* Going back to New York, he played at CONNIE'S INN in HARLEM in 1929 and performed on stage in a musical revue, *HOT CHOCOLATES*, at the Hudson Theatre on Broadway. By the mid-1930s, Armstrong was earning $8,000 per week. He divorced Hardin in 1938. With his fourth wife, Lucille, he purchased an 11-room, two-and-half-story, red brick row house in 1943 in Corona, New York, in the borough of Queens.

In 1936, Armstrong performed with Bing Crosby in the film *Pennies from Heaven,* played a major role in the film *New Orleans* in the 1940s with Billie Holiday, and appeared in *Artists and Models, Going Places,* and *Every Day's a Holiday,* all in 1937; *Cabin in the Sky* (1942); *Pillar to Post* (1945); *The Strip, Glory Alley, A Song Is Born, The Glenn Miller Story, The Five Pennies, High Society,* and *Jazz on a Summer's Day,* in 1958; *La Paloma, The Night Before the Premiere,* and *Auf Wiedersehen,* all German films in 1959; *A Girl, a Guitar and a Trumpet* in Denmark in 1959; *Paris Blues* with Paul Newman, Sydney Poitier, and Diahann Carroll (1960); *Where the Boys Are* (1965); *A Man Called Adam* (1966); and *Hello Dolly* (1969) with Barbra Streisand. Armstrong also played the character Bottom on stage in *Swingin' the Dream* (1939). In all, the trumpeter Armstrong appeared in 24 motion pictures.

During the 1930s, his performances included engagements with Luis Russell's orchestra at Frank Sebastian's Cotton Club in California. In July 1932, he embarked on his first European trip. It was during this visit to the London Palladium that Daniel Louis "Satchelmouth" Armstrong got the nickname "Satchmo." An editor named P. Mathison Brooks could not precisely articulate "Satchelmouth" and started to call him "Satchmo." He returned to Europe in 1933 for a tour that lasted until January 1935.

Critics noted the emotional force of Armstrong's trumpet playing, which literally blew out his top lip, and his gruff voice and "scat" singing. To soothe his lips, he was given a lifetime supply of salve by the Franz Schuritz Company. Armstrong won appreciation as a popular singer with the hits *Mack the Knife* (1956) and *Hello Dolly* (1964). His raspy rendition of *What a Wonderful World* (1968) became the theme song for the film *Good Morning, Vietnam* in 1987. His personal favorite was *It's Sleepy Time Down South,* and he closed every show with it throughout his career.

In January 1944, during the bop era, the *Esquire* magazine jazz music polls recognized Armstrong as a top soloist, who later won a number of times for best vocalist and trumpeter. Recognized as well in international magazine polls, he celebrated his victory by playing the first jazz program at the Metropolitan Opera House in New York. He later played Carnegie Hall in 1947. He then assembled a group called the All Stars—with pianist Earl Hines, bass player Milt Hinton, drummer Cozy Cole, and others—with whom he toured France in 1948, Japan in 1954, Ghana in 1956, and Spoleto, Italy, in 1959. He also recorded during this period tributes to the legendary musicians W. C. HANDY and FATS WALLER on Columbia records and duets with song stylist Ella Fitzgerald and pianist Oscar Peterson on Verve records.

Punctuating his performances with broad grins and growls, Armstrong seemed to be perpetually happy until it came to Jim Crow segregation, such as when white citizens rioted to prevent black students from integrating schools in Little Rock, Arkansas in 1957. He spoke out against such incidents, and doing so at times cost him engagements. Those African Americans who viewed Armstrong as a modern-day minstrel saw his public protests against racism as his redeeming shining moment. He refused to visit foreign countries as a representative of the United States because of the extreme racism practiced in the South. In the eyes of many he became a champion in the battle for civil rights.

A heart attack in 1959 forced Armstrong to reduce his performance activities. Nevertheless, with the increasing success of the late 1950s Civil Rights movement, he began once more to perform outside the United States. Between 1961 and 1967, the U.S. State Department sponsored Armstrong in goodwill concert tours for America, resulting in sellout concerts around the world. Thousands attended an open-air concert in Africa, and President Kwame Nkrumah of Ghana gave a reception for Armstrong at his guest house. "Satchmo," now an ambassador for jazz music, also traveled during this decade to Mexico, Australia, New Zealand, Hong Kong, Korea, Japan, Hawaii, India, Hungary, Holland, Sweden, and Denmark. He played before 93,000 jazz enthusiasts in the Budapest Football Stadium.

A second heart attack in 1969 prevented Armstrong from continuing to play with the energy and productivity of earlier years. Yet, for a man with a weak heart, he had a big heart. His Louis Armstrong Educational Foundation, with funds derived from his royalties, helped support music education programs in public schools, a pediatric music therapy program at Beth Israel Hospital, and the Lincoln Center Jazz for Young People Concerts directed by trumpeter and composer Wynton Marsalis. For this, and for influencing generations of jazz musicians, he was endearingly called "Pops." By 1983, the Louis Armstrong Educational Foundation had given away $10 million.

Despite doctors' orders that he should stop performing, Armstrong continued working. He sang at the Shrine Auditorium in Los Angeles, appeared in a special *Salute to Satch,* costarred with Pearl Bailey on stage, did a benefit concert in London, and played the Empire Room at the Waldorf-Astoria in New York. He suffered another heart attack on March 5, 1971, and died in his sleep on July 6, 1971. He was survived by his fourth wife, Lucille. His second wife, Lil Hardin, died on August 27, 1971, while playing a concert in tribute to "Satchmo" at Chicago's Civic Center Plaza.

In 2002, the Armstrong archives were placed in the Rosenthal Library of Queens College, part of the City University of New York system, at 65-30 Kissena Boulevard in Flushing, Queens, New York.

Further Reading

Armstrong, Louis. *Louis Armstrong, in His Own Words: Selected Writings.* New York: Oxford University Press, 1999.

Armstrong, Louis, and Leslie Gourse. *Louis' Children: American Jazz Singers (updated).* Lanham, Md.: Rowman and Littlefield Publishers, Inc. 2001.

Curtis, Nancy C., Ph.D. *Black Heritage Series: An African-American Odyssey and Finder's Guide.* Chicago and London: American Library Association, 1996.

Thompson, Bertram, trans. *Louis Armstrong: The Definitive Biography.* New York: Peter Lang Publishing, Inc., 1999.

— Sandra L. West

art and the Harlem Renaissance

The art of African Americans in the 1920s went through an evolution on canvas, in murals at black college campuses and other public buildings, through sculpture, through photography, and in FOLK ART, to emerge as the unique, timeless art of the Harlem Renaissance.

The GREAT MIGRATION of African Americans was a vital ingredient in the creation of this new art. In droves, especially during the 1920s and 1940s, African Americans left lives of poverty and racism in the South for more promising opportunities in such Northern locations as Detroit, CHICAGO, and NEW YORK CITY. The result was cultural intermingling, cultural exchange, cultural exploitation, and cultural genius that unleashed a raw artistry. Previously, the creativity of African Americans in the South had been expressed through front-porch storytelling, folk art sculpture, quilting, plantation dancing, and fine and craft arts.

Rhodes Scholar Dr. ALAIN LOCKE and *CRISIS* editor Dr. W. E. B. DU BOIS helped provide social and educational guidance for the migrating and developing artists of the *NEW NEGRO* movement. In his speech, "Criteria of Negro Art," Du Bois referred to the experience of the New Negro in the new land as a race with ". . . new stirrings; stirrings of the beginning of a new appreciation of joy, of a new desire to create, of a new will to be. . . ." He encouraged the black artist to seize upon this exciting time to honor the Negro past with an accurate self-portrait for future generations. Du Bois also saw art as propaganda and encouraged the new artists to use their gifts as political tools.

Dr. Locke pointed out in the *New Negro* anthology that blacks must "be seen through other than the dusty spectacles of past controversy. "The black artist was the primary catalyst by which to dispel the myth that the Negro had no cultural heritage or worthy lineage," Locke wrote.

Not all black visual artists fully agreed with Dr. Locke's and Dr. Du Bois's interpretation of their roles as black artists. They did not want to exchange one yoke for another, and this feeling was equally dominant among younger black writers, such as those who edited the literary journal *FIRE!!* In visual art quarters, for just one example, award-winning painter PALMER COLE HAYDEN started his career by creating caricatures of black people that did not sit well with the masses of dignified New Negroes.

Most artists understood the necessity of using culture to help elevate the political and social status of African Americans. They chronicled the history of black life before and during the American experience and showed that the Negro's abilities and quest for the American Dream were equal to those of his white brother. As the artists created, a modern school of art was born that depicted blacks devoid of garish caricature, idiotic buffoonery, or rural romanticism. The artwork included instead a painful but extraordinary history time line that extended into antiquity. Artists painted religious scenes presenting expressions of faith and sculpted momentous figures reflecting hope and determination. They photographed high-stepping young dancers at Harlem dance halls. They painted wall after wall of black heroes, to educate and empower their people, and of black migrants moving north during the Great Migration.

Among the artists of the era, JACOB ARMSTEAD LAWRENCE and ROMARE BEARDON, ARCHIBALD JOHN MOTLEY, JR., META VAUX WARRICK FULLER, and AARON DOUGLAS produced works that defined the Harlem Renaissance. The aforementioned are very well-known names, but the era was teeming with talent that also included the contributions of lesser known figures such as William Edouard Scott and Charles Sebree.

William Edouard Scott (1884–1964), born in Indianapolis, Indiana, was a muralist and apprentice to expatriate painter

HENRY OSSAWA TANNER in PARIS. Scott won first prize for a mural he created for the Chicago Shakespeare Festival in 1907, and he went on to paint many murals in public buildings around the country. He won a HARMON FOUNDATION gold medal in 1927. Four years later, he won a Rosenwald Fellowship to go to Haiti and paint the indigenous people, producing such works as *Haitian Man.*

Charles Sebree (1914–58) illustrated books for the Harlem Renaissance writers and worked on a WORKS PROGRESS ADMINISTRATION (WPA) project. Born in Madisonville, Kentucky, Sebree worked for the Esel Division of the Illinois Federal Art Project, a division of the WPA, from 1936 to 1938. Sebree painted *The Clown* and illustrated *The Lost Zoo,* written by poet COUNTEE CULLEN. Sebree's work was included in the art collection of the SCHOMBURG CENTER FOR RESEARCH IN BLACK CULTURE.

As evidenced by this poster for the Harlem Community Art Center, sponsored by the Works Progress Administration Federal Art Project, ca. 1936 to 1938, members of the general community and professional artists alike enjoyed exploring their visual creativity during the Great Depression. *(Library of Congress, Prints & Photographs Division [LC-USZC2-5383])*

Equally productive artists who contributed to the New Negro movement were Ronald C. Moody, Henry Bozeman Jones, John Wesley Hardwick, Frank Joseph Dillon, Samuel Joseph Brown, Jr., and William Braxton.

Ronald C. Moody (1900–84) was a sculptor born in Jamaica, West Indies, who moved to London in 1923. In 1938, he participated in the Harmon Foundation exhibition. His most noted works are *Wohin* (1935), *Midonz* (*Goddess of Transmutation,* 1937), and *Tacet* (1938).

Henry Bozeman Jones (1889–1963) of Philadelphia, Pennsylvania, was an illustrator of children's books who held a solo exhibition in 1933 at the 135th Street Branch of the New York Public Library. As a painter, he exhibited nature scenes and religious works at Harmon Foundation shows in 1929, 1930, 1931, and 1933.

John Wesley Hardwick (1891–1968) of Indianapolis, Indiana, won the Harmon Foundation bronze medal in fine arts in 1927, and in 1933 he won a prize for outstanding artwork in the Indiana State Exhibition. He painted murals in the Indianapolis area. An undated oil painting by Hardwick, *Salt Lick Creek-Brown County,* is in the collection of the Indiana State Museum.

Frank Joseph Dillon (1866–1954) of Mt. Holly, New Jersey, painted still life portraits and designed stained glass windows. He also won an Honorable Mention in the 1929 Harmon Foundation art shows.

Samuel Joseph Brown, Jr., (1907–) was born in Wilmington, North Carolina, and grew up in Philadelphia where he still resided in 2002. Brown produced abstract and realistic watercolors for the Federal Art Project of the WPA from 1933 to 1935.

William Braxton (1878–1932) is considered one of the first African-American expressionist painters. He was born in WASHINGTON, D.C., worked as a valet and Pullman porter, and produced *Seascape, Portrait of Ira Aldridge,* and *Portrait of Alexander Pushkin.* Aldridge was one of the leading Shakespearean actors of the 19th century, and Pushkin was a major African-Russian poet. Braxton's major work, *Figural Study,* is now in the collection of the Schomburg Center for Research in Black Culture.

Photographers of the Harlem Renaissance included the legendary JAMES VAN DER ZEE, Addison Scurlock, P. H. Polk, Hansen Austin, King Daniel Ganaway, and Morgan and Marvin Smith. These black photographers established small studios in the black community. They supplied black newspapers and mainstream magazines with candid yet complementary documentation of black America: the stylish middle class, the high achievers, the honest working class, and the glittery entertainers.

Addison Scurlock (1883–1964) was the official photographer at HOWARD UNIVERSITY in Washington, D.C. As such, he captured the essence of that community's black, educated middle class. He opened his first studio in 1911 and operated it with his wife and sons until his death. His sons, Robert and George, still maintained the Scurlock Studios in 2002.

Photographer P. H. Polk (birth date presently unknown) opened his first studio at Tuskegee Institute in Tuskegee, Alabama, in 1927. In 1928, he joined the faculty of Tuskegee's Photography Department and later became its head. He photographed prominent visitors to the Institute such as singer/actor and humanitarian PAUL ROBESON and made a series of photographs of scientist George Washington Carver.

Hansen Austin (1910–96) was a Caribbean, grassroots photographer who chronicled 1930s Harlem life. Born in the Virgin Islands, Austin moved to New York in 1928. A musician as well as a visual artist, he played drums in local Harlem nightclubs and took pictures of neighborhood street scenes. He served in World War II as a photographer's mate, 2nd class, with the U.S. Navy and Office of War Information. After the war, he returned home to Harlem to open a studio on West 135th Street. His work was published in the *AMSTERDAM NEWS, NEW YORK AGE, African Express,* and *People's View.* More than 20,000 of his photographs are in the private collection of the Schomburg Center for Research in Black Culture.

King Daniel Ganaway (1883–unknown) was a prizewinning photographer in the 1930s. Born in Murfeesboro, Tennessee, he moved to Chicago in 1914. In 1918, Ganaway won first prize in the John Wanamaker Annual Exhibition of photographs. He was staff photographer for *The Bee,* a black Chicago weekly newspaper, and is well known for his scenes of Chicago's industrial neighborhoods and waterfront. Ganaway's photography was exhibited in the "Century of Progress" exposition in 1933.

Prolific social and political photographers Marvin and Morgan Smith were twins born on February 16, 1910, in Nicholasville, Kentucky, the only children of Charles Smith and Allena Hutchinson Smith. When they graduated from Dunbar High School in 1933, they relocated to New York, found employment as laborers with the WPA, and helped to create the Shakespeare Garden in Central Park. They studied at the Savage School of Arts and Crafts at 315 West 126th Street, administered by sculptor AUGUSTA FELLS SAVAGE, and joined the artistic THREE-O-SIX crowd at 306 West 141st Street in Harlem, led by CHARLES HENRY ALSTON. They submitted their photographs of Harlem life to the *PITTSBURGH COURIER*, the Baltimore *Afro-American,* and the New York *Amsterdam News* and were paid $1.50 per image.

Their career took off in 1937 when Morgan won the *New York Herald Tribune* Kodak amateur photography contest and was offered a position as photographer for the *AMSTERDAM NEWS.* In 1939, they opened their first studio at 141 West 125th Street, next to the APOLLO THEATRE, and stayed at this location until 1968.

The Morgan brothers are noted for their snapshots of the first black trooper in New York City, the first black woman juror, and the stars who worked at the Apollo Theatre. They snapped the New York Black Yankees versus the Philadelphia Stars in 1936; inaugural poet Maya Angelou in her early career as a dancer with PEARL PRIMUS; artist RICHMOND BARTHÉ with his bust of Abraham Lincoln; the legendary Nat King Cole Trio in 1940; and the high-flying, tap dancing NICHOLAS BROTHERS in 1937. Marvin worked as chief petty officer of photography in the navy during World War II and was the first African American to attend the Naval Air Station School of Photography and Motion Pictures at Pensacola, Florida. He returned home to work in the news service Morgan had established to provide photographs to the black press. In 1942, Morgan worked as the photographer for the *People's Voice,* a weekly edited by ADAM CLAYTON POWELL, JR., pastor of ABYSSINIAN BAPTIST CHURCH, and New York's charismatic congressman.

The twins, who believed that black history was made every day and made sure they were on hand to record it, worked so well as a team that they did not allow publishers to know which one of them took a photo. Instead, they labeled their work "M. Smith," or "M. & M. Smith." Theirs was always a collective effort. They were adamant about not displaying the black community in a disparaging light, and refused lucrative photo assignments—such as a photographic study of black street gangs—that might have increased their personal salary significantly but also shamed their community. Morgan Smith died in 1993, and Marvin died on November 9, 2003.

The work of the artists of this era was published profusely in the important periodicals of the day, including *Crisis, OPPORTUNITY,* and *New Masses.* In addition to painting, sculpting, and photography, the arts explosion during the Harlem Renaissance included a profound development of community art organizations, some of which exist into the 21st century. The Harmon Foundation, Harlem Arts Guild, HARLEM COMMUNITY ART CENTER, SOUTH SIDE COMMUNITY ART CENTER in Chicago (still existing in 2002), and the Augusta Savage Art Workshop are a few organizations founded during the cultural flowering of the Harlem Renaissance.

Further Reading

Miers, Charles, ed. *Harlem Renaissance: Art of Black America.* New York: Harry N. Abrams, Inc., 1994.

Porter, James A. *Modern Negro Art.* Washington, D.C.: Howard University Press, 1992.

Powell, Richard J. *Black Art and Culture in the 20th Century.* London: Thames and Hudson Ltd., 1997.

Powell, Richard J., and David A. Bailey. *Rhapsodies in Black: Art in the Harlem Renaissance.* Berkeley: University of California Press, 1997.

Reynolds, Gary A., and Beryl J. Wright. *Against The Odds: African-American Artists and the Harmon Foundation.* Newark N.J.: The Newark Museum, 1989.

— Sandra L. West

Artis, William Ellisworth (1914–1977) *sculptor*

William Ellisworth Artis studied at the Harlem studios of legendary sculptor AUGUSTA FELLS SAVAGE during the 1930s, participated in HARMON FOUNDATION exhibitions, and is best known for his sensitive terra-cotta depictions of African-American children.

Artis was born in Washington, North Carolina, in 1914, but relocated to NEW YORK CITY in 1927. A natural educator, he taught sculpture, arts, and crafts at the 135th Street branch of the Harlem YMCA from the time he was in high school until 1941.

He studied sculpture and pottery under Augusta Savage at her studio school. Artis was a participant in the Harmon Foundation exhibition in 1933 where he won the John Hope Prize in sculpture. Among his notable works is *Head of a Girl* (1933). Because he was a Harmon Foundation winner, Artis received a scholarship to the Art Students League (1933–34) and studied ceramics at the Craft Students League and the Greenwich House Ceramic Center (1936–38).

On a Harmon Foundation fellowship in 1946, Artis toured black southern colleges to demonstrate the art of sculpture. He was awarded a coveted Julius Rosenwald Fellowship at Tuskegee Institute but, determined to get a solid formal education, Artis attended the New York State College of Ceramics at Alfred, New York (1940 and 1946–47). In 1950 he received a B.F.A. from Syracuse University and an M.F.A. in 1951. Additionally, he received a B.A. in 1955 from Nebraska State College and studied on the graduate level at Pennsylvania State University from 1956 to 1959.

Artis served as professor of ceramics at Nebraska Teachers College (1956–66) and professor of art at Mankato State College in Minnesota (1966–75). He died in 1977. His work is included in many collections, including those at Atlanta University, HOWARD UNIVERSITY, FISK UNIVERSITY, and the National Portrait Gallery of the Smithsonian Institution.

Further Reading

MacKlin, A. D. *Biographical History of African-American Artists, A–Z.* Lewiston, N.Y.: Edwin Mellen Press, 2000.

Powell, Richard J. *Black Art: A Cultural History (World of Art Series).* New York and London: Thames and Hudson, 2003.

Reynolds, Gary, and Beryl J. Wright. *Against The Odds: African-American Artists and the Harmon Foundation.* Newark, N.J.: The Newark Museum, 1989.

— Sandra L. West

Association for the Study of Negro Life

The Association for the Study of Negro Life was founded on September 9, 1915, in CHICAGO, by renowned historian CARTER GODWIN WOODSON to establish an organization dedicated to the research and development of information regarding peoples of African descent. Now known as the Association for the Study of Afro-American Life and History, Incorporated, the organization was created with Woodson's hope that it would help promote "harmony between the races by acquainting the one with the other."

The initial meeting of the Association for the Study of Afro-American Life and History was held at the Wabash Avenue Young Men's Christian Association (YMCA) on South Side Chicago. In addition to Woodson, its founding members were YMCA director A. L. Jackson, insurance man J. E. Stamps, educator W. B. Hartgrove, and Dr. George Cleveland Hall. The association was incorporated on October 3, 1915, under the laws of WASHINGTON, D.C. Three months later, Woodson began publishing the *Journal of Negro History.* The journal has served since as both an organ promoting the goals of the association and an ongoing record of the contributions of blacks to history.

From the day of its founding, financing the organization remained a challenge and Woodson provided funds primarily out of his own income from teaching and from the sale of his books and articles. In 1920, he started Associated Publishers to strengthen the organization's finances by publishing and selling his own works and those of other scholars writing about the history of Africans and African Americans. To help him meet the demands of operating a publishing company, a journal, and teaching responsibilities, Woodson hired the writer LANGSTON HUGHES as his personal assistant in 1925.

In February 1926, the Association for the Study of Afro-American Life and History observed its first Black History Week. Created specifically to acknowledge, celebrate, and encourage achievements in black history, the original week was officially expanded to a month in 1976 as part of the country's bicentennial celebrations. Woodson made a practice of assigning a theme to the annual observance and handing out informational packets on black history, a tradition that is still practiced by the association in modern times.

The association celebrated its 20th anniversary with a meeting in Chicago in 1936. Joining Woodson for the event were sociologist E. Franklin Frazier and researcher Vivian G. Harsh. Also in 1936, educator Mary McLeod Bethune became president of the association. Under her leadership, the organization published its first *Negro History Bulletin* in 1937. It was presented as an instructional tool for teachers. Bethune remained president of the association until 1951, a year after Woodson's death.

The Association for the Study of Afro-American Life and History is currently headquartered in Silver Spring, Maryland. In 2002 it had a membership of 2,500. It is headed by President Dr. Gloria Harper Dickinson, Vice President Mrs. Shirley Kilpatrick, and Executive Director Irena Webster.

Further Reading

Durden, Robert Franklin. *Carter G. Woodson: Father of African American History.* Berkeley Heights, N.J.: Enslow Publishers, Incorporated, 1998.

Woodson, Carter G., and Kunjufu, Jawanza (introduction). *The Miseducation of the Negro.* Chicago: African American Images, 2000.

— Aberjhani

Atlanta University See ART AND THE HARLEM RENAISSANCE.

Austin, Hansen See ART AND THE HARLEM RENAISSANCE.

Autobiography of an Ex-Colored Man, The

Author, composer, and political activist JAMES WELDON JOHNSON published *The Autobiography of an Ex-Colored*

Man anonymously in 1912 and, with the help of arts patron CARL VAN VECHTEN, reissued it under his name in the 1920s.

James Weldon Johnson was an extremely versatile man. Active in Republican Party politics in 1904, by 1906 he was appointed U.S. consul to Puerto Cabello, Venezuela, by President Theodore Roosevelt. While in Venezuela, Johnson wrote his only novel, *The Autobiography of an Ex-Colored Man,* a narrative about race relations and "passing," the practice of light-complexioned African Americans identifying themselves as white although they are of African ancestry. When the novel first appeared, sales were sluggish and reviews tepid. With its second publication during the *NEW NEGRO* movement, the spelling of the word *"Ex-Colored"* in the title was changed to *"Ex-Coloured."* Johnson's renown—he was by then the director of the NATIONAL ASSOCIATION FOR THE ADVANCEMENT OF COLORED PEOPLE—improved the reception of the book.

The nameless, main male character of the book is light-skinned enough to "pass" for white, yet identifies with his mother's black race until he witnesses a mob of whites setting fire to a black man in the South. Traumatized, the young man is so plagued with feelings of humiliation associated with his race that he, once buoyed by aspirations of becoming a musical composer, "passes" into the life of a white businessman. He then finds himself overwhelmed with feelings of failure, shame, and low self-esteem. Johnson wrote the novel not to add to the canon of literature about "passing" but to spotlight the social prejudice and economic injustice that allowed "passing" to be a consideration at all.

In the definitive anthology *The New Caravan,* the editors wrote: "This novel is definitely a forerunner: Southern rural life seen in its own terms, the Bohemian life of Negroes in New York, and the problem of 'passing' are done with quiet realism."

According to literary critic Addison Gayle, Jr., "*The Autobiography of an Ex-Coloured Man* is a conservative document, leaning heavily toward the ideology of the black middle class. Yet Johnson is a racial conservative who wishes to lend credence to characters drawn in the fiction of Griggs [Sutton E. Griggs] and Du Bois [W. E. B. DU BOIS]—characters who, though different from the black poor, are proud of their racial heritage. Unlike Fauset [JESSIE REDMOND FAUSET], he does not frown upon the desire of the mulatto class for assimilation; like her, however, he argues that those with attributes similar to those of whites comprise among themselves a unique, specific group, and it is here, not in the white world, that such people belong."

Upon its initial publication, much of the public thought the 1912 novel was actually Johnson's personal history; to eliminate this confusion he wrote his memoir, *Along This Way,* in 1933. During the Black Arts Movement of the 1960s and 1970s, African Americans rediscovered *The Autobiography of An Ex-Coloured Man,* and Robert A. Bone, a literary critic and editor of *The Negro Novel in America,* applauded Johnson as "the only true artist among the early Negro novelists."

Further Reading

Bone, Robert A. *The Negro Novel in America.* New Haven, Conn.: Yale University Press, 1965.

Brown, Sterling, A. Davis, P. Arthur, and Ulysses Lee. *The Negro Caravan: Writings by American Negroes.* New York: The Dryden Press Publishers, 1941.

Metzger, Linda, senior ed. *Black Writers: A Selection of Sketches from Contemporary Authors.* Detroit, London: Gale Research, 1989.

Smith, Valerie. *Self-Discovery and Authority in Afro-American Narrative.* Cambridge: Harvard University Press, 1991.

Tobert-Rouchaleau, Jane, and Nathan I. Huggins (ed.) *James Weldon Johnson: Author.* Broomall, Penn.: Chelsea House Publishers, 1991.

— Sandra L. West

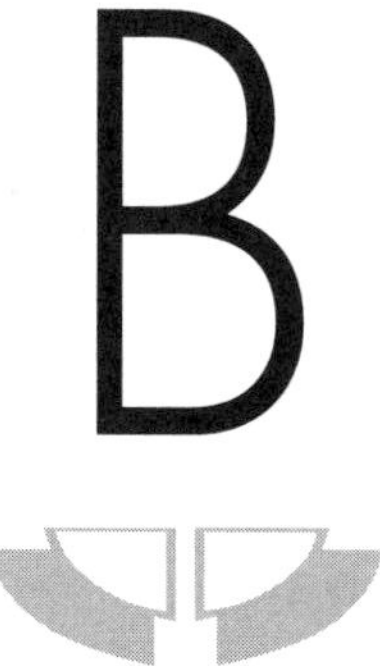

back-to-Africa movement

Attempts to transport free African Americans and slaves from the United States back to Africa and other areas grew into a full-scale movement with the establishment of the American Colonization Society in 1817 and the advocacy of Martin Robinson Delany during the late 1800s. The idea was later associated with the MARCUS GARVEY movement in the 1920s and remained a point of reference for BLACK NATIONALISM during the late 1900s.

The American Colonization Society settled its first group of 80 former slaves and free blacks in Liberia in 1820. The society's motives were questioned by various blacks who believed it wished primarily to remove free African Americans as an obstacle to the enslavement of all blacks in the United States. Despite this, blacks continued to emigrate under the auspices of the American Colonization Society. In 1847, however, enough had settled in Liberia for them to declare independence from the organization. The passage of the Fugitive Slaves Act in 1850 further encouraged African Americans to emigrate if possible and by 1852 approximately 7,500 African Americans had left the United States for Liberia.

Martin Robinson Delany, a physician who along with Frederick Douglass coedited the abolitionist newspaper the *North Star,* was among those free African Americans who distrusted the American Colonization Society. In 1852, Delany authored *The Condition, Elevation, Emigration and Destiny of the Colored People of the United States,* calling for the emigration of blacks to South America and the West Indies. His book was among the first to present a detailed analysis of the African-American presence in the United States. Throughout the 1850s, he participated in several emigration conferences.

In 1859, Delany traveled to Liberia to visit Alexander Crummell, a black priest and educator who had emigrated to the settlement in 1853. From Liberia, he went to Nigeria where he signed a treaty with the government allowing African Americans to settle there. Returning to the United States, Delany began the process of organizing an emigration party to Nigeria when the Civil War started and he was commissioned as a major, becoming the highest-ranking black officer in the Union army. Following the Civil War, Delany worked with the Freedman's Bureau in South Carolina and participated in politics but remained ambivalent about African Americans staying in the United States.

Alexander Crummel, whom W. E. B. DU BOIS would eulogize in *THE SOULS OF BLACK FOLK*, remained in Liberia until 1872 with periodic trips back to the United States. While in Liberia, he published *The Relations and Duties of Free Colored Men in America to Africa* in 1861 and *The Future of Africa* in 1862. Crummel was also instrumental in the development of the country's school system and upon his return to the United States advocated for African Americans a balance of industrial and higher education.

Bishop Henry McNeal Turner of the African Methodist Episcopal (AME) Church was more conservative than radical when elected to the Georgia legislature in 1869 and 1870. However, his own expulsion from the legislature after his first election, ongoing attempts by white legislators to deprive blacks of racial equality, and a steady increase in the murder of African Americans by LYNCHING, all served to convince Turner that it would be a mistake for African Americans to depend on the U.S. government for protection or recognition as American citizens with rights equal to those of whites. After delivering before the Georgia legislature a speech in which he refused "to cringe before any party, nor stoop to beg them for my rights," Turner began advocating emigration in 1870. He in turn noted Haiti, New Mexico, and Africa as possible destinations for African Americans. In 1876, he took a controversial position as vice president of the American Colonization Society. Upon the society's discontinuation, he established the International Emigration Society in 1892. Turner made at least four trips to

Africa during the 1890s, helping some 22 African Americans to settle there in 1895 and 325 more in 1896. In addition, he established AME churches in Liberia and Sierra Leone. At the beginning of 1900, some 12,000 African Americans had relocated to Africa.

Neither the Trinidadian Henry Sylvester Williams nor W. E. B. Du Bois adopted Turner's call for emigration to Africa at the first PAN AFRICAN CONGRESS in London in 1900. Delegates to the congress were concerned primarily with fostering cooperation among and an awareness of peoples of African descent no matter where they were. The two concepts became more linked, however, with the rise of Marcus Garvey and his UNIVERSAL NEGRO IMPROVEMENT ASSOCIATION just after WORLD WAR I. With the publication and worldwide distribution of his newspaper, the *NEGRO WORLD*, and the establishment of a shipping fleet, the Black Star Line, Garvey took Pan-Africanism from proposal to reality. While the Black Star Line was used mainly as a cargo and cruising line rather than one offering permanent transport to Africa, Garvey did popularize the notion of a return to African values and "Africa for Africans." In the 15th article of his *Declaration of the Rights of the Negro Peoples of the World,* he put "on record our most solemn determination to reclaim the treasures and possession of the vast continent of our forefathers." Though such statements generally addressed the conditions of those blacks living in countries colonized or occupied by white governments, journalists interpreted and reported them as advocating the emigration of all African Americans to Africa. Critics like GEORGE SCHUYLER and A. PHILIP RANDOLPH ridiculed Garvey as the promoter of a seemingly preposterous idea. Garvey himself sought permission to establish a small settlement of technologically trained blacks in Liberia but was denied. Following his deportation from the United States for charges of mail fraud, he returned for a time to his native Jamaica and then moved to England without once visiting Africa before his death in 1940.

During the 1960s, many individual black nationalists did relocate to various parts of Africa, but members of the movement generally looked to Africa for cultural and spiritual substance to strengthen their political ideology in regard to greater autonomy in the United States. The move back to Africa was made via the adoption of traditional forms of African dress, native African languages like Swahili, and greater familiarization with African foods, customs, and history.

Further Reading

Kadalie, Modibo. *Internationalism, Pan-Africanism and the Struggle of Social Classes.* Savannah Ga.: One Quest Press, 2000.

Van Deburg, William L., ed. *Modern Black Nationalism: From Marcus Garvey to Louis Farrakhan.* New York: New York University Press, 1997.

White, John. *Black Leadership in America, from Booker T. Washington to Jesse Jackson.* New York: Longman, 1994.

— Aberjhani

Baker, George See FATHER DIVINE.

Baker, Josephine (1906–1975) *singer, dancer*

After winning acclaim for performances in *SHUFFLE ALONG* and *CHOCOLATE DANDIES* in the United States, Josephine Baker moved to Paris, where she became an international star and earned France's Legion of Honor and the Medallion of the City of PARIS.

Josephine Baker was born into abject poverty on June 3, 1906, in Kansas City, Missouri. She left home at the age of 13 to work as a dresser and adjunct dancer in a traveling show.

Baker's initial dancing efforts were thwarted because she was considered too thin and too dark-skinned, but she eventually became an intermittent chorus girl with the touring company of *Shuffle Along* (1921). The embryonic Baker was in good company in *Shuffle Along* with entertainer FLORENCE MILLS, actor and scholar PAUL ROBESON, composer JOHN ROSAMOND JOHNSON, and composer WILLIAM GRANT STILL. Producers NOBLE SISSLE and EUBIE BLAKE were so impressed with her star quality and impromptu comedic abilities that she was headlined in their next effort, *Chocolate Dandies* (1924), originally titled *In Bamville.*

Baker's familiar comic routine of dancing out of step with arms akimbo and eyes crossed landed her a chorus line role in

Josephine Baker became the ultimate African-American expatriate when she gave up her U.S. citizenship to live as an international star, advocate for racial equality, and celebrated veteran of the French Resistance. She is shown here in a December 1932 publicity photo for her review "La Joie de Paris" at the Casino de Paris. *(Associated Press/Casino de Paris)*

Plantation Revue (1925). She brought down the house with her stand-in rendition of "Dinah," much to the distress of the show's regular vocal star, ETHEL WATERS.

In 1925, Baker traveled to PARIS with the show *La Revue nègre.* For the show, she wore nothing more than a pink flamingo feather. She later starred at the *Folies-Bergère.* Her primitive, risqué routines were less appreciated in NEW YORK CITY, however, conflicting as they did with Dr. W. E. B. DU BOIS's and Dr. ALAIN LOCKE's dignified *NEW NEGRO* philosophy. After performing in a production of *ZIEGFELD FOLLIES* in New York in 1936, she left the city to return to more appreciative audiences in France. There, she made a lucrative living in jazz clubs and revues, introducing French audiences to the Charleston and the Black Bottom dance crazes and immortalizing the songs "Yes, We Have No Bananas" and "Two Loves Have I."

With her marriage to Jean Lion in 1937, Baker became a French citizen. The couple divorced just more than a year later.

During World War II, Baker worked with the Free French forces in North Africa. For her wartime services to France, she was awarded the Legion of Honor, the Rosette of the Resistance, and the Medallion of the City of Paris.

Baker married Jo Bouillon in 1947 and with him adopted 12 children of various races. They separated in 1960.

Experiencing financial disaster as she tried to maintain her family, Baker returned to the United States for a successful tour in 1973. She enjoyed a triumphant return to stardom in Europe with the production of *Josephine,* a show that celebrated her life and career. She died on April 12, 1975, four days after *Josephine* opened in Paris. Thousands of people filled the streets of Paris to mourn her passing and honor her 50th anniversary in the city.

Further Reading

Altman, Susan, *The Encyclopedia of African-American Heritage.* New York: Facts On File, 1997.

Baker, Jean-Claude, and Chris Chase. *Josephine Baker: The Hungry Heart.* 1993. Reprint, New York: Cooper Square Press, 2001.

Rose, Phyllis. *Jazz Cleopatra: Josephine Baker in Her Time.* New York: Vintage Press, 1989.

Shack, William A. *Harlem in Montmartre, a Paris Jazz Story Between the Great Wars.* Berkeley: University of California Press, 2001.

— Sandra L. West

Bannarn, Henry

See THREE-O-SIX.

Barnes, Albert Coombs (1872–1951) *art collector, writer*

Dr. Albert Coombs Barnes, a collector of European and African art, founded the Barnes Foundation and wrote articles for *OPPORTUNITY* magazine and the special Harlem edition of *SURVEY GRAPHIC* magazine.

Albert Coombs Barnes was born on January 2, 1872, in Philadelphia, Pennsylvania. He attended Central High School and earned a medical degree from the University of Pennsylvania. His invention of an antiseptic called Argyrol made him a millionaire.

In 1922, he established the Barnes Foundation in Merion, Pennsylvania. The Barnes Foundation was an art collection composed of work by the finest European painters, from Matisse to Degas, and African art.

Barnes's interest in African art led to his meeting in 1923 with philosopher and HOWARD UNIVERSITY professor Dr. ALAIN LOCKE, NATIONAL ASSOCIATION FOR THE ADVANCEMENT OF COLORED PEOPLE assistant secretary WALTER WHITE, and *Opportunity* editor CHARLES SPURGEON JOHNSON. Because of his relationships with these Harlem Renaissance leaders, he was asked to write articles on African art for leading African-American publications such as *Opportunity.* Barnes wrote "Contribution to the Study of Negro Art in America" for *Survey Graphic* magazine in 1925, a special edition devoted to African-American culture, and "Negro Art and America" for Locke's anthology, *The NEW NEGRO.*

In "Negro Art and America," Barnes notes the Harlem Renaissance as, "one of the events of our age which no seeker for beauty can afford to overlook." He wrote that the Negro had outstanding characteristics that prevailed in his art: emotional

Art patron Albert Barnes established the Barnes Foundation in 1922 to preserve and promote the fine art of various cultures, including that of African Americans. He is shown here in 1940. *(Library of Congress, Prints & Photographs Division, Carl Van Vechten Collection [LC-USZ62-131766])*

endowment, imagination, and individual expression. He also observed that the art of African Americans survived the horrors of slavery and continued to be extraordinary into the Harlem Renaissance years because it was "an achievement, not an indulgence."

Albert C. Barnes died on July 24, 1951. He bequeathed his art collection to Lincoln University in Pennsylvania, alma mater of Harlem Renaissance poet LANGSTON HUGHES.

Further Reading

Locke, Alain, ed. *The New Negro: Voices of the Harlem Renaissance.* New York: Touchstone, 1997.

Miers, Charles, ed. *Harlem Renaissance: Art of Black America.* New York: Harry M. Abrams, 1994.

— Sandra L. West

Barron's Exclusive Club

Opened during the early 1920s, Barron's Exclusive Club was one of the leading entertainment centers in HARLEM and a forerunner to such cabarets as the COTTON CLUB, SMALL'S PARADISE, and CONNIE'S INN.

Businessman Barron D. Wilkins established the club on West 134th Street at SEVENTH AVENUE. Wilkins had operated a number of such facilities in Harlem since moving there in 1903. One of them was the Little Savoy on 35th Street.

While it catered primarily to affluent whites, Barron's Exclusive Club lived up to its name by serving a wealthy clientele that included white and black celebrities. Some of its regular patrons were BERT WILLIAMS, JACK JOHNSON, NOBLE SISSLE, EUBIE BLAKE, entertainer Al Jolson, actress Joan Crawford, and the mobster Jack Diamond. Guests were required to wear formal or semiformal evening attire, with men dressed in jackets and ties and women wearing gowns. It was a common practice for individual customers to throw hundreds of dollars in change on the floor to express their approval of favored entertainers.

One such entertainer was Valaida Snow, a singer who went on to perform in a number of musical revues. Ada Smith, who received her famous nickname, BRICKTOP, from Wilkins when he was visiting CHICAGO some years before, was a featured performer at the Exclusive Club in 1922. Through her influence, FLORENCE MILLS also became one of the club's principal attractions but soon left to join the cast of *SHUFFLE ALONG*. Bricktop was instrumental as well in persuading DUKE ELLINGTON and his Washingtonians to relocate from WASHINGTON, D.C., to Harlem, and work at Barron's Exclusive Club. Eventually, Bricktop left the club to headline at Connie's Inn just prior to moving to PARIS and opening her own club.

In May 1924, Wilkins was reportedly shot and killed at the age of 63 by a man known as "Yellow Charleston." In addition to being well known for his Barron's Exclusive Club, he was also known as a financier of black baseball teams, an early backer of Jack Johnson, and a philanthropist to many in the Harlem community.

Further Reading

Haskins, James. *Black Music in America: A History Through Its People.* New York: Welcome Rain Publishers, 2000.

Riss, Thomas L. *Just Before Jazz.* Washington, D.C.: Smithsonian Institution Press, 1994.

— Aberjhani

Barnett-Aden Gallery See WASHINGTON, D.C.

Barrow, Joseph Louis See LOUIS, JOE.

Barthé, Richmond (1901–1989) *painter, sculptor*

HARMON FOUNDATION exhibitor Richmond Barthé was a self-taught watercolorist and a sculptor whose work depicted busts of legendary visual artists and historical figures.

Richmond Barthé was born on January 28, 1901, in Bay St. Louis, Mississippi. He was only one month old when his father, Richmond Barthé, died. His mother, Clementine Raboteau, was influential in nurturing his early artistic talent. When young Richmond was just an infant, he reportedly was intrigued with the Old English letters on the front page of the *New Orleans Times Picayune* newspaper. His mother supplied him with paper and pencils to practice copying the letters.

Barthé grew up in Missouri, Mississippi, and Louisiana. Throughout these years, he continued to practice copying, advancing from letters to comic strips, and began to paint at the age of six. His first works were shown at the County Fair in Mississippi. He was 12 years old when he dropped out of school in the seventh grade.

At the age of 18, he won a blue ribbon from the County Fair in NEW ORLEANS for his pen-and-ink rendition of a woman reclining and surrounded by drapery. An art critic from the *New Orleans Times Picayune* was so taken with the drawing that he tried to get Barthé into art school until discovering he was black and would not be admitted.

While working as a butler, Barthé was given a set of oil paints by his employer. He painted the head of Jesus Christ and donated it to Rev. Harry Kane of the local Catholic Church for the church's May Festival. Rev. Kane in turn helped Barthé enroll at the School of the Art Institute in Chicago and paid his tuition. Living with his Aunt Rose and working at a restaurant, Barthé attended the school from 1924 to 1928. In 1925, he exhibited in two one-man shows in NEW YORK CITY at the Delphic Studios and Caz-Delbos Gallery.

Originally a painter who leaned toward watercolor, Barthé was accidentally introduced to sculpture at the Art Institute. In 1927, during Negro History Week, he exhibited two sculptured heads at the Chicago Women's Club, and they were so well-received that he was asked to produce more. He accepted commissions to create busts of the Haitian freedom fighter Toussaint L'Ouverture and the artist HENRY OSSAWA TANNER. The acclaim that arose from the production of these commissioned sculptures resulted in a one-man show in

Chicago and a Rosenwald Fellowship. In 1929, 1931, and 1933, he participated in Harmon Foundation exhibitions. Working in clay, bronze, and stone, his works during the GREAT DEPRESSION included *Portrait of Harold Jackson* (1929), *Blackberry Woman* (1932), and *African Dancer* (1933), the latter two pieces purchased by the Whitney Museum of American Art in New York.

From 1937 to 1938, under the U.S. Treasury Art Project, Barthé completed large scale bas-reliefs on religious themes from the play *GREEN PASTURES* for the Harlem River Houses apartment complex in New York. On July 28, 1939, First Lady ELEANOR ROOSEVELT took note of Barthé in her column in the *New York World-Telegram:* "Artists are always sensitive people who appreciate the hardships of others. The stories of the Spanish refugees made such an impression on Richard Barthé, the sculptor, that he has given his sculptured figures of two Spanish refugee children as a contribution to the Negro People's Committee for Spanish Refugee Relief. His only stipulation is that the proceeds go to resettle a Spanish family in Mexico."

In 1946, Barthé received the first commission given to an African American for a bust slated for New York University's Hall of Fame. In 1947, he served on a committee to help modernize the sculpture in the Catholic churches of the United States.

Barthé's paintings, busts, and dance-related sculptures are in the collections of the Museum of African-American Art in Los Angeles and the SCHOMBURG CENTER FOR RESEARCH IN BLACK CULTURE in HARLEM. His work can be found in galleries and private collections all over the world, from Austria to the Virgin Islands.

Richmond Barthé died on March 6, 1989, in Pasadena, California at the age of 88.

Further Reading

Bailey, David A., and Paul, Gilroy. *Rhapsodies in Black: Art of the Harlem Renaissance.* Berkeley: University of California Press, 1997.

Powell, Richard J. *Black Art and Culture in the Twentieth Century.* New York: Thames and Hudson, 1997.

— Sandra L. West

Basie, Count (William Basie) (1904–1984) *pianist, bandleader*

Bandleader Count Basie was a master of the SWING SOUND and instrumental in bringing the big band movement to HARLEM in the 1930s.

He was born William Basie in Red Bank, New Jersey, on August 21, 1904. As a child, he studied music with his mother and was later influenced by pianists Earl "Fatha" Hines, Teddy Wilson, and FATS WALLER.

Basie began his career in vaudeville and as an accompanist for silent movies. He later learned to play the organ by watching Waller play at the *LINCOLN THEATER* in Harlem. In 1927, Basie played with the Gonzelle White show on the Keith Circuit in Kansas City, Missouri, a "home" of the BLUES. In 1928, he became the pianist for Walter Page's band, the Blue Devils, then joined Bennie Moten's group a year later.

When Moten died in 1935, Basie and saxophonist Buster Smith formed the Buster Smith and Basie Barons of Rhythm at the famous Reno Club in Kansas City. The Barons also broadcast from the Reno Club to radio station WXBY. Members of this band included tenor saxophonist Lester Young and drummer Jo Jones. The nine-piece Barons of Rhythm were truly rhythmic, swinging blues tunes boldly into what would come to be known as a "big band sound." Basie would play piano with the rhythm section alone. His style was minimalist and so unique that he was given the nickname "Count" to denote a high stature in the JAZZ world just below that of COTTON CLUB bandleader DUKE ELLINGTON.

The Barons of Rhythm played the Grand Terrace in CHICAGO and made their way to NEW YORK CITY in the 1930s, where they expanded to 15 members and introduced their big band sounds to Harlem. They opened at Roseland in New York in 1936 and made their first recording for Decca records in January 1937. The band's vocalists included Helen Humes, BILLIE HOLIDAY, and Pearl Bailey. The orchestra enjoyed success until World War II brought on economic stress, and a bad contract with Decca prevented Basie from receiving royalties for hits like "One O'Clock Jump," "Jumping at the Woodside," and other classic recordings of the era.

Basie pulled his group back together in 1952, began a long association with the Birdland nightclub in New York, and toured Europe in 1955. Band personnel during this period included trumpet players Thad Jones and Joe Newman as well as singer Joe Williams, who recorded the hit "Every Day" in 1955. Basie's orchestra was the first black band to play the Waldorf-Astoria Hotel in New York in 1957. During the 1960s, Basie accompanied popular vocalists Tony Bennett and Sammy Davis, Jr., in concerts and on recordings.

Count Basie's band received many awards from the music community, including *Esquire* magazine's Silver Award for best big band in 1945; *Down Beat* magazine's Readers Poll as best big band in 1955, 1957, 1958, 1959, and 1961; and as a best dance band in 1962 and 1963. Like the trumpeter and raspy voiced vocalist LOUIS ARMSTRONG, Count Basie's Orchestra was featured in a number of movies, including *Stage Door Canteen* (1943), *Blazing Saddles* (1974), and the video *The Last of the Blue Devils* (1991).

When Count Basie died on April 26, 1984, the band continued to perform under the leadership of longtime personnel: Thad Jones from 1985 to 1986, Frank Foster from 1986 to 1995, and Grover Mitchell in 1995.

Further Reading

Feather, Leonard, and Ira Gitler. *The Biographical Encyclopedia of Jazz.* New York: Oxford University Press, 1999.

Lowe, Jacques, with Bob Blumenthal and Cliff Preiss. *Jazz: Photographs of the Masters.* New York: Aristan, 1995.

— Sandra L. West

Bates, Ad See THREE-O-SIX.

Bearden, Romare (1914–1988) *painter*
Romare Bearden started his art career in the early 1930s, became a member of the Harlem Artists Guild, and by the 1940s was recognized as one of the leading abstract painters of the 20th century.

Romare Bearden was born in rural Mecklenberg County, North Carolina, on September 2, 1914. To escape the harshness of racial discrimination, his family traveled to Canada and Pennsylvania before settling in HARLEM, on West 131st Street in NEW YORK CITY, where Romare was raised.

Bearden's mother, Bessye, was a politically astute woman who founded the Negro Women's Democratic Association. His father, Howard, was a pianist. Among their friends were the composer DUKE ELLINGTON and performing artist PAUL ROBESON.

Bearden was introduced to art as a child through a young friend, Eugene, in Pittsburgh. Eugene, who died in his teens, drew pictures of houses without fronts and in which one could see what was going on in each room. He and Bearden often spent afternoons drawing together, and Bearden later memorialized this rite of passage in a collage entitled *Farewell to Eugene* (1978).

As a Harlem youth, Bearden studied mural painting under his cousin CHARLES HENRY ALSTON at the HARLEM COMMUNITY ART CENTER. A stellar student who once thought of becoming a physician, Bearden attended Lincoln University and Boston University (where he was a star pitcher on the baseball team and drew a cartoon series "Beanpot" for the student magazine). In 1935, he graduated from New York University (where he drew political cartoons for *Medley,* a student publication) with a B.S. degree in education.

He also studied at the University of Pittsburgh; American Artists School; Art Students League; Columbia University, New York (1943); and the Sorbonne in PARIS (1950–1951). While in Paris, an endeavor financed by the G.I. Bill that stemmed from his service in the U.S. Army, Bearden studied art, literature, and philosophy. He also befriended legendary painters Matisse and Miro, two of his influences.

When Bearden returned to the United States, he worked as a songwriter and as a political cartoonist for the *Baltimore Afro-American.* After a stint with college baseball and transient thoughts of a medical career, Bearden returned to art.

Back in Harlem, Bearden joined the Harlem Artists Guild and met with other artists at THREE-0-SIX, a gathering place on 141st Street. He began as a watercolorist and was fascinated with Picasso and the Cubist movement with its origins in African art. He experimented with the geometric forms and structures of the movement. In 1941, Bearden had his first one-man show at Three-O-Six. He exhibited 24 works, from gouaches to drawings, most of them reflective of the social conditions of African Americans in the rural South and urban North.

To support himself, Bearden worked as a caseworker for the New York City Department of Welfare. He rented a studio at 33 West 125th Street in a building where visual artist JACOB ARMSTEAD LAWRENCE and poet CLAUDE MCKAY, both pillars during the Harlem Renaissance, lived just down the hall. There, Bearden painted memories of North Carolina and scenes of Harlem. He also gave parties on 125th Street at which McKay, poet LANGSTON HUGHES, and dancers and musicians would perform. His exhibitions during this period included shows at the Carnegie Museum in Pittsburgh 1937; the Harlem Art Center in 1939; and a group exhibit, "American Negro Art from the 19th and 20th Centuries," at the Downtown Gallery in 1941.

Starting in 1942, Bearden had served three years in the army in support of World War II. While in the military, he had participated in the shows "New Names in American Art" and "Ten Hierographic Paintings by Sgt. Romare Bearden" at The G Place Gallery in WASHINGTON, D.C., in 1944. Upon his return from the war, he exhibited a series, *The Passion of Christ,* at Kootz Galleries on 15 East 57th Street, that sold out. He continued to have successful shows at Kootz and at the Whitney Museum of American Art, then located at 10 West Eighth Street.

In 1953, following a sojourn in Paris, Bearden suffered a mental breakdown. He recovered in 1954 and married Nanette Rohan. Bearden then began to experiment with the collage form, a color art form supplemented with newspaper and magazine articles, that made his art a national treasure. He photographed the collages, then blew them up in size. This style is known as photomontage and proved so financially lucrative that Bearden quit his job and worked on his art full-time.

Bearden excelled in many different styles throughout his long career. By the 1960s, he worked often with collage and photomontage, producing *Projection* in 1964. His themes included texts from the Bible and classical literature, memory, music (especially jazz piano), nature, women, and southern ritual. Due to his own participation in the 1960s Civil Rights movement, and the influences of his politically savvy mother, social awareness was etched indelibly into his canvas.

Working with artists ERNEST CRICHLOW and Norman Lewis, Bearden also founded the CINQUE GALLERY in New York during the 1960s as a tribute to the professional unity and creative spirit of the Harlem Renaissance.

In 1987, President Ronald Reagan awarded the National Medal of Arts to Bearden. In 1988, Bearden coauthored with Harry Henderson *A History of African-American Artists from 1972 to the Present.*

Romare Bearden succumbed to cancer on March 11, 1988. His papers are collected at the Archives of American Art, Smithsonian Institution, Washington, D.C. In 2003–2004 the National Gallery held a major retrospective.

Further Reading

Fine, Ruth E., Romare Bearden, and Jacqueline Francis. *The Art of Romare Bearden.* New York: Abrams, 2003.

Leininger-Muller, Theresa A. *New Negro Artists in Paris: African American Painters and Sculptors in the City of Light, 1922–1934.* Piscataway, New Jersey: Rutgers University Press, 2000.

Schwartzmann, Myron, August Wilson, and Romare Bearden. *Romare Bearden: His Life and Art.* New York: Harry N. Abrams, Inc., 1990.

— Sandra L. West

"Begin the Beguine" See BIG BAND ERA.

Bennett, Gwendolyn Bennetta (1902–1981)
writer, graphic artist
Among the numerous creative individuals who participated in the Harlem Renaissance, Gwendolyn Bennetta Bennett stands out as an artist, poet, essayist, and editor of "The Ebony Flute," a column in *OPPORTUNITY: A JOURNAL OF NEGRO LIFE.*

Gwendolyn Bennett was born on July 8, 1902, in Giddings, Texas. Her parents, Joshua Robin and Maime Franke Bennett, were teachers. They divorced when their only child was five or six years old. As a single parent, Maime Bennett left teaching to secure a cosmetology position at a finishing school in WASHINGTON, D.C. Joshua Bennett abducted Gwendolyn during a parental visit when she was eight years old, settled in Harrisburg, Pennsylvania, remarried, and moved the family to Brooklyn, New York, where he died in 1926.

Gwendolyn Bennett was educated in the elementary schools of Washington, D.C., and Harrisburg. She graduated from Brooklyn's Girls' High School in 1921, where she was the first black contributor to the literary and drama societies. She won a prize for a poster she designed, wrote lyrics for the class graduation song, wrote the graduation speech, and penned poetry.

Though she loved poetry, in 1921 Bennett studied fine arts at Columbia University's Teachers College in NEW YORK CITY. Unable to endure the racism she encountered, she stayed at the university for only two years. She then transferred to Pratt Institute in Brooklyn, studied art and drama, and graduated in 1924.

Bennett's poem, *To Usward,* published in the May 1924 issue of *CRISIS* magazine, is an observation of the literary renaissance in progress at the time and a call to literary freedom. Bennett made her public debut as a poet when she recited *To Usward* at the March 21, 1924, CIVIC CLUB DINNER spearheaded by *Opportunity* editor CHARLES SPURGEON JOHNSON. The dinner—originally designed to celebrate the publication of JESSIE REDMOND FAUSET's novel *There Is Confusion* and to give promising writers and established publishers a place to network—is noted as the celebratory launching of the Harlem Renaissance era. In *To Usward,* Bennett encouraged emerging writers to be still "as ginger jars" upon a shelf and to create "conscious of the strength in unity."

Bennett's first job after graduation from Pratt was as an instructor in watercolor and design at HOWARD UNIVERSITY in Washington, D.C., in 1924. With a $1,000 scholarship from the DELTA SIGMA THETA sorority, in June of 1925, Bennett left Washington to study art at Académie Julian, Académie Colarossi, and Ecole du Pantheon in PARIS, France. She studied French at the Sorbonne and associated with writer Gertrude Stein, singer PAUL ROBESON, and scientist ESLANDA CARDOZO GOODE ROBESON.

Though experienced in watercolor and fabric (batik) arts, in 1926 she returned to HARLEM to become assistant editor of *Opportunity* magazine at the NATIONAL URBAN LEAGUE. From 1926 to 1928, she was assistant editor for "The Ebony Flute" column, commenting on the activities of black artists. Also from 1927 to 1928, she periodically returned to Howard University as an art instructor. Throughout the 1920s, her poetry, short stories, and articles appeared in a range of periodicals, including *The MESSENGER,* Palms, and *FIRE!!.* Most of her poems appeared in *Opportunity* from 1923 to 1926. She also contributed poetry to various anthologies, including *The Book of American Negro Poetry,* edited by JAMES WELDON JOHNSON in 1922; *Anthology of Magazine Verse for 1925 and Yearbook of American Poetry,* edited by WILLIAM STANLEY BEAUMONT BRAITHWAITE in 1926; *Caroling Dusk: An Anthology of Verse by Negro Poets,* edited by COUNTEE CULLEN in 1927; and *The Poetry of Black America: Anthology of the Twentieth Century,* edited by Arnold Adoff in 1973. Her poetry was described as "delicate" and "poignant" by James Weldon Johnson but was assessed as "race conscious" by STERLING ALLEN BROWN in *Negro Poetry and Drama* and *The Negro in American Fiction.*

Bennett was also an essayist. *Howard University Record* published her "The Future of the Negro in Art" (December 1924) and "Negroes: Inherent Craftsmen" (February 1925). *Crisis* magazine (June 1935) published "Rounding the Century: Story of the Colored Orphan Asylum and Association for the Benefit of Colored Children in New York City." And "The American Negro Paints" appeared in *Southern Workman* (January 1928).

Bennett's years in New York were socially and professionally fruitful. She illustrated covers for *Crisis* and *Opportunity* magazines from 1923 to 1931. She also helped edit the short-lived journal *Fire!!* and maintained a friendship with colorful folk writer ZORA NEALE HURSTON, who lived in her building at 43 West 66th Street. In addition, she dated journalist GEORGE SCHUYLER, befriended *Fire!!* editor WALLACE THURMAN, and became a member of the Harlem Writers Guild with poets COUNTEE CULLEN, LANGSTON HUGHES, and ERIC DERWENT WALROND.

When Bennett returned to her teaching responsibilities at Howard, she fell in love with Morehouse graduate and Howard medical student Alfred Joseph Jackson. Because Bennett was a professor, their romance evoked scandal. Bennett's resignation was accepted, and she married Jackson on April 14, 1928.

When Jackson returned to his Eustis, Florida, hometown to practice medicine, Bennett taught art and English at Tennessee State College, then later joined him. Moving south presented them with problems. Jackson struggled with his practice. To supplement their income, Bennett taught Spanish in the local Lake County School for $50 a month. With no cultural society to engage her, she stopped writing. Bennett encouraged her husband to take the New York medical examination, which he passed, and they moved to Hempstead, Long Island. Jackson, however, died in the early 1930s.

Following her husband's death, Bennett worked with the WORKS PROGRESS ADMINISTRATION's Federal Art Project as assistant director in 1937. The next year, she served as director of sculptor AUGUSTA FELLS SAVAGE's HARLEM COMMUNITY ART CENTER.

Bennett's association with Savage, who subscribed to the philosophy of MARCUS GARVEY, drew charges of COMMUNISM against her. By the 1940s, she left the Harlem Community Art Center and established the Jefferson School for Democracy and the George Washington Carver School. Both schools were shut down by the House Committee on Un-American Activities.

Bennett later married Richard Crosscup, a Harvard graduate and English teacher at Carver. They moved to Kutztown,

Pennsylvania, where they opened an antique store. Crosscup died in January 1980 and Bennett on May 30, 1981.

Further Reading

Hines, Darlene Clark, ed. *Facts On File Encyclopedia of Black Women in America.* New York: Facts On File, 1997.

Huggins, Nathan Irvin, ed. *Voices from the Harlem Renaissance.* New York: Oxford University Press, 1994.

Lewis, David Levering. *When Harlem Was in Vogue.* New York: Vintage Books, 1982.

Wilson, Sondra Kathryn, ed. *The Crisis Reader.* New York: Modern Library, 1999.

— Sandra L. West

Bentley, Gladys (Bobbie Minton) (1907–1960)

singer

Gladys Bentley was unique among entertainers of the Harlem Renaissance as an openly lesbian singer who dressed in male clothes and, like BESSIE SMITH, sang risqué lyrics.

Born on August 12, 1907, in Pennsylvania, Gladys Bentley left home when she was 16 years old to sing at the Mad House, a Harlem nightclub on 133rd Street. Her stage name at this time was Bobbie Minton.

Bentley, who had an alto voice, later performed at the Clam House, CONNIE'S INN, and BARRON'S EXCLUSIVE CLUB. Her beginning $35-a-week salary quickly rose to $125. She headlined at the Clam House, which was known to be a homosexual and lesbian hangout on 133rd Street, the street itself being known as JUNGLE ALLEY. Connie's Inn at 2221 SEVENTH AVENUE was originally named Shuffle Inn in honor of the dynamite musical revue *SHUFFLE ALONG*. It was one of the top clubs in Harlem during the 1920s and was also part of the 11 clubs that did business in Jungle Alley. Barbara's Exclusive Club was an establishment Bentley owned during the 1930s.

Gladys Bentley had an unusual style of singing. Accompanying herself on the piano, she yodeled and growled through such standard tunes as "St. James Infirmary," "Alice Blue Gown," and "Sweet Georgia Brown," adding as she sang her own risqué lyrics. She recorded on the Okeh record label in the 1930s.

Bentley's way of dressing was also a draw. Weighing 400 pounds, she wore elegant, male evening clothes: bow ties, top hats, and tuxedos. She was as bold in her personal life as she was in her stage life. She donned a tuxedo to marry her female lover in a civil ceremony, then married a sailor, then married a newspaper columnist, and was the focus of an *Ebony* magazine article (August 1952) entitled, "I Am a Woman Again."

Gladys Bentley died on January 18, 1960.

Further Reading

Hughes, Langston. *The Big Sea.* 1940, Knopf. Reprint, New York: Hill and Wang, 1964.

Watson, Steve. *The Harlem Renaissance: Hub of African-American Culture, 1920–1930.* New York: Pantheon Books, 1995.

— Sandra L. West

big band era

The expansive, brassy sound of the big band era was a musical phenomenon that induced Americans to dance in felt skirts and saddle shoes in the late 1920s and 1930s.

People in HARLEM took the big band sound seriously, and white groups claimed a stake in the music. Glenn Miller, Benny Goodman, Artie Shaw, and brothers Tommy and Jimmy Dorsey represented successful white big bands that often featured black singers. Big bands were extremely popular, as *Downbeat* magazine documented, until after World War II.

Big bands were exactly that: ensembles of 14 members or more. They played in almost every major city that had a large African-American population and—although so popular that they established a national trend—encountered problems as monumental as their horn sections. Transportation, the military draft, and a crippling union strike all created great difficulties for big band members and their fans.

Groups generally traveled across the country in cars and buses. The rationing of gasoline often curtailed mobility, especially between 1942 and 1945 when the United States was involved with World War II. Patriotism was high and big band musicians Miller, Shaw, and others chose to perform for the military rather than pursue their individual music careers.

A strike by the American Federation of Musicians Union on August 1, 1942, prevented the manufacturing of recordings until September 1943, which put a dent in the music industry. Band leaders DUKE ELLINGTON, COUNT BASIE, and Goodman worked with recording companies Columbia and Victor but could not record for more than two years. When their already existing recordings played on the radio, the musicians received no royalties. Record companies Columbia and Victor did not settle until November 1944. They and other record companies contributed monies into a union fund for those records sold during the period of non-recording.

Instrumentalists remained inactive for years because of the strike, but vocalists were not part of the union and were free to do as they chose. Without a big band behind them, singers performed with nonunion, amateur musicians or with backup a cappella vocal groups. The vocalists were extremely successful because they filled the gap created by the strike. At this time, such legendary white songsters as Doris Day, Bing Crosby, and Frank Sinatra rose to prominence by singing popular ballads.

Songs of the big band era were smooth and sentimental. Tommy Dorsey's band employed Sinatra and the Pied Pipers, a group that included Jo Stafford, and they hit it big with "I'll Never Smile Again," recorded on May 23, 1940. Another early "sweet" big band era song was "Marie," written by Irving Berlin in 1928 and introduced in the film *My Awakening* (1928). Master crooner Rudy Vallee popularized "Marie" on radio and an RCA Victor recording in 1928. In 1937, Dorsey's band recorded "Marie" and sold more than a million copies. It was Dorsey's first major recording success. "Marie" survived after the war in a musical called *The Fabulous Dorseys,* produced by United Artists in 1947. Shaw's band had a victory with "Begin the Beguine," a song noted for its unusual musical entrance: it started with a hard downbeat on the first bar and had clashing cymbals. "Begin the Beguine," words and music by the prolific Cole Porter, debuted in the musical stage comedy *Jubilee* in 1935.

Another challenge to the big band era was the cabaret tax of 1941. The tax impacted the clubs that allowed dancing. Such facilities were forced by law to pay 30 percent of their profits in taxes. Thus, in order to stay alive, clubs hired the more compact, less expensive combos with three horns instead of the larger bands with 14 members.

Following World War II, the popularity of big band music declined. Record sales were not particularly profitable for musicians, and those who still enjoyed the music could view performances of it on television without going out to pay for it. Moreover, many of the musicians who had created the music were aging and less inclined to travel across the country. They felt stifled, and in 1946 alone eight major big bands disintegrated, including Goodman's and Dorsey's.

The music of bebop and rhythm and blues gradually replaced the sounds of the big band era. Big band enthusiasts, however, enjoyed a number of revivals in the 1950s.

Further Reading

Kernfield, Barry, ed. *The Blackwell Guide to Recorded Jazz, 2nd Edition.* Cambridge, Mass.: Blackwell Publishers, 1995.

Schoener, Allon, ed. *Harlem on My Mind: Cultural Capital of Black America 1900–1968.* New York: Random House, 1968.

Yanow, Scott. *Swing.* San Francisco: Miller Freeman Books, 2000.

— Sandra L. West

Bishop, Hutchens C., Rev. See SAINT PHILIP'S EPISCOPAL CHURCH.

Blackbirds of 1928

Starting out as an all-black musical revue at HARLEM's Alhambra Theatre on West 126th Street and Seventh Avenue, *Blackbirds* grew into an international hit that generated a series of successful shows.

Debuting at the Alhambra in 1926, *Blackbirds* was the theater's first major musical presented to attract a black audience and brought to an end the management's discriminatory JIM CROW practices. It was produced by Lew Leslie, a white promoter who previously produced all-black shows in London and New York. With a triumphant six-week run at the Alhambra, *Blackbirds* bypassed the traditional practice of touring other states and then returning to New York for a Broadway debut. It traveled instead to Europe, where it played for a year, and its stars became international celebrities.

The show featured the talents of singer FLORENCE MILLS, dancer BOJANGLES ROBINSON, dancer Earl "Snakehips" Tucker, and comic Johnny Hudgins. Its music was composed by Jimmy McHugh with lyrics by Dorothy Fields, both white. Its hit songs included "Dig-a Dig-a Do" and "I Can't Give You Anything but Love," the latter recorded by both ETHEL WATERS and LOUIS ARMSTRONG. The celebrated Mills Brothers recorded other songs from the show. The success of *Blackbirds* allowed Hudgins to remain in Paris and star in a subsequent show at the famed Moulin Rouge. It inspired the press to draw comparisons between JOSEPHINE BAKER and Mills, frequently indicating Mills was the more superior artist.

The triumph of *Blackbirds* in Paris and London had virtually guaranteed the same success on Broadway when in 1927 Mills died unexpectedly following an appendectomy. Several performers were brought in to compensate for the loss of Mills. When *Blackbirds of 1928* opened May 9 at the Liberty Theatre, its lineup included ADELAIDE HALL, Aida Ward, Elizabeth Welch, and Eloise Uggams, mother of the famous entertainer Leslie Uggams. Robinson remained with the cast, drawing praise for his second-act dance, "Doin' the New Low-Down." Added to the show was a song called "A Memory of You," a tribute to Mills that was sung by Ward. The show's music was considered one of its stronger features, but it received some negative criticism for its old-styled vaudeville humor depicting blacks made up in blackface as they stole chickens or walked terrified through graveyards.

The death of Mills had generated fear that *Blackbirds of 1928* would fail. The show, however, ran for 518 performances. In 1930, Lew Leslie revived his show to feature not only an all-black cast but an all-black team of writers. *Blackbirds of 1930* boasted the music of EUBIE BLAKE and the lyrics of Andy Razaf. Flournoy Miller wrote the book for the show. Filling out the cast were Ethel Waters, the song and dance comedy team of Buck and Bubbles, and Miller. The 1930 version of the show opened September 1 at the Majestic Theatre in Brooklyn. It later moved to Broadway for a run of 62 weeks.

The show continued to attract audiences with productions in 1933 and 1939.

Further Reading

Hatch, James V., and Bernard L. Peterson, Jr. *Profiles of African American Stage Performers and Theatre People, 1816–1960.* Westport, Conn.: Greenwood Publishing Group, 2000.

Spencer, Jon Michael. *The New Negroes and Their Music: The Success of the Harlem Renaissance.* Knoxville: University of Tennessee Press, 1997.

— Aberjhani

Black Jews See COMMANDMENT KEEPERS.

Black Hebrews See COMMANDMENT KEEPERS.

black humor

Black humor was a mainstay of the emerging African-American culture of the 1920s, 1930s, and 1940s. It found expressions through a diversity of mediums ranging from nightclub comics and Broadway stars to the literary works of writers like EULALIE SPENCE, ZORA NEALE HURSTON, GEORGE SCHUYLER, and LANGSTON HUGHES.

Black humorists working in theater at the beginning of the 1900s had to face the challenge of remaining funny while breaking away from an established minstrel show tradition. Minstrelsy ridiculed the appearance and physical features of African Americans with white and black performers wearing makeup that darkened their faces and whitened their mouths until their lips appeared much larger than normal. It also stereotyped the characters of African Americans by presenting them as incorrigible thieves, lazy beyond belief, unintelligent, and cowardly.

The image of African Americans presented through humor began to change gradually during the 1890s with productions that focused more on the musical and dancing abilities of African-American performers while also casting them in shows with structured plots and themes. One of the first of these shows was *Oriental America,* produced by John W. Isham in 1896, followed by Bob Cole's *A Trip to Coontown* in 1898, and *Clorindy, The Origin of the Cakewalk,* by Will Marion Cook and Paul Laurence Dunbar, in 1898.

The move away from minstrelsy continued in the next decade with shows by the team of Bob Cole, JOHN ROSAMOND JOHNSON, and JAMES WELDON JOHNSON. The highly successful comedy duo of GEORGE WALKER and BERT WILLIAMS, who achieved success on Broadway and in Europe with shows like *Bandanna Land,* continued the tradition of performing in blackface. However, Williams was a master of the double entendre song in which he often mixed humor with bitter political criticism. Addressing white audiences attending his show *In Dahomey* in 1903, Williams sang with serious conviction and intention when admonishing whites to take care how they spoke to their servants because, "You may be talking to a king." His desire to establish a black theater to explore a wide range of drama and comedy was well known. In 1908, Rosamond Johnson and Bob Cole contributed material to *Mr. Lode of Koal,* a show that displayed Williams's talents without reference to the minstrel genre.

Johnson and Cole, and Walker and Williams, paved the way for a new group of dancing comedians that gained fame on Broadway and stages worldwide. Aubrey Lyles and Flournoy Miller made show business history when they combined their dancing and comic talents with the musical finesse of EUBIE BLAKE and NOBLE SISSLE to create the 1921 hit *SHUFFLE ALONG.* Dancing comic teams Rufus Greenlee and Thaddeus Drayton, Buck and Bubbles, and many others followed Lyles and Miller's example to create a tradition of such performers.

Whereas minstrelsy died a slow but definitive death on the musical stage, it lingered longer in old vaudeville, nightclubs, and circus acts. In the 1920s, the comedian PIGMEAT MARKHAM, who later would gain fame at the APOLLO THEATRE and in the movies, was among the last of the black comedians to serve their apprenticeship in vaudeville shows that still required blackface and relied on ridicule and heavy sexual suggestiveness rather than sublety for humorous appeal. BUTTERBEANS AND SUSIE, a husband and wife team who got married as part of their first performance together, also pushed ridicule and sexual suggestiveness but more in reference to marriages than to race itself. Moreover, the couple diversified their performance by dancing and singing the BLUES. MOMS MABLEY was a performer who broke completely with the blackface tradition. She won over audiences at the LAFAYETTE THEATER, the COTTON CLUB, and Apollo with her own brand of wry folk humor as opposed to raw obscenity or self-degradation. Blackface itself remained a part of the fading vaudeville circuit until the GREAT DEPRESSION and faded completely as younger black performers protested against it in the 1940s.

The RACE RECORDS industry of the 1920s also relied on black humor for record sales. In addition to recordings by Butterbeans and Susie, renowned "empress of the blues" BESSIE SMITH and "queen of the moaners" CLARA SMITH recorded songs lampooning the pitfalls of relationships. They recorded a number of duets in which one woman would beg the other to keep the husband she had stolen instead of giving him back.

Among the emerging black writers of the 1920s and 1930s, humor in the form of racial satire and sly folk wisdom was often a fundamental element of their work. The poetry of COUNTEE CULLEN and Langston Hughes laughed at the ironies of racism as much as they protested it or even ignored it altogether while simply affirming their African-American heritage. In addition to the folk humor prevalent in his poetry, Hughes exercised unbridled satire in *The Em-Fuehrer Jones,* his comic take on Eugene O'Neill's prizewinning play *The EMPEROR JONES.* In his famous series of short stories featuring the character Jesse B. Semple, Hughes celebrated what he saw as the ability of African Americans to simultaneously cry over and laugh at the hardships of life in America. Zora Neale Hurston also used humor in both short stories and plays.

Eulalie Spence was a prolific playwright, director, and literary critic who rejected the notion that her art should serve principally as propaganda to further black causes as spelled out by cultural leaders like W. E. B. DU BOIS and ALAIN LOCKE. She opted instead, in works like *Foreign Mail* and *The Starter, A Comedy of Harlem Life,* to explore and lampoon the customs and rituals of daily living among African Americans in HARLEM. Spence's comic vision won her a number of literary awards, including those presented by *CRISIS* and *OPPORTUNITY* magazines.

PITTSBURGH COURIER editor George Schuyler also used the stage for satirical works. His play *The Witch Hunt*—like Pulitzer-winner Arthur Miller's *The Crucible,* which was written after it—examined the hysteria that often gripped Americans at the mention of the word COMMUNISM. Schuyler's most enduring satirical work, however, and the most enduring of its kind to come out of the Harlem Renaissance, was his 1931 novel, *Black No More.* Borrowing literary techniques from science fiction and social realism, Schuyler poked fun at the attitudes of blacks and whites toward race by spinning a yarn about a scientist who discovers a way to turn blacks white. He does so with a number of unforeseen and comical results.

Through the political sophistication of writers like Schuyler and Spence and the comic artistry of masters like Moms Mabley, black humor continued to evolve and remains a fundamental element of black culture.

Further Reading

Jackson, Pamela F. *Black Comedy: A Critical Anthology of Plays, Interviews and Essays.* New York: Applause Theatre Book Publishers, 1997.

Lowe, John. *Jump at the Sun: Zora Neale Hurston's Cosmic Comedy.* Champaign: University of Illinois, 1999.

Watkins, Mel, ed. *African American Humor: The Best Black Comedy from Slavery to Today.* Chicago: Chicago Review Press, 2002.

— Aberjhani

Black Nationalism

Developing at the same time as the BACK-TO-AFRICA MOVEMENT, Black Nationalism proposed that African Americans should establish a governmental and social system as separate as possible from that of whites.

The back-to-Africa movement of the 1800s was advocated in part by whites attempting to remove free blacks as obstacles to institutional slavery. In contrast, various African Americans viewed Black Nationalism as a logical alternative to both avoiding slavery and attempts to integrate or reintegrate themselves into African societies. They did not favor integration into American society, as Frederick Douglass did. Martin Robinson Delany, Douglass's coeditor of the *North Star,* suggested African Americans reestablish themselves in South America or the West Indies. Delany presented his proposal for the emigration of African Americans at conventions throughout the 1850s and in his groundbreaking 1952 book, *The Condition, Elevation, Emigration and Destiny of the Colored People of the United States.*

Whether within the United States or outside of it, Black Nationalism focused primarily on the political, social, cultural, and economic autonomy of black populations. In the 1890s, the rising number of African Americans murdered by LYNCHING caused Georgia State Representative Henry McNeil Turner to champion the move back to Africa. Also disturbed by the threat of lynching, Bishop Lucius Henry Holsey, the founder of Augusta's Paine College, advocated "establishing a black state." With more than two dozen towns populated and governed by African Americans during the 1910s, Oklahoma gave some credence to the possibility of a black state. The TULSA OKLAHOMA RIOT, however, destroyed one of the most affluent black communities in American history and raised doubts about the coexistence of such communities alongside white communities.

The West Indian Cyril Briggs, writing for the *AMSTERDAM NEWS*, took note of political changes in Eastern Europe and published an editorial suggesting African Americans consider the example of those Europeans claiming independence. Briggs, who founded the AFRICAN BLOOD BROTHERHOOD and was closely allied with supporters of COMMUNISM, continued to advocate the idea of black statehood as he wrote for the *Crusader.* His views changed, however, with the rise of MARCUS GARVEY, whom Briggs criticized severely in his editorials. Herbert Harrison, also affiliated with supporters of communism, founded the International Colored Unity League in 1924 specifically to research the establishment of a black state on American soil.

In the 1930s, Elijah Muhammed succeeded Nation of Islam leader Wallace D. Fard and combined Black Nationalism with religion. Under Muhammed's leadership, the Nation of Islam acquired extensive farmland in Michigan and established a national chain of stores, restaurants, and bakeries. The organization expanded until it became one of the most powerful black-controlled economic and political institutions since Garvey's UNIVERSAL UNITED NEGRO IMPROVEMENT ASSOCIATION. The Nation of Islam both emphasized and demonstrated self-sufficiency, pride in black culture, and racial autonomy.

During the 1960s, Malcolm X lent even greater influence to the Nation of Islam prior to his break with the organization and became a powerful spokesperson of African Americans as a nation already established within a nation. The Black Panther Party took a similar stance. They also stressed the need for self-protection and stirred controversy by publicly bearing arms to protect themselves and members of black communities.

Black Nationalism, like the back-to-Africa movement, is characterized in the 21st century more by cultural and intellectual study than by political action.

Further Reading

Kadalie, Modibo M. *Internationalism, Pan-Africanism and the Struggle of Social Classes.* Savannah, Ga.: One Quest Press, 2000.

Smethurst, James E. *The New Red Negro: The Literary Left and African American Poetry, 1930–1946.* New York: Oxford University Press, 1999.

— Aberjhani

Black Unit of the Federal Theater Project, Works Progress Administration

As part of President FRANKLIN DELANO ROOSEVELT's New Deal initiatives, the Works Progress Administration (WPA) Arts Project established in 1935 a Federal Theater Project (FTP) that allowed thousands of unemployed actors, directors, and visual artists to remain employed within their field during the GREAT DEPRESSION. Many African Americans were able to maintain their careers in the dramatic arts or to start them in earnest through the FTP's Black Units.

With much of the country struggling daily for such basics as food and shelter, WPA administrator Harry Hopkins had to convince the U.S. Congress that it was not a waste of money to pull $27 million out of the $5 billion WPA budget and apply it toward the arts. Although he eventually won his case, the battle to retain funding for the arts remained a constant one (much as it does in the 21st century) throughout the FTP's five-year existence.

Hopkins appointed former Vassar professor Hallie Flanagan as director of the FTP. A strong believer in theatrical experimentation, cultural inclusiveness, and local control of productions, Flanagan divided the FTP into 10 regions, each with its own director, throughout the United States. These included specialty units geared toward Hispanics, Yiddish-speaking populations, French, Italians, children, and African Americans.

In her concerns over how best to present African-American theater through the FTP, Flanagan had to wrestle with many of the same issues faced by black leaders in the 1920s. W. E. B. DU BOIS, ALAIN LOCKE, and CHARLES SPURGEON JOHNSON had all dealt with the questions of whether black theater should be left to its own devices as a form of art inherently capable of influencing U.S. society for the better or if it should be consciously employed to serve as a vehicle for racial propaganda. Unlike Flanagan, however, they had never had the use of millions of government dollars to explore possible answers to these questions. To help her devise plans for the Black Units, Flanagan met with renowned actress ROSE MCCLENDON, director John Houseman, and other members of the theater community. McClendon's input was particularly valued not only because of her standing as a superlative actress in black theater but also as a director of the HARLEM EXPERIMENTAL THEATER, a board member of the Theatre Union, and cofounder of the Negro People's Theatre. The latter would eventually become part of the Black Units.

Toward the end of 1936, some 17 Black Units had been formed in such areas as Los Angeles, Oakland, Seattle, Boston, New Jersey, and Connecticut. CHICAGO's Black Unit boasted both a minstrel outfit and a dramatic company. In New York, there were at least four black companies: the LAFAYETTE THEATER Unit, the Black Youth Unit, the African Dance Unit, and the Vaudeville Unit. The Lafayette Theater, after two decades as Harlem's premier entertainment showplace, was well on its way to permanent abandonment until the FTP took it over, and many aspiring black playwrights and actors worked for the first time in the profession with the Black Youth Unit.

Moreover, with the bulk of its budget going toward salaries, the FTP had more African Americans on its payroll than any other employer in Harlem. Aside from the expected musicians, artists, actors, and directors, the units also employed general stagehands, researchers, lighting technicians, sound engineers, business managers, and various clerical assistants.

The question of local leadership was particularly important in New York, where African Americans had already established a strong theatrical tradition and stood to either lose or gain a tremendous amount according to who represented them. The very real restrictions of racist JIM CROW practices reportedly prompted McClendon to nominate white director John Houseman to serve as the New York Black Unit's director. McClendon and others reasoned that Houseman, who had directed an all-black cast in Gertrude Stein's *Four Saints in Three Acts,* would be able to bypass such restrictions as segregated buildings and having his suggestions automatically ignored. Accepting the position, Houseman brought with him a team that included future film director Orson Welles and two black assistants, Edward Perry and Carlton Moss.

To satisfy the demands of both conservatives and modernists, Houseman formed a classical company and an experimental company at the Lafayette. The group began its run of theatrical productions with Frank Wilson's *Walk Together, Chillun,* followed by RUDOLPH FISHER's *The Conjure Man Dies.* The New York Black Unit hit its stride, however, with a modernized production of *Macbeth* that became popularly known as *Voodoo Macbeth.* An overhaul of the Shakespeare classic performed with a Haitian setting, the idea was conceived by Welles's wife Virginia and executed to raving reviews by

The Black Unit of the Federal Theater Project's production of *Haiti* was one of their most politically charged and popular plays. This poster is from 1938. *(Library of Congress, Prints & Photographs Division [LC-USZC2-5469])*

Welles, Houseman, and a cast of more than 100 black actors. The FTP's *Macbeth* was one of the most anticipated productions ever to play Harlem. The show sold out for its opening night, April 14, 1936, and remained sold out for 59 performances. At the end of its Harlem run, it played another two weeks downtown before going on a tour of seven major cities.

Macbeth was successful enough that it allowed both Houseman and Welles to move on to bigger and better things. After producing one more play for the Lafayette, *Turpentine* by Gus Smith and Peter Morell, Houseman and Welles left the Harlem unit to pursue other FTP projects. A team of three blacks took their place: Carlton Moss, Gus Smith, and the West Indian Harry Edward.

The FTP often found itself challenged by the question of which plays to produce and which ones to keep off the stage. While it encouraged black playwrights to produce plays based on black experiences, such plays were set aside when considered too offensive, toward either blacks or whites, or too politically inflammatory. One such play was *Ethiopia.* Described as a living newspaper, a form of drama in which actors recited reports of current events interspersed with speeches and other sources, *Ethiopia* was considered too effective as an editorial on the United States's failure to more forcefully address Italy's invasion of the country. Fear of political embarrassment or a federal reprimand convinced the FTP to cancel the production.

Theodore Ward's *Big White Fog* barely escaped the cancellation of its Chicago production when both the FTP and members of the black community expressed strong doubts about the play's focus on Garveyism and its earthy portrayal of a black urban family's daily hardships. While the play did enjoy a short successful run, it never received the full backing that Ward felt would have made it a major play nationally.

The FTP was often accused of being a haven for COMMUNISM, proponents of which were known to work in theater as they did in many cultural outlets. In 1939, the congressional House Committee on Un-American Activities accused the FTP, and its Black Units in particular, of being overrun by Jews, radicals, blacks, and condescending New York cultural elitists. Congressional cuts in funding ended the program the same year.

Noah: A Human Comedy was one of numerous plays produced by black units of the Federal Theater Project in the 1930s. *(Library of Congress, Prints & Photographs Division [LC-USZC2-5380])*

Further Reading

Craig, E. Quita. *Black Drama of the Federal Theatre Era: Beyond the Formal Horizons.* Boston: University of Massachusetts Press, 1980.

Favor, J. Martin. *Authentic Blackness: The Folk in the New Negro Renaissance.* Durham, N.C.: Duke University Press, 1999.

Fraden, Rena. *Blueprints for a Black Federal Theatre 1935–1939.* New York: Cambridge University Press, 1996.

Mangione, Jesse. *The Dream and the Deal: the Federal Writers Project, 1935–1943.* Syracuse, N.Y.: Syracuse University Press, 1996.

— Aberjhani

Black Wall Street See TULSA, OKLAHOMA, RIOT.

Blake, Eubie (James Hubert Blake) (1883–1983)

composer, songwriter

James Hubert "Eubie" Blake coproduced the 1921 hit *SHUFFLE ALONG*, a musical revue that many felt officially started the Harlem Renaissance, and he maintained a career that lasted well into the 1970s when his songs were featured in another musical, *Bubbling Brown Sugar.*

James Hubert "Eubie" Blake was born on February 7, 1883, in Baltimore, Maryland. His parents, Emily Johnston Blake and John Sumner Blake, were former slaves.

Eubie Blake, as he became popularly known, had exceptionally long fingers and for a time considered the word JAZZ as obscene. His first attempt to play music was on his family's organ. He received piano lessons at the age of six. Then, as a teenager, he ventured out to play ragtime at local brothels and clubs. He composed his first RAGTIME tune, "Charleston Rag," in 1899. Scott Joplin, often referred to as the "king of ragtime," was one of Blake's contemporaries.

In 1915, Blake formed a partnership with the singer and lyricist NOBLE SISSLE. The musical duo wrote "It's All Your Fault," which became a hit when recorded by the white songstress of the BLUES tradition, SOPHIE TUCKER. In 1921, Blake and Sissle, along with the comedy team of Flournoy Miller and Aubrey Lyles, wrote the triumphant *Shuffle Along.* The musical revue featured FLORENCE MILLS, PAUL ROBESON, JOSEPHINE BAKER, the music of *HALL JOHNSON* and composer WILLIAM GRANT STILL. *Shuffle Along* proved such a success in NEW YORK CITY that eventually three national touring companies of the revue were in operation at the same time. Harlem Renaissance poet LANGSTON HUGHES wrote in his autobiographical *The Big Sea* that "it was the musical revue, *Shuffle Along,* that gave a scintillating send-off to that Negro vogue in Manhattan . . . *Shuffle Along* was a honey of a show." Some of the timeless songs from the Broadway hit are "Shuffle Along," "Love Will Find a Way," and "I'm Just Wild about Harry." The last of these became the campaign song for President Harry Truman.

After the success of *Shuffle Along,* Blake composed scores for other musicals: *CHOCOLATE DANDIES* (1924), *Blackbirds of 1930* (1930), *Shuffle Along of 1933* (1933), *Swing It* (1937), and *Shuffle Along of 1952* (1952). A benchmark Blake song from *Blackbirds of 1930* is "Memories of You."

The energetic Blake conducted music for the United Service Organization Hospital during World War II, put himself back in school at the age of 66 to study theory and composition at New York University and, in 1969, went into the recording studios to produce an album, *The Eighty-Six Years of Eubie Blake.* At age 89 in 1972, Blake inaugurated his own record company. In 1978, *Eubie,* a revue based on his music, had a successful Broadway run.

Eubie Blake was the recipient of many honors. In 1981, he was awarded the Presidential Medal of Freedom. He received honorary doctorate degrees from Brooklyn College in New York, Dartmouth College in New Hampshire, Rutgers University in New Jersey, and the New England Conservatory of Music in Massachusetts.

The phenomenal Eubie Blake died on February 12, 1983, five days after his 100th birthday.

Further Reading

Hughes, Langston. *The Big Sea.* New York: Hill & Wang, 1995.

Jasen, David A., and Gene Jones. *Spreadin' Rhythm Around, Black Popular Songwriters, 1880–1990.* New York: Schirmer Books, 1998.

— Sandra L. West

blues

The blues, a secular music form created by African Americans to express the anguish, humor, and challenges of their lives, was popularized and evolved during the Harlem Renaissance through the talents of such performers as MA RAINEY (Gertrude Malissa Nix Pridgett Rainey), CLARA SMITH, BESSIE SMITH, and Mamie Smith. It was a music that also found its way into the literature of the period and became at times a dividing line between the tastes of the black masses and the black intelligentsia.

The blues possess a very distinctive sound. Though there are improvisations upon the basic theme, blues is usually characterized by a 12-bar 3-line stanza, more specifically a 12-bar iambic lyric bar with two unaccented lines and one accented line; a primary line, a repetition of that primary line; and a new third line. The all-important third line usually delivers lyrics of gritty pathos or tongue-in-cheek humor. The lyrics often combine heartbreaking sadness with straightforward honesty. The pace of the blues is typically unhurried. The tone can be melancholy and mournful, but it can also be humorous and profound. Candor and emotional depth constitute the blues aesthetic.

There are, generally, three types of blues songs: country or rural, city or classic, and urban. According to black music historian Eileen Southern in *The Music of Black Musicians: A History,* country blues involves one singer with his guitar; city blues was sung by women during the Harlem Renaissance years with a piano or orchestra; and urban blues, played with electric guitars and more modern instruments, developed in the 1940s . Examples of country or rural blues singers who played guitar during the 1920s were Blind Lemon Jefferson (1897–1930) and Huddie "Leadbelly" Ledbetter (1888–1949). City blues singers include Bessie Smith, and urban blues is still played by B. B. King.

The themes of blues songs include earthy sexuality, the fickleness of love, marital infidelity, misery, and tales of conflict between lovers. The songs expose the many injustices black people have faced. But, more often, the blues mourns a failed love affair or departed lover. An example of the latter is "How Long Blues" (1928), in which the singer wails: "You have left me singin' those how long blues."

NEW ORLEANS, Louisiana; Memphis, Tennessee; CHICAGO, Illinois; and the Mississippi Delta are popularly held as major birthplaces of the blues. There are actually a Delta school of blues singing (country blues) and a Chicago sound, but generally speaking, the blues resulted from spirituals and work songs sung by black people on plantations and workplaces all over the South during the 1800s. As blacks in the early 20th century participated in the GREAT MIGRATION, leaving plantations for more industrialized areas within the United States, they carried the blues with them.

Some of the early blues interpreters were W. C. HANDY, who wrote "Memphis Blues" in 1909, and Ma Rainey, who recorded "See, See Rider" in 1924. Rainey was called the "Mother of the Blues," and Handy the "Father of the Blues." Bessie Smith, known as "Empress of the Blues," recorded "Downhearted Blues" in 1923. A noted deep-rooted blues singer was Mamie Smith with her Jazz Hounds. Smith recorded "Harlem Blues" in 1920, a song that was immensely popular and profitable. Other blues singers of the 1920s included Bertha "Chippie" Hill, Sara Martin, Sippie Wallace, and Clara Smith. Smith was known as the "Queen of the Moaners." JAZZ singer BILLIE HOLIDAY later wrote and immortalized "Fine and Mellow" in a melding of blues and jazz tones. And, in more contemporary years, Muddy Waters (McKinley Morganfield) sung the mischievously titled blues "Hoochie Coochie Man" in the 1950s.

The predominate instrument of the blues singer is the guitar, though the piano and full orchestra were later introduced when the blues evolved under the influence of jazz and the SWING SOUND in the 1930s. By the 1940s, the blues took on a faster beat. The stanzas, pace, themes, and instruments of blues songs were often supplemented by vocal "props" from growls to train bells.

When performing with an orchestra, blues singers often employed the call and response style developed among West Africans and African Americans. In this style, the sound of a musical instruments follow the vocals of the singer in a call and response manner. The vocalist calls out lyrics, and the instrumentalist responds. Examples of the call and response genre can be found in Jimmy Rushing's 1939 "Goin' to Chicago Blues," and Joe Williams's 1955 "Every Day (I Have the Blues)," both performed with the COUNT BASIE band.

The blues also entered the films and literature of the Harlem Renaissance years. The movie *St. Louis Blues* in 1929 featured the blues singing of Bessie Smith. CARL VAN VECHTEN, arts patron and author of the novel *NIGGER HEAVEN,* wrote the article "The Black Blues" for *Vanity Fair* in 1925. Van Vechten wrote that the blues were the "Negro's prayer to a cruel Cupid." LANGSTON HUGHES, quoted in Van Vechten's article, described the music as "sad, sadder even than the Spirituals. . . ." Hughes himself remains well known for his bouncy blues poetry about the human condition, particularly those poems in his book *The Weary Blues.* WILLIAM WARING CUNEY also used the blues as an element of poetry about black life.

It should be noted, however, that as popular as the blues was, it was not the music of such *NEW NEGRO* movement proponents as *CRISIS* magazine editor Dr. W. E. B. DU BOIS, philosophy professor Dr. ALAIN LOCKE, and poet and educator STERLING ALLEN BROWN. An English professor at HOWARD UNIVERSITY in WASHINGTON, D.C., Brown was disparaged by his colleagues because he appreciated blues music and authored blues poetry, traits that endeared him to his students.

Du Bois, author of the Talented Tenth philosophy, omitted from the NATIONAL ASSOCIATION FOR THE ADVANCEMENT OF COLORED PEOPLE publication materials pertaining to the blues. The music with its "victim" mentality, risqué scenes, and ribald humor was deemed, by his dismissal of it, as music that the community of educated strivers and uplifters of the race did not need.

Dr. Alain Locke discusses spirituals—as a black folk music—in his definitive anthology *The New Negro* (1925). But there is neither an assessment of the popular, big-money-making blues form nor hope for it in the grander scheme of things. In the dignified *New Negro* mandate, according to Locke, there was no room for the blues, even when it came in the form of Hughes's *The Weary Blues,* Handy's *St. Louis Blues,* or George Gershwin's American concerto, *Rhapsody in Blue.* Nevertheless, the music remains to this day one of the most popular in the world.

Further Reading

Adler, Mortimer J., ed. *The Negro in American History I. Black Americans 1928–1968.* Chicago: Encyclopædia Britannica Educational Corp., 1969.

Anderson, Paul Allen. *Deep River: Music and Memory in Harlem Renaissance Thought.* Duke: Duke University Press, 2001.

Gates, Henry Louis, Jr., ed. *The Norton Anthology of African American Literature.* New York and London: W.W. Norton, 1997.

Harrison, Daphne Dural. *Black Pearls: Blues Queens of the 1920s.* Piscataway, New Jersey: Rutgers University Press, 1988.

King, B. B., with David Ritz. *Blues All Around Me: The Autobiography of B. B. King.* New York: Avon Books, 1996.

— Sandra L. West

Blumstein's Department Store See HARLEM.

Bolling, Leslie Garland (1898–1955) *sculptor*

Leslie Garland Bolling was a self-taught sculptor whose wood carvings depicted ordinary, everyday people. Excelling at this FOLK ART, his work was included in the private collection of Harlem Renaissance writer and arts patron CARL VAN VECHTEN.

Leslie Garland Bolling was born in Surry County, Virginia, on September 16, 1898. His father was Clinton C. Bolling, a blacksmith, and his mother was Mary Bolling.

Leslie Bolling was educated at Hampton Normal and Agricultural Institute (now Hampton University) from 1916 to 1918. He graduated from the Academy Department of Virginia Union University in 1924. Working as a porter at Everett Waddey Stationery Store in RICHMOND, Bolling married his first wife, Julia V. Lightner, in 1928 and his second, Ethelyn M. Bailey, in 1948. He did not have any children.

Bolling had no formal art instruction, but he turned his woodcarving hobby into a serious pursuit in 1926, at a time when "whittling" was enjoying a national revival. Using a jackknife and the soft wood of the female poplar tree, he created an average of only six pieces a year. Between 1933 and 1937, Bolling created a seven-piece series entitled *Days of the Week.* The series included small detailed carvings of expressive people performing ordinary chores: *Aunt Monday* washed clothes in a tub, and *Mama on Saturday* removed the bird roasted for Sunday from the oven. Art patron Van Vechten acquired for his collection Bolling's well-known *Cousin-on-Friday,* a piece that shows a domestic worker scrubbing a floor.

Aside from his *Days of the Week* series, Bolling's works include *Red Cap, The Workman, A Study of Curves, The Runner, Puff Sleeves, Portrait Bust of a Friend, President Roosevelt, Mrs. Roosevelt, My Idol, Figure Reclining No. 1, Figure Reclining No. 2,* and *Bunny.* He reportedly carved 51 pieces in his lifetime.

In 1933, Bolling exhibited at the National Negro Exhibition of the Smithsonian Institution, encouraged by HOWARD UNIVERSITY art historian John A. Porter and Howard University art professor James V. Herring. In 1935, he had a one-man show at the Richmond Academy of Arts (now Virginia Museum of Fine Arts), the first person of color to do so. In 1940, a photograph of his work appeared in *The Negro in Art* by ALAIN LOCKE, published by Howard University, and that same year he carved a bust of operatic contralto MARIAN ANDERSON after her performance in Richmond. He exhibited extensively with the HARMON FOUNDATION in NEW YORK CITY and with its traveling shows from 1934 to 1940: the William D. Cox Gallery in New York (1937); the Hampton,Valentine Museum, Virginia Artists' Exhibition (1934); the Richmond Artists' Exhibition (1934); the New Jersey State Museum (1935); and the Texas Centennial Celebration of 1936.

Bolling was the first black artist to exhibit at Richmond's white museum, and he was reportedly instrumental during the 1930s in initiating the first WORKS PROGRESS ADMINISTRATION funded community art center for black people in the South. Richmond was known at the time as the Harlem of the South, and Bolling helped establish there the Craig House Art Center on 17th Street, a facility similar to the famous HARLEM COMMUNITY ART CENTER and the SOUTH SIDE COMMUNITY ART CENTER in Chicago. He taught wood carving there from 1931 to 1941.

Bolling left Richmond for Pennsylvania, then lived in New York during the 1950s. He was represented there by the Cox gallery and died in New York on September 27, 1955. He was buried in Richmond.

Further Reading

Bearss, Sara B., John T. Kneebone, J. Jefferson Looney, Brent Tarter, and Sandra Gioia Treadway, eds. *Dictionary of Virginia Biography, Volume 2.* Richmond: The Library of Virginia, 2001.

Reynolds, Gary A., and Beryl J. Wright. *Against The Odds: African-American Artists and the Harmon Foundation.* Newark, N.J.: The Newark Museum, 1989.

— Sandra L. West

Bontemps, Arna (Arnaud Wendell Bontemps)

(1902–1973) *writer, editor, librarian*

A children's author, historian, novelist, and editor, Arna Bontemps was a multifaceted writer and librarian who secured a number of significant literary papers for FISK UNIVERSITY.

Born on October 13, 1902, in Alexandria, Louisiana, Arnaud Wendell Bontemps was part of an African-American, Catholic family of French lineage. His father was Paul Bismark Bontemps, a successful brick mason and trombonist with Claiborne Williams's JAZZ band. His mother was Maria Carolina Pembroke, a teacher and dressmaker who died when Arna was young. His maternal grandmother, Sarah Pembroke, nicknamed him Arna. The Bontemps lived on Ninth and Winn Streets in Alexandria but, because of growing anti-black sentiment, in 1906 moved to the Watts area of Los Angeles, California. They converted to the Seventh-Day Adventist faith.

Arna attended Ascot Avenue School in Los Angeles, and he graduated from San Fernando Academy in 1920. His father, who wanted Arna to become a bricklayer, restricted his son's relentless reading because he considered it unhealthy. Arna loved Robert Louis Stevenson's novel *Treasure Island* and any books he could find about black heroes. He wanted to immerse himself in black culture and write about it, a thought that horrified his father.

To please his father, Bontemps enrolled in Pacific Union College, a Seventh-Day Adventist institution in Napa City, California, as a premed major. He later changed his major to English when he decided to become a writer. Graduating in 1923, he obtained a job at the Los Angeles Post Office where he befriended WALLACE THURMAN, the future novelist and editor of *FIRE!!* magazine. Thurman encouraged Bontemps to relocate to HARLEM, just as he planned to do himself, if he really wanted to write. Bontemps moved to NEW YORK CITY shortly after his first poem "Hope" was published in *THE CRISIS: A RECORD OF THE DARKER RACES* (August 1924).

Reaching Harlem, he rented living quarters at Fifth Avenue and 129th Street and acquired a teaching position at Harlem Academy, a Seventh-Day Adventist Church School on SEVENTH AVENUE and 127th Street. One of his students was Alberta Johnson of DuPont, Georgia. They married in 1926 and became parents of six children: Joan, Paul, Poppy, Camille, Constance, and Arna. Bontemps wrote poetry, attended receptions at the DARK TOWER salon on 136th Street, and met LANGSTON HUGHES, who would become his lifelong friend.

Bontemps and Hughes exchanged more than two thousand letters during their 40-year friendship. Both were born in 1902, both came from literate families, and both had fathers who rejected black culture and abhorred their sons' decision to write. They were also physically similar. Poet COUNTEE CULLEN's father, Rev. Frederick A. Cullen, supposedly could never tell Bontemps and Hughes apart.

Bontemps, like Hughes, did not attend the legendary CIVIC CLUB DINNER in 1924. However, he did join the Harlem Writers Guild and was a member of Georgia Douglas Johnson's literary salon in WASHINGTON, D.C., along with Hughes and novelist JEAN TOOMER.

Bontemps won many awards for his work based on historical, religious, and personal literary themes. In 1926 he won *OPPORTUNITY* magazine's Pushkin Prize for the poem "Golgotha Is a Mountain." John W. Word III later set this poem to music. *Crisis* magazine published "Dirge" in May 1926. In 1927, Bontemps won the Pushkin Prize for "The Return" and the first place *Crisis* poetry prize for "Nocturne at Bethesda." Twenty-three of Bontemps' poems written during the 1920s are collected in *Personals* (1963).

Bontemps earned only \$5 to \$8 per poem. When patronage from wealthy individuals withered, leaving writers without supplemental economic support, Bontemps began to write novels. His first was *God Sends Sunday* (1931) about a black jockey. Bontemps and Cullen later molded it into a play called *St. Louis Woman.* After writing *God Sends Sunday,* Bontemps

Arna Bontemps, shown here in 1939, was one of the most prolific and influential writers and editors of the Harlem Renaissance. *(Library of Congress, Prints & Photographs Division, Carl Van Vechten Collection [LC-USZ62-100865])*

moved to Alabama to teach at Oakwood Junior College. Oakwood administrators chastised his literary lifestyle and ordered him to burn his books. Fleeing Alabama, he moved in with his father in California and completed a story called "A Summer Tragedy " (1932), which won *Opportunity's* literary prize.

Surrounded by his own talkative children, Bontemps found his niche in children's literature, which he oftentimes coauthored with Hughes. *Popo and Fifina* (1932) was illustrated by Harlem Renaissance cartoonist E. SIMMS CAMPBELL. *You Can't Pet a Possum* was published in 1934, *The Pasteboard Bandit* in 1935, and *Sad Face Boy* in 1937.

A historical novel about the Prosser slave insurrection, *Black Thunder,* was published in 1936, while *Drums at Dusk,* another historical novel, was published in 1939.

In the 1940s, Bontemps cowrote W. C. HANDY's *Father of the Blues: An Autobiography,* moved to Illinois, and began graduate studies at the University of Chicago. Previously a Harlem Renaissance participant, he now became a member of the CHICAGO Renaissance (1935–50). He worked with the Illinois Writers' Project and South Side Writers' Group, befriended novelist RICHARD NATHANIEL WRIGHT *(Black Boy, Native Son)* and in 1943 earned a master's degree in library science. Bontemps became head librarian of Fisk University and inaugurated a Langston Hughes Renaissance Collection that included works by Toomer and Cullen.

In 1945, Bontemps published a biographical series, *We Have Tomorrow,* and (with Jack Conroy of the Illinois Writers' Project) wrote a study of black migration, *They Seek a City,* revised in 1966 as *Any Place but Here.* With Conroy in 1942, Bontemps wrote three juvenile novels, including *Fast Sooner Hound,* and in 1949 he edited *The Poetry of the Negro* with Hughes.

By 1956, when he was awarded the Jane Addams Award for *The Story of the Negro,* Bontemps was a two-time recipient of the Julius Rosenwald Fellowship for writing and a John Simon Guggenheim Fellow. With Hughes, he edited *The Book of Negro Folklore* in 1958. He then completed two books about George Washington Carver, as well as *Frederick Douglass: Slave, Fighter, and Freeman* (1959).

In 1965, Bontemps retired from Fisk. Later, he taught at the University of Illinois, published *Great Slave Narratives,* lectured at Yale University, and curated their JAMES WELDON JOHNSON Collection. He returned to Fisk in 1971 as writer-in-residence and edited *The Harlem Renaissance Remembered* in 1972.

Bontemps died on June 4, 1973. The Arna Bontemps African American Museum and Cultural Arts Center in Alexandria was founded in 1988.

Further Reading

Fleming, Robert E., ed. *James Weldon Johnson and Arna Wendell Bontemps: A Reference Guide.* New York: Macmillan Publishing Company, Inc., 1978.

Jones, Kirkland C. *Renaissance Man from Louisiana: A Biography of Arna Wendell Bontemps.* Westport, Conn.: Greenwood Press, 1992.

Nichols, Charles H., ed. *Arna Bontemps–Langston Hughes Letters 1925–1967.* New York: Dodd, Mead & Company, 1980.

— Sandra L. West

Bottomland

Rather than a true musical revue, *Bottomland* was tailored to showcase the music of the Clarence Williams Trio during the summer of 1927 at Broadway's Princess Theatre. Playing 21 performances there, it also played the Savoy Theatre in Atlantic City, New Jersey.

A popular radio and recording group for Okeh Records, the Clarence Williams Trio was one of several entertainment ventures headed by Williams. It included Williams, his wife Eva Taylor, a former cast member of the 1921 hit musical *SHUFFLE ALONG,* and Sara Martin.

Bottomland, Williams stated in various interviews, was the result of requests from fans of the Clarence Williams Trio to see their favorite group perform live. Williams wrote the book, music, and lyrics for the show himself. With more singing than actual acting, the show told the story of May Mandy Lee, who leaves her southern home in Bottomland to join a friend working as a singer in NEW YORK CITY. She arrives in the city only to discover that her friend, instead of living the life of glamour described in her letters, is actually suffering from alcoholism and struggling through performances in rundown clubs. Although critics dismissed the show as too insubstantial for Broadway, they and audiences alike applauded such featured songs as the title "Bottomland" and "Shootin' the Pistol." In addition to the Clarence Williams Trio, singer Katherine Henderson and a chorus of eight children also performed in *Bottomland.*

A native of NEW ORLEANS, Williams was much more successful as a composer and music publisher than producer. He became well-known for such songs as "Tain't Nobody's Business If I Do." "Sugar Blues," "West End Blues," and "Baby, Won't You Please Come Home." He was also a prominent recording director who influenced the careers of BESSIE SMITH, KING OLIVER, LOUIS ARMSTRONG, Sidney Bechet, and many others.

Further Reading

Slout, William L. *Broadway's Poor Relations: Plays of Repertoire and Stock, 1920–1930.* San Bernardino, Calif.: Borgo Press, 1999.

Steyn, Mark. *Broadway Babies Say Goodnight: Musicals Then and Now.* New York: Routledge Publishing, 2000.

— Aberjhani

Braithwaite, William Stanley Beaumont

(1878–1962) *poet, editor*

William Stanley Beaumont Braithwaite, a self-educated man, contributed to the Harlem Renaissance as a poet, literary critic, editor of poetry anthologies, and publishing house founder.

William Braithwaite was born in Boston, Massachusetts, on December 6, 1878. At the age of 12, he was forced to leave school to work and support the family, following the death of his father, William Smith Braithwaite. He was home-schooled for the balance of his early education by his mother, Emma DeWolfe Braithwaite.

He worked as a typesetter in a print shop and in a bookstore surrounded by classics; there, he began to read the poetry of John Keats and William Wordsworth. In the late 1800s, he became a member of the AMERICAN NEGRO ACADEMY, a literary and intellectual society in WASHINGTON, D.C. By 1903, he began to write essays on nature—such as "Twilight: An Impression," published in *CRISIS* magazine (April 1912)—and verse that was more classical and romantic than racial. One example was "Scintilla," which was published in *Crisis* magazine in April 1915. Aside from readings of the early novels of JESSIE REDMOND FAUSET, Braithwaite was a conservative critic of Harlem Renaissance writers. He analyzed the history of African Americans in American literature in an essay called "The Negro in Literature" for *Crisis* magazine (September 1924).

In 1904, Braithwaite published *Lyrics of Life and Love.* Four years later, *The House of Falling Leaves, with Other Poems* was published. From 1909 to 1929, he was literary editor of the *Boston Transcripts.* He published the annual *Anthology of Magazine Verse and Yearbook of American Poetry* from 1913 to 1929. In 1918, the NATIONAL ASSOCIATION FOR THE ADVANCEMENT OF COLORED PEOPLE recognized Braithwaite by awarding him the SPINGARN MEDAL

His career continued in 1919 when he wrote *The Story of the Great War,* one of several contributions to WORLD WAR I literature by African-American writers. In 1921, he instituted the B. J. Brimmer Publishing Company and served as its editor until the company filed for bankruptcy in 1927. He was appointed professor of creative literature at Atlanta University in 1935, and he served on the editorial board of *Phylon* magazine, a sociological journal founded by W. E. B. DU BOIS at the university. *Phylon* published his autobiography, *The House Under Arcturus,* in 1941.

Retiring in 1945, Braithwaite moved to HARLEM. He published his *Selected Poems* in 1946 and *The Bewitched Parsonage,* a biography of the literary Bronte family, in 1950. He died on June 8, 1962.

Further Reading

Posnock, Ross. *Color and Culture: Black Writers and the Making of the Modern Intellectual.* Cambridge, Mass.: Harvard University Press, 1998.

Wintz, Cary D., ed. *The Politics and Aesthetics of "New Negro Literature."* New York: Garland Publishing, 1996.

— Sandra L. West

Brawley, Benjamin Griffith (1882–1939) *writer, poet, social historian*

Benjamin Griffith Brawley edited the well-received *The Negro Genius* in 1937. Among the era's myriad defenders and patrons, however, he was often a scathing critic of Harlem Renaissance writers.

Benjamin Griffith Brawley was born in Columbia, South Carolina, on April 22, 1882. His father was Edward Brawley and his mother Margaret Dickerson Brawley.

Brawley received his B.A. from Atlanta Baptist College (now Morehouse College) in 1901. He earned a second B.A. from the University of Chicago in 1906, and an M.A. from Harvard University in 1908. After Harvard, he became a HOWARD UNIVERSITY professor circa 1910, a professor of English at Morehouse College in 1912, taught at Shaw University circa 1920, and returned to Howard in 1931. In between teaching, in 1921 he was ordained a Baptist minister and pastored in Massachusetts for one year.

Brawley was one of the most productive anthologists of the period, publishing the following: *The Negro in Literature and Art in the United States* (1910); *A Short History of the American Negro* (1913); *The Negro in Literature and Art* (1918); *A Social History of the American Negro* (1921); *New Survey of English Literature* (1925); *Negro Builders and Heroes* (1937); and the popular *The Negro Genius* (1937). A poem, "The Freedom of the Free," subtitled "Emancipation Exposition Poem," was published in *CRISIS: A RECORD OF THE DARKER RACES* (November 1913). He wrote an essay about Rev. John Jasper of RICHMOND, VIRGINIA, and his legendary 1880 sermon "The Sun Do Move" for *The Negro Caravan* (1941).

As a critic, Brawley often lashed out against Harlem Renaissance writers. Upon the publication of the explicit literary journal *FIRE!!*, produced by WALLACE THURMAN and LANGSTON HUGHES in 1926, Brawley stated: "If Uncle Sam ever finds out about it, it will be debarred from the mails." When Hughes's *Fine Clothes to the Jew* was published in 1927, Brawley brashly critiqued the book as "the sad case of a young man of ability who has gone off on the wrong track altogether." However, when ERIC DERWENT WALROND's *Tropic Death* debuted in 1926, Brawley conceded: "It is hardly too much to say that in a purely literary way, it is the most important contribution made by a Negro to American letters since the appearance of [Paul Lawrence] Dunbar's *Lyrics of Lowly Life.*"

Benjamin Brawley died on February 1, 1939.

Further Reading

Lewis, David Levering. *When Harlem Was in Vogue.* New York: Vintage Books, 1982.

Mitchell, Angelyn, ed. *Within the Circle: An Anthology of African American Literary Criticism from the Harlem Renaissance to the Present.* Durham, N.C.: Duke University Press, 1994.

— Sandra L. West

Braxton, William See ART AND THE HARLEM RENAISSANCE.

Bricktop (Ada Beatrice Queen Victoria Louise Virginia Smith) (1894–1984) *entertainer, nightclub hostess*

After starting out as a teenage vaudeville performer, Bricktop grew into an internationally celebrated nightclub singer, hostess, and owner, who operated a succession of clubs in France, New York, Mexico City, and Rome.

Bricktop was born Ada Beatrice Queen Victoria Louise Virginia Smith on August 14, 1894, in Alderson, West Virginia. Her father, Thomas Smith, ran a barbershop, which catered to

Bricktop left New York to enjoy a successful career as an international hostess managing nightclubs in Paris and Rome. She is shown here in Paris in 1934. *(Library of Congress, Prints & Photographs Division, Carl Van Vechten Collection [LC-USZ62-99870])*

whites only, and he was generally considered a prominent citizen in Alderson. He died four years after Bricktop's birth. Her mother, Hattie E. Thompson Smith, was of Scotch-Irish descent and often impressed upon her daughter the belief that they were members of the "first families of Virginia."

Following the death of Thomas Smith, Hattie Smith moved her family to CHICAGO where she operated boardinghouses while raising her four children. Bricktop attended Chicago's integrated public schools until leaving at age 16 to go on tour with the vaudeville team of Miller and Lyles in 1912. Learning singing, dancing, and comedy, she continued her apprenticeship with a number of acts, including McCabe's Georgia Troubabors, the Kinky Do Trio, the 10 Georgia Campers, and the Panama Trio. The last featured Bricktop with Cora Green and FLORENCE MILLS. She also caught the eye of one JACK JOHNSON and performed at his "Café Champ."

She spent extended periods in California and Vancouver before moving on to NEW YORK CITY in 1922. There she worked at the BARRON'S EXCLUSIVE CLUB, run by Barron Wilkins, the man who nicknamed her Bricktop for the fiery red color of her hair. As its name implied, the Exclusive Club was among the most fashionable on the Harlem night scene and brought Bricktop in contact with many of the period's most celebrated talents. However, it was while visiting WASHINGTON, D.C., that she became aware of DUKE ELLINGTON's Washingtonians and arranged for them to play the Exclusive. She later left the Exclusive to headline at CONNIE'S INN.

Bricktop's increasing renown as a performer extended far enough that EUGENE JACQUES BULLARD, a native Georgian who fought for the French in WORLD WAR I, invited her in 1924 to take over as the house singer at Le Grand Duc in PARIS. She replaced Florence Jones, who until then was the only professional black female singer performing in Paris and who had moved to another club. Despite the fact that Le Grand Duc turned out to be a much smaller venue than anticipated, and Jones had taken the club's business with her, Bricktop stuck with the job. Eventually, Paris's American community gravitated toward her, and she became successful enough to open her own club, The Music Box, in 1926. She later took over Le Grand Duc itself and subsequently opened larger and larger clubs then named after her: Bricktop's.

In her 1983 autobiography, written with cultural historian James Haskins, Bricktop credits the American songwriter-composer Cole Porter for her extraordinary success. Both by promoting her club among his famous and affluent friends, and by arranging for Bricktop to give lessons on the Charleston at their private parties, Porter helped her evolve from a hired performer to a celebrated cabaret owner and hostess. Her customers were often considered her friends and came to include some of the most recognized names in 20th century art, literature, and politics, among them the Prince of Wales, F. Scott Fitzgerald, Pablo Picasso, ETHEL WATERS, Kay Boyle, and Man Ray. So strongly did members of America's "Lost Generation" identify with the atmosphere maintained at Bricktop's that it became commonplace for writers like Evelyn Waugh, Ernest Hemingway, and LANGSTON HUGHES to refer to the club and the woman when writing about their experience of 1920s Paris.

She married NEW ORLEANS saxophonist Peter Duconges in 1929. The couple separated several years later but remained married until Duconges's death in 1967. With her establishment in Paris, Bricktop's became an international community center for white and black Americans in France. As such, she was able to help the young JOSEPHINE BAKER make her transition to Paris upon her arrival there in 1925. She teamed up with the English-born soprano Mabel Mercer in 1931, and the two women worked together until 1938. The name Bricktop itself became both a kind of collateral and an institution which its owner was able to move from country to country whenever necessary.

The GREAT DEPRESSION which had been strangling the U.S. economy since 1929 caught up with Paris in the mid-1930s, and Bricktop was forced to close her club in 1936. Like other Americans in Europe in 1939, Bricktop was driven from France during the beginning rumblings of World War II. Returning to New York, she met with friends she had known in Paris, including Porter and Mercer. She was not, however, able to duplicate the success she'd enjoyed overseas and in 1943 moved to Mexico City. There, she recaptured some of the grandeur of her Parisian years at The Minuet and Chavez's.

She left Mexico City in 1949 with the intent of returning in a few days to renew her working permit. That plan was dropped when she met white BLUES singer Hugh Shannon in New York and they decided to head for Europe. She reopened Bricktop's in Paris only to find that the war had changed both the city of Paris and the quality of Americans who now came to the city. Whereas she had previously been sheltered from racism by the cosmopolitan attitudes of her affluent friends, she found herself subjected to it by a different class of Americans who often brought their racism with them and encouraged French citizens to adopt a similar behavior toward African Americans.

Bricktop managed to keep her Paris location open for a single entertainment season before moving on to Rome. With Hollywood doing steady business shooting films in Italy, she again catered to a glamorous crowd consisting of such individuals as Ella Fitzgerald, LOUIS ARMSTRONG, Frank Sinatra, Shirley MacLaine, King Farouk, and the Duke and Duchess of Windsor.

Declining health and the competitive nature of the night club business led to Bricktop's partial retirement in 1964 at the age of 69. Money inherited from her sister Blonzetta's dealings in real estate left her financially secure enough to spend her last years visiting friends and, well into her 80s, making guest appearances at various clubs and on television. She died in New York City in 1984.

Further Reading

Bricktop, with James Haskins. *Bricktop.* New York: Welcome Rain Publishers, 2000.

Hill, Anthony D. *Pages From the Harlem Renaissance: A Chronicle of Performance.* New York: Peter Lang Publishing, 1996.

— Aberjhani

Brooks, Gwendolyn (Gwendolyn Elizabeth Brooks Blakely) (1917–2000) *poet*

Illinois poet laureate Gwendolyn Brooks published poems in *CRISIS: A RECORD OF THE DARKER RACES* and *OPPORTUNITY* during the 1930s. She also won the 1950 Pulitzer Prize in poetry for her volume *Annie Allen,* the first African American and the youngest poet, male or female, to do so. She was three years old when the 1920s Harlem Renaissance blossomed but became a participant in the movement through its midwestern counterpart, the CHICAGO Renaissance, that immediately followed HARLEM's in 1935. During her 60-year career, Brooks authored more than 20 books and influenced generations of writers and readers throughout two major literary periods.

Brooks was born on June 7, 1917, in Topeka, Kansas, when her schoolteacher mother, Keziah Corinne Wims Brooks, returned to her family home to give birth. Her father, David Anderson Brooks, was a musician and janitor, whom his more assertive wife sometimes overshadowed. In later years, as if to endow him with voice, Brooks named her chapbook publishing company after her father. The David Company published *Winnie* (1988), in tribute to Winnie Mandela, "Mother Africa," social worker and wife of Nelson Mandela.

Brooks's mother often said that her daughter, who as a child read the poets T. S. Eliot, Ezra Pound, and Wallace Stevens, would grow up to be a "lady Paul Laurence Dunbar." She once rebuked her daughter's elementary school teacher, who didn't believe Brooks had produced a well-written composition, with, "She can write better than you."

Brooks began writing poetry at the age of seven and was published in the *CHICAGO DEFENDER* while still a child. When she became an adolescent, she met Harlem Renaissance writers JAMES WELDON JOHNSON and LANGSTON HUGHES. Hughes, who also wrote for the *Chicago Defender,* befriended Brooks and confirmed her gifts as a poet.

Brooks attended Hyde Park High School, Wendell Phillips High School, and graduated from Englewood High School. In 1936, she graduated from Wilson Junior College (now Kennedy-King). She once worked as a secretary for a fortune-teller in Chicago and for a time as a domestic worker, but by 1934 she was a part-time staffer at the *Chicago Defender,* where she contributed almost 100 poems in a weekly poetry column. She taught poetry workshops and creative writing at Northeastern Illinois University, Elmhurst College, and the University of Wisconsin. She taught at Columbia College in Chicago in 1963.

In 1938, the same year her terse poem "Miss Corley's Maid" was published in *Opportunity,* she met poet Henry Blakely II at a young council meeting sponsored by the NATIONAL ASSOCIATION FOR THE ADVANCEMENT OF COLORED PEOPLE. They married one year later and had two children, Nora and Henry Blakely III. They were separated from 1969 to 1973, and Blakely died in July 1996.

Brooks wrote poems about everyday black people and their world. She celebrated black women who wore their hair in its natural "nappy" state and wrote about southern immigrants who stood idly on northern street corners, little boys learning about honor, abortions, and life in cramped Chicago kitchenettes. Her most anthologized poem, "We Real Cool," was written after she walked past a neighborhood pool hall filled with players who probably should have been in school. Her first poetry collection, *A Street in Bronzeville,* set in a Chicago neighborhood, was published in 1945 during the literary era of "urban realism."

Hughes wrote of *A Street in Bronzeville* in his review for *Opportunity* magazine: "several reasons why I find it enormously to my liking immediately come to mind. First, I think it is her great simplicity—I know what every one of her poems is about at a single reading. Second, I think it is her picture-power—I see the places and people she writes about. Third, it is no doubt because of my own sense of identity with her subject matter—me, a Negro, dweller in furnished rooms and kitchenettes, a product of the black belts of our big middle-western industrial cities, Kansas City, Chicago, Cleveland."

In 1950, she won the Pulitzer for *Annie Allen.* A natural sonneteer, she placed urban themes in classical poetic form and wrote in a lean fashion. During the 1960s Black Arts movement (BAM), Brooks evolved dramatically. In April 1967, she attended the Second FISK UNIVERSITY Writers Conference, led by poet Amiri Baraka (LeRoi Jones). After experiencing the fierce self-affirmation of young black poets at Fisk, she removed her books from the control of white publishers and put them in the hands of black publishers. She began to cultivate a wider audience of black readers. Whether encountering blacks in taverns or pool halls, she would write poetry about them.

She established the Illinois Poet Laureate Awards in 1969 for elementary and high school writers, and she awarded cash prizes to the children from her own pocket. "Kindness," she often said, was her "religion." She gave wholeheartedly of herself—"until it hurt"—at hospitals, schools, libraries, drug rehabilitation centers, and prisons.

Haki R. Madhubuti (Don L. Lee), chairman emeritus of The Gwendolyn Brooks Center for Creative Writing at Chicago State University, as well as poet, publisher, and founder of Third World Press, recalled that Brooks had "taken the alphabet and poetically structured a new language." With this language, she was influenced and nurtured by late Harlem Renaissance writers, authored more than 20 books, and inspired generations of writers and readers throughout the Chicago Renaissance and the Black Arts Movement. She wrote fiction, children's books, autobiographies, and nonfiction, including the following: *Maud Martha* (1953), *The Bean Eaters* (1960), *Selected Poems* (1963), *In the Mecca* (1968), *Riot* (1969), *The Tiger Who Wore White Gloves* (1970), *Report from Part One* (1972), *A Capsule Course in Black Poetry Writing* (1975), *Young Poet's Primer* (1980), *Blacks* (1987), *Coming Home Children* (1992), *Report From Part Two* (1996), and *In Montgomery* (2001), published posthumously.

Her many commendations include poet laureate of Illinois (1969–2000), service as the 29th poetry consultant to the Library of Congress (1985–86), and more than 75 honorary doctorates.

Gwendolyn Brooks died on December 3, 2000. Madhubuti eulogized in *Black Issues in Higher Education:* "That other poets have championed good writing and literature, have exposed evil in the world, have contributed mightily of personal revenues to the young, to the would-be-writers, to students and to the institutions of common good is without a doubt. However, the only poet who had made it her mission to incorporate all of this and more into a wonderful and dedicated lifestyle is Gwendolyn Brooks."

Further Reading

Kent, George E. *A Life of Gwendolyn Brooks.* Lexington: University Press of Kentucky, 1990.

Madhubuti, Haki R. *Say That the River Turns: The Impact of Gwendolyn Brooks.* Chicago: Third World Press, 1987.

Mootry, Maria K., and Gary Smith, eds. *A Life Distilled: Gwendolyn Brooks, Her Poetry and Fiction.* Urbana and Chicago: University of Illinois Press, 1987.

Tate, Claudia, ed. *Black Women Writers at Work.* New York: Continuum, 1983.

— Sandra L. West

Brooks, Shelton (1886–1975) *songwriter*

Shelton Brooks composed a number of songs that became major hits for entertainers during the Harlem Renaissance and made him one of the most successful songwriters of the era.

Brooks was born on May 4, 1886, in Amesburg, Ontario, Canada. His family migrated to Detroit, Michigan, when he was 15 years old.

A fan of vaudeville entertainment, Brooks attended shows in performance halls. In 1910, he met white BLUES performer SOPHIE TUCKER in one of these halls and sang for her "Some of These Days," a song he had written, which may have been modeled after a similar 1905 tune by Frank Williams. Tucker adopted the song for herself and it became one of her most popular numbers. With the success of the song, she and Brooks began a friendship that lasted years.

In 1911, the songwriter emerged as a performer in *Dr. Herb's Prescription, or It Happened in a Dream,* a musical comedy at CHICAGO's Pekin Theatre. During this same period, he also worked as a drummer with Danny Small's Hot Harlem Band, and in 1915 he conducted a syncopated orchestra in Chicago's Grand Theater, a facility that provided entertainment for African Americans.

In 1916, Brooks wrote another hit, "Walkin' the Dog," that inspired a dance of the same name. "Walkin' the Dog," the origin of which is also attributed to dancer John Sublett, was later fashioned into a dance hit by Junior Walker and the All-stars during the 1960s.

The song that made Brooks a household word was "Darktown Strutters' Ball," published in 1917 and recorded by the Original Dixieland Jazz Band. The song received international attention when, in 1919, it was recorded by famed military band leader Lieutenant James Reese Europe's 369th Infantry Band. Europe was stationed in France during WORLD WAR I, and his band had played a crucial role in the introduction of JAZZ to France and the rest of Europe.

During the 1920s and 1930s, Brooks added to his repertoire with the recording of "Darktown Court Room," a comedy record that sold more than 80,000 copies. He sang and danced in *Miss Nobody from Starland* (1920) and *K of P* (1923). He also performed with the international star FLORENCE MILLS in the musical *From Dixie to Broadway* and traveled across Europe in *Blackbirds* (1932), another stage musical.

Shelton Brooks died on September 6, 1975.

Further Reading

Morgan, Thomas L. *From Cakewalks to Concert Halls: An Illustrated History of African-American Popular Music from 1895 to 1930.* Washington, D.C.: Elliott & Clark, 1992.

Spencer, John Michael. *The New Negroes and Their Music: The Success of the Harlem Renaissance.* Knoxville: University of Tennessee Press, 1997.

— Sandra L. West

Brotherhood of Sleeping Car Porters

The members of the Brotherhood of Sleeping Car Porters, led by A. PHILIP RANDOLPH, battled one of the largest corporations in America for a decade before winning official recognition as the country's first major all-black union.

From 1859 to 1900, George M. Pullman built a business empire on the strength of technological innovation, America's ongoing expansion toward the west coast, and cheap labor in the form of newly freed slaves in need of a means for survival. As travel by train evolved into the dominant means of cross-country transportation during the latter half of the 1800s, Pullman recognized the need for improved facilities to accommodate passengers taking trips that became longer and longer, lasting throughout the day and often overnight. The train compartments in which passengers made these trips were little more than covered wagons designed for rails. They provided neither restroom facilities nor refreshments of any kind, let alone sleeping quarters. Through a succession of experiments starting in 1859, Pullman designed the luxurious Pullman Car. Modeled to provide the comforts of a hotel while speeding from one state to another, the cars showcased velvet-lined interiors, furniture imported from Europe, chandeliers, silk curtains, foldaway beds, restrooms, and glittering mirrors. In 1868, the Delmonico Dining Car joined the lineup and passengers were able to add exceptional meals to their travel experience.

As the Pullman Company grew, so did its competitors with their own luxury cars. Pullman sought to gain an edge for his company by hiring former slaves trained as genteel servants to cater to his customers' every need during their journey. In addition to such expected services as carrying passengers' bags onto the train, escorting them to their seats, preparing their sleeping accommodations when appropriate, and providing requested items, they generally were obligated by company policy to comply with whatever request was made by any given passenger. Among their duties was to wear a smile at all times whether they felt inclined to or not. Providing five-star hotel quality service earned the Pullman porters the title "The Ambassadors of Hospitality."

On the one hand, the Pullman Company provided a much-needed employment opportunity both for former house slaves at odds with where to go or what to do in the wake of the Civil War and for a country facing the flip side of the same dilemma, which was what to do with such individuals. On the other hand,

As editor of the *Messenger* and leader of the Brotherhood of Sleeping Car Porters, A. Philip Randolph helped lay the foundation for the success of the 1950s and 1960s Civil Rights movement. This photo was taken ca. 1911 or 1912. *(Library of Congress, Prints & Photographs Division [LC-USZ62-97538])*

the rules by which the Pullman porters had to perform their jobs often turned them into targets in more ways than one. White children and college students in particular were fond of having the porters perform monkey-like antics for their amusement or splattering with food the uniforms that the porters were required to maintain as spotless as possible. Yet by company rules, the porters were forbidden to complain or refuse any request. The lengths to which they went to satisfy the demands of white customers became so extreme that by 1900 the Pullman porter had become a fixed stereotype of American culture much on par with that of the minstrel show performer. Posters and cartoons lampooning the porters were not uncommon.

Attacks on dignity aside, the Pullman porters also had to contend with a number of professional challenges on a regular basis. They worked an average of 400 hours per month and, on a train ride lasting several days, were allowed only three hours sleep their first night out and less than that on subsequent nights. They were required to spend hours for which they were not paid preparing for journeys or remaining on call. They also often had to perform their own jobs as well as those of conductors, yet they were generally denied promotion to conductor status. And, unlike their white counterparts, black porters were not allowed to live in the company-sponsored planned community known as Pullman, or Pullmantown, Illinois, just outside CHICAGO.

Though its founder died in 1897, the Pullman Company enjoyed nonstop growth, buying out its competitors until it represented an empire that included some 12,000 African-American employees. The first major challenge to the empire did not come from its black workers but instead from the white residents of Pullmantown; their lives were much like northern versions of the southern sharecropper who remained perpetually in debt to his landlord employer. The workers were represented by the labor socialist Eugene V. Debs and his American Railway Union, which welcomed as a member anyone employed by a railroad company. In 1894, Debs called for a strike and national boycott against the Pullman Company. For his leadership and the riots that supposedly resulted from it, Debs received a six-month jail sentence. Employees of the Pullman Company, black and white, received the very clear message that the company was antiunion and any Pullman worker joining a union would be promptly dismissed and replaced.

Whereas the first generation of Pullman porters were newly freed slaves grateful just for an opportunity to survive, an entirely different breed had entered the picture going into the 1920s. Notions of cultural integrity, racial equality, and racial pride were much touted by promoters of the *NEW NEGRO*, a movement intent on distancing itself as far as possible from the kind of BOOKER TALIAFERRO WASHINGTON accommodationist image as yet represented by Pullman porters. The newer generation of porters enjoyed extending the tradition of their forerunners' legendary elegance and deportment, but they resented spending 400 hours on the rails every month for roughly 17 cents per hour, without payment for overtime, earning them $68 and regular abuse.

Unable to let the situation continue as it was, three Pullman porters, considered exemplary representatives of the field, chose to take a risk against the odds. Ashley Totten, Roy Lancaster, and William Des Verney decided the Pullman porters needed a union and that A. Philip Randolph was the man to help them establish it. The charismatic Randolph had actually made his way from Florida to NEW YORK CITY intending to become an actor. However, when approached by the embattled Pullman porters, he had already helped start a half dozen unions that eventually folded. He had also gained a reputation as one of the powerful editors, along with Chandler Owen, of the *MESSENGER*, subtitled as the "only radical Negro magazine in America." He did not support the call for black involvement in WORLD WAR I, criticized the United States for its tolerance of racism and discrimination, and encouraged blacks to defend themselves against LYNCHING. While his uncompromising stance caused government officials to dub him "the most dangerous Negro in America," his work on behalf of the Pullman porters prompted those whom he represented to call him "Chief" or "the Saint."

At first Randolph refused to become involved in the plight of the porters. Acknowledging that their condition was a serious one, he stated he was not the man to help them establish a union. When no one else stepped forward, he decided he had no other choice. On August 25, 1925, some 500 railroad porters, hotel workers, and dining car personnel gathered at the HARLEM Elk Lodge meeting hall on 129th Street to join Randolph in the creation of the first black-controlled union, the Brotherhood of Sleeping Car Porters.

Fully aware of the Pullman Company's antiunion policy and its previous victory over Eugene Debs, Randolph did not expect the company to calmly recognize the Brotherhood of Sleeping Car Porters. He immediately turned the *Messenger* into a publication organ for the new union's grievances and set out across the United States to build support and membership for it. Milton P. Webster took charge of the Chicago branch; E. J. Bradley headed the St. Louis chapter; and "Dad" Moore took on the Oakland division. The men anticipated a long hard battle for recognition by the Pullman Company, but none expected it to take them through the GREAT DEPRESSION and last an entire decade.

The fight for the Brotherhood of Sleeping Car Porters' right to union representation absorbed the lives of nearly all those involved. The union saw its membership swing back and forth between four and three figures. A Ladies Auxiliary to the union was created to garner family and community support for the struggle. The men who formed its leadership more often than not went without salaries and sacrificed jobs and homes out of dedication to their cause. Randolph himself depended on collections taken up on his behalf to provide fare for traveling from city to city. He was on the road when first his mother died and later his brother.

The Brotherhood of Sleeping Car Porters took a major step toward victory in 1934 when they succeeded in becoming the first all-black union admitted into the international ranks of the American Federation of Labor (AFL). They moved closer with the United States Congress's 1934 Railway Labor

Act, which essentially outlawed the Pullman Company's ban on hiring workers affiliated with unions. In 1935, the company was forced into a dramatic showdown vote in which 8,316 porters voted the Brotherhood as its official union of representation over 1,422 for the Pullman Company. In 1937, the Brotherhood became the first black union to sign a labor contract with a major corporation. The porters' work hours were reduced from 400 per month to 240, they received a salary increase with payment for overtime, and they earned the right to redress any unfair loss of employment.

The porters' triumph set the stage for the organization of other black workers and it also established a platform for the Civil Rights movement of the 1950s and 1960s. In 1978, the Brotherhood of Sleeping Car Porters merged with the larger and more modern Brotherhood of Railway and Airline Clerks.

Further Reading

Arnesen, Eric. *Brotherhoods of Color, Black Railroad Workers and the Struggle for Equality.* Cambridge, Mass.: Harvard University Press, 2001.

Bates, Beth Tompkins. *Pullman Porters and the Rise of Protest Politics in Black America, 1925–1945.* Chapel Hill: University of North Carolina Press, 2000.

Bulhe, Mari Jo, Paul Buhle, and Dan Georgakas. *Encyclopedia of the American Left.* New York and Oxford: Oxford University Press, 1998.

Quarles, Benjamin. *The Negro in the Making of America.* New York: Simon and Schuster, 1996.

— Aberjhani

Brown Buddies

Brown Buddies debuted at the Liberty Theatre on October 7, 1930, and ran for 113 performances to become one of the first popular black musical reviews of the 1930s.

Brown Buddies drew on the experiences of African Americans during WORLD WAR I to tell the story of a black army unit that was from St. Louis and served in France. The show included an extended song and dance tribute to Young Men's Christian Association (YMCA) entertainers and a celebratory return of heroes to St. Louis. Included in the cast were BOJANGLES ROBINSON, ADELAIDE HALL, the Red and Struggy comedy team, Putney Dandridge, and Ada Brown.

While critics offered a mixture of reviews regarding *Brown Buddies* as a Broadway musical, nearly all praised the work of Bojangles Robinson and Adelaide Hall. Robinson, by then already an entertainment legend in HARLEM and elsewhere, added to his stature by appearing in the show after being accidentally shot by a Pittsburgh policeman. Robinson had actually brandished his famed gold-plated gun to stop a mugging when the police arrived and mistook him for the robber. Despite his wound, audiences and critics marveled at his ability to focus on and dance with his feet as if they were partners separate from him rather than part of his anatomy.

Adelaide Hall, by then a seasoned performer from such shows as *SHUFFLE ALONG* and *RUNNIN' WILD*, drew repeated praise for her recital of such songs as "My Blue Melody" and "Give Me a Man Like That."

Further Reading

Brantley, Ben. *The New York Times Book of Broadway on the Aisle for the Best Plays of the Last Century.* New York: St. Martin's Press, 2001.

Miller, Scott. *Rebels with Applause: Broadway's Groundbreaking Musicals.* Portsmouth, New Hampshire: Heinemann, 2001.

— Aberjhani

Brown, Charlotte Eugenia Hawkins (Lottie Hawkins) (1883–1961) *educator, activist, writer*

A highly accomplished educator, Charlotte Eugenia Hawkins Brown founded the Alice Freeman Palmer Memorial Institute in 1901, became the only black woman elected to the Twentieth Century Club in Boston in 1928, and authored a book on etiquette in 1941.

Charlotte Eugenia Hawkins Brown was born Lottie Hawkins on the Hawkins plantation in Henderson, North Carolina, on January 11, 1883. (Her birth month has also been recorded as June.) Her mother, Caroline Francis Hawkins, was a former slave who learned to read at Shaw University in Raleigh shortly after emancipation. Her brother was named Mingo. When her biological parents separated, her mother moved the family to Boston, Massachusetts.

Brown matriculated from Allston Allison Grammar School in Cambridge, where she was the graduation speaker. She attended Cambridge English High and Latin School. Changing her name to Charlotte Eugenia, she enrolled at Massachusetts State Normal School with financial aid from Alice Freeman Palmer, the second president of Wellesley College. Throughout her life she studied at Simmons College and at Boston, Harvard, and Temple Universities. She later received honorary degrees from Howard, Lincoln, and Wilberforce Universities and, in 1944, was chosen as an honorary member of the Wellesley College Alumnae Association.

She taught for $30 a month in 1901 at Bethany Institute in McLansville, North Carolina. Her aspiration, however, was to open her own school, as BOOKER TALIAFERRO WASHINGTON had done with Tuskegee Institute in Alabama. In addition to academics, she wanted to design a curriculum that included social skills, for she believed civility and gentility would help eliminate racism. In 1902, her dream was realized with the financial support of Palmer, and the Palmer Institute was founded in Sedalia, North Carolina. She was married in 1911 to Edmund S. Brown, a Harvard graduate, later divorced, and returned to the school's helm until 1952. She then served as financial director until 1955.

Brown's civil rights activism is a matter of public record, and her writings and official papers are collected in libraries throughout the South and at Radcliffe College. Before the modern Civil Rights movement of the 1960s, she entered a North Carolina coffee shop, requested service, and was indeed served without incident. In 1920, driven from a proper seat on a southern train, she sued and won the lawsuit in court.

Brown was genteel, almost to a fault, but her writing reflected a spirit of protest. "Mammy: An Appeal to the Heart of the South," was published by Boston's Pilgrim Press in 1919. The short story, which does not have a happy ending, portrays a female slave after emancipation who, upon the selfish demand of her employer, decides to stay in service and starve with, defend, and protect his family, even though death comes to her for doing so. "Mammy" was anthologized in the 1988 edition of *Afro-American Women Writers, 1748–1933.*

Her nonfiction is indicative of the manner in which she lived and taught. The undated "A Biography" is part of the Schlesinger Library of Women in America at Radcliffe College, along with the essay "My Theory of Public Speaking." Another essay, "Cooperation Between White and Colored Women," was published in *Missionary Review of the World* (June 1922). Her benchmark piece, *The Correct Thing to Do, to Say, to Wear,* was published by Boston's Christopher Publishing House in 1941, was revised in 1965, and was reprinted by the Charlotte Hawkins Brown Foundation in 1990.

Her official papers are housed at Radcliffe, but records on this pioneering woman can also be found at the Greensboro Public Library, the Thomas F. Holgate Library at Bennett College, and the W. C. Jackson Library at the University of North Carolina at Greensboro.

Charlotte Hawkins Brown died on her birthday, January 11, in 1961.

Further Reading

Hubbard, Dolan, ed. *Recovered Writers/Recovered Texts: Race, Class, and Gender in Black Women's Literature.* Knoxville: University of Tennessee Press, 1977.

Wadelington, Charles W. "What One Young African American Woman Could Do: The Story of Dr. Charlotte Hawkins Brown and the Palmer Memorial Institute," *Tar Heel Junior Historian,* Fall 1995.

— Sandra L. West

Brown, Hallie Quinn (1845–1949) *educator, writer, orator*

One of the most accomplished educators of her generation, Hallie Quinn Brown gained international renown as a lecturer, advocate of women's rights, promoter of civil rights, and author.

Brown was born on March 10, 1845, the fifth of six children born to former slaves Thomas Arthur Brown and Frances June Scroggins Brown. After purchasing his freedom, her father provided for his family by working as the steward of a riverboat.

At the age of 19, Brown moved with her family to Chatham, Ontario, where she was educated until the age of 25. She then moved with her family to Ohio. There, she attended Wilberforce University and graduated in 1873. From 1875 to 1879, she taught in the public school system of Dayton, Ohio, and pioneered a night school program for adults. Brown published her first book, *Bits and Odds: A Choice Selection of Recitations,* in 1880. In Columbus, Ohio, she served as dean of Allen University from 1885 to 1887 while simultaneously attending and graduating from Chautauqua Lecture School.

Brown joined the staff of BOOKER TALIAFERRO WASHINGTON's Tuskegee Institute in Alabama in 1892 and until 1893 filled the position of "lady principal." She returned to Wilberforce as professor of elocution for a year before undertaking a five-year lecture tour of Europe. Sponsored partly by the famed abolitionist Frederick Douglass, Brown addressed the British Women's Temperance Association and was appointed representative to the 1897 International Congress of Women.

Like IDA BELL WELLS-BARNETT, Brown was a forerunner in the black women's clubs movement. From 1905 to 1912, she served as president of the Ohio Federation of Colored Women's Clubs. During the same period, she returned to Wilberforce University as professor of elocution and in 1910 traveled as a representative to the Missionary Society of the African Methodist Conference in Edinburgh, Scotland.

She was elected leader of the National Association of Colored Women in 1920. As such, she was instrumental in the preservation of Frederick Douglass's home in Washington, D.C., and also in increasing scholarship funds available to black women. At the 1920 Council of Republican Women in Ohio, Brown was elected vice president. In the same year, she published her book, a manual on presentations called *First Lessons in Public Speaking.* It was the first such book ever published by an African American.

Throughout the 1920s *NEW NEGRO* movement, Brown refrained from writing the kinds of literary works, such as JEAN TOOMER's *Cane* or JESSIE REDMOND FAUSET's *There Is Confusion,* that gave the Harlem Renaissance its cultural thrust. She opted instead to produce works of instructional or historical value and published *The Beautiful: a Story of Slavery,* in 1924; *Tales My Father Told,* in 1925; and *Our Women: Past, Present, and Future,* also 1925. Her most popular work, *Homespun Heroines and Other Women of Distinction, Biographies of 60 Black Women Born in the U.S. and Canada from 1745 to 1900,* was published in 1926, while *Ten Pictures of Pioneers of Wilberforce* appeared in 1937.

In the 1920s and 1930s Brown also lent her voice to the increasing rise from women across the United States in protesting the lynching of African Americans.

Brown never married and she dedicated her life to her work. Wilberforce University recognized her many achievements in 1936 by awarding her an honorary doctorate in law. She died on September 14, 1949, at the age of 104. The Hallie Quinn Brown Community House in St. Paul, Minnesota, and the Hallie Quinn Brown Memorial Library at Wilberforce are named in her honor.

Further Reading

Bracey, Ernest N. *Prophetic Insight: The Higher Education and Pedagogy of African Americans.* Lanham, Maryland: University Press of America, 2001.

Kates, Susan. *Activist Rhetorics and American Higher Education, 1885–1937.* Carbondale, Ill.: Southern Illinois University Press, 2001.

Winegarten, Ruth, and Sharon Kahn. *Brave Black Women: From Slavery to the Space Shuttle.* Austin: University of Texas, 1997.

— Aberjhani

Brown, Sterling Allen (1901–1989) *poet, educator*
Author and editor of several important academic works, including the anthology *The Negro Caravan,* Sterling Allen Brown was one of HOWARD UNIVERSITY's most prominent and influential professors.

Sterling Allen Brown was born in WASHINGTON, D.C. on May 1, 1901, at Sixth and Fairmount Streets, N.W., next door to the present location of the Howard University School of Social Work. His father, Sterling Nelson Brown, a former slave, was a writer, minister at Lincoln Temple Congregational Church, onetime member of the District of Columbia Board of Education, and professor of religion at Howard from the late 1880s to 1929. His mother was Adelaide Allen Brown, valedictorian of her graduating class at FISK UNIVERSITY.

Brown's home environment was saturated with literature, philosophy, and history. His mother recited to her son the verses of Henry Wadsworth Longfellow, Robert Burns, and Paul Laurence Dunbar while she performed house chores. Dunbar was a family friend. Because of his father's academic and civic connections, regular house guests who influenced young Sterling included college founder BOOKER TALIAFERRO WASHINGTON, abolitionist Frederick Douglass, sociologist Dr. W. E. B. DU BOIS, and editor of the *NEW NEGRO* anthology, ALAIN LOCKE.

At Dunbar High School, Brown studied with a number of exceptional African-American teachers, including Frederick Douglass's grandson Haley Douglas; poet and playwright ANGELINA EMILY WELD GRIMKE; later-to-be *CRISIS* literary editor JESSIE REDMOND FAUSET; and Neville Thomas, president of the Washington, D.C. branch of the NATIONAL ASSOCIATION FOR THE ADVANCEMENT OF COLORED PEOPLE (NAACP). After graduating from Dunbar with honors in 1918, Brown won a minority students scholarship to a white college, Williams, where he read Fyodor Dostoyevsky and Leo Tolstoy, began to write poetry about rural people in the countryside that surrounded the college, and listened to the BLUES voice of Mamie Smith. He joined Phi Beta Kappa in 1921, won the Graves Prize for his essay "The Comic Spirit in Shakespeare and Molière," and graduated cum laude from Williams in 1922. He earned his master's degree in English from Harvard University in 1923. At Harvard, he discovered a text that would redefine his writing life: *Modern American Poetry* (1921) by Louis Untermeyer. Through this book, he was introduced to Carl Sandburg, Robert Frost, and other poets who took risks with language.

Editors began to publish Brown's own poetry in the early 1920s. Some of these poems appeared in *The Book of American Negro Poetry* (1922), edited by JAMES WELDON JOHNSON; *Caroling Dusk: An Anthology of Verse by Negro Poets* (1927); edited by COUNTEE CULLEN; and *Negro* (1934), edited by NANCY CUNARD. During this same period, Brown won three major literary awards from *OPPORTUNITY* magazine, sponsored by the NATIONAL URBAN LEAGUE. In 1922, he won second prize for a poem about ROLAND HAYES. In 1927, he captured first prize for the poem "When de Saints Go Ma'ching Home" and third prize, shared with Frank Horne, for an essay titled "The Plight of Certain Intellectuals."

Brown assumed his first teaching assignment at Virginia Seminary and College in Lynchburg (1923–26), where he taught rhetoric and literature. After three years, he began teaching literature at Lincoln University in Jefferson City, Missouri (1926–28).

Brown married Daisy Turnbull in September 1927, and they had one son, John L. Dennis. Remaining in the South, he accepted a position at Fisk, his mother's alma mater, in Tennessee (1928–29). He then went to Howard University as a professor of English in 1929. Brown's colleagues frowned upon his fondness for the blues, JAZZ, Negro spirituals, and the folk literature he had learned to love and which he started writing while teaching in the South. Although his colleagues considered him "low brow," his students revered him for the time he shared with them and his open appreciation for black culture and FOLK ART. Sterling Brown taught students who led the 1960s and 1970s Black Arts movement. Among them were Black Power activist Stokely Carmichael (Kwame Toure); president of Ghana, Kwamé Nkrumah; actor/producer/writer Ossie Davis; poet Lucille Clifton; and writer Amiri Baraka (LeRoi Jones).

Brown completed additional graduate study from 1931 to 1932 at Harvard and wrote groundbreaking class papers but did not complete the requirements for his Ph.D. Two of the class papers written by Brown at Harvard that indicate his inclination toward ethnic character and voice are "Plays of the Irish Character: A Study in Reinterpretation" (1932) and "Negro Character as Seen by White Authors" (1933).

Drawing upon his earlier experiences in the South, Brown published his landmark poetry volume, *Southern Road,* in 1932. Brown wrote the volume using natural, rural dialect and with the invigorating spirit of the *New Negro* movement, as opposed to the "old Negro" of early 1900s dialect poet Paul Laurence Dunbar. To Brown, the rural Negro was a folk hero. The non-pretentious, well-orchestrated collection, embellished with snippets of blues tunes and Negro spirituals that his Howard University colleagues found offensive, was illustrated by E. SIMMS CAMPBELL, black cartoonist of *Esquire* magazine fame. *Southern Road* is divided into three parts, with each section dedicated to a different person. For example, Part 1, "Road So Rocky," is dedicated to Harlem Renaissance poet ANNE BETHEL BANNISTER SPENCER. Each chapter is introduced by an epigram taken from his favorite music.

The introduction for the 1930s edition of *Southern Road* was written by James Weldon Johnson, director of the NAACP, and coauthor of "LIFT EVERY VOICE AND SING." Johnson wrote that Brown had "infused his poetry with genuine characteristic flavor by adopting as his medium the common, racy, living speech of the Negro in certain phases of *real* life." Alain Locke hailed Brown as the folk poet of the *New Negro* movement and highly praised *Southern Road:* "The discriminating few (reviewers of *Southern Road*) go further; they hail a new era in Negro poetry, for such is the deeper significance of this volume."

Some of the poems in *Southern Road* were previously published in *The Carolina Magazine, Contempo, Crisis, Ebony and Topaz, Folk Say, New York Herald Tribune, Books, Palms, Theatre Arts Monthly,* and *Color.* And the volume itself sold well. However, Brown's publisher decided not to reprint it and to reject his second manuscript. The dual rejection caused Brown to become depressed.

Brown served as an editor for the Negro Affairs division of the WORKS PROGRESS ADMINISTRATION's FEDERAL WRITERS' PROJECT from 1936 to 1939. In that capacity, he collected folklore, contributed the essay "The Negro in Washington" to *Washington, City and Capital* (1937), and inaugurated the study *The Negro in Virginia* (1940). He also became a staff member of the Carnegie-Myrdal Study of the Negro (1939). Additionally, he published *The Negro in American Fiction* (1937), *Negro Poetry and Drama* (1937), and the classic anthology *The Negro Caravan* (1941), edited with Ulysses Lee and Arthur P. Davis. Editor Willard Thorp included selections of Brown's work in *A Southern Reader* (1955). In addition to poetry, he published reviews and essays for *New Republic, The Nation, Journal of Negro Education,* and *Phylon.*

Brown retired from Howard in 1969. His acknowledged masterpiece, *Southern Road,* was finally republished in 1975 and his second book of poetry, *The Last Ride of Wild Bill and Eleven Narratives,* came out the same year. His 40 years of service at Howard were punctuated with visiting professorships at the University of Illinois, University of Minnesota, New York University, New School for Social Research, Sarah Lawrence College, and Vassar College. He was elected to the Academy of American Poets and was named poet laureate of the District of Columbia. Members of the Black Arts movement, as well as former students of Brown who felt he deserved greater recognition, literally demanded that Howard University award him an honorary doctorate in 1971.

Sterling Allen Brown, black vernacular poet, died of leukemia on January 13, 1989.

Further Reading

Brown, Sterling A., and Arthur P. Davis, eds. *The Negro Caravan.* New York: Arno Press, 1970.

Gabbin, Joanne V., ed. *Sterling A. Brown: Building the Black Aesthetic Tradition.* Charlottesville: University of Virginia Press, 1994.

Gates, Henry Louis, Jr., and Cornel West. *The African American Century: How Black Americans Have Shaped Our Country.* New York: The Free Press, 2000.

Sanders, Mark A. *Afro-Modernist Aesthetics and the Poetry of Sterling A. Brown.* Athens: University of Georgia Press, 1999.

— Sandra L. West

Brownies' Book

The *Brownies' Book* was an early magazine for African-American children. Its purpose was "to make colored children realize that being colored is a normal beautiful thing, to make them familiar with the history and achievements of the Negro race, and to make them know that other colored children have grown into beautiful, useful, and famous persons."

Brownies' Book: A Monthly Magazine for Children of the Sun, its full and proper title, was produced by the NATIONAL ASSOCIATION FOR THE ADVANCEMENT OF COLORED PEOPLE, which also published *CRISIS: A RECORD OF THE DARKER RACES,* under the editorship of W. E. B. DU BOIS, JESSIE REDMOND FAUSET, and Augustus Granville Dill. It debuted in January 1920 in NEW YORK CITY. Published as a monthly, it cost 15 cents per issue, was approximately 24 pages long, and focused on children's stories, poetry, music, plays, history, and profiles.

One section of *Brownies' Book* was "The Grown-Ups Corner," in which C. M. Johnson wrote about the need to instill "race love" into African-American children. Uniquely, *Brownies' Book* was cowritten by children; for instance, Ruth Marie Thomas, at age 17, interviewed actor CHARLES SIDNEY GILPIN. And the magazine featured a photo of children who participated in the Silent Protest Parade of 1917. The covers of *Brownies' Book* were illustrated by exceptional artists such as Marcellus Hawkins.

Though young people contributed poetry and artwork, the work of adults was also part of the magazine. Novelist NELLA LARSEN wrote fiction for *Brownies' Book,* and the poems "Fairies" and "Winter Sweetness" by LANGSTON HUGHES were published in the January 1921 issue.

Brownies' Book was not the first magazine published specifically for black children. In 1887, Amelia Etta Johnson edited *Joy* for African-American children. On December 1921, due to lackluster community support, Du Bois's "labor of love" for African-American children was published for the last time. The established tradition continued in the 1970s and 1980s when *Ebony* magazine published *Ebony Jr!*

Further Reading

Johnson, Abby Arthur, and Ronald Maberry Johnson. *Propaganda and Aesthetics: The Literary Politics of Afro-American Magazines in the Twentieth Century.* Amherst: University of Massachusetts Press, 1979.

Johnson-Feelings, Diane. *The Best of the Brownies' Book.* New York: Oxford University Press, 1996.

— Sandra L. West

Bubbles, John (John William Sublett) (1902–1986)

dancer

Forming one-half of the song-and-dance team, Buck and Bubbles, John William Sublett performed in several hit stage musicals, including *PORGY AND BESS,* and taught dance from a wheelchair when he was 80 years old.

John William Sublett was born on February 19, 1902, in Louisville, Kentucky. He began dancing as a child and at the age of eight created a dance routine called "Walking the Dog." That routine evolved into a popular dance and likely inspired SHELTON BROOKS and SOPHIE TUCKER's 1916 hit song of the same name. One year later, Sublett's family migrated to Indianapolis to help further his dancing career.

Entertainer John W. Bubbles created the role of Sportin' Life for George Gershwin's folk opera *Porgy and Bess*. He is shown here in a 1935 photo. *(Library of Congress, Prints & Photographs Division, Carl Van Vechten Collection [LC-USZ62-114802])*

At the age of 10, Sublett joined with a kindred spirit, six-year-old Ford Lee Washington, to form a song-and-dance act called Buck and Bubbles. Sublett then took on the role of singer for the twosome.

As they matured, Buck (Washington) and Bubbles (Sublett) worked in several menial and sports areas. They worked as jockeys, carnival dancers, and as bat boys for the Louisville Colonels baseball team, part of the NATIONAL NEGRO BASEBALL LEAGUE. However, they continued dancing. After some years, the teenagers moved to HARLEM to participate in the feted Hoofers' Club, where tap dancers, like JAZZ musicians at late-night clubs, held "jam sessions." Initially, veteran hoofers (tap dancers) ridiculed Bubbles's efforts. Two years later, however, he perfected a style known as the "rhythm tap" and gained greater acceptance.

Because Washington was younger than Sublett, the older performer legally adopted the younger. They became the first black entertainment duo to appear at the Palace Theater in New York City. Billing themselves as Buck and Bubbles, Washington and Sublett danced in *Raisin' Cane* in 1923 and *BLACKBIRDS OF 1928*. In 1935, Sublett appeared as the character Sportin' Life in the now classic folk opera *Porgy and Bess*. His lifelong tap dance partner, Washington, also performed in the opera.

Although confined to a wheelchair in his later years, John William "Bubbles" Sublett became an enthusiastic dance instructor. He died May 18, 1986.

Further Reading

Jasen, David A., and Gene Jones. *Spreadin' Rhythm Around, Black Popular Songwriters, 1880–1930.* New York: Schirmer Books, 1998.

Watson, Steven. *The Harlem Renaissance: Hub of African-American Culture, 1920–1930.* New York: Pantheon Books, 1995.

— Sandra L. West

Bullard, Eugene Jacques (1895–1961) *aviator, expatriate*

As a member of France's renowned Lafayette Flying Corps fighting in WORLD WAR I, Eugene Jacques Bullard became the first African-American fighter pilot and, living in PARIS, exemplified the life of black expatriates in Europe.

Born October 9, 1895, in Columbus, Georgia, Bullard was the seventh of 10 children born to Josephine Thomas Bullard and William O. Bullard. Three of Bullard's siblings died in infancy. The remaining were Pauline, Hector, Ben, McArthur, Jacques, and Leona. William Bullard was born in the final years of American slavery and as an adult worked as a river merchant trader and laborer to support his large family. Josephine Bullard died in 1902 when her son Eugene was six years old.

Bullard attended elementary school in Columbus until the age of 11, when he ran away from home and made his way to north Georgia, working intermittently as a stable hand, jockey, and errand boy. Making his way in 1912 from Atlanta to Norfolk, Virginia, he stowed away on a German merchant steamship that carried him to Scotland. There, he worked as a street performer while periodically taking night classes and training as a boxer. He traveled to England where he joined a vaudeville act called Belle Davis's Freedman's Pickaninnies and befriended the accomplished welterweight boxer Aaron L. "Dixie Kid" Brown. Through Brown, Bullard met JACK JOHNSON and other black fighters then celebrated in Europe for their boxing prowess. He also became part of a community of black expatriates who had opted to immigrate to England rather than join the GREAT MIGRATION of African Americans moving from the South to the North in the United States.

Fighting in matches arranged by Brown and touring Europe with Belle Davis's act, Bullard went to Paris and settled there in 1914. His travels had allowed him to learn some German and enough French to act as a translator for visiting Americans. On his 19th birthday, October 9, 1914, he joined the French Foreign Legion to combat the advance of German troops prior to the United States's direct involvement in World War I. Bullard first served as a machine gunner on France's western front. Defending the historic city of Verdun, he sustained severe wounds to his face and legs until the Red Cross removed him from the battlefield. For his valor, he was awarded France's Croix de Guerre, the first of 15 medals he would receive for his services to the country in two world wars.

Unable to return to ground combat, Bullard obtained his pilot's license with the French Air Force on May 5, 1917, and in August of that year returned to Verdun as the first African-American combat pilot. Bullard flew almost two dozen missions and reportedly downed five enemy aircraft. His flying career, however, was cut short after several months when white American military officials complained to French officials that Bullard should not be allowed to fly because of his race. This type of racist JIM CROW reasoning was something white Americans would try to impart to the French throughout the following decades as the latter, in contrast to the general American public, came to celebrate various aspects of black culture. Bullard, as an expatriate, would repeatedly find the relative equality he enjoyed in Paris challenged by whites from the United States. In addition to ending Bullard's career with the French Air Force, the U.S. military prohibited him, as it did all blacks at the time, from flying with the U.S. Army Air Corps.

After the end of World War I, Bullard returned to Paris, where for two decades he managed and owned several businesses, including the Le Grand Duc nightclub, the L'Escadrille Bar, and Bullard's Athletic Club. He also played the drums part-time for a JAZZ combo and helped foster the popularity of the music in France. He was instrumental in bringing singer and hostess BRICKTOP to Paris, and his associates included JOSEPHINE BAKER, LANGSTON HUGHES (whom he hired as a dishwasher) LOUIS ARMSTRONG, FATS WALLER, and NOBLE SISSLE.

On July 17, 1923, Bullard married the French countess Marcelle Straumann. The couple had two daughters, Jacqueline, born in 1924, and Lolita Josephine, born in 1927. Their son, Eugene, Jr., was born in 1926 but died in infancy. When the couple divorced in 1935, Bullard retained custody of his daughters.

Bullard again fought for his adopted country in World War II, serving as an underground resistance agent and as a machine gunner. French officials eventually decided it was too dangerous for Bullard to remain in the country, and he traveled to Spain and Portugal, where he boarded a ship and returned to the United States on July 18, 1940. A year later he was successful in getting his daughters out of France, and the family settled in an apartment in HARLEM.

Bullard's loyalty to France never diminished, and he helped organize in the United States such groups as Free French and France Forever in support of the country's war efforts. In 1954, he returned to Paris as a French war veteran to participate in the city's Bastille Day ceremonies. In 1959, on his 64th birthday, he was inducted as a Knight of the French Legion of Honor. Bullard died in NEW YORK CITY on October 12, 1961.

Further Reading

Lloyd, Craig. *Eugene Bullard, Black Expatriate in Jazz-age Paris.* Athens: University of Georgia Press, 2000.

Shack, William A. *Harlem in Montmartre: A Paris Jazz Story Between the Great Wars.* Berkeley: University of California Press, 2001.

— Aberjhani

Burke, Selma (1900–1995) *sculptor*

Artist Selma Burke excelled at sculpting figures from African-American history and holds the distinction of having etched the image of an American president for the head of a U.S. dime.

Burke was born in Mooresville, North Carolina, in 1900 and, in her adult years, lived in a barn in New Hope, Pennsylvania.

She was educated at St. Agnes Training School for Nurses in Raleigh, North Carolina; Women's Medical College in North Carolina; and Columbia University in NEW YORK CITY, where she earned a Ph.D. (circa 1936–41). During the 1930s, she attended Sarah Lawrence College and supported herself as a model.

Burke studied under master sculptors Maillol in PARIS, France, and Povolney in Vienna, Austria. A social activist, when Hitler marched into Austria, she fled with a half-million dollars in jewels stitched into her clothing to deliver to the Quaker refugee offices in America.

During the 1940s, Burke immortalized the image of "New Deal" President FRANKLIN DELANO ROOSEVELT on the U.S. dime coin. She also sculpted a bronze bust of Roosevelt, unveiled by President Harry S. Truman in 1945, which stands on display at the Recorder of Deeds Building in WASHINGTON, D.C. Her major exhibitions include Julian Levy Galleries, New York, 1945.

Founder of the Selma Burke Art Center in Pittsburgh, Pennsylvania, she was once married to Harlem Renaissance poet CLAUDE MCKAY. Her second husband, architect Herman Kobbe, who designed the Pennsylvania barn they lived in, died in 1955.

Burke's major sculpture, *Uplift,* was installed at the Pearl S. Buck Foundation Center in Perkasie, Pennsylvania, in 1991. In 1994, she received a federal commission to sculpt the likeness of social activist Rosa Parks, considered to be the "mother of the modern Civil Rights movement." But before she could undertake the work, Burke, who lost both feet to diabetes, died on September 2, 1995. As a tribute, Selma Burke Day is celebrated in North Carolina, the state of her birth.

Further Reading

Miers, Charles, ed. *Harlem Renaissance: Art of Black America.* New York: Harry N. Abrams, 1994.

— Sandra L. West

Burleigh, Harry Thacker (1866–1949) *singer, composer*

Classically trained Harry Thacker Burleigh gained prominence during the Harlem Renaissance as baritone soloist at NEW YORK CITY's St. George's Episcopal Church in HARLEM, as well as a composer and arranger of Negro spirituals.

Harry Thacker Burleigh was born on December 2, 1866, in Erie, Pennsylvania. The grandson of a blind slave, Burleigh won a scholarship to New York's National Conservatory of Music in 1892. At the conservatory, he studied voice, double bass, and timpani. Antonin Dvorak, the school's director, planned to incorporate Negro spirituals into his composition, *Symphony from the New World,* and Burleigh sang spirituals for him over the course of two years.

In the middle of the sometimes roguish Harlem Renaissance, Burleigh used his voice in service to his God. In 1894, he began a 40-year tenure as baritone soloist at St. George's Episcopal Church. For the time, his performance of Negro spirituals, or "sorrow songs," as *CRISIS* editor W. E. B. DU BOIS classified them, was an innovation. After a short-lived period of indignation and surprise, the elitist white congregation and church choir soon began to enjoy the songs. In 1902, Burleigh became the sole black member of the choir at Temple Emanu-El in New York, and he stayed 25 years. A humble man who took his faith and his music seriously, Burleigh did not care whether he sang in a church or synagogue.

Burleigh sang in concert halls as well as sacred chapels. He participated in the Coleridge-Taylor Festival in *Hiawatha* in WASHINGTON, D.C., and in CHICAGO in 1906. Traveling extensively, he gave concerts in Europe and America.

Burleigh did not neglect the other side of the musical talent that he nurtured at the Conservatory. In 1900, he joined the music publishing firm of Ricordi and Sons in New York to compose fine art songs. As editor and arranger, he composed 90 ballads and 50 choral pieces. He created 50 arrangements of Negro spirituals for soloists and violinists, and he composed works of art for pianists.

He arranged the songs in *Afro-American Folksongs* (1914) and *Jubilee Songs of the United States of America* (1916), two musical books written by H. E. Krehbiel. One of the songs was the immortal "Deep River." In 1929, Burleigh published his own book of arrangements, *Old Songs Hymnal.*

Burleigh won the NATIONAL ASSOCIATION FOR THE ADVANCEMENT OF COLORED PEOPLE'S SPINGARN MEDAL in 1917 and received honorary degrees from Atlanta and Howard Universities. In Indiana, a singing group specializing in the performance of Negro spirituals was named in his honor: the Harry T. Burleigh Association.

Harry Burleigh died on September 12, 1949.

Further Reading

Anderson, Jervis. *This Was Harlem: A Cultural Portrait, 1900–1950.* New York: Farrar Straus Giroux, 1981.

Floyd, Samuel A., ed. *Black Music in the Harlem Renaissance: A Collection of Essays.* Knoxville: University of Tennessee Press, 1994.

— Sandra L. West

Burroughs, Margaret Taylor Goss See CHICAGO.

Butterbeans and Susie
(Jodie Edwards) (ca. 1900–1967)
(Susie Hawthorn Edwards) (1896–1963) *comedians*

Jodie Edwards and Susie Hawthorne launched a comedy career that spanned more than three decades when the couple accepted $50 to get married on stage as part of a publicity stunt in Greenville, South Carolina, on May 15, 1917.

Susie Hawthorn was born in 1896 in Pensacola, Florida. Jodie Edwards was born circa 1900 in Marietta, Georgia.

Adopting the stage names Butterbeans and Susie, the couple continued their career following their stage wedding with engagements at the Douglass Theater in Macon, Georgia, and developed a battle of the sexes routine similar to that of their predecessors, Stringbeans and Sweetie. They were seasoned vaudeville performers by the time they began headlining at such venues as the APOLLO THEATRE and the COTTON CLUB, and they expanded their act to include singing and dancing.

The duo, described as the "monarchs of laughter and blues," appeared on bills that featured such top-notch performers as LENA HORNE, COUNT BASIE, the NOBLE SISSLE Band, and BILLIE HOLIDAY. Susie's appearance on stage was generally an elegant contrast to Butterbeans's, who often performed in blackface, and whose trademark costume was tight pants and a derby hat clearly too small for his head. The couple exchanged patter that moved back and forth between comical insults, woeful laments, and material that was heavily sexually suggestive. Susie supplied the BLUES singing talent and they combined song with chatter through such numbers as BESSIE SMITH's "I Need a Little Hot Dog for My Roll," and the popular "When the Real Thing Comes Along."

Part of Butterbeans's performance was a dance known as the itch, sometimes called the heebie jeebies. It was performed with his hands in his pockets scratching wildly at some hidden cause of irritation. He also routinely performed the Black Bottom, a dance that made it to Broadway in George White's production of *Scandals of 1926.* The CAKEWALK was another popular dance that he and Susie worked into their act.

In addition to putting on such stage shows as *That Gets It* and the *Butterbeans and Susie Revue,* the couple enjoyed a recording career. During the 1920s, they released *When My Man Shimmies* on Okeh Records. Backing them up on the recording were JAZZ greats KING OLIVER and Clarence Williams. Their final album in 1962 was the self-titled *Butterbeans and Susie.* The recordings are now available as collector's items in two separate volumes. Moreover, their contribution to modern music is acknowledged on the 1996 release *The Roots of Rap.*

Butterbeans and Susie did not achieve the kind of crossover success that made television and movie audiences celebrate the career of the legendary MOMS MABLEY. They were, however, recognized and honored during the 1950s for their contributions to black entertainment. Susie died on December 5, 1963, in CHICAGO. Butterbeans continued to perform until his death from heart failure while walking onstage at the Dorchester Inn outside Chicago on October 28, 1967.

Further Reading

Finn, Julio. *The Bluesman: The Musical Heritage of Black Men and Women in the Americas.* Northampton, Virginia: Interlink Publishers Group, 1998.

Hamalian, Leo, and James V. Hatch. *The Roots of African American Drama.* Detroit: Wayne State University Press, 1991.

Huggins, Nathan. *Voices from the Harlem Renaissance.* New York: Oxford University Press, 1976.

— Aberjhani

C

cakewalk

On American slave plantations during the mid-1800s, the cakewalk developed as a dance performed by blacks satirizing the formal balls and mannerisms of white slave owners. Whites viewing the dance generally perceived the exaggerated strutting, stretched necks, and improvised kicks of the black couples as a form of play and awarded the most entertaining couple with a prize cake.

Variations of the cakewalk were sometimes performed as harvest rituals, and slaves were known to provide the prize cake themselves.

While its beginnings are generally associated with the slave plantation, as Eric J. Sundquist observed in *To Wake the Nations,* it may have had its beginnings in Africa: "In addition, the dance carried with it the remembered and transmitted patterns of a festive celebration of life, not of enslavement and death, the echoes of an inherited African beginning."

In an ironic twist of culture, history, and race, white minstrel performers made up in blackface adopted the cakewalk to entertain American audiences in the 1880s and 1890s. With burnt cork or other darkening agents smeared on their faces, the performers unknowingly presented a parody of themselves. The dance became a routine feature of the minstrel shows in which black people were often portrayed as childish and moronic.

The cakewalk began to boom in popularity during the 1890s and evolved into something of a staple in musical theater. Blacks themselves were featured in a number of shows, a trend that helped provide employment for them in musical theater. One such show was *Black Patti's Troubadours* in 1896, headed by opera soprano turned troupe leader Sissieretta Jones. Another was Bob Cole and William Johnson's 1897 spoof of *A Trip to Chinatown,* renamed *A Trip to Coontown.*

Public enthusiasm for the cakewalk was so strong that national competitions for it were held at New York's Madison Square Garden. Its impact on national culture may be determined from the caption on an 1899 advertisement for a competition: "A popular diversion of the colored people. In which white persons manifest great interest." The steps of the dance also influenced the composition and playing of RAGTIME music.

Poet Paul Lawrence Dunbar and composer WILL MARION COOK sought to add a touch of stylistic class to the dance when they featured it in the 1898 musical *Clorindy, or the Origin of the Cakewalk,* performed at the Casino Theater Roof Garden in New York. With its showcasing of music by the classically trained Cook, the show was viewed as something of a deathblow to minstrelsy, which had been waning in appeal throughout the 1890s. Cook and Dunbar gave the dance another boost in 1903 along with BERT WILLIAMS and GEORGE WALKER in their musical *In Dahomey.* A runaway success on Broadway, it went on to play London for eight months and made the cakewalk an international phenomenon.

The dance came close to equaling the tango in popularity by 1915. Though elements of it influenced other dances, it gradually faded during the 1920s.

Further Reading

Perplner, John O. *African American Concert Dance: The Harlem Renaissance and Beyond.* Champaign: University of Illinois Press, 2001.

Sundquist, Eric J. *To Wake the Nation.* Cambridge, Mass.: Belknap Press of Harvard University Press, 1993.

— Aberjhani

Calloway, Blanche

See CALLOWAY, CAB.

Calloway, Cab (Cabell Calloway) (1907–1994)

singer, bandleader

A former pre-law student in CHICAGO, Cab Calloway left college to become the premier JAZZ orchestra conductor at the aristocratic COTTON CLUB during the Harlem Renaissance and one of the most well-known musicians of the SWING era.

Cabell "Cab" Calloway was born on Christmas Day in 1907 in Rochester, New York, and raised in Baltimore, Maryland. During his early days in Baltimore, he sang with a group called the Melody Boys quartet. As a teenager, he lived in Chicago with a sister named Blanche who sang in the musical revue *Plantation Days.* When Blanche learned that the show needed to replace a performer, she helped her brother get the job. At the end of the tour, Calloway registered as a pre-law student at Crane College. In 1925, he dropped out to play drums and sing at Dreamland Cabaret. Soon afterward he began conducting a band, the Albanians, at the Sunset Café.

In 1929, Calloway took his band to HARLEM, in NEW YORK CITY, where they performed at the SAVOY BALLROOM but were not offered an extended engagement. He then joined the MISSOURIANS, a swing band that was already considered one of the best. Invited to fill in for DUKE ELLINGTON and his orchestra at the Cotton Club, Calloway became an instant hit. He later enjoyed a brief engagement at the Plantation Club before the club was destroyed by mob violence. Calloway returned to the Cotton Club and remained there until 1932.

Having helped Cab Calloway get his start in the music industry, Blanche Calloway also moved to New York and played frequently at the Ciro Club. She formed a band called Blanche Calloway's Joy Boys and toured with them until 1938.

Cab Calloway's elaborate, two-hour-long floor shows were punctuated with songs that personified the light-skinned black women in the club's famous chorus line: "She's Tall, She's Tan, and She's Terrific," and "Cotton Colored Gal of Mine," were among the audience's favorites. Performing in complete formal tuxedo dress, Calloway danced, jumped up and down, leaped from the orchestra platform, and shook his long, straight hair as he went into a frenzy. Audiences cheered his displays of self-abandon. The two-hour show often included dancing by the fluid Earl "Snakehips" Tucker and a song by a female singer. One of the most memorable featured female singers at the Cotton Club was LENA HORNE.

Changing outfits as often as 12 times a night, Calloway owned at least 40 zoot suits ranging in price from $150 to $225. The average suit cost the average man on the street approximately $34.

Calloway was an early expert at the style of singing known as SCATTING lyrics. His most famous scat was "Hi-dee hi-dee hi-dee ho," taken from his benchmark song, "MINNIE THE MOOCHER," written in 1931 by Irving Mills and Calloway. "Minnie the Moocher" became a classic to which audiences all over the world responded until Calloway was dubbed the "hi-de-ho man." Another Calloway trademark was "Jumpin' Jive," which also incorporated scat lyrics. In 1934, Mills and Calloway cowrote the popular song "Jitterbug."

During the 1930s, 1940s, and into the 1950s, when Calloway was not on the bandstand he performed in movies or on the radio. He appeared in *The Big Broadcast* (1933), *International House* (1933), *The Singing Kid* (1936), *Stormy Weather* (1943), *Sensations of 1945* (1945), and *St. Louis Blues* (1958).

Cab Calloway, shown here ca. 1933, enjoyed stardom as a headliner at the Cotton Club and major bandleader of the swing era. *(Library of Congress, Prints & Photographs Division, Carl Van Vechten Collection [LC-USZ62-115133])*

He also did the vaudeville radio show *Quizzicale* on NBC'S Blue Network in 1942.

After years of touring Europe and America, Calloway played the character Sportin' Life in the African-American folk opera *PORGY AND BESS* in 1952. He toured with stage and screen star Pearl Bailey's *Hello, Dolly!* in the 1960s.

As a trendsetter, Calloway helped create the black slang and zesty language called jive talk that characterized the swing era. Working with writer Ned Williams, Calloway produced *Professor Cab Calloway's Swingformation Bureau* (1945) and *The Cab Calloway Hepster's Dictionary* (1938). The dictionary offered a compilation of era slang and terms used by Harlemites and jazz musicians during the 1920s and 1930s. Some of the terms are "faust," meaning an ugly girl; "mezz," for supreme or genuine; and "slide your jib," meaning to talk freely. In 1976, he wrote his autobiography, entitled *Of Minnie the Moocher and Me.*

Cab Calloway died on November 8, 1994.

Further Reading

Anderson, Jervis. *This Was Harlem: A Cultural Portrait, 1900–1950.* New York: Farrar Straus Giroux, 1981.

Peretti, Burton W. *The Creation of Jazz: Music, Race, and Culture in Urban America (Music in American Life).* Chicago: University of Illinois Press, 1992.

— Sandra L. West

Campbell, E. Simms (Elmer Simms Campbell)

(1906–1971) *writer, cartoonist*

E. Simms Campbell, as he preferred to be known, won a national art award in 1926 while still in high school, illustrated books for authors ARNA BONTEMPS and LANGSTON HUGHES, and became a leading cartoonist of the Harlem Renaissance. An African American, he was known for his white female character "Cutie," one of the most popular cartoons of the 20th century.

Born Elmer Simms Campbell in St. Louis, Missouri, on January 2, 1906, his father was a high school principal and his mother a painter who encouraged her son to develop his creative gifts. The family migrated to CHICAGO, where Campbell played halfback on the football team at Englewood High School and was editorial cartoonist for the *"E" Weekly.* Through his work on the school newspaper, he attracted national attention in 1926 with his award-winning Armistice Day cartoon. In the cartoon, Campbell illustrated a soldier kneeling in front of his comrade's grave. His caption read, "We've Won, Buddy!"

At the age of 14, Campbell attended the University of Chicago. He also studied at the Art Institute of Chicago and at the Art Students League in NEW YORK CITY in 1932. At the Art Institute, Campbell freelanced for *College Comics* magazine. In New York, he freelanced for *OPPORTUNITY* magazine and mainstream publications, including *Saturday Evening Post. Esquire,* a commercial magazine whose audience was predominately white men, seized upon his talent and signed him to a long contract. It was an unusual employment situation for a black man in the 1930s when relations between black and white people were not at their best. But *Esquire* published Campbell's illustrations in every issue from 1933 to 1958. He also created the magazine's mascot, *Esky.* Campbell's cartoon illustrations were so sought after that, by the 1950s, his work appeared in the pages of *Esquire*'s competition, *Playboy.*

Campbell's best known cartoon characters were the *Sultan* and *Cutie. Cutie,* by far the most popular of the two, was a voluptuous redhead, an unusual character for a black man to draw in the 1930s, largely due to the controversies regarding INTERRACIAL INTERACTION at the time. *Esquire*—in accordance with the standards of the day and to avoid losing white advertisers and white readers who might, in protest, pull advertisements out of the magazine or discontinue subscriptions—did not publicize Campbell's race. They simply wanted him to keep drawing *Cutie* and to keep creating entertaining gags and jokes.

The inspiration for *Cutie* began in 1922, when Campbell drew a turkey and sold the illustration for 75¢. According to Campbell: "The slim-legged, full-hipped, lusty red-headed woman grew out of a turkey. . . . Because it was the first thing I ever drew back in St. Louis." He created *Cutie* as a redhead because "red reproduces well. Nearly every magazine in America uses red. . . . And almost every flat (apartment, house) in the world has some red in it. That's why she's a red head. . . . I sell a commodity. I sell what people want."

Campbell also worked with book publishers. He illustrated *Popa and Fafina,* a popular children's book written by Harlem Renaissance poets Arna Bontemps and Langston Hughes. He also illustrated a collection of poetry, *We Who Die & Other Poems* by Binga Dismond, during the same period.

Campbell's drawing ability was supplemented by his writing talent. For *Esquire* he wrote articles on JAZZ, the BLUES, and dance, and these pieces were accompanied by his own drawings. He wrote the essay "Early Jam" for *The Negro Caravan,* the scholarly anthology about black cultural life in NEW ORLEANS, edited by HOWARD UNIVERSITY professor and poet STERLING ALLEN BROWN. A music aficionado, he enjoyed a close relationship with singer and bandleader CAB CALLOWAY.

E. Simms Campbell continued to win awards after capturing national attention in 1926 for the Armistice Day cartoon. He won several student prizes at the Art Institute of Chicago; awards at the Minneapolis exhibitions in 1924 and 1925; the *St. Louis Post-Dispatch* black and white contest in 1928; and the Hearst Prize in 1936.

Elmer Simms Campbell died on January 27, 1971.

Further Reading

Bailey, David A., and Paul Gilroy. *Rhapsodies in Black: Art of the Harlem Renaissance.* Berkeley: University of California Press, 1997.

Brown, Sterling A., Arthur P. Davis, and Ulysses Lee, eds. *The Negro Caravan.* New York: The Dryden Press, 1941.

— Sandra L. West

Cane See TOOMER, JEAN.

Cardozo, W. Warrick (William Warrick Cardozo)

(1905–1962) *research scientist*

A pioneer in the field of research for medical conditions pertaining to African Americans, Dr. William Warrick Cardozo in the 1930s achieved landmark success in his revolutionary research on sickle-cell anemia.

William Warrick Cardozo was born on April 16, 1905, in WASHINGTON D.C. His father was Francis Cardozo, Jr., a school principal.

W. Warrick Cardozo, as he was known, received his medical education at Ohio State University. He completed his internship at City Hospital in Cleveland, Ohio, his residency at Provident Hospital in CHICAGO, Illinois, and was awarded dual fellowships in the field of pediatrics at both Provident and Children's Memorial.

Warrick received a research grant from ALPHA PHI ALPHA FRATERNITY to study sickle-cell anemia, a disease that results in a shortage of red blood cells. Through his research, Warrick made the following discoveries: that sickle-cell anemia is inherited; it is found predominately in African Americans, particularly children; not all people with the sickled-shape blood cell have anemia; and the disease is not automatically fatal. In 1937, his research findings were published in *Archives of Internal Medicine* and established a foundation for the modern treatment of the disease.

Warrick continued to research and help develop treatments for health problems pertaining to black people. In addition to his private practice, he became an adjunct professor, Pediatrics Division, at the HOWARD UNIVERSITY College of Medicine and Freedmen's Hospital in Washington, D.C., and worked as a school medical inspector for the district's board of health for 24 years.

Dr. Cardozo died on August 11, 1962.

Further Reading

Kranz, Rachel, and Philip Koslow, Jr., *The Biographical Dictionary of African Americans.* New York: Facts On File, Inc., 1999, 35.

— Sandra L. West

Carolina Magazine

Like *SURVEY GRAPHIC* magazine in its special HARLEM edition in 1925, *Carolina Magazine,* the official literary publication of the student body at the University of North Carolina, also produced special editions devoted exclusively to the creative works and culture of the *NEW NEGRO*. The editions appeared in May 1927 and April 1929.

The editor of *Carolina Magazine*'s May 1927 issue was Lewis Alexander. Born on July 4, 1900, in the intellectually stimulating district of WASHINGTON, D.C., Alexander was an actor, director, and poet. He attended HOWARD UNIVERSITY, where he was a member of the Howard Players. He also attended the University of Pennsylvania. In addition, he performed with the ETHIOPIAN ART PLAYERS in *Salome* and *The Comedy of Errors* on Broadway. He directed productions at the Ira Aldridge Players of the Grover Cleveland School and the Randall Community Center Players, both in Washington, D.C.

As a poet, Alexander specialized in the Japanese haiku. His work was included in COUNTEE CULLEN's *Caroling Dusk, An Anthology of Verse by Negro Poets* (1927). His poems in that volume were "Negro Woman," "Africa," "Transformation," "The Dark Brother," "Tanka I-VIII," "Japanese Haiku," and "Day And Night."

For the first special edition of *Carolina Magazine,* Alexander organized essays and poetry of well-known and second-echelon writers. Among them was "The Message of the Negro Poets," an essay by Dr. ALAIN LOCKE of Howard University, and an essay on BLUES lyrics by CHARLES SPURGEON JOHNSON, the editor of *OPPORTUNITY* magazine. Also included was a pen and ink drawing by ALLAN RANDALL FREELON.

The volume was heavy with contributions from poets, including LANGSTON HUGHES, author of *The Weary Blues;* WILLIAM WARING CUNEY, author of the poem, "No Images"; STERLING ALLEN BROWN of Howard University; award-winning poet ARNA BONTEMPS; Edward Silvera; literary editor for *CRISIS* magazine JESSIE REDMOND FAUSET; Mae V. Cowdery; poet and dramatist ANGELINA EMILY WELD GRIMKE; John F. Matheus; Carrie W. Clifford; *Black Opals* coeditor Nellie Rathborne Bright; Donald Jeffrey Hayes; James H. Young; literary SALON leader Georgia Douglas Johnson; and ALICE DUNBAR-NELSON.

The April 1929 edition of *Carolina Magazine* included only plays by black dramatists. Those writers and their plays were theater anthologist WILLIS RICHARDSON's *The Idle Head;* John F. Matheus's *Black Damp;* MAY MILLER's *Scratches;* and EULALIE SPENCE's *Undertow.*

Harlem Renaissance writers who continued to publish in the accommodating *Carolina Magazine* following its special Harlem Renaissance issues included May Miller, who contributed her short story "Door Stop" (May 1930).

Further Reading

Johnson, Abby Arthur, and Ronald Maberry Johnson. *Propaganda and Aesthetics: The Literary Politics of Afro-American Magazines in the Twentieth Century.* Amherst: University of Massachusetts Press, 1979.

Kellner, Bruce, ed. *The Harlem Renaissance: A Historical Dictionary for the Era.* Westport, Conn.: Greenwood Press, 1984.

— Sandra L. West

Catlett, Elizabeth Alice (1915–) *sculptor*

Elizabeth Alice Catlett, a sculptor, painter, and printmaker, worked for the Public Works of Art (PWA) branch of the WORKS PROGRESS ADMINISTRATION (WPA) during the GREAT DEPRESSION and produced a series of works focusing on women as her subject. Like AARON DOUGLAS at FISK UNIVERSITY, she was, at Dillard University in Louisiana, part of the first generation of black WPA artists to teach and chair art departments in the black university system.

Elizabeth Catlett was born in WASHINGTON, D.C., in 1915. Like many eager black students of the era, Catlett was a victim of educational discrimination. She was rejected by the then all-white Carnegie Institute of Technology in Pittsburgh, Pennsylvania, before she turned to a black school in her native city. She graduated cum laude with a B.A. degree from HOWARD UNIVERSITY in 1936. She befriended artists LOIS MAILOU JONES and JAMES LESESNE WELLS, as well as art historian James A. Porter. She earned an M.A. in fine arts from the University of Iowa in 1940, where she roomed with the poet and novelist MARGARET ABIGAIL WALKER. She also studied ceramics at the Art Institute of CHICAGO and lithography at the Art Students League in NEW YORK CITY.

Catlett excelled in lithographics and paintings, and she is well known for her sculpture, especially of women and children, which she created from bronze, limestone, and mahogany. Some of her noted works are *Negro Woman* (1938), *Negro Girl* (1939), and *In Harriet Tubman I Helped Hundreds to Freedom* (1946).

In the 1940s, she met, befriended, and was influenced by some of the foremost intellectuals and artists of the day: *CRISIS* magazine editor W. E. B. DU BOIS; writer LANGSTON HUGHES; novelist RALPH WALDO ELLISON of *Invisible Man* fame; visual artists JACOB ARMSTEAD LAWRENCE and AARON DOUGLAS; and human rights activist and performing artist PAUL ROBESON. Also during this time, she taught at George Washington Carver High School, an alternative night school in HARLEM, and received the Rosenwald Fellowship to work in Mexico.

Catlett married the muralist CHARLES WILBERT WHITE in the early 1940s, but the couple divorced after several years together. In 1947, she married Mexican artist Francisco Mora.

In Mexico at Taller de Grafica Popular, as a guest artist she worked on prints that documented and inspired the political struggles of the masses. She spoke out against the second-class citizenship of women of all races and nationalities. The U.S. government branded her a leftist for this outspokeness, and she spent three days in a Mexican jail. She eventually renounced her American citizenship.

She chaired the sculpture department at the Universidad Nacional Autonoma de Mexico from 1958 to 1976. In 1971, she was Mexican delegate to the Cuban Women's Federation. Catlett was also part of the 1960s Civil Rights movement in the United States. Exhibitions of her work have been held at the University of Iowa, Iowa City, Iowa, in 1939; Downtown Gallery, New York, in 1940; American Negro Exposition in 1940, where she won the Sculpture Award; and Atlanta University, Atlanta, Georgia, in 1942. She completed in 2001 a 15-foot bronze sculpture in tribute to author RALPH WALDO ELLISON, and named it *Invisible Man*, after the author's highly acclaimed novel.

In 2002, Elizabeth Catlett was living in New York, where she continued to create art and speak out on human rights issues. Her papers are collected in the Papers of African-American Artists at the Smithsonian Institution, Washington, D.C.

Further Reading

Herzog, Melanie. "Elizabeth Catlett in Mexico: Identity and Cross-Cultural Intersections in the Production of Artistic Meaning." *International Review of African American Art* 11, no. 3, 1994.

Miers, Charles, ed. *Harlem Renaissance: Art of Black America.* New York: Harry N. Abrams, 1994.

— Sandra L. West

Chicago Art League

See DAWSON, CHARLES CLARENCE.

Chicago Bee, The

See CHICAGO.

Chicago

As the Harlem Renaissance developed in NEW YORK CITY, it helped generate a similar movement in Chicago, Illinois. Lasting officially from 1935 to 1950, the Chicago Renaissance was getting underway just as the Harlem Renaissance was fading.

Chicago was founded in the late 1780s by Jean-Baptiste Pointe DuSable (1745–1818), a Haitian fur trader born to an African slave woman and a French sailor. Very much like its sister city, New York, Chicago claimed a hefty influx of southern immigrants during the GREAT MIGRATION in the early 1900s, when thousands of African Americans moved north from Arkansas, Alabama, Louisiana, Mississippi, and other southern states.

African Americans moving to the North did not escape discrimination and violence resulting from racial tension. The RED SUMMER OF 1919, consisting of approximately 25 race riots and 76 lynchings, devastated many lives throughout the United States. The best known event was a six-day riot that erupted in Chicago following the stoning and subsequent drowning of an African-American teenager after he drifted into the swimming section reserved for whites.

LYNCHING and employment discrimination in the South played a huge part in the migration. "Every time a lynching takes place in a community down South you can depend on it that colored people will arrive in Chicago within two weeks," noted T. Arnold Hill, head of the Chicago NATIONAL URBAN LEAGUE branch. The *CHICAGO DEFENDER* reported to its southern readers that daily wages could increase by 100 percent. Thus, southerners earning $2.50 or less per day fled the South and packed themselves into Chicago's South Side district, Bronzeville. Chicago's more prominent migrants bought property and summered at an all-black resort, Idlewild, in nearby Michigan, where author Charles Chestnutt and *CRISIS* magazine editor W. E. B. DU BOIS were neighbors.

Musically, Chicago became known as the home of the BLUES, the place of origin for the musical style described as boogie-woogie, and a JAZZ capital during the 1920s. During this era, the South Side's entertainment business, like HARLEM's, was at an all-time high with an abundance of nightclubs. Entertainment facilities included the Apex Club, Deluxe Café, Pekin Inn, Dreamland, Lincoln, Schiller's, the Grand Terrace Ballroom, and Vendome. World-class musicians, predominantly instrumental immigrants from melodically rich NEW ORLEANS, performed in "the Windy City" and created a Chicago sound. KING OLIVER'S Creole Jazz Band made the first recording by a black band at the Paramount Company in Chicago in 1923.

Trumpeter LOUIS ARMSTRONG—who was Oliver's protégé—and his Hot Five and Hot Seven performed at the Vendome and recorded in Chicago between 1925 and 1928. Pianist Earl "Fatha" Hines played a "trumpet piano" style with Armstrong's Hot Five and Hot Seven bands. Hines's right hand played the melody in octaves, and his left hand played what sounded like an orchestra's rhythm section. Hines later led an orchestra at the Grand Terrace Ballroom.

Other musicians that played Chicago's clubs were pianists Lil Hardin Armstrong (Louis Armstrong's wife) and FATS WALLER; clarinetist Sidney Bechet; guitarist Johnny St. Cyr; and such then up-and-coming white jazz musicians as drummer Gene Krupa and bandleader Benny Goodman. Harlem Renaissance historian DAVID LEVERING LEWIS noted that the music of Chicago had "more of the wail of the blues in it than its New York counterpart." Consequently, those musicians who made the employment transition from Chicago to Harlem often had a hard time adjusting to the musical requirements of the city.

JELLY ROLL MORTON and his Red Hot Peppers also played in Chicago and made a series of recordings from 1926 to 1928. Clarinetist Johnny Dodds and his group the Chicago Footwarmers recorded in Chicago as well during the late 1920s.

The boogie-woogie piano style originated in Chicago much the way STRIDE PIANO originated in Harlem. Musicians Jimmy Yancey (1894–1951), Clarence "Pinetop" Smith (1904–29), Meade Lux Lewis (1905–64), and Albert Ammons (1907–49) all excelled at the musical form. Developing out of the blues, the boogie-woogie style allowed pianists to play bass notes at different pitch levels. Among the more popular boogie-woogie songs were *Pine Top Boogie* and *Honky-Tonk Train Blues.* Ammons, Lewis, and Pete Johnson, another pianist, performed boogie-woogie concerts in Chicago.

Just as the Harlem Renaissance was defined largely by such publications as the *CRISIS, MESSENGER,* and *OPPORTUNITY* magazines, Chicago also boasted a number of influential periodicals. The *Chicago Defender,* founded by ROBERT ABBOTT, was Chicago's leading newspaper and, with a national circulation, was directly linked to the success of the Great Migration. Another important black publication in Bronzeville was the *Chicago Bee,* located at 3647 South State Street in the Chicago Bee Building, constructed by publisher Anthony Overton during 1929–31. The community newspaper went out of business in the 1940s. The Chicago Bee's Art Deco building was restored and, in April 1986, registered in the National Register of Historic Places. Since May 1996, the building has been used as the Chicago Bee Branch of the Chicago Public Library, and a Family Literacy Center sponsored by DePaul University and the Chicago Public Library.

From sociological writers to journalists and poets, the writers that resided in Chicago at one point or another were numerous. They included CHARLES SPURGEON JOHNSON, ARNA BONTEMPS, GWENDOLYN BROOKS, MARGARET ABIGAIL WALKER, and RICHARD NATHANIEL WRIGHT. Brooks, Walker, and Wright were responsible for ushering in the era of "urban realism" so prominent in black literature in the 1940s and 1950s.

Johnson is predominantly known as the visionary editor of *OPPORTUNITY* magazine at the New York Urban League office. However, just before he left the Chicago Urban League in September 1922, where he was associate executive secretary, he

Some African Americans established enclaves in sections of large northern cities, as exemplified by this bar in the South Side of Chicago. *(Library of Congress)*

wrote *The Negro in Chicago: A Study of Race Relations and a Race Riot.* The 700-page report was, on paper, coauthored by Graham Romeyn Taylor but was, historians note, actually the monumental work of Johnson.

Moving to Chicago in the fall of 1935 to complete his master's degree in library science at the University of Chicago, Bontemps was a seven-year member of the Harlem Renaissance who, after living in Alabama and California for short periods of time, appreciated the comradeship of Chicago's South Side Writers' Group. At the writers conclave he met Wright, Frank Marshall Davis, Theodore Ward, and Margaret Walker. By the time of his Chicago residence, Bontemps had already published his novel *God Sends Sunday* (1931) and had won poetry awards in 1926 and 1927 from the *Crisis* and *Opportunity* magazines. He completed *Black Thunder* (1936) in Chicago. In 1939, Bontemps worked as a supervisor on the Illinois Writers' Project, a division of the WORKS PROGRESS ADMINISTRATION (WPA). After two years there, he completed *The Negro in Illinois.*

Because Bontemps lived and worked through both the Harlem and Chicago renaissance periods and wrote about them, he is regarded as a historian of both those periods. In his essay "Famous WPA Authors, "published in *Negro Digest,* June 1950, he wrote: "Chicago was definitely the center of the second phase of Negro literary awakening. . . . Harlem got its renaissance in the middle & 'twenties, centering around the *Opportunity* contests and the Fifth Avenue Awards Dinners. Ten years later Chicago reenacted it on WPA without finger bowls but with increased power."

Working with Jack Conroy, the white editor of the radical journal *New Anvil,* Bontemps published a history of the Great Migration, based on Illinois Writers' Project documents, called *They Seek a City.* When Bontemps completed his graduate studies, he left Chicago in 1943 for FISK UNIVERSITY in Nashville, Tennessee.

The first African American and the youngest poet to win a Pulitzer Prize, Gwendolyn Brooks is one of the most distinguished members of the Chicago Renaissance. Her first poetry collection, *A Street in Bronzeville,* set in the Chicago neighborhood of Bronzeville, was published in 1945. In 1950, she won the Pulitzer Prize for poetry for *Annie Allen.* During her 60-year career, she authored more than 20 books, and she influenced generations of writers and readers from the Chicago Renaissance and into the 1960s and 1970s Black Arts movement.

Before Margaret Walker's epic poem *For My People* and her novel *Jubilee* became literary classics, she worked on the Federal Writers' Project in Chicago in the 1930s. *Poetry: A Magazine of Verse* published Walker's work several times during the late 1930s. Her collection *For My People* won the Yale Younger Poets' Award in 1942.

A leading figure among the Chicago school of writers, Richard Wright moved to the city in December 1927, joined the literary Chicago John Reed Club, and united with the Communist Party in Chicago in 1933. He was admitted to the Illinois Federal Writers' Project in April 1935 and worked as publicity agent for the Chicago Federal Negro Theatre from September to November, 1936. Wright, originally from Mississippi, wrote *Lawd Today* while living in Chicago in 1935, though the book was not published until 1963. His acknowledged masterpiece, the novel *Native Son,* was set in Chicago and published in 1940.

Other Chicago Renaissance authors of note were Margaret Essie Danner, Frank Marshall Davis, Theodore Ward, Elizabeth Lindsay Davis, and Frank Yerby.

Danner, a native of Pryorsburg, Kentucky, attended Chicago's Loyola University and Northwestern University. In 1945, she received second prize in the Poetry Workshop of the Midwestern Writers Conference. In 1951, she published "Far from Africa" in *Poetry: The Magazine of Verse,* for which she was awarded a John Hay Whitney fellowship. Her work focused mainly on African culture.

Frank Marshall Davis, a poet, moved to Chicago from Kansas in 1927 to work as a journalist. He worked for the Associated Negro Press (now National Newspaper Publishers' Association, NNPA). His poetry collection *Black Man's Verse* (1935) earned him a grant from the Julius Rosenwald Foundation. He also wrote *I Am the American Negro* (1937), *Through Sepia Eyes* (1938), and *47th Street Poems* (1948).

Theodore Ward was a playwright. The Federal Theatre Project produced his *Big White Fog* in 1938. And Chicago activist Elizabeth Lindsay Davis authored *Lifting as They Climb* (1933), the first national history of the black women's club movement.

For many years, the general public did not know that Frank Yerby was a black novelist because, in addition to his biracial background, his novels focused on white characters. He graduated from Paine College in 1937 and received a master's degree in English from Fisk University in 1938. He later studied English at the University of Chicago for nine months as a Ph.D. candidate before leaving without the degree. Like Bontemps and Wright, Yerby took advantage of the Federal Writers' Project to further develop his literary skills while earning payment for the same. Yerby went on to achieve widespread success as an author of "pulp," or general popular, fiction. His first novel, a Southern historical romance titled *The Foxes of Harrow* (1946), made him a millionaire. It was made into a movie in 1951.

As Harlem writers convened at the Harlem Writers' Guild and similar groups, the South Side Writers' Group met weekly at the Lincoln Center on Oakwood Boulevard. Members included Bontemps, Frank Davis, Walker, Ward, and Wright. And visual artists such as Hughie Lee-Smith and ARCHIBALD JOHN MOTLEY, JR., were among the many supporters of the SOUTH SIDE COMMUNITY ART CENTER that continued to operate in 2002 from the same address it had in the late 1930s.

Because of the Harlem Renaissance's national and international influence, which extended as far as West Africa, and because Chicago's artistic era came so close behind New York's, it might appear that the Harlem Renaissance simply spilled into the Midwest. However, as one of the capitals of jazz and the blues, and home to numerous writers, artists, and influential business ventures, the Chicago Renaissance developed as a unique and independent movement in its own right.

Further Reading

Altman, Susan. *The Encyclopedia of African-American Heritage.* New York: Facts On File, Inc., 1997.

Parks, Carole A., ed. *NOMMO: A Literary Legacy of Black Chicago 1967–1987.* Chicago: OBAC Writers' Workshop, 1987.

Mullen, Bill V. *Popular Fronts: Chicago and African-American Cultural Politics, 1935–46.* Champaign: University of Illinois Press, 1999.

Sochen, June, ed. *The Black Man and the American Dream: Negro Aspirations in America, 1900–1930.* Chicago: Quadrangle Books, 1971.

Southern, Eileen. *The Music of Black Musicians: A History.* New York: W.W. Norton and Co., Inc., 1971.

— Sandra L. West

Chicago Defender

The *Chicago Defender,* a newspaper destined to grow into one of America's most influential publications during the first half of the 20th century, made its humble debut as a four-page publication the size of a leaflet with a circulation of 300 on March 4, 1905. With an investment of 25¢ to supply his new publication with paper and pencils, Georgia native ROBERT ABBOTT became the publisher, writer, business manager, and circulation department of what he proudly billed as "The World's Greatest Weekly."

Abbott had initially set his professional sights on a career in law after graduating from Virginia's Hampton Institute in 1896 and from CHICAGO's Kent Law School in 1899. However, Abbott was told he was too dark to exercise favorable influence as a lawyer in Chicago, and he met with similar barriers of prejudice in Gary, Indiana, and Topeka, Kansas. It was then that he turned to a trade he had learned in part working alongside his stepfather, John J. Sengstacke, while growing up in Savannah, Georgia.

Abbott kept his new publication afloat with the assistance of his landlady, Mrs. Harriet Plummer Lee, and her daughter, who provided meals for him and allowed him to employ her home as if it were his very own newspaper office.

By 1910, the *Chicago Defender's* circulation and profits had increased enough for Abbott to hire his first full-time employee, reporter J. Hockley Smiley. Abbott and Smiley made a close study of the sensationalistic and yellow journalism techniques employed in the publications of Randolph Hearst and Joseph Pulitzer. Their decision to adapt those techniques to their own use marked a departure from the generally more conservative approach to journalism practiced by most African-American weeklies. The result was stories and headlines that focused on every aspect of the black community while simultaneously identifying the atrocities of racism as an ongoing threat to the community. The paper adopted an uncompromising militancy with its attacks on JIM CROW racism, disfranchisement, and LYNCHING.

The paper's circulation jumped to 90,000 in 1917 and by 1920 that number had tripled, with more than 60 percent of the *Chicago Defender's* readers living outside of Chicago. Offices were established in London and New York, with Bessie Bearden, mother of famed artist ROMARE BEARDEN, holding the position of New York editor for the paper during the 1920s.

The *Chicago Defender,* with the elegant 5'6" Abbott leading the charge, took on a powerful history-altering role when it went beyond reporting the GREAT MIGRATION out of the South and started encouraging it by enticing southern African Americans to make their way to the North where they at least could enjoy the opportunity, if not a guarantee, to improve their lives. This encouragement was backed up by advertisements for jobs that had become exceptionally abundant during WORLD WAR I, with white American males entering the draft and white immigrants temporarily barred from entering the country. Northern companies in need of laborers were happy to advertise in a newspaper that helped them to drain the South of its cheap labor pool. Southern African Americans weary of poverty, Jim Crow, and the threat of lynching, were happy to learn such intense conditions of racism were not universal.

Abbott's call to African Americans in the South peaked with a campaign that became known as the Great Northern Drive of May 15, 1917. The drive was promoted and organized by the *Chicago Defender* as a single day on which southern African Americans were to participate in a mass exodus out of the South. To accomplish this, the newspaper obtained agreements from railroads to add extra passenger cars to their trains for May 15, and many offered special "excursion rates" as well. Northern merchants sent representatives armed with contracts to the South to secure work agreements from many blacks even before they boarded a train. The *Chicago Defender* published schedules, fares, and information on various modes of available transportation. Among the other newspapers joining the *Defender* in its rallying cry were the *NEW YORK AGE,* the *Christian Recorder,* and the *Dallas Express.*

News of the drive alarmed the southern white community. White officials in some towns simply confiscated tickets from local African Americans planning trips north. Travelers were arrested on exaggerated charges, and at least two distributors of the *Chicago Defender* were killed for distributing the paper. Nevertheless, the offices of the *Chicago Defender* filled with mail from African Americans seeking more information about the drive and praising Abbott's militant stand against racism. The precise number of African Americans who left the South as part of the May 15 drive can probably never be known, but thousands reportedly did make their way onto a northbound train that day, and many who did not were seen traveling by horse and wagon, in boats, and by foot. The idea of black southerners migrating North for greater opportunities to improve the quality of their lives became a fixed one that kept African Americans on the move well into the 1960s.

Neither southerners in particular nor the U.S. government in general tended to remain calm in the face of the *Chicago Defender's* militancy. Abbott did not echo W. E. B. DU BOIS's cry for blacks to "close ranks" and set aside racial grievances during World War I but instead published constant reminders that both black soldiers and civilians were frequent targets of white violence. His unrelenting crusade to publicize that specific truth resulted in interrogations from the U.S. Bureau of Investigations and charges that he was collaborating with the German enemy. The newspaper's political agitation was cited as one cause of

Under the editorship of Robert Abbott, the *Chicago Defender,* which the newsboy pictured here is selling in 1942, had become one of the most militant and successful black-owned newspapers of the 1920s. *(Library of Congress, Prints & Photographs Division. [LC-USW3-000698-D])*

the summer of 1919 riots. Oddly, both white southerners and the government blamed the *Chicago Defender* for stirring unrest among the races rather than attributing the riots to the practices of racial discrimination and murdering blacks. They moved to block the paper's distribution through the postal service and, when failing to do so legally, would delay the delivery of the publication or destroy it. Nor was it uncommon for entire bundles of the *Chicago Defender* to disappear from newsstands or other distribution points. Consequently, those southern African Americans who did get a copy of the newspaper often secretly circulated it among neighbors and friends.

As it maintained strong local and national circulation throughout the 1930s and 1940s, the *Chicago Defender* won the distinction of becoming the first black unionized newspaper and the first integrated black newspaper. It also made Abbott the first black publisher to become a millionaire. Moreover, its pages became home to the work of some of the most influential writers of the era. Following the loss of her own newspaper, the *Memphis Free Speech,* IDA BELL WELLS-BARNETT contributed a number of times to the *Chicago Defender.* Her story for the *Defender* on Dr. LeRoy C. Bundy, a black dentist accused of helping incite the 1917 St. Louis riots, moved readers to send in contributions totaling some $1,500 to pay for his legal defense and ultimate freedom. Works by Du Bois also appeared in the paper. LANGSTON HUGHES's *Simple Stories* made their debut in the publication, and GWENDOLYN BROOKS published poetry in it as a teenager.

After Abbott's death in 1940, his nephew John H. Sengstacke became its publisher and editor. Sengstacke took the bold step, on February 5, 1956, of turning the weekly *Chicago Defender* into the *Chicago Daily Defender,* making it the world's largest black-owned daily newspaper. He expanded his publications into a roster that included the *Louisville Defender* and Memphis's *Tri-State Defender.* Sengstacke, prior to his death in 1997, was also one of the founders of the National Newspaper Publishers Association and spent several terms as its president.

Like other newspapers, both black and white, in the 21st century, the *Daily Defender* has had to compete with the expansive communication world of radio, television, and computers. Dropping from the quarter of a million circulation of its high point in the 1920s and 1930s, it has maintained since the 1970s a circulation of 30,000.

Further Reading

Maxwell, William J. *New Negro, Old Left: African American Writing and Communism Between the Wars.* New York: Columbia University Press, 1999.

Simmons, Charles A. *The African American Press.* Jefferson, N.C.: McFarland & Company, 1998.

— Aberjhani

Chittlin' Circuit See THEATER OWNERS BOOKING AGENCY; WASHINGTON, D.C.

Chocolate Dandies (In Bamville)

Making its New York debut on September 1, 1924, at the Colonial Theatre, *Chocolate Dandies* was lyricist NOBLE SISSLE and composer EUBIE BLAKE's follow-up to their history-making musical comedy, *SHUFFLE ALONG.*

Sissle and Blake were still enjoying the success of *Shuffle Along* while planning and writing their new show. After splitting with their previous creative partners, Aubrey Lyles and Flournoy Miller (who had written a second show of their own, *RUNNIN' WILD*), Sissle and Blake enlisted the talents of comedian Lew Payton to help write the book for their new show. They also employed composers Spencer Williams and Chris Smith to provide supplemental music. The show was produced by Bert C. Whitney.

Prior to its New York debut, *Chocolate Dandies* went on tour under the name *In Bamville.* Touted as Sissle and Blake's latest hit musical, it debuted as *In Bamville* at the Lyceum Theatre in Rochester, New York, on March 10, 1924, only two months after the close of *Shuffle Along.* It remained on the road for 24 weeks, moving on to Pittsburgh, Chicago, Detroit, and other cities before returning to New York as *Chocolate Dandies.*

Like *Shuffle Along, Chocolate Dandies* showcased "clean humor," dynamic dancing, and the music of Sissle and Blake. Its story was told through a fantasy sequence in which a man dreams he has won a large amount of money at the racetracks and become his town's most influential citizen. He then wakes to a completely different reality. Among the show's most outstanding features was a horse race with three live horses competing on a treadmill.

Unlike its predecessor, *Chocolate Dandies* did not have to rely on secondhand costumes. Its cast of more than 100 performers were dressed in tailor-made outfits that made critics compare the show to ZIEGFELD FOLLIES productions. The *Chicago Herald* and a number of other newspapers decided such a comparison was not flattering because it supported a repeated charge that *Chocolate Dandies* was "too white" and lacked the elements that made superior black entertainment. As an exception to this critical rule they cited the antics of JOSEPHINE BAKER in her role as a comic chorus line girl. In all, critics and audiences were divided over how good the show was or was not, with many proclaiming it was far superior to *Shuffle Along* and others stating the exact opposite. For his part, Eubie Blake maintained throughout the rest of his career (which lasted until he died at age 100) that his score for *Chocolate Dandies* included the best work he had ever done. The press often cited the songs "Dixie Moon," "Sons of Old Black Joe," "Thinking of Me," and "Jassamine Lane" as highpoints of the show.

Along with Blake on piano, *Chocolate Dandies* starred Sissle in the role of Dobby Hicks. It also included Lew Payton as the main character Mose Washington, the comic dancer Johnny Hudgins, singer Lottie Gee, the Four Harmony Kings with PAUL ROBESON, LENA HORNE in the chorus line, and the perfectly pitched singer Valaida Snow. For his performance, Hudgins was hailed as the new BERT WILLIAMS.

Chocolate Dandies's 100-plus cast made it difficult for the show to regularly turn substantial profits, and cast members, including Sissle and Blake, saw their salaries periodically cut to help the show meet operating expenses. The show did not come close to *Shuffle Along*'s 1921 record-setting run of 504 performances, but it did make it through 96 before closing in May 1925.

Further Reading

Hay, Samuel A. *African American Theatre: A Historical and Critical Analysis.* New York: Cambridge University Press, 1994.

Spencer, Jon Michael. *The New Negroes and Their Music: The Success of the Harlem Renaissance.* Knoxville: University of Tennessee Press, 1997.

— Aberjhani

Cinque Gallery

The Cinque Gallery in New York City was established in February 1969 to honor the creative spirit of the Harlem Renaissance of the 1920s and the federally funded arts projects of the 1930s. It was founded and incorporated by artists ROMARE BEARDEN, a collagist; ERNEST CRICHLOW, a figurative painter; and NORMAN LEWIS, an abstract expressionist painter.

Bearden, Lewis, and Crichlow hoped that, with the opening of the Cinque Gallery, they would be able to supplement the space available for African-American artists to show their work. They noted that whereas various African-American colleges and universities exhibited works by African-American artists, mainstream art galleries were less apt to do so. Therefore, they defined the official mission of Cinque Gallery as follows: to support the growth and development of artists of color, including painters, sculptors, ceramists, printmakers, and photographers.

The art gallery was inaugurated in February because of the month's designation as Black History Month by CARTER GODWIN WOODSON, the "father of black history." It was named in honor of an African man, Joseph Cinque. Leader of the famous *Amistad* mutiny, Cinque and his fellow countrymen were charged with piracy, then negotiated their freedom in an American court of law in March 1841. They won their case and the kidnapped Africans sailed back to Sierra Leone in November 1841.

A legacy institution, the Cinque Gallery was originally located in the New York Public Theatre on Lafayette Street and relocated several times before moving in June 1988 to its final space at 500 Broadway, Suite 504, New York City, in the Soho district. Ernest Crichlow, the only member of the founding group still living in 2002, was at that time the gallery's artistic director. After decades of service, Cinque Gallery closed in November 2003.

Further Reading

Brown, Kevin, and Nathan I. Huggins, eds. *Romare, Bearden.* Broomall, Pa.: Chelsea House Publishers, 1994.

Miers, Charles, ed. *Harlem Renaissance: Art of Black America.* New York: Harry N. Abrams, 1994.

— Sandra L. West

Civic Club dinner

More than 100 publishers, magazine editors, artists, and writers gathered at NEW YORK CITY's Civic Club on March 21, 1924, to acknowledge and celebrate the emerging abundance of black creative talent.

The publication of *There Is Confusion,* a novel by JESSIE REDMOND FAUSET, is often cited as the occasion for the Civic Club dinner but extended research indicates the idea for the dinner evolved out of discussions among individuals who gathered weekly for intellectual exchange at the SALON held in the home of Georgia Douglas Johnson in WASHINGTON, D.C. Following the cultural current of the times, participants in the group established similar meetings upon moving to New York.

The Civic Club, a short distance from Fifth Avenue on 12th Street, was known for its then liberal policy of allowing the races and genders to mix as they pleased. The racial element of the club was important to help establish a cultural community consisting not only of black writers with talent but white publishers with outlets for the same. Moreover, white writers who had lent their pens to interpreting the significance of the African-American experience were also considered important and invited to attend the event. The guest list, drawn up by OP-

PORTUNITY magazine editor and the dinner's host, CHARLES SPURGEON JOHNSON, included Eugene O'Neill, Ridgely Torrence, Zona Gale, H. L. Mencken, and Clement Wood, all of them established white authors of the period.

The appointed master of ceremonies for the affair was ALAIN LOCKE. The philosopher and scholar had already served as mentor to several of the writers recognized at the dinner, and many were looking to him to provide further intellectual leadership to the new generation of black writers and artists. Paul Kellogg, editor for *SURVEY GRAPHIC* magazine wrote to Locke and expressed his vision of what he believed the growing movement in black culture could achieve: "We are interpreting a racial and cultural revival in the new environment of the northern city; interpreting the affirmative genius of writers, thinkers, poets, artists, singers and musicians, which make for a new rapprochement between the races at the same time that they contribute to the common pot of civilization."

As if to draw a very clear line between the past and the future, Locke used the dinner as an opportunity to thank such venerable veterans of African-American letters as W. E. B. DU BOIS and JAMES WELDON JOHNSON for the literary contributions they had made and upon which the younger writers hoped to build. Addressing the assembly in turn were WALTER WHITE, J. Montgomery Gregory, Jessie Fauset, and Carl Van Doren. As the editor of *Century Magazine,* Van Doren's comments were particularly striking in his description of the African-American condition as an aesthetic advantage to black artists. Concluding the occasion's program were poetry readings by COUNTEE CULLEN and GWENDOLYN BENNETTA BENNETT. Of those writers later recognized as principal contributors to the Harlem Renaissance, JEAN TOOMER, CLAUDE MCKAY, LANGSTON HUGHES, and ZORA NEALE HURSTON were not present at the dinner. Toomer had been invited but elected not to attend. McKay and Hughes were out of the country, and Hurston had not yet made her inimitable entrance into New York.

Appreciative of all he had seen and heard during the dinner, Paul Kellogg approached Charles Johnson to inform him that he would like to devote an entire issue of *Survey Graphic* to the work of the new writers. Johnson passed on to Alain Locke the task of actually collecting the work to appear in the magazine and reserved for his own responsibility that of alerting black writers and artists throughout the country that a new black cultural movement was under way. The edition of *Survey Graphic* featuring the younger generation of black artists sold out two printings and garnered a readership of more than 40,000. It also laid the groundwork for the *NEW NEGRO*, also edited by Alain Locke and destined to become the defining text of the Harlem Renaissance.

With the Civic Club dinner having set the stage, the movement advanced further with the establishment of literary prizes for plays, essays, poetry, and short stories published in *Opportunity* and *CRISIS: A RECORD OF THE DARKER RACES* magazines. White publishers backing the works of black writers often saw themselves both as assisting the cause of such writers and simultaneously providing American literature overall with a much-needed shot of new energy and inspiration.

Further Reading

Hutchinson, George. *The Harlem Renaissance in Black and White.* Cambridge and London: The Belknap Press of Harvard University Press, 1995.

Lewis, David Levering. *W. E. B. Du Bois, Biography of A Race 1868–1919.* New York: Henry Holt and Company, 1993.

Watson, Steven. *The Harlem Renaissance, Hub of American Culture, 1920–1930.* New York: Pantheon Books, 1995.

— Aberjhani

Cole, Allen

See ART AND THE HARLEM RENAISSANCE.

Coleman, Anita Scott (Elizabeth Stepleton Stokes) (1890–1960) *writer*

Anita Scott Coleman, a productive poet and short story writer whose work explored women's issues, wrote frequently for *CRISIS: A RECORD OF THE DARKER RACES* and *Half-Century Magazine* during the Harlem Renaissance.

Anita Coleman was born in 1890 in Guaymas, Sonora, Mexico. Her father was a Cuban who purchased the freedom of her mother, an enslaved African.

After graduating from New Mexico Teachers College, Coleman taught school in Los Angeles. In addition, she wrote short stories for the NATIONAL ASSOCIATION FOR THE ADVANCEMENT OF COLORED PEOPLE's (NAACP) journal, *Crisis* magazine, and for the NATIONAL URBAN LEAGUE's (NUL) *OPPORTUNITY* magazine. She published poetry under a pseudonym.

Crisis published Coleman's "El Tisco" (March 1920), "Three Dogs and a Rabbit: A Story of Passing Memory" (January 1926), "Unfinished Masterpieces" (March 1927), and "Two Old Women A-Shopping Go! A Story of Man, Marriage and Poverty" (May 1933). *Opportunity* published "Cross Crossings Cautiously" (June 1930) and "The Eternal Quest" (August 1931).

The radical *MESSENGER* journal, edited by A. PHILIP RANDOLPH, also published Coleman's work: "The Brat" appeared in April 1926, "Silk Stockings" in August 1926, "G'Long, Old White Man's Gal" in April 1928, and "White Folk's Nigger" in May 1928.

Though well-published in prominent periodicals alongside legendary literary figures, Coleman's stories more frequently appeared in *Half-Century Magazine,* which was published in Chicago (1915–25). Its subtitle was "A Colored Monthly for the Businessman and the Homemaker." The interests of its readers, generally educated and biracial, evolved around obtaining the American Dream and maintaining social status. Popular columns were "What They Are Wearing" by Madame F. Madison and "Health Talks" by Dr. Julian Lewis. Monthly topics ran under the headings of "General Race News," "Classy Fiction," "Business," "Fashion," and "Fun." Anita Scott Coleman contributed regularly to the "Classy Fiction" department. Her "Love's Power" appeared in "Classy Fiction" in the May 1919 edition; "Phoebe Goes to a Lecture" in June 1919; "Billie Settles the Question" in August 1919; "Phoebe and Peter Up North" in February 1919; "The Nettleby's New Year" in January 1920; "Jack Arrives" in February 1920; "Rich Man, Poor

Man" in May 1920; and "The Little Grey House" published in July/August 1922. Additionally, "The Hand That Fed" appeared in *Competitor,* December 1920. With poetry anthologized in *Negro Voices* (1938) and *Ebony Rhythm* (1948), she published *Small Wisdom* (1937) and *Reason for Singing* (1948) under the pseudonym of Elizabeth Stepleton Stokes.

In contrast to what some consider the male-dominated focus of the Harlem Renaissance and the works of women authors like JESSIE REDMOND FAUSET and NELLA LARSEN, who wrote about middle-class domestic drama, Anita Scott Coleman wrote stories about self-sacrificing women, the harsh economic plight of single working women, the anguish of newly migrated blacks, and cruel INTERRACIAL INTERACTIONS.

Coleman died in 1960, one year before her poetry volume, *The Singing Bells,* was published.

Further Reading

Hubbard, Dolan, ed. *Recovered Writers/Recovered Texts: Race, Class, and Gender in Black Women's Literature.* Knoxville: University of Tennessee Press, 1997.

Russell, Sandi. *Render Me My Song: African-American Women Writers from Slavery to the Present.* San Francisco: Harper Book, 2001.

— Sandra L. West

Colored American Magazine

The *Colored American Magazine,* published in Boston, Massachusetts, and NEW YORK CITY, at the beginning of the 20th century, was the most widely distributed black-oriented journal prior to the establishment of the *CRISIS: A RECORD OF THE DARKER RACES,* edited by W. E. B. DU BOIS, in 1910. One of the magazine's editors, PAULINE ELIZABETH HOPKINS, emerged as a noted Harlem Renaissance writer, and the magazine itself proved an early, successful black business with black investors. It documented Boston, home of *Saturday Evening Quill* writers, as a city of wealthy, black intellectuals.

The first issue of *Colored American* was published in May 1900. It sold for 15¢ per copy with an annual subscription rate of $1.50. Its circulation in 1905 reached 15,000. It was published by the Colored Cooperative Publishing Company at 232 West Canton Street in Boston. Advertisers sold watches with Frederick Douglass images and hair-straightening products. The long subtitle of the "monthly magazine of merit" also described its purpose: "An Illustrated Monthly Devoted to Literature, Science, Music, Art, Religion, Facts, Fiction and Traditions of the Negro Race. A Co-operative Journal by Prominent Negro Statesmen, Scientists and Teachers, Together with Other Celebrated Authors."

Walter W. Wallace founded the magazine, and Hopkins, whose short story "Mystery Within Us" appeared in the inaugural issue, was editor of the women's pages. Hopkins later became a literary editor who published the work of ANGELINA EMILY WELD GRIMKE.

The magazine is noted as a predecessor of the modern-day, similarly styled *Ebony. Colored American* published 17 volumes before its demise in November 1909.

Further Reading

Allen, Carol. *Black Women Intellectuals: Strategies of Nation, Family, and Neighborhood in the Works of Pauline Hopkins, Jessie Fauset and Marita Bonner.* New York: Garland Publishing, 1998.

Johnson, Abby Arthur, and Ronald Maberry Johnson. *Propaganda and Aesthetics: The Literary Politics of Afro-American Magazines in the Twentieth Century.* Amherst: University of Massachusetts Press, 1979.

— Sandra L. West

Commandment Keepers

Affiliated with Jamaican leader MARCUS GARVEY'S UNIVERSAL NEGRO IMPROVEMENT ASSOCIATION (UNIA), the Commandment Keepers were a religious organization that embraced the Jewish/Hebrew tradition. Two of its founders were Arnold Josiah Ford and Arthur Wentworth Matthew.

Arnold Josiah Ford was a UNIA leader who adopted Judaism, learned Hebrew, and, in 1924, founded Beth B'nai Abraham, a black Jewish assembly in HARLEM.

Arthur Wentworth Matthew was born in Nigeria in 1892 and settled in St. Kitts, British West Indies, before relocating to Harlem in 1911. In Harlem, Matthew joined and became a minister in the Church of the Living God, the Pillar and Ground of the Truth, located at 29 West 131st Street. This congregation had originally been founded by Mother Lena Lewis Tate, also a Garveyite.

Black Hebrews in general became part of America's religious community around the turn of the 20th century. The Church of God and Saints in Christ was organized in Belleville, Virginia, in 1905, and the Church of God was founded in Philadelphia in 1915. During the 1920s and 1930s, a group of multi-denominational southern immigrants and African Caribbeans from every island, especially Jamaica, held gatherings in Harlem. This melting pot of people of African descent was reflected in diverse religious institutions throughout Harlem, from Protestant congregations to FATHER DIVINE cults, including denominations of Black Hebrews, also known as Black Jews. In the midst of the religious mix, a group of West Indians established their religious intentions.

In 1919, Matthew founded the Commandment Keepers Church of the Living God, located at 1 East 123rd Street, and became its bishop. Through his meeting and subsequent friendship with Ford in the 1920s, Rabbi Matthew learned Orthodox Judaism, the Hebrew language, and Hasidic rituals.

When Ford's congregation, Beth B'nai Abraham, experienced financial problems in 1930, Ford transferred his congregation to Matthew's watch. Ford then relocated to Ethiopia and never returned to the United States.

A tenet of the Black Hebrew is the belief that Black Hebrews are part of the lost tribes of Israel. With his combined congregations, Rabbi Matthew prospered and expanded his teachings to include all that Ford had taught him about the religion, the language, and the existence of the Falashas, the black Jews of Ethiopia. By 1935, Matthew declared his congregation the Falashas in America and received official recognition from

Ethiopian emperor Haile Selassie. He inaugurated a Hebrew school and trained future Black Hebrew leaders at the Ethiopian Hebrew Rabbinical College in Harlem.

The belief system of Black Jews combines Judaism with African and African-American traditions. The Commandment Keepers strive to practice moral restraint, dignity, and strong parental authority in the home. They observe the rituals and holidays of ancient Jewish traditions. Their form of worship is called Sephardic, which originated with the Jews in Spain and Portugal and came to black people via Latin America and the West Indian islands. The Commandment Keepers keep Sabbath on Friday evenings and Saturday mornings. Men wear skullcaps. They observe Jewish dietary rules, such as eating kosher foods. They perform a ritual washing of their feet and sing gospel hymns, as in the African-American religious tradition. Through these rituals, performed in a solemn manner, they identify with both the persecution of non-black Jews and former African slaves in America. Like non-black Jews, they learn Hebrew, study scripture from the Talmud and Old Testament, and learn Jewish history.

Rabbi Matthew also observed the esoteric Jewish practice known as the cabala and was acknowledged as a healer. Matthew, a graduate of the Jewish Theological Seminary, died in 1973. His grandson, Rabbi David M. Dore, a graduate of Yeshiva University, led the Commandment Keepers in 2002. The organization at that time was located at 31 Mount Morris Park West in Harlem, near Fifth Avenue, in the John and Nancy Dwight mansion. An Italian Renaissance structure, the mansion served as a sanatorium until it was converted into the Jewish synagogue in 1962.

Black Jews view white Jews as Jews of a different tribe, though relations between the two groups are cordial. Black Hebrews who migrate to Israel have, in modern times, experienced difficulty assimilating into the culture because they were not considered as "real" Jews.

As of the 1970s, membership in the Commandment Keepers denomination in metropolitan New York and the Northeast numbered approximately 3,000. In the United States, 44,000 Black Hebrews congregated in temples such as the House of Judah in Wetumpka, Alabama, and the Temple of Love in Miami, Florida.

Further Reading

Dolkart, Andrew S., and Gretchen S. Sorin. *Touring Historic Harlem: Four Walks in Northern Manhattan.* New York: New York Landmarks Conservancy, 1997.

Raboteau, Albert J. *A Fire in the Bones: Reflections on African-American Religious History.* Boston: Beacon Press, 1995.

Smith, Jonathan Z., ed. *The HarperCollins Dictionary of Religion.* San Francisco: HarperSanFrancisco, 1995.

— Sandra L. West

communism

African Americans fighting for civil rights during the 1900s often found themselves working in alliance, sometimes reluctantly, sometimes gratefully, with adherents to an American brand of communism.

The Russian Revolution of October 1917 inspired the formation of several American communist groups that eventually united within a single political party. The more radical members of Latvian-American Socialists and the Socialist Propaganda League broke away from their parent organizations in late 1917 to form the Friends of New Russia. Further changes and experiments in political tactic and ideology produced the Communist Party of Americana and the Communist Labor Party in 1919. A decade later, these would evolve into the Communist Party, U.S.A.

From its beginning, the Communist Party placed among its priorities the struggles of African Americans, both because of their obvious political plight as members of a racially oppressed group and because of their potential membership in the new party. While most African Americans shared a general distrust of communism, fearing manipulation by the group and a loss of individuality, many believed its principles were a sound solution for the divisions of race, class, and gender that so frequently stirred unrest in the country. Even those who did not adopt communism in practice welcomed the intellectual stimulation of discussing its political potential in contrast to socialism or capitalism.

HARLEM became home to a number of believers who, if not outright card-carrying communists, became affiliates who interacted with communists to the degree that communists supported black causes. The former editor of NEW YORK CITY's *AMSTERDAM NEWS* and founder of the AFRICAN BLOOD BROTHERHOOD, Cyril Briggs, promoted worker rights combined with black nationalism and Pan-Africanism in a monthly magazine called the *Crusader* from 1918 to 1922. Briggs, a native of the West Indies, published every literary form and covered subjects ranging from sports to business. The *Crusader*'s contributors included CLAUDE MCKAY, T. Thomas Fortune, and Paul Laurence Dunbar. The magazine was largely a political organ for the African Blood Brotherhood, a group of black men and women who believed in retaliation against white mob violence, advocated self-government for African Americans, and went back and forth between supporting and not supporting MARCUS GARVEY. Briggs openly advocated an Americanized communist system for the United States and worked with various communist organizations throughout his life.

PAUL ROBESON, LANGSTON HUGHES, and W. E. B. DU BOIS each championed communism as a tool for political discourse and analysis applicable to African America, if not as a political system likely to replace capitalism. Robeson gained world renown for lending his voice in song and speech to the rights of workers all over the world and became so revered in Russia that a mountain was named after him. Du Bois lost faith in any hope for integration in the United States and joined the Communist Party before departing America in 1961 to live his final years as a citizen of Ghana.

Harlem's famed religious leader, the enigmatic FATHER DIVINE, was frequently criticized for accepting communist support of his Peace Mission program, aimed at feeding, clothing, and housing the poor. He nevertheless honored the support he received by riding with a contingent of his followers in parades promoting communist causes.

Throughout the 1930s the Communist Party lent its backing to black causes. In a Harlem hit very hard by the GREAT DEPRESSION, the organization coordinated protests against rent evictions and in many instances were able to have families reinstated in their homes. The members also participated in relief demonstrations when it became evident that government monies allocated for public relief too often failed to make its way into black hands. Harlem resident Benjamin J. Davis ran openly as a "Black Communist" for a Harlem city council seat and won.

The group scored a major public relations coup when its International Labor Defense (ILD) branch beat out the NATIONAL ASSOCIATION FOR THE ADVANCEMENT OF COLORED PEOPLE (NAACP) to represent the nine black youth accused of raping two white women in the SCOTTSBORO TRIAL. Communist newspapers, as well as many black-owned newspapers, contrasted the NAACP's indecisiveness about the significance of the case with the ILD's constant attentiveness to the young men and their families. Communist members of the National Negro Congress did not present themselves as representatives of the Communist Party but became such a dominating element within the congress that A. PHILIP RANDOLPH and other more socialist-leaning individuals withdrew from it. Steadfastly aligning itself with black political groups, the Communist Party went on record in opposition to Italy's 1935 invasion of Ethiopia.

As might be expected, the communists generally established a strong presence in various unions and were particularly active within the American Federation of Labor.

Moreover, branches such as the Southern Youth Conference and Civil Rights Congress helped lay the groundwork for the Civil Rights movement of the 1950s and 1960s. The Civil Rights Congress developed out of a merger among the ILD, members of the National Negro Congress, and the National Federation for Constitutional Liberties. Starting in 1946, the Congress picked up where the ILD had left off with its defense of African Americans in cases and locales where mob violence was more likely to triumph over any attempts at justice. Toward that end, they successfully defended a black truck driver named Willie McGee whose white lover decided to scream rape when her husband learned of their affair. They also defended Rosa Ingram and her two sons, who, under assault by a white tenant farmer, defended themselves and killed him.

Bayard Rustin, who joined the Youth Communist League in 1936, was a major participant in A. Philip Randolph's March on Washington and, with many others, remained an important behind-the-scenes organizer of the Civil Rights movement.

Internal disputes and structural problems had already begun to weaken the Communist Party even before the era of McCarthyism, when right-wing extremists sought to purge the United States of any active communist influence. However, the campaign to portray American communists as affiliates of the Soviet Union and the greatest possible threat to American security forever changed the image of U.S. communists from politically militant to militarily dangerous.

Nevertheless, black radicals during the 1960s Black Power movement found substantial support for their agenda in a struggling but still active Communist Party. Ironically, the dissolution of the Soviet Union in 1989 created a ripple effect just as the October Revolution had done in 1917. Just as the Soviet Union lost its center and, reportedly, continues to experience social chaos in the early 21st century, the Communist Party U.S.A. gradually followed suit and quietly dissolved in 1991. Despite its less than glorious conclusion, the contributions of the Communist Party to the struggles of African Americans were many.

Further Reading

Maxwell, William J. *New Negro, Old Left: African American Writing and Communism Between the Wars.* New York: Columbia University Press, 1999.

Smethurst, James E. *The New Red Negro: The Literary Left and African American Poetry, 1930–1946.* New York: Oxford University Press, 1999.

Solomon, Mark. *The Cry Was Unity: Communists and African Americans, 1917–1936.* Jackson: University of Mississippi Press, 1998.

— Aberjhani

Connie's Inn

Music revues that attracted talent scouts from Broadway and helped launch the careers of such musical greats as LOUIS ARMSTRONG and FATS WALLER made Connie's Inn one of the most popular night clubs in HARLEM during the 1920s.

Connie's Inn was formerly known as a basement club called the Shuffle Inn. Trading in his delicatessen for a shot at the entertainment business, German immigrant Connie (Conrad) Immerman teamed up with his brothers George and Louie to open Connie's Inn. With the LAFAYETTE THEATRE beside them and a popular musician's hangout known as The Barbeque located above them, the new club benefited from a steady stream of both potential patrons and talent. However, like the COTTON CLUB and more than half a dozen other entertainment facilities in Harlem at the time, Connie's Inn welcomed white patrons but not black ones.

Located at SEVENTH AVENUE and 132nd Street, the club won a reputation as the first stop for white entertainment-seekers out for a fun-filled night in Harlem. Just outside the club was the fabled TREE OF HOPE, a supposed living talisman for entertainers seeking work or hoping for an exceptional performance. Inside was space enough to hold fewer than 300 people and an interior that resembled a small village complete with a miniature church. Considered among the more expensive clubs in Harlem, an individual check could easily come to $14 and the tab for a party of four more than $50.

As with all of the racially exclusive clubs, what made the high prices and tight space at Connie's Inn worthwhile was the superb black entertainment. Connie's Inn featured dancers and a black orchestra that rivaled the Cotton Club's. When the Immerman brothers noted the impact BRICKTOP was having at BARRON'S (Wilkins's) EXCLUSIVE CLUB, they wooed her to their own with a salary offer she found irresistible. Another headliner was comedian MOMS MABLEY.

Connie's Inn also enjoyed the talents of the gifted musician Thomas "Fats" Waller, who had been a delivery man for Immerman's delicatessen business. Working with Andy Razaf, Waller wrote and performed in the review *Connie's Hot Chocolates.* It also featured Louis Armstrong performing "Ain't Misbehavin" and "Can't We Get Together." An indication of the bigger things to come in Waller's career, the review dropped Connie's from its title and went to Broadway as *HOT CHOCOLATES.*

Harlem Hotcha starred Earl "Snakehips" Tucker, a dancer whose swiveling hips rather than tapping feet mesmerized the customers at Connie's Inn. Unique talent that he was, Tucker also performed *Harlem Hotcha* at the Lafayette. Among the other revues presented at the club were *Connie's Inn Frolics* and *Hot Feet.*

Members of the ZIEGFELD FOLLIES, heiress Gertrude Vanderbilt, publisher Max Schuster, Harry K. Thaw, and numerous others poured in from downtown to enjoy the shows at Connie's Inn and were sometimes influential in moving those shows to Broadway.

In the early 1930s, the Immermans moved Connie's Inn to a downtown location. There, they produced one of their last great revues, *Stars Over Broadway,* which starred BILLIE HOLIDAY and featured BESSIE SMITH as a temporary fill-in for Holiday when she was ill.

The GREAT DEPRESSION forced Connie's Inn to close and the Immerman brothers to obtain individual employment.

Further Reading

Floyd, Samuel A., ed. *Black Music in the Harlem Renaissance: A Collection of Essays.* Knoxville: University of Tennessee Press, 1994.

Roberts, John W. *Odunde Presents: From Hucklebuck to Hip-Hop.* Collingdale, Pa.: DIANE Publishing Company, 1997.

— Aberjhani

Cook, Will Marion (Will Marion) (1869–1944)

composer, musician

Will Marion Cook abandoned his formal training as a classical musician to compose music for RAGTIME, JAZZ, and one of the first successful black stage productions, *Clorindy, or The Origin of the Cakewalk,* with dialect poet Paul Laurence Dunbar.

Will Marion Cook was born on January 27, 1869, in WASHINGTON, D.C., to educated and accomplished parents. His father, John H. Cook, was a lawyer who graduated from Howard University's first law class in 1871. His mother, a teacher, graduated from Ohio's Oberlin Conservatory in 1865.

Cook studied violin at Oberlin when he was just 13 years old. A prodigy, he also studied at the University of Berlin and at the National Conservatory of Music in NEW YORK CITY, where he was a classmate of singer and composer HARRY THACKER BURLEIGH. In 1895, he made his concert debut playing the violin at Carnegie Hall and in 1890 he directed a chamber orchestra.

Cook entered the field of musical theater with the assistance of the most noted black poet of his era, Paul Laurence Dunbar, primarily a dialect poet, and husband to Harlem Renaissance poet ALICE DUNBAR-NELSON. Cook composed the music and Dunbar created the lyrics for an African-American folk opera called *Clorindy, or The Origin of the Cakewalk,* in 10 solid hours. The CAKEWALK was a popular dance that evolved out of entertainment among blacks on southern plantations. Cook's folk opera, full of comedy, songs, and dances, angered the composer's refined mother, who exclaimed: "I've sent you all over the world to study and become a great musician and you return such a nigger!"

Clorindy produced the hit song "Darktown Is Out Tonight" and starred Ernest Hogan. Hogan performed the encore-raising tune "Who Dat Say Chicken in Dis Crowd." The musical opened on July 5, 1898, at the Casino Theater Roof Garden in New York. It was such a landmark success that Cook said: "I was so delirious that I drank a glass of water, thought it was wine and got gloriously drunk. . . . "

Cook married Abbie Mitchell, a singer and dancer in the show. They had one son, Mercer.

Outside of musical theater, the classically trained violinist composed songs under the pseudonym Will Marion. He organized the Clef Club's Syncopated Orchestra, a group of 125 black musicians; acted as composer-in-chief and musical director for Broadway shows written by the comedy and minstrel team of BERT WILLIAMS and GEORGE WALKER; and, in 1918, toured Europe with his group called the Southern Syncopaters, also known as the New York Syncopated Orchestra. When he returned to New York, he conducted the Clef Club Orchestra, featuring as a lead singer the bass vocalist and human rights activist PAUL ROBESON.

Cook lived in the exclusive HARLEM neighborhood of STRIVER'S ROW from 1918 to 1944. He died in New York on July 19, 1944.

Further Reading

Anderson, Jervis. *This Was Harlem: A Cultural Portrait, 1900–1950.* New York: Farrar Straus Giroux, 1981.

Fitzpatrick, Sandra, and Maria R. Goodwin. *The Guide to Black Washington: Places and Events of Historical and Cultural Significance in the Nation's Capital.* New York: Hippocrene Books, 1990.

Morgan, Thomas L. *From Cakewalk to Concert Halls: An Illustrated History of African-American Popular Music from 1895 to 1930.* Washington, D.C.: Elliott & Clark, 1992.

— Sandra L. West

Cooper, Anna Julia (Anna Julia Haywood)

(1858–1964) *educator, writer*

One of the earliest black feminists, Anna Julia Cooper was an educator and forerunner of the Harlem Renaissance who both helped lay the foundation for the *NEW NEGRO* movement of the 1920s and, while in her late 60s, made significant contributions to it.

Anna Cooper was born Anna Julia Haywood in slavery on August 10, 1858 (some sources say 1859), in Raleigh, North Carolina, to a slave mother, Hannah Stanley, and a white father, her mother's master. In 1869, she graduated from St. Augustine Normal and Collegiate Institute (now St. Augustine's College) in Raleigh, where, still a student herself and only nine years old, she was a teacher. She married the Rev. George Cooper in 1877 but was widowed two years later. She was one of three black female alumnae in the entire United States when she graduated from Oberlin College with a B.A. in 1884 and an M.A. in 1887.

In the 1890s, Cooper edited the women's pages of *Southland Magazine,* lectured on women's issues with poet ALICE DUNBAR-NELSON, and authored *A Voice From the South by a Black Woman of the South* (1892), her major publication. At the turn of the century, Cooper was a central element in the intellectual renaissance of WASHINGTON, D.C.: she was a delegate at the first PAN AFRICAN CONGRESS in London, along with Dr. W. E. B. DU BOIS; was reportedly the only woman to participate in the male-dominated AMERICAN NEGRO ACADEMY; and helped lead the Washington Colored Woman's League. In 1901, she became principal at the elitist M Street High School in Washington (later the Dunbar School). After teaching there since 1887, Cooper was forced to resign—some records report she was fired—in 1906.

The termination of Cooper's services, whether she was fired or resigned, was called "The M Street School Controversy." One account of the incident states that Cooper was released because of a romantic involvement with a male boarder in her house, a teacher named John Love. Another states that conflict arose when Cooper refused to support the recommendation of white educational administrators to utilize vocational training for all black students in Washington, D.C. Cooper was reportedly then forced out and resumed teaching at Lincoln University near Philadelphia, the future alma mater of LANGSTON HUGHES, from 1906 to 1910.

In 1914, Cooper began doctoral studies at Columbia University. In 1925, at the age of 67, she earned a Ph.D. from the Sorbonne in PARIS, France. She was only the fourth African-American woman to obtain such a degree. She published two nonfiction works in Paris: *L'attitude de la France a l'égard de l'esclavage pendant la revolution* and *Charlemagne: Voyage à Jerusalem et à Constantinople,* both in 1925. Also in 1925, she published the autobiographical *The Third Step* and returned to Washington, D.C., to open a school in her own home for the area's academically disadvantaged young, working adults. That school, Frelinghuysen University, operated into the 1930s. Also in the 1930s, she wrote the essays "The Humor of Teaching" (November 1930) and "Angry Saxons and Negro Education" (May 1938) for *CRISIS: A RECORD OF THE DARKER RACES.* Twenty-one years later, she self-published *The Life and Writings of the Grimke Family* (1951).

Former slave Anna Julia Cooper died on February 27, 1964, at the age of 105.

Further Reading

Busby, Margaret, ed. *Daughters of Africa: An International Anthology of Words and Writings by Women of African Descent From the Ancient Egyptian to the Present.* New York: Pantheon Books, 1992.

Roses, Lorraine Elena, and Ruth Elizabeth Randolph. *Harlem Renaissance and Beyond: Literary Biographies of 100 Black Woman Writers 1900–1945.* Boston: G. K. Hall, 1990.

— Sandra L. West

Cooper, Ralph (1908–1992) *entertainer*

An entertainment mainstay at the APOLLO THEATRE for half a century, Ralph Cooper excelled as an actor, movie producer, comic, dancer, choreographer, and radio personality.

Cooper was born in NEW YORK CITY on January 16, 1908. His career got underway in 1916 when he was included in the cast for *Darktown Follies* at the LAFAYETTE THEATRE in HARLEM. In the 1920s, he formed one half of a dance act with Eddie Rector and appeared in a string of hit musicals, including *RUNNIN' WILD* in 1923, *DIXIE TO BROADWAY* in 1924, *Tan Town Topics* in 1926, and *BLACKBIRDS OF 1928.* He also at the height of the JAZZ age led two bands: the San Domingoes and the Kongo Knights.

At the beginning of the 1930s, Cooper joined the growing movement in independent black films spearheaded by OSCAR MICHEAUX and the LINCOLN MOTION PICTURE COMPANY. While he would later become involved as a producer and writer of films, he started out acting in the 1930 films *Gang Smashers* and *Mr. Smith Goes Ghost.*

Juggling films with his stage career, Cooper also began producing an Amateur Night show at the Lafayette Theatre in April 1933. Amateur Night featured singers, dancers, comedians, and a variety of entertainers seeking recognition or a fun night out. The event proved successful enough that Cooper was able to host alternate Amateur Nights at the Lafayette and the Harlem Opera House. After the reopening of the Apollo Theatre around 1933, Cooper moved his show there in 1935 and introduced what has since become a legend in the history of American entertainment.

From its beginning, every Wednesday from 11 P.M. to midnight, Amateur Night at the Apollo Theatre attracted individuals of exceptional talent who later achieved phenomenal success. Among them were PEARL BAILEY, Sarah Vaughan, Ella Fitzgerald, and Leslie Uggams. Cooper first heard BILLIE HOLIDAY perform at the Hot-Cha club while having dinner there and afterward invited her to perform on Amateur Night at the Apollo. She became one of the theater's most successful singers and subsequently one of jazz music's pioneering icons.

Cooper also maintained a regular position with the Apollo as its emcee on other nights as well. His versatility as a performer allowed him often to participate in skits with comedians such as MOMS MABLEY and PIGMEAT MARKHAM.

He continued as well to act in films, performing in *White Hunter* in 1936 and *Bargain with Bullets* in 1937. In addition, Cooper joined an independent black film production company called Million Dollar Productions and both performed in and produced the film *Dark Manhattan* in 1937. Similarly, in 1938, he was one of the producers of *The Duke Is Tops* and performed in it with LENA HORNE and DUKE ELLINGTON. He appeared in 1940 in *Am I Guilty* and *Gang War,* accumulating enough film credits that he was nicknamed "The Bronze Bogart."

Cooper's continuing work at the Apollo made him one of the most well known individuals in Harlem and one of the most respected personalities in show business. He continued throughout the latter half of the 1900s to host amateur nights and provide some of the world's biggest stars with their introductions to show business. Such celebrated names as Michael Jackson and the Jackson Five, Luther Vandross, James Brown, the Isley Brothers, Patti LaBelle, and many others participated in Amateur Night or headlined at the Apollo Theatre under the direction of Cooper.

The famed emcee remained active in Hollywood toward the end of the century by serving as a consultant for a film on the COTTON CLUB in 1984, producing the television shows *Harlem Spotlight* and *Fifty-seventh Street* in 1987. He died in Harlem on April 4, 1992.

Further Reading

Cooper, Ralph. *Amateur Night at the Apollo: Ralph Cooper Presents Five Decades of Great Entertainment.* New York: Harper Trade, 1990.

Hawkins, Fred W. *Resources for Vintage Black Movies and Videos.* Campbell, California: iUniverse, Incorporated, 2000.

— Aberjhani

Cortor, Eldzier (1916–) *painter*

Artist Eldzier Cortor was a cartoonist who worked with the WORKS PROGRESS ADMINISTRATION (WPA) and explored Afrocentric themes through his paintings, especially those of women.

Eldzier Cortor was born in the Tidewater area of Richmond, Virginia, on January 10, 1916. In 1917, his parents moved the family to the South Side of CHICAGO, Illinois. Attending Englewood High School, one of his classmates was CHARLES WILBERT WHITE, later widely acclaimed as a muralist.

As a child, Cortor read the "Bungleton Green" comic strip in the *CHICAGO DEFENDER*, and he was an early fan of African-American cartoonist E. SIMMS CAMPBELL. At Englewood High, Cortor experimented with cartoon drawing. He finished high school in the evenings and enrolled in night courses at the School of the Art Institute of Chicago. He eventually became a day student there, where another classmate was fellow artist and future playwright Charles Sebree.

At the Art Institute of Chicago, where Cortor studied from 1937 to 1938, he learned anatomical drawing, composition, and formal techniques of painting. An early instructor, Kathleen Blackshear, introduced him to African art at the Field Museum, an influence that showed up in his later art forms. Another influence was the 19th-century French realists, also known as "the commentators of the common people." These were Dutch and Flemish painters. Later he studied at the Institute of Design, Columbia University, in NEW YORK CITY and at Pratt Graphic Art Center, in Brooklyn, New York. Cortor worked with colored pencils and pen and ink to produce watercolors, oils, and etchings.

During the GREAT DEPRESSION, when the federal government funded the WPA, Blackshear worked with Cortor to help him qualify as an easel painter in the Federal Art Project of the 1930s and 1940s. In the WPA, he met ARCHIBALD JOHN MOTLEY, JR., an artist who also encouraged him in his work. Cortor's creative output at this time included the paintings *She Didn't Forget* (1930), *Night Letter* (1938), and *Signs of Times* (1940).

Through the Illinois Federal Arts Project (1938–39), Cortor was assigned to the SOUTH SIDE COMMUNITY ART CENTER. Here, and later at the Illinois Arts and Crafts Project, he met poet GWENDOLYN BROOKS, sculptor ELIZABETH ALICE CATLETT, photographer Gordon Parks, novelist RICHARD NATHANIEL WRIGHT, and painter Hughie-Lee Smith. He organized exhibitions for the artists, taught art classes, and produced paintings.

In the 1940s, Cortor was awarded a Guggenheim Fellowship and a Julius Rosenwald Fund Fellowship. On the advice of Horace Cayton, author of *Black Metropolis,* working at the time on the WPA Federal Writers' Project, Cortor traveled to the Georgia–South Carolina Sea Islands, land of the Gullah language, and to Cuba, Jamaica, and Haiti. In these countries, he sketched and painted and, once back in the United States,

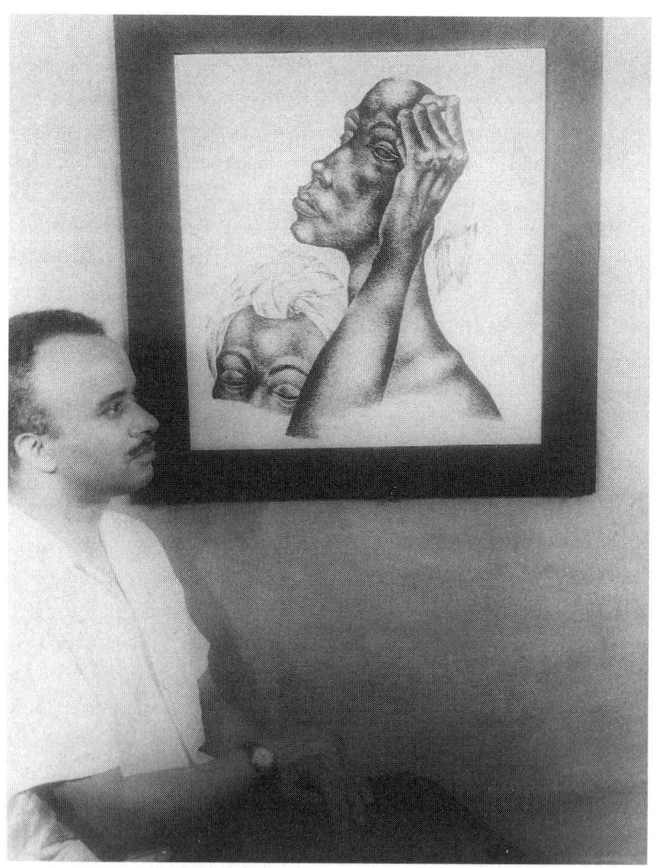

Eldzier Cortor, shown here in 1959, was among the black artists to emerge out of Chicago's cultural renaissance. *(Library of Congress, Prints & Photographs Division, Carl Van Vechten Collection)*

transferred some of these very free and sometimes elongated images into etchings, lithographs, and woodcuts at the Bob Blackburn Printmaking Studio in New York.

Cortor's style, symbols, and themes are unique. He pays tribute to boxers, dancers, and African-American women, all types of everyday people involved in everyday activities. His paintings often include symbolic items: a letter, Bible, or photo of a blues singer to indicate time, place, and history, or to arouse curiosity, queries, and conversation.

Further Reading

Beckman, Wendy. *Artists and Writers of the Harlem Renaissance.* Berkeley Heights, N.J.: Enslow Publishers, Inc., 2002.

Lewis, Samella, *African American Art and Artists.* Berkeley: University of California Press, 1990.

— Sandra L. West

Cotter, Joseph Seamon, Jr. (1895–1919) *poet, journalist, playwright*

Although he died at a young age, Joseph Seamon Cotter, Jr., contributed to the Harlem Renaissance as a poet, playwright, and, like ALICE DUNBAR-NELSON, as a journalist whose work forms an important part of the African-American canon of WORLD WAR I literature.

Joseph Cotter, Jr., was born on September 2, 1895, in Louisville, Kentucky. His father was JAMES SEAMON COTTER, SR., a poet, educator, and civic leader. His mother, a teacher, was Maria F. Cox.

After graduating in 1911 from Louisville Central High School, Cotter, Jr., entered FISK UNIVERSITY in Nashville, Tennessee. While there, he worked on the *Fisk Herald,* a monthly literary journal. During his sophomore year, he was stricken with tuberculosis and returned home to Louisville. Back in Louisville, he accepted a position as a journalist on the *Leader* and began to make his mark as a poet.

In his poetry, Joseph Cotter, Jr., focused on themes that addressed World War I, racism, racial identity, love, death, and nature. He wrote "To Florence," influenced by the death of his sister, Florence Olivia Cotter, also a Fisk student. She died of tuberculosis in December 1914. He wrote a number of poems about the controversial World War I, including "Sonnet to Negro Soldiers" and "O, Little David, Play on Your Harp." Cotter, Jr., avoided the dialect style of his father and Paul Laurence Dunbar and instead experimented with free verse and, in "Rain Music," rhythmic styles. His poems were published in *A.M.E. Zion Quarterly Review* (1920–21) and the *CRISIS: A RECORD OF THE DARKER RACES* (1918).

While infirmed with tuberculosis he wrote a 30-page volume of poetry, *The Band of Gideon,* published by Cornhill Publishing Company in 1918. It included one of his best known free verse poems, "The Mulatto to His Critics." The volumes *Out of the Shadows* (1920) and *Poems* (1921) were published posthumously.

Cotter, Jr.'s most significant work, a play entitled *On the Fields of France,* was published in the June 1920 edition of *Crisis* magazine, one year after his death. The surrealistic, single-act play about World War I denotes a nonhostile relationship between two officers, one white and one black, in PARIS, France. Cotter, Jr., did not serve in the war but maintained a correspondence on it with his friend, Abraham Simpson, the youngest black captain to serve in the war. In view of the controversy that brewed over whether or not, and how, blacks should serve in World War I, *On the Fields of France* presented a study of black and white soldiers fighting under the same flag and finding common ground even as racial discrimination raged back home. The two soldiers contemplate the depth and damage of racism to their native country, consider the friendship they might have enjoyed in the states had racism not been part of their socialization, and die hand in hand.

Joseph Seamon Cotter, Jr., died of tuberculosis on February 3, 1919.

Further Reading

Brown, Sterling A., Arthur P. Davis, and Ulysses Lee, eds. *The Negro Caravan.* New York: The Dryden Press, 1941.

Hatch, James V., ed. *Black Theatre U.S.A.: Plays by African Americans from 1847 to Today.* New York: Free Press, 1996.

Peterson, Bernard L., Jr. *Early Black American Playwrights and Dramatic Writers.* New York: Greenwood Press, 1990.

— Sandra L. West

Cotter, Joseph Seamon, Sr. (1861–1949) *poet, educator, civic leader*

Adhering to the self-help philosophy of Tuskegee Institute founder BOOKER TALIAFERRO WASHINGTON, writer Joseph Seamon Cotter, Sr., founded an independent black community in Kentucky and authored verse chronicling the achievements of both Washington and W. E. B. DU BOIS, editor of the *CRISIS: A RECORD OF THE DARKER RACES.*

Joseph Cotter was born on February 2, 1861, near Bardstown, Kentucky. His father, of Scotch-Irish ancestry, was Micheil J. Cotter. His mother, Martha Vaughn Cotter, was black. His mother taught him to read when he was three. He left school in the third grade to work and help his family. Cotter later attended night school for 10 months. He then worked as a ragpicker and prizefighter before becoming a teacher. His first position as an educator was at Western Colored School in 1889. He married a fellow teacher, Marie F. Cox, on July 22, 1891. They had three children: Leonidas, Florence Olivia, and JOSEPH SEAMON COTTER, JR., noted poet and playwright of the Harlem Renaissance era. All of the Cotter offspring died young, predominantly from tuberculosis contracted during their college years.

In 1891, following Washington's self-help philosophy, Cotter, Sr., established a black community near Louisville called "Little Africa." He also founded the Paul Laurence Dunbar School, named after the poet with whom he shared a friendship based upon their love of literature and dialect verse. Cotter was principal of the school from 1893 to 1911. He further distinguished himself as principal of the Samuel Coleridge-Taylor School (1911–42) in Louisville, Kentucky, won election to the Louisville Board of Education in 1938, and instituted storytelling contests at the town's public libraries. Cotter memorialized his own community development work in a pamphlet on *The Twenty-fifth Anniversary of the Founding of Colored Parkland or "Little Africa"* (1934).

Joseph Cotter, Sr., wrote history plays, short stories, and six volumes of poetry. His benchmark poem is "The Tragedy of Pete," a folk ballad. His first collection of poetry, *A Rhyming* (1895), included Italian sonnets and dialect forms, influenced by Dunbar. His second collection, *Links of Friendship* (1898), includes the poem "The Negro's Loyalty," about African Americans in the Spanish-American War, in addition to "Answer to Dunbar's 'After a Visit'" and "Answer to Dunbar's 'A Choice.'" *A White Song and a Black One* (1909) was republished in 1975 by AMS Press. *Collected Poems of Joseph S. Cotter, Sr.,* debuted in 1912 but was published in a modern edition by Books for Libraries Press in 1971. *Sequel to "The Pied Piper of Hamelin" and Other Poems* (1939) includes "The Race Welcomes Dr. W. E. B. Du Bois as Its Leader." The title poem of the *Hamelin* collection was Cotter's response to "The Pied Piper" by Robert Browning.

Cotter was deeply influenced by Washington, as evidenced by his four-act play *Caleb, the Degenerate* (1901). The play, with 14 characters including an unnamed ensemble of boys and girls of the Industrial School—indication of homage to Washington—reflects the black college founder's views on self-help and manual arts education over liberal arts education for black people. This history play depicts the times, experiences, and needs of the black community at the dawn of the 20th century.

Cotter also wrote short stories and in 1912 published *Negro Tales.* Containing the story "Caleb," *Negro Tales* is his only collection of short fiction. Cotter, Sr., worked until the end of his life, producing *Negroes and Others at Work and Play* (1947), poems and short stories published just two years before his death.

Cotter's teaching and civic work was highly regarded, and his poetry appeared in the major periodicals of the day. His poem "Shakespeare's Sonnet" appeared in *Crisis* magazine in September 1923, and his humorous "Tragedy of Pete" won a prize from *OPPORTUNITY* magazine in the 1920s.

Joseph Cotter Seamon, Sr., died on March 14, 1949.

Further Reading

Beckman, Wendy Hart. *Artists and Writers of the Harlem Renaissance.* Berkeley Heights, N.J.: Enslow Publishers, 2002.

Hatch, James V., ed. *Black Theater, U.S.A. Forty-Five Plays by Black Americans 1847–1974.* New York: The Free Press, 1974.

— Sandra L. West

Cotton Club

The Cotton Club held the distinction of being known simultaneously as one of HARLEM's most glamorous nightclubs and one of its most notorious.

Founded in 1918, the club was known originally as the Douglas Club. In 1920, heavyweight boxing champion JACK JOHNSON turned it into one of Harlem's premier showplaces and named it the Club Deluxe. However, the business venture failed under Johnson and he sold it to Owney Madden.

Madden was, reportedly, a gangster who used the club as an East Coast distribution center for his own brand of bootleg beer. Such known criminal types as Al Capone, Sam Sellis, and the club's manager, George "Big Freddy" Demange, were readily associated with the establishment.

The criminal element provided only one source of the club's notoriety. Another was its JIM CROW policy barring blacks from patronizing the club while hiring the cream of black entertainment to perform for its exclusively white audiences. Those audiences included some of the most celebrated names in NEW YORK CITY and Hollywood, including heiress Emily Vanderbilt, singer and actor Bing Crosby, actor Jimmy Durante, composer Irving Berlin, bandleader Paul Whiteman, and Mayor Jimmy Walker. Writer and patron CARL VAN VECHTEN was welcomed to enjoy the club when alone or with other whites but was turned away when in the company of black friends. The prejudicial treatment incensed Van Vechten enough that at one point he threatened to boycott the club. One black woman who successfully challenged the club's discriminatory policy and entertained her friends there whenever she liked was the millionairess A'LELIA WALKER.

The Cotton Club was not the only one in Harlem that catered to whites while excluding blacks within their own neighborhood. There were a dozen such entertainment spots, including three of the Cotton Club's primary competitors: CONNIE'S INN, SMALL'S PARADISE, and BARRON'S EXCLUSIVE CLUB. The owners of these clubs reasoned that they were providing safe environments for whites to visit and enjoy Harlem without the presumed threat of interracial or gang violence.

Notoriety to the side, the Cotton Club offered enough in the way of first-class entertainment to earn it the title "Aristocrat of Harlem." Joseph Urban, whose innovative artistry proved crucial to the success of the ZIEGFELD FOLLIES, designed the Cotton Club's main showroom. Patrons walked into a double-tiered space containing seating that was surrounded by palms and jungle decor, while the scenery onstage would evoke memories of the old South with cotton plants and slave cabins. European dishes and soul food alike filled out the menu with prices considered high but worthwhile by those who could afford them. The main attraction was its lineup of powerhouse black entertainers. Gracing its stage on a regular basis were some of the most outstanding performers of the era. BOJANGLES ROBINSON and the NICHOLAS BROTHERS danced at the club. A 16-year-old LENA HORNE danced and sang there while her mother shielded her from the seedier aspects of the place's business. ETHEL WATERS, hearing Horne sing "STORMY WEATHER" in her dressing room, suggested the young woman might do well as a singer for NOBLE SISSLE's band. Horne took that advice and did indeed shine with Sissle's orchestra. Waters herself was recruited from the club by Irving Berlin, who made her at the time the highest paid black woman on Broadway, commanding a salary of $1,000 a week, when he cast her in *As Thousands Cheer.*

The club was famed as well for its chorus line, a group of women required to be at least five feet six inches tall, above average in beauty, capable as dancers, and very light in complexion. One of the first darker complexioned women to join the chorus line was LOUIS ARMSTRONG's future wife, Lucille. Ironically, Armstrong himself was considered too dark to perform at the club. The $25 per week that the dancers received was higher than average, and at times white dancers reportedly attempted to pass for lighter complexioned blacks to earn the better salary.

DUKE ELLINGTON and CAB CALLOWAY provided the club with musical entertainment that other musicians and composers traveled from across the country and around the world to enjoy as well as study. Starting in the late 1920s, Ellington and his band began a five-year stint with the Cotton Club. During that time, the band made 200 recordings and went national with broadcasts over the CBS radio network. The club's Jim Crow policy toward black patrons disturbed Ellington to the point that he finally approached its management with the argument that it was ludicrous for the families of performers to be barred from their shows. The restriction was lifted with the stipulation that blacks would not mix with whites but attend and leave with blacks only.

When Ellington took his band on the road in 1931, he left the Cotton Club in the capable musical hands of Cab Calloway. Known for his signature party-shout, "Hi-dee hi-dee hi-dee ho!" Calloway was already a regular stand-in for Ellington and continued to ensure as much attendance at the club as his predecessor.

As with clubs like Connie's Inn and the APOLLO THEATRE, a staple of the Cotton Club's entertainment was a series of miniature revues featuring a variety of acts performing along the same theme. Most of the Cotton Club's shows were written and produced by Jimmy McHugh, Lew Leslie (the producer of *BLACKBIRDS*), Harold Arlen, Ted Kohler, and Dorothy Fields. Among their shows were *Between the Devil and the Deep Blue Sea* and *Rhythmania,* both in 1931; *Minnie the Moocher's Weddin' Day,* in 1932; and *Stormy Weather,* featuring Ethel Waters, in 1933.

Club owner Owney Madden's underground activities eventually caught up with him, and in 1933 he was sentenced to imprisonment at Sing Sing. The Harlem branch of the Cotton Club closed in 1936 and moved to Broadway. In 1978, some 42 years later, the club reopened in Harlem with a still-energetic Cab Calloway among the headliners. Currently owned by John Beatty, the club features the music of the Melvin Sparks Band.

Further Reading

Haskins, James S. *The Cotton Club.* New York: Hippocrene Books, 1994.

Waggoner, Susan. *Nightclub Nights: Art, Legend, and Style 1920–1960.* Italy: Rizzoli International Publications, 2001.

— Aberjhani

Covarrubias, Miguel (1904–1957) *artist, illustrator*

Mexican-born Miguel Covarrubias excelled at the art of caricature and was one of the most popular illustrators during the Harlem Renaissance years.

Born in 1904, Miguel Covarrubias migrated from Mexico to HARLEM in 1923. He immediately took an interest in the creative culture of the uptown village. The mainstream magazine *The American Mercury* (November 1927) noted his arrival and his celebrity as well as how smitten he was by "the color, the rhythm, the incomparable vitality of Negro life, especially as it exists in the theatres, on the streets, in the cabarets."

Like poet LANGSTON HUGHES and folklorist ZORA NEALE HURSTON, Covarrubias became a charge under the support of CHARLOTTE OSGOOD MASON, a PATRON known as "Godmother" to those whom she assisted in their careers.

Covarrubias developed into a principal caricaturist of the era. Caricature is, according to *The American Heritage Dictionary* (1983), "a representation, especially a pictorial, in which a subject's distinctive features or peculiarities are exaggerated for comic or grotesque effect." The images he created were often exaggerated likenesses of talented individuals on their way to becoming Harlem Renaissance icons, including "Father of the Blues" W. C. HANDY and theatrical performer FLORENCE MILLS. His caricature of a dancing arts patron, CARL VAN VECHTEN, author of *NIGGER HEAVEN,* made Van Vechten look almost like an African-American man.

His spare and "bald" approach to illustration was printed by leading publishers of the day. Alfred A. Knopf published Covarrubias's books of caricatures, *The Prince of Wales and Other Americans* (1925) and *Negro Drawings* (1927). When W. C. Handy wrote *Blues* in 1926, a collection of musical compositions published by Boni and Liveright, Covarrubias drew the illustrations for the book. The red, black, and yellow cover of Hughes's *The Weary Blues* (1925) was Covarrubias's caricature of a black piano player, and his depiction of a jazz singer was included in Dr. ALAIN LOCKE's *The New Negro* (1925). Covarrubias's illustrations also appeared in the conventional periodicals *Vanity Fair* and *The New Yorker.* In addition, he designed book dust jackets for such established classics as Harriet Beecher Stowe's *Uncle Tom's Cabin.* His representative 1928 caricature, *Dancing Couple,* juxtaposes exceedingly dark skin, hair, and clothing against ultra-white eyes, teeth, and exaggerated palms of black dancers performing the Charleston, one the era's most popular dances.

Returning to Mexico in the 1930s, Covarrubias wrote several books on the arts and anthropological studies. He died on February 4, 1957.

Further Reading

Anderson, Jervis. *This Was Harlem: A Cultural Portrait, 1900–1950.* New York: Farrar Straus Giroux, 1983.

Kellner, Bruce, ed. *The Harlem Renaissance: A Historical Dictionary for the Era.* Westport, Conn.: Greenwood Press, 1984.

— Sandra L. West

Cox, Ida (1896–1967) *singer*

Starting out as a child acting in minstrel shows, performer Ida Cox rose to stardom as one of the most successful BLUES singers of the 1920s and 1930s, forming and starring in her own road shows.

Ida Cox was born Ida Prather. Sources vary on the exact place and date of her birth but most cite Knoxville, Tennessee, or Toccoa, Georgia, and put her birth date at February 25, 1896.

Running away from home as a child, Ida joined a succession of minstrel shows, troupes of performers who wore makeup that exaggerated the appearance of African Americans and ridiculed the behavior of blacks. A fading tradition at the time, the shows she joined included White and Clark Black and Tan Minstrels; the Rabbit Foot Minstrels; and the Florida Cotton Blossom Minstrels. As a member of the troupes, she portrayed the character Topsy from *Uncle Tom's Cabin,* the classic abolitionist novel by Harriet Beecher Stowe.

In 1920 she married Adler Cox, a member of the Cotton Blossom Minstrels, and years later she married an organist, Jesse "Tiny" Crump.

During the 1920s, Ida Cox became part of the RACE RECORDS industry, singing blues on the Paramount record label and the vaudeville circuit. She also performed as a featured "girl singer" with such renowned JAZZ musicians as JELLY ROLL MORTON and LOUIS ARMSTRONG. Like a number of female blues singers, Cox produced several road shows of her own, including *Raisin' Cain* and *Dark Town Scandals.* She was known on the entertainment circuit as the "Sepia Mae West." By 1939, she commanded enough status as a star to stage her concert "From Spirituals to Swing" at Carnegie Hall.

Cox was still performing in the 1960s, and in 1961 she recorded *Blues for Rampart Street* with jazzman Coleman Hawkins. She was stricken with cancer and died on November 10, 1967.

Further Reading

Finn, Julio. *The Bluesman: The Musical Heritage of Black Men and Women in the Americas.* Northampton: Virginia Interlink Publishers Group, 1998.

Kellner, Bruce. *The Harlem Renaissance: A Historical Dictionary for the Era.* Westport, Conn.: Greenwood Press, 1984.

— Sandra L. West

Crescent Theatre

HARLEM's Crescent Theatre, built in 1909 on 135th Street, was the first in NEW YORK CITY to provide entertainment principally for African Americans and the only one until the LINCOLN THEATRE opened later the same year.

Like the LAFAYETTE THEATRE later on, the Crescent was initially managed by the business team of Martinson and Nibus, who operated an alcohol enterprise. They hired comedian Eddie Hunter to help promote the theater during its early years, and Hunter took advantage of the opportunity by writing and producing a number of his own shows. His *Goin' to the Races* was one of the first productions to use a screen onstage to create the effect of a moving and talking picture. In addition to *Goin' to the Races,* Hunter also staged *Why Husbands Leave Home, The Battle of Who Run,* and other shows. He later won some acclaim as author of the Broadway production *HOW COME?*

With the Lincoln Theatre also opening in 1909 and the Lafayette Theatre starting its business in 1912, the Crescent expanded its program to include such quality entertainment as H. Lawrence Freeman's opera *The Tryst.* It also created a house ensemble called the Crescent Players in 1914. The stock company included singer Edmona Addison, the former vaudeville duo Hodges and Lauchmere, actor Willard Pugh, and actors Ophelia Muse and Clarence Muse. The company staged a production of *Another Man's Wife* and other plays before leaving after approximately a year to form the Lafayette Players.

Increasing competition forced the Crescent Theatre out of business just prior to WORLD WAR I.

Further Reading

McDaniels, Pellom, and Marcus Allen. *My Own Harlem.* Shawneer Mission, Kansas: Addax Publishing Group, 1998.

Peterson, Bernard L., Jr. *The African American Theatre Directory, 1816–1960.* Westport, Conn.: Greenwood Press, 1997.

— Aberjhani

Crichlow, Ernest (1914–) *painter*

Figurative painter Ernest Crichlow, cofounder of the CINQUE GALLERY in NEW YORK CITY, worked on the Federal Arts Project of the WORKS PROGRESS ADMINISTRATION (WPA) and became well known for his depictions of motherhood and African-American children.

Ernest Crichlow was born in 1914 in New York City. He was educated at New York University and the Art Students League.

During the 1930s, Crichlow worked on the Federal Arts Project in North Carolina and in New York. As was the case with ELIZABETH ALICE CATLETT at Dillard University in Louisiana and AARON DOUGLAS at FISK UNIVERSITY in Nashville, Tennessee, Crichlow was a WPA worker who transferred his experience into academic teaching at Shaw University in Raleigh, North Carolina.

During the 1930s, he exhibited at the HARLEM COMMUNITY ART CENTER and the Federal Gallery in New York. Among Crichlow's most noted works are *Young Boy* and *The White Fence.*

In 1969, he cofounded the Cinque Gallery in New York City with fellow Harlem Renaissance artists ROMARE BEARDEN and NORMAN LEWIS. Cinque Gallery was founded and incorporated by the three in February of 1969 in the spirit of the renaissance of the 1920s and the federally funded arts projects of the 1930s.

Letters, photographs, sketchbooks, and other printed material pertaining to the life and creativity of Ernest Crichlow and Norman Lewis are collected at the Smithsonian Institution, Papers of African-American Artists, in Washington, D.C. Crichlow, the only founding member of the Cinque Gallery still living in the early 21st century, was at the time its artistic director.

Further Reading

Bearden, Romare, and Harry Henderson. *A History of African American Artists: From 1792 to the Present.* New York: Pantheon Books, 1993.

Powell, Richard J. *Black Art and Culture in the 20th Century.* New York: Thames and Hudson, 1997.

— Sandra L. West

Crisis: A Record of the Darker Races

The official magazine of the NATIONAL ASSOCIATION FOR THE ADVANCEMENT OF COLORED PEOPLE (NAACP), a civil rights organization, the *Crisis: A Record of the Darker Races* began publication in 1910 and became, under the editorship of Dr. W. E. B. DU BOIS, one of the premier journals of the Harlem Renaissance.

The stated purpose and mission of the *Crisis* was to generate among its readers intellectual discussions on race and to "defend, praise, and instruct black people." The magazine's name came from a poem by James Russell Lowell called "The Present Crisis." In his autobiography, Du Bois said of his editorial role: "With *The Crisis,* I essayed a new role of interpreting to the world the hindrances and aspirations of American Negroes." True to its mission and title, the *Crisis* reported on the LYNCHING epidemic of the period, touted black intellectual achievement, and encouraged creativity. *Crisis* accomplished its mission to defend, praise, and instruct through published social essays, conference reports, visual art, photographs, news on black colleges, book and theater reviews, appraisals of sophisticated musical events, poetry, fiction, and children's pages.

Regular monthly sections were "Along the Color Line" and "The Horizon," from which Du Bois reported on major events and local personalities. In "The Burden," Du Bois reported on events of black oppression, such as lynching. In "Men of the Month," he included photographs and biographies of male and female leaders. At the time, photographs of black people in publications were an uncommon sight. Mainstream white newspapers did not publish photographs of black people unless they were criminals. Black newspapers published photographs of black entertainment celebrities. Thus, *Crisis* took a bold stand by adding photographs of accomplished black people. "Opinion" directed itself to the topic of race. "The Health of Black Folk," "Color Caste in the United States," "The Right to Work," and "Our Class Struggle" were sections created in 1933.

A controversial aspect of the *Crisis* was Du Bois's editorials. One of the most debated was "Close Ranks" (July 1918), a piece that encouraged blacks to "forget our special grievances and close our ranks" with like-minded nonblacks.

If the *Crisis* started out as a magazine of social and political thought, it soon became a major literary effort. Du Bois and NAACP secretary JAMES WELDON JOHNSON viewed the magazine's publication of creative works as critical to the struggle for racial equality in America. The first poem published in *Crisis* was "Jim Crow," by LESLIE PINCKNEY HILL in 1911. The first work of fiction published was in April 1912, "The Doll" by novelist Charles Chestnutt of *The House Behind the Cedars* fame. LANGSTON HUGHES's first published poem, "The Negro Speaks of Rivers," appeared in the June 1921 edition. And in April 1922, JEAN TOOMER's poem "Song of the Sun," later included in his novel *Cane,* was published. *Cane* (1923) has often been noted as the first novel of the Renaissance era. The *Crisis* published in its March and April 1926 issues "The Broken Banjo," a play by WILLIS RICHARDSON, plus work by African-Russian activist and poet Alexander Pushkin, and essays on Japanese haiku. The magazine also employed visual artists to illustrate its covers, among them AARON DOUGLAS, a celebrated muralist.

At the *Crisis,* Du Bois surrounded himself with accomplished editors and writers: WILLIAM STANLEY BEAUMONT BRAITHWAITE, JESSIE REDMOND FAUSET, Johnson, and WALTER WHITE. Braithwaite was a member of the 1910 *Crisis* editorial board. In 1912, Fauset served as director of the "What to Read" department and in 1919 as literary editor. Johnson, already renowned as the lyricist for "LIFT EVERY VOICE AND SING" and the author of *THE AUTOBIOGRAPHY OF AN EX-COLORED MAN,* contributed important poems and essays. White's background made him an invaluable member of the staff because his very light complexion allowed him to "pass" and infiltrate white mobs to investigate lynching activities.

The *Crisis* was, for most of its years, a solid business venture. The first issue of 16 five-inch-by-eight-inch pages premiered on November 1, 1910, with 1,000 copies. By 1911, circulation was at 16,000. The June 1919 edition sold 104,000 copies, largely because of Du Bois's WORLD WAR I composition, "Essay Toward a History of the Black Man in the Great War." By 1918, the magazine saw its income jump from $6,500 to $57,000, and it was circulating all over the United States and abroad. February 1920 circulation reduced to 72,000, though its income reached $77,000. In 1921, its average circulation was 50,000, but by 1924 it fell to 35,000 due to the 1923 publication debut of *OPPORTUNITY* magazine, the official publication of the conservative NATIONAL URBAN LEAGUE. Its income in 1924 was $46,000. In 1930 and 1931, 18,000 was the average circulation. In 1932, circulation dropped to less than 14,000, and it never again regained the large numbers seen in 1919.

The cost of the magazine from 1910 to 1919 was 10¢ a copy. In December 1919, the per issue price was increased to 15¢ for 64 pages. By 1916, it was a self-supporting venture, which meant that *Crisis* was able to pay for publicity, utility bills, and salaries for clerical workers, business manager, and editor. Advertising came from black businesses and colleges. White advertisers shunned the *Crisis,* the U.S. Congress frowned upon it, and even some blacks were afraid to be caught reading it. Nevertheless, it was a success financially, politically, and culturally. From 1910 to 1934, the magazine's publishing bill to the NAACP was never more than $2,000.

Du Bois used the power of his office to organize conferences, initiate awards, and start other publications. He organized a PAN AFRICAN CONGRESS in 1919, 1921, 1923, and 1927; published the *BROWNIES' BOOK* magazine for children in 1921; and sponsored a symposium, "The Negro in Art," in February 1926. He also initiated a program to present monthly literary prizes sponsored by various patrons, including Amy Spingarn, for whom the Spingarn Award was named, and novelist Charles W. Chestnutt. Among the many recipients of awards was playwright Ruth Ada Gaines-Shelton, who won $40 and the Spingarn Award for her comedy *The Church Fight* in 1925. The comedy focused on hypocrisies in the black church and was published in May 1926 in the *Crisis.*

In 1932 and 1933, Du Bois proposed that the magazine enlist a council of writers, including NELLA LARSEN and CLAUDE MCKAY, as readers and book reviewers. The proposal faltered, and Du Bois left the magazine in 1934. Returning in 1944, he remained four years more before final retirement.

Crisis continues to publish into the 21st century under the banner of Crisis Publishing Company, separate from the NAACP organization itself.

Further Reading

Du Bois, W. E. B. *The Autobiography of W. E. B. Du Bois.* New York: International Publishers, 1968.

Rampersad, Arnold. *The Art & Imagination of W. E. B. DuBois.* New York: Schocken Books, 1990.

Wilson, Sondra Kathryn, ed. *The Crisis Reader: Stories, Poetry, and Essays from the NAACP's Crisis Magazine.* New York: The Modern Library, 1999.

— Sandra L. West

Crite, Allan Rohan (1910–) *painter*

During the 1920s, artist Allan Rohan Crite painted neighborhood scenes and images of wealthy African Americans to create a unique visual historical record of the black population in Boston, Massachusetts.

Born in Plainfield, New Jersey, in 1910, Allan Crite was reared in the Roxbury area of Boston, Massachusetts. He attended vocational art classes at Boston Latin and English High School. Between 1929 and 1935, he studied at the School of the Museum of Fine Arts in Boston, where he was awarded a scholarship and worked as a furniture decorator and illustrator. He also studied at the Massachusetts School of Art.

Crite's illustrations were published in *OPPORTUNITY;* the *CRISIS: A RECORD OF THE DARKER RACES; SURVEY GRAPHIC;* the *Boston Globe;* and *The Art of Seeing* (1925), a book written by Charles Woodbury, with whom Crite studied at the Children's Art Center in Boston. He also painted scenes of black people working and playing in their neighborhoods during the 1920s and 1930s. These neighborhood depictions later served as historical documentation of the African-American community throughout the Harlem Renaissance and GREAT DEPRESSION years in the city of Boston. His work was presented at the Boston Society of Independent Artists in 1929.

Crite was also among those artists who worked with the WORKS PROGRESS ADMINISTRATION in the 1930s. He eventually published all of his black-and-white drawings from the period in a book series, one of which is titled *Were You There When They Crucified My Lord?* (1944). In 1930 to 1932 and in 1935, Crite's work went on exhibit at the HARMON FOUNDATION in NEW YORK CITY. Toward the end of the 1930s, Crite's attention turned from colorful portraits of neighborhood people and middle-class activities to black-and-white drawings of religious themes. Some of his notable works during this period are *Beneath the Cross of St. Augustine* and *City of God.* However, in *One of Our Exhibitions and Teas* (1939), a painting he created for artist LOIS MAILOU JONES, he continued his observations of the black middle class with this portrayal of well-appointed black guests at a Boston reception.

His masterpiece, *Three Spirituals,* was published in a book titled *Three Spirituals from Earth to Heaven* in 1948. He further completed religious works for, among others, the chapel of Massachusetts Institute of Technology, Grace Church in Martha's Vineyard in Massachusetts, and the Holy Cross Church in Morrisville, Vermont.

In 1968, Crite continued his education by obtaining a B.A. in extension studies from Harvard University. In 2002, he continued to reside in Boston. His papers, an oral history interview conducted circa 1979–1980, are in the collection of Papers of African-American Artists, Smithsonian Institution, Washington, D.C.

Further Reading

Bailey, David A., and Paul Gilroy. *Rhapsodies in Black: Art of the Harlem Renaissance.* Berkeley: University of California Press, 1997.

Powell, Richard J. *Black Art and Culture in the 20th Century.* New York: Thames and Hudson, 1997.

— Sandra L. West

Cubism See DOUGLAS, AARON.

Cullen, Charles A., Rev. See SALEM METHODIST CHURCH.

Cullen, Countee (Countee Leroy Porter) (1903–1946) *poet, editor, writer*

Prizewinning poet Countee Cullen published more of his verse in mainstream publications than any of his Harlem Renaissance contemporaries. And, although one of the leaders of the *NEW NEGRO* movement, he held that the poetry of African Americans was more influenced by their Americanisms than by their African heritage.

Countee (pronounced Count-TAY) Leroy Porter was born on May 30, 1903. His birthplace is generally cited as Louisville, Kentucky, though Baltimore and NEW YORK CITY have also been cited. Reportedly, relatives later took him to New York. He became Countee Cullen when Rev. Frederick Asbury Cullen and his wife, Carolyn Belle Mitchell Cullen, adopted him in 1918, the year of his previous guardian's death. Rev. Cullen was a former teacher, served as president of the Harlem Branch of the NATIONAL ASSOCIATION FOR THE ADVANCEMENT OF COLORED PEOPLE (NAACP), and pastored SALEM METHODIST CHURCH, later Salem United Methodist Episcopal Church in HARLEM. Mrs. Cullen was a devout Christian and full-time homemaker.

The adoption of Countee Cullen was unusual in that he not only became the son of Rev. and Mrs. Cullen but also a "ward" of the church. Following the death of Cullen's natural parents, church members convinced the Cullens to adopt him. Noting his intelligence and diligent Sunday school attendance at Salem, the members offered to help raise and educate him. They did so well into Cullen's adulthood.

Cullen proved to be an academic scholar and a literary prodigy. At the predominately white DeWitt Clinton High School, from which he graduated in 1921, his writing was influenced by the classic poets John Keats and A. E. Housman. At age 19, with high-pitched voice and supposed homosexual mannerisms, Cullen entered New York University and was elected to the Phi Beta Kappa Honor Society.

Cullen wrote poetry throughout his school years. His work garnered major attention from the *CRISIS: A RECORD OF THE DARKER RACES*, edited by W. E. B. DU BOIS, who described Cullen as a genius. The *Crisis* published "Dad," "Bread and Wine," and "Sonnet to Her" in the November 1922, June 1923, and March 1927 editions, respectively.

In 1925, Cullen's work received national attention when he won *Poetry* magazine's John Reed Memorial Prize for "The Ballad of the Brown Girl." Two years later, the poem would be issued as an illustrated book bearing the same title.

Cullen's first collection of poetry was called *Color,* published in 1925, and reviewed all over the world. On January 21, 1926, the London edition of the *New York Times Literary Supplement* recorded: "What makes it of primary importance in estimating his quality as a poet is that he compels the savage and bitter details of color conflict to serve an imaginative purpose and symbolize a spiritual conflict which is common to all mankind." And ERIC DERWENT WALROND, who would gain fame as the author of a story collection called *Tropic Death,* wrote for the March 31, 1926, edition of *New Republic:* "Ordained is a pretty bloaty word, but if there ever was a poet ordained by the stars to sing of the joys and sorrows attendant upon the experience of thwarted black folk placed in wretched juxtaposition to our Western civilization, that poet is Countee Cullen."

Additionally in 1925, Cullen won the Witter Byner Prize for poetry for "Poems," the Amy Spingarn Award from the *Crisis* for "Two Moods of Love," and second prize in the *Palm* Poetry Contest for "Wisdom Cometh with the Years."

Continuing his education, Cullen obtained a master's degree from Harvard in 1926. The same year, he went to work as assistant editor at *OPPORTUNITY: A JOURNAL OF NEGRO LIFE*, at the offices of the NATIONAL URBAN LEAGUE, a conservative civil and human rights organization that specialized in securing employment opportunities for African Americans. At *Opportunity,* he wrote an arts column called "The Dark Tower." In it, he stirred controversy when he lauded white poet Robert Frost and suggested, in his review of *The Weary Blues* by LANGSTON HUGHES, that the black poet refrain from being a "racial artist." Heiress and arts patron A'LELIA WALKER adopted the column's name for the SALON she held at her NEW YORK CITY mansion, the DARK TOWER, a gathering place for society people, writers, painters, dancers, singers, and other creative individuals. Cullen wrote a portion of his poem "To The Dark Tower" on the walls of the salon.

Countee Cullen, shown here in 1941, was one of the first poets of the Harlem Renaissance to receive national recognition. *(Library of Congress, Prints & Photographs Division, Carl Van Vechten Collection [LC-USZ62-42529])*

In 1926, Cullen continued to win awards as he captured second prize in the *Crisis* Poetry Contest for "Thoughts in a Zoo." The following year, he published his second volume of poetry, *Copper Sun,* illustrated by Charles Cullen. Moreover, he earned a Guggenheim Fellowship that enabled him to study in PARIS, received the HARMON FOUNDATION's first gold medal for literature, and edited *Caroling Dusk: An Anthology of Verse by Negro Poets.*

One of most important anthologies of the period, *Caroling Dusk* presented the poetry of 38 writers, including ARNA BONTEMPS; Paul Laurence Dunbar and ALICE DUNBAR-NELSON; young playwright JOSEPH SEAMON COTTER, JR.; WILLIAM WARING CUNEY, whose *No Images* is still a much anthologized classic; JEAN TOOMER, the reluctant leading novelist at the time; Langston Hughes; Georgia Douglas Johnson, leader of literary salon society in WASHINGTON, D.C.; militant writer CLAUDE MCKAY; and child prodigy Lula Lowe Weeden, who was nine years old. The editor's prefatory notes laid bare his controversial perception: "As heretical as it may sound, there is the probability that Negro poets, dependent as they are on the English language, may have more to gain from the rich background of English and American poetry than from any nebulous atavistic yearnings toward an African inheritance."

Caroling Dusk drew reviews from all over the country. An unauthored review in the books section of *New York Herald Tribune* on November 27, 1927, noted: "There are some admirable qualities about Mr. Cullen's compilation of Negro poetry and prime among them is the space that he gives to young and heretofore hardly known writers." *Caroling Dusk* was republished in 1955 and 1993.

In 1928, Cullen fused two influential "society" families when he married Nina Yolande Du Bois, daughter of W. E. B. Du Bois. The groomsmen were predominantly poets, including Hughes. Following the wedding at his father's church and reception at the Dark Tower, Yolande returned to her job in Maryland while Cullen returned to his at *Opportunity.* Cullen then sailed to Paris with his high school friend, Harold Jackman, instead of with his bride. Du Bois and Cullen divorced in 1930, one year after he published his third collection of poetry, *The Black Christ and Other Poems,* and a personal travel essay about his impressions of PARIS, France, "Countee Cullen to His Friends," in *Crisis* (1929).

Cullen in fact enjoyed several church-underwritten vacations to Paris, traveling with his father from 1928 to 1934. His mother was not fond of travel and did not accompany them.

In 1932, Cullen wrote *One Way to Heaven,* a love story and satire on Harlem intellectuals that also lay bare what Cullen perceived of as the hypocrisy of the black church. Among the novel's main characters were Sam Lucas, a one-armed gambler who pretended to be "saved" at revivals; Mattie, a religious convert who fell in love with him; and Constancia Brown, an upper-class biracial woman who refused to "pass" for white. Cullen satirized MARCUS GARVEY's BACK-TO-AFRICA MOVEMENT, highbrow book clubs, self-important public orators, and haughty black nationalists. *One Way to Heaven* was not successful, and though Cullen translated *Medea* (1935), an updated version of the classic Greek drama, and published *The Medea, and Some Poems* (1937), he never wrote another adult novel.

Offered a position in Nashville, Tennessee, to teach at FISK UNIVERSITY, Cullen chose to remain in New York to teach English, French, and creative writing at Frederick Douglass Junior High School (1934–45). At this point in his life, his work as a poet began to decrease, while his efforts at playwrighting and writing juvenile literature increased. Literary critics decried the "low" timbre of *One Way to Heaven* and the alleged lack of growth and maturity in his poetry.

One such critic was BENJAMIN GRIFFITH BRAWLEY. Conservative and African American, Brawley published *The Negro Genius* (1934), in which he applauded *The New Negro* by ALAIN LOCKE, congratulated *Opportunity* editor CHARLES SPURGEON JOHNSON on the *Ebony and Topaz* anthology, and praised the works of WILLIAM STANLEY BEAUMONT BRAITHWAITE and JAMES WELDON JOHNSON. However, he charged Cullen's poetry with intermittent "lapses in taste" and "artificiality."

In this critical climate, Cullen coauthored with Owen Dodson a one-act play entitled *The Third Fourth of July* (*Theatre Arts,* August 1946). He also adapted Arna Bontemps's novel *God Sends Sunday* into the musical *St. Louis Woman.* It was not, however, staged until March 1946, three months after Cullen's demise. When *St. Louis Woman* opened on Broadway, it transformed singer Pearl Bailey into a bona fide celebrity.

For juvenile readers Cullen created *The Lost Zoo* (1940) and *My Lives and How I Lost Them* (1942), about his cat. In his later days, he collected his verse in *On These I Stand: An Anthology of the Best Poems of Countee Cullen,* not published until 1947.

Cullen stood out from fellow Harlem Renaissance poets because he published in more mainstream publications than any of them. In addition to *Crisis, Opportunity,* and the *MESSENGER,* which were prominent African-American publications of the day, his work was also included in such mainstream periodicals as *Vanity Fair, The Bookman, The American Mercury, The Century, Folio, Harper's, Les Continents, Poetry,* SURVEY *GRAPHIC,* and *The World Tomorrow.* His themes were religion, death, nature, love, and the African-American condition, though he shunned racial topics in the middle of his literary career. His most noted poems include "What Is Africa to Me" and "Yet Do I Marvel," the latter posing Cullen's poignant question to his Creator: "Yet do I marvel at this curious thing:/To make a poet black, and bid him sing?"

Despite the loose and free clothing fashions of the era (see FASHION AND THE HARLEM RENAISSANCE), Cullen habitually wore formal vested suits and tight neckties customary of the proper, reserved Victorian intelligentsia. Nevertheless, this extremely traditional man was known to "dance like the devil" at social gatherings and earned the envy of his colleagues with his agility on the dance floor. He suffered from chronic high blood pressure and died of uremic poisoning on January 9, 1946, at the age of 42. He left a widow, Ida Mae Roberson, whom he married on September 27, 1940, and with whom he amassed a priceless art collection, which they bequeathed to the Hampton University Art Museum. Cullen's funeral was officiated by his father at Salem, where one of the pallbearers was Harold Jackman.

Further Reading

Bontemps, Arna. *The Harlem Renaissance Remembered.* New York: Dodd, Mead & Company, 1972.

Cullen, Countee, ed. *Caroling Dusk: An Anthology of Verse by Black Poets of the Twenties.* New York: Carol Publishing Group, 1993. Original publishing date 1927.

Early, Gerald L. *My Soul's High Song: The Collected Writings of Countee Cullen, Voice of the Harlem Renaissance.* New York: Doubleday and Company, 1991.

Ferguson, Blanche E. *Countee Cullen and the Negro Renaissance.* New York: Dodd, Mead & Company, 1966.

— Sandra L. West

Cunard, Nancy (1896–1965) *editor*

Considered an avant-garde member of the Harlem Renaissance, Nancy Cunard was a white British subject who in 1934 compiled and edited the controversial *Negro: An Anthology,* founded an alternative publishing company in the late 1920s, and scandalized two continents with her personal relationships with black people.

Nancy Cunard was born in 1896 in Neville Holt, located in Leicestershire, outside of London, England. Her father was Sir Bache Cunard, of the Cunard shipping family. Her mother, Lady Cunard, was born Maud Burke in the United States. Nancy Cunard always called her mother "Her Ladyship."

Cunard grew up an only child surrounded by governesses. Her mother, a society woman, attempted to raise her daughter in a manner she felt appropriate to their social background. Nancy Cunard, however, developed a greater interest in poetry, poets, painters, and conversations about JAZZ music and left-wing politics. A debutante ball and marriage to a young Guards officer, Sidney Fairbairn, failed to change her interests. The marriage failed, and Cunard moved to PARIS, France, in 1920.

In Paris, she quickly found friends among the literati and continued to write poetry, as she had done in England. She published several poetry volumes, including *Outlaws* (1921), *Sublumary* (1923), and *Parallax* (1925). Her book sales were fair, but the art she inspired in others was phenomenal. So striking did Cunard's stark white skin and piercing eyes appear to others that she often became the subject of their work: the artists Brancusi sculpted her likeness, Kokoschka painted her, and Curtis Moffit photographed her.

In 1926, Cunard visited her cousin Victor Cunard in Venice. Here, she met the first African Americans she had ever seen. One of them was Henry Crowder. Through issues of the *CRISIS: A RECORD OF THE DARKER RACES* and *The Liberator,* Crowder, a pianist and composer formerly with a group called The Alabamians, educated Cunard about the condition of African Americans and of people of African descent around the world. He told her about W. E. B. DU BOIS and WALTER WHITE as well as giving her lessons in HARLEM's unique vocabulary. She began to collect African art and, in 1928, established the Hours Press.

After her education from Crowder, Cunard became incensed at England's oppressive treatment of its black-populated colonies in the West Indies. The notion of white superiority among Caucasian peers infuriated her, as did the lack of opportunities for black people in America and other countries. Consequently, she declared a personal war on racism, and to fight her battle she chose to create a weapon in the form of a book: *Negro: An Anthology.*

In preparation for *Negro* (the working title was *Color*), Cunard and Crowder sailed to the United States to meet members of the Negro intelligentsia in and around Harlem. Du Bois and White, both officials of the NATIONAL ASSOCIATION FOR THE ADVANCEMENT OF COLORED PEOPLE (NAACP), promised to write essays for *Negro,* and several of Crowder's former teachers from the South also promised to help Cunard with articles on black southern education. Cunard lived in Harlem for a time, traveled to Jamaica and Cuba to complete research for the book, wrote articles for the *Crisis,* sided with COMMUNISM on every political issue, and scandalized both Harlem and England with her intimate relationship with Crowder.

Negro appeared on February 15, 1934. A small British firm printed 1,000 copies. Years later, London was bombed and the publishing house was destroyed, along with all the extra copies of Cunard's anthology. As a result, original copies are, today, very rare.

Negro informed its readers of the politics, culture, and history of not only African Americans but of blacks throughout the African diaspora. Included were "I, Too, Sing America" by Harlem Renaissance poet LANGSTON HUGHES; "Dr. BOOKER T. WASHINGTON: Negro Educationalist and Founder of the Tuskegee Institute" by Rev. Arthur E. Massey; "Characteristics of Negro Expression" by Harlem Renaissance anthropologist ZORA NEALE HURSTON; "The Negro Student in the U.S.A" by Gabriel Carritt; "The Ku Klux Klan in Indiana" by Dr. Sarah Frances Chenault; "Negro Music in Porto Rico" by Harlem Renaissance music critic Maud Cuney Hare; "Jamaica—The Negro Island" by Nancy Cunard; and "There Is No White Superiority" by Anthony Butts.

To Cunard's dismay, the book did not receive the number of reviews she had hoped it would. Outside of a few unsympathetic notices from the British press, the *AMSTERDAM NEWS* in Harlem and *The New Republic* were the only publications to write about it. Henry Lee Moon of the *Amsterdam News* noted her "definite Communist bias," and he agreed with Cunard's view that the case of the SCOTTSBORO TRIAL was not an "isolated instance of race terrorization" but a "link in a whole system of oppression." *The New Republic* wrote: "Miss Cunard views the Negro in his relations with the white world with singularly rare insight. For her . . . the Negro . . . is a man, an American, a worker, handicapped, to be sure, by the pernicious color-phobia of America, but nevertheless fundamentally akin to other workers."

In what may be viewed as a testament to Cunard's sincerity and diligence toward her subject, Toni Cade Bambara wrote in her foreword to Hurston's *The Sanctified Church* that the great painter Salvador Dali once exclaimed: "The Negro! What do I know about the Negro? Everything! I've met Nancy Cunard."

Cunard's Hours Press closed in 1931. In 1935, she and Crowder separated and they never saw each other again. He died in the late 1940s. Cunard continued writing and publishing until her death on March 17, 1965.

Further Reading

Chishol M., Anne. *Nancy Cunard: A Biography.* New York: Viking Penguin, 1981.

Cunard, Nancy. *Negro: An Anthology.* New York: Continuum, 1996. Previously published by F. Ungar, 1970. Originally published in 1934.

Douglas, Ann. *Terrible Honesty, Mongrel Manhattan in the 1920s.* New York: Farrar, Straus and Giroux, 1995.

— Sandra L. West

Cuney, William Waring (1906–1976) *poet*

William Waring Cuney was a poet and editor whose poem "No Images" won first prize in the *OPPORTUNITY* magazine contest of 1926 and went on to become one of the most anthologized in American literature.

William Cuney was born on May 6, 1906, in WASHINGTON, D.C. His father was Norris Cuney II, and his mother Madge Louise Baker.

Like fellow Harlem Renaissance poet LANGSTON HUGHES, Cuney was educated at Lincoln University as well as at HOWARD UNIVERSITY. He also studied music at the New England Conservatory of Music in Boston, and voice at the Conservatory in Rome. Aside from writing poetry, he authored songs and broadsides, including: *The Alley Cat Brushed His Whiskers, Two Poems: "Darkness Hides His Throne" (and) "We Make Supplication,"* and *Women and Kitchens.*

Moreover, Cuney published poetry and literary criticism in the *CRISIS: A RECORD OF THE DARKER RACES*; *Harlem Quarterly; Negro Quarterly;* and *Black World.* His first collected volume of poetry, *Chain Gang Chant,* was published in 1930.

Cuney served as a technical sergeant in the U.S. Army during World War II and spent several years in the South Pacific. Returning to the States, he teamed with Hughes and Bruce M. Wright in 1954 to coedit the *Lincoln University Poets: Centennial Anthology, 1854–1954.*

A second collection of Cuney's work, *Puzzles,* was published in 1960, and a third, *Storefront Church,* in 1973. Folk singer Joshua White recorded Cuney's protest poems on an album titled *Southern Exposure.*

Cuney's poem, the short and poignant "No Images," however, is considered his principal work. One of the most anthologized poems in American literature, it concerns a uniquely beautiful black woman who thinks that: ". . . her brown body/Has no glory" because her life is full of drudgery and "dish water gives back no images." This and other works by Cunard are included in the primary anthologies of the era: *American Negro Poetry; An Anthology of Magazine Verse for 1926; Negro Caravan; Caroling Dusk; Cavalcade; Book of American Negro Poetry; Negro Poets and Their Poems;* and *Beyond the Blues.*

Cuney died on June 30, 1976.

Further Reading

Bontemps, Arna. *The Harlem Renaissance Remembered.* New York: Dodd, 1972.

Smethurt, James E. *The New Red Negro: The Literary Left and African American Poetry, 1930–1946.* New York: Oxford University Press, 1999.

— Sandra L. West

D

Daddy Grace See GRACE, DADDY.

Dandridge, Dorothy (1922–1965) *actress, singer*
Dorothy Dandridge grew up while the initial wave of blacks working in Hollywood began to make their mark in film, and she emerged from the second wave to become the first African-American woman nominated for an Academy Award for best leading actress. Born on November 9, 1922, in Cleveland, Ohio, Dandridge was the second of Cyril Dandridge and Ruby Butler Dandridge's two children, both daughters. While still pregnant with their second daughter, Ruby Dandridge decided that life within the boundaries of a traditional marriage was not something she wanted, and she separated from her husband, Cyril. Just as her father, George Butler, had done with her, Ruby Dandridge taught her young daughters the basic mechanics of showmanship. With the help of Geneva Williams, Ruby Dandridge trained her daughters to become professional singers and dancers. She took particular notice of Dorothy's talent when, not yet in grade school, she volunteered to recite a poem by Paul Laurence Dunbar, filling in for her mother at a function when the latter was too tired to keep the engagement. By the time they were teenagers, they had teamed up with a friend to form the Dandridge Sisters.

Consisting of Dorothy, older sister Vivian Alferetta Dandridge, and friend Etta Jones, the Dandridge Sisters made a strong enough name for themselves to win bit parts that showcased their talents in several films, including *A Day at the Races* (1937, prior to Jones's joining the sisters), *Irene* (1940), and *Going Places* (1939). Impressed by their talent, well-known musician LOUIS ARMSTRONG convinced his manager Joe Glaser to help the trio secure work, and in 1938 they played a long run at NEW YORK CITY's COTTON CLUB, which helped launch their club careers nationally and internationally.

While Ruby Dandridge remained instrumental in the promotion of her daughters' careers, she also worked hard to establish for herself a career that included work as a character actress on film, stage, and such radio programs as the *Judy Canova Show* and the *Gene Autry Show.*

The early success of the Dandridge Sisters was often overshadowed by the emotional and physical abuse that Dorothy and Vivian Dandridge reportedly suffered at the hands of Geneva Williams, who generally disciplined and traveled with them while Ruby pursued her professional goals. Dandridge began to emerge as a single act at age 18 when she signed on for a stage production of *Meet the People* (1940). She followed that success with noted appearances in such films as *Four Shall Die* and *Sun Valley Serenade* (1941).

At age 19, Dandridge married 21-year-old Harold Nicholas of the famed NICHOLAS BROTHERS in 1942, gaining further independence from her show business family and its attendant traumas. The following year saw the birth of Harolyn Suzanne Nicholas, the couple's only child, who was born with brain damage attributed to an insufficient supply of oxygen during her birth. Their daughter's condition became a point of pained friction between Dandridge and Nicholas and would remain throughout Dandridge's life a haunting source of guilt and regret. Her marriage to Nicholas ended with divorce in 1950.

Dandridge teamed up with music arranger and coach Phil Moore to begin her solo club career in Las Vegas in 1949. Despite the humiliation of discriminatory practices in white-owned clubs of the period, Dandridge was well on her way to developing the style of nightclub act for which she would soon become world famous. By 1951, she had appeared in two more movies, *Tarzan's Peril* and *The Harlem Globetrotters,* and established the pattern of alternating work in film and clubs that would characterize her performance career. By moving back and forth between the two, she was able to bypass the kind of stereotypical roles generally offered black women during that time.

She achieved the ranks of stardom when director Otto Preminger cast her for the title role in *Carmen Jones* (1954). The film was the first major all-black Hollywood musical since *Cabin in the Sky* and *Stormy Weather* a decade before. It proved a powerful vehicle for the talents of such major and future stars as Harry Belafonte, Pearl Bailey, Diahann Carroll, and Brock Peters. Playing opposite Belafonte, Dandridge portrayed the assertively independent Carmen, a role that signaled a definitive break from Hollywood's image of black women represented, ironically, by the very types of character roles often played by Ruby Dandridge, the star's mother. The performance made her a contender for the Academy Award for best actress, pitting her against Judy Garland, Audrey Hepburn, Jane Wyman, and Grace Kelly (who won it for *The Country Girl*). Prior to Dandridge, the only black women nominated for Academy Awards were Ethel Waters and Hattie McDaniel, both as supporting actresses. McDaniel actually won it for her role as Mammy in *Gone With the Wind* (1939).

Riding the history-making success of *Carmen Jones,* Dandridge became an even bigger draw on the international nightclub circuit, playing such venues as New York's Waldorf Empire Room and London's Café de Paris. However, she primarily considered herself to be a dramatic actress and had to cope with the inevitable challenge of being so within an industry that often cited her talent but rarely chose to employ it with the same frequency as it did her white counterparts. She nevertheless went on to make more than a half dozen other films, including *PORGY AND BESS* (1959) with Sidney Poitier and her final movie, *The Murder Men* (1961; presented on American television as *Blues for a Junkman*).

Following a series of romances, a second failed marriage, and the institutionalization of her daughter, Dandridge suffered repeated bouts of severe depression leading to alcoholism and a dependency on the antidepressant drug Tofranil. She was found dead from an overdose of Tofranil on September 8, 1965. Whether her death was accidental or a suicide has never been determined.

In 1997, film historian Donald Bogle published *Dorothy Dandridge,* the definitive biography of the actress. In 1999, actress Halle Berry starred as Dandridge in an HBO movie of her life titled *Introducing Dorothy Dandridge.* For her portrayal of Dandridge, Berry won both the Golden Globe and an Emmy Award. Moreover, in 2002, Berry, also a native of Cleveland, became the first African American to win the Academy Award for best actress, so honored for her role in the film *Monster's Ball.* An emotional Berry paid tribute to Dandridge in her acceptance speech.

Actress and singer Dorothy Dandridge in 1954 became the first black actress nominated for an Academy Award for best leading actress, an award that eluded black actresses until Halle Berry won it in 2002. She is shown here in 1954. *(Library of Congress, Prints & Photographs Division, NYWT&S Collection [LC-USZ62-109664])*

Further Reading

Bogle, Donald. *Blacks in America's Films and Television: An Illustrated Encyclopedia.* New York: Simon and Schuster, 1989.

———. *Dorothy Dandridge: A Biography.* New York: Harper Trade, 1996.

Dandridge, Dorothy, and Earl Conrad. *Everything and Nothing: The Dorothy Dandridge Tragedy.* New York: HarperCollins, 2000.

— Aberjhani

Danner, Margaret Essie See CHICAGO.

Dark Tower, The

The Dark Tower salon, hosted by arts patron A'LELIA WALKER Robinson, daughter of millionaire beauty culturist MADAME C.J. WALKER, provided a fashionable gathering place for the literary and artistic community of the Harlem Renaissance.

The salon was located on the ground floor of the 108 West 136th Street mansion purchased by Madame Walker in 1916. A'Lelia Walker named it the Dark Tower Tea Club from the "The Dark Tower" monthly column written by poet COUNTEE CULLEN for *OPPORTUNITY* magazine.

The 1928 formal invitation to the grand opening of the salon read: "We dedicate this tower to the aesthetes. That cultured group of young Negro artists, composers and their friends. A quiet place of particular charm. A rendezvous where they may feel at home to partake of a little tidbit amid pleasant, interesting atmosphere. Members only and those whom they wish to bring will be accepted. If you choose to become one of us you may register when first attending 'The Dark Tower . . . ' Open nine at eve 'til two in the morning."

Visitors included editors, publishers, poets, visual artists, and performance artists for dinners, receptions, a card game of bridge, and dancing. Writers held critique sessions to help them prepare their work for publication.

Regular attendees were arts patron and photographer CARL VAN VECHTEN; writer LANGSTON HUGHES, who once came with his mother Carrie Clark and the arts patron, CHARLOTTE OSGOOD MASON; poet-artist RICHARD BRUCE NUGENT; teacher Harold Jackman, intimate friend of Cullen and pallbearer at his funeral; writers JAMES WELDON JOHNSON and WALTER WHITE; *Opportunity* prizewinner Helene Douglass Johnson; actress and singer FLORENCE MILLS; and singer and actor PAUL ROBESON. Artistic college students were invited to the Dark Tower on Saturdays during summer break. And, when Cullen married Yolande Du Bois, daughter of editor and political activist W. E. B. DU BOIS, their wedding reception was held at the Dark Tower.

The salon was lavishly decorated in rosewood furniture. There was a grand piano painted gold, a sky-blue Victrola, rose-colored curtains, and on the walls were written two poems: "From the Dark Tower" by Cullen and sections of "The Weary Blues" by Hughes. Additionally, a painting by AARON DOUGLAS hung on the wall.

Though Walker was a millionaire, the Dark Tower was not a free enterprise. Membership was cited in the opening invitation as one dollar a year. To check one's hat or coat cost 15¢, coffee was 10¢, sandwiches were 50¢, and lemonade cost 25¢.

Hughes, in his autobiography *The Big Sea,* remembers A'Lelia Walker as the "the joy-goddess of Harlem's 1920s." She operated the Dark Tower for a year and then leased the mansion to the city of New York for use as a health center. The Dark Tower closed November 1928, two years before Walker's death. Eulogizing both, Hughes wrote:

"That was really the end of the gay times of the New Negro era in Harlem, the period that had begun to reach its end when the crash came in 1929 and the white people had much less money to spend on themselves, and practically none to spend on Negroes, for the depression brought everybody down a peg or two. And the Negroes had but few pegs to fall."

Further Reading

Hughes, Langston. *The Big Sea.* New York: Hill and Wang, 1995.

Ottley, Roi, and William J. Weatherby, eds. *The Negro in New York: An Informal Social History 1626–1940.* New York: Praeger Publishers, 1969.

Watson, Steve. *The Harlem Renaissance: Hub of African-American Culture, 1920–1930.* New York: Pantheon Books, 1995.

— Sandra L. West

Daughters of the American Revolution

See ABYSSINIAN BAPTIST CHURCH; ANDERSON, MARIAN.

Davis, Elizabeth Lindsay

See CHICAGO.

Davis, Frank Marshall

See CHICAGO.

Dawson, Charles Clarence (1889–1981) *painter*

Charles Clarence Dawson, a muralist with the WORKS PROGRESS ADMINISTRATION (WPA) during the 1940s, exhibited his work with the HARMON FOUNDATION, wrote and illustrated juvenile literature, and founded a club for black artists in CHICAGO.

Charles Dawson was born on a plantation in Warrenton, Georgia, in 1889. As he grew up, Dawson drew pictures of the rural workers. He was later educated at Tuskegee Institute in Alabama and, in 1907, migrated to NEW YORK CITY. There, he worked as an elevator operator and attended evening sessions at the Art Students League. While at the Art Students League, then at the Art Institute, where he studied when he moved to Chicago, he continued to develop his portrayals of rural workers.

In Chicago, Dawson worked as a freelance painter and illustrator. In 1917, the Arts and Letters Society sponsored the exhibition for black artists. It featured Dawson and his fellow painters William Farrow, William Harper, and ARCHIBALD JOHN MOTLEY, JR.

Participating in the entrepreneurial spirit of the times, Dawson founded the Chicago Art League as the *NEW NEGRO* movement developed in the 1920s. The Chicago Art League served as a club for black artists that met at the Wabash Avenue YMCA, a comparable social, artistic, and education venture to the Harlem Arts Guild, over which muralist AARON DOUGLAS presided.

In 1929, Dawson exhibited *Quadroon Madonna* in the Harmon Foundation art show. He later sold *Quadroon Madonna* to the Negro Salon at Roosevelt High School in Gary, Indiana.

Watercolor and pencil were among Dawson's favorite mediums, and he used these to produce, in addition to his images of farmworkers, many depictions of black children. One of his most noted is *The Last Marble* (1929).

Working for the WPA during the GREAT DEPRESSION, Dawson painted murals for the NATIONAL URBAN LEAGUE Social Work exhibition at the Century of Progress exhibit held in Chicago in 1933. In addition, he premiered a collection of his work at the Findlay Art Galleries and at the Illinois Host House the same year. Also in 1933, he wrote, illustrated, and self-published a picture book for children called the *ABC of Great Negroes.*

Dawson died in 1981. His letters, photographs, business records, and writings are stored at the DuSable Museum of African-American History in Chicago, Illinois, and are included in the Papers of African-American Artists, Smithsonian Institution, Washington, D.C.

Further Reading

Bearden, Romare, and Harry Henderson. *A History of African Artists: From 1792 to the Present.* New York: Pantheon Books, 1993.

Miers, Charles, ed. *Harlem Renaissance: Art of Black America.* New York: Harry N. Abrams, 1994.

— Sandra L. West

Day, Caroline Bond Stewart

See LITERATURE AND THE HARLEM RENAISSANCE; *OPPORTUNITY.*

Delaney, Beauford (1901–1979) *painter*

An emotionally troubled but genial man who befriended participants in the Harlem Renaissance, Beauford Delaney was a portrait painter and instructor for the WORKS PROGRESS ADMINISTRATION (WPA) who eventually joined the community of black expatriates in PARIS, France.

Beauford Delaney was born in Knoxville, Tennessee, on December 30, 1901, three years before his equally artistic brother, JOSEPH DELANEY. His mother, Delia Johnson, had been born into slavery in RICHMOND, Virginia. In addition to doing laundry and cleaning homes for a living, she sewed, quilted, and sang. His father, John Samuel Delaney, had been born in Bristol, Tennessee. He had married Delia on April 9, 1885, and moved to Knoxville where he accepted a position as assistant minister of the Methodist Episcopal Church. The family moved to Jefferson City when Rev. Delaney became pastor of the Boyd Chapel Methodist Church. He then returned in 1915 to his original church in Knoxville, where the Delaney family lived at 815 East Vine Street.

Beauford was the eighth of 10 children. His early goal was to become a singer but this gave way, despite a distinguishing baritone voice, to his leanings toward visual art. His early efforts included the creation of Sunday school cards and figures molded from the red Knoxville clay. He sketched daily in a pad, attended school, and with his brother Joseph worked at the Vine Street Café and Shoe Shop as a shoemaker's apprentice and general helper. Beauford also painted signs for a store on Gay Street, where the shop's proprietor, Mr. Willis, commissioned Beauford to paint a seascape and provided the art supplies to do so. The resulting painting, *Tennessee Seascape* (1922), so impressed Willis that he introduced Beauford to a local artist, Lloyd Branson, who was also impressed.

Branson, an avowed Confederate, had designed the Knoxville flag. However, he offered Delaney lessons in impressionistic painting in exchange for his services as a porter in Branson's studio in the Tennessee Theater Building on Gay Street.

Delaney produced a second painting in 1922 called *Tennessee Landscape.* In 1923, while still a teen and with Branson as his PATRON, Beauford left Knoxville to study at the Massachusetts Normal Art School, the South Boston School of Art, and the Copley Society. He lived and studied in Boston from 1923 to 1929. While there, he met poet COUNTEE CULLEN, who had already published poems in the *CRISIS: A RECORD OF THE DARKER RACES* and *OPPORTUNITY* magazines and was studying for his master's degree at Harvard. The two remained lifelong friends. Delaney's paintings were among the collection that Cullen and his wife Ida gave to the Hampton University Art Museum in Virginia upon their deaths.

Delaney moved to NEW YORK CITY in 1929 and joined the artistic revolution taking place in HARLEM. He took a position at the Billy Pierce Dancing School where he drew portraits of dancers. His portrait of Billy Pierce was called *The Dancing Master of Broadway* and was published in the May 1930 edition of *Opportunity* magazine. It won first prize in the Whitney Museum art show.

Delaney quickly made friends with people whose artistic and intellectual contributions defined the Harlem Renaissance. Among them were *Crisis* magazine editor W. E. B. DU BOIS, jazz musician LOUIS ARMSTRONG, and performer ETHEL WATERS. He also became close friends with sculptor SELMA BURKE, writer Henry Miller of *Tropic of Cancer* fame, and writer James Baldwin, who, like Delaney, eventually left New York for Paris.

Taking advantage of the organizational and artistic opportunities of the day, Delaney joined the Harlem Artists Guild, painted in the studio of his artist-friend CHARLES HENRY ALSTON, and created pastel and charcoal portraits of his intellectual and artistic associates. Musician and composer W. C. HANDY urged Delaney in the 1930s to create a series of drawings of African-American JAZZ musicians. Working at a variety of odd jobs to support himself, Delaney continued to paint and exhibit his work throughout New York. Moving out of Harlem, he in turn lived in stark studios on Downing Street and Greene Street in Greenwich Village in lower Manhattan.

In the 1930s, like many other artists during the GREAT DEPRESSION, Delaney obtained a position with the WPA. He taught art in a WPA-sponsored adult art project in Brooklyn and earned $23 a week. He also continued to produce and exhibit his own work, including *Joseph Delaney* in 1933.

He held exhibits at the following: the Whitney Studio Club; the 135th Street Branch of the New York Public Library; Independent Artists Exhibit at Grand Central Palace; Washington Square Outdoor Exhibit; Harmon College Art Association Traveling Exhibition of 1934–1935; International Art Center Show at Roerich Museum in 1935; and Studio Museum in Harlem. The author Henry Miller found Delaney inspiring and wrote about him in the 1945 essay, "The Amazing and Invariable Beauford Delaney."

Like EUGENE JACQUES BULLARD, JOSEPHINE BAKER, and BRICKTOP before him, Delaney left New York for Paris in 1953. Although often acknowledged as an immensely talented artist, Beauford Delaney was plagued by mental illness. He died in a hospital for the mentally ill in Paris on March 25, 1979.

Among Delaney's most celebrated paintings are *Portrait of a Man* (1943), *Greene Street* (1946), *Washington Square* (1952), and *Rosa Parks* (1970). His work is in the Collections of the Ewing Gallery at the University of Tennessee, Clark-Atlanta University Art Gallery, and the Whitney Museum of American Art.

Further Reading

Leeming, David. *Amazing Grace: A Life of Beauford Delaney.* New York: Oxford University Press, 1998.

Theresa A. Leininger-Muiller. *New Negro Artists in Paris: African American Painters and Sculptors in the City of Light, 1922–1934.* Piscataway N.J.: Rutgers University Press, 2000.

— Sandra L. West

Delaney, Joseph (1904–1991) *artist*

The younger brother of painter BEAUFORD DELANEY, Joseph Delaney was also an artist and won acclaim producing works that portrayed the wealthy as well as scenes common to everyday city life.

Joseph Delaney was born in 1904 in Knoxville, Tennessee. Unlike Beauford, who knew he wanted to paint from the time he was a child, Joseph did not become attracted to art until 1930. Once he made the decision, he moved to New York to study at the Art Students League. There, he met the artists Jackson Pollock and Thomas Hart Benton. Studying under Benton at the Art Students League, he was greatly influenced by Benton's multicultural street scenes. One painting from the period that shows Benton's influence is *His Last Known Address* (1934). Delaney also studied at the London School of Art in WASHINGTON, D.C.

From 1936 to 1939, Joseph Delaney worked on the New York Federal Arts Project of the Works Progress Administration (WPA). From 1936 to 1940 he worked on the Index of American Design at the Metropolitan Museum of Art, painting and recording American decorative arts. In addition, he painted portraits of wealthy patrons. His noted works include *Penn Station at Wartime* (1943) and *Waldorf Cafeteria* (1945).

Joseph Delaney went to PARIS, France, in 1979 when his brother, Beauford, died there. He then returned to the United States to accept an artist-in-residency at the University of Tennessee in Knoxville in 1985.

Joseph Delaney died in Knoxville on November 21, 1991.

Further Reading

Beckman, Wendy Hart. *Artists and Writers of the Harlem Renaissance.* Berkeley Heights, N.J.: Enslow Publishing, 2002.

Leeming, David. *Amazing Grace: A Life of Beauford Delaney.* New York: Oxford University Press, 1998.

— Sandra L. West

Delta Sigma Theta Sorority, Inc.

Differences of opinion between senior members of ALPHA KAPPA ALPHA SORORITY, the first Greek-lettered black sorority in the United States, and 22 underclassmen led to the formation of the Delta Sigma Theta Sorority at HOWARD UNIVERSITY in the fall of 1913.

The dissenting sorority members were dissatisfied with such issues as Alpha Kappa Alpha's legal status and the sorority's choice of emblems and priorities. Their motion to institute change within the then four-year-old sorority was effectively challenged by Nellie Quander, who after the division oversaw the incorporation of Alpha Kappa Alpha.

The members of the newly formed Delta Sigma Theta were Oceola M. Adams, Marguerite Y. Alexander, Winona C. Alexander, Ethel C. Black, Bertha P. Campbell, Zephyr C. Carter, Edna B. Coleman, Jessie M. Dent, Frederica C. Dodd, Myra D. Hemmings, Olive C. Jones, Jimmie B. Middleton, Pauline O. Minor, Vashti F. Murphy, Naomi S. Richardson, Mamie R. Rose, Eliza P. Shippen, Florence L. Toms, Ethel C. Watson, Wertie B. Weaver, Madree P. White, and Edith M. Young.

From the outset, the members of Delta Sigma Theta not only sought to achieve scholastic excellence but aimed to establish themselves as academic leaders. They did so by consistently earning higher grade point averages and the recognition that accompanies such a feat. Their academic achievements were combined with political activism, and in 1913 they joined the Women's Suffragette March in the battle for women's right to vote.

The new sorority successfully attracted some of the era's most dynamic agents for social change. Three of its most outstanding members were educators and civil rights activists Mary McLeod Bethune and Mary Church Terrell and entertainer LENA HORNE.

In the 1930s in the wake of the infamous SCOTTSBORO TRIAL, in which nine young black men were falsely accused of raping two white women, the sorority dared to protest the outrage. In the same decade, they created their National Library Project, turning buses into bookmobiles and traveling throughout the South to increase literacy among African Americans. While such an endeavor might appear tame by 21st century standards, in the 1930s black women were still targets for both sexual abuse and the violence of LYNCHING, which had yet to be outlawed. To present oneself as a progressive African American in rural southern areas was to make oneself susceptible to considerable danger. In addition to the drive to increase literacy, Delta Sigma Theta successfully provided scholarships ranging from $100 to $500 at the same time the United States was struggling to free itself from the strangling grip of the GREAT DEPRESSION.

The organization remained strong in its political vigilance during the 1950s. In addition to voicing its own protest against second-class citizenship, the sorority supported those arrested during sit-ins and marches by providing funds to bail them out of jail.

Toward the 1980s and 1990s, Delta Sigma Theta, Inc., combined its traditional roles with modern concerns and designed a roster of programs focusing on rites of passage, dramatizing the process of maturation, women's rights, global consciousness, the black diaspora, economic development in the black community, mental health, social actions, and tutorials in arts and letters as well as other subjects.

The sorority has also continued to attract such exceptional achievers as the following: Barbara Jordan, Judith Jamison, Wilma Rudolph, Shirley Caesar, Nancy Wilson, Nomzamo Winnie Mandela, Johnetta C. Cole, Camille Cosby, Ruby Dee, Aretha Franklin, Paula Giddings, and Nikki Giovanni.

Further Reading

Bracey, Ernest N. *Prophectic Insight: The Higher Education and Pedagogy of African Americans.* Lanham, Md.: University Press of America, 2001.

Giddings, Paula. *In Search of Sisterhood: Delta Sigma Theta and the Challenge of the Black Sorority Movement.* New York: William Morrow, 1994.

— Aberjhani

Dillon, Frank Joseph

See ART AND THE HARLEM RENAISSANCE.

Dixie to Broadway

Dixie to Broadway, debuting on October 29, 1924, at the Broadhurst Theatre in NEW YORK CITY, extended the tradition of black musical revues established by *SHUFFLE ALONG* in 1921.

The revue was produced and directed by Lew Leslie, and it starred FLORENCE MILLS, who starred as well in Leslie's *Plantation Revue, Dover to Dixie,* and *Blackbirds of 1926.* Leslie also cowrote the show along with Tom Howard, Sidney Lazarus, and Walter DeLeon. Grant Clark, Roy Turk, George W. Meyer, and Arthur Johnson wrote the music and lyrics for the show. Will Vodery arranged and conducted the music.

Dixie to Broadway started out in Europe as a show called *From Dover to Dixie.* In this original version, it featured white American and British performers as well as African Americans. As such, it was culturally balanced. However, upon its return to the United States, white producer Leslie dropped the British and white American components of the show to capitalize on the then growing trend in black musicals. The two-act program emphasized scenes with such titles as "Evolution of the Colored Race," "Dixie Dreams," and "Jungle Nights in Dixieland."

The revue also provided Mills with the second production by Leslie geared toward making her a major star comparable to BERT WILLIAMS, the first black performer featured in the ZIEGFELD FOLLIES. In addition to Mills, it also starred Maud Russell, Cora Green, Shelton Brooks, and Hamtree Harrington. Critics often singled out dancer Johnny Nit for his performance.

Among the show's most celebrated songs was "I'm a Little Blackbird Looking for a Bluebird," which became Mills's signature piece and guaranteed a standing ovation every time she sang it. Another was "Mandy, Make Up Your Mind," which Mills sang dressed as a groom to would-be bride Alma Smith. "Put Your Old Bandanna On," and "Dixie Dreams" became favorites as well, as did "He Only Comes to See Me Once in a While," which was sung by Cora Green.

Further Reading

Lamb, Andrew. *150 Years of Popular Musical Theatre.* New Haven, Conn.: Yale University Press, 2001.

Mordden, Ethan. *Make Believe: The Broadway Musical in the 1920s.* New York: Oxford University Press, 1997.

— Aberjhani

Dorsey, Thomas Andrew (Georgia Tom Dorsey, Barrelhouse Tom, Texas Tommy) (1899–1993)

pianist, singer, composer

Recognized as "the Father of Gospel Music," Thomas Andrew Dorsey composed more than 1,000 BLUES, rhythm and blues, and gospel songs to become the first African American inducted into the Nashville Songwriters International Hall of Fame.

Thomas Andrew Dorsey was born on July 1, 1899, in rural Villa Rica, Georgia. Both his parents were sharecroppers, but his father, Rev. T. Madison Dorsey, was also a traveling revivalist preacher in the Baptist church. His mother, Etta Plant Dorsey, was a church organist. Seeking a better life, the deeply religious, musical family moved to Atlanta, Georgia, in 1908.

In Atlanta, Dorsey was drawn to the urban blues of BESSIE SMITH as well as MA RAINEY, the "mother of the blues." He dropped out of school in the fourth grade and, by the time he was 12, had developed enough competence as a pianist to play the blues at RENT PARTIES, dance halls, and bordellos. Dorsey joined the GREAT MIGRATION of African Americans moving out of the South to the North and Midwest, and he relocated to CHICAGO in 1916. He attended Chicago's College of Composition and Arranging. While working as an agent for Paramount Record Company, he began to write music.

Dorsey wrote his first blues composition, "If You Don't Believe I'm Leaving, You Can Count the Days I'm Gone," in 1920. However, plagued by clinical depression in 1921, he wrote religious music partly to remain inspired and composed the tune "We Will Meet Him in the Sweet By and By," a song that is still popular in the 21st century. He completed his first gospel song, "If I Don't Get There," in 1922. Gospel is defined as a form of very energetic black American music derived from the spiritually aggressive singing in church worship services—especially those observed at the end of the 19th century in the Pentecostal church, in which "shouting," "speaking in tongues," and "holy dancing" were widely accepted practices.

Steeped in both blues and gospel traditions, Dorsey originally remained a composer, singer, and pianist of nonreligious, worldly blues songs, working with the Whispering Syncopators Band and in a Chicago speakeasy owned by gangster Al Capone. Dorsey's blues arrangement for "Riverside Blues" was recorded by JAZZ musician KING OLIVER in 1923 and became Dorsey's first hit song. In 1924, he joined Rainey's Wild Cat Jazz Band and toured with her for two years on the THEATER OWNERS BOOKING AGENCY (TOBA) circuit.

On August 1, 1925, Dorsey married Nettie Harper. Mrs. Dorsey became Ma Rainey's wardrobe mistress in order to work and travel with her husband.

During his early musical career in Chicago, he performed under several names: Georgia Tom Dorsey, Barrelhouse Tom, and Texas Tommy. As Georgia Tom, working with guitarist Hudson "Tampa Red" Whittaker, with whom he recorded many songs between 1928 and 1932, Dorsey wrote and sang sexually suggestive songs including "Pat My Bread," "You Rascal You," and "Somebody's Been Using That Thing." "It's Tight Like That" (1928), another in that genre, sold 7 million copies.

Although he became a millionaire, Dorsey suffered a second attack of depression in 1928. He then returned to composing music for the church but began to fuse the lusty rhythms of the blues with the more staid tones of the church. The end result was a bluesy gospel melody, a style that was for years known as a "Dorsey," meaning a down-home, uninhibited blues meshed with consecrated lyrics that spoke to the hearts of spiritually inclined people. Dorsey's songs were printed on small sheets, called "ballets," and each sheet sold for a few pennies. However, conventional choir directors all over the nation declined to perform his 1928 gospel composition, "If You See My Savior, Tell Him That You Saw Me," until soloist Willie Mae Fisher successfully sang it at the Golden Jubilee meeting of the conservative National Baptist Convention in 1930. In 1931, he organized the world's first gospel chorus at Ebenezer Baptist Church and the Chicago Gospel Choral Union. By 1932, with the success of "If You See My Savior, Tell Him That You Saw Me" fresh in the minds and hearts of Chicago residents, Dorsey was asked to establish a gospel chorus at Chicago's Pilgrim Baptist Church. This chorus was accompanied by piano, an unusual addition because at the time many church singers, especially touring groups and male choruses, sang a cappella.

On August 26, 1932, Dorsey's wife, Nettie, died in childbirth and their newborn son died the next day while Dorsey was in St. Louis on a trip to promote gospel music. The tragedy marked a major turning point in the composer's life. Dorsey said of that time, "I needed help; my friends and relations had done all they could for me. I was failing, and I did not see how I could live." He survived his grief by writing a song called "Precious Lord, Take My Hand," which has since become a healing balm for generations of people.

One week after writing "Precious Lord, Take My Hand," the song was performed at Chicago's Ebenezer Baptist Church and received with unbridled enthusiasm. It has been translated into more than 50 languages and recorded by many gospel artists, including Mahalia Jackson, Roy Rogers and Dale Evans, Aretha Franklin, and James Cleveland. It was the favorite gospel song of 1960s civil rights activist Rev. Dr. Martin Luther King, Jr., who requested that Mahalia Jackson should sing it at his funeral if he died before her, which he did in 1968. National Public Radio (NPR) named the song as one of the 20th century's most memorable compositions.

Grieving heavily after the deaths of his wife and son, Dorsey converted completely to the religious training of his childhood. He never again penned blues or risqué songs. He established the Dorsey House of Music in Chicago in 1932, becoming the first independent publisher of gospel music. He toured with gospel greats Mahalia Jackson and Sallie Martin. Dorsey also founded and presided over the National Convention of Gospel Choirs and Choruses in 1933. As a minister of gospel music, Dorsey wrote a song especially for Mahalia Jackson called "There'll Be Peace in the Valley," equal in fame to "Precious Lord, Take My Hand," in 1937. He also wrote "Never Turn Back," "When I've Done My Best," "Hide Me in Thy Bosom," "Search Me, Lord," "Rock Me," and "Standing Here Wondering Which Way to Go." In 1937, he returned to the National Baptist Convention and, without the controversy of previous years, directed a gospel choir, "Dorsey" style. Because of his impact upon black religious music, along with fellow Chicagoans Mahalia Jackson and Sallie Martin (star of the Parisian *Gospel Caravan* in 1979), many view Chicago as the origin of black gospel music. Likewise, many consider Dorsey as "the Father of Gospel Music."

Dorsey joined the Nashville Songwriters International Hall of Fame in 1979. In the 1980 documentary film *Say Amen, Somebody,* his contributions and influence on the gospel tradition once again placed him at the forefront of musical quarters. In 1982, he was inducted into both the Georgia Music Hall of Fame and the Gospel Music Association's Living Hall of Fame. The Thomas A. Dorsey Archives were opened at FISK UNIVERSITY, in Nashville, Tennessee, in August 1982.

Thomas Dorsey died on January 23, 1993, at the age of 93.

Further Reading

Gates, Henry Louis, Jr., and Cornel West. *The African American Century: How Black Americans Have Shaped Our Century.* New York: The Free Press, 2000.

Harris, Michael W. *The Rise of Gospel Blues: The Music of Thomas Andrew Dorsey in the Urban Church.* New York: Oxford University Press, 1994.

Southern, Eileen, *The Music of Black Americans: A History, Third Edition.* New York: W.W. Norton, 1997.

Watkins, T. H. "Through the Storm." *American Legacy* 4, no. 4, 1999, 12–14.

— Sandra L. West

Douglas, Aaron (1899–1979) *muralist*

A principal illustrator for the *NEW NEGRO* anthology edited by ALAIN LOCKE, the *CRISIS: A RECORD OF THE DARKER RACES*, and *OPPORTUNITY* magazine, Aaron Douglas created work that epitomized the creative spirit of the Harlem Renaissance. Because of his extensive history and mural paintings, and because of his leadership skills with the Harlem Artists Guild, he was called "the father of African-American art."

Aaron Douglas was born on May 26, 1899, in Topeka, Kansas. Noticing his creative gifts when he was a child, his mother encouraged his artistic talent. His determination to develop that talent increased after Douglas saw the work of the master painter HENRY OSSAWA TANNER.

After serving in WORLD WAR I, Douglas was commissioned to create a mural for Club Ebony in HARLEM in 1920. Enrolling at the University of Nebraska, he received a B.A. in fine arts from the school in 1922. He also studied privately during the 1920s with German portraitist WINOLD REISS, who encouraged him to use African motifs in his art work and to consider painting murals to depict the hardships and accomplishments of his people.

Before moving to NEW YORK CITY in 1925, Douglas taught art at Lincoln High School in his hometown. In 1925, he was the only African-American visual artist featured in the *New Negro* anthology, a work often referred to as the defining text of the Harlem Renaissance. He also designed the dust jacket for JAMES WELDON JOHNSON's *God's Trombones: Seven Negro Sermons in Verse* in 1927; LANGSTON HUGHES's *The Weary Blues* in 1926; and Johnson's *THE AUTOBIOGRAPHY OF AN EX-COLOURED MAN* in 1928. Douglas's illustrations often graced the covers of the *Crisis,* the official publication of the NATIONAL ASSOCIATION FOR THE ADVANCEMENT OF COLORED PEOPLE (NAACP); *Opportunity* magazine, the official publication of the NATIONAL URBAN LEAGUE; and *Vanity Fair,* a mainstream periodical.

In 1929, Douglas created a mural for the Sherman Hotel College Inn Ballroom. In 1931, he painted a mural—currently

Artist Aaron Douglas provided illustrations for much of the writing produced during the Harlem Renaissance, including a number of those illustrations featured in the *New Negro* anthology. Shown here is *The Negro Speaks of Rivers (for Langston Hughes),* 1941, pen and ink on paper. *(The Walter O. Evans Collection of African-American Art)*

at Bennett College in North Carolina—that has been given many names, including the *Alfred Stern Mural,* the *Aaron Douglas Mural, Spirits Rising,* and *Harriet Tubman.* In 1934, he painted a series of murals for the 135th Street COUNTEE CULLEN Branch of the New York Public Library as a project for the WORKS PROGRESS ADMINISTRATION (WPA).

Aaron Douglas served as president of the Harlem Artists Guild in the mid 1930s. The Guild grew out of the need for African-American artists to organize in order to receive a fair share of WPA funds, a cruel fact of economic and artistic discrimination initially addressed by activist and sculptor AUGUSTA FELLS SAVAGE. The guild met at the Harlem YMCA on 135th Street. Members included CHARLES HENRY ALSTON, GWENDOLYN BENNETTA BENNETT, ERNEST CRICHLOW, BEAUFORD DELANEY and JOSEPH DELANEY, PALMER COLE HAYDEN, JACOB ARMSTEAD LAWRENCE, and NORMAN LEWIS.

Douglas was a master painter of the common man, an illustrator and muralist who created woodcuts and African masks, experimented with cubism, and painted in colorful oils, but he sometimes used only the colors of black and white. Among his most celebrated works are *Self-Portrait* (1925), *Listen, Lord—A Prayer* (1925), *The Negro in An African Setting* (1933), *Triborough Bridge* (1935), *Evolution of the Negro Dance* (1935), and *Alta* (1936).

In the late 1930s, with the assistance of South Carolina photographer and portrait painter EDWIN AUGUSTUS HARLESTON, Douglas created murals for FISK UNIVERSITY in Nashville, Tennessee. He became known as a "pioneering Africanist," though as he and wife Alta admitted in later years when he became a member of the Civil Rights movement, some of his murals were influenced by COMMUNISM.

In 1939, Douglas joined the staff of Fisk University and there became a professor of art and the art department chairperson. He furthered his own education in 1944 at the Teachers College of Columbia University and at the Académie Scandinave in PARIS, France.

Heading Fisk's library while Douglas taught there was Harlem Renaissance writer ARNA BONTEMPS. And CHARLES SPURGEON JOHNSON, formerly of the National Urban League and *Opportunity* magazine, was president of the university.

The "father of African-American art" retired from the department chairmanship at Fisk in 1966. He died on February 2, 1979.

Further Reading

Bailey, David A., and Paul Gilroy. *Rhapsodies in Black: Art of the Harlem Renaissance.* Berkeley: University of California Press, 1997.

Kirschke, Amy Helene. "The Depression Murals of Aaron Douglas: Radical Politics and African American Art." *International Review of African American Art* 12, no. 4, (1996).

———. *Aaron Douglas: Art, Race and the Harlem Renaissance.* Jackson: University Press of Mississippi, 1995.

Pierce, Aaronetta. "Aaron Douglas at 100." *International Review of African American Art* 17 no. 2 (2000).

— Sandra L. West

Douglas, Lena See HOLT, NORA.

Downhearted Blues See HUNTER, ALBERTA.

Du Bois, Shirley Lola Graham (Lola Bell Graham, Shirley Graham DuBois) (1896–1977)

biographer, playwright, activist

Playwright, biographer, and librettist Shirley Lola Graham Du Bois founded *Freedomways* journal and directed the Negro Unit of the Chicago Federal Theatre. A Pan-Africanist, she was also the second wife of W. E. B. DU BOIS.

She was born on November 11, 1896, in Indianapolis, Indiana, and baptized as Lola Bell Graham. Some records indicate her birth date as November 11, 1906. Her father was David Andrew Graham, a minister. Her mother was Etta Bell Graham.

Upon graduation from Lewis and Clark High School in Spokane, Washington, Graham was named class poet and wrote a prizewinning essay on BOOKER TALIAFERRO WASHINGTON. Unable to afford college, she married Shadrach T. McCanns and had two sons: David (deceased) and Robert Graham McCanns (renamed David Du Bois). She and McCanns divorced in the 1920s.

Following her marriage, Graham's education spanned two continents as she traveled with her father. When Reverend Graham went to Liberia to administrate a school, she settled in PARIS, from 1926 to 1928, to study music. She received a certificate from the Sorbonne in 1929 and taught music at Morgan State College (now Morgan State University) in Baltimore, Maryland. She then graduated from Oberlin College in 1934 with a B.A. and in 1935 with an M.A.

Graham entrusted her sons to the care of their grandparents and began to write. With her background in music, she created several plays and operas. She wrote her first play, *Tom-Tom,* in 1932. Crafted into a 16-scene opera, it dramatized the historical Middle Passage voyage from Africa to America and was produced by the Cleveland Summer Opera Company in July 1932, the first all-black opera and the first staged opera by a black female.

While developing her craft as a playwright, from 1935 to 1936 Graham taught music and arts, serving as chair for the fine arts department at Tennessee State College in Nashville. She then directed the Negro Unit of the Chicago Federal Theatre from 1936 to 1938. She published the essays "Spirituals to Symphonies" in *Etude* magazine (November 1936) and "Towards an American Theatre" in *Arts Quarterly 1* (October–December 1937).

In 1938, members of the KARAMU HOUSE in Cleveland, where LANGSTON HUGHES first began experimenting with drama, performed Graham's *Coal Dust* and in 1942 *Elijah's Raven.* CHICAGO's Federal Theatre Project staged her *Little Black Sambo* and *The Swing Mikado* in 1938, and Boston's Expression Company produced *Track Thirteen* in 1940. Graham's growing list of accomplishments earned her a Julius Rosenwald Fellowship at the Yale University School of Drama in 1940.

Graham accepted an appointment as field secretary for the NATIONAL ASSOCIATION FOR THE ADVANCEMENT OF COLORED PEOPLE (NAACP) in 1942 and remained in the position for two years. The period coincided with the same time frame during which W. E. B. Du Bois returned to the organization after having retired from it the previous decade, and the two became mutually admiring coworkers.

She began in 1944 to publish a series of biographical works, beginning with *Dr. George Washington Carver: Scientist.* She followed that with *There Once Was a Slave,* an adult historical novel based upon the life of abolitionist Frederick Douglass. Called "the best book combating intolerance in America," *There Once Was a Slave* earned her the Julian Messner Award for $6,500 in December 1946.

On February 14, 1951, Graham married the widowed W. E. B. Du Bois. In 1961, Pan-Africanists Shirley Graham Du Bois and W. E. B. Du Bois renounced their U.S. citizenship. They moved to Ghana, West Africa, where they became citizens in 1963. W. E. B. Du Bois died on August 27 of the same year.

In 1964, Shirley Graham Du Bois founded *Freedomways,* an intellectual journal, and became founding director of Ghana Television. In 1968, she moved to Beijing (Peking), China, where she served as English editor of the Afro-Asian Writers Bureau.

DuBois wrote several articles for *Black Scholar* magazine in 1970, including "Egypt Is Africa," published in two parts in May and September, and "The Struggle in Lesotho," published in November. Du Bois also completed a biography of civil rights activist Rosa Parks in 1973 and two biographical books about her second husband: *His Day Is Marching On: A Memoir of W. E. B. Du Bois* (1971) and *A Pictorial History of W. E. B. Du Bois* (1976), published by Johnson Publishing Company, an African-American house in Chicago.

Du Bois died in Peking (Beijing), China, on March 27, 1977.

Further Reading

Horne, Gerald. *Race Woman: The Lives of Shirley Graham DuBois.* New York: New York University Press, 2000.

Roses, Lorraine Elena, and Ruth Elizabeth Randolph, eds. *Harlem Renaissance and Beyond: Literary Biographies of 100 Black Woman Writers 1900–1945.* Boston: G. K. Hall, 1990.

— Sandra L. West

Du Bois, W. E. B. (William Edward Burghardt Du Bois, W. E. B. Du Bois, W. E. B. DuBois) (1868–1963)

sociologist, historian, writer, editor

William Edward Burghardt Du Bois was a major sociologist, historian, writer, editor, political activist, and cofounder of the NATIONAL ASSOCIATION FOR THE ADVANCEMENT OF COLORED PEOPLE (NAACP). During the Harlem Renaissance and through his editorship of *CRISIS* magazine, he actively sought and presented the literary genius of black writers for the entire world to acknowledge and honor.

Du Bois was born on February 23, 1868, in Great Barrington, Massachusetts. His father, Alfred Du Bois, was a former Civil War soldier who left his family when his son was still a toddler. His mother, Mary Silvina Burghardt Du Bois, died in 1884, shortly after her son graduated at the top of his class from Great Barrington High School.

Although he had been raised in a white, virtually nonracist New England environment, Du Bois chose to attend college at black, southern FISK UNIVERSITY. It was at Fisk that he developed a deeper awareness of himself as an African American, and he graduated from there in 1888.

Following his attendance at Fisk, Du Bois enrolled at Harvard University in his native state. Because he had graduated from a black southern school deemed of lower quality than

Harvard, Du Bois was forced to start as a junior even though he had earned a bachelor's degree from prestigious Fisk. In 1890, he received a second bachelor's degree with a *cum laude* designation from Harvard. He was one of five graduating seniors to deliver a commencement address. He acquired a master's degree from Harvard in 1891. Concentrating on history and sociology at the University of Berlin in Germany from 1892 to 1894, Du Bois received his Ph.D. from Harvard in 1895. He set the standard for a series of Harvard Historical Studies with the 1896 publication of his dissertation, *The Suppression of the African Slave-Trade to the United States of America, 1638–1870.*

Du Bois then taught languages and literature for a year in 1895 at Wilberforce University in Ohio. He accepted a research assignment from the University of Pennsylvania in Philadelphia in 1896, producing a landmark case study that would be published in 1899 as *The Philadelphia Negro,* the first such study of an African-American community.

Also in 1896, he married Nina Gomez. Their son Burghart Gomer Du Bois, born in 1897, died as an infant. Their daughter, Nina Yolande, born in 1900, would later marry and divorce one of the most celebrated poets of the Harlem Renaissance, COUNTEE CULLEN.

In 1897, Du Bois moved to Atlanta University in Georgia to teach economics and history. That same year, he became a charter member of the AMERICAN NEGRO ACADEMY, founded in WASHINGTON, D.C., by the Episcopal minister and Pan-Africanist Alexander Crummell. In 1900, he joined the Trinidadian Henry Sylvester Williams and Bishop Alexander Walters London to help coordinate the first PAN-AFRICAN CONGRESS.

Living in Atlanta, Du Bois felt imprisoned by the JIM CROW segregation laws and customs of the South. Growing up in Great Barrington, he had experienced rare occasions of a white person making him feel uncomfortable with remarks about his African heritage, but there had been no Jim Crow laws to abide by. As if to write his way out of the box that white segregationists wanted to put him and his people in, Du Bois published his now classic work *THE SOULS OF BLACK FOLK* in 1903. A collection of penetrating essays examining the nature of racism in America and the plight of African Americans, the book became a best-seller and in many ways served as a principal spark for the 1920s *NEW NEGRO* movement. JAMES WELDON JOHNSON, CLAUDE MCKAY, LANGSTON HUGHES, ALAIN LOCKE, JESSIE REDMOND FAUSET, and numerous others all later acknowledged their debt to Du Bois's work. *The Souls of Black Folk* also presented a formidable challenge to the accommodationist political philosophy and leadership of BOOKER TALIAFERRO WASHINGTON. In doing so, it prepared the way for Du Bois himself to achieve black leadership status on a national and international scale.

With the publication of his essay titled "The Talented Tenth"—which was included in the anthology *The Negro Problem: A Series of Articles by Representative American Negroes of Today,* only months after *The Souls of Blacks Folk* caught the public's attention—Du Bois further defined the solutions to black leadership in the United States. Specifically, his Talented Tenth concept called for the development of "the Best of this race that they may guide the Mass away from the contamination and death of the Worst, in their own and other races." He noted that while Booker T. Washington criticized such individuals, the staff of his Tuskegee Institute was filled with people, including Washington's wife, who had studied the same liberal arts courses at Fisk University as Du Bois. The quest to identify and empower those African Americans of exceptional ability would prove one of the central principles behind the Harlem Renaissance.

In 1905, Du Bois founded the NIAGARA MOVEMENT at Niagara Falls, New York, where under his leadership more than two dozen African-American men gathered to formulate racial strategies and alternatives to the tactics of Booker T. Washington. The group met again at Harper's Ferry, West Virginia, in 1906 and, as it grew, continued to hold annual conferences until 1908. These political empowerment meetings were forerunners to the establishment of the NAACP, initiated in 1909 by black and white leaders interested in obtaining and maintaining civil and human rights for black people. Du Bois resigned from Atlanta University in 1907. He moved to NEW YORK CITY in 1910 to work with the NAACP as director of publicity and research, join the board of directors, and edit the magazine *Crisis: A Record of the Darker Races.* A year later he published his first novel, a study in social realism called *The Quest of the Silver Fleece.*

One of Du Bois's chief concerns as editor of the *Crisis* was LYNCHING and antilynching legislation, a topic Booker T. Washington would rarely address. Du Bois, on the other hand, kept a running tally of lynching activity in the *Crisis.* The issue was only one of many on which the two leaders disagreed. As the founder of Tuskegee Institute, Washington taught black students domestic and industrial arts. Du Bois thought this curriculum too limited and fought for the intellectual development of black people through an expanded liberal arts program. Following Washington's death in 1915, DuBois grew into greater prominence as a leader, and through the pages of *Crisis* magazine his ideas on education, racial equality, and black culture influenced millions of African Americans and white Americans.

Du Bois, however, often found himself at odds with another black leader: MARCUS GARVEY, the founder of the UNIVERSAL NEGRO IMPROVEMENT ASSOCIATION (UNIA). Discord between the two leaders began in 1915, when Du Bois visited Jamaica as a "good faith" guest of UNIA and proclaimed that Jamaica had no race problems. The statement angered Garvey, and when visiting the New York NAACP offices in 1916, he criticized the organization for having a majority of white staff members. With Du Bois writing in the *Crisis* and Garvey writing in the *NEGRO WORLD*, their intolerance of each other grew into a much-publicized war of insults, reported in the *NEW YORK AGE*, the *AMSTERDAM NEWS*, and the *MESSENGER*. It continued until Garvey was deported from the United States in 1927 on charges of mail fraud.

Whereas Du Bois and Garvey criticized each other's style of leadership, both agreed that people of African descent throughout the world should establish some measure of political unity. Garvey made his contribution to that effort through his UNIA organization, his *Negro World* publication, and the Black Star Line shipping fleet. Du Bois made his by continuing to support the Pan-African Congress, attending a second one in 1919 in Paris and a third in 1921 in London.

As editor of the the *Crisis,* Du Bois grew so influential that he was able to persuade thousands of African Americans to set aside racial grievances and support the country's war efforts in WORLD WAR I. The *Crisis* magazine became one of the highest circulating periodicals in the United States, reaching a peak of 100,000 during the war and leveling off to almost 40,000 in the mid-1920s.

Like CHARLES SPURGEON JOHNSON of the NATIONAL URBAN LEAGUE'S *OPPORTUNITY* magazine, ALAIN LOCKE of HOWARD UNIVERSITY, and *Crisis* magazine's literary editor, Jessie Redmond Fauset, Du Bois became increasingly aware of the black literary talent gathering in New York and joined his colleagues for the official launch of the *New Negro* movement at the CIVIC CLUB DINNER on March 21, 1924. With the success of the dinner and the resulting "Harlem Edition" of *SURVEY GRAPHIC* magazine, *Crisis* began to feature the Amy Einstein Spingarn Prizes in Literature and Art. The prizes helped to attract, develop, and promote some of the most outstanding writers of the era, including EULALIE SPENCE, DOROTHY WEST, RUDOLPH FISHER, WILLIS RICHARDSON, and ELOISE ALBERTA VERONICA BIBB THOMPSON. They also helped to spawn such organizations as the theatrical troupe the KRIGWA PLAYERS.

In his 1926 essay, *Criteria of Negro Art,* Du Bois stated his belief that black art and propaganda should go hand in hand, promoting a concept with which various Harlem Renaissance artists would repeatedly disagree. Nevertheless, Du Bois himself remained one of the most prolific of the era's writers and one of its most dedicated propagandists. Having published the collections of essays *Darkwater* in 1920, and *The Gift of Black Folk* in 1924, he went on to publish his second novel, the romantic fantasy *Dark Princess,* in 1928.

Citing the financial difficulties of publishing a magazine during the GREAT DEPRESSION as well as ideological conflicts with fellow NAACP board members, Du Bois resigned from the *Crisis* in 1934 and returned to Atlanta University to chair its department of sociology.

Continuing to author influential works, in 1935 Du Bois published a revisionist history of southern reconstruction titled *Black Reconstruction.* In 1939, he published *Black Folk: Then and Now,* and in 1940, *Dusk of Dawn: An Autobiography of a Concept of Race.* In the latter, he fostered the notion of a "voluntary segregation" that indicated he no longer believed as strongly in the concepts of racial integration he had advocated as a board member of the NAACP. Despite this, in 1944, he again left Atlanta University for New York City and worked once more with the NAACP, remaining there until 1948.

His support of Pan-Africanism grew stronger, and in 1945, he was elected international president of the fifth Pan-African Congress held in Manchester, England. DuBois's first wife, Nina Gomez, died in 1950 and he married his second wife, the writer and former NAACP field secretary SHIRLEY LOLA GRAHAM DU BOIS, in 1951.

Like PAUL ROBESON, with whom Du Bois shared an interest in COMMUNISM as an ideological tool for addressing racism in the United States, Du Bois became a target of Senator Joseph McCarthy's 1950s campaign against political subversion in general and communism in particular. Accused of subversion for advocating a ban on nuclear weapons, Du Bois was acquitted of the charges in 1951. However, also like Robeson, Du Bois's passport was revoked for some seven years. At the end of the suspension of his passport, Du Bois embarked on a world tour and, in Moscow in 1959, received the Lenin Peace Prize.

As an author, Du Bois's output barely waned even in the face of extreme political adversity. He produced a second biography, *In Battle for Peace,* in 1952. In 1957, he published *The Black Flame,* the first of a fictional trilogy, followed by *Mansart Builds a School* in 1959 and *Worlds of Color* in 1961.

Disillusioned by his home country's failure to eradicate racism from American society, Du Bois embraced communism,

Educator, political advocate, and author W. E. B. Du Bois, shown here in 1946, dedicated his life to obtaining social and political equality for human beings all over the world. *(Library of Congress, Prints & Photographs Division, Carl Van Vechten Collection [LC-USZ62-42528])*

renounced his American citizenship, and in 1963, at the invitation of President Kwame Nkrumah, moved with his wife to Accra, Ghana. There, he had resumed work on plans to publish a four-volume reference titled *Encyclopaedia Africana* when he died on August 27, 1963, the eve of his native country's largest civil rights demonstration, the 1963 March on Washington.

Du Bois's most comprehensive biographical work, *The Autobiography of W. E. B. Du Bois,* was published posthumously in 1968. Appointed executor of his literary estate, historian Herbert Aptheker the following decade released *The Complete Published Works of W. E. B. Du Bois,* a series that totaled some 36 volumes. In 1999, the celebrated scholars Kwame Anthony Appiah and Henry Louis Gates, Jr., honored Du Bois's vision of an *Encyclopaedia Africana* with the publication of *Africana: The Encyclopedia of the African and African American Experience.* The massive 2,095-page volume was dedicated to Du Bois and Nelson Rolihlahla Mandela.

Further Reading

Du Bois, W. E. B., and David Levering Lewis (foreword). *Black Reconstruction in America, 1860–1880.* New York: The Free Press, 1998.

Fontenot, Chester, ed., Mary A. Morgan, and Sarah Gardner. *W. E. B. Du Bois and Race: Essays Celebrating the Centennial Publication of the Souls of Black Folk.* Macon, Ga.: Mercer University Press, 2001.

Horne, Gerald, and Mary Young, eds. *W. E. B. Du Bois: An Encyclopedia.* Westport, Conn.: Greenwood Publishing Group, Inc., 2001.

Huggins, Nathan, ed. *W. E. B. Du Bois: Writings.* New York: The Library of America, 1986.

Lewis, David Levering. *W. E. B. Du Bois: The Fight for Equality and the American Century, 1919–1963.* New York: Henry Holt, 2001.

Sundquist, Eric J., ed. *The Oxford W. E. B. Du Bois Reader.* New York: Oxford University Press, 1996.

— Sandra L. West and Aberjhani

Dunbar-Nelson, Alice (Alice Ruth Moore)

(1875–1935) *poet, journalist*

Alice Dunbar-Nelson stands with journalist IDA BELL WELLS-BARNETT in the history of black literature as one of only a few African-American female diarists and in her own right as an accomplished poet, playwright, journalist, and political activist.

She was born Alice Ruth Moore in NEW ORLEANS, Louisiana, on July 19, 1875. Her father was a sailor named Joseph Moore. Her mother, Patricia Moore, was a seamstress.

In 1892, she graduated from Straight University (now Dillard) and began teaching in New Orleans. She later received an M.A. at Cornell University in New York and studied for a time at the Pennsylvania School of Industrial Art and the University of Pennsylvania.

Moore's writing career began with "Appointed, Some Points of View," a column for the *Daily Crusader* in 1894. She published a collection of poems, short stories, and essays called *Violets, and Other Tales* in 1895. The following year, her family moved to Medford, Massachusetts, where she wrote for local publications. Paul Laurence Dunbar, the most popular and influential black poet of the early 20th century, began to correspond with her after taking note of her work and photograph in Boston's *The Monthly Review.* In 1897, she moved to 33 Poplar Street in Brooklyn, NEW YORK CITY. While working as a teacher, she helped establish White Rose Mission, later White Rose Home for Girls in HARLEM.

On March 8, 1898, she married Dunbar and moved with him to WASHINGTON, D.C., where she continued to write about love and nature. Her poem "Rainy Day" was published in Elmira, New York's *Advertiser* in September 1898. She then published *The Goodness of St. Rocque, and Other Stories,* 14 tales of Creole life in New Orleans, in 1889.

At the turn of the century, Moore's work was widely known. Her play "The Author's Evening at Home" was published in *Smart Set* (September 1900); a story "The Little Mother" appeared in *Standard Union* (March 1900); and *Leslie's Weekly* (December 12, 1901) ran a second story titled "The Ball Dress." *Lippincott's* (December 1902) published a poem by her called "Summit and Vale." In 1902, the same year her marriage dissolved, she sold the love story "A Foreordained Affair" to the *Chicago Recorder.*

Divorced, Moore moved to Delaware to teach at Howard High School in Wilmington. There, she wrote academic articles such as "Training of Teachers of English" for *Education* magazine (October 1908). Her 1910 marriage to Henry Arthur Callis was kept a secret because married female teachers were not expected to work. They divorced a year later.

She returned to fiction, writing "Hope Deferred" for *CRISIS: A RECORD OF THE DARKER RACES* in September 1914. During the same period, she wrote articles for *The A. M. E. Church Review* and edited *Masterpieces of Negro Eloquence: The Best Speeches Delivered by the Negro from the Days of Slavery to the Present Time* (1914).

Dunbar-Nelson reportedly engaged in romantic relationships with men and women before marrying journalist Robert J. Nelson in 1916. The marriage signaled a turning point in Dunbar-Nelson's life. Through her union with Nelson and through club work with Mary Church Terrell and the National Association of Colored Women, she became involved in political activities. With her husband, Dunbar-Nelson copublished the *Advocate* in Wilmington, Delaware.

Continuing to write for other periodicals, she produced a two-part article, "People of Color in Louisiana," for *The Journal of Negro History* (October 1916 and January 1917), and the poem, "Violets," for *Crisis* (August 1919).

Dunbar-Nelson's focus turned to the issue of war when *Mine Eyes Have Seen,* a wartime drama produced on April 10, 1918, at Dunbar High School in Washington, was published in *Crisis* the same year. In 1919, her article "Negro Women in War Work" appeared in *Emmett J. Scott's Official History of the American Negro in World War I.* "I Sit and Sew," printed in *The Dunbar Speaker and Entertainer and Negro Poets and Their Poems* (1920), addressed the issue of females denied the opportunity to participate in WORLD WAR I.

Politically inspired, she founded a chapter of the Circle of Negro War Relief and served as a field representative for the Women's Commission on the Council of Defense. She was the first African-American woman to become a member of the Republican State Committee and was relieved of teaching duties because of her political activities. She served, in 1920, as chairperson of the League of Colored Republican Women and helped establish the Industrial School for Colored Girls in Marshalltown, Delaware. In 1921, she chaired the publicity committee of the National League of Colored Republican Women and Anti-Lynching Crusaders.

In 1921, she began a diary that she discontinued until 1926, then started again and continued through to 1931. Her published writings continued to develop in a political and historical vein, including the poem "To Madame Curie" in Philadelphia's *Public Ledger* (August 1921) and "Politics in Delaware" in *OPPORTUNITY* magazine (November 1924).

From 1926 to 1930, she wrote three columns: "Une Femme Dit" for the *Pittsburgh Courier;* "So It Seems—To Alice Dunbar-Nelson," and "As in a Looking Glass," for the *Washington Eagle,* in which she reviewed works by the writers LANGSTON HUGHES, CLAUDE MCKAY, and NELLA LARSEN.

In 1927, Dunbar-Nelson wrote several essays for the radical journal the *MESSENGER*: "Woman's Most Serious Problem," "Textbooks in Public Schools: A Job for the Negro Woman," and "Facing Life Squarely," for the March, May, and July issues, respectively.

Even as her poetry was anthologized—"April Is on the Way" in *Ebony and Topaz* (1927) and "Forest Fire" in *Harlem: A Forum of Negro Life* (November 1928)—Dunbar-Nelson continued her political activism. From June 1, 1928, and into the 1930s, she worked, under Harlem Renaissance poet LESLIE PINCKNEY HILL, as executive secretary of the American Interracial Peace Committee (AIPC). When Robert Nelson was appointed, in January 1932, to the Pennsylvania State Athletic Commission by Governor Gifford Pinchot, he and his wife left Delaware. Dunbar-Nelson, known to sell her jewelry to pay utility bills, became part of Philadelphia's elite with membership in book societies and social clubs. Shortly before her demise on September 18, 1935, she wrote "Try Golden Rule Next," which appeared in the June 1, 1935, issue of the *AMSTERDAM NEWS*.

Further Reading

Alexander, Eleanor. *Lyrics of Sunshine and Shadow: The Tragic Courtship and Marriage of Paul Laurence Dunbar and Alice Ruth Moore.* New York: New York University Press, 2001.

Hull, Gloria T., *Color, Sex and Poetry: Three Women Writers of the Harlem Renaissance.* Bloomington and Indianapolis: Indiana University Press, 1987.

Hull, Gloria T., ed. *Give Us Each Day: The Diary of Alice Dunbar-Nelson.* New York: W.W. Norton, 1984.

— Sandra L. West

Dunham, Katherine (Kaye Dunn) (1909–)

choreographer, anthropologist

Katherine Dunham combined science and art to forge an exceptional career as a choreographer, writer, and anthropologist, creating in the process a treasured legacy of culture.

Dunham was born on June 22, 1909, in Joliet, Illinois. Her mother, Fanny June Taylor, was of mixed French Canadian and Native American ancestry, and her father, Albert M. Dunham, Sr., was a musician and businessman. Her elder sibling was Albert M. Dunham, Jr.

Dunham's natural mother died in 1914 and her father married Annette Poindexter. When Annette Poindexter Dunham separated from Albert Dunham, her stepchildren eventually joined her. Following graduation from high school, Dunham attended Joliet Junior College. She moved to CHICAGO in 1928 and there worked as a librarian while pursuing her education. Attending the University of Chicago, she received a B.A., M.A., and Ph.D. in cultural anthropology.

Working with choreographers Ruth Page and Mark Turbyfill, Dunham opened a dance studio in the early 1930s and started her own dance troupe, the Bal Negres. One of her earliest productions was an adaptation of RICHARD BRUCE NUGENT's prose poem, *Sahdji,* originally published in the *NEW NEGRO* anthology edited by ALAIN LOCKE. WILLIAM GRANT STILL composed the music for the ballet, and it was staged at the Eastman School of Music on May 22, 1931.

In 1933, Dunham danced her first leading role in Ruth Page's "La Guiabless." She went on to perform in 1934 both at the Chicago World's Fair and for the Chicago Opera Company.

A Rosenwald Fellowship in 1936 allowed Dunham to travel to Haiti, where she performed research for her doctoral thesis and began a lifelong relationship with the people and culture of the island. Moving beyond objective research, Dunham actually became an initiate of Vodun (Voodoo) and joined a community of Maroons.

Already known as a dancer, Dunham worked on the 1939 productions of the musicals *Le Jazz Hot* and *Tropics,* which established her as a gifted choreographer who fused African-American, African, and Caribbean cultural themes. Her success not only took her to Broadway and allowed her to travel with her troupe on a worldwide tour but opened the door to a side career in film. In 1940, she appeared in *STORMY WEATHER* along with BOJANGLES ROBINSON, LENA HORNE, CAB CALLOWAY, and the NICHOLAS BROTHERS. She also performed the same year in *Cabin in the Sky.*

Dunham married theatre manager John Thomas Pratt on July 10, 1941. The couple had a daughter named Marie Christine.

Dunham's interests and career continued to expand, and she opened the Katherine Dunham School of Arts and Research in NEW YORK CITY in 1943. In time she would establish branches of the school in PARIS, France, other parts of Europe, and the Caribbean. With the publication of *Journey to Accompong* in 1946, Dunham gained attention as an author capable of blending poetic artistry with the acute observations of the anthropologist she had trained to become. Along the same lines, as Dunham continued to tour with her troup, she collected from around the world African and Caribbean cultural artifacts that had been removed from their original locations.

In 1959, Dunham published an autobiographical work titled *A Touch of Innocence,* chronicling her young adulthood

Choreographer Katherine Dunham, shown here in 1940, created numerous original works in dance and also established herself as an accomplished author. *(Library of Congress, Prints & Photographs Division, Carl Van Vechten Collection [LC-USZ62-93100])*

with straightforward honesty. She gave her last Broadway performance in 1962 in a production of *Banboche.* The following year she became the first African-American woman to work with the New York Metropolitan Opera when she choreographed a production of the classic *Aida.* In 1965, she presented the last performance of her dance company.

The various artifacts Dunham collected in her travels were numerous enough in 1967 that she was able to house them in the Katherine Dunham Dynamic Museum, established in 1967 in Alton, Illinois. Among her many collectibles are ceremonial masks, work tools, musical instruments, ritual costumes, sculptures, and rare cloth.

Dunham also authored the fictional *Kasamance: A Fantasy,* and coauthored a play called *Ode to Taylor Jones* in 1967. She also wrote a number of articles, short stories, and scripts for foreign television, sometimes using the pseudonym Kaye Dunn. Moreover, having been made an honorary citizen of Haiti, Dunham described her relationship with the country's people and culture in *Island Possessed,* a book published in 1969.

Dunham's contributions as a performing artist, writer, teacher, and anthropologist have been recognized and honored in many ways. A television special, *Divine Drumbeats: Katherine Dunham and Her People,* aired in 1980. In 1983, she was among those honored at the annual Kennedy Center Awards. In 1986, she received the Distinguished Service Award of the American Anthropological Society. And in 1987, her peers staged *The Magic of Katherine Dunham* in tribute to her at the Alvin Ailey American Dance Theatre in New York.

Possibly the most significant testimony to the artist and scientist's life and work is the ongoing operation of the Katherine Dunham Dynamic Museum, reestablished in East St. Louis, Missouri, in 1969, when Ms. Dunham relocated there to serve as a consultant and instructor. The Doris Duke Charitable Foundation in 2001 donated $1 million to the Library of Congress for a two-year program supporting the Katherine Dunham Legacy Project to procure her archives and papers. As of 2002, Ms. Dunham was still listed as the executive director of her museum, and Jeannelle Stovall was listed as the associate director.

Further Reading

Aschenbrenner, Joyce. *Katherine Dunham: Dancing a Life.* Chicago: University of Illinois Press, 2002.

Ramsay, Burt. *Alien Bodies: Representations of Modernity, Race and Nation in Early Modern Dance.* New York: Routledge Press, 1998.

— Aberjhani

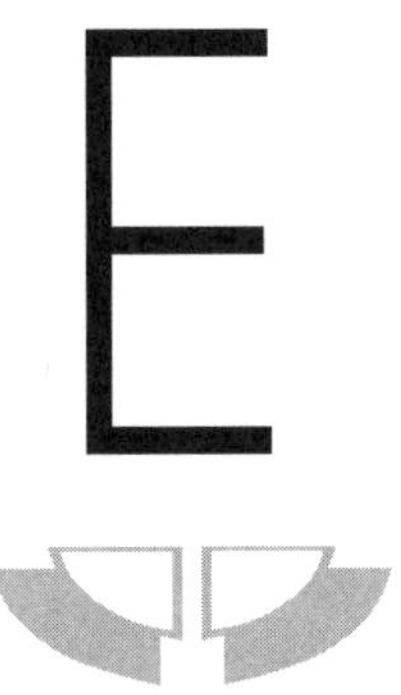

Eastman, Max (1883–1969) *editor, patron*

Max Eastman emerged out of a group of NEW YORK CITY radicals known as the Greenwich Village Left to become one of the leading writers, editors, and critics of the 1900s.

Eastman was born on January 12, 1883, in Canandaigua, New York, to Annis Bertha and Samuel Eastman. Both his parents were ministers. In 1905, he graduated from Williams College, in Williamstown, Massachusetts, and later taught philosophy at Columbia University for four years.

In 1910, Eastman founded the first Men's League for Women's Suffrage. Along with his sister Crystal, he was a member of the Greenwich Village Left, a group of white New York radicals that championed artistic innovation, social experimentation, and equality between the sexes and races. Included in the group were political activist Emma Goldman, radical journalist John Reed, and photographer Alfred Stieglitz.

From 1913 to 1917, Eastman edited the radical magazine *The Masses,* founded in 1911 by socialist Piet Vlag. Drawing political fire with its stand against WORLD WAR I, *The Masses* gave way to a new magazine, *The Liberator,* in 1918. As coeditors of *The Liberator,* Max Eastman and Crystal Eastman at first sought to provide an outlet for John Reed's explosive reports on the Bolshevik revolution. The magazine expanded to include coverage of the Mexican Revolution and the MARCUS GARVEY movement as well. Moreover, it provided a showcase for the work of such writers as JEAN TOOMER, JAMES WELDON JOHNSON, Georgia Douglas Johnson, John Dos Passos, LANGSTON HUGHES, and CLAUDE MCKAY.

McKay in particular developed both a strong professional relationship with *The Liberator* and a literary friendship with Eastman. They met in 1919, and each expressed admiration for the other's work. Eastman was impressed enough by McKay's poetry that he published a full spread of it in *The Liberator*'s July 1919 issue. Whereas other editors had backed off publishing McKay's now signature poem, "IF WE MUST DIE," Eastman featured it just as the RED SUMMER OF 1919—so-called because of the violent riots that ripped through American cities that summer—was approaching its zenith. With Eastman's departure for Europe in 1922, McKay became one of the editors for *The Liberator* and lobbied for an increase in the magazine's African-American content. His own contributions to it, prior to the magazine becoming the *Worker's Monthly* in 1924, equaled more than 40 poems and a dozen essays and reviews. Eastman later wrote the preface for McKay's poetry collection, *Harlem Shadows.* McKay lived with the editor and his second wife, Eliena Krylenko, while completing his novel, *HOME TO HARLEM.* Throughout McKay's career, Eastman provided occasional financial assistance and professional support.

Journeying through Europe in the 1920s, Eastman befriended the Bolshevik leader Leon Trotsky and later served as Trotsky's American literary agent and translated his *Third History of the Russian Revolution* (1932) and *The Revolution Betrayed* (1937). Eastman also wrote several books criticizing the developing Soviet Union, publishing *Since Lenin Died* in 1925 and *Stalin's Russia and the Crisis in Socialism* in 1939.

In 1941, he joined *Reader's Digest* as a roving editor. Of his own works, he wrote the autobiographical volumes *Enjoyment of Living* in 1948 and *Love and Revolution: My Journey Through an Epoch* in 1965.

Eastman was married three times: to the poet and actress Ida Rauh, in 1911; to Russian artist and dancer Eliena Krylenko, in 1924; and to Yvette Szekely, in 1958. He died in Bridgetown, Barbados, on March 25, 1969.

Further Reading

Hutchinson, George. *The Harlem Renaissance in Black and White.* Cambridge and London: The Belknap Press of Harvard University Press, 1995.

A longtime friend of Claude McKay, Max Eastman lent support to writers and artists of the Harlem Renaissance as an editor and sometime patron. He is shown here in 1955 in front of a portrait painted by his wife. *(Library of Congress, Prints & Photographs Division, NYWT&S Collection [LC-USZ62-115118])*

O'Neill, William L. *The Last Romantic: A Life of Max Eastman.* Somerset, N.J.: Transaction Publishers, 1991.

— Aberjhani

economy and the Harlem Renaissance

The GREAT MIGRATION of African Americans leaving the South during the early 1900s was fueled to a large degree by their desire to share in "the American Dream" of potential economic prosperity for anyone seeking it. That dream was one black southern immigrants felt they could realize only in the West and in the more industrialized and liberal North, far from the South where the extreme apartheid practices known as JIM CROW deprived them of basic civil and human rights.

During slavery, the kidnapped African in America was not allowed to own property, including him- or herself. After emancipation, the freed African American had to adapt to such concepts and practices as owning one's home and receiving payment for one's labor. By contrast, during the Harlem Renaissance in the late 1920s, almost 30 percent of all African Americans had indeed adapted and reportedly owned the homes in which they lived.

However, in HARLEM in 1927, out of 2,326 apartments checked by the NATIONAL URBAN LEAGUE (NUL), investigations revealed that for those Africans who paid rent for their dwellings, the monthly cost for them was higher than the monthly rent for whites living in NEW YORK CITY. The Urban League reported that the average monthly rent for a black family was $56, paid out of an annual income of $1,300, or approximately $108 a month. White families paid on the average $32 for monthly rent from an annual income of $1,570, or approximately $131 a month. In short, whereas blacks had to pay about half of their monthly income for rent, whites paid just over 25 percent of their monthly income for the same.

Nevertheless, despite the drawbacks, employment opportunities for African Americans in the North were much more abundant than they were in the South. In New York City alone, there were 600 public school teachers. Although the retail industry was generally restricted to whites, African Americans were able to work in subway construction or the field of chemistry, a sharp contrast to the agrarian and domestic jobs available to them in the more severely segregated South. Moreover, as the northern black population increased and African Americans took advantage of educational opportunities as well as employment opportunities, they gradually entered such areas as banking, insurance, real estate, taxi service, garage service, and arts and letters.

Cultural endeavors as forms of employment provided better than average salaries and lifestyles for those participants in the *NEW NEGRO* movement who excelled at their chosen art, among them: W. E. B. DU BOIS, the editor of the *CRISIS: A RECORD OF THE DARKER RACES*; HOWARD UNIVERSITY professor of philosophy and favored charge of art patrons ALAIN LOCKE; and concert performer MARIAN ANDERSON. Singer and dancer FLORENCE MILLS earned, at the time of her untimely death in 1927, $3,500 a week. Author COUNTEE CULLEN, in 1932, one of the worst years of the GREAT DEPRESSION, could live off of his writing, profiting a high of $707 in royalties plus monies from teaching and lecturing engagements.

Still, Harlem had a high percentage of working-class people, including factory workers, elevator operators, Pullman porters, and maids. In 1939, 80 percent of all black women workers were domestics. A maid earned $7 to $8 a week and a laundry worker $10 a week. The salary of a porter during the 1930s was $89.50 a month. These were the people who held RENT PARTIES and took in boarders in order to meet their monthly obligations and close the gap between incomes and expenditures.

Rent parties were, literally, social gatherings held to generate money to pay the rent. The parties were held on Saturday or Thursday nights with admission fees ranging from a dime to 50¢. A menu of favored foods and live entertainment provided by masters of STRIDE PIANO provided many families with an important supplement to their regular jobs. Likewise, those who operated a basement SPEAKEASY provided affordable alternatives to the more expensive and segregated big business clubs in JUNGLE ALLEY while profiting substantially from such a venture.

Families who took in boarders sometimes rented the same mattress or couch twice to different boarders: first, to a boarder who worked during the day and slept at night, then second, to a boarder who worked the night shift and slept during the day.

Disparities to the side, the economic condition of African Americans in the North represented a vast improvement over the average farm laborer's income of several dollars per week and life in a sharecropper's shack.

Further Reading

Bascom, Lionel C., ed. *A Renaissance in Harlem: Lost Voices of an American Community.* New York: Avon, 1999.

Lewis, David Levering. *When Harlem Was in Vogue.* New York: Vintage Books, 1982.

Sochen, June, ed. *The Black Man and the American Dream: Negro Aspirations in America, 1900–1930.* Chicago: Quadrangle Books, 1971.

Jones, Eugene Kinckle. "The Negro's Opportunity Today." *Opportunity* Magazine, January 1928, 10–12.

Wintz, Cary E. *Black Culture and the Harlem Renaissance.* Houston, Texas: Rice University Press, 1988.

— Sandra L. West

Edmonds, Sheppard Randolph (1900–1983)

dramatist

Randolph Edmonds's achievements as a director, playwright, and educator won him widespread acceptance as the unofficial "Dean of Black Academic Theatre."

Edmonds was born Sheppard Randolph Edmonds on April 30, 1900 to sharecropper parents in Lawrenceville, Virginia. He attended the former St. Paul's Normal and Industrial School, graduating as class valedictorian and earning prizes in English and history in 1921. Edmonds continued his education at Oberlin College, in Oberlin, Ohio. There, he organized the Dunbar Forum as a cultural outlet for black students, and the group produced several of his early plays. He graduated from Oberlin in 1926.

Edmonds's career as a playwright began in 1922 with the one-act folk play *Job Hunting,* for which he won honorable mention in *OPPORTUNITY* magazine's drama competition. From 1922 to 1926, he produced a series of one-act plays examining the issues of the era. Among the most powerful was *A Merchant in Dixie* (1923), in which a white businessman and a black member of the NATIONAL ASSOCIATION FOR THE ADVANCEMENT OF COLORED PEOPLE (NAACP), once childhood friends, confront each other as adults. Randolph's *Doom* was a one-act play that seemingly challenged the radical spirit behind the *NEW NEGRO* philosophy and championed the economic and racial philosophies of BOOKER TALIAFERRO WASHINGTON.

In 1926, *CRISIS: A RECORD OF THE DARKER RACES* magazine awarded Edmonds two honorable mentions in its drama competitions. The first was for his interracial drama *Illicit Love.* The second was for *Peter Stith,* which examined the increasing distance between the values of urban and rural African Americans in the 1920s. Edmonds took another honorable mention from *Opportunity* magazine in 1927 for *Bleeding Heart,* a sentimental take on American slavery. The playwright also enjoyed some popular success with *Sirlock Bones,* a comedy that entertained the audience at the APOLLO THEATRE in 1928.

Edmonds had produced enough work in 1930 to publish a collection entitled *Shades and Shadow.* A second collection, *Six Plays for a Negro Theatre,* followed in 1934. *The Land of Cotton and Other Plays,* his third collection, was published in 1942.

Edmonds maintained an affiliation with academic theater throughout his career. In 1931, he directed the drama program at Morgan College in Baltimore while also working with the local KRIGWA PLAYERS. In his work with that group, he produced plays by Georgia Douglas Johnson, WILLIS RICHARDSON, and MAY MILLER.

He enrolled at Columbia University in NEW YORK CITY in 1934 to obtain his master's degree in English and drama. He then took a fellowship to study at the Yale University School of Drama and followed that with study and travels in England, Ireland, Scotland, and Wales.

From 1935 to 1944, he directed the Dillard Players' Guild at Dillard University in NEW ORLEANS and spearheaded the formation of the Southern Association of Dramatic and Speech Arts. In a brief stint as a Special Divisions military officer during World War II, he produced shows for black troops at Ft. Huachuca, Arizona.

Edmonds accepted the chair of the drama department at Florida A & M in 1948, a position he held for 20 years and which, in conjunction with his continuing writing career, earned him the title, "Dean of Black Academic Theater."

He married the writer and director Irene Colbert in 1931. The couple had two children: Henriette Edmonds and S. Randolph Edmonds, Jr. After the death of his first wife, in 1968, Edmonds returned to his hometown of Lawrenceville and there married Ana Manson Turner.

In 1974, he wrote a history of the black American theater called *Blacks in the American Theatre, 1700–1970.* His many contributions to that subject were recognized two years earlier with a Special Citation from the American Theatre Association. Edmonds died on March 28, 1983.

Further Reading

Caponi, Gena Dagel, ed. *Singnifyin(G), Sanctifyin' and Slam Dunking: A Reader In African American Expressive Culture.* Amherst: University of Massachusetts Press, 1999.

Mitchell, Angelyn, ed. *Within the Circle: An Anthology of African American Literary Criticism from the Harlem Renaissance to the Present.* Durham, N.C.: Duke University Press, 1994.

— Aberjhani

Edmondson, William (1874–1951) *sculptor*

The first black solo exhibitor in the history of the Museum of Modern Art (MOMA) in NEW YORK CITY, William Edmondson carved tombstones for the black community in Nashville, Tennessee, and created visionary sculpture of animals and angels.

Edmondson was born in 1874 near Nashville in the Hillsboro Road area of Davidson County, Tennessee. His parents,

George and Jane, were former slaves. A simple man, William Edmondson worked as a janitor at the Women's Hospital (now Baptist Hospital) in Nashville from 1908 to 1931.

At the end of his official workday, Edmondson labored in his yard to create tombstones from abandoned blocks of limestone. Using chisels and files that he made, he carved angels and animals on the tombstones that his church members asked him to create for deceased loved ones in the rural church cemetery. In addition to the tombstones he designed and sold to church and other community members, he carved such biblical characters as *Preacher* (1930s), which is now in the collection of the University of Tennessee in Knoxville, and *Speaking Owl* (1937). Other subjects included figures of young brides; popular personalities such as First Lady ELEANOR ROOSEVELT; the characters Porgy and Bess from the African-American folk opera; and garden ornaments such as birdbaths.

Louise Dahl-Wolfe, a photographer visiting from New York, discovered Edmondson at work on his tombstones and figures. She photographed his work and presented the photographs to the director of MOMA, who quickly signed Edmondson to exhibit at the museum. Edmondson's first show, in 1937, was a solo exhibit, which was both unusual and an honor for a fledgling folk artist. It was also the first time MOMA exhibited the work of any black artist in a solo show.

FOLK ART is the name given to work by artists who are self-taught or formally uneducated. It is also termed primitive or "outsider" art and is created by common, everyday folk as opposed to university-educated professionals or those who had capital, unlike Edmondson, to register for art workshops. The painting of peasant scenes, woodcarving, and pottery are also examples of folk art.

After the well-received MOMA exhibition, Edmondson was—much to his surprise—designated an artist, something he did not know he was until others said so. As an artist, he was then affiliated with the WORKS PROGRESS ADMINISTRATION (WPA) from 1939 to 1941.

Following his primary exhibit, Edmondson's surprisingly sophisticated owls, angels, and figures were shown at the Nashville Art Gallery (1941), the Nashville Artist Guild (1951), the Willard Gallery, New York (1964 and 1971), the Tennessee Fine Arts Center (1964), the Montclair Art Museum (1975), and the Tennessee State Museum (1981).

The works of William Edmondson are collected in the Cheekwood Fine Arts Center in Nashville and the Newark Museum in New Jersey. He died on February 7, 1951.

Further Reading

Edmondson, William. *The Art of William Edmondson.* Jackson: University Press of Mississippi, 2000.

Livingston, Jane, and John Beadsley. *Black Folk Art in America, 1930–1980.* Jackson: Corcoran Gallery of Art, University Press of Mississippi-Jackson, and The Center for the Study of Southern Culture, 1982.

Ollman, John E., ed. *Miracles: The Sculpture of William Edmondson.* Janet Fleisher Gallery, 1994.

— Sandra L. West

Ellington, Duke (Edward Kennedy Ellington)

(1899–1974) *jazz pianist, composer*

Edward Kennedy Ellington, who once dreamed of becoming a painter, became instead a JAZZ pianist and composer of more than 1,000 orchestra arrangements, creating musical revues, an opera, film scores, suites of sacred music, television productions and helping establish the SWING SOUND. He was nicknamed "Duke" because of the elegant clothes he wore.

Edward Kennedy Ellington was born into middle-class comfort on April 29, 1899, in WASHINGTON, D.C., to Daisy Kennedy Ellington and James Edward Ellington. His mother was a domestic and his father a butler who also operated a part-time catering enterprise. He began piano lessons at age six and, with the help of a succession of mentors, became skilled enough to work as a professional musician by the time he was a teenager. His original professional plan, however, was to become an artist, and toward that end he studied commercial art at the Armstrong Manual Training School. Deciding that music held greater appeal for him, Ellington left art school before graduating in order to pursue his career as a professional musician.

At the age of 17, Ellington composed his first song, "The Soda Fountain Rag," the name taken from his job as a soda jerk. He was inspired by the RAGTIME music that was popular then and influenced by the STRIDE PIANO performances of HARLEM musicians James P. Johnson and Willie the Lion Smith. He also studied with composers WILL MARION COOK and Will Vodery. He formed a group called "The Duke's Serenaders, Colored Syncopaters" in 1918 and with it played throughout Washington, D.C., and Virginia.

On March 11, 1919, Ellington married Edna Thompson and they had one son, named Mercer. Though only 19 years old, Ellington had done well enough for himself as a musician to purchase a home for his new family.

With the assistance of club hostess and singer BRICKTOP, Ellington moved with his group to NEW YORK CITY to play at the Kentucky Club and soon won acceptance at some of the most popular clubs in Harlem, including CONNIE'S INN and BARRON'S EXCLUSIVE CLUB. In 1927, when jazz pioneer KING OLIVER turned down a job at the COTTON CLUB, Ellington was hired for the position. Ellington and his band remained at the famed entertainment facility for five years as "Duke Ellington and His Famous Cotton Club Orchestra," creating a musical dynasty.

The music Ellington played at the Cotton Club was known as "jungle music," a sound achieved by using horn mutes to imitate the sounds of jungle animals. The white patrons of the Cotton Club, which was one of more than a dozen nightclubs that initially catered to whites only, found jungle music entertaining. However, Ellington continued to create artful compositions that fell more into the category of jazz and classical music. Ellington himself never liked the word *jazz* or any categorization of music as a particular style. He maintained that there was only good music or bad music.

Toward the end of the 1920s, Ellington's marriage to Edna Thompson dissolved, although they never officially divorced and Ellington did not remarry. He became somewhat notorious for declaring "music is my mistress," a phrase he later used as the title of his autobiography.

Initially managing his career himself, Ellington hired the white songwriter and music publisher Irving Mills as his agent around 1928. Mills's contract with Ellington entitled him to 45 percent of those earnings by the group from jobs he arranged. One of the deals he obtained for Ellington's band was a recording contract on the Columbia Records label. Ellington maintained his partnership with Mills for 14 years. It ended following disputes over Mills's alleged rights to credit and royalties for works by Ellington, who severed his ties with Columbia as well.

In addition to recording a series of groundbreaking records during his tenure at the Cotton Club, Ellington also made live radio broadcasts and his group emerged in the early 1930s as America's leading jazz band. Upon Ellington's departure from the Cotton Club in 1931, CAB CALLOWAY and the MISSOURIANS became the club's house band while Ellington embarked on national and international tours. In 1933, the band toured England, where Ellington was hailed as a "genius."

By the early 1940s, he created the first of many jazz suites: "Black, Brown and Beige" debuted at Carnegie Hall in 1943. Suites that followed were the sacred "The River"; "Symphony in Black: A Rhapsody of Negro Life"; and "Paris Blues," which was a film score. Critics found it difficult to classify Ellington, who at times wrote jazz compositions based on European classical music, such as his African-American version of Peter Tchaikovsky's *Nutcracker Suite.* Moreover, in addition to his works in jazz, he composed sacred and classical music for entire orchestras, writing the intricate, demanding scores down on paper. He may have played "jungle music" in a segregated nightclub in the 1920s, but Ellington developed throughout the 1930s and 1940s into a serious artist concerned with philosophical, purposeful music.

Ellington also infused his jazz compositions with Cuban and Latin musical forms, and he orchestrated his musicians to achieve a unified sound that became known as the "Big Band Sound," an innovation also claimed by bandleader and clarinetist Benny Goodman. Some of Ellington's better known works are "Satin Doll," "Sophisticated Lady," "Don't Get Around Much Anymore," "Do Nothin' Til You Hear from Me," "In a Sentimental Mood," "Take the 'A' Train" and "Lush Life" (both written by Ellington's pianist-arranger, William

Among the acknowledged masters of jazz, Duke Ellington, here performing at the Hurricane in 1943, is recognized as the genre's greatest composer. *(Library of Congress, Prints & Photographs Division [LC-USW3-023967-D])*

"Billy" Strayhorn), and "Perdido" and "Caravan" (written by Ellington's trombonist, Juan Tizol).

Ellington nurtured his orchestra members so that many remained with him for decades, and he regularly told audiences all over the world, "I love you madly." Musicians who performed with Ellington included violinist Ray Nance, vocalist Joya Sherrill, alto saxophonist Johnny Hodges, trumpeter James "Bubber" Miley, trumpeter Rex Stewart, tenor saxophonists Ben Webster and Paul Gonsalves, baritone saxophonist Harry Carney, trumpeter Charles "Cootie" Williams, bassist Jimmy Woode, and jazz vocalist Ivie Marie Anderson. Anderson won renown for introducing the song "It Don't Mean a Thing (If It Ain't Got That Swing)" in 1931. Anderson employed SCATTING, the improvisational vocal jazz technique of the era, and not only introduced to the public one of the most popular songs of the Harlem Renaissance era but sang "All God's Children Got Rhythm" in the Marx Brothers film *A Day at the Races* in 1937. Noted as one of Ellington's all-time favorite vocalists, Anderson died in 1949.

Another innovative musician who contributed greatly to the Ellington sound was William Alonzo "Cat" Anderson. Cat Anderson, a master of the upper registers, could make his trumpet growl like a real person, an important factor in Ellington's music. Author of *The Cat Anderson Trumpet Method: Dealing with Playing in the Upper Register,* he performed with Ellington from 1944 to 1947. His high register trumpet features predominantly on Ellington's "The Far East Suite."

Though he neither ascribed to COMMUNISM, nor was identified as the subject of an official bureau investigation, nor ever posed an acknowledged threat to U.S. security, the Federal Bureau of Investigation (FBI) maintained a file on Ellington that indicated they suspected he was a Communist sympathizer. File number 100-434443 contained newspaper clippings of Ellington's engagements. For example, one clipping read that Ellington was scheduled to play at the Golden Gate Ballroom on October 24, 1943, in a "Davis Victory Show" to pay tribute to Benjamin J. Davis, Jr., Communist Party candidate for the City Council of New York. The file also holds clippings of Ellington's concerts in the Soviet Union. Despite the implications, he was, by his own admission, not a political man. In the 1950s, he stated, "I've never been interested in politics in my whole life, and I don't pretend to know anything about international affairs. . . ."

His significance as a serious composer grew more evident in 1959 when Ellington won three Grammys at the second annual Grammy Awards. Winning all three for the film score of *Anatomy of a Murder,* Ellington won in the categories for Best Musical Composition, Best Soundtrack, and Best Pop Performance by a Dance Band.

Duke Ellington died on May 24, 1974, while working on an opera. His son, Mercer Ellington, took over the band until his own death in 1996. A granddaughter, Mercedes, survives and heads the Duke Ellington Foundation.

Neither Ellington's death nor that of his son lessened the impact of the composer's music on the world. In 1999, celebrations were held worldwide in honor of the centennial of Ellington's birth. In 2000, at the 42nd Annual Grammy Awards, Ellington won two posthumous awards: in the category of Best Historical Jazz Album, he won for *The Duke Ellington Centennial Edition—The Complete RCA Victor Recordings* (1927–73), and in the category for Best Traditional Pop Vocal Performance, he won for "Bennett Sings Ellington—Hot and Cool," with vocals by Tony Bennett.

Further Reading

Curry, George E. "FBI Kept an Eye on Duke for Decades." *Emerge,* April 1999.

Ellington, Edward Kennedy. *Music Is My Mistress.* New York: Doubleday, 1973.

Rattenbury, Ken. *Duke Ellington: Jazz Composer.* New Haven, Conn.: Yale University Press, 1993.

Seymour, Gene. "The Genius of Duke Ellington." *Emerge,* April 1999.

Stewart, Rhonda. "In the Tradition." *Emerge,* April 1999.

Tucker, Mark, ed. *The Duke Ellington Reader.* New York and Oxford: Oxford University Press, 1993.

— Sandra L. West

Ellison, Ralph Waldo (1913–1994) *writer*

Famed as a critic and for his internationally acclaimed novel, *Invisible Man,* Ralph Ellison began writing during the concluding years of the Harlem Renaissance but, despite a close association with author LANGSTON HUGHES and an affinity for JAZZ, considered his work separate from that of the *NEW NEGRO* movement rather than an extension of it.

Ralph Waldo Ellison was born on March 1, 1913, to Oklahoma City pioneers Lewis Alfred Ellison and Ida Millsap Ellison. A businessman and former soldier with a passion for literature, Lewis Ellison named his son after the American author Ralph Waldo Emerson with the hope that the name would endow him with a similar love and talent for literature. Ellison's younger sibling was named Herbert.

After his father's death when Ellison was three, his mother continued to encourage his intellectual development by later providing him with magazines discarded by employers in her work as a domestic. Among the magazines she presented him was *Vanity Fair,* the same publication in which CARL VAN VECHTEN during the 1920s promoted the works of Langston Hughes, JAMES WELDON JOHNSON, BESSIE SMITH, ETHEL WATERS, and others associated with the Harlem Renaissance.

Although Ida Ellison eventually remarried twice, Ralph Ellison's childhood was essentially one of poverty that forced his mother to constantly relocate while generally raising her sons alone. Attending Oklahoma City's Frederick Douglass School at the elementary and high school levels, Ellison became a student of music. He learned to play the trumpet for his high school band as well as with local jazz bands.

Ellison graduated from the Frederick Douglass School in 1932. He then joined the legions of men and women who rode illegally on freight trains during the GREAT DEPRESSION to travel to Alabama. There, he enrolled in Tuskegee Institute, the vocational training center founded by BOOKER TALIAFERRO

WASHINGTON. At Tuskegee, he continued his formal study of music and developed an interest in sculpture while pursuing literature as a valued hobby. His reading of T. S. Eliot's "The Wasteland" is often cited as a catalyst in Ellison's recognition of literature as a medium capable of triggering transcendent experience for both readers and writers. While attending Tuskegee, Ellison briefly met HOWARD UNIVERSITY professor of philosophy and editor of the *New Negro* anthology ALAIN LOCKE.

Approaching his senior year at Tuskegee, Ellison traveled in 1936 to NEW YORK CITY, where he hoped to earn money to continue his education and to study sculpture with AUGUSTA SAVAGE. In New York, he met Alain Locke for the second time. With Locke was Langston Hughes, to whom he introduced Ellison. The contact with Hughes developed into a friendship that would last decades and through which Ellison was introduced to writings by left-wing authors. Moreover, Hughes also introduced Ellison to the artist RICHMOND BARTHÉ, who further assisted Ellison in becoming acclimated to New York City.

Rather than returning to Tuskegee as he first had planned, Ellison soon settled in HARLEM. Again through Langston Hughes, in 1936 Ellison met RICHARD WRIGHT, with whom he also formed a close literary friendship. Working with DOROTHY WEST and Marian Minus in 1937 on the *New Challenge* magazine, Wright was instrumental in the publication of a book review by Ellison, his first essay in such a journal. The following year, Ellison began to contribute regularly to the communist-influenced magazine *New Masses* (see also COMMUNISM). Writing for *New Masses,* he gained a reputation as an insightful observer and skilled interpreter of social trends and issues in American society.

On September 17, 1938, Ellison married performing artist Rose A. Poindexter. They separated after less than a year together but did not officially divorce for another six years.

Also in 1938, Ellison joined the WORKS PROGRESS ADMINISTRATION'S (WPA) New York City branch of the FEDERAL WRITERS' PROJECT (FWP). Like other writers affiliated with the FWP, he gathered for its archives biographies, profiles of communities, historical research, folklore, and reports on various social and cultural practices among African Americans. Among those with whom Ellison worked at the FWP were Dorothy West, CLAUDE MCKAY, STERLING BROWN, who headed the Negro Affairs Division of the FWP, WILLIAM WARING CUNEY, and RICHARD BRUCE NUGENT.

Ellison began in 1939 working on *Slick,* his first novel, from which a section called "Slick Gonna Learn" was later published in *Direction* magazine. Although the novel remained unpublished, Ellison wrote throughout the early 1940s a series of critical essays for influential journals that increased his renown and influence as a writer. In addition, in 1942 he edited the *Negro Quarterly* with Angelo Herndon, the radical labor leader whose life had been the subject of Langston Hughes's one-act play *Angelo Herndon Jones.* In his editorials, reviews, and essays, Ellison often described works by Harlem Renaissance writers as lacking in ideological content or aesthetic formulation. He championed Langston Hughes for his exploration of black folk culture but criticized other Harlem Renaissance writers for producing flawed literary works based on that of their white counterparts, echoing an observation previously voiced by writer WALLACE THURMAN.

Ellison began in 1943 a two-year stint in the Merchant Marines during World War II. That same year, he wrote for the *New York Post* an account of the HARLEM RIOT that tore through the community on June 20.

Following his divorce from Poindexter in 1945, Ellison married Fanny McConnell Buford in 1946. Initially an aspiring writer herself, Fanny Ellison gave up her literary pursuits to work as a secretary and maintain a steady income while her husband worked from 1945–52 on his second novel, *Invisible Man.*

Prior to its publication, sections of *Invisible Man* appeared in the journals *48: Magazine of the Year, Horizon,* and *Partisan Review.* Upon its publication, as with most literary works eventually declared masterpieces, critics were divided over the book's merits and qualities. W. E. B. DU BOIS, who at the height of the Harlem Renaissance had championed the propaganda potential of black literature over its artistic value, predictably found Ellison's novel too heavy on aesthetic structure and too light on racial militancy. By contrast, many of those whites to whom Ellison had become a leading literary and cultural critic hailed the novel as a literary triumph. The book is essentially the story of a young African-American man's struggle to determine his own identity and destiny in a society unsupportive of black men's lives. Capable of being read on many different levels, Ralph Ellison, in one of his most famous essays, "Change the Joke and Slip the Yoke," described the book as his hero's "memoir, . . . one long, loud rant, howl and laugh."

The novel went on in 1953 to win the prestigious National Newspaper Publishers' Russworm Award, the National Book Award, and a certificate of recognition from the *CHICAGO DEFENDER.* Following those in 1954 was the Rockefeller Foundation Award. The overwhelming success of *Invisible Man* allowed Ellison to launch a career as an educator and to elevate his already formidable standing as a public intellectual. Whereas fellow writers such as Wright, Chester Himes, and James Baldwin relocated to PARIS, France, to practice their craft, Ellison in 1955 received a Prix de Rome Fellowship that allowed him to live and work for two years in Italy. Upon his return to the United States, he continued teaching at various colleges and universities while also engaging in important debates on African-American and American culture.

A collection of Ellison's essays was published under the title *Shadow and Act* in 1964. In 1965, a *New York Herald Tribune Book Week* poll recognized Ellison as one of the top ten most influential novelists in the United States and *Invisible Man* as the most substantial and distinguished novel published by an American author after World War II. He was awarded the Medal of Freedom in 1969 and France's Chevalier de l'Ordre des Arts et Lettres in 1970.

A second novel on which Ellison reportedly worked throughout the 1960s was destroyed in a fire in 1967. Almost two decades later, in 1986, he published a second collection of essays titled *Going to the Territory.* He continued to publish essays, interviews, and excerpts from a novel in progress up until his death in New York City on April 16, 1994.

Appointed literary executor of Ellison's estate, John Callahan published *The Collected Essays of Ralph Ellison* as part of Random House's Modern Library series in 1995 and a collection of short fiction titled *Flying Home and Other Stories* in 1996. *Juneteenth,* a novel culled from the reportedly epic story on which Ellison was working when he died, was published in 1999. Sculptor ELIZABETH CATLETT in 2000 produced a 15-foot-monument called *Invisible Man* in tribute to Ellison. Professor of English Lawrence Jackson in 2002 published the first major biography of the author, titled *Ralph Ellison: Emergence of Genius,* detailing the first half of Ellison's life.

To commemorate the fiftieth anniversary of the publication of *Invisible Man,* biographer Arnold Rampersad, author Horace Porter, editor John Callahan, and moderator Paula Moya held a symposium on the novel at Stanford University, California, April 24, 2002. Rampersad, the award-winning biographer of Langston Hughes, was at that time working on a full-scale biography of Ellison.

Further Reading

Ellison, Ralph. *Invisible Man.* New York: Random House, Inc., 2002.

Ellison, Ralph and Murray, Albert. *Trading Twelves: The Selected Letters of Ralph Ellison and Albert Murray.* New York: Knopf Publishing Group, 2001.

Fabre, Michel. *The Unfinished Quest of Richard Wright.* Urbana and Chicago: University of Illinois Press, 1993.

Graham, Maryemma, and Amritjit Singh, eds. *Conversations with Ralph Ellison.* Jackson: University Press of Mississippi, 1995.

Jackson, Lawrence. *Ralph Ellison: Emergence of Genius.* New York: John Wiley & Sons, Inc., 2002.

Porter, Horace A. *Jazz Country: Ralph Ellison in America.* Iowa City: University of Iowa Press, 2001.

— Aberjhani

Emperor Jones, The

Debuting in 1920, *The Emperor Jones* was the first dramatic Broadway play to feature a black man in the title role. Starring CHARLES SIDNEY GILPIN, the play was written by white playwright Eugene O'Neill, who in the same year of its production won a Pulitzer Prize for another play, *Beyond the Horizon.*

O'Neill was a member of a group of playwrights and actors who called themselves the Provincetown Players. Originally based in Provincetown, Massachusetts, the group relocated to Greenwich Village around 1915 and made it their goal to create works that were innovative, realistic, and socially provocative. *The Emperor Jones* was one of several experimental works in which O'Neill (who eventually would win four Pulitzers and a Nobel Prize for his contributions to American theater) tackled race relations in the United States. He had already expressed his interest in the subject in *Bound East* (1913), *The Moon of the Carribbees* (1918), and *The Dreamy Kid* (1919). He would revisit the issue again in *All God's Chillun Got Wings* (1924) and *The Iceman Cometh* (1939).

Coming only a year after the RED SUMMER OF 1919, *The Emperor Jones* was close to an act of subversion with its portrayal of a black man tempted, corrupted, and ultimately destroyed by his desire for symbols of white power.

By the time he took on the role of Emperor Jones, Charles Gilpin was a veteran of minstrel shows, CHICAGO's Pekin Theater, and NEW YORK CITY's LAFAYETTE THEATRE and LINCOLN THEATRE. For his performance, Gilpin was awarded the SPINGARN MEDAL by the NATIONAL ASSOCIATION FOR THE ADVANCEMENT OF COLORED PEOPLE (NAACP) in 1921.

PAUL ROBESON placed his inimitable stamp on the title role of *The Emperor Jones* when the play was revived in 1925. He further went on to star in the movie based on the play in 1933. As a film, *The Emperor Jones* was among the first wave of movies to feature blacks in leading roles.

The play remains a favorite of small company productions and at festivals honoring O'Neill's work.

Further Reading

Black, Stephen A. *Eugene O'Neill: Beyond Mourning and Tragedy.* New Haven, Conn.: Yale University Press, 2002.

O'Neill, Eugene. *Complete Plays 1913–1920.* New York: Viking Press, 1988.

— Aberjhani

entertainment and Harlem

HARLEM's growth and development as the largest African-American community in the United States gave rise to one of the most dynamic and celebrated entertainment centers in the world.

The departure of blacks from the South at the beginning of the GREAT MIGRATION in the early 1900s and their relocation in Harlem coincided with a productive period of building construction in NEW YORK CITY. Townhouses and theaters initially intended to benefit Harlem's white community were left to the migrating blacks when whites departed large sections of the area. Consequently, African Americans inherited upon the departure of whites such elegant and well-equipped theaters as the LAFAYETTE THEATRE, the LINCOLN THEATRE, and the ALHAMBRA BALLROOM. Prior to increased population of blacks in Harlem, managers of theaters as a general rule practiced JIM CROW segregation that required African Americans to attend shows on certain days or restricted their seating to the balcony.

As black patronage increased, most of these theaters remained under the ownership of whites but were sometimes, as in the case of the Lafayette, managed by blacks to plan shows appealing to black audiences. Efforts to attract and satisfy such audiences on a regular basis increased the available venues for such traditional vaudeville acts as MOMS MABLEY, BUTTERBEANS AND SUSIE, and PIGMEAT MARKHAM. They and numerous other black singers, dancers, comedians, and actors were no longer restricted to a series of one-night performances in the small-town one-room clubs known as juke joints, the SPEAKEASIES springing up in the North, or the segregated clubs and hotels located along the east coast. The theaters of Harlem by the mid-1910s became an African-American version of Broadway and the goal to which black performers aspired.

Influential in this development was Lester Walton, a drama critic for the *NEW YORK AGE* who worked as a manager at the Lafayette Theatre. Determined to bring serious theatrical entertainment to Harlem, Walton staged the hit musical *Darktown Follies* at the Lafayette Theatre and began to draw crowds from Broadway to uptown as early as 1914. The following year he helped Aubrey Lyles and Flournoy Miller achieve their first big success with a production of *Darkydom* some six years before they teamed up with NOBLE SISSLE and EUBIE BLAKE to create the record-setting Broadway musical, *SHUFFLE ALONG*.

The standards Walton set at the Lafayette were noted and duplicated by surrounding theaters that not only featured the best of black vaudeville but offered black productions of classic works by Shakespeare and new experimental pieces by writers and composers such as Paul Laurence Dunbar, Scott Joplin, WILLIS RICHARDSON, and ALEXANDER ROGERS.

While Harlem's theaters were not the setting for the birth of RAGTIME, JAZZ, or the BLUES, they did promote these musical forms in a manner that helped to elevate them to the status of cultural treasures. Musical great FATS WALLER learned to play the organ as an accompanist for silent films prior to developing into one of the acknowledged masters of STRIDE PIANO. BESSIE SMITH, CLARA SMITH, Mamie Smith, and other blues singers headlined at Harlem theaters in shows they often produced themselves. When the record industry began in the 1920s to produce RACE RECORDS, blues singers created a new entertainment market that generated hundreds of millions of dollars in sales for Columbia Records and other major white-owned companies before the boom in such records slowed down at the start of the GREAT DEPRESSION. These singers were championed and celebrated in Harlem more than almost anywhere else at the time, and they provided the American culture with one of its most enduring musical legacies.

Along with increasing the impact of black music on U.S. musical culture, theaters and nightclubs in Harlem provided Broadway with some of its most successful shows and performers. The hit Broadway musicals *LIZA* in 1922, *BLACKBIRDS* featuring FLORENCE MILLS in 1926, and *HOT CHOCOLATES* with Fats Waller and LOUIS ARMSTRONG were all staged in Harlem prior to making successful Broadway runs. Moreover, Lester Walton's dream of establishing an authentic performing arts tradition—featuring a wide range of drama, comedy, and dance—was realized with the formation of a series of theatrical groups that worked out of library basements and community centers. These included the HARLEM SUITCASE THEATER founded by LANGSTON HUGHES, the KRIGWA PLAYERS sponsored by *CRISIS: A RECORD OF THE DARKER RACES* magazine, the Negro Experimental Theater, and the BLACK UNIT OF THE FEDERAL THEATER PROJECT sponsored by the WORKS PROGRESS ADMINISTRATION.

With stride piano, musicians in Harlem made a singular contribution to the evolution of jazz, the development of the SWING SOUND, the culture of RENT PARTIES, and popular dance. Mastered by pianists in Harlem largely to distinguish them from other musicians in the United States, stride piano included elements of improvisation that heavily influenced jazz in the 1920s and a noted syncopation that helped define the swing sound in the 1930s and 1940s. As such music, featuring the works of DUKE ELLINGTON, COUNT BASIE, and CHICK WEBB, dominated radio shows broadcast out of New York, it set the trend followed by the rest of the country. It also created such a powerful black musical culture in Europe that many African Americans migrated there—joining blacks such as EUGENE JACQUES BULLARD, who had gone to France at the beginning of WORLD WAR I—and became celebrated musicians, dancers, hostesses, athletes, writers, and artists.

With trends in music came trends in dance. The number-one dance craze of the 1920s, the Charleston, like much of the North's developing black musical culture, came out of the South but did not become an international phenomenon until it was popularized in the black musicals *LIZA* and *RUNNIN' WILD*. Once it was made popular in New York City, with many of its more expert performers giving lessons in Harlem, it spread to England and France and throughout Europe. In PARIS, the much-celebrated BRICKTOP supplemented her income as a nightclub hostess by providing lessons on the Charleston to Europeans and white American expatriates. A dance more of a Harlem original was the Lindy Hop. More physically demanding than the Charleston, the Lindy Hop did not enjoy the same international stature. It was, however, popular enough in its own right that major dance halls such as the SAVOY BALLROOM and the Alhambra sponsored special events and reserved seating space just for the more accomplished dancers.

Harlem gained a reputation as "The Nightclub Capital of the World" in the 1920s and maintained that reputation for decades with the establishment of such clubs as the COTTON CLUB, BARRON'S EXCLUSIVE CLUB, Gladys' Clam House, and CONNIE'S INN. Whereas these clubs provided their patrons with elegant settings and superior entertainment, they provided black performers with the opportunity to excel as creative artists and establish a performance industry comparable to that created by blues singers and race records. A dancer at the Cotton Club, for example, made an average of $25 a week, about three times the amount earned by the average black domestic or hotel worker. Musicians earned a good deal more and were able to increase their incomes with studio recordings and tour dates. If there was a downside to Harlem's thriving nightclub scene, it was the fact that many of the clubs, particularly those operated in JUNGLE ALLEY, were owned by white gangsters who used the facilities to traffic illegal sales of alcohol and other drugs. Moreover, at least a dozen of the better-known clubs practiced racial discrimination against black customers as part of their general policy. Despite this, the clubs were incubators for a number of world-class acts, including DOROTHY DANDRIDGE, ETHEL WATERS, CAB CALLOWAY, the NICHOLAS BROTHERS, and LENA HORNE.

If any single entertainment facility symbolized the sheer abundance and quality of talent either produced in or nurtured by Harlem, it was the APOLLO THEATRE. The Apollo showcased everything from the pioneer feature films of black producer OSCAR MICHEAUX to international headliners and neophytes

One of the most popular performers during the mid-1920s and early 1930s in Harlem, Earl "Snake Hips" Tucker was a favorite dancer in nightclub shows and on Broadway. *(Photograph and Prints Division, Schomburg Center for Research in Black Culture, The New York Public Library, Astor, Lenox and Tilden Foundation)*

presented on its amateur night. Despite boasting the appearance of such acts as Ella Fitzgerald, CHARLIE PARKER, BILLIE HOLIDAY, JOSEPHINE BAKER, emcee RALPH COOPER, and numerous other major stars, the Apollo became a place where the community of Harlem itself became part of the performance. The theater gained renown worldwide for its critical feedback during shows and its penchant for joining performers in call and response exchanges. Unlike the majority of clubs in Jungle Alley or such first-rate theaters as the Lafayette, the Apollo still stands as a unique entertainment showcase for local, national, and international black talent.

With what is currently recognized as a triumphant revitalization effort in Harlem, the community remains both a source of celebrated performers and a treasured venue for them.

Further Reading

Hill, Anthony D. *Pages from the Harlem Renaissance: A Chronicle of Performance.* New York: Peter Lang Publishing, 1996.

Krasner, David. *A Beautiful Pageant: African American Theatre, Drama, and Performance in the Harlem Renaissance, 1910–1927.* New York: Palgrave Macmillan, 2002.

Shack, William A. *Harlem in Montmartre, a Paris Jazz Story Between the Great Wars.* Berkeley: University of California Press, 2001.

— Aberjhani

Ethiopian Art Players

Performing a variety of modern works, the Ethiopian Art Players were one of the most progressive African-American theater groups of the 1920s.

The Ethiopian Art Players were known in turn as the Chicago Folk Theatre and the Colored Folk Theatre before taking on their more modernist name. The group was founded by director and organizer Raymond O'Neil and sponsored in part by Mrs. Sherwood Anderson. Unlike the KRIGWA PLAYERS, the Ethiopian Art Players did not restrict themselves to a creed calling for works by, for, and about African Americans only. Their reported goals were to produce works of a universal nature appealing to all audiences; to inspire both whites and blacks to create dramatic works on the African-American experience; and to help establish theatrical organizations similar to their own in other cities.

The Ethiopian Players obtained WILLIS RICHARDSON's play, *The Chip Woman's Fortune,* after ALAIN LOCKE's Howard Players at HOWARD UNIVERSITY were denied permission to perform it. W. E. B. DU BOIS suggested that Richardson contact O'Neil regarding the play. *The Chip Woman's Fortune,* in addition to eventually becoming the first dramatic work by an African American produced on Broadway, became one of three plays with which the Ethiopian Art Players made their debut. The other two were a jazz version of Shakespeare's *Comedy of Errors* and *Salome* by Oscar Wilde. The triple bill debuted in CHICAGO in January 1923, went on to play in WASHINGTON, D.C., in April of the same year, and was staged at the LAFAYETTE THEATRE in May 1923. It played Broadway's Frazee Theatre for a week before returning to the Lafayette.

Among the members of the Ethiopian Players were Sidney Kirkpatrick, Marion Taylor, and Evelyn Preer, who later starred in a number of movies produced by OSCAR MICHEAUX.

Further Reading

Alexander, Michael. *Jazz Age News.* Princeton, N.J.: Princeton University Press, 2001.

Hay, Samuel A. *African American Theatre: A Historical and Critical Analysis.* New York: Cambridge University Press, 1994.

— Aberjhani

Europe, James Reese

See SISSLE, NOBLE.

F

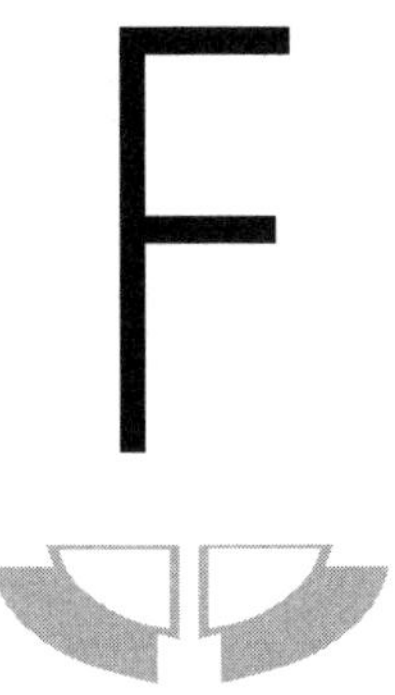

fashion and the Harlem Renaissance

One of the most fashionable epochs of the 20th century, the Harlem Renaissance was a period that saw people dressed in brogues, the chemise dress, feathered hats, zoot suits, garter belts, embroidered dressing gowns, red silk stockings, and the creations of an African-American designer named Ann Lowe.

At the dawn of the 20th century, proper or sophisticated African Americans adopted the formal and Victorian style of clothing worn by the general American public. The men wore practical one-piece, woolen underwear with a buttoned flap at the derriere, and long-waisted jackets as outerwear. Women wore boned corsets under their street length, bustled dresses with high-laced collars. Though lacy and elegant, the clothing was somber in color with skirts long enough to conceal even the slightest view of an ankle.

During the late 1800s and early 1900s, when NEW YORK CITY's black community lived in the area of 53rd Street between Sixth and Eighth Avenues, right before the uptown migration to HARLEM, dress for black and white males included great attention to detail. Harlem Renaissance historian Jervis Anderson reports that African-American men were seen socially in ". . . frock coats, vests, and wide-bottom trousers . . . shirts, fastened with studs, had detachable stiff collars and cuffs, made of linen, celluloid, cotton, or paper . . . watch chains . . . straw hats were commonly worn in summer, and derbies (or "high dicers") in winter . . . carried walking sticks . . . wore high boots polished with Bixby's Best Blacking."

Poor and rural African Americans wore bandannas and overalls, in accordance with the sweaty field work they performed during the week. On Sundays, however, they practically paraded to church in their "Sunday-go-to-meeting-suits," oftentimes wearing shoes for the first time that week. As work garb, both men and women wore the bibbed overalls, the forerunner of the 21st century's popular blue jeans. In both JEAN TOOMER's celebrated book *Cane* and in ZORA NEALE HURSTON's equally celebrated *Their Eyes Were Watching God,* women wear overalls. In both books, the overalls symbolize the women's personal strength over femininity, illustrating that they are, as Toomer puts it in *Cane,* "strong as any man." Though sometimes included in Harlem Renaissance literature, usually in a "country" or rural scene of a novel, overalls did not constitute a uniform worn by the *NEW NEGRO*. For them, overalls represented a chattel system they preferred to forget.

Regardless of their social or financial status, people of African descent placed importance on fashion, quite possibly because as field slaves, and even during 20th-century sharecropping, they had little or no choice regarding what they wore. They often worked naked or near naked, or they were forced to wear torn, hand-me-down items. Experimental and influential with style, African Americans took what little they had and embellished it with ingenuity and glamour.

After the Victorian era, African Americans were encouraged by the freedom of the arts movement, the growth of industry, and the geographical and spiritual release of the GREAT MIGRATION. From 1920 to 1940, Black America's clothing scene took a dramatic turn from the prim and proper. During the Harlem Renaissance, and particularly in Harlem itself, African Americans wore clothing that was far from somber. Two exceptions to that rule were W. E. B. DU BOIS, the editor of the *CRISIS: A RECORD OF THE DARKER RACES*, who was ever reserved in his watch chain, suit, and vest, and conservative poet COUNTEE CULLEN, who wore the same "uniform of the intelligent class." Most others enjoyed modern fashions, from underwear to outerwear, with reckless abandon and trendiness.

As the black community moved to Harlem, uptown's SEVENTH AVENUE became known as "the Great Black Way." Throughout the 1920s, for the Seventh Avenue Easter parades and after-church strolls in Harlem, smart black men wore white gloves and velvet-collared Chesterfield coats. On their arms were women dressed in wide hats garlanded with flowers, modest

Dressed to the height of fashion, three members of the Northeasterners, a group of socialites dedicated to community service, are shown here in 1927 standing on Seventh Avenue. They are, from left to right: Edith Scott, Louise Swain, and Helen Corbin. *(Photographs and Prints Division, Schomburg Center for Research in Black Culture, The New York Public Library, Astor, Lenox and Tilden Foundation)*

veils, open-toed slippers, and the low-slung dress, possibly with a ribbon at the hip. One dress style was known as a chemise, slung low on the hips, and another was the lacy georgette. Popular by the 1930s was the trendy beret hat with stand-up or egret feather, though the 1920s cloche, a close-fitting number usually made of felt or wool, was extremely popular for casual wear and was worn jauntily pulled down over the eye.

African Americans also demonstrated respect for their heritage through a style of leopard-skin coats symbolizing the great power of the well-known African animal. Leopard-skin coats appeared in Harlem Renaissance literature as the trendy thing to wear.

Boned corsets gave way to garter belts, and fancy dressing gowns evolved into house robes, known in the 21st century as housecoats or bathrobes. Silk stockings, held up by garters, were also extremely popular. The gifted and prolific author LANGSTON HUGHES often described dancing women dressed in red stockings in his JAZZ poems. In his novel *The Blacker the Berry,* WALLACE THURMAN noted chorus girl dancers who would roll silk stockings down below their knees. By the 1940s, a popular color of stockings for black women was called "red fox."

During the Victorian era, following the biblical mandate, long hair on a woman had been considered a source of beauty and vanity and was not supposed to be cut. However, when high-necked and laced Victorian collars gave way to V-necked, low-hipped chemise dresses during the *New Negro* Renaissance, long hair lost its appeal. Thurman, once more in *The Blacker the Berry,* describes his protagonist Emma Lou as brushing "boyishly bobbed" hair. Among the young jazz set, the short hair was not only acceptable but was often employed as a symbol of women's liberation from restricting mores of Victorian society. Still, as Jean Toomer reported in *Cane,* the bob was an unacceptable hairstyle for someone like a teacher because a teacher, or a woman in another traditionally conservative occupation, was expected to uphold an image of social respectfulness and propriety. The cost of a short bobbed hairdo was about 50¢ at a barbershop, a far cry from the average $20 haircut of more contemporary times.

Black men during the 1920s generally wore their hair brushed straight down and back. Some had their naturally curly, kinky hair straightened or "conked," a chemical procedure using an application of lye on the hair and scalp. This hairstyle is also examined in Thurman's novel, where a pianist at a RENT PARTY is described as having pomaded "slicked-down hair." By the time Langston Hughes wrote his *Jesse B. Simple* stories in the 1940s, male hairstyles, for the average non-entertainer, were less chemically treated. In "Conversation on the Corner," Simple removes his hat to reveal a short cut, not straightened, oiled, or "conked," with about an inch or two high in front "in a kind of brush."

Facial hair was also dictated by fashion. During the era of slavery in America, black men were not allowed to wear a mustache because it was considered a symbol of manhood. Within the Harlem Renaissance years, a thin, abbreviated mustache, carefully drawn and coifed, and as worn by COTTON CLUB bandleader DUKE ELLINGTON, became the vogue.

Color was a crucial and liberating element during the Harlem Renaissance. [Even dressing gowns were theatrical and exotic.] Harlemites adopted exquisite materials like silk and taffeta with bold colors, much like the majestic madras headwraps of the free black women of color in Louisiana and the Caribbean. NELLA LARSEN presented a survey of styles in her novel *Quicksand:* "There were batik dresses in . . . indigo, orange, green, vermilion, and black: dresses of velvet and chiffon in screaming colors, blood-red, sulfur-yellow, sea-green. . . ."

By the 1940s, the jazz age had made a strong impact on the fashion industry. The clothing of young and "hip" black men was just as expressive as the music. The zoot suit defined the 1940s for black urban youth. Trousers were pleated with high waists. The suit jacket was 36 inches long with a fly front, padded shoulders that stuck out three and a half inches, and two breast pockets plus slashed side pockets. Author Frank Marshall Davis defined the zoot suit as "a form of visual protest." To complete this suit, the fashionable male wore pointed-toe shoes, in tan calfskin or colored suede, and a porkpie-shaped or six-inch crown hat. Band leader CAB CALLOWAY owned more than 40 zoot suits ranging in price from

$150 to $225. The more ordinary zoot suit for the everyday man on the street cost $33.50.

Padded shoulders were also added to suits and blouses worn by women. Severe, padded business suits and sultry evening dresses with padded shoulders were featured in movies when worn by 1940s movie stars Joan Crawford and Cotton Club song stylist LENA HORNE. In the 1980s, the style became popular again.

Shoes were an important part of one's wardrobe during the period. Types of shoes included loafers, sandals, and for some, even tennis shoes. Surveying a group of men in *The Blacker the Berry,* Emma Lou notes that, "Rubber heels were out of fashion. Hard heels, with metal heel plates were the mode of the day. . . ." Men also wore black custom-made brogues or two-toned, white-and-tan shoes called spats. Women wore high-heeled patent leather oxfords, penny loafers, and stacked, wedge-heeled shoes, many with ankle straps and large buckles, to achieve the "modern" look dictated by the new, trendy era.

A notable African-American designer during the period, especially during the 1940s, was Ann Lowe, who designed clothes only for those listed on the social register. In 1920, Lowe owned a dress shop called Annie Cohen in Tampa, Florida. Lowe's shop was the leading salon in town. She created gilded gowns, with thousands of hand-stitched beads and sequins, for elite belles attending Tampa's annual Gasparilla Festival. In New York in 1928, Lowe worked for exclusive shops such as Henri Bendel, Neiman Marcus, and I. Magnin. In 1950, she opened her own salon, Ann Lowe's Gowns, and in 1953 designed the wedding gown in which Jacqueline Lee Bouvier married Senator (later President) John F. Kennedy.

As famous as Bill "Bojangles" Robinson was for his work as a dancer, radio personality, and film star, he was nearly as renowned for his fashionable attire, such as this suit worn by the entertainer and later placed on exhibit at the Black History Museum & Cultural Center of Virginia. *(Black History Museum & Cultural Center)*

With its innovations, boldness, and definitive styles, fashion during the Harlem Renaissance proved one of the most dynamic fashion epochs of the 20th century.

Further Reading

Anderson, Jervis. *This Was Harlem: A Cultural Portrait, 1900–1950.* New York: Farrar Straus Giroux, 1981.

Gates, Henry Louis, Jr., ed. *The Norton Anthology of African-American Literature.* New York and London: W. W. Norton, 1997.

Hughes, Langston. *The Best of Simple.* New York: American Century Series, Hill and Wang, 1961.

Peacock, John. *20th Century Fashion: The Complete Sourcebook.* London: Thames & Hudson, 1993.

— Sandra L. West

Father Divine (George Baker, Jr., Reverend M. J. "Father" Divine) (1879–1965) *religious leader*

Calling himself Father Divine, George Baker established the Peace Mission in NEW YORK CITY during the GREAT DEPRESSION and developed a large following of people who looked upon him as a human embodiment of divinity.

Father Divine's origins, like that of many self-styled religious leaders, have been the source of much debate. The most extensive documentation on him, however—including that provided by Jill Watts in *God, Harlem, U.S.A., The Father Divine Story*—places his birth in Rockville, Maryland, in 1879. Born George Baker, Jr., he was one of several children born to Nancy Smith Baker and George Baker, Sr. Baker, Jr., obtained a basic elementary education as a child and grew up with a strong appreciation for the teachings of the black church.

As a young adult, Baker moved to Baltimore in 1899 and there earned his living as a gardener while also teaching Sunday school. He then moved to Pennsylvania, where he met men who referred to themselves as "divine messengers." In Pennsylvania, at the turn of the 20th century, Baker joined a group led by Sam Morris, who called himself Father Jehovia. Referred to as "messenger" by Morris, Baker later aligned with a group called "Lift Ever, Die Never," directed by John Hickerson, also known as St. John the Divine Hickerson. Through these exposures, Baker was introduced, like GARLAND ANDERSON and CHARLOTTE OSGOOD MASON, to an ideology known as New Thought, which in part stressed the mental application of divine will to achieve miraculous results.

As a "messenger" of New Thought, Baker embarked on a tour of the South during the 1910s just as the GREAT MIGRATION of African Americans moving North was beginning to increase. In Georgia, Baker proclaimed himself God and was arrested by the police because his outdoor services were deemed a public nuisance. Booked as "John Doe, alias God," he served two months in jail. Departing Georgia in 1914, he relocated to New York City where he served under Hickerson, established his own church in Brooklyn, and proclaimed himself God.

In 1919, Baker married Peninah, called Sister Penny, and purchased a home in Sayville, Long Island. In this wealthy

Father Divine moved to Harlem at the beginning of the Great Depression and established a number of "Heavens" as part of his peace mission movement. Shown here in 1941 is the entrance to one such "Heaven" on the East Side of Manhattan. *(Library of Congress, Prints & Photographs Division [LC-USF34-012896-D])*

neighborhood, there were many domestic workers from HARLEM, and he successfully recruited them, in addition to some of their wealthy white employers, as followers. Baker was an integrationist and civil rights advocate, though most of his Long Island neighbors did not like the idea of black and white followers. While Sister Penny cooked free dinners, Baker preached, and his ministry grew. In 1930, Baker officially took the name of Father Divine, Reverend M. J. "Father" Divine.

On November 15, 1931, Father Divine and 80 of his communicants were arrested for disturbing the peace in Sayville. He was sentenced to a year in the county jail plus a $500 fine. When the judge died of a heart attack three days after the trial, Father Divine said, "I hated to do it," a statement that added to his growing mystique as a living divine presence. His conviction was overturned and his membership in his church increased with many believing he truly was a black messiah, a God on earth who had the power of life and death over others. After a huge banquet held at Rockland Palace Ballroom in Harlem, Father Divine expanded his outreach to include the black uptown village, and his ministry became known as the Peace Mission. The banquets were an integral part of the worship service because they demonstrated that "Father" could take care of those who were loyal to him. Each banquet was a multicourse feast, including more than six varieties of vegetables and stuffed sausage as well as veal and various breads and desserts. It was a demonstration before his followers, he said, that "God will provide."

The belief system of Baker's nondenominational church was built upon on a strict moral code. Followers refrained from alcohol, drugs, and tobacco. They could not partake of race hatred, profanity, hair-straightening, or buying household items on the installment plan. They had to refute crime and violence. Sexual abstinence was required even between husband and wife. As such, followers rarely had children and those who were born were raised communally at the church's farm by substitute parents. Men and women were segregated by sex in hotels, in nighttime sleeping arrangements, and in worship services.

In the worship services, called "Heaven," songs were sung and impromptu sermons delivered. Scripture readings from the Bible were not utilized, and Father Divine was the only speaker, without the benefit of traditional clergy. Nondenominational incorporated churches of the Divine Movement had annual meetings where a president, secretary, treasurer, and board of trustees were elected, all subject to approval by Father Divine. The Divine brand of theology was a combination of Pentacostalism, African-American Christianity, Methodism, and Catholicism, but mostly the power of positive thinking to achieve prosperity and salvation.

Father Divine's Peace Mission was especially popular in the 1930s and 1940s because it responded to the economic needs of people impoverished by the Great Depression. The movement was noted for providing jobs, low-cost food, and shelter to its members. The organization purchased apartment houses in Harlem, grocery stores, barbershops, and a coal business. It operated shoe-shine stands and dry cleaners. Their food shops served dinners for 15¢. Divine, who referred to himself as "the written word," promised his followers that he would " . . . bless you, give you homes for your bodies, rest for your souls. . . . " Much to the chagrin of established clergy at mainstream black churches who felt that he was a sham, Father Divine's Peace Mission successfully fed and clothed many living in Harlem and elsewhere.

The Peace Mission established two newspapers to promote its philosophy, the *Spoken Word* and *New Day.* Continuing to expand, the organization's operations spread to Australia, Sweden, England, Germany, Austria, and Switzerland.

The Divine Movement also captured the imagination of local politicians. When FIORELLO HENRY LA GUARDIA was a mayoral candidate, on November 4, 1933, he attended a Rockland Palace banquet to seek divine counsel. Father Divine endorsed voting and encouraged his followers to participate in the political process. Interestingly, communicants were allowed to register to vote under assumed names rather than birth names. The Peace Mission became a political force.

Legal problems persisted, however, and on April 20, 1937, Father Divine and one of his followers, "Faithful Mary," were involved in a scandal. Two white men confronted them and were beaten. Allegations of sex, assault, and blackmail arose. Father Divine fled to Connecticut but was brought back to New York. A white follower, John West Hunt, was arrested for taking a young female follower, "Miss Delight Jewel," across state lines for sexual purposes. Faithful Mary defected and made charges regarding Father Divine's actual sex life and accusations that followers had been blackmailed. She eventually, however, rejoined the organization.

Even with his image tarnished, Father Divine remained a wealthy leader. In 1938, he purchased the Krum Elbow estate in Hyde Park, New York. President FRANKLIN DELANO ROOSEVELT was his neighbor. In 1941, Father Divine received a gift of a 32-room PHILADELPHIA mansion from a wealthy white follower, John De Voute. He fled to this mansion to escape prison when he was found in contempt of court after refusing to pay $5,000 to a female follower whom he, allegedly, defrauded.

With his headquarters moved to Philadelphia and the Harlem headquarters defunct, membership declined in the Peace Mission even as scandal repeatedly occurred. Father Divine's wife, Sister Penny, died in 1943, and he married Ednah Rose Ritchings in April 1946. A 21-year-old white stenographer and follower from Canada, she became known as "Sweet Angel" and "Mother Divine." According to Father Divine, she was his former wife, Sister Penny, reincarnated. The announcement filled newspapers and attracted new followers. As a result, Father and Mother Divine amassed a fortune. In 1953, they purchased a 73-acre estate in Merion, Philadelphia, and called it "Kingdom of Peace."

Upon Father Divine's death on September 10, 1965, he left $10 million in assets, and Mother Divine was to be in charge of the Peace Mission movement. A $300,000 shrine was built in 1966 to house his body at the Woodmount estate in Pennsylvania. Followers continued to visit the estate and shrine where worship services were held by Mother Divine. Membership lists for the Peace Mission were never made available to the public, but a 1978 *New Day* contained a mailing list of nine thousand. One remaining example of Father Divine's outreach mission is the Divine Hotel in Newark, New Jersey, which in the early 21st century still provided low-cost shelter for men and women.

Further Reading

Anderson, Jervis. *This Was Harlem: A Cultural Portrait, 1900–1950.* New York: Farrar, Straus, Giroux, 1981.

Payne, Wardell Jr., ed. *Directory of African American Religious Bodies: A Compendium by the Howard University School of Divinity.* Washington, D.C., Howard University Press, 1991.

Smith, Jonathan Z. *The HarperCollins Dictionary of Religion.* San Francisco: HarperSanFrancisco, 1995.

Watts, Jill. *God, Harlem, U.S.A., The Father Divine Story.* Berkeley: University of California Press, 1992.

Weisbrot, Robert. *Father Divine and the Struggle for Racial Equality.* Champaign, Ill.: University of Illinois Press, 1983.

— Sandra L. West

Fauset, Arthur Huff (1899–1983) *anthropologist, writer, editor*

In addition to writing anthropological studies, Arthur Huff Fauset edited a black interest literary magazine, wrote prizewinning short stories, and authored juvenile literature during the Harlem Renaissance in the city of PHILADELPHIA.

Arthur Huff Fauset was born in Flemington, New Jersey, on January 20, 1899. His father was Rev. Redmond Fauset and his mother Belle Huff, Rev. Fauset's second wife. His half-sister was JESSIE REDMOND FAUSET, often described as midwife to the emerging black writers of the era, a novelist, and literary editor of *CRISIS: A RECORD OF THE DARKER RACES.*

Arthur Fauset received his B.A., an M.A., and a Ph.D. from the University of Pennsylvania. He taught and served as an administrator in the public school system of Pennsylvania from 1918 to 1946. His wife, Crystal Byrd Fauset, was the first African-American woman elected to the Pennsylvania legislature.

As a literary writer, Fauset's areas of interest included historical nonfiction and short stories. *Crisis* magazine published his story "A Tale of the North Carolina Woods" in

1922. Another story, "Symphonesque," won the O. Henry Memorial Award in 1926 and was anthologized in *For Freedom: A Biographical Story of the American Negro* in 1927.

During the *NEW NEGRO*'s era of PATRONS, Huff received support to produce his literary output from Mrs. CHARLOTTE OSGOOD MASON, who led and financed a stable of writers that included LANGSTON HUGHES, ALAIN LOCKE, and ZORA NEALE HURSTON. In 1927, he shared editorial responsibilities for *Black Opals,* a middle-class literary journal, with Nellie Rathborne Bright, a teacher in Philadelphia, with whom he coauthored a children's history book, *America: Red, White, Black, Yellow* (1969).

In addition, Fauset was a Fellow in the American Anthropological Association. He collected folklore for *Folklore of Nova Scotia* (1931), wrote *Sojourner Truth, God's Faith Pilgrim* (1938), and authored *Gold Gods of the Metropolis: Negro Religious Cults of the Urban North* (1970).

Arthur Huff Fauset died on September 2, 1983.

Further Reading

Fauset, Arthur Huff, Barbara Diane Savage (foreword), and John F. Szwed (introduction). *Black Gods of the Metropolis: Negro Religious Cults of the Urban North.* Philadelphia: University of Pennsylvania Press, 2001.

Lewis, David Levering. *When Harlem Was in Vogue.* New York: Vintage Books, 1982.

— Sandra L. West

Fauset, Jessie Redmond (ca. 1884–1961) *poet, editor, novelist*

Noted literary editor for *CRISIS: A RECORD OF THE DARKER RACES*, Jessie Redmond Fauset was a central figure of the Harlem Renaissance who wrote about the black middle class, helped shape the work of other writers, and hosted parties where guests were required to speak in French.

Jessie Fauset was born on April 27, 1884, in Snow Hill, New Jersey (formerly Fredericksville, now Lawnside), near Camden, circa 1882 to 1886. Her father was Rev. Redmond Fauset, a minister in the African Methodist Episcopal Church. Her mother was Annie Seamon Fauset. Her half brother, ARTHUR HUFF FAUSET, coedited *Black Opals* literary journal with Nellie Rathborne Bright in Pennsylvania during the Renaissance era. The family moved when Fauset was very young, and she grew up in an all-white neighborhood in PHILADELPHIA, Pennsylvania.

Fauset was the sole black student at Philadelphia High School for Girls. Following high school graduation, Bryn Mawr College discouraged Fauset from attending because of her race but made it possible for her to obtain a scholarship to Cornell University. In 1905, she became the first black woman to graduate from Cornell and the first black woman elected to Phi Beta Kappa. She earned an M.A. in 1919 from the University of Pennsylvania, attended the Sorbonne at the University of Paris, and due to the mentorship of *Crisis* magazine editor W. E. B. DU BOIS, taught summer school at FISK UNIVERSITY in Tennessee, his alma mater.

Because of racism, Fauset could not secure a teaching position in Philadelphia. She worked, instead, as a public school teacher at Douglass High School in Baltimore, Maryland, and taught French at M Street High School in WASHINGTON, D.C., until moving to HARLEM in 1919 to work with DuBois as literary editor of *Crisis.* She also edited and was primary writer for the *BROWNIES' BOOK*, a magazine for black children cofounded by Du Bois. She earned $100 per month in this position.

Throughout her teaching and editorial years, Fauset wrote poems, essays, novels, and short stories that dealt with racism, sexism, and the lives of middle-class blacks. Her early poems were lyrical and feminine: "Rondeau," and "Again It Is September" were published in *Crisis* of April 1912 and September 1917 respectively. During the 1920s *NEW NEGRO* movement, she published many more poems in *Crisis,* including "Oriflamme" (January 1920) and "LaVie C'est LaVie" (July 1922).

She also authored fiction including "Emmy," serialized in the December 1912 and January 1913 issues of *Crisis,* and "Double Trouble" in *Crisis* of August and September 1923.

As literary editor for the *Crisis* magazine and a prolific novelist in her own right, Jessie Redmond Fauset was a leading figure of the Harlem Renaissance. *(Library of Congress, Prints & Photographs Division)*

Fauset's nonfiction, such as "New Literature on the Negro," "Impressions of the Second Pan-African Congress," "What Europe thought of the PAN-AFRICAN CONGRESS," and "The Symbolism of Bert Williams," appeared in *Crisis* during the early 1920s.

As literary editor for the *Crisis,* Fauset actively promoted the writing careers of LANGSTON HUGHES, COUNTEE CULLEN, JEAN TOOMER, and CLAUDE MCKAY. Hughes, the most widely published poet in *Crisis* history, referred to Fauset as a "midwife" of the younger Renaissance writers. In the pages of *Crisis,* Fauset also exposed black America to the literature of French-speaking African and African-Caribbean authors.

Fauset, who experienced difficulty in securing publishers for her work, wrote four major novels. The first was *There Is Confusion* (1922). Though it is rarely noted, CHARLES SPURGEON JOHNSON's March 1924 CIVIC CLUB DINNER was partially designed to celebrate the publication of this book, which was published in 1924. The 1925 *NEW NEGRO* anthology, which was edited by ALAIN LOCKE and resulted from the Civic Club Dinner, included Fauset's *The Gift of Laughter,* an essay on the comedian BERT WILLIAMS.

Fauset was a cultured, genteel woman. She gave parties at her home at 1945 SEVENTH AVENUE and 142nd Street in Harlem where she requested that guests speak in French. The younger writers she nurtured found this stifling at times but were generally as fond of Fauset as they were intimidated by Du Bois. She officially left the *Crisis* in 1926 and returned to NEW YORK CITY in 1927 to teach, until 1944, at DeWitt Clinton High School.

Fauset published her second novel, *Plum Bun: A Novel Without a Moral,* in 1929. Like her previous novel, *Plum Bun* was set in Philadelphia, where before, during, and after the Harlem Renaissance there lived a large, literate, and sophisticated black middle class. *OPPORTUNITY* magazine (September 1929) book reviewer GWENDOLYN BENNETTA BENNETT observed that Fauset, "writes with a quaint charm about Philadelphia. There is a tenderness of touch that Miss Fauset bestows upon the scenes. I found particular pleasure in her apt, yet subdued, picture of Sunday afternoon in a middle-class Negro home. Her descriptions of New York scenes in the latter part of the book never ring with the same fervor that these earlier scenes do."

Also in 1929, Fauset married Herbert Harris, an insurance broker. She published her third novel, *The Chinaberry Tree: A Novel of American Life,* in 1931, and her fourth, *Comedy, American Style,* in 1933.

She and Harris moved to Montclair, New Jersey, in 1940. At about the same time, she stopped writing. When Harris died in 1958, Fauset returned to Philadelphia, where she died on April 30, 1961.

Further Reading

Allen, Carol. *Black Women Intellectuals: Strategies of Nation, Family, and Neighborhood in the Works of Pauline Hopkins, Jessie Fauset and Marita Bonner.* New York: Garland Publishing, 1998.

Gloster, Hugh M. *Negro Voices in American Fiction.* Durham: University of North Carolina Press, 1948.

Jenkins, Wilbert. "Jessie Fauset: A Modern Apostle of Black Racial Pride." *The Zora Neale Hurston Forum 1, no. 1,* 1986, 14–24.

Wall, Cheryl A. *Women of the Harlem Renaissance.* Bloomington, Ind.: Indiana University Press, 1995.

— Sandra L. West

Fax, Elton (1909–) *artist*

Elton Fax was born on October 9, 1909, in Baltimore, Maryland. He was educated at Syracuse University, receiving his B.F.A. in 1931. He taught art at Claflin University in South Carolina from 1935 to 1936, and at the Harlem Arts Center in 1939. Two of his most noted works are *Steelworker* and *Contemporary Black Leaders.* He showed at Baltimore Art Museum in 1939 and the American Negro Exposition in 1940. From 1949 to 1956, he was a chalk-talk artist for the *New York Times* Children's Book Program. "Chalk-talks" are lectures in which the artist illustrates with drawings. Fax also authored an illustrated travelogue called *Through Black Eyes: Journeys of a Black Artist to East Africa and Russia* and has written and/or illustrated other books. The Elton Fax Papers, from 1930 to 1974, are housed with the New York Public Library. His art is part of the collection at Virginia State University in Petersburg.

Further Reading

Driskell, David. *Elton Fax "Drawings from Africa,"* Catalog, Art Gallery, Fisk University, 1968.

Fax, Elton C. *Through Black Eyes: Journeys of a Black artist to East Africa and Russia.* New York: Dodd, Mead, 1970.

— Sandra L. West

Federal Writers' Project (FWP)

Part of FRANKLIN DELANO ROOSEVELT's New Deal efforts to combat unemployment during the GREAT DEPRESSION of the 1930s, the Federal Writers' Project was established by the WORKS PROGRESS ADMINISTRATION (WPA) and employed thousands of writers, researchers, editors, and librarians.

The Federal Writers' Project began in May 1935. It was one of several programs included under the Works Progress Administration's Federal Project Number One. The Federal Arts Project, the Federal Music Project, and the Federal Theater Project were also part of the program.

Henry G. Alsberg, a former writer for *The Nation* magazine, served as national director of the Federal Writers' Project, which had branches in every state. Alsberg's team of national administrators and editors was headquartered in WASHINGTON, D.C. The U.S. Congress oversaw funding for the program and over a period of seven years provided it with more than $27 million. Although it managed at one point to employ close to 7,000 people, only 106 of these were black. *Native Son* author RICHARD NATHANIEL WRIGHT, poet and novelist CLAUDE MCKAY, novelist and folklorist ZORA NEALE HURSTON, novelist RALPH WALDO ELLISON, and poet Robert Hayden all found employment with the project. In addition to writers and editors, the program also employed such white-collar professionals as lawyers, teachers, and ministers.

The Federal Writers' Project established offices for a number of programs, including the compilation of local histories, folklore collections, nature studies, ethnic studies, and a series of travel guides. The *American Guide Series* was one of the project's most influential and enduring accomplishments. Picking up where the *Baedeker* travel guides had left off in 1914, the *American Guide Series* produced maps and narrative guides for each of the then 48 states and American territories, Alaska and Puerto Rico. They also published guidebooks to outstanding communities, central highways, and such major cities as NEW ORLEANS, Los Angeles, San Francisco, and NEW YORK CITY. The guidebook to Washington, D.C., titled *Washington: City and Capitol,* was one of the largest published, with 1,141 pages.

The Historical Records Survey began as a branch of the Federal Writers' Project but eventually developed into an independent office. As its name implies, the Historical Records Survey played a crucial role in the preservation of American history. Directed by Luther Evans, the survey office cataloged and analyzed inventories of state and county records while providing detailed narratives on the value of such records. It also collected a variety of church records, manuscripts, indexes of portraits in public buildings, and bibliographies of texts on history and literature.

The Folklore Collections department of the Federal Writers' Project maintained a number of operations designed to document the past and contemporary lives of Americans. Heading the department were John A. Lomax, Benjamin A. Botkin, and Morton Royce. Their collection of "life histories" provided detailed accounts of life during the Great Depression in both rural and urban areas. While recording the many ways that people coped with the Great Depression, the life histories also documented such everyday customs as marriage ceremonies, holiday celebrations, farming techniques, recreation, and funeral customs. Moreover, they placed on file collections of everyday folk expressions, folk songs, stories, and traditional beliefs.

Another branch of the Folklore Collections department was the Office of Negro Affairs, headed by poet and educator STERLING ALLEN BROWN. Between 1935 and 1939, this division interviewed more than 2,000 former slaves to produce one of the most substantial records available on the experience of African Americans during slavery. The validity of these records is sometimes held in question because many of those interviewing the former slaves were whites who sometimes wrote their own interpretations of what the subjects were saying rather than what they in fact had said. Nevertheless, the collected narratives provide rare insight into the daily lives of American slaves, noting the clothes they wore, their diets, housing, and family lives. During the 1970s, George P. Rawlins published a comprehensive 41-volume set of the narratives titled *The American Slave: A Composite Autobiography.*

The advent of World War II forced Congress to halt funding for the Federal Writers' Project in October 1939. Alsberg resigned from his position as national director, and John D. Newsome took over as individual states began to provide funding for the project. Following the bombing of Pearl Harbor in 1941, the Federal Writers' Project was absorbed into the Writers Unit of the War Services Division. In that capacity, writers produced recreational guides for military personnel. In 1943, the program ended completely along with all others associated with the Works Progress Administration.

Today the Library of Congress houses some 300,000 field reports, oral testimonies, collected correspondences, graphs, charts, memoranda, manuscripts, and field notes compiled by its writers. Intended from the beginning to provide future generations with a source of materials that they might use for creative reconstructions of the past, the work is used by many modern writers, scholars, and educators for precisely that purpose.

Further Reading

Baker, Ronald L. *Homeless, Friendless, and Penniless: The WPA Interviews with Former Slaves Living in Indiana.* Bloomington: Indiana University Press, 2000.

Mangione, Jesse. *The Dream and the Deal: The Federal Writers' Project, 1935 to 1943.* Syracuse, N.Y.: Syracuse University Press, 1996.

— Aberjhani

Fetchit, Stepin (Lincoln Theodore Monroe Andrew Perry) (1902–1985) *actor*

Stepin Fetchit was Hollywood's first black actor to receive a studio contract along with feature billing for his movies.

Fetchit was born Lincoln Theodore Monroe Andrew Perry on May 30, 1902, in Key West, Florida. Until he was 12, Fetchit attended a Catholic boarding school. He left to work in show business and joined the *Royal American Shows' Plantation Revues.* Teaming up with a partner named Ed Lee, the two entertainers formed a comic duo and called themselves "Step and Fetch It: Two Dancing Fools from Dixie." When the partnership dissolved, Fetchit retained the stage name for himself and became a popular performer on the THEATER OWNERS BOOKING AGENCY (TOBA) circuit.

When a talent scout for Fox Pictures caught Fetchit's act, he offered him a contract with the movie studio. While many actors had to give up their profession during the GREAT DEPRESSION, Fetchit rose from obscurity to the status of a bona fide star with at least 30 movies to his credit between 1927 and 1939. He would perform in more than 40 before the end of his career. Fetchit started out in such films as *In Old Kentucky* (1927) and *The Ghost Talks* (1929). He drew the attention of producers and critics alike with his performance as a slave named Gummy in the 1929 movie *Hearts in Dixie.* Fetchit went on to star as Joe in the original 1929 movie version of *Show Boat.*

During the 1930s, Fetchit starred in films opposite some of Hollywood's biggest white stars. In 1934, he shared the screen with Spencer Tracy in *Marie Galante.* In the same year he performed with the classic Hollywood child actress Shirley Temple in *Stand Up and Cheer.* He worked with Temple again in the 1939 movie *Dimples.* Fetchit also teamed up with the celebrated humorist and ZIEGFELD FOLLIES star Will Rogers for a series of movies during the mid-1930s: *Judge Priest, David Harum, The County Chairman,* and *Steamboat 'Round the Bend.*

Although Fetchit was clearly triumphant as an individual performer, his career was marked by a great deal of controversy. At one point, Fox Pictures released him from his contract on charges basically amounting to a lack of professional conduct only to re-sign him in a fanfare of publicity celebrating his return. Critics applauded Fetchit as a performing artist for his impeccable timing, precise choreography, and ability to endow the image of a stereotypical minstrel "coon" with human depth and vulnerability. The fact that nearly every role Fetchit played was that of a quintessential coon raised protest from such organizations as the NATIONAL URBAN LEAGUE (NUL) and the NATIONAL ASSOCIATION FOR THE ADVANCEMENT OF COLORED PEOPLE (NAACP). In these roles, Fetchit generally played a slave or servant with minimal intelligence, dubious moral discretion, and lacking in any apparent sense of dignity or self-respect. In nearly every film his eyes bulged, he spoke in broken monosyllables, and he walked with a lazy dragging shuffle. Moreover, his character routinely suffered both verbal and physical abuse at the hands and feet of whites.

Yet for all of the degradation Fetchit tolerated on-screen, off-screen he reportedly lived in a manner glamorous and opulent enough to match, or even surpass, that of many of his white counterparts. With a fleet of cars, clothing imported from around the world, Asian servants, and a half dozen houses, he lived at the opposite extreme of the characters he played. This extravagant lifestyle led him to file for bankruptcy with debts totaling $4 million while he had less than $200 in the bank.

Fetchit's popularity began to wane in the late 1930s, and he all but disappeared during the 1940s, at that time appearing in a few all-black films without the kind of distribution, high profiling, or high salaries he had commanded in Hollywood. In 1952, he again shared billing with a major actor, starring in *Bend of the River* with James Stewart. And in 1954, he was cast in *The Sun Shines Bright.* Although the public seemed to be rejecting Fetchit, it ironically embraced a number of imitators who owed their film careers largely to Fetchit's pioneering performances. Actor Willie Best adopted the pseudonym Sleep 'n' Eat to match the descriptive Stepin Fetchit. Mantan Moreland extended the image of the wide-eyed terrified Negro through a series of 1940s *Charlie Chan* movies.

A 1968 television documentary titled *Black History: Lost, Stolen, or Strayed,* narrated by Bill Cosby, summed up Fetchit's career as one that had been used to perpetuate negative stereotypes of African Americans and thus had stalled racial progress. Fetchit countered that assessment with the observation that his work had helped others establish careers in Hollywood and made it possible for images of African Americans to evolve in Hollywood films.

Among Fetchit's last films were *Amazing Grace,* the 1974 tribute to MOMS MABLEY, and *The Dog Who Saved Hollywood,* in 1976. He died in Woodland Hills, California, on November 19, 1985.

Further Reading

Bogle, Donald. *Toms, Coons, Mulattoes, Mammies, and Bucks: An Interpretative History of Blacks in American Films.* New York: The Continuum Publishing Company, 1997.

Guerrero, Ed. *Framing Blackness: The African American Images in Film.* Philadelphia: Temple University Press, 1993.

— Aberjhani

Fire!!: A Quarterly Devoted to the Younger Negro Artists

Fire!!: A Quarterly Devoted to the Younger Negro Artists was an avant-garde magazine edited and published in 1926 by Harlem Renaissance novelist and playwright WALLACE THURMAN.

Discontented with the staid mandate of the *NEW NEGRO* movement, a group of young writers decided to publish an exotic literary quarterly as an alternative to such established black publications as *CRISIS: A RECORD OF THE DARKER RACES*, the official publication of the NATIONAL ASSOCIATION FOR THE ADVANCEMENT OF COLORED PEOPLE (NAACP); *OPPORTUNITY* magazine, published by the NATIONAL URBAN LEAGUE; and the *MESSENGER*, produced by labor leader A. PHILIP RANDOLPH.

It is uncertain whether poet LANGSTON HUGHES or writer and illustrator RICHARD BRUCE NUGENT originally proposed the publication of *Fire!!* Hughes, in his autobiography, *The Big Sea,* implies that the event was a group decision among ZORA NEALE HURSTON, AARON DOUGLAS, John P. Davis, Nugent, GWENDOLYN BENNETTA BENNETT, himself, and Thurman. The magazine's title, however, was likely derived from a line in a Hughes poem that appeared in the introductory pages of the journal: "Fy-ah (Fire) gonna burn ma soul!" Hughes noted that the word *fire* as a journal title was critical: "the idea being that it would burn up a lot of the old dead, conventional Negro-white ideas of the past, *épater le bourgeois* into a realization of the existence of the younger Negro writers and artists, and provide us with an outlet for publication not available in the limited pages of the small Negro magazines then existing, the *Crisis, Opportunity,* and the *Messenger*—the first two being house organs of interracial organizations, and the latter being God knows what."

Thurman, fresh from an editing position at the *Messenger,* assumed editorial responsibilities for *Fire!!* Financial backers who also served as associate editors were Hughes, Nugent, Davis, and Bennett. Another financial backer was visual artist Douglas, called "a pioneering Africanist" by Harlem Renaissance leader ALAIN LOCKE. Each backer promised to donate $50 to the start-up publication costs, but most did not honor their commitment. *Fire!!*, therefore, started out in debt. PATRONS who later donated money to help settle its cost included writer ARTHUR HUFF FAUSET, brother of JESSIE REDMOND FAUSET and coeditor of *Black Opals* literary journal in PHILADELPHIA, and CARL VAN VECHTEN, the author of *NIGGER HEAVEN.*

Original office space for the magazine was at 17 Gay Street in the Greenwich Village section of NEW YORK CITY. Due to its publishers financial difficulties, *Fire!!* headquarters moved into Thurman's HARLEM apartment in a rent-free building at 267

Fire!!, published and edited by a group of the Harlem Renaissance's younger writers and artists, represented an attempt on their behalf to inject into the movement more individual creativity and less political propaganda. *(Carrington Papers, Moorland-Spingarn Research Center, Howard University)*

West 136th Street. The building, "christened" NIGGERATI MANOR by novelist and anthropologist Hurston, was then home for several indigent but prolific artists: Hurston, Nugent, and Hughes among them.

The interior walls of Niggerati Manor were red and black, and Douglas, later an acclaimed muralist, used these same colors for the cover of *Fire!!* Thurman obtained printing on credit from the upscale black printing business, Service Bell. The magazine cost $1,000 to produce. At one dollar per issue, and in the New Negro era, the antiestablishment audience *Fire!!* required for survival was not plentiful or prosperous enough.

Fire!! included short stories, a play, and poetry, with many contributions seemingly more coarse and vulgar than the next. "Cordelia the Crude," a story written by Thurman, about a 15-year-old prostitute, provided the basis for Thurman's 1929 Broadway play, *Harlem.* Nugent contributed "Smoke, Lilies and Jade, A Novel, Part I," about a hallucinatory experience under the opium drug. A short story, "Wedding Day," by Bennett, examined a black boxer's hatred for white people. A play by Hurston, called *Color Struck,* included a CAKEWALK dance contest. Poetry submissions included "Elevator Boy" by Hughes; "From the Dark Tower" by COUNTEE CULLEN; "Southern Road" by Helene Johnson; "Length of Moon" by ARNA BONTEMPS; "The Death Bed" by WILLIAM WARING CUNEY; "Streets" by Lewis Alexander; and "Jungle Taste" by Edward Silvera.

Reviews of the magazine were largely unsupportive. Two mainstream publications, *Bookman* and *Saturday Review of Literature,* duly and without enthusiasm noted its debut. *Crisis* editor W. E. B. DU BOIS expressed outrage even as he tried to give support to the writers' efforts. *The Baltimore Afro-American* expressed extreme disgust: "I have just tossed the first issue of *Fire* into the fire," the *Afro* reviewer wrote. Cullen was criticized for obscuring beautiful poetic thought in "superfluous sentences," and Douglas for spoiling "three perfectly good pages and a cover with his pen and ink hudge pudge [sic]." Literary critic BENJAMIN GRIFFITH BRAWLEY said: "If Uncle Sam ever finds out about it, it will be debarred from the mails."

Hundreds of unsold copies were burned in an accidental apartment fire. Thurman spent four years paying the printing bills for the magazine, and *Fire!!*—born November 1926 at Niggerati Manor—never saw a second edition.

Further Reading

Hughes, Langston. *The Big Sea.* New York: Hill & Wang, 1995.

Lewis, David Levering. *When Harlem Was in Vogue.* New York: Vintage Books, 1982.

Watson, Steven. *The Harlem Renaissance: Hub of African-American Culture, 1920–1930.* New York: Pantheon Books, 1995.

— Sandra L. West

Fisher, Rudolph (Rudolph John Chauncey Fisher)

(1897–1934) *writer*

Trained as a physician, Rudolph Fisher won acclaim as one of the most versatile and brilliant of the Harlem Renaissance writers, authoring stories and novels that examined the comical as well as the tragic aspects of life in HARLEM.

Rudolph John Chauncey Fisher was born on May 9, 1897, in WASHINGTON, D.C. His father was Rev. John Wesley Fisher and his mother Glendora Williamson Fisher. His siblings were a brother named Joseph and a sister named Pearl. The Fisher family moved to NEW YORK CITY in 1903. When Rev. Fisher accepted a pastorate in Rhode Island, they moved to Providence in 1905.

Rudolph Fisher grew up in Providence and graduated from Classical High School with honors. Attending Brown University, he was a well-rounded student, earning awards in German studies, oratory, and writing. He was also elected to the Phi Beta Kappa honorary society. He graduated from Brown with honors in 1919 and earned a master's degree in biology from the university in 1920. He graduated summa cum laude from HOWARD UNIVERSITY Medical School in 1924. He then interned at Freedmen's Hospital and, from 1925 to 1927, continued his medical studies at Columbia University's College of Physicians and Surgeons under a research fellowship.

Fisher obtained a position working in the X-ray division of the New York Department of Health. In 1924, he married Jane Ryder, a teacher. They had one son, Hugh, born in 1926.

As would any physician, Fisher wrote scientific articles, but he also arranged musical scores for spirituals sung by PAUL ROBESON and attended literary parties given by arts patron REGINA ANDREWS with poet LANGSTON HUGHES. While still a medical school senior, he wrote his first short story, "The City of Refuge." Published in the *Atlantic Monthly* (February 1925), it explored the plight of "green" southern immigrants who met with disaster in northern cities. The story was anthologized in *Best Short Stories in 1925, American Negro Short Stories* (1966), and *Black Literature in America* (1971).

Atlantic Monthly also accepted Fisher's story "Ringtail" for its May 1925 issue. The serialized "High Yaller" debuted in *CRISIS: A RECORD OF THE DARKER RACES* in November 1925 and was anthologized in *Cavalcade: Negro American Writing From 1760 to the Present* (1971). Concerning light-skinned blacks antagonized in their own communities, "High Yaller" won *Crisis* magazine's Amy Spingarn Award in 1925.

Atlantic Monthly, which had published essays by W. E. B. DU BOIS before they were collected into a single volume for *THE SOULS OF BLACK FOLK,* continued to feature Fisher's work in 1927. Fisher's "The Promised Land," a story of family divisiveness, and "Blades of Steel," a picture of the cutthroat world of Harlem gamblers, appeared in the magazine in January and August. His stories "The Backslider" and "Fire by Night" were published in *McClure's* (August and December 1927). "Blades of Steel" was included in *Anthology of American Negro Literature* (1929).

Fisher wrote his first novel, *The Walls of Jericho,* in 1928. *The Walls of Jericho* ushered in a period in which fiction cut into the attention that was, up to this time, given to poetry. ALAIN LOCKE, editor of *The New Negro* (1925), wrote in *OPPORTUNITY* (January 1929) that Fisher's novel is notable for its "art of social analysis." It was also, many observed, notable for its comic portrayal of life in Harlem.

During the 1930s, Fisher wrote "Common Meter" for the *Baltimore Afro-American* (February 1930) and "Miss Cynthie" for *Story* magazine (June 1933). The latter has been republished in a variety of anthologies, including *Dark Symphony: Negro Literature in America* (1968).

In 1932, Fisher published his second novel, *The Conjure-Man Dies: A Mystery Tale of Dark Harlem,* widely considered as the first black mystery novel ever written. It was adapted for the stage by Fisher prior to his death and performed by the Federal Theater Project's Negro Union in March and April 1936, at Harlem's LAFAYETTE THEATRE as a project of the WORKS PROGRESS ADMINISTRATION (WPA). The Cleveland Federal Theatre also produced the play in 1936, and the Gilpin Players at KARAMU HOUSE theater staged it in 1938.

Rudolph Fisher died on December 26, 1934, after three surgeries for a stomach disorder caused by the X rays he worked with. A first lieutenant in the reserve medical corps of the historical 369th regiment, the HARLEM HELLFIGHTERS, the literary medical doctor was given a military funeral.

In the early 21st century, Rudolph Fisher's work was generating a renaissance all its own. Almost 70 years after his death, and since his stories first appeared in the 1920s and 1930s in *Atlantic Monthly, Story* magazine, the *Crisis,* and numerous anthologies, a new generation of literary scholars began to reevaluate and promote his stories and novels. In addition, his adaptation of *The Conjure Man Dies* was scheduled for a revival at Woodie King's New Federal Theatre in New York City.

Further Reading

Andrews, William L., ed. *Classic Fiction of the Harlem Renaissance.* New York: Oxford University Press, 1994.

Bone, Robert A. *The Negro Novel in America.* New Haven, Conn.: Yale University Press, 1965.

Harper, Phillip Brian. "Passing for What? Racial Masquerade and the Demands of Upward Mobility." *Callaloo* 21, no. 2 (1998): 381–397.

Tignor, Eleanor Q. "Rudolph Fisher, Harlem Novelist." *Langston Hughes Review* 1, no. 2 (1982): 13–22.

— Sandra L. West

Fisk Jubilee Singers (1867–1913) *performance artists*
In the course of helping to raise operating funds for FISK UNIVERSITY, the Fisk Jubilee Singers introduced the world to African-American sacred music and to the plight of the newly emancipated slave.

The Fisk Jubilee Singers were a group of emancipated slaves seeking formal education. All had registered for classes at the new university in Tennessee and had become friends in the school choir under the direction of Charles L. White. Fisk was composed of several one-story frame buildings. It opened in 1866–1867 and was in dire financial straits. At the request of White, university treasurer and music instructor, the choir of 1867 organized into the Fisk Jubilee Singers and, on October 6, 1871, embarked upon a challenging international and domestic tour to secure $20,000 for the school.

The original members of the Jubilee Singers were Hinton D. Alexander, Maggie Carnes, Isaac P. Dickerson, Georgia Gordon, Benjamin M. Holmes, Jennie Jackson, Julie Jackson, Mabel Lewis, Frederick J. Loudin, Maggie Porter, America W. Robinson, Thomas Rutling, Ella Sheppard, Minnie Tate, Benjamin W. Thomas, and Edmund Watkins. ROLAND HAYES performed with the chorus during one of their later domestic tours.

The determined musical director, White carried his singers on an extensive and tiring tour. They sang all over the United States and the world, touring as far as England and Scotland, to meet their financial goal. Most of the singers became so exhausted they could not return to academia. Voices were forfeited, health deteriorated, and lives were lost on the years-long journey. Their supreme sacrifice, however, secured Fisk's future.

In addition to achieving their monetary goal, the singers introduced Europe to the plight of the African American through songs of sorrow and songs of joyful liberation, including "Nobody Knows the Trouble I See, Lord!" "Didn't My Lord Deliver Daniel," "Many Thousand Gone," "Deep River," and "Steal Away." And they ushered in an era of traveling African-American choirs such as the HALL JOHNSON Negro Choir. Jubilee Hall, named in their honor, was built on the university's campus in 1875.

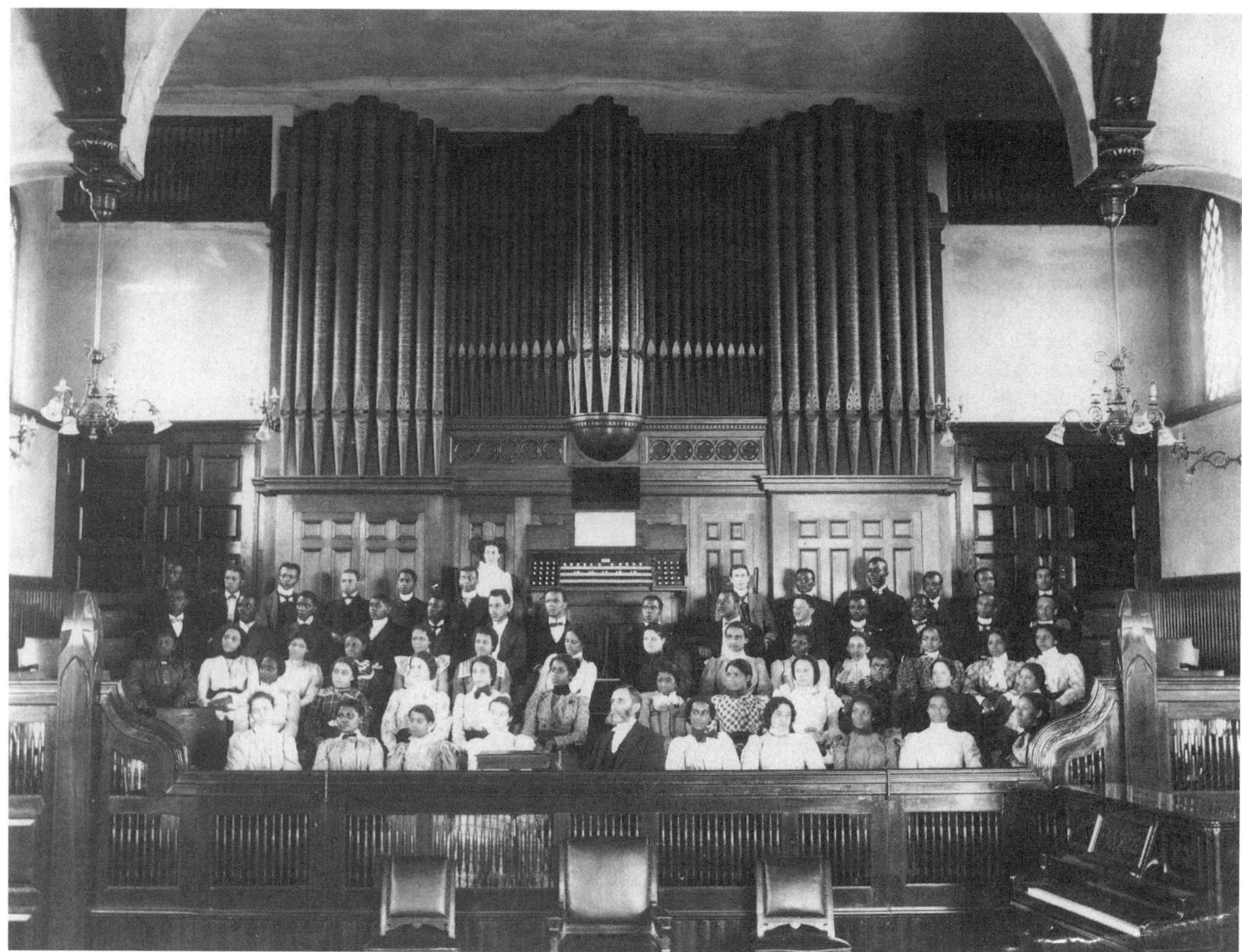

Founded in Nashville, Tennessee, in 1865, Fisk University stands as one of the most prestigious traditionally black colleges in the United States. Pictured here is its choir (around 1899). *(Library of Congress, Prints & Photographs Division [LC-USZ62-49404])*

The Jubilee Singers remain part of Fisk's contemporary history.

Further Reading

Favor, J. Martin. *Authentic Blackness: The Folk in the New Negro Renaissance.* Durham, N.C.: Duke University Press, 1999.

Ward, Andrew. *Dark Midnight When I Rise: The Story of Jubilee Singers Who Introduced the World to the Music of Black America.* New York: Farrar, Straus & Giroux, 2000.

— Sandra L. West

Fisk University

One of the few nonvocational educational institutions created for African Americans in the 1800s, Fisk University in Nashville, Tennessee, is home to the renowned FISK JUBILEE SINGERS and alma mater to some of the most accomplished participants in the Harlem Renaissance.

Purchased for $16,000, Fisk University opened in January 1866 and was chartered in 1867. It was founded by the abolitionist American Missionary Association (AMA) and the Western Freedmen's Aid Commission. The university was named for General Clinton B. Fisk of the Freedmen's Bureau in Tennessee.

The university is home of the Fisk Jubilee Singers, whose incredible story honors one of the oldest buildings on campus, Jubilee Hall. Their saga of touring to raise funds for Fisk was told in *The Story of the Jubilee Singers; With Their Songs.* In addition to Jubilee Hall, another early building is Carnegie Library, designed by Moses McKissak in 1908. McKissak was an African-American architect whose family established a tradition of practicing architecture in Tennessee.

Fisk University was founded upon the premise that "there were no inherent racial differences in educational potential." As such, the curriculum was strictly academic and rigorous. Student enrollment its first year numbered one thousand. Most were former slaves who had to begin academic work on an elementary level. It took some of them 10 years to complete both the primary and collegiate courses. Fisk's first graduating class was in 1875.

Among its notable graduates are W. E. B. DU BOIS, cofounder of the NATIONAL ASSOCIATION FOR THE ADVANCEMENT OF COLORED PEOPLE (NAACP) and author of the *SOULS OF BLACK FOLK*, and JAMES WELDON JOHNSON, coauthor of the song referred to as the Negro National Anthem, "LIFT EVERY VOICE AND SING." The founder of Tuskegee Institute, BOOKER TALIAFERRO WASHINGTON, was a staunch advocate of vocational education yet sent his daughter to Fisk to study Latin and Greek. The school was also alma mater to Washington's wife. Contemporary graduates include poet Nikki Giovanni and historian John Hope Franklin.

Following his departure from the NATIONAL URBAN LEAGUE (NUL) and his position as editor of *Opportunity* magazine in 1928, CHARLES SPURGEON JOHNSON joined Fisk as chair of its social sciences department. Johnson, one of the "fathers" of the Harlem Renaissance, became in 1947 the university's first black president. Similarly, after his departure from the NAACP, James Weldon Johnson taught English at Fisk beginning in 1931. Muralist AARON DOUGLAS started his career as an art professor at Fisk in 1937.

Moreover, distinguished Harlem Renaissance leaders became the first generation of renowned professors at black universities around the country, especially in the previously underserved area of fine art. Writer ARNA BONTEMPS *(God Sends Sunday)*, literary and historical contributor to the Harlem and CHICAGO renaissance periods, was appointed head librarian at Fisk. Bontemps established the school's CARL VAN VECHTEN collection and secured valuable manuscripts, books, and art that are still available to researchers today.

Further Reading

Richardson, Joe M. *A History of Fisk University, 1865–1946.* Tuscaloosa: University of Alabama Press, 2002.

Savage, Beth L., ed. *African American Historic Places.* Washington, D.C.: The Preservation Press, 1994.

— Sandra L. West

folk art

Whereas painted historical scenes of the African-American past, African-inspired sculpture, and ethnic murals were almost mandated art forms for professional artists during the Harlem Renaissance, a number of significant folk artists produced noteworthy work during the 1930s. Some of the major talents

Jubilee Hall, the front of which is viewed here from the south, was named for the famous Jubilee Singers of Fisk University, who toured the world to raise funds for the school. *(Library of Congress, Prints & Photographs Division, [HABS, TENN, 19-NASH, 7A-1])*

among them were WILLIAM EDMONDSON, LESLIE GARLAND BOLLING, and HORACE PIPPIN.

Folk art emerged predominately from the work of slaves, and it includes such forms as wood carving, grave decoration, quilting, pottery, and iron works. Thus, folk artists were not, in the main, products of urban areas. They were born in and created their work in states such as Georgia, Alabama, Louisiana, and Mississippi. Folk artist/sculptor William Edmondson, for example, was born near Nashville, Tennessee, and lived there all of his life.

One definition of folk art offered by art critic Regenia A. Perry describes it as, "primitive, untutored, outsider, isolate, visionary, mystic, self-taught . . . created by artists who have little or no artistic training and work outside mainstream art movements." The fundamental features of folk art include "flatness of form, a tendency toward overall surface patterning, tipped-up perspective, inaccurate scale relationships, incorrect anatomical proportioning, drawing subjects from memory rather than preliminary sketches, and a bold use of unmixed colors."

Because folk artists are "untutored" by definition, they usually had other types of employment, mostly menial labor, during their early years and entered their creative phases late in life. Or they may have been injured on a job and turned to the creation of art in order to spend their time constructively and develop a way to express themselves. Thus, several African-American folk artists were "discovered" during what would be termed as retirement years, or when they were disabled. One case in point is Mose Tolliver, born in 1919 in Montgomery, Alabama. Immobilized due to a job-related accident, Tolliver began to paint in 1973 at the age of 54. Often at that point of life, the formally educated visual artist might be on the second tier of their career, teaching or chairing an academic art department at a college, as in the case of muralist AARON DOUGLAS, in addition to producing his or her own art work.

The tools of the artistic trade in other genres may be sable brushes and stretched canvas, but the folk artist tended to make his or her own tools or to use very simple instruments already available from nature, junkyards, garbage cans, or other unlikely places. Leslie Garland Bolling carved small images such as *A Workman* (1936) from pieces of a poplar tree with a common pocketknife. Tolliver utilized metal rings from containers of beer and soda instead of conventional, "store-bought" picture hangers. Minnie Evans (1890–1987) used wax crayons to create landscapes and Jimmie Lee Suddoth, born 1918 in Alabama, mixed sugar and mud to manufacture his own paint.

The folk artist also tended to have a strong religious bent. Sister Gertrude Morgan (1900–1980) of Louisiana continuously painted wedding ceremony scenes that depicted herself and God. She painted on mayonnaise jars, window shades, and other unlikely canvases. One of Edmondson's most renowned pieces is *Preacher* (1930s). The majority of folk art themes, however, are of everyday people, events, and symbols. Edmondson carved doves, mermaids, and images of athletes such as boxer Jack Johnson from limestone. Horace Pippin, who started his artistic career after he was disabled in the military, painted a domestic scene of a family playing a game in *Domino Players* (1943). Pippin worked in oils but painted on plain composition board. Bolling's most celebrated output was the *Days of the Week* series, depicting *Aunt Monday* washing clothes, *Sister Tuesday* completing her ironing task, and so on.

A significant portion of African-American folk art was documented by the WORKS PROGRESS ADMINISTRATION (WPA) during the 1930s and 1940s.

Further Reading

Livingston, Jane, and John Beardsley. *Black Folk Art in America, 1930–1980.* Jackson: University Press of Mississippi for the Corcoran Gallery of Art, Jackson and the Center for the Study of Southern Culture, 1982.

Perry, Regenia. "Contemporary African American Folk Art: An Overview." *International Review of African American Art* 11, no. 1, 1993.

— Sandra L. West

folk literature

Folk literature, including folktales, is primarily considered that of the oral tradition but refers equally to written text and, during the Harlem Renaissance, played a major role in works by writers like JAMES WELDON JOHNSON, JEAN TOOMER, and ZORA NEALE HURSTON.

In the oral tradition of folk literature, extravagant stories may be handed down from generation to generation or through the lyrics and legends found in blues songs. In the written tradition, stories, novels, and plays draw upon peasant scenes, the ways of common folk, indigenous speech patterns, or religious belief systems.

In *Cane* (1923), hailed as the first fictional masterpiece of the Harlem Renaissance, Jean Toomer included songs transcribed from the actual speech patterns of the black peasantry in Sparta, Georgia. James Weldon Johnson wrote *God's Trombones: Seven Negro Sermons in Verse* (1927), based on sermons inspired by the King James Bible and delivered in the poetic, metaphorical, emotional oratory of the old-time folk preacher. Zora Neale Hurston drew upon the folk tradition of her native Eatonville, Florida, when she wrote *Their Eyes Were Watching God* (1937). In that folk culture, it was tradition for the town's men to gather on the porch of the general store and tell stories, often very tall stories, about their many exploits.

In Marc Connelly's play and film *THE GREEN PASTURES* (1930), black people sang in celestial choirs, held a fish fry in Heaven, and followed a black preacher named "De Lawd." Though imaginary, these scenes pulled on the myths, traditions, and speech patterns of the African-American community. For instance, the use of the phrase "De Lawd" instead of "The Lord" is a display of the valid dialect referred to as Black English. Likewise, Dubose Heyward's play *Porgy* (1927), on which the folk opera *PORGY AND BESS* was later based, utilized the language of the Gullah people of South Carolina and Georgia's coastal islands. Gullah is a blend of African languages and Southern dialect that resembles Caribbean patterns of language.

Folk literature colorfully displays a "sighting" of African-American culture through sayings, dances, community customs and the like, though a portion of the literature, such as *The Green Pastures,* was obviously written to entertain and amuse white people who bemusingly thought the life of the African-American peasantry to be "quaint." On the whole, however, exceptional and important black folk literature constitutes a substantial portion of the greater body of black literature produced during the Harlem Renaissance.

Further Reading

Valade, Roger M., III. *The Essential Black Literature Guide.* Detroit: Visible Ink, 1996. Published in Association with the Schomburg Center for Research in Black Culture.

Gates, Henry Louis, Jr., ed. *The Norton Anthology of African American Literature* New York: W. W. Norton, 1997.

— Sandra L. West

Freelon, Allan Randall (1895–1960) *painter*

Allan Randall Freelon, one of the few traditionalist painters of the Harlem Renaissance, edited the literary magazine *Black Opals* and held exhibitions with the HARMON FOUNDATION.

Allan Freelon was born in 1895 in PHILADELPHIA. Awarded a scholarship in approximately 1912, Freelon attended and graduated from the Pennsylvania Museum and School of Industrial Art. He went on to receive a master's degree in fine art from the Tyler School at Temple University in Philadelphia.

Freelon's entire work history was with the Philadelphia Board of Education. He was an instructor in 1919 and, by 1922, became art supervisor for elementary and secondary education.

Freelon was a member of the Philadelphia artists and writers who were compliant with the mandates of the *NEW NEGRO* movement; however, ALAIN LOCKE, editor of the *The New Negro Anthology (1925)* and a reformer who advocated strong social content in the work of black artists, labeled Freelon a traditionalist. It was not until 1935, at the Arthur U. Newton Galleries in NEW YORK CITY, that Freelon broke with traditionalism and submitted to the themed exhibit an arresting drawing entitled "Art Commentary on Lynching." Before the widely publicized exhibit on LYNCHING, Freelon was a serene painter of traditional harbor scenes. He painted the harbor at Gloucester, Massachusetts, and exhibited various harbor scenes in the Harmon Foundation art shows of 1928 and 1931.

A member of Philadelphia's black intellectual elite, Freelon edited a journal, *Black Opals,* that was affiliated with a literary society of the same name. Members of the *Black Opals* family included ARTHUR HUFF FAUSET and Nellie Rathborne Bright.

Freelon exhibited throughout his career—from Atlanta University in 1934 to HOWARD UNIVERSITY in 1940—and remained art supervisor with the Philadelphia Board of Education until his retirement. He died in 1960.

Further Reading

Bailey, David A., and Paul Gilroy. *Rhapsodies in Black: Art of the Harlem Renaissance.* Berkeley: University of California Press, 1977.

Reynolds, Gary A., and Beryl J. Wright. *Against the Odds: African-American Artists and the Harmon Foundation.* Newark: The Newark Museum, New Jersey, 1989.

— Sandra L. West

Frogs, The

A group of African-American professional performing artists, The Frogs were founded in HARLEM in 1908 to provide support for each other's work and that of emerging black performers.

The founding members of The Frogs were comedian GEORGE WALKER, elected president of the organization; composer and performer JOHN ROSAMOND JOHNSON, vice president; director and librettist Jesse A. Shipp, treasurer; lyricist Cecil Mack, secretary; songwriter ALEXANDER ROGERS, historian; actor Tom Brown, house committee chairman; comic and dancer BERT WILLIAMS, art committee; playwright and comic Bob Cole, art committee; performer Samuel Corker, Jr., auditing committee; musician James Reese Europe, librarian; and critic and promoter Lester A. Walton (of the *NEW YORK AGE*) house committee.

Beneath a photograph of The Frogs in *Black Magic,* a pictorial history of blacks in the performing arts, LANGSTON HUGHES and Milton Meltzer describe them as "most of the best black talent" in show business at the time.

The Frogs took their name from Greek drama and mythology, borrowing from a fable by Aesop and a play by Aristophanes in which the comic writer satirized the more cynical playwright, Euripides. While not overtly political, the name implies a rejection of the more somber accommodationist teachings of Tuskegee Institute founder BOOKER TALIAFERRO WASHINGTON in favor of the more creative spirit that would characterize the *NEW NEGRO* movement in the following decades.

Aside from their assistance to struggling black entertainers and each other, The Frogs annually raised funds for a variety of charities by hosting a vaudeville and social dance called "The Frolic of the Frogs" at the Manhattan Casino. The affair cost 50¢ to enter, started late in the evening, and lasted throughout the night. The organization's famed members promenaded around the dance floor for their guests, acknowledged women with various courtesies, and presented awards to those dressed in costumes best representing the spirit of the occasion. In 1913, the event spawned a separate fund-raising revue called *The Frog Follies,* which was produced by Rosamond Johnson, James Reese Europe, and WILL MARION COOK.

The Frogs' charitable gestures, as well as its members' fame, made them well known in Harlem, and they sponsored events in the community up until the mid-1920s. Much of the organization's vitality and drive were lost with the deaths of founding members George Walker, Bob Cole, James Reese Europe, and Bert Williams.

Further Reading

Hill, Anthony D. *Pages from the Harlem Renaissance: A Chronicle of Performance.* New York: Peter Lang Publishing, 1996.

Peterson, Bernard L., Jr. *The African American Theatre Directory, 1816–1960.* Westport, Conn.: Greenwood Press, 1997.

— Aberjhani

Fuller, Meta Vaux Warrick (1877–1968) *sculptor*

Sculptor Meta Vaux Warrick Fuller was a recluse whose art drew heavily on African themes and folktales and expressed the emotions of deep anguish and solitude that characterized her life.

Meta Vaux Warrick was born in PHILADELPHIA, Pennsylvania, on June 9, 1877. Her mother, Emma Jones Warrick, was a beautician. Her father, William H. Warrick, was a barber and caterer.

Warrick's unusual middle name came from one of her mother's beauty salon customers. Mrs. Vaux, an upper-class white woman, was the daughter of Senator Richard Vaux and suggested that the latest Warrick child be named after her family. With middle-class domestic surroundings and the name of a well-heeled political white family, Meta Vaux Warrick was groomed to be a proper, sheltered, Victorian gentlewoman.

Her art education and art influences began at home. Her older sister, who later became a beautician like her mother, had an interest in art and kept clay that Meta was able to play with. Her brother and grandfather entertained and fascinated her with endless horror stories. These influences partly shaped her sculpture as she eventually progressed into an internationally trained artist known as "the sculptor of horrors."

At age 18, Warrick won a three-year scholarship to the Pennsylvania Museum and School for Industrial Art. In 1898, her sculpture, *Procession of the Arts and Crafts,* won the school's George K. Crozier Prize. She graduated in 1899 with honors.

After gradation, she sailed to PARIS, France, to study. There, Warrick ran head-on into racial discrimination at the American Women's Club, where even though she had made reservations she was refused lodging. Painter HENRY OSSAWA TANNER, a family friend, found lodging for her and introduced her to his circle of friends.

In Paris, Warrick studied at the Academie Colaross, at the Ecole des Beaux Arts, and with figure painter Raphael Collin. In 1902, she exhibited sculpture at S. Bing's L'Art Nouveau and met and studied with master sculptor Auguste Rodin. Of her plaster sketch entitled *Man Eating His Heart,* Rodin remarked, "My child, you are a sculptor; you have the sense of form in your fingers." Another friend met in Paris, and one who evolved into a lifelong confidant, was intellectual W. E. B. DU BOIS, later noted for his editorship of the magazine *CRISIS: A RECORD OF THE DARKER RACES.* Du Bois, a Pan-Africanist, encouraged Warrick to utilize African and African-American themes in her work. In 1903, just before Warrick returned to the United States, two of her works, *The Wretched* and *The Impenitent Thief,* exhibited at the Salon in Paris.

When Warrick returned to Philadelphia in 1903, gallery dealers rejected her work because of her race and because, they said, it was "domestic." Though private galleries turned her down, the federal government commissioned her to do a sculpture that depicted black progress for the Jamestown Centennial Exhibition, and she exhibited at the Pennsylvania Academy of Fine Arts in 1906.

In 1907, Warrick married Dr. Solomon Carter Fuller. Of Liberian birth, Dr. Fuller became the first black psychiatrist in the world. When they married, he was on staff in the pathology department at Westboro State Hospital in Massachusetts. The couple settled in Framingham, Massachusetts, and had three sons. White neighbors resented the presence of the black family, tried to remove them via petition, and isolated them from neighborhood affairs. Meta Fuller built a studio in the back of her house, something Dr. Fuller was totally against, and in between domestic duties sculpted less powerful, traditional religious scenes, even though she was estranged from her church due to the racial bigotry of parishioners.

Fuller again exhibited at the Pennsylvania Academy of Fine Arts in 1908 and 1920. In 1922, she showed at the Boston Public Library, and her work was included in an exhibition for the Tanner League held in the studios of Dunbar High School in WASHINGTON, D.C.

The federal commissions kept her employed, but she was neither encouraged nor nurtured, as she had been in Paris where her artistic genius was exalted. Moreover, a suspicious fire in 1910 destroyed the warehouse in which was housed most of the work she had created for 16 years. Fuller was, at that point in her life, financially dependent upon her family, socially detached from African-American contacts, and desolate about her career.

Meta Vaux Warrick Fuller is best known for sculpture that depicts the horrors and sadness of African-American life. These include: *Ethiopia Awakening* (1914), *Mary Turner: A Silent Protest Against Mob Violence* (1919), and *Talking Skull* (1937). *Ethiopia Awakening,* drawn from Egyptian sculptural concepts, represented her statement on black consciousness in Africa and in the United States. *Mary Turner* was her response to the lynching of a black woman from Valdosta, Georgia. And *Talking Skull* explored issues of life and death within the context of an African folktale.

Dr. Fuller lost his eyesight and died in 1953. Meta Vaux Warrick Fuller died on March 13, 1968, at Cushing Hospital in Framingham.

Further Reading

Hoover, Velma J. "Meta Vaux Warrick Fuller: Her Life and Art." *Negro History Bulletin* 40, no. 2, March–April (1997): 678–681.

Leininger-Muller, Theresa A. *New Negro Artists in Paris: African American Painters and Sculptors in the City of Light, 1922–1934.* Piscataway, N.J.: Rutgers University Press, 2000.

— Sandra L. West

Garvey, Marcus (Marcus Mosiah Garvey)
(1887–1940) *political advocate, publisher*

In his worldwide efforts to help people of African descent achieve political and economic autonomy, Marcus Garvey established one of the largest and most influential organizations geared toward such efforts in black history.

Born on August 7, 1887, in St. Ann's Bay, Jamaica, Garvey was the youngest of 11 children. However, nine of his siblings died during childhood and, aside from his parents, he grew up with his older sister, Indiana. His mother, Sarah Garvey, and his father, Marcus Garvey, Sr., were both descended from Jamaica's famed rebel fighters, the Maroons. Garvey, Sr., was a skilled mason, a farmer, and the owner of a sizable personal library that allowed him to sometimes serve as a lawyer for his friends and neighbors.

Young Marcus Garvey grew up as a colonial in a Jamaica still governed by Britain, which meant that a population of approximately 15,000 whites exercised rule over 168,000 of mixed ancestry and more than 630,000 blacks. The association of color with power was one Garvey never forgot, and he often charged that worse than color prejudice between the races was that color prejudice that existed among the members of the black race itself.

Garvey became an apprentice printer by the time he reached his teens and at 14 ended his formal education. At the age of 20, he moved to Kingston. There, he worked in a printing shop with his godfather and advanced to become the youngest foreman printer in the city. He underwent one of his first tests as a leader when the printers' union went on strike for higher wages. The strike failed and cost Garvey his job. He wound up blacklisted and skeptical regarding labor politics. He eventually found another job in a government printing office.

Kingston also provided Garvey with exposure to a culture where individuals often engaged in eloquent public debate over the state of their affairs. He studied and adopted modes of oratorical skill practiced in such common places as on the waterfront, in churches, in stores, and in barbershops, which later served him well when persuading others to his political way of thinking. He studied poetry in the same manner and eventually used it to such powerful effect in his speeches that W. E. B. DU BOIS, one of his severest critics, placed him among the more dynamic leaders of his time based solely on his eloquence.

In 1910, Garvey took his printing skills a step further and published his first newspaper, *Garvey's Watchman.* While he did achieve a circulation of 3,000, *Garvey's Watchman* proved the first in a line of newspapers intended to represent blacks living in the British island empire but ultimately proved to be short-lived. The second was *La Nacion,* founded in Costa Rica where he worked as a timekeeper on the United Fruit Company's banana plantation. In Costa Rica, Garvey witnessed what he reported as British indifference to the severe working conditions of West Indian immigrant laborers. Through the pages of *La Nacion* he attempted to hold the British consul accountable for those conditions. Moving to Panama, he saw a similar situation regarding Jamaican laborers working on the Panama Canal and created the newspaper *La Presna* to file reports on the plight of his countrymen.

The image of people of color laboring under extreme conditions to realize the goals of Europeans was repeated many times over as Garvey traveled through Ecuador, Colombia, Nicaragua, and Honduras. In 1911, he returned to Jamaica before traveling to England in 1912 to join his sister Indiana, who was working there as a nursemaid.

In England, Garvey joined the staff of the pan-African journal *African Times and Orient Review,* published by an Egyptian nationalist named Duse Mohammed Ali. Exposure to Ali and others at *African Times* expanded Garvey's awareness of racial conditions worldwide. It also introduced him to the philosophies of BOOKER TALIAFERRO WASHINGTON, whose

Despite the fatal flaws of his organization, UNIA founder Marcus Garvey, shown here in 1923, gained the largest following of any black leader of his era. *(Library of Congress, Prints & Photographs Division [LC-USZ62-109626])*

ideas on black self-reliance were supported by Ali. As Garvey put it, reading *Up from Slavery* generated for him an epiphany during which he realized his true calling to become "a race leader."

Up from Slavery also provided Garvey with a living hero in the form of Washington himself. He stated full agreement with Washington's assessment that the oppressive political and economical condition of blacks was less important than the black race's own willingness to work hard, improve itself, and earn the respect of other races. Garvey developed with Washington a correspondence that resulted in an invitation to visit Washington's stronghold, the Tuskegee Institute. Washington died before Garvey's visits to Tuskegee in 1916 and 1923, and much of his admiration for the older leader later turned to somewhat scornful criticism. In refuting the accommodationist teachings of Washington, Garvey spoke often of the *NEW NEGRO* several years prior to the publication of ALAIN LOCKE's anthology of the same title.

Still greatly inspired by Washington in 1914, Garvey returned to Jamaica to establish his UNIVERSAL NEGRO IMPROVEMENT ASSOCIATION (UNIA) and African Communities League. The UNIA was designed to construct and maintain economic and cultural links between the communities of the black diaspora. With a firm foundation in Jamaica, Garvey arrived in the United States on March 23, 1916. Reportedly on a visit to give lectures and raise funds to build an industrial school in Jamaica, Garvey became outspoken concerning what he called a lack of black leadership in the United States. Instead of returning to Jamaica, he completed a tour of almost 40 states and then went to NEW YORK CITY. With assistance from the city's West Indian population, he shifted the base of his operations from Jamaica to HARLEM, where he opened the first U.S. branch of UNIA.

The year 1919 proved a pivotal one for Marcus Garvey. By his estimates, the membership in the UNIA had grown to almost 4 million. Branches were forming throughout the United States as well as in South America, the West Indies, and Central America. He purchased a large auditorium on 138th Street in Harlem, named it Liberty Hall, and used it for UNIA-sponsored events, political as well as social and religious. He also started the Negro Factories Corps, which not only produced an extensive line of commodities in the United States and abroad but provided jobs for thousands of black workers.

Moreover, Garvey founded the *NEGRO WORLD*, destined to become the most successful newspaper of his publishing career and one of the most successful black periodicals of the 1920s, lasting well until 1933. The newspaper's motto declared it was "A Newspaper Devoted Solely to the Interests of the Negro Race." On the strength of that promise, backed with articles on black history and culture, stories detailing events surrounding the UNIA, and front-page editorials by Garvey, the paper reached a circulation of 200,000. Editions were published in English, French, and Spanish with distribution in Latin America, the Caribbean, and Africa. Just as the U.S. government at times blamed ROBERT ABBOTT's *CHICAGO DEFENDER* for unrest in the United States, so did the British name Garvey's *Negro World* as one cause of the 1919 race riots that swept through Jamaica, Trinidad, and British Honduras.

Also in 1919, Garvey launched one of UNIA's most ambitious projects: his now legendary Black Star Shipping Line. With a fleet of four used ships, the stated purpose of the Black Star Shipping Line was to conduct a Pan-African shipping trade among the United States, the West Indies, Africa, and Latin America. It was also made available to blacks for business and pleasure trips without the stigma of JIM CROW racism that characterized transportation services offered by whites. Garvey's critics writing in the black and white press sought to ridicule him by charging that the ships had been purchased to transport African Americans "back to Africa." Amy Jacques Garvey, Marcus Garvey's second wife, stated that the only return to Africa advocated by her husband was a spiritual one. The leader did, however, seek permission to establish a colony of skilled blacks in Liberia to contribute to the country's and the African continent's ongoing development. He was not allowed to do so.

So persuasive was Garvey in his call for blacks to rise to the challenge of a glorious destiny that his followers often called him the "Black Moses" or even John the Baptist. The UNIA, by the mid-1920s, had achieved the unprecedented feat of opening 700 branches in 38 states and 200 more in the international community, making it the largest organization on record dedicated to the economic and political advancement of people of African descent. As Garvey himself became more influential, he also became more daring. In 1921, he met with Edward Young Clarke, the Ku Klux Klan's Imperial Kleagle of Georgia. Reasoning in terms of the autonomy it would allow blacks, Garvey remarked that he agreed with Clarke's stand on a separation of the races, targeting Africa for blacks and the United States for whites. The statement was widely publicized and Garvey's critics interpreted it as an endorsement not just of philosophy but of the practice of LYNCHING promoted so vigorously by the Ku Klux Klan during that period. Owen Chandler of the *MESSENGER* stated in a headline that Garvey had become the "Messenger Boy of the White Ku Klux Kleagle."

Controversy over Garvey's public statements had less of an impact on the organizations he had created than mismanagement and weaknesses within the structures themselves. Operational expenses and extensive maintenance required for the ships of the Black Star Line placed the operation in debt for $500,000 after limited sailing for four years. The UNIA with its network of factories began accumulating debt that eventually hit $200,000. Any opportunity to reverse these trends ended when Garvey and three of his associates were arrested in 1922 on charges of mail fraud. The charges were based on information provided to the Bureau of Investigation (later the Federal Bureau of Investigation [FBI]) largely by Cyril V. Briggs through his monthly magazine, *The Crusader,* an organ of the radical group AFRICAN BLOOD BROTHERHOOD.

Garvey spent three months in New York City's Tombs Prison in 1923. On February 8, 1925, he entered the Atlanta Penitentiary, where he stayed two years. Originally sentenced to serve four years, the sentence was commuted by President Calvin Coolidge. In December 1927, Garvey was deported from the United States as an alien convicted of a felony. For a time, he held various public offices in Jamaica and tried to regain the earlier strength of his UNIA organization there but failed to win the kind of support he had received in the United States. In 1934, he moved to London, where he died on June 10, 1940, at the age of 52.

Garvey's first marriage was to Amy Ashwood. In 1922, he married for the second time to Amy Jacques Garvey, who led a national campaign for her husband's release from prison when he was arrested. In addition to serving as associate editor for the *Negro World,* she published two volumes of Garvey's speeches, entitled *Philosophy and Opinions of Marcus Garvey,* in 1923 and 1925. The couple had two sons, Marcus, Jr., and Julius. When Garvey moved to London, his wife chose to remain in Jamaica. In 1963, she wrote his biography, *Garvey and Garveyism.*

Further Reading

Cronon, E. David. *The Black Moses: The Story of Marcus Garvey and the Universal Negro Improvement Association.* Madison: University of Wisconsin Press, 1972.

Martin, Tony. *Amy Ashwood Garvey: Pan-Africanist, Feminist, and Wife Number One.* Dover, Mass.: Majority Press, Inc., 1999.

Van Deburg, William L., ed. *Modern Black Nationalism: From Marcus Garvey to Louis Farrakhan.* New York: New York University Press, 1997.

— Aberjhani

general community and the Harlem Renaissance

African Americans relocated from the South to the North as part of the GREAT MIGRATION, and workers such as truck drivers, cooks, Pullman porters, longshoremen, maids, and street peddlers using pushcarts or horse carts made up the general community of HARLEM during the Harlem Renaissance. They were also hairdressers, and laundry workers who handled 12-pound irons and worked 54 hours a week and 10 hours a day for $10 a week.

By contrast, those who created and sustained the Harlem Renaissance, or Negro Renaissance as leading participant LANGSTON HUGHES referred to it, were black writers, visual artists, championship athletes, scholars, nightclub singers, bandleaders, and middle-class blacks with income and aspiration enough to live year-round on SUGAR HILL and to summer in the black resort of Idlewild.

Hughes, often called the "poet of the people," enjoyed his familiarity with the everyday man on the street. He was often surrounded by the accomplishments and affected mannerisms of the "Niggerati," Harlem's noveau literati (as coined by folklorist ZORA NEALE HURSTON), and all the cultural propaganda of the glittery Harlem Renaissance. However, his interests and writings were devoted to the common folk of working-class origins. According to Hughes, "The ordinary Negroes hadn't heard of the Negro Renaissance. And, if they had, it hadn't raised their wages any. . . ."

Still, members of the general community in Harlem were the subject of a series of interviews conducted by writers employed

Black-owned newspapers proliferated during the Harlem Renaissance, making newsboys like the one seen here a common sight in black communities across the country. This photo was taken by Gordon Parks in 1943. *(Library of Congress, Prints & Photographs Division [LC-USW3-023997-E])*

Street peddlers and shop merchants added vitality to the growing community of Harlem during the 1910s, 1920s, and beyond. This photo was taken by Gordon Parks in 1943. *(Library of Congress, Prints and Photographs Division [LC-USW3-023989-E])*

with the FEDERAL WRITERS' PROJECT (FWP) of the WORKS PROGRESS ADMINISTRATION (WPA) in the 1930s. Harlem writers included a prolific Vivian Morris, Herb Boyd (*AMSTERDAM NEWS*), future novelist RALPH WALDO ELLISON (*Invisible Man*), prizewinning fiction writer DOROTHY WEST (*The Living Is Easy*), and others during the GREAT DEPRESSION.

The writers documented Harlem's employment trends, social activities, names of businesses, and regular PATRONS of local "watering holes" like Eddie's Bar on 147th and St. Nicholas. Those interviewed lived during the Harlem Renaissance but were not "of" the Harlem Renaissance. In the face of others more public and prosperous, they were "voiceless." Economically boxed in by low-paying, nonunion jobs, there were laborers who at times found release in the political teachings of MARCUS GARVEY or the spiritual teachings of men like DADDY GRACE and FATHER DIVINE. Likewise, they hosted gay, uninhibited, risqué RENT PARTIES more out of applied economic necessity than for pure social pleasure.

Harlem Renaissance and WPA scholar Lionel C. Bascom reports in his work *A Renaissance in Harlem: Lost Voices of an American Community* that in 1939, 80 percent of all black women workers were domestics. They held largely the same jobs they had held in the rural South and during slavery. Whereas Pullman porters earned $89.50 to $112.50 a month,

Harlem domestics earned $6 to $8 dollars a week. In 1938, if a domestic worker secured a part-time job—and jobs often started as part-time and then developed into full-time positions with part-time compensation—wages were set at $3.20 a week with a 40¢ finder's fee that the worker paid the employment agency. To pay rent and other expenses, domestics labored up to 10 hours per day without the benefits of Social Security or other forms of job security. In their own interest, they created the Domestic Workers Union Local 149 AF of L (American Federation of Labor) and A. PHILIP RANDOLPH's BROTHERHOOD OF SLEEPING CAR PORTERS & Maids were born.

Domestics were called "Thursday Girls," because Thursday was their only day off. Sometimes, these hard-working mothers and wives of Harlem received only half a Thursday off. On this day, they ran personal errands and perhaps enjoyed entertainment at a SPEAKEASY or dance hall like the SAVOY. Also, to make ends meet on the average $50–$60 a month rent-gouged Harlem apartments the working class occupied, rent parties were held on Thursday. They were also held on Saturday, when the working class received their pay.

Another enterprise used to supplement incomes was the buffet flat. These involved serving food and alcoholic drinks, gambling, and renting out apartment rooms for sexual liaisons. Card games alone could earn the host or hostess of a buffet flat $28 in one night. Some maids quit their domestic jobs and, overlooking the illicit aspects of the enterprise, ran buffet flats full time.

Another working-class commodity during the Harlem Renaissance years was the peddler. Among them were the members of the Pushcart Peddlers' Colony, who scavenged garbage cans for automobile parts and old magazines to sell to the American Junk Dealers, Inc., located adjacent to the colony at West 134th Street and Park Avenue. Others were street criers and vendors who sold a variety of fruits and vegetables on the streets of Harlem.

To attract the attention of potential buyers, street vendors invented songs, hollers, and chants, all in poetic style, about their products: chicken, ham, greens, pork chops, rice, beans, etc. A fish vendor might holler out: "I got shad/Ain't you glad?" or a vegetable peddler, "I got vegetables today/So don't go away." As they sold their wares, they changed language and demeanor in accordance with the neighborhood they occupied at the time; for example, in a neighborhood of southern black immigrants from Alabama, a peddler could sing, "I got yellow yams/From Birmingham." Comparable rhymes would be used to address people in West Indian, Jewish, or Spanish-speaking areas. Street vendors formed a vivacious addition to the neighborhood culture.

Harlem's working-class blacks celebrated when "Brown Bomber" JOE LOUIS became world champion, they took pride in the international stardom of FLORENCE MILLS, and they could do the latest dances performed on Broadway stages in black musical revues. But the poor did not usually buy books or oil paintings. They did not attend literary soirees at the home salon of REGINA ANDREWS, intellectual discussions at the Harlem branch library, or art exhibitions sponsored by the HARMON FOUNDATION (see also SALONS). They were not active participants in the dazzle of the Harlem Renaissance and, buried under the demands of daily necessities, likely did not realize the full social and historic significance of the artistic times in which they lived.

Further Reading

Bascom, Lionel C., ed. *A Renaissance in Harlem: Lost Voices of an American Community.* New York: Avon, 1999.

Clark-Lewis, Elizabeth. *Living In, Living Out: African American Domestics and the Great Migration.* New York: Kodansha International, 1996.

Greenberg, Cheryl Lynn. *"Or Does It Explode?" Black Harlem in the Great Depression.* New York and Oxford: Oxford University Press, 1991.

Wintz, Cary D. *Black Culture and the Harlem Renaissance.* Houston, Texas: Rice University Press, 1988.

— Sandra L. West

Gilpin, Charles Sidney (1878–1930) *actor, singer*

For his portrayal of the title character in the debut of Eugene O'Neill's *EMPEROR JONES*, Charles Gilpin won acclaim as one of the greatest actors of his time.

Charles Sidney Gilpin was born on November 20, 1878, in RICHMOND, VIRGINIA. He was the youngest of 14 children born to a nurse, Caroline Gilpin, and a steel-rolling mill laborer, Peter Gilpin. Until the age of 12, he attended the St. Francis School for Catholic Colored Children. He then took on an apprenticeship as a printer at the *Richmond Planet* newspaper.

In the 1890s, Gilpin moved to PHILADELPHIA, where he juggled a number of jobs that included singing, dancing, and performing comedy routines in bars. His talents as a performer led him into vaudeville, but racism barred him from performing drama. He later maintained that acting was not something for which he necessarily felt a calling but one of the means by which he was able to support himself. Among the other means were working as a printer, in a barbershop, as a railroad porter, and in minstrel shows.

He made his way to CHICAGO where he worked at the Pekin Theater and became one of the original members of the Pekin Players. As part of that group, he performed with veteran entertainers Lottie Grady and Lena Marshall in such plays as *The Mayor of Dixie, The Man Upstairs,* and *The Idlers.* In 1915, he moved to New York. There, he maintained jobs in luxury apartment buildings as an elevator worker and switchboard operator while also working periodically with GEORGE WALKER and BERT WILLIAMS, the Lafayette Players of the LAFAYETTE THEATRE, and the Lincoln Players.

Gilpin landed his first major role in 1919 when British playwright John Drinkwater cast him to play Reverend William Custis in his play *Abraham Lincoln.* By all accounts, the role was an extremely flawed interpretation of the great abolitionist Frederick Douglass. Yet just as unanimous was the opinion that Gilpin had managed to transcend his material and draw from it a powerful and memorable performance. Pulitzer and future

Nobel Prize–winning playwright Eugene O'Neill was persuaded enough by Gilpin's dramatic powers to cast him in the lead role for his experimental play *The Emperor Jones.*

The role was one of the most substantial ever afforded a black man on an American stage and extraordinary for both its political implications and its artistic structure. Composed largely of a monologue that drives the principal action and character of the play, the sustained balance of concentration and physical exertion required of the lead actor was considerable. Gilpin accepted the challenge with the play's debut on November 3, 1920, at the Provincetown Playhouse. Gilpin was recognized immediately as a performer with rare and even overwhelming dramatic gifts. The only actor with whom reviewers could later make comparisons was Ira Aldridge, who in the previous century had abandoned the United States to enjoy a celebrated international career.

The Emperor Jones enjoyed a lengthy run on Broadway, and for his performance Gilpin received the 1921 SPINGARN MEDAL presented by the NATIONAL ASSOCIATION FOR THE ADVANCEMENT OF COLORED PEOPLE to an African American for exceptional contributions to the black race. He also won acclaim from the Drama League as one of the top 10 people who did the most for American theater in 1920. The Drama League's recognition was somewhat marred when Gilpin's attendance at its recognition dinner was heatedly protested because of his race. Gilpin chose to attend regardless, and the dinner took place without disruption. Race and racism, however, would continue to play a significant part in Gilpin's fate as an actor and help fuel the alcoholism that would contribute to his demise.

While Gilpin remained with the production of *The Emperor Jones* on Broadway, his disagreements with O'Neill over the use of demeaning terms caused him to leave the play before it debuted in London. Though Gilpin was acknowledged as one of the greatest actors of his era, his career stalled. He remained active performing occasional parts in black theater and later started a theater company in Cleveland, but he also returned to the more reliable income sources of running elevators and working a switchboard. In 1924, he played the role of a minister in the play *Roseanne.* He lost the lead role in a Hollywood production of *Uncle Tom's Cabin* when he refused to play it in a stereotypical manner.

Gilpin was never able to regain the level of fame he won with *The Emperor Jones.* The play was revived in 1925 with PAUL ROBESON as the title character, and most people associate the play and the subsequent movie based on it with Robeson. As lauded as stage productions of *The Emperor Jones* were on Broadway, it was less so in HARLEM. Audiences there, sometimes described as the toughest critics in America, often viewed the title character as more comic than tragic or noble and laughed throughout the play rather than sitting spellbound by suspense. LANGSTON HUGHES clearly appreciated its comic possibilities and employed them in his spoof of the play, *The Em-Fuehrer Jones.*

Nevertheless, in an assessment of his dramatic creations, O'Neill stated that of all the actors with whom he had worked, Gilpin was the only one who had fully captured and interpreted his character exactly as he thought it should be.

Frustrations stemming from a lack of outlets for his talents, coupled with alcoholism, caused Gilpin to suffer a breakdown. He died on May 6, 1930, at Eldridge Park, New Jersey. In 1941, the city of Richmond recognized the actor as one of its most famous sons and named its first low-income housing project, Gilpin Court, after him.

Further Reading

Curtis, Susan. *The First Black Actors on the Great White Way.* Columbia: University of Mississippi Press, 1998.

Douglas, Ann. *Terrible Honesty: Mongrel Manhattan in the 1920s.* New York: Farrar, Straus, and Giroux, 1995.

— Aberjhani

Grace, Daddy (Marcelino Manoel daGrace, Charles Manoel Grace, Sweet Daddy Grace)

(ca. 1881–1960) *religious leader*

Bishop Charles M. "Sweet Daddy" Grace, known as both a revered prophet and as a religious cult leader from 1940 to 1960, founded the United House of Prayer for All People in 1919–21.

Daddy Grace was born Marcelino Manoel DaGraca on January 25, 1881 (year of birth approximate), on the island of Brava in the Portuguese-controlled Cape Verdean Islands near West Africa. His mother was named Delomba and his father Emmanuel DaGraca. In 1903, the family migrated to New Bedford, Massachusetts. Marcelino Manoel DaGraca then became known as Charles Manoel Grace, an anglicization of his Portuguese name.

As a young man, Grace worked in a grocery store and as a cook on the Southern Railway. Though he converted from Catholicism to Methodism by 1921, he eventually gravitated toward the Holiness-Pentecostal Church. Grace joined the Nazarene Church in Wareham, Massachusetts, until the congregation divided. Feeling "called to preach," he led a faction of that church into the first United House of Prayer for All People on Kempton Street in New Bedford, Massachusetts. Dates on the founding of the church vary between 1919 and 1921. The church adopted a mission of dutiful community service and was housed in a building painted red, white, and blue, the same colors as Grace's automobile. As led by Daddy Grace, the United House of Prayer became known for a charismatic form of worship called "shouting." This early church and the entire chain of House of Prayer churches that followed were based upon Pentecostal, Catholic, Baptist, and African traditions and rituals. Between 1921 and 1926, Houses of Prayer were established in a dozen eastern cities.

A member of the predominantly black congregants was taught to believe the following: "I am God's child, and God is Colorless." They followed the teachings of the Bible and were baptized not in a river but under a water hose. Bishop Daddy Grace charged one dollar for each baptism, "watering" thousands of converts at one time until he had a following of more than 3 million people at the church's highest point in the 1930s and 1940s. An *AMSTERDAM NEWS* article reported, "Daddy Grace to Use Fire Hose on 300" as late as July 28, 1956.

The congregants opened each service with the internationally known hymn "Amazing Grace" and worshiped according to Psalm 150 from the Old Testament, loudly and physically, accompanied by a brass band that played BLUES and JAZZ. During the GREAT DEPRESSION of the 1930s, Bishop Grace fed congregants and allowed the homeless to stay in his mansion. He built schools and provided employment for many.

Bishop Grace established *Grace Magazine* in 1945 to advocate material success among his followers. In 1949, the HARLEM-based United House of Prayer for All People established a community cafeteria. This 2,000-seat church on the corner of Eighth Avenue and 125th Street is known as the Mother House in Harlem or "Sweet Honey, Heaven Harlem."

Grace's ministry challenged the organization of another alternative religious leader, FATHER DIVINE. Because Grace built his empire upon religious and spiritual beliefs that challenged the status quo of Christianity and black ministers throughout Harlem and the United States, there are contradicting perceptions of him. The question at that time and one pondered in the modern era is whether or not Daddy Grace was genuinely helpful and sincere in his ministry.

Daddy Grace died on January 12, 1960, in Los Angeles, California. He is buried in Pine Grove Cemetery in New Bedford. Two nickels are glued to the steps of his tomb, possibly in homage to his penniless state in 1922 and to the materialistic foundation of the church he established. At the time of his death, his personal worth was approximately $6 million. The original House of Prayer church burned down in 1972 and was rebuilt in 1975. There are currently about 110 Houses of Prayer in the United States, with more in Egypt, England, Cape Verde, and Portugal.

Further Reading

Davis, Lenwood G. *Daddy Grace: An Annotated Bibliography.* Westport, Conn.: Greenwood Press, 1992.

Favor, J. Martin. *Authentic Blackness: The Folk in the New Negro Renaissance.* Durham, N.C.: Duke University Press, 1999.

— Sandra L. West

Great Depression

Alerted to the danger of economic instability by the Wall Street crash on October 23, 1929, American government officials who expected danger to pass in a short period of time were stunned when the country entered a debilitating depression lasting for all of 10 years.

Millions of white Americans had cultivated lifestyles of comfort and upward mobility during the so-called Roaring Twenties, but the Great Depression introduced them to experiences of poverty that few had ever thought possible. For the people of HARLEM and African Americans throughout the United States, the period represented both an extension of the apartheid conditions under which they had already been living and new opportunities to combat those very same conditions.

Convinced that wholesale prices and shares had dropped as low as they could during the last days of October 1929, the republican Herbert Hoover's presidential administration found itself dealing with a quandary of international proportions as the initial decrease continued right up until the 1932 presidential election. With Wall Street's failure, foreign trade, commercial productivity, and employment all took a painful dive. Those who had significant amounts of money in banks began withdrawing it, thousands of banks themselves had to shut down, families lost their homes, and individuals lost their jobs. Many who once made shopping for groceries or clothing a social event wound up standing in soup lines and picking items out of dump heaps. An estimated 25 percent of the country's workforce was not working. For African Americans in major cities such as NEW YORK CITY, PHILADELPHIA, CHICAGO, and Detroit, the unemployment rate was usually estimated as double that of white Americans. With the closing of entire factories and the loss of mainstream business positions, whites who had been accustomed to such jobs began to work in lower-paying positions, such as doormen and elevator operators, formerly reserved for blacks. While such adjustments meant a reduction in pay for the whites involved, it meant a complete loss of employment for the blacks involved. Furthermore, many whites who until the depression had been able to employ blacks as servants now had to relinquish that luxury and blacks who had depended on those positions had to seek other possibilities for employment.

With continued economic decline and the very real fact of hunger cramping people's stomachs, Americans went to the polls in 1932 and chose to take the former governor of New York, Democrat FRANKLIN DELANO ROOSEVELT, up on his offer of what he called "a New Deal for the forgotten man at the bottom of the economic pyramid." To implement his New Deal, Roosevelt introduced a series of legislative and executive actions that tackled different aspects of the nation's economic crisis. The May 12 Federal Emergency Relief Act placed $500 million directly in the hands of states, cities, and counties. It later paved the way for the Civil Works Administration, a program that allowed millions of unemployed workers to escape the suffocating sense of idleness by accepting minimal wages for such tasks as maintaining parks, building schools, constructing roads, and cleaning sewers. The June 16 National Recovery Industrial Act provided regulatory standards to help failed industries recover and operate in a manner that protected workers with restricted work hours and minimal earning levels while improving industrial efficiency. One of the most important programs to fall under its umbrella was the WORKS PROGRESS ADMINISTRATION, which in addition to securing employment for the average laborer did the same for artists, writers, and musicians. The Agricultural Adjustment Act and the Emergency Farm Mortgage Act restored some of the financial strength farmers had lost and helped reduce the threat of property loss. The May 27 Truth in Securities Act tackled the regulation of the banks and stock exchange. Two years later,

Details are unknown regarding the precise activities of the group known as the Wall Street Boys, seen here in 1925 in attire indicating financial affluence, but they are believed to have been one of many business clubs formed in Harlem to help blacks achieve economic prosperity prior to the Great Depression. *(Photographs and Prints Division, Schomburg Center for Research in Black Culture, The New York Public Library, Astor, Lenox and Tilden Foundation)*

the Social Security Act would introduce the federal system of unemployment and old age insurance system on which generations would depend long after the depression.

The above programs were never intended to be permanent solutions to America's economic and political problems. They were, however, expected to provide those families in need with a fighting chance for survival during a time when survival could not be taken for granted. Whether blacks in Harlem and elsewhere in the United States benefited from them was often a matter of debate. As Cheryl Lynn Greenberg stated in "Or Does It Explode?", her excellent study of the community, Harlem during the 1920s "crumbled into a slum while optimists noticed only advancement. It lived in depression before the Depression." In short, the extreme levels of unemployment and difficulties in meeting everyday living expenses were already standard features among Harlem's mixed black population of native New Yorkers, southern blacks, Puerto Ricans, Jamaicans, and West Indians. Its cause had not been Wall Street's fluctuating markets but pure unbridled racism. Nevertheless, the depression impacting on everyone did further the damage already suffered in Harlem: by the end of 1932 the average family in the community, even with every able body working, barely pulled in $1,000 a year; unemployment escalated even further.

In many ways, the depression created a platform of social grievances that whites had no choice but to share with blacks. Roosevelt's reforms provided concrete tools with which blacks could now address their condition. The fact that relief was known to be available helped encourage blacks to further organize and fight for the same. Such organization had already begun before the New Deal when blacks in 1930 followed Chicago's lead and adopted the "Don't Buy Where You Can't Work" campaign to combat discriminatory hiring practices in Harlem. The Harlem Housewives League made sure discriminating store owners in the community got their message by directing black consumers to shops that had at least one black clerk. ADAM CLAYTON POWELL, SR., as the head of Harlem's Citizen's Committee on More and Better Jobs, advocated boycotts against discriminating stores, and the NATIONAL ASSOCIATION FOR THE ADVANCEMENT OF COLORED PEOPLE (NAACP) maintained an ongoing dialogue with business owners to push for nondiscriminatory hiring. If these efforts did not end discriminatory hiring altogether, they did often provide blacks who were more than qualified for the job to obtain work as clerks.

As the decade of the 1930s progressed, so did the depression. The relief allotments that made it possible for many to survive did not necessarily make it possible for them to thrive: the amounts provided, while clearly preferable to nothing, was generally less than needed to meet requirements for such combined monthly expenses as food, clothing, and utilities. Dwellings designed for a single family continued to shelter two or three instead. Young adults barely making $6 to $15 a week often left home so their income would not disqualify other family members for relief aid in one form or another. The prolonged conditions of poverty and overcrowding gave way to a rise in delinquency and disease. Blacks in Harlem compared to whites suffered disproportionately from tuberculosis, pneumonia, infant mortality, maternal mortality, and homicide. One sign that conditions were not improving was the HARLEM RIOT of 1935.

To help step up the battle against depression ills, members from various black political organizations combined their collective clout to form the National Negro Congress (NNC) in 1935. In an attempt to present a national united front against American racism, the NNC succeeded for a time in lining up beneath its banner the NATIONAL URBAN LEAGUE, the International BROTHERHOOD OF SLEEPING CAR PORTERS, the Communist Party, and the NAACP. Its goal was a worthy one, as it stated, not to override existing black political organizations but "to accomplish unity of action" between them. In addition to addressing those problems related directly to the depression, the NNC's agenda included the adoption of a federal anti-LYNCHING law, protection of southern blacks' voting rights, and opposition to "war and fascism, the attempted subjugation of Negro people in Ethiopia, the oppression of colonial nations throughout the world; for the independence of Ethiopia."

The closing years of the 1930s saw the United States increasingly funding war-affiliated industries to help supply its allies with armaments. As the country made its way toward full participation in World War II in 1941, demand for labor (both civilian and military) began to increase. The growing signs of economic prosperity were slower to reach black communities as battles were once again waged to participate in the developing boom, including the war itself. That meant blacks in Harlem still had to contend with disproportionately high unemployment rates and challenging living conditions. However, the battles they and other blacks had already fought during the height of the depression had won for them membership in unions, greater access (though not total) to job training programs as well as some jobs themselves, and a degree of rent control. Though many at the beginning of the 1940s still remained on government relief, they were politically better equipped to slowly improve the quality of their lives.

Further Reading

Greenberg, Cheryl Lynn. *Or Does It Explode? Black Harlem in the Great Depression.* New York: Oxford University Press, 1991.

Holloway, Jonathan Scott. *Confronting the Veil: Abram Harris, Jr., E. Franklin Frazier, and Ralph Bunche, 1919–1941.* Durham: University of North Carolina Press, 2002.

— Aberjhani

Great Migration

The racist practices of JIM CROW, the murder of African Americans in the form of LYNCHING, and increased job opportunities in the northern and western United States motivated millions of American blacks to leave the South during the movement known as the Great Migration.

African Americans began the massive exodus from the South as early as the Civil War. During that time, individual men, women, and families departed the region where whites had fought to keep them in slavery and migrated to where they had fought to liberate them from slavery. Federal troops assigned after the war to safeguard the rights of newly freed slaves ensured their freedom until withdrawal of the troops in 1876. Left in place of the troops were the Black Codes, a set of laws that made it illegal for blacks to own farmland or live independently without being employed by a white person. Many interpreted the Black Codes, which also allowed whites to whip blacks for punishment, as an extension of slavery without use of the word.

In addition to setting their sights as far north as Canada, many African Americans began to make their way west. Led by Benjamin "Pap" Singleton from 1875 to 1880, a group of 7,500, calling itself the "exodusters," made its way from Tennessee to Kansas. Various groups in turn journeyed from southern states to Colorado, Mexico, Nebraska, Iowa, the Dakota Territory, and Oklahoma. Estimates of the number of blacks departing the South from 1870 to 1890 run as high as 41,500, and those leaving during the 1890s were more than 100,000. Newspapers such as the *Wesley Cyclone* and the *Colored Visitor* spread the word that blacks were both needed and welcomed in other areas of the country. The availability of land and rumor of oil not only drew African Americans to Oklahoma but led to the establishment of such black townships as Langston in 1891 and Boley in 1904.

The near reinstatement of slavery with the Black Codes coincided with increases of mob violence against blacks. Public whippings and the rape of black women and men were almost merciful compared to the lynchings that left their burned and mutilated bodies hanging from trees, tossed to the sides of roads, or cut up and distributed as souvenirs. Lynching was clearly retaliation for the Civil War, and by 1900 more than 2,000 African Americans had been murdered in that manner. It was not

Conditions of extreme poverty and racism forced many African Americans in the rural South to run businesses or live in shacks like the store pictured here in Belle Glade, Florida, in 1945. Millions fled these conditions during the Great Migration. *(National Archives, 180-16N-6435)*

uncommon for news of a lynching to inspire half or more of a town's black population to vacate it as quickly as possible.

Added to the threat of lynching was the 1896 Supreme Court decision in the case of *Plessy v. Ferguson.* Legalizing "separate but equal" public facilities in the United States, the ruling set the stage for the practice of Jim Crow throughout the country. Much less harsh than the Black Codes, it nevertheless made it easy for white America to ignore the very unequal realities of black life. With Jim Crow the legal rule of the day, various forms of discrimination became commonplace in the South and North but were generally taken to greater extremes in the South. The lack of proper schools, unbridled prejudice on behalf of the courts, the assumption of white superiority, and the specter of lynching all combined to produce a steady stream of African Americans moving out of the South.

The stream turned into a flood from 1910 to 1920. Prior to that time, most African Americans had left the South motivated by fear and fairly vague notions of greater opportunities for social and political advancement. However, the boom in jobs created by WORLD WAR I, coupled with the wartime ban on foreign immigration, and a campaign launched by black newspapers urging blacks to leave the South en masse, established a true and structured northern migration. Newspapers such as the *CHICAGO DEFENDER*, the *PITTSBURGH COURIER*, and the *NEW YORK AGE* all published editorials urging blacks to come north and provided information on how to do so. The papers informed its readers about the availability of jobs in private industries as well as those driven by the demands of the war. They published train schedules, fare information, and letters from blacks throughout the South seeking assistance coordinating their journey. Possibly even more important, they were exposed to the bold militant writings of such men as the *Chicago Defender's* ROBERT ABBOTT and W. E. B. DU BOIS of the *CRISIS: A RECORD OF THE DARKER RACES*, each of whom dared to call the genocidal practices of southern racism by its name and inspired their readers to fight it rather than accommodate it.

The newspaper campaign hit its peak when Abbott engineered the Great Northern Drive of May 15, 1917, designating a single day for southern African Americans to depart the South all at once. With labor recruiters on hand signing up potential workers at train stations and offering free tickets, many blacks did exactly as Abbott and other black editors recommended. Some drove their own cars, some went in horse-drawn wagons, and some spent weeks walking and hitching rides until they reached their northern destination.

The ravages of nature also played a major part in driving blacks north. Floods in Alabama, Mississippi, and elsewhere in the South had done more than deprive many people of their incomes; they had deprived them of their homes and lives. Cotton farmers throughout the South lost thousands of acres and millions of dollars to the destruction caused by the beetle known as the boll weevil.

The bulk of African Americans leaving the South lived primarily in the rural areas of Georgia, South Carolina, Alabama, Florida, Mississippi, and Louisiana. Rather than attempt the longer journey north, some simply moved from rural areas to southern cities. Southern urban centers such as Jacksonville, Savannah, Atlanta, Charleston, and New Orleans all saw their black populations increased by 10,000 or more at the start of the 1920s.

Those who did go north settled primarily in the larger cities such as CHICAGO, NEW YORK CITY, Detroit, PHILADELPHIA, Pittsburgh, Cleveland, Cincinnati, and Columbus. Chicago's black population jumped from 40,000 in 1910 to 165,000 in 1920. New York's made a similar leap, up from 100,000 in 1910 to approximately 210,000 in 1920, with a sizable fraction of that number moving straight to HARLEM.

More than the simple availability of work was the opportunity to earn enough to actually live. Workers in the South typically made 40¢ to $1.75 on a daily basis, earning for a full week's labor what most workers in the North earned in a single day. Also numerous fields were not open for blacks in the South where they could even try to earn more. By contrast, the North was putting black workers in furniture factories, munitions

The northern urban environment, such as that represented by the typical street scene in Harlem pictured here in 1943, presented a sharp contrast to the rural poverty in which many blacks lived and ultimately abandoned in search of better living conditions. *(Library of Congress, Prints & Photographs Division [LC-USW3-031113-C])*

plants, canning factories, office positions, laundries, the steel industry, garment factories, automobile plants, and railroad companies. It was true blacks often got the more dangerous and less glamorous positions within these fields, but it was also true that they were able to voice their grievances in political discourses without fear of being murdered for doing so.

The shift of black migrants from the South to the North and West meant a loss of one of the South's most treasured resources. Though African Americans were no longer slaves, they had still remained a form of cheap labor on which the fortunes of many white families had been built and continued to rest. Seeing that labor source disappear before their eyes brought reactions of violence from some and attempts at compromise from others. Not vanishing altogether, lynching would level off in the late 1920s and begin a steady decline from that point on.

In the North, the growing presence of blacks in the labor force and the neighborhood generated competition for paychecks and housing. The friction often heated up into riots, with blacks and whites clashing in the streets. The Springfield, Illinois, riots of 1908 inspired the call for a renewed dedication to racial equality that eventually led to the formation of the NATIONAL ASSOCIATION FOR THE ADVANCEMENT OF COLORED PEOPLE (NAACP). The RED SUMMER of 1919 saw conflicts between the races in more than two dozen American cities. The worst of these was in Chicago, where 38 people died and thousands lost their homes.

Responses to the Great Migration varied throughout its duration. The NATIONAL URBAN LEAGUE was created in 1911 mainly to help African Americans new to the urban North make the transition as smoothly as possible. On the other hand, representatives attending the 26th Annual Tuskegee Conference in 1917 urged blacks to stay where they were and put their energies into developing a diversity of crops and establishing new southern townships.

The mixture of rural culture transferred to urban environments generated a creative vitality that found its way into styles of cooking, music, dance, and literature. Writers such as ZORA NEALE HURSTON not only came from the South but made it a principal element of their art. Celebrated artist JACOB ARMSTEAD LAWRENCE painted an entire series depicting different aspects of the Great Migration—from people waiting in crowded train stations to recent black migrants confronting northern versions of white racism. The political clout of those hundreds of thousands of blacks who previously had been denied voting rights became evident as well. The 1932 presidential elections marked the first time African Americans shied away from loyalty to Abraham Lincoln's Republican Party and looked to the Democrats for improvements in their social, political, and economic situations.

Although the end of WORLD WAR I brought for black men and women the inevitable loss of jobs with the return of white troops, that did not stop the Great Migration north. The numbers decreased in the 1930s as the GREAT DEPRESSION forced black and white Americans to take to roads leading all over the country in search of means for survival. As it had during World War I, the lag picked up again during World War II when the demand for labor increased once more. The move toward the West Coast, particularly California, was as strong this time around as that going North. With the end of the war, the migration movement remained steady well into the 1950s. During that decade, an estimated million and a half African Americans left the South. The numbers decreased significantly during the 1960s. Toward the end of the 1900s, many African Americans began returning to the South to reclaim their families' American roots.

Further Reading

Arnesen, Eric J. *African Americans and the Great Migration.* New York: St. Martin's Press, 2002.

Lawrence, Jacob. *The Migration Series.* Washington, D.C.: The Rappahannock Press in Association with The Phillips Collection, 1993.

Lemann, Nicholas. *The Promised Land: The Great Black Migration and How It Changed America.* New York: Vintage Books, 1992.

— Aberjhani

Green Pastures, The

The 1930 Pulitzer Prize–winning play *The Green Pastures* featured an all-black cast and stirred both praise and controversy as it ran through more than 600 performances on Broadway and almost 2,000 more on tour across the United States.

The play was written by white authors Marc Connelly and Roark Bradford. It was based on stories Bradford, who grew up on a plantation, wrote for the *New York World* and published in book form as *Ol Man Adam and His Chillun* in 1928. Connelly had a reputation as a writer of satirical plays written with George S. Kaufman; both were members of the famed NEW YORK CITY literary group the Algonquin Round Table.

Directed by Connelly, *The Green Pastures* presented stories from the Old Testament narrated in black dialect by a rural southern black preacher. A cast of some 60 black actors performed the biblical dramas of Adam and Eve, Noah, Moses, the passion of Christ, and other biblical stories. These were presented in such then modern-day settings as an Elks Lodge and at a fish fry presided over by "De Lawd."

Among those playing the figures from the Old Testament were Wesley Hill as the angel Gabriel, Inez Richardson Wilson as Eve, and Alonzo Fenderson as Moses. One of its most celebrated stars, in the role of the Lord, was RICHARD B. HARRISON, a 65-year-old newcomer to the professional stage. Until taking on the role of the Lord, Harrison had toured black churches, schools, and clubs while giving recitals from the Bible and Shakespeare. To master the black dialect spoken by his divine character, he was coached by a white tutor. Harrison then went on to make the curtain call for 1,568 performances. He died while preparing for the show's revival in 1935.

LANGSTON HUGHES described *The Green Pastures* as a mark of decline signaling an end to the achievements in black culture that took place throughout the 1920s. W. E. B. DU BOIS, on the other hand, called the play "the beginning of a new era" in American art for blacks and whites. Critics were divided over whether it was an extremely flawed commentary on black religion, with characters that were more simpleminded than wise or pious, or a profound statement on humanity's relationship with God.

Following its Broadway closing in 1931, *The Green Pastures* went on five national tours, playing in 200 cities in 39 states. In the South, controversy over the play centered more around JIM CROW racial segregation than theology or literary exactitude. Officials in Lubbock, Texas, banned the play because they did not want the black cast to use the only facilities in the town capable of accommodating its performance: a high school for white students only. A local law in Tampa, Florida, forbade blacks from buying tickets to the show so that members of the company had to devise ways to sneak them in.

In England, the office of Lord Chamberlain ruled the play was blasphemous because it had an actor playing God and for that reason it was banned. A production in Sweden was put on with Swedish actors in blackface and at least one performance became the target of eggs thrown on the stage.

The Green Pastures returned to Broadway in 1935, and in 1936 the play was made into a movie starring Rex Ingram as the Lord. Costarring with Ingram were Oscar Polk and EDDIE "Rochester" ANDERSON, who gained fame on radio and television as white entertainer Jack Benny's black sidekick, "Rochester."

The play enjoyed another revival in 1951. By then, its characters were viewed largely as negative stereotypes and the Committee for the Negro in the Arts waged a protest against the production. Ironically, an earlier critic of the play, celebrated actor and director Ossie Davis, found himself in the role of the angel Gabriel. The play continued to generate new life in 1957 when the Hallmark Hall of Fame series produced for television a version starring Frederick O'Neal and Eddie Anderson.

Further Reading

Davis, Ossie, and Ruby Dee. *With Ossie and Ruby: In This Life Together.* New York: William Morrow, 1998.

Elam, Harry J., and David Krasner, eds. *African American Performance and Theatre History: A Critical Reader.* New York: Oxford University Press, 2000.

— Aberjhani

Grimké, Angelina Emily Weld (1880–1958) *poet, playwright*

Angelina Emily Weld Grimké, whose work incorporated controversial themes on gender, was a poet and an early black playwright of note.

Angelina Emily Weld Grimké was born into privilege and middle-class comfort on February 27, 1880, in Boston, Massachusetts. Her father, Archibald Henry Grimké, was a lawyer. Her mother, Sarah Eliza Stanley Grimké, came from a prominent white family. Author of *The Light of Egypt,* Sarah Grimké abandoned her family when Angelina was three years old. The celebrated abolitionist sisters, Angelina Grimké Weld and Sarah Grimké, adopted Archibald as their nephew because they shared the same surname. Consequently, Archibald named his daughter in honor of the famous "aunt."

Angelina Emily Weld Grimké was still a child when she wrote a poetic tribute to a forgotten soldier, "The Grave in the Corner," for Massachusett's *Norfolk County Gazette* (May 27, 1893). She attended Fairmount School in Hyde Park; Carlton Academy in Northfield, Minnesota; Cushing Academy in Ashburnham, Massachusetts; and Girls' Latin School. She earned a physical education degree in 1902 from Boston Normal School of Gymnastics (later Department of Hygiene, Wellesley College).

In 1902, she taught physical education at Armstrong Manual Training School in WASHINGTON, D.C., transferred to the English department at M Street H (later Dunbar High), and continued there until retirement. She studied English at Harvard University from 1904 to 1910.

In 1909, Grimké penned "El Beso," a poem about romantic love between women, which was published in *Transcript* (October 1909). The poem is considered autobiographical and likely refers to Grimké and her fellow teacher and playwright Mary Burrill. Both women wrote about similar themes and published their works in the same journals.

Although controversial, Grimké's writing found an audience. Her poetry was published in *OPPORTUNITY* and *CRISIS: A RECORD OF THE DARKER RACES*, as well as anthologized in the *NEW NEGRO* (1925), *Caroling Dusk* (1927), and *Ebony and Topaz* (1927). But it was *Rachel,* her play about LYNCHING and racism, that sealed Grimké's reputation as a writer.

Rachel was published by the Cornhill Company. In 1919, Grimké entered into an agreement with Cornhill to receive $300, 25 free author copies, 50 percent of gross receipts up to 700 copies, and 20 percent of gross receipts afterward. After two other original titles—*The Pervert* and *Blessed Are the Barren*—the three-act play was staged on March 3–4, 1916, at Myrtill Minor Normal School in Washington under the auspices of the Drama Committee, District of Columbia branch, NATIONAL ASSOCIATION FOR THE ADVANCEMENT OF COLORED PEOPLE (NAACP). On April 26, 1917, it was presented in NEW YORK CITY at Neighborhood Playhouse, and again on May 24, 1917, in Cambridge, Massachusetts, at St. Bartholomew's Church.

The play met with strong criticism from Iowa's *Grinnell Review* (January 1921): "Exaggeration spoils this play. Had Miss Grimké's negroes been less shabby-genteel, their tragedy would have been more convincing." However, critic Arthur P. Davis called *Rachel* "the first successful stage drama to be written by a Negro." After *Rachel,* Grimké's "The Closing Door" (1919) and "Goldie" (1920) appeared in *Birth Control Review.*

Grimké's longtime friend, Mary Burrill, died in 1946. Outside of her relationship with Burrill, the timid Grimké enjoyed a degree of sisterly friendship with Marita Bonner and JESSIE REDMOND FAUSET through Georgia Douglas Johnson's literary SALON in Washington, D.C. When she retired from teaching in 1933, she stopped writing. She died at home, 208 West 151st Street in HARLEM, on June 10, 1958.

Further Reading

Davis, Arthur P. *From The Dark Tower: Afro-American Writers 1900 to 1960.* Washington, D.C.: Howard University Press, 1974.

Hull, Gloria T. *Color, Sex, and Poetry: Three Women Writers of the Harlem Renaissance.* Bloomington and Indianapolis: Indiana University Press, 1987.

— Sandra L. West

Gwathmey, Robert, Jr. (1903–1988) *painter*

Robert Gwathmey was a white, southern, social realist painter, who was prominent during the 1930s and 1940s. He depicted in his art the lives of rural African Americans and worked as a muralist for the WORKS PROGRESS ADMINISTRATION (WPA).

Robert Gwathmey, Jr., was born of Welsh heritage on January 24, 1903, in Manchester, Virginia, near RICHMOND. His father, Robert Gwathmey, Sr., was a railroad engineer who was killed in a locomotion explosion. His mother, Eva Mortimer Harrison, was a public school teacher.

Gwathmey attended John Marshall High School in Richmond, studied for one year at the Maryland Institute of Design in Baltimore from 1925 to 1926, and graduated from the Pennsylvania Academy of Fine Arts in 1930. From the Pennsylvania Academy he won the Cresson scholarship, which enabled him to study during the summer months in Europe in 1929 and 1930. He taught art at several colleges, including Temple University in PHILADELPHIA from 1930 to 1932, and Cooper Union from 1942 to 1968, where he influenced contemporary African-American artist Faith Ringgold.

On November 2, 1935, Gwathmey married photographer Rosalie Hook of Charlotte, North Carolina. After living in Philadelphia and Europe, they returned to North Carolina to have their son, Charles, in 1938. Gwathmey was a Southerner but did not believe in the racist JIM CROW practices of his region. Through his travels, he became involved in leftist politics and began to see his homeland, and the way the South treated blacks, as if he had never really seen it before. He destroyed all of his previous work and began to create anew from his political worldview, using pencil, oils, and watercolors.

In 1939, Gwathmey received a commission from the WPA to paint *The Countryside* (1939–1941), a mural for the post office in Eutaw, Alabama. In 1944, he won a Rosenwald Foundation fellowship that enabled him to live, for three months, on a North Carolina tobacco farm and paint. He depicted toiling black sharecroppers, southern village scenes, and LYNCHING. His works include *Street Scenes* (1938); *Land of Cotton* (1939); *Sun-Up* (1948); *Shanties* (1951); and a series of paintings of the World Series for *Sports Illustrated* (1957).

Gwathmey did not paint blacks in a romantic way. He was a realist and used his art to protest injustice. Realism, or social realism, is the unsentimental and authentic representation of people, places, and things in a work of art. Other realist artists during the Harlem Renaissance were painter WILLIAM HENRY JOHNSON and muralist CHARLES WILBERT WHITE.

In 1946, Gwathmey had a one-man exhibit at the American Contemporary Art (ACA) Gallery in NEW YORK CITY. Social reformer PAUL ROBESON, at the time under investigation for alleged ties to COMMUNISM, wrote the introduction for the catalog of Gwathmey's work. In 1949, the black artistic community offered him the position of principal speaker at the opening of Atlanta University's Eighth Annual Exhibition of Painting and Sculpture by Negro Artists.

His post office mural, *The Countryside,* caused a controversy during the Black Power movement of the 1960s and 1970s when young, black revolutionaries interpreted Gwathmey's depiction of African Americans as subservient or demeaning and called for its removal.

Robert Gwathmey died on September 21, 1988.

Further Reading

Kammen, Michael. *Robert Gwathmey: The Life and Art of a Passionate Observer.* Chapel Hill and London: The University of North Carolina Press, 1999.

— Sandra L. West

H

Half Century See HOPKINS, PAULINE ELIZABETH.

Hall, Adelaide (1901–1993) *singer*

Entertainer Adelaide Hall recorded the 1927 JAZZ classic "Creole Love Call," sang in several hit musical revues during the Harlem Renaissance, and performed for the last time at the age of 90.

Born in Brooklyn on October 20, 1901, Adelaide Hall was the daughter of a music teacher at Pratt Institute in NEW YORK CITY. She grew up in HARLEM and was barely out of her teens when she made her performance debut in the hit musical *SHUFFLE ALONG*, followed by an appearance in *RUNNIN' WILD* in the early 1920s. She then toured Europe in *Chocolate Kiddies* and appeared in *Desires of 1927.*

Along with LOUIS ARMSTRONG and ETHEL WATERS, Hall was one of the early pioneers of jazz singing and in 1927 recorded the innovative "Creole Love Call" with bandleader and composer DUKE ELLINGTON. She was also one of the featured "girl" singers at the celebrated COTTON CLUB, where Ellington and his band reigned for half a decade.

Hall achieved further fame in 1928 when she became one of the singers to take the place of FLORENCE MILLS, upon Mills's death, in the successful musical *BLACKBIRDS OF 1928*.

During the 1930s, she toured with jazz great Art Tatum and moved to London. There, she starred in *The Sun Never Sets* and established her own radio program. As late as the 1950s, she worked on Broadway in *Jamaica* (1957) with LENA HORNE, who had also performed at the Cotton Club in the 1930s.

Hall's soprano made memorable several tunes: "I Can't Give You Anything but Love," "Ill Wind," "Baby I Must Have That Man," and "Drop Me Off in Harlem." She continued to record songs into the 1970s. In 1988, she enjoyed a triumphant one-woman show at Carnegie Hall and in 1992 received Britain's Gold Badge from the Academy of Songwriters, Composers, and Authors.

One of those incomparable stars of long life, Adelaide Hall performed until she was 90 years old. She died in London on November 7, 1993.

Further Reading

Anderson, Jervis. *This Was Harlem: A Cultural Portrait, 1900–1950.* New York: Farrar, Straus, Giroux, 1981.

Kellner, Bruce, ed. *The Harlem Renaissance: A Historical Dictionary for the Era.* Westport, Conn.: Greenwood Press, 1984.

Watson, Steven. *The Harlem Renaissance: Hub of African-American Culture, 1920–1930.* New York: Pantheon Books, 1995.

— Sandra L. West

Hampton University See MUSEUMS, AFRICAN-AMERICAN UNIVERSITY.

Handy, W. C. (William Christopher Handy) (1873–1958) *composer, music publisher*

Classically trained as a musician, W. C. Handy composed some of the most popular, recognizable BLUES songs in America and became known as the "Father of the Blues."

William Christopher "W. C." Handy was born in Florence, Alabama, in a simple log cabin on November 16, 1873. His grandparents had been slaves, though his grandfather was also a minister. His mother, Elizabeth Brewer Handy, was a freed slave who played the guitar. His father, Charles Bernard, was a Methodist minister.

W. C. Handy had a true musician's education, though it was not formal. He attended public schools in Florence, studied music with Y. A. Wallace, a FISK UNIVERSITY graduate, and played religious songs on the organ. He also studied the cornet. In 1893, Handy organized a quartet that sang at the CHICAGO Columbian Exposition (World's Fair), and he toured the South, Cuba, and

Mexico with his own band. In addition, he played the cornet with Mahara's Minstrels, eventually becoming the leader of the troupe. During that time, Handy's nickname was "Fess," which was short for "professor," because he was so learned about music.

In 1898, Handy married Elizabeth Price. They settled in Memphis, Tennessee, and had six children.

In 1902, he formed marching and dance bands that became popular in Clarksville, Mississippi. He also managed, in the first decade of 1900, a "bootleg business" in which he supplied the black population with black periodicals that were banned or otherwise frowned upon by the local white townspeople. The newspapers were the *CHICAGO DEFENDER*, *Indianapolis Freeman*, and *Voice of the Negro*.

Throughout his travels, studies, and work responsibilities, Handy read, listened to music, and wrote. He read *First Lessons in Harmony* and *Moore's Encyclopedia of Music*. He listened to folk melodies, wrote notes down in his pad, and began to write music of his own while documenting popular American music. He also taught music at the Teacher's Agricultural and Mechanical College for Negroes in Huntsville, Alabama. Moreover, in 1907 he began to work with Harry Pace in Memphis, with the Pace & Handy Music Company, which they eventually moved to NEW YORK CITY.

In 1909, Handy wrote a campaign song for Ward H. "Boss" Crump's mayoral election bid for the city of Memphis. When Handy's band played the song at street rallies for Crump, the people danced to it. Crump won the election, but Handy had a difficult time publishing the song and was cheated out of his royalties because of JIM CROW racial discrimination. Originally titled "Mr. Crump," the song was finally published in 1912 as "Memphis Blues." Singer and band leader NOBLE SISSLE noted that "Memphis Blues" was a groundbreaking song that inspired dancers Vernon and Irene Castle to create a dance called the "Bunny Hug," soon afterward named the "Fox Trot."

Through his many arrangements and published blues compositions, William Christopher Handy, shown here in 1947, became known as the "Father of the Blues." *(Library of Congress, Prints & Photographs Division, Carl Van Vechten Collection [LC-USZ62-42531])*

Compositions that followed included "St. Louis Blues" (1914); "Yellow Dog Blues" (1914); "Joe Turner Blues" (1915); and "Beale Street Blues" (1917). "St. Louis Blues," with the first lines, "I hate to see de evening sun go down," was written in sad recall of LYNCHINGS in the South. It was also a reminder of those times when, after playing a "gig," whites would caution Handy not to let the sun go down with him still in "their" town, threatening violence if he procrastinated. "Beale Street Blues" was inspired by a tired black male pianist in a café on Beale Street in Memphis, Tennessee. Handy thought that the indefatigable piano player "represented his race" well.

With his band, the Mahara Minstrels, Handy went on tour and relocated to New York in 1918. RACE RECORDS, recordings by black artists, were popular in the 1920s, and Handy and Pace published and recorded them at the Black Swan Recording Company in HARLEM. Among his own compositions during that period were "Careless Love" (1921) and "Aunt Hagar's Blues" (1922).

The 1929 film *St. Louis Blues*, produced by Warner Brothers, dramatized Handy's musical composition of the same name. The title song was sung by BESSIE SMITH. "St. Louis Blues" has since become one of the most recorded songs in the history of music, and it garnered a political history of its own: King Edward VIII of England requested a performance of it on Scottish bagpipes, and it became the Ethiopian (African) battle hymn in the 1930s. Though Handy experienced difficulty retrieving royalties for "Memphis Blues," the "St. Louis Blues" continued to provide him with $25,000 every year well into the 1950s.

As a collector, W. C. Handy assembled music in *Blues: An Anthology* (1926) and *W. C. Handy's Collection of Negro Spirituals* (1938). He also wrote *Negro Authors and Composers of the United States* (1936).

Handy lost his sight in 1943, two years after he published his autobiography, *Father of the Blues*, and just before his last book was completed, *Unsung Americans Sung* (1944). Father of the Blues was cowritten by Harlem Renaissance author ARNA BONTEMPS.

His wife of many years died in 1937, and Handy wed Irma Louise Logan in 1954 when he was 80 years old. W. C. Handy, "Father of the Blues," died four years later on March 28, 1958. In 1969, Handy's likeness was placed on a commemorative postage stamp by the U.S. Postal Service. The city of Memphis paid tribute to the composer by naming W. C. Handy Park, on Beale Street, after him.

Further Reading

Adler, Mortimer J., ed. *The Negro in American History I. Black Americans 1928–1968.* Encyclopædia & Chicago: Britannica Educational Corp., 1969.

Altman, Susan. *The Encyclopedia of African-American Heritage.* New York: Facts On File, Inc., 1997.

Handy, W. C., and Arna Bontemps, ed. *Father of the Blues.* New York: DeCapo Press, 1985. Original: 1941.

Gussow, Adam. "Make My Getaway": The Blues Lives of Black Minstrels in W. C. Handy's Father of the Blues." *African-American Review* 35, no. 1 (Spring 2000): 5–28.

Kranz, Rachel, and Philip J. Koslow. *The Biographical Dictionary of African Americans.* New York: Facts On File, Inc., 1999.

Southern, Eileen. *The Music of Black Musicians, A History.* New York: W.W. Norton, 1971.

— Sandra L. West

Happy Rhones

Among the first entertainment facilities to make the transition from a bar and saloon style of presentation to a more elegant setting, Happy Rhones during the 1910s and 1920s helped pioneer modern nightclub entertainment in HARLEM and throughout the United States.

Located at LENOX AVENUE and 143rd Street, Happy Rhones featured a luxurious decor designed to attract affluent customers. The club's management also made it a point to hire waitresses and hosts to lavish individual attention upon their customers at a time when other facilities did not offer such service. Particularly significant was the club's initiation of the tradition of floor shows in Harlem. Long before CONNIE'S INN or the COTTON CLUB became world famous for shows that made stars of individuals like DUKE ELLINGTON, DOROTHY DANDRIDGE, and FATS WALLER, Happy Rhones featured such shows as part of its regular entertainment. NOBLE SISSLE, cocreator of the hit musical *SHUFFLE ALONG*, served at one point as one of the hosts for the club's entertainment. In addition, FLETCHER HENDERSON and his orchestra helped make the club a favorite gathering place for lovers of JAZZ.

Among the distinguished clientele that Happy Rhones successfully attracted were ETHEL WATERS, BOJANGLES ROBINSON, W. C. HANDY, FLORENCE MILLS, LANGSTON HUGHES, ALBERTA HUNTER, and a variety of white entertainers from Broadway shows and the ZIEGFELD FOLLIES.

Further Reading

Favor, J. Martin. *Authentic Blackness: The Folk in the New Negro Renaissance.* Durham, N.C.: Duke University Press, 1999.

Waggoner, Susan. *Nightclub Nights: Art, Legend, and Style 1920–1960.* Italy: Rizzoli International Publications, 2001.

— Aberjhani

Hardin, Lillian

See ARMSTRONG, LOUIS.

Hardwick, John Wesley

See ART AND THE HARLEM RENAISSANCE.

Harlem

Considered a haven for Africans, African Caribbeans, and African Americans during the early 1900s, the northern area of NEW YORK CITY known as Harlem, near the Hudson River and East 125th Street, was founded in 1658 by Peter Stuyvesant as part of a Dutch settlement called Nieuw Haarlem.

African Americans in New York City did not always call Harlem "home." They gravitated to the uptown village over time, usually seeking better housing. During the 1800s, black people lived in lower Manhattan on Broome, Spring, Sullivan, Thompson, and Bleecker Streets. This section later became known as the Greenwich Village and Washington Square area, a "bohemian" district of poets and various creative artists. They lived in this neighborhood because in Washington Square and on Fifth Avenue's lower portion lived wealthy white families with whom many blacks were employed as butlers and maids. Living in Greenwich Village allowed them to be near their jobs.

By 1890, the black population moved into the upper 20s and lower 30s west of Sixth Avenue; then, in 10 years, to the north around West 53rd Street. A hub of the neighborhood was the Marshall Hotel at 127–129 West 53rd Street, where Sunday dinners were served, modern JAZZ bands played, and discussions were held on the status of black life and culture. The Negro population, some like the famous poet Paul Laurence Dunbar, dressed in their very best to partake of it all.

Around 1900 to 1915, black people began to move into Harlem. In approximately 1910, the 60,534 black people who had lived throughout the borough of New York City increased to 175,000 who lived solely in Harlem. They came from Georgia, the West Indies, Africa, Panama, Florida, and places throughout the southern United States. During the early part (1910) of the GREAT MIGRATION, with the heaviest part of migration coming in 1915, New York City became a haven for a variety of people of African descent. The NATIONAL URBAN LEAGUE (NUL), using the 1923 federal census, cited 183,428 African Americans living in Harlem, though the Information Bureau of the United Hospital Fund quoted 300,000.

LYNCHING, lack of employment opportunities, the denial of voting rights, and poor educational opportunities motivated many African Americans to migrate from the South and settle in such northern locales as Harlem. In the Southern states, the majority of rural blacks were sharecroppers who lived in shanties, or shacks, that did not belong to them. Home ownership or habitable housing in general was something denied many African Americans, even though there was in fact a black middle home-owning class in the South. They nevertheless were bound, as all American blacks were, by the apartheid system of JIM CROW laws and customs. Moreover, the atrocious practice of murdering African Americans by lynching was a frequent event that usually went without the arrest of the murderers. And whereas employment openings were severely restricted for African Americans in the South, they were fairly plentiful in the North, particularly during WORLD WAR I. Many African Americans relocating to Harlem found employment in factories, as teachers in public schools, as bookkeepers, and as lawyers—opportunities that were all but closed to the average southern rural black.

Blacks also left the South in droves because the educational system was unequal and education not compulsory. Eugene Kinckle Jones of the National Urban League observed that in 1920, in New York City, $66 per year was spent on every child, white or black, for education, in sharp contrast to the $1.25 per year spent in South Carolina on one black child. Southern farm children were educated in one-room schoolhouses and were allowed to attend class only after working with their families in the fields.

ALAIN LOCKE, professor of philosophy at HOWARD UNIVERSITY and editor of the *NEW NEGRO* (1925), noted: "A railroad ticket and a suitcase, like a Baghdad carpet, transported the Negro peasant from the cottonfield and farm to the heart of the most complex urban civilization. Here in the mass, he must and does survive a jump of two generations in social economy and of a century and more in civilization."

Locke noted further that "Harlem has the same role to play for the New Negro as Dublin has had for the New Ireland or Prague for the New Czechoslovakia." After many moves from downtown to uptown, and with the influx of blacks from the South and the islands, New York's black population converged in what used to be Nieuw Haarlem—now called Harlem and nicknamed "Little Africa." It became a "city within a city," "about 50 blocks long (from 110th Street), seven to eight blocks wide, and with as many as 5,000 to 7,000 people living in a single block."

Aside from "Little Africa," Harlem acquired several other names. JAMES WELDON JOHNSON, coauthor of the "Negro National Anthem," called Harlem "Black Manhattan" and authored a social history under that title. Johnson wrote: "So here we have Harlem—not merely a colony or a community or a settlement—not at all a 'quarter' or a slum or a fringe—but a black city located in the heart of white Manhattan, and containing more Negroes to the square mile than any other spot on earth. . . ." Militant poet CLAUDE MCKAY called Harlem the "Negro Metropolis." By the mid-1920s, the black metropolis was internationally known as the hub of African-American life and culture and the official headquarters of the New Negro movement.

The original uptown village, when still heavy with German, Irish, and Jewish residents, was full of large apartment buildings and brownstones, and because the Lenox Avenue Subway had not yet been constructed, the buildings were not rented to capacity. White landlords were losing money. A former mortician named Philip A. Payton promised the landlords of these large, under-occupied buildings that he could fill them up with African-American tenants and he did so, which did not concern white residents in the area until black families spread west of LENOX AVENUE. Payton formed the Afro-American Realty Company and bought and leased houses for blacks like himself. SAINT PHILIP'S EPISCOPAL CHURCH also bought houses and made them available to their black congregation. And other black realtors, groups of African-Caribbean relatives, and black business ventures followed suit. However, 1920s studies from the National Urban League show that black families paid 47 percent more for rent than white families.

Even so, at the height of the *New Negro* movement in the late 1920s, Harlem boasted luxurious black neighborhoods in SUGAR HILL and STRIVER'S ROW, as well as a thriving cabaret business in JUNGLE ALLEY. Its residents included legions of writers and other creative artists, from poet LANGSTON HUGHES to short story writer RUDOLPH FISHER, who made the community richer by their presence and contributions.

Throughout the 1930s, African-American tenants and homeowners in the community continued to increase, and by the end of the decade, 30 percent of the apartment buildings lacked proper bathrooms. White residents moved out in droves, leaving black residents with high rents that had to be supplemented by boarders and rent parties (see also RENT PARTY). Black Baptist churches replaced white Lutheran churches, cabarets opened for business, societies were established for the social and economic benefit of its latest citizens, and Harlem became a community of vibrant color, cultural energy, and (unfortunately) crime.

The new residents of Harlem were black, but the immediate businesses in the community did not reflect their existence. In 1930, blacks in the same year owned less than 19 percent of the 10,300 businesses in Harlem, and most of the employees were part-time workers. Of the businesses, there were only 258 black-owned retail stores in Manhattan. Most of these were grocery stores and lunch counters. An exception to these was The Hobby Horse book shop, located at 205 West 136th Street, where books by black authors were sold. The owner, Douglas Howe, encouraged young writers and visual artists by stocking their books and displaying their art work in his shop. One of the visual artists who had a Hobby Horse shop exhibition was James Allen, a popular photographic chronicler of Harlem scenes. Howe was well known for his business card and advertisements that deftly played on his last name, "Howe About Books?"

Another Harlem business, Blumstein's Department Store at 230 West 125th Street, served as a reminder, during the 1930s, that racial segregation in the United States was not limited to the South. Built by German immigrant Louis Blumstein in 1898, Blumstein's was a full-scale department store. Though it accepted the business of the black residents, the store did not hire black people for anything other than menial jobs. In 1934, the Citizens League for Fair Play started an economic boycott against the store. The boycott was endorsed by more than 50 churches and organizations, including the ABYSSINIAN BAPTIST CHURCH, where both ADAM CLAYTON POWELL, SR., and JR., pastored; Mother A.M.E. Zion Church; Ephesus Seventh Day Adventist Church, which author ARNA BONTEMPS attended when a Harlem resident; Yoruba Literary Club; Students Literary Association of St. Mark's Episcopal Church; Premier Literary Circle; Garvey Club of New York, Inc.; the *NEW YORK AGE;* and the Negro Lodge Elks. The theme of the boycott was "Don't Buy Where You Can't Work." It was so successful that similar barriers in the North were torn down.

Blumstein's became the first urban store to use a black Santa Claus during the Christmas holiday season and the first to use black mannequins.

During the 1920s and 1930s, Harlem experienced lavish parades sponsored by MARCUS GARVEY's UNIVERSAL NEGRO IMPROVEMENT ASSOCIATION, crime waves, race riots, economic boycotts against business establishments that would not hire blacks, the GREAT DEPRESSION, and Easter parades up and down SEVENTH AVENUE. In more modern times, the community, like many others, has suffered from illicit drug traffic that has killed more young black people than the number lost in the Vietnam War, and renovation projects have both succeeded and failed.

Through it all, there remains no place in the world quite like Harlem. In the early 21st century, it continues to be a leading jazz center, home of the legendary APOLLO THEATRE and the SCHOMBURG CENTER FOR RESEARCH IN BLACK CULTURE. Brownstones are undergoing renovation, and several writers' guilds remain active. One of the largest black bookstores in the United States, Hue-Man, announced its relocation from Colorado to Harlem. Old Navy, an updated version of the Army and Navy clothing stores, opened on 125th Street. Upscale coffee shops—one a Starbucks owned by Los Angeles Lakers legend Erwin "Magic" Johnson—and clothing shops abound, plus 2,700-seat movie theaters and jazz clubs. The *Amsterdam News* continues to publish every week, and the Harlem Writers Guild, founded during the renaissance, still convenes at the Schomburg. Old tenement buildings have been demolished and rehabilitated. Monthly rents have increased from the average $50 of the Harlem Renaissance era for a five-room walk-up on West 119th Street between Fifth and Lenox, to $1,500 a month for a one-bedroom apartment at Lenox Towers apartments on 135th Street.

In addition, former President William Jefferson Clinton brought national attention to Harlem when he secured office space in the Adam Clayton Powell, Jr., State Office Building, adjacent to the prestigious Studio Museum in Harlem. The Harlem Boys Choir, Ebony Opera, the Dance Theatre of Harlem, and Barbara Ann Teer's tireless theater efforts still provide the kind of superlative cultural performances that added

125th Street has long been one of Harlem's principal thoroughfares. Shown here ca. 1910 to 1920, looking west from Seventh Avenue, one sees a prosperous, busy community. *(Library of Congress, Prints & Photographs Division)*

The site of theaters, restaurants, shops, and apartments, Harlem's 125th Street (shown here in 1943) thrived with the influx of African Americans to the community in the 1920s and 1930s. *(Library of Congress, Prints & Photographs Division [LC-USW3-031112-C])*

to the community's renown during the renaissance. In short, Harlem in the modern era continues to boom.

Further Reading

Bascom, Lionel C., ed. *A Renaissance in Harlem: Lost Voices of an American Community.* New York: Avon, 1999.

Cantor, George. *Historic Landmarks of Black America.* Detroit: Gale Research, 1991.

Dolkart, Andrew S., and Gretchen S. Sorin. *Touring Historic Harlem: Four Walks in Northern Manhattan.* New York: Landmarks Conservancy, 1997.

Hughes, Langston, and John Henrik Clarke, eds. *Harlem: A Community in Transition.* New York: Citadel Press, 1964.

Johnson, James Weldon. *Black Manhattan.* New York: Knopf, 1930.

Kellner, Bruce, ed. *The Harlem Renaissance: A Historical Dictionary for the Era.* Westport, Conn.: Greenwood Press, 1984.

Lindo, Nashoremeh N. R. *Harlem 1900–1940: An African-American Community. An Exhibition Portfolio.* New York: The Schomburg Center for Research in Black Culture, The New York Public Library. A Project of the Schomburg Center Schools Program made possible by RJR Nabisco Inc., 1991.

McKay, Claude. *Harlem: Negro Metropolis.* New York: 1940. Reprint, New York: Harcourt Brace, 1968.

Sochen, June, ed. *The Black Man and the American Dream: Negro Aspirations in America, 1900–1930.* Chicago: Quadrangle Books, 1971.

Wintz, Cary D. *Black Culture and the Harlem Renaissance.* Houston, Texas: Rice University Press, 1988.

— Sandra L. West

Harlem Artists Guild

See DOUGLAS, AARON.

Harlem Community Art Center

Established by sculptor AUGUSTA FELLS SAVAGE and sponsored by the WORKS PROGRESS ADMINISTRATION (WPA), the Harlem Community Art Center on 135th Street provided classes for thousands of HARLEM residents during the GREAT DEPRESSION. It operated from 1937 to 1942.

First Lady ELEANOR ROOSEVELT was among those who participated in the opening festivities for the Harlem Community Art Center. The facility eventually became so successful that it expanded to include additional space at 306 West 141st Street. One of the primary reasons for the center's exceptional impact was the quality of its many illustrious instructors. Two of those instructors were ELTON FAX and NORMAN LEWIS. Both Augusta Savage and, later, GWENDOLYN BENNETTA BENNETT served as directors. It was considered by many to be the best of the WPA art centers.

Further Reading

"Narratives of African American Art and Identity." Available online. Downloaded October 16, 2002. URL: http://www.artgallery.umd.edu/driskell/exhibition/sec3/sava_a_02.htm.

New Deal Network. "Harlem Community Art Center, NY." Available online. Downloaded October 16, 2002. URL: http://newdeal.feri.org/library/2_7_6h.htm.

— Sandra L. West

Harlem Experimental Theater

The Harlem Experimental Theater became in 1929 the second in a line of theater groups that performed out of the Harlem Library Little Theater located in the basement of the 135th Street Branch of the New York Public Library. The first group of players was the KRIGWA PLAYERS, founded by W. E. B. DU BOIS and REGINA ANDREWS.

The founding members of the Harlem Experimental Theater were: Regina Andrews, Dorothy Peterson, Harold Jackman, Theopilus Lewis, Ira D. Reid, JESSIE REDMOND FAUSET, and William Jackson. Peterson was appointed the group's first executive director and Andrews became its second. Jackman, often cited as a friend to COUNTEE CULLEN and other Harlem Renaissance figures, directed several of the theater's plays.

While the Harlem Experimental Theater followed the same cultural philosophy as the Krigwa Players and promoted works by and about African Americans, they did feature at their start *The No Count Boy* by white playwright Paul Green. As noted in various studies on the Harlem Renaissance, the period supposedly did not produce any known black playwrights that achieved the stature of its more renowned poets and novelists. Members of the Harlem Experimental Theater took it upon themselves to fill that gap with their own creations.

Andrews wrote several plays produced by the group and directed by Jackman. Her plays, produced from 1931 to 1932, included *Climbing Jacob's Ladder,* a play that portrayed a lynching that took place while people prayed in church, *The Man Who Passed,* and *Underground.* Works by some of the other playwrights were Harry Camp's *The Prodigal Son,* Robert Dorsey's *Get Thee Behind Me Satan,* and George Cogman's *Little Stone House,* all in 1932.

The Harlem Experimental Theater players left the basement of the Harlem Library Little Theater and relocated to St. Philip's Parish House on West 134th Street shortly before disbanding. The Harlem Library Little Theater then became home for a short time to the Harlem Players. Continuing the tradition of producing works by black writers, the Harlem Players staged *Taxi Fare* by the artist RICHARD BRUCE NUGENT and Rose McClendon, *Sacrifice* by Carlton Moss and Richard Huey, and *Burning the Mortgage* by William Jackson.

Further Reading

Peterson, Bernard L., Jr. *The African American Theatre Directory, 1816–1960.* Westport, Conn.: Greenwood Press, 1997.

— Aberjhani

Harlem Globetrotters

Originally named The Savoy Big Five, the Harlem Globetrotters were founded in 1927 by Abe Saperstein as a new kind of basketball team that combined athletics and comedy.

The name Savoy Big Five likely came from the marquee of the SAVOY BALLROOM, a dance and music club popular during the Harlem Renaissance. The Harlem Globetrotters would later also become known as the "Ambassadors of Goodwill" because of their international celebrity.

When the Globetrotters were formed in 1927, the National Basketball Association (NBA) was racially segregated. Unlike the NATIONAL NEGRO BASEBALL LEAGUE, in basketball there was no organized league for African-American athletes. Thus, Abe Saperstein drafted his ball club, predominantly, from black college teams.

Saperstein used reverse segregation to hold the Globetrotters together: he threatened to boycott the NBA, wherever they were playing, if they considered integrating their teams. No drafts of African Americans were allowed, according to Saperstein. He wanted to keep his players to himself. His threats were viable until 1950–51, when the Boston Celtics drafted Chuck Cooper and integrated the sport of basketball in the United States.

Saperstein was as tough on his players as he was on the association. He paid them relatively poorly, from $500 to $600 a month, then forbid them to go to the higher paying NBA. He outlawed jump shots because he thought that the jump shot was a "defilement" of the game. Saperstein also forced veteran Globetrotter players to try out for the team every fall. The players stayed with the team because the Globetrotters were, for African-American players until the 1950s, the only professional game in town. Moreover, Saperstein, for all his rigidity, was termed a "loyal friend."

Appreciative crowds filled sports arenas to capacity all over the world to see the Harlem Globetrotters play. Being a Globetrotter was very much like being part of an athletic, traveling circus. The team played before popes, dictators, and royal families. They played on such nontraditional "courts" as bullrings, fish markets, and at the bottom of a drained swimming pool. Their game would start out as traditional competitive basketball, then would change into "clowning" or hilarious antics. Since they were basically a well-oiled comedy routine with extraordinary athletic skills, the Globetrotters played against "Class B" teams such as the New York Nations or the Chicago Demons. On the Harlem Globetrotters court, all was in jest. They performed to their theme song, "Sweet Georgia Brown."

Among the most popular Globetrotter "clowns," as they were called, were Meadowlark Lemon and Goose Tatum. After the 1950s, several NBA players emerged from the Globetrotters bench, including NBA superstar Wilt Chamberlain.

Abe Saperstein died in 1966. The Globetrotters were sold for $3.7 million to Potter Palmer, George Gillett, and John O'Neil. The salary for a Globetrotter in the modern era rose to approximately $70,000 per year. Women were introduced in the lineup in 1986. The first female Globetrotter was Lynette Woodard.

In patriotic red, white, and blue uniforms, the Globetrotters have played in more than 89 countries before more than 75 million people. At 75 years old, they are a holdover from "The Golden Age of Sports" and continue to delight audiences into the 21st century.

Further Reading

African-American Biography, 2. Detroit: UXL, 1994, 320–22.

Bloom, John, and Michael Nevin Willard, eds. *Sports Matters: Race, Recreation, and Culture.* New York: New York University Press, 2002.

Wilkes, John D. *The Harlem Globetrotters.* Broomall, Pa.: Chelsea House Publishers, 1997.

— Sandra L. West

Harlem Hellfighters

The Harlem Hellfighters, aptly named by German soldiers, were the first Americans to fight on French soil in WORLD WAR I. Distinguishing itself in battle, the black regiment won high French military honors and returned to the United States to a triumphant homecoming.

Originally members of the 15th New York, a National Guard regiment, the unit was organized as early as June 1913 by a bill passed in the state legislature to form an infantry of African-American soldiers. Years after the bill had passed, Colonel William Haywood, a New York Public Service Commissioner and former veteran of the Spanish-American War, made a public call to enlist black men for the infantry.

Official recruitment began on June 29, 1916. Haywood concentrated on enlisting men from HARLEM, the Williamsburg section of Brooklyn, and San Juan Hill. He recruited from neighborhood sites, such as the cigar store on the corner of 131st Street and SEVENTH AVENUE. By October 1916, 10 companies of 65 men each were formed and ready for training.

Without an armory in which to train, the unit drilled at the Lafayette Dance Hall on 132nd Street and Seventh Avenue. They dug trenches to simulate the wartime theater in the backyards of tenements in Harlem and Brooklyn. The new recruits were not issued rifles; they drilled with broomsticks on Morningside Avenue and were given the New York Infantry flag as standard issue.

Several well-known civilians enlisted, most notably James Reese Europe, NOBLE SISSLE, and BERT WILLIAMS. Europe had recently organized the first existing musicians' union. Musicians that were part of the Clef Club also joined the infantry. Sissle was a composer and bandleader who became the infantry drum major. Williams, a famous comedian and actor, was a former captain of the California National Guard. The infantry was to have one of the finest bands in the U.S. Army.

At the onset of the war, the troops were stationed in tents at Van Cortland Park until dispatched to Camp Wadsworth in Spartanburg, South Carolina, for combat training. There, they were met with racial hostility from the southern town and white troops. The war department had considered it a mistake to send northern blacks to the South and had planned to keep black Americans from fighting. They preferred to see war fought by whites. The volatile situation caused the regiment of black men to deport prematurely to France without the benefit of combat training.

In November 1917, the 15th New York Infantry embarked for France from the Hoboken, New Jersey, Pier 3 shipyard on the *Pocahontas*—nameless at the time. They landed in Brest, France, on December 26, 1917. They were besieged by a snowstorm, an outbreak of German measles, and a hostile reception from the U.S. Marines. The only wartime regiment to go to war under a state flag, for one and a half months they worked as laborers, stevedores, woodchoppers, mechanics, and trench diggers. The men's morale began to suffer, and they asked when they would be allowed to fight.

While the majority of the unit labored, the band was sent on a tour of France. Under the directorship of James Reese Europe, the band provided France with its first taste of African-American JAZZ. They became popular with the French allies.

In response to the declining morale of his men, Haywood petitioned General Pershing to reassign the regiment. With the Germans 60 miles outside of their country, the French needed reinforcements. As a result, the 15th New York was assigned to the French 4th Army. It was not until this assignment that the unit was given a federal designation: the 369th Regiment d'Infanterie Etats Unis (United States Infantry).

Under the French, the New York soldiers were issued French grenades, bayonets, rifles, and machine guns. The equipment was different and older than that used in the U.S. Army. The black soldiers adapted their technique for throwing grenades from urban sandlot baseball games, and in grenade-throwing practice they surpassed their French instructors. They also excelled at use of the bayonet and learned the French language quickly.

The 369th went into action in the spring of 1918 in the Bois d'Hauze, Champagne sector, and remained on the front lines for 191 consecutive days. Two members showed particular valor in combat: Private Henry Johnson, a redcap from Albany, New York, and Needham Roberts of Trenton, New Jersey. Johnson and Roberts were sent to a listening post several yards advanced of the trenches occupied by their comrades to warn of possible attack by Germans. While on post, Roberts was attacked and wounded, but he held the enemy at bay by lobbing hand grenades. The German raiding party continued to attack and were able to capture Roberts. As Roberts was carried off to the German lines, Johnson rushed the enemy with a bolo knife, single-handedly creating such a diversion and inflicting so many casualties that Roberts was released. For their bravery they were awarded the Croix de Guerre, the highest French military medal for valor. Both men recovered from their wounds and returned home, but they were neither compensated nor recognized by the U.S. government.

Ironically, while fighting for the principles of justice and democracy, the black regiment was subject to German propaganda. Pamphlets dropped on the trench-bound soldiers warned them that they were fighting for democratic principles that would not be extended to them in America. Undaunted by German attempts to undermine their purpose, the regiment took their responsibility as American citizens to heart. It was the Germans who began to call the 369th "hellfighters" for their fighting spirit.

In the combat zone in the Argonne Forest, the 369th held a thin line of defense. In an area about four miles long, their battle continued. No German was able to get into their trenches and the offensive stalled. A total of 200 Hellfighters were killed and 800 wounded. They ran farther and faster than any other regiment and won all battles against the Germans. They never lost a prisoner, a trench, or a foot of ground. They served on the front lines longer than any other regiment by at least five days. The 369th was the first to reach the Rhine River and occupied three German towns.

The entire 369th Regiment, 171 men, were individually awarded the Croix de Guerre. Two soldiers received the Congressional Medal of Honor, nine the Legion d'Honneur, 10 the Distinguished Service Cross, and eight the American Citation for Gallantry. They returned home triumphantly in February 1919. Lead by their famous band, they marched up Fifth Avenue in NEW YORK CITY in a victory parade from Greenwich Village to Harlem in a French phalanx formation of 16 abreast. Europe played only French marches, not the jazz that the crowd expected. All New York celebrated the victory. In Harlem, especially, the Hellfighters were enthusiastically welcomed back with pride and jubilation.

The Harlem Hellfighters saw the first and longest service of any American regiment as part of a foreign army, even with less training than any American unit before going into action. However, when the parade was over and the decorated men returned to private life in their homeland, they discovered that JIM CROW racial segregation was still an ugly and limiting reality.

An early account of the regiment was written in 1936 by Arthur W. Little in *From Harlem to the Rhine: The Story of New York's Colored Volunteers,* and a chronicle of the regiment is preserved by the 369 Historical Society at the museum of the 369th Veterans Association at 2366 Fifth Avenue, at 142 Street, in NEW YORK CITY.

Further Reading

Harris, Bill. *The Hellfighters of Harlem: African American Soldiers Who Fought for the Right to Fight for Their Country.* New York: Avalon Publishing Group, 2002.

Katz, William. *Harlem Hellfighters.* New York: HarperCollins Publishers, 2002.

— Karen E. Johnson

Harlem Hospital

With just 54 beds occupying a three-story wooden building on East 120th Street in NEW YORK CITY, Harlem Hospital opened for business in 1887. Its purpose was to serve indigent transfer patients on their way to other facilities and to act as an emergency branch of the larger Bellevue Hospital.

By 1900, the need for 100 beds was clear, and the hospital moved to LENOX AVENUE on 136th and 137th streets in HARLEM. On April 13, 1907, it relocated to an even newer facility with 150 beds. At the beginning of the hospital's operations, black patients were not in the majority, and its staff did not include black doctors. The hospital hired several black nurses in 1917, but white nurses responded to this personnel action by resigning from their posts.

During and after WORLD WAR I, Harlem experienced a huge influx of black southern immigrants. The new community members expressed outrage at the hospital's biased hiring practices. Led by Rev. ADAM CLAYTON POWELL, SR., activist pastor of the ABYSSINIAN BAPTIST CHURCH, and other leaders, the community protested, rallied, and demanded that the hospital hire more black medics.

Bending to the community's wishes, in 1919, Dr. Louis T. Wright was appointed clinical assistant in the Out-Patient Department. He began work in this mundane position on January 1, 1920, the first African-American physician in the history of New York City hospitals. Similar to the 1917 walkout of white nurses, four white doctors resigned to protest Wright's appointment. Dr. Casmo D. O'Neil, the administrator responsible for Wright's selection, was demoted. Harlem Hospital added three more African-American visiting physicians to the staff in January 1926, and Dr. Wright, at the low end of administration, was given the title of assistant visiting physician. With these adjunct appointments, Harlem Hospital still lacked a tenured or house-staff African-American physician. Dr. Wright, still the assistant visiting physician, took a civil service examination, earned a promotion, and in 1928 became the first African-American police surgeon of the City of New York.

By 1929, there were 64 doctors and surgeons at Harlem Hospital. Seven of them were African-American. One of the African-American doctors was Dr. Aubre de L. Maynard, the first black intern on the house staff. Also, Dr. Peter Marshall Murray was appointed at this time as a provisional assistant adjunct visiting gynecologist.

Morale at the hospital and in the community was low, and racial hostility was teeming because African-American physicians were not appointed to responsible, desirable, tenured positions. In 1931, five black doctors were fired from the hospital. This action instigated a public protest led by Rev. ADAM CLAYTON POWELL, JR., of Abyssinian Baptist Church, and the five were reinstated

In accordance with the trend of painting murals for institutions during the Harlem Renaissance, CHARLES HENRY ALSTON and HALE ASPACIO WOODRUFF, with helpers EDWIN AUGUSTUS HARLESTON and twin photographers Marvin and Morgan Smith, painted a mural entitled "Magic and Medicine" (1937) on the internal walls of the Harlem Hospital. The mural depicts the history of medicine, but it created a major

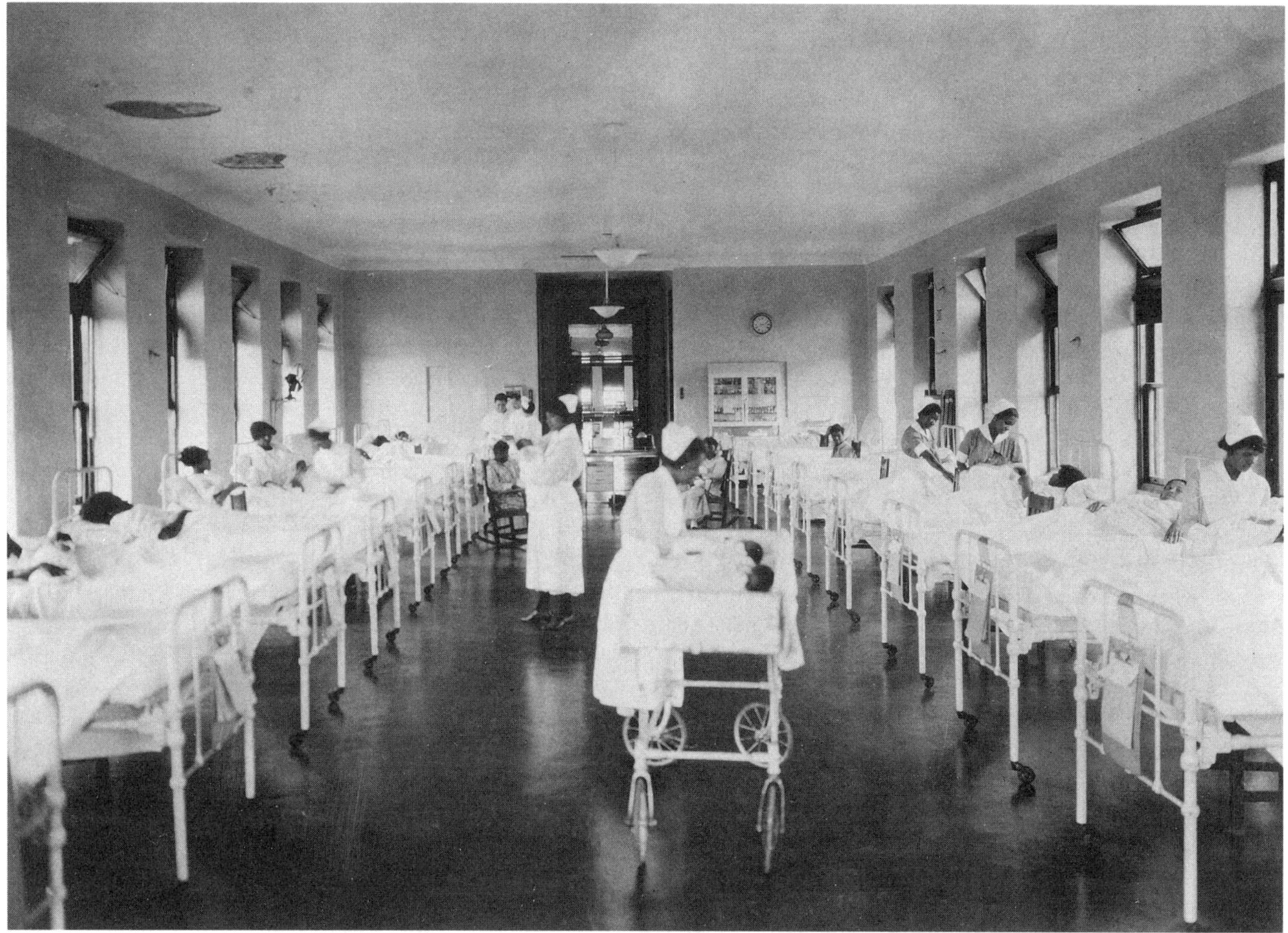

The site of many controversies regarding racist hiring practices and proper medical care for African Americans in its earlier years, the Harlem Hospital developed from a 54-bed facility in 1887 to a major medical center in the 1900s. *(Photographs and Prints Division, Schomburg Center for Research in Black Culture, The New York Public Library, Astor, Lenox and Tilden Foundations)*

public controversy because of the primitive manner in which the history was represented. The style allegedly was not in the spirit of the dignified, enlightened NEW NEGRO.

In 1934, Dr. Wright became the second black physician admitted to fellowship in the American College of Surgeons, the first being the eminent Dr. Daniel Hale Williams. In 1943, Dr. Wright was made director of the Department of Surgery. When he died in 1952, the directorship to the department of surgery was given to Dr. Maynard.

By 2002, Harlem Hospital had become the largest in Harlem with some 400 beds, a modern Urgent Care Center, and specialized critical care units for the treatment of burns and asthma.

Further Reading

Maynard, Aubre de L. *Surgeons to the Poor: The Harlem Hospital Story.* New York: Appleton-Century Crofts, 1978.

Savitt, Todd L., Dr. "Black Doctors: A Strong Medicine to Take in the New South." *Crisis,* January/February 2001, 26–30.

— Sandra L. West

Harlem Riots

Rumors and strained social conditions combined to create two of HARLEM's most destructive riots, in 1935 and 1943, as residents of the community responded violently against the very conditions often portrayed in the music, art, and writings of the Harlem Renaissance.

At the center of the riot in Harlem on March 19, 1935, was a Puerto Rican adolescent named Lino Rivera who was accused of shoplifting a penknife at K. S. Kress and detained by the store's owner and an investigating policeman. As the policeman began to escort Rivera toward the back of the store, reportedly for questioning and to avoid interference, a bystander screamed out that they were taking the young man downstairs to beat him. Although the store owner asked the policeman to release Rivera, the charge of brutality echoed throughout Harlem until it became a charge of murder. By early evening, a full-scale riot had ensued to protest the killing of a young black man.

Up and down the main thoroughfares of Harlem, people broke the windows of 300 primarily white-owned businesses.

Advocates of COMMUNISM circulated flyers stating that Rivera had been violently beaten, and looters gathered goods throughout the commercial district. Business and property damages totaled $2 million. More than 100 people were arrested and three black men were killed, two of them described as looters shot through the chest by policemen. More than 500 policemen filled the community; a number of them were injured by bottles and stones tossed from upper-floor windows. Despite officials' attempts to inform rioters that Rivera was very much alive and uninjured, violence took over the streets until four the next morning.

On March 21, 1935, the *New York Times* reported that black leaders, trying to understand what caused the riot, all agreed that it involved a lot more than a boy's desire for a penknife: "the basic cause is economic maladjustment; segregating and discrimination against Negroes in the matter of employment." In 1935, the midpoint of the GREAT DEPRESSION, Harlemites suffered an unemployment rate of 50 percent. Yet what monies were available for spending ultimately went to the white shop owners—the very ones whose businesses were looted—who collected black dollars but generally refused to hire black workers. Moreover, it was widely acknowledged that the cost of rent and various goods tended to run higher in the black community than the cost for comparable spaces and goods elsewhere in NEW YORK CITY. Feeling the pinch of economic straits as they did, many families doubled or tripled up on apartment space simply to survive. Some blocks contained as many as 3,000 to 4,000 residents. Not surprisingly, disease became a major health issue, yet in a community of some 200,000 people, the HARLEM HOSPITAL was equipped with only 273 beds and 50 bassinets.

A biracial Mayor's Commission on Conditions in Harlem, established by Mayor FIORELLO HENRY LA GUARDIA, held 25 hearings and listened to 160 witnesses to determine the causes and implications of the 1935 riot. ALAIN LOCKE traveled from Howard University to review and confirm the committee's findings. Committees were established to make recommendations for better educational facilities and job opportunities. However, eight years later, a more severe riot once again tore the community apart.

As with the riot of 1935, the riot that occurred on June 20, 1943, began with a dispute involving two individuals and grew into one that engulfed the whole of Harlem. Marjorie Polite was staying at the Braddock Hotel when she decided its bathroom facilities were inadequate and that she wanted to check out. When she requested that a hotel employee return a dollar tip she said she had given him, the employee contended he had never received such a tip and the two began arguing. Because the hotel had previously been raided for prostitution, an officer named James Collins was on "Raided Premises Duty" and attempted to arrest Polite. Florine Roberts was also at the Braddock Hotel, visiting her son Robert Bandy on leave from the army. Demanding the release of Polite, Mrs. Roberts also confronted Patrolman Collins. The patrolman reportedly wound up struggling with Mrs. Roberts and her son, who struck the policeman, then ran, and was shot in the back. With the arrival of police backup, Collins and Bandy were both taken to Sydenham Hospital, where Bandy's wound proved to be minor.

Shortly after the incident, the story spread that a black soldier had been trying to protect his mother when he was shot and killed by a white policeman. Crowds gathered at the Braddock Hotel, police headquarters, and Sydenham Hospital. Police addressed the groups with assurances that Bandy was alive and well. Rumor insisted otherwise and by 11 P.M. store windows were again breaking in Harlem. Gunfire rang through the streets as stores were looted and burned. With doors torn from their hinges and glass shattered, old and young alike were seen gathering food, clothing, household items, and various luxuries.

Black leaders rode on municipal sound trucks asking residents to maintain order and announcing that Bandy had not been killed but was only slightly wounded. La Guardia called for unity over the radio and restricted entrance to Harlem to its residents only. Arranging for emergency food and supplies for the area, he stressed that the riot was not a "race riot" per se but one instigated by criminal elements taking advantage of the Collins/Polite/Bandy incident. While all did not agree with his assessment of the nature of the riot, most did agree that he provided effective leadership when it happened.

By the time the chaos receded the next morning, Eighth Avenue, SEVENTH AVENUE, and 125th Street had become rivers of debris. The death count doubled that of the 1935 riot with six black people killed this time around. Some 200 were injured and almost 600 arrested. Estimates of property damage ran as high as $5 million.

Conditions leading up to the 1943 riot were similar to the ones that helped spark the Harlem riot in 1935. One huge difference was a riot in Detroit that only two months before had ended with the deaths of 25 African Americans and nine European Americans. More than 700 people were injured and property damage came to $2 million. Like other major northern and midwestern cities, Detroit had been feeling the strain of adjusting to an increased black population—approximately 50,000 from 1940 to 1943—and accommodating the production demands of World War II. NATIONAL ASSOCIATION FOR THE ADVANCEMENT OF COLORED PEOPLE (NAACP) leader WALTER WHITE, city commissioner ADAM CLAYTON POWELL, JR., and Mayor La Guardia all expressed concern prior to the June 20 riot that Harlem could easily go the way of Detroit, and steps were taken to prevent exactly such an event. Various leaders and civic groups publicly advocated for racial harmony in New York. Walter White and Wendell Willkie joined with celebrities and known literary personalities to produce a series of nationally broadcast radio programs promoting harmony between the races. Famed *Invisible Man* author RALPH WALDO ELLISON wrote an account of the riot for the *New York Post.*

In addition to the slum-like conditions under which many Harlem citizens were already living, a series of events occurred that, according to various observers, added intolerable insult to already grievous injury. Although Stuyvesant Metropolitan

Life Insurance Company had a reputation for flagrant racism, it was awarded a $50 million contract to construct project homes initially targeted for African Americans but then rumored to be for whites. The company stated that it had no intentions of renting to blacks and refused to adopt an antidiscrimination clause, threatening to abandon the project if forced to do so. Mayor La Guardia, who generally maintained a strong reputation for political fairness among New York's black population, suffered a loss in credibility over the issue when he failed to reprimand the company and supported its receipt of the contract. Further frustration in Harlem's black community came when the U.S. Navy rented Hunter College for use in training the Women's Reserve of the U.S. Naval Reserve (WAVES). Again, the issue became one of local government appearing to sanction the discriminatory practices of an organization known for the same—in this case, the WAVES. Still, an event that the community took more personally was the NYPD's closing of the popular SAVOY BALLROOM on charges of prostitution.

Preventive measures did not stop the riot from occurring, but many felt they helped decrease the damage that was done. The riot convinced La Guardia to adopt an earlier proposal to establish a biracial committee on race relations. The Office of Price Administration opened a branch in Harlem to investigate the long-standing charges of overpricing in the community. The Savoy Ballroom was reopened. Twenty-one years would pass before another major riot hit Harlem, during the Civil Rights movement in 1964.

Further Reading

Capeci, Dominic J., Jr. *The Harlem Riot of 1943.* Philadelphia: Temple University Press. 1977.

Curtis, Lynn A., and Fred R. Harris, eds. *Locked in the Poorhouse: Cities, Race, and Poverty in the United States.* Lanham, Md.: Rowman and Littlefield, 2000.

Jackson, Lawrence. *Ralph Ellison: Emergence of Genius.* New York: Wiley, 2002.

— Aberjhani

Harlem Suitcase Theater

The Harlem Suitcase Theater was founded by LANGSTON HUGHES in 1937 as a form of proletariat theater based largely on productions Hughes had seen while traveling in Russia.

Helping Hughes establish the group were Hilary Phillips, who acted as its director; Thomas Richardson, the executive director; and LOUISE THOMPSON PATTERSON. Patterson helped provide backing from the labor fraternity known as the International Workers Order (IWO). Their first base of operations was the IWO's Community Center on West 125th Street.

The Harlem Suitcase Theater based its name on the minimal props, reportedly capable of fitting inside a small suitcase (a piano being the exception), used by the group for its productions. The plays were often done without scenery or curtains. In addition to providing the kind of African-American plays theatergoers rarely experienced on Broadway, the group's goal was to produce theater reflecting the voice of the masses. It specifically targeted HARLEM audiences and employed Harlem actors. Prices to attend the performances were on a par with those to attend a movie.

Between 1937 and 1938, the Harlem Suitcase Theater staged six plays by Hughes, all of them studies in the kind of balance the writer managed to achieve between humor and serious politics. *Don't You Want to be Free?* was a musical drama exploring African-American history up to contemporary times. It achieved the distinction of becoming one of the longest running plays in the Harlem community with 135 performances. The play benefited from direction by its author and a cast that featured Robert Earl Jones, father of celebrated actor James Earl Jones.

The group also staged Hughes's *Angelo Herndon Jones,* examining the real-life case of a man condemned to 27 years on a chain gang for leading a protest against unemployment; *The Em-Fuehrer Jones,* satirizing Adolf Hitler and Eugene O'Neill's *EMPEROR JONES;* Little Eva's End, lampooning Harriet Beecher Stowe's *Uncle Tom's Cabin; Limitations of Life,* parodying the movie *Imitation of Life;* and *De Organizer,* a blues opera that was composed with RAGTIME pianist James P. Johnson and focused on attempts to organize sharecropper labor (this opera was performed in December 2002 with Johnson's score, once assumed lost).

Works by other playwrights were also performed by the Harlem Suitcase Theater. Among these were *The Slave* by Elizabeth Yates; *The Man Who Died at Twelve O'Clock* by Paul Green; *Young Man of Harlem* by Powell Lindsay; and *Fuente Ovejuna,* a play by Lope de Vega translated by Dorothy Peterson and Hughes. A lack of funding prevented the scheduled dramatization of a play based on RICHARD NATHANIEL WRIGHT's story *Fire and Cloud.*

With the conclusion of productions by the Harlem Suitcase Theater in 1939, Hughes went on to establish two other theater groups. In 1939, he formed the New Negro Theater in Los Angeles, and in 1941, the Skyloft Players in Chicago.

Further Reading

Hamalian, Leo, and James V. Hatch. *Lost Plays of the Harlem Renaissance 1920–1940.* Detroit: Wayne State University Press, 1996.

Krasner, David. *A Beautiful Pageant: African American Theatre, Drama, and Performance in the Harlem Renaissance, 1910–1927.* New York: Palgrave Global Publishing, 2002.

— Aberjhani

Harleston, Edwin Augustus (1882–1931) and Elise Beatrice Forrest Harleston (1891–1971)

artists, photographers

Husband and wife Edwin Augustus Harleston and Elise Beatrice Harleston, a true example of the creative and entrepreneurial spirit that pervaded the Harlem Renaissance era, did not live in HARLEM, but together they photographed images of key Harlem Renaissance figures.

Edwin Augustus Harleston was born on March 14, 1882, to Louise Moultrie and Edwin G. Harleston in Charleston, South Carolina. His father owned three funeral homes in South Carolina and Florida. Elise Beatrice Forrest Harleston was born on February 8, 1891, to Elvira Moorer and Augustus Forrest in Charleston, South Carolina. Her father was an accountant.

Edwin Harleston received a scholarship to attend Avery Normal Institute (now Avery Research Center) in Charleston. Elise Forrest also attended Avery, a private boarding school for black children, established by the American Missionary Association.

Edwin Harleston left Charleston in 1900 to attend Atlanta University, where he befriended two professors. One was W. E. B. DU BOIS, later editor of *CRISIS: A RECORD OF THE DARKER RACES*, and the other George A. Towns. Towns's daughter, Grace, was one of Harleston's first models. She later became the first black woman in the Georgia legislature. Edwin Harleston continued his education at the School of the Museum of Fine Arts in Boston, then returned to Charleston to assist with the family business.

When Elise Forrest graduated from Avery in 1910, she began to teach in a rural school. She met Edwin Harleston in 1913, three years before he founded the Charleston branch of the NATIONAL ASSOCIATION FOR THE ADVANCEMENT OF COLORED PEOPLE (NAACP) and fought the law that prohibited blacks from teaching in city schools.

To be of assistance in the family business, Edwin studied embalming in NEW YORK CITY and Elise worked in an orphanage on Long Island, New York. Already acquainted with W. E. B. Du Bois, Edwin Harleston also befriended JAMES WELDON JOHNSON in New York and through both NAACP officials sometimes obtained commissions for his work.

When the couple returned to Charleston in 1918, they cofounded the Harleston Studio on 118 Calhoun Street. To hone her skills, Elise returned to New York to study photography at the E. Brunel School of Photography. In 1921, the couple married. She continued studies at Tuskegee Institute with C. M. Battey, the "dean of black photographers," and he at the Art Institute of CHICAGO. Elise worked as the primary photographer and Edwin painted portraits from the photographs. Their subjects over the years included poet LANGSTON HUGHES and NAACP executive MARY WHITE OVINGTON.

Edwin Harleston received an Amy Spingarn Award in 1925 from *The Crisis* for *Ouida,* a portrait of his wife. In 1930, he not only assisted AARON DOUGLAS with murals for the library at FISK UNIVERSITY but painted a portrait of Douglas for Fisk. He also won the ALAIN LOCKE Prize for portrait painting from the HARMON FOUNDATION in 1931, the year of his death. The portrait was called *The Old Servant.*

Elise Harleston's photograph *Mr. Wigfall* became an Edwin Harleston painting entitled *The Bible Student* that appeared on the cover of *OPPORTUNITY* magazine, January 1924. When Edwin died, Elise left Charleston, studied at the Atlanta School of Social Work, and moved to Baltimore. There she married John J. Wheeler, a high school teacher who died in 1943. Elise Forrest Harleston, one of black America's first female photographers, died in 1971.

Further Reading

Gentry, Mae W. "Portrait of an Artist." *The Atlanta Journal/The Atlanta Constitution,* 8 December 1996, sec. M3.

Bailey, David A., and Paul Gilroy. *Rhapsodies in Black: Art of the Harlem Renaissance.* Berkeley: University of California Press, 1997.

— Sandra L. West

Harmon Foundation

The Harmon Foundation was established in 1922 by William E. Harmon to promote the works of African-American visual artists.

William E. Harmon, who died in 1928, was a wealthy, white real estate magnate who was encouraged to serve as a philanthropist by ALAIN LOCKE, philosopher at HOWARD UNIVERSITY and editor for the *NEW NEGRO* in 1925. The stated mission of the foundation was to "assist in the development of a greater economic security for the race." To do so, Harmon sponsored an annual national competition, an exhibition, and an award program for African-American artists. Exhibitions traveled around the country, but in New York they were featured at the International House on Riverside Drive. Prize money was awarded to winners in the general amount of $400.

The Harmon Foundation shows were premier events for the African-American artist. Press releases soliciting black artists went out for every show, but response was often small. Only 19 visual artists responded to the inaugural call in 1926. Among them was the janitor at the Harmon Foundation, PALMER COLE HAYDEN, who became the first gold-medal winner. The bronze award went to HALE ASPACIO WOODRUFF. In 1927, LAURA WHEELER WARING and William Edouard Scott won gold medals, and John Wesley Hardrick won the bronze. ARCHIBALD JOHN MOTLEY, JR., won the gold and MAY HOWARD JACKSON the bronze in 1928. Other prizewinners came to include RICHMOND BARTHÉ, SARGENT CLAUDE JOHNSON, LOIS MAILOU JONES, and EDWIN AUGUSTUS HARLESTON.

By 1933, the last year of the competition, artist responses came in from CHICAGO to Copenhagen, and more than 400 entries were exhibited at the International House.

In 1944, the Harmon Foundation fell under the direction of Mary Beattie Brady. Brady organized an exhibition entitled "Portraits of Outstanding Americans of Negro Origin." Two portraits included among the many were *George Washington Carver* (1942) by Betsey Graves Reneau and *Marian Anderson* (1944) by Laura Wheeler Waring. In 1967, 41 of the 50 portraits in the original exhibition at the Smithsonian Institution were given to the National Portrait Gallery by the Harmon Foundation.

The work of the foundation did not progress without harsh criticism. The artists felt the foundation was paternal. The foundation was condemned because it was segregated—for African-American artists only—and because the range of talents went unevenly from amateur to professional. Though the foundation was established as "an experimental service for human welfare" and encouraged artists to develop a style "devoid of academic or Caucasian influences," it was alleged that the foundation was condescending toward the work of black artists. Some considered this the case when foundation officials pointed out, in what could be considered a racist judgment, the "humor" and "rhythm" in a black artist's work as opposed to serious, nationalistic intentions. And, though viewing patrons increased through the years, few came to buy.

When the Harmon Foundation closed shop in 1967, its amassed collection was dispersed among the art museums of African-American colleges and universities.

Further Reading

Beckman, Wendy Hart. *Artists and Writers of the Harlem Renaissance.* Berkeley Heights, N.J.: Enslow Publishers, 2002.

Reynolds, Gary A., and Beryl J. Wright. *Against the Odds: African-American Artists and the Harmon Foundation.* Newark, N.J.: The Newark Museum, 1989.

— Sandra L. West

Harrison, Richard B. (1864–1935) *orator, actor*

With minimal acting experience, Richard B. Harrison successfully performed one of the most controversial roles in Broadway history, playing God in the Pulitzer Prize–winning play *The* GREEN PASTURES.

Harrison was born on September 28, 1864, to fugitive slaves who left the United States to live in freedom in Canada. He was educated in the public schools of Ontario. Harrison later moved to Detroit and held a variety of jobs that included work as a waiter, dishwasher, police station handyman, and railroad porter. To supplement his income, both while in Canada and in the United States, Harrison gave recitals from Shakespeare and the Bible for black audiences at clubs, schools, and churches. He also later taught speech and elocution at black colleges.

Harrison became an acquaintance of the renowned black poet Paul Laurence Dunbar, who reportedly wrote two plays, though not produced, for him in 1899. The first was a three-act comedy called *Robert Herrick,* based on the life of the English lyric poet of the same name. The second was a one-act drama called *Winter Roses.*

In 1922, Harrison went on tour with a musical organization known as the Clef Club Orchestra. Organized by WILL MARION COOK, the orchestra also included PAUL ROBESON. In 1925, he helped GARLAND ANDERSON publicize and finance *APPEARANCES*, the first full-length drama by an African American to play Broadway, with a reading of the play at the Waldorf Astoria Hotel in NEW YORK CITY.

Harrison went from straightforward recitals to performance in 1923 when he joined the Lafayette Players for a production of *Pa Williams' Gal,* by Frank Wilson, at the LAFAYETTE THEATRE. In addition to Harrison and the author, the two-act drama also starred ROSE MCCLENDON.

The year 1930 proved to be a pivotal one for Harrison. He performed in OSCAR MICHEAUX's silent movie *Easy Street,* and he recited scripture in a musical program with HARRY THACKER BURLEIGH. He was working as the director of church festivals in HARLEM for the New York Federation of Churches when, at the age of 65, he was chosen to play "de Lawd" in *The Green Pastures* by Marc Connelly.

Based on the 1928 book, *Ol Man Adam and His Children,* by Roark Bradford, *The Green Pastures* was Connelly's folk dramatization of stories from the Old Testament. The play was written in Connelly's interpretation of southern African-American dialect, and Harrison was tutored by a white actor for his part. *The Green Pastures,* featuring an all-black cast, opened on February 26, 1930, at the Mansfield Theatre on Broadway and ran for 640 performances. Closing on Broadway in 1931, it went on the road for five national tours, playing 200 cities in 39 states. Connelly won the 1930 Pulitzer Prize for the play, and in 1935 it returned to Broadway for another successful run. For his portrayal of "de Lawd," Harrison was awarded the SPINGARN MEDAL in 1931 by the NATIONAL ASSOCIATION FOR THE ADVANCEMENT OF COLORED PEOPLE.

Despite the success of *The Green Pastures,* Harrison became an object of controversy among both whites and blacks for his role as the Lord. Many whites resented the notion of a black man portraying God, and different towns in the South either prohibited performances of the play altogether or banned blacks from attending it. African Americans pressured cast members to refuse to perform in theaters that practiced JIM CROW segregation. When African Americans in WASHINGTON, D.C., asked cast members not to perform at the city's National Theatre because it did not admit blacks, some of the cast members went on strike and were fired for doing so. Harrison chose to perform and was heavily criticized for that decision.

Harrison played his role in *The Green Pastures* for 1,568 performances without missing a single curtain call. He was preparing for the 1935 revival of the play when he died on March 14 in New York.

Further Reading

Hill, Anthony D. *Pages from the Harlem Renaissance: A Chronicle of Performance.* New York: Peter Lang Publishing, 1996.

Peterson, Bernard L., Jr., and James V. Hatch. *Profiles of African American Stage Performers and Theatre People, 1816–1960.* Westport, Conn.: Greenwood Publishing Group, 2000.

— Aberjhani

Hayden, Palmer Cole (Peyton Cole Hedgeman) (1890–1973) *painter*

Palmer Cole Hayden, the "janitor who painted," was to visual art what author ZORA NEALE HURSTON was to literature—an artist who used his craft to explore and document African-American folklore.

Palmer Cole Hayden was born Peyton Cole Hedgeman in Wide Water, Virginia, on January 15, 1890. His parents were James and Nancy Hedgeman.

Peyton's name changed to Palmer in 1914 when he enlisted in the army during WORLD WAR I. His commanding sergeant could not pronounce Peyton Cole Hedgeman, so he called him Palmer Cole Hayden instead, and the name stuck.

Hayden never had substantial employment. Before he entered the service, he worked on the railroad. In 1919, home from World War I, he worked in New York, part-time, as a house cleaner, postal clerk, porter, and janitor. In 1925, he furthered his education at Cooper Union in NEW YORK CITY and at the Boothbay Colony in Maine.

In 1926, when he was working as a janitor in the basement of the HARMON FOUNDATION, he entered a piece of his art into the foundation's art show and was awarded first prize, the William E. Harmon Award and Gold Medal in Fine Art. His prize was $400. With medal in hand, he went on to exhibit at the Boothbay Art Colony, at the Civic Club in New York, and completed an oil painting entitled *Fétiche et Fleurs.*

In 1927, Hayden received $3,000 from an arts patron (see also PATRONS). With this money, he went to PARIS, France, and stayed for five years painting and studying with Clivette Lefever at the Ecole des Beaux-Arts. By 1928, he was exhibiting on both sides of the Atlantic. He had a one-man show at the Berheim-Jeune Gallery in Paris, and he participated in "The Exhibition of Fine Arts: Production of American Negro Artists," sponsored by the Harmon Foundation in January 1928.

In 1929, Hayden's work was included in an exhibition at the Smithsonian Institution in WASHINGTON, D.C., and in 1933 he was awarded $100 and the Mrs. John D. Rockefeller Prize for *Fétiche et Fleurs.* Also in 1933, he exhibited at the Cooperative Art Market in New York and at the HARLEM COMMUNITY ART CENTER. Like most artists of the era, he joined the WORKS PROGRESS ADMINISTRATION (WPA) from 1934 to 1938.

Hayden maintained menial jobs to devote more time to his art. He painted sophisticated landscapes, florals, and ghetto scenarios. He painted scenes of rural black people and, sometimes, black people cruelly ensconced in the grin and posture of a minstrel; such caricatures did not fit the mandate of the Harlem Renaissance's *NEW NEGRO* to produce artistic works reflecting racial pride and dignity. Eventually, when the criticism started to annoy and embarrass him, he began to develop an interest in a more serious, nontheatrical, non-satirical black subject matter. His most ambitious work in this vein was the *John Henry Series,* which he completed in 1954.

The bulk of Hayden's work now belongs to the Museum of African-American Art in Los Angeles, California. Palmer Cole Hayden died in New York on February 8, 1973.

Further Reading

Bearden, Romare, and Harry Henderson. *A History of African American Artists: From 1792 to the Present.* New York: Pantheon Books, 1993.

McElroy, Guy, Sharon Patton, and Richard Powell, eds. *African-American Artists, 1880–1987, Selections from the Evans-Tibbs Collection.* Washington, D.C.: Smithsonian Institution Traveling Exhibition Service, in Association with University of Washington Press, Seattle and London, 1989.

— Sandra L. West

Hayes, Roland (1887–1976) *classical vocalist*

One of the first black classical music performers to achieve international fame, Roland Hayes's many achievements in music earned him the 1924 SPINGARN MEDAL, awarded by the NATIONAL ASSOCIATION FOR THE ADVANCEMENT OF COLORED PEOPLE (NAACP).

The son of a former slave, Roland Hayes was born June 3, 1887, in Curryville, Georgia. He was raised in Chattanooga, Tennessee. When his father died, young Hayes stopped attending primary school to work in a foundry to support his mother. He enjoyed singing, participated in the church choir, and, without knowing anything about classical vocalists, instinctively learned as much about music as he could. A visiting Oberlin College student played for him the recordings of master soloists Caruso, Sembrich, and Eames. When Hayes heard the rich quality of their voices, he said that he was "born again" and decided to become a concert singer.

At the age of 18, with $50 in his pocket and only a fifth-grade education, Hayes hoped to make his way to Oberlin in Ohio, but the lack of money forced him instead to register at FISK UNIVERSITY in Tennessee. There, he studied voice under Jennie A. Robinson for four years—the last three years on

Tenor Roland Hayes, shown here in 1954, was one of the first African Americans to sustain a career in classical music. *(Library of Congress, Prints & Photographs Division, Carl Van Vechten Collection [LC-USZ62-114533])*

scholarship—provided an operatic voice to silent films in movie theaters, and gave recitals in town.

He also traveled to Massachusetts to sing a concert series with the famed FISK JUBILEE SINGERS. An arts patron, Henry H. Putnam, helped him with auditions and soon, in 1911, Hayes moved to Boston to study privately with voice coach Arthur Holland. He also worked as a waiter and as a messenger at the Hancock Life Insurance Company while giving concerts at area black churches. With his jobs and fledgling career as a classical tenor, he supported himself and his mother, who moved to Boston to live with him.

Hayes's first professional concert was in 1912 at Steinhart Hall in Boston. Thereafter, he formed and toured with the Hayes Trio, which included baritone William Richardson and pianist William Lawrence. In 1914, he sang duets with HARRY THACKER BURLEIGH. He gave a recital at Jordan Hall in Boston in 1915, and another at Boston's Symphony Hall in 1917. He and Burleigh worked together again in 1918 when Hayes sang in New York's Aeolian Hall with Burleigh at the piano. Hayes performed songs composed by Burleigh and Samuel Coleridge-Taylor, another African-American classical artist.

In 1917, he sponsored himself in two recitals at Symphony Hall in Boston. He then studied and sang in Europe in 1920. While there, he was asked to appear before the king and queen of England, and he performed for them songs in French, German, and Italian. He returned to New York's Town Hall in December 1923 as a leading figure in the field of music. Hayes's repertoire was classical and always included Negro spirituals arranged by such African-American composers as WILLIAM GRANT STILL. He performed before sellout audiences at Town Hall and Carnegie Hall.

Performing in 1924 in Berlin, Germany, before a crowd that heckled him, Hayes patiently waited until they finished, began singing, and wooed the crowd with his love and respect for the music. During this same period, upon returning to America, he gave 125 concerts across the country. For his renown and acknowledged superior performance skills, he received the Spingarn Medal for achievement in 1924. In 1926, he purchased the Georgia farm where his mother had been enslaved.

Roland Hayes arranged the spirituals he sang in his concerts into a collection called *My Songs: Aframerican Religious Folksongs,* published in Boston (1948). His biography, *Angel Mo' and Her Son, Roland Hayes,* was written by MacKinley Helm (1942).

Universities showered Hayes with doctorates: Fisk in 1932, Morehouse in 1945, HOWARD UNIVERSITY in 1950, and others. He received France's Purple Ribbon for "services to French music" in 1949. Hayes taught music at Boston University in 1950 and, at age 75, gave a benefit concert for black college scholarships at Carnegie Hall in New York.

Roland Hayes died on New Year's Eve, 1976, in Brookline, Massachusetts.

Further Reading

Anderson, Paul Allen. *Music and Memory in Harlem Renaissance Thought.* Durham, N.C.: Duke University Press, 2001.

Kellner, Bruce, ed. *The Harlem Renaissance: A Historical Dictionary for the Era.* Westport, Conn: Greenwood Press, 1984.

Spencer, Jon Michael. *The New Negroes and Their Music: The Success of the Harlem Renaissance.* Knoxville: University of Tennessee Press, 1997.

— Sandra L. West

Hayford, Gladys May Casely (Aquah Laluah)

(1904–1950) *poet*

An African poet published in *CRISIS: A RECORD OF THE DARKER RACES, OPPORTUNITY* magazine, and several major anthologies, Gladys May Casely Hayford created poetry that symbolized the spirit of the PAN-AFRICAN CONGRESS and NEGRITUDE movements shared by many African and African-American writers during the Harlem Renaissance.

Gladys May Casely Hayford (Aquah Laluah, her African name) was born on May 11, 1904, in Axim, Gold Coast, West Africa. Her father was Joseph Casely Hayford, a Ghanian lawyer and leader in the Pan-African movement. Her mother was Adelaide Smith Casely Hayford, founder of Girls' Vocational School in Freetown, Sierra Leone.

Hayford was fluent in English and Fanti, studied at Colwyn Bay College in Wales, and instead of continuing her studies at Radcliffe College, joined a Berlin JAZZ troupe. She taught African folklore and literature at the Girls' Vocational School.

She wrote, "to show those who are prejudiced against color, that we deny inferiority to them, spiritually, intellectually and morally; and to prove it." Her poetry included "Creation" (*MESSENGER,* May 1926); "Mammy" (*Messenger,* 1926); "Nativity" (*Opportunity,* January 1927); "Rainy Season Love Song" (*Opportunity,* September 1927); "A Poem" (*Opportunity,* July 1928); and "The Palm Wine Seller" (*Journal of Negro Life,* February 1930).

Her work, rich with African images, was well received by Harlem Renaissance anthologists. "The Serving Girl" appeared in *Golden Slippers* (1941), edited by ARNA BONTEMPS; "Nativity," "Rainy Season Love Song," and "The Serving Girl" were selected for *Caroling Dusk* (1927), edited by COUNTEE CULLEN; and "The Palm Wine Seller" appeared in *Negro Poets and Their Poems* (1923).

Stricken with blackwater fever, Hayford died in 1950.

Further Reading

Hubbard, Dolan, ed. *Recovered Writers/Recovered Texts: Race, Class, and Gender in Black Women's Literature.* Knoxville: University of Tennessee Press, 1997.

Roses, Lorraine Elena, and Ruth Elizabeth Randolph, eds. *Harlem Renaissance and Beyond: Literary Biographies of 100 Black Women Writers 1900–1946.* Boston: G. K. Hall, 1990.

— Sandra L. West

Hearts in Dixie

In 1929, Fox studios released the first all-black sound musical, *Hearts in Dixie,* just two years after the first talkie, *The Jazz Singer,* appeared in 1927.

Hearts in Dixie was directed by Paul Sloane, who had written and directed more than two dozen silent films before taking on the project. The screenplay was written by Walter Weems, and the film was produced by William Fox.

Hearts in Dixie was a romanticized portrait of African-American life on a southern plantation following the Civil War. Despite the apparent slave-like living and working conditions of the blacks in the film, the characters were sublimely joyful. The movie served largely as a vehicle for showcasing African-American music and dance. It was also important as a film addressing black culture in general. Moreover, it allowed the Fox Studio to release a black musical before its competitor, Metro-Goldwyn-Mayer, which later in the same year released its all-black musical *Hallelujah.*

Sloane featured a team of veteran vaudeville and black theater performers in *Hearts in Dixie.* They included Clarence Muse as Uncle Nappus; STEPIN FETCHIT as Gummy; Gertrude Howard as Emmy; Clifford Ingram as Rammey, and Mildred Washington as Trailia. For Washington, the film actually represented a transition from the silent era. Prior to *Hearts in Dixie,* she had performed in *Tenderfeet* and *The Shopworn Angel* in 1928.

Clarence Muse had performed during the 1910s with both the LINCOLN THEATRE and the LAFAYETTE THEATRE. Muse was also a composer who wrote one of LOUIS ARMSTRONG's signature pieces, "When It's Sleepy Time Down South." For him, *Hearts in Dixie* was the beginning of a film career that would last well into the 1970s and include such classics as *Showboat, PORGY AND BESS,* and *Buck and the Preacher.*

Hearts in Dixie also provided Stepin Fetchit with one of his first significant roles as he honored a contract with Fox Studios that made him the biggest black film star of the 1930s. Despite the controversy that would surround his portrayal of modern minstrel-type "coons," he went on to star in nearly three dozen films throughout the GREAT DEPRESSION.

Further Reading

Elam, Harry J., and David Krasner, eds. *African American Performance and Theatre History: A Critical Reader.* New York: Oxford University Press, 2000.

Peterson, Bernard L. *A Century of Musicals in Black and White.* Westport, Conn.: Greenwood Publishing Group, 1993.

— Aberjhani

Henderson, Fletcher (James Hamilton Fletcher Henderson, Jr.)

(1897–1952) *pianist, arranger, bandleader*

Fletcher Henderson helped launch the big-band SWING SOUND, arranged music for Benny Goodman's orchestras, and was a key member of the Black Swan Record Company under the PACE PHONOGRAPHIC RECORD CORPORATION in HARLEM.

Fletcher Hamilton Henderson, Jr., was born into middle-class comfort on December 18, 1897, in Cuthbert, Georgia. When he was six years old, his mother taught him to play the piano. His parents were educators and did not allow Henderson to play JAZZ or RAGTIME, the dominant musical forms of the day.

Henderson graduated from Atlanta University with a degree in chemistry and mathematics. He relocated to NEW YORK CITY in 1921 to work in a chemistry laboratory, and he also worked part-time as a song demonstrator for Harry Pace and W. C. HANDY's publishing company. When Pace and Handy dissolved their partnership, Henderson continued to work with Pace's newly formed Black Swan Record Company, the nation's first black record company.

At Black Swan, Henderson worked as recording manager and as full-time accompanist for blues singers BESSIE SMITH, MA RAINEY, ALBERTA HUNTER, and ETHEL WATERS. In addition, he organized the Black Swan Troubadors, a traveling band.

In 1924, Henderson married Leora Meoux, a classical trumpet player who had performed with the LAFAYETTE THEATRE Orchestra. They settled on 139th Street in Harlem where band leader CAB CALLAWAY and blues singer Smith often visited them.

Outside of Black Swan, Henderson and his orchestra played at Club Alabam and the Roseland Ballroom. He recruited trumpeter LOUIS ARMSTRONG for his 10-piece ensemble in 1924. Armstrong taught Mrs. Henderson how to play a "hot jazz trumpet." The orchestra's style was a combination of ragtime and the European classics Henderson learned in Georgia. It was also influenced by the style of his co-arranger, Don Redman. The entire band was enhanced by Armstrong's signature solos, especially on the songs "Sugar Foot Stomp" and "Dippermouth Blues."

Jazz historian Amiri Baraka (LeRoi Jones) noted that "Henderson reached his Negro audience mostly via records because even when he got his best band together (with Coleman Hawkins, Louis Armstrong, Don Redman, et al.), he was still playing at Roseland, which was a white club." Another musical star who performed with the orchestra was FATS WALLER.

After the GREAT DEPRESSION, Henderson's big band disbanded. He arranged songs for Tommy and Jimmie Dorsey. His wife, Leora Meoux, formed a musical group called the Vampires. Henderson sold his band's arrangements to swing-era bandleader Benny Goodman in 1935, and he worked with Goodman, dubbed by some as the "King of Swing," as an arranger and sextet-pianist until 1939.

Henderson introduced an innovation in jazz that required orchestras to perform by switching the main instruments in the rhythm section from tuba to bass and from banjo to guitar, a technique that influenced the music well into the 1940s.

In 1950, Fletcher Henderson's sextet performed at Café Society in New York.

He died on December 29, 1952.

Further Reading

Baraka, Amiri (Jones, LeRoi). *Blues People: Negro Music in White America.* New York: William Morrow, 1963.

Stowe, David W. *Swing Changes: Big-Band Jazz in New Deal America.* Boston: Harvard University Press, 1994.

— Sandra L. West

Herring, James Vernon See MUSEUMS, AFRICAN-AMERICAN UNIVERSITY.

Herring, James W. See ART AND THE HARLEM RENAISSANCE.

Hill, Leslie Pinckney (1880–1960) *educator, poet*
Leslie Pinckney Hill, a poet and dramatist who earnestly adhered to HOWARD UNIVERSITY philosophy professor ALAIN LOCKE's mandate for *NEW NEGRO* literature, held the distinction of being the first poet published in the *CRISIS: A RECORD OF THE DARKER RACES*, edited by W. E. B. DU BOIS.

Leslie Hill was born in Lynchburg, Virginia, on May 14, 1880. He attended high school in East Orange, New Jersey. Hill received from Harvard University a B.A. in 1903 and an M.A. in 1904.

Firm in his conviction that education was the key to racial progress and harmony, in 1904 Hill began his long career as a teacher of English and education courses at Tuskegee Institute, working under Tuskegee founder BOOKER TALIAFERRO WASHINGTON. He was appointed and served as principal of Manassas Industrial Training School in Virginia from 1907 to 1913. From 1913, he worked as principal of the Institute for Colored Youth, which in turn became Cheyney Training School for Teachers (1914), Cheyney State Normal School (1920), and Cheyney State Teachers College (1951). He was also chairman of the American Inter-Racial Peace Committee (AIPC), a subsidiary organization of the American Friends (Quakers) Service Committee, where poet and journalist ALICE DUNBAR-NELSON worked in her capacity as executive secretary.

Once *Crisis* editor W. E. B. Du Bois decided to include literature in the magazine, Hill's poem "The Teacher" earned the honor of "first poem published" in January 1911. Another poem, "Vision of a Lyncher," was published in *Crisis* in January 1912. Though Hill's name is not as well known as ARNA BONTEMPS or COUNTEE CULLEN, *Crisis* critic WILLIAM STANLEY BEAUMONT BRAITHWAITE considered him among the best of the New Negro poets.

In 1921, Hill authored *Wings of Oppression,* a collection of 69 poems in standard verse that stressed the endurance of the black race. A play, *Toussaint L'Ouverture: A Dramatic History,* written in poetic form about the Haitian slave and freedom fighter, followed in 1928. He wrote the biblical drama *Jethro* in 1931. Literary critic Edward O. Ako contends that Hill did not pick his dramatic subjects without due consideration. He maintains that Hill consciously wrote a dramatic account of such a strong historical figure as Toussaint L'Ouverture (Louverture), a symbol of liberation for black people within the diaspora, because of the principles of racial pride and uplift advocated by Locke and Du Bois. Hill responded: "A worthy literature reared upon authentic records of achievement is the present spiritual need of the race." Leslie Hill died on February 16, 1960.

Further Reading

Ako, Edward O. "Leslie Pinckney Hill's Toussaint L'Ouverture." *Phylon,* Vol. XLVIII, no. 3, 1987, pp. 190–95.

Johnson, Abby Arthur, and Ronald Maberry Johnson. *Propaganda and Aesthetics: The Literary Politics of Afro-American Magazines in the Twentieth Century.* Amherst: University of Massachusetts Press, 1979.

— Sandra L. West

Holiday, Billie (Eleanora Fagan, "Lady Day") (1915–1959) *jazz vocalist, songwriter*
One of the outstanding pioneers in JAZZ vocals, Billie Holiday achieved stardom performing with several noted jazz bands and singing such classic songs as "God Bless the Child" and "Strange Fruit."

Billie Holiday was born Eleanora Fagan on April 7, 1915, probably in Philadelphia. Some biographers cite her birth name as Eleanora Fagan Gouch or Eleanora Gouch McKay. Actually, McKay was the last name of a man she married. Holiday changed her name from Eleanora when she began her professional career, and musician Lester Young, a member of the COUNT BASIE Band, gave her the name "Lady Day" in the 1930s to symbolize the manner in which she sang the BLUES.

Billie Holiday's father was Clarence Holiday, a guitarist in FLETCHER HENDERSON's band. Her mother, Sadie Fagan, was a teenager when Billie was born. While Billie was an infant, Sadie moved to Baltimore, where her family lived. Billie attended public school in Maryland. She was sexually assaulted at the age of 10, and at age 12 left Maryland for NEW YORK CITY. She worked there, for a time, as a prostitute.

Holiday started singing professionally at the age of 15 in nightclubs in HARLEM'S JUNGLE ALLEY. Arranger John Hammond claims that he discovered her: "Early in 1933 . . . I dropped in at Monette Moore's place on 133rd Street. . . . I was expecting to hear Monette, a fine blues singer. Instead, a young girl named Billie Holiday was substituting. . . . She was not a blues singer, but she sang popular songs in a manner that made them completely her own. She had an uncanny ear, an excellent memory for lyrics, and she sang with an exquisite sense of phrasing. . . . I decided that night that she was the best jazz singer I had ever heard."

After singing on 133rd Street, she worked in front of an exacting but appreciative audience at Harlem's APOLLO THEATRE and recorded with Benny Goodman's band in 1933. She formed Billie Holiday and Her Orchestra and recorded with Theodore "Teddy" Wilson from 1935 to 1939, surrounded by stellar musicians Lester Young, Roy Eldridge, Johnny Hodges, and Ben Webster. She then made a series of recordings with Young and earned recognition around the world. A bona fide star, she lent her voice to the soundtrack of the film *Symphony in Black* in 1935 and toured with the Basie band in 1937. She spent nine months, beginning in 1938, with the white, swing band of Artie Shaw, making her contribution to the SWING SOUND and the BIG BAND ERA. With these musicians she recorded songs that sold voluminously: "Mean to Me," "He's Funny That Way," "More Than You Know," and others.

Billie Holiday, shown here in 1949, remains celebrated as one of the foremost interpreters of jazz and blues. *(Library of Congress, Prints & Photographs Division, Carl Van Vechten Collection [LC-USZ62-109626])*

Traumatized by racist JIM CROW laws and graphic scenes of LYNCHING, Holiday in 1939 recorded "Strange Fruit," a song written by Lewis Allen (Abel Meeropol). Considered by many as the first song to openly protest the practice of murdering blacks by hanging them from trees and burning them, Holiday's record company, Columbia, feared the controversy it could generate and at first refused to let her record it. Holiday's recording of the song has since become recognized as one of the most powerful and poignant classics in the entire canon of jazz.

In the 1940s, Lady Day sang with a string orchestra on the Decca record label. She performed "Fine and Mellow" in concert halls, sang "Lover Man" for servicemen in the United Service Organizations (USO) during World War II, and completed a soundtrack for *New Orleans* (1947).

Holiday toured Europe with Jazz Club U.S.A. in 1954 and worked at the first Newport Jazz Festival the same year. In 1956, she wrote her autobiography, *Lady Sings the Blues,* with William Duffy, from which the 1972 film starring songstress Diana Ross and matinee idol Billy Dee Williams was created. As a songwriter, Holiday composed "God Bless the Child" with songwriter Arthur Herzog, after an argument with her mother, and "Don't Explain," after an incident regarding her husband's infidelity. She popularized "Foggy Day," "Say It Isn't So," and provided the voice for the film *The Sound of Jazz* (1957).

Suffering from alcohol and drug addiction, Holiday often recorded in the studio with a glass of whiskey in her hand. Onstage or off, she was, more times than not, "high" on heroin and stumbled rather than walked. Her love affairs were unhealthily indiscriminate, with male lovers and female lovers, and she chain-smoked. Toward the end of her life, her looks changed dramatically. Her voice cracked over notes, and she forgot lyrics she had been singing for years. A tragic addict, Billie Holiday died on July 17, 1959.

Further Reading

Altman, Susan. *The Encyclopedia of African-American Heritage.* New York: Facts On File, 1997.

Anderson, Jervis. *This Was Harlem: A Cultural Portrait, 1900–1950.* New York: Farrar, Straus, Giroux, 1982.

Clarke, Donald. *Billie Holiday: Wishing on the Moon.* New York: Da Capo Press, 2002.

Griffin, Farah Jasmine. *If You Can't Be Free, Be a Mystery: In Search of Billie Holiday.* New York: The Free Press, 2001.

Jackson, Reuben. "That Holiday Spirit." *Crisis,* December/January 1998.

Margolick, David, and Cassandra Wilson (foreword). *Billie Holiday, Café Society, and a Cry for Civil Rights.* Philadelphia, Pa.: Running Press, 2000.

Nicholson, Stuart. *Billie Holiday.* Boston: Northeastern University Press, 1997.

Southern, Eileen. *The Greenwood Encyclopedia of Black Music: Biographical Dictionary of Afro-American and African Musicians.* Westport, Conn.: Greenwood Press, 1982.

Wilson, Calvin. "Recordings Immortalize Lady Day's Immense Legacy." *Emerge,* April 2000.

— Sandra L. West

Holloway, Lucy Ariel Williams (1905–1973) *poet, musician*

A concert pianist, educator, and poet, Lucy Ariel Williams Holloway won the *OPPORTUNITY* magazine poetry prize competition in 1926, and she bears the honor of having a school in Mobile, Alabama, named after her.

Lucy Ariel Williams, who used her middle name Ariel Williams, was born on March 3, 1905, in Mobile, Alabama. Her father was Dr. H. Roger Williams, a physician, pharmacist, and poet. Her mother, Fannie Brandon, was a school teacher.

She attended Emerson Institute in Mobile, completed her high school years in the preparatory department of Talladega College in 1923, and received a B.A. in music from FISK UNIVERSITY in Nashville, Tennessee, in 1926. She received a bachelor's degree in music, piano, and voice from the Oberlin Conservatory of Music.

Williams's career was divided among literature, music, and education, but it was through literature that she made her contribution to the Harlem Renaissance. She contributed five poems to the national publications *Opportunity* and *CRISIS: A*

RECORD OF THE DARKER RACES from 1926 to 1935. Her dialect poem on the GREAT MIGRATION, "Northbound," won the *Opportunity* contest of 1926 and was anthologized in *Caroling Dusk* (1927). In only four short lines, the poem captured the essence of African Americans' dreams for a better life in the North: "Since Norf is up/ An' Souf is down,/ An' Hebben is up,/ I'm upward boun'."

During the GREAT DEPRESSION, Williams extended her musical studies with Fred Waring and at Columbia University in NEW YORK CITY during the summers. As a concert pianist, Williams rarely gave recitals outside of Mobile, which resulted in regional recognition instead of national acclaim. As a music educator, however, she was director of music at North Carolina College in Durham from her Oberlin graduation until 1932. She taught music at Dunbar High School in Mobile from 1932 to 1936 and at Fessenden Academy in Florida from 1936 to 1937.

In 1936, she married Joaquin M. Holloway, a postal employee. They had one son, Joaquin, Jr. She continued her teaching career at Lincoln Academy in Kings Mountain, North Carolina, from 1938 to 1939, returning to Dunbar High in 1939.

The anthology *Golden Slippers* (1941), edited by Harlem Renaissance poets COUNTEE CULLEN and ARNA BONTEMPS, republished Holloway's poem "Northbound." In addition, the poem was used as part of a textbook for the State Teachers' College in Mobile, Alabama.

From the 1940s until 1973, Holloway served as supervisor of music in the Mobile public schools. In addition to directing music, she published "E for Excellent" in *Music Educator's Journal* in January 1955. In the same year, she published her first poetry collection, *Shape Them Into Dreams,* with Exposition Press.

Lucy Ariel Williams Holloway died in 1973. The Ariel Williams Holloway School located at 625 Stanton Road in Mobile, Alabama, is named in her honor.

Further Reading

Giovanni, Nikki. *Shimmy Shimmy Shimmy Like My Sister Kate: Looking at the Harlem Renaissance Through Poems.* New York: Henry Holt, 1996.

Roses, Lorraine Elena, and Ruth Elizabeth Randolph. *Harlem Renaissance and Beyond: Literary Biographies of 100 Black Woman Writers 1900–1945.* Boston: G. K. Hall, 1990.

— Sandra L. West

Holt, Nora (Lena Douglas) (1890–1974) *music critic*

In 1918, Nora Holt became the first black woman to earn a master of music degree at the Chicago Musical College. She was a music critic for several black publications during the Harlem Renaissance and served as the model for a major character in CARL VAN VECHTEN's 1926 novel, *NIGGER HEAVEN.*

Nora Holt was born Lena Douglas in 1890 in Kansas City, Kansas. At the age of 15, she married musician Sky James. Divorcing James, she entered a succession of marriages, including unions with politician Philip Scroggins and barber Bruce Jones. She also pursued her education, earning a B.A. from Western University and working as a singer while also obtaining a position as a music critic for the *CHICAGO DEFENDER.* She then pursued her graduate studies at the Chicago Musical College and in 1918 became the first black woman to earn a master of music degree from the school. She founded the National Association of Negro Musicians and edited and published the magazine *Music and Poetry.*

She entered a fourth marriage, with George Holt, and changed her name to Nora. An elderly, affluent businessman, George Holt died after three years of marriage, when his wife was only 30. Nora Holt became a wealthy widow with large blocks of stock in the Liberty Life Insurance Company. Following her fourth husband's demise, she married Joseph L. Ray, a Pennsylvania businessman, in 1923. This marriage lasted 19 months. With her entourage of former husbands and an assortment of single and married lovers in between her marriages, Holt became the model for Van Vechten's haughty character, Lasca Sartoris in his controversial 1926 novel, *Nigger Heaven.*

During the 1930s, Holt supported herself in France, England, Japan, and China as a singer. When she returned to the

Music critic Nora Holt, shown here in 1955, was as famous for her own performances as she was infamous for a succession of marriages to wealthy older men. *(Library of Congress, Prints & Photographs Division, Carl Van Vechten Collection [LC-USZ62-114530])*

United States in 1938, she first settled in California, where she served on the Board of Education in Los Angeles. She then returned to New York in 1943 to critique music for the *AMSTERDAM NEWS* and the *New York Courier.* From 1953 to 1964, she also conducted the Nora Holt Concert Showcase on radio station WLIB. She retired in California in 1964 and died on January 25, 1974.

Further Reading

Reed, Bill. *Hot from Harlem: Profiles in Classic African American Entertainment.* Los Angeles: Cellar Door Books, 1998.

Watson, Steven. *The Harlem Renaissance: Hub of African-American Culture, 1920–1930.* New York: Pantheon Books, 1995.

— Sandra L. West

Home to Harlem

Written by Jamaican author CLAUDE MCKAY, *Home to Harlem* was the first best-seller by any black novelist during the Harlem Renaissance. Together with RUDOLPH FISHER's *Walls of Jericho* and Julia Peterkin's *Scarlet Sister Mary,* all published in 1928, *Home to Harlem* ushered in a period in which a new focus on fiction balanced the attention that until then had been given almost exclusively to poetry.

McKay, known for such militant poetry as "IF WE MUST DIE," wrote about the pagan characteristics of his people and the more sensuous elements of NEW YORK CITY life in *Home to Harlem.* He used SPEAKEASIES and barbershops as urban landscape for the sporting lives of strapping black longshoremen, dining car cooks, and waiters to whom casual love affairs are paramount. The novel describes the carnal adventures of Jake, who has just returned "home to Harlem" from WORLD WAR I, and his buddies, Gin-Head Susy of Brooklyn and the fat black Zeddy. Although it sold well in 1928, it did not sit well with black leaders and reviewers of the era's journals.

MARCUS GARVEY, a Jamaican like McKay, edited the radical *NEGRO WORLD* and was a staunch supporter of McKay's unflinching, nationalistic poetry. However, Garvey wrote in *Negro World* (September 29, 1928) that *Home to Harlem* "is a damnable libel against the Negro."

James W. Ivy reviewed *Home to Harlem* for the *MESSENGER* (May/June 1928): "Those who objected to *NIGGER HEAVEN* (by CARL VAN VECHTEN) will, if they are honest, howl with rage when they read *Home to Harlem* . . . a story of the so-called common nigger; and pimps, bulldykers, faggots, 'snoweaters,' wild parties, razor fights, and sluttish women, are all written of in a free and open manner . . . beautiful but frank to the verge of cruelty."

W. E. B. DU BOIS wrote in *CRISIS: A RECORD OF THE DARKER RACES* (June 1928) that although portions of the novel are beautiful and fascinating, "Claude McKay's *Home to Harlem* . . . for the most part nauseates me, and after the dirtier parts of its filth I feel distinctly like taking a bath."

However, younger writers such as LANGSTON HUGHES and WALLACE THURMAN admired the book and felt inspired enough by it to write novels of their own.

Further Reading

Vincent, Theodore G., ed. *Voices of a Black Nation: Political Journalism in the Harlem Renaissance.* San Francisco: Ramparts Press, 1973, pp. 352–60.

Winston, James, and Claude McKay. *A Fierce Hatred of Injustice: Claude McKay's Jamaican Poetry of Rebellion.* London: Verso, 2001.

— Sandra L. West

Hopkins, Pauline Elizabeth (Sarah A. Allen)

(1859–1930) *novelist, literary editor*

Pauline Elizabeth Hopkins was a playwright, novelist, and magazine editor whose career began when she won an essay contest sponsored by America's first black playwright.

Born in 1859 in Portland, Maine, Pauline Hopkins was raised in Boston, Massachusetts, by her parents, Sarah Allen and Northrup Hopkins. Pauline Hopkins later assumed her mother's name as her pseudonym.

At age 15, before graduating from Boston's Girls High School, Hopkins won $10 in an essay competition sponsored by William Wells Brown (author of the play *Clotel*) for black students. Her essay was titled "Evils of Intemperance and Their Remedies."

After the contest, Hopkins's literary interests turned to playwriting, most likely due to Brown's influence on her. In 1879, her family formed the Hopkins Colored Troubadours and performed her musical drama *Slaves' Escape; or, the Underground Railroad* (later named *Peculiar Sam; or, the Underground Railroad*) in July 1880 at Oakland Garden in Boston. A realist, Hopkins studied stenography and worked for the Bureau of Statistics governmental agency and as a personal stenographer for Republican Party members from 1892 to 1899.

Hopkins continued to evolve as a writer, and her short story "The Mystery Within Us" was published in *Colored American*'s inaugural issue, May 1900. It was the first in a long line of collaborations between author and periodical, including "As the Lord Lives, He Is One of Our Mother's Children" (November 1903). By *Colored American*'s second number, she was writing for its women's pages. From 1900 to 1903, the Colored Co-Operative Publishing Company, owner of *Colored American,* serialized her first novel, *Contending Forces: A Romance Illustrative of Negro Life in the North and South.* When the magazine changed owners in 1903, Hopkins was hired as literary editor. Under her tenure, the works of Frances E. W. Harper and ANGELINA EMILY WELD GRIMKE were published.

Hopkins also assumed leadership in the business end of publishing. She formed the Colored American League to gain subscriptions for the magazine, and readership of *Colored American* jumped to 15,000. However, when the magazine moved to NEW YORK CITY, Hopkins was fired because of her political leanings.

During her four years at *Colored American,* she published three additional novels: *Hagar's Daughter: A Story of Southern Caste Prejudice; Winona: A Tale of Negro Life in the South and Southwest;* and *Of One Blood; or, The Hidden Self.* The latter novel was serialized under her pseudonym, Sarah A. Allen.

Winona: A Tale of Negro Life in the South and Southwest and *Of One Blood; or, The Hidden Self* dealt with interracial romance. Publication of these novels caused a rash of subscription cancellations by white readers.

With an abiding faith in a classical, non-manual-arts education as the key to her people's complete liberation and uplift, Hopkins wrote historical essays that exemplified "the Negro genius." She wrote "Toussaint L'Ouverture: His Life and Times" for *Colored American* (November 1900); "The Dark Races of the Twentieth Century," a series in *Voice of the Negro* (February 1905–July 1905); "Famous Men of the Negro Race," a series in *Colored American* (February 1901–September 1902); "Famous Women of the Negro Race," a series in *Colored American* (November 1901–October 1902); and *A Primer of Facts Pertaining to the Early Greatness of the African Race and the Possibility of Restoration by Its Descendants, With Epilogue,* which she produced under her own Cambridge-based publishing company, P. E. Hopkins, in 1905. Also for *Voice of the Negro,* founded in January 1904, Hopkins wrote an article titled "The New York Subway" (December 1905).

In 1916, *New Era* magazine, published by New Era Publishing Company in Boston, hired Hopkins as editor. For them she wrote a novella, "Topsy Templeton" (February 1916), and biographies of prominent clergy (March 1916). When *New Era* folded shortly thereafter, she left literary life and returned to stenography at the Massachusetts Institute of Technology.

Literary critic Mary Helen Washington wrote that Hopkins, "enlisted (her) fiction in the battle to counter the negative images of blacks and women." She was a leading playwright, historical essayist, and editor, yet she died in obscurity on August 13, 1930, from burns suffered in a domestic fire.

Further Reading

Allen, Carol. *Black Women Intellectuals: Strategies of Nation, Family, and Neighborhood in the Works of Pauline Hopkins, Jessie Fauset and Marita Bonner.* New York: Garland Publishing, 1998.

Roses, Lorraine Elena, and Ruth Elizabeth Randolph, eds. *Harlem Renaissance and Beyond: Literary Biographies of 100 Black Women Writers 1900–1945.* Boston: G. K. Hall, 1990.

— Sandra L. West

Horne, Lena (1917–) *actress, singer*

Successfully avoiding the stereotypical roles assigned to most black actresses during the 1940s, Lena Horne became one the most accomplished actresses of that era and subsequently won acclaim as an enduring star of film, Broadway, concerts, and radio.

Horne was born Lena Calhoun Horne on June 30, 1917, to Edna Scottron Horne and Edwin Teddy Horne in Brooklyn, NEW YORK CITY. Her father, although the son of a well-established black middle-class family, was a gambler who left his family when Horne was three. Her mother was an actress who toured with the LAFAYETTE THEATRE's Lafayette Players.

Horne was raised during her earliest years by her paternal grandparents, Edwin and Cora Calhoun. Her grandfather helped her develop an appreciation for drama and music. Her grandmother, a social worker, was an active member of the NATIONAL ASSOCIATION FOR THE ADVANCEMENT OF COLORED PEOPLE (NAACP) and enrolled Horne in the organization before she was five years old.

She attended Brooklyn Ethical Culture School before going to live and tour with her mother throughout the South. For several years, they lived alternately in Miami, Florida, and Macon, Ft. Valley, and Atlanta, Georgia. She returned to Brooklyn at age 13 and attended the Girls High School. Following the death of her grandparents, she lived for a time with a family friend named Laura Rollock, who obtained singing and dancing lessons for Horne. She was living with her mother and stepfather, Miguel Rodriguez, when she quit school to join the chorus line at the famed COTTON CLUB. At the Cotton Club, she earned $25 a week alongside such entertainers as DUKE ELLINGTON, ETHEL WATERS, CAB CALLOWAY, and Jimmie Lunceford. Because of her age, her mother acted as chaperone during each of her performances, and both her father and stepfather frequented the sometimes rowdy club to protect Horne.

Performing "As Long as I Live," she sang at the club for the first time when another singer canceled. Shortly afterward, in 1934, she debuted on Broadway in the all-black production of *Dance With Your Gods.* The following year, at the suggestions of Flournoy Miller and Ethel Waters, she joined the NOBLE SISSLE Society Orchestra. As a vocalist with Sissle, cocreator of the 1921 Broadway hit *SHUFFLE ALONG*, Horne went on tour throughout the United States and further developed her performance skills.

At age 18, Horne married aspiring politician Louis Jones and the couple had two children, Gail and Teddy. Conflicts over the demands of Horne's career caused them to separate shortly after their son's birth. Horne was allowed custody of her daughter, Gail, while Jones kept their son, Teddy.

In 1938, Horne joined the cast of Lew Lesley's *Blackbirds* revue. In 1939, she went on tour with white bandleader Charlie Barnet, recording for the band a hit single called "Good for Nothing Joe." During the same year, she became a featured vocalist at New York's Café Society Downtown. There, she worked with pianist Hazel Scott and big-band leader COUNT BASIE. She also enjoyed a friendship with PAUL ROBESON and WALTER WHITE, who would encourage her when the opportunity came to go to Hollywood, California.

Horne first ventured into film in 1938, when she played RALPH COOPER's wife in the independently produced *The Duke Is Tops,* which starred Duke Ellington. In the early 1940s, she moved to Hollywood and became the first black actress to sign a seven-year contract with a major studio, Metro-Goldwyn-Mayer. Moreover, with her father, Edwin Horne, assisting in the negotiations, Horne stipulated that she would not play roles that were stereotypical or demeaning to black women in any way. Earning a salary of $200 a week, she filmed *Panama Hattie* and *Harlem on Parade* in 1942. In these musicals, her roles were more like cameo appearances in which she sang, then departed. While waiting to film a more substantial role in

Cabin in the Sky, Horne performed at the Savoy Plaza in New York and for the first time won national critical acclaim in both *Time* and *Life* magazines.

Returning to Hollywood, Horne took on a lead role as a temptress named Georgia Brown, a role performed for the stage by KATHERINE DUNHAM, in *Cabin in the Sky.* Starring with her were EDDIE ANDERSON, Ethel Waters, and Rex Ingram. Ironically, *Cabin in the Sky* was released in 1943, the same year that Horne also starred for 20th Century Fox in the film that would provide her signature song, *STORMY WEATHER.* A loose musical biography of BOJANGLES ROBINSON, *Stormy Weather* celebrated black music of the 1920s and 1930s. In addition to Horne and Robinson, it also featured Cab Calloway, FATS WALLER, Katherine Dunham, and the NICHOLAS BROTHERS.

Horne's emergence as a star actress during World War II made her a favorite among military men, and like other Hollywood stars she went on tours of United Servicemen's Organizations (USO) to help maintain positive morale. When she protested against the continuing racist treatment of African-American servicemen, her studio canceled her tour. Horne, however, opted to finance the tour herself and continued to entertain troops.

Despite a successful run of films and tours throughout Europe during the 1940s, Horne's Hollywood career stalled in the 1950s. She became a target of the Communist scare engineered by Senator Joseph McCarthy, and her name was placed on the Red Channels blacklist of performers suspected of aiding COMMUNISM. Horne was identified largely because of her friendship with Paul Robeson, her outspokenness regarding racism, and her affiliation with a group called the Progressive Citizens of America. Denied work in film, television, and recording, Horne returned to Broadway. In 1956, she starred with Ricardo Montalban in *Jamaica.* Horne eventually returned to films with *Meet Me in Las Vegas* in 1956 and *Death of a Gunfighter* in 1969. By 1978, when she played the good witch Glinda in *The Wiz* and inspired a new generation of African Americans with her performance of "If You Believe," she had become an entertainment icon.

Horne became an honorary member of DELTA SIGMA THETA at the invitation of sorority president Jean Noble in 1960. In 1963, she joined James Baldwin, Lorraine Hansbury, Harry Belafonte, Dr. Kenneth Clark, and others, in a meeting with Robert Kennedy to help assess the state of African America.

The loss of her father, her son, and her second husband, Lennie Hayton, during the early 1970s caused Horne to suffer for a time from a deep depression. Nevertheless, in 1974, she toured England and the United States with Tony Bennett. In 1981, Horne starred in her one-woman Broadway show, *Lena Horne: The Lady and Her Music.* The show ran for more than a year and won two Grammy Awards, a Tony Award, and the New York Drama Critics Circle Award.

Horne received an honorary doctorate from HOWARD UNIVERSITY in 1980 and another from Yale University in 1998. In 1983, she received the NAACP's SPINGARN MEDAL. For more than 50 years, she has been featured on *Ebony Magazine*'s annual listing of the most beautiful people.

Performing artist Lena Horne, shown here in 1941, refused to play roles she felt were demeaning to African Americans and became one of the first black actresses to negotiate her career on her own terms. *(Library of Congress, Prints & Photographs Division, Carl Van Vechten Collection [LC-USZ62-116600])*

Further Reading

Babo, Jacqueline. *Black Women as Cultural Leaders.* New York: Columbia University Press, 1995.

Handy, D. Antoinette. *Black Women in American Bands and Orchestras.* Lanham, Md.: Scarecrow Press, 1999.

Howard, Brett. *Lena Horne.* Los Angeles: Holloway House Publishing, 1991.

Knight, Arthur. *Disintegrating the Musical: Black Performance and American Musical Film.* Durham, N.C.: Duke University Press, 2002.

— Aberjhani

Hot Chocolates

Hot Chocolates was one of many floor shows that FATS WALLER and Andy Razaf wrote specifically for CONNIE'S INN at SEVENTH AVENUE and 132nd Street in HARLEM until its success earned the show a place off-Broadway at the Hudson Theatre.

An expanded version of *Hot Chocolates* debuted at the Hudson on June 20, 1926. Staged by Leonard Harper, who staged most of the shows at Connie's Inn, *Hot Chocolates* featured a book and lyrics by Razaf with music by Waller and Harry Brooks. It also showcased the talents of Jazzlips Richardson, a somewhat gymnastic dancer whose performance always drew raves from the audience and reviewers alike. Dancing was considered a strong point in *Hot Chocolates.* In addition to Richardson, the show spotlighted a waltzing husband and wife team from the Bahamas named Paul and Thelma Meeres, a chorus line of female dancers, a second line of male dancers known as the Bon Bon Buddies, and an exotic dancer named Louise Cook.

Several of the show's songs became instant hits and are considered classics of the JAZZ Age. These include "Black and Blue," "Can't We Get Together," and "Sweet Savannah Sue." Another song, "Ain't Misbehavin'," became Waller's signature piece. LOUIS ARMSTRONG, CAB CALLOWAY, Margaret Simms, and other cast members all sang it at various points throughout the show. It later became the title of another Broadway show constructed around Waller's music and personality, as well as the name of a biography of the musician.

As physically demanding a show as *Hot Chocolates* was, the cast fell into a routine of performing it twice a night almost every night of the week. They would first put the show on downtown at the Hudson, then travel uptown to perform a slightly scaled-down version at Connie's Inn. Reviewers marveled that the dancers could maintain such high levels of creative stamina throughout an entire evening at two different venues. Waller, moreover, continued to record while performing with the show and remained a favorite on the RENT PARTY scene. Armstrong also did double duty while performing in the show with additional appearances at the LAFAYETTE THEATRE.

Hot Chocolates played through 219 performances before going on the road. In 1929, it played for a time at the Alhambra Theatre. It was revived for Broadway in 1935.

Further Reading

Johnson, Anne E. *Jazztap: From African Drum to American Feet.* New York: Rosen, 1999.

Peterson, Bernard L. *A Century of Musicals in Black and White.* Westport, Conn.: Greenwood Publishing Group, 1993.

— Aberjhani

Hotel Theresa

During the 1940s, the Hotel Theresa was known as the Waldorf of HARLEM and served as home to many of the outstanding African-American celebrities who lived in or often visited the community.

The Hotel Theresa building is located at 2082–2096 ADAM CLAYTON POWELL, JR., Boulevard, on SEVENTH AVENUE and 125th Street in Harlem. It was built in 1913 by Gustave Seidenberg, a maker of cigars, whose wife's name was Theresa. The building was designed by George and Edward Blum and displays geometric patterns with white terracotta embellishment.

The hotel maintained a JIM CROW racial segregation policy in the 1930s when there was a still sizable white, middle-class Harlem community to support such a policy. Gradually, however, the hotel lost money as the neighborhood's population changed to reflect the GREAT MIGRATION of blacks from the South and Caribbean. The hotel administration decided to open its doors to African-American visitors and residents in 1940, even as midtown hotels continued to maintain a whites-only policy.

The Theresa was a 13-story hotel of 300 rooms. During the 1940s, rooms cost $8 a night. Because the Theresa was close to the APOLLO THEATRE, legions of entertainers such as JAZZ pianist COUNT BASIE and COTTON CLUB featured singer LENA HORNE called Hotel Theresa home when they were working. One of the most famous athletes to stay at the Theresa was the "Brown Bomber," JOE LOUIS. In 1948, when Louis won his bout with Jersey Joe Walcott, Harlemites mobbed the lobby and streets so that traffic was backed up for miles. The Theresa was the boxer's "Victory Headquarters."

The Theresa had permanent residents and rented office space. Office space was assigned to A. PHILIP RANDOLPH for the 1940s March on Washington movement, which was later aborted. Comedian MOMS MABLEY maintained an apartment at the Theresa, and the gossipy Theresa Bar was a regular beat for black newspaper reporters.

One family in residence during the 1940s was William Harmon Brown and his wife Gloria Brown. A manager for the Hotel Theresa, William Brown opened the building's roof and named it the Skyline Ballroom. The spot became a dancing venue for black socialites. The halls of the Theresa were a playground for the Browns' son, Ronald H. Brown, who later became chairman of the Democratic Party and U.S. Secretary of Commerce during the William Jefferson Clinton presidency. Ron Brown later died in office in a plane crash in 1996.

When African Americans became welcome at majority hotels, the Theresa's popularity waned, and in 1953 it was sold. New manager Andy Kirk had been leader of the Twelve Clouds of Joy, a band popular during the SWING SOUND era. Proving that it was down but not out, on September 18, 1960, the Hotel Theresa hosted Cuba's Communist leader Fidel Castro and his 40-member entourage, who were incensed that they had been asked to pay $10,000 up front at the midtown Shelburne Hotel. Castro's visitors at the Theresa included Russian prime minister Nikita Khrushchev, Harlem Renaissance poet LANGSTON HUGHES, Beat Generation poet Allen Ginsberg, and Minister Malcolm X, whose Organization of Afro-American Unity had an office in the hotel. With all the celebrity glitter surrounding Castro's business at the United Nations and visit to the Hotel Theresa, it was almost like the establishment's glory days of the 1940s, as Castro racked up a bill for $15,000.

The grand Hotel Theresa was sold in 1966 for $1.25 million. It has been an office building since 1970.

Further Reading

Dolkart, Andrew S., and Gretchen S. Sorin. *Touring Historic Harlem: Four Walks in Northern Manhattan.* New York: New York Landmarks Conservancy, 1997.

Scherman, Tony. "The Theresa." *American Legacy,* Winter 1998.

— Sandra L. West

Howard University

Named after Freedmen's Bureau commissioner Oliver Otis Howard, Howard University was founded in 1866 by a group of whites affiliated with the First Congregational Society of

WASHINGTON, D.C. In the twentieth century, Howard developed into a stronghold of proponents of W. E. B. DU BOIS's "Talented Tenth" philosophy.

A citadel of black firsts and a mainstay of black academic and cultural sophistication in Washington, D.C., Howard University is located on Georgia Avenue in northwest Washington's Shaw neighborhood. Prior to, during, and after the Harlem Renaissance, some of the most influential minds in black America were associated with this university on the hill. These included philosopher ALAIN LOCKE, playwright WILLIS RICHARDSON, folklorist ZORA NEALE HURSTON, playwright MAY MILLER, and numerous others.

Howard University installed its first black president, Dr. Mordecai Johnson, in 1926. Unlike other black universities during the 1920s and 1930s, the university's faculty was predominately African American. The exceptionally accomplished Rhodes Scholar Alain Locke edited the *NEW NEGRO* anthology (1925) and, along with Du Bois and *OPPORTUNITY* magazine editor CHARLES SPURGEON JOHNSON, spearheaded the Harlem Renaissance. The author of *Southern Road,* STERLING ALLEN BROWN; biology researcher and the first recipient of the SPINGARN MEDAL, ERNEST EVERETT JUST; sculptor MAY HOWARD JACKSON, and their colleagues taught students who often strove to fulfill Du Bois's call for the Talented Tenth of those African Americans with the exceptional ability, insight, and determination to help their race advance. In addition, they designed departments, held chairmanships, and won national and international awards and acclaim. All of this led Howard University, with more professional departments than any other black campus, to become known as the National Negro University.

Many of the campus buildings at Howard denote the school's rich history. Among its more notable structures are the Howard University Hospital, which until 1975 was known as Freedmen's Hospital; the Founders' Library; the Andrew Rankin Memorial Chapel; and the Ira Aldridge Theater.

From 1894 to 1898, Freedmen's Hospital came under the administration of the eminent black surgeon Dr. Daniel Hale Williams (1858–1931), who founded Provident Hospital in CHICAGO and performed the first successful open heart surgery in 1893. World famous blood plasma researcher Dr. Charles Drew (1905–50) served as a professor and head of surgery at Howard University Medical School in the 1930s.

Founders' Library houses the renowned Moorland-Spingarn Research Center (founded in 1946), a large and comprehensive collection on black history and culture amassed from the separate collections of Dr. Jesse E. Moorland (1863–1940), a Howard alumnus, and NATIONAL ASSOCIATION FOR THE ADVANCEMENT OF COLORED PEOPLE (NAACP) executive Arthur B. Spingarn.

Howard was one of the first universities to offer a campus art gallery. Howard professor James V. Herring initiated the campus art department in the 1920s, the first such department in the entire black college system. An art gallery bearing his name occupies the building behind the Ira Aldridge Theater. The theater itself is home to the Howard Players, a dramatic group formed during the Harlem Renaissance. In 1930, the Andrew Rankin Memorial Chapel became home to the Howard University Gallery of Art.

For its list of accomplished instructors and students and its historical impact, Howard remains known by its motto: The Capstone of Negro Education.

Further Reading

Fitzpatrick, Sandra, and Maria R. Goodwin. *The Guide to Black Washington: Places and Events of Historical and Cultural Significance in the Nation's Capital.* New York: Hippocrene Books, 1990.

Lewis, David Levering. *When Harlem Was in Vogue.* New York: Vintage Books, 1982.

Locke, Alain. *The New Negro: Voices of the Harlem Renaissance.* New York: Simon and Schuster, 1997. Original copyright 1925.

— Sandra L. West

How Come?

Joining the list of hit musical revues featuring African Americans during the 1920s, *How Come?* debuted at the APOLLO THEATRE on 42nd Street on April 16, 1923.

The show was written by Eddie Hunter, who during the 1910s had headlined as a comedian at the CRESCENT THEATRE in HARLEM. There, he had written and starred in such shows as *Why Husbands Leave Home* and *Subway Sal.* His cowriters for *How Come?* were composer and music arranger Will Vodery, Henry Creamer, and Ben Harris.

In *How Come?* Hunter presented a twist on the standard vaudeville skit of blacks stealing chickens. Instead of losing chickens, the members of the Mobile Chicken Trust are robbed by their former treasurer, who then sets up a bootleg operation to repay the group.

In addition to Hunter, *How Come?* starred Sidney Bechet, who was beginning to gain fame as a JAZZ saxophonist and clarinetist; the veteran vaudeville team Chapelle and Stinnette; and dancer Johnny Nit, whose talent drew comparisons to that of BOJANGLES ROBINSON.

How Come? helped increase the popularity of the Charleston, introduced on Broadway the year before in *LIZA*, with two songs: the *Charleston Cut-Out* and *Charleston Finale.* The show ran for 32 performances.

Further Reading

Davis, Lee. *Scandals and Follies: The Rise and Fall of the Great Broadway Revue.* New York: Limelight Editions, 1998.

Woll, Allen. *Black Musical Theatre, From Coontown to Dreamgirls.* New York: Da Capo Press, 1989.

— Aberjhani

Hughes, Langston (James Mercer Langston Hughes) (1902–1967) *writer*

James Mercer Langston Hughes was a prolific writer whose literary output spanned the Harlem Renaissance of the 1920s, the Black Arts movement of the 1960s, and several different genres. A poet laureate also known as the Dean of Negro Writers, his vast body of creativity embraced the short story, novel, libretto, drama, autobiography, and essay.

James Mercer Langston Hughes, known as Langston Hughes, was born on February 1, 1902, in Joplin, Missouri. His lineage includes grandfather Charles Langston, a conductor in the Ohio Underground Railroad, and grandfather Lewis Sheridan Leary, active in John Brown's raid at Harper's Ferry. His parents were James Nathaniel Hughes and Carrie Mercer Langston Hughes.

Hughes's early life was unstable. He grew up predominantly in Lawrence, Kansas, but before completing grade school in 1915 he had lived in Buffalo, New York; Cleveland, Ohio; Lawrence, Kansas; Topeka, Kansas; and Colorado Springs, Colorado. This instability came from marital discord between his parents. His father, prevented from taking the bar exam in Oklahoma because of his race, abandoned his family. To avoid the racist apartheid practices of JIM CROW in the United States, he moved first to Cuba, then Mexico, where he became a lawyer. His son was left with an ailing, artistic mother and a stern grandmother.

Carrie Mercer Langston Hughes was a teacher who wrote poetry and took her son to literary society meetings and plays. Mary Sampson Patterson Leary Langston was Hughes's maternal grandmother. He lived with her in Lawrence, Kansas, where she passed down to him, through the oral tradition, stories about slavery and abolition.

As a child, Hughes enjoyed the poetry of Paul Laurence Dunbar and Carl Sandburg. Beginning to write himself, he was designated the class poet upon graduation from grammar school in Lincoln, Illinois. Later, at Central High School in Cleveland, Ohio, he wrote for the school papers, edited the senior yearbook, and wrote short stories, plays, and poetry. He wrote "When Sue Wears Red," his first jazz poem, while still in high school.

In 1919, when Hughes was 18, he traveled to Mexico to visit his father. En route, on a train crossing the Mississippi River, he wrote "The Negro Speaks of Rivers," later published in *CRISIS: A RECORD OF THE DARKER RACES* (June 1921). His father did not encourage his son's writing but wanted him to study engineering. Nevertheless, by the time the younger Hughes left Mexico in 1921, he had completed a significant body of work, taught English at a Mexican finishing school, and learned German and Spanish. He also agreed to study engineering at Columbia University in NEW YORK CITY.

Drawn to life in HARLEM, Hughes left Columbia in 1922 and continued to write. His poem "The South" was published in *Crisis* (June 1922), and his first story, "Mexican Games," was published in *BROWNIES' BOOK*, a journal for African-American children edited by W. E. B. DU BOIS and JESSIE REDMOND FAUSET. In February 1923, *Crisis* also published his poem "When Sue Wears Red."

Hughes performed various odd jobs, working as a delivery boy for a florist and as a mess boy on a freighter that never left port. He joined the crew of the S.S. *Malone* in 1923 and for six months traveled to West Africa, Holland, Italy, and Paris. He witnessed African folklife firsthand in Senegal, and he listened to the BLUES and JAZZ contributions of black expatriate musicians in nightclubs in PARIS, France.

Hughes returned to America in 1924 and moved to WASHINGTON, D.C., to live with his mother. He worked for a short time there as a clerk for the ASSOCIATION FOR THE STUDY OF NEGRO LIFE, founded by CARTER GODWIN WOODSON, the Father of Negro History, who edited *The Journal of Negro History* and created Negro History Week, now Black History Month.

In 1925, Hughes accepted a job as busboy at the Wardman Park Hotel. He recognized poet Vachel Lindsay in the hotel's dining area and placed three poems on his plate: "Jazzonia," "Negro Dancers," and "The Weary Blues." Excited by the poems, Lindsay arranged for a news story on the busboy poet. Between 1925 and 1926, Hughes's work appeared in *Vanity Fair* magazine and won poetry contests sponsored by *The Crisis* and *Opportunity* magazine, the official publication of the NATIONAL URBAN LEAGUE, a conservative civil rights organization.

Hughes traveled regularly from Washington to New York to enjoy both the cultural activities centered in Harlem and a good party. At these parties, he met the head of the NATIONAL ASSOCIATION FOR THE ADVANCEMENT OF COLORED PEOPLE (NAACP), JAMES WELDON JOHNSON; his assistant, WALTER WHITE; white arts patron and author of the controversial novel *NIGGER HEAVEN*, CARL VAN VECHTEN; and a poet with whom he would exchange more than 2,000 letters over a 40-year friendship, ARNA BONTEMPS.

From 1925 to 1930, Hughes published prose in the *MESSENGER*, produced by A. PHILIP RANDOLPH, and *NEGRO WORLD*, published by activist MARCUS GARVEY as a vehicle for his UNIVERSAL NEGRO IMPROVEMENT ASSOCIATION (UNIA). Hughes was also a founding member of the DARK TOWER, a group that held literary receptions and meetings in the New York mansion of millionaire A'LELIA WALKER. At the Dark Tower, Hughes, poet COUNTEE CULLEN, and other writers discussed the evolution of poetry and read and critiqued each other's works in preparation for publication.

Hughes gained audiences around the world as he wrote essays for magazines in Asia and Moscow and as his poetry was translated into foreign languages. In this period, two volumes of Hughes's poetry were published, *The Weary Blues* (1926) and *Fine Clothes to the Jew* (1927), by Alfred A. Knopf. Hughes published much of his most important work with Knopf, but throughout his very long career he also published with Golden Stair Press, Troutbeck Press, International Workers Order, Negro Publication Society of America, Musette Publishers, Macmillan, Hill & Wang, Random House, and Simon & Schuster, among others.

The Weary Blues, with an introduction by Van Vechten, was reviewed by *PORGY AND BESS* author DuBose Heyward in the August 1, 1926, *New York Herald Tribune:* "Always intensely subjective, passionate, keenly sensitive to beauty and possessed of an unfaltering musical sense, Langston Hughes has given us a 'first book' that marks the opening of a career well worth watching." *Fine Clothes to the Jew* was another matter. When it was published, the *PITTSBURGH COURIER* ran a huge headline in capital letters: "LANGSTON HUGHES' BOOK OF POEMS TRASH."

Hughes began a poetry-reading tour in 1927. He read his poems at Princeton University in New Jersey and at FISK UNIVERSITY in Tennessee and embarked on a black church tour throughout the Deep South. His voice was a monotone, but audiences responded well to his work. On these tours, he used his poetry to address such issues as Jim Crow segregation, the lack of self-esteem among black people, racial injustice in courtrooms, and unfair housing policies.

Hughes won prizes and scholarships for his varied writings: religious plays, humorous short stories, and sharp, biting, social essays. He won an Amy Spingarn prize from *The Crisis,* and first prize from Witter Bynner's Intercollegiate Undergraduate Poetry Contest in 1926. A scholarship from arts PATRON Spingarn underwrote his formal education at Lincoln University in Pennsylvania, a black college from which he would graduate in 1929.

One of the most influential essays of Hughes's early career was published in June 1926 in *The Nation.* Hughes wrote "The Negro Artist and the Racial Mountain" in response to an essay by GEORGE S. SCHUYLER titled "The Negro-Art Hokum." In his essay, Hughes expressed open disdain—and perhaps distrust—of the black intelligentsia. Most important, he articulated a theory of the black aesthetic as a value system with political implications that provided fuel for the Harlem Renaissance. The essay also became one of the defining texts of the NEGRITUDE movement sweeping through France, the Caribbean, and Africa. It would influence several other literary movements as well and dignify Hughes's work until his death.

In 1927, Arts patron CHARLOTTE OSGOOD MASON began to supplement Hughes's income with an allowance of $150 per month. For her patronage, Mason required Hughes to write her a letter every day. She insisted that he read contemporary literary journals and paid for his subscriptions as well as for his writing supplies. "Godmother," as Mason was called by Hughes and folklorist ZORA NEALE HURSTON, also supported by Mason, required her wards to write exotic literature only, a demand Hughes could not meet. Conflict arose when he and Hurston clashed over their combined authorship of a folk comedy called *MULE BONE,* a project that Mason had sponsored, and that ultimately ended Hughes and Hurston's relationship.

The GREAT DEPRESSION that began in 1929 put a dent into the gaiety and prosperity of the Harlem Renaissance, but Hughes continued to write and publish in different forms. For his first novel, *Not Without Laughter,* written in 1930, he won approving reviews in the mainstream press and the 1931 Harlem Gold Award for Literature. Reviewing *Not Without Laughter* for the August 6, 1930, *Nation* magazine, V. F. Calverton wrote: "It is significant because even where it fails, it fails beautifully, and where it succeeds—namely, in its intimate characterizations and in its local color and charm—it succeeds where almost all others have failed."

Hughes also continued to publish volumes of poetry: *The Negro Mother and Other Dramatic Recitations* (1931), *Dear Lovely Death* (1931), *The Dream Keeper and Other Poems* (1932), and *Scottsboro Limited: Four Poems and a Play* (1932). With his friend Arna Bontemps, he published the popular children's book *Popo and Fifina* (1932).

In addition to giving recitals in Cuba and Haiti, Hughes traveled in 1932 with fellow author DOROTHY WEST, political activist LOUISE THOMPSON PATTERSON, and more than two dozen others to the Soviet Union to make a film called *Black and White.* The movie *Black and White* was not successful, but Hughes stayed in the Soviet Union from 1932 to 1933. He then traveled all over Europe and the Caribbean and networked with such literary icons as Nicolás Guillén in Cuba.

By the mid-1930s, Hughes had collected short stories in *The Ways of White Folks* (1934), and his first play, *Mulatto,* had a successful run on Broadway. Supported for years by grants and fellowships from the Guggenheim Foundation, the American Academy of Arts and Letters, and the Rosenwald Fund, Hughes wrote other plays: a comedy, *Little Ham* (1936), and the historical drama *Emperor of Haiti* (1936). He was economically free to establish the HARLEM SUITCASE THEATER in 1938, the New Negro Theater in Los Angeles the following year, and Skyloft Players in CHICAGO in 1942. While in Chicago, he encouraged a young black poet named MARGARET ABIGAIL WALKER in her literary efforts

Though primarily known as a poet, part of Hughes's fame stems from his autobiography, *The Big Sea* (1940); a bluesy poetry volume, *Shakespeare in Harlem* (1942); an attack on racial segregation, *Jim Crow's Last Stand* (1943); and a character he invented in 1942, Jesse B. Simple.

Simple was a product of the GREAT MIGRATION, which during the 1940s saw an increase in blacks migrating from southern states to northern industrial cities. Hughes's character Simple, like African Americans in real life, received encouragement to leave southern tobacco and cotton fields from such journalists as ROBERT ABBOTT, editor of the *CHICAGO DEFENDER.* The plight of Harlem-based Simple with his satiric comments as he deftly handled the ups and downs of northern living became a weekly column in the *Chicago Defender* starting on February 13, 1943.

Black America laughed at Simple's antics and, starting in 1950, the Simple newspaper tales grew into books: *Simple Speaks His Mind* (1950) and *Simple Takes a Wife* (1953). In 1957, the play *Simple Stakes a Claim* was presented on Broadway and in Hollywood. The collection *The Best of Simple* was published in 1961. Historian John Henrik Clarke wrote in *Freedomways* that Simple was, "a latter day Aesop whose fables are as entertaining as they are meaningfully true. . . . In his own earthy approach to American race problems he says more in a few sentences than some Ph.D. authorities have said in a small mountain of books."

Having learned German and Spanish when living with his father, Hughes translated with Mercer Cook in 1947 "Masters of the Dew," by Roumain. He also translated Nicolás Guillén's "Cuba Libre" in 1948 with Ben Frederick Carruthers, and Federico Garcia Lorca's "Romancero Gitano" in 1951.

Moreover, during the same period, while maintaining his productivity as an author, Hughes worked as poet-in-residence at Atlanta University in 1947 and taught at the Laboratory School at the University of Chicago in 1949. In 1947, he wrote the lyrics for the Kurt Weill and Elmer Rice creation *Street Scene,* an American opera. He also wrote two little known books of poetry: *Fields of Wonder* (1947) and *One-Way Ticket* (1949). In addition, he created the libretto for *Troubled Island* (1949), an opera in three acts, by black composer WILLIAM GRANT STILL. With Bontemps, Hughes edited *The Poetry of the Negro, 1746–1949,* a volume that continued to sell profusely in 2002.

Hughes, like PAUL ROBESON, LENA HORNE, W. E. B. Du Bois, and others, was called before the House Committee on Un-American Activities established by Senator Joseph McCarthy in the early 1950s. In question was Hughes's affiliation with people and organizations supportive of COMMUNISM. Hughes was adamant that he had never been a party member. He nevertheless had to answer publicly for radical verse he had written and published in the Soviet Union, including *A Negro Looks at Soviet Central Asia,* published by the Cooperative Publishing Society of Foreign Workers in 1934. Following the decline of McCarthyism, Hughes wrote about his experiences in the Soviet Union in *I Wonder as I Wander* (1956), his second autobiography.

On his own, Hughes started a "first" and "famous" book series for juveniles, including *The First Book of Negroes* (1952) and *Famous Negro Music Makers* (1955). He wrote about Harlem in *The Sweet Flypaper of Life* (1955), inspired by the photographs of Roy DeCarava. In 1957, he set one of his Simple tales to music in *Simply Heavenly* (1957).

During the 1960s, the Black Arts movement (BAM) demanded a more anti-western type of black literature. Hughes was an nationalist who sought to raise black consciousness through his writing. He fought for his freedom as an artist and, in 1960, won the NAACP's SPINGARN MEDAL. One of his most popular plays, *Black Nativity,* was presented in New York in 1961 during the Black Arts movement and continues to be staged every Christmas season in black community theaters across the country.

Langston Hughes, shown here in 1943, authored works in virtually every literary genre to become one of the Harlem Renaissance's most prolific and enduring writers. *(Library of Congress, Prints & Photographs Division [LC-USW3-033841-C])*

He edited several volumes, including *Poems from Black Africa* (1963) and *New Negro Poets: U.S.* (1964) with a foreword by poet GWENDOLYN BROOKS. Nevertheless, he and his work were deemed out of step by BAM writers. Still, ever the elder statesman of the black written word, Hughes continued to produce his own work and influence that of other writers.

In his last years, he wrote a book-length poem titled *Ask Your Mama* (1962) and attended literary conferences in Uganda and Nigeria, where black African writers viewed his work as important to the empowerment of the entire diaspora of African people. In 1966, Hughes was designated an "historic figure" at the First World Festival of Negro Arts in Dakar, Senegal. His last book, *The Panther and the Lash* (1967), was about the Civil Rights movement and was published after his death.

The prolific Hughes never married. His home from 1947 to 1967 was 20 East 127th Street in Harlem. He had no children. His sexuality has been challenged, discussed, and made the subject of a play and a movie by Isaac Julien, a black film director from London. *Looking for Langston* is a film about black gay life during the Harlem Renaissance, Hughes's share in that lifestyle, and his apparent love for black men as evidenced through a series of unpublished poems he wrote to a black male lover named "Beauty." The estate of Hughes moved to have the film blocked in the United States. It was shown in 1989, after which the estate asked Julien to soft-pedal the poems.

By his death, Hughes had published 16 books of poetry, two novels, seven collections of short stories, two autobiographies, nine children's books, and five works of nonfiction, including pictorial histories of black America. He translated works of Spanish authors and wrote 30 plays, plus opera librettos, and scripts for radio, television, and film. An opera titled *De Organizer,* written by Hughes with music by Ragtime composer James P. Johnson in 1940, was revived in 2002. The opera's music had been lost for some 60 years until located by music professor James Dapogny.

Throughout his artistic career, Hughes's main concern, true to his beginnings as a product of the Harlem Renaissance, was the uplift of his people. Using prose and poetry, he confronted racial stereotypes, protested social conditions, and expanded African America's image of itself. A "people's poet" who sought to reeducate both audience and artist, Hughes wrote the story of his people in the musical language of blues and jazz, advocated the cultural nationalism of African-American poets, and lifted the theory of the black aesthetic into reality.

Langston Hughes died on May 22, 1967.

Further Reading

Berry, Faith, ed. *Good Morning Revolution: The Uncollected Social Protest Writing of Langston Hughes.* Lawrence Hill, 1973.

———. *Langston Hughes: Before and Beyond Harlem.* New York: Citadel Press, Carol Publishing Group, 1983.

Clarke, John Henrik. "Langston Hughes and Jesse B. Simple," *Freedomways,* Spring 1968, 167–9.

Hughes, Langston. *The Big Sea.* New York: Alfred A. Knopf, 1940.

Klotman, Phyllis R. "Jesse B. Simple and the Narrative Art of Langston Hughes," *The Journal of Narrative Technique,* January 1973, 66–75.

Nichols, Charles H., ed. *Arna Bontemps–Langston Hughes Letters: 1925–1967.* New York: Dodd, 1980.

Rampersad, Arnold. *The Life of Langston Hughes: Volume I: 1902–1941: I, Too, Sing America.* New York: Oxford University Press, 1986.

— Sandra L. West

Hunter, Alberta (1895–1984) *blues singer*

Blues singer Alberta Hunter achieved initial success during the RACE RECORD boom of the 1920s only to abandon performing for decades before reemerging in the 1970s as a star singer of rare interpretative ability and phrasing.

Alberta Hunter was born on April 1, 1895, in Shelby County, Memphis, Tennessee. She left home at the age of 11 and made her way to CHICAGO. There she developed into a singer, performing at Dago Frank's Club, Hugh Hoskins's club, the Panama Club, and the Dreamland Cabaret.

During the 1920s in NEW YORK CITY, she continued to sing in cabarets and in 1922 acted in *Dumb Luck* with ETHEL WATERS. She also wrote BESSIE SMITH's first hit record, "Downhearted Blues," which in 1923 sold more than a million copies. Like Bessie Smith, CLARA SMITH, and Waters, Hunter enjoyed a successful recording career during the rise of the black music industry. Her songs included "A Good Man Is Hard to Find," "Loveless Love," and "Beale Street Blues." She recorded on the PACE PHONOGRAPHIC RECORD CORPORATION's Black Swan, Paramount, Gennett, Okeh, Victor, Decca, and Bluebird record labels. Sometimes she recorded under a pseudonym: Josephine Beatty or May Alix.

According to composer and pianist EUBIE BLAKE, Hunter's performance was convincing to the point that, "you felt so sorry for her you wanted to kill the guy she was singing about."

In 1928, Hunter played Queenie in the hit Broadway musical *Showboat,* along with PAUL ROBESON, and replaced international celebrity JOSEPHINE BAKER in the musical revue the *Folies Bergères.* She was so popular that celebrated composer Noel Coward wrote a song called "I Travel Alone" specifically for her.

During the 1930s, Alberta Hunter appeared again with Waters in *Mamba's Daughters* (1939) and toured with the United Services Organization (USO) during World War II. In 1956, Hunter retired from the stage and began a second career as a practical nurse. At the age of 82, she returned to the stage and was rediscovered in 1977. She became a regular star attraction at The Cookery in New York's Greenwich Village and, like DOROTHY WEST in the 1990s, was celebrated as one of the great talents to have emerged during the Harlem Renaissance and survived until the latter half of the 1900s.

Alberta Hunter died in New York City on October 17, 1984.

Further Reading

Dahl, Linda. *Stormy Weather: The Music and Lives of a Century of Jazzwomen.* New York: Limelight Editions, 1996.

Taylor, Frank C., and Gerald Cook. *Alberta Hunter: A Celebration in Blues.* New York: McGraw-Hill Companies, 1987.

— Sandra L. West

Hurston, Zora Neale (1891–1960) *writer, folklorist, anthropologist*

The writing career of Zora Neale Hurston spanned nearly 40 years, producing essays, folklore, short stories, novels, plays, articles on anthropology, and autobiography. She cut a literary path that celebrates folk traditions and the cultural heritage of African Americans.

From birth to death, Hurston's life was filled with inconsistencies and controversy. Both her birthplace and age remain questionable. Hurston maintained that she was born in Eatonville, Florida, her idyllic childhood home. Family records, however, indicate that the Hurstons moved there shortly after her birth in Alabama on January 7, 1891. Hurston refuted this and other records throughout her lifetime. She routinely lied about her age, and her autobiography, *Dust Tracks on a Road* (1942), never mentions the failure of her two very brief marriages—to Herbert Sheen in 1927 and Albert Price III in 1939.

Hurston's belief that she could write her own destiny and rewrite her history was sparked in Eatonville, the first self-governing black town incorporated in the United States. There, during her formative years, she grew up amid numerous examples of independence and self-determination. Her hometown environment colored her outlook on both life in America and an individual's possibilities for success. Consequently, it became a rich source for much of her writings.

Groomed by her mother, former educator Lucy Ann (Potts) Hurston, to meet life assertively, Hurston's forwardness often incited debate. Zora's mother encouraged her children to speak out and set high goals. Zora's father, the Reverend John Hurston, however, vigorously criticized this position. A tenant farmer and Eatonville's three-time mayor, he remained vigilant toward potential dangers facing outspoken blacks. He warned his daughter, "It did not do for Negroes to have too much spirit." Sandwiched by these opposing perspectives, the eight Hurston children grew up in an atmosphere ripe for lively interaction.

The siblings thrived on the five-acre, greenery-rich estate anchored by the eight-room house in which they lived. Their stability, however, was rocked by Lucy Hurston's death when Zora was about 13. Uprooted and shipped to a Jacksonville, Florida, boarding school, Hurston's world quickly unraveled. On the heels of her father's hasty remarriage, she found her education abruptly interrupted. John Hurston, at his new wife's urgings, discontinued tuition payments, forcing his daughter to be dismissed from school.

In lodging limbo for years afterward, Hurston was shuffled among relatives and friends. Seeking to support herself by working as a domestic, she could not attend school regularly. Always fascinated by books and the new worlds they unfolded, she yearned for reading material and constantly searched for literary treasures.

For more than a year, the education-starved teen worked as a maid and wardrobe assistant for an actress touring with a theatrical troupe. This job fed Hurston's hunger for literary exposure and travel. She flourished in the actors' company. With ready access to opera and books, Hurston's appreciation of literature intensified.

After her employer left the tour in Baltimore, Maryland, Hurston settled there and entered night school. Two years later, in 1918, she completed high school at Morgan Academy, then enrolled in WASHINGTON, D.C.'s HOWARD UNIVERSITY. Amid some of the nation's most intellectually gifted blacks, Hurston's exceptional ability to engage the academic elite in extended discussions made an impression on professors and students alike. At Howard, she became known for spirited exchanges, leading one professor to characterize her as a "rough edged diamond."

She was admitted to the university's exclusive literary club, Stylus. In May 1921, the organization published Hurston's first story, "John Redding Goes to Sea," in its magazine. Under the tutelage of Harvard- and Oxford-educated professor ALAIN LOCKE, Hurston continued to develop her craft. Still, after spending five years in Washington, she managed to finish less than two years of coursework. Again, financial need preempted her studies, as she spent the bulk of her time working as a manicurist. Though low on tuition funds, Hurston remained high on creative resources and wrote several short stories and a play, *Color Struck.*

Novelist, folklorist, and anthropologist Zora Neale Hurston was one of the most gifted and prolific of the Harlem Renaissance writers. *(Archives, Moorland-Spingarn Research Center, Howard University)*

Practically penniless and jobless, she moved to NEW YORK CITY in 1925 and managed immediately to associate with the emerging cultural movement that spawned the Harlem Renaissance. Hurston gained recognition when her stories appeared in Locke's the *NEW NEGRO*, an anthology of works by Harlem Renaissance writers and artists. She garnered acclaim as well when sociologist CHARLES SPURGEON JOHNSON published her play and story "Spunk" in *OPPORTUNITY: A JOURNAL OF NEGRO LIFE*. She also joined LANGSTON HUGHES, WALLACE THURMAN, RICHARD BRUCE NUGENT, and other writers to produce *FIRE!!*, a single-issue literary magazine focused on black culture.

Hurston's distinction as a major Harlem Renaissance writer who hailed from the rural southeastern United States further spotlighted her works. Her intimate knowledge of black folklife endeared her to many colleagues, although her trademark earthiness distressed others. Despite her sometimes disruptive boisterousness, Hurston's imagery-rich stories won her a scholarship to complete her education at New York's Barnard College.

Adding to the general stir over Hurston was her flat refusal to politicize her early writings by adopting the prevailing notions driving African-American social reform. For decades, she would remain steadfast in a position she voiced in "How It Feels to Be Colored Me," an essay published in 1928. In it, she boldly disowned any notion of obsessing over the supposed downtrodden state of blacks and affirmed her color-blind belief in self-determination.

After receiving a B.A. in 1928, Hurston began graduate studies in anthropology at Columbia University. Guided by anthropologist Franz Boas, she returned to Eatonville and Alabama to collect black folklore. The resulting volume of tales, *Mules and Men,* published in 1935, reflected two milestones in the scientific field. Never before had such stories been gathered and published by an African-American woman. Nor had any anthropologist native to a culture engaged in its study, in keeping with the standard practice of maintaining emotional distance for the sake of objectivity.

While awaiting the publication of *Mules and Men,* Hurston wrote and produced a critically popular but financially disastrous Broadway musical. In its wake, she sought sanctuary in Eatonville, where she wrote a few short stories but ended up impoverished. Eventually, one story, catching the interest of a publisher, grew into her first novel, *Jonah's Gourd Vine.* Published in 1934, it explores the conflict that middle-class blacks faced when working to reconcile two opposing worldviews of human sexuality. Although mainstream critics praised the book, some African Americans objected to *Jonah's Gourd Vine*'s folklore content. Ultimately, Hurston's only financial gain from the book was the $200 advance she received.

To support herself, Hurston then taught drama for a short while at a Daytona Beach college and for the WORKS

PROGRESS ADMINISTRATION's Federal Theater Project. Also, she received a Rosenwald Fellowship to earn a doctorate in anthropology but defaulted by not attending classes. Her interest in folk culture as the source of anthropological study had waned. Instead, she used it purely for journalistic, dramatic, and fictional purposes.

Upon publication, her folklore collection *Mules and Men* received mixed reviews. Whites praised it for authentically celebrating the oral tradition and lifestyle of southern rural blacks. However, black intellectuals, most notably Howard University poet and professor STERLING ALLEN BROWN, lashed out at Hurston for caricaturing her people. They saw the collection of traditional stories, songs, games, and customs as counterproductive to the goals of the New Negro movement. Harlem Renaissance leaders viewed its unflattering depictions as an affront since they passionately maintained that articulate, talented blacks were obligated to uplift the race and raise the social conscience. They argued that Hurston's tales ignored the harsher truths of her subjects' lives, concentrating instead on the lighter side of their world.

Undaunted by the negative criticisms, Hurston, supported by two Guggenheim Fellowships, traveled throughout the southern United States and to the Caribbean to study folk culture. In Haiti, she was an active observer by day and a creative writer by night, producing in just seven weeks what was to become a classic in American literature, *Their Eyes Were Watching God.* This novel also evoked white praise and incited black disapproval. Even her former mentor Alain Locke stated that the book's folklore weakened its story line—a black American woman's search for self-determination through establishing and maintaining a free sexual identity.

Hurston published *Tell My Horse,* a collection of Haitian and Jamaican folklore, in 1938, and her third novel, *Moses, Man of the Mountain,* in 1939. The latter, presenting a retelling of the biblical tale of Moses from a black perspective, elicited similar sets of opposing reviews.

Even her autobiographical *Dust Tracks* drew conflicting criticisms. An unconventional blend of autobiography and anthropology, it presents both Hurston's folk and intellectual perspectives. She peppers this personal chronicle with folk expressions and narratives. The book's exclusion of certain personal details also generated concern.

Hurston's unshakable individualism continually riled her African-American contemporaries. She expressed unpopular stances on key sociopolitical issues of her day. In *Dust Tracks,* she decried anyone who belabored racial injustice. Blacks disliked her walking a racial tightrope, often spouting conciliatory remarks for her white audience while offering blacks less tolerant views. Among the affronts to blacks were statements seeming to support segregation. As a result, many African Americans, including members of the NATIONAL ASSOCIATION FOR THE ADVANCEMENT OF COLORED PEOPLE (NAACP), denounced Hurston.

In white literary circles, however, *Dust Tracks* won awards for promoting race relations. Due to the memoir's welcome reception among whites, notable mainstream magazines, including the *Saturday Evening Post,* sought Hurston to write commentaries and articles on black culture. She also reviewed plays, musicals, and books.

While these writings remained apolitical, during the same period, in pieces published in the *Negro Digest,* Hurston openly discussed racism. At first, her comments were not scathing. Instead, they focused on discrimination as a consequence of white disillusionment. Eventually, though, in the article "Crazy for This Democracy," Hurston unleashed criticism of America's exploitation of certain ethnic groups. Then, in another article, she suggested that publishing companies' stereotypes of blacks limited the development of her writing.

Because of her demand as a contributing writer, Hurston earned enough to purchase a houseboat and lived on it in Florida for several years. During that time she wrote her final novel, *Seraph on the Suwanee.* Published in 1948, it was both a continuation of and a stark departure from the style of writing for which she was renowned. *Seraph on the Suwanee* is a story about southern folklife, but that of whites. The book depicts a poor woman's journey from low self-esteem and despair to a discovery of self-worth. Hurston wrote *Seraph on the Suwanee* to debunk the myth that blacks could not effectively write about whites. This novel also received a mixed response.

By the 1950s, Hurston was again in financial straits. Though she continued to write, she worked temporarily as a freelance journalist, librarian, substitute teacher, and even again as a maid. Because of her erratic income, she moved often. After drifting from one small Florida town to the next, the Saint Lucie County Welfare Home in Fort Pierce became her final residence, following a debilitating stroke on October 29, 1959. Hurston died destitute on January 28, 1960.

Further Reading

Boyd, Valerie. *Wrapped in Rainbows: The Life of Zora Neale Hurston.* New York: Scribner, 2003.

Hurston, Zora Neale, and Carla Kaplan, ed. *Zora Neale Hurston: A Life in Letters.* New York: Doubleday, 2002.

Jones, Sharon L. *Rereading the Harlem Renaissance: Race, Class, and Gender in the Fiction of Jessie Fauset, Zora Neale Hurston, and Dorothy West.* Westport, Conn.: Greenwood, 2002.

Lowe, John. *Jump at the Sun: Zora Neale Hurston's Cosmic Comedy.* Champaign: University of Illinois, 1997.

Meisenhelder, Susan Edwards. *Hitting a Straight Lick with a Crooked Stick: Race and Gender in the Work of Zora Neale Hurston.* Tuscaloosa: University of Alabama Press, 2001.

— Iris Formey Dawson

I

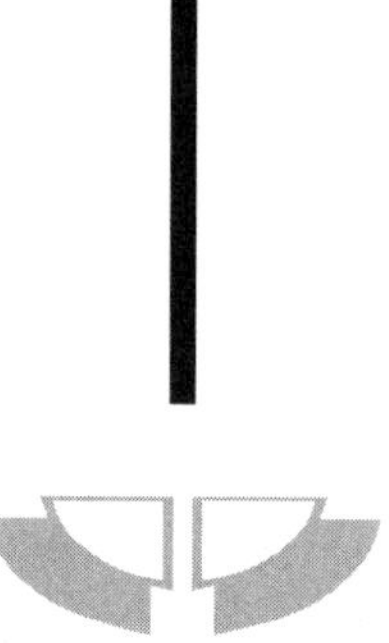

"If We Must Die"

A poem published at the height of the RED SUMMER OF 1919, when violent riots resulted in hundreds of deaths and the destruction of property throughout the United States, "If We Must Die" catapulted author CLAUDE MCKAY to international fame.

"If We Must Die" initially appeared in the July 1919 issue of the radical *Liberator* magazine edited by patron and author MAX EASTMAN. Part of a two-page spread in the magazine, it was featured beside six other poems by McKay, including "A Roman Holiday," "The Capitalist at Dinner," and "The Little People." The poems, like those published three years later in McKay's book of verse, *Harlem Shadows,* introduced a new tone of militancy to the poetry published by blacks at the time.

Riots caused deaths and destruction in more than two dozen cities the summer McKay wrote "If We Must Die." At the time, the poet worked as a dining car waiter for the Pennsylvania Railroad and stated that during his travels he observed a high degree of anxiety and tension among African Africans. "We stuck together, some of us armed," he stated, "going from the railroad station to our quarters. . . . We never knew what was going to happen." After writing the poem, McKay recited it to his fellow railroad workers and was surprised at the deep emotional response it generated. Encouraged by their reaction, he submitted "If We Must Die" and other poems to *The Liberator.*

Following its appearance in *The Liberator,* "If We Must Die" was published next in the *MESSENGER,* edited by A. PHILIP RANDOLPH and Chandler Owen. Within a month, the poem was republished in weekly and monthly periodicals across the United States, and McKay became the most famous black poet in the country. The poem itself, however, does not allude specifically to black people, and various groups struggling against political oppression adapted McKay's words to their own causes, frequently quoting the famous final lines: "Like men we'll face the murderous, cowardly pack, Pressed to the wall, dying, but fighting back!"

In addition to helping to boost the sales of McKay's own 1922 volume of poetry, *Harlem Shadows,* "If We Must Die" was also included in JAMES WELDON JOHNSON's anthology *The Book of American Negro Poetry.*

Addressing a joint session of the United States during World War II, British prime minister Winston Churchill recited "If We Must Die" to underscore his country's determination to resist defeat by Nazi Germany. It thereafter became a rallying cry of the allied forces. Churchill reportedly neglected to acknowledge McKay as the author of the poem.

It again surfaced as a rallying cry in 1971 when inmates of the Attica state prison in New York circulated copies of the poem with their own writings in protest of penal conditions. "If We Must Die" remains a standard inclusion for anthologies of 20th-century black literature. Moreover, as recently as 2002, a recital of the poem was included on the compact disc *Cookie: The Anthropological Mixtape* by musician Meshell Ndegeocello.

Further Reading

Hathaway, Heather. *Caribbean Waves! Relocating Claude McKay and Paule Marshall.* Bloomington: Indiana University Press, 1999.

Winston, James, and Claude McKay. *A Fierce Hatred of Injustice: Claude McKay's Jamaican Poetry of Rebellion.* London: Verso Publishing, 2001.

— Aberjhani

interracial interaction and the Harlem Renaissance

Interaction between blacks and whites in the United States throughout the first half of the 1900s ran the gamut from the intimacy of affectionate personal relationships to the murderous violence of riots and LYNCHING.

With the apartheid system of JIM CROW sanctioned by both legislation and social custom in the United States, the division of blacks and whites was an ongoing political and personal issue during those decades preceding, including, and following the Harlem Renaissance. Whereas the South was routinely vilified for such racist extremes as hanging blacks from trees and burning them alive, the lesser racism of segregation in such public accommodations as restaurants, hotels, and transportation was common in every region of the country. Interracial marriages, along with the aggressive political advocacy of the NATIONAL ASSOCIATION FOR THE ADVANCEMENT OF COLORED PEOPLE (NAACP) and protests of the black press, proved one of the principal threats, and thus challenges, to apartheid in the United States.

Marriage between blacks and whites in the 1920s and 1930s in particular was viewed alternately as a threat to the survival of the white race and as a means of reinvigorating it. White patron CHARLOTTE OSGOOD MASON championed the works of ZORA NEALE HURSTON, ALAIN LOCKE, and other African Americans because she believed the culture of people of African descent was essential to restore vitality to the culture of white America. Black satirist GEORGE S. SCHUYLER and his wife, white Texas aristocrat Josephine Cogdell, shared a belief in what they termed racial hybridization, theorizing that the biracial offspring of a mixed marriage would prove superior to the offspring of a same-race marriage. In the case of their celebrated daughter, child prodigy and concert pianist Philippa Schuyler, the theory seemed to bear out.

In direct opposition to the beliefs of the Schuylers and Charlotte Osgood Mason were the proponents of eugenics, who then held that biracial marriages between blacks and whites would result in the decline of intelligence and other presumed superior qualities in whites. Eventually, they reasoned, it would destroy the white race altogether. Advocates for eugenics in the 1920s managed successfully to either pass or reinforce existing laws banning interracial marriages in some 30 states, extending a tradition of such legislation started by Maryland in 1664. In addition to Maryland, the states included Alabama, Arkansas, Arizona, California, Colorado, Delaware, Florida, Georgia, Indiana, Iowa, Kentucky, Louisiana, Mississippi, Missouri, Montana, Nebraska, Nevada, North Carolina, North Dakota, Oklahoma, Oregon, South Carolina, South Dakota, Tennessee, Texas, Utah, Virginia, West Virginia, and Wyoming.

Proponents of eugenics were also often affiliated with the hundreds of lynchings of black men, women, and youths that took place during the 1920s.

The issues at hand in many ways were exemplified by the 1925 case of a young biracial woman named Alice Jones and her husband, Kip Rhinelander, heir to a New York real estate fortune. Rhinelander's family charged that the 21-year-old heir had been deceived regarding his 24-year-old wife's race and attempted to have their marriage annulled. This attempt failed when it was reasoned that Jones could not have deceived Rhinelander because the couple had been nude together, and the examinations of a jury revealed that without clothing Jones's race was evident enough. The Rhinelander family's defense then changed, holding that such a marriage threatened the white gene pool as well as the Rhinelander—and by extension the white race's—monetary fortune. Separated from her husband, Jones countersued the Rhinelander family for approximately $32,000 and a monthly allowance. The couple officially divorced in 1929.

Despite a well-established movement against integration in general and interracial marriages in particular, a number of the era's well-known musicians, artists, writers, and athletes did enter into biracial marriages either in the United States or outside the United States. Among them were EUGENE JACQUES BULLARD, JACK JOHNSON, CHARLIE PARKER, JEAN TOOMER, WALTER WHITE, and RICHARD NATHANIEL WRIGHT.

Likewise, a number of celebrated friendships between blacks and whites provided the necessary mixture of talent, financial resources, publicity, and performance venues that made the Harlem Renaissance possible. The black comedian BERT WILLIAMS and the white comedian Eddie Cantor were both stars of the ZIEGFELD FOLLIES, and when not on stage they would find restaurants that did not enforce a Jim Crow policy in order to share time together. W. E. B. DU BOIS and Joel Spingarn, JAMES WELDON JOHNSON and CARL VAN VECHTEN, Charlotte Osgood Mason and Alain Locke, each enjoyed friendships that directly impacted the *NEW NEGRO* movement. Both as a friend of CLAUDE MCKAY and as an admirer of his work, white editor MAX EASTMAN placed his publication and his assistance as a PATRON at McKay's disposal. Similarly, celebrated white author Waldo Frank did the same on behalf of Jean Toomer. The relationship between the British-born NANCY CUNARD and black musician Henry Crowder was largely responsible for a number of published works on black culture by Cunard.

Those works produced by writers of the Harlem Renaissance focused less on interracial friendships or marriages per se than they did on the offspring of such relationships. A major exception to that observation are the novels of PAULINE ELIZABETH HOPKINS. The dilemma of being biracial in American society formed the basis for some of the era's most accomplished works, including James Weldon Johnson's novel *AUTOBIOGRAPHY OF AN EX-COLORED MAN;* Langston Hughes's hit Broadway play, *Mulatto;* and NELLA LARSEN's novel, *Passing.* Jean Toomer's literary montage, *Cane,* explored the subject somewhat more than other works. However, interracial relationships themselves would receive far more extensive treatment in such novels as Chester Himes's *Pinktoes* in 1961 and James Baldwin's *Another Country* in 1962.

It should be noted that while whites often made funds and publishing outlets available to blacks, they in turn often profited from black culture itself. The playwrights Ridgeley Torrence and Eugene O'Neill looked to the experience of African Americans for material to revitalize what they considered a stagnant American theatre. O'Neill in particular incorporated elements of the black experience into a series of his dramatic works, most notably *THE EMPEROR JONES,* which starred in turn black performers CHARLES SIDNEY GILPIN and PAUL ROBESON in the title role. The same was true for George Gershwin in his collaboration with Dubose Heyward to create the classic folk opera *PORGY AND BESS.*

Marc Connelly and Roark Bradford's very successful musical adaptation of the New Testament, *The GREEN PASTURES*, also capitalized on black culture at the same time that it employed and promoted black actors.

As the cultural and social interaction between black and whites increased, the move to block interracial marriages lost much of its drive, and nearly half those states that passed legislation against such unions in the 1920s repealed their laws in the 1950s and early 1960s. Almost all of the remaining states repealed their laws banning interracial marriage when the U.S. Supreme Court declared them unconstitutional in the 1967 case of *Loving v. Virginia.* The number of biracial marriages then rose from 51,000 in 1960 to 65,000 in 1970. The number reached 121,000 in 1980; 231,000 in 1990; and in 2002 was estimated at 450,000.

The last states to remove all clauses barring biracial marriages from their laws were South Carolina in 1998 and Alabama in the year 2000.

Further Reading

Moran, Rachel F. *Interracial Intimacy: The Regulation of Race and Romance.* Chicago: University of Chicago Press, 2001.

Sollors, Werner, ed. *Interracialism, Black-White Intermarriage in American History, Literature, and Law.* New York: Oxford University Press, 2000.

— Aberjhani

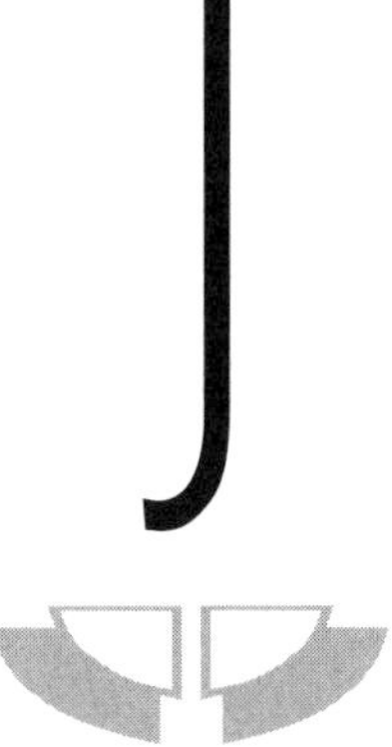

Jackson, May Howard (1877–1931) *sculptor*

An art instructor at HOWARD UNIVERSITY in WASHINGTON, D.C., for several years, May Howard Jackson created busts of famous individuals such as Dr. W. E. B. DU BOIS and Paul Laurence Dunbar.

May Howard Jackson was born in 1877 in PHILADELPHIA, Pennsylvania. She was educated at J. Liberty Tadd's Art School in Pennsylvania and at the Pennsylvania Academy of Fine Arts. Jackson was the maternal aunt and, for a time, foster mother of sculptor SARGENT CLAUDE JOHNSON when he became an orphan.

She married Sherman Jackson, a high school principal at M Street School (later Dunbar High School) in Washington, D.C., in 1902. In the same year, Jackson established a private art studio that she would maintain throughout her adult life. She taught sculpture and modeling from life subjects in 1922 at Howard University.

Jackson's forte was the sculptured bust of prominent individuals. Her work includes *Paul Laurence Dunbar* (1919); *W. E. B. Du Bois* (1929); *Kelly Miller* (1929); and *JEAN TOOMER* (no date). Dunbar was a dialect poet well known for verse such as *When Malindy Sings;* Du Bois cofounded the NATIONAL ASSOCIATION FOR THE ADVANCEMENT OF COLORED PEOPLE (NAACP); Miller, a former slave, was a member of the illustrious society of scholars the AMERICAN NEGRO ACADEMY, with BOOKER TALIAFERRO WASHINGTON and Du Bois. Toomer is renowned as the author of *Cane,* considered the first novel and one of the most celebrated books of the Harlem Renaissance. Jackson also produced such black thematic sculpture as *Mulatto Mother and Her Child* (1929) and *Shell-Baby* (1929).

Art historian James A. Porter, in the 1940s, stated that Jackson's work held "no great originality in any of the pieces she attempted." ALAIN LOCKE, editor of the *NEW NEGRO* (1925), believed that because Jackson did not go the route of the expatriate artist to study in Europe or otherwise work outside the academic environment, she stifled her credibility as an artist.

Jackson's work was exhibited at the National Academy of Design, the New York Emancipation Exposition, and the National Academy of Art in NEW YORK CITY.

She died in 1931.

Further Reading

Robinson, Jontylye Theresa. *Bearing Witness: Contemporary Works by African- American Women Artists.* Atlanta and New York: Spelman College and Rizzoli International Publications, Inc., 1996.

Wall, Cheryl A. *Women of the Harlem Renaissance.* Bloomington: Indiana University Press, 1995.

— Sandra L. West

jazz

The enduring polyphonic musical idiom known as jazz combined RAGTIME, the BLUES, and traditions of European music to create a distinctly American music that developed in the cities of the South, West, and Midwest, most notably NEW ORLEANS, CHICAGO, San Francisco, and St. Louis. Jazz during the Harlem Renaissance grew into such a powerful expression of creativity, culture, and personality that for many the 1920s became known as the Jazz Age.

One may say that in its essence jazz evolved out of the black American's creative instinct, specifically a legacy of his African heritage, for inventing new forms of musical expression by absorbing and reinterpreting musical elements from different cultures. That creative impulse is readily apparent in any study of the genesis of what sociologist W. E. B. DU BOIS described as the Sorrow Songs, the now traditional African-American spirituals that adapted the hymns of the white American Protestant to the work songs and laments of the slave to create one of the most unique and original bodies of music in the history of American culture. A similar musical synthesis occurred with the creation of ragtime when African Americans blended such traditional European musical forms as polkas, waltzes, and marches with the African's gift for percussion to generate the innovative rhythm known as syncopation that became a chief characteristic of ragtime and, later, of the SWING SOUND.

Played primarily on the piano, ragtime in the 1890s was composed by blacks and whites who sold their compositions as SHEET MUSIC and on piano rolls. A precursor of the phonograph record, piano rolls were perforated rolls of paper that unwound upon a mechanical device attached to a piano and designed to duplicate the sound of human performance. Ragtime introduced to American and European popular music culture the intertwining, sustained, and progressive rhythmic quality known as syncopation. Ragtime composers such as Tom Turpin, the Savannah, Georgia, native who wrote "Harlem Rag" in 1897, and the Texas-born Scott Joplin, who wrote his million-selling classic "Maple Leaf Rag" in 1899, experimented with variations in style and melody. Their compositions broke with the more singularly patterned forms of European music and paved the way for the incorporation of such musical elements as combative contrast, discontinuity, and improvisation, all of which would become defining qualities of jazz.

Even as ragtime was approaching the peak of its expression and popularity, jazz was beginning to take form in St. Louis, Savannah, Memphis, Kansas City, and other urban centers of the South and Midwest. The city with the most substantial claim to the title of the birthplace of jazz, however, is generally acknowledged to be New Orleans.

A mainstay of jazz was and is its inclusion of musical influences from different cultures. Of all the cities where the music began to develop, none were as diverse in cultural influences as New Orleans. Nor were any as liberal in allowing people of African descent to observe both publicly and privately a number of dance rituals and spiritual practices associated with African cultures. Dance rituals in particular, often held in public squares and referred to as circle dances or ring shouts, were characterized by animated drumming, impromptu utterances similar to those associated with voodoo ceremonies, and an energetic dancing inspired and driven by the drumming. Added to the powerful foundation of transplanted African culture in New Orleans were the musical influences of the French, the Germans, the Caribbean, the Spanish, and others to a lesser but still significant degree.

Music as a whole in the overall culture of New Orleans generally formed a more dominant element than in most American cities. As a part of backyard family gatherings, church ceremonies such as funerals and weddings, public holidays, picnics, and everyday entertainment, it constituted an abiding presence. Individuals who played banjos, cornets, drums, guitars, or trumpets, as well as those who joined together to form brass bands, were common in every segment of the city.

With music serving as such an integral part of New Orleans culture, the city produced both the man most often described as the first jazz musician, Buddy Bolden, and the man who claimed to have invented jazz, JELLY ROLL MORTON. More than likely, both musicians were only two of many who played the music but also proved more aggressive in their experimentation with it. Not all who played or enjoyed the music flaunted that fact because more conservative individuals and organizations considered it vulgar or profane, an affront to standard marches, hymns, and waltzes. Bolden, a cornetist, composed a song called "Buddy Bolden's Stomp" that was virtually outlawed because of its references to local society and politics. Bolden gained fame as a musician in the late 1890s and first decade of the 1900s. As jazz increased in popularity, he became known as the father of jazz, and his music, though never recorded, was an influence on those who eventually carried jazz into the mainstream of popular culture.

Jelly Roll Morton claimed to have invented jazz around 1902, when he was 12 years old and performing in the brothels of New Orleans's legendary Storyville district. Whereas his invention of jazz is open to much debate, Morton was in fact the first musician to publish a jazz arrangement with his composition "Jelly Roll Blues" in 1915. Moreover, he did go on to create dozens of recognized masterpieces of the genre.

Aside from acknowledging New Orleans natives Buddy Bolden and Jelly Roll Morton as important figures associated with the beginnings of jazz, New Orleans was home to a number of others whose talents further refined and advanced the new music. In this, the sheer number of such gifted musicians, New Orleans again surpassed other cities. Among those who lived there and eventually traveled to spread the music around the country and the world were cornet player KING OLIVER; trombonist, cornet player, and bandleader Kid Ory; cornet player Sidney Bechet; and trumpeter LOUIS ARMSTRONG.

Morton, King Oliver, Ory, and Armstrong all took their music on the road and, by the time of WORLD WAR I, had relocated to Chicago. There, they played what became known as Chicago Dixieland Jazz and influenced an entire generation of white musicians who would also adopt and adapt the music for their own audiences. In addition to playing the music at hotels, in restaurants, bars, and private parties, musicians played jazz in the pit orchestras of theaters such as Chicago's Metropolitan and Vendome. Among those white musicians who adapted the jazz of black musicians from New Orleans and went on to become accomplished musicians in their own right were trumpeter Bix Beiderbecke, who performed in turn with the Wolverine Orchestra, the Frankie Trunbauer Band, and the Jean Goldkette Orchestra; and Benny Goodman, who would eventually rival COUNT BASIE for the title of King of the SWING SOUND.

That progressive whites embraced and celebrated jazz as readily as blacks indicated the democratic nature of the music. Jazz came to represent a break with tradition, namely Victorianism, something that proponents of early 1900 modernism greatly favored. By its very improvisational nature, jazz tended to celebrate all music by including all music so that an original composition by someone like pianist Earl Hines, also prominent in Chicago, might feature a short sampling of Mozart followed by another of the blues before reverting back to the original song. The improvisational aspect of jazz also allowed players to perform in rhythms counter to or complementary of the dominant melody so that soloists had the opportunity to express through the music their individual artistry and personality. In that sense, more important than one's blackness or whiteness was the uniqueness of one's creative musical vision.

Just as musicians from New Orleans were saturating Chicago and other cities with jazz, bandleader James Reese Europe and singer and lyricist NOBLE SISSLE introduced France and its allies to the music in their roles as members of an infantry band. The band performed goodwill concerts throughout France, and Sissle wrote a number of songs, most memorably "To Hell with Germany," that French regiments adopted as rallying cries. Moreover, black expatriate and French World War I hero EUGENE JACQUES BULLARD was known to perform with a jazz combo in PARIS in between flying combat missions.

Noble Sissle returned from the war to team up with his partner EUBIE BLAKE just as various musicians were making their way to NEW YORK CITY and HARLEM, both to take advantage of the growing entertainment industry there and to participate in jam sessions with other musicians. Sissle and Blake, along with Flournoy Miller and Aubrey Lyles, utilized jazz music as well as jazz dance to create their 1921 history-making Broadway hit, *SHUFFLE ALONG*. The noted creative genius of *Shuffle Along* and the exuberant vitality of the production drew record crowds of blacks and whites to the Cort Theatre on 63rd Street for more than 500 consecutive weeks before going on the road for an equally successful national tour. For writer LANGSTON HUGHES, it was this show that marked the beginning of the Harlem Renaissance. For many others, it and America's victory in World War I marked the beginning of the Jazz Age. And *Shuffle Along* did, in fact, create on Broadway a vogue for musicals featuring the culture and presence of African Americans that lasted throughout the 1920s.

Viewing dances such as the Charleston and Black Bottom on stage, whites often hired black professional entertainers to teach the dances at private parties and clubs. Part of the celebrity enjoyed by both BRICKTOP and JOSEPHINE BAKER in Paris was their willingness and ability to teach Europeans and wealthy white American expatriates African-American dances performed to jazz.

As the popularity of ragtime began to wane and that of jazz and the blues increased, pianists in Harlem invented a form of playing called STRIDE PIANO that in many ways bridged the gap between the musical forms. With stride piano, such rightly celebrated musicians as James P. Johnson, Willie "The Lion" Smith, and FATS WALLER basically played standard ragtime with one hand while playing counter rhythms and injecting snatches of different musical styles with the other. Stride piano became the music of preference at Harlem RENT PARTIES, SPEAKEASIES, and many of the community's increasing number of clubs.

Inevitably, jazz impacted on the writings and visual art of the *NEW NEGRO* movement that in 1926 announced its presence and intent first with the publication of the *SURVEY GRAPHIC* Special Harlem Edition, then with the publication of the *New Negro* anthology, edited by ALAIN LOCKE. *The New Negro* anthology recognized the growing power of jazz as a cultural force in its bibliography, citing the compositions *Jazz Sonata,* by George Antheil; *Krassy Kat, a Jazz Pantomime,* by John Alden Carpenter; *Jazz Symphony Based on Negro Blues,* by Albert Chiaffarelli; and, among others, *The Seven Deadly Arts, a Jazz Ballet,* by Eastwood Lane. It also included GWENDOLYN BENNETTA BENNETT's poem "Song" and two jazz poems by Langston Hughes, "Jazzonia" and "Nude Young Dancer."

The journalist and historian James A. Rogers contributed an essay titled "Jazz at Home" to the *New Negro* anthology. Rogers observed in his essay that, "The true spirit of jazz is a joyous revolt from convention, custom, authority, boredom, even sorrow—from everything that would confine the soul of man and hinder its riding free on the air." He further theorized that jazz received its name from the black Chicago trombonist Jasbo Brown. According to the essay, Brown, like King Oliver, was skilled at muting his trombone with a derby hat and making it "talk." Audiences thrilled by this performance would shout out, "More, Jasbo. More, Jas, more," thus giving the music its name.

Aside from the aforementioned literary works, jazz would also be celebrated in novels by CLAUDE MCKAY, DOROTHY WEST, CARL VAN VECHTEN, F. Scott Fitzgerald, RALPH WALDO ELLISON, and numerous others. Moreover, the musicians, their lifestyle, and their art would become favorite subjects for the paintings of such artists as ROMARE BEARDON and JACOB ARMSTEAD LAWRENCE.

The music itself continued to evolve during the middle and late 1920s as glamorous clubs and ballrooms sprang up not only to showcase the talents of superior musicians and bands but also to provide venues for jazz dance enthusiasts to enjoy themselves. The clubs of JUNGLE ALLEY, such as the COTTON CLUB and CONNIE'S INN, became notorious for featuring superior black musicians and dancers while exercising a JIM CROW segregation policy that allowed only whites to enjoy the entertainment. Most of the dance ballrooms, however, did not place such restrictions on INTERRACIAL INTERACTION and leaned toward a policy of mixed audiences. The discriminating factor in ballrooms like the SAVOY was whether or not one could dance the Charleston, the Lindy Hop, the Strut, or the Black Bottom.

The clubs and ballrooms created important platforms for such bands and individual performers as FLETCHER HENDERSON and His Orchestra; the CHICK WEBB Band, which would introduce the world to the phenomenal Ella Fitzgerald; the MISSOURIANS and CAB CALLOWAY; the DUKE ELLINGTON Orchestra; and FESS WILLIAMS and His Royal Orchestra.

At the beginning of the 1920s, blues songs rather than jazz recordings were the driving commercial force behind the RACE RECORD boom that made singers like BESSIE SMITH and ETHEL WATERS famous and relatively wealthy. However, as the decade progressed, a number of significant recordings served to demonstrate the music's depth, flexibility, and increasing range of appeal. Two of its earliest pioneers, Morton and Oliver, both made important recordings in 1923. Among Morton's recordings that year were "Grandpa's Spells" and "Kansas City Stomp." Oliver recorded "Dippermouth Blues" and "Tears." Fletcher Henderson released "Hop Off" and "Whiteman Stomp" in 1927. In the same year, Duke Ellington teamed up with the pioneering female jazz vocalist ADELAIDE HALL to record "Creole Love Call," one of the first to employ the human voice as an instrument particularly conducive to jazz techniques. Through SCATTING and other vocal experiments, such singers as Fitzgerald, Sarah Vaughan, and BILLIE HOLIDAY would further increase the potential of the human voice as an instrument of jazz. In 1928, Louis Armstrong recorded "West End Blues" and joined with Bessie Smith to record "Empty Bed Blues."

The popularity of jazz spread not only as musicians moved from city to city but also through live broadcasts from both clubs and radio stations. With the release of a number of recordings, live radio broadcasts, and a five-year stint as the house band for the Cotton Club, by the time of the GREAT DEPRESSION Duke Ellington and his orchestra had become the most popular jazz band in the United States. While Fletcher Henderson laid much of the foundation for the swing sound with arrangements for his own band and for Benny Goodman, it was Duke Ellington who announced the arrival of the next stage in jazz music with "It Don't Mean a Thing If It Ain't Got That Swing."

Swing music ushered in the era of the BIG BAND, which changed jazz from the product of small ensembles to that of virtual orchestras consisting of 15 to 30 members or more. The swing sound magnified the basic elements of jazz while also setting the stage for solo musicians and vocalists, providing them with a framework in which each complemented the strength of the other. Count Basie, Benny Goodman, Cab Calloway, and others were leading figures of the swing era throughout the 1930s and 1940s.

With each succeeding decade of the 1900s, jazz continued to expand and evolve as new instrumentalists and vocalists, black and white, women and men, contributed their interpretations of it and advanced the canon and culture of the music. CHARLIE PARKER, Dizzy Gillespie, Sarah Vaughn, and Billy Eckstine were among the central creators of bebop jazz in the 1940s. From bebop the music developed into cool jazz, hard bop, free jazz during the Civil Rights movement of the 1960s, jazz fusion, postmodern jazz, smooth jazz, and other forms prevalent in 2000.

One of the controversies surrounding jazz in 2002, debated at conferences, in books, and on radio, was whether the music was founded by African Americans or white Americans. The best answer, significantly enough, is likely that provided by James A. Rogers in *The New Negro.* In it, he pointed out that both blacks and whites have traditionally performed and enjoyed jazz, but the music itself originated indisputably out of the African and African-American experience. Moreover, even a general cursory study of the music's history makes it clear that those who engineered its greatest advances have also been African American. Or, in the words of the French novelist, jazz musician, and critic Boris Vian, who wrote in 1953, "jazz's teeming qualities reflect those of the fifteen million Blacks who, bullied and terrorized, carved themselves, by dint of their tears and labors, a place in the Benighted States."

All controversy aside, true to its democratic nature, jazz in the modern era continued to absorb, transform, and be transformed by different musical cultures, including its much celebrated Latino and Asian influences.

Further Reading

Dahl, Linda. *The Music and Lives of a Century of Jazzwomen.* New York: Limelight Editions, 1996.

Driggs, Frank, and Harris Lewine. *Black Beauty, White Heat: A Pictorial History of Classic Jazz, 1920–1950.* New York: Da Capo Press, 1995.

Ellison, Ralph, and Robert O'Meally, eds. *Living with Music.* New York: The Modern Library, 2001.

Elmore, Charles J. *All That Savannah Jazz.* Savannah, Ga.: Savannah State University, 1999.

Enstice, Wayne, and Paul Rubin. *Jazz Spoken Here: Conversations With 22 Musicians.* New York: Da Capo Press, 1994.

Shack, William A. *Harlem in Montmartre: A Paris Jazz Story Between the Great Wars.* Berkeley: University of California Press, 2001.

— Aberjhani

Jim Crow

The term *Jim Crow* evolved out of a variety of cultural expressions and legislative actions until it came to represent the system of separation by color or race practiced throughout the United States from the latter half of the 1800s to the 1960s.

As a cultural expression the term referred to both a song and a dance practiced by slaves in the United States in the 1800s. It was later personified as an actual character featured in minstrel shows during the late 1800s.

Despite the emancipation of American slaves in 1865, a succession of legislative acts and Supreme Court rulings upheld the notion that blacks and whites would live in greater harmony if they lived as separately as possible. At the core of such reasoning was the belief that whites were innately superior to blacks, and too much interaction between the two groups would somehow contaminate the former. The hard-won freedom of African Americans was all but nullified by the body of laws called Black Codes that were adopted by southern states in the years immediately following the Civil War. While the codes granted former slaves such rights as marriage within one's race and the ownership of limited amounts of land, many of them also restricted the types of professions that blacks could pursue, required employment with a white person, and allowed African Americans to be beaten by whites for any perceived transgression, among other measures.

The official political status of African Americans swung back and forth between full equality and legislated inequality, or apartheid. The Thirteenth Amendment in 1865, the Fourteenth Amendment in 1866, and the Fifteenth Amendment in 1870, along with Civil Rights Acts in 1866 and 1875, combined to place black Americans on the same footing as white Americans. However, the Black Codes, for a time at least, effectively countered those measures and were reinforced by the U.S. Supreme Court's ruling in *Plessy v. Ferguson* in 1896. That ruling, in a case specifically targeting public transportation, announced that separate but equal public facilities for the races were legal. As such, it provided the legal justification for and encouragement of the various forms of racial discrimination and segregation that would plague the United States for the next half century.

Jim Crow segregation impacted every sphere of life in the United States. Religious observation, education, entertainment, personal relationships, politics, shopping, housing, military service, and employment were all determined by skin color. At its mildest, the result was pained humiliation. At its most extreme, it was murder in the form of LYNCHING, disproportionate rates of disease due to a lack of medical facilities specifically for blacks, and excessive sentencing for blacks in the courts. To avoid the public humiliation of Jim Crow practices, most blacks limited their interaction with whites as much as possible. MADAME C. J. WALKER had a movie theater included in her company's Indiana plant to avoid the discriminatory practice of white-owned theaters. The NATIONAL ASSOCIATION FOR THE ADVANCEMENT OF COLORED PEOPLE (NAACP) was started in large measure to dismantle the legal and social structures of Jim Crow.

The era of Jim Crow has often been described as absurd because of the many incongruent and irrational situations it produced. For example, white partygoers were privileged to be entertained at clubs in black neighborhoods such as Harlem and by black entertainers such as DUKE ELLINGTON while consciously avoiding socializing with blacks in the very same establishments.

In his autobiography *The Big Sea,* LANGSTON HUGHES recounts traveling through Savannah, Georgia, and going into a restroom reserved for whites in order to purchase a *Sunday New York Times* because the restroom for blacks did not have a newsstand. Upon leaving the restroom, he is stopped by a white policeman who forbids him to exit the whites-only section even though he is already in it, while simultaneously forbidding him to go back into the restroom. Hughes's only remaining option is to hop onto the nearby railroad tracks and walk the rails back to the boarding platform, laughing as he does so at the stupidity of the situation. Many of those who could not laugh at such incidents during the 1920s made their way overseas to PARIS. There, they joined a group of black and white American expatriates, including black soldiers and musicians who had remained in France after WORLD WAR I, who were free to ignore color differences.

World War I and World War II provided opportunities for organizations such as the NAACP and newspapers such as the *PITTSBURGH COURIER* to dramatize the hypocrisy of Americans

Racially segregated public facilities were a common feature of the system of apartheid known as Jim Crow in the first half of the 20th century in the United States. Here a man must use the "colored" entrance to a movie theater in Mississippi in 1939. *(Library of Congress, Prints & Photographs Division [LC-USZ62-115416])*

fighting abroad for democracy while African Americans continued to suffer discrimination in their homeland, not to mention within the very armed forces in which they served. In 1948, President Harry S. Truman agreed that blacks in the military at least would no longer be subject to segregation and issued Executive Order 9981 to abolish racial separation in the armed forces.

Labor leader A. PHILIP RANDOLPH's success in establishing the BROTHERHOOD OF SLEEPING CAR PORTERS as the first black-run union to negotiate a contract with a major company provided a modern platform for the discussion of racial inequalities. Moreover, in 1954, the NAACP scored a direct hit against the 1896 *Plessy v. Ferguson* ruling in their case *Brown v. Board of Education, Topeka, Kans.* Specifically addressing the inequality of educational facilities for African Americans, the Supreme Court ruled that such facilities were inherently unequal under segregation. That ruling, combined with Rosa Parks's refusal to relinquish her bus seat to a white passenger, ushered in the 1950s and 1960s Civil Rights movement.

With millions of black and white Americans protesting the ongoing Jim Crow system, the U.S. Congress in the 1960s effectively removed any remaining legal foundations for segregation. The 1960 Voting Rights Act outlawed attempts to deprive African Americans of their right to vote, and the 1964 Civil Rights Act made discrimination in federal hiring, public accommodations, transportation, and other areas illegal.

Further Reading

Dinley, Jane E., and Glenda E. Gilmore. *Jumpin' Jim Crow.* Princeton, N.J.: Princeton University Press, 2000.

Hoskins, Charles Lwanga. *Yet with a Steady Beat.* Savannah, Ga.: The Gullah Press, 2001.

— Aberjhani

Johnson, Charles Spurgeon (1893–1956) *sociologist, editor*

The editor of *OPPORTUNITY* magazine and research director for the NATIONAL URBAN LEAGUE in NEW YORK CITY, Charles S. Johnson, along with JESSE REDMOND FAUSET, ALAIN LOCKE, JAMES WELDON JOHNSON, and W. E. B. DU BOIS, was one of the principal leaders behind the Harlem Renaissance.

Johnson was born in Bristol, Virginia, on July 24, 1893. His mother was Winfred Branch Johnson and his father Charles H. Johnson, pastor of the Lee Street Baptist Church for some 42 years. The senior Johnson was the son of a slave and a white man who provided him as a child with the same religious education he gave Johnson's white half-brother. He later sent him to Richmond Institute, where he graduated in 1883. Charles S. Johnson was the first of five children born to Charles H. and Winfred. The others were his sisters Lillie, Sarah, and Julia and his brother, Maurice.

Johnson attended Bristol's public elementary school for blacks before going on to graduate from the Wayland Academy preparatory school in Richmond. Following Wayland, he attended Virginia Union University, graduating from there with a B.A. in 1916.

Joining the GREAT MIGRATION of African Americans leaving the South and going North, Johnson moved in 1917 to continue his studies at the University of CHICAGO. There, he studied with Robert E. Park, a former ghostwriter for BOOKER TALIAFERRO WASHINGTON. Park impressed upon Johnson the idea of using "publicity as a means of social reform and social control," a concept that Johnson later adapted and applied to his strategy for launching the Harlem Renaissance. Although Johnson completed his studies and received his Ph.B. (bachelor of philosophy) from the University of Chicago in 1918, he and Park remained friends and colleagues who often shared ideas on race relations in the United States throughout the years.

Johnson joined the 803d Pioneer Infantry American Expeditionary Forces in France during WORLD WAR I. Serving as a sergeant major with his unit, he participated in combat at Meuse-Argonne before returning to the United States in 1919.

Upon his arrival in Chicago, Johnson was caught up in one of the worst riots of what eventually was called the RED SUMMER OF 1919. The latest in a series of riots that swept through cities across the United States, the Chicago riot proved one of the most destructive, with dozens of people killed, hundreds injured, and thousands of homes destroyed. When Governor Frank O. Lowden established a Chicago Commission on Race Relations to determine the underlying causes of the violence, Johnson was appointed associate executive secretary for the commission. He devised its research strategy and wrote the bulk of the resulting document, *The Negro in Chicago: A Study of Race Relations and a Race Riot,* published some three years later. The commission concluded that the riot stemmed from inadequate housing for African Americans, prejudicial law enforcement against blacks, and racist hiring practices. They were all issues that the larger northern cities had to confront as the Great Migration continued well throughout the 1920s and several decades thereafter. They were also part of the general JIM CROW racism practiced throughout the United States at the time.

Johnson joined the staff of the Chicago branch of the NATIONAL URBAN LEAGUE in 1920. In the same year, on November 6, he married Marie Antoinette Burgette, a librarian and teacher from Milwaukee. The couple, who remained married until Johnson's death, would have four children: Charles Spurgeon II, born in 1921; Robert Burgette, 1922; Patricia Marie, 1924; and Jeb Vincent, 1931.

Moving to New York City in 1921, Johnson became director of the National Urban League's Department of Research and Investigation. In 1923, he took on the editorship of the League's newly founded periodical, *Opportunity, A Journal of Negro Life.* As editor of *Opportunity,* Johnson attempted through his editorials to dismantle the numerous racial myths used to justify racist treatment of blacks and notions of racial superiority entertained by whites.

Initially, *Opportunity* magazine featured primarily sociological surveys, research data, and accompanying explanatory essays. However, like Jessie Fauset and W. E. B. Du Bois at *CRISIS* magazine, the main publicity organ for the NATIONAL ASSOCIATION FOR THE ADVANCEMENT OF COLORED PEOPLE (NAACP),

Johnson began to take greater notice of the black writers and artists settling in HARLEM as well as of the increasing general interest in black culture. Looking for ways to make a positive impact on race relations, Johnson reasoned that literature and the visual arts were areas open to expansion and use as tools to help generate change in the overall negative attitudes of white Americans toward African Americans. Toward that end, Johnson began to feature fiction and poetry in *Opportunity* magazine and worked with HOWARD UNIVERSITY philosophy professor Alain Locke to obtain materials by such then emerging writers as COUNTEE CULLEN and GWENDOLYN BENNETTA BENNETT. Although Johnson believed literature and art could affect race relations, he did not suggest that artists should intentionally restrict their work to propaganda. He believed, somewhat like Locke, that freedom for blacks could be found in "the surrounding beauty of our lives, and in recognition that beauty itself is a mark of the highest expression of the human spirit."

To formally announce the beginnings of a black renaissance, Johnson arranged a CIVIC CLUB DINNER where black writers, artists, and intellectuals could meet with white writers and publishers to share insights as well as publishing resources. Johnson elected Locke to serve as master of ceremonies for the occasion and dubbed the philosophy professor "dean of the younger school of writers." Among those attending the affair on March 21, 1924, were NAACP board member Joel Spingarn, *Crisis* editor Du Bois, NAACP director and author James Weldon Johnson, *EMPEROR JONES* author Eugene O'Neill, and publisher Oswald Garrison Villard. Locke paid tribute to Johnson and Du Bois as venerable forerunners of the new group of younger writers, and they in turn made short presentations on their hopes for the new movement. He acknowledged as well the publication of *There Is Confusion,* the new novel by Jesse Fauset. And there was, in fact, some confusion for those who thought the occasion would be devoted solely to publicizing Fauset's novel, including Fauset herself. While JEAN TOOMER, LANGSTON HUGHES, and CLAUDE MCKAY were all traveling at the time, each was acknowledged as a formidable talent. Countee Cullen and Gwendolyn Bennett, along with several others, read from their works to considerable applause.

The editor of *SURVEY GRAPHIC* magazine was so moved by the gathering at the Civic Club that he offered to devote an issue of the magazine to works by the writers he had seen and heard about. The special Harlem edition of the *Survey Graphic* magazine was published in March 1925. Material from it formed the nucleus of *The NEW NEGRO* anthology, to which Johnson contributed the essay "New Frontage on American Life." The Civic Club Dinner also set the stage for the establishment of monthly literary prizes that would be awarded by both *Crisis* and *Opportunity* magazines. While Langston Hughes was absent from the initial event, he did attend the first *Opportunity* awards banquet and there met Johnson for the first time. He also won first prize in the poetry awards for his poem "The Weary Blues."

In addition to sponsoring contests and introducing authors to publishers, Johnson maintained a file on artists and writers throughout the United States and used it to maintain contact with them and encourage them in their creative pursuits. He would assist them with finding employment, patronage, housing, and scholarships. Hughes, Cullen, ZORA NEALE HURSTON, ERIC DERWENT WALROND, NELLA LARSEN, AARON DOUGLAS, and many others cited Johnson as a principle motivator and worker behind the more public accomplishments of the Harlem Renaissance.

Editor, writer, and sociologist Charles S. Johnson, shown here ca. 1935 to 1945, was a principal architect of the Harlem Renaissance. *(Library of Congress, Prints & Photographs Division, [LC-USW3-019352-C])*

Johnson concluded his work as editor of *Opportunity* with the publication of *Ebony and Topaz* in 1928. An anthology of works by the talented individuals he had helped get their start, it also featured satirist GEORGE S. SCHUYLER, sociologist E. Franklin Frazier, psychologist Allison Davis, and publisher John P. Davis.

Leaving *Opportunity,* Johnson accepted a position as sociology department head at FISK UNIVERSITY in Nashville, Tennessee. For the next 28 years, his work revolved around field research devoted to the study of African-American life and race relations in the South. Through the establishment of seminars and the education of young black sociologists, Johnson successfully established Fisk University as a major research center. Moreover, he opened the doors of the university to employment for James Weldon Johnson, E. Franklin Frazier, Aaron Douglas, and ARNA BONTEMPS. He brought his friend and mentor Robert Park during his final years to the university as well.

Johnson emerged as a prominent social scientist and author in his own right with the 1930 publication of *The Negro in American Civilization: A Study of Negro Life and Race Relations in the Light of Social Research.* The book provided an extensive profile of family life, employment, education, religion, and housing as related to blacks in the United States at the beginning of the GREAT DEPRESSION.

Johnson extended his research in 1930 to labor conditions in Liberia. Assisting him on the assignment was John F. Matheus, author of the short story "Fog" in the *New Negro* anthology. Traveling to Africa, Johnson and Matheus met with Countee Cullen and PAUL ROBESON in France, where the international NEGRITUDE movement inspired by the Harlem Renaissance was getting under way. Johnson gathered enough research in Liberia to write a book titled *Bitter Canaan,* but it was not published until after his death.

In 1934, he published a study of some 600 black families in rural Arkansas called *Shadow of the Plantation.* The following year he presented a report called *The Collapse of Cotton Tenancy.* The report detailed the flaws and racial inequities of the southern sharecropping systems as well as the failure of FRANKLIN DELANO ROOSEVELT's New Deal programs to fully correct such problems. Johnson was appointed a member of Roosevelt's Special Committee on Farm Tenancy, and his report laid the groundwork for the 1937 Farm Security Administration, instituting reform for farmers, tenants, and laborers. In addition to serving as an adviser for Roosevelt, Johnson formally advised presidents Herbert Hoover and Dwight D. Eisenhower.

Johnson published a groundbreaking study of black youth in the South called *Growing Up in the Black Belt* in 1941. Along with *Shadow of the Plantation,* it is considered one of his most important contributions to the field of African-American sociology. He further contributed to the field in 1943 with *Patterns of Negro Segregation.*

In 1946, Johnson became the first African American appointed president of Fisk University. During his tenure, he continuously increased the school's financial endowment and employed its sociology department to help stimulate racial progress in the United States. Throughout his career, he received a number of awards and honorary degrees, including honorary doctorates from the University of Glasgow, Howard University, and Harvard University. In 1954, he provided an assessment of his years in Harlem in an essay titled *The Negro Renaissance and Its Significance.* He described the movement as "that sudden and altogether phenomenal outburst of emotional expression, unmatched by any comparable period in American or Negro American history."

Johnson died on October 27, 1956, in Louisville, Kentucky, while traveling from Nashville to New York.

Further Reading

Lewis, David Levering, ed. *The Portable Harlem Renaissance Reader.* New York: Penguin, 1995.

Robbins, Richard. *Sidelines Activist: Charles S. Johnson and the Struggle for Civil Rights.* Oxford: University Press of Mississippi, 1996.

— Aberjhani

Johnson, Georgia Douglas See SALONS.

Johnson, Hall (1888–1970) *composer*

Composer Hall Johnson established the Hall Johnson Negro Choir in the tradition of the FISK JUBILEE SINGERS of FISK UNIVERSITY. They performed in the popular play *THE GREEN PASTURES* (1936) and represented the United States at the International Festival of Fine Arts in Berlin in 1951.

Hall Johnson was born on March 12, 1888. He was raised in Athens, Georgia, and his father was an elder in the African Methodist Episcopal Church. Johnson attended Knox Institute in Georgia; Atlanta University in Georgia; Allen University in South Carolina; and the Hahn School of Music. He went on to study at the University of Pennsylvania in PHILADELPHIA, the Institute of Musical Art, and the University of Southern California.

When Johnson arrived in NEW YORK CITY in 1914, he played violin in James Reese Europe's Tempo Club Orchestra. Europe became conductor for the HARLEM HELLFIGHTERS jazz band in France during WORLD WAR I. In 1921, he played in the orchestra for the musical revue *SHUFFLE ALONG* and was a violist in the Negro String Quartet that appeared with ROLAND HAYES at Carnegie Hall in 1925.

Composer and music director Hall Johnson, shown here in 1947, modeled his Hall Johnson Negro Choir after the Fisk Jubilee Singers, and with them he went on a number of successful tours as well as performing in major stage productions and films. *(Library of Congress, Prints & Photographs Division, Carl Van Vechten Collection [LC-USZ62-108272])*

Hayes was a classical vocalist but, because he had so revered the music, ended all of his concerts and recitals with Negro spirituals. Influenced by Hayes, Johnson, also a classically trained musician, formed a choral group in 1925. One of his goals was to sing spirituals and elevate the diction and overall execution of gospel and spiritual music to a classical art form. His efforts earned him the Caspar Holstein Prize for composition in 1925 and 1927.

The Hall Johnson Negro Choir was soon in demand to record, sing in Hollywood films, and perform in dramatic plays. The choir recorded with the RCA Victor Company in 1928 and in 1930 sang in the dramatic play, *The Green Pastures.* Its renown increasing, the choir won the HARMON FOUNDATION Award in 1931. The singers contributed to the film version of *The Green Pastures* in 1936. The Hall Johnson Negro Choir also sang in 126 performances of a folk play by Johnson titled *Run, Little Chillun.* The play was revived in 1935.

Johnson organized two festivals in the 1940s—the Negro Festival Chorus of Los Angeles (1941) and the Festival Chorus of New York City (1946). In 1951, his Hall Johnson Choir represented the United States at the International Festival of Fine Arts in Berlin. As a composer, Johnson wrote *Son of Man,* a cantata; *FiYer,* an operetta; *The Green Pastures Spirituals;* and several other spirituals, including "Honor, Honor," "Ride on, King Jesus," and "Crucifixion."

For his many musical contributions, Hall Johnson received the New York Handel Medal in 1970, as well as an honorary doctorate of music from the Philadelphia Academy of Music.

Johnson died on April 30, 1970.

Further Reading

Kellner, Bruce, ed. *The Harlem Renaissance: A Historical Dictionary for the Era.* Westport, Conn.: Greenwood Press, 1984.

Ward, Andrew. *Dark Midnight When I Rise, The Story of the Jubilee Singers Who Introduced the World to the Music of Black America.* New York: Farrar, Straus and Giroux, 2000.

— Sandra L. West

Johnson, Jack (John Arthur Johnson) (1878–1946)

boxer

Heavyweight boxing champion John Arthur Johnson made headlines in the 1910s and 1920s as much for his boxing record as for his business dealings, marriages, and interracial relationships.

John Arthur Johnson, later known as Jack Johnson, was born on March 31, 1878, in Galveston, Texas. Because of his slight size at birth, he was nicknamed Lil' Arthur. He was one of seven children born to Tina Johnson and Henry Johnson. His father was a minister and caretaker of a public school building. Rev. Henry Johnson was a full-blooded African who could trace his lineage to the Coromantee nation on the Gold Coast in Africa.

John Arthur Johnson dropped out of school in the fifth grade to work and help support his family. When he was 14 years old, he was so intrigued with stuntman Steve Brodie, famous for leaping from the Brooklyn Bridge, that he stowed away on a boat that he thought was heading for NEW YORK CITY just to meet him. The boat took young Johnson to Florida instead. He eventually made it to New York by peeling potatoes to pay his boat passage. After meeting Brodie, they became friends. Johnson then moved on to Boston. There, he worked as a stable boy and broke his leg. When Brodie heard of Johnson's misfortune, he traveled to Boston, saw to Johnson's medical needs, and sent him back home to his family in Galveston.

Still in his teens, Johnson took a job on the docks. Because the older dock workers often physically fought each other, he followed their lead and learned to defend himself with his fists. He became a fair dock fighter and took up boxing as a sport. Around the same time, he finished grammar school. He then moved to Dallas where he found work in a carriage-painting shop. His boss, Walter Lewis, was an amateur boxer. Johnson was 15 years old when they began to work out together.

He returned to Galveston for his first fight against a boxer named Joe Lee. Johnson won after 16 rounds. A boxer named Bob Johnson then offered the area fighters $25 to go four rounds with him. Fresh from his victory over Lee, young Jack Johnson stayed the four rounds and won the $25. He afterward remained in bed for two weeks because of intense body pain.

In 1897, Johnson officially became a professional boxer. He relocated to Springfield, Illinois, to join a boxing club. In a battle royal with five boxers in the ring, Johnson emerged victorious by knocking out his four opponents. Johnny Connors became his manager and good friend. Under Connors's tutelage, Johnson fought a white boxer named Klondike in CHICAGO in May 1899 but was knocked out in the fifth round.

At six feet and one-quarter-inch tall, and 195 pounds, Johnson joined the Joe Walcott sparring camp in New York. From the early 1900s, he fought and defeated the formidable African-American boxers of the era: Joe Jeanette, Sam Longford, and Sam McVey. He knocked out Bob Fitzsimmons in 1906, after which white boxers refused to compete with Johnson. White boxer Tommy Burns, however, was the heavyweight champion and had no choice but to fight Johnson in order to defend his title.

In front of 40,000 spectators, Johnson defeated Tommy Burns in Sydney, Australia, on December 26, 1908. To blacks during this era, Johnson's knockout punch was a definitive response to JIM CROW racism both in the ring and out. They were jubilant, especially when the police had to stop the fight in the 14th round because Johnson was beating Burns so badly. The white community was incensed at Johnson's physical domination of Burns. For them, this was not a mere sports battle. For them, white superiority was at stake. To make matters worse, Johnson had taunted Burns in the ring.

After the Burns competition, Johnson knocked out James Jeffries in Reno, Nevada, on July 4, 1910. The 15-round fight was hailed as the "fight of the century." The purse was $101,000. It had been rumored that if Jeffries did not win, Johnson would be killed. Again, Jeffries was a white man of considerable strength and reputation. Johnson, cocky and arrogant, flaunted his victory.

Blacks in communities like HARLEM saw Johnson's win as their win over white domination, and race riots erupted around

Controversial and outspoken, Jack Johnson, shown here ca. 1910 to 1915, was the first African American to win the heavyweight boxing championship. *(Library of Congress, Prints & Photographs Division [LC-USZ6-1823])*

the nation and internationally. Rioting occurred in WASHINGTON, D.C.; Kansas City; New York; and other cities. In Chattanooga, Tennessee, a black man thrust a newspaper containing an account of Johnson's victory into the face of several white men and was promptly attacked by the men. Newsreels showing the fight were banned from theaters because it was thought that seeing it again would incite bloodshed. In Jamaica, the following song was sung among black islanders: "Hif wasn't for the referee/ Jack Johnson woulda kill Jim Jeffrey/ Right, left, and the upper cut/One lick, ina Jeffrey gut."

Members of the white community expressed their desire for a "great white hope" who could stop Johnson's domination of white men in the ring.

Johnson's personal life also generated controversy. Although romantically involved with black women, three of his four wives were white women at a time when such INTERRACIAL INTERACTION was generally frowned upon. This racial preference became part of his overall legacy. He married his first wife, a black woman named Mary Austin, in 1898. He married Etta Terry Duryea, a socially prominent white woman of Spanish origin, on January 18, 1911. Duryea later committed suicide. Johnson was 34 years old and his third wife, Lucille Cameron, was 18 when they married on December 3, 1912. His fourth wife was Irene Pineau, with whom he was photographed in the 1920s.

Johnson's earnings as an athlete allowed him to purchase and invest in a number of businesses. In 1912, he bought the Cabaret de Champion at 42 W. 31st Street in Chicago. The cabaret later appeared in a painting called *Saturday Night* (1935) by ARCHIBALD JOHN MOTLEY, JR. He also invested in clubs in Harlem.

In 1913, as Johnson traveled with his third wife, he was arrested and found guilty of violating a law against "white slavery," defined as the transporting of white women across state lines for decadent purposes (sexual activity). While on bond from his prison sentence, Johnson escaped to Europe. Still physically commanding, in Europe he lost income and boxing skills due to a lack of training, a lack of work, and too much of the nightlife that he enjoyed.

During this period, Jess Willard emerged as the "great white hope" for which many whites had literally prayed. Thirty thousand people attended Johnson's fight against Willard at the Oriente Race Track in Havana, Cuba, in 1915. After 25 uneventful rounds, in the 26th round, Willard defeated Johnson with a knockout. Some speculated that Johnson allowed Willard to win.

Johnson received $35,000 for the fight in Cuba. He remained in Europe and occasionally fought in exhibition matches. When he returned to the United States in 1920, he was jailed on the white slavery charge. In Leavenworth federal prison, where he spent one year and one day, he became the athletic director. He was respected and treated well in prison. When released, he did not box professionally. He lectured on politics and race and joined the Huberts Museum and Flea Circus in New York's Times Square.

Johnson's business life was also in a shambles. He lost the liquor licenses to several nightclubs he owned in Chicago and Harlem. Some reports state that Johnson rented the Club Deluxe in Harlem, and some reports say he owned it. In either case, he lost it to gangsters, popularly known as "the mob." The building in which Club Deluxe was located was originally called the Douglas Casino, constructed around 1918 on the northeast corner of 142nd Street and LENOX AVENUE. On the street floor was the Douglas Theatre, the site of films and vaudeville acts, and one flight up was a dance hall, unused until around 1920. Johnson, an amateur cellist who loved music and other entertainments, took the Douglas Casino and turned it into an intimate supper club, the Club Deluxe. It was large enough to hold 400 to 500 people. The club failed until gangster Owney Madden, backed by legendary Chicago mobster Al Capone, acquired it as an east coast outlet for a beer product that bore his name. Taking it over from Johnson, he reopened the Club Deluxe in 1923 as the segregated "whites only" COTTON CLUB, the most popular nightclub during the Harlem Renaissance.

With a prison record, several failed marriages, abortive business investments, and his boxing career behind him, Johnson continued to spend money and live affluently. In June 1946, he purchased an expensive Lincoln-Zephyr. On June 10th, while driving in North Carolina on his way to New York, Jack Johnson crashed into a power pole and died. He was buried in Graceland Cemetery in Chicago. Thousands of people attended the funeral.

The "king of the ring" was posthumously inducted into the Boxing Hall of Fame in 1954. Jack Johnson's tumultuous story was made into a stage drama and a film, *The Great White Hope,* starring James Earl Jones and Jane Alexander, in the 1970s.

Further Reading

Chalk, Ocania. *Pioneers of Black Sport.* New York: Dodd, Mead and Company, 1975.

Gates, Henry Louis, Jr., and Cornel West. *The African American Century: How Black Americans Have Shaped Our Century.* New York: The Free Press, 2000.

Rust, Edna, and Art Rust, Jr. *Art Rust's Illustrated History of the Black Athlete.* New York: Doubleday, 1985.

— Sandra L. West

Johnson, James P. See STRIDE PIANO.

Johnson, James Weldon (1871–1938) *writer, political activist*

Through his multiple achievements as educator, writer, and political activist, James Weldon Johnson not only helped lay the foundation for the cultural arts movement known as the Harlem Renaissance but became one of its principal participants.

Johnson, born on June 17, 1871, was the eldest of two sons born to James Johnson and Helen Dillet Johnson. His father was a self-educated man who had been born free in Virginia. The elder Johnson spoke Spanish fluently and spent part of his youth working as a waiter in NEW YORK CITY. He later moved to Jacksonville, Florida, where his sons were born, and where he worked as headwaiter for the St. James Hotel. Helen Johnson was born in Nassau, the Bahamas, and grew up in New York. She was one of the first African Americans to teach in Jacksonville.

Johnson and his brother, JOHN ROSAMOND JOHNSON, grew up in an atmosphere of music, bilingual conversation, and travel. Because at the time, Jacksonville schools for blacks offered classes no higher than the eighth grade, Johnson's parents sent him to Atlanta University in Atlanta, Georgia, at the age of 16. There, he completed high school, then entered college. During the summer of his freshman year, he taught school in the rural community of Hampton, Georgia. His exposure to the community strengthened his sense of a race consciousness and helped inspire much of his later writings. He graduated from college with a B.A. in 1894, later obtaining his M.A. in 1904.

Following his graduation from Atlanta University, Johnson accepted an appointment in 1894 as principal of Jacksonville's Stanton High School, where he had attended grammar school and his mother had taught. During his tenure, he added two more grades to the school's system. He also became the first African American in Florida to pass the state's bar exam and founded its first black-owned daily newspaper, *The Daily American.* Although the paper lasted less than a year, it provided Johnson with a platform to exercise his literary skills and address issues relevant to Jacksonville's African-American community.

Moving to New York in the late 1890s, Johnson began a second career as the cowriter of hit songs and musicals with his brother, J. Rosamond Johnson. They teamed up to write a number of hit songs for some of the most popular white entertainers and shows of the era. Some of their better-known compositions were "Under the Bamboo Tree," "Congo Love Song," "Maiden With the Dreamy Eyes," and "My Castle on the Nile." In 1900, Johnson wrote the lyrics and his brother composed the music for "LIFT EVERY VOICE AND SING," a song that has since become known throughout the United States as the black national anthem. Even during Johnson's lifetime, it became traditional for African Americans to sing it in schools, churches, and at various official gatherings. The brothers also formed a partnership with Bob Cole, a leading comic, lyricist, and playwright. The trio billed themselves as the Ebony Offenbachs. While Johnson penned lyrics and librettos, his brother and Cole performed onstage in a series of Broadway shows, most notably *Shoo-Fly Regiment* in 1906 and *The Red Moon* in 1908.

Throughout his adult life, Johnson balanced multiple careers and in 1902 returned to college to study English and drama at Columbia University. In 1904, he cowrote for Theodore Roosevelt a campaign song titled, "You're All Right, Teddy." The song, along with BOOKER TALIAFERRO WASHINGTON's recommendation, earned Johnson a diplomatic post as consul to Venezuela in Puerto Cabello. He took a second diplomatic post in 1909 in Corinto, Nicaragua, and remained in consular service until 1913. At the same time that he served as a consul, he continued to write and in 1907 began publishing poetry in various magazines.

He married Brooklyn native Grace Nail in 1910. Nail was from a family that made a fortune dealing real estate in HARLEM during the GREAT MIGRATION north.

In 1912, Johnson wrote and published anonymously the novel *THE AUTOBIOGRAPHY OF AN EX-COLORED MAN.* The novel was, and still is, considered groundbreaking for its psychological and geographical profiling of African Americans during the early 1900s. It essentially tells the story of a black man who is light complexioned enough to live as, or "pass" for, a white person. He is initially unaware of his racial identity but, once he discovers it, he sets out to learn more about his heritage and takes some pride in it. However, he finds life as a black person too restricting and oppressive so opts to pass for white instead. In the end, he concludes that passing was the "lesser" of his possible choices. Beyond the storyline, Johnson's examination of RAGTIME, biracial marriages, BLACK HUMOR, and color prejudice among African Americans within the context of his biographical novel was something new in American literature. Although the impact of the novel was minimal when first published in 1912, it nevertheless joined such works as *THE SOULS OF BLACK FOLKS* by W. E. B. DU BOIS and *The Conjure Woman*

James Weldon Johnson, shown here in 1932, became one of the most commanding figures of the Harlem Renaissance in his multiple roles as a lyricist, editor, historian, novelist, and director of the NAACP. *(Library of Congress, Prints & Photographs Division, Carl Van Vechten Collection [LC-USZ62-42498])*

by Charles W. Chestnutt as an important predecessor to those literary works produced by blacks during the 1920s.

Leaving the consular service in 1913, Johnson settled in Harlem and joined the staff of the *NEW YORK AGE*. He wrote a regular column called *Views and Reviews* in which he tackled such issues as LYNCHING, voting rights, and discriminatory employment practices. Deeply impressed by Johnson's insights and background, W. E. B. Du Bois and Joel Spingarn offered him a position with the NATIONAL ASSOCIATION FOR THE ADVANCEMENT OF COLORED PEOPLE (NAACP) as the organization's field secretary. Until then, Johnson was more a proponent of Booker T. Washington's accommodationist theories of racial progression. Following Washington's death, however, in 1915, Johnson joined the NAACP in 1916. A year following his appointment as field secretary, Johnson worked with Du Bois to organize the historic Silent Parade. It included some 10,000 people marching through New York to peacefully yet dramatically protest violence against African Americans during the East St. Louis riots of 1917. It was at the time the largest mass protest demonstration ever conducted by African Americans.

As field secretary for the NAACP, Johnson traveled throughout the United States, just as A. PHILIP RANDOLPH would do on behalf of the BROTHERHOOD OF SLEEPING CAR PORTERS, to establish new branches of the organization primarily in black communities. Johnson is credited with virtually single-handedly increasing the NAACP's membership from 9,000 when he joined in 1916 to 90,000 in 1920. More than demonstrating Johnson's leadership capabilities, the increased membership also shifted the bulk of power in the NAACP from the hands of whites into that of African Americans. On one journey to establish a branch in Atlanta, Johnson met WALTER WHITE and later offered him the position of assistant field secretary.

The NAACP recognized Johnson's extraordinary achievements by making him the organization's first black executive secretary in November 1920. Throughout the full decade that he held the position, Johnson extended and strengthened a number of programs the NAACP already had in place. A well-known and highly visible personality in his own right, he used his position as executive secretary to further articulate and popularize the concept of blacks and whites working together to overcome the blight of racism in the United States. He changed the NAACP's organizational structure by decreasing its reliance on volunteers and increasing its employment of professionals. He also increased the organization's use of the media to heighten public sensitivity to what he termed the mental and physical abuses of racist JIM CROW practices throughout the country.

One of the practices he attacked most vigorously was that of lynching. Like IDA BELL WELLS-BARNETT before him, he published regular reports on incidents of lynching. Just prior to taking on the position of executive secretary, he published one report based on his and Walter White's firsthand investigations of the practice called *Thirty Years of Lynching*. In 1920, he put the full strength of the organization and his personal lobbying effort behind support for the Dyer Anti-Lynching Bill. The bill passed the House of Representatives with a vote of 230–119 on January 11, 1921, but failed to pass the Senate. Even so, the highly publicized controversy over the bill did help the white American public to redefine lynching as an aberration of the law rather than as an implementation of it.

Johnson stuck to the NAACP's strategy for battling racism through the courts themselves. Among its most significant victories under his leadership was the 1924 *Nixon v. Herndon* case, which challenged the practice in El Paso, Texas, of restricting primary election voting to whites only. The Supreme Court ruling on the case declared such restrictions in El Paso unconstitutional and paved the way for further victories culminating in 1944 in the abolishment of all racially restricted primary elections.

Johnson continued to steer the NAACP through the 1920s JAZZ age until his resignation in 1931. At the same time, he also continued to cultivate his own literary career and that of the emerging writers and artists of the Harlem Renaissance. In 1922, he edited the *Book of American Negro Poetry*, fairly establishing the tradition of black literature anthologies and setting the precedent for ALAIN LOCKE's *NEW NEGRO* collection two years later. In 1925 and 1926, he coedited with his brother Rosamond *The Book of American Negro Spirituals* and *The Second Book of American Negro Spirituals* respectively. Upon meeting CARL VAN VECHTEN in the mid-1920s, the two discovered they shared a birthday, June 17, and a taste for cosmopolitan culture that made them close friends. When he read *The Autobiography of an Ex-Colored Man,* Van Vechten recommended it to publisher Alfred A. Knopf for republication and wrote a foreword for the novel. Previously published anonymously, the novel now had Johnson's acquired fame as a leader and poet as well as the endorsement of Van Vechten to ensure much stronger sales than before. Johnson also introduced Van Vechten to LANGSTON HUGHES and obtained his influence in the publication of works by Hughes, NELLA LARSEN, RUDOLPH FISHER, and others.

Continuing to add works of his own to the growing canon of the Harlem Renaissance, Johnson published *God's Trombones, Seven Sermons in Verse,* in 1927, and *Black Manhattan* in 1930. The latter proved to be one of the most detailed accounts of African-American culture in New York during the 1920s and also something of a small homage to Johnson's brother Rosamond. In 1933, he published an authentic autobiography called *Along This Way;* an examination of race relations called *Negro Americans, What Now?* in 1934; and *St. Peter Relates an Incident of the Resurrection Day* in 1935.

Following his departure from the NAACP, Johnson first accepted a position as professor of creative literature at FISK UNIVERSITY in Tennessee and then accepted a second similar position at New York University. He taught both courses and continued to write until he was killed in an accident when his car collided with a train while he was vacationing in Maine.

In 2000, African Americans throughout the United States observed the 100th anniversary of Johnson's song "Lift Every Voice and Sing" with performances of the song and tributes to Johnson's life.

Further Reading

Byrd, Rudolph P., and Carl Van Vechten. *Generations in Black and White.* Athens: The University of Georgia Press, 1997.

Price, Kenneth M., and Lawrence J. Oliver, eds. *Critical Essays on James Weldon Johnson.* Woodbridge, Conn.: G.K. Hall and Co., 1997.

Wilson, Sondra Kathryn. *In Search of Democracy: The NAACP Writings of James Weldon Johnson, Walter White, and Roy Wilkins (1920–1970).* New York: Oxford University Press, 1999.

— Aberjhani

Johnson, John Rosamond (1873–1954) *composer, performing artist*

John Rosamond Johnson was one of the most prolific composers and accomplished performers of the late 1800s and early 1900s. He was also a founding member of several influential organizations devoted to supporting African Americans in the performing arts.

Johnson was born in 1873, the second son of James Johnson and Helen Dillet Johnson. His older sibling was noted author and civil rights advocate JAMES WELDON JOHNSON.

Unlike most people of African descent living in the United States during the mid-1800s, Johnson's father was born in freedom in Virginia rather than in slavery. His mother was also born free in the Bahamas and raised in NEW YORK CITY. His father was a self-educated man who spoke fluent Spanish and worked as a headwaiter at the St. James Hotel in Jacksonville. His mother was one of the first black teachers in Jacksonville. Both parents raised their sons to appreciate literature, music, and diverse languages.

Johnson received his formal musical training in the 1890s at the New England Conservatory of Music in Boston. While still a student, he performed in 1896 on Broadway at the Wallack Theatre in *Oriental America.* The all-black musical, produced by John W. Isham, was one of the first to break away from the minstrel show tradition of portraying blacks as dim-witted and infantile.

By the end of the 1890s, Johnson was composing music and experimenting with ideas for shows of his own. He encouraged his brother James to write lyrics, and in 1899 the two wrote a comic opera called *Tolosa,* or *The Red Document.* They failed in their attempts to have the opera produced but won the admiration and support of theatrical producer Oscar Hammerstein. They continued to work on their music and in 1900 wrote "LIFT EVERY VOICE AND SING" for a program held in observance of Abraham Lincoln's birthday. Following its debut, the song became known as the black national anthem, and African Americans began singing it as a matter of routine at official gatherings.

The brothers also formed a partnership with performer Bob Cole. Well known for his minstrel show character of Willie Wayside, Cole was also a talented playwright and lyricist. Cole and the Johnson brothers called themselves the Ebony Offenbachs when working as a team writing shows and songs. With Hammerstein's influence helping them gain recognition, they contributed a number of songs to popular Broadway shows geared toward white audiences, including the hit shows *The Belle of Bridgeport, The Sleeping Beauty and the Beast,* and *The Supper Club.* Among their more popular songs were "My Castle on the Nile," "Nobody's Looking but the Owl and the Moon," "Congo Love Song," and "I Must Have Been A-Dreaming." In addition, they helped Theodore Roosevelt win the presidential election with their 1904 campaign song, "You're All Right, Teddy."

While continuing to write for others, Rosamond Johnson and Cole also created a stage act of their own. In 1905, they became international stars when they played the Palace Theatre in London for six weeks. In 1906, they performed in the *Shoo-Fly Regiment* at the Bijou Theatre on Broadway. The show featured "the most beautiful dusky chorus in the world," according to their advertisements for it, and offered a musical interpretation of blacks fighting in the Spanish-American War. The team scored another Broadway hit in 1908 with *Red Moon.*

Johnson and Cole also contributed songs to the CHICAGO-based Pekin Stock Company's production of *The Husband* in 1908. In the same year, they became founding members of the FROGS, a group of black performing artists who joined together to help sponsor and promote works by African Americans. Other founding members included comedian GEORGE

Composer and arranger J. Rosamond Johnson, shown here in 1933, was one of the early pioneers of black musicals on Broadway and cowrote "Lift Every Voice and Sing," a song commonly referred to as the African-American national anthem. *(Library of Congress, Prints & Photographs Division, Carl Van Vechten Collection)*

WALKER, composer James Reese Europe, and performer BERT WILLIAMS. Although some viewed Johnson and Cole as competition for the highly successful team of Willams and Walker, they actually wrote a show for Williams called *Mr. Lode of Kole.* Designed to showcase Williams's dancing and comedic skills, it was one of the great comedian's last productions before the death of his partner and prior to his becoming a main attraction for the ZIEGFELD FOLLIES.

The Johnson and Cole partnership ended in 1911 when Cole died by drowning. Many of those who had performed in their shows went on to form companies for the LINCOLN THEATRE and LAFAYETTE THEATRE. Johnson later accepted an appointment from Oscar Hammerstein to serve as musical director of the Grand Opera House in London. Around the same time, he married Nora Floyd.

The composer served in 1917 as conductor of the singing orchestra for white playwright Ridgely Torrence's trilogy of *Plays for a Negro Theatre: Rider of Dreams, Granny Maumee,* and *Simon the Cyrenian,* in which actor and political activist PAUL ROBESON made his stage debut. In 1925 and 1926, Johnson again worked with his brother James to edit and publish *The Book of Negro Spirituals* and *The Second Book of Negro Spirituals,* respectively. In addition to compiling and preserving spirituals, Johnson, like HARRY THACKER BURLEIGH, also constructed musical arrangements for some 150 spirituals. He performed many of these in 1927 on tour in England with the singer Taylor Gordon.

In 1935, Johnson originated the role of Frazier in George Gershwin's folk opera *PORGY AND BESS.* And in 1937, he published a collection of his songs entitled *Roll Along in Song.* In the same year that his brother James died in a car accident, 1938, Johnson became a founding member of the Negro Actors Guild of America, Incorporated. NOBLE SISSLE, W. C. HANDY, and Rex Ingram were among those who helped organize the guild. In 1941, Johnson joined ETHEL WATERS, LENA HORNE, and EDDIE ANDERSON as part of the cast for *CABIN IN THE SKY.*

Johnson died in HARLEM on November 11, 1954. His composition "Lift Every Voice and Sing" remains one of the most performed songs in the United States.

Further Reading

Byrd, Rudolph P., and Carl Van Vechten. *Generations in Black and White.* Athens: University of Georgia Press, 1997.

Johnson, James Weldon. *Black Manhattan.* New York: Da Capo Press, 1991.

— Aberjhani

Johnson, Malvin Gray

See ART AND THE HARLEM RENAISSANCE.

Johnson, Sargent Claude (1887–1967) *sculptor*

A HARMON FOUNDATION award-winning sculptor, Sargent Claude Johnson produced works influenced by African and Mexican culture, and worked as a state-level supervisor for the Federal Arts Project in the 1930s.

Sargent Claude Johnson was born on October 7, 1887, in Boston, Massachusetts. His father, Anderson, was a Swede. His mother, Lizzie Jackson, was of Cherokee Indian and African-American descent. His parents' marriage dissolved, leaving Johnson and his five brothers and sisters orphaned in 1902. His uncle, Sherman William Jackson, a high school principal in WASHINGTON, D.C., and his uncle's wife, sculptor MAY HOWARD JACKSON, for a time took care of the Johnson children.

The young artist and his siblings eventually moved from their uncle and aunt's home in Washington to the home of their maternal grandparents in Alexandria, Virginia. Soon after arriving in Virginia, his sisters were sent to a school in Pennsylvania, and Johnson and his brothers were sent to a school administered by the Sisters of Charity in Worcester, Massachusetts.

Leaving Massachusetts, Johnson spent a brief time in Chicago with relatives, then in 1915 registered at the avant-garde A. W. Best School of Art and the California School of Fine Arts. In California, he married Pearl Lawson in 1915. In 1920, he worked as an artist printing photographs for Willard E. Worden and in 1921 as a framer for Valdespino Framers.

Johnson's daughter, Pearl Adele, was born in 1923. He received an award from the San Francisco Art Association for *Pearl* (1925), a sculpture done in honor of his daughter. He and his wife later separated in 1936.

Johnson exhibited with the San Francisco Art Association from 1925 to 1931 and the Harmon Foundation from 1926 to 1935. From the Harmon Foundation, he won the Otto H. Kahn award in 1927, the Harmon Bronze Medal in 1929, and the Robert C. Ogden award in 1933. He also received an award from the foundation for *Sammy* (1928), a sculpture created in the image of Edwin Gordon, son of NATIONAL ASSOCIATION FOR THE ADVANCEMENT OF COLORED PEOPLE member Walter Gordon.

Some of Johnson's most noted early works are *Elizabeth Gee* (1928) and *Negro Woman* (1933). His passion for African and Mexican culture is evident in these pieces, as is the importance he placed on portraying his people in a dignified manner.

During the GREAT DEPRESSION, Johnson held a number of exhibits: at the Art Institute of Chicago (1930); with Malvin Gray Johnson and RICHMOND BARTHÉ at the Delphic Studios in New York (1935); at the Baltimore Museum (1939); and at the American Negro Exposition (1940).

During the depression he also worked for the Federal Arts Project as an artist, senior sculptor, assistant supervisor, assistant state supervisor, and state supervisor. The San Francisco Art Association presented him with an award for *Forever Free* (1935). In 1937, he created a redwood organ screen for the California School for the Blind. He won more awards for the lithographs *Black and White* (1938) and *Chester* (1939).

In 1939, Johnson carved two eight-foot-high Inca sculptures for the Golden Gate International Exposition in San Francisco. Also during this time, he created a mosaic mural for the Maritime Museum in the city. The Sunnydale Housing Project in San Francisco is another "museum" for the work of Sargent Johnson: for the housing development's playground, he sculpted green and gray animals, including a duck and a grasshopper.

From the 1940s to the 1960s, Johnson traveled to Mexico to study archaeology and art. In this period, he produced 100 panels and plates and received several significant commissions, including a wall-sized enamel mural for Richmond, California's City Hall Chambers (1949).

His wife, Pearl Lawson Johnson, died in 1964. Sargent Claude Johnson died in San Francisco on October 10, 1967.

Further Reading

Dallas Museum of Art. *Black Art: Ancestral Legacy.* Dallas: Dallas Museum of Art, 1989.

Johnson, Sargent Claude. *Oral History Interview, 1964.* The Papers of African-American Artists, Smithsonian Institution, Washington, D.C.

— Sandra L. West

Johnson, William Henry (1901–1970) *painter*

Artist William Henry Johnson created more than 1,200 works throughout his career, taught at the HARLEM COMMUNITY ART CENTER, and was a HARMON FOUNDATION exhibitor.

William Johnson was born on March 13, 1901, in Florence, South Carolina. His mother was Alice Smoot Johnson, an employee of the Young Women's Christian Association (YWCA). Johnson's father reportedly was a white man, but shortly after his birth his mother married a black man named William Johnson, who was a railroad fireman. After having two sons and two daughters with Alice Johnson, William was crippled and no longer able to work.

With the family's finances in dire straits, William Henry Johnson worked to help support his mother and step siblings and did not complete high school. He copied cartoons from the newspaper and dreamed of becoming an artist.

In 1918, Johnson moved to NEW YORK CITY to escape the limits of southern JIM CROW racism and to make his mark in the art world. He stayed in HARLEM with his uncle, Willie Smoot, a Pullman porter, and his wife, Rebe. Johnson worked as a cook, sent money to his family in Florence, and in 1921 enrolled at the School of the National Academy of Design.

He excelled in painting at the school and attended summer school at the Cape Cod School of Art in Provincetown, Massachusetts. Although he graduated in good standing from the design school in 1926, he did not win the school's major travel prize. His instructor, realist painter Charles W. Hawthorne, suspected that his student did not win the award because of racism. Therefore, Hawthorne himself raised money for Johnson's trip and the student sailed for France.

In France, Johnson settled in Cagnes-sur-Mer, painting the countryside and still lifes. He had his first one-man show in 1927 at the Students and Artists Club on the Boulevard Raspail. Among his influences was French modernist Paul Cezanne. In Paris, Johnson met expatriate African-American artist HENRY OSSAWA TANNER and a Swedish textile artist, Holcha Krake, his future wife.

Johnson moved back to New York in 1930, entered the Harmon Foundation competition, and won the foundation's gold medal and $400 prize. One of the judges was sculptor META VAUX WARRICK FULLER. Johnson's work was included in the foundation's traveling exhibit, "Exhibit of Fine Arts by American Negro Artists," that went through major cities in the United States during 1930–31. While in New York, he met Harlem Renaissance philosopher ALAIN LOCKE, editor of the *NEW NEGRO* (1925), and poet LANGSTON HUGHES.

He returned to South Carolina to visit his father, had several exhibits during the 1930 visit, and painted *Landscape with Sun Setting, Florence, S.C.* (1930). Having lived in New York and France, Johnson deemed himself a "free" man and had forgotten that Florence, South Carolina, was a small town in a racist state where in 1930 his very existence was suspect. Like any free man and exuberant artist would do, Johnson set up his easel in the midst of town and painted a picture of the town's brothel, *Jacobia Hotel* (1930). Having acted beyond those racial and social boundaries established by Jim Crow, Johnson and his painting were promptly put in jail.

Upon his release, he returned to Europe and married Krake in Denmark. Through much of the 1930s, they traveled through Germany, France, and Tunisia, absorbing artistic styles and exhibiting their art.

In 1938, Johnson and his wife returned to New York, where he began work on a series of religious and cultural paintings. Some of the titles were *Jesus and the Three Marys* and *I Baptize Thee.* Quite different from landscapes and still lifes, this colorful documentation of African-American life, culture, and religious experience also included paintings of children playing games in Harlem and of stylishly dressed Harlem residents. They marked a new development in style for Johnson.

During the late 1930s–40s, Johnson taught at the Harlem Community Art Center, created in volume, and exhibited widely. His work, however, was not met with enthusiasm and was criticized for being exaggerated, highly stylized, and disturbing.

Holcha Johnson died on January 13, 1943, of breast cancer. William Henry Johnson suffered from mental illness caused by syphilis. He spent the last 23 years of his life in Central Islip State Hospital in New York and died there on April 13, 1970.

The Harmon Foundation, which had collected Johnson's art during the early 1930s, donated 1,154 pieces of his work to the National Collection of Fine Art, now called the National Museum of American Art; 20 pieces to the Oakland Museum in California; and additional pieces to the Library of Congress and various black colleges and universities. The papers of William H. Johnson are in the Archives of American Art, Smithsonian Institution, WASHINGTON, D.C. The papers cover the years 1922–46 and include clippings from Swedish, Danish, and Norwegian newspapers and magazines, the prenuptial agreement between Johnson and his wife, exhibition announcements, and gallery guest books.

Further Reading

King-Hammond, Leslie. "No Ordinary American Painter: William Henry Johnson (1901–1970)." *The International Review of African-American Art 9,* no. 4 (1991).

Leininger-Muller, Theresa A. *New Negro Artists in Paris: African American Painters and Sculptors in the City of Light, 1922–1934.* Piscataway, N.J.: Rutgers University Press, 2000.

— Sandra L. West

Jones, Henry Bozeman See ART AND THE HARLEM RENAISSANCE.

Jones, Lois Mailou (1905–1998) *painter*

Influenced by the culture of Haiti and Africa, artist and educator Lois Mailou Jones created in the impressionist style and maintained a vigorous output of paintings, designs, and illustrations for six decades.

Lois Mailou Jones was born on November 3, 1905, in Boston, Massachusetts. Her father, Thomas Vreeland Jones, attended night classes at Suffolk Law and received his law degree at age 40 in 1915 while working as the superintendent of a large office building. Her mother was Caroline Dorinda Adams, a beautician. Originally from Paterson, New Jersey, Thomas and Caroline migrated to Cambridge, Massachusetts, and settled in Boston soon after their marriage in 1896.

Lois Mailou Jones studied at the High School of Practical Arts in Boston; Boston Normal Art School; the School of the Museum of Fine Arts in Boston; Teachers College, Columbia University in NEW YORK CITY; HOWARD UNIVERSITY in WASHINGTON, D.C.; Académie Julian in PARIS; and École des Beaux-Arts in PARIS.

As a youth, Jones worked after school as a costume and mask designer at the Ripley Studios in Boston. As an adult, she taught art at Palmer Memorial Institute in Sedalia, North Carolina, and later, in 1930, at Howard University. At Howard, along with Professor James Vernon Herring, James Amos Porter, and JAMES LESESNE WELLS, all visual artists of note, Jones had the opportunity to help design the new art program for the university, initiated by Herring. In addition to teaching and writing curriculum, she exhibited with the HARMON FOUNDATION in New York in 1930–31, winning honorable mention for her *Negro Youth* in 1931.

During the summers, Jones vacationed on Martha's Vineyard in Massachusetts with sculptor META VAUX WARRICK FULLER and composer HARRY THACKER BURLEIGH, who encouraged her to go to Paris for further study. Jones secured funds from the General Education Board Fellowship and sailed for France on September 1, 1937. She studied at Académie Julian, and exhibited at the Salon de Printemps of the Société des Artistes Français.

When Jones returned to the United States, she exhibited at the Robert Vose Galleries in Boston in 1939 and was greatly influenced by Rhodes scholar and philosopher ALAIN LOCKE, one of the principal leaders of the *NEW NEGRO* movement, who encouraged her to document Negro life in her art. This she did during the 1940s in *Jennie, The Pink Tablecloth,* and *Meditation.*

In 1953, Lois Mailou Jones married the noted Haitian graphic artist and designer Louis Vergiaud Pierre-Noel and was invited by the Haitian government to serve as guest instructor at the Centre d'Art and the Foyer des Arts Plastiques. In 1969, Jones received a grant from Howard University to go to Africa and interview African artists. As she traveled, studied, and grew artistically, Jones's style progressed from that of the impressionists to the decorative artists, to a style influenced by Haitian and African culture.

Jones exhibited widely, including at the American Negro Exposition in CHICAGO; Barnet-Aden Gallery in Washington, D.C.; the 135th Street Branch of the New York Public Library; Atlanta University; and Corcoran Gallery of Art. Her awards include the Boston Museum of Fine Arts Award, 1927; the Robert Woods Bliss Landscape Award in Oil Painting Award, Corcoran Gallery, 1941; the Lubin Award, 1947; the Award of the National Museum of Art, Washington, D.C., 1947; the Haitian Government Decoration and Order of Achievement in Art, 1954; and the Washington Society of Artists Award. Jones retired from Howard University in 1977.

There are many references to 1997 as the death date of Lois Mailou Jones, but according to the *Encyclopædia Britannica,* the correct date is June 9, 1998, in Washington, D.C.

Further Reading

Benjamin, Tritobia H. "Color, Structure, Design: The Artistic Expressions of Lois Mailou Jones." *The International Review of African-American Art* 9, no. 4 (1991): 28–40.

Henkes, Robert. *The Art of Black American Women: Works of 24 Artists of the 20th Century.* Jefferson, N.C.: McFarland, 1993.

— Sandra L. West

Jungle Alley

Also known as The Jungle, or Beale Street, Jungle Alley was a stretch of HARLEM nightclubs and restaurants located on 133rd Street between SEVENTH AVENUE and LENOX AVENUE.

Known as much for their JIM CROW segregation policies as for the superior entertainment they provided, Jungle Alley's famed nightclubs included BARRON'S EXCLUSIVE CLUB, CONNIE'S INN, the COTTON CLUB, the Catagonia Club, and SMALL'S PARADISE. Although located in the heart of black Harlem, the clubs that comprised Jungle Alley were designed for patronage by affluent whites who desired black entertainment in what they considered a relatively safe and controlled atmosphere. Consequently, even without the enforced color barrier, the average Harlem resident would likely have declined to patronize such clubs due to their higher prices. Those who could afford them, however, were allowed to enjoy entertainment by such now legendary figures as DUKE ELLINGTON and his orchestra, ETHEL WATERS, CAB CALLOWAY, LENA HORNE, LOUIS ARMSTRONG, the NICHOLAS BROTHERS, and FATS WALLER.

Many of those visiting Jungle Alley were Broadway entertainers and producers, such as SOPHIE TUCKER and George Gershwin, who often studied and then adapted black styles of music and dance for their own shows. Politicians such as the future mayors Jimmie Walker and FIORELLO HENRY LA GUARDIA also met and socialized with various constituents in Jungle Alley.

Because many of the clubs were either owned by mob bosses or heavily influenced by them, Jungle Alley was a place where access to alcohol during the Prohibition 1920s was easy. Likewise, such illicit drugs as cocaine and marijuana were also readily available.

The Nest Club, the interior of which is viewed here, was among those located in Jungle Alley and specializing in entertainment for white visitors to Harlem. *(Photograph and Prints Division, Schomburg Center for Research in Black Culture, The New York Public Library, Astor, Lenox and Tilden Foundation)*

LANGSTON HUGHES criticized the kind of glamorized nightlife offered in Jungle Alley as an affront to Harlem citizens who were denied entry into the clubs while their neighborhood became a "playground" for wealthy whites. Nevertheless, his friend CARL VAN VECHTEN was one of those who frequented the clubs and wrote about them in both essays and his celebrated novel, *NIGGER HEAVEN*. The renown of the musicians who performed there as well as its more scandalous elements helped establish and increase Harlem's reputation as one of the great entertainment centers of the world.

Further Reading

Favor, J. Martin. *Authentic Blackness: The Folk in the New Negro Renaissance.* Durham, N.C.: Duke University Press, 1999.

Watson, Steven. *The Harlem Renaissance, Hub of African-American Culture, 1920–1930.* New York: Pantheon Books, 1995.

— Aberjhani

Just, Ernest Everett (1883–1941) *research biologist*
A prolific science writer and researcher, in 1915 Ernest Everett Just became the first African American to receive the SPINGARN MEDAL presented by the NATIONAL ASSOCIATION FOR THE ADVANCEMENT OF COLORED PEOPLE (NAACP), for his outstanding accomplishments in biology.

Ernest Everett Just was born on August 14, 1883, in Charleston, South Carolina. His father, Charles Fraser Just, died in 1887 from alcoholism. His mother was Mary Mathews Cooper Just, a dressmaker and teacher who founded a black farm settlement, Maryville, named in her honor. The family lived at 103 Calhoun Street and 28 Inspection Street in Charleston.

Ernest Just was educated at South Carolina State College from 1894 to 1900, and at Dartmouth College, from which he graduated in 1907 with top honors in history and biology.

Just began his professional career as an English professor at HOWARD UNIVERSITY in WASHINGTON, D.C., in 1907. However, because scientists were sorely needed and his grades were exemplary in biology, the president of Howard persuaded him to do graduate studies in biology, which he did from 1908 until 1916 when he received his doctorate in biology at the University of CHICAGO. During the summers, Just studied at the Marine Biology Laboratory at Woods Hole, Massachusetts. When he returned to Howard, fortified by science studies and with his advanced degree, he headed the medical school's department of physiology from 1912 to 1920.

Just was a highly driven researcher and writer who penned articles for a variety of scholarly journals, a practice many black researchers and scientists did not follow. In 1912, he contributed "The Relation of the First Cleavage Plane to the Entrance Point of the Sperm" to *Biological Bulletin 22.*

Also in 1912, Just married Ethel Highwarden. They had three children.

Just was chosen to receive the first Spingarn Medal awarded by the NAACP, both because of his exceptional accomplishments and because the organization was looking for a means and an individual to help prove its commitment to the struggle for racial equality.

His research continued, and his published works included the following: "The Susceptibility of the Inseminated Egg to Hypotonic Sea-Water: A Contribution to the Analysis of the Fertilization-Reaction," in *Anatomical Record* 20 (1921); "Science and Human Needs," *Howard Medical News* 1 (1925); "Methods for Experimental Embryology with Special Reference to Marine Invertebrates," *Collecting Net* 3 (1928); "On the Origin of Mutations," *American Naturalist* 66 (1932); "On the Rearing of *Ciona intestinalis* under Laboratory Conditions to Sexual Maturity," *Carnegie Institution of Washington Yearbook* 33 (1934); and "On Abnormal Swimming Forms Induced by Treaatment of Eggs of *Strongylocentrotus* with Lithium Salts and Other Means," *Anatomical Record* 78 (1940).

In 1930, Just was elected vice president of the American Society of Zoologists for his work in cell structure and fertilization of the female egg by the male sperm. In 1936, he was elected to the Washington Academy of Sciences.

He received research grants from philanthropist Julius Rosenwald and the National Research Council. However, Howard president Mordecai Johnson preferred Just remain primarily in the classroom and reportedly wanted to use Just's grant money to train other black scientists. Because of these obstacles to his research, and because of racism toward black scientists in the United States, Just relocated to Europe in the 1930s to work in European laboratories. In 1939, he wrote *The Biology of the Cell Surface,* which proved to be controversial because it combined philosophy, physics, and biology.

Weary of being told that since he was black he had to work only in the interest of the black community, Just remained in Europe. Having divorced his first wife, he married German biologist Hedwig Schnetzler in 1939. He did not return to Howard University until 1940, when Adolph Hitler's racist policies became a direct threat to him and his wife.

Just was elected to the New York Academy of Sciences in 1941 and died on October 27 of that year.

Further Reading

Manning, Kenneth R. *Black Apollo of Science: The Life of Ernest Everett Just.* New York: Oxford University Press, 1983.

Spangenburg, Ray, and Kit Moser. *African Americans in Science, Math, and Invention.* New York: Facts On File, 2003.

— Sandra L. West

K

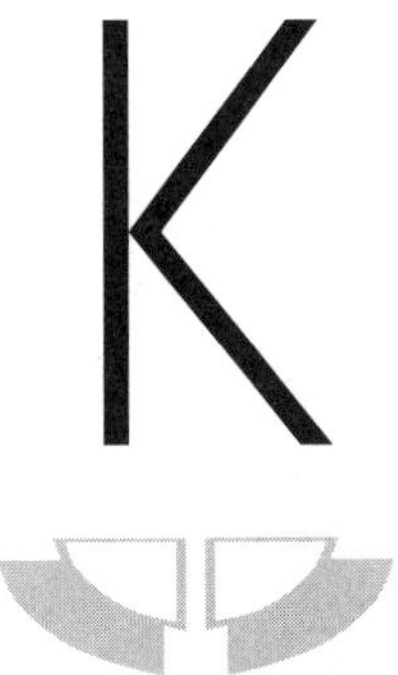

Kappa Alpha Psi Fraternity, Inc.

Like the founding members of ALPHA PHI ALPHA at Cornell University in 1906, the small number of African Americans attending Indiana University in Bloomington, Indiana, recognized the advantages of starting a fraternity to support each other's academic and professional pursuits. Former HOWARD UNIVERSITY students Elder Diggs and Byron K. Armstrong acted on that recognition by establishing Alpha Kappa Nu on January 5, 1911.

Joining Diggs and Armstrong in the formation of the new fraternity were Guy L. Grant, Ezra D. Alexander, Edward G. Irvin, Paul W. Caine, George Edmonds, John M. Lee, Henry T. Asher, and Marcus P. Blakemore.

Diggs was elected the group's first Grand Polemarch and held that position for six years. As such, he oversaw the fraternity's incorporation under the name Kappa Alpha Nu but by proclamation had it changed to Kappa Alpha Psi on April 15, 1915. Diggs would later go on to enjoy a career as a distinguished educator. However, he was also among those who answered W. E. B. DU BOIS's call to "close ranks" during WORLD WAR I and volunteered for the new black officers training camp in Des Moines, Iowa. He was commissioned as a lieutenant and served in Europe with the 368th Infantry.

Following Kappa Alpha Psi's formation at Indiana University, the organization began to expand, and chapters were created between 1911 and 1914 at the University of Illinois, Indianapolis Alumni, the University of Iowa, and Pennsylvania's Lincoln University. Chapters were further established nationwide from 1914 to 1918. In 1921, the *Kappa Alpha Psi Journal* became a monthly publication that helped promote the fraternity's principles of striving to achieve and serve.

Kappa Alpha Psi used the opportunity of its first national convention in 1922 to kick off a national service program called Guide Right. Geared toward helping youth master academics and determine professional goals, the program became one of the fraternity's primary tools for maintaining an active presence in the black community throughout the 1900s.

The 1950s and 1960s saw the organization lending its support to such civil rights initiatives as the Montgomery bus boycott, more stringent civil rights legislation, and the Black Power movement. In the case of the Montgomery bus boycott, Kappa Alphi Psi made a particularly significant contribution in the form and person of Rev. Ralph Abernathy, one of its members. The group also acknowledged the need for stronger leadership skills among black men in all fields and developed the Kappa Instructional Leadership to fill that need.

To help safeguard those gains made by African Americans during the 1960s, the organization joined the Leadership Conference on Civil Rights held in the 1970s. As it continued to grow and develop in the 1980s, the Kappa Alpha Psi Foundation was established to help generate funding to support undergraduate housing and scholarships. It announced the expansion of its political concerns in 1985 by using its 66th national convention to stage a march of 4,000 on the South African embassy in protest of that country's racist JIM CROW practices during that time.

In 1991, Kappa Alpha Psi took up residence in its new international headquarters in PHILADELPHIA. Entering the 2000s, its members participate in a number of partnerships with such community organizations as Habitat for Humanity, the Children's Miracle Network, and the Salvation Army. Following in the footsteps of the fraternity's founders have been an exceptional number of gifted athletes, entertainers, politicians, and businessmen. Among them are the following: former Cleveland mayor Carl Stokes, astronaut Dr. Bernard A. Harris, Jr., former Los Angeles mayor Tom Bradley, tennis champion and humanitarian Arthur Ashe, businessman and minister Leon Sullivan, author Lerone J. Bennett, Jr., Dallas Cowboys most valuable player Larry Brown, New York City Abyssinian Baptist Church pastor Calvin O. Butts, attorney Johnnie L. Cochran, and BET founder and CEO Robert Johnson.

Further Reading

Bennett, Jr., Lerone, and Charles White. *The Shaping of Black America: The Struggles and Triumphs of African Americans, 1619–1990s.* New York: Viking Penguin, 1993.

Bracey, Ernest N. *Insight: The Higher Education and Pedagogy of African Americans.* Maryland: University Press of America, 2001.

— Aberjhani

Karamu House

Founded in 1916 by Oberlin College graduates Russell and Rowena Woodham Jelliffe, the Karamu House in Cleveland, Ohio, is now the oldest community organization dedicated to the exploration and celebration of African-American culture.

The organization began as a six-member group called the Dumas Dramatic Club. Its initial focus was on children's theater produced through an agency described as the Playhouse Settlement. With the increased influx of African Americans into the Cleveland area during the GREAT MIGRATION, the organization grew to include a number of writers, actors, dancers, and artists. While dedicating itself to an exploration and advancement of African-American culture, the group also stressed racial inclusiveness and welcomed works by both black and white individuals.

Members of the organization met black actor CHARLES SIDNEY GILPIN in 1923 following his celebrated portrayal of the *EMPEROR JONES* and in 1927 changed their name to the Gilpin Players.

As a youth in Cleveland, LANGSTON HUGHES visited the organization often and befriended its founders, the Jelliffes. They eventually produced a number of his plays, including *Little Ham, Joy to my Soul, Shakespeare in Harlem,* and *Drums of Haiti.* The last later became *Troubled Island,* Hughes's opera with composer WILLIAM GRANT STILL. Other productions of works by writers of the Harlem Renaissance have included *Compromise,* by WILLIS RICHARDSON; *Sermon in the Valley,* by ZORA NEALE HUSTON; and *St. Louis Woman,* by COUNTEE CULLEN and ARNA BONTEMPS.

In 1941, the Gilpin Players became the Karamu Players under the Karamu House, *karamu* being a Swahili word indicating a place to gather in the community for enjoyment and feasting. Until the early 1940s, the Jelliffes had directed all their theater productions themselves but thereafter began to employ others. The couple retired in 1963. Ruben Silver, Junius Edwards, and Gerald Marans are some of the other directors who have helped the Karamu House grow in prominence.

Continuing to develop its repertoire throughout the latter half of the 20th century, the Karamu House produced works as diverse as *A Midsummer Night's Dream* and *Macbeth,* by William Shakespeare; *Così fan tutte,* an opera by Mozart; *A Raisin in the Sun,* by Lorraine Hansberry; and *The Birthday Party,* by Harold Pinter. Dr. Benno D. Frank helped the Karamu House develop a musical ensemble that went on to perform a number of modern classics: *The King and I; Amahl and the Night Visitors;* and *Lost in the Stars.*

Performers affiliated with the Karamu House have become so renowned that they have often been "loaned out" to assist other companies with their productions. Various Broadway productions, the Cleveland Playhouse, and the Jewish Community Center Hall Theatre have all borrowed the residential talents of the Karamu House. Some of its more famous members are Nolan Bell, Ivan Dixon, Mildred Smith, Robert Guillaume, and Isabel Cooley.

In May 1996, the Karamu Players presented their first full production of Hughes and Hurston's play, *MULE BONE.* After writing the play together in 1930, Hurston and Hughes disagreed over its authorship, and it was never produced while they lived. The Karamu Players' production was directed by Sarah May and starred Nile Rivers, Kyle Primous, and Sonya Leslie.

The Karamu House in 2001 was located at 2355 E. 89th Street in Cleveland. In addition to its Karamu Performing Arts Theatre, it conducted an early childhood development center, drama theater for youth, a speakers' bureau, a variety of cultural events, and classes in music, dance, and photography.

Further Reading

Elam, Harry J., and David Kinsner, eds. *African American Performance and Theatre History: A Critical Reader.* New York: Oxford University Press, 2000.

Gill, Glenda E. E. *No Surrender! No Retreat! African American Pioneer Performers of Twentieth Century American Theatre.* New York: St. Martin's Press, 2000.

— Aberjhani

Keep Shufflin'

Hoping to duplicate the success they had enjoyed with *SHUFFLE ALONG* in 1921, Aubrey Lyles and Flournoy Miller took their show *Keep Shufflin'* on the road in 1928.

Starting out with a trial run at Philadelphia's Gibson's Theatre, *Keep Shufflin'* returned to NEW YORK CITY for its debut at Daly's 63rd Street Theatre, where the original *Shuffle Along* had also premiered in the city.

Keep Shufflin' was in many ways a reprise of *Shuffle Along,* which meant it was another ingenious extension of Lyles and Miller's vaudeville skit *The Mayor of Dixie.* The musical brought back their characters Sam Peck and Steve Jenkins, who in *Shuffle Along* had competed for the mayor's office. In *Keep Shufflin',* the comical pair were benevolent would-be bank robbers literally dreaming up schemes to make themselves and everyone else rich. They conclude, however, that such an abundance of money would ultimately make it valueless and their good intentions prove futile. Although the press interpreted the show's story line as a negative attack on COMMUNISM, Miller and Lyles maintained any political connotations were coincidental and their interest was solely in the comic value of the story.

Advertisements for *Keep Shufflin'* boasted that the show featured the original *Shuffle Along* orchestra. However, neither EUBIE BLAKE nor NOBLE SISSLE, cocreators of the original, were part of the show's lineup. For the music component of their show, Lyles and Miller turned to the talents of composer and director Jimmy Johnson, famed pianist FATS WALLER, musician

Clarence Todd, and the lyricists Henry Creamer and Andy Razaf. The team composed almost two dozen numbers for some 75 dancers and singers. *Keep Shufflin'* was produced by the gambler Arnold Rothstein, whose creative input often tended to clash with the ideas of Lyles and Miller.

The show spawned several hit songs, including "Harlem Rose," "How Jazz Was Born," and "Give Me the Sunshine," the last written by Con Conrad and sung by Jean Starr. However, the audience and critics alike took special note of the piano duets performed by Fats Waller and Jimmy Johnson during intermissions. Rather than simply filling a gap in between the primary performances, Waller and Johnson's nightly improvised takes on the songs "Sippi" and "Willow Tree" became principal draws for the show. Command for the songs grew so great that Victor Records invited the duo to record them.

In addition to Lyles, Miller, and Waller, *Keep Shufflin'* also showcased the talents of dancers Byron Jones and Blanche Calloway, sister of bandleader CAB CALLOWAY.

Keep Shufflin' moved from Daly's 63rd Street Theatre to the Eltiage Theatre on 42nd Street to remain in production for a run of 104 performances. It closed in September 1928.

Further Reading

Malone, Jacqui. *Steppin' on the Blues: The Visible Rhythms of African American Dance.* Champaign: University of Illinois Press, 1996.

Peterson, Bernard L. *A Century of Musicals in Black and White.* Westport, Conn.: Greenwood, 1993.

— Aberjhani

Krigwa Players

Operating out of the basement of the 135th Street branch of the New York Public Library, the Krigwa Players launched a national theater movement focusing on black audiences, black performers, and black culture within black communities.

The idea for the Krigwa Players grew out of meetings conducted by the Drama Committee of the NATIONAL ASSOCIATION FOR THE ADVANCEMENT OF COLORED PEOPLE (NAACP). In its review of means to use drama as a tool to promote greater racial equality, the committee developed the *CRISIS: A RECORD OF THE DARKER RACES* literary awards. Out of these evolved the Crisis Guild of Writers and Artists, composed of the winners of the contests. CRIGWA became an acronym for the Crisis Guild of Writers and Artists. It in turn was changed to Krigwa and eventually came to describe a theater, a theatrical group, and a theatrical movement.

The Krigwa Little Theater was established in the basement of the same library where the playwright and librarian REGINA ANDREWS was employed. The Krigwa Players were led by W. E. B. DU BOIS and directed by Charles Burroughs. Members of the group included sometime director Harold Jackman, artist AARON DOUGLAS, playwright EULALIE SPENCE, Ira D. Reid, Ardella Dabney, Thomas Mosely, Frank Horn, and Richard J. Huey.

In addition to directing the players, Burroughs also wrote *Black Man: A Fantasy,* the group's premier production. Staged in 1925, *Black Man: A Fantasy* was an intentionally prophetic work designed to both inspire and predict the future achievements of African Americans in drama, art, music, and literature.

The Krigwa Players's affiliation with *Crisis* magazine's literary awards provided them with precisely the kind of black-oriented drama Du Bois wanted the group to perform. Aside from its premier production in 1925, the group also put on WILLIS RICHARDSON's *The Broken Banjo,* which took first place in the *Crisis* play awards. In 1926, the group produced Georgia Douglas Johnson's play *Blue Blood,* which won an honorable mention in the *OPPORTUNITY* magazine awards. In 1927, the Players staged Eulalie Spence's *A Fool's Errand,* a play that won the National Little Theatre Tournament Samuel French award for the best unpublished play in the contest.

With the Krigwa Players well established in New York, the group spread to establish branches in Baltimore, Maryland; WASHINGTON D.C.; New Haven, Connecticut; and other cities. Among the works produced by the branch in Washington were Eulalie Spence's *The Hunch* and a number of plays by Willis Richardson. The latter was one of the founders of the Washington branch.

In 1927, the New York branch of the Krigwa Players abandoned the Krigwa Little Theater following a disagreement over Du Bois's reported appropriation of prize monies won by Spence for her play *A Fool's Errand* but then used by Du Bois to cover the costs of staging the play. The Krigwa Little Theater continued to serve as a starting point for a succession of theater groups, including the HARLEM EXPERIMENTAL THEATER and the HARLEM SUITCASE THEATER. Various branches of the Krigwa Players continued to stage works until the beginning of the 1930s.

Further Reading

Hill, Anthony D. *Pages From the Harlem Renaissance: A Chronicle of Performance.* New York: Peter Lang, 1996.

— Aberjhani

L

Lafayette Theatre

Originally constructed by Meyer Jarmulowsky in 1912 to accommodate white audiences, the 2,000-seat Lafayette Theatre soon began to provide quality entertainment for HARLEM's growing black population.

The theater was leased by two white businessmen, alcohol dealers Martinson and Nibus, who were also owners of the CRESCENT THEATRE. Noting Harlem's changing racial makeup, *NEW YORK AGE* drama critic Lester Walton saw in the Lafayette an opportunity to do big business in the kind of black entertainment Broadway mostly ignored. Setting out to establish a venue for the best of black talent, he achieved exactly that while turning the Lafayette into what writer Ted Andrews called "the granddaddy of all black theaters."

Establishing the theater as a place for first-rate musical stage entertainment, Walton booked a relatively unknown road show called *The Darktown Follies,* and soon both blacks in Harlem and whites outside of Harlem began packing the theater to see it. According to JAMES WELDON JOHNSON, writing in *Black Manhattan,* the success of this unexpected hit marked the beginning of whites traveling from downtown to uptown on a regular basis in search of black entertainment. Based on a merger of shows by J. Leubrie Hill and ALEXANDER ROGERS, *The Darktown Follies* enjoyed a run of several months at the Lafayette. Florenz Ziegfeld was thrilled enough by the show's finale, titled "At the Ball," that he purchased the rights to it and several songs for performance in his own ZIEGFELD FOLLIES.

A steady, solid lineup of musical entertainment encouraged Walton to add dramatic works to the theater's programs. He hired a number of veteran entertainers formerly associated with the shows of GEORGE WALKER and BERT WILLIAMS, the duo of Cole and Johnson, and the Anita Bush Stock Company. The group became known as the Lafayette Players and balanced productions of comedy and drama at the theater for seven years, racking up some 250 productions. For straightforward quality musical entertainment, the Lafayette boasted such headliners as famed JAZZ trumpeter LOUIS ARMSTRONG, BLUES singer BESSIE SMITH, dancer BOJANGLES ROBINSON, the Mills Brothers, ETHEL WATERS, and CAB CALLOWAY. For dramatic fare, the Lafayette Players put on such plays as *The Octoroon, Dr. Jekyll and Mr. Hyde, The Three Musketeers,* and *Madame X.* Classics were presented weekly, and for the 300th anniversary of Shakespeare's death, the company put on a production of *Othello* starring E. S. Wright and Margaret Brown. In addition to producing black versions of Broadway hits, the players also put on a number of plays by black playwrights.

Between 1915 and 1919, the newly formed Quality Amusement Circuit (QAC) made the Lafayette part of a chain of black theaters in the East and Midwest. The Lafayette Players quadrupled their output by creating three more groups and touring the QAC on a regular basis. Walton teamed with composer WILL MARION COOK to create a show called *Darkydom* that first toured the circuit outside New York and then returned for a triumphant run at the Lafayette. Walton left the management of the Lafayette to Robert Levy for several years and returned as the United States was entering WORLD WAR I.

The Lafayette Theater and QAC continued to maintain a high level of success until business began to decline in 1921 and the QAC sold its interests in the theater. The theater underwent at least two changes in management during the 1920s. The Coleman Brothers dropped the more serious dramatic acts from the lineup and concentrated on the foolproof drawing power of musicals. Frank Schiffman, working with his sons, followed much of the same pattern, with vaudeville acts and movies thrown in as well. Even with its reduced offerings, it was still a home to major stars of the era. FATS WALLER staged his show *Tan Town Topics* there, and Bessie Smith added to her legend with *Mississippi Days.* Feeling the full impact of the GREAT DEPRESSION in 1932, the theater functioned primarily as a movie house with an occasional musical production.

However, like other American enterprises, the entertainment industry benefited from President FRANKLIN DELANO ROOSEVELT's New Deal. In the case of the Lafayette, the theater became home to New York's African-American segment of the WORKS PROGRESS ADMINISTRATION's (WPA) Federal Black Theater and Black Youth Theater. During the mid-1930s, the numbers of blacks employed at the theater at any given time ranged from 500 to 750. Moreover, the employees were not only actors and writers but theater maintenance crews, records managers, shop carpenters, clerks, and directors. The program's first directors, both white, were future Academy Award winners: John Houseman, who won for his supporting role in *Paper Chase,* and George Orson Welles, who won for his screenplay of *Citizen Kane.* The directors thereafter were black: Edward Perry, Carlton Moss, and H. F. V. Edward. In addition to providing jobs at such a crucial time, the WPA project also provided blacks with a form of professional experience often denied them in the private sector. As a result, some were later able to apply their experience on Broadway and in Hollywood.

The WPA groups produced works by both black and white writers. George Bernard Shaw reportedly found black interpretations of his works, such as *Androcles and the Lion,* exciting theatrical experimentation. Eugene O'Neill, on the other hand, ironically in view of his use of African Americans as subject matter, reportedly preferred African Americans not to stage his plays on their own. Works by black writers that the WPA group produced included COUNTEE CULLEN and ARNA BONTEMPS's adaptation of RUDOLPH FISHER's *The Conjur Man Dies.*

Following the departure of the Federal Theater Project from its premises in 1939, the Lafayette lost its prominence as a place of high entertainment and shut down theatrical production. The original building subsequently found new life in the form of a church. Such, however, was the strength of the reputation and history of the old Lafayette Theatre proper, that a new group of actors and playwrights later borrowed its name and called themselves the New Lafayette Theater.

Further Reading

Hay, Samuel A. *African American Theatre: A Historical and Critical Analysis.* New York: Cambridge University Press, 1994.

Thomas, Lundeana M. *Barbara Ann Teer and the National Black Theatre: Transformational Forces in Harlem.* New York: Garland Publishing, 1997.

— Aberjhani

La Guardia, Fiorello Henry (1882–1947) *politician*
Presiding as mayor of NEW YORK CITY for three consecutive terms, Fiorello Henry La Guardia led the city through one of its most politically volatile as well as productive periods.

La Guardia was born on December 11, 1882, the son of an Italian father named Achille Luigi La Guardia and a Jewish immigrant mother, Irene Cohen, from Austria-Hungary. Although born in New York's Greenwich Village, La Guardia grew up in Arizona, New Mexico, and Italy.

From 1900 to 1906, he served as a consular official in Budapest and Hungary. Upon his return to the United States in 1907, La Guardia accepted a position with the Immigration Station at Ellis Island. In his work as a consular and immigration official, La Guardia learned to speak some half dozen languages, including Yiddish, French, Italian, and German. He also attended the New York University Law School while working for the Immigration Service and won his admittance to the bar in 1910.

La Guardia made an unsuccessful bid for the U.S. Congress in 1914. However, running on the Republican ticket in 1916, representing Greenwich Village, he became the first Italian American elected to Congress. The very next year, he joined the U.S. Air Force following the United States's entry into WORLD WAR I and commanded fighters on the Italian-Austrian front.

He resumed political life in 1919 as president of New York's board of aldermen. La Guardia regained his congressional seat in 1922 and maintained it until 1932. As a congressman, he backed pro-labor initiatives and sponsored the Norris-La Guardia Act to block injunctions in labor disagreements. His decade-long tenure as a congressman provided him with firsthand knowledge and experience of government processes at the federal level and his association with then governor of New York FRANKLIN DELANO ROOSEVELT ensured a degree of access to the future president that few mayors enjoyed.

In 1929, in his first attempt to become the mayor of New York, La Guardia lost to Jimmy Walker, who had first been elected in 1926 and was the favorite of the Tammany Hall political machine. Walker, however, was forced to leave office in the midst of scandals involving his political and personal life. With John P. O'Brien completing Walker's term toward the end of 1933, La Guardia won the November elections on the Fusion ticket and was sworn in as New York's 99th mayor on January 1, 1934.

Like other U.S. cities in 1934, New York was suffering the ravages of the GREAT DEPRESSION when La Guardia became its mayor. It was also suffering the impact of political corruption that had become commonplace while Walker was in office. La Guardia openly challenged and defeated the collective of political and mob bosses who were known to divert public funds and resources toward their own interests. Presiding over a city with a population of 7 million people, he presented himself as a champion of the city's diverse ethnic groups: Hispanics, African Americans, and his own double heritage, Jews and Italians.

Among La Guardia's top priorities upon occupying the mayor's office was balancing a municipal deficit of $30 million. He stabilized the city's economy by initiating a series of minimal taxes while simultaneously acquiring relief funds through Roosevelt's New Deal program to finance a number of important construction projects. La Guardia consistently fought for and obtained funding to construct more than a dozen housing projects, 60 parks, and more than 100 bridges and highways, upgrading the city's public transportation to a level never before achieved. He also obtained funding to repair its docks and improve and extend the city's subway system.

Mayor Fiorello La Guardia and a throng of New Yorkers gather on D day in Madison Square, on June 6, 1944. *(Library of Congress, Prints & Photographs Division [LC-USW3-054077-C])*

In his attempts to ensure representation of New York's African-American community, La Guardia often communicated with officials of the NATIONAL ASSOCIATION FOR THE ADVANCEMENT OF COLORED PEOPLE (NAACP), particularly its director, WALTER WHITE, and periodically attended community meetings in HARLEM. He also created the New York Housing Authority partly as a measure to investigate and counter the development of slum conditions in Harlem. His personal rapport and reputation, however, did not prevent the HARLEM RIOTS of 1935 and 1943.

Ostensibly, the riot on March 19, 1935, was sparked by the apprehension of an Hispanic youth named Lino Rivera accused of shoplifting. It was generally understood that the real causes of the riot were such issues as unemployment, overcrowded housing, poverty, and insufficient medical care. Occurring only a year after La Guardia had been elected to office, the riot caused the death of three black men, more than 100 arrests, and business and property damages totaling $2 million. La Guardia hoped to prevent another such a event by establishing the biracial Commission on Conditions in Harlem to conduct interviews and hold hearings on the causes of the riot. HOWARD UNIVERSITY professor ALAIN LOCKE was brought in to assess the committee's findings and pronounced what nearly everyone already knew: that the citizens of Harlem were in need of more facilities for education, employment, and health care.

The second riot occurred on June 20, 1943, during La Guardia's third and final term as mayor. Stemming from a conflict between a white policeman named James Collins and a black soldier named Robert Bandy over the attempted arrest of one Marjorie Polite, the riot got under way when false rumors spread that Collins had killed Bandy for trying to protect his mother. The result was a night of destruction that ended with six people dead, 200 injured, nearly 600 arrested, and property damages running to estimates of $5 million. La Guardia's immediate response to news of the riot as it progressed was to address the situation on the radio, arrange for emergency supplies to the area, and restrict entrance to Harlem until order had been restored.

In 1945, La Guardia announced his retirement from city government. Part of his legacy to New York was a new city charter that revised the structure of city government and the now famous LaGuardia Airport, which opened for business in 1939. He was also a pioneer in the establishment of policies for equal opportunity employment and housing practices prior to those eventually adopted by the national government.

In 1946, he was appointed director of the United Nations Relief and Rehabilitation Administration and hosted a weekly radio show. He was a nationally known figure when he died September 20, 1947.

Further Reading

Jeffers, H. Paul. *The Napoleon of New York: Mayor Fiorello La Guardia.* New York: John Wiley and Sons, 2002.

Kerik, Bernard B., and John Botte. *In the Line of Duty: A Tribute to New York's Finest and Bravest.* New York: HarperCollins Publishers, 2001.

— Aberjhani

Larsen, Nella (1891–1964) *novelist*

Nella Larsen wrote two of the most critically acclaimed novels of the Harlem Renaissance, yet her moment in the spotlight was brief and is often overlooked in many literary circles.

Nella Larsen was born Nellie Walker on April 13, 1891, in CHICAGO, Illinois. Her mother, Marie Hansen Walker, was Danish, and her father, Peter Walker, was by all accounts a Danish West Indian. She would later write that her father died when she was two. Her mother then married Peter Larsen, and the family moved into Chicago's Danish community. Another version of her story states that after her sister Anna was born in 1893, Larsen's father elected to pass into the white race, at first changing his name to Larson. Later the spelling became Larsen. The birth certificate for Nella Larsen identified her as "colored," and thus began the checkered life of this "mystery woman" of the Harlem Renaissance.

Larsen grew up in Chicago in a household with her parents and younger sister Anna. Birth records indicate that Anna was born in 1893, two years after Nella, and Anna's father is listed as Peter Larsen. The Chicago census of 1910 lists Anna as Marie's only child. During this same time, school records for Nella list her father as her guardian, as if her mother disappears from her life at this point.

The South Side Chicago neighborhood in which Larsen grew up was known for its diverse population, and her mixed parentage seemed to be of no real concern. However, the family then moved to a neighborhood where apparently Anna fit in, with regard to color, and Nella did not.

In an effort to expose Nella to an environment more conducive to her development, her parents enrolled her at FISK UNIVERSITY in Nashville, Tennessee, in the fall of 1907. At the time, the student body was made up of students of mixed race and of middle social class. Many were future doctors, lawyers, and teachers. Larsen attended the Normal Department, a three-year certification program. At this point in her life, she had moved from her family situation, in which the question of her color raised concern, into another situation made up of the black elite. This is probably when she was forced to deal with the race issues that made up most of her adolescent life.

On May 3, 1919, Larsen married Dr. Elmer S. Imes, a physicist. She was 28, he was 36. Imes had completed a doctorate in physics the year before at the University of Michigan at Ann Arbor.

At the time of their marriage, Imes was a research physicist for Burrows Magnetic Equipment Corporation in NEW YORK CITY, where he worked until 1926. Later he became a research engineer. At the end of 1929, Imes returned to Fisk University, his alma mater, to chair the physics department.

Larsen was working as a nurse and librarian in New York when she and her husband befriended the writers and artists living in HARLEM. It was also then that she began to write. She became a novelist at the historic moment when African Americans were beginning to come into their own in terms of literary accomplishment. From the start of her transformation from librarian to writer, she ranked novels at the highest level of creativity.

In January and April 1926, she published two short stories in *Young's Magazine:* "The Wrong Man" and "Freedom" bore the pseudonym Allen Semi—Nella Imes in reverse. Three months after the second story appeared, she announced she was writing a novel.

With the publication of *Quicksand* in 1928 and *Passing* in 1929, Nella Larsen established a reputation as one of the leading novelists of the Harlem Renaissance. The critical response to *Quicksand* was generally enthusiastic—particularly by black reviewers, who expressed relief that it was not another novel about the seamy side of black life, which is how many had described *NIGGER HEAVEN* by CARL VAN VECHTEN in 1926 and CLAUDE McKAY's *HOME TO HARLEM* in 1928. Instead, it was the story of Helga Crane, an educated black woman unable to find her niche in the world. And like JAMES WELDON JOHNSON's *AUTOBIOGRAPHY OF AN EX-COLORED MAN*, it examined the psychological challenges of living as a biracial individual in the United States. In that regard, it was the first novel to examine such a condition from the perspective of a black woman.

Her second novel, *Passing,* is the story of Irene Westover Redfield, a mulatto woman who attempts to pass for white but meets with tragedy when her husband discovers that she is black. *Passing* both examined a fascination of the era and prefigured the trend of the tragic mulatto that would appear in such Hollywood films as the classic *Imitation of Life.*

Larsen wrote *Passing* during a period of her life when she was coping with two unresolved issues: marriage and economic stability. These themes are threaded throughout her second novel, which shares a number of similarities with *Quicksand.* Both are stories about and psychological explorations of mulatto life.

The last piece of fiction she published was a short story called "Sanctuary," which appeared in the January 1930 issue of *Forum.* It was one of her strongest statements about race, and the sole piece of dialect fiction that Larsen published in her career. However, after the story appeared in *Forum,* some accused Larsen of plagiarism. The story, they claimed, was an exact copy of a story by Sheila Kaye-Smith called "Mrs. Adis," published in a book called *Joanna Godden Married and Other Stories.* "Mrs. Adis" had not only been included in Kaye-Smith's collection of short stories but had also been published originally in the January 1922 issue of *Century* magazine. It seems more likely that Nella possessed something akin to a photographic memory, and for that reason "Sanctuary" contains so many similarities to "Mrs. Adis." The only difference was that Larsen had made a racial story out of her work; the plot was the same as Kaye-Smith's, and the dialogue in some places is almost identical.

In 1930, Larsen became the first woman of color to receive a Guggenheim Fellowship. The $2,500 grant could not have come at a better time. She was in the midst of marital problems. Her husband had returned to teaching at Fisk University, and she decided to join him to attempt a reconciliation. However, it did not work, and she and Imes divorced in 1933.

Larsen seemed to intentionally break off communication in the 1930s with friends who knew her as a writer. By 1935, the surviving writers of Harlem's literati had lost track of her. The people she associated with after 1940 knew her only as a nurse who revealed very little about her private life or past experiences.

On March 30, 1964, Nella Larsen Imes was found dead in her Manhattan apartment. The medical examiner determined the cause of death to be congestive heart failure. Missing from the official report was any mention that Nella Larsen Imes was the novelist Nella Larsen of Harlem Renaissance fame.

Further Reading

Davis, Thadious M. *Nella Larsen, Novelist of the Harlem Renaissance: A Woman's Life Unveiled.* Baton Rouge: Louisiana State University Press, 1994.

Larson, Charles R. *Invisible Darkness: Jean Toomer & Nella Larsen.* Iowa City: University of Iowa Press, 1993.

— Vaughnette Goode

Lawrence, Jacob Armstead (1917–2000) *painter*
The only visual artist to win the SPINGARN MEDAL presented by the NATIONAL ASSOCIATION FOR THE ADVANCEMENT OF COLORED PEOPLE (NAACP), Jacob Armstead Lawrence portrayed African-American neighborhoods and epic African-American history narratives on multi-paneled works.

Jacob Armstead Lawrence was born in Atlantic City, New Jersey, on September 7, 1917. His mother, Rose Lee Lawrence, a native of Virginia, was a domestic worker. His father, Jacob, a native of South Carolina, was a cook on a railroad line. He had a sister named Geraldine and a brother named William.

When Jacob Lawrence was a toddler, the family moved from New Jersey to Easton, Pennsylvania, a coal-mining town. There, his parents separated. His mother found work in NEW YORK CITY, and the children were put into foster care in Pennsylvania. When Jacob was 13 years old, he and his siblings were reunited with their mother in HARLEM.

The Harlem neighborhood in which Rose Lee Lawrence settled with her children contained violent street gangs. To help keep her children out of trouble and off the urban streets, she took them to ABYSSINIAN BAPTIST CHURCH for worship services and family activities. She also enrolled them in the local after-school program, Utopia House, one of the first community centers in Harlem funded by federal dollars from President FRANKLIN DELANO ROOSEVELT's WORKS PROGRESS ADMINISTRATION (WPA) initiative. At the center, the Lawrence children participated in soap carving, leather work, woodwork, and painting.

Utopia was set up in the 135th Street library. At the center were two notable African-American artists, JAMES LESESNE WELLS and CHARLES HENRY ALSTON, who noticed young Jacob's developing talent. Wells was a painter and director of the after-school program. Alston was a muralist and sculptor. Alston later organized the Utopia Neighborhood Center, which Jacob also joined.

Lawrence spent a few years in the High School of Commerce but, at age 16, dropped out to work at a laundry and a printing plant. Working, he supported his mother and siblings, painted, and visited the Metropolitan Museum of Art, where he fell in love with art of the early Italian Renaissance, a style that influenced his later paintings. He painted neighborhood scenes and urban residents under the admiring eyes of Alston and AUGUSTA FELLS SAVAGE, sculptor and director of the WPA-funded Harlem Arts Workshop. The Harlem Arts Workshop, located at the 135th Street library, was a major center for cultural activity. Here, Lawrence met Harlem Renaissance poet COUNTEE CULLEN and Professor Charles Seifert. Seifert taught African-American history at the library and suggested that Lawrence focus on African-American history and paint the struggles of African-American people.

Lawrence adopted Alston as his mentor and virtually lived with him at THREE-O-SIX—306 West 141st Street—where sculptor Henry Bannarn also lived and where Lawrence rented space in Alston's studio.

In the mid-1930s, Lawrence produced *Street Scene-Restaurant* (1936–38) and *Street Orator* (1937) among other neighborhood scenes. He then left New York City to work with the Civilian Conservation Corps (CCC), building a dam in Middletown, New York. In 1937, he returned to New York City to accept a two-year scholarship to the American Artists School and to exhibit his paintings at the Harlem Artists Guild studio.

In 1938, Jacob Lawrence had a one-man show at the Harlem Young Women's Christian Association (YWCA) and began working with the WPA's Federal Arts Project, courtesy of the diligent Augusta Savage. For his work on the Federal Arts Project, Lawrence was paid $23.86 a week.

The next year, Lawrence debuted 41 paintings called the *Toussaint L'Ouverture Series* at the Baltimore Museum of Art. François Dominique Toussaint L'Ouverture (or Louverture) was an African Caribbean from Haiti, a self-educated slave, martyr, and freedom fighter. The series won second place in the 1940 American Negro Exposition. Heeding Dr. Seifert's suggestion that he should paint scenes from black history,

Lawrence followed his *Toussaint L'Ouverture Series* with a 63-work series on Frederick Douglas and Harriet Tubman. Douglas (1817–1895) was a legendary abolitionist and author of *My Bondage, My Freedom,* and Tubman (1820–1913) led more than 300 slaves to freedom via the Underground Railroad, earning the name "Moses of her People." On the Douglas and Tubman series, for the first time Lawrence used casein tempera, a water-based paint applied to gesso that resulted in a startling vividness.

In 1940, Jacob Lawrence received a Julius Rosenwald Fund Fellowship Award. He rented a Harlem studio for $8 a month and began work on *The Migration of the Negro,* his benchmark creation. The epic work of sixty paintings depicted the GREAT MIGRATION when millions of African Americans, among them his own parents, fled the limiting JIM CROW racism of the South for the "promised land" of better opportunities in northern states. Created in the stark unsentimental style of realism, one of the many images is of a LYNCHING, with a man hanging from a tree and a weeping woman huddled on the ground. Working until the series was completed, Lawrence did not stop until he had used up all of the paints on his palette.

The Migration of the Negro was an immediate success. It was featured in *Fortune* magazine and shown at the Downtown Gallery on December 7, 1941. The even-numbered panels were purchased by the New York Museum of Modern Art. The odd-numbered panels were purchased by the Phillips Memorial Gallery (now Phillips Collection) in WASHINGTON, D.C. The panels are reunited for travel exhibits.

In 1941, Jacob Lawrence married fellow artist Gwendolyn Knight. Just two years later, Lawrence entered military service. During World War II, he served as a steward's mate for the U.S. Coast Guard, stationed in St. Augustine, Florida. He later served as a petty officer, a position that offered him time to paint, and created a 48-work series called *War* (1946) about life on a Coast Guard ship. When Lawrence was released from military service in 1946, he taught at Black Mountain College in North Carolina and started work on another series, a 14-work project about World War II.

In 1947, *Fortune* commissioned him to create a series on the theme of opportunities for African Americans in the postwar South, a request that resulted in *In the Heart of the Black Belt,* reproduced in the magazine's August 1948 edition.

Lawrence then suffered a nervous breakdown, and in October 1949, he admitted himself into Hillside Hospital in Queens, New York, to receive rest and treatment for stress. He stayed at the hospital for nine months, creating a nine-work series called *Sanitarium* that was exhibited at the Downtown Gallery in October 1950.

From the 1950s to the 1970s, Lawrence taught and painted commemorative works. During this time, his style changed again. Influenced by the modern Civil Rights movement, his paintings of blacks and whites working together to ease racial tensions in the United States were drawn sharply and done in shades of gray, a far cry from the vibrant reds, yellows, and blues of his earlier works. While continuing to paint, he taught at Pratt Institute in Brooklyn, New York; the Art Students League in New York City; and at Brandeis University in Waltham, Massachusetts. He was also artist-in-residence at California State University at Hayward in 1969 and claimed the same position at the University of Washington in Seattle in 1970, which he held until resigning in 1983.

Painting historical events as well as scenes of everyday black life, artist Jacob Lawrence, shown here in 1941, is now recognized as one of the most accomplished American painters of the 20th century. *(Library of Congress, Prints & Photographs Division, Carl Van Vechten Collection [LC-USZ62-95743])*

The NAACP recognized the exceptional quality and ongoing legacy of Lawrence's work by presenting him with the Spingarn Award in 1970. In 1972, he created a poster for the 1972 Summer Olympic Games in Munich, Germany. He further produced in 1977 a print of President Jimmy Carter's inauguration; a mural for HOWARD UNIVERSITY entitled *Exploration* in 1980; and, in 1984, a poster for the 75th anniversary of the NATIONAL URBAN LEAGUE.

Lawrence was also an illustrator and author of juvenile literature. The books he illustrated are *Aesop's Fables* (University of Washington Press, 1997) and *Toussaint L'Ouverture: The Fight for Haiti's Freedom* (Simon and Schuster, 1996). He wrote *The Great Migration* (HarperTrophy, 1995); *Story Painter: The*

Life of Jacob Lawrence (Chronicle Books, 1998); and *Harriet and the Promised Land* (Aladdin Paperbacks, 1997).

Jacob Lawrence died on June 9, 2000. A memorial service was held on September 28, 2000, at the Riverside Church in New York City. It featured the music of Johann Sebastian Bach and a vocalist who sang an African-American sorrow song, "I Don' Feel No-Ways Tired." At the service, Pulitzer and Nobel Prize–winning author Toni Morrison paid moving tribute to Lawrence. The printed program for the memorial noted that, "Jacob Lawrence seized beauty—whether it lay in an environment of heartbreak, survival or triumph. He seized beauty, manhandled it and made us know it too."

Further Reading

Jackson, Sandra. "In Memoriam: Jacob Lawrence 1919–2000." *Black Issues Book Review,* November–December 2000.

Lawrence, Jacob. *The Migration Series.* Washington, D.C.: The Rappahannock Press, 1993.

Nesbett, Peter T., and Michelle Du Bois. *The Complete Jacob Lawrence.* Washington: University of Washington Press, 2000.

Nesbett, Peter T., and Michelle Du Bois, eds. *Over the Line: The Art and Life of Jacob Lawrence.* Washington: University of Washington Press, 2000.

Valentine, Victoria. "Real Life, True Color: The Art of Jacob Lawrence." *The Crisis,* July/August 2001.

— Sandra L. West

Lee, Canada (Lionel Canegata) (1906–1952)

violinist, jockey, boxer, actor

Canada Lee, born Lionel Canegata, became a celebrated actor late in life, and he originally flourished as a nightclub owner, an accomplished musician, and an award-winning athlete in horse racing and boxing.

Canada Lee was born in HARLEM on March 3, 1906, to West Indian parents. Impatient with formal education, he dropped out of school. He loved music, however, and studied violin under JOHN ROSAMOND JOHNSON, brother of JAMES WELDON JOHNSON and coauthor of "LIFT EVERY VOICE AND SING." Johnson's young student entertained audiences at Aeolian Hall in NEW YORK CITY but decided he wanted more excitement out of life.

Lee ran away from school and home at the age of 14 to become a professional jockey at Saratoga Raceway in northern New York State. Jockeys are well established in African-American history. Blacks learned the sport on southern plantations, and by the late 19th and early 20th centuries, blacks dominated the profession. African-American Isaac Murphy won the Kentucky Derby in 1884, 1887, and 1890. Willie Simms and Jimmy Winkfield achieved notoriety for their racing accomplishments from 1875 to 1902.

Canada Lee joined the tradition of African-American jockeys by racing on half-mile tracks at Jamaica, Aqueduct, and Belmont in New York, and on the Canadian circuit for two years. In his first race, he finished second. In his second race, he finished first. He retired when he gained too much weight to race professionally.

After Lee returned home to Harlem, a friend suggested that he try boxing, another sport that, for blacks, originated on the plantation. Slaves of unusual physical fortitude were often groomed to fight other slaves on neighboring plantations. In the ring, the former jockey became a welterweight champion. He won the metropolitan, state, intercity, and national welterweight titles. He turned professional in 1926–27 and changed his name from Lionel Canegata to Canada Lee. Rated highly as a boxer, he was popular with Harlem fans and appeared many times at Madison Square Garden. A detached retina, however, forced his retirement from the ring in 1933.

The athletic Lee turned back to his artistic beginning. He orchestrated music as a bandleader, operated a nightclub, and participated in dramatic plays at the Harlem Young Men's Christian Association (YMCA), an association funded by the WORKS PROGRESS ADMINISTRATION (WPA) as were many Harlem community art centers at the time. Canada Lee profited from his work on the stage in Harlem. In 1936, he played Banquo in the BLACK UNIT OF THE FEDERAL THEATER PROJECT's all-black production of *Macbeth.* His performance was critically acclaimed. On Broadway, he played *Othello* and the classic character Bigger Thomas in *Native Son,* the stage adaptation of RICHARD WRIGHT's best-selling novel.

Athlete and actor Canada Lee starred in the 1940 stage adaptation of Richard Wright's novel *Native Son.* *(Library of Congress, Prints & Photographs Division, Carl Van Vechten Collection [LC-USZ62-95743])*

Lee's performance in *Native Son* was noted as "the most vital piece of acting on the current stage." Playing Bigger Thomas became his benchmark performance and secured his career as a professional actor. The former jockey and boxer progressed to Hollywood movies: *Keep Pinching* (1939), *Farmer Henry Browne* (1942), *Lifeboat* (1944), *Body and Soul* (1947), *Lost Boundaries* (1949), and *Cry, the Beloved Country* (1951).

Unfortunately, when the House Committee on Un-American Activities (HUAC) began its investigation into the Hollywood motion picture industry during the McCarthy hearings after World War II, Lee was identified as a member of the Communist Party. Though he denied the accusation, he was "blacklisted" by the United States government and his acting career was terminated. In April 1952, a harassed and frazzled Lee wrote a letter to WALTER WHITE of the NATIONAL ASSOCIATION FOR THE ADVANCEMENT OF COLORED PEOPLE (NAACP): "I can't take it anymore. I am going to get a shoeshine box and sit outside the Astor Theatre. My picture *[Cry, the Beloved Country]* is playing to capacity audiences and, my God, I can't get one day's work."

Canada Lee died shortly thereafter on May 9, 1952, at the age of 46.

Further Reading

Fleischer, Nathaniel. *Black Dynamite I.* New York: C. J. O'Brien, 1947.

Hawkins, Fred W. *Resources for Vintage Black Movies and Videos.* Campbell, Calif.: iUniverse, Inc., 2000.

Yearwood, Gladstone Lloyd. *Black Film as a Signifying Practice: Cinema, Narration, and the African American Aesthetic Tradition.* Lawrenceville, N.J.: Africa World Press, 2000.

— Sandra L. West

Lenox Avenue (Malcolm X Boulevard)

Originally named for a prominent 1800s European-American family, Lenox Avenue was and remains a primary thoroughfare in HARLEM and one of the widest avenues in NEW YORK CITY.

During the late 1800s, the tree-lined area was known for its elegant brownstone houses, especially between 122nd and 123rd streets. While the Harlem Renaissance was taking place, Lenox Avenue was the street where folklorist and anthropologist ZORA NEALE HURSTON, a student at the time, went to measure the heads of blacks, as directed by her Barnard College anthropology professor, Dr. Franz Boaz.

Lenox Avenue was also home to the white-patrons-only COTTON CLUB, the fledgling version of the world-renowned SCHOMBURG CENTER FOR RESEARCH IN BLACK CULTURE, and HARLEM HOSPITAL. In addition, it was the location of several ornate houses of worship that moved from downtown to the prospering urban village of Harlem as the population became increasingly African-American, as well as other classical and historical edifices. In the 1940s, the GGG Studio, workplace of the exceptional photographer and urban life historian JAMES VAN DER ZEE, was located at 272 Lenox Avenue on the ground floor of a rowhouse.

A peanut vendor peddles his goods in 1938 on Lenox Avenue, one of Harlem's busiest and most famous commercial areas. *(Library of Congress, Prints & Photographs Division [LC-USF34-015794-E])*

A northern extension of New York City's Sixth Avenue that stretches parallel to the Hudson River, Lenox Avenue was officially renamed Malcolm X Boulevard in 1987 in honor of the respected minister and human rights leader. Born Malcolm Little (1925–1965) and known as Detroit Red during his crime and prison years, Little converted to the Muslim faith in the Nation of Islam and became Malcolm X, a fiery teacher with a razor sharp intellect. His evolution from drug use and hatred of the white "devils" (as he called white people early in his career), to his role as an internationally recognized leader is recounted in *The Autobiography of Malcolm X,* written by Alex Haley (who also wrote *Roots*) and in the film *Malcolm X* by director Spike Lee.

Malcolm X Boulevard remains central to the economic, cultural, and real estate boom in 21st-century Harlem.

Further Reading

Dolkart, Andrew S., and Gretchen S. Sorin. *Touring Historic Harlem: Four Walks in Northern Manhattan.* New York: New York Landmarks Conservancy, 1997.

Haley, Alex. *The Playboy Interviews.* New York: Ballantine Books, 1962.

Hughes, Langston. *The Big Sea.* New York: Hill and Wang, American Century Series, 1964. Original: New York: Knopf, 1940.

— Sandra L. West

Lenox Club

Located on LENOX AVENUE and 143rd Street, the popular Lenox Club offered high-quality entertainment for a mixed crowd of blacks, whites, show business celebrities, and everyday laborers.

Whereas nearly all of the more luxurious clubs located in JUNGLE ALLEY purposely priced entry fees and menu items beyond the budget of the average HARLEM resident, the Lenox Club's manager, Jeff Blount, used a sliding scale on prices for many of his customers. Consequently, a hotel clerk or waiter could enjoy the same entertainment as the Lenox Club's celebrity clientele, one of whom was ETHEL WATERS.

With a black orchestra and the capacity to seat approximately 400, the Lenox Club was also unique in its policy on integration. Rather than following the general rule of JIM CROW segregation observed by many of the more luxurious nightclubs, patronage at the Lenox Club was integrated, with blacks usually outnumbering whites.

The club was also known to stay open all night and, instead of closing on late-night Sundays, continued to operate past midnight and offered a Monday morning breakfast dance. Instead of the customary dollar and half-dollar coins tossed at the feet of dancers and entertainers in other leading clubs, patrons at the Lenox Club tossed rolled bills at their favorite dancers.

Cast members from such shows as *BLACKBIRDS* and *HOT CHOCOLATES* variously entertained at the club and went there to be entertained as well.

Further Reading

Haskins, James S. *Black Dance in America: A History Through Its People.* New York: Harper Collins, 1991.

Steven, Craig, and Steven Wilder. *In the Company of Black Men: The African Influence on African American Culture in New York City.* New York: New York University Press, 2001.

— Aberjhani

Lewis, David Levering (1936–) *historian*

With the publication of *When Harlem Was in Vogue* in 1981, historian David Levering Lewis became one of the foremost chroniclers of the Harlem Renaissance and later achieved the distinction of winning two Pulitzer Prizes for biographies on W. E. B. DU BOIS, one of the era's principal figures.

Lewis was born May 25, 1936, in Little Rock, Arkansas. Enrolling at FISK UNIVERSITY in Nashville, Tennessee, in 1952, he graduated Phi Beta Kappa in 1956. Lewis continued his education at Columbia University in NEW YORK CITY, there earning a master's degree in American history in 1958. He then earned his doctorate in French history at the London School of Economics and Political Science in 1962.

In the U.S. Army from 1960 to 1962, Lewis served overseas at Landstuhl, Germany, where he also participated in the University of Maryland Overseas Education Program. He then spent a year as a lecturer at the University of Ghana before returning to the United States as a lecturer at HOWARD UNIVERSITY in WASHINGTON, D.C. He joined the staff of Morgan State College in 1966 and in 1970 was appointed associate professor of history.

Also in 1970, Lewis published his first major book, *King: A Biography,* on the life of slain civil rights leader Martin Luther King, Jr. He demonstrated the scope of his interests as an historian with the 1974 publication of *Prisoners of Honor: The Dreyfus Affair,* and *District of Columbia: A Bicentennial History* in 1976.

Culling previously untapped sources in the form of letters, rare manuscripts, and original interviews with individuals who lived during the Harlem Renaissance, Lewis published *When Harlem Was in Vogue* in 1981. The work was a groundbreaking one for its layered analyses of the community, politics, racial climate, and cultural achievements that characterized HARLEM during the JAZZ Age. Moreover, it was published by Alfred A. Knopf, one of the most prolific publishers of Harlem Renaissance authors during the 1920s.

Lewis published his fifth book, *The Race to Fashoda: European Colonialism and African Resistance in the Scramble for Africa,* in 1988.

Receiving a Guggenheim Foundation Fellowship to study the life of W. E. B. Du Bois, Lewis's research carried him to the former Soviet Union before he completed *W. E. B. Du Bois: Biography of a Race, 1868–1919,* and published it in 1993. The first of two volumes, the biography proved a critical success and

David Levering Lewis, the winner of two Pulitzer Prizes for his two-volume biography on W. E. B. Du Bois, is recognized as one of the foremost authorities on the Harlem Renaissance. *(Courtesy of David Levering Lewis)*

went on to win more than half a dozen major awards, including the Society of American Historians' Francis Parkman Prize; the Ralph Waldo Emerson Prize of the Phi Beta Kappa Society; and the Pulitzer Prize.

Having achieved recognition as a leading authority on the Harlem Renaissance and Du Bois, Levering edited a series of W. E. B. Du Bois readers for Henry Holt and Company as well as the *Portable Harlem Renaissance Reader* for the Penguin Books series.

In 2000, Lewis published *W. E. B. Du Bois: The Fight for Equality and the American Century, 1919–1963,* the second volume of his acclaimed biography on the political leader. Once again, the biography was championed by critics, with many proclaiming that the two volumes had successfully restored Du Bois's legacy to its proper place in American and world history. With the second volume, Lewis achieved in April 2001 the unprecedented feat of winning consecutive Pulitzers for a double-volume biography.

As of 2002, Lewis was Martin Luther King Jr. professor of history at Rutgers University and was at work on *W. E. B. Du Bois: An Encyclopedia.*

Further Reading

Du Bois, W. E. B., and David Levering Lewis, ed. *W. E. B. Du Bois: A Reader.* New York: Holt, 1995.

Lewis, David Levering. *W. E. B. Du Bois: Biography of a Race, 1868–1919.* New York: Holt, 1993.

Lewis, David Levering. *W. E. B. Du Bois: The Fight for Equality and the American Century, 1919–1963.* New York: Holt, 2000.

— Aberjhani

Lewis, Norman (1909–1979) *artist*

Norman Lewis participated in a succession of cultural arts movements, beginning with that of the Harlem Renaissance in the 1930s, and he eventually won recognition as the first major African-American abstract expressionist painter.

Lewis was born July 23, 1909, in HARLEM, NEW YORK CITY. His family was among the first blacks to live in Harlem while it was still a predominantly white community. As a youth, Lewis worked as a presser, cook, and elevator operator. Following the advent of the GREAT DEPRESSION in 1929, he spent three years as a seaman stationed in South America.

In 1933, Lewis met the sculptor and advocate AUGUSTA SAVAGE. He worked with Savage for two years out of a basement studio known as Savage's Uptown Art Laboratory. In addition to providing Lewis for the first time with studio space to practice his art, the Uptown Art Laboratory also brought him into contact with many influential writers and artists. Author CLAUDE MCKAY, singer ROLAND HAYES, photographer and writer CARL VAN VECHTEN, and many others on occasion visited the studio.

In 1934, Lewis joined Savage and artist CHARLES ALSTON to help found the famed THREE-O-SIX alliance of artists at 306 West 141st Street. A year later, he teamed up with JOSEPH DELANEY, BEAUFORD DELANEY, ROMARE BEARDEN, and others to establish the HARLEM ARTISTS GUILD, founded to monitor the distribution of WORK PROGRESS ADMINISTRATION (WPA) funds to African-American artists.

At the same time that Lewis met and worked with other artists, he continued his education by attending New York's Columbia University and John Reed Club Art School until 1935. He generally maintained that he financed his education by gambling but noted in interviews that he also received a scholarship to attend the John Reed Club Art School. In 1935, however, he began teaching at Public School 139 and at the HARLEM COMMUNITY ART CENTER. Painting, teaching, and cultural and political activism became the dominant pattern of his adult life.

Lewis's art during the mid-1930s was identified as social realism, a depiction of semi-defined images that often served as commentary on the political status of African Americans. Works along these lines included the *Washerwoman* and *The Yellow Hat* in 1936. His paintings in 1940 were among those featured as part of Tate Gallery's *Art of The American Negro* exhibit in CHICAGO.

Aside from his association with artists linked to the Harlem Renaissance, Lewis also formed creative ties with such then avant-garde artists as Lee Krasner, Jackson Pollock, and Willem de Kooning. Moreover, during World War II, he experimented with works in the style of European modernist painters Wassily Kandinsky, Pablo Picasso, and Georges Braque. Following the war, he ventured further into modernism by adopting the style of abstract expressionism, a form of painting he felt to be more commensurate with his individual creative vision. In 1943, he designed a war relief poster for the communist-influenced Congress of Industrial Organization (CIO).

Lewis continued to explore abstract expressionism in such paintings as *Composition Number One* in 1945 and *Fantasy* in 1946. His work was featured with that of several other painters in 1946 at New York's Marian Willard Gallery. The following year, he held his first solo exhibit at the gallery, beginning a professional association that would last 18 years.

In 1950, Lewis was the only African American whose work was included in the *Artists Sessions* exhibit at Studio 35. Among the other artists were his long-time associates Willem de Kooning and Robert Motherwell. He continued to both enjoy solo exhibits of his work and to accumulate honors recognizing his achievements. He won honorable mention in 1952 at the 10th Annual American Drawing exhibit sponsored by the Virginia Museum in Norfolk, and in 1955 he won the Popularity Prize at the Carnegie International Exhibition.

In support of the 1960s Civil Rights movement, Lewis joined fellow African-American artists HALE WOODRUFF, Bearden, and others in 1963 to form a cultural collective called Spiral. In 1964, he held his last solo exhibition at the Willard Gallery and moved to California. He then produced *The Processional,* one of his most famous paintings, in 1965. A visual interpretation of the Civil Rights movement done in contrasting lines of black and white, the painting was viewed by many as both a powerful political statement and a superior creative work in its own right.

As a tribute to the cultural legacy of the Harlem Renaissance, Lewis worked with artists Bearden and ERNEST CRICHLOW to cofound the CINQUE GALLERY in New York City in 1969. He also continued to garner widespread recognition for his individual work, winning the American Academy of Arts and Letters Award in 1970 and the National Institute of Arts and Letters Award in 1971.

Lewis returned to New York as an instructor for the Arts Students League in 1972. That same year, both the National Endowment for the Arts and the Mark Rothko Foundation awarded him individual artist grants. He received a John Solomon Guggenheim Memorial Foundation fellowship in 1975. The first major retrospective of his work, *Norman Lewis, a Retrospective,* was held at the City University of New York.

Lewis died in New York City on August 27, 1979. His work, however, continued to receive attention, and in 1989 the Kenkeleba Gallery in New York presented an exhibit titled *Norman Lewis: From the Harlem Renaissance to Abstraction.* In 1998, officials at the SCHOMBURGH CENTER FOR RESEARCH IN BLACK CULTURE featured Lewis's work in a catalogue of black 20th-century artists. The Studio Museum in Harlem; Wadsworth Antheneum in Hartford, Connecticut; and the Dayton Art Institute in Dayton, Ohio, all hosted an exhibit of the artist's work in 1998.

Further Reading

Gibson, Ann. *Norman Lewis: From the Harlem Renaissance to Abstraction Exhibition Catalogue.* New York: Kenkeleba Gallery, 1989.

Jones, Kellie. *Norman Lewis: The Black Paintings Exhibition Catalogue.* Newark, N.J.: Rutgers University Press, 1895.

Jordan, Denise M. *Harlem Renaissance Artists.* Portsmouth, N.H.: Heinemann Library, 2002.

Ludington, Townsend, Thomas Fahy, and Sarah P. Reuning, eds. *A Modern Mosaic: Art and Modernism in the United States.* Durham: University of North Carolina Press, 2000.

— Aberjhani

Liberia

See BACK-TO-AFRICA MOVEMENT.

"Lift Every Voice and Sing"

The song "Lift Every Voice and Sing," written by JAMES WELDON JOHNSON and JOHN ROSAMOND JOHNSON in 1900 for a program honoring the birthday of Abraham Lincoln, has since been adopted by African Americans as the unofficial "Negro National Anthem."

James Weldon and J. Rosamond Johnson were brothers born in Jacksonville, Florida, in 1871 and 1873, respectively. Their father, James Johnson, was a self-taught headwaiter who was fluent in Spanish. Helen Dillet Johnson, their mother, was one of the first black teachers in Jacksonville. Both parents passed on to their sons an appreciation for literature, music, and other cultural arts.

James Weldon Johnson graduated from Atlanta University in Georgia in 1894. He returned home to Jacksonville, where he became a school principal, founded the city's first black daily newspaper, and passed the bar exam. Rosamond Johnson attended the New England Conservatory of Music in Boston, Massachusetts, graduating from there around 1897. The brothers moved to NEW YORK CITY in the late 1890s and there established themselves as successful songwriters, with James writing lyrics and Rosamond composing music for Broadway shows featuring white performers. They combined their talents with those of the comedian and playwright Bob Cole to create a number of successful shows featuring black performers.

Composed at the beginning of their songwriting career, "Lift Every Voice and Sing" made its debut at a school in Jacksonville as part of a program honoring the birthday of Abraham Lincoln. At the time, the Emancipation Proclamation issued by Lincoln to free African Americans in the Confederate States from slavery was only 37 years old, and celebrations observing the former president's birthday were common throughout the United States. On one of the earliest published editions of the song, the Johnson brothers dedicated it to the great black spokesman BOOKER TALIAFERRO WASHINGTON. James Weldon Johnson received a diplomatic appointment to Venezuela in part because of Washington's influence and remained a Washington loyalist until the leader's death in 1915. In 1916, Johnson became field secretary for the NATIONAL ASSOCIATION FOR THE ADVANCEMENT OF COLORED PEOPLE (NAACP), and in 1920 the organization published "Lift Every Voice and Sing" and the "Battle Hymn of the Republic" on flip sides of a single sheet of a paper.

The song grew in popularity as the Johnson brothers each achieved distinction in his chosen field: Rosamond as a composer and performer, and James as an author and political activist. They coedited *The Book of Negro Spirituals* in 1925 and *The Second Book of Negro Spirituals* in 1926. By the end of the 1920s, the general African-American public had begun referring to "Lift Every Voice and Sing" as the Negro National Anthem. It became routine, and in many instances required, to sing it at official gatherings in churches, schools, clubs, and civic organizations throughout the country. In recent times, it remained the closing theme song for many black-owned and black-music-oriented radio stations throughout the country. In the year 2000, black fraternities and organizations all over the United States sponsored programs in honor of the song's 100th anniversary.

Further Reading

Wesley, Doris A., and Wiley Price. *Lift Every Voice and Sing.* St. Louis: University of Missouri Press, 1999.

Wilson, Sondra Kathryn. *In Search of Democracy: The NAACP Writings of James Weldon Johnson, Walter White, and Roy Wilkins (1920–1977).* New York: Oxford University Press, 1999.

— Aberjhani

Lincoln Motion Picture Company

Actor Noble Johnson teamed up with his brother George Johnson, a postal worker, and several others to form the Lincoln

Motion Picture Company, the first movie production company managed by African Americans, on May 24, 1916.

Born on April 18, 1881, in Marshall, Missouri, Noble Johnson grew up in Colorado Springs, Colorado. His movie career began in 1915 with a bit part in the film *A Western Governor's Humanity* and continued in 1916 with a part in *Kinkaid, Gambler.*

Recognizing the potential of working through his own production company, Johnson formed the Lincoln Motion Picture Company with himself as president, brother George as director of marketing; actor Clarence Brooks as secretary; Dudley A. Brooks, assistant secretary; and pharmacist Dr. James J. Smith as vice president. Valued at almost $16,000, the company was incorporated in California on January 20, 1917.

The Lincoln Motion Picture Company released its first film, *The Realization of a Negro's Ambition,* in 1916, two years before OSCAR MICHEAUX would release his feature-length film *The Homesteader.* With Noble both acting and producing, *The Realization of a Negro's Ambition* borrowed on the literary themes of Charles Dickens and the racial philosophy of BOOKER TALIAFERRO WASHINGTON, founder of Tuskegee Institute, now Tuskegee University. It presented a former Tuskegee student who overcomes racism in the Los Angeles oil industry through selfless acts of valor and faith. Not only is he rewarded with financial assistance from a wealthy white philanthropist but he also gains financial independence and wins the hand of his female costar. The movie was screened at the annual Washington-sponsored National Negro Business League conference and won some support from the so-called Tuskegee Machine. With its network of churches, schools, black businesses, and newspapers, the Tuskegee Machine would prove helpful in marketing black films that would not be shown in white-owned commercial theaters.

The Lincoln Motion Picture Company continued its productions in 1917 with *A Trooper of Troop K.* Like *The Realization of a Negro's Ambition, A Trooper of Troop K* refuted the popular image of African American men as imbecilic and untrustworthy, depicting them instead as courageous self-sacrificing soldiers of the U.S. Cavalry battling to protect the country's western borders.

The company followed *A Trooper of Troop K* with *The Law of Nature* in 1917, *A Man's Duty* in 1919, and its final film, *By Right of Birth,* in 1921.

Throughout its existence, the company had to contend with the challenge of limited outlets for its films. Marketing director George Johnson made it a point to win the support of black newspaper editors so they would in turn recommend the films to black theater owners as well as hotel managers, school personnel, club members, or virtually any group of people that could secure space for the screening. George Johnson at times personally carried the films to different venues throughout the Midwest and West, sat with audiences through their screening, then collected the company's percentage of earnings.

While president of the Lincoln Motion Picture Company, Noble Johnson continued to act in films for other producers, performing in *The Dolan of New York* in 1917, *Bull's Eye* in 1918, and *The Adorable Savage* in 1920, among others. His multiple business roles eventually created conflicts, and he turned over the presidency of the Lincoln Motion Picture Company to Dr. Smith.

Following the dissolution of the Lincoln Motion Picture Company in 1921, Noble Johnson continued his film career as a screenwriter and an actor of astonishing versatility, performing at times as a Native American, African, Egyptian, West Indian, or Hispanic character. He entered the era of talking movies in a string of supporting roles with some of Hollywood's most accomplished stars, including appearances in *Moby Dick* with John Barrymore in 1930; *The Mummy* with Boris Karloff in 1932; *Wee Willie Winkie* with Shirley Temple in 1937; and *The Ghost Breakers* with Bob Hope in 1940.

In all, Noble Johnson appeared in some 119 films. His career lasted until the mid-1960s. He died on January 9, 1978, in California.

Further Reading

De Angelis, Gina. *Black Filmmakers.* Broomall, Pa.: Chelsea House Publishers, 2001.

Hawkins, Fred W. *Resources for Vintage Black Movies and Videos.* Campbell, California: iUniverse, 2000.

Yearwood, Gladstone Lloyd. *Black Film as a Signifying Practice: Cinema, Narration, and the African American Aesthetic Traditions.* Lawrenceville, New Jersey: Africa World Press, 2000.

— Aberjhani

Lincoln Theatre

During the 1910s and 1920s, HARLEM's Lincoln Theatre was one of the few in NEW YORK CITY that focused on African-American entertainment for African Americans. It was also one of more than a dozen such theaters across the country that shared the same name.

The Lincoln started out as one of the earliest types of movie theater, known as a nickelodeon, and was originally called the Nicklette. As the Nicklette, the management exercised the JIM CROW policies that either restricted or altogether forbid the attendance of blacks at the theater. When a Cuban businesswoman named Maria C. Downs bought and expanded the theater in 1909, she abolished the racist policy and adopted one of open attendance. She also hired a black man named Eugene Elmore, known by patrons as Frenchy, to manage the theater.

Downs offered Harlem residents a full slate of entertainment that included vaudeville-style comedy, *BLUES* singers, new films daily, and new full-length plays on a weekly basis. The Lincoln did well enough that a new theater was constructed in 1915 and its former seating capacity of 300 was increased to 850. The entertainment lineup then boasted a chorus line as well as a seven-piece black orchestra.

Performers entertaining the audience at the Lincoln included the comedy team of Eddie Hunter and Thomas Chappelle. Writing and producing skits for the theater on a weekly basis allowed Hunter to gather material that he later would extend into such full-length plays as *HOW COME?* and *What Happens When the Husband Leaves Home.*

The theater's management was progressive enough that it put on *Treemonisha,* the opera by Scott Joplin, for a single performance in 1915.

A number of performance troupes spent time at the Lincoln Theatre, starting with the Anita Bush Players in 1915. An actress, dancer, and director, Bush led her group through performances of *The Count of Monte Cristo, Dr. Jekyll and Mr. Hyde,* and Shakespeare's *Othello.* She refused, however, to change her troupe's name to the Lincoln Players and left the Lincoln for an engagement with the LAFAYETTE THEATER. The new Lincoln Stock Company got its proper start in 1916 with a group led by Clarence Muse. Like Bush, Muse and company eventually left for the Lafayette. Moreover, Muse himself went on to enjoy an acting career that encompassed film throughout the GREAT DEPRESSION of the 1930s and television in the 1950s.

A third temporary resident theater group was the Ida Anderson Players. A salary dispute caused Anderson to separate briefly from her performers, but they reunited as the National Colored Players and transferred their act to the West End Theatre.

With or without regular stock players, the Lincoln provided ongoing quality entertainment with a variety of musical revues and individual performers. Blues legends Mamie Smith, BESSIE SMITH, and MA RAINEY all played the theater. The comedians Billy Higgins and Emmett Anthony brought their own brand of the ZIEGFELD FOLLIES to the theater with their *Creole Follies* in 1922 and 1923. And a female impersonator named Andrew Tribble brought his production, *Ophelia Snow from Baltimo',* to the theater in 1928 and 1929.

FATS WALLER was a regular at the Lincoln and often played accompaniment for such singers as ETHEL WATERS. DUKE ELLINGTON and His Orchestra also became favorites at the Lincoln.

In 1929, Downs sold the theater to Frank Schiffman, who already owned interests in the Harlem Opera House and the Lafayette. Ceasing the production of dramatic works at the Lincoln, Schiffman concentrated on presenting variety shows, movies, and revues. In 1932, he closed the theater while preparing to move his base of operations to the new APOLLO THEATRE.

Further Reading

Lemon, Ralph. *Geography: Art/Race/Exile.* Hanover, N.H.: University Press of New England, 2000.

Reed, Bill. *Hot from Harlem: Profiles in Classic African American Entertainment.* Los Angeles: Cellar Door Books, 1998.

— Aberjhani

literature and the Harlem Renaissance

The literature of the Harlem Renaissance sprang from a motivation to write about black heroes and heroic episodes from American history as well as the need for African Americans to express a franker and deeper revelation of the black self.

Writer and Harlem Renaissance historian ARNA BONTEMPS divided the literary aspects of the era into two phases: phase one (1921–24) represented the period of primarily black propaganda; and phase two (1924–31) connected Harlem writers to the white intelligentsia with its access to established publishing companies.

The propaganda phase of literature created during the Harlem Renaissance, orchestrated by W. E. B. DU BOIS, interpreted by ALAIN LOCKE, and compounded by the politician MARCUS GARVEY and his BACK-TO-AFRICA MOVEMENT, involved publication of *THE CRISIS: A RECORD OF THE DARKER RACES* and *OPPORTUNITY: A JOURNAL OF NEGRO LIFE.* The assigned mission of these periodicals was, among several, to reveal the humanity of—and, thereby, validate—the African-American race through the strength of its arts and letters.

Although the propaganda period of the Harlem Renaissance is placed from 1921 to 1924, PAULINE ELIZABETH HOPKINS observed as early as 1900 that art was "of great value to any people as a preserver of manners and customs—religious, political, and social. It is a record of growth and development from generation to generation. No one will do this for us; we must ourselves develop the men and women who will faithfully portray the inmost thoughts and feelings of the Negro with all the fire and romance which lie dormant in our history. . . ." William Pickens extended Hopkins's observation in 1922: "It is not simply that the white story teller will not do full justice to the humanity of the black race; he cannot."

The publication stage of the epoch was particularly historic because, according to Harlem Renaissance historian DAVID LEVERING LEWIS, no more than five African Americans had published significant literary writings between 1908 and 1923. Those writers were Sutton Grigg (*Pointing the Way,* 1908); W. E. B. Du Bois (*The Quest of the Silver Fleece,* 1911, and *Darkwater,* 1920); JAMES WELDON JOHNSON (*THE AUTOBIOGRAPHY OF AN EX-COLORED MAN,* 1912); CLAUDE MCKAY (*Harlem Shadows,* 1922); and JEAN TOOMER (*Cane,* 1923).

As the renaissance progressed, especially after modern young writers met mainstream publishers at the CIVIC CLUB DINNER of 1924, and black-interest journals and mainstream magazines began to widely publish the poetry and fiction of black writers, the slim list of pre-1924 names expanded. It came to include and seal into notoriety the following: LANGSTON HUGHES *(The Weary Blues);* poet and literary SALON arts patron Georgia Douglas Johnson; poet WILLIAM WARING CUNEY ("No Images"); dramatists MAY MILLER *(Scratches)* and WILLIS RICHARDSON *(The Chip Woman's Fortune);* Frank Horne *(Letters Found Near a Suicide);* George Henderson *(Ollie Miss);* Mae V. Cowdery *(We Lift Our Voices);* ZORA NEALE HURSTON *(Mules and Men);* COUNTEE CULLEN *(Color);* Juanita Harrison *(My Great Wide Beautiful World);* JESSIE REDMOND FAUSET *(There Is Confusion);* DOROTHY WEST, Florence Marion Harmon, Alvira Hazzard, and other female writers of the *Saturday Evening Quill;* playwright and novelist Mercedes Gilbert *(Ma Johnson's Harlem Rooming House);* WALLACE THURMAN *(Infants of Spring);* Bontemps *(God Sends Sunday);* and numerous others of every caliber.

William H. Ferris, literary editor of *NEGRO WORLD,* stated that the responsibility of the Negro novelist of the 1920s was to create fiction that depicted Africa as a powerful civilization and novels that added to the exalted status of the race. This mandate was more or less adhered to, even though the issue of blacks "passing" for white was publicly addressed in NELLA LARSEN's novel, *Passing* (1927), and the effects of denying one's race was explored in GEORGE S. SCHUYLER's satirical novel, *Black No More* (1931).

Among others not enraptured by the output of the period's writers, the era had a detractor in Theophilus Lewis. A critic for the *MESSENGER* (October 1926), Lewis wrote that the Harlem Renaissance was no Harlem Renaissance to him, spirituals were not musical art, African-American musicians were not first-rate, and most black fiction writers, except for the experimental author of *Cane,* were mediocre.

Outside the realm of fiction, and a school of plays later anthologized by dramatist Richardson, poetry actually led the literary form of the Harlem Renaissance. It was extremely popular and widely produced. The critical Lewis, ironically, was truly fascinated by the era's poetry, a literary art well practiced by Hughes, Bontemps, Cullen, McKay, and AARON DOUGLAS. HOWARD UNIVERSITY professor and 1930s folk poet STERLING ALLEN BROWN wrote in *Negro Poetry and Drama* that five main areas of interest existed in Harlem Renaissance poetry: (1) a discovery of Africa as a source for racial pride (which coincided with the BACK-TO-AFRICA MOVEMENT of Garvey); (2) a use of black heroes and heroic episodes from American history; (3) propaganda of protest; (4) a treatment of the black masses, frequently of the folk and less often of the workers, with more understanding and less apology; and (5) franker and deeper self-revelation. These principles were clear in Brown's own treatment of the black rural masses as folk heroes and in the race-pride poetry of Walter Everette Hawkins *(Thus Speaks Africa).* They were also evident in Waring Cuney's revelation of self-obligation to acknowledge and accept black beauty on its own terms in "No Images." Likewise, they informed Hughes's objection to JIM CROW regulations in "Merry-go-Round," and his post–Harlem Renaissance poem, "Birmingham Sunday (September 15, 1963)," a protest against the hate-crime assassination of four little black girls in an Alabama church.

Not every black writer sought to observe racial, historical, or cultural pride in their work. Ethel Caution-Davis's poetry transcended race. She wrote poems about nature, religion, and, in the pre-mall days of the Harlem Renaissance, about the joys of shopping. Her work was anthologized in WILLIAM STANLEY BEAUMONT BRAITHWAITE's *Anthology of Magazine Verse for 1926,* won a *Crisis* literary award in 1927, and was included in Turner Cromwell's *Readings from Negro Authors* in 1931.

The Harlem Renaissance officially burned out in the wake of the GREAT DEPRESSION. The depression severely limited economic support for writers from arts patrons and all but halted expensive publishing ventures for literary works, so the commercial and financial demise of the Harlem Renaissance was obvious. On an individual level, the collapse can be authenticated in the 1930s experiences of Hughes, Bontemps, and Cullen, for just three examples of what was certainly happening to everyone else. Hughes took his poetry tour, so successful in America's South in the 1920s, abroad to Chile and Haiti, and settled for a time in Russia, where he wrote radical verse. Bontemps turned away from creating poetry, for which he earned $5 to $8 per verse, to write more lucrative historical fiction and children's literature. The royalty checks of Cullen, the Harlem Renaissance poet most widely published in mainstream journals, dropped from $707 in 1932 to $147 in 1938. Still, and in spite of decreased economic backing, the philosophy and influence of Harlem Renaissance literature lived on to inspire future generations.

Further Reading

Bontemps, Arna. *The Harlem Renaissance Remembered.* New York: Dodd, Mead & Company, 1972.

Brown, Sterling A. *The Negro in American Fiction and Negro Poetry and Drama.* New York: Arno Press & The New York Times, 1969.

———. Arthur P. Davis, Ulysses Lee, eds. *The Negro Caravan.* New York: Dryden Press, 1941.

Gates, Henry Louis, Jr. "The African American Century: 100 Years of Pioneering Achievements." *Black Issues Book Review,* November–December 1999, 34.

Gayle, Addison, Jr., ed. *The Black Aesthetic.* Garden City, N.Y.: Anchor Books, 1972.

Griffith, Farah Jasmine. "The Ambivalence of Abundance." *Black Issues Book Review,* November–December 1999.

Moses, Wilson Jr. "The Lost World of the Negro, 1895–1919: Black Literary and Intellectual Life Before the Renaissance." *Black American Literature Forum,* 21, no. 1–2, 1987.

Vincent, Theodore D., ed. *Voices of a Black Nation.* San Francisco: Ramparts Press, 1973.

— Sandra L. West

Liza

Liza debuted November 27, 1922, at Daly's 63rd Street Theatre and then changed locations to the Nora Bayes Theater on 44th Street and ran for 172 performances, making it the most successful black musical revue to play the 1922–23 Broadway season. It also became the first such musical to play Broadway at the peak of the theater season as opposed to the off-season months of summer.

With its book by Irving C. Miller and music by Maceo Pinkard, *Liza* had its trial run as a show named *Bon Bon Buddy, Jr.,* in HARLEM. Although the musical *RUNNIN' WILD* would later receive credit for popularizing the Charleston, the most popular dance of the 1920s, it was actually introduced on Broadway by Maude Russell and Rufus Greenlee dancing in *Liza* to Maceo Pinkard's composition *The Charleston Dance.*

Liza borrowed heavily from its hit predecessor, *SHUFFLE ALONG,* in both format and story line. It blends political intrigue with romance in a mythical southern town where the funds established to build a statue in honor of the town's former mayor have somehow disappeared and have to be recovered. In addition to Russell and Greenlee, the musical starred dancer Eddie Rector, actress Margaret Sims, and dancers Dewey Weinglass and Thaddeus Drayton.

Liza was the fourth in a string of hit black musicals started by *Shuffle Along* in 1921. It helped maintain both public and critical interest in the black musicals that followed; including *Runnin' Wild*, *HOW COME?*, and *BLACKBIRDS*.

Further Reading

Davis, Lee. *Scandals and Follies: The Rise and Fall of the Great Broadway Revue.* New York: Limelight Editions, 1998.

Stearns, Jean, and Marshall Stearns. *Jazz Dance.* New York: Da Capo Press, 1994.

— Aberjhani

Locke, Alain (1886–1954) *philosopher, educator, editor*
An accomplished philosopher and editor of the *NEW NEGRO* anthology, Alain Locke worked to advance the causes of African-American culture in virtually every field, including literature, music, visual art, and theater.

Locke was born on September 13, 1886. He was the only son of a mother and father descended from distinguished African-American families in PHILADELPHIA. His mother was an educator and his father a HOWARD UNIVERSITY law school graduate who died before Locke was seven years old.

Attending public schools in Philadelphia, Locke enrolled at Harvard University in 1904 and, like W. E. B. DU BOIS before him, studied with noted philosopher William James. He became a member of Phi Beta Kappa and graduated magna cum laude in 1907. Locke gained national renown when he became the first African-American Rhodes Scholar at Oxford University, from which he received a B.A. in 1910. He then attended the University of Berlin, also like Du Bois, from 1910 to 1911. Through his education and international travels, Locke became fluent in French and German.

Returning to the United States, Locke accepted the position of professor of philosophy at Howard University and eventually became head of the philosophy department. Except for a brief separation from the university during the mid-1920s, Locke would maintain his position for some 25 years, helping the university to start its theater group, the Howard Players, and its journal, the *Phylon Review.* He would also teach classes at FISK UNIVERSITY and the City College of New York.

In 1916, Locke published his first book, *Race Contacts and Interracial Relations.* He published *The Problem of Classification in Theory Value* in 1918. During the same year, Locke received his Ph.D. from Harvard University.

By 1919, Locke had already begun working with ideas of racial and cultural inclusion applicable to American concepts of democracy as opposed to the actual practice of JIM CROW segregation in the United States. At the same time that he hoped to help strengthen democracy as both concept and practice, Locke also expressed intent to "vindicate the Negro" from charges of inferiority and the overall legacy of American slavery. Toward that end, like MARCUS GARVEY and others, he began to champion the "New Negro" and, like Du Bois, sought out those talented African Americans who could join him in his battle to help win what he called "culture-citizenship" in the United States. These African Americans included composers, painters, actors, singers, and writers. Locke had also begun to advise such individuals that in order to create enduring works of art they would need to achieve mastery on two levels: the first being mastery of form and technique; and the second being mastery of mood and spirit. Insofar as form and technique were involved, Locke advised artists to allow a European influence on their works. In regard to mood and spirit, he advised the cultivation of an African influence.

In 1922, Locke met JEAN TOOMER, soon to become the celebrated author of *Cane,* and arranged for the publication of Toomer's poem, "Song of the Son," in *CRISIS: A RECORD OF THE DARKER RACES* magazine. Similarly, Locke also met author CLAUDE MCKAY and arranged for the publication of his work in the *Liberator* magazine. Locke's role as an unofficial agent and publicist for emerging writers and artists of the Harlem Renaissance would prove much like that of CARL VAN VECHTEN's. In 1923, he began corresponding with LANGSTON HUGHES after reading poems by Hughes in the *Crisis.*

Locke and Hughes toured Europe together in 1924. In Paris, they met René Maran, the Goncourt Prize–winning author of the novel *Batouala,* and began an association that would eventually help spark the NEGRITUDE movement in France, the Caribbean, and Africa. In the French newspaper *Les Continents,* Maran published Locke's article *New African-American Poetry* and through it introduced Europe to the Harlem Renaissance. Maran eventually published works by COUNTEE CULLEN, Hughes, McKay, and many others. In addition, he and Locke arranged SALONs in which they introduced Harlem Renaissance writers and artists to such founding members of Negritude as Leopold Sengho, Aimé Cesaire, and the Nardal sisters, Jeanne and Paulette.

Locke himself regularly reviewed the works of black writers and artists in essays published in *OPPORTUNITY* magazine. While Du Bois wrote for the *Crisis* and advocated the use of art as a tool for political propaganda, Locke published essays that promoted creativity as a liberating force in and of itself. Regardless of their divergent views on the proper uses of art and beauty, both men participated in the 1924 CIVIC CLUB DINNER held in NEW YORK CITY to formally announce the onset of a renaissance in African-American culture centered in HARLEM. In addition to such emerging black writers as JESSIE REDMOND FAUSET and veteran authors like JAMES WELDON JOHNSON, a number of white publishers, editors, and writers also attended the event. Paul Kellogg of the *SURVEY GRAPHIC* magazine was particularly impressed by the assembled talent and invited Locke, who was master of ceremonies for the dinner, to edit an edition of the magazine focusing on African-American culture. Locke titled the March 1925 issue of the magazine *Harlem, Mecca of the New Negro* and included works of poetry, fiction, and nonfiction representing a diversity of styles and perspectives. Locke later added more material to that published in the *Survey Graphic* to create *The New Negro* anthology, the book generally recognized as the definitive text of the Harlem Renaissance. The anthology introduced developing talents such as RICHARD BRUCE NUGENT and GWENDOLYN BENNETTA BENNETT at the same time that it paid tribute to venerable forerunners Du Bois and James Weldon Johnson.

Through his numerous articles and essays published on both sides of the Atlantic, Locke continued to promote and showcase African-American culture. In 1927, he coedited, with Montgomery Gregory, *Plays of Negro Life,* the first anthology of African-American drama. He also edited *Four Negro Poets* to provide greater exposure for several writers featured in *The New Negro.*

Following a lecture he presented on African art in 1927, Locke met CHARLOTTE OSGOOD MASON, a wealthy 72-year-old white widow with a deep interest in "primitive" peoples and culture. Mason became Locke's PATRON and sponsored him on trips around the world. She also added substantially to Locke's collection of African art. Moreover, through Locke, Mason became a patron for Hughes, writer and folklorist ZORA NEALE HUSTON, artist AARON DOUGLAS, and many others.

Working with the HARMON FOUNDATION in 1928, Locke assisted in the production of the first of a series of all-black art exhibitions, held at the International House in New York. The exhibit featured almost 100 paintings, sculptures, drawings, and other works by African-American artists. Throughout his career, Locke would maintain an affiliation with black visual artists and have an impact on the careers of LOIS MAILOU JONES and JACOB ARMSTEAD LAWRENCE.

Likewise, Locke championed African-American music and in 1931 persuaded the composer WILLIAM GRANT STILL to set to music Richard Bruce Nugent's prose poem *Sahdji,* taken from *The New Negro* anthology. Still's music transformed the work into a ballet performed by the KATHERINE DUNHAM dance troupe. In 1932, Locke himself was made the subject of a work of art when WALLACE THURMAN cast him as Dr. Parkes in his novel, *Infants of the Spring.*

Locke became one of the founders of the Associates in Negro Folk Education during the mid-1930s. Like CARTER GODWIN WOODSON's Associated Publishers, the association was established to publish scholarly works on African-American culture and history. Locke served as editor as of its Brown Booklet series and in 1936 authored two of its titles—*Negro Art: Past and Present* and *The Negro and His Music.* The latter was one of the first to discuss in some detail various types of black music and musicians, particularly those that played fundamental roles during the Harlem Renaissance.

In 1940, Locke produced one of his most enduring titles in the form of *The Negro in Art: A Pictorial Record of the Negro Artists and the Negro Theme in Art.* In 1942, he coedited *When Peoples Meet: A Study in Race and Culture Contacts.* The American Association for Adult Education elected Locke to serve as its first black president in 1945, a position he maintained until 1947.

Retiring from his chair at Howard University in 1953, Locke was awarded an honorary doctorate in humane letters. He died of heart disease in June 1954 while working on *The Negro in American Culture,* a book he did not complete but hoped would serve as a summation of his knowledge of African Americans.

Locke has been described as everything from "one of the principal midwives of the Harlem Renaissance" to "the father of the New Negro" because of his indelible impact on the movement. He was also, however, one of the most widely published philosophers of his time, and conferences were held annually to discuss his ideas on democracy, pragmatism, cultural pluralism, and other aspects of his work. One of the best known of these conferences took place at Temple University in Locke's hometown of Philadelphia. Moreover, acting on a suggestion by Leonard Harris of Purdue University, the American Philosophical Association Conference founded the Alain Locke Society in Boston in December 1994.

Philosopher and editor Alain Locke, along with W. E. B. Du Bois, Jessie Redmond Fauset, and Charles S. Johnson, was one of the central leaders of the Harlem Renaissance and editor of the movement's definitive anthology, *The New Negro. (Alain Locke Collection, Moorland-Spingarn Research Center, Howard University)*

Further Reading

Harris, Leonard. *The Critical Pragmatism of Alain Locke.* Lanham, Md.: Rowman and Littlefield, 1999.

Harris, Leonard, ed. *Philosophy of Alain Locke: The Harlem Renaissance and Beyond.* Philadelphia: Temple University Press, 1991.

Washington, Johnny. *A Journey into the Philosophy of Alain Locke.* Westport, Conn.: Greenwood Press, 1994.

— Aberjhani

Louis, Joe (Joseph Louis Barrow, Brown Bomber) (1914–1981) *boxer*

So physically powerful that he was called the "Brown Bomber," Joe Louis became one of the greatest boxing champions in history during the GREAT DEPRESSION and was widely recognized as a symbol of freedom for African Americans and Americans in general.

Joseph Louis Barrow was born on May 13, 1914, in Lafayette, Alabama. His father, Munn Barrow, was a sharecropper. His mother, Lillie Reese, was a laundress. When Munn Barrow died, Lillie Reese married Patrick Brooks. Joining the GREAT MIGRATION of African Americans moving north, the family relocated to Detroit, Michigan, in search of a better life.

As a youth, Joe sold papers and shined shoes to earn money. At age 16, he became a sparring partner in a gymnasium. He quickly progressed through the amateur ranks but chose to work for Ford Motor Company rather than box professionally at that time. However, three months after he accepted a job on the plant assembly line, he changed his name to Joseph Louis and turned professional. His trainer was Jack Blackburn and, after eight victories, Joe Louis was known as the "Brown Bomber" of Detroit. After Louis knocked out Stanley Poreda and Lee Ramage, he became nationally known.

Heavyweight champion Joe Louis, shown here in 1941, became a symbol of triumph over bigotry and racism in America during the Great Depression. *(Library of Congress, Prints & Photographs Division, Carl Van Vechten Collection [LC-USZ62-42521])*

On June 25, 1935, Louis defeated Primo Carnera in NEW YORK CITY. Fifteen thousand African Americans showed up at Yankee Stadium for the event. Louis then fought Max Baer on September 24 and, by the end of 1935, had fought 14 bouts and earned $368,000.

The Brown Bomber won easily over Jack Sharey, Eddie Simms, and Bobby Pastor. On June 19, 1936, he suffered his first defeat at the hands of the German and former world champion, Max Schmeling. It was a defeat that many viewed and described in the press as a strike by German militarism against American democracy.

Harlem Renaissance poet LANGSTON HUGHES wrote in his autobiography, *I Wonder as I Wander,* that as he traveled through HARLEM via SEVENTH AVENUE he witnessed, "grown men weeping like children, and women sitting on the curbs with their heads in their hands."

Two months later Louis knocked out Jack Sharkey in a bout at Yankee Stadium. In June of 1937, he emerged victorious over Jim Braddock at Comiskey Park in Chicago and became the heavyweight champion of the world. To celebrate, 100,000 jubilant Harlem residents poured into the streets with drums, horns, and cowbells. Louis fought again, this time barely squeaking out a victory over Tommy Farr, in August 1937 at Yankee Stadium.

In June of 1938, Louis had a return bout with Schmeling, a bout that had strong political overtones for leaders of the free world. Schmeling was an avowed follower of the German dictator Adolf Hitler and like him an avowed white supremacist. President FRANKLIN DELANO ROOSEVELT told Louis that America was counting on him to win the boxing match, which Louis accomplished by knocking Schmeling out within two minutes of the first round. Battered, Schmeling was hospitalized, and he quickly returned to Germany. Louis earned $1 million from the fight.

Louis ruled the ring for 10 years after the Schmeling battle. Winning against Billy Conn in 1941, he then entered the army during World War II as an exhibition boxer. He defeated Jersey Joe Walcott in 1946, one year after his October 1, 1945, discharge from the military.

Joe Louis retired from professional boxing on March 1, 1949. He tried to make a comeback, but Rocky Marciano knocked him out on October 26, 1951. In a 71-bout career, Joe Louis lost three fights.

Money and medical woes claimed the end of Louis's life. The Internal Revenue Service claimed he had not paid enough taxes. He established the Joe Louis Food Franchise Corporation in 1969, but the business failed. In 1970, he suffered a nervous breakdown and spent five months at the Colorado Psychiatric Hospital and the Veterans Administration Hospital in Denver. By 1977, he was wheelchair bound and had surgery for an aneurysm. In 1980, he received a pacemaker for his heart, and on April 12, 1981, Joe Louis died. In 1993, the "Brown Bomber" continued to make headlines when the U.S. Postal Service issued a Joe Louis commemorative postage stamp.

Further Reading

Altman, Susan. *The Encyclopedia of African-American Heritage.* New York: Facts On File, 1997.

Anderson, Jervis. *This Was Harlem: 1900–1950.* New York: Farrar, Straus, Giroux, 1982.

Gates, Henry Louis, Jr., and Cornel West. *The African American Century: How Black Americans Have Shaped Our Century.* New York: The Free Press, 2000.

— Sandra L. West

Lyles, Aubrey See *SHUFFLE ALONG.*

lynching

African Americans murdered by the mob violence known as lynching numbered in the thousands during the first half of the 1900s, and the practice was one of the major driving forces behind the GREAT MIGRATION that took blacks out of the South and into the North, Midwest, and West.

In the 1780s, a judicial officer in Virginia named Charles Lynch supposedly provided the practice with its name, through his endorsement of personal interpretations and administrations of the law. Following the Civil War, the practice took on a distinctly racial aspect. Whereas white abolitionists or genuine criminals had formed the majority of lynch victims prior to the Civil War, following the war those numbers had continued to shift, with the murder of whites steadily decreasing and that of blacks increasing.

The number for blacks in 1892 was particularly high; the figures range from 161 to 292. Aside from the growing numbers was the macabre horror of lynching itself. The most frequent victim was a black male falsely accused of raping a white woman and who was then abducted, hanged from a tree, castrated, burned, and shot. Such incidents sometimes became social events during which whites often had picnics. Body parts of the lynched individual were sometimes taken for souvenirs; black men's severed penises when not kept by someone else were typically placed in the victim's mouth. Invitations to view this spectacle were often sent to people in neighboring towns. And while such obvious elements as the Ku Klux Klan were known to participate in lynchings, as time went on, so, increasingly, were general citizens as well as key community, political and social figures. Participants were never arrested for killing blacks in this manner.

Frederick Douglass, IDA BELL WELLS-BARNETT, ROBERT ABBOTT, and the NATIONAL ASSOCIATION FOR THE ADVANCEMENT OF COLORED PEOPLE (NAACP) all placed the eradication of lynching at the top of their political agendas. With the publication of *A Red Record: Tabulated Statistics and Alleged Causes of Lynchings in the United States,* journalist Wells-Barnett debunked the myth of black male sexual aggression as the principal cause of lynchings. More significant in her assessment were economic factors and the refusal of white males to accept consensual relationships between white women and black men. The issue proved a major political stumbling block for BOOKER TALIAFERRO WASHINGTON, who fairly avoided it until near the end of his career when he began publishing annual reports on lynching.

Lynching, the practice of murdering African Americans, was accepted in many white communities, especially in the Deep South, during the first half of the 20th century. *(Library of Congress, Prints & Photographs Division [LC-USZ62-35347])*

Conversely, *CHICAGO DEFENDER* publisher Robert Abbott and the editors of such publications as the *NEW YORK AGE, AMSTERDAM NEWS*, and *MESSENGER* frequently reported on the nonstop atrocity of lynching and the failure of one U.S. president after another to directly address the issue. Combined with the promise of better opportunities for education and employment during WORLD WAR I, black editors emphasized the futility of remaining in a region where it was basically legal to murder blacks and encouraged African Americans to relocate to the North and Midwest.

JAMES WELDON JOHNSON and WALTER WHITE of the NAACP also compiled a series of reports on lynching that they used to dramatize the reality and horror of the practice. White proved particularly effective at gathering such information because his white appearance allowed him to infiltrate racist groups and gather firsthand information from them. Writing for *CRISIS: A RECORD OF THE DARKER RACES* magazine, White described one incident during which Mrs. Mary Turner, eight months pregnant, was beaten, hung from a tree, burned, then cut open. The child she had been carrying was then also murdered.

While secretary of the NAACP during the 1920s, Johnson placed the bulk of the organization's resources behind support for the Dyer Anti-Lynching Bill of 1921. The initiative passed the House of Representatives but failed to garner sufficient votes in the Senate. Controversy and public debate over the proposal allowed the NAACP to further inform the public about lynching. Black millionaire MADAME C. J. WALKER contributed thousands of dollars to the NAACP specifically to fund its campaign against lynching.

Like the Great Migration and the politics of MARCUS GARVEY, lynching became unavoidable subject matter for the works of various writers and artists. The painter JACOB ARMSTEAD LAWRENCE, filmmaker OSCAR MICHEAUX, actor PAUL ROBESON, writer JEAN TOOMER, and numerous others all addressed the issue in their artistic works. Many felt BILLIE HOLIDAY summed up the physical, spiritual, and political anguish of lynching in her now classic recording "Strange Fruit."

By 1930, almost 4,000 African Americans were known to have lost their lives to lynchers. Although lynchings took place in the North as well as the South, the states with the worse records by far were southern, with Mississippi, Georgia, Texas, Louisiana, Alabama, Florida, and Tennessee possessing the highest figures.

Various presidents denounced lynching when addressing black leaders, but it was not until President Harry S. Truman was elected in 1945 that definitive legal action was taken to prevent lynchings. Truman's Executive Order 9808 made it unlawful for individuals or groups to administer punishments or vengeance at their personal discretion. Instances of lynching steadily decreased until vanishing throughout the 1950s and 1960s as the Civil Rights movement gained momentum and African Americans further secured their basic political rights.

Further Reading

Dray, Philip. *At the Hands of Persons Unknown: The Lynching of Black America.* New York: Random House, 2002.

Miller, Ericka M. *The Other Reconstruction: Where Violence and Womanhood Meet in the Writings of Ida B. Wells-Barnett, Angelina Weld Grimke, and Nella Larsen.* New York: Garland Publishing, 1999.

Wexler, Laura. *Fire in a Canebrake: The Last Mass Lynching in America.* New York: Scribner, 2003.

— Aberjhani

M

Mabley, Moms (Jackie Mabley, Loretta Mary Aiken) (1897–1975) *comedian*
The first African-American woman to achieve national status in standup comedy as a single act, Jackie "Moms" Mabley helped pave the way for the many black women working in modern comedy. Mabley was born Loretta Mary Aiken on March 19, 1897, in Brevard, North Carolina, to very industrious parents. Her father ran several businesses to sustain his large family, and her mother maintained a boardinghouse operation while also caring for her children.

Mabley received her introduction to the world of entertainment in Cleveland, Ohio, where she went to live as a teenager following a series of traumatic events. When she was 11, her father died in a fire truck explosion. As an adolescent, she was raped twice and became pregnant both times. In the latter years of her career, she would speak with poignant honesty as a guest on talk shows about the older black man and the white sheriff who fathered her children. At the advice of her grandmother, she left the children with two women in order to pursue a career. In Cleveland, she met Canadian Jack Mabley, the man whose name would provide her stage identity.

Still a teenager, Mabley entered the world of vaudeville with the comic duo Buck and Bubbles. She later teamed up with BUTTERBEANS AND SUSIE, the husband and wife vaudeville act that gave Mabley her big break when they invited her to join them for a performance in Pittsburgh, Pennsylvania. By doing so, they helped launch a career that would span some six decades and encompass nightclubs, movies, recordings, and television. Their association extended to NEW YORK CITY, where Mabley came into her own as a nightclub act, performing at such venues as CONNIE'S INN and the famed COTTON CLUB during the 1920s and the APOLLO THEATRE during the 1930s. She shared billing with some of the biggest names of the period, including LOUIS ARMSTRONG, CAB CALLOWAY, COUNT BASIE, and DUKE ELLINGTON. She and ZORA NEALE HURSTON teamed up in 1931 for the Broadway play *Fast and Furious: A Colored Review in 37 Scenes.* In one skit, she and Hurston entertained their audience as cheerleaders.

Early in her career, Mabley created the character of an elderly woman who wore flower-print housedresses and addressed her audience as "my children" while dispensing satirical observations in the language of folk wisdom and humor. Although she became known for such wry observations as "The only thing an old man can do for me is bring a message from a young one," Mabley avoided the raunchier brand of humor often employed by her male counterparts. Her nightclub success was a professional and social triumph in terms of her ability to win acceptance as a single black female comic. It was a tremendous personal triumph following a youth filled with tragedy.

In 1933, Mabley made her movie debut in one of the first so-called race films, PAUL ROBESON's *THE EMPEROR JONES*. Her work in films went on to include *Killer Diller* (1948) and *Boarding House Blues* (1948). She made *Amazing Grace* (1974) a year before her death, working alongside fellow veterans of entertainment Butterfly McQueen, STEPIN FETCHIT, and Slappy White. Although Mabley was clearly in poor health when she made *Amazing Grace,* the film served as an apt tribute to the pioneer comedian.

Both television and the recording industry opened their doors to Mabley in the 1960s. Her recording of *Moms Mabley at the U.N.* sold more than a million albums to earn her a gold record. She built on her initial recording success throughout the 1960s with such albums as *Moms Mabley at the Geneva Conference* and *Moms Mabley—The Funniest Woman in the World.* By the end of the decade, she had placed her vintage brand of humor on some 20 albums.

She became a favored guest on talk shows and in 1969, along with Leslie Uggams and Woody Allen, helped launch the premiere of *The Merv Griffin Show.* She made appearances as well on *The Tonight Show, The Smothers Brothers, The Flip Wilson Show,* and the *Grammy Awards.*

After starting out earning $85 a week for her early performances at the Apollo, in the 1960s going into the 1970s she was commanding $8,500 per week.

Mabley died on May 23, 1975, at the age of 78 in White Plains, New York.

Further Reading

Gill, Glenda. *No Surrender! No Retreat! African-American Pioneer Performers of 20th Century American Theatre.* New York: St. Martins Press, 2000.

Williams, Elsie Arlington. *The Humor of Jackie Moms Mabley: An African American Comedic Tradition.* New York: Garland Publishing, 1995.

— Aberjhani

Markham, Pigmeat (Dewey Markham)

(1906–1981) *comedian*

Among the last of those African-American comedians trained in the minstrel comedy tradition, Dewey Markham obtained stardom as a headliner at the APOLLO THEATRE, in film, as a recording artist, and as a 1960s television personality.

Markham was born in Durham, North Carolina, on April 18, 1906. His career as an entertainer began at the age of 13 when he left home to join a circus.

Throughout the early 1920s, Markham performed in various carnivals and traveling shows. These specialized in the then rapidly fading tradition of the minstrel show, which had become popular during the late 1800s and emphasized humor based on negative parodies of African Americans. Black and white performers in the minstrel tradition used burnt cork to darken their faces and white makeup to paint on oversized mouths. The tradition also, however, showcased such popular dances as the CAKEWALK and musical innovations such as RAGTIME. One of the first minstrel shows in which Markham performed was the *Gonzel White Minstrel Show.* Until joining it, he was known by the nickname "Black Rock." After joining the show, he gained some popularity performing a song called "Sweet Papa Pigmeat" and thereafter became known as Pigmeat Markham.

In addition to the *Gonzel White Minstrel Show,* Markham also performed throughout the South with *Jeff Murphy's Carnival, Dr. Andrew Payne's Medicine Show, A. G. Allen's Mighty Minstrels,* and the *Florida Blossoms.* In the last, he distinguished himself with his performance of the Sand Dance, in which he and a partner would shuffle through sand spread across the stage floor. Comedic and innovative dance would later prove to be trademarks of Markham's performances at the Apollo.

Markham moved to HARLEM in 1927 and regularly played such venues as the LAFAYETTE THEATRE and the Alhambra Theatre. During the 1930s he also joined a lineup of comics at the Apollo Theatre that included his sometimes partner RALPH COOPER, MOMS MABLEY, and BUTTERBEANS AND SUSIE. The same dancing skills, ribald style of humor, and gift for pantomime that Markham honed during his minstrel show days won him numerous fans at the Apollo. He became one of the acknowledged masters of comical dances, and his act often included performances of such popular dances as the Suzy-Q, the Cakewalk, the Black Bottom, and Truckin'. Although the last dance was popularized by the NICHOLAS BROTHERS at the COTTON CLUB, Markham insisted that he invented it.

The NATIONAL ASSOCIATION FOR THE ADVANCEMENT OF COLORED PEOPLE (NAACP) criticized Markham's and other comics' use of blackface, but he continued the practice until challenged by younger comedians in the 1940s. Markham began his stint at the Apollo on a salary of $75 a week, becoming so successful that during the middle of the GREAT DEPRESSION he headlined at the theatre for four consecutive years. In addition to his dance routine, his act included the traditional minstrel skit featuring a terrified black man walking through a graveyard or haunted house. Many felt Markham's superior pantomime skills elevated the skits to forms of true dramatic art.

Throughout the 1940s, Markham appeared in a number of all-black films. In 1940 alone, he was in four films: *Am I Guilty?, Swanee Showboat, One Big Mistake,* and *Mr. South Goes Ghost.* He performed in *That's My Baby* in 1944, *Fight That Ghost* and *House Rent Party* in 1946, and *Junction 88* in 1947.

Markham continued to perform at the Apollo for some 40 years, sharing the bill with some of the greatest entertainers of the era, including FATS WALLER and BILLIE HOLIDAY, whom he literally pushed into the spotlight when stage fright prevented her from moving. In the 1950s, he became a nationally and internationally recognized star. During the 1960s, he made frequent television appearances on such variety programs as the *Ed Sullivan Show.* During the 1968–69 broadcasting season, he became a regular on the hit comedy program *Rowan and Martin's Laugh-in.* It was on that show that he and Sammy Davis, Jr., popularized what became Markham's signature line: "Here comes the judge." The line became so popular that in 1968 it provided Markham with a Top 20 novelty hit record. It also helped him earn a salary of $5,000 a week playing Lake Tahoe and Las Vegas with Davis.

Like Moms Mabley and Butterbeans and Suzy, Markham recorded a number of albums throughout his comedy career. Of the 16 known records he made, *Crap Shootin' Reverend* and *Would the Real Pigmeat Markham Please Stand Up* remain available.

Markham died in New York on December 13, 1981.

Further Reading

Gregory, Dick. *Callus on My Soul: A Memoir.* Atlanta: Longstreet Press, 2000.

Kallen, Stuart A. *Great Male Comedians.* Detroit, Mich.: Gale Group, 2001.

— Aberjhani

Mason, Charlotte Osgood (1855–1945) *patron*

Charlotte Osgood was a white 72-year-old widow when she took on the role of PATRON to a group of black writers and artists in 1927.

Born into a wealthy family in 1855 as Charlotte van der Veer Quick, she was the second wife of a noted physician named Rufus Osgood Mason. Dr. Mason was a strong believer in parapsychology who expressed his theories in such publications as *Telepathy and the Subliminal Self.* A number of his patients believed he had cured them by means of psychic healing and out of gratitude supplied his widow with trust funds that she was able to dispense among her favored protégés.

Charlotte Mason subscribed to her husband's beliefs and was convinced that Native Americans and African Americans, to her mind the "younger races unspoiled by white civilization," were rich sources of powerful primitive, creative, and spiritual energies necessary to renew America. She had spent time among Native Americans and assisted in the publication of Natasha Curtis's *The Indians' Book,* a volume that she would frequently reference when encouraging her African-American charges to protect their own racial link to what she called African primitivism.

Mason met ALAIN LOCKE, editor of the *NEW NEGRO* anthology, in 1927 following a lecture he had presented on African art. In exchange for his cultural influence and intellectual companionship, Mason subsidized works of African art collected by Locke and for 13 years sponsored him on trips back and forth to Europe. They shared a passion for black music and often exchanged critiques of such musicians as WILLIAM GRANT STILL, DUKE ELLINGTON, and ROLAND HAYES. Locke also acted as intermediary between Mason and younger black writers and artists whom he felt were worthy of her patronage, introducing them to her at her Park Avenue penthouse. Among those Mason met and came to influence through Locke were: AARON DOUGLAS, MIGUEL COVARRUBIAS, ZORA NEALE HURSTON, CLAUDE MCKAY, and LANGSTON HUGHES. Mason asked that they not identify her publicly and that they address her as "Godmother." While an offer was made to assist PAUL ROBESON, the celebrated performance artist decided against it.

Langston Hughes was already an award-winning poet and author of *The Weary Blues* when he met Mason in the spring of 1927. At their first meeting she presented him with a gift of $50 and toward the end of the year established for him a monthly allowance of $150 along with open accounts for clothing and other needs. She extended her generosity even further by financing the education of Hughes's foster brother, Gwyn, at a school in Springfield, Massachusetts. For his part, Hughes often escorted Mason to musical revues and dinners. He also allowed her to critique his works in progress, and she edited, as well as provided a stenographer for, his novel *Not Without Laughter.* Mason's willingness to provide Hughes with financial stability as well as her knowledgability forged a powerful bond between the poet and the patron.

An equally, if not more, powerful bond was formed between Mason and Zora Neale Hurston, who met the patron in the fall of 1927. Hurston gladly catered to Mason's sense of cultural and spiritual leadership, claiming a special bond of psychic communication between them. The two women signed a contract whereby Mason would pay Hurston $200 per month and purchase a car for her to drive through the South and collect folklore comparable to that in *The Indians' Book.* At one point, she suggested Hughes join Hurston as she collected the material. The two worked together for a time, both collecting materials and discussing ideas for a proposed folk opera to be called *MULE BONE.* Plans for the project ended when Hughes severed his relationship with Mason to retain creative control of his writings and Hurston claimed the proposed work solely as her own. Hurston's own relationship with Mason ended in late 1932.

Like Hughes, Aaron Douglas could not abide another controlling his creative endeavors and broke with Mason for that reason.

Locke remained a confidant to the patron until her death at age 90 in 1945.

Further Reading

Berry, Faith. *Langston Hughes: Before and Beyond Harlem.* New York: Citadel Press, 1992.

Meisenhelder, Susan Edwards. *Hitting a Straight Line with a Crooked Stick: Race and Gender in the Work of Zora Neale Hurston.* Tuscaloosa: University of Alabama Press, 2001.

— Aberjhani

Matthew, Arthur Wentworth, Rabbi

See COMMANDMENT KEEPERS.

McClendon, Rose (1884–1936) *actor*

A star of Broadway plays by LANGSTON HUGHES and Paul Green, Rose McClendon was one of the most accomplished and respected black actors of the 1920s and 1930s.

McClendon was born Rosalie Virginia Scott on August 27, 1884, in Greenville, South Carolina. Joining the flow of African Americans beginning to make their way North during the GREAT MIGRATION, she moved with her family to NEW YORK CITY just after 1900. In 1916, she married Henry P. McClendon, a chiropractor who also pulled shifts as a railroad porter.

McClendon first expressed serious interest in theater by directing and acting in productions at St. Mark's African Methodist Episcopal Church. Her professional ambitions were strengthened considerably when she won a scholarship to study at the American Academy of Dramatic Arts. By 1924, she had developed her talents enough to share the stage with CHARLES SIDNEY GILPIN in *Roseanne,* and she later performed with PAUL ROBESON in the same play. Critics praised her performance when she played opposite Jules Bledsoe in *Deep River* in 1926. She again won strong reviews along with Bledsoe in Paul Green's Pulitzer Prize–winning play *In Abraham's Bosom.* She took the role of Serena in Dorothy Heyward's stage adaptation of her husband DuBose Heyward's novel *Porgy* (Ira Gershwin's version, *PORGY AND BESS,* would come later).

Despite initial doubts about performing in Hughes's play *Mulatto,* McClendon did join the cast for what became the longest running Broadway play by an African American up to that point. Pneumonia eventually forced McClendon to resign from the play and she was replaced by Mercedes Gilbert.

In addition to garnering acclaim for her onstage performances, McClendon often served as a representative of the theater community. Along with Dick Campbell, she organized the Negro People's Theater in Harlem. She also served as a board member of the Theater Union and as director of the HARLEM EXPERIMENTAL THEATER.

Such was her renown that when Federal Theater Projects (FTP) administrator Hallie Flanagan began to establish the New York performance units, she met with McClendon to draw up plans for the BLACK UNIT OF THE FEDERAL THEATER PROJECT. It was also McClendon who nominated white director John Houseman to run the HARLEM units—both so that blacks who had primarily been actors would be able to learn from an experienced director and so Houseman could sidestep discriminatory practices when handling business for the unit. She worked with Houseman and Flanagan to establish antisegregation policies for the FTP. Under these, the Black Units would not perform before segregated audiences, nor would company members accept segregated seating or segregated hotel accommodations when traveling.

In 1935, COUNTEE CULLEN updated the classic *Medea,* by Euripides, as a vehicle for McClendon. Plans were under way for production when McClendon died of pneumonia on July 12, 1936. Shortly after her death, the Black Unit of the Federal Theater Project she had championed scored its greatest victory with a Haitian version of Shakespeare's *Macbeth.*

Actress Rose McClendon poses in 1935 as Medea, a role updated for her by the poet Countee Cullen. *(Library of Congress, Prints & Photographs Division, Carl Van Vechten Collection [LC-USZ62-131767])*

Dick Campbell, his wife Muriel Rahn, and George Norford started the Rose McClendon Players and Workshop in 1938 as a memorial to the late actor. Attempting to strengthen community theater, the organization had its offices and taught classes at the 134th Street New York Public Library Branch in Harlem. Among its founding members were the now famous husband and wife acting team of Ossie Davis and Ruby Dee, as well as Frederick O'Neal and Helen Marling. With Campbell as its artistic director, the group put on a number of successful comedies, dramas, one-act plays, and full-length presentations. Two of its more outstanding full-length plays were *A Right Angle Triangle* by Ferdinand Voteur and *Joy Exceeding Glory* by George Norford, both produced in 1939.

The McClendon Players disbanded at the onset of World War II. Many of its members went on to join the ranks of the American Negro Theatre.

Further Reading

Tanner, Jo A. *Dusky Maidens: The Odyssey of the Early Black Dramatic Actress.* Westport, Conn.: Greenwood, 1992.

— Aberjhani

McDaniel, Hattie (1895–1952) *actress, singer*

For her portrayal of Mammy in the 1939 epic movie *Gone With the Wind,* Hattie McDaniel became the first African American to win an Academy Award.

McDaniel was born on June 10, 1895, in Wichita, Kansas, the 13th child of Susan Holbert McDaniel and Baptist minister Henry McDaniel. She grew up in Denver, Colorado, where as a teenager she sang in black minstrel shows and performed in high school plays and musicals. In 1910, she left high school to travel and perform with her father's troupe, the *Henry McDaniel Minstrel Show.*

A versatile performer, she later sang with a group called the Melody Hounds and performed vaudeville comedy. As a singer, she was often compared to SOPHIE TUCKER, and as a comic compared to BERT WILLIAMS. A songwriter as well, she was among those artists who worked with the Okeh record label during the RACE RECORDS boom of the 1920s. McDaniel toured on a variety of entertainment circuits, including Pantages, Orpheum, Elks, and the THEATER OWNERS BOOKING AGENCY. When necessary, she worked odd jobs as a maid, an experience that provided useful insights for the roles she would later play in Hollywood films.

In 1931, McDaniel moved with her brother Sam and sister Etta, also entertainers, to Los Angeles. She worked on several radio programs, including *the Eddie Cantor Show,* *AMOS 'N' ANDY,* *The Optimistic Do-Nuts,* and *Hi-Hat Hattie.* The last featured her as a willful maid prone to following her own inclinations as opposed to anyone's orders and added further to the persona she would perfect on screen.

McDaniel broke into film with the 1932 movie *The Gold West.* During the same year she performed with Hollywood icon Marlene Dietrich in *Blonde Venus,* a film in which her character was something of a heroine, helping Dietrich and her son to elude police and an abusive husband. Throughout the 1930s, McDaniel both established and distinguished herself in such movies as *The Judge Priest,* with STEPIN FETCHIT and Will Rogers in 1934; *The Mad Miss Manton,* with Barbara Stanwyck in 1935; *The Little Colonel,* with Shirley Temple, also in 1935; and *Showboat,* as Queenie, with PAUL ROBESON.

While McDaniel, like other black actors of the era, often played the role of a servant, she did so in such a nonsubservient and self-possessed manner that her performances stood out, and roles were sometimes written specifically as vehicles for her talent. Whereas during the GREAT DEPRESSION Hollywood was willing to champion and encourage the audaciousness of McDaniel's characters, it was far less supportive of such qualities in roles for black men; a progressive actor such as Paul Robeson had to work outside the United States to star in films portraying him as a nonsubservient and self-asserting black man. On the other hand, Stepin Fetchit, who worked with McDaniel in the aforementioned *Judge Priest* and in the 1939 film *Zenobia,* soared to stardom in roles portraying black men as lazy, sycophantic, and extremely dim-witted.

Nevertheless, it was McDaniel's ability to transcend the stereotype mold of her characters that won her the part of Mammy. *Gone With the Wind,* based on the bestselling 1936 novel by Margaret Mitchell, was one of the most anticipated films of its time. Directed by Victor Fleming and produced by David O. Selznick, it starred the celebrated white actors Vivien Leigh and Clark Gable. As Mammy to Leigh's Scarlett O'Hara in the film, Hattie McDaniel created a character that did not simply serve a white family but directed the course of its social and moral actions. Ironically, portraying such a character required McDaniel to refrain from displaying any sense of inferiority, yet the NATIONAL ASSOCIATION FOR THE ADVANCEMENT OF COLORED PEOPLE (NAACP) criticized it as one more highly visible demeaning role stereotyping black women. Although the charge disturbed McDaniel, she countered it by pointing out that she herself was much better off making $7,000 a week playing a maid than making $7 a week working as one. Her performance earned her the Academy Award for best supporting actress. Leigh also won for best actress and Fleming for best director.

In addition to McDaniel, *Gone With the Wind* also featured the talents of black performers Butterfly McQueen and EDDIE "ROCHESTER" ANDERSON.

McDaniel's career continued to thrive following her Academy Award. In 1946, she played Aunt Tempy in Walt Disney's *Song of the South,* and in 1949 she performed in *Family Honeymoon.* In 1947, she returned to radio with the nationally broadcast show *Beulah,* in which she again played an independent-minded maid. She was the first African American to star in such a show and every week drew some 20,000 listeners. In 1950, *Beulah* became the first television situation comedy to star a black woman. However, it was ETHEL WATERS who first took the role to television. McDaniel, suffering from cancer, attempted the part as the second Beulah, and Louise Beavers filled in when McDaniel's illness forced her to leave the show.

McDaniel reportedly was married briefly four times. She was also a member of SIGMA GAMMA RHO. The actress died on October 26, 1952, in Woodland Hills, California.

Further Reading

Jackson, Carlton. *Hattie: The Life of Hattie McDaniel.* Madison, Wisc.: Madison Books, 1993.

Klotman, Phyllis Rauch. *Frame by Frame: A Black Filmography.* Bloomington: Indiana University Press, 1997.

— Aberjhani

McDonald, Henry See SPORTS AND THE HARLEM RENAISSANCE.

McKay, Claude (Festus Claudius McKay)

(1889–1948) *writer*

Having established himself as an award-winning poet in his native Jamaica, Claude McKay became, during the 1920s, one of the most militant authors of fiction and verse in the United States and Europe.

McKay was born on September 15, 1889, the youngest of 11 children, eight of whom lived to adulthood, in the Sunny Ville sector of Clarendon Parish in Jamaica. His parents, Hannah Ann Elizabeth Edwards McKay and Thomas Francis McKay, were fairly prosperous farmers. His mother was a descendant of Madagascans and his father, who passed on to his son a strong sense of ancestral pride, a descendant of West Africa's Ashanti tribe. The other McKay children were Uriah Theodore, Matthew, Rachel, Thomas Edison, Nathaniel, Reginald, and Hubert.

McKay began his elementary education at Mt. Zion Church and was later tutored by his oldest brother, Uriah Theodore, who taught in a school near Montego Bay. His brother noted McKay's love of literature, introduced him to the works of classic English authors, and encouraged him when he began to write poetry of his own.

In 1907, McKay moved away from home to train as a woodworker in Brown's Town. While there, he befriended Walter Jekyll, an English musician and collector of island folklore. Jekyll also encouraged McKay's writing and introduced him to such authors as Charles Baudelaire and Walt Whitman. Most significantly, Jekyll persuaded McKay to compose verse in his native dialect rather than formal English.

McKay left Brown's Town for a position with the constabulary in Kingston, Jamaica's capital. Unlike the relatively harmonious daily life he had experienced growing up in Sunny Ville, the overt displays of racial oppression he witnessed in Kingston prompted him to leave his job after a year and return home. He continued to write and with Jekyll's assistance in 1912 published two volumes of poetry: *Songs of Jamaica* and *Constab Ballads.* Each book demonstrated the dominant qualities for which McKay would become known throughout his literary career. The poems in *Songs of Jamaica* were noted for

McKay's lyrical celebration of life among black peasants on a beautiful tropical island. Those in *Constab Ballads* illustrated his political concern with racial prejudice and oppression. For his work, McKay became the first black to win the Jamaican Institute of Arts and Sciences Award.

Using the money that came with his literary award, McKay immigrated to the United States in 1912. Disembarking in South Carolina, he made his way to BOOKER TALIAFERRO WASHINGTON's Tuskegee Institute, where he attempted to study agriculture for approximately two months before transferring to Kansas State College. At Kansas State, he read W. E. B. DU BOIS's *SOULS OF BLACK FOLK* and in 1914 left the college to move to NEW YORK CITY.

In New York, McKay married Eulalie Imelda Lewars on July 30, 1914. The couple had a daughter named Ruth Hope but were separated before McKay ever saw her. Remaining in New York, the writer for a time ran his own restaurant, then worked alternately as a longshoreman, porter, and barman. He immersed himself in life in both HARLEM and Greenwich Village. Through the latter in particular, he entered into what was described as a bohemian lifestyle that advocated equality among social classes as well as among the races and sexes. It also included experimentation in open relationships and bisexuality that became the norm for McKay for the rest of his life.

McKay's associates soon included the writer Waldo Frank, who would assist JEAN TOOMER in his career, and NATIONAL ASSOCIATION FOR THE ADVANCEMENT OF COLORED PEOPLE official Joel Spingarn. Both men were affiliated with *Seven Arts* magazine and published in it McKay's first American poems, "The Harlem Dancer" and "Invocation," under the pseudonym Eli Edwards. The poems earned McKay immediate renown and he began to publish works in the *CRISIS: A RECORD OF THE DARKER RACES, NEGRO WORLD*, and the *MESSENGER*.

He met the editors of the *Liberator* magazine, MAX EASTMAN and his sister Crystal Eastman, in 1919. Impressed by each other's work, Max Eastman and McKay became close friends. In July 1919, during the period of violent riots known as the RED SUMMER, Eastman published in the *Liberator* a two-page spread of McKay's poetry that included the title "IF WE MUST DIE." The poem seemed to speak directly to the loss of black lives in riots across the country and particularly to those lost in CHICAGO in the very month the magazine was published. It was reprinted in newspapers and magazines throughout the United States and brought Claude McKay international fame. During the same period, McKay helped establish the COMMUNISM-influenced organization the AFRICAN BLOOD BROTHERHOOD, headed by journalist Cyril Briggs.

In the fall of 1919, McKay left the United States for Europe, traveling through Holland, Belgium, and England. He settled in London long enough to write for the Communist newspaper *Worker's Dreadnought*, publishing articles there under different pseudonyms. He also published some two dozen poems in *Cambridge* magazine, extending his international reputation as a poet. While in England, his poetry collection *Spring in New Hampshire and Other Poems* was published and was well received in the United States.

He returned to the States in 1921 and accepted a position as associate editor at the *Liberator*. His editorship at the *Liberator* brought McKay in contact with some of the most gifted black writers of the period, including Georgia Douglas Johnson, LANGSTON HUGHES, Jean Toomer, and JAMES WELDON JOHNSON, with whom McKay would remain friends until Johnson's death in 1938. McKay attempted at the *Liberator* to establish an editorial policy requiring the magazine to devote 10 percent of its editorial space to issues pertaining to blacks, but he was defeated in this proposal. He left the magazine in August 1922.

McKay was able to publish more than three dozen of his poems and articles in the *Liberator* prior to his departure. His reputation as a major black poet further increased with the publication of 13 of his poems in James Weldon Johnson's anthology *The Book of American Negro Poetry* in 1922. In his introduction to McKay's work, Johnson described him as "the poet of rebellion" and "the poet of passion." Moreover, McKay's own *Harlem Shadows*, with an introduction by Max Eastman, was also published in 1922. The book's lyrical evocation of black life in Harlem balanced with the subversive tones of such poems as "If We Must Die" brought McKay wide recognition as a poet of serious intent and exceptional ability. For that reason, many view *Harlem Shadows* as the book that started the 1920s black literary renaissance rather than Jean Toomer's *Cane*, portions of which McKay published in the *Liberator*. McKay himself, however, along with James Weldon Johnson, Langston Hughes, ALAIN LOCKE, and others, all acknowledged their literary debt to Du Bois's *Souls of Black Folk*, published in 1903.

Despite the acclaim heaped upon him for *Harlem Shadows*, McKay did not remain in the United States to bask in literary stardom. JESSIE REDMOND FAUSET, JOHN ROSAMOND JOHNSON, James Weldon Johnson, WALTER WHITE, and other well-wishers threw a good-bye party for him as he set sail in 1922 for Russia. Twelve years would pass before his return to the United States.

In Russia, McKay was greeted as a diplomat of African America and addressed the Fourth Congress of the Communist Party on the commitment of Communist leaders in America to racial equality for blacks. Winning popularity with party officials as well proletariat citizens, McKay wrote for the Soviet press a series of articles that were gathered into a book called *Negroes in America* and published in Russia. His farewell poem to the country, *Petrograd: May Day, 1923*, was translated and published in the newspaper *Pravda*.

From Russia, McKay traveled to Berlin, Germany, where he met Alain Locke for the first time and sent articles back to the *Crisis* magazine in New York. He also met with extreme financial difficulties and often wrote to the bibliophile and historian ARTHUR SCHOMBURG for assistance collecting his royalties, procuring loans, and selling articles. Toward the end of 1923, McKay moved to PARIS. After bouts with severe illness, he earned his living modeling and working as a script reader while working on a novel. He met Jane and Paulette Nardal, two sisters whose salons in Paris would help start the

NEGRITUDE literary and art movement, which would continue to grow with visits to France from other black writers and artists. Award-winning novelist René Maran, who would also publish works by Locke, Hughes, and Cullen, published translations of McKay's poetry in his magazine *Les Continents.*

McKay endured periods of extreme poverty and illness, including respiratory disease and syphilis, before completing his first novel accepted for publication. Published by Harper and Brothers in 1928, while McKay was still in France, his novel *Home to Harlem* became the first American best-seller by a black author. It also stirred controversy equal to that surrounding the publication of *NIGGER HEAVEN* by CARL VAN VECHTEN in 1926. *Home to Harlem* focused on the story of a military deserter named Jake and an aspiring writer named Ray as each pursued his pleasures and suffered his fate in Harlem. In Jake, McKay embodied the presumed natural freedom and virility of the instinctual black self versus the apparently unnatural and disempowered efforts of the Americanized intellectual self. This dichotomy between the instinctive and intellectual response to living as a person of color within a society dominated by whites was a theme Mckay would explore in each of his novels. With its uninhibited portrayal of lovers at play and war, *Home to Harlem* drew disapproval from Du Bois, who said it made him feel the need to take a bath, and cheers from Langston Hughes, who called it "the flower of the Negro Renaissance, even if it is no lovely lily." In two months, the book went through five printings, and its success inspired McKay to write another novel.

Banjo: A Story Without a Plot was McKay's second novel, published in 1929. Though it sold considerably less in the United States than *Home to Harlem,* its depiction of black laborers in Europe made the novel one of the fundamental texts of the developing Negritude movement. PAUL ROBESON later made it into a movie called *Big Fella.* McKay traveled to Spain and Morocco to continue writing. He followed *Banjo* with a collection of stories called *Gingertown* in 1932 and with a third novel, titled *Banana Bottom,* in 1933. *Banana Bottom* is generally acknowledged as McKay's strongest work of fiction. In it, McKay tells the story of an independent-thinking young black woman's odyssey through western and native cultures as well as her self-determined sexual liberation. While critically successful, sales of *Banana Bottom,* like those of many other literary works, suffered from the continuing onslaught of the GREAT DEPRESSION throughout the 1930s.

On February 1, 1934, McKay returned to New York after more than a decade of living abroad. Although respected for the literary work he had accomplished, he was unable to earn a living from his writings and in 1936 joined the WORK PROGRESS ADMINISTRATION'S FEDERAL WRITERS' PROJECT, maintaining employment with the program for three years. Joining him at the Federal Writers' Project in New York in 1937 were the future author of *Invisible Man,* RALPH ELLISON, and the soon-to-be famous author of *Native Son,* RICHARD NATHANIEL WRIGHT.

A Long Way from Home, McKay's autobiography, was published to approving reviews in 1937 but did not rekindle his earlier popularity. As demands for his writings declined and his health began to deteriorate, McKay drew closer to the Catholic community. Through his former Federal Writers' Project coworker Ellen Tarry, he developed relationships with members of the Catholic-sponsored Friendship House in Harlem. In 1940, he published *Harlem: Negro Metropolis,* a collection of essays inspired by his increasing interest in Catholicism.

Author Claude McKay wrote the first best-selling novel, *Home to Harlem,* by an African American. *(Library of Congress, Prints & Photographs Division, Carl Van Vechten Collection [LC-USZ62-105919])*

Starting in 1942, illness required McKay to spend more and more time in hospitals. He nevertheless managed to work briefly for the Office of War Information in New York before moving to Chicago in 1944. With the help of his friend Mary Keating, he secured a position with a branch of the Catholic Youth Organization as a consultant on race relations. McKay renounced his previous support of the Communist Party and on October 11, 1944, was baptized as Roman Catholic. He died of heart failure on May 22, 1948, at the age of 58 in Chicago.

A volume of *Selected Poems* by Claude McKay was published in 1953 with an introduction by renowned philosopher John Dewey and a biographical portrait of McKay by his old friend Max Eastman. McKay's work remains among the most studied and anthologized in African-American literature.

Further Reading

Tillery, Tyrone. *Claude McKay: A Black Poet's Struggle for Identity.* Amherst: University of Massachusetts Press, 1995.

Winston, James, and Claude McKay. *A Fierce Hatred of Injustice: Claude McKay's Jamaican Poetry of Rebellion.* London: Verso Publishing, 2001.

Wintz, Cary D., ed. *The Politics and Aesthetics of "New Negro Literature."* New York: Garland Publishing, 1996.

— Aberjhani

Messenger

Founded in 1917 and edited by union leaders A. PHILIP RANDOLPH and Chandler Owen, the *Messenger* was a militant, socialist, and irregularly published magazine that featured the work of many Harlem Renaissance poets, writers, and artists.

The editors described the magazine with several different subtitles, all strident in tone, calling it in turn: "The Only Radical Negro Magazine in America"; "A Journal of Scientific Radicalism"; and "The World's Greatest Negro Monthly." The last subtitle adopted for the *Messenger* was "New Opinion of the Negro." It focused primarily on news regarding business, education, politics, WORLD WAR I, political cartoons, trade unions, theater, poetry, short stories, music, and LYNCHING, all in an aggressive, uncompromising voice. And the editors asserted that they exercised a courage and a perception that the *CRISIS: A RECORD OF THE DARKER RACES* and *OPPORTUNITY: A JOURNAL OF NEGRO LIFE* did not dare display.

The stated mission and purpose of the *Messenger*, published by The Messenger Publishing Company at 230 William Street in NEW YORK CITY, was "to create and crystallize sentiment against the present unrighteous conditions through an organized educational campaign; to compile and distribute literature and to conduct public lectures on the vital issues affecting the colored people's economic and political destiny; to appraise men and measures in public life; to examine, expose and condemn cunning and malicious political marplots in the legislative, judicial and executive departments of the city, state and nation; fearlessly to criticize and to denounce selfish and self-styled leaders; to devote our influence uncompromisingly to the advocacy of all principals to the endorsement of all men, and to the support of all movements working for justice and progress."

In 1919, some 100,000 subscribers paid $1.50 to receive the magazine for a year, or one dollar to receive it for eight months. A single copy sold at 15¢ and consisted of approximately 23 pages.

Specific and regular sections of the politically charged *Messenger* included "Economics and Politics," "Education and Literature," "Open Forum," "Book Review," "Who's Who," "Sports," "The Theatre," "The Critic," and a column by the revolutionary historian James A. Rogers. It featured such empowering editorials as one entitled "IF WE MUST DIE." Accompanied by CLAUDE MCKAY's poem of the same name, the editorial stated: "The NEW NEGRO has arrived with stiffened back bone, dauntless manhood, defiant eye, steady hand and a will of iron." Similarly, the magazine's articles fearlessly presented a different attitude from those in the *Crisis* and *Opportunity*—*Messenger* contributors delighted in taking potshots at the ideology of *Crisis* editor W. E. B. DU BOIS—and addressed such controversial issues as "Organizing The Negro Actor," "Socialism: The Negroes' Hope," and "The Failure of the Negro Church."

Even reviews and essay contests had an insolent edge to them. In a 1926 column entitled "The Theater: The Souls of Black Folks," by Theophilus Lewis, the author irreverently dissected the icon, songbird, and darling of Broadway FLORENCE MILLS, whom he reported was "going stale." In 1927, the *Messenger* held an essay contest, asking New York blacks why they liked HARLEM. Contest winner Ira De A. Reid of 136th Street wrote that Harlem was likable not because it was a "Mecca" for blacks but because it was the "Maker of a New Negro," and because of its bums as well as social leaders. She added that Harlem, with its "strained family relations . . . lack of social direction . . . " is "life, Life, LIFE. We suck its breast and enjoy it."

Unabashedly socialist, the *Messenger*'s advertisements reflected its political outlook. Among them was one for "Mill House, A Country School for Colored Children and Others, A Libertarian International School, in Marlborough, New York."

Comments on the magazine came from every quarter: "I want to express to you my pleasure at the publication of a magazine, edited by colored men, that makes as its cornerstone the solidarity of labor, and the absolute need of the Negro's recognizing this solidarity," wrote MARY WHITE OVINGTON, a white board member of the NATIONAL ASSOCIATION FOR THE ADVANCEMENT OF COLORED PEOPLE (NAACP) in New York. The president of the NAACP in WASHINGTON, D.C., Archibald H. Grimké, also a major participant in the intellectual society AMERICAN NEGRO ACADEMY, added that "We . . . are thankful that we have such fearless and able periodicals as *The Messenger* and *The Liberator* to dare to speak out NOW when others grow silent and submit to be muffled."

However, in 1921, the U.S. Department of Justice reported to the U.S. Senate that "*The Messenger*, the monthly magazine published in New York, is by long odds the most able and most dangerous of all the Negro Publications." As if to confirm this report, A. Philip Randolph turned the *Messenger* into a major weapon in his battle to win union representation for the BROTHERHOOD OF SLEEPING CAR PORTERS and other black workers. Although the magazine folded in 1928, Randolph and the porters won their battle in 1937.

Further Reading

Danky, James P., and Maureen E. Hady, eds. *African-American Newspapers and Periodicals: A National Bibliography.* Cambridge: Harvard University Press, 1998.

Johnson, Abby Arthur, and Ronald Maberry Johnson. *Propaganda and Aesthetics: The Literary Politics of Afro-American Magazines in the Twentieth Century.* Amherst: University of Massachusetts Press, 1979.

Smethurst, James E. *The New Red Negro: The Literary Left and African American Poetry, 1930–1946.* New York: Oxford University Press, 1999.

The Messenger. Kraus Microform, Millwood, N.Y., Volume 1–10, no. 5, November 1917–May/June 1928, 6702-001, Microfilm #0001742.

— Sandra L. West

Metcalfe, Ralph Harold (1910–1978) *track and field sprinter*

Ralph Harold Metcalfe won a reputation as "the world's fastest human," along with silver medals in the 100-meter dashes in the 1932 and 1936 Olympics.

Ralph Harold Metcalfe was born on May 30, 1910, in Atlanta, Georgia. He became an outstanding sprinter while growing up in CHICAGO and as a student at Marquette University in Milwaukee, Wisconsin. He had a long stride and was noted for strong finishes. In at least eight 100-meter dashes, he tied the world record of 10.3 seconds. He also tied the world record of 20.6 seconds in the 200-meter dash.

Metcalfe's 100-meter dash at the 1932 Olympics in Los Angeles ended in a virtual dead heat with Eddie Tolan, both men finishing in 10.38 seconds. After hours of deliberation, the judges determined that Tolan won by about an inch. Metcalfe won a silver medal in the 199-meter dash and a bronze medal in the 200-meter dash at the 1932 Games. Eddie Tolan (1909–1967), his great rival, became the first black sprinter to win two Olympic gold medals in 1932.

Metcalfe was a member of the American 4×100-meter relay team that won a gold medal at the 1936 Olympic Games in Berlin. He finished second in the 100-meter dash, winning another silver medal. The victor in these games, a tenth of a second faster, was JESSE OWENS, who won four gold medals.

After his retirement in 1936, Metcalfe attended the University of Southern California, graduating with an M.A. in 1939. He then engaged in a long political career, serving as a Chicago alderman and Democratic ward committeeman, then as a U.S. congressman from Illinois. The "world's fastest runner," who lost only five times in the 100 and three times in the 200 during his five years of competition, became a coach and political science instructor in addition to a politician.

Metcalfe died on October 10, 1978.

Further Reading

Bloom, John, and Michael Nevin, ed. *Sports Matters: Race, Recreation, and Culture.* New York: New York University Press, 2002.

Page, James A. *Black Olympian Medalists.* Colorado: Libraries Unlimited, 1991.

— Sandra L. West

Micheaux, Oscar (1884–1951) *novelist, filmmaker*

In his efforts to inspire African Americans to make economic gains and live practical, virtuous lives, Oscar Micheaux wrote seven novels and produced more than 40 films, including the first all-black feature films of both the silent and the sound film era.

Micheaux was born in Metropolis, Illinois, on January 2, 1884, the fifth of 13 children born to Bell Willingham and Calvin Swan Michaux (original spelling of family name). The senior Michaux was a prosperous farmer who moved his family from rural Illinois to Metropolis to ensure an education for his growing family. In 1901, Michaux and his wife migrated with their family to Great Bend, Kansas. The 17-year-old Oscar moved to CHICAGO where he lived with an older brother and worked alternately shining shoes and as a Pullman porter on the railroad.

Micheaux took advantage of homesteading opportunities in South Dakota in 1905, moving there to work as a ranger and farmer. Around 1911, he married Orlean M. McCracken, a union that reportedly failed due to interference from McCracken's minister father. Micheaux drew heavily upon his experiences as a homesteader and young husband for his first novel, *The Conquest, the Story of a Negro Pioneer.* To pay for the publication of the book, he sold advance copies to neighbors and various business interests. Micheaux dedicated the book "To the Honorable BOOKER T. WASHINGTON." Oscar Devereaux, the hero of the book, is easily recognizable as Micheaux himself and demonstrates the kind of industriousness and economical aspirations that Washington encouraged all African Americans to practice as a means of gradually advancing the black race. Despite his avowed allegiance to the teachings of Washington, Micheaux's control over his creative output and his flexibility as artist also placed him very much in line with both W. E. B. DU BOIS's concept of the "Talented Tenth" and ALAIN LOCKE's description of the *NEW NEGRO.*

With the monies made from the sales on his first novel, Micheaux established the Western Book and Supply Company to publish his next two books: *The Forged Note: A Romance of the Darker Races* in 1915, and *The Homesteader* in 1917. *The Forged Note* further fictionalized Micheaux's biography with an account of his attempts to market his first novel. *The Homesteader* proved a reworking of his first novel, *The Conquest,* with the addition of a then highly controversial theme that Micheaux would explore further in several of his films: interracial romance.

As pleased as he was with *The Homesteader* as a novel, it struck Micheaux that his story would make a powerful film, and he set out in 1918 to teach himself the craft of producing films. Toward that end, he learned to write a script, direct actors, raise capital for production, and distribute his films both throughout some 700 black-oriented theaters in the United States and internationally. Transforming his previous publishing company into the Micheaux Book and Film Company, he filmed a silent version of *The Homesteader* in 1918. It was the first feature-length film by a black company and grossed $5,000. It also provided Micheaux with the means to tackle his next film project: *Within Our Gates.*

As with his first film, Michaeux wrote, produced, directed, and distributed *Within Our Gates* in 1919. He also made a cameo appearance in his film. From the beginning, Michaeux made it clear that his films were meant to provide alternatives to the stereotypical negative portrayals of African Americans in Hollywood films. He intended *Within Our Gates* specifically as a black response to the unapologetically racist film *Birth of a Nation,* produced by D. W. Griffith in 1915. Micheaux's film starred an actress he would feature in at least nine titles, Evenlyn Preer, a former vaudeville performer who had also been a member of the Lafayette Players. *Within Our Gates* told the story of a beautiful, virtuous young black woman of mixed racial ancestry who, following the end of a romance, works selflessly alongside a school's founder to raise funds for the institution. Contrary to the one-dimensional or nonexistent portrayals of black love relationships in films of the era, Micheaux portrayed several complex romantic relationships with a black woman as the principal object of beauty and desire. The film also explored interracial attraction and contained a LYNCHING scene that resulted in protests that caused it to be banned in some cities.

Along with his *The Gunsaulus Mystery* in 1921, and *Lem Hawkins Confession* in 1935, *Within Our Gates* was Micheaux's film interpretation of the well-known Leo M. Frank murder trial. Not only the first recorded case of a Jew being lynched in the United States, the trial also marked the first time a southern white man was found guilty based on the testimony of a black man. Based largely on the testimony of African-American Newt Lee, Leo M. Frank was convicted of murdering 14-year-old factory worker Mary Phagan. After Frank was tried, convicted, and placed in prison, a mob broke into the prison in 1913 and removed and lynched him. Political advocate MARY WHITE OVINGTON paid tribute to Phagan in her poem "Mary Phagan Speaks." No known copies of *Within Our Gates* were thought to have survived until a Spanish version, known as *La Negra,* was discovered and restored in the 1980s, then retranslated into English.

In 1924, Micheaux provided PAUL ROBESON with his first screen appearance in *Body and Soul.* The following year, he produced a study of the life of MARCUS GARVEY called *Marcus Garland.* He released *The Exile* in 1931. A remake of his first film based on his novel *The Homesteader, The Exile* was the first full sound film produced by an African American.

In addition to providing continual work for such actors as Robert Earl Jones, the father of modern Hollywood icon James Earl Jones, Micheaux's films and books created a detailed record of both rural and black urban life during the 1910s, 1920s, 1930s, and 1940s. To keep his production company afloat during the GREAT DEPRESSION, he joined forces with Frank Schiffman of the APOLLO THEATRE.

Micheaux returned to writing novels in 1944 with *The Wind from Nowhere,* followed by *The Case of Mrs. Wingate* in 1945, *The Story of Dorothy Stanfield* in 1946, and *The Masquerade* in 1947. His last film was a three-hour effort in 1948 called *The Betrayal.* Often described as a critical success but a box office failure, the film was Micheaux's final attempt to perfect the story he had originally told in *The Homesteader.*

Micheaux married for the second time in 1928 to actress Alice Russell. The couple lived on Morningside Drive in HARLEM until Micheaux's death in Charlotte, North Carolina, on March 26, 1951.

In 1994, the University of Nebraska Press began to republish Micheaux's novels, starting with *The Conquest.* As of 2001, some 10 of his films are known to exist. Micheaux has become something of a cult figure in Hollywood, and directors such as Spike Lee, Tim Reid, and Robert Townsend cite him as a significant influence. In addition to the establishment of an Oscar Micheaux Theatre in Buffalo, New York, an Oscar Micheaux Award is presented annually in Oakland, California. He also has a star on the Hollywood Boulevard Walk of Fame.

Further Reading

Bowser, Pearl. *Writing Himself Into History: Oscar Micheaux, His Silent Films, and His Audiences.* Piscataway, N.J.: Rutgers University Press, 2000.

Green, J. Ronald. *Straight Lick: The Cinema of Oscar Micheaux.* Bloomington, Ind.: Indiana University Press, 2000.

VanEpps-Taylor, Betti Carol. *Oscar Micheaux, A Biography.* Rapid City, S.D.: Dakota West Books, 1999.

— Aberjhani

Miller, Flournoy See *SHUFFLE ALONG.*

Miller, May (1899–1995) *playwright, poet*

May Miller grew up in the culturally enriched environment of HOWARD UNIVERSITY in WASHINGTON, D.C., to enjoy a literary career producing plays, fiction, and poetry for nine decades.

Miller was the third child of Annie Mae Butler, a teacher at Baltimore Normal School, and Kelly Miller, a professor of sociology and dean of arts and sciences at Howard University. The Millers raised their family in the university's John M. Langston House, where they frequently received such visitors as Paul Laurence Dunbar, Georgia Douglas Johnson, W. E. B. DU BOIS, BOOKER TALIAFERRO WASHINGTON, and WILLIAM STANLEY BEAUMONT BRAITHWAITE. Both her parents and their friends encouraged the young Miller in her study of literature and writing. At Dunbar High School she also received instructions in drama from the playwrights May Burrill and ANGELINA EMILY WELD GRIMKE.

Johnson in particular became one of Miller's mentors, and Miller became one of the Saturday Nighters and Round Table members who met for discussions at Johnson's home. JEAN TOOMER, LANGSTON HUGHES, and ZORA NEALE HURSTON, with whom Miller developed a literary friendship, also attended the discussions. Miller was with Johnson when the latter died in 1966.

Following her graduation from Dunbar High School, Miller attended Howard University. Graduating with honors in 1920, she received during the graduation ceremony an award for her play, *Within the Shadows,* and was treated to a performance of it as part of the proceedings. Miller went on to study poetry and drama at American and Columbia universities. She accepted a teaching position at Frederick Douglass High School in Baltimore, Maryland, and there taught English and speech for 20 years. She married postal worker John Sullivan, who encouraged her literary goals.

Miller had begun experimenting with the possibilities of writing, producing, and acting in plays while still a teenager. In the 1920s, she concentrated on one-act plays and in 1925 won third prize for *The Bog* in the *OPPORTUNITY* magazine's play competition. In 1926, the magazine awarded her an honorable mention for her play *The Curs'd Thing.* Continuing to focus on the one-act play, by the end of the 1930s Miller had produced 20 such dramas. The works were performed at schools and churches throughout Baltimore as well as in university theaters across the United States. One of her most popular plays, *Riding the Goat,* was produced by several different companies in the late 1920s and early 1930s, including the KRIGWA PLAYERS, who performed it in Baltimore in 1932.

In 1930, Miller teamed up with fellow playwright WILLIS RICHARDSON to edit the collection *Plays and Pageants of Negro Life.* Containing several of her own plays, the collection demonstrated Miller's and Richardson's belief in the use of drama to educate audiences about African-American history and foster a greater appreciation for it. The two playwrights again worked together in 1935 when they edited *Negro History in Thirteen Plays.* Miller's work as an editor as well as a playwright continued to generate interest in her work nationwide. In 1933, her antilynching play, *Nails and Thorns,* won an award in a drama competition at Southern University in Baton Rouge, Louisiana. In *Nails and Thorns,* an exceptional work for its time, the author exercised a unique perspective as a black writer examining the moral consequences of the LYNCHING of an African American on a white family.

Whereas Miller had no qualms about producing plays for political and educational purposes, she believed poetry was a genre designed to communicate a more individually artistic vision, and after 1943 she ceased working in theater to concentrate on her poetic vision. Journals that published her poetry included *CRISIS*, Phylon, the *Nation,* the *New York Times,* and the *Antioch Review.* Starting in 1959, she published seven volumes of poetry: *Into the Clearing* (1959), *Poems* (1962), *Not That Far* (1973), *The Clearing and Beyond* (1974), *Dust of Uncertain Journey* (1975), *Halfway to the Sun* (1981), and *The Ransomed Wait* (1983). In 1964, she shared author credits with Katie Lyle and Maude Rubin for *Lyrics of Three Women.*

In the tradition of her parents and friend Georgia Douglas Johnson, Miller hosted a salon for writers and artists to gather at her home on S Street in Washington, D.C. Some of those who joined the discussions were Frank Horne, GWENDOLYN BROOKS, Charles Sebree, Owen Dodson, and Toni Morrison.

Miller died in Washington, D.C., on February 8, 1995, at the age of 96.

Further Reading

Gavin, Christy, and C. James Trotman, eds. *African American Women Playwrights: A Research Guide.* New York: Garland Publishing, 1999.

Russell, Sandi. *Render Me My Song: African-American Women Writers from Slavery to the Present.* San Francisco: Harper Books, 2001.

— Aberjhani

Mills, Florence (1895–1927) *entertainer*

Singer, dancer, and actor Florence Mills appeared in two classics of black vaudeville before the age of 10 and was the most celebrated black performer in the United States and Europe when she died at the young age of 32.

Mills was the youngest of three children, all daughters, born to Nellie Simon and John Winfrey. Her parents were former slaves who labored as tobacco workers. Her mother later became a laundress and her father a day laborer. Her older sisters, with whom she would later perform for a time, were Olivia and Maude.

Mills's abilities were recognized as early as age four when she was given a walk-on part in the first Broadway musical produced by African Americans, Bob Cole's and William Johnson's *A Trip to Coontown,* in 1899. Four years later, she joined BERT WILLIAMS and GEORGE WALKER for the tour of their show *Sons of Ham,* in which the eight-year-old Mills sang "Miss Hannah from Savannah."

She moved with her family to NEW YORK CITY around 1905 and as a teenager performed with her siblings as The Mills Sisters. Touring the THEATER OWNERS BOOKING AGENCY (TOBA) circuit throughout the South, Mills witnessed and experienced acts of racist cruelty she never forgot, and in time she used her celebrity status to quietly wage protest against them.

Mills met U.S. (Slow Kid) Thompson, a comedian and dancer, while still on the vaudeville circuit. Once married, they made it a point to work in the same shows and toured the Keith Circuit with a group called the Tennessee Ten. Mills made the transition out of vaudeville when she became a cabaret performer with the future international hostess and performer BRICKTOP at the Panama Club in CHICAGO. Along with Cora Green, she and Bricktop formed a group called the Panama Trio and were fairly successful until Bricktop departed for New York. They reunited when Mills also went to New York and worked with Bricktop at the BARRON'S EXCLUSIVE CLUB in HARLEM.

Mills arrived in New York in 1921 just as NOBLE SISSLE and EUBIE BLAKE's musical, *SHUFFLE ALONG,* was on its way to making show business history. When one of its principal stars, Gertrude Saunders, left the show for other opportunities, Bricktop recommended Mills as a replacement to Harriet Toy Sissle, Noble Sissle's first wife, who in turn took the suggestion to her husband. Sissle and Blake both had doubts about the contrast of Mills's "flute-like" voice with that of Saunders's earthier delivery. They had, in fact, written several of the show's key songs specifically for Saunders. Nevertheless, Mills's debut performance drew 18 encores and launched one of the most spectacular careers of the 1920s JAZZ Age.

Following *Shuffle Along*'s Broadway run of more than 500 shows, Mills bypassed an offer to join the ZIEGFELD FOLLIES and opted instead to accept a contract performing for Lew Leslie's PLANTATION CLUB. There, she performed with composer Will Vodery's Plantation Orchestra and worked with Leslie to develop the *Plantation Review.* Despite charges that the *Plantation Review* contained risqué humor bordering on the vulgar, it set the stage for Mills's first trip to England in 1923 to perform in *Dover Street to Dixie* at the prestigious London Pavilion. English protesters against the show, presumably acting on the assumption that it was imported racism, were literally overcome by Mills's performance. Upon hearing her sing, protests against the review ceased. The British press hailed Mills as a creative genius and "the most artistic person London had ever had the good fortune to see."

Dover Street to Dixie turned out to be something of a trial run for *Dixie to Broadway,* which in 1924 had a successful two-month run back in New York. With *Shuffle Along,* the *Plantation Review, Dover Street to Dixie,* and *Dixie to Broadway* all part of her credits, Mills commanded a weekly salary of almost $4,000 in the mid-1920s.

Mills's voice was inevitably described by reviewers in fairly ethereal terms. Sissle and Blake said she possessed the rare quality of being "lovable," while JAMES WELDON JOHNSON wrote that "her voice was full of bubbling, bell-like, bird-like tones." A petite and graceful woman, it was by nearly all accounts the manner in which she used her voice mattered more than its actual quality. The man called "the dean of black composers," WILLIAM GRANT STILL, found himself so enchanted by Mills's talent that in 1926 he featured her as a soloist for his three-movement suite, *Levee Land.*

That year—1926—was also the year Mills enjoyed her greatest triumph starting with the debut of her show *BLACKBIRDS* at the ALHAMBRA THEATRE in Harlem. Performing with BOJANGLES ROBINSON, Johnny Hudgins, and Earl "Snakehips" Tucker, Mills's appearance in *Blackbirds* helped end the discrimination against black patrons attending performances by black entertainers at the Alhambra. The show introduced the song that would become her signature, "I'm a Little Blackbird Looking for a Bluebird." It also included the now classic "I Can't Give You Anything but Love" and "Dig-a Dig-a Do."

With a string of successful Broadway shows and appearances in Europe, performer Florence Mills had achieved international stardom and become a favored Harlem celebrity when she died in 1927 at the age of 32. *(Photographs and Prints Division, Schomburg Center for Research in Black Culture, The New York Public Library, Astor, Lenox and Tilden Foundations)*

Blackbirds went from Harlem to Europe, where it played in PARIS and London for a total of 11 months. In Paris, it was impossible for Mills to avoid comparisons to expatriate star and former costar from *Shuffle Along,* JOSEPHINE BAKER. Whereas the press touted Mills as the greater performer, Mills herself and Baker generally expressed admiration and fondness for each other.

In England, Mills sealed her reputation as a rare and consummate entertainer with sold-out performances and frequent interviews with the press. Her status in Europe and the United States increased as reports came out that the Prince of Wales attended her show repeatedly until he had seen it nearly two dozen times. Yet for all the attention and adulation heaped upon her, Mills retained a humble sense of service on behalf of African Americans. Addressing an audience at Picadilly Cabaret, she spoke openly about the pains of racism and the need for greater racial equality. Talking with a reporter from the *London Express,* she explained her hope that "my own success will make people think better of other colored folk."

Mills vacationed in Germany before preparing for the Broadway debut of *Blackbirds* and returned to New York in October 1927 to a heroine's welcome. The *Inter-State Tattler* stated unabashedly: "It is not too much to say that some of us even worship her, for it is only a step from the pedestal of a heroine to the immortality of a goddess."

After postponing an appendectomy as long as she could, Mills had the surgery in late October 1927. She died a week later on November 1. Her death made international headlines, and the people of Harlem mourned her loss by the thousands. A eulogy written by Bill Robinson was read by Fred Moore of the *NEW YORK AGE* at the Mother Zion Church. More than 100,000 people insisted on viewing her body as it lay in state for four days, and more than twice that many filled the streets during her funeral.

The Florence Mills Theatrical Society was founded in the performer's memory to raise funds to build a retirement home for black entertainers. When *BLACKBIRDS OF 1928* opened on Broadway the following year, Aida Ward sang a song newly added to the show, *A Memory of 1927,* in honor of Mills.

Further Reading

Gill, Glenda E. E. *No Surrender! No Retreat! African-American Pioneer Performers of Twentieth Century American Theatre.* New York: St. Martin's Press, 2000.

Marks, Carole, and Diana Edkins. *The Power of Pride: Stylemakers and Rulebreakers of the Harlem Renaissance.* New York: Crown Publishing Group, 1999.

Reed, Bill. *Hot From Harlem: Profiles of Classic African American Entertainment.* Los Angeles: Cellar Door Books, 1998.

— Aberjhani

"Minnie the Moocher"

Written by COTTON CLUB bandleader CAB CALLOWAY and composer Irving Mills in 1931, "Minnie the Moocher" was the first major hit for Cab Calloway's Cotton Club Orchestra and was adopted as the band's theme song.

So popular and successful was "Minnie the Moocher" that it subsequently generated several recorded sequels, a short film, and an autobiography.

Calloway and Mills combined styles and influences from several popular songs of the era to compose "Minnie the Moocher." The team used a traditional BLUES song called "St. James Infirmary," plus two then popular songs entitled "Minnie the Mermaid" and "Willie the Weeper," as models for their own. Despite the song's repeated and seemingly comic refrain, "Hi-dee hi-dee hi-dee ho," the song was actually the tale of a tragedy. Its title character, described by Calloway as "a low-down hoochy coocher," is a tough but sincere and generous woman whose involvement with a drug addict named "Smoky" leads her to become the same. In acknowledgment of her downfall, Calloway ends the song with the lament, "Poor Min, poor Min." The song provided a pointed commentary on the drug culture that entered with the JAZZ Age of the 1920s and in many cases remained a part of the club scene in the United States.

In 1932, Harold Arlen and Ted Koehler, who also composed "Stormy Weather," wrote "Minnie the Moocher's Wedding Day," the first follow-up to the original song. It employed much of the same drug imagery as its predecessor. In the same year, filmmaker Dave Fleisher directed a short animated film named after the song and featuring the now classic cartoon character Betty Boop. Calloway provided vocals for the film.

Enough bands and individual artists have recorded and dramatized "Minnie the Moocher" that Calloway in his autobiography, *Of Minnie the Moocher and Me,* credits the song's royalties with helping him to build a fortune. Among those who recorded it were DOROTHY DANDRIDGE and the Dandridge Sisters in 1940.

In addition to Arlen and Koehler's song, other recorded sequels to "Minnie the Moocher" were "Big-Mouth Minnie," in 1938, by Calloway, Andy Razaf, Walter Thomas, and Joe Davis; and "Minnie Grew Up Overnight," by Calloway, Hall Seeger, and Buster Harding.

Aside from his "Minnie the Moocher" recordings, Calloway enjoyed a number of hits that became standards of the time. Among them were "The Jitterbug" in 1934, written by Calloway, Mills, and Ed Swayzee; and "The Jumpin' Jive" in 1939, by Calloway, Frank Froeba, and Jack Palmer. "Minnie the Moocher," however, remains his most enduring musical creation, and videos and compact discs featuring the internationally known song and character are generally available throughout the United States.

Further Reading

Kanfer, Stefan. *Serious Business: The Art and Commerce of Animation in America from Betty Boop to Toy Story.* New York: Da Capo Press, 2000.

Travis, Dempsey Jerome. *Cab Calloway.* New York: Urban Renewal Press, 1994.

— Aberjhani

Missourians, The

Originally from Kansas City and St. Louis, Missouri, The Missourians became one of NEW YORK CITY's top jazz bands during the 1920s and, as CAB CALLOWAY's COTTON CLUB Orchestra, one of the top SWING bands in the United States during the 1930s.

The band was founded in 1923 as Wilson Robinson's Synchopators. Trombonist DePriest Wheeler and drummer Leroy Maxey remained with the group as it evolved throughout the decade, moving to New York in 1926 and becoming the SAVOY BALLROOM's house band under the direction of Lockwood Lewis. In addition to Wheeler and Maxey, its members included trumpeters Lamar Wright, Reuben Reeves, and R. Q. Dickerson; trombonist Harry White; saxophonists Walter Thomas, Bill Blue, and Andy Brown; bassist Jimmy Smith; banjoist Charley Stamps; and pianist Earres Prince.

The Missourians became known for an energetic, aggressive style of jazz that helped to develop and define the big band sound of swing music. Among their early recordings were "Prohibition Blues," "Swingin Dem Cats," and "St. James Infirmary." On May 4, 1929, they teamed up with Cab Calloway to compete in a six-band Battle of Jazz held at the Savoy. Their opponents were FESS WILLIAMS and the Royal Flush Orchestra; the Cotton Club Orchestra; the Ike Dixon Band; the Happy Pals Band; and the DUKE ELLINGTON Orchestra. With Calloway as their guest vocalist, the Missourians won the event performing "Tiger Rag."

In 1930 Calloway formed a more permanent partnership with the Missourians after performing in Connie's *HOT CHOCOLATES*. Accepting an invitation to replace the Duke Ellington Orchestra at the Cotton Club, The Missourians and Calloway became the Cab Calloway Cotton Club Orchestra. In March 1931, they recorded "MINNIE THE MOOCHER." The song sold more than a million copies and became both Calloway's signature song and the band's theme song.

The Missourians recorded and toured with Calloway throughout the GREAT DEPRESSION.

Further Reading

Jensen, Everette, and Norma Miller. *Swingin' at the Savoy: The Memoirs of a Jazz Dancer.* Philadelphia: Temple University Press, 2001.

Reed, Bill. *Hot from Harlem: Profiles in Classic African American Entertainment.* Los Angeles: Cellar Door Books, 1998.

— Aberjhani

Morton, Jelly Roll (Ferdinand Joseph Lamothe)

(1890–1941) *musician*

One of the early innovators of RAGTIME music, Jelly Roll Morton helped establish the foundation for JAZZ and SWING with energetic performances and compositions that blended such diverse musical traditions as black spirituals, the BLUES, Hispanic folk music, NEW ORLEANS Creole, Caribbean music, and classical European.

Morton was born Ferdinand Joseph Lamothe on October 20, 1890, in New Orleans, to Louise Monette and Edward J. Lamothe. He later adopted the last name of the man who became his stepfather, Ed Morton. Both his parents were light-complexioned Creole, and throughout his life Morton often referred to himself as white rather than black.

Morton's childhood years were spent in a house on Frenchmen Street in what was known as New Orleans's Third Municipality. He started playing the guitar by the age of six but later chose the piano as his preferred musical instrument. He added to his natural abilities studying music in St. Benedict, Louisiana, at St. Joseph's Seminary College. At the age of 12, Morton was accomplished enough to earn $100 a night playing in the brothels of New Orleans's Storyville district. He was still a teenager when he played at the 1904 St. Louis World Fair and toured throughout the United States. He learned to supplement his income as a pianist by singing and performing comedy in vaudeville, hustling pool, and playing cards.

He played clubs in NEW YORK CITY in 1911 and in 1912 formed a band in CHICAGO. In 1915, Morton became the first musician to publish a jazz arrangement with the publication of his composition "Jelly Roll Blues." In the same year, he moved to California and from there embarked on tours in Vancouver, Alaska, and Mexico. During that period, in California he met Anita Gonzales, the woman with whom he maintained a relationship for more than two decades and identified as his common-law wife.

Morton made his first professional recordings on the Gennett Recording label in Richmond, Indiana, in 1923. There, he recorded a number of songs that illustrate both the versatility and the individualism that marked Morton as a pioneer of the jazz solo piano. These included: "The Pearls," "Kansas City Stomp," "Grandpa's Spells," and "King Porter Stomp." From 1926 to 1930, Morton recorded steadily with Victor Records in Chicago and New York. During that time, he produced such now classic works as "Wild Man Blues," "Black Bottom Stomp," and "Dead Man Blues."

During the 1920s Morton also gained a reputation for conceit that sometimes made it difficult to find musicians willing to work with him, though much of his best work was done with his own ensemble, the Red Hot Peppers. He contended to have founded jazz in 1902, called himself the best pianist in the world, and accused others of stealing his compositions. He was fond of flashing large rolls of money as well as a diamond-studded tooth. He was also known, at different times, to supplement his income by acting as a pimp.

During the 1930s, Morton moved back and forth between the west and east coast, playing engagements in clubs as well as managing one in WASHINGTON, D.C. Demand for his talents decreased with the rise of swing music and the advent of the GREAT DEPRESSION. Nevertheless, in the summer and December of 1938, he made some 52 records consisting of more than 100 pieces for the Fold Music Archives of the Library of Congress. Working with Alan Lomax, in addition to his music, Morton provided commentaries on the history of jazz and analyses of his specific playing style. Among the songs he recorded were "The Naked Dance," "Whinin' Boy Blues," and "Ballin' the Jack." From his work with Morton and additional interviews with acquaintances, Lomax wrote the first major biography on the musician, *Mister Jelly Roll,* published in 1950. While this biography is generally considered a definitive work on Morton's life, data recently discovered by Lawrence Gushee and Philip Pastras have provided further insights and clarifications regarding the musician's life.

Because Morton's was a mercurial temperament that embodied both profound creativity and illicit practices, he has often been viewed as one of the most controversial figures in the history of American music. With growing studies of his work, he is now increasingly considered to have been a genius.

Morton died on July 10, 1941, in Los Angeles. He left most of the royalties from his recordings to Anita Gonzales, who was with him at his death. Gonzales died on April 24, 1952.

Further Reading

Lomax, Alan. *Mister Jelly Roll: The Fortunes of Jelly Roll Morton, New Orleans Creole and Inventor of Jazz.* Berkeley: University of California Press, 2001.

Pastras, Philip. *Dead Man Blues: Jelly Roll Morton Way Out West.* Berkeley: University of California Press, 2001.

— Aberjhani

Motley, Archibald John, Jr. (1891–1981) *painter*

A painter of varied scenes from African-American culture, Archibald John Motley, Jr., part of the CHICAGO contingent of the Harlem Renaissance and one of the most brilliant colorists of the era, was still a student when he first exhibited his work at the Arts and Letters Society in 1917.

Archibald John Motley, Jr., was born in 1891 in NEW ORLEANS, Louisiana. His father, Archibald John Motley, Sr., was a Pullman porter who wanted his son to become a doctor. His mother, Mary F. Huff Motley, was a teacher. When his family migrated from Louisiana, they settled at 350 West 60th Street in the Englewood section of Chicago.

Motley's childhood activities included everything from attendance at Olivet Baptist Church to hanging out at Rick's Pool Room. He was educated at the School of the Art Institute of Chicago (SAIC). There he participated in the first show in Chicago to exhibit works by black artists, the Arts and Letters Society exhibit of 1917. He received Class Honorable Mention for oil portraiture in 1918.

Motley's theme was black people engaging in various activities in different environments. He loved JAZZ and a good party but had a quiet side that came out in a series of portraits he painted in the 1920s. *The Octoroon* (1922) and *The Octoroon Girl* (1925) are very quiet and elegant portraits of beautiful African-American women. He experimented with depictions of Vodun (Voodoo) in 1927. Motley made the first page of the *New York Times* in 1928 after his one-man exhibition at the New Gallery at 600 Madison Avenue in NEW YORK CITY and continued his series on black women with *Aline: An Octoroon.* In 1929, *The Octoroon Girl* won the HARMON FOUNDATION Gold Medal.

Living in PARIS in 1929, Motley painted *The Jockey Club,* which also included black people. He further painted black couples—with the women adorned in pearls—dancing on a crowded nightclub floor (*Blues,* 1929), and a charismatic man and woman kicking up their heels in a cabaret in *Saturday Night* (1935). The real-life cabaret that Motley drew from for *Saturday Night* was Cabaret de Champion at 42 West 31st Street in Chicago, a facility owned by boxer JACK JOHNSON in 1912. As always, his canvas included vibrant red.

Motley joined the WORKS PROGRESS ADMINISTRATION (WPA) in 1935 and became an artist-in-residence at HOWARD UNIVERSITY in WASHINGTON, D.C. Howard commissioned him to paint murals in Douglas Hall. Since that time, the murals have been painted over and are lost to the contemporary viewer. Motley continued to paint and exhibit until his death in 1981.

Further Reading

Leininger-Muller, Theresa A. *New Negro Artists in Paris: African American Painters and Sculptors in the City of Light, 1922–1934.* Piscataway, N.J.: Rutgers University Press, 2000.

Robinson, Jontyle Theresa. *Art of Archibald J. Motley, Jr.* Chicago: Chicago Historical Society, 1991.

— Sandra L. West

Mule Bone

Mule Bone, the product of a brief partnership between writers ZORA NEALE HURSTON and LANGSTON HUGHES, was the first African-American comedy written by African Americans outside the minstrel show tradition.

Hughes was in the process of promoting his new drama, *Mulatto,* when New York Theater Guild founder Theresa Helburn expressed interest in a comedy about African Americans. Discussing the idea with Hurston, the two writers decided in 1930 to tackle the project together. Aware of the historical significance should they succeed, they initially kept their plans secret.

The team worked at a boardinghouse in Westfield, New Jersey. Typing the manuscript for them was stenographer LOUISE THOMPSON PATTERSON, whose services were paid for by CHARLOTTE OSGOOD MASON, the PATRON known to Hughes and Hurston as "Godmother." The writers utilized for the basis of their comedy a black folk story from a collection gathered by Hurston. Reportedly, Hughes worked on its plot structure and character development while Hurston developed the dialogue.

They finished drafts for the first and third acts of a three-act comedy with a partial draft and notes for a second act. Hurston then traveled south, taking the incomplete work with her and agreeing to complete the draft for the second act. With that understanding between them, Hughes involved himself in other projects.

Juggling possible titles for their play, Hurston and Hughes chose the more comical *Mule Bone* over the more dramatic *Bone of Contention.* The play revolves largely around two friends who are also entertainers, Jim and Dave. They argue over a beautiful young woman named Daisy until Jim hits Dave in the head with a mule bone. In the original folk story, the argument is between two hunters over a turkey. The townspeople consider the blow from the mule bone so violent that they hold a trial in a church where Baptists and Methodists take different sides in the argument. Jim is run out of town, where he encounters both Daisy and his friend Dave. The friends argue again over Daisy but in the end decide that giving up their life as entertainers would be too big a sacrifice for marriage. They resume their friendship and encourage Daisy to find a local man more capable of working a traditional job and supporting her in the manner she would prefer. The friends then depart with Jim playing the guitar and Dave dancing along railroad tracks.

With Hurston in the South, Hughes traveled to Cleveland where he spent time with his family and underwent a tonsillectomy. He was attending a play at Cleveland's KARAMU HOUSE when Rowena Jelliffe, codirector of the House, informed him that the Gilpin Players were preparing to produce a black folk comedy by Zora Neale Hurston called *Mule Bone.* Jelliffe was stunned to learn that Hughes had coauthored the play just as Hurston was surprised to learn that Jelliffe was considering producing it.

During a cross fire of telephone messages, letters, and telegrams, Hughes learned that Hurston had forwarded a slightly altered version of the play to writer CARL VAN VECHTEN without informing Van Vechten that Hughes had coauthored it. Van Vechten, who often promoted African-American writers, passed the play onto different agencies until the Samuel French theatrical agency acted on it and sent it to Cleveland. Confusion and controversy escalated over the play until Hurston claimed sole ownership of it. She had, in fact, secretly copyrighted the play solely in her name with the title *De Turkey and de Law.* While hoping Hurston and Hughes would somehow resolve the issue, Jelliffe continued making plans for the Gilpin Players to stage a production of *Mule Bone* at the Theatre of Nations under the auspices of the *Cleveland Plain Dealer* newspaper.

Van Vechten, philosopher and editor ALAIN LOCKE, and lawyer Arthur Spingarn were all consulted on the matter. Van Vechten was primarily interested in the historical importance of the play and hoped to see it produced at any cost. Locke, who had introduced Hughes to Charlotte Mason, was reportedly nurturing a grudge against Hughes for ending the relationship with Mason and chose to side with Hurston. Spingarn advised both Hughes and Hurston to avoid litigation. When Jelliffe compared Hughes's copy of the original play to the one she had received citing only Hurston as the author, she wrote Spingarn that the work was clearly a collaborative effort between the writers and stated further that Hurston had treated Hughes "very badly."

Hurston declined Hughes's offer to grant her two-thirds ownership of the play. She accused Hughes of trying to obtain royalties from the play for Patterson and stated that the play would never be produced. Her command stood for 60 years until Michael Schultz, some 31 years after Hurston's death in 1960, and 24 years after Hughes's in 1967, produced it at Lincoln Center in 1991 with BLUES master Taj Mahal singing Hughes's songs. Mahal also recorded Hughes's song to make them available on CD. In addition, the play did finally get its Cleveland production at the Karamu Performing Arts Center in May 1996. Directed by Sarah May, it starred Nile Rivers as Jim, Kyle Primous as Dave, and Sonya Leslie as Daisy, with music by "Mississippi" Charles Bevels.

Further Reading

Fabre, Genevieve, and Michel Feith. *Temples for Tomorrow: Looking Back at the Harlem Renaissance.* Bloomington: Indiana University Press, 2001.

Hurston, Zora Neale. *Mule Bone.* New York: Harper Collins, 2000.

— Aberjhani

museums, African-American university

The artistic assets of several historically black colleges and universities (HBCUs) in the United States constitute a virtual "who's who" of Harlem Renaissance art and artists and provide a uniquely definitive view of the era.

Art museums at black colleges had extremely humble beginnings. The Hampton University Art Museum in Virginia began with a handful of simple items but stands today as a leading facility among all black college art museums. In terms of Harlem Renaissance art holdings, art instruction, annual exhibitions, and art degree programs, Hampton University, Atlanta University, HOWARD UNIVERSITY, and FISK UNIVERSITY are some of the most artistically endowed universities within the HBCU group.

Hampton University

The art museum at Hampton University (formerly Hampton Normal and Agricultural Institute in Virginia) has one of the strongest collections of Harlem Renaissance and other art of all the HBCUs in the United States. The collection started in 1868 with a few modest objects from Hawaii.

In August 1868, General Samuel Chapman Armstrong, the university's founder, started the museum collection with samples of coral, lava, and other "curiosities" found in Hawaii, where he had been raised. With these items, Armstrong initiated a museum that he hoped would expand the education of his 15 African-American agricultural and technical students, especially in the academic disciplines of world geography, world cultures, and world history.

By 1870, Armstrong's interest in a diverse education gave way to an African studies program at Hampton, and the museum acquired African materials. When in 1879 fire destroyed Academic Hall, home of the early museum, the African articles and identifying inventory were also destroyed. However, as the museum was rebuilt in the 1880s, two alumni contributed ample replacements.

Alumnus Ackrel F. White presented to the museum objects he had acquired while a missionary in Sierra Leone, West Africa, during the 1870s. In 1911, another alumnus made a generous presentation. Dr. William H. Sheppard, a missionary from 1890 to 1910 in what was then known as Zaire, conferred upon Hampton articles he had acquired on his African journey. With acquisitions from Sierra Leone and the 400 items from the Sheppard Collection, the museum was fully restored.

In 1878, and for the next 45 years, Hampton officials began collecting Native American art for the museum as they registered and educated 1,300 Native American boarding students from 65 different tribes. Still, with a sharp focus on African-American art, in 1894 the museum acquired two paintings by HENRY OSSAWA TANNER. One of them was the masterful *The Banjo Lesson.*

By the time of the Harlem Renaissance in the 1920s, the art museum founded to expand the basic education of agricultural students and to foster racial pride in African Americans, Native Americans, and other ethnic groups was the only art museum in the South that welcomed African Americans as patrons.

During the 1960s—1967 especially—art museum holdings at select HBCUs grew by the hundreds. Paintings, works on paper, and sculptures were donated to the schools from the collection of the now-defunct HARMON FOUNDATION. Included in this art for Hampton were works by Harlem Renaissance artists HALE ASPACID WOODRUFF; PALMER COLE HAYDEN; ARCHIBALD JOHN MOTLEY, JR.; WILLIAM HENRY JOHNSON; SARGENT CLAUDE JOHNSON; AARON DOUGLAS; and JACOB ARMSTEAD LAWRENCE.

Since 1978, more than 500 pieces have been added, including work by LOIS MAILOU JONES. In 1986, the museum purchased the Countee and Ida Cullen Art Collection of 29 paintings and sculptures from six major 20th-century artists who were friends of the Harlem Renaissance poet and his wife. Further, the university museum has actively acquired artwork created by Hampton University graduates John T. Biggers, Samella S. Lewis, ELIZABETH ALICE CATLETT, and others.

Hampton University by 2002 offered a major in museum studies. The Hampton University Museum contained more than 9,000 objects and works of art in its collection, offered museum programs to the community, and published the *International Review of African-American Art* founded in 1982.

Atlanta University

In 1942, Hale Woodruff, muralist and art instructor at Spelman College in Atlanta, Georgia, initiated an annual art exhibition at nearby Atlanta University. Exhibits were held from April 1942 to April 1970 and resulted in the acquisition of works by major artists for the university's collection. Exhibition awards were granted in the amounts of $50 to $250. The first show captured 107 paintings. Sixty-seven artists exhibited their works. That inaugural year, winners were William Carter of CHICAGO, Illinois; Frederick Flemister of Atlanta, Georgia; and Edward I. Loper of Wilmington, Delaware, for oil painting. CHARLES HENRY ALSTON of NEW YORK CITY and LOIS MAILOU JONES of WASHINGTON, D.C., won for watercolors. Judges included Woodruff and AARON DOUGLAS, Harlem Renaissance painter and a professor at Fisk University, and others.

The Atlanta University Art Collection grew as a direct result of the annual exhibitions and corporations that gave pieces of art to the collection. Harlem Renaissance artists in the Collection include *Two Alone* by CHARLES WILBERT WHITE, *Young Girl* by ELIZABETH CATLETT, and *The Quiet One* by WILLIAM ELLISWORTH ARTIS.

Howard University

Located in the Shaw neighborhood of Washington, D.C., Howard University was the first African-American university to open an art gallery devoted to contemporary art. It was also the place where many notable black artists who emerged during the Harlem Renaissance or worked on Works Progress Administration (WPA) art projects exhibited their work and taught the next generation of visual artists.

Although Hampton University Art Museum had begun operating in 1868, the Howard University Gallery of Art became in 1928 the first art gallery in a black educational institution devoted to contemporary and international arts. In addition to pieces by African and African-American artists, the Howard collection contained substantial examples of Chinese and Japanese art, with James V. Herring and James A. Porter as the first directors.

Howard invested early on in a full-service art department. In 1921, the school officials established a degree program. Professor Herring directed the program for artists. A staunch realist, he passed the technique on to his students, teaching them to paint everything that they saw. The students dared not create an urban or rural landscape without depicting every tree and everything else that came within their vision. Because many of them hailed from the rural south, the outhouse, or outside bathroom, was part of their reality. As such, so many of Herring's students included the rural outhouse in their work that during his tenure Howard University became known as "The Outhouse School."

In 1943 Herring cofounded the Barnet-Aden Gallery. Black artists who had a difficult time exhibiting their work in mainstream galleries during the period between the Harlem Renaissance years and the Black Arts movement of the 1960s found a place at the Barnet-Aden Gallery. Herring and Alonzo J. Aden, gallery co-owners, created art and initiated artistic academic institutions still enjoyed in the early 21st century. Aden served for 10 years as curator of the Howard University Gallery of Art and died in 1961. The Washington, D.C., Barnet-Aden Gallery has since closed.

Artist, critic, and art historian James A. Porter received his bachelor's degree in art in 1926 from Howard and was appointed assistant professor the following year. He was married to Dorothy Porter, Howard librarian, archivist, and scholar of African-American literary societies.

Notable Harlem Renaissance artists taught and received their education at Howard. Lois Mailou Jones studied there and, from 1930 to 1977, taught courses in design and watercolor painting. JAMES LESESNE WELLS taught at Howard, and MAY HOWARD JACKSON instructed students in sculpture for several years.

In 1935, Archibald Motley, Jr., was artist-in-residence at the school, a residency made possible by the U.S. Department of the Treasury Art Project, a division of the WPA. Unfortunately, the murals Motley created in the Frederick Douglass Building at Howard no longer exist.

Sculptor Elizabeth Catlett graduated cum laude from Howard in 1936. ALLAN RANDALL FREELON had a one-man show at Howard in 1940. Hughie Lee-Smith had a major exhibition at the university, and his works are included in the private collection there. The work of painter and sculptor Margaret Taylor Burroughs, equally known for her writing and institutional building skills, can also be found in the school's collection.

Fisk University

Located in Knoxville, Tennessee, Fisk University began its art collection in 1876 with African and Native American art that was housed in the basement of the university's theology building.

Sculptor Elizabeth Catlett, a visiting instructor in the Art Department at Fisk in 1943, and her husband Charles Wilbert White also contributed to the development of black college museums. While Catlett served as an educator, White completed the mural *The Negro's Contribution to Democracy* for one of the assembly halls at the school.

The legacy of Aaron Douglas is apparent in several areas of Fisk. Philosopher ALAIN LOCKE, an art collector and editor of the *NEW NEGRO*, cited Douglas as the premier artist of the Harlem Renaissance. In 1939, Douglas was named to the faculty of Fisk and later became head of its Department of Art Education. The Aaron Douglas Papers are in Fisk's Special Collections, and the Fisk University Collection of African-American Art houses his mural series, *The Symbolic Negro History Series,* painted in the 1930s in the Erastus Milo Cravath Library (now the administration building). Douglas received assistance on this mural from painter and photographer EDWIN AUGUSTUS HARLESTON of South Carolina. Also included in the Fisk Collection are photographs taken by Harlem Renaissance photographer and writer CARL VAN VECHTEN.

In 2002 Fisk was also home to works by WILLIAM HENRY JOHNSON, James A. Porter, Elizabeth Catlett, and Charles White.

In addition to those institutions already mentioned, a number of other colleges and universities maintain significant collections: the small museum at Virginia Union University in Richmond includes Thornton Dial folk art originals, and Hale Woodruff painted the eminent *Amistad Murals* at Talladega College in Alabama. Significant collections have also been deposited at Spelman College in Atlanta, Georgia; at Morgan State College in Baltimore, Maryland; and at Dillard University in Baton Rouge, Louisiana.

Further Reading

Bailey, David A., and Paul Gilroy. *Rhapsodies in Black: Art of the Harlem Renaissance.* Berkeley: University of California Press, 1997.

Beckman, Wendy Hart. *Artists and Writers of the Harlem Renaissance.* Enslow Publishers, 2002.

Coleman, Floyd. "Black Colleges and the Development of an African-American Visual Arts Tradition." *The International Review of African-American Art* 11, 1994.

Powell, Richard, and Jock Reynolds. *To Conserve a Legacy: American Art from Historically Black Colleges and Universities.* Andover, Mass.: Addison Gallery of American Art, 1999.

— Sandra L. West

National Association for the Advancement of Colored People (NAACP)

One of the boldest experiments in the struggle to obtain social and political equality for African Americans began when William English Walling, MARY WHITE OVINGTON, and Henry Moscowitz, three white Americans, met in Walling's Manhattan apartment in 1909 to discuss strategies for countering the rise of mob violence against blacks in the United States.

Somewhat accustomed to such violence in the South, they had all been stunned when on September 3, 1908, it took a particularly vicious swing toward the North in Springfield, Illinois, the birthplace of Abraham Lincoln. Fueled by an unfounded charge of rape, the riot raged for two days. During that period, two black men were lynched and four whites were killed. Property damage reached nearly a quarter-million dollars, and hundreds of blacks (some estimate 2,000) fled the city of Lincoln's birth and burial to save their lives. Walling arrived in Springfield just as the National Guard was called in to restore order, and he wrote an article entitled "Race War in the North" and published it in the *Independent* newspaper. Walling's article warned that the Springfield riot was an indication that the United States must either return to "the spirit of the abolitionists" or prepare for a race war likely to engulf the entire nation.

Ovington, a social worker and writer, and Moscowitz, also a social worker and an immigrant Jew from Russia, felt strongly enough about Walling's journalistic outcry that they decided literary protest was no longer enough. Further meetings brought in Oswald Garrison Villard, publisher of the *New York Evening Post* and future publisher of *The Nation.* The group decided to publish on February 12, 1909, the centennial of Lincoln's birth, a call for a conference that would deal head-on with the reality of American racism. Drafted by Villard, the statement was issued for "believers in democracy to join in a National Conference for the discussion of present evils, the voicing of protests, and the renewal of the struggle for civil and political liberty."

Signing the document were sixty political progressives, including W. E. B. DU BOIS, IDA BELL WELLS-BARNETT, Bishop Alexander Walters, Mary Church Terrell, William Lloyd Garrison, and Francis J. Grimké. In response, a two-day conference got under way May 29, 1909, at the Henry Street Settlement in New York with more than two dozen presenters speaking for up to 15 minutes each on the issues of racial intolerance, "scientific" studies proving the equality of the races, disfranchisement, mob violence, segregation, and enforcement of the Fourteenth and Fifteenth Amendments. The conference ended with a hopeful crowd gathered at Cooper Union. Established over the two days of the event was a committee of 40 members that formed the nucleus of the new National Negro Committee. The new organization was glad to welcome into its fold members of the recently defunct NIAGARA MOVEMENT. Moreover, it chose to act with caution and elect committee members known for their progressiveness yet not so radical that the embryonic organization would draw fire from the man likely to become its principal critic—BOOKER TALIAFERRO WASHINGTON.

The National Negro Committee got down to the business of tightening its organizational structure during its second meeting from May 12 to 14 in 1910. For its first president, the committee chose Moorfield Storey, a former president of the American Bar Association and influential Boston lawyer. Walling took on the role of executive committee chairman; John E. Milholland, treasurer; Villard, disbursing treasurer; and Du Bois, director of publicity and research. It also then took on the name by which it has been known ever since: the National Association for the Advancement of Colored People (NAACP).

Incorporating as an organization in 1911, the NAACP stated in its published principles that its mission was to end illegal and violent acts against blacks, dismantle the JIM CROW system of separate public facilities for the races, pursue equal opportunities in public education for black children, and to establish the fact of freedom for African Americans to go along with the word itself. To do this, the members said simply, "The only means we can employ are education, organization, agitation, publicity—the force of an enlightened public opinion."

Villard allowed the NAACP to operate for a time rent-free out of the offices of the *New York Post.* Branches were established immediately in such cities as Boston, WASHINGTON, D.C., and CHICAGO.

As the NAACP director of publicity and research, Du Bois also took on the editorship of the association's primary organ of communication, the *CRISIS: A RECORD OF THE DARKER RACES.* The move took him out of Atlanta University and placed him at the helm of what would become one of the most influential periodicals in America during the first half of the 20th century. Its goal was, declared Du Bois in an editorial, to "record important happenings and movements in the world which bear on the great problem of inter-racial relations, and especially those which affect the Negro-American." It would also serve in the decades to follow as a literary showcase for those writers whose work would eventually make up the core of the Harlem Renaissance canon.

At the top of the NAACP's agenda was employing the court system to battle the discriminatory practices that had basically become an accepted aspect of everyday life in the United States. One of the first cases to test the organization's strength was that of Pink Franklin in 1910. During an ongoing dispute with his landlord regarding payment for rent, a sheriff entered Franklin's home in the middle of the night without a warrant and was killed in the resulting confrontation. Without examination of the facts or adequate legal representation, Franklin was sentenced to death. The NAACP intervened to obtain a reduced sentence of life imprisonment. Later, Franklin was released altogether.

With Joel E. Spingarn joining its ranks in 1910, the NAACP took on and won a string of individual cases focusing on discriminatory practices in theaters and restaurants. Like Du Bois's, Spingarn's role in the fight to balance race relations would be a dual one consisting of political advocacy and the literary support of black writers during the 1920s. Renowned as a literary critic, not only would he encourage such publishers as Alfred A. Knopf and Harcourt Brace to publish the works of black writers but his wife Amy would also help finance the studies of LANGSTON HUGHES at Pennsylvania's Lincoln University.

With a growing need to develop branch offices and increase membership nationwide, the association hired JAMES WELDON JOHNSON to serve as field secretary. His work throughout the country produced both a steady increase in membership—growing from approximately 3,000 in 1913 to more than 90,000 in 1920—and a growing pile of data on the persistent practice of LYNCHING. Spearheading the NAACP's push to outlaw such mob violence, Johnson persuaded enough congressmen to treat the matter seriously to get an antilynching bill passed by the House of Representatives, voting 230–119 on January 11, 1921. He was less successful when it came to the Senate, and the antilynching bill never became an actual law.

WALTER WHITE left Atlanta to join the NAACP as an assistant to Johnson but distinguished himself as one of the association's most accomplished leaders after succeeding Johnson in 1930. Prior, however, to settling down to the business of serious advocacy and lobbying, White penned two novels: *The Fire in the Flint* (1922) and *Flight, the Story of A Girl Who "Passes"* (1924).

As executive secretary of NAACP, in 1934 White lost the services of Du Bois, who returned to Atlanta University. White nevertheless went on to become one of the foremost consultants on issues of race in New York City and the United States. Mayor FIORELLO HENRY LA GUARDIA during the GREAT DEPRESSION of the 1930s depended heavily on White's analyses of conditions in Harlem and racial disturbances throughout the country. In 1941, he joined forces with labor leader A. PHILIP RANDOLPH to protest racist hiring in the government-financed defense industry and military. By backing Randolph's threat to lead a march of 100,000 workers on Washington, D.C., they persuaded President FRANKLIN DELANO ROOSEVELT to institute the Fair Employment Practices Committee, obtaining for the first time federal intervention in the economic plight of blacks. Five years later, White headed a delegation to address President Harry S. Truman regarding the unabated violence against blacks, and specifically the lynching of African-American soldiers, following World War II. With the signing of Executive Order 9808, President Truman outlawed "the action of individuals who take the law into their own hands and inflict summary punishment and wreak personal vengeance."

The NAACP scored one of its most significant victories in May 1954. The organization combined different cases on behalf of black elementary and high school students from Delaware, Virginia, South Carolina, and Kansas to present the landmark case known as *Brown v. the Board of Education.* Arguing that separate educational facilities for the African-American children included in the suit were inherently inferior, or not equal as required by law, the NAACP took its case all the way to the Supreme Court. There, the chief justices determined that segregation in elementary and high schools was unconstitutional due to the inherent inequality of a segregated school system. The decision overturned the 1896 *Plessy v. Ferguson* ruling, which had sanctioned "separate but equal facilities" and set the stage for the JIM CROW system the NAACP had committed itself to destroying. Though the ruling specifically addressed segregation in public elementary and high schools, its implications were not lost on the larger public, which understood its applicability to such areas as colleges, housing, theaters, and other facilities.

Though it remained a formidable force for racial equality, in the 1960s the NAACP's influence within the black community began to dwindle. With the growing stature of such charismatic leaders as Martin Luther King, Jr., and Malcolm X, along with the more militant proponents of the Black Power movement, the NAACP found itself more and more in supporting roles rather than central ones. It nevertheless continued to honor its original agenda by reporting on and legally addressing the issues of discriminatory hiring practices and the segregation that no longer had legal foundation but was still practiced throughout much of the country.

From its humble beginnings in Walling's apartment, going into the 21st century the NAACP operates as an international organization with upward of 2,200 affiliates throughout the United States, Japan, and Germany. The association maintains a very active presence among Washington lobbyists and in 1999 helped pass a bill to award Rosa Parks the Congressional Gold Medal in recognition of her contribution to the struggle for civil rights. Recognizing the impact of President Bill Clinton's administration, the NAACP lobbied against impeachment articles to remove Clinton from office due to controversy stemming from his relationships with Paula Jones and Monica Lewinski.

Kwesi Mfume, a former five-time member of Congress and head of the Congressional Black Caucus, served as its president and chief executive officer in 2003. Educator and former senator Julian Bond was at that time chairman of its national board of directors.

Further Reading

Bennett, Jr., Lerone, and Charles White. *The Shaping of Black America: The Struggles and Triumphs of African Americans, 1619–1990s.* New York: Viking Penguin, 1993.

Hutchinson, George. *The Harlem Renaissance in Black and White.* Cambridge and London: Belknap Press of Harvard University, 1995.

Ovington, Mary White. *Black and White Sat Down Together: Reminiscences of an NAACP Founder.* New York: Feminist Press of the City University of New York, 1996.

Wilson, Sondra Kathryn. *In Search of Democracy: The NAACP Writings of James Weldon Johnson, Walter White, and Roy Wilkins (1920–1977).* New York: Oxford University Press, 1999.

— Aberjhani

National Negro Baseball League (Negro Leagues)

The National Negro Baseball League was started in 1920 by Andrew "Rube" Foster in CHICAGO, Illinois, and played to thousands of fans across the country until 1960. By that time major league baseball had ended its JIM CROW discrimination practices and included black players.

Andrew "Rube" Foster, one of the best pitchers of his time, was a former manager and owner of the Chicago American Giants. He earned the nickname of "Rube" when his team defeated that of Rube Wadell, a white pitcher, in an exhibition game in 1902. Foster organized the National Negro Baseball League, popularly known as the Negro Leagues, because, as far back as 1859, black players had been banned from some teams. In his attempt to do something positive for blacks while remaining independent of white economic control, Foster created African-American athletic entrepreneurship.

In 1920, National Negro Baseball League franchises began operating in cities with large black populations, including NEW YORK CITY, New York; Newark, New Jersey; PHILADELPHIA, Pennsylvania; St. Louis, Missouri; Cleveland, Ohio; Memphis, Tennessee; Kansas City, Missouri; and Baltimore, Maryland. The National Negro Baseball League consisted of the Kansas City Monarchs, Indianapolis ABC's, Dayton Marcos, Chicago Giants, Chicago American Giants, Detroit Stars, St. Louis Giants, and the Cuban Giants. Other National Negro Baseball League teams included the Newark Eagles, Newark, New Jersey's National Negro League Team; and the Newark Bears, the city's International Minor League Team, which started in the 1930s.

By 1923, the Negro Leagues proved successful and innovative, playing games across the United States. The league invented night baseball and the use of shin guards. Its success prompted white businessmen to form a rival league called the Eastern Colored League, which included the Philadelphia Hilldales, Cuban Stars, Brooklyn Royal Giants, Atlantic City Bacharach Giants, Baltimore Black Sox, and New York Lincoln Giants.

The standings of the National Negro Baseball League, and exploits of black athletes in general, were followed in black-owned newspapers around the country. White-oriented newspapers rarely mentioned these events but between 1919 and 1929, sports coverage in black newspapers such as the *CHICAGO DEFENDER, PITTSBURGH COURIER*, and *Washington Bee* expanded from several columns to two or three pages.

The two leagues played in the first Negro World Series in 1924. The Kansas City Monarchs of the National Negro Baseball League won over the Hilldales of the Eastern Colored League. An annual All-Star game began in 1933. The teams became the pride of their communities, regularly attracting large enough attendance for most franchises to post substantial profits. The black teams played in stadiums leased from the magnates of organized white baseball when their teams were scheduled on the road. African-American fans packed the stands to watch the athletic performances of star players like Josh Gibson, Cool Papa Bell, Buck Leonard and John Henry Lloyd, to name a few.

A lack of financial backing during the GREAT DEPRESSION caused both black leagues to collapse in 1932. The following year, a second Negro National League was established and the biggest annual event in black baseball, the East-West All-Star game, was inaugurated. Moreover, black teams from the Midwest and South formed the Negro American League in 1937.

The legendary Jackie Robinson spent one year in the Negro Leagues, in 1945, before breaking the color line in major league baseball with a contract to play for the Montreal Royals, a minor-league affiliate of the Brooklyn Dodgers, in 1947. The acceptance of Robinson into the league ended more than 60 years of segregation in major league baseball. However, the integration of baseball also marked the end of independent, lucrative, Negro baseball organizations, and in 1960 all of the Negro leagues ended.

One of the members of the Negro leagues written about the most was Satchel Paige, who played in major league baseball near the end of his career. Paige and Josh Gibson are included in "The Legends of Baseball" stamps issued in July 2000 by the U.S. Postal Service. Also, many members of the National Negro League have now been inducted into baseball's Hall of Fame. A star of the Kansas City Monarchs, Turkey Stearns, entered the National Baseball Hall of Fame as recently as July 2000.

Further Reading

Holway, John. *The Complete Book of Baseball's Negro Leagues: The Other Half of Baseball History.* Fern Park, Fla.: Hastings House Publishers, 2001.

Izenberg, Jerry. "Way Too Late: A Baseball Great Takes His Place in History." *The Star-Ledger,* July 18, 2000, 55.

Loverro, Thom. *The Encyclopedia of Negro League Baseball.* New York: Facts On File, 2003.

Riley, James A., ed. *The Biographical Encyclopedia of the Negro Baseball Leagues.* New York: Carroll and Graf, 2002.

Robinson, Frazier "Slow." *Catching Dreams: My Life in the Negro Leagues.* New York: Syracuse University Press, 1999.

— Sandra L. West

National Urban League (NUL)

Three organizations dedicated to helping African Americans make effective transitions from southern states to northern urban environments combined forces in 1911 to form the National Urban League (NUL): the National League for the Protection of Colored Women; the Committee for the Improvement of Industrial Conditions Among Negroes in New York; and the Committee on Urban Conditions Among Negroes.

The oldest of the institutions was the National League for the Protection of Colored Women. It was established in 1905 by Frances Keller and Mrs. Ruth Standish Baldwin, a widowed PATRON who would often give her voice and resources to the causes of social equality in early 20th-century America. Among the principal motives behind the formation of the National League for the Protection of Colored Women were reports of young African-American women arriving from the South in large northern cities and quickly falling prey to schemes luring them into prostitution or other illegal activities. The league sought to contact such women as quickly as possible upon their arrival, preferably at the train station, and initiate the process of helping them obtain housing, jobs, and even training for industrial employment.

The Committee for the Improvement of Industrial Conditions Among Negroes in New York was established in 1906. Baldwin and Dr. George E. Haynes, a FISK UNIVERSITY graduate and the first African American to receive a doctorate from Columbia University, started the Committee on Urban Conditions Among Negroes in 1910. The latter committee took it upon itself to obtain training and education for social workers to address African-American and urban-related problems throughout the country.

Like the NATIONAL ASSOCIATION FOR THE ADVANCEMENT OF COLORED PEOPLE (NAACP), the National Urban League operated with a biracial board of advisers. Unlike the NAACP, the league took a more grassroots approach to solving the problems of newly urban blacks by rendering social services targeting their immediate relief; by contrast, the NAACP relied heavily on litigation and increased public awareness of such issues. It was Baldwin who stated the league's social philosophy: "Let us work not as colored people nor as white people for the narrow benefit of any group alone, but together, as American citizens, for the common good of our common city, our common country."

The transition from three organizations into one took place under the leadership of the league's first president, Edwin R. A. Seligman. He was followed by Baldwin, Dr. Haynes, and Eugene Kinckle Jones, who remained its executive secretary for 23 years, from 1918 to 1941. The organization in the 1920s set up 42 branches in cities across the country, maintaining its national office in NEW YORK CITY and a southern field office in Atlanta.

The National Urban League sought to accomplish its objectives by engaging issues at multiple levels. In addition to gathering data for the league's own use, its Department of Research and Investigation made such information available to speakers, writers, and anyone seeking solutions to the same race-related conditions as themselves. Its National Industrial Relations Department utilized bulletins and other forms of publicity to obtain employment for highly qualified blacks as well as to inform general laborers about the availability or nonavailability of jobs in specific fields. The league also maintained community houses where it conducted classes and workshops on such fundamentals as health education, personal hygiene, etiquette, professional conduct, and styles of dress. In what was perhaps one of its more progressive programs, the league managed a network of fellowships to ensure training for black social workers at the New York School of Social Work, the University of Pittsburgh, and other academic institutions. It also held scholarships at Pennsylvania's School of Social and Health Work.

In 1923, the National Urban League launched *OPPORTUNITY: A JOURNAL OF NEGRO LIFE.* Opportunity was edited by CHARLES SPURGEON JOHNSON, a sociologist and graduate of the University of Chicago. The publication adopted the same social science focus as its parent organization, which meant it published articles and studies examining in depth the plight of African Americans. However, Johnson was also a shrewd observer of the cultural scene and published as well as encouraged the works of emerging black writers. As a literary critic, he often advocated poetry and fiction that drew on urban realism to portray the lives of the black masses.

While maintaining its social science approach to the resolution of African America's economic and social problems, the National Urban League often lent its support to more politically aggressive organizations in the 1950s and 1960s during the push to secure civil rights. Unable to participate directly in protests because of its nontaxable status, the league more often engaged in such activities as planning strategies and other forms of support. Whitney M. Young, executive director of the league in 1966, went before Congress to urge passage of the proposed Civil Rights Act of 1966. Young also introduced a 10-point Marshall Plan which President Lyndon B. Johnson's administration took into serious consideration when implementing its own War on Poverty legislation.

Toward the end of the 20th century, with the GREAT MIGRATION long behind it, the National Urban League's primary concern was no longer the fate of blacks moving into northern cities. With significant gains in the acquisition of civil rights and improved employment and education among blacks, the organization continued its social service agenda with a focus still on such issues as housing and health but also dealing more in depth with the modern challenges of widespread teenage pregnancy, unemployment among black youth, and fluctuating black turnout at the voting polls. *Opportunity* lasted only until 1949, and the league's State of Black America Report was adopted in 1976 under the leadership of Vernon Jordan, who became its fifth executive director in 1972 following the death of Young.

Programs geared toward helping youth prepare to live professionally rewarding and financially sound lives continued to receive strong attention with John E. Jacob at the head of the league from 1982 to 1994 and from Hugh B. Price leading the organization in 2002. The league notes that one of its major challenges in modern times is to ensure that resources and opportunities remain available to African Americans during what many are describing as a transitional period of globalization.

Further Reading

Bennett, Lerone, Jr., and Charles White. *The Shaping of Black America: The Struggles and Triumphs of African Americans, 1619–1990s.* New York: Viking Penguin, 1993.

Moore, Jesse T. *A Search for Equality: The National Urban League, 1910–1961.* University Park, Pa.: Pennsylvania State University Press, 1989.

Staff, National Urban League. *Black Americans and Public Policy: Perspectives of the National Urban League.* New York: National Urban League, 1988.

— Aberjhani

Negritude

Leon Damas, Leopold Senghor, and Aimé Césaire were students in PARIS, France, when they launched the movement known as Negritude. At a time when European politics and ideals dominated the globe, Negritude was dedicated to the preservation and promotion of African values and culture for people of African descent.

Founders Damas, Senghor, and Césaire first released what became known as "the great black cry" in the pages of *L'Etudiant Noir,* or *The Black Student* magazine. The students drew strength for their inspiration from earlier Caribbean and French Martinican writers as well as those of the HARLEM RENAISSANCE. The works of Haitian poets Oswald Durand and Massilou Coicou were particularly influential. So were those of the French Martinican poet, novelist, and biographer René Maran, whose *Batouala* won France's much-coveted Goncourt Prize in 1921 and was the first novel by a Franco African to present a critical portrait of French colonists.

It was Senghor who introduced his fellow students to modern French literature and that of African-American writers. French translations of CLAUDE MCKAY's *Banjo,* JAMES WELDON JOHNSON's *God's Trombones,* and LANGSTON HUGHES's *The Negro Artist and the Racial Mountain* served as literary models and statements of independent black thought. The students were fortunate enough to occasionally meet some of the Harlem writers at literary SALONS hosted by Paulette Nardal in the early 1930s.

Born in Senegal in 1906, Senghor served in the French army during WORLD WAR II and spent two years as a German prisoner of war. He published his first collection of poetry, *Songs of Darkness,* the same year he was elected deputy from Senegal to the French National Assembly. The simultaneous events marked a trend of literary pursuit and public service that would characterize the lives of all three Negritude founders. His second poetry collection, *Black Host,* was published in 1945. In 1960, he was elected president of Senegal (a position he held until 1980) and in 1961 won the Poets and Artists of France's International Grand Prize for Poetry for his volume, *Nocturnes.*

From French Guiana, Damas was born in 1912 and died in 1980. His 1937 *Pigments* was the first poetry volume published by a member of the movement and contained lines so politically volatile that it was banned in West French Africa. Rather than encouraging Africans to join France's political causes, Damas suggested Africans "leave the Krauts in peace" and look to the liberation of their own homelands. He published a prosework entitled *Return From Guiana* in 1938 and from 1945 to 1951 held the office of French assembly deputy from Guiana. Toward the end of his life, Damas worked on a French biography of Hughes and original translations of Hughes's poetry.

The French Martinican Césaire, born in 1913, composed *Cahier d'un Retour au Pays Natal,* known in the West as *Return to My Native Land,* during the early 1930s, and in it he introduced the world to the term *Negritude.* While segments of the poem appeared in French "little magazines" such as *Volontés* in 1938 and 1939, it was published in book form in 1944 with a French-English version in 1947. The work drew the attention of cultural critic André Breton, who immediately hailed it as a surrealist masterpiece and wrote for it a preface that brought greater attention to both Césaire and the Negritude movement. It also helped the surrealists to regain the flagging momentum of their own movement and prompted famed author Jean-Paul Sartre to debate the kinship and merits of both Surrealism and Negritude.

Césaire went on to win acknowledgment as one of the most significant 20th-century black authors writing in French. He and his wife Suzanne Césaire, along with René Menil, edited the magazine *Tropiques* from 1941 to 1943 as a vehicle to promote native culture and assert African identity. His work gained in critical acceptance and garnered awards as he continued to publish poetry, wrote plays on historical African figures, and authored essays on surrealism and other cultural movements.

The writer was elected to the twin post of mayor of Martinique's capital city, Fort-de-France, and deputy to the French National Assembly in 1944. He was a member of the French Communist Party from 1944 to 1956.

Negritude grew to embrace a large number of black artists and writers in West India, Africa, and the United States. African-American RICHARD NATHANIEL WRIGHT made his move from the states to France in 1948, the same year the magazine *Presence Africaine* was founded to further champion and explore the more positive attributes of black culture. Always of keen interest to members of the movement were racial events in America, and such incidents as the SCOTTSBORO TRIAL and

One of the founding members of the Negritude movement, Leopold Senghor, shown here in 1963, has been celebrated worldwide as a gifted lyrical poet and former president of Senegal. *(Library of Congress, Prints & Photographs Division, NYWT&S Collection [LC-USZ62-112307])*

the Montgomery bus boycott were both discussed and adopted as subject matter for poems, essays, and fiction. The movement maintained its strength with the publication of Frantz Fanon's 1952 *White Skin, Black Masks.* Writers, artists, and statesmen further expanded its impact with the first Congress of Negro Artists and Writers held in Paris in 1956 and a second Congress held in Rome in 1958.

In 2003, in a three-part documentary of Césaire's life entitled *Aimé Césaire, A Voice for History,* he spoke of the Negritude movement as one encompassing not only black culture and black people but the greater spectrum of human beings and experience. On Senghor's 90th birthday in 1996, people worldwide honored him as a statesman, poet, and spiritual visionary. He died on December 20, 2001, in Normandy, France.

Further Reading

Arnold, A. James. *Modernism and Negritude: The Poetry and Poetics of Aime Cesaire.* Campbell, Calif.: iUniverse, Inc., 1998.

Kadalie, Modibo. *Internationalism, Pan-Africanism and the Struggle of Social Classes.* Savannah, Ga.: One Quest Press, 2000.

Richardson, Michael, and Krzysztof Fijalkowski. *Refusal of the Shadow: Surrealism and the Caribbean.* London: Verso Books, 1996.

Sharpley-Whiting, T. Denean. *Negritude Women.* Minneapolis: University of Minnesota, 2002.

Soyinka, Wole. *The Burden of Memory, the Muse of Forgiveness.* New York: Oxford University Press, 1999.

— Aberjhani

Negro Leagues See NATIONAL NEGRO BASEBALL LEAGUE.

Negro World

Based in HARLEM and distributed internationally, *Negro World* was a political and literary weekly newspaper published by the UNIVERSAL NEGRO IMPROVEMENT ASSOCIATION (UNIA), led by the BACK-TO-AFRICA MOVEMENT advocate MARCUS GARVEY.

Marvus Garvey's mission for *Negro World* was grounded in a black aesthetic: black authors must be loyal to and proud of their race and deliver that message to their people through "healthy and decent literature." Sections of *Negro World* were written in French and Spanish to accommodate black West Indians fluent in those languages. The weekly, with an impressive circulation of 200,000 during its heyday, published stinging black nationalist articles and verse and was a forerunner in the area of literary competitions.

Garvey became the first editor of *Negro World* in 1919. Subsequent editors between 1920 and 1927 came from a long line of distinguished journalists and academicians: William H. Ferris, Hubert H. Harrison, ERIC DERWENT WALROND, T. Thomas Fortune, John Edward Bruce, H. G. Mudgal, Robert T. Browne, and Garvey's wife, Amy Jacques Garvey. Ferris, *Negro World*'s literary editor, had educational credentials from Harvard and Yale. Harrison was an intellectual and writer. Walrond, associate editor from 1921 to 1923, authored the highly praised fiction collection *Tropic Death.* Fortune, a former speechwriter for BOOKER TALIAFERRO WASHINGTON and founder of the *NEW YORK AGE*, was known as "the dean of Afro-American journalists." Bruce founded the Negro Society for Historical Research in 1911. Mudgal was a columnist for *Negro World.* Browne, associate editor during the early 1920s, had been president of the Negro Library Association of NEW YORK CITY (1914). Garvey's wife, a political activist and short-story writer, served as associate editor on an occasional basis.

As with the *CRISIS: A RECORD OF THE DARKER RACES*, official publication of the NATIONAL ASSOCIATION FOR THE ADVANCEMENT OF COLORED PEOPLE (NAACP), and *OPPORTUNITY: A JOURNAL OF NEGRO LIFE*, official publication for the NATIONAL URBAN LEAGUE (NUL), both principal periodicals during this epoch, *Negro World* devoted itself to the burgeoning literature of the *NEW NEGRO* by publishing poems, book reviews, literary criticism, short stories, and theater reviews.

While *Crisis* and *Opportunity* offered well-documented and now-legendary literary dinners and awards, *Negro World* had public relations strategies geared toward using literature to raise race consciousness. It was achieved in part by presenting free books to newspaper subscribers. One of these books was *From Superman to Man* by J. A. Rogers, a West Indian historian and staunch Garveyite whose several controversial titles were the most reviewed books in the newspaper's history.

Though the famed CIVIC CLUB DINNER, *Crisis* magazine awards, and *Opportunity* magazine awards have gone down in Harlem Renaissance history, *Negro World* was actually a forerunner in literary marketing and competitions. *Negro World* officials held literary events four years before the editors of *Crisis* and *Opportunity* held theirs. *Negro World* contests were structured around themes such as "How to Unite the West Indian and American Negroes." Garvey, Ferris, and Bruce performed as the judges. In 1921, 36 cash prizes were dispersed for poetry, essays, and short stories, among them a $100 first prize to Walrond for his short story "A Senator's Memories," under Garvey's "Africa Redeemed" literary category.

The love of literature, and the realization that literature could and must motivate, unite, and honor all black people within the black diaspora, was resolute among UNIA members and *Negro World* readers. The author of an April 1922 *Negro World* editorial suggested that at its next convention the UNIA commission a black scholar to write a history of black literature. And in 1922, Garvey attempted to launch a separate magazine, *Blackman,* as a literary aside for *Negro World,* but it did not succeed.

Frequent contributors to *Negro World* included illustrious names of the period: ARTHUR SCHOMBURG, Casper Holstein, and CARTER GODWIN WOODSON. During the 1920s, Schomburg served as president of the AMERICAN NEGRO ACADEMY, an intellectual and literary society. Holstein was a Harlem gangster with West Indian roots who helped support the UNIA financially.

"Poetry for the People" was a popular component of *Negro World* from 1920 to 1922. The poetry published in the magazine dealt with such militant issues as the demise of the Ku Klux Klan (KKK) and BLACK NATIONALISM. J. R. Ralph Casimir of Dominica, West Indies, and Charles H. Este of Montreal, Canada, contributed poetry regularly to *Negro World* and coordinated UNIA literary clubs in their respective communities. Other contributors included Ethel Trew Dunlap, a UNIA member in CHICAGO; avant-garde poet Leonard I. Brathwaite of New York; and Sgt. Lucian B. Watkins of Virginia, whose work was anthologized in *The Book of American Negro Poetry* (1922). Sculptor AUGUSTA FELLS SAVAGE, a Garveyite, contributed her poem "Supplication" to a 1922 edition of the magazine. And folklorist and novelist ZORA NEALE HURSTON published several pieces in *Negro World,* including the poem "Night" in 1922.

John Edward Bruce, who authored "The Negro in Poetry" (1923), wrote literary essays for *Negro World.* Among stock book reviewers for the magazine were: Walrond, Schomburg, Rogers, and MARY WHITE OVINGTON, chairman of the board of directors for the NAACP. Although a white woman, Ovington wrote the "Book Chat" column for *Negro World* from 1921 to 1923. In 1922, she reviewed *The Lynching Bee and Other Poems* by William Ellery Leonard. Woodson, founder of the ASSOCIATION FOR THE STUDY OF NEGRO LIFE, published a column in *Negro World* from 1931 to 1932.

Charges of mail fraud against Garvey and UNIA stifled all operations of organization, including the newspaper's. Garvey was jailed and deported to Jamaica, and *Negro World* ceased publication in 1933.

Further Reading

Johnson, Abby Arthur, and Ronald Maberry Johnson. *Propaganda and Aesthetics: The Literary Politics of Afro-American Magazines in the Twentieth Century.* Amherst: University of Massachusetts Press, 1979.

Kornweibel, Theodore, Jr. *Seeing Red: Federal Campaigns Against Black Militancy, 1919–1925.* Bloomington: Indiana University Press, 1991.

Martin, Tony. *Literary Garveyism: Garvey, Black Arts and the Harlem Renaissance,* Dover, Mass.: The Majority Press, 1983.

— Sandra L. West

New Negro

The term *New Negro* denoted a philosophy, movement, and book indicating a conscious effort on behalf of African Americans to destroy the public image of themselves as ex-slaves incapable of self-determination and to promote the public image of American blacks as industrious and independent. Whereas the "old negro" in American public opinion may have been subservient, sycophantic, illiterate, criminal, and even savage, the New Negro would be intellectually informed, racially proud, creative, and individualistic.

The term *New Negro* first appeared as the *new nigger* in various folktales that circulated throughout the South during the Reconstruction era following the Civil War. It was generally used to describe a black individual who was no longer willing to comply with orders issued by whites. Toward the end of the 1800s, BOOKER TALIAFERRO WASHINGTON and others promoting Washington's strategy for the economic advancement of blacks through industrial training often used the phrase *New Negro*. The editors of black-owned newspapers also used the term to note outstanding achievements by African Americans that clearly marked them as something other than an inferior race. Although his philosophy was generally interpreted as one designed to accommodate American racism, in 1900 Washington contributed an essay to a book titled *A New Negro for a New Century,* suggesting that his political aim was more toward compromise than accommodation.

The New Negro often meant different things to different individuals and organizations. To author and sociologist W. E. B. DU BOIS, writing in 1903 in his classic *The SOULS OF BLACK FOLK,* it meant claiming one's full humanity through the agencies of higher education, then making worthwhile contributions to American society. He further stressed that African Americans would have to target their most talented individuals, a Talented Tenth, to reverse those social and political losses incurred by slavery. In his words, the Talented Tenth of the Negro race must be made leaders of thought and missionaries of culture among their people. Such talented missionaries of culture included the Broadway show writing team of JOHN ROSAMOND JOHNSON, JAMES WELDON JOHNSON, and Bob Cole, whose hit musicals during the early 1900s broke with the blackface minstrel tradition and paved the way for the successful black musicals of the 1920s. Brothers Rosamond and James Weldon Johnson also provided African Americans with the song they would adopt as a virtual anthem of the New Negro, "LIFT EVERY VOICE AND SING." Originally composed for a celebration of Abraham Lincoln's birthday, performances of the song went on to become a standard feature of programs in black churches, schools, private clubs, and civic organizations. In black-owned newspapers such as Thomas T. Fortune's *NEW YORK AGE* and ROBERT ABBOTT's *CHICAGO DEFENDER*, the voice of the New Negro was often militant in tone. Fortune and Abbott both, as well as journalist IDA BELL WELLS-BARNETT, led an aggressive campaign against the practice of murdering African Americans by LYNCHING. In response to lynching, they proposed self-defense as well as relocation out of the South by way of the GREAT MIGRATION north as opposed to depending on a system of justice that clearly did not view whites murdering blacks as a crime.

In his 1916 publication, *The New Negro,* William Pickens of the NATIONAL ASSOCIATION FOR THE ADVANCEMENT OF COLORED PEOPLE (NAACP) not only noted that the New Negro had arrived but also suggested African Americans monitor and update "The Renaissance of the Negro Race." MARCUS GARVEY, writing in the *NEGRO WORLD* and speaking all over the United States as the president of the UNIVERSAL NEGRO IMPROVEMENT ASSOCIATION (UNIA), promoted his idea of the New Negro as one who obtained economic independence, took pride in his African heritage, and demonstrated BLACK NATIONALISM and Pan-Africanism. Many felt that the basic tenet of the New Negro was best expressed by CLAUDE MCKAY's poem, "IF WE MUST DIE," published in the radical magazine *The Liberator* during the RED SUMMER OF 1919, when violent race riots claimed the lives of blacks and whites throughout the United States. In its own way, "If We Must Die" came to serve as much as an anthem as "Lift Every Voice and Sing." More than a poem advocating physical self-defense against such atrocities as lynching, which it clearly does, McKay's words underscored the New Negro's determination to advance on all fronts regardless of opposition.

Equal to the spirit of determination, militancy, pride, and self-sufficiency that characterized the New Negro was that of celebration so evident in RAGTIME, JAZZ, and the BLUES, the dominant forms of American musical expression during the 1920s. EUBIE BLAKE and NOBLE SISSLE's *SHUFFLE ALONG* became a celebrated Broadway smash in 1921 precisely because it was what in modern times would be called a "feel good" jazz and ragtime musical, one that by nearly all accounts had an inspiring and regenerative effect. JELLY ROLL MORTON, ETHEL WATERS, FATS WALLER, KING OLIVER, and many others expressed through their music an exuberance that ignored or defied the dehumanizing realities of JIM CROW apartheid prevalent in both the South and the North.

The varying elements and definitions of the New Negro began to congeal in the works of emerging writers and artists who joined the Great Migration north and made their way to NEW YORK CITY, CHICAGO, WASHINGTON, D.C., and other urban centers. Many of these writers and artists, among them COUNTEE CULLEN, RUDOLPH FISHER, LANGSTON HUGHES, and JESSIE REDMOND FAUSET, found outlets and cash prizes for their literary works through the pages of *CRISIS: A RECORD OF THE DARKER RACES* and *OPPORTUNITY* magazines. Taking note of the abundance of creative talent centered in Harlem, HOWARD UNIVERSITY philosophy professor ALAIN LOCKE worked with *Opportunity* editor CHARLES SPURGEON JOHNSON to host a CIVIC CLUB DINNER designed to announce officially the onset of a New Negro movement or renaissance.

Attending the dinner at the Civic Club was a mixture of black and white editors, novelists, poets, playwrights, publishers, artists, educators, and political advocates. Acting as master of ceremonies, Locke presided over a program that acknowledged the groundbreaking work of such authors as Du Bois and Johnson, applauded Fauset's new novel, *There Is Confusion,* and featured recitals by Cullen and GWENDOLYN BENNETTA BENNETT. Among those attending the dinner was the editor of *SURVEY GRAPHIC* magazine, Paul U. Kellogg, who was so impressed by the proceedings that he invited Locke to edit a special edition of his magazine focusing on the emerging black renaissance. The edition of the *Survey Graphic* edited by Locke was called "Harlem, Mecca of the New Negro," and showcased the work of most of those black writers who attended the Civic Club Dinner. With Joel Spingarn and other PATRONS purchasing copies of the special edition *Survey Graphic* by the thousands for distribution in schools and as gifts for friends, the issue far surpassed the magazine's normal circulation rate. Publishers Albert and Charles Boni became convinced the material featured in the magazine would make a worthwhile book and contacted Kellogg and Locke to discuss the idea. Before 1925 ended, Locke had gathered and edited enough additional material to produce the defining black literary work of the era, *The New Negro* anthology.

His goal, Locke stated in the foreword to *The New Negro,* was "to document the New Negro culturally and socially, to register the transformations of the inner and outer life of the Negro in America." In doing so, he identified the "old Negroes" as sociologically constructed "Uncle Toms," "aunties," "mammies," or "Sambos," a politically and economically dependent race that might be described collectively as "the sick man of American Democracy." The New Negro was one who operated with the dual purposes of bringing new leadership to modern America and "rehabilitating the race in world esteem from that loss of prestige for which the fate and conditions of slavery have so largely been responsible." He illustrated his point in *The New Negro* anthology with sections on the black renaissance; black youth; fiction; poetry; drama; music; sociology; history; and Pan-Africanism, examined at the book's conclusion in Du Bois's article "The Negro Mind Reaches Out."

In addition to featuring works by those individuals who had attended the Civic Club Dinner, *The New Negro* included poetry and fiction by JEAN TOOMER, ZORA NEALE HURSTON, and Claude McKay. Toomer, however, was not particularly pleased with his inclusion in *The New Negro,* partly, he stated, because he had not given Locke permission to use his work. Other reasons involved Toomer's perception of himself as multiracial, which conflicted with anything identifying him as Negro, whether New or not. His life following the publication of *Cane* in 1923 was spent among Europeans and American whites who generally knew nothing of his black ancestry. While he acknowledged the New Negro movement as a significant American event, he did not acknowledge it as a relevant personal one.

Balancing the literary works of some three dozen writers featured in *The New Negro* were images of African sculptures and masks. Further enhancing these were nearly a dozen illustrations by AARON DOUGLAS.

Upon its publication, *The New Negro* received substantial promotional and critical support from V. F. Calverton, the editor of *Modern Quarterly* magazine. Calverton not only wrote positive reviews for *Opportunity* and *The Nation* magazines but invited Charles S. Johnson, Du Bois, Locke, and Hughes to continue the New Negro campaign by publishing additional works by them in *Modern Quarterly.* H. L. Mencken, the normally satirical editor of *American Mercury,* lauded the book as a symbol of African Americans' "bold decision to go it alone."

While *The New Negro* anthology gave substance to Locke's and others' vision of a renaissance in progress, the movement itself took on other forms. FLORENCE MILLS working in theater in the mid-1920s and LENA HORNE in Hollywood during the 1940s both used their status as celebrities to challenge negative stereotypes of blacks and promote more positive images. Likewise, novelist and filmmaker OSCAR MICHEAUX, who as a youth was inspired by the teachings of Booker T. Washington, created a visual library of more than 40 films celebrating the virtues and diversities of African Americans. Composer WILLIAM GRANT STILL completed his Afro-American Symphony, the first by a black man to be performed by a major American symphony, in 1932 with an expressed intent to help "vindicate the Negro." The philosophy was one that motivated Still up until the conclusion of his career in 1978.

Moreover, while many have maintained that the New Negro movement was largely an indulgence in elitism among black intellectuals of the 1920s and 1930s, educators at traditionally black high schools and colleges throughout the United States during the latter half of the 1900s often employed its general philosophy to motivate their students to set and achieve goals beyond the expected.

Further Reading

Favor, J. Martin. *Authentic Blackness: The Folk in the New Negro Renaissance.* Durham, N.C.: Duke University Press, 1999.

Washington, Robert E. *The Ideologies of African American Literature: From the Harlem Renaissance to the Black Nationalist.* Lanham, Md.: Rowman and Littlefield, 2001.

Wintz, Cary D., ed. *The Politics and Aesthetics of "New Negro Literature."* New York: Garland Publishing, Incorporated, 1996.

— Aberjhani

New Orleans

Founded as a French colony in 1718 on the banks of the Mississippi River, New Orleans came under Spanish rule from 1767 to 1800 before reverting to the French and finally, as part of the Louisiana Territory in 1803, becoming part of the United States. With a port that served as a major link to Latin America and the Caribbean, and with its strong French and Spanish influences, New Orleans grew into a major urban center reflecting a blend of cultures that made it unique among American cities.

That uniqueness turned New Orleans into a center of JAZZ long before WORLD WAR I. It is renowned as the home of Congo Square, a founding center of African-American dance; the Tenderloin, later Storyville, district that produced jazz innovators LOUIS ARMSTRONG and JELLY ROLL MORTON; the traditional jazz funeral called "The Second Line"; and the New Orleans Rhythm Kings.

Congo Square

Congo Square, originally Congo Plains, located at the intersection of Rampart and St. Peter streets near New Orleans's French Quarter, served during slavery as the site of antebellum slave dances. Under the surveillance of their white owners, African slaves were allowed to perform African songs and dances, and to play drums and gourds on Sundays in this public space until 1851. The dances influenced later styles: the Bamboula dance performed by the slaves evolved into the African-American 20th-century dance called the "flat-footed Shuffle."

The Congo Square dances, and the music to which they were performed, helped generate the creation of jazz itself.

Class-Conscious New Orleans

In the late 1880s and early 1900s, class-conscious New Orleans bands were separated by the skin color of the musicians who originally resided in different neighborhoods. Members of the Creole bands were light complexioned, came from a mixed ancestry of African and French, and lived in the downtown French-speaking section of town. One such group, the Onward Brass Band, played the music that Creoles requested: concert music, marches, and quadrilles (square dance music). Skilled at reading music, some of them had taken lessons from the French Opera House orchestra.

The uptown bands were dark in skin tone and on Sunday evenings in Lincoln Park filled the neighborhood with lively music in an un-genteel fashion. They could not read music and were proud of that fact. They played "with the heart" and thought that formal education would hinder their improvisational abilities. One leader of the uptown bands was Charles "Buddy" Bolden (1868–1931), whose specialty song was "Bucket's Got a Hole in It." A favored composer was Morton, who composed "New Orleans Blues," which many of the city's bands loved and played. KING OLIVER headed the Creole Jazz Band during the 1920s and with it migrated successfully to CHICAGO. Oliver also mentored Louis "Satchmo" Armstrong to help him become the first outstanding soloist of jazz. Armstrong was native to the Tenderloin Storyville area of New Orleans.

The Tenderloin

In the Tenderloin, where JIM CROW segregation laws forced the Creole and black musicians to live in same area, they learned to play music collectively on the main Basin Street, a street immortalized in "Basin Street Blues." The Tuxedo dance hall, from which the Tuxedo Brass Band evolved, was the neighborhood's most popular. As the musicians communicated and urged each other on to try new things, the music changed. They threw timidity to the wind and began to use mutes, fashioned from plungers or pop bottles. The more they experimented, the more the sound of New Orleans jazz developed and evolved.

The area known as the Tenderloin evolved and became known as Storyville.

The Second Line

The Second Line is a spiritual and musical tradition with African roots prevalent from the 1880s to the Harlem Renaissance years and into the 1950s. It was especially prominent in the indigent Storyville neighborhood, in which trumpeter and jazz vocalist Armstrong grew up.

The Second Line originated with the West African belief that the spirit of the deceased is "active" and should be placated. This foundation is apparent in the traditional New Orleans jazz funeral where the life of the deceased is celebrated with raucous music in addition to the somber expression of mourning. A customary Second Line includes a march from church to gravesite. At the church, musicians play religious hymns such as "Just a Closer Walk with Thee," in strict, nonimprovisational fashion. After the church service and/or when the body is entrusted to the earth, the bandleader directs the procession away from the gravesite or church, without playing music, then, after reaching a respectful distance, begins to play jazz. The band's dignified grand marshal—wearing white gloves, black tuxedo, black hat, and holding an umbrella—initiates a march into the streets of the town. A "second line" of spectators joins the procession; animated, dancing, strutting, clapping, hollering, and generally "appeasing" the spirit of the deceased.

When first adopted, the Second Line was a final service exclusively for jazz musicians and members of secret societies. Band members came from the ranks of social clubs. During the early 19th century, benevolent societies were initiated to take

The famed French Quarter, shown here ca. 1920 to 1924, in New Orleans reflects only one of the city's many diverse cultural influences. *(Library of Congress, Prints & Photographs Division [LC-USZ62-112758])*

care of the living and the dead, and social-aid clubs were formed to pay for bands to play at weddings and funerals. During the 1930s, the entire band was usually paid $2.50, plus food and drink.

Jelly Roll Morton wrote that the Second Line band "would get started and you would hear the drums, rolling a deep, slow rhythm. A few bars of that and then the snare drummer would make a hot roll on his drums and the boys in the band would just tear loose, while the second line swung down the street, singing . . . ," and the band would also sing "When the Saints Go Marching In" or "Didn't He Ramble?"

Bands that played jazz funerals in New Orleans included the Tonic Triad Band, the Tuxedo Brass Band, the Olympic Brass Band, and the Eureka Brass Band. During the 1920s and 1930s, William Etienne Pajaud, Sr., owner of the Music Box Club on Canal and Prieur Streets in New Orleans, played trumpet with the Eureka Brass Band and led it for a time. Among the Eureka Brass Band members were Joseph "Cle" Frazier on snare drum; Robert "Son Few Clothes" Lewis on bass drum; Manual Paul, tenor saxophone; and Harold Dejan, alto saxophone.

Pajaud, Sr., died in May 1960. His only offspring, William E. Pajaud, Jr., born on August 3, 1925, in New Orleans, matured into a visual artist. Pajaud, Jr., documented the Second Line tradition in the painting "White Gloves" in 1989; his father's funeral in "Parade Rest" in 1992; and "Eureka Funeral and Second Line" in 2000. These and other renditions of the New Orleans jazz funeral tradition by Pajaud, Jr., are housed at M. Hanks Gallery, 3008 Main Street in Santa Monica, California. Photographs depicting the New Orleans tradition are held at the Hogan Jazz Archive, Tulane University.

New Orleans Rhythm Kings

In the world of jazz, a music noted by many musical scholars as "African-American classical music," the Rhythm Kings were unique because they were not black. Originally named the Friars' Inn Society Orchestra, in 1921 they became the first group of white jazz musicians to capture the attention and respect of the music-savvy people of New Orleans. Original members of the group included: Paul Mares (cornet); George Brunis (trombone); Leon Roppolo (clarinet); Jack Pettis (saxophone); Lon Black (banjo); Steve Brown (bass); and Frank Snyder (drums). Pianist Jelly Roll Morton played with this band in 1923. Among the recordings made by the New Orleans Rhythm Kings during the mid-1920s were "Maple Leaf Rag" and "Tin Roof Blues." The music blended a textured jazz sound of soft clarinet and sizzling trombone that was popular until 1925.

In addition to the New Orleans Rhythm Kings, there were dozens of other bands in New Orleans: the Onward Brass Band; the Excelsior String Band dance ensemble, which included violin or mandolin; and a variety of small string bands that utilized a guitar and played for neighborhood functions.

Following the GREAT MIGRATION, New Orleans's old Storyville district emerged as a black entertainment area. The public lot known as Congo Square was overtaken in 1930 when the Municipal Auditorium was constructed on the site. Although the time-honored custom of the Second Line began to change along with American music in the 1970s when many youth broke with the tradition, it continued in fragmented form into the 21st century. The city remains a major seat of jazz culture and home to some of the music's most renowned performers and innovators.

Further Reading

Bloom, Gary W. "New Orleans Marches to a Different Beat." *American Visions,* October/November 1998.

Emery, Lynne Fauley. *Black Dance in the United States from 1619 to 1970.* Palo Alto, Calif.: National Press Books, 1972.

Hanks, Eric. "A Song for His Father: William Pajaud and the Jazz Funeral Tradition." *The International Review of African American Art* 17, no. 2, 2000.

McRae, Barry. *The Jazz Handbook.* Boston: G. K. Hall & Co., 1989.

Savage, Beth, editor. *African American Historic Places.* Washington, D.C.: The Preservation Press, 1994.

Southern, Eileen. *The Music of Black Musicians: A History.* New York: W.W. Norton & Company, 1971.

Touchet, Leo, and Ellis Marsalis. *Rejoice When You Die: The New Orleans Jazz Funeral.* Baton Rouge: Louisiana State University Press, 1998.

— Sandra L. West

Newsome, Mary Effie Lee (1885–1979) *writer, librarian*

As a poet, illustrator, and writer of prose, Mary Effie Lee Newsome was one of the most frequent contributors to the *CRISIS: A RECORD OF THE DARKER RACES* and the *BROWNIES' BOOK* magazines published by the NATIONAL ASSOCIATION FOR THE ADVANCEMENT OF COLORED PEOPLE (NAACP) in the 1920s.

Newsome was born Mary Effie Lee on January 19, 1885, in PHILADELPHIA. She was one of five children born to Mary Elizabeth Ash Lee and Benjamin Franklin Lee. Her father held a variety of positions, working at one point as an editor and later becoming a bishop. He lived with his family for a time in Texas before moving to Ohio. There, he eventually was appointed president of Wilberforce University.

Newsome attended high school in Ohio before enrolling at Wilberforce University in 1901 and graduating in 1904. She went on to study for a year at the Oberlin College Academy until 1905 and spent another year at the Philadelphia Academy of Fine Arts from 1907 to 1908. Three years later she enrolled at the University of Pennsylvania and remained there until 1914.

Her career as a poet began in 1917 with the publication of materials in *Crisis* magazine, then edited by W. E. B. DU BOIS. For nearly two decades, Newsome would publish more than a hundred poems in the *Crisis.*

On August 4, 1920, she married Reverend Henry Nesby Newsome. The couple moved to Birmingham, Alabama, where Newsome started the Boys of Birmingham Club. Returning to Wilberforce, Ohio, she worked as a librarian at the Central State College Elementary School before accepting a position as librarian at Wilberforce University's College of Education.

While contributing poems to *Crisis* magazine, Newsome also began in the early 1920s publishing poems, short prose, and illustrations in the NAACP's *Brownies' Book,* a publication designed specifically for African-American children. In 1926, she won honorable mention in the *Crisis* magazine poetry competition for her poem *The Bird in the Cage.* She chose, however, to publish the poem under the pseudonym "Johnson Ward." The following year, her work was anthologized in *Caroling Dusk,* edited by COUNTEE CULLEN. Toward the latter part of the 1920s, she edited *Crisis* magazine's *The Little Page* dedicated to children readers.

ARNA BONTEMPS included work by Newsome in his 1941 anthology, *Golden Slippers.* In 1944, the ASSOCIATION FOR THE STUDY OF NEGRO LIFE published Newsome's own collection, *Gladiola Gardens: Poems of Outdoors and Indoors for Second Grade Readers.* In her poems written for children, Newsome generally presented playful sketches of nature and fantasy. In those addressed to adults, she explored issues involving racial oppression.

Newsome remained a librarian at Wilberforce until retiring in 1963. She died on May 12, 1969.

Further Reading

Longmeadow Press Staff. *The Workings of the Spirit: The Poetics of African American Women's Writing.* Stamford, Conn.: Longmeadow Press, 1995.

Russell, Sandi. *Render Me My Song: African-American Women Writers from Slavery to the Present.* San Francisco: Harper Books, 2001.

— Aberjhani

New York Age

The *New York Age* was founded by T. Thomas Fortune as the *New York Freeman* in 1884 and became a forerunner of the militant African-American weeklies established in the early 1900s.

Fortune was born in slavery October 3, 1856, in Marianna, Florida, to Emanuel and Sarah Jane Fortune, both of whom were of mixed ancestry. With the Emancipation Proclamation providing freedom in 1865, Fortune later worked as a young man for WASHINGTON, D.C.'s black weekly, the *People's Advocate,* while also studying law during the night at HOWARD UNIVERSITY. He had not yet turned 30 when he wrote two important books: *Black and White: Land, Labor and Politics in the South,* and *The Negro in Politics.*

Moving with his wife, Carrie Smiley, to NEW YORK CITY in 1881, Fortune juggled a number of jobs with different black weekly newspapers. At the *New York Sun,* he held a position as printer and staff member while also working part time for the *Rumor.* He advanced steadily at both papers, eventually taking over the editorship at the *Rumor* and changing its name to the *Globe.* Among its contributors from across the country was the young W. E. B. DU BOIS. As with most black newspapers of the period, the *Globe* suffered from economic instability and Fortune sidestepped its eventual collapse in part by starting the *New York Freeman* in 1884. His brother Emanuel changed the name of the paper to the *New York Age* in 1887 and served as its editor until his death in 1889, when Fortune took it over once again.

From its outset, the *New York Age* displayed little tolerance for the ongoing practices of racism and segregation. Fortune was one of the earlier advocates for the desegregation of grade schools in New York. He also calmly suggested that it was both natural and desirable for African Americans to defend themselves against white mob violence. After losing her own newspaper, the *Memphis Free Press,* to mob violence in 1892, IDA BELL WELLS-BARNETT joined forces with the *New York Age.* In addition to her considerable skills as a journalist, she provided the paper with her subscription list, for which Fortune presented her with 25 percent of its ownership. The exchange provided Wells-Barnett with a new base of operations and Fortune with an extension of his readership into the Memphis area. In June 1892, they very boldly featured on the front page of the *Age* a seven-column story by Wells detailing instances of LYNCHING with names, dates, places and the nature of accusations against those murdered. Fortune printed 10,000 copies for distribution throughout America.

His paper in the 1890s maintained a national circulation of 6,000 and was read by blacks and whites. It also enjoyed the good fortune of advertising contracts from national white businesses. These allowed it to avoid the early death of most post–Civil War black newspapers and in the following century join the ranks of those battling for full African-American citizenship. After winning its reputation for militancy, however, the *Age* lost much of it when Fortune lent his support to BOOKER TALIAFERRO WASHINGTON both as a journalist and as a ghost writer.

Though personal setbacks caused Fortune to sell the *New York Age* in 1907, the paper went on to join the *CHICAGO DEFENDER* and the *PITTSBURGH COURIER* in the push for the GREAT MIGRATION, urging southern blacks to make their way north for greater economic and social opportunities.

Despite its promotion of black middle class values and its critique of both socialism and radical COMMUNISM, the *New York Age* was among those black newspapers that the government investigated for possible "sedition" during WORLD WAR I. Acting on a clause in the wartime Espionage Act, the government sought, though it failed, to prohibit publication of the paper should it prove that it was promoting riots, revolution, or political rebellion in any manner contrary to any U.S. law.

In addition to his trailblazing work as a journalist, Fortune cocreated along with 50 other African Americans the Afro-American League in CHICAGO in 1890. His league set the stage for the NIAGARA MOVEMENT and the NATIONAL ASSOCIATION FOR THE ADVANCEMENT OF COLORED PEOPLE (NAACP). In 1923, the man who had given the *New York Age* its start took on the editorship of the *NEGRO WORLD* for MARCUS GARVEY'S UNIVERSAL NEGRO IMPROVEMENT ASSOCIATION (UNIA) organization. Prior to his death in PHILADELPHIA, June 2, 1928, the National Negro Press Association bestowed upon him the honorary title of "Dean of Negro Journalism." Fortune's former home in New Jersey is now a National Historic Landmark listed in the State and National Register of Historic Places.

Further Reading

Kobre, Reva H., and Sidney Kobre. *A Gallery of Black Journalists Who Advanced Their Race . . . and Our Nation.* Norfolk, Va.: United Brothers and Sisters Communications Systems, 1999.

Thornbrough, Emma Lou. *T. Thomas Fortune: Militant Journalist.* Chicago: University of Chicago Press. 1972.

— Aberjhani

New York City

Recognized universally as one of the greatest cities in the world, New York City was a major focal point for the cultural and political movements that made up the Harlem Renaissance during the first half of the 1900s.

Currently with a population in excess of 8 million, New York City originated as a chain of trading posts established by the Dutch in 1610. The Dutch West India Company entered into a 24-year charter for rights to trade in the land they originally called New Netherland. In 1625, they created a settlement that they called New Amsterdam. (The island was originally controlled by the Manhattan band of the Lenni Lenape, Delaware giving the city its later name). Negotiating on behalf of the West India Company, Peter Minuet reportedly purchased the land from Native Americans for goods worth some 60 gilders. Other settlers added Long Island to New Amsterdam in 1626 and Staten Island to the settlement in 1670.

Virtually from the time of its founding, blacks maintained a presence in the new colony largely as slaves tending crops for the Dutch. As the trading of furs and meats increased, New Amsterdam developed into an important commercial center and attracted such religious groups as Jews, Quakers, Catholics, Lutherans, and Puritans. In 1664, King Charles II of England claimed the territory for his brother, the Duke of York, and renamed it New York.

With an influx of French settlers during the 1680s, the city's population swelled to 5,000 by 1700. A decade later, approximately 250 free African Americans were part of that population. A thriving industry grew up around shipping, lumbering, tavern-keeping, and the operation of general stores as the city continued to grow. However, half the city was destroyed by fire and it lost some 66 percent of its population during the Revolutionary War in the 1770s and 1780s. New York nevertheless emerged victorious in 1790 when it was proclaimed the new nation's first capital.

The city, with a population grown to 124,000 in 1810, made a number of important advances throughout the 1800s. New York was a stronghold of abolitionists and 33 percent of its black population was already free when it abolished slavery altogether in 1827. The 1840s saw the beginnings of a theater district that came to include such landmarks as the Park Theatre, the Bowery, Broadway, Astor, and others. Numerous high schools were constructed during the 1850s, and in 1857 Frederick Law Olmstead and Calvert Vaux created their design for Central Park. The city increased its area and population with the acquisition of sections of the Bronx in 1874 and 1895. The Brooklyn Bridge was completed in 1883, and in 1886, Frenchmen Edouard-René Lefebvre de Laboulaye and designer Frédéric-Auguste Bartholdi presented New York with the Statue of Liberty, one of the country's most definitive symbols of freedom and democracy. Brooklyn and Queens joined Manhattan, Staten Island, and the Bronx in 1898 to complete the five boroughs that make up modern-day New York. With the immigration of British, Germans, Irish, Italians, and Eastern Europeans to the city during the 1800s, its population at the beginning of the 1900s totaled more than 3,400,000.

Adding to the population growth during the first decade of the 1900s was a steady stream of African Americans making their way out of the South at the beginning of what later came to be known as the GREAT MIGRATION. Whereas in 1890, the city's black population was approximately 10,500, it rose by 1910 to approximately 95,000. The ongoing murder of African Americans by the mob violence called LYNCHING, limited opportunities for education and employment, and the overall domination of JIM CROW racism in the South encouraged blacks to seek their fortunes elsewhere. In addition to New York, northern and midwestern urban centers such as CHICAGO, Detroit, PHILADELPHIA, Pittsburgh, and Cleveland would all see a dramatic rise in their black populations for the entire first half of the 20th century.

As New York's population continued to grow, the city itself did the same with the design and construction of many of the skyscrapers that would become one of its chief characteristics. The 612-foot Singer Building went up in 1908 followed by the Metropolitan Tower at 657 feet in 1909 and the Woolworth Building at 792 feet in 1903. Manhattan's business district developed into one of the world's leading financial centers, and the city enjoyed a dominant status in the fields of shipping, publishing, communications, manufacturing, and commercial retail. Construction of the city's fabled subway system also got under way in the first decade of the 20th century. In short, New York at the beginning of the 1900s was one of the first modern metropolises. Accordingly, writers such as Sinclair Lewis, Edith Wharton, Theodore Dreiser, and John Reed found much within the city to celebrate and criticize.

New York had already begun to rival such cultural giants as Paris and London when BERT WILLIAMS, GEORGE WALKER, JAMES WELDON JOHNSON, and JOHN ROSAMOND JOHNSON moved there from the Midwest and the South, respectively. Drawn by the possibilities that the world of New York theater held as an outlet for their creative talents, Williams and Walker became the first blacks to sustain a successful career as a comedy and dance team on Broadway. Walker went on to become a major star with the ZIEGFELD FOLLIES. And the Johnson brothers teamed up with Bob Cole to write a string of successful musicals for white performers as well as several for themselves. James Weldon Johnson's early contributions to musical theater in New York helped set the stage for the success of black musicals during the 1920s. Similarly, his fictional *AUTOBIOGRAPHY OF AN EX-COLORED MAN*, along with W. E. B. DU BOIS's 1903 *SOULS OF BLACK FOLK*, was one of the major precursors to the *NEW NEGRO* literary movement.

Racial conflicts stemming from the changing demographics of northern urban centers and the ongoing violence of Jim Crow apartheid all over the United States inspired the creation of both the NATIONAL ASSOCIATION FOR THE ADVANCEMENT OF COLORED PEOPLE (NAACP) and the NATIONAL URBAN LEAGUE (NUL) in New York. The former launched its war against racism in the United States by constantly publicizing the atrocities of the practice and sponsoring court cases against them. The National Urban League dealt more directly with those African Americans relocating from a rural environment to an urban one by providing professional guidance on everything from personal grooming to obtaining housing and employment.

New York, along with Kansas City and Chicago, also became one of the major centers for the development of RAGTIME, the BLUES, and JAZZ. More than New York's most popular musical form during the 1910s, ragtime was also the driving musical expression behind the sales of SHEET MUSIC produced by the city's publishing houses and the development of radio and phonographs. The acknowledged "King of Ragtime," Scott Joplin, moved to the city in 1915. It was there that he staged the first presentation of his folk opera, *Treemonisha,* at the LINCOLN THEATRE in HARLEM.

One of the founding fathers of jazz, JELLY ROLL MORTON, moved in and out of New York during the 1910s and 1920s. His individual style helped bridge the gap between ragtime and jazz. Along with EUBIE BLAKE, NOBLE SISSLE, FATS WALLER, KING OLIVER, LOUIS ARMSTRONG, and many others, he turned the city into one of the locations where jazz took firm root and grew into a major form of musical art. In addition, it was jazz musicians who later popularized the term "Big Apple" as a nickname for New York.

The RACE RECORD industry that popularized the blues was centered in New York as well. The noted "Father of the Blues" W. C. HANDY and Harry Pace established their music publishing company there before Pace went on his own to create PACE PHONOGRAPHIC RECORD CORPORATION and Black Swan Records. It was the first black-owned record label in the United States and one of the more successful in the 1920s to focus on music featuring black singers. The success of "The Empress of the Blues" BESSIE SMITH on Columbia Records and Mamie Smith on Okeh Records prompted major white-owned record companies to create their own specialty labels for black singers. In addition to establishing a new professional outlet for black entertainers, the blues added yet one more thriving industry to New York City.

The city also quite literally provided the stage for a decade-long run of black Broadway musical hits beginning with *SHUFFLE ALONG,* the show that LANGSTON HUGHES cited as the beginning of the Harlem Renaissance, in 1921. The hits continued with *LIZA* in 1922 and *RUNNIN' WILD* in 1923. In addition, shows such as *DIXIE TO BROADWAY* in 1924 and *BLACKBIRDS* in 1926 made FLORENCE MILLS the United States's first black female international superstar. Unlike JOSEPHINE BAKER, who made PARIS her base of operations, Mills remained in New York and further added to the city's growing reputation as one of the major entertainment capitals of the world.

Home to the Statue of Liberty, world-famous skyscrapers, and Harlem, New York City provided the central location, cultural vitality, and vital resources that made the Harlem Renaissance possible. Manhattan's skyline is seen here from Brooklyn in a 1936 lithograph by Louis Lozowick. *(Library of Congress, Prints & Photographs Division [LC-USZ62-98241])*

Just as the music, politics, and theater that defined the Harlem Renaissance were based largely in New York, virtually every major writer affiliated with the movement either lived in the city at some point or, like HOWARD UNIVERSITY professor of philosophy ALAIN LOCKE, visited frequently enough that the city became for them a second home. As previously noted, James Weldon Johnson first moved to New York at the turn of the century and enjoyed a career as a Broadway composer. He left to serve as a U.S. consul in Venezuela and Nicaragua. He returned to accept a position with the *NEW YORK AGE* prior to joining the staff of the NAACP in 1916. Likewise, W. E. B. Du Bois left Atlanta University to relocate to the city and take on the editorship of the NAACP's *CRISIS* magazine. JEAN TOOMER, CLAUDE MCKAY, Langston Hughes, ZORA NEALE HURSTON, RUDOLPH FISHER, and ERIC DERWENT WALROND were not natives of New York but all made their way there to participate in its thriving black culture and opportunities for a better quality of life. When California failed to provide WALLACE THURMAN and ELOISE ALBERTA VERONICA BIBB THOMPSON with anything comparable to the *New Negro* movement they saw taking place in New York, both left the west coast for the east. Similarly, MARCUS GARVEY transferred the world headquarters for the UNIVERSAL NEGRO IMPROVEMENT ASSOCIATION from Jamaica to Harlem in New York.

In WORLD WAR I as well as World War II, New York proved a critical center for the manufacturing of wartime goods and materials. Its harbors and shipping industry proved the same. With an ongoing stream of immigrants to New York throughout the 1900s, the opening of the United Nations Building in 1953, and the occupation of the 110-story World Trade Center in 1970, the city grew into not just a major American city but a major world city.

It became the focus of world outrage and heartbreak on September 11, 2001, when terrorists destroyed the World Trade Center by flying two commercial airliners directly into the structures. Part of a plot that included an attack on the Pentagon in Washington, D.C., the death toll from the World Trade Center collapse was approximately 2,900. In the aftermath, New York mayor Rudy Guiliani was cited for providing exceptional leadership in a time of extreme crisis, and citizens of the city inspired the world with their displays of unity, hope, and courage. The city in 2003 continued to heal even as it has continued to grow and inspire since its founding.

Further Reading

Jackson, Kenneth T. *The Encyclopedia of New York City.* New Haven, Conn.: Yale University Press, 1995.

Lankevich, George J. *American Metropolis: A History of New York City.* New York: New York University Press, 1998.

Steven, Craig, and Steven Wilder. *In the Company of Black Men: The African Influence on African American Culture in New York City.* New York: New York University Press, 2001.

— Aberjhani

Niagara Movement (1905–1909)

BOOKER TALIAFERRO WASHINGTON's powerful leadership of African-American people at the the turn of the 20th century ran into its first institutionalized opposition from those he sought to represent when 29 men traveled from throughout the United States to meet, elaborate on, and document their grievances, thus founding the Niagara Movement.

Meeting on the Ontario, Canada, side of Niagara Falls, the men convened from July 11 to July 13, 1905. Led by educator W. E. B. DU BOIS and newspaperman William Monroe Trotter, the assembly included doctors, lawyers, educators, editors, and civil administrators. They formed an impressive representation of Du Bois's Talented Tenth, those intellectually advanced African Americans whom Du Bois theorized would lift his race above its oppressed status. Du Bois's recorded credentials for the meeting had him listed already as the noted author of *SOULS OF BLACK FOLK*, cited him as a Fellow of the American Association for the Advancement of Science, a member of the International Law Society, and secretary of the National Afro-American Committee. One affiliation he no longer claimed was with Washington's Committee of Twelve, from which he had resigned the previous year.

Trotter was editor of the *Boston Guardian* and a former schoolmate of DuBois's. He was passionate enough about his disagreements with Washington's political and educational formulas for racial progress that he shouted them out while Washington was delivering a speech in Boston in 1903. The action cost Trotter a month in jail and a permanent place on Washington's list of enemies among his people.

Also included in the group of 29 were the lawyer and former alderman of Cambridge, Massachusetts, Clement G. Morgan; medical director of PHILADELPHIA's Douglass Hospital, Dr. N. F. Mossell; editor of one of the country's most influential black newspapers, *Voice of the Negro,* T. Max Barber; and author of *The Aftermath of Slavery* and field secretary of the Constitution League, William A. Sinclair.

The group drew up a Declaration of Principles that tackled without inhibitions the issues of discriminatory hiring practices, JIM CROW segregation in transportation and housing, judicial reform, health care for blacks, and the responsibilities of black citizens. Without placing Washington's actual name in the line of fire, the Niagara Movement stated demands and observations in a tone and language that contrasted sharply with Washington's conservative philosophy of racial accommodation and left little doubt what their aim or target was. Whereas Washington was prone at times to chiding blacks for behavior he felt inappropriate or reckless, the Niagara Movement chose to "congratulate the Negro-Americans on certain undoubted evidences of progress in the last decade, particularly the increase of intelligence." And while Washington urged patience and tolerance in the face of racial discrimination, the Niagara Movement disavowed any sense of compromise: "discrimination based simply on race or color is barbarous, we care not how hallowed it be by custom, expediency or prejudice." Believing that Washington's tactics were leading blacks backward, the group declared, "Persistent manly agitation is the way to liberty, and toward this goal the Niagara Movement has started and asks the cooperation of all men of all races."

Du Bois was voted general secretary of the organization and Trotter headed its press and public opinion committee. Despite some debate over the issue, the men decided womanly agitation might also serve their political agenda and chose to include women in their conference the following year.

The Niagara Movement was not something Booker T. Washington took lightly. Du Bois's potential as a rival for Washington's authority beyond the classrooms of Tuskegee University in Tennessee became evident enough both with Du Bois's resignation from the Committee of Twelve and the publication of *Souls of Black Folk* in which the younger man took the elder to task in the essay, *Of Mr. Booker T. Washington and Others.* From the Niagara Movement's first meeting, Washington deployed assistants to report on the group's activities and used his considerable influence with the white press to block any publicity on the group. He also reportedly discouraged various philanthropists and officials from providing funds for the organization throughout its short life span of five years. Moreover, his opposition was intense enough that members of the Niagara Movement were sometimes caused to lose their jobs beneath the impact of Washington's disapproval and would find themselves struggling for further employment.

White social worker and part-time journalist MARY WHITE OVINGTON was one observer of America's racial plight who often balanced herself between Washington's camp and Du Bois's. Writing for the *New York Evening Post* in 1906, Ovington covered both the second Niagara Movement meeting, held at Harper's Ferry, and Washington's Negro Business League meeting. Ovington attempted to present the Niagara Movement's ideas and activities in such a manner that they appeared more reasonable than militant. A future founder of the NATIONAL ASSOCIATION FOR THE ADVANCEMENT OF COLORED PEOPLE (NAACP), she strived for objectivity while writing about Washington, but her personal ideology was already moving in its own more radical direction. Ovington proved influential as well in gaining for the organization the assistance of Oswald Garrison Villard, grandson of the famed abolitionist and *Liberator* editor William Lloyd Garrison and very much a champion for racial equality in his own right. Like Ovington, he would also help the NAACP get under way.

The Niagara Movement continued to meet annually in various historical locations, including Ohio's Oberlin College in 1908, until 1909. Its members headed chapters in more than three dozen states, and estimates of its peak membership range from 400 to 800 in 1907 and 1908. With Washington's opposition to the organization and a lack of funding and support among blacks and whites alike, it slowly began to dissolve. It also suffered from the bane of any organization in need of unity: in-house bickering. Du Bois's disagreements with Trotter at times flared up in public, and the latter abandoned official affiliation with the Niagara Movement after two years. Even so, the Niagara Movement did enjoy some small successes when calling for boycotts of discriminatory public functions, battling disfranchisement in specific towns, such as Baltimore, and protesting the screening of *The Clansman* in CHICAGO.

By February 1909, the foundation had been laid to establish the NAACP and in lieu of holding a Niagara Movement conference in 1910, Du Bois advised its members to join the newer organization.

Further Reading

Lewis, David Levering. *W. E. B. Du Bois: Biography of a Race 1868–1919.* New York: Henry Holt and Company, 1993.

— Aberjhani

Nicholas brothers (Fayard Nicholas) (1914–) (Harold Nicholas) (1921–2000) *dancers*

Fayard Nicholas and his younger brother Harold combined the athletics of acrobatics, the grace of ballet, and the jazz precision of tap to astound audiences for more than six decades. The sons of pianist Viola Nicholas and drummer Ulysses Nicholas, Fayard was born on October 28, 1914, and Harold on March 17, 1921. Their only other sibling was a sister named Dorothy.

Viola and Ulysses were established performers and bandleaders at the Standard, a black vaudeville theater in PHILADELPHIA. Growing up in such an environment, Fayard and Harold routinely enjoyed the stage antics and talents of various performers, including the singer ADELAIDE HALL and the great LOUIS ARMSTRONG. For them, the dance routines they began to work out when Fayard was 12 and Harold five were in many ways a form of play, and the quality of exuberant playfulness so evident in their act later on would help draw audiences around the world. Their parents recognized their talents early and felt strongly enough about their potential to both promote and manage their sons, something Viola Nicholas would continue to do after her husband's death.

The larger public received its initial exposure to the brothers' talents in 1931 when fans of the *The Horn and Hardart Kiddie Hour* radio program tuned in to hear their professional debut, the sound of their feet tapping out rhythm. The following year they joined the glittering lineup of entertainers working at the COTTON CLUB, where Harold would meet his future wife DOROTHY DANDRIDGE. Such was the magnitude of their appeal and audiences' respect for the sheer excellence of their performances that the Cotton Club's standard rule of forbidding its black entertainers to mix with its white audience was set aside as patrons requested and received their company at their tables.

While they worked as one of the Cotton Club's starring acts until 1939, their work expanded to include movies, radio, and clubs and theaters on the international circuit. In the same year as their Cotton Club debut, they appeared in *Pie Pie Blackbird* with Nina Mae McKinney and EUBIE BLAKE's orchestra. Movie producer Samuel Goldwyn caught one of their performances at the Cotton Club and cast them in Eddie Cantor's musical *Kid Millions.* Throughout the 1930s and 1940s their talents would be showcased in numerous films, including *The Big Broadcast of 1936, Down Argentine Way* (1940), *Sun Valley Serenade* (1941), and *Orchestra Wives* (1942). Among the most famous of their films was *STORMY WEATHER* (1943), featuring LENA HORNE and BOJANGLES ROBINSON. The Nicholas brothers' staircase routine, punctuated by seemingly impossible splits, is one that still awes both audiences and students of the medium.

Despite the recognition and top billing that made them bona fide stars, the Nicholas brothers were denied the kind of full-length feature opportunities provided such Hollywood prodigies as Shirley Temple or other male dancers such as Gene Kelly and Fred Astaire. They were simply presented in a sequence in which they often proved the highlight of the movie, then disappeared. Commenting in 1985 on the lack of full-length scripts for him and brother Fayard, Harold Nicholas observed of the movie studios, "I'm sure they probably wanted to give us maybe some roles, but it would've been probably roles as a boot black that came out to dance or something. Or a role, as a whatever, you know, a house boy or something that dances around the house or something. So rather than to accept anything like that, we said, 'Well, we'll dance. Just let us dance.'"

Both brothers married their first wives during the early 1940s. Both marriages concluded with divorce. Fayard married Geraldine Pate and Harold married Dorothy Dandridge. Later, Fayard married Vicky Barron. Harold's next marriage was to Elayne Patronne, then later still to Rigmor Newman.

With the decline of America's interest in musicals during the 1950s, the Nicholas brothers took their high-powered presentation to the stages of Europe. Upon their return to the States in the 1960s, they were recognized as the veteran performers of show business they were and made the round of guest appearances on variety shows.

A documentary on the brothers called *We Sing, We Dance: The Nicholas Brothers* is broadcast periodically on Public Broadcast System stations, and the Arts and Entertainment cable network offers a biographical video on the duo. Their impact upon the generations of dancers that followed them has been both profound and diverse, with talents such as Mikhail Baryshnikov, Michael Jackson, and Savion Glover all acknowledging their influence. In the foreword to Constance Valis Hill's book on the dancers, *Brotherhood in Rhythm,* Gregory Hines notes that should anyone attempt a movie version of their lives, "the dance numbers would have to be computer generated."

For his choreography work on the Broadway show *Black and Blue* (1989), Fayard received the distinguished Tony Award. For his performance in *Stompin' at the Savoy,* Harold received the Bay Area Critics Circle Award. Both brothers were inducted in 1986 into the Apollo Theatre Hall of Fame, received an Ebony Lifetime Achievement Award in 1987, and stood among the recipients of the Kennedy Center Honors in 1991. In their seventh decade as celebrated performers, they were awarded a star on the Hollywood Boulevard Walk of Fame.

The youngest of the brothers, Harold Nicholas, died on July 3, 2000, following surgery on his heart and legs. In the early 21st century, elder brother Fayard continued to live in Los Angeles and still made occasional guest appearances at events, including the 2002 Costa Mesa/Orange County Classical Jazz Festival in California.

Further Reading

Dunham, Katherine. *Black Dance: From 1619 to Today.* Princeton, N.J.: Princeton Book Company, 1991.

Hill, Constance Valis. *Brotherhood in Rhythm: The Jazz Tap Dancing of the Nicholas Brothers.* New York: Oxford University Press, 2000.

— Aberjhani

Niggerati Manor

Niggerati Manor, an apartment building on 136th Street in HARLEM during the Harlem Renaissance, housed a group of avant-garde African-American literary and visual artists. As such, the building has been justly declared "the headquarters of the Harlem Renaissance's vanguard wing."

The creative literary, or "literati," population of this building was further classified as "niggerati" by folklorist and anthropologist ZORA NEALE HURSTON. A resident of the manor herself, Hurston meshed the words "literati" and "nigger," the latter a racial slur often used as a kinship term between African Americans, to produce the term "niggerati." However, in poet LANGSTON HUGHES's autobiography *The Big Sea,* he states that the *Messenger* editor, novelist and manor resident WALLACE THURMAN, a dark-skinned, insecure man who was exceptionally critical of his race, coined the term "niggerati" to describe authors of *NEW NEGRO* literature, especially those who lived in Harlem.

According to the New York Landmarks Conservancy, Niggerati Manor, part of a set of row houses that boasted stained glass windows, was located at 267 West 136th Street, right next door to the office building of the conservative civil rights organization the NATIONAL URBAN LEAGUE (NUL). Number 267 has since been demolished. It was an apartment building divided into rooms (a rooming house) and run by Iolanthe Sydney. Interestingly, in *The Big Sea,* Hughes writes that in 1926 he lived with Thurman in a rooming house on 137th Street, not 136th. On one thing history can agree: Sydney refused to charge rent to the artist residents of "267." She believed, it appears, that when artists were not harassed with such realities as monthly rent responsibilities, they worked better because they were "freed" to produce significant works of visual art and literature.

The walls of Niggerati Manor were painted in an eccentric color scheme of black and red. Compared to the more conservative authors such as poet COUNTEE CULLEN and novelist JESSIE REDMOND FAUSET, the residents of Niggerati Manor were so unconventional that *Black Opals* coeditor ARTHUR HUFF FAUSET noted: "The 267 House artists claimed to be much more in tune with what Hughes (Langston) described as 'those elements within the race which are still too potent for easy assimilation.'" Fauset and Hughes meant, no doubt, an assimilation into traditionalist, *New Negro* publications such as the *CRISIS: A RECORD OF THE DARKER RACES*, and *OPPORTUNITY* magazine, as well as into traditions of conservative visual art.

Niggerati Manor residents included Thurman (*Infants of the Spring*); Hurston, (*Their Eyes Were Watching God*); muralist painter AARON DOUGLAS; Hughes (*The Weary Blues*); and writer and painter RICHARD BRUCE NUGENT. Together, the "potent" artists of the Manor, under the editorship of Thurman, produced a bohemian, explicit, literary journal called *FIRE!!* The publication blasted the established literary tenets, shocked black and white readers, and lasted for only one edition. The residence itself—a main "character" in Thurman's novel *Infants of the of Spring,* noted as the last novel of the Harlem Renaissance—sported homoerotic murals painted on the interior walls by Nugent.

Further Reading

Dolkart, Andrew S., and Gretchen S. Sorin, *Touring Historic Harlem: Four Walks in Northern Manhattan.* New York: New York Landmarks Conservancy, 1997.

Hughes, Langston. *The Big Sea.* New York: Hill and Wang, 1964. Original: New York: Knopf, 1940.

Lewis, David Levering. *When Harlem Was in Vogue.* New York: Vintage Books, 1982.

— Sandra L. West

Nigger Heaven

The August 1926 publication of *Nigger Heaven,* by white author CARL VAN VECHTEN, created extensive controversy at the same time that it further promoted the causes of the *NEW NEGRO*, African Americans dedicated to the cultural and political advancement of their people.

During the 1910s Van Vechten gained fame as a critic of music and drama for the *New York Times* and the *New York Press,* respectively. He later became well established as an author of both nonfiction and fiction that provided detailed portraits of America's developing JAZZ Age.

From the mid-1910s going into the 1920s, Van Vechten immersed himself into African-American culture through the nightlife offered by HARLEM and through friendships with such prominent individuals as JAMES WELDON JOHNSON, WALTER WHITE, LANGSTON HUGHES, PAUL ROBESON, and others. Whether Van Vechten cultivated these friendships to exploit them for literary purposes is a matter of debate. It is, however, a matter of record that he viewed the emerging culture of a growing HARLEM as important literary material and publicly urged black authors to take advantage of it before a white writer, such as himself, could do the same.

By 1925, Van Vechten saw no reason to hold off any longer and wrote his friend Gertrude Stein in France that he was ready "to start my Negro novel." Anticipating the backlash likely to come, Van Vechten sought support for *Nigger Heaven* prior to its publication from those African Americans he had befriended and whose careers he had helped advance. He conferred with James Weldon Johnson on the controversial title and decided it was suitable based on the many ways in which it could be interpreted, as well as its obvious explosive quality. The phrase was in fact a fairly common one used to describe the upper floor theater balcony seats that JIM CROW segregation forced blacks to occupy. In the context of Van Vechten's novel it would come to symbolize Harlem as a black society surprisingly similar to, but separate and unequal from, that of whites. Van Vechten pointed out further that the word *nigger,* according to what he had observed in Harlem and according to what many note to this day, could be employed by blacks with either derision or affection, depending on who used the word and how.

Walter White, who named his son after Van Vechten, wrote a column for the *PITTSBURGH COURIER* to announce the coming publication of the book and detailed Van Vechten's many contributions to African-American writers, artists, and entertainers. And although the editor of the *CRISIS: A RECORD OF THE DARKER RACES* would later denounce the book as an affront to blacks and whites alike, prior to its publication the magazine announced that artist AARON DOUGLAS had been commissioned to provide an illustration for the novel's cover.

Charles Van Vechten, the author's father, had rejected the Jim Crow attitudes of his times and raised his son to address blacks as equals. The artistic value of the title chosen by his son meant nothing to him and he begged him to change it. The book with its controversial title went on sale in August 1926 and became an immediate bestseller. In four months it went through nine printings, and in two years it went through 14 with translations into 10 different languages.

From the outset, *Nigger Heaven* was described as a melodramatic romance that some said was greatly inferior to Van Vechten's earlier novels, such as *Peter Whiffle: His Life and Works* and *The Tattooed Countess.* Nevertheless, the novel commanded attention more as a kind of journalistic exposé than a superior literary performance. The view of a multilayered black culture that Van Vechten offered whites through his novel was one that very few had ever experienced. Yet the desire for such an exposure had been increasing ever since the Broadway hit *SHUFFLE ALONG* began the trend of white New Yorkers seeking out black entertainment.

On its surface, Van Vechten's novel told the story of a young black couple caught in a tug-of-war between personal ambition, racism, and the conflicting elements of black culture that came with the influx of African Americans into Harlem during the GREAT MIGRATION. While the novel provided a voyeuristic peep inside nightclubs where people danced the Black Bottom and the Charleston, it also made many whites for the first time aware of an emerging black intelligentsia. If on the book's first page readers met a questionable character called Scarlet Creeper, they later met the very refined Mary Love, who vacationed in Italy and read books by such modern black authors as JEAN TOOMER, JESSIE REDMOND FAUSET, CLAUDE McKAY, and Van Vechten's friends, Johnson and White.

The supposed seedier aspects of the novel, which many said were fairly tame compared to some real-life situations in Harlem at the time, caused such black newspapers as the *CHICAGO DEFENDER* and the *Pittsburgh Courier* to dismiss the book as an insult while the latter pulled its ads for it. Satirist GEORGE S. SCHUYLER, however, an editor for the *Courier,* championed the novel as realistic and successful on its own terms. COUNTEE CULLEN and W. E. B. DU BOIS both concluded their friendship with Van Vechten for a number of years upon reading *Nigger Heaven.* Ironically, Du Bois often had and would still encourage black writers to employ literature as propaganda, and many read *Nigger Heaven* as exactly that: propaganda promoting racial equality disguised as a novel about blacks in Harlem.

NELLA LARSEN and a number of other black writers expressed admiration to the point of envying Van Vechten's accomplishment, stating openly that they wished one of them had written it instead. Claude McKay's *Home to Harlem* drew comparisons to the novel, but McKay made it clear that his book had been written independent of any influence from Van Vechten.

Despite controversy surrounding the novel, its success did help generate worldwide interest in Harlem, and tourists traveled from all over to see the famed "black capitol of the world." Van Vechten found himself cast into the role of a reluctant spokesperson on behalf of blacks and turned to White and Johnson to present the speeches that others asked him to give.

Further Reading

Van Vechten, Carl. *Generations in Black and White.* Athens: University of Georgia Press 1997.

———. *Flashes on Genius: African American Portraits.* Athens, Ga.: Hill Street Press, 2001.

— Aberjhani

Nugent, Richard Bruce (1906–1987) *illustrator, writer*

Richard Bruce Nugent contributed erotic illustrations and stories to publications during the Harlem Renaissance, served on the editorial staff of the bohemian literary journal *FIRE!!*, and outlived every member of the Harlem Renaissance except DOROTHY WEST.

Richard Bruce Nugent was born on July 2, 1906, in WASHINGTON, D.C., to parents Pauline Minerva and Richard H. Nugent. He left Washington, D.C., and relocated to HARLEM when he was 13 years old. In NEW YORK CITY, he worked a variety of jobs: errand boy, bellhop at the all-women's Martha Washington Hotel, iron worker, designer, and elevator operator. He called himself Richard Bruce so that his middle-class family would not be able to recognize him as the creator of erotic, homosexual literature and illustrations.

Nugent's *Sahdji* appeared in ALAIN LOCKE's anthology the *NEW NEGRO*, in 1925. After its publication, he and Locke adapted the story for the stage with *Sahdji: An African Ballet,* staged in 1932 at the Eastman School of Music, with a score by WILLIAM GRANT STILL and choreography by KATHERINE DUNHAM. Nugent was also the associate editor of the short-lived, avant-garde magazine *Fire!!,* edited by WALLACE THURMAN, to which he contributed erotic illustrations and the story "Smoke, Lillies and Jade." His illustrations appear as well in Thurman's second magazine, *Harlem,* on which he served as an editor. In addition, poetry by Nugent appeared in COUNTEE CULLEN's anthology *Caroling Dusk* (1927), and in *OPPORTUNITY* magazine.

Nugent worked with Thurman, who was very self-conscious about his swarthy skin tone, on several literary projects. They became close friends. A consummate bohemian, Nugent sometimes slept under Thurman's bed if he did not find a bench in Washington Square on which to spend the night. But when they first met, Nugent, a light-skinned black man, was so aghast at the darkness of Thurman's skin that he walked away from him. Thurman later portrayed Nugent as Paul Arbian, a major character in his 1932 novel *Infants of the Spring.*

Nugent lent his dramatic persona to the stage with DuBose Heyward's play *Porgy* and toured the United States and abroad with it for several years. During the WORKS PROGRESS ADMINISTRATION (WPA) era of the 1930s, he worked with the FEDERAL WRITERS' PROJECT, Federal Arts Project, and the Federal Theater Project. In the liberal 1960s, when many of his Harlem Renaissance colleagues were ill, retired from the arts, or dying, he cofounded the Harlem Cultural Council, which included Dancemobile and Jazzmobile components that New York neighborhoods enjoy to this day.

Nugent was openly homosexual, and he introduced the homosexual life into the art and literature of the Harlem Renaissance. He died on May 27, 1987, decades after Harlem Renaissance colleagues LANGSTON HUGHES, Countee Cullen, and ARNA BONTEMPS.

Further Reading

Nugent, Richard Bruce. *Selections from the Work of Richard Bruce Nugent.* Durham N.C.: Duke University Press, 2002.

Watson, Steven, *The Harlem Renaissance: Hub of African-American Culture, 1920–1930.* New York: Pantheon Books, 1995.

— Sandra L. West

O

Oliver, King (Joseph Oliver) (1885–1938) *musician*
Cornetist King Oliver was one of the leading pioneers of Chicago-style JAZZ and NEW YORK CITY's Jazz Age as well as a major influence on trumpeter LOUIS ARMSTRONG.

Oliver was born Joseph Oliver on May 11, 1885, on a plantation in Donaldsville, Louisiana. He grew up in NEW ORLEANS, where he worked as a yard boy and, due to an accident, lost sight in one eye. Inspired by New Orleans's many street musicians, Oliver began playing the trombone but gave it up for the cornet. He was particularly influenced by cornetist Charles "Buddy" Bolden, cited as one of the legendary founders of jazz.

During the 1910s, Oliver performed at dances, in parades, and with a variety of brass bands, including the Magnolia Band, the Eagle, and the Melrose Brass Band. He led a band of his own in 1915. For the next two years, he performed at Pete Lala's Café with the Kid Ory Band. In recognition of his superior musicianship, Kid Ory dubbed Oliver "King." The young Louis Armstrong adopted Oliver as his mentor and often sat outside the café to enjoy and study his music.

During WORLD WAR I, Oliver moved to CHICAGO where he played in both the Bill Johnson Band and Lawrence Duhe's New Orleans Jazz Band. Through his extended engagement with Duhe at Chicago's Lincoln Gardens (previously the Royal Garden Café), Oliver gained a reputation for his improvisational solos and stylistic phrasings. He took over the band in 1922 and renamed it the Creole Jazz Band. He hired Louis Armstrong as a second cornetist and Lil Hardin, who would become Mrs. Armstrong in 1924, as a featured vocalist. Clarinetist Johnny Dodds also joined the band. Bix Beiderbecke and other white musicians adapted the music of the Creole Jazz Band and that of JELLY ROLL MORTON, who worked in Chicago in 1923, to develop the Chicago music known as Dixieland Jazz.

Oliver and his Creole Jazz Band began in 1923 to embark on a series of recordings that established them as the first jazz band to produce such an extended body of work. Like Morton, with whom Oliver recorded in 1924, the Creole Jazz Band recorded on the Paramount and Gennett labels, moving later to Okeh Records, Columbia Records, and the Vocalion Company RACE RECORDS. Before his actual move to New York, musicians and jazz lovers in HARLEM began buying and discussing Oliver's records shortly after their release in 1923. Among the musical innovations that made Oliver stand out was his use of such devices as rubber plunger cups to mute or alter the sound of his horn. "Dippermouth Blues," "West End Blues," and "Dr. Jazz" became some of his better-known songs.

Despite his recording success and influence among younger musicians, Oliver lost most of his more experienced band members, including Louis Armstrong, during the mid-1920s. On May 15, 1927, he made his debut at the SAVOY BALLROOM with the Dixie Syncopators. After a successful two-week engagement at the Savoy, the managers of the COTTON CLUB invited Oliver and his band to work as their house orchestra. They disagreed, however, over the financial conditions, and the job went instead to DUKE ELLINGTON and his orchestra. However, that year Oliver and the Dixie Syncopators did enjoy the success of their record "Someday Sweetheart," which was recorded on Vocalion and sold a million copies.

In 1929, Oliver's health began to deteriorate and he sometimes employed others to perform solos for recordings under his name. "Sweet Like This" and "Too Late," both recorded in 1929, are two of the final recordings attributed to Oliver himself.

Oliver continued to form bands and tour the South during the early 1930s, living for a time in Nashville, Tennessee. He made his last recordings in 1931. Around 1936, Oliver settled in Savannah, Georgia, where he played for local dances and worked odd jobs to support himself. Following a newspaper report that Oliver was living in somewhat destitute circumstances, Armstrong visited his former mentor in Savannah in August 1937. Oliver died in Savannah on April 8, 1938.

Further Reading

Bisso, Ray. *Jelly Roll Morton and King Oliver.* New York: First Books Library, 2001.

Elmore, Charles J. *All That Savannah Jazz.* Savannah, Ga.: Savannah State University, 1998.

Porter, Eric. *What Is This Thing Called Jazz: African American Musicians as Artists, Critics, and Activists.* Berkeley: University of California Press, 2002.

— Aberjhani

Omega Psi Phi Fraternity

The Omega Psi Phi Fraternity secured its place in the history of African-American fraternities on November 17, 1911, at HOWARD UNIVERSITY, when it became the first Greek-letter organization founded on the campus of a black college.

The originators of the new fraternity were undergraduates Edgar Love, Frank Coleman, and Oscar Cooper. They formed the organization with the assistance of biologist Ernest E. Just, the man who in 1915 would become the first recipient of the SPINGARN MEDAL presented by the NATIONAL ASSOCIATION FOR THE ADVANCEMENT OF COLORED PEOPLE (NAACP).

Omega Psi Phi adopted its organization letters from the initials of the Greek phrase meaning, "friendship is essential to the soul." The guiding principles they chose for its members were scholarship, manhood, perseverance, and uplift. On December 15, 1911, the fraternity began the business of organizing with 14 charter members. Love was elected president, Cooper secretary, and Coleman treasurer.

Although the members of the fraternity were certain about their aim and goals, the administration at Howard University was not and on March 8, 1912, rejected their first proposed charter. The rejection marked the beginning of a two-year struggle. During that time, the fraternity fought for recognition by posting notices announcing its formation all over the campus, negotiating via faculty representatives, and meeting face-to-face with the administration. A principal issue of debate was whether the fraternity should be restricted to a local one as the faculty preferred, or whether it should be allowed national status as the organization desired. The battle ended with its national status recognized and the organization's incorporation on October 28, 1914.

Following its incorporation, additional chapters were formed at Lincoln University in Pennsylvania, in Boston, and in Nashville. With the United States's entry into WORLD WAR I and the country's establishment of a black officers training camp in Des Moines, Iowa, Omega Psi Phi instituted a war chapter to support the country's military efforts.

Founding members Love and Coleman both made contributions to the war efforts as military officers. Love served as an army chaplain before later becoming a bishop in the Methodist church. Coleman later became a professor of physics and department head at Howard University. Cooper, the third founding member, became a doctor.

World War I also saw the beginning of the fraternity's official publication, the *Oracle* magazine. Those goals and aspirations set forth by Omega Psi Phi attracted a number of the era's most progressive individuals, including the inventor of the blood plasma bank, Dr. Charles R. Drew, and key Harlem Renaissance figures—writer STERLING ALLEN BROWN, writer LANGSTON HUGHES, and historian CARTER GODWIN WOODSON. It was at the fraternity's national conference in Nashville in 1920 that Woodson first proposed the observance of National Achievement Week, the annual event that would eventually develop into Black History Month. Later, members of the fraternity would take out life memberships in Woodson's ASSOCIATION FOR THE STUDY OF NEGRO LIFE.

By 1923, Omega Psi Phi had nearly four dozen chapters across the United States. In the 1930s, the organization put the strength of its numbers behind the push to make certain African Americans got their fair share of the employment opportunities offered through New Deal government relief programs during the GREAT DEPRESSION. Members worked in unison with such groups as the International Brotherhood of Red Caps, the NAACP, the Southern Black Conference, and the NATIONAL URBAN LEAGUE.

In 1949, the corporation reached a milestone with the purchase of its first headquarters building in WASHINGTON, D.C. Around the same time it recognized the contributions of one of its former members when it named a scholarship fund after Dr. Charles R. Drew.

The economic support and development of black communities occupied much of the fraternity's concern during the 1940s. In the 1950s and 1960s, that concern translated into active participation in sit-ins, marches, and the endorsement of lobbies supporting civil rights legislation.

All three of Omega Psi Phi's founders, Love, Coleman, and Cooper, were on hand when the corporation continued its move forward with the dedication of its new international headquarters in Washington, D.C., in 1964.

Continuing to exercise its dedication to community service, in 1976 the fraternity implemented Operation Big Vote, a drive to register as many people as possible for that year's presidential elections. It also completed a goal to make a $250,000 contribution to the United Negro College Fund and dedicated itself to making a contribution of $50,000 to the fund each year thereafter.

Omega Psi Phi entered the 2000s with a lineup of programs designed to assist the homeless, provide tutoring for high school students, recognize and reward academic excellence among youth, and assist the elderly.

Some of the fraternity's better-known achievers are as follows: political advocate Rev. Jesse Jackson, journalist Carl Rowan, medical researcher Dr. Perry Julian, entertainer and educator Dr. Bill Cosby, astronaut Charles Bolden, former Virginia governor Lawrence Douglas Wilder, basketball greats Michael Jordan and Shaquille O'Neal, comedian Joe Torry, former NAACP director Roy Wilkins, and Moorehouse College president emeritus Benjamin E. Mays.

Further Reading

Hoskins, Charles Lwanga. *Yet with a Steady Beat.* Savannah, Ga.: The Gullah Press, 2001.

O'Neal, Shaquille. *Shaq Talks Back: The Uncensored Word on My Life and Winning in the NBA.* New York: St. Martin's Press, 2001.

— Aberjhani

Opportunity: A Journal of Negro Life

Sociologist and editor CHARLES SPURGEON JOHNSON launched *Opportunity: A Journal of Negro Life,* in January 1923 as the official publication of the NATIONAL URBAN LEAGUE (NUL), a conservative self-help and support organization that forged a strong link between Harlem Renaissance writers, editors, and publishers.

A sociologist educated at the University of Chicago, Charles S. Johnson joined the CHICAGO branch of the National Urban League in 1921 as its director of research. Transferring to New York, he established *Opportunity* magazine at a point when the *CRISIS: A RECORD OF THE DARKER RACES* was near the peak of its success as one of the most read black-oriented magazines in the United States. W. E. B. DU BOIS, editor of the high-flying *Crisis,* the official publication of the NATIONAL ASSOCIATION FOR THE ADVANCEMENT OF COLORED PEOPLE (NAACP), had just returned from a trip abroad when the rival *Opportunity* debuted. He was flabbergasted by the publication's intrusion. Not only did Johnson successfully establish *Opportunity* but he became a principal mentor for Harlem Renaissance artists.

Johnson regularly scoured periodicals for names of black writers and maintained profiles on all he found. He held informal literary meetings with these emerging writers and invited them to visit NEW YORK CITY. When they arrived, he introduced them to his secretary, Ethel Ray Nance, and her roommate, librarian REGINA ANDREWS. Nance and Andrews's apartment at 580 St. Nicholas Avenue was a haven for literary artists. They hosted parties for the established artistic community, and for newcomers they provided referrals for jobs, publications, and a home-cooked meal.

Andrews and graphic artist and poet GWENDOLYN BENNETTA BENNETT saw a need to create a platform for emerging artists and encouraged Johnson to do so. The time, they felt, was right. In the 20 years prior to 1924, according to historian DAVID LEVERING LEWIS, the literary output of African Americans was powerful but small. Titles published during the period included *Pointing the Way* by Sutton Grigg in 1908; *The Quest for the Silver Fleece* by W. E. B. Du Bois in 1908; *THE AUTOBIOGRAPHY OF AN EX-COLORED MAN* by JAMES WELDON JOHNSON in 1912; *Harlem Shadows* by CLAUDE MCKAY in 1922; and *Cane* by JEAN TOOMER in 1923.

After the important efforts of Grigg, DuBois, Johnson, McKay, and Toomer came a tremendous flood of poetry and fiction. To celebrate these literary accomplishments and announce the publication of JESSIE REDMOND FAUSET's novel, *There Is Confusion,* Johnson hosted the CIVIC CLUB DINNER on March 21, 1924. The event officially heralded the arts-patron-fueled Harlem Renaissance and, later, the *Opportunity* literary awards. At the dinner, emerging and established writers met socially with publishers, editors, and potential PATRONS. Johnson also wanted the dinner to jump-start sales of the new books. While some have minimized Johnson's contributions and influence during the *NEW NEGRO* movement, writer ZORA NEALE HURSTON remarked that the Harlem Renaissance "was (Johnson's) work, and only his hush-mouth nature had caused it to be attributed to many others."

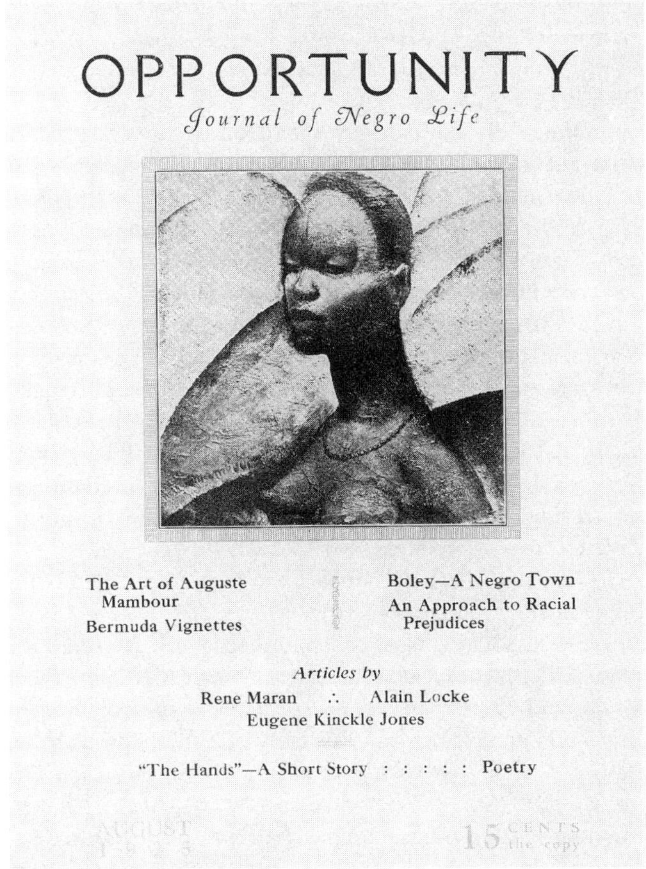

OPPORTUNITY

Journal of Negro Life

The Art of Auguste Mambour

Bermuda Vignettes

Boley—A Negro Town

An Approach to Racial Prejudices

Articles by

Rene Maran ∴ Alain Locke

Eugene Kinckle Jones

"The Hands"—A Short Story : : : : : Poetry

AUGUST 1 9 2 5

15 CENTS the copy

Through its awards programs for visual and literary artists, *Opportunity* magazine became a principal showcase for the writers and artists of the Harlem Renaissance. *(Alain Locke Collection, Moorland-Spingarn Research Center, Howard University)*

With a strong stable of writers, and with Johnson's philosophy that black art and literature could help eradicate racism, the *Opportunity* literary awards began in 1924. Harlem gambler and mobster Caspar Holstein, who had a penchant for black arts, provided part of the funding for the awards. CARL VAN VECHTEN, himself a journalist and novelist *(NIGGER HEAVEN)*, was also a dedicated *Opportunity* arts patron. Literary award judges included author Fannie Hurst, dramatic critic Robert C. Benchley, and editor John Farrar.

Among the many *Opportunity* literary award winners were Caroline Bond Stewart Day and Brenda Ray (Francke) Moryck. Day's short story "The Pink Hat" won third prize in the 1926 contest. "The Pink Hat" was about a black woman who successfully passes for white under the protection of her wide pink hat and decides, after a crisis, that she is quite content being black after all. Moryck, a columnist for the *Baltimore*

Afro-American and *New Jersey Herald* newspapers, won second prize in 1926 for "A Man I Know," an essay about *Opportunity* editor Johnson. She also won honorable mention in 1927 for "When a Negro Sings."

One of the magazine's frequent contributors was Eunice Roberta Hunton Carter, who published four short stories in *Opportunity* magazine: "Digression" (December 1923); "Replica" (September 1924); "Who Gives Himself" (December 1924); and "The Corner" (April 1925). Her book reviews also found an audience through *Opportunity*'s pages and in May 1929 she critiqued WALLACE THURMAN's controversial novel *The Blacker the Berry.* (An attorney, Carter later accepted the position of secretary of the Committee on Conditions in Harlem at the request of Mayor FIORELLO HENRY LA GUARDIA following the HARLEM RIOTS in 1935. In August 1935, Special Prosecutor Thomas E. Dewey appointed her to a grand jury investigation into organized crime and, that same year, also appointed her deputy assistant district attorney for New York County.)

Opportunity regularly published a column called "Our Book Shelf." Among books reviewed were *Not Without Laughter* by LANGSTON HUGHES (September 1930); *Paul Robeson Negro* by ESLANDA CARDOZO GOODE ROBESON (September 1930); and *The Captain's Daughter* by the "father of modern Russian literature," African-Russian writer Alexander Pushkin (January 1930). *Opportunity* book reviewers included journalist ALICE DUNBAR-NELSON and poet STERLING ALLEN BROWN.

Johnson surrounded himself with exemplary editorial talent: philosopher ALAIN LOCKE, poet ERIC DERWENT WALROND, and bibliophile ARTHUR SCHOMBURG, for whom the SCHOMBURG CENTER FOR RESEARCH IN BLACK CULTURE is named. They published in the magazine such articles as "Elizabeth Prophet: Sculptress" by COUNTEE CULLEN (July 1930); and "Once More the Germans Face Black Troops" by Claude McKay (November 1939). The February 1939 issue featured verse by Hughes, Verna Avery, Marcus R. Christian, GWENDOLYN BROOKS, and James Dykes. Brooks became, in 1950, the youngest winner of the coveted Pulitzer Prize in poetry and the first African-American recipient.

Unlike *Crisis* magazine, *Opportunity* was not self-supporting but dependent upon the National Urban League for its existence. Circulation, at its peak, reached 11,000 in 1928. During the 1930s and 1940s, the price of one copy was 15¢. *Opportunity* continued to publish in 2002 with a focus on economic development for black Americans.

Further Reading

Johnson, Abby Arthur, and Ronald Maberry Johnson. *Propaganda and Aesthetics: The Literary Politics of Afro-American Magazines in the Twentieth Century.* Amherst: University of Massachusetts Press, 1979.

Wilson, Sondra Kathryn, ed. *Opportunity Reader: Selections from the Urban League's Opportunity Magazine.* New York: Random House, Inc., 1999.

Wilson, Sondra Kathryn. "Reading Opportunity." *Opportunity,* February 2000.

— Sandra L. West

Outhouse School, The

See MUSEUMS, AFRICAN-AMERICAN UNIVERSITY.

Ovington, Mary White (1865–1951) *political advocate, author*

A lifelong advocate for racial equality and women's rights, Mary White Ovington was one of the original founders of both the NATIONAL URBAN LEAGUE (NUL) and the NATIONAL ASSOCIATION FOR THE ADVANCEMENT OF COLORED PEOPLE (NAACP).

The daughter of Ann L. Ketchum Ovington and Theodore Tweedy Ovington, Mary White Ovington was born on April 11, 1865, in Brooklyn, NEW YORK CITY. The Ovingtons were descendants of abolitionists, and Mary was the third of four children. Her brother Charles Ketchum was born in 1856, sister Adele in 1861, and sister Helen in 1870.

Ovington attended the Packer Collegiate Institute from 1881 to 1891 before entering Harvard Annex, later known as Radcliffe College, in 1894, remaining there for two years. While at Packer, she was inspired to consider working in race relations when she heard a presentation by the famed abolitionist Frederick Douglass at Brooklyn's Plymouth Church.

In 1893, Ovington accepted a position as registrar for the Pratt Institute in Brooklyn, and in 1895 she cofounded the Institute's Greenpoint Settlement. During her tenure as the head social worker for the Greenpoint Settlement, she toured slum areas in London and further resolved to correct such living conditions in the United States. She left the Greenpoint Settlement in 1903 when she was awarded a fellowship for social work at Mary Kingsbury Simkhovitch's Greenwich House in Manhattan. During the same year, she heard BOOKER TALIAFERRO WASHINGTON speak at the Manhattan Social Club and eventually became one of Washington's political acquaintances.

Ovington began in 1904 to research in depth the political and social conditions of African Americans. She worked with the PATRON Ruth Standish Baldwin and Francis Keller to help establish the National League for the Protection of Colored Women and the Committee for Improving the Industrial Condition of Negroes in New York. Six years later these organizations combined with the Committee on Urban Conditions Among Negroes to form the National Urban League, an organization dedicated to helping those blacks moving out of the South during the GREAT MIGRATION adjust to living conditions in the urban North.

Touring the South, Ovington visited Virginia's Hampton Institute in 1904 and the following year visited Atlanta University, where she met W. E. B. DU BOIS. Also in 1905, she joined the Socialist Party and remained a socialist throughout her life. In 1906, she went on journalism assignments for Oswald Garrison Villard's *New York Evening Post,* reporting on both Washington's National Negro Business League meeting in Atlanta and on Du Bois's NIAGARA MOVEMENT convention at Harper's Ferry in West Virginia.

Ovington found herself at the center of controversy in 1908 when she attended a multiracial dinner held at New York's Cosmopolitan Club. Newspapers across the United

Pictured here in 1920 with W. E. B. Du Bois following a ceremony to present the Spingarn Medal awarded by the National Association for the Advancement of Colored People (NAACP), Mary White Ovington was one of the organization's founders and primary policy makers. *(Library of Congress, Prints & Photographs Division [LC-USZ62-33796])*

States reported on the fact that she had dined among African-American men. The *Savannah News* in Savannah, Georgia, described her as the "high priestess" of the event who could lead younger white women "astray" in a den of miscegenation (see INTERRACIAL INTERACTION).

Of longer lasting significance for Ovington in 1908 was her response to *Race War in the North,* a story by William English Walling on a race riot in Springfield, Illinois, one of the worst the country had ever experienced. Ovington took Walling's call for a return "to the spirit of the abolitionists" literally. She, Walling, and social worker Henry Moscowitz, a Jewish immigrant from Russia, met in Walling's apartment to plan a call to political action. They worked with Oswald Garrison Villard to publish a call for a "renewal of the struggle for civil and political liberty." Their call was answered in the form of a National Conference on the Negro organized by a National Negro Committee, first in 1909 and again in 1910. During the second conference, the National Negro Committee adopted the name National Association for the Advancement of Colored People, and Ovington served briefly as its acting executive secretary. Joining her as founding members of the NAACP were a number of former members of the Niagara Movement, including DuBois. Among Ovington's early achievements on behalf of the NAACP was coauthoring the organization's first antilynching pamphlet and extending the work of IDA BELL WELLS-BARNETT by helping initiate its antilynching program.

Ovington's extensive research on the lives of African Americans culminated in 1911 in the publication of a book called *Half a Man: The Status of the Negro in New York.* A groundbreaking work for its time, it was adopted as required reading for college sociology classes. Ovington continued to publish throughout the 1910s, producing a children's novel called *Hazel* in 1913 while writing frequently for the *CRISIS: A RECORD OF THE DARKER RACES*, the *New Republic,* the *New Review,* the *Masses,* and A. PHILIP RANDOLPH's *MESSENGER*. She gained some literary renown in August 1915 when the *New Republic* published her poem "Mary Phagan Speaks," in which she dramatized the voice of a 14-year-old girl who had been murdered. Her short story "The White Brute," in which she assigned to white males the stereotype more frequently attributed to black men, brought her further fame upon its publication in the *Masses* in November. Aside from her literary pursuits and political activism, she often served as a patron to black students from the American South and various parts of Africa.

In 1919, Ovington became chairman of the NAACP's board of directors, a position she would maintain for some 13 years. As chairman, she became one of the organization's most powerful members, influencing its policies on such vital issues as tactics for combating the racist JIM CROW practices of the time, acknowledging the accomplishments of black women, and selecting the recipients of the SPINGARN MEDAL, the award presented annually by the NAACP in recognition of outstanding achievements in race relations. She also traveled extensively on visits to NAACP chapters in every region of the country.

Moreover, Ovington remained productive as an author during the 1920s. She published a second children's novel, *The Shadow,* in 1920, along with an anthology for black children titled *The Upward Path.* Noting the growing number of published books by African Americans, she began to write a column called *Book Chat* in 1921 and in it reviewed such works as WALTER WHITE's *Fire in the Flint,* JAMES WELDON JOHNSON's *Book of Negro Verse,* and CARL VAN VECHTEN's *NIGGER HEAVEN.* In 1923 she published a play, *The Awakening,* and in 1927, *Portraits in Color,* literary profiles of influential black leaders, including Du Bois, Johnson, White, MARCUS GARVEY, and others. *Zeke,* her second children's novel, was published in 1931, and her second play, *Phyllis Wheatley,* in 1932.

Also in 1932, Ovington resigned as chairman of the NAACP's board of directors and took on the position of its treasurer. She began in September of the same year writing for the *Baltimore Afro-American* a series of articles called *Reminiscences, or Going Back 40 Years.* In these, she recounted her development as a political activist and landmark events in the struggle for racial equality. She remained one of the NAACP's principle policy makers until 1940 and kept her position as treasurer of the organization until 1947. Her autobiography and history of the NAACP, *The Walls Came Tumbling Down,* was published in 1947.

Ovington died in 1951. Commemorating her life and contribution to the black struggle for civil rights, the *Baltimore Afro-American* reran her series, *Reminiscences.*

Further Reading

Ovington, Mary White. *Black and White Sat Down Together.* New York: Feminist Press at the City University of New York, 1995.

Wedin, Carolyn. *Inheritors of the Spirit.* New York: John Wiley and Sons, 1998.

— Aberjhani

Owens, Jesse (James Cleveland Owens, J. C. Owens) (1913–1980) *track and field athlete*

Jesse Owens, cited as "the world's fastest man" in track and field, won four gold medals at the 1934 Olympic Games in Berlin and drew the indignation of Germany's leader, Adolf Hitler, whose military aggressiveness and policy of white supremacy overshadowed the Olympics.

Jesse Owens was born James Cleveland Owens on September 12, 1913, in Oakville, Alabama. His parents, Henry and Emma Owens, were sharecroppers. His family called him J. C., for the initials of his first and middle names. When he was eight years old, the family migrated to Cleveland, Ohio. The young J. C. got the name Jesse because an elementary school teacher in Cleveland could not audibly distinguish the similarly sounding "J. C." from "Jesse." She called him Jesse, and the name stuck.

Owens was frail and sickly as a child, but he enjoyed running. To help support his family, he took odd jobs on which he could run, which he did as a grocery delivery boy, a freight car loader, and shoe shiner. Owen's gym class coach, Charlie Riley, noticed Owens's running talent and offered to train him in the mornings so that he could run on the school track team. At Cleveland East Technical High School, Jesse Owens became a track star. As a senior, he tied the world record in the 100-yard dash with a time of 9.4 seconds. He tied this record again running in the Interscholastic Championships in CHICAGO. While in Chicago, he also leaped a distance of 24 feet 9 $^5/_8$ inches in the broad jump.

In 1933, following high school, Owens attended Ohio State University during the era of JIM CROW racial segregation and worked three jobs to support himself. He was forced to live off campus with other African-American athletes instead of being allowed to live in the main dorm facilities. Nor was he allowed to eat in restaurants with his white Ohio State teammates; he was forced instead to eat at blacks-only restaurants and to sleep in blacks-only hotels.

Because of his speed in track and field competitions, Owens earned the nickname Buckeye Bullet. On May 25, 1935, at a Big Ten meet in Ann Arbor, Michigan, Owens, although suffering pain from a back injury, set three world records and tied a fourth, all in a span of 45 minutes.

At the 1936 Olympics in Berlin, Germany, Owens participated in the long jump against German athlete Lutz Long. Germany's chancellor, Adolf Hitler, a white supremacist, referred to the 10 black athletes at the games as "subhuman." He thought the German athletes could crush the black athletes. Owens defeated Long and set a record that stood for 25 years. The victory disturbed Hitler. In the same Olympics, Owens won gold medals in the 100-meter sprint, the 200-meter sprint, and the 400-meter relay. The German crowd loved Owens, but Hitler publicly snubbed him. It was a snub that made headlines around the world.

Owens returned to the United States a hero. He received a ticker-tape parade in NEW YORK CITY. Yet, even with a partial college background, he was unable to find a job to support himself and complete his formal education. Forced to drop out of college, he worked as a janitor, performed on stage as a tap dancer with BOJANGLES ROBINSON, and made speeches on behalf of Alf Landon, the Republican presidential candidate.

Eventually Owens did complete college, left professional sports, and worked at jobs ranging from a WORKS PROGRESS ADMINISTRATION (WPA) official in Cleveland, Ohio, to director of his own public relations firm. In the latter capacity, he earned $100,000 a year in speaking engagements.

Owens supported the Republican Party when most African Americans were Democrats. During the Black Power movement of the late 1960s, he opposed a black boycott of the Olympics, much to the chagrin of many black people. Owens also authored two books: the biographical *Blackthink* in 1970 and *I Have Changed* in 1972. He remained "ambassador of sports" for the U.S. State Department, received a Presidential Medal of Freedom from President Gerald Ford in 1971, the Living Legend Award from President Jimmy Carter in 1979, and the Congressional Gold Medal, posthumously, from President George Bush in 1990.

Jesse Owens died on March 31, 1980 in, Phoenix, Arizona.

Further Reading

Altman, Susan. *The Encyclopedia of African-American Heritage.* New York: Facts On File, 1997.

Page, James A. *Black Olympian Medalists.* Colorado: Libraries Unlimited, 1991.

Steele, Philip. *Jesse Owens.* Portsmouth, New Hampshire: Heinemann Library, 2001.

— Sandra L. West

Pace Phonographic Record Corporation

The Pace Phonographic Record Corporation, founded in 1921, was the first record company owned and operated by African Americans.

The founder of the company was Harry H. Pace, who was born on January 6, 1884, in Covington, Georgia, and who died on July 26, 1943, in CHICAGO. Pace's first business venture was a printing company that he started with W. E. B. DU BOIS, one of his former professors at Atlanta University. He and Du Bois published the first African-American illustrated journal, the *Moon Illustrated Weekly.* In 1909, Pace entered the music publishing world with the man often called "the father of the blues," W. C. HANDY. The team moved their business, the Pace and Handy Music Company, in 1918 from Memphis to NEW YORK CITY. They dissolved their partnership in 1921, the same year Pace founded the Pace Phonographic Record Corporation.

Pace established his company shortly after Mamie Smith began the craze for RACE RECORDS in 1920 with her hit song "That Thing Called Love" on Okeh Records. To cash in on the new trend, Pace hired pianist and composer FLETCHER HENDERSON as his recording manager and WILLIAM GRANT STILL as his music arranger and director. He also maintained a strong relationship with his former teacher Du Bois by providing him with a seat on the company's board of directors.

Aiming to accommodate popular and sophisticated tastes in black music, the company focused on piano and violin solos, blues, spirituals, novelty songs, and ballads issued on its Black Swan Label. Pace named the label after Elizabeth Taylor Greenfield, the first black concert singer in the United States. Bypassing the talents of BESSIE SMITH, whose work would earn Columbia Records a small fortune, the Pace Corporation recorded instead the Broadway troupe the Four Harmony Kings, vaudevillian Katie Crippin, sopranos Revella Hughes and Florence Cole, and baritone C. Carroll Clark. ALBERTA HUNTER joined the company as performer and songwriter, recording "Bring Back the Joys" in 1921. In the same year, ETHEL WATERS recorded Hunter's "Down Home Blues," composed with Lovie Austin, and gave the company its first big hit. Following up the song's success, Waters and Henderson went on tour for six months as part of a group called the Black Swan Troubadours.

Pace's company motto stated very boldly that it was "The Only Genuine Colored Record—Others Are Only Passing for Colored." Despite this proclamation, white-owned record companies with labels devoted solely to black artists dominated the market until the Pace Phonographic Record Corporation went bankrupt in December 1923. Nevertheless, while it operated, the company helped elevate blues musicians to professional status and forced the hand of its white competitors to invest more advertising dollars in black-owned newspapers.

After the company's closure, Pace moved to Chicago. There, he helped Supreme Liberty Life Insurance Company become one of the biggest African-American-owned businesses in the United States.

Further Reading

Handy, D. Antoinette. *Black Women in American Bands and Orchestras.* Lanham, Md.: Scarecrow Publishing, 1999.

Kebede, Ashenafi. *Roots of Black Music: The Vocal, Instrumental and Dance Heritage of Africa and Black America.* Lawrenceville, N.J.: Africa World Press, 1995.

Spencer, Jon Michael. *The New Negroes and Their Music: The Success of the Harlem Renaissance.* Knoxville: University of Tennessee Press, 1997.

— Aberjhani

Paige, Satchel See NATIONAL NEGRO BASEBALL LEAGUE.

Pan-African Congress

Black scholars and statesmen from around the world established the Pan-African Congress to promote greater political, cultural, and economic unity among peoples of African descent on an international scale. Different groups of Pan-Africanists have repeatedly debated the feasibility of a "return to Africa" (see MARCUS GARVEY).

The idea of people of African descent supporting each other on a global level found an early champion in Martin R. Delaney, Frederick Douglass's coeditor of the *North Star* and author of *The Condition, Elevation, Emigration of the Colored People of the U.S., Politically Considered* (1852). In addition, Bishop Henry McNeal Turner, convinced by his experience in the Georgia state legislature that African Americans would never achieve racial equality, helped sponsor 200 African Americans' journey to Liberia in 1878. Educator Alexander Crummell met with like-minded individuals at the CHICAGO Congress on Africa in 1893 to explore the pros and cons of forging stronger links with the international African community.

That community voiced its concerns as a collective of 33 men and women from Canada, the United States, Europe, Africa and the Caribbean attended the first Pan-African Congress in London, on July 23–25, 1900. Trinidadian Henry Sylvester Williams was a principal organizer of the event. Bishop Alexander Walters of the African Methodist Episcopal Zion (A.M.E.Z.) Church and an affiliate of the National Afro-American Council served as the congress's presiding officer. W. E. B. DU BOIS was appointed its secretary. Though he did not attend, BOOKER TALIAFERRO WASHINGTON was a supporter of Pan-Africanism in general and of the congress in particular, circulating flyers to urge attendance at the latter. The congress served mostly to establish a Pan-African Association that confirmed communication and a sense of solidarity among those involved.

The second Pan-African Congress was held in PARIS, on February 19–21, 1919, at the same time that the Paris Peace Conference convened to bring about an end to WORLD WAR I. From the start of U.S. involvement in the war, the issue of racism (which often took the form of genocide) and democracy had been a resounding one and the 1919 Pan-African Congress followed up on it, demanding to know how people of African descent could expect to benefit from the war's end.

Attending the congress were some 57 delegates from 16 different countries. Along with Blaise Diagne of Senegal, who served as president of the congress, Du Bois played a more substantial role than he did during the congress of 1900. As editor of the *CRISIS: A RECORD OF THE DARKER RACES*, and an executive board member of the NATIONAL ASSOCIATION FOR THE ADVANCEMENT OF COLORED PEOPLE (NAACP), he was also in Europe to research and investigate the treatment of African-American soldiers. However, he was equally passionate, if not more so, about Pan-Africanism, which he compared to Zionism and described as "the centralization of the race effort and the recognition of a racial fount." His "Resolutions of the Pan-African Congress" articulated the congressional delegates' primary focus. Included were calls for indigenous peoples of color to retain ownership of their land; the cessation of capitalistic exploitation of such people; educational programs financed by the state to provide classes for technical training and other skills, taught and developed in the context of indigenous peoples' native language; unhindered development of native cultures and religion; self-government; and protection by the League of Nations against colonialism.

The congress provided a stronger foundation for such meetings in the future and solidified a network of advocates for racial equality all over the world. Wheels were also set in motion to one day create a permanent Pan-African Congress Headquarters in Paris.

A third Pan-African Congress convened in London, Brussels, and Paris from August 28 to September 6, 1921. With Diagne and Du Bois once again at the helm, 113 delegates attended. Topping the 1921 agenda was the congress's petition to the League of Nations to help colonial peoples obtain greater autonomy in their homelands. While some called for a complete removal of the European presence from the African continent, others felt such a withdrawal should be gradual to allow a preparatory period of adjustment. Along those lines, the congress composed a manifesto entitled "To the World," and within it demanded the independence of such countries as Abyssinia, Liberia, Haiti (then under U.S. occupation), and the Dominican Republic.

The Pan-African Congress remained active with further conventions in 1923, 1945, and 1974.

Pan-Africanism in 2001 was perhaps strongest on the African continent where organizations such as the Pan-Africanist Congress of Azania was working to develop a "United States of Africa with all who pay their only allegiance to Africa being accepted as Africans." The organization was founded in Soweto on April 6, 1959, with the Rev. Dr. Stanley Mogoba as president.

Moreover, African-American citizens of St. Helena, South Carolina, declared an alliance with refugees and statesmen from Sierra Leone on May 20, 1999, to exert pressure upon the U.S. Congress to amend the U.S. policy on military intervention in Africa. The Sierra Leone refugees had been caught in the middle of a civil war instigated by rebels procuring diamonds and other minerals from the country for export to Europe and America. Emory Campbell, the director of St. Helena's historic Penn Center, hosted the conference on behalf of the "Friends of Sierra Leone" at the center. Then Georgia state representative Cynthia McKinney was one of the alliance's strongest supporters.

Further Reading

Aptheker, Herbert. *A Documentary History of the the Negro People in the United States, Volume 3.* New York: Carol Publishing Group, 1993.

Kadalie, Modibo M. *Internationalism, Pan-Africanism, and the Struggle of Social Classes.* Savannah, Ga.: One Quest Press, 2000.

— Aberjhani

Paris

From the 1920s to the 1940s, and even well into the 1970s, Paris, France—often called the City of Light—provided a haven of racial and creative freedom for African-American artists. Lucrative, satisfying careers such as the dancing art of JOSEPHINE BAKER were established in Paris, something that could not have been possible in the race-obsessed United States.

Even before the Harlem Renaissance, African Americans traveled to Paris, especially for conferences, and were awed by the independence and encouragement they experienced there. In NEW ORLEANS, Louisiana, early in the 19th century, a Paris-educated Creole named Armand Lanusse organized a black literary society called Les Cenelles. Members of the society sailed to Paris to study because people of color were not allowed to pursue literary education in Louisiana.

Among a significant stream of early African-American visitors to Paris were playwright William Wells Brown *(Clotel; or, The President's Daughter)* and Tuskegee Institute founder BOOKER TALIAFERRO WASHINGTON. Brown went to Paris in 1849 as a fugitive slave, one of the 12 Massachusetts delegates to the Peace Congress, traveling with Rev. Alexander Crummel, founder of the AMERICAN NEGRO ACADEMY. When he addressed the Congress, Brown's host welcomed him with, "I hope you feel yourself free in Paris." He contributed to a school of African-American travel writing with his *Sketches of Places and People Abroad,* in which he discusses his time in Paris.

Through the years, many black artists, including painter HENRY OSSAWA TANNER, migrated to Paris and never returned to America. Tanner claimed France as his home in 1891 and died there in 1937. Booker T. Washington visited the Paris studio of Tanner in the 1890s and diplomatically declared to the world what Tanner already knew: "Here in France no one judges a man by his color. The color of the face neither helps nor hinders." Yet Washington also observed that while many French appreciated the creativity of African Americans and, in the main, were sympathetic to early abolitionist efforts, many also viewed the African American as a lazy beast.

The city of Paris, France, became a place of refuge for biracial Americans during slavery and at the time of the Harlem Renaissance for black musicians, fine artists, writers, and others seeking opportunities to practice their craft free from American racism. The outdoor café at Place du Tertre in Montmartre, seen here in 1956, was typical of Parisian culture. *(Library of Congress, Prints & Photographs Division [LC-USZ62-126993])*

Prior to the Harlem Renaissance, the community of African-American travelers to Paris was fairly wealthy. One member of this community was Mary Church Terrell, who became president of the National Association of Colored Women. Terrell's family's affluence allowed her to visit frequently between 1888 and 1921 for a cultural education in Parisian art galleries and a formal education in Berlin. Terrell noted: "The country in which I was born and reared and have lived is my fatherland, of course, and I love it genuinely but my motherland is dear, broad-minded France in which people with dark complexions are not discriminated against on account of their color."

JAMES WELDON JOHNSON ("LIFT EVERY VOICE AND SING"), brother JOHN ROSAMOND JOHNSON, and performance partner Bob Cole were successful young songwriters when they visited London and Paris in 1905. Writing in his autobiography, *Along This Way,* James Weldon Johnson described the sense of liberation many blacks experienced going to France: "I recaptured for the first time since childhood the sense of being just a human being. . . . I was suddenly free: free from a sense of impending discomfort, insecurity, danger; free from the conflict with the Man-Negro dualism and the innumerable maneuvers in thought and behavior that it compels; free from the problem of the many obvious or subtle adjustments to a multitude of bans and taboos; free from special scorn, special tolerance, special condescension, special commiseration; free to be merely a man."

Education in Paris was an important "draw" for American blacks who could not further their education or attend schools of their choice back in the states. The "father of black history," CARTER GODWIN WOODSON, spent one semester at the Sorbonne in Paris—circa 1908, while earning his M.A. from the University of Chicago—before he returned to the United States to inaugurate the ASSOCIATION FOR THE STUDY OF NEGRO LIFE and *The Journal of Negro History.*

William Monroe Trotter, editor of *The Boston Guardian,* sailed to France in 1919 on a freighter called *Yarmouth,* the same freighter MARCUS GARVEY purchased for his BACK-TO-AFRICA MOVEMENT. Trotter's travel experiences were very much contrary to those of the wealthy Terrell. He had been refused a passport and was forced to travel incognito to France as a menial laborer even though he was, in fact, a delegate to the National Equal Rights League and secretary of the Race Petitioners, Versailles Peace Conference.

Trotter's close friend, W. E. B. DU BOIS, also traveled to Paris in 1919, where he helped conduct the PAN-AFRICAN CONGRESS. Of partial French heritage, though born and raised in Massachusetts, the editor of *CRISIS: A RECORD OF THE DARKER RACES,* called Paris "the greatest of the world's cities." He returned many times, including in 1921, to stage another Pan-African Congress.

At the close of WORLD WAR I, when Paris actually and officially became known as a land of freedom for blacks, especially black artists, it was generally in view of their harmonious introduction to the African American through the presence of the hard-fighting, JAZZ-playing black soldiers called the HARLEM HELLFIGHTERS. A number of African Americans, like EUGENE JACQUES BULLARD, who fought for France in World War I, remained there after the war to form a stable and supportive community of African-American expatriates.

During the Harlem Renaissance years, the love affair between African Americans and Paris intensified because the literate, cultured French well appreciated the talents of black writers, jazz musicians, and visual artists who were not always acknowledged in their own land. Paris had an attitude conducive to the making of art, getting things done, and living life to the fullest. Harlem Renaissance poet and novelist CLAUDE MCKAY *(HOME TO HARLEM)* left for Europe in 1922 and spent the bulk of the Harlem Renaissance period in France. While there, he was once refused admission to a Paris nightclub because he was a dark-skinned African-Caribbean man, and American whites on vacation objected to his presence. Nevertheless, McKay loved French literature and remained in France to write several of his own books, including the celebrated *Home to Harlem,* until 1934. He never forgot, however, and never feared to discuss, the hard-to-accept, little acknowledged fact (by African Americans) of the exploitation of Africans by the French.

JEAN TOOMER *(Cane)* went to the country in 1924 to study at the Institute for the Harmonious Development of Man with the educator and mystic George Ivanovitch Gurdjieff. Toomer returned to the country several times while preparing to become an instructor for American branches of the institute.

Unlike most *NEW NEGRO* writers and artists who championed the culture and civility of Paris, LANGSTON HUGHES *(The Weary Blues)* was less enchanted with the city. He traveled to Paris from Africa in 1924, looking for work, with only $7 in his pocket. A black jazz musician informed him that, "'Less you can play jazz or tap dance, you'd just as well go back home." Hughes wrote his friend COUNTEE CULLEN, who would have a love affair with Paris: "Kid, stay in Harlem! The French are the most franc-loving . . . hard-faced, hard-worked, cold and half-starved set of people I've ever seen in my life. . . . And do they like Americans of *any color?* They do not!! . . . Little old New York for me! But the colored people here are fine, there are lots of us."

Exceptional among the "us" that Hughes referred to were Josephine Baker, a former star of *SHUFFLE ALONG,* and BRICKTOP, a former headliner at clubs in Harlem. Both rose to prominence as entertainers in Paris and, like Tanner before them, made it their home (although Bricktop would return to the United States during World War II). Baker would achieve a level of international success rare for anyone in any country, and she became a French citizen and war hero before dying in Paris in 1975.

Educator ANNA JULIA COOPER (*A Voice from the South by a Black Woman of the South,* 1892), intellectual and early feminist, earned her doctorate from the Sorbonne in 1925 when she was approximately 65 years old. She then returned to WASHINGTON, D.C., and in her living room opened Frelinghuysen University, an urban basic-skills academy to help the functionally illiterate working class members of her neighborhood. GWENDOLYN BENNETTA BENNETT traveled to Paris as an art student in 1925 and experienced homesickness but wrote in her diary that her patriotism grew as a result of her trip. Her year in Paris yielded the short stories "Wedding Day" and "Tokens."

When NATIONAL ASSOCIATION FOR THE ADVANCEMENT OF COLORED PEOPLE (NAACP) official WALTER WHITE won a Guggenheim fellowship in 1927 and moved to the French Rivera, his family's eight-room villa cost $250 a year with a maid at only $16 a month and a bottle of whiskey at $2.40. The whiskey was a real bargain considering the year 1927 was part of the alcohol-free Prohibition Era in the United States. And maids were generally paid $44 per month in the United States.

Harlem Renaissance author Countee Cullen *(Color)* visited Paris several times with his father, and following his wedding to Du Bois's daughter Nina Yolanda, he traveled there with his friend Harold Jackman. In 1928, he traveled to the city on a Guggenheim fellowship. Cullen studied French literature at the University of Paris and the French language at the Alliance Française, going there every summer during the 1930s before he returned to Harlem to teach French at Frederick Douglass Junior High School Number 139. Paris inspired a number of compositions by Cullen: the poem "To France" was published in *OPPORTUNITY* magazine in August 1932, and his essay "Countee Cullen on French Courtesy," in *Crisis* in June 1929.

English poet and anthologist NANCY CUNARD (*Negro,* 1934) and African-American musician Henry Crowder visited Paris in 1931. Though an interracial couple, they were not harassed as they would have been in most American cities at the time.

The "free air" and wild applause of Paris attracted African Americans and other people of African descent long after the Harlem Renaissance. A colony of artistic black people continued to develop there. Urban realist novelist and haiku poet RICHARD NATHANIEL WRIGHT, a leader during the CHICAGO Renaissance, left for Paris in the 1950s and never moved back to the United States, citing racism for his departure from his homeland. Pianist and television host Hazel Scott, wife of Rev. ADAM CLAYTON POWELL, JR., pastor of the ABYSSINIAN BAPTIST CHURCH, lived in Paris in the 1960s. Harlem native and famed essayist James Baldwin *(Nobody Knows My Name)* became a resident of St. Paul de Vence in the south of France. And Harlem Renaissance painter BEAUFORD DELANEY also claimed France as home during France's "heyday" of appreciation for black culture.

Though relations have been historically rich between Paris and African Americans, in the 1980s a French fascist party called the National Front declared racism "patriotic." Black Parisians and visiting African Americans alike witnessed increased police brutality and employment discrimination against people of color even as many French continued to appreciate expressions of black creativity. Tyler Stovall, author of *Paris Noir: African-Americans in the City of Light,* reported in his 1996 book that almost 2,000 African Americans still lived in Paris, the largest number of blacks in any Continental European city.

Further Reading

Fabre, Michel. *From Harlem to Paris: Black American Writers in France, 1840–1980.* Urbana and Chicago: University of Illinois Press, 1991.

Griffin, Farah J., and Cheryl J. Fish, eds. *A Stranger in the Village: Two Centuries of African-American Travel Writing.* Boston: Beacon Press, 1998.

Mack, Tara. "Racisme déjà vu: Paris' Image as a Haven for Black Americans May Be Fading." *Emerge,* June 2000.

Shack, William A. *Harlem in Montmartre: A Paris Jazz Story Between the Great Wars.* Berkeley: University of California Press, 2001.

Stovall, Tyler. *Paris Noir: African-Americans in the City of Light.* Boston and New York: Houghton Mifflin Company, 1996.

— Sandra L. West

Parker, Charlie (Charles Christopher Parker, Jr., "Bird") (1920–1955) *jazz musician*

Through his work as a soloist and in partnership with trumpeter John Birks "Dizzy" Gillespie, saxophonist Charlie Parker revolutionized 1940s SWING music to create the modern style of JAZZ known as bebop.

Parker was born Charles Christopher Parker, Jr., on August 29, 1920, in Kansas City, Kansas, to Adelaide Bailey Parker and Charles Parker, Sr. His father was a dancer and singer who by a previous marriage had at least one other son, John Parker, when the future musician was born. Parker Senior separated from his family when his youngest son was about nine and had little interaction with him afterward.

Parker's mother was both African- and Native American, of the Choctaw tribe. She raised her son in Kansas City, Missouri, across the river from where he had been born. In Kansas City, Parker attended Crispus Attucks Elementary School, Charles Sumner Elementary School, and Lincoln High School. His mother purchased his first saxophone, a used alto, for $45 when he was 11. Some four years later, he joined for a time a student band called the Deans of Swing.

Kansas City during Parker's youth was governed by the openly corrupt administration of Mayor Tom Pendergast. Criminal activity was commonplace and hard drugs readily available. The city was also a major center for jazz where bandleader COUNT BASIE and legendary saxophonist Lester "Prez" Young often worked and participated in jam sessions in all-night clubs. In this mixed environment of music, political corruption, and uninhibited nightlife, Charlie Parker was introduced to heroin and other drugs at the age of 15. The drug would affect his artistry, health, and career throughout his life.

Parker was motivated to improve his musicianship when, to signal that he was not ready to play professionally, an older musician tossed a cymbal at his feet during an informal jam session. Parker then spent the summer of 1937 with the George Lee Band playing jobs at Ozark Mountain resorts. At the same time, he bought and studied records featuring solos by Lester Young. His mastery of Young's solos gained him greater respect and he joined a band led by Henry "Buster" Smith, who also played alto saxophone and became a mentor to Parker. When Smith relocated to NEW YORK CITY, Parker, in 1939, did the same. He worked a variety of odd jobs in New York, including playing at the Parisian Dance Hall, while also sitting in on jam sessions at such HARLEM nightspots as Dan Wall's

Chili House and Clark Monroe's Uptown House. During this period, he experienced an aesthetic leap in which he "learned to play the thing I'd been hearing. I came alive."

His increased experience among musicians in New York made him a much-sought-after musician upon his return to Kansas City. There, he joined the Jay McShann Band and helped revive its career with his newly expanded ideas on musical arrangements. Around the same time, he first met Dizzy Gillespie in Kansas City. He toured extensively with Jay McShann for two years, traveling to Dallas, CHICAGO, and returning to New York for engagements at the SAVOY BALLROOM, the APOLLO THEATRE, and other venues.

Parker's addiction to heroin made it difficult for him to sustain professional relationships, and he went through several periods of drifting from one band to another, including playing at one point with the NOBLE SISSLE Orchestra and pianist Earl Hines's big band. In 1944, he joined one of the most progressive bands in jazz history, teaming up with bandleader and singer Billy Eckstine, Dizzy Gillespie, vocalist Sarah Vaughan, and drummer Art Blakey. Eschewing the established music of swing and performing instead songs with titles like "Do-Bop-Sh-Bam," Eckstine's group became the first big band to play bebop.

Parker and Gillespie continued to define the sound of bebop on recordings in 1945 for Guild Records. In February 1945, they recorded as the Dizzy Gillespie Sextet the songs *Grooving High; All the Things You Are;* and *Dizzy Atmosphere.* In May, under the name the Dizzy Gillespie Quintet, they recorded: *Salt Peanuts; Lover Man; Shaw 'Nuff;* and *Hot House.* In each of these Parker began to demonstrate the densely contracted rapid bursts of improvisations on rhythm, harmonies, and melodies that gained him a large following among both fans and fellow musicians. He, Gillespie, and pianist Thelonius Monk further established bebop as a significant new form of jazz in clubs on New York's 52nd Street where they played both solo and combo performances.

Following club dates with Gillespie and recordings for Dial Records in 1946, Parker, suffering from drug withdrawal, was arrested on charges of suspected arson and public nudity. He was sentenced to a minimum of six months at the Camarillo State Hospital in California. He was released with the help of his future biographer, Ross Russell, after seven months.

Returning to New York in 1947, Parker recorded a number of sessions for Dial Records and put together a quintet of musicians that included the young trumpeter Miles Davis, drummer Max Roach, pianist Duke Jordan, and bassist Tommy Potter. With occasional alternate personnel, the quintet remained Parker's principal creative foundation for the next three years.

Throughout the late 1940s and early 1950s, Parker was voted favorite alto saxophonist in readers' polls for *Metronome, Esquire,* and *Down Beat* magazines. In 1949, he performed at Carnegie Hall and the International Festival of Jazz in Paris, where he met the renowned philosopher Jean-Paul Sartre. In November 1949, Parker became the first modern jazz soloist, heading an ensemble called Charlie Parker and Strings, to record using a background of woodwinds and strings. Among the songs he recorded on Mercury Records were "Summertime" and "April in Paris." Parker's status as one of the preeminent jazzmen of his time increased with the opening of Birdland, a club named in his honor.

Charlie Parker, along with Dizzy Gillespie, was one of the principal founders of bebop jazz and remains recognized as one of the music's most dynamic and influential innovators. *(Library of Congress, Prints & Photographs Division, NYWT&S Collection [LC-USZ62-120470])*

In 1950, Parker played concerts in Sweden and Denmark. From 1951 to 1953, his New York cabaret license, required for musicians to work at clubs in the city, was revoked. The Apollo Theatre was one of the few entertainment centers at which he could still play. Parker made his final recording, an interpretation of songs by Cole Porter, in 1954. In March 1955, he performed publicly for the last time at Birdland.

Parker married four times. He was 15 when he married his first wife, Rebecca Ruffin, in 1936, and 18 when their son Francis Leon Parker was born. He and his first wife reportedly were still married when he also married Geraldine Scott in 1943. Divorcing his first two wives, he married Doris Sydnor in 1948. At the time of his death, he was in a common-law marriage with Chan Richardson. They had two children, a daughter named Pree, who died in 1954, and a son named Baird. On March 12, 1955, at the age of 34, Parker died of stomach ulcers, liver disease, and a heart condition.

Further Reading

Gray, Martin. *Blues for Bird.* Santa Monica, Calif.: Santa Monica Press, 2001.

Peretti, Burton W. *The Creation of Jazz: Music, Race, and Culture in Urban America (Music in American Life).* Chicago: University of Illinois Press, 1992.

Woideck, Carl. *Charlie Parker, His Music and Life.* Ann Arbor: University of Michigan Press, 1996.

— Aberjhani

patrons

Various patrons who supplemented the incomes and resources of African Americans during the 1910s through the 1940s contributed significantly to the success of the Harlem Renaissance's cultural revolution.

In many ways, the early 1900s tradition of philanthropists contributing to African-American causes began with BOOKER TALIAFERRO WASHINGTON, a man who did not identify himself with the more progressive ideas of such leaders as W. E. B. DU BOIS but whose affiliation with wealthy whites helped him procure a $2 million endowment for the school he founded, the Tuskegee Institute in Tuskegee, Alabama. Washington's program of progress in moderation and accommodationism for African Americans won the support of such millionaires as Andrew Carnegie, George Eastman, John D. Rockefeller, and Henry C. Rogers. Washington also allied himself with a number of politicians, churches, newspapers, and businesses that armed him with a virtual political machine that he was able to employ however he chose. It also made him for a period the most powerful black man in the United States.

Those writers and artists struggling to establish political, economic, and artistic autonomy during the 1920s and 1930s did not assemble anything so formidable as Washington's powerful network. They did, however, enjoy extensive assistance from a number of sources. Joel, Amy, and Arthur Spingarn were Jews who not only helped finance the careers of such individuals as Du Bois and LANGSTON HUGHES but also donated legal and administrative services to the NATIONAL ASSOCIATION FOR THE ADVANCEMENT OF COLORED PEOPLE (NAACP). Upon publication of the 1925 *SURVEY GRAPHIC* focusing on Harlem's emerging modern culture, the Spingarns purchased hundreds of copies of the magazine to distribute to friends and organizations across the country. One of the family's lasting contributions has been the SPINGARN MEDAL awarded annually by the NAACP in recognition of an individual African American's contributions to the struggle for racial equality.

One of the most well-known patrons of the era was CHARLOTTE OSGOOD MASON, a wealthy widow who asked not to be identified and preferred that her charges call her "Godmother." With ALAIN LOCKE acting as intermediary between Mason and younger writers and artists, the widow became "Godmother" to ZORA NEALE HURSTON, AARON DOUGLAS, CLAUDE MCKAY, Langston Hughes, and others. In addition to providing monthly allowances for her would-be protégés, Mason directed their creative works and even edited Hughes's novel *Not Without Laughter.* While the younger individuals eventually severed their relationship with Mason in order to maintain control of their work, Locke retained his relationship with the patron until her death. She provided him with trips to Europe and added to his collection of African art for some 13 years. Estimates of her financial contribution to writers and artists range from $50,000 to $75,000, or half a million dollars by modern standards.

Self-made millionaire MADAME C. J. WALKER and her daughter A'LELIA WALKER were among the few African Americans able to assist the careers of others on a large scale. Through her international business empire, Madame C. J. Walker helped thousands establish their own beauty salons and schools. She was more prone to helping foster independence rather than offering donations yet did occasionally finance literary prizes and upon her death left two-thirds of her fortune to charities. Her daughter A'Lelia, following Madame Walker's death, turned their Harlem town house and Hudson River mansion into gathering places for the creatively gifted and the socially liberal. By making luxury and good times available to all, she became a legendary personality and muse who inspired numerous creative works.

Few had the vision, energy, or resources to promote African-American culture in the manner of CARL VAN VECHTEN. Aside from writing articles in support of black culture and offering prize monies for literary competitions sponsored by *OPPORTUNITY* magazine, Van Vechten was directly involved in the publication of works by JAMES WELDON JOHNSON, WALTER WHITE, Hughes, AARON DOUGLAS, RUDOLPH FISHER, and a number of others. Moreover, Van Vechten provided a lasting legacy in the form of an extensive photographic record of accomplished African Americans. The inheritor of a million-dollar trust fund at the beginning of the GREAT DEPRESSION, the white and gay Van Vechten was able to devote himself to what he called his "violent passion for things Negro" and through photographs honor individuals he viewed as geniuses of his era.

Other individuals, such as the editor and writer MAX EASTMAN, who befriended and helped support Claude McKay, and Elizabeth Marbury, who assisted DOROTHY WEST and WALLACE THURMAN, made contributions that were not necessarily large in scale but crucial at the time to the recipients involved.

The HARMON FOUNDATION offered a different kind of patronage. Locke and Du Bois both sought assistance for black artists from the foundation, which held annual exhibitions and provided monetary awards. These cash prizes allowed visual artists such as WILLIAM HENRY JOHNSON and others to develop their creative gifts and sometimes travel to Europe for additional study and exposure. At the advent of the Great Depression in 1930, privately sponsored patronage decreased significantly, and the WORKS PROGRESS ADMINISTRATION (WPA) was established by the federal government to help artists continue earning a living with their creativity.

Further Reading

Bundles, A'Lelia Perry. *On Her Own Ground: The Life and Times of Madame C. J. Walker.* New York: Simon and Schuster, 2001.

Hutchinson, George. *The Harlem Renaissance in Black and White.* Cambridge: The Bellnap Press of Harvard University Press, 1995.

— Aberjhani and Sandra L. West

Patterson, Louise Thompson (1901–1999)

political activist

Louise Thompson Patterson was the wife of WALLACE THURMAN and served as a literary assistant to LANGSTON HUGHES and ZORA NEALE HURSTON prior to becoming an influential member of the Communist Party U.S.A.

Patterson was born Louise Thompson in 1901 in CHICAGO but spent most of her youth relocating to the different cities in California where her stepfather was able to find employment as a chef. Her family settled in Oakland in 1919, and Patterson enrolled at the University of California in Berkeley. While there, she was greatly impressed and influenced by a lecture on race and racism presented by W. E. B. DU BOIS. In 1923, she graduated from the university with a degree in economics and secondary studies in Spanish. Racially nondistinct, Thompson's very light complexion and her fluency in Spanish allowed her when she chose to pass for Spanish or white, primarily to avoid discrimination in hiring practices.

Thompson returned to Chicago following her graduation and there worked briefly for a black-owned law firm while also taking graduate courses at the University of Chicago. In 1925, she moved to Pine Bluff, Arkansas, where she accepted a teaching position. The next year she taught business administration at the Hampton Institute in Virginia. Siding with students opposed to the excessively controlling policies of the institution, she supported a strike against the administration and left her position there.

A scholarship to the New York School for Social Work, granted by the NATIONAL URBAN LEAGUE (NUL), allowed Patterson to move to NEW YORK CITY in 1928. Deeply interested in the *NEW NEGRO* movement under way in the city and across the country, Thompson befriended various writers and artists through her acquaintance with AARON DOUGLAS and his wife Alta.

Meeting the novelist and playwright Wallace Thurman, Thompson accepted a temporary job assisting him with the preparation of his manuscripts. When Thurman, who suffered from alcoholism and tuberculosis, became ill, Patterson helped nurse him back to health. They were married on August 22, 1928. Six months later, however, Thompson filed for divorce on grounds of incompatibility due to Thurman's homosexuality. The couple separated and made arrangements for alimony settlements but were still legally married when Thurman died on December 22, 1934.

CHARLOTTE OSGOOD MASON, a patron who through ALAIN LOCKE provided financial assistance for many black writers and artists, hired Thompson in 1929 as a stenographer to help Langston Hughes complete his novel *Not Without Laughter.* The next year, Thompson assisted both Hughes and Zora Neale Hurston with the completion of their play, *MULE BONE.* The trio worked together at a boardinghouse in Westfield, New Jersey. Disputes over the authorship of the play arose when Hurston expressed her belief that Hughes and Thompson were having an affair and attempting to deprive her of her proper share in its ownership. The play, consequently, was never produced while its authors were alive.

Thompson began to work with a politically and socially progressive organization called the Congregational Education Society in New York in 1930. Working with the artist AUGUSTA FELLS SAVAGE, she formed a group called The Vanguard and helped develop the HARLEM chapter of the Friends of the Soviet Union. Increasingly affiliated with supporters of COMMUNISM, Thompson organized in 1930 a voyage of some 30 African Americans to Russia to make a film titled *Black and White.* Based in Moscow, the Meschrabpom Film Corporation sponsored the trip. Among those participating in the venture were DOROTHY WEST and Hughes. Upon its arrival in Russia, the group learned that the intended movie script could not be used because of its erroneous depiction of African-American life. The film was canceled and most of the party returned to the United States after 10 days. Thompson provided her account of the experience in an essay titled "With Langston Hughes in the USSR."

Thompson officially joined the Communist Party U.S.A. in 1933 when she became the assistant secretary for the National Committee for the Defense of Political Prisoners. She gave public talks on the SCOTTSBORO TRIAL and took a full-time position with the International Workers Order. Her organizational activities led to her arrest in 1934 in Birmingham, Alabama, where she spent a night in jail.

Thompson and Hughes remained lifelong friends, and in 1938 she helped him establish the HARLEM SUITCASE THEATER by providing the International Workers Order Community Center as a base of operations. Four years later, Hughes dedicated his book of poetry, *Shakespeare in Harlem,* to Thompson.

In 1940, Thompson married William Patterson, a civil rights lawyer and associate of W. E. B. Du Bois and PAUL ROBESON. Patterson was also a leading member of the Communist Party U.S.A. and would serve as executive director of its Civil Rights Congress from 1946 to 1956. Joining her husband and others on the Civil Rights Congress, Louise Thompson Patterson helped provide defense for such historical civil rights cases as that of the Chicago teenager Emmett Till, murdered in Mississippi for addressing a white female, and Rosa Lee Ingram, a black sharecropper in Georgia who in self-defense killed her white assailant.

Working with such notables as Shirley Graham and author Alice Childress, Patterson remained an active member of the Civil Rights Congress throughout the 1950s. She died on August 27, 1999, in New York City.

Further Reading

Maxwell, William J. *New Negro, Old Left: African-American Writing and Communism Between the Wars.* New York: Columbia Universe Press, 1999.

Smethurst, James E. *The New Red Negro: The Literary Left and African American Poetry, 1930–1946.* New York: Oxford University Press, 1999.

— Aberjhani

Paul Laurence Dunbar Apartments

The Paul Laurence Dunbar Apartments, named for the noted 19th-century poet and one-time husband of ALICE DUNBAR-

NELSON, were the first garden-style cooperative apartments for black residents in HARLEM. Dunbar (1862–1906), named to the AMERICAN NEGRO ACADEMY, was one of the first black poets to make a living from his writing; he wrote, among other things, *Majors and Minors* (1895) and *The Sport of the Gods* (1902).

The Dunbar Apartments were constructed in 1926 by Roscoe Conklin Bruce, apartment manager and son of Blanche Kelso Bruce, the Reconstruction-era black senator from Mississippi. Construction was financed by PATRON John D. Rockefeller, Jr., of the politically liberal and wealthy Rockefeller dynasty. The 511-unit complex occupies an entire city block, five acres, at 2588 ADAM CLAYTON POWELL, JR., Boulevard, formerly SEVENTH AVENUE, between 149th and 150th streets. The apartments consist of six U-shaped, brown brick buildings centered on a sunny flowered courtyard that contained a playground. A children's nursery was located in the basement of the apartment building and, on the ground floor, the Dunbar National Bank, also underwritten by Rockefeller.

Before the GREAT DEPRESSION, a four-room apartment in this area rented for $67.50 while rent for a six-room apartment ranged from $84 to $99. After the depression, rent receded by $20. (See HARLEM.) The complex was a cooperative, and tenants were expected eventually to purchase their apartments.

Named after the celebrated poet, playwright, and novelist Paul Laurence Dunbar, the Dunbar Apartments, at 246 W. 150th Street, were among the modern constructions built in Harlem during the Harlem Renaissance. *(Library of Congress, Prints & Photographs Division, HABS, NY,31-NEYO,118-3)*

During its Harlem Renaissance heyday, illustrious residents included poet COUNTEE CULLEN and illustrator E. SIMMS CAMPBELL. Arctic explorer Matthew A. Henson (1866–1955) was also a resident of the Dunbar Apartments. Henson was a member of the team of explorers, led by Lt. Robert Peary, who discovered the North Pole. It was he who planted the U.S. flag at the site upon its discovery. In Henson's honor, a commemorative plaque is affixed to the Seventh Avenue entrance of the complex, where he resided from 1925 until his death in 1955.

The Dunbar Apartments' management staff published a newspaper called the *Dunbar News* that kept residents informed regarding the social status of visitors, celebrity dinner guests, and deaths among the Dunbar Apartments' populace. The publication also printed poetry, occasionally verse by the famous LANGSTON HUGHES (*Dunbar News* of October 7, 1931), who lived nearby at 20 East 127th Street from 1947 until his death in 1967. MADAME C. J. WALKER, millionaire beauty culturist, operated a beauty parlor next door to the complex.

Dunbar National Bank, the first bank in Harlem to hire African-American tellers and managers, opened in September 1928 with all white board members. Located at Eighth Avenue and 150th Street, the bank did, by April 6, 1929, have three African-American trustees. Those members were Dr. Robert Russa Moton, principal of Tuskegee Institute; Roscoe C. Bruce, manager of Dunbar Apartments; and Alderman Fred R. Moore, editor of the *NEW YORK AGE*. Dunbar National Bank did not survive the fragile economic period caused by the stock market crash of 1929–30 and Great Depression. The Dunbar Apartments, however, still stood as of 2002.

Further Reading

Curtis, Nancy C. *Black Heritage Series: An African American Odyssey and Finder's Guide.* Chicago and London: American Library Association, 1996.

Dolkart, Andrew S., and Gretchen S. Sorin. *Touring Historic Harlem: Four Walks in Northern Manhattan.* New York: New York Landmarks Conservancy, 1997.

Kellner, Bruce, ed. *The Harlem Renaissance: A Historical Dictionary for the Era.* Westport, Conn: Greenwood Press, 1984.

Lewis, David Levering. *When Harlem Was in Vogue.* New York: Vintage Books, 1982.

— Sandra L. West

Peace Mission See FATHER DIVINE.

Perry, Lincoln Theodore Monroe Andrew See FETCHIT, STEPIN.

Phal, Louis (Baye "Battling Siki") See SPORTS AND THE HARLEM RENAISSANCE.

Phi Beta Sigma Fraternity, Inc.

In addition to paving the way for its own chapters, the formation of the first black Greek-lettered organization, ALPHA PHI ALPHA FRATERNITY also paved the way for the variety of fraternities that would follow. The Phi Beta Sigma Fraternity added its name to the growing number of black college fraternities and sororities on January 9, 1914.

A. Langston Taylor's dream to start a new fraternity took root while he was still in high school and grew into a reality when he and fellow founders Leonard Morse and Charles I. Brown met at the WASHINGTON, D.C., branch of the YMCA to form the new Phi Beta Sigma Fraternity. Adopting as their motto, "Culture for Service and Service for Humanity," the new fraternity soon accepted nine initiates into its ranks. Taylor, having issued the call for the formation of the organization, was elected its president.

Though eight years behind Alpha Phi Alpha in its creation, Phi Beta Sigma began to expand and by the 1920s had more than two dozen chapters on campuses throughout the United States. As with most politically aware African-American groups of the era, the fraternity criticized the American government for turning a blind eye to the ongoing atrocities of LYNCHING in the country. It also exercised solidarity with the PAN-AFRICAN CONGRESS, the international collective of black leaders who held a series of conferences in PARIS, in its condemnation of the U.S. occupation of Haiti. In addition, the members instituted a Bigger and Better Business Program to help foster economic development and growth in black communities.

Despite the illustrious history of its older brother fraternity, the Alphas, Phi Beta Sigma successfully recruited a number of the most influential figures of the Harlem Renaissance. A. PHILIP RANDOLPH, George Washington Carver, ALAIN LOCKE, and JAMES WELDON JOHNSON all pledged their brotherhood to the fraternity.

Throughout the 20th century, Phi Beta Sigma lent its support to many of the most progressive movements in the African-American community. While millions agonized over the rightness or wrongness of the 1995 Million Man March, the fraternity assisted in its organization and helped sponsor an event that has since moved beyond controversy into celebrated achievement. It has further exercised political advocacy in campus and community voter registration drives. Its historical focus on economic stability in black communities evolved into a National Federal Credit Union owned and operated in Washington, D.C., by members of the fraternity.

Initiatives under its social action program include an ongoing promotion of literacy and a definitive stance against teen pregnancy.

The appeal of the organization to distinguished individuals has also continued, and well-known members of the present era include eight-term New York Congressman Edolphus Towns, former president of Ghana Kwame Nkrumah, actor Blair Underwood, actor Morris Chestnut, Congressman John Lewis, professional basketball player Karl Malone, and author and political activist Huey P. Newton.

Further Reading

Bracey, Ernest N. *Prophetic Insight: The Higher Education and Pedagogy of African Americans.* Lanham, Md.: University Press of America, 2001.

— Aberjhani

Philadelphia and the Harlem Renaissance

A stronghold of abolitionists during the 18th and 19th centuries, Philadelphia, Pennsylvania, developed a community of free African Americans prior to the Civil War and, along with NEW YORK CITY and CHICAGO, became during the 20th century one of the primary centers of the Harlem Renaissance.

A sizable and influential society of "old Philadelphians" was created in part when escaped slaves fled to Columbia, Pennsylvania, from Virginia circa 1819 and eventually settled in the city. They managed to educate themselves, buy homes, and achieve a cultural distinction that set them apart.

The free black community of Philadelphia developed in the midst of the abolitionist and black church movements. The American Anti-Slavery Society met in Philadelphia's Adelphi Hall in 1834 and represented a major force in the movement to end slavery. Free blacks themselves became financially empowered enough to establish self-help institutions and challenge slavery. Former slave Richard Allen organized the African Methodist Episcopal (AME) Church based on principles of abolition and rebellion in November 1787. The church matured to establish Wilberforce University in Ohio, Allen University in South Carolina, *The A.M.E. Church Review* in Tennessee, and other African-American educational and literary institutions.

Other early institutions established by Philadelphia's community of free blacks were The Free African Society, founded in 1787 by Absalom Jones and Allen, which provided medical care and funeral services; the Underground Railroad and Philadelphia Vigilance Committee, established to assist escaped slaves; the Philadelphia Library Company of Colored Persons (January 1, 1833); the Rush Library Company and Debating Society (March 1, 1837); the Demosthenean Institute, publisher of *Demosthenean Shield* newspaper (January 10, 1839); *The National Reformer* newspaper (1841), edited by William Whipper; the Minerva Literary Association (October 1834); the Edgeworth Literary Association (circa 1830s–1840s); and the Gilbert Lyceum (January 1841), a reading club.

By the 1920s, privileged black Philadelphians—teachers, doctors, and lawyers who rarely ventured outside of their own "class"—with their educational and literary prowess were well equipped to contribute to the Harlem Renaissance. They did so through periodicals and cultural organizations that included *Brown American* magazine, the Beaux Arts Club, and *Black Opals* literary journal.

Brown American Magazine

The goal that *Brown American* magazine (1936–45) expressed to its readership was "to succeed against all odds." Among the regular features in the magazine were "Negro Education in the

Philadelphia was a major center of black culture both prior to the Harlem Renaissance and during it. Pictured here in 1916 is a night view of the one of the city's main thoroughfares with the glowing tower of its City Hall. *(Library of Congress, Prints & Photographs Division [LC-USZ62-98734])*

United States" and "The Working Front." Magazine articles included "Get Trained for America's Tomorrow" and "That Future Day Shall Be Different." Notables who wrote regularly for, or were featured in, *Brown American* were W. E. B. DU BOIS, editor of the national *CRISIS: A RECORD OF THE DARKER RACES;* JAMES WELDON JOHNSON, official of the NATIONAL ASSOCIATION FOR THE ADVANCEMENT OF COLORED PEOPLE (NAACP); and MARIAN ANDERSON, opera star and Philadelphia native. *Brown American* published five volumes before its demise in 1945.

The Beaux Arts Club

Being an isolated group, Philadelphia's elite literary populace gathered into small cultural clusters to write, paint, and discuss their art. One of these clusters was the Beaux Arts Club. The club was different from most artistic groups in Harlem because it was based upon class distinctions. The club's roster included the very young poet and visual artist Mae Virginia Cowdery and society columnist and nature writer Evelyn Crawford Reynolds. Both were members of Philadelphia's black bourgeoisie and contributors to the archives of Harlem Renaissance literature and journalism.

Mae Virginia Cowdery

Mae Virginia Cowdery (1909–53) lived in the affluent Germantown section of the city and was educated at the Philadelphia School for Girls. Her father, Lemuel Cowdery, was a caterer and post office clerk. Her mother was a social worker and director of the Bureau for Colored Children. While she was still in high school, three of Cowdery's poems were published in *Black Opals* literary journal (Spring 1927). After graduation, she attended Pratt Institute in New York as a design and art student.

In New York, she befriended poet LANGSTON HUGHES and ALAIN LOCKE. At Locke's insistence, Cowdery submitted poetry to *Crisis* and *OPPORTUNITY;* her work appeared in both periodicals between 1927 and 1930. She also published in *CAROLINA MAGAZINE* and *Unity.* CHARLES SPURGEON JOHNSON, editor of *Opportunity,* included Cowdery's poem "Dusk" in his 1927 anthology, *Ebony and Topaz.* Her work was also anthologized in *The Negro Genius,* edited by BENJAMIN GRIFFITH BRAWLEY. In 1927, she won the Krigwa Poetry Prize for "Longings" and, upon doing so, was photographed for the cover of *Crisis* (January 1928). A short story, "Lai-Li," was published in *Black Opals* (Spring 1928).

Cowdery produced promising work during her short life, coming to the attention of Harlem Renaissance "officials" through poems about love, nature, and death. She published *We Lift Our Voices and Other Poems* in 1936. Class-conscious Beaux Arts Club members described her as "bohemian." Unfulfilled and isolated from the staid Philadelphia arts community, she committed suicide in 1953.

Evelyn Crawford Reynolds

Evelyn Crawford Reynolds (1900–91) was also a member of Philadelphia's Beaux Arts Club. Reynolds was an educated woman who worked as a teacher, as did the majority of Philadelphia's middle and upper class. She graduated from Girls High, was further educated at Temple University, and taught in the Bureau of Recreation. She married Hobson Richmond Reynolds, a mortician, politician, and court judge.

Employed as a community services social worker, Reynolds also wrote for two newspapers popular among black Philadelphians, the *PITTSBURGH COURIER* and the *Philadelphia Tribune.* In addition, she authored volumes of poetry regarding nature and God, with few about racial discrimination. These included *No Alabaster Box* (1936), *To No Special Land: A Book of Poems* (1953), and *Put a Daisy in Your Hair* (1963). Her publications stood out from other work created by Beaux Arts Club members because she, with an unbridled zeal for public relations and social acknowledgement, employed the founder of Bethune-Cookman College, Mary McLeod Bethune, and opera star Anderson to write forewords for her.

Under the pseudonym Eve Lynn, Reynolds gained notoriety by writing a society column geared to black professionals. Her column was titled "Eve Lynn Chats 'bout Society and Folks."

Black Opals Literary Magazine

Black Opals (1927–28) was Philadelphia's principal literary magazine. Preceded by Philadelphia's *McGirt's Magazine*

(1905–09), *Black Opals* was similar to Harlem's *FIRE!!* (1927) in diminutive size, artistic covers, erratic distribution, and short life span. Given its sedate Philadelphia foundation and audience, however, it was not as avant-garde or sexually explicit as *Fire!!* Philadelphia's black literary community generally favored works focused on "respectability, temperance, moral uplift, cultural improvement, family pride, and economic stability," genteel characteristics associated with Locke's *NEW NEGRO* movement.

Black Opals was a "little magazine" about 16 pages per issue, five by eight inches in size, and enlivened by poetry and short stories. Among its Philadelphia contributors, in addition to Cowdery, were ARTHUR HUFF FAUSET, brother of *Crisis* literary editor JESSIE REDMOND FAUSET, and Nellie Rathborne Bright. Fauset and Bright served as coeditors of the magazines. He contributed an essay, "Symphonesque," to the defiant *Fire!!* that later won the O. Henry Memorial Award (1926). Bright's poem "Longings," appeared in the 1927 number, and a line from the poem, ". . . flame like fire in black opals," gave the journal its name. Jessie Fauset contributed poetry with French titles, a language in which she was fluent.

Black Opals also published works by Marita Bonner and GWENDOLYN BENNETTA BENNETT that further placed it among noteworthy Harlem Renaissance literary publications. Bonner, a member of the Saturday Nighters SALON in WASHINGTON, D.C., run by poet Georgia Douglas Johnson, was an essayist for the journal. Poet and illustrator Bennett was guest editor of *Black Opal*'s second issue. Visual artist ALLAN RANDALL FREELON was the magazine's artistic director. Freelon won awards from *Crisis* and *Opportunity* for the journal covers and illustrations. *Black Opals* was insulated, however, as were its class-conscious writers. Its audience was limited, possibly by design to remain as exclusive as its contributors felt themselves to be. But, just as Du Bois avidly read and encouraged Boston's Saturday Evening Quill writers, he introduced *Black Opals* to *Crisis* readers in 1927. Nevertheless, *Black Opals* was "put to bed" for the last time in 1928.

Idabelle Yeiser

Another active member of Philadelphia's *New Negro* movement, also recognized by the Harlem branch of the movement and published in *Black Opals,* was Idabelle Yeiser. Idabelle Yeiser was born around 1897 in either Philadelphia, Pennsylvania, or Montclair, New Jersey. She graduated from the State Normal School in Montclair, matriculated at the University of Pennsylvania, and earned a Ph.D. in French from Columbia University. After traveling to Africa and France in 1925 and 1926, the bilingual Yeiser settled in Philadelphia to teach school and develop culturally balanced grade-school programs in all academic disciplines.

Yeiser published academic papers, essays, poems, and short stories during the Harlem Renaissance and beyond. In the 1920s, her work appeared in *Crisis* and *Opportunity* magazines. She published the story "An Echo from Toulouse, France" in the July 1926 *Crisis.* Her essay "Letters" won first prize in the *Opportunity* contest of 1927. "Letters," a travel article based upon her experiences in Algiers, Biskra, and Tunis, Africa, also appeared in the Christmas 1927 edition of *Black Opals.* It was one of the era's examples of travel writing, a genre also utilized by Harlem Renaissance poet COUNTEE CULLEN.

Known as an "intellectual poet," she wrote *Moods: A Book of Verse* in 1937. *Moods* is a collection of sonnets and free verse, set in five themed portions: Nature, Children, Miniatures, Love, and Philosophy. The poems are free of racial overtones, not unusual for Philadelphia Renaissance literati, though Harlem-influenced authors such as CLAUDE MCKAY were unabashedly militant in much of their poetry.

In 1943, Yeiser presented a paper at the Harvard University Workshop in Intercultural Education for the Harvard Graduate School of Education entitled "The Curriculum as an Integrating Force for Ethnic Variations." In 1947, she published *Lyric and Legend,* her second poetry collection. The focus of *Lyric and Legend* was world peace. One of the poems, "What Price Peace," had been published in the February 1944 issue of *Unity* magazine.

Philadelphia and the Works Progress Administration (WPA)

After the Harlem Renaissance proper, when the GREAT DEPRESSION took its toll on the entire nation, the WORKS PROGRESS ADMINISTRATION (WPA) organized employment programs for artists and writers. Philadelphians participated in the programs from 1936 to 1942 through its Federal Theater Project (FTP), Federal Arts Project (FAP), and Federal Music Project (FMP).

Philadelphia's FTP, also called the WPA Colored Theater Project, presented the well-regarded musical revues *Truckin' Along, So What?,* and the dramatic *Jericho* at the Walnut Street Theatre. The FAP developed a fine-print workshop, the only one of its type in the nation, and participating black artists such as LAURA WHEELER WARING exhibited their works from Pittsburgh to San Francisco. The FMP's Civic Symphony Orchestra shattered the existing color line. Black performers—contralto Mary Denby and pianist Clyde Winkfield among them—performed before appreciative integrated audiences three years before contralto Marian Anderson, denied access to Constitution Hall by the racist Daughters of the American Revolution (DAR), gave her open-air concert on April 19, 1939, at the Lincoln Memorial in Washington, D.C.

With its cultured black writers, artists, educators, and publications, Philadelphia added important talent and creative substance to the Harlem Renaissance.

Further Reading

Graham, Lawrence Otis. *Our Kind of People: Inside America's Black Upper Class.* New York: Harper Collins, 1999.

Jarvis, Arthur R. "Opportunity, Experience, and Recognition: Black Participation in Philadelphia's New Deal Arts Projects, 1936–1942." *The Journal of Negro History,* February 2000.

Jubilee, Vincent. *Philadelphia's Afro-American Literary Circle and the Harlem Renaissance.* Philadelphia: University of Pennsylvania, 1980.

Major, Geraldyn Hodges. *Black Society.* Chicago: Johnson Publishing Co., 1976.

Roses, Lorraine Elena, and Ruth Elizabeth Randolph. *Harlem Renaissance and Beyond: Literary Biographies of 100 Black Women Writers 1900–1945.* Boston: G. K. Hall & Co., 1990.

— Sandra L. West

Pippin, Horace (1888–1946) *painter*

Described as a creator of "primitive," or nonacademic, art, Horace Pippin lost the use of one of his arms in WORLD WAR I but continued to produce paintings of religious scenes, military incidents, and "pleasant memory" art.

Horace Pippin, son of a domestic worker, was born on February 22, 1888, in West Chester, Pennsylvania. He was educated at Merry Green Hill School, a one-room schoolhouse. At school, Pippin was severely discouraged from creating art. He would write a simple word, such as "cat," draw a picture to accompany the word, and was promptly chastised for his methods of learning and creating. He had to stay after school for these creative outbursts and was beaten when he returned home for being insubordinate in class.

Throughout Pippin's youth, he won awards and sold his art to members of his community. In response to a magazine advertisement, he drew a funny face and won a box of crayons, a box of watercolors, and two paintbrushes. At a Sunday school festival he drew biblical scenes on muslin doilies and sold them to ladies in the village.

At the age of 14, Pippin took a job as a porter at a hotel to help support his mother, who was ill. He worked at the hotel for seven years instead of going to art school. He then worked in 1913 for a moving company in Paterson, New Jersey, and in 1916 as a moulder for Brake Shoe Company in Mahwah, New Jersey. When the United States entered World War I, he joined the U.S. Army.

In the army in 1917, he became Corporal Horace Pippin of the famous 369th Regiment, also known as the HARLEM HELLFIGHTERS. He fought and sketched pictures of his comrades and of the French landscape. During a skirmish, he was shot in the right arm, the arm he painted with, and in January 1919 was sent back home to West Chester on a hospital ship. He was discharged on May 22, 1919. He, and every man in the 369th, was awarded the Croix de Guerre award for heroic service.

Pippin then married a widow, Jennie Ora Featherstone Wade, who had a son. They lived on his small pension and her wages from taking in laundry.

In 1929, the one-armed artist taught himself to draw again by supporting his limp right arm with an iron poker. The first picture he painted in this manner was *Losing the Way.* Pippin also patiently painted the famous *The End of the War: Starting Home* with the poker and carved a frame for it. It took him three years to complete. He visualized in his mind for a considerable length of time what he wanted to compose before he actually executed the painting, which he did using very simple colors—brown, amber, yellow, black, white, and green. Pippin would "work my foreground from the background," so that his work would appear multidimensional. Such was his method, he said, for "bringing out my work."

Art critic Christian Brinton and art collector ALBERT COOMBS BARNES took note of Pippin's work. Brinton encouraged Holger Cahill to put Pippin's paintings into an exhibit called "Masters of Popular Painting" in June 1938. Barnes invited Pippin to study art at the Barnes Foundation but the artist, who avowed that he painted from his "heart and mind," refused the education. "To me it seems impossible for another to teach one of art," he said.

The self-taught artist exhibited his work at the Downtown Gallery, Chicago Arts Club, San Francisco Museum of Art, and the Carnegie Institute Museum of Fine Art in Pennsylvania.

Horace Pippin died of a stroke on July 6, 1946, two weeks before his wife.

Further Reading

Bearden, Romare, and Harry Henderson. *Six Black Masters of American Art.* New York: Zenith Books/Doubleday, 1972.

Beckman, Wendy Hart. *Artists and Writers of the Harlem Renaissance.* Berkeley Heights, N.J.: Enslow Publishers, 2002.

— Sandra L. West

Pittsburgh Courier

One of the first major African-American newspapers, the *Pittsburgh Courier* started out in 1907 as a literary showcase for the work of an aspiring poet, Edwin Nathaniel Harleston, who worked as a security guard for the H. J. Heinz food packing plant.

With enough time on his hands to entertain himself at work by writing poetry, Harleston accumulated enough poems that he was encouraged to begin a four-page leaflet-sized paper called *A Toiler's Life.* He printed 10 copies of each edition and sold as many as he could at five cents each. Like ROBERT ABBOTT with his *CHICAGO DEFENDER* just two years earlier, Harleston held the positions of editor, writer, business manager, and circulation manager for his publishing enterprise.

However, even at 10 copies per edition, *A Toiler's Life* didn't begin to make the kind of impact for which Harleston had hoped until he brought in a number of coworkers and associates to help with its management. Edward Penman, Hepburn Carter, Scott Wood, Jr., Harvey Tanner, and Robert Lee Vann in 1909 provided the paper with an organizational structure and a diversified voice. The following year, *A Toiler's Life* became incorporated as the *Pittsburgh Courier.* The new management team, however, fell apart following disputes over profit shares and several, including Harleston, quit the publication. The man left to steer the *Pittsburgh Courier* to a level of success rivaling that of the *Chicago Defender* was Robert Lee Vann.

Vann was born on August 20, 1879, in Ahoskie, North Carolina, to a former slave named Lucy Peoples. He attended Virginia Union University in RICHMOND and later graduated from the Western University of Pennsylvania at Pittsburgh. He had begun to establish himself as a lawyer in Pittsburgh's African-American community when his position at the *Pitts-*

burgh Courier quickly evolved from that of a part-time interest to a full-time occupation.

Taking on the paper's editorship in 1910, Vann sidestepped the sensationalistic focus of the more militant black newspapers or the more scandal-oriented white newspapers. He instead turned his attention to the social conditions of the black community, stressing the need for blacks to obtain an education to help better themselves individually and collectively. Like other black papers, he pointed out the ongoing atrocities of JIM CROW racism and the silent sanctioning of genocide in the form of LYNCHING, but he also expanded the paper's scope to include articles on society news, entertainment, and sports. A front-page column called "The Camera" advised African Americans on the best ways to handle their finances, and space was often provided for stories tackling the need for improved health and medical resources.

As the GREAT MIGRATION gained steam and Pittsburgh's black population increased along with that of other major northern cities, the *Courier* featured a section called *News from Back Home* and its circulation enjoyed a steady climb. With the onset of the United States's entry into WORLD WAR I in 1917, Vann supported black involvement in the war as a means of obtaining greater racial equality in America. His moderate stance on this point spared the *Courier* the charge of sedition and communist affiliation that prompted government investigations of the *Chicago Defender,* A. PHILIP RANDOLPH's *the MESSENGER*, and the *NEW YORK AGE*.

In 1925, one the most prolific and controversial black writers of the era, GEORGE S. SCHUYLER, accepted an assignment from the *Courier* to tour the former Confederate south and write a column on his experiences and observations. His reports on lynching and his satirical takes on racism reportedly helped the paper pick up 10,000 new subscriptions and won Schuyler a full-time editorial position. Describing himself as a black conservative, Schuyler's journalism employed a form of negative criticism to motivate blacks to seek change. His works of fiction, such as *Black Empire,* serialized in the *Courier* from 1936 to 1938, presented blacks in alternative versions of history. Schuyler remained with the *Courier* until a negative editorial that he wrote on Martin Luther King, Jr.'s Nobel Prize win resulted in his resignation.

By the end of the 1920s, the *Courier*'s circulation topped the 100,000 mark, surpassing 150,000 in the 1930s and topping 200,000 in the 1940s. It published more than a dozen editions, including in New York, Louisiana, and Texas. Both W. E. B. DU BOIS and WALTER WHITE contributed works to the paper. Famed historian Joel A. Rogers presented in its pages historical information geared toward reversing negative stereotypes of African Americans. Along those same lines, the *Courier* denounced the popular 1930s *AMOS 'N' ANDY* radio show for its unflattering image of blacks and petitioned to have it taken off the air. Cartoonist and future expatriate Ollie Harrington sent photographs from the front lines of World War II back to the paper, and ZORA NEALE HURSTON took on its courtroom beat to cover a murder trial.

Ira F. Lewis began working at the *Courier* as a staff writer in 1914, worked his way up to managing editor, and, at Vann's request, took over after Vann died on October 24, 1940. By the time of his death, Vann had risen to prominence not only as the editor of the *Courier* but as a national representative for the NATIONAL ASSOCIATION FOR THE ADVANCEMENT OF COLORED PEOPLE (NAACP) and as assistant to the U.S. attorney general in the Justice Department. His considerably influential political contacts helped safeguard the distribution of the *Courier* so that it bypassed the kind of tampering that caused bundles of the *Chicago Defender* to be destroyed or lost. Ironically, Vann's death came half a year after his Chicago rival Abbott's.

Lewis picked up on the trail of journalistic advocacy where Vann left off and in 1942 kicked off the Double V campaign, demanding the United States grant African Americans full and unconditional civil rights in recognition of their defense of the country in the first world war and now the second. The campaign spread to other newspapers and expanded to include songs, dances, buttons, and posters to gain the full support of the black community and the full attention of the government.

The newspaper also broke new ground in its coverage of African Americans in sports. Not only did the paper raise the cry for desegregation in the major leagues but also deployed journalists to travel with such figures as Jackie Robinson and file reports on both their exceptional athletic performances and the treatment they received as African Americans throughout the country.

The *Courier,* publishing now as the *New Pittsburgh Courier,* has remained a newspaper with a strong voice representing African-American interests, but its circulation began to decline following Lewis's death in 1948. John Sengstacke, Abbott's nephew and the inheritor of the *Chicago Defender,* bought the paper in 1965.

Further Reading

Kornweibel, Theodore, Jr. *Seeing Red: Federal Campaigns Against Black Militancy, 1919–1925.* Bloomington: Indiana University Press, 1998.

Simmons, Charles A. *The African American Press.* Jefferson, N.C.: McFarland and Company, 1998.

Washburn, Patrick S. *A Question of Sedition: The Federal Government's Investigation of the Black Press During World War II.* New York: Oxford University Press. 1986.

— Aberjhani

Plantation Club

Originally known as the Café de Paris, the Plantation Club was founded by white producer Lew Leslie in the mid-1920s and showcased the talents of African Americans in musical revues prior to their debut on Broadway and the international stage.

The Plantation Club itself was located on Broadway and 50th Street in NEW YORK CITY. One of its first major successes was Leslie's production of the *Plantation Revue* in 1922. The show was largely a musical variety production designed to capitalize on the trend created by *SHUFFLE ALONG* in 1921. It also aimed to draw on the appeal of its star, FLORENCE MILLS, who had helped *Shuffle Along* achieve its record-setting run of more than 500 Broadway performances. The *Plantation Revue* made its theatrical debut at the 48th Street Theater on July 17, 1922. It later played the LAFAYETTE THEATRE as well.

The following year the club debuted *Dover Street to Dixie* before taking the show to London. After a triumphant run there, it returned to Broadway as *Dixie to Broadway.*

In addition to Mills, the Plantation Club featured ETHEL WATERS, JOSEPHINE BAKER, BOJANGLES ROBINSON, LENA HORNE, and many others, making it the only Broadway facility consistently featuring black entertainers.

In 1930, a second Plantation Club was scheduled to open for business in HARLEM on 126th Street off of LENOX AVENUE with CAB CALLOWAY and his orchestra as its featured act. However, the owners of the COTTON CLUB reportedly vandalized the facility before it could open in order to prevent it from competing with their business. (Cab Calloway was there and reported it in his autobiography, *Of Minnie the Moocher and Me.* The Schiffman family gave similar reports in their book on the Apollo Theatre.)

Further Reading

Davis, Lee. *Scandals and Follies: The Rise and Fall of the Great Broadway Revue.* New York: Limelight Editions, 1998.

Van Hoagstraten, Nicholas. *Lost Broadway Theatres.* Princeton, N.J.: Princeton Architectural Press, 1997.

— Aberjhani

Polk, P. H.

See ART AND THE HARLEM RENAISSANCE.

Pollard, Fritz

See SPORTS AND THE HARLEM RENAISSANCE.

Popel, Esther A. B. (Esther Shaw) (1896–1958)

educator, poet

A popular speaker on the developing women's club circuit, Esther Popel was also an educator fluent in four languages, a participant in literary SALONS, and a frequent contributor of poetry to *OPPORTUNITY* magazine and *CRISIS: A RECORD OF THE DARKER RACES* from 1925 to 1934.

Esther Popel was born in 1896 in Harrisburg, Pennsylvania. She attended Central High School in Harrisburg and graduated Phi Beta Kappa from Dickinson College in Carlisle, Pennsylvania, in 1919. She married William A. Shaw, who died in 1946, and had one daughter, Patricia Shaw Iversen.

At Dickinson, Popel excelled in languages, speaking French, German, Latin, and Spanish. She wrote six plays for young people that are lost to modern readers and taught French and Spanish at Shaw Junior High School and Francis Junior High School in WASHINGTON, D.C.

Outside of teaching, Popel joined the literary salon held on Saturdays at poet Georgia Douglas Johnson's home in the district. There, she associated with writers LANGSTON HUGHES, Marita Bonner, and others while eating cake, sipping wine, and discussing poetry. Popel's poetry was lyrical, religious, and political. "Kinship," for example, published in *Opportunity* (January 1925) defends the biblical account of creation and rebukes evolutionists "who idly boast/That man has come from things akin/To apes. . . . " *Opportunity* also published "Bagatelle" (November 1931); "Blasphemy American Style" (December 1934); "Credo" (January 1925); "Little Grey Leaves," a gentle, haiku-like poem (September 1925); "October Prayer" (October 1933); and "Theft" (April 1925). "Flag Salute," a racial and political poem about LYNCHING, was published in *Crisis* (August 1934).

Popel's lectures to women's groups and social essays were sometimes published. "Our Thirteenth—in Ohio, 1936" was included in the *Journal of the National Association of College Women* (1936). She presented *Personal Adventures in Race Relations* at the Women's Club in Lawrenceville, New Jersey; it was then published by the Woman's Press of the YMCA in 1946. The *Journal* (1933–34) printed Popel's "The Tenth Milestone."

Esther Popel died in 1958.

Further Reading

Hubbard, Dolan, ed. *Recovered Writers/Recovered Texts: Race, Class, and Gender in Black Women's Literature.* Knoxville: University of Tennessee Press, 1997.

Russell, Sandi. *Render Me My Song: African-American Women Writers from Slavery to the Present.* San Francisco: Harper Books, 2001.

— Sandra L. West

Porgy and Bess

Having first won popularity as a novel and dramatic play, *Porgy and Bess* debuted as a folk opera featuring an all-black cast on September 30, 1935, at the Colonial Theatre in Boston, Massachusetts. It went on to make its NEW YORK CITY debut on October 10, 1935, at the Alvin Theatre and ran there for 124 performances.

White South Carolina native (Edwin) DuBose Heyward was inspired to write his 1925 novel, *Porgy,* after reading a news article about a crippled Charleston beggar who had been accused of assault. Prior to writing the novel, Heyward had sold insurance and written two volumes of poetry; after writing it, he would author four more novels and at least one more play. Heyward initially rejected the idea of a stage version of his novel but was won over when he viewed the draft for such a version, written in secret by his wife, Dorothy Heyward.

After the Heywards worked together to complete their play, the first stage version of *Porgy* was produced by the Theatre Guild in October 1927. It featured the talents of the celebrated black actress ROSE McCLENDON, Frank Wilson, Evelyn Ellis, and Jack Carter. The play ran for a total of two years in New York and London.

George Gershwin was already the famed and wealthy composer of *Rhapsody in Blue* and *An American in Paris* when he first contacted Heyward in 1926 to suggest turning his novel into an opera. Agreeing upon the idea of the opera, neither acted on it until 1932 when Gershwin again contacted Heyward. Gershwin then began working on the project in 1933 and in 1934 traveled with Todd Duncan, who would star as Porgy in the opera, to South Carolina. There, Gershwin immersed himself as deeply as possible in the culture of that region's Gullah population, a group of African Americans living on coastal islands and long recognized as having retained more Africanisms, or patterns of African speech and culture, than any other group of blacks in the United States. Visiting schools, plantations, and churches, Gershwin studied and absorbed the various forms of the music that would go into his opera: BLUES, JAZZ, church shouts, spirituals, and work songs. However, rather than simply record and use what he heard, Gershwin utilized their influence to compose his own music.

While George Gershwin composed the opera's music, his brother Ira and Dubose Heyward wrote its libretto and lyrics. The result was a folk opera in which nearly every song became an American classic, including *Summertime; A Woman Is a Sometime Thing; O, I Got Plenty O' Nutttin';* and *It Ain't Necessarily So.* The opera stuck largely to the novel and stage play's original story. It is mainly that of the crippled beggar Porgy, who gets around town in a goat cart, and his seemingly impossible love for Bess, who already has a boyfriend named Crown. A series of events and mishaps leads Porgy to kill Crown and causes Bess to think twice about the value of Porgy's love for her. Before anything further can develop between them, Bess leaves for New York with Sportin' Life and Porgy is left to pursue them in his goat cart.

Among the stars of the 1935 opera debut were HOWARD UNIVERSITY voice instructor Todd Duncan as Porgy, soprano Anne Brown as Bess, Warren Coleman as Crown, and vaudeville veteran JOHN BUBBLES (William Sublett) as Sportin' Life, a role originally intended for bandleader CAB CALLOWAY (he would play it in a later production). Also playing the part of the lawyer in the opera was the composer (and brother of JAMES WELDON JOHNSON) JOHN ROSAMOND JOHNSON. Ruby Elzy performed the role of Serena in the opera.

The fact that *Porgy and Bess* was written by two Jewish brothers and a white South Carolinian stirred some controversy over the authenticity of its portrayal of black life and culture. James Weldon Johnson, as he did with CARL VAN VECHTEN's *NIGGER HEAVEN*, defended the opera as a valid work of art. DUKE ELLINGTON and WILLIAM GRANT STILL criticized it as a watered-down version of the real thing.

The folk opera took on new life when it was revised by Cheryl Crawford in 1941. After much of the opera's singing was changed to spoken dialogue, the show doubled its original New York run to eight months and toured some 26 cities across the country. It made its European debut in Copenhagen in March 1943 and from there toured more than two dozen counries worldwide.

Samuel Goldwyn produced a film version of *Porgy and Bess* in 1959. Directed by Otto Preminger, it starred DOROTHY DANDRIDGE, Sidney Poitier, Pearl Bailey, Sammy Davis, Jr., and Diahann Carroll.

Recognized as a genuine "American classic," *Porgy and Bess* productions are often staged throughout the world.

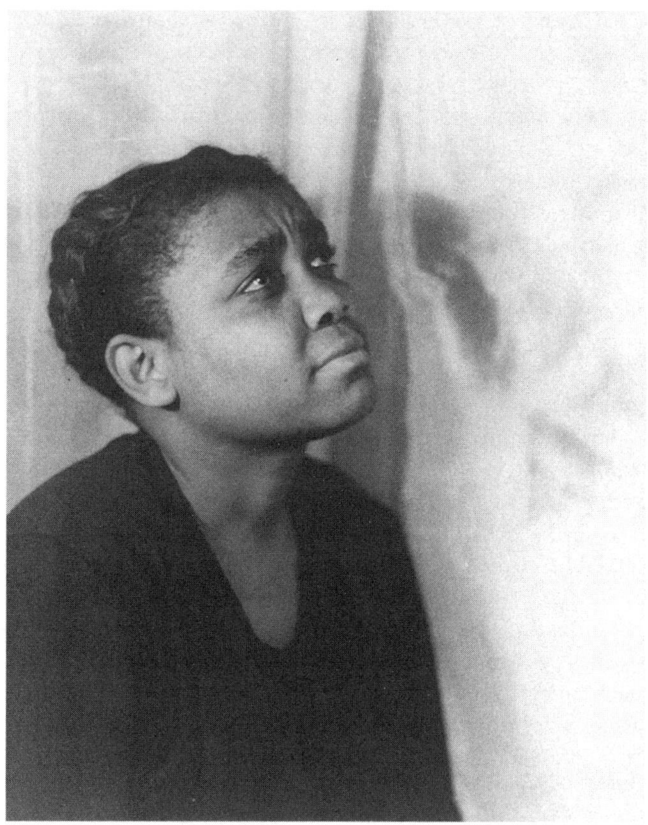

Actress Ruby Elzy, shown here in 1935, originated the role of Serena in *Porgy and Bess*. *(Library of Congress, Prints & Photographs Division, Carl Van Vechten Collection [LC-USZ62-114448])*

Further Reading

Burton, Fisher D. *Porgy and Bess.* Coral Gables, Fla.: Opera Journeys Publishing, 2000.

Hutchisson, James M., and William Baer, eds. *Dubose Heyward: A Charleston Gentleman and the World of Porgy and Bess.* Oxford: University of Mississippi Press, 2000.

— Aberjhani

Porter, James Amos See ART AND THE HARLEM RENAISSANCE.

Powell, Adam Clayton, Jr. (1908–1972) *minister, author, politician*

Heir to his father's position as pastor of the ABYSSINIAN BAPTIST CHURCH in NEW YORK CITY, Adam Clayton Powell, Jr., rose to prominence as a persuasive orator, a U.S. congressman, and the author of several noted books.

Adam Clayton Powell, Jr., was born in New Haven, Connecticut, on November 29, 1908, to Mattie Fletcher Powell and ADAM CLAYTON POWELL, SR. A sibling, Blanche, died when he was 18 years old. Powell, Jr., was a poor student at City College of New York, and in 1926 his frustrated parents sent him to Colgate University in upstate New York.

In contrast to Powell, Sr., described as a race man who was very proud of his people and willing to work on their behalf, Powell, Jr., took advantage of his very light complexion to pass for white at Colgate. His true racial identity was not discovered until he pledged to a white fraternity that checked his background. One of only four black students at the university, he graduated from Colgate in 1930. He became a part-time student at Union Theological Seminary, joined his father as assistant pastor at Abyssinian in 1930, and graduated with a master's degree in religious studies from Columbia University in 1932.

No longer avoiding his racial identity as he did in college, Powell, Jr., grew incensed at the JIM CROW racism that dominated American society. Battling against it, he helped his father provide food, fuel, and clothing for Harlem families during the GREAT DEPRESSION. From the pulpit, he led boycotts against bus companies that did not hire black workers and helped form the Coordinating Committee on Employment. In 1930, he publicly protested HARLEM HOSPITAL's overtly discriminatory policy against hiring black medical staff. His protests resulted in an interracial staff and training program for black nurses and doctors. In 1931, he protested at City Hall against the firing of five black Harlem Hospital doctors until they were reinstated. In 1932, he supported the defense in the SCOTTSBORO TRIAL. The defendants, known as the Scottsboro Boys, were nine black Alabama youths who had been sentenced to death for allegedly raping two young white women.

Against his family's wishes, Powell, Jr., married COTTON CLUB dancer Isabel Washington in 1933. In 1937, he became full pastor at Abyssinian Baptist Church, a transition that divided the congregation both because of his wife's background as a dancer and because of Powell, Jr.'s, radical affiliation with COMMUNISM. Despite all this, and just as his father had predicted to dubious members of the church, Powell, Jr., took up where his father had left off and launched Abyssinian into a second era of social activism.

Powell, Jr., was reportedly an exciting, animated preacher who enjoyed fancy clothes and nightlife. Consequently, his congregation included gamblers, bootleggers, numbers runners, and women from the Cotton Club chorus line. In one famous sermon, he borrowed a slogan from a billboard cigarette advertisement—"I'd Walk a Mile for a Camel"—and asked his congregation how far they would walk for Jesus. He was also known for growling, with a cigar in his mouth, the phrase, "Keep the faith, baby," which delighted his audiences.

For 10 years, starting in 1935, he wrote a column called "Soap Box" for the New York *AMSTERDAM NEWS*. Through this column, he attacked racial discrimination wherever he

Adam Clayton Powell, Jr., seen here with wife Hazel Dorothy Scott on their wedding day in 1945, succeeded his father as pastor of Abyssinian Baptist Church in 1937. *(Library of Congress, Prints & Photographs Division, NYWT&S Collection [LC-USZ62-124573])*

saw it. With Reverend John Johnson of St. Martin's Episcopal Church, Powell, Sr., and labor activist Sufi Hamid, Powell, Jr., adopted the slogan "Don't Buy Where You Can't Work" as they boycotted 125th Street department stores. From 1939 to 1940, he picketed against the exclusion of black workers at the New York World's Fair and won hundreds of jobs for them. He also gained jobs for black workers at Consolidated Edison and New York Telephone Company. His activism earned him the nickname "Fighting Adam," and in 1941 he easily won a seat on the New York city council. He was the city's first black councilman.

In 1942, he founded a newspaper, *People's Voice.* Novelist RICHARD NATHANIEL WRIGHT *(Native Son)* occasionally worked on the newspaper, from his home in PARIS, France, as did cartoonist Ollie Harrington, from Germany. Powell, Jr., also began work on his first book, *Marching Blacks: An Interpretive History of the Rise of the Black Common Man* (1945).

Continuing to advance in his political career, the charismatic Powell, Jr., in 1944 ran for the seat of the newly designed 22nd Congressional District in HARLEM and became the first black congressman since the Reconstruction era following the Civil War. During this same period, Powell, Jr., divorced his first wife and in 1945 married jazz pianist Hazel Scott, a West Indian. After having a son, Adam III, with Hazel Scott, the couple divorced and he married Yvette Diego in 1960. With Diego, he had a son named Adam IV.

As Congressman Powell, he tried to pass the Powell Amendment, a bill that would end federal funding of segregated schools. In 1960, he was appointed to the House Committee on Education and Labor, through which he passed 48 bills, including the Minimum Wage Bill. His congressional years were tumultuous: He was expelled from Congress in 1967 for insulting a woman and reinstated in 1969. His fame often infuriated his colleagues, and his chronic absence from his post enraged his constituents.

He left Congress in 1970 when Harlem would no longer support him and retired from Abyssinian Baptist Church in 1971. He moved to the Bahamas and died on April 4, 1972, in Miami, Florida. In honor of this ostentatious religious and political leader, New York City renamed a portion of SEVENTH AVENUE as Adam Clayton Powell, Jr., Boulevard.

Further Reading

Gore, Robert L., Jr. *We've Come This Far: The Abyssinian Baptist Church: A Photographic Journal.* New York: Stewart, Tabori & Chang, 2001.

Hampton, Charles V. *Adam Clayton Powell, Jr.: The Political Biography of an American Dilemma.* New Haven, Conn.: Cooper Square Publishers, 2002.

Haygood, Wil. *King of the Cats: The Life and Times of Adam Clayton Powell, Jr.* New York: Houghton Mifflin, 1994.

Powell, Adam Clayton, Jr. *Adam by Adam: The Autobiography of Adam Clayton Powell, Jr.* New York: Kensington Publishing, 2002.

Williams, Lea E. *Servants of the People: The 1960s Legacy of African American Leadership.* New York: St. Martin's Press, 1998.

— Sandra L. West

Powell, Adam Clayton, Sr. (1865–1953) *minister, political advocate*

The father of famed U.S. Congressman ADAM CLAYTON POWELL, JR., and a prominent political activist in his own right, Adam Clayton Powell, Sr., led the congregation of the ABYSSINIAN BAPTIST CHURCH from 1908 to 1937. In that time, Powell more than tripled the church's membership, turning it into the largest and one of the most politically influential Protestant congregations in the United States.

Adam Clayton Powell was born the son of Anthony and Sally Dunning Powell in Franklin County, Virginia, on May 5, 1865. Both his parents had been slaves. He attended Wayland Seminary (now Virginia Union University) in RICHMOND from 1888 to 1892, working in coal mines and as a waiter and janitor to pay his tuition. After graduation from Wayland, Powell, Sr., attended Yale University School of Divinity in Connecticut and served as pastor of Immanuel Baptist Church in New Haven. He married Mattie Fletcher, and their son, Adam Clayton Powell, Jr., was born November 29, 1908.

Adam Clayton Powell, Sr., began his ministry at Abyssinian Baptist Church in December 1908. The oldest black Baptist church in NEW YORK CITY, Abyssinian was founded in 1808 when a group of African Americans and Ethiopian merchants quit the First Baptist Church out of protest against its practice of JIM CROW racial discrimination. When Powell assumed leadership of the church, it had a membership of 1,600 and was indebted for more than $100,000.

Preaching a social gospel, the new minister discussed current political events every week in church. He became one of the founders of the NATIONAL URBAN LEAGUE (NUL), a leader in the NATIONAL ASSOCIATION FOR THE ADVANCEMENT OF COLORED PEOPLE (NAACP), a lecturer on INTERRACIAL INTERACTION, and an organizer of the Silent Protest Parade in HARLEM in 1917.

In 1923, Powell, Sr., moved his congregation from the wooden building it occupied on Worth Street and built its current neo-Gothic structure, with community house, at 136–142 West 138th Street in Harlem. The contemporary church address is 132 W. 138th Street. The cost of the new structure was $325,000. He opened the first church-based community recreation center in Harlem and encouraged his congregation to follow his lead and relocate from downtown Manhattan to the new black village of Harlem, where black people were now residing and prospering. By the 1930s, Abyssinian Baptist Church had become one of the most financially successful in the United States with more than 10,000 members, a social and religious education program, and a reputation as a catalyst for change in the African-American community.

At the beginning of the GREAT DEPRESSION, in a December 1930 sermon titled, "A Hungry God," Powell, Sr., stated that, "We clothe God by clothing men and women." With that observation, he convinced his congregation to donate thousands of dollars to help clothe poor Harlemites and to pledge 5 percent of their income for four months toward this same cause. He himself donated $1,000 of his salary, during a three-month period, to help alleviate unemployment in Harlem. He also opened soup kitchens and fed thousands of hungry people during the depression years, led an economic boycott against Blumstein's Department Store on 125th Street when that business refused to hire black clerks, and campaigned for better jobs and city services for black people.

Powell, Sr., retired from Abyssinian in 1937 and handed the official reins of the church over to his son, Adam Clayton Powell, Jr. He died on June 12, 1953.

Further Reading

Gore, Robert L., Jr. *We've Come This Far: The Abyssinian Baptist Church: A Photographic Journal.* New York: Stewart, Tabori and Chang, 2001.

Williams, Lea E. *Servants of the People: The 1960s Legacy of African American Leadership.* New York: St. Martin's Press, 1998.

— Sandra L. West

Primus, Pearl (1919–1994) *dancer, choreographer, anthropologist*

Like KATHERINE DUNHAM, Pearl Primus merged an interest in anthropology and art to create a unique blend of dance merging the African, African-American, and Caribbean cultures.

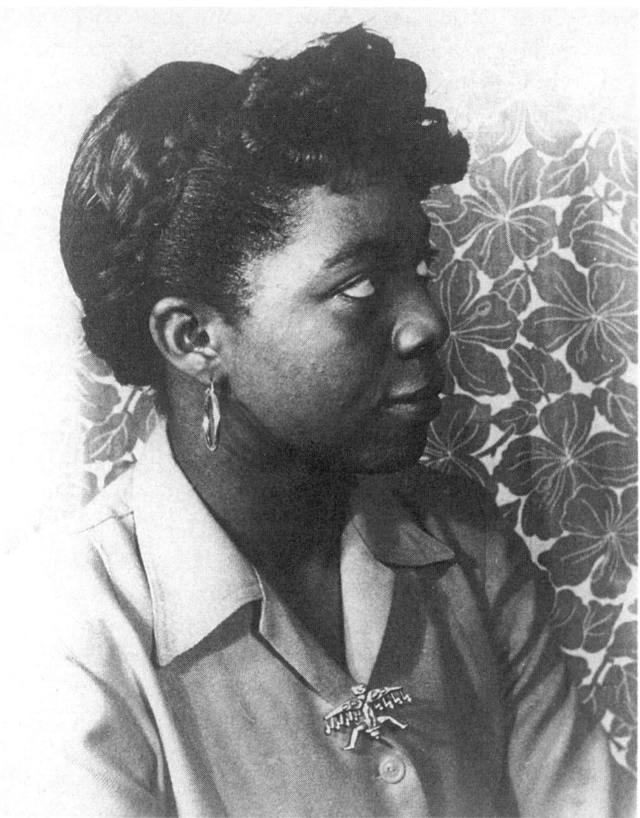

Pearl Primus, shown here in 1943, successfully blended traditional African dance with pointed references to modern race relations. *(Library of Congress, Prints & Photographs Division, Carl Van Vechten Collection [LC-USZ62-127352])*

Pearl Primus was born in Trinidad, West Indies, on November 29, 1919. Her family moved to NEW YORK CITY when she was two years old.

Primus originally planned to pursue a medical career, and in 1940 she graduated from Hunter College with a degree in biology and premedical studies. At Hunter, she became involved with a dance collective, won a scholarship with the New Dance Group, and produced her first choreographic work, *African Ceremonial,* in 1943. Examining racial and social issues through emotional physical movement, in 1943 she designed *Strange Fruit,* about a woman's response to LYNCHING. The following year, she choreographed *The Negro Speaks of Rivers,* based on the well-known poem by Harlem Renaissance writer LANGSTON HUGHES.

In 1948, Primus won a Rosenwald Fellowship to study dance in Africa, where she directed Liberia's Performing Arts Center. Developing a devout attachment to the continent, she became known as "Omowale," a name meaning "child has returned home." Returning to the United States, She married dancer Percival Borde in 1953 and founded the Pearl Primus Dance Language Institute in New York City.

In 1974, Primus combined African and Caribbean dance cultures to choreograph *Congolese Wedding,* which was produced for the Alvin Ailey American Dance Theater. She completed her doctorate in educational sociology and anthropology from New York University in 1978. She went on to teach dance and anthropology at Hunter and other universities throughout the country and world. In 1979, she produced *Michael, Row Your Boat Ashore,* about the 1960s church bombing in Birmingham, Alabama, that killed four young girls as they attended Sunday school.

From 1982 to 1984, Primus served as director of the Cora P. Maloney College at the University of Buffalo. She received many awards during her lifetime, including the Star of Africa from the Liberian Government, an honorary doctorate from Spelman College, and the National Medal of Arts.

Pearl Primus died on October 29, 1994, in New Rochelle, New York.

Further Reading

Welsh-Asante, Kariamu, ed. *African Dance: An Artistic, Historical and Philosophical Inquiry.* Lawrenceville, N.J.: Africa World Press, 1996.

Wright, Patricia. "The Prime of Miss Pearl Primus." *Contact,* February 1985.

— Sandra L. West

Prophet, Nancy Elizabeth (1890–1960) *sculptor*

Trained in PARIS and the United States to become a classical sculptor, Nancy Elizabeth Prophet won international recognition for her work while struggling to excel and earn a living as an artist.

Nancy Elizabeth Prophet was born in 1890 in Warrick, Rhode Island, the offspring of an African-American mother and Native American father. Her parents encouraged her to pursue work as a teacher or domestic, but she was determined to become an artist.

Nancy Prophet married Francis Ford of Maryland in 1915. Ford was attending Brown University at the time of their marriage but did not graduate. He was 34 years old; she was 24. In 1918, Prophet graduated from the Rhode Island School of Design with a certificate in freehand drawing and painting.

Supported by the sponsors who purchased her work, Prophet earned enough money to sail to Paris in 1922 and she stayed there for 10 years. In Paris she studied at the Ecole des Beaux Arts; participated in the Salon d'Automne in 1924 and 1927; exhibited in the Paris August Salons of 1925 and 1926; and in the Salon des Artistes Français of 1929. While in Paris she also received the HARMON FOUNDATION Award in 1929 for her sculpture *Head of a Negro.* She received good reviews in Paris, though she sketched studies more often than she painted full portraits or completed sculptures. She befriended Harlem Renaissance poet and travel writer COUNTEE CULLEN in the Paris studios of expatriate painter HENRY OSSAWA TANNER, a fertile meeting ground for black artists who visited or relocated to France.

In 1932, Prophet returned to the United States and exhibited at the Boston Society of Independent Artists, the Vose Galleries in Boston, and the Art Association of Newport, Rhode Island. She won the Richard S. Greenough Prize for her wood sculpture of a head, *Discontent* (1930). Her wood carving *Congolaise* (1931) is now in the collection of the Whitney Museum of American Art.

At the urging of *CRISIS: A RECORD OF THE DARKER RACES* editor Dr. W. E. B. DU BOIS, in 1933 Prophet moved to Atlanta, Georgia, to teach at Atlanta University. She spent just one year at the university before going to teach at neighboring Spelman College, where she remained until 1944. Leaving Atlanta to return to Providence in her home state, she was unable to find a teaching position. Prophet then suffered a nervous breakdown and was hospitalized. Upon her release from the hospital in 1958, she accepted a job as a maid for the Carly family in Providence. She worked for the family for six months and died a pauper in 1960.

Further Reading

Dallas Museum of Art. *Black Art: Ancestral Legacy.* Dallas: Dallas Museum of Art, 1989.

Leininger-Miller, Theresa A. *New Negro Artists in Paris: African American Painters and Sculptors in the City of Light, 1922–1934.* New Brunswick, N.J.: Rutgers University Press, 2000.

— Sandra L. West

Public Works of Art Project (PWAP) See WORKS PROGRESS ADMINISTRATION.

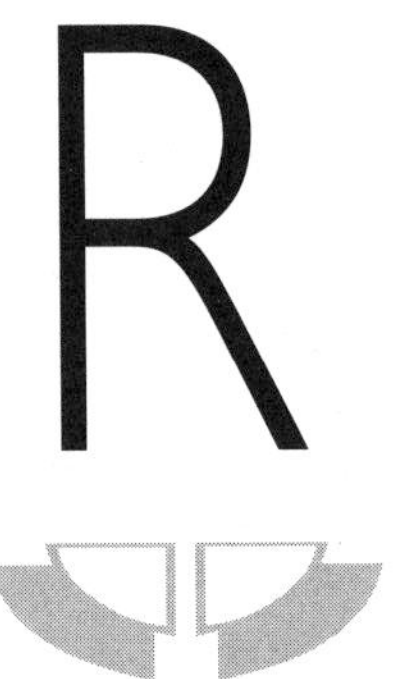

race records

Phonographic recordings by African Americans marketed for the first time to reach black audiences created a new industry known as race records in the 1920s.

Until 1920, a small number of African Americans made recordings primarily for historical rather than entertainment purposes. Broadway performers BERT WILLIAMS and GEORGE WALKER had the distinction of being the first African Americans known to make a record when they recorded several folk and popular show tunes in 1901 for the Victor Company. The FISK JUBILEE SINGERS made a series of recordings from 1902 to 1917. And ROLAND HAYES recorded for the English branch of Victor Records in 1920 but was denied permission for the recordings to be released.

However, it was white BLUES singer SOPHIE TUCKER's cancellation of a recording session with Okeh Records that led to an actual demand for music by black performers. Tucker had to cancel an agreement to record for Okeh after learning that doing so would violate a contract she had with another company. Because of Tucker's dilemma and the absence of another white singer to take her place, black songwriter Perry Bradford convinced Okeh Records to allow a black singer to record the song. The decision to do so was a difficult one because record companies did not believe whites would buy songs recorded by blacks. Bradford, on the other hand, pointed out that millions of African Americans would buy such songs. With that in mind, Mamie Smith took over for Tucker and recorded "You Can't Keep a Good Man Down" backed by "That Thing Called Love" on February 14, 1920. Encouraged by the moderate success of that effort, Okeh brought Smith back into the studio several months later to make a second recording, "Crazy Blues." Selling at the then substantial price of $1, "Crazy Blues" sold 75,000 copies in one month and by the year's end had reached sales of a million and a half copies.

As Mamie Smith continued to sing and record, both African Americans and white Americans continued to buy her records. Recognizing that they had come upon an untapped market, Okeh brought in other black performers to make records. FATS WALLER, KING OLIVER, Edith Wilson, CLARA SMITH, James P. Johnson, LOUIS ARMSTRONG, and numerous others all made their way into the Okeh studios.

Moreover, other white record companies established labels to market black music specifically to black Americans. Among them were the Vocalion Company, Gennett, Paramount, and Victor. This growth in companies eager to sell black music opened the recording industry's doors to newcomers and veterans alike. MA RAINEY, BESSIE SMITH, ALBERTA HUNTER, JELLY ROLL MORTON, Trixie Smith, and Sippi Wallace found an outlet for their talents away from stages and road shows. As it happened, this demand for black music coincided with the development of radio in the United States, and through that medium more people were exposed to the music of African Americans than ever before.

Race records became known throughout the 1920s by several names, including Negro records, coloured records, and popular blues songs. While most of the companies distributing them were white-owned, a few black-owned record companies did cash in on the boom as well. One of the more successful was Black Swan Records, part of the PACE PHONOGRAPHIC RECORD CORPORATION started by Harry Pace after he split with his former partner, W. C. HANDY. The Black Swan label was named in honor of the United States's first black concert singer, Elizabeth Taylor Greenfield, and its board of directors included *CRISIS: A RECORD OF THE DARKER RACES* editor W. E. B. DU BOIS and music arranger WILLIAM GRANT STILL. Gifted JAZZ musician and bandleader FLETCHER HENDERSON worked as the company's recording manager. One of the first singers signed by Black Swan was ETHEL WATERS, who gave the company a hit with "Down Home Blues" and "Oh Daddy." Waters, Henderson, and dancer Ethel Williams formed a group called the Black Swan Troubadors and took their talents on tour for a year. The label also recorded the Four Harmony Kings, the group that helped make *SHUFFLE ALONG* a hit show on Broadway, and concert sopranos Revella Hughes and Florence Cole Talbert.

Lesser known singers sometimes got their big breaks through field recordings, conducted using portable devices on locations where proper studios were not available. Such was largely the case in the South, where aspiring singers recorded the equivalent of a modern-day demo in churches, schools, hotel rooms, or clubs.

Sales on race records shot past $100 million in 1927. For many of those companies promoting them, such as Columbia with its star singer Bessie Smith, those sales meant the difference between profits and foreclosure. Most of the singers, however, only earned $25 to $50 per recording. Whereas Mamie Smith negotiated a deal to receive royalty percentages on her recordings, most others, like Bessie Smith, did not. Without royalty payments, for singers race records served largely as a form of advertisement to ensure attendance at concerts and shows.

The GREAT DEPRESSION considerably slowed the rise of race records until sales dropped to less than 7 million in the early 1930s. They nevertheless paved the way for the extraordinary success of black rhythm and blues artists during the latter half of the 1900s.

Further Reading

Davis, Angela Y. *Blues Legacies and Black Feminism: Gertrude "Ma" Rainey, Bessie Smith and Billie Holiday.* New York: Knopf, 1999.

Haskins, James. *Black Music in America: A History Through Its People.* New York: Welcome Rain Publishers, 2000.

— Aberjhani

ragtime

The music of ragtime developed out of late 1800s minstrel shows, black folk dances, and saloons of the Southwest to become the dominant musical form in the United States during the early 1900s.

The initial growth of ragtime was fueled in part by the popularity of the black folk dance, later to be popularized on stages across the world, known as the CAKEWALK. The more popular the high-stepping and exaggerated antics of the cakewalk became, the greater became the demand for music by which to perform it. Traditional popular songs and adopted European musical styles such as the waltz did not match the animated movements of the cakewalk, elements of which have been traced back to African origins.

As entertainment music played in saloons and whorehouses, ragtime was first composed primarily for the piano and later included brass instruments and vocals. It generally consisted of three to four sections containing 16 measures, each composed of a syncopated melody backed by a steady rhythm, or march. Variations on this pattern in time produced classical ragtime, novelty ragtime, and the STRIDE PIANO perfected in HARLEM during the 1920s. It also, eventually, gave birth to its replacement, JAZZ.

Theories abound on the precise origin of the term *ragtime,* and they range from attempts to describe the piecing together of different melodies to the driving syncopation considered ragtime's chief characteristic. While the music was generated in public entertainment establishments, it became equally popular in individual homes through the use of printed SHEET MUSIC and the piano. During the late 1800s and until the mid-1900s, Americans purchased sheet music and pianos the way contemporary consumers purchase stereos and compact discs. Production of the classic piano increased through the first decade of the 1900s, and production of the player piano began. The innovative player piano used a perforated roll of paper attached to a device that manipulated and played the piano in lieu of an individual striking the keys. As the phonograph and radio were developed during the 1910s and 1920s, the music that made its way from the piano roll to these more modern mechanisms was ragtime. It was also the music that the collective group of publishers known as Tin Pan Alley promoted more than any other.

White composer Theodore H. Northrup wrote the first published ragtime, entitled "Louisiana Rag," in 1897. The first published ragtime composition by a black man was "Harlem Rag" by Tom Turpin the same year. A native of Savannah, Georgia, Turpin later moved to St. Louis, where he operated the Rosebud Bar, wrote numerous ragtime compositions, and hosted ragtime competitions. One of the musicians Turpin befriended and whose musical development he influenced was Scott Joplin, the man crowned "king of the ragtime composers."

Joplin was born in Bowie County, Texas, on November 24, 1863, and died on April 1, 1917, in NEW YORK CITY. The offspring of a musical family, Joplin grew up surrounded by the sounds of black folk music and received further training in European classical music. Like WILLIAM GRANT STILL after him, Joplin's musical experiments combined African-American folk music with elements from European romanticism to create operas, ballets, waltzes, and the music for which he became most famous, ragtime. His 1899 composition, "Maple Leaf Rag," sold more than half a million copies in sheet music by 1907 and eventually more than a million. It was the song that introduced the school of classical ragtime, which lasted until the music's novelty and stride piano period in the 1920s. Joplin became an acknowledged master of ragtime and continued to compose such outstanding works as "The Cascades" in 1904 and "Fig Leaf Rag" in 1908. He moved to New York in 1915 and there staged the first presentation of his folk opera *Treemonisha,* in Harlem's LINCOLN THEATRE. For his contributions to American music, Joplin was posthumously awarded a Pulitzer Prize in 1976.

Ragtime was so entrenched as America's principal music during the 1910s that European composers openly acknowledged its growing impact on their work. Likewise, black musicians such as James Reese Europe and NOBLE SISSLE took ragtime to France during WORLD WAR I and showcased it in concerts and parades designed to boost the morale of U.S. and allied troops. During the same period, Sissle's future partner in the production of 1921's *SHUFFLE ALONG*, EUBIE BLAKE, played ragtime at high society affairs as well as Harlem RENT PARTIES. Often attending such parties in Harlem was ragtime enthusiast and renowned future composer of the folk opera *PORGY AND BESS*, George Gershwin. JAMES WELDON JOHNSON and his brother JOHN ROSAMOND JOHNSON made their contribution to the genre with such songs as "Under the Bamboo Tree" and "Congo Love Song."

Both a prolific composer and influential performer of ragtime, NEW ORLEANS native JELLY ROLL MORTON toured and recorded throughout the United States, most notably in California; CHICAGO, Illinois; New York City; and WASHINGTON, D.C. Morton's very individual style of ragtime incorporated the original music's syncopation and marches but included diverse elements bordering on improvisation that hints at the creation of jazz; for that reason it is viewed as a viable bridge between the two musical forms. In the mid-1920s, Morton took advantage of the growth in RACE RECORDS to record several songs with his ensemble, the Red Hot Peppers. These included "Smokehouse Blues," "Kansas City Stomp," and "Grandpa's Spells." He joined the stride pianists in New York in 1928.

The performance style of playing known as stride piano was at once an extension of ragtime and a signature mark that separated Harlem's better piano players from those from anywhere else. Among its masters were the much-celebrated James P. Johnson, Luckey Roberts, Willie "the Lion" Smith, and FATS WALLER. Through their compositions, recordings, and performances, very often on Broadway, ragtime remained a vital force in American music even as SWING and jazz began to supplant it in the 1920s, 1930s, and 1940s.

Various composers and musicians maintained an interest in ragtime throughout the 1900s; the music and its era spawned a number of notable literary works as well as films. E. L. Doctorow's novel *Ragtime* was published in 1975 and later made into both a movie and stage production featuring the music of Scott Joplin. Radio stations, journals, publishing houses, and annual festivals dedicated solely to the promotion of ragtime remain active in the 21st century.

Further Reading

Badger, Reid. *A Life in Ragtime: A Biography of James Reese Europe.* Nashville, Tenn.: Replica Books, 2001.

Jasen, David A. A., and Gene Jones. *Black Bottom Stomp: Eight Masters of Ragtime and Early Jazz.* New York: Routledge, 2001.

— Aberjhani

Rainey, Ma (Gertrude Pridgett) (1886–1939) *blues singer*

One of the earliest performers of the BLUES, Ma Rainey built a solid base of black fans throughout the rural South before joining the GREAT MIGRATION of African Americans moving north in the 1920s and emerging as the celebrated "mother of the blues."

Rainey was born April 26, 1886, in Columbus, Georgia. She was the second of five children born to Ella and Thomas Pridgett, performers in what was then a thriving minstrel show tradition. Pridgett made her performance debut at the age of 12 when she sang in a talent show. Performing as a teenager in various stage productions, she reportedly began singing the blues before audiences in 1902 at the age of 16. Her renditions of the blues at that time have since been recognized as the first public performances of the blues by a female artist.

On February 2, 1904, Pridgett married Will Rainey, a comic whose act, like that of many black entertainers of the era, also included singing and dancing. Billing themselves as "Ma and Pa Rainey: The Assassinators of the Blues," the couple toured for more than a decade with such shows as the Rabbit Foot Minstrels, Tolliver's Circus and Musical Extravaganza, and the Silas Greene Show. Increasingly successful, they helped promote the careers of numerous others, including BUTTERBEANS AND SUSIE and BESSIE SMITH, with whom Ma Rainey shared a close relationship, often described as romantic in nature.

The Raineys separated around 1916 and Ma Rainey developed as a soloist on the THEATRE OWNERS' BOOKING AGENCY (TOBA) circuit. Working on the TOBA circuit, she began touring the Northeast and Midwest as well as additional venues in her native South. After singing professionally for two decades, Rainey signed a recording contract with Paramount Records in 1923. Along with Mamie Smith, Bessie Smith, ETHEL WATERS, CLARA SMITH, and others, she became one of the major stars of the RACE RECORDS industry that increased the popularity of the blues, JAZZ, and RAGTIME during the 1920s.

Rainey's first recorded songs in 1923 were: "Jelly Bean Blues," "Barrel House Blues," "Walking Blues," "Broken-Hearted Blues," and "Countin' the Blues," the latter with LOUIS ARMSTRONG and FLETCHER HENDERSON. She followed those in 1924 with a number of songs eventually considered classics of the genre: "These Dogs of Mine," "Lucky Rock Blues," "Ma Rainey's Mystery Record," "Lawd Send Me a Man Blues," and "See See Rider Blues."

In all, Rainey recorded close to 100 songs for Paramount between 1923 and 1928. She generally worked with the most acclaimed musicians of the era. In addition to the aforementioned Armstrong and Henderson, she also worked with gospel music pioneer THOMAS DORSEY, jazz great Coleman Hawkins, and NEW ORLEANS jazz legend Kid Ory. Moreover, she made a series of recordings working with Lovie Austin's Blues Serenaders and her own back-up musicians, the Georgia Band and the Jub Jug Washboard Band, which endowed Rainey's music with a quality of rural authenticity that she never lost.

The sale of her records added to the glamour of Ma Rainey's showmanship in live performances. On stage, she routinely made her entrance through a giant phonograph (precursor to the modern stereo system). In addition to sparkling sequined gowns and soft feathers, she wore a necklace and earrings fashioned out of gold eagle dollar coins.

Whereas the race record industry went into decline with the advent of the GREAT DEPRESSION in 1929, Ma Rainey maintained her career by continuing to produce and travel with her own shows. She also invested in two vaudeville theaters in Rome, Georgia, a venture that allowed her in 1933 to retire comfortably in her birthplace of Columbus. She died there December 22, 1939.

Ma Rainey's contributions to American music were recognized in 1983 when she was inducted into the Blues Foundation Hall of Fame and in 1990 when she was inducted into the Rock and Roll Hall of Fame.

Further Reading

Davis, Angela Y. *Blues Legacies and Black Feminism: Gertrude "Ma" Rainey, Bessie Smith, and Billie Holiday.* New York: Pantheon Books, 2002.

Friedwald, Will. *Jazz Singing: America's Great Voices From Bessie Smith to Bebop and Beyond.* New York: Da Capo Press, Inc., 1996.

Krasner, David. *Beautiful Pageant: African American Performance, Theater and Drama in the Harlem Renaissance, 1910–1927.* New York: Palgrave Publishers, 2002.

Reed, Bill. *Hot from Harlem: Profiles in Classic African American Entertainment.* Los Angeles: Cellar Door Books, 1998.

— Aberjhani

Randolph, A. Philip (Asa Philip Randolph)

(1889–1979) *political activist*

An influential editor, labor organizer, and civil rights advocate, Asa Philip Randolph helped lead African Americans through five decades, from the 1920s to the 1960s, in the struggle for racial equality.

Randolph was born on April 15, 1889, in Crescent City, Florida, the son of Elizabeth Robinson Randolph and his minister father, James Randolph. He grew up in Jacksonville, where he graduated from Cookman Institute. In 1911, Randolph joined the millions of African Americans migrating to cities in the North and moved to NEW YORK CITY with hopes of becoming an actor. He abandoned his theatrical ambitions in the course of juggling numerous odd jobs while simultaneously attending New York City College at night.

Randolph's formal courses included classes in history, political science, economics, philosophy, and history. However, he also received an extensive education in socialism, at the time a growing political movement in the United States, through his independent studies and affiliation with socialist organizations on his college campus. Socialism became the ideological tool Randolph would employ to analyze and address the political and economic status of African Americans.

In 1914, Randolph married beauty shop owner Lucille Green, whose support would prove essential during Randolph's battle to gain official recognition for the BROTHERHOOD OF SLEEPING CAR PORTERS.

In 1917, Randolph joined with fellow black socialist Chandler Owen to start the *MESSENGER*, which presented itself as the "only radical Negro magazine in America." Through the *Messenger,* Randolph and Owen addressed the full spectrum of political issues affecting African Americans, from policies issuing out of the White House to scathing critiques of black leadership. In a tone of recognition and condemnation that was likely influenced by his father's sermons, Randolph summed up President Woodrow Wilson's administration as one that was self-serving and class-biased. Without overtly saying he wished the president would die, he stated calmly enough that no tears would be shed if he did. Randolph viewed BOOKER TALIAFERRO WASHINGTON as self-deluded and was never able to take MARCUS GARVEY seriously, often referring to him as a clown. While W. E. B. DU BOIS in his fashion was at least as radical as Randolph, the latter was skeptical of the former because of his affiliation with the NATIONAL ASSOCIATION FOR THE ADVANCEMENT OF COLORED PEOPLE (NAACP) and that organization's moderate approach to achieving racial equality. He also disagreed with Du Bois's call to "close ranks" during WORLD WAR I because he felt the war was an issue between capitalist powers with no interest in the welfare of the working masses, in which he included African Americans. His concern was more with African Americans protecting themselves from LYNCHING; like ROBERT ABBOTT of the *CHICAGO DEFENDER*, he advocated a policy of self-defense.

Although he would later denounce COMMUNISM as a serious threat to African-American causes, Randolph initially celebrated and supported the Russian Revolution of 1917 as a victory for workers. By linking the struggle of African Americans to that of workers worldwide, he felt, blacks would benefit from a network of allies emphasizing political solidarity over racial division. He and Owen were so outspoken in their call for political change in the United States that the two were arrested for two days during a speech engagement in Cleveland, Ohio.

More than voicing his opinion about political issues, Randolph sought to contribute solutions by helping groups of black workers form union and trade organizations. As if rehearsing for the larger battles to come, Randolph established a number of labor organizations, such as the Friends of Negro Freedom in 1920 and the United Negro Trades in 1923, which were promising but ultimately short-lived. In 1925, he addressed a meeting at the Elk Lodge in Harlem where 500 railroad porters, hotel workers, and dining car attendants were hoping Randolph would lead them in the creation of the first black-controlled union, the Brotherhood of Sleeping Car Porters.

The challenge was one that Randolph at first doubted he could meet. It would entail months of travel across the country to build a union composed of African Americans employed by the Pullman Railroad Company, one of the largest and richest companies in the country. Even with a substantial body of members, he would still have to fight for the union's recognition by a company that was staunchly antiunion. Yet the plight of the porters struck Randolph not only as clearly unjust but also indicative of the kind of conditions black workers faced all over the country. The Pullman porters were often required to work back-to-back shifts for days and nights on end with little or no rest, made to perform two separate jobs without additional pay, and required to accept whatever manner of abuse an individual categorized as a customer might heap upon them. Randolph reasoned that a victory for the porters would open

A. Philip Randolph's many years as a dedicated advocate for the rights of workers and African Americans made him one of America's most influential and revered black leaders. He is shown here speaking at the March on Washington for jobs and freedom, August 28, 1963. *(Library of Congress, Prints & Photographs Division)*

the door to improved labor conditions for blacks in all vocations. Over a course of 10 years, Randolph waged a war of nerves, faith, and endurance against the Pullman company.

Elected president of the Brotherhood of Sleeping Car Porters, Randolph used the *Messenger* as an organ for the new union and regularly publicized the conditions they were fighting against as well as the rights they were fighting for. He and his regional representatives, in cities like CHICAGO, Illinois, and St. Louis, Missouri, in the beginning achieved success with a membership that grew rapidly into the thousands. When the Pullman company fought back, however, with job terminations, threats, and the creation of their own puppet union designed to protect the interests of the company, the membership dwindled. The union, like the rest of the country, suffered a further blow with the onset of the GREAT DEPRESSION. Working without a salary and at one point without an office, Randolph's Brotherhood of Sleeping Car Porters remained more an idea than a reality. Still, those porters who insisted on continuing the battle became along with Randolph living symbols of heroism and integrity. Their first major step toward victory occurred in 1934 when the porters won admission into the internationally recognized American Federation of Labor. The 1934 Railway Labor Act further increased their strength by making it illegal for the Pullman company to discriminate against workers affiliated with unions. The following year the Pullman company was forced to recognize the Brotherhood of Sleeping Car Porters as the official representative of the majority of its black employees. In 1937, the brotherhood became the first black union to obtain a contract with a major U.S. corporation.

As he had hoped 10 years earlier, triumph for the Brotherhood of Sleeping Car Porters led to a recognition of black workers' rights in a variety of fields. It also secured Randolph's position as one of the most influential black leaders in the United States. At the 1936 National Negro Congress held in Chicago, Randolph was elected president of a body of black leaders representing almost 600 organizations. It was not the goal of the congress to replace any of these organizations but to present a united front of organizations dedicated to such issues as federal action against lynching, recognition of the hardships of black farmers, and equal distribution of government relief funds issued as part of President FRANKLIN DELANO ROOSEVELT's New Deal program, opposition to war, and complete social and political equality for African Americans. Ralph Bunche, ALAIN LOCKE, ADAM CLAYTON POWELL,

JR., and John P. Davis were among the delegates. As members of the Congress affiliated with communism became more influential, Randolph protested their involvement and resigned in 1940.

With the advent of World War II in Europe in 1939, Randolph turned his attention to discrimination in the military and those industries that received government funds in support of the war effort. Joining forces with WALTER WHITE of the NAACP and T. Arnold Hill of the NATIONAL URBAN LEAGUE (NUL), Randolph met with President Roosevelt to request federal intervention ensuring that African Americans would receive the same opportunities as anyone else for jobs in the defense industries. Roosevelt's initial failure to commit himself to any such action prompted Randolph to start a march on Washington movement, calling for 10,000 African Americans to march and dramatize their protest in the nation's capital. To avoid the complications of such a march during wartime, Roosevelt issued Executive Order 8802 outlawing discriminatory hiring practices in U.S. defense industries. The Committee on Fair Employment Practices was established to enforce the order, and the march on Washington was duly canceled.

Randolph modified the radicalism that had characterized editorials in the 1920s and, like Martin Luther King, Jr., after him, practiced his version of Mohandas Gandhi's philosophy of nonviolent protest. His League for Nonviolent Civil Disobedience Against Military Segregation was founded in 1948 to emphasize the incongruity of maintaining a racially separated military when blacks had defended the United States in two world wars. President Harry Truman signed Executive Order 9981 to end segregation in the military the same year.

Despite significant political gains for African Americans during the 1950s, the discrimination that still existed in housing, voting rights, and employment prompted Randolph to renew his call for a march on Washington in 1963. Political activist Bayard Rustin and civil rights leader Martin Luther King, Jr., worked with Randolph to organize the peaceful demonstration dedicated to "jobs and freedom." A quarter of a million peaceful demonstrators participated in the event, marking the largest mass demonstration for the rights of African Americans in U.S. history. Randolph, at 74 years old, crowned four and a half decades of leadership with his keynote speech advocating renewed dedication to the struggle for civil rights. Introducing nine other speakers, he ended with Martin Luther King, Jr., who delivered his famous "I Have a Dream" speech.

Acknowledging Randolph's lifelong struggle for racial equality in America, President Lyndon B. Johnson awarded him the Presidential Medal of Freedom in 1964. Randolph died in New York on May 16, 1979.

Further Reading

Pfeffer, Paula F. *A. Philip Randolph, Pioneer of the Civil Rights Movement.* Baton Rouge: Louisiana State University Press, 1996.

Reef, Catherine. *A. Philip Randolph: Labor Leader and Civil Rights Crusader.* Springfield, Ill.: Enslow Publishers, 2001.

— Aberjhani

Rang Tang

Rang Tang was one of the most successful black musical revues of the late 1920s, opening in July 1927 and closing in January 1928 after a run of 119 performances.

Much of *Rang Tang*'s success, following such short-lived shows as *Bottomland* and ETHEL WATERS's *Africana* the same year, was due to the talents of the dancing comedy team Flournoy Miller and Aubrey Lyles. Miller and Lyles had cowritten and also costarred in *SHUFFLE ALONG*, the musical that in 1921 started the trend in black as well as white musical revues on Broadway.

Rang Tang was in many ways simply another version of *Shuffle Along* in that it, like the latter, focused on the antics of Sam and Steve, two characters from the mythical southern locale of Jimtown. In *Rang Tang,* the two are on the lam from creditors and make their way by plane to Africa. Once there, they encounter the queen of Sheba, assorted warriors, and a treasure of diamonds. Taking possession of the diamonds, they return to America to live the life of their dreams.

The book and libretto for *Rang Tang* was written by Kaj Gynt with music by Ford Dabney and lyrics by Jo Trent. In addition to Miller and Lyles, it starred a number of dancers who by then were established veterans of black musicals on Broadway. Among them were Mae Brown, Lavinia Mack, and Byron Jones.

Further Reading

Lamb, Andrew. *150 Years of Popular Musical Theatre.* New Haven: Yale University Press, 2001.

Mordden, Ethan. *Make Believe: The Broadway Musical in the 1920s.* New York: Oxford University Press, 1997.

— Aberjhani

Red Summer of 1919

Riots throughout the summer of 1919 occurred in 25 U.S. cities, including Omaha, Nebraska; WASHINGTON, D.C.; Longview, Texas; PHILADELPHIA, Pennsylvania; Knoxville, Tennessee; and CHICAGO, Illinois; creating the most destructive confrontations between Americans since the Civil War. Nearly a hundred African Americans lost their lives and countless others were injured during this period, which writer and composer JAMES WELDON JOHNSON described as the Red Summer.

The violence was the culmination of a series of events. Often cited as the principal factor was the social atmosphere created by the GREAT MIGRATION, that massive exodus of African Americans from the southern United States to the northern, which roughly began in 1910. By the time 1919 arrived, blacks were convinced that the North offered much better opportunities for jobs, housing, education, and relief from the apartheid practices of JIM CROW. However, where blacks saw themselves taking advantage of opportunities, many northern whites saw the arrival of blacks as competition.

Nevertheless, after participating in WORLD WAR I, African Americans were instilled with a stronger sense of their right to compete or fight for their share of opportunities. Participation in the war also reduced the tolerance of both African Americans and many European Americans for the more overt forms of racism, particularly the practice of lynching. Although some whites were reportedly hung and mutilated, the number of blacks to suffer LYNCHING (which generally was not treated as a crime) was much higher. By 1919, more than 3,000 African-American men and women had been lynched following the end of the Civil War. The threat of such an event was rarely far from the considerations of the average black person in 1919.

With tensions constantly mounting on both sides of the color line, the flow of blood that made the summer of 1919 red could almost be expected. Only two years before then, a more compact version of 1919's carnage erupted in St. Louis in what was clearly identified as white-on-black mob violence.

While the body counts were scattered throughout the nation in 1919, the death toll in Knoxville reached seven; in Washington, D.C., it hit six; and in Longview, four. Of the 25 cities involved, Chicago was hit the hardest. The city had been in a state of unrest following a series of random bombings directed at blacks and ongoing struggles between laborers vying for equal representation in unions. That unrest escalated into full-scale pandemonium on July 27 when a 17-year-old black youth named Eugene Williams swam into a section of Lake Michigan Beach supposedly reserved for whites only. A mob of enraged whites hurled stones at Williams, causing the young man to drown.

Instead of ending the threat of uncontrolled violence, the arrival of policemen at Lake Michigan Beach further sparked it when they failed to arrest any of the whites that witnesses reported had thrown the stones at Williams. What followed was five days of attacks and counterattacks throughout Chicago. Some 38 African Americans were killed, hundreds of blacks and whites were injured, more than a thousand people lost their homes, and businesses were shut down. It was not until the state militia entered the fray that the city-turned-war zone resumed some semblance of order.

The Red Summer dispelled any illusions entertained by blacks or whites that racial violence in America was a solely southern phenomenon. Moreover, leaders across the board took note that blacks involved in the riots throughout the country were markedly unlike the passive victims of the past. Indeed, it was as if they had taken their defiant cue from a poem, published that very same hot July in *The Liberator:* CLAUDE MCKAY's "IF WE MUST DIE," with its famous closing lines:

> Like men we'll face the murderous, cowardly pack,
> Pressed to the wall, dying, but fighting back!

Further Reading

Aptheker, Herbert. *A Documentary History of the Negro People in the United States: 1910–1932.* New York: Carol Publishing Group, 1993.

Brown, Gregory. *The East St. Louis Race Riot.* Milwaukee: The Black Holocaust Society, 1999.

Grant, Joanne. *Black Protest.* New York: Fawcett World Library, 1968.

— Aberjhani

Reiss, Winold (1886–1953) *painter*

Winold Reiss was a portrait painter from Germany who immigrated to the United States and sought to capture on canvas his perception of the dignity of Native Americans, Asian Americans, and African Americans, influencing in the process the work of Harlem Renaissance artists.

Winold Reiss was the son of another artist, Fritz Reiss. He was born in Germany in 1886 and moved to NEW YORK CITY in 1913. In the United States, he worked for the Great Northern Railway to promote the West by creating realistic portraits of Native Americans on calendars and railroad posters.

Reiss's work is distinctive and pure in line. His drawings appear to illuminate the inner selves of his subjects at a time when minstrel implications and racial caricatures were typical. Among his extremely serene and dignified portraits of significant Harlem Renaissance figures are ALAIN LOCKE, literary critic and editor of *The NEW NEGRO* (1925); W. E. B. DU BOIS, cofounder of the NATIONAL ASSOCIATION FOR THE ADVANCEMENT OF COLORED PEOPLE (NAACP) and editor of *The CRISIS: A RECORD OF THE DARKER RACES*; ROLAND HAYES, tenor; and poet LANGSTON HUGHES, author of *Weary Blues.*

German-born painter Winold Reiss excelled in illustrations depicting the culture of various ethnic groups, such as his drawing of African Americans seen here and the graphics he contributed to the *New Negro* anthology. *(Library of Congress, Prints & Photographs Division [LC-USZC4-5687])*

Aside from employing Harlem Renaissance writers and artists as subjects, Reiss also worked alongside them, helping AARON DOUGLAS to develop his distinctive style for evoking African and African-American culture in his images. He also worked with Douglas and MIGUEL COVARRUBIAS to provide the graphics and illustrations for *The New Negro* anthology.

Fascinated by indigenous people, Reiss lived in Montana among the Blackfoot Indians. He opened a school at Glacier National Park in Montana and taught there. He also taught in New York. FISK UNIVERSITY in Nashville, Tennessee, acquired work of Winold Reiss in 1951 by way of one of Reiss's former students, muralist Douglas.

Reiss's entire portrait collection of Harlem Renaissance figures is owned by the National Portrait Gallery in WASHINGTON, D.C. Reiss died in Montana in 1953.

Further Reading

Bailey, David A., and Paul Gilroy. *Rhapsodies in Black: Art of the Harlem Renaissance.* Berkeley: University of California, 1997.

Beckman, Wendy Hart. *Artists and Writers of the Harlem Renaissance.* Berkeley Heights, N.J.: Enslow Publishers, 2002.

— Sandra L. West

Renaissance Big Five, "The Rens"

See SPORTS AND THE HARLEM RENAISSANCE.

Renaissance Casino and Ballroom

Located on West 138th Street in HARLEM, the Renaissance Casino and Ballroom stood unique among such comparable entertainment centers as the Roseland Ballroom, the SAVOY BALLROOM, and the LINCOLN THEATRE.

The Renaissance divided its entertainment activities between two floors. The bottom level served primarily as a movie and live performance theater that offered entertainment for entire families. The upper level, on the other hand, generally featured more adult-oriented activities with some all-inclusive exceptions such as sports events. A small-scaled casino, dinners, concerts, and dances were also held on the second floor. Like other entertainment facilities of the era, the various activities were generally offered on different days and nights of the week planned to avoid similar offerings by its competitors. Toward this end, the Renaissance Casino and Ballroom often set aside specific evenings for dancers wanting to perfect their moves for such dances as the black bottom, the lindy hop, or the Charleston. It also featured the more progressive JAZZ and RAGTIME performers in the mode of KING OLIVER, FESS WILLIAMS and his Royal Flush Orchestra, and FLETCHER HENDERSON's pioneering SWING SOUND band.

The facility was owned by African Americans and managed by the W. C. Roach Company. Popular in the 1920s, its very name has often generated an association of the theater and ballroom with the Harlem Renaissance.

Further Reading

Bascom, Lionel C. *A Renaissance in Harlem, Lost Voices of an American Community.* New York: Avon, 1999.

Petersen, Bernard L., Jr. *The African American Theatre Directory, 1816–1960.* Westport, Conn.: Greenwood Publishing Group, 1997.

— Aberjhani

rent party

Black residents of HARLEM during the 1920s responded in part to the double challenge of higher than average rents and lower than average incomes with the unique social and entertainment phenomenon known as the rent party.

As the name implies, rent parties were held (and in some communities are still held) to help raise money to pay rent and avoid the ugly spectacle of a family seeing its belongings tossed out onto the street for lack of payment.

Residents of Harlem generally had to face rent costs that were $20 to $30 higher than those paid by whites for apartments of similar design and with the same number of rooms. This practice of rent gouging remained a principal bone of contention until attempts to regulate rents were instituted in the 1930s. The hardship was one deeply felt within a community where the average family managed to take in approximately $1,300 annually and had to use half of that for rent alone. By contrast, the average white family earned about $1,600 per year but only paid a quarter of its income on rent.

To help offset the economic imbalance, Harlemites began hosting parties on Thursdays and Saturdays to raise whatever funds were needed for rent due the next week. These ventures proved successful enough that many began to hold the parties on any night of the week, whether rent was due or not, to supplement their salaries as housekeepers, elevator operators, and other occupations. Holding such a party meant transforming the living room or parlor, and possibly a bedroom or dining room, into a miniature dance hall with the more oversized furniture shoved out of the way and smaller chairs lined up against the walls. Word of the parties was spread by rhyming advertising jingles printed on business cards or leaflets and distributed on the street. Those who did not receive such an ad could recognize the location of a rent party by the red, blue, or pink lightbulb shining in the window.

The cost of admission to rent parties ranged from a dime to half a dollar, with the average price being 25¢. Once inside, partygoers could also sidestep the law prohibiting the sale of alcohol and purchase bathtub gin or corn liquor. Also on sale would be a feast of such foods as fried chicken, black-eyed peas with rice, collard greens, potato salad, pork chops, and cabbage. The quieter side of a rent party took place from about 10 P.M. to midnight, while one of the biggest draws to the party got under way after midnight: live music and cut-loose dancing. At a minimum, a good piano player entertained at rent parties, and very often a three-piece combo would provide the music. It was also common for professional musicians to drop in after their performances at clubs and cafés. The dancing could last easily until the next morning, with revelers working their way through the Charleston, the Black Bottom, Strut, Stomp, Slow Drag, or Lindy Hop. Mostly it was the kind of uninhibited dancing that lent itself well to sexual flirtations but sometimes became part of a contest. The all-night marathons were more likely to take place on a Thursday or Saturday night because many had the following days off from work and could recuperate at their leisure.

To many of those blacks newly arrived in Harlem from the South, the red, blue, or pink lightbulbs signaling a rent party in progress were something of a throwback to the juke joints back home. Just as it had indicated a place of social gathering and retreat from the harshness of racism down South, it indicated the same up North.

Moreover, rent parties were not restricted to lower-class workers. Everyone from professionals fresh from their jobs to the formally attired social elite would arrive for a late night filled with rowdy dance, continuous live music, and a menu of the original "soul food."

Whereas most rent parties functioned precisely as originally intended, some turned into something very different and served instead as covers for so-called buffet flat pleasure houses. The primary pleasures offered at those particular gatherings were prostitution and gambling.

Further Reading

Bascom, Lionel C. *A Renaissance in Harlem.* New York: Avon, 1999.

Favor, J. Martin. *Authentic Blackness: The Folk in the New Negro Renaissance.* Durham, N.C.: Duke University Press, 1999.

— Aberjhani

Richardson, Willis (1889–1977) *playwright*

When the curtains went up on May 17, 1923, at the Frazee Theater on Willis Richardson's *The Chip Woman's Fortune,* it marked the first time that a nonmusical play by a black writer was produced on Broadway.

Willis was born on November 5, 1889, in Wilmington, North Carolina, to Willis Wilder and Agnes Harper Richardson. In 1898, his parents left Wilmington to escape the riots that erupted there over voting rights for blacks. They moved to WASHINGTON, D.C., where Richardson attended Dunbar High School. He was encouraged to write by the playwright Mary Burrill and the historian CARTER GODWIN WOODSON.

Graduating from high school in 1910, Richardson was unable to take advantage of a scholarship that he won to attend HOWARD UNIVERSITY but pursued his studies in poetry and drama through a correspondence school. He accepted a job working as a clerk with the U.S. Bureau of Printing and Engraving, a position he held until retiring in 1954. In 1914, he married Mary Ellen Jones. The couple had three children: Jean Paula, Antonella, and Noel Justine.

Reflecting on a performance of ANGELINA EMILY WELD GRIMKE's play *Rachel,* which he saw in 1916, Richardson wrote *The Hope of a Negro Drama* in 1919. It became one of the first essays by a black writer to critique the state of African-American theater. In the essay, Richardson acknowledged the value of drama as a tool of protest but suggested the spiritual qualities of African Americans held greater promise for serious black drama. He set to demonstrate his theories by publishing a series of dramatic children's sketches in *the BROWNIES' BOOK,* a children's magazine published by the NATIONAL ASSOCIATION FOR THE ADVANCEMENT OF COLORED PEOPLE (NAACP). His first play for adults, *The Deacon's Awakening,* was produced in St. Paul, Minnesota, in 1921.

Hoping to have his work performed by Howard University's Howard Players, Richardson met with the group's codirectors, ALAIN LOCKE and Montgomery Gregory. They were denied permission to produce the plays based on the university president's assessment that Richardson's work was too racially inflammatory. W. E. B. DU BOIS directed the playwright to Raymond O'Neil's ETHIOPIAN ART PLAYERS in CHICAGO. The group staged Richardson's *The Chip Woman's Fortune* in Chicago, Illinois, took it on the road to Washington, D.C., then staged it as part of a triple bill at the LAFAYETTE THEATRE in HARLEM. When the drama moved to Broadway for a week in May 1923, Richardson became an African-American cause for celebration across the nation.

Following the Broadway triumph of *The Chip Woman's Fortune,* the Howard Players produced Richardson's *Mortgaged* in 1924. The play was later put on by the Dunbar Dramatic Club and took fourth place in a drama tournament in Plainfield, New Jersey. Over the next two years, his work continued to garner awards while being performed by some of the most acclaimed black little theater groups of the time. Both the Gilpin Players and the KRIGWA PLAYERS performed his play *Compromise.* The Krigwa Players also put on Richardson's *The Broken Banjo,* which won *CRISIS: A RECORD OF THE DARKER RACES* magazine's Spingarn literary prize. In the same year, 1925, his *Fall of the Conjurer* won honorable mention in the *OPPORTUNITY* magazine awards. In 1926, he won a $100 award for *Boot-Black Lover,* and the Negro Art Players performed his *Room for Rent.*

In addition to his plays, Richardson continued to publish essays, poetry, and stories. He also turned his hand to editing and in 1930 published the collection *Plays and Pageants from the Life of the Negro.* In 1935, he teamed up with MAY MILLER to coedit *Negro History in Thirteen Plays.* A final volume of his plays, *The King's Dilemma and Other Plays for Children,* was published in 1956.

Richardson was one of the Saturday Nighters who met at the S Street SALON hosted by Georgia Douglas Johnson in Washington. The group met weekly and included Locke, STERLING ALLEN BROWN, Owen Dodson, ALICE DUNBAR-NELSON, and many others who sometimes traveled from New York and other parts of the country to participate in discussions on literature, race, and various cultural matters.

Recognized and honored as one of the greatest black playwrights of his era, Richardson is often described as having been "ahead of his time." Many believe he is the great black playwright of the Harlem Renaissance who simply was never recognized as such while he lived, though he wrote some four dozen plays, including six three-act plays, addressing everything from fantasies for children to dramas on black history and black family life. His works were performed in Atlanta, Georgia; Baltimore, Maryland; New York City; Cleveland, Ohio, and many other cities. Richardson died on November 8, 1977.

Further Reading

Gray, Christine Rauchfuss. *Willis Richardson, Forgotten Pioneer of African-American Drama.* Westport, Conn.: Greenwood Press, 1999.

Hay, Samuel A. *African American Theatre: A Historical and Critical Analysis.* New York: Cambridge University Press, 1994.

— Aberjhani

Richmond, Virginia (Harlem of the South)

The all-black Jackson Ward neighborhood in Richmond, Virginia, was so culturally rich, capitalistically focused, and economically sound during the Harlem Renaissance that it became nationally known as the HARLEM of the South.

During the 1920s, Jackson Ward's Second Street, located off Richmond's main Broad Street, was the hub of JAZZ music and industrious black entrepreneurship. On it, and the surrounding blocks that made up Jackson Ward, black businesses included vendors who sold fruit and vegetables from horse-driven buggies, print shop operators, morticians, shoe shine stands, and horseshoeing and construction companies. Also operating in the area were furniture stores, grocers, Dr. Williams's pharmacy, a watch repair shop, beauty salons, and Dr. Foster's dental practice. Insurance companies developed out of burial societies and beneficial societies established immediately after slavery were also plentiful.

Included among the businesses was a blacks-only elementary school and a library for black readers. In addition, the Second Street area supported at least three newspapers: *The Reformer, The Daily Planet,* and the *St. Luke Herald.* The newspa-

Folk artist Leslie Garland Bolling contributed to Richmond's cultural renaissance both as an artist and a teacher at the Craig House Art Center, a facility steeped in history, as the sign seen here indicates. This was the only art center for black youth in the South sponsored by the WPA. The building continues to stand in the Church Hill neighborhood. *(photo by Sandra L. West)*

pers, like such northern counterparts as the *PITTSBURGH COURIER* and the *AMSTERDAM NEWS*, encouraged thrift, crusaded against LYNCHING, and reported on black social events. The area's hospital was named the Gilpin Hospital, after Dr. Z. Gilpin, a relative of actor CHARLES SIDNEY GILPIN, who won the SPINGARN MEDAL for his performance in the original stage production of the *EMPEROR JONES*.

The Harlem of the South prospered with hotels and theaters. The Hippodrome, at 528 N. Second Street, featured such film entertainment as movies by OSCAR MICHEAUX and live stars straight from NEW YORK CITY. DUKE ELLINGTON, COUNT BASIE, and BILLIE HOLIDAY are just a few of the era's stars to perform at the Hippodrome, the Booker T. Theatre, the Maggie L. Walker theater, and other Jackson Ward locations.

According to the *Richmond Afro-American* of July 19, 1938, the U.S. Census Department counted 274 "colored" hotels, with Virginia claiming nine of them. On Second Street alone, there was the Biltmore, Slaughter's, and the Apollo Hotel. Flagg's Hotel opened in 1875. Miller's Hotel opened in 1903. Neverett A. Eggleston, Sr., owned and operated the Eggleston Motel on Second Street during the lively era when celebrities performed at the Hippodrome Theatre, right down the block, and stayed at his two-story establishment.

Among those entertainers from the area to achieve renown were the gospel group the Harmonizing Four, tap dancer Pleasant "Snowball" Crump, and the legendary BOJANGLES ROBINSON. Johnson's Happy Pals, a 10-piece big band formed in 1927, was considered among the best of the SWING SOUND performers, and in 1929 they went to New York, where they defeated the Duke Ellington Orchestra and others in a big band contest at the SAVOY BALLROOM.

Second Street also had its version of JUNGLE ALLEY with the Happy Land, Waltz Dream, and Black and Tan nightclubs. Moreover, it boasted dance halls, ballrooms, and juke joints such as Jackson's Beer Garden. The True Reformers' Hall held concerts and boxing matches promoted by George Fry, who in the 1920s also managed the Richmond Giants, a NATIONAL NEGRO BASEBALL LEAGUE team. Casino-type gambling took place at Capital City Lodge. All the Jackson Ward businesses did well enough that cars, buggies, and people clogged the streets from the opening of the business day to the predawn closings of the juke joints.

With its many thriving businesses, Richmond was a black bankers' town. Millionaire Maggie Lena Walker, the first African-American president of a chartered bank, presided over the St. Luke Penny Savings bank. In its more prosperous days, the Commercial Bank, True Reformers, Mechanics Savings Bank, Nickel Savings, and Second Street Savings—all black owned and operated—coexisted in Jackson Ward. Several of the aforementioned merged into Consolidated Bank & Trust Company—known in the neighborhood as "Maggie Walker's bank"—which in 2002 still handled savings accounts and issued loans from their Marshall & First Streets address, with a million dollars in assets. One of the failed banks was Mechanics Savings, led by *Daily Planet* publisher John Mitchell, which closed in 1922 with assets of $500,000.

The Harlem of the South was torn asunder, geographically and emotionally, in the 1950s when the Richmond-Petersburg Turnpike was built. Between 1970 and the mid-1980s, half of the area's black and longtime residents moved from the area. In 1989, only 1,600 people lived in Jackson Ward and only one-fourth of that number owned their own homes. In homage to what was, and to what many hope will exist again, as of 2002 Second Street had been the site of the famous Second Street Festival, a "memory lane gala," for 11 consecutive years.

Further Reading

"Census Department Lists 274 Hotels." *The Richmond Afro-American,* July 19, 1938.

Ives, Patricia Carter. "Jackson Ward Became Center of Black Activity." *The Richmond Afro-American and Richmond Planet,* January 29, 1983.

Mitchell, Tom. "Second Street Was the Hub of Life and Hope for Richmond's Blacks." *Richmond Dispatch,* March 13, 1989.

— Sandra L. West

Robeson, Eslanda Cardozo Goode (1896–1965)

chemist, activist, writer

A biographical and historical writer, an international activist, and an actress, Eslanda Cardozo Goode Robeson in 1923 became the first black analytical chemist ever employed at a major NEW YORK CITY medical institution. She was also the wife of performing artist and political activist PAUL ROBESON.

Eslanda Cardozo Goode, named for her mother, was born on December 15, 1896, in WASHINGTON, D.C. Her father was John Goode, a clerk in the U.S. War Department, and her mother was a beauty culturist. Her lineage can be traced to Francis Lewis Cardozo, South Carolina's first black secretary of the treasury, during the early 1800s. John Goode died when Eslanda, nicknamed Essie, was six years old. Her mother moved their family to New York to escape Washington's segregated educational system.

Eslanda Goode, her daughter, studied at the State University of Illinois and majored in chemistry at the Teachers College of Columbia University in New York. While a student, she met Paul Robeson, then a law student at Columbia, and the two married in 1921.

Continuing her studies in chemistry at Columbia Presbyterian Medical Center, she graduated from the school in 1923. Afterward, she accepted a position there as supervisor of the laboratory in the surgery and pathology department, becoming the first black analytical chemist ever employed by the hospital. She resigned from this position in 1925 to accompany her husband to London, where he was starring in *The EMPEROR JONES*.

The couple spent a decade (1928–39) in London. During this time, Eslanda Robeson bore one son, Paul, Jr. In addition, she wrote a revealing biography titled *Paul Robeson, Negro* (1930); worked as her husband's manager; studied anthropology at London University from 1935 to 1937; performed a minor role in the movie "Big Fella" (1938), adapted from CLAUDE MCKAY's novel *Banjo;* and attended the London

School of Economics in 1938. A selection from *Paul Robeson, Negro* was included in the important anthology *The Negro Caravan,* and the book was reviewed in *OPPORTUNITY: A JOURNAL OF NEGRO LIFE*. The exposé stirred controversy in HARLEM society. According to Harlem Renaissance scholar DAVID LEVERING LEWIS, Eslanda wrote that she was responsible for her husband's success and professed, "Paul was very lazy." He, in response, abandoned her for a time.

In the 1940s, Robeson continued as a writer with the publication of *African Journey* (1946) and emerged as an international activist. She helped inaugurate the Council on African Affairs (1941), a lobby group for African independence. She earned a Ph.D. in anthropology from Hartford Seminary (1945); wrote a pamphlet for the Council on African Affairs—"What Do the People of Africa Want" (1945)—which criticized American ignorance about Africa; and coauthored *American Argument,* about the role of women in society, with her friend novelist Pearl S. Buck *(The Good Earth)*.

In addition, Robeson served as a delegate to the San Francisco conference that led to the formation of the United Nations. In 1951, she boldly disrupted a session of the United States Genocide Conference with pointed questions and lengthy documents pertaining to domestic terrorism committed against black Americans.

After she was reunited with her husband, the couple traveled in 1938 during the Spanish Civil War to Spain, where Eslanda visited the wounded. They then traveled to the Soviet Union and China, communicating with masses of laborers everywhere they went.

Leaning toward left-wing politics, in 1949 the Robesons were accused of treason and were called to defend themselves before Senator Joseph McCarthy's Senate subcommittee. When the committee interrogated Eslanda Robeson about her sympathies regarding COMMUNISM, she turned the tables and cross-examined them about America's racist JIM CROW treatment of black Americans. The Robesons' passports were seized. Paul, who had sung for antifascist troops in Spain in 1935 and who would later accept the Stalin Peace Prize (1952), was forced into artistic exile. In the 1950s, the family's income plummeted from a 1947 high of $104,000 per year to $2,000 until the restrictions against them were lifted in 1958.

Through the years, she publicly opposed European fascism and in the 1960s protested against the U.S. war in Vietnam. In Germany, she fought for women's rights—as she did all over the world—and for her advocacy was awarded in 1963 the German Peace Medal and Clara Zitkin Medal.

Eslanda Robeson died on December 13, 1965.

Further Reading

Lewis, David Levering. *When Harlem Was in Vogue.* New York: Vintage Books, 1982.

Ransby, Barbara. "Eslanda Goode Robeson, Pan-Africanist." *SAGE: A Scholarly Journal on Black Women,* III, no. 2, 1986.

Robeson, Susan. *The Whole World in His Hands: A Pictorial Biography of Paul Robeson.* New York: Citadel Press, 1981.

— Sandra L. West

Robeson, Paul (1898–1976) *performing artist, political activist*

Paul Robeson's achievements as an athlete, intellectual, performing artist, and political activist have made him one of the most accomplished figures in African-American history. Born on April 9, 1898, in Princeton, New Jersey, Robeson was the youngest of William Drew Robeson and Maria Louisa Bustill Robeson's five children.

William Robeson was born into slavery in North Carolina but made his way to freedom through the Underground Railroad by the time he was 15. He took advantage of his hard-won independence to obtain an elementary education and then work his way through college. Graduating from an all-black university in Pennsylvania, he alternately worked as a minister and coachman. Maria Robeson came from a prominent PHILADELPHIA family and worked as a teacher. The Robesons set high standards for their children, refusing to accept a segregated school system as a reason for personal failure or mediocrity. Although Maria Robeson died when Paul was only six, William Robeson often sat with his son, going through lessons page by page, to help ensure his scholastic success.

Graduating as an honor student at the age of 17 from Somerville High School in Somerville, New Jersey, Robeson won a four-year scholarship to attend Rutgers College in New Brunswick, New Jersey. He was only the third African American

In addition to winning fame as an athlete, scholar, singer, and political advocate, Paul Robeson, seen here as *Othello* in 1944 was one of the most acclaimed Shakespearean actors of his time. *(Library of Congress, Prints & Photographs Division, Carl Van Vechten Collection [LC-USZ62-111185])*

to attend the school. Balancing his college career between sports and academics, Robeson excelled in both. His participation in Rutgers' athletics programs was met with a forceful resistance that resulted in a broken nose, a dislocated shoulder, and painful discouragement. However, weighing 190 pounds and standing six-foot-three, he challenged the racism exhibited by his teammates and eventually won their respect and admiration. He was named twice to the All-American football team. In addition to those in football, he won letters in baseball, basketball, and track and field, accumulating a total of 15 by the time he graduated. Academically, he became a champion debater and was elected to both the Phi Beta Kappa society and Cap and Skull.

Graduating from Rutgers with high honors in 1919, he served as class valedictorian. In his address, entitled "The New Idealism," Robeson spoke the words that could have formed the creed by which he would live the rest of his life: "Neither the old time slavery, nor continued prejudice need extinguish self-respect, crush manly ambition, or paralyze effort." He continued his education at Columbia University Law School and, while still a student, married Eslanda Cardozo Goode in 1921. The couple's only son, Paul, Jr., would be born six years later. Though he obtained his law degree as planned, Robeson did not work long in his chosen profession: He quit his law firm when a white secretary refused to take dictation from him because he was black.

His law career behind him, Robeson immersed himself more completely in the performing arts for which he would become world famous. He had already moved to HARLEM after graduating from Rutgers and in 1920 made his acting debut with the lead role in a play called *Simon the Cyrenian,* from the white poet Ridgely Torrence's *Plays for a Negro Theater.* He later followed that performance with a role in Mary Hoyt Wiborg's play *Taboo* (later called *Voodoo*). After graduating from Columbia he expanded his performance skills to include singing at Harlem's COTTON CLUB.

Robeson's son noted in Dick Russell's "Black Genius" that while his father "was still in law school, he began going to the Harlem gatherings at the houses of JAMES WELDON JOHNSON, JOHN ROSAMOND JOHNSON, and W. E. B. DU BOIS. In the beginning he would sit and listen, asking questions, absorbing everything. And every once in a while he would speak up about something, and *they* would listen."

Also listening to Robeson was the Pulitzer Prize–winning playwright Eugene O'Neill. Robeson starred in three plays by O'Neill: *All God's Chillun Got Wings* (1924); *THE EMPEROR JONES* (1925); and *The Hairy Ape* (1931). He also starred in Jerome Kern and Oscar Hammerstein II's *Showboat* (1928) giving a rendition of "Ol' Man River" so powerful it won him instant fame and acclaim. He made history in 1930 when he followed in the footsteps of legendary black actor Ira Aldridge to open in Shakespeare's *Othello* at the Savoy Theater in London. Robeson was not only the first black man to play the role since Aldridge but was fortunate enough to receive coaching on Shakespearean elocution from Amanda Ira Aldridge, the late actor's daughter. He took the role to Broadway in October 1943 where it ran until June 1944 for a critically acclaimed and unprecedented run of 296 performances.

At the same time that he grew in prominence as a stage actor, Robeson developed equally celebrated careers as a singer and film star. Accompanied by pianist Lawrence Brown, he enjoyed in 1926 a successful tour of concerts featuring performances of such Negro spirituals as "Deep River" and "Go Down Moses," employing arrangements of these spirituals by HARRY THACKER BURLEIGH and others. Robeson was among the first to present a concert made up entirely of Negro spirituals and helped preserve this musical form (currently undergoing a resurgence in popularity through such modern presentations as Robert Sims's *Three Generations*). Robeson eventually added to his repertoire folk songs from around the world and in 1941 was listed among the top 10 highest paid concert performers.

As a film actor, Robeson was the only black performer during the 1930s to work steadily on both sides of the Atlantic, making movies in America and in England. Black director OSCAR MICHEAUX gave Robeson his first American film role in *Body and Soul* (1925), which was also among the first independently produced black films. In his first foreign film, *Borderline* (1930), Robeson was able to mix business with family pleasure by working with his wife, Eslanda. In 1937 he starred in *Big Fella,* an adaptation of CLAUDE MCKAY's novel *Banjo.*

His movie career remained productive throughout the 1930s, and his screen presence became a commanding one that many felt transcended his actual roles. Among his most noted portrayals are those of the title character in the screen adaptation of *The Emperor Jones* and Joe in *Showboat.* Robeson, however, stated for the record that he found most of his film work dissatisfying. This was largely because his perception and projection of his characters as strong, proud black men was often made into something very different through editing and the addition of scenes he knew nothing about until viewing the finished product. Nevertheless, he expressed some pride in two films shot outside America: *Song of Freedom* (1938) and *The Proud Valley* (1941). Though he lent his voice to the narration of the movie *Native Land* (1942), his last screen appearance was with ETHEL WATERS and EDDIE ANDERSON in *Tales of Manhattan* (1942).

Robeson's disappointment in the failure of moviemakers to provide more substantially positive roles for him led the actor to delve more deeply into his African heritage. He felt most of the images he had encountered of the African race in America, including those he had helped construct for movies, depicted a people with minimal intelligence and qualities more akin to those of pets than human beings, but what he found through his own investigations was quite different. He not only studied several African languages at the University of London but got to know such future African statesmen as Kenya's Jomo Kenyatta and Nigeria's Nnamdi Azikiwe. He discovered a heritage rich with culture, history, noble traditions, and powerful spiritual values. It was a discovery that inspired him to raise his voice in something more than song as he began to publicly address the impact of racism on people of color throughout the world. To help African countries in particular gain independence from European rule, he and Max Yergan founded the Council on African Affairs in 1937.

Moreover, through his contact with laborers in England and the people of Russia, Robeson began to view the discrimination practiced against African Americans as an extension of oppression against workers in general. His fluency in some 25 languages allowed him to lend the full strength of his oratorical and musical skills to the articulation of working class people's struggles worldwide. Audiences of thousands came to hear him speak and sing at gatherings for coal miners, auto workers, war protesters, black soldiers, and others. He became very popular in Russia and cited that country as a place where Africans could live on an equal footing with Europeans. Half a century before the world turned its collective attention to the plight of an imprisoned Nelson Mandela, Robeson dared to speak out against the blatant injustice and cruelties of South Africa's apartheid.

He was particularly outspoken when it came to the United States's tolerance for the practice of LYNCHING and to the participation of blacks in American wars. His outspokenness drew the attention of the House Committee on Un-American Activities, which held hearings to investigate the political loyalties of Robeson and others suspected of being communists. Asked if he were a communist, Robeson refused to identify himself as such and defended his right to explore and express political options. Labeling him a threat to national security, the U.S. State Department rescinded Robeson's passport from 1950 to 1958. His freedom to travel abroad, he was told, would be granted only if he refrained from giving public speeches while doing so, something to which he would not agree.

The public divided over its support of Robeson. Many feared some form of political retaliation from the U.S. government, such as the loss of their livelihood, if they sided with the great performer during this period that became known as the McCarthy era. At the time, Senator Joseph McCarthy of Wisconsin succeeded in convincing Americans that communism had corrupted and was on the verge of overtaking the country. Ossie Davis, a friend of Robeson's, was among those blacks called before a federal court to testify on the threat of communist subversion and recalled the following in *With Ossie & Ruby,* his memoir with wife Ruby Dee: "Many Americans, who had been so proud of Paul's status as a spokesman up till now—white folks who used him as the prime example of what America had accomplished in the way of race relations, and black folk who used him as the prime example of what we could do given half a chance—found themselves embarrassed, if not frightened."

In the same year that Robeson regained his passport, 1958, he gave his first major concerts in years, singing in New York, Moscow, and London. By then, however, the wear and tear of constant political battle had begun to take its emotional toll. Although he continued to tour and record for several more years, in the early 1960s his public appearances became fewer. He was not one of those singled out as a leader during the growing Civil Rights movement of that time. His final public appearance was at a Student Nonviolent Coordinating Committee (SNCC) benefit dinner.

When he died at age 77 on January 23, 1976, Paul Robeson was one of the most celebrated men in African-American history. His honors included recognition as a top male vocalist in countries around world; honorary degrees from colleges and universities worldwide; the NAACP SPINGARN MEDAL (1945); the naming of Russia's Mount Robeson in his honor (1949); the Stalin Peace Prize presented to him by W. E. B. Du Bois; the publication of his autobiography, *Here I Stand* (1958); and the NATIONAL URBAN LEAGUE's annual Whitney M. Young Memorial Award (1972).

Further Reading

Peterson, Bernard L., Jr., and James V. Hatch. *Profiles of African American Stage Performers and Theatre People, 1816–1960.* Westport, Conn.: Greenwood Publishing Group, 2000.

Robeson, Paul. *Here I Stand.* 1958. Reprint, Boston: Beacon Press, 1988.

Robeson, Susan. *The Whole World in His Hands: A Pictorial Biography of Paul Robeson.* New York: Citadel Press, 1981.

— Aberjhani

Robinson, Bojangles (Luther Bill Robinson)

(1878–1949) *dancer*

Possibly the most well known tap dancer of the 20th century, Luther Bill "Bojangles" Robinson is renowned for dancing up and down stairs in 14 films and numerous stage shows during the Harlem Renaissance and GREAT DEPRESSION. He was known alternately as the Honorary Mayor of HARLEM, "Mr. Bojangles," and "Mr. Show Business."

Luther Robinson was born in RICHMOND, VIRGINIA (the Harlem of the South) on May 25 or 28, 1878. He lived at 915 North Third Street in Jackson Ward with his father, Maxwell, a machinist, and mother Maria, a choir director. His parents died when he was seven years old. Luther and his brother William were raised by their paternal grandmother, Bedilia Robinson, a former slave who abhorred and disallowed dancing.

After a juvenile brawl with his brother, Luther announced that he was assuming his brother's name, Bill, and that his brother would thereafter be known as Percy. Thus, Luther Robinson became Bill Robinson. The name Bojangles, likely a southern version of another name, was also acquired in Richmond. Reportedly, young Robinson stole a tall beaver hat from a hat repair shop owned by Leon J. Boujasson, a name similar in sound to Bojangles. When he boldly wore the hat in the neighborhood, his neighbors hollered out a call and response song, slightly mispronouncing the shop owner's name so that it came out: "Who took Bojangles hat? Why, Bojangles took it." The name Bojangles stuck from that point. Robinson's other childhood nickname was Snowball.

As a youth, Robinson worked as a shoe shine boy for 5¢ a shine and at times stole, gambled, and fought. Guns and knives became part of his daily costume. Against his grandmother's wishes, he danced in the streets for pennies, especially the "buck-and-wing" dance—with his neck held stiff and arms and

Dubbed the unofficial mayor of Harlem, Bojangles Robinson, shown here in 1933, was one of the community's most distinguished entertainers and residents. *(Library of Congress, Prints & Photographs Division, Carl Van Vechten Collection [LC-USZ62-114512])*

legs flapping like a bird's. He dropped out of school in the second grade to run away to WASHINGTON, D.C., and secured a job as a stable hand. He also worked as a dancer in vaudeville for 50¢ a night and formed a street-based dancing and singing partnership with a young white boy who later became a famous blackface minstrel singer: Al Jolson.

Robinson danced all of his life but did not reach celebrity status until middle age. In the 1890s, he played a small stage part in *The South Before the War,* later tapping solo as "The Dark Cloud of Joy." In 1900, Robinson danced in *In Old Kentucky* and performed for tips at the Douglass Club in Harlem, where black entertainers would come to jam after their regular shows. In 1918, Robinson introduced the stair step routine into his act in *Jazz Dance.* The routine was so phenomenal that he tried for years to patent it but could not. In addition to the stair step tap routine, Robinson could run backward faster than any man in show business: 75 yards in 8.2 seconds. On stage, he was extremely demanding. If his dancing partner made more than three mistakes, he fired him or her on the spot.

Robinson achieved a rare level of stardom. When *Blackbirds of 1927* headliner FLORENCE MILLS died following an appendix operation, Robinson was cast in *BLACKBIRDS OF 1928*—performing with slithery Earl "Snakehips" Tucker. In *Blackbirds of 1928,* he achieved fame by tap-dancing up and down a five-step set of stairs in formal dress that included tailed coat and top hat. Garnering praise for this performance from *Vanity, Graphic,* and *The Nation,* he became the most popular dancer in Harlem. He won increasing renown for his dance skills, ready smile, an infectious personality that pulled audiences into whatever he was doing, and his deep need to help his fellow man. On the strength of this smashing economic success that took him over half his lifetime to acquire, Robinson moved into the brand new, exclusive PAUL LAURENCE DUNBAR APARTMENTS.

Blackbirds ran for 518 performances on Broadway. It was Robinson's first true hit, and he was 50 years old with legs and feet—including an irritating bunion—that still performed as if he was 16. Robinson returned to vaudeville in 1929 with *HOT CHOCOLATES* at CONNIE'S INN in Harlem.

An eccentric man of many extremes, Robinson danced wearing split clogs, the most unusual shoes in the business. The clogs were professionally made—for increased flexibility and the delicate tap touch Robinson was known for—by Aiston Shoe Company in CHICAGO. They had a wooden heel slightly higher than the leather heel on an ordinary street shoe. Robinson wore out 30 pairs of dancing shoes per year. He was fastidious in regard to his clothing and traveled with one trunk for suits and another for shoes.

Despite his personal extremes, Robinson was such a public-spirited humanitarian that his own pockets were often bare. According to his biographers, Haskins and Mitgang, "If he saw a family being dispossessed, when he could he would pay their back rent, pay some street men to carry their belongings back into their apartment, and move them back into shelter." He was just as caring about his hometown. In Richmond's Jackson Ward where he grew up, there was a dangerous intersection at the corner of Leigh and Adams Streets at which children crossed on their way to school. Robinson's gift of $1,240.70 made it possible to install four streetlights at the intersection. A statue of Robinson, in tap dance position with the stair steps, as always, was later placed on the same corner.

The dancer made his film debut in 1930 in *Dixiana.* At the same time, he continued his stage career, performing during the Great Depression in *BROWN BUDDIES* (1930); *Hot from Harlem* (1932), which two years later became *Goin' to Town;* and *Blackbirds of 1933.* He also taught tap dance to wealthy New York socialites, including tobacco heiress Doris Duke. He danced as well in *Harlem Is Heaven* (1933), featuring the orchestra of EUBIE BLAKE, and *Black Orchids* (1934).

As the unofficial mayor of Harlem, in 1934 Robinson saved the famous TREE OF HOPE, an elm tree that stood at SEVENTH AVENUE and 131st Street. Some people believed that if they rubbed its bark and made a wish, the wish would come true. Celebrities, especially, flocked to this tree. When Seventh Avenue was widened, the beloved but diseased Tree of Hope was cut down. Another healthier tree was planted in its place but Robinson, aware of how much the tree meant to the community, placed the stump of the old Tree of Hope at the entrance of LAFAYETTE THEATRE. It was later moved to the stage of the historic APOLLO THEATRE, where amateurs rubbed it for good luck before performing. In 1935, Robinson was officially crowned "mayor of Harlem" in the film *Hooray for Love.*

His movie career continued with *In Old Kentucky* (1935). He went on to dance in the films *The Little Colonel* (1935); *The Littlest Rebel* (1935); *Just Around the Corner* (1938); and *Rebecca of Sunnybrook Farm* (1938), all with child star Shirley Temple. He appeared as well in this period in *The Big Broadcast of 1937,* featuring white vaudeville comedians George Burns and Gracie Allen.

It was because of his films with child star Shirley Temple, in which he was usually cast as a stereotypical grinning butler, porter, or other role submissively serving a white character, that black people began to call Robinson an "Uncle Tom." This name-calling haunted Robinson to his death and beyond, especially during the 1960s–70s Black Arts movement, when his legacy was practically annihilated.

He performed the role of the emperor in *The Hot Mikado* (1939), a remake of a Gilbert and Sullivan operetta produced by the WORKS PROGRESS ADMINISTRATION (WPA) Federal Theater of Chicago. *The Hot Mikado* was staged at the 1939 World's Fair. And in 1943, he starred in the successful films *STORMY WEATHER* and *Cabin in the Sky* with singer LENA HORNE.

Robinson was also a star of radio in the 1940s. Over the airwaves, he sang songs from his films and stage shows and told memorable jokes and famous one-liners such as "I haven't been this proud since I was colored."

Although greatly accomplished, Robinson was an illiterate man who could not read at all. His wife, Fannie, who had trained as a pharmacist, read his scripts to him at the kitchen table, and he committed them to memory. Yet, the word *copacetic*—meaning that everything was "fine" or "all right"—was one that he made famous and that found a permanent home in the dictionary. Every day of his life, he ate four to eight quarts of vanilla ice cream, yet he remained a perfect size 38 at all times. Scars and bullet holes from sundry altercations covered his body.

Robinson was a millionaire four times over up to the last year of his life—earning $6,600 a week at the height of his career—yet died penniless because he was a heavy gambler and dedicated philanthropist. He danced in benefits for the Lafayette Theatre and Catholic Charities. The COTTON CLUB had a soup kitchen operation during the depression, and Robinson provided bags of groceries for people who came to the club for food. He danced on Times Square for a cancer benefit and in a tribute to baseball star Jackie Robinson.

For his generosity and talent, people revered Bill Bojangles Robinson. On his 61st birthday, crowds cheered as he danced down Broadway from Columbus Circle to 44th Street. His graceful, light tap was so authentic that white dance stylist Fred Astaire choreographed a special routine called "Bojangles of Harlem."

Bojangles Robinson died on November 25, 1949. On November 27, 32,000 people viewed his body in state at the 369th Regiment Armory on Fifth Avenue and 142nd Street; 13,000 visited ABYSSINIAN BAPTIST CHURCH on West 138th Street, where his funeral service was held; and another 50,000 stood on New York's Duffy Square and Times Square as the funeral motorcade made its way past Broadway to Evergreen Cemetery. New York public schools were closed so children could grieve, and the flags of Harlem and Broadway were at half-mast in his honor. Honorary pallbearers included boxer JOE LOUIS, JAZZ great DUKE ELLINGTON, orchestra leader NOBLE SISSLE, and blues composer W. C. HANDY. Among the mourners were New York mayor Paul O'Dwyer, Manhattan borough president Hugo Rogers, Chief Magistrate Edgar Bromberger, Parole Commissioner Samuel J. Battle, Manhattan borough president-elect Robert F. Wagner, Jr., and Tammany Hall leader Carmine DeSapio. Robert Merrill of the Metropolitan Opera and the New York Fire Department Glee Club provided music. Rev. ADAM CLAYTON POWELL, JR., delivered Robinson's eulogy.

Further Reading

Gates, Henry Louis, Jr. *The African American Century: How Black Americans Have Shaped Our Century.* New York: The Free Press, 2000.

Haskins, Jim, and N. R. Mitgang. *Mr. Bojangles: The Biography of Bill Robinson.* New York: William Morrow and Company, 1988.

Marks, Carole, and Diana Edkins. *The Power of Pride: Stylemakers and Rulebreakers of the Harlem Renaissance.* New York: Crown Publishing Group, 1999.

— Sandra L. West

Rogers, Alexander (1876–1930) *lyricist, playwright*

Alexander C. Rogers wrote lyrics for and performed in some of the most successful stage musicals starring African Americans during the early 1900s.

Born in 1876 in Nashville, Tennessee, Rogers began his career in theater as a member of the creative team that produced shows for BERT WILLIAMS and GEORGE WALKER, two of the most successful performers of the era and black pioneers on NEW YORK CITY's Broadway. One of Rogers's first jobs with the celebrated Walker and Williams was in their hit 1902 musical *In Dahomey.* In addition to writing lyrics for the show, Rogers performed in it as an intelligence officer. The musical also marked the development of a creative partnership between Rogers and the author of the play's book, Jesse A. Shipp.

In 1906, Rogers and Shipp coauthored Williams and Walker's *Abyssinia,* and in 1907 they teamed up to write one of Williams and Walker's most successful shows, *Bandanna Land.* Rogers also wrote with Williams himself a number of the comedian's most remembered songs, including "I May Be Crazy, but I Ain't No Fool"; "Why Adam Sinned"; and "I'm a Jonah Man." In 1908, Rogers joined Williams, Walker, Shipp, James Reese Europe, JOHN ROSAMOND JOHNSON, and several others as founders of the THE FROGS, an organization dedicated to supporting blacks in the performing arts.

Rogers authored lyrics for *A Trip to Africa,* one of the Black Patti Troubadour shows around 1909. He coauthored in 1913 *Old Man's Boy,* one of the early plays to star CHARLES SIDNEY GILPIN, who later would win fame for his performance in *THE EMPEROR JONES.* Rogers also enjoyed considerable success in 1913 with a musical called *The Darktown Follies,* which he cowrote with J. Leubrie Hill. The production ran for several months at the LAFAYETTE THEATRE, caught the attention of major critics, and drew a good share of Broadway theatregoers uptown to HARLEM. JAMES WELDON JOHNSON, writing in *Black Manhattan,* credited the show with starting the trend of white patrons going nightly to Harlem in search of black-oriented entertainment. Among those who saw the show was Florenz Ziegfeld, who went with Bert Williams. Ziegfeld was so impressed by the show's finale that he bought the rights to it for his own show, the ZIEGFELD FOLLIES.

Although he continued to write, on April 5, 1917, Rogers performed in two of the plays featured in Ridgely Torrence's *Three Plays for Negro Theatre.* He played Dr. Williams in *The Rider of Dreams* and later Pilate in *Simon the Cyrenian.* The latter starred performing artist and political activist PAUL ROBESON in his stage debut in 1920.

In 1919, Rogers joined C. Luckeyth Roberts as one of the principal writers for the Quality Amusement Corporation. Based at the Lafayette Theatre, the corporation represented a circuit of theaters located in the North and on the East Coast. Shows written by Rogers for the corporation included *Follies of the Stroll, Baby Blues,* and *This and That.*

Rogers continued writing until his death in New York on September 14, 1930.

Further Reading

Peterson, Bernard L., Jr. *The African American Theatre Directory, 1816–1960.* Westport, Conn.: Greenwood Press, 1997.

Smith, Eric Ledell. *Bert Williams: A Biography of the Pioneer Black Comedian.* North Carolina: McFarland and Company, 1992.

— Aberjhani

Roosevelt, Eleanor (Anna Eleanor Roosevelt)

(1884–1962) *first lady, humanitarian*

Through her work as a spokesperson for the rights of women and advocate for the rights of African Americans, Eleanor Roosevelt redefined the role and potential impact of presidential first ladies.

Roosevelt was born Anna Eleanor Roosevelt in NEW YORK CITY on October 11, 1884, to Elliott Roosevelt and Anna Hall Roosevelt. Her father was the younger brother of President Theodore Roosevelt. Her mother died in 1892 when Roosevelt was eight. Suffering from severe alcoholism, her father was confined to a sanitarium and died two years after her mother.

Following her parents' deaths, Roosevelt was raised by her maternal grandmother, who sometimes gently teased her for being shy and withdrawn. Her education consisted of private tutoring until she was 15, when she was sent to Allenswood School in England. In 1902, she became a social worker in New York.

On March 17, 1905, she married FRANKLIN DELANO ROOSEVELT, her fifth cousin. Her uncle Theodore Roosevelt, who had been elected president the previous November, gave her away. Of the Roosevelts' six children, five grew to adulthood: Anna Eleanor Roosevelt, born in 1906; James Roosevelt, 1907; Elliott Roosevelt, 1910; Franklin D. Roosevelt, Jr., 1914; and John Aspinwal Roosevelt, 1916.

While she, like her husband, was born into a family that could boast a number of political leaders, Roosevelt's own entrance into the world of politics came with her husband's election to the New York Senate in 1911 and his appointment as assistant secretary to the U.S. Navy in 1916. Her involvement became more direct in 1921 when her husband contracted polio and was paralyzed in both legs. She personally aided and supervised his recovery over a period of three years until he regained limited use of his legs. The paralysis initially convinced Franklin Roosevelt that he could no longer serve as a public official. However, Eleanor Roosevelt convinced him otherwise and began to give public presentations and interviews herself in order to help him remain politically aware and active. While performing as her husband's political assistant and informant, Roosevelt evolved into an influential public personality in her own right. She publicly rejected the idea that COMMUNISM posed an immediate threat to the United States and informed women that in order to achieve equality they "must learn to play the game as men do."

With his political confidence restored, Franklin Roosevelt won the governorship of New York in 1929 and remained governor until 1933. On November 8, 1932, he won the first of four presidential elections that would place the Roosevelts in the White House until 1945. Being in a wheelchair had no impact on President Roosevelt's administrative abilities, but it did obviously affect his mobility. Eleanor Roosevelt, on the other hand, did more than compensate for that particular drawback by traveling extensively throughout the country, visiting military bases, civil rights organizations, religious groups, and children's organizations. She wrote a syndicated column called "My Day" in which she offered insights on national events as well as points of etiquette. She served as cochairman of the Office of Civil Defense and remained active in the National Youth Administration created by the New Deal. In regard to the latter, she worked often with her close friend Mary McLeod Bethune, who was appointed director of minority affairs for the administration. Bethune was also founder of the National Council of Negro Women, and she and Roosevelt often conferred on strategies for addressing problems pertaining to women, black and white.

Whereas President Roosevelt rarely took a public stance against JIM CROW racism, Eleanor Roosevelt did so frequently enough that many began to consider her an unofficial ambassador to African America. Her outspokenness drew repeated criticism from the South, where whites accused her of undermining that region's traditional social and racial structure. In 1939, she made one of her most famous protests against racism when she resigned from the Daughters of the American Revolution following the organization's refusal to allow celebrated opera singer MARIAN ANDERSON to perform at the Constitution Hall in WASHINGTON, D.C. In addition to resigning from the organization, Roosevelt then helped arrange for Anderson to perform in front of 75,000 people on the steps of the Lincoln Memorial.

When President Roosevelt died on April 12, 1945, during his fourth term in office, Eleanor Roosevelt announced that her own career as a public servant had ended as well. In 1946, however, Roosevelt accepted an appointment from President Harry S. Truman to serve as a member of the first U.S. delegation to the United Nations. She became chairman of the UN Commission on Human Rights and helped author the Declaration of Human Rights. She remained with the United Nations until 1952.

Roosevelt wrote her first autobiography, *This I Remember,* in 1949, and in 1958 wrote her second, *On My Own.* In 1961, she wrote the more definitive: *The Autobiography of Eleanor Roosevelt.* In that same year, she accepted from President John F. Kennedy a second appointment to the United Nations, remaining with the organization until 1962.

Roosevelt died of bone marrow tuberculosis on November 7, 1962, in New York City.

Further Reading

Black, Allida. *Casting Her Own Shadow: Eleanor Roosevelt and the Shaping of Postwar Liberation.* New York: Columbia University Press, 1996.

Burns, MacGregor James, and Susan Dunn. *The Three Roosevelts: Patrician Leaders Who Transformed America.* New York: Grove/Atlantic Incorporated, 2001.

Cook, Blanche Wiesen. *Eleanor Roosevelt, 1884–1933, Vol. 1.* New York: Penguin, 1993.

———. *Eleanor Roosevelt: The Defining Years, 1933–1938, Vol. 2.* New York: Penguin, 2000.

— Aberjhani

Roosevelt, Franklin Delano (1882–1945) *U.S. president*

Serving a historic four terms as president of the United States from 1933 to 1945, Franklin D. Roosevelt implemented a system of economic recovery and reform that permanently altered American society on nearly every level. Its impact on African Americans has often been described as second in historical importance only to the Emancipation Proclamation.

The son of James Roosevelt and Sara Delano Roosevelt, the future president was born on January 30, 1882, in Hyde Park, New York. His father was a lawyer and part-time businessman wealthy enough to afford a private railroad car. His mother was a sixth cousin to her husband and came from a wealthy family in Newburgh, New York. The Roosevelt family included a number of influential political leaders, both in the past and contemporary with Franklin. Among Roosevelt's distant cousins were former president Ulysses S. Grant; former president Zachary Taylor; British prime minister Winston Churchill; and the 26th U.S. president, Theodore Roosevelt.

Roosevelt was privately tutored as a youth and went to school for a brief period in Nauheim, Germany. His studies included German, French, music, and dance. He graduated from Groton Preparatory School in 1900 and from Harvard University in 1904. He studied law at Columbia Law School and withdrew from the school after passing his bar exam in 1907. He then joined the law firm of Carter, Ledyard, and Milburn in NEW YORK CITY.

While attending Columbia, Roosevelt married ELEANOR ROOSEVELT on March 17, 1905. She was his fifth cousin and a niece of then President Theodore Roosevelt, who gave away the bride. Five of the couple's six children grew to maturity: Anna Eleanor Roosevelt, born in 1906; James Roosevelt, 1907; Elliott Roosevelt, 1910; Franklin D. Roosevelt, Jr., 1914; and John Aspinwal Roosevelt, 1916.

Roosevelt's political career began in earnest with his election to the New York State Senate in 1911. Although he lost his seat in 1914, his career continued to expand with an appointment during WORLD WAR I as assistant secretary of the navy, a position he held until 1920. He afterward returned to practicing law until he was stricken by polio in 1921. The disease left him paralyzed in both legs, and for a time he considered withdrawing completely from a life of political service. With the help of his wife Eleanor, he underwent therapy and rehabilitation for three years before regaining a limited use of his legs. While the disease forced Franklin Roosevelt to reduce his political activities, it simultaneously forced his wife Eleanor to overcome her own shyness and fill the void created by her husband's absence with more and more public appearances of her own. She began to give frequent interviews and speeches on every topic, from the role of women in politics to antique furniture and COMMUNISM. As she grew into a political force in her own right, she also kept her husband informed about the political and social attitudes of those she addressed.

In 1929, Franklin Roosevelt returned to politics with a successful run for the governorship of New York. Roosevelt's tenure as governor from 1929 to 1933 coincided with FIORELLO HENRY LA GUARDIA's last five years in the House of Representatives. The two leaders established a political rapport that served La Guardia well when he was elected mayor of New York City and Roosevelt was elected president of the United States.

Roosevelt won his first term as president of the United States on November 8, 1932, with 472 electoral votes, over his incumbent Republican opponent Herbert Hoover's 59. Roosevelt ran for the presidency at a time when the United States and much of the world was in one of the worst economic slumps it had ever experienced, the GREAT DEPRESSION. The crash of Wall Street in October 1929 had ushered in a period of economic decline resulting in the failure of thousands of businesses, bank closures, loss of employment for millions, and loss of properties. In addition, many families were broken apart as various members took to the rails in search of employment or other means of survival. The Hoover administration successfully dodged blame for the crisis but failed to implement any means of countering it. Roosevelt campaigned on the promise of a New Deal, offering a fresh economic start not only for the businessman who had lost heavily on Wall Street but for the common laborer who had had little to begin with.

Roosevelt's New Deal took the form of a series of sweeping presidential acts that completely changed the manner in which Americans relate to their government and established the foundation for the modern-day welfare and social security systems. Two of the most popular programs established through the New Deal were the Civilian Conservation Corps in 1933 and the WORKS PROGRESS ADMINISTRATION (WPA) in 1935. Both provided forms of employment that benefited workers as well as the country. More than 100,000 public buildings were constructed under the program, more than half a million miles of road, and some 75,000 bridges. Additionally, it included the Federal Arts Project, which allowed artists, actors, and writers to practice their specific craft, some for the first time. RICHARD NATHANIEL WRIGHT, DOROTHY WEST, ARNA BONTEMPS, MARGARET ABIGAIL WALKER, and many others took advantage of the program.

The 1933 National Industrial Act, the 1934 National Housing Act, the 1933 Federal Emergency Relief Administration, and the Social Security Act of 1935 did not address the needs of African Americans specifically but did not exclude them either. Most African Americans of the period simply included themselves in Roosevelt's acknowledgment of "the common man." While African Americans at the local level were often discriminated against when applying for such New Deal programs as relief funds, such instances were addressed and frequently corrected through the agencies of the NATIONAL ASSOCIATION FOR THE ADVANCEMENT OF COLORED PEOPLE (NAACP), the NATIONAL URBAN LEAGUE (NUL), and the government itself, which found in Eleanor Roosevelt a constant advocate for racial equality. Moreover, while President Roosevelt administered his programs, he also used the radio for his now famous fireside chats to address Americans directly regarding the state of the country and his plans for economic and social recovery.

The New Deal's Wagner Act provided A. PHILIP RANDOLPH and the BROTHERHOOD OF SLEEPING CAR PORTERS with the political leverage they needed to become the first black union recognized by a major American company. However, during World War II, Randolph and Roosevelt clashed when, in a meeting that included NAACP leader WALTER WHITE, the president refused to order the integration of the armed services. When Randolph threatened a march of 100,000 African Americans on the White House, Roosevelt compromised with Executive Order 8802, banning discriminatory hiring practices in the defense industry. He further strengthened the order with the establishment of the Committee on Fair Employment Practices. The economic impact of Executive Order 8802 on African Americans as a whole was unprecedented and set off a second GREAT MIGRATION with millions of blacks making their way to the west coast to work in the defense industry.

Roosevelt's defense of the common American combined with his bold vision for economic reform ensured his reelection for a second term, in 1936, a third, in 1940, and a fourth, in 1944. He died during his fourth term, on April 12, 1945, in Warm Springs, Georgia, four months before the end of World War II.

Further Reading

Dorn, Linda. *The Roosevelt Cousins.* New York: Random House, 2001.

Maney, Patrick J. *The Roosevelt Presence: The Life and Legacy of FDR.* Berkeley: University of California Press, 1998.

Van Rijn, Guido. *Roosevelt's Blues: African American Blues and Gospel Songs on Franklin D. Roosevelt.* Jackson: University of Mississippi Press, 1996.

— Aberjhani

Runnin' Wild

The comedy and dance team of Flournoy Miller and Aubrey Lyles followed up on the history-making success of their 1921 Broadway hit, *SHUFFLE ALONG*, with a second hit musical revue, titled *Runnin' Wild.*

After a short trial run in WASHINGTON, D.C., *Runnin' Wild* debuted in NEW YORK CITY on October 29, 1923, at the Colonial Theatre on Broadway and 62nd. With its dancers performing the Charleston to a song of the same name, composed by James P. Johnson and Cecil Mack, *Runnin' Wild* increased the popularity of the dance and turned it into a national and international entertainment phenomenon.

The show itself focused on the same kind of black vaudeville humor and black music that made *Shuffle Along* a hit and that created a string of such Broadway productions throughout the 1920s. However, in the case of *Runnin' Wild,* nearly all agreed that the show owed its successful eight-month run to its version of the Charleston. Whereas Maude Russell and Rufus Greenlee had performed the Charleston earlier on Broadway in the musical *LIZA*, *Runnin' Wild* provided it with a larger showcase featuring a female chorus line and a trio of male dancers called the Dancing Redcaps. Moreover, the dance as presented in *Runnin' Wild* included improvisations by Lyles and Miller.

Runnin' Wild was produced by George White. In addition to the talents of Lyles and Miller, it also starred singers ADELAIDE HALL and Elisabeth Welch; novelty dancers Tommy Woods and George Stamper; and tap dancers Lavinia Mack and Mae Barnes.

Further Reading

Reed, Bill. *Hot from Harlem: Profiles in Classic African American Entertainment.* Los Angeles: Cellar Door Books, 1998.

Stearns, Jean, and Marshall Stearns. *Jazz Dance.* New York: Da Capo Press, 1994.

— Aberjhani

S

Saint Philip's Episcopal Church

St. Philip's is the oldest African-American Episcopal congregation in NEW YORK CITY and was designed by the first black architects registered in the states of New York and New Jersey.

The history of St. Philip's evolution reflects the same pattern of migration as that of African Americans in New York City. The church was initially constructed in 1818 and located downtown, where the majority of black people once lived in the city. It first moved from Centre Street to Mulberry Street, then Mulberry to West 25th Street, and in 1909, to its final home at 210–216 West 134th Street in HARLEM.

The modern neo-Gothic, Roman brick and terra-cotta church and parish house was designed by Vertner Tandy and George W. Foster, Jr. Tandy was the first black architect registered in New York State and also designed MADAME C. J. WALKER's palatial mansion, Villa Lewara, located on the Hudson River. Foster was one of two black architects registered in New Jersey.

The story of the purchase of the 134th Street property represents only one saga of northern style JIM CROW racial and real estate discrimination. Because Harlem landlords in 1909 often discriminated against black people who wanted to purchase property, St. Philip's administrator, Rev. Hutchens C. Bishop, bought the property in his own name under the pretense that he was white. Light enough in complexion to bypass any challenge to his purchase of the land, Bishop obtained it without incident, then transferred ownership to the church. The St. Philip's Episcopal Church family subsequently built a number of apartment houses on 135th Street.

Unlike the emotional, charismatic ceremonies observed in storefront churches where many southern migrants felt most comfortable, St. Philip's formal Episcopal mode of worship was called a high service. It presented teaching instead of preaching from the pulpit, the use of white-robed acolytes, weekly communion sacraments instead of monthly ones, emotionless straightforward singing, and the use of fragrant incense when the rector blessed the fold. Parishioners were middle class, professional, and biracial. This was the church of the early black bourgeoisie.

Further Reading

Favor, J. Martin. *Authentic Blackness: The Folk in the New Negro Renaissance.* Durham, N.C.: Duke University Press, 1999.

Haynes, George E. "The Church and the Negro Spirit." *The Survey Graphic* Harlem Number, March 1925.

— Sandra L. West

Salem Methodist Church (Salem United Methodist Church)

An example of the progressive black church growth and pioneering ecumenical leadership in HARLEM during the *NEW NEGRO* movement, Salem Methodist Church was founded by Frederick Asbury Cullen, the adoptive father of poet COUNTEE CULLEN. The church was the setting for both Countee Cullen's marriage to Nina Yolanda Du Bois and the poet's funeral.

Salem began as a mission of St. Mark's Methodist Episcopal Church in 1881 under Rev. Charles Albright. According to *The Chronicle,* Salem's contemporary history journal, in April 1902, Rev. Frederick Asbury Cullen was appointed to St. Mark's as assistant pastor prior to founding and assuming leadership of Salem Methodist Church.

Frederick Cullen was born in Somerset County, Maryland, during the 1800s. His father was Isaac Cullen, who died when his son was just two months old. His mother, Emmeline Cullen, then moved her family to Baltimore.

As a child, Frederick Cullen attended the State Normal School and Sharpe Street Methodist Episcopal Church, circa 1894. He later taught school in Fairmount, Maryland, and entered Morgan College (now Morgan State University) to study theology. While still at Morgan, he administrated two churches: Boyer's Chapel and Willis Chapel, both in Catlin, Maryland. Cullen was ordained an elder in 1900, served at Siloan Church in Chester, Pennsylvania, and was assigned to Salem, a Harlem, NEW YORK CITY mission, on April 18, 1902.

The mission occupied a storefront at 250 St. Nicholas Avenue, near 122nd Street, where Rev. Cullen delivered his first sermon on April 20, 1902. The collection for that day was 19¢. Attempting to expand his small congregation, Cullen went out into neighborhoods and actively solicited people. He played marbles with children on Harlem sidewalks, then invited the children and their families to church.

In August 1902, the growing Salem congregation relocated to 232 West 124th Street. The two-room church, which Cullen rented, also served as the pastor's residence. A fire forced the congregation to rebuild the church, and it remained on 124th Street until 1908. In that year, the New York City Missionary and Church Extension Society of the Methodist Episcopal Church purchased for Salem six to eight private houses at 102–194 West 133rd Street, near LENOX AVENUE. The congregation raised $15,000 as partial payment of the debt. At that time, during a general conference, Salem was separated from St. Mark's and declared an independent church.

The extra rooms were critical to Rev. Cullen's civic focus for the growing church. During his tenure he established many auxiliaries and programs designed in modern terms to nurture "the whole person," not unusual by contemporary standards but groundbreaking for its time. He held workshops and Sunday afternoon lyceums in the meeting rooms. Among those invited to speak at these gatherings were labor leader A. PHILIP RANDOLPH, bibliophile ARTHUR SCHOMBURG, historian J. A. Rodgers, and WALTER WHITE of the NATIONAL ASSOCIATION FOR THE ADVANCEMENT OF COLORED PEOPLE (NAACP).

The church also organized its Salem Crescent Athletic Club at the new site. Designed for neighborhood children, the athletic club provided a variety of athletic competitions in the city and as far away as Europe. In addition, Rev. Cullen established the Brotherhood, Altar Guild, Golden Leaf Circle, Floral Circle, Salem Benevolent Society, and several usher boards. He initiated a band of junior officers to help young people learn about official church positions. He also organized at Salem a boy scout troop, altar boys and acolytes, and the Phyllis Wheatley Club. The Wheatley club held formal teas at the HOTEL THERESA every February as a church fund-raiser.

Rev. Cullen, who authored *From Barefoot Town to Jerusalem,* initiated Salem's monthly publication, *The Announcer.* The periodical not only contained community and church news but also featured advertisements from church and community organizations. Such a journalistic business venture within the church was virtually unheard of in the early part of the 20th century.

The Salem congregation remained on 133rd Street for 16 years. It then, in September 1924, purchased the white Methodist Episcopal Church at 129th Street and SEVENTH AVENUE at a cost of $258,000, as recorded in the *SURVEY GRAPHIC* (March 1925) essay "The Church and the Negro Spirit." In 2002, Salem United Methodist Church was still located at 2190 ADAM CLAYTON POWELL, JR., Blvd. (formerly Seventh Avenue).

With no children of their own, Rev. Cullen and his wife adopted Countee Cullen when he became an orphan and attended Sunday school at Salem.

Further Reading

Anderson, Jervis. *This Was Harlem: A Cultural Portrait, 1900–1950.* New York: Farrar, Straus, Giroux, 1981.

Reynolds, Linda A., ed. *Salem United Methodist Church: A Chronicle 1902–1922.* New York: The Salem United Methodist Church History Committee (undated).

— Sandra L. West

salons

Writers, visual artists, performers, educators, and others interested in cultural events during the Harlem Renaissance often gathered in meetings known as salons, where they discussed various ideas and sometimes displayed their work. Such meetings formed an integral and substantial part of the *NEW NEGRO* movement.

Salons among participants in the Harlem Renaissance varied in their degree of formality or informality. Some resembled the conservativeness of an upper-class English gathering, while others were closer to simple "hang-out sessions" where like-minded individuals freely enjoyed each others' talents and intelligence. Among blacks, the salons offered an environment where talent and intelligence were not qualities that had to be proven, as professional black creative artists of the era often felt they had to do in regard to white America, but qualities that could be taken for granted. Moreover, such environments sometimes functioned like prep schools in which future writers were reared.

Virtually every major participant in the Harlem Renaissance either periodically hosted salons or attended them. In many ways, NIGGERATI MANOR was a nonstop salon with its many financially struggling but exceptionally brilliant residents frequently interacting with each other on one level or another. Among them were RICHARD BRUCE NUGENT, ZORA NEALE HUSTON, AARON DOUGLAS, and WALLACE THURMAN. The latter lampooned the tradition of salons in his 1932 satirical novel, *Infants of the Spring.* In one famous scene, young writers and artists gather to discuss a black cultural agenda with A. L. Parkes, a character modeled after HOWARD UNIVERSITY professor ALAIN LOCKE. Also present in the scene are some half dozen other Harlem Renaissance writers and artists presented as characters debating cultural politics.

Standing in contrast to Niggerati Manor was heiress A'LELIA WALKER's the DARK TOWER, named after a column by author COUNTEE CULLEN, specifically as a gathering place for the culturally inclined. She called it "my contribution" to the era. Located in a 136th Street mansion initially purchased by her millionaire mother, MADAME C. J. WALKER, the tower featured literary quotes on its walls and displays of rare books along with art by Aaron Douglas. Attendees included entertainer FLORENCE MILLS, author and political activist JAMES WELDON JOHNSON, PATRON and writer CARL VAN VECHTEN, and performing artist ETHEL WATERS. The Dark Tower functioned as a restaurant as well as a cultural outlet. While meals were served in one area, a literary critique might be taking place in another and a card game or piano recital in yet another. Remaining open only for a year, the Dark Tower closed in 1928.

More typical of the salons were those hosted by such writers and educators as REGINA ANDREWS and JESSIE REDMOND FAUSET, both of whom held salons with the intent of helping others recognize and develop their talents. Andrews opened her home on SUGAR HILL to aspiring creative artists in much the same manner that she opened the basements of the libraries where she worked to help establish such theater groups as the KRIGWA PLAYERS and HARLEM EXPERIMENTAL THEATER. PHILADELPHIA native Jessie Redmond Fauset required those attending her salon to speak French. Her role as hostess on such occasions complemented and supplemented her role as literary editor for the *CRISIS: A RECORD OF THE DARKER RACES*.

In WASHINGTON, D.C., poet and playwright Georgia Douglas Johnson hosted one of the most famous and well-attended salons of the era. Johnson not only opened her home for salons but for writing workshops in which aspiring writers developed ideas and actual works. Those writers based in NEW YORK CITY often made it a point to visit the Johnson home when traveling through Washington or periodically visited the city specifically to attend the salon. Some historians maintain that the idea for the CIVIC CLUB DINNER that launched the literary aspect of the Harlem Renaissance originated out of discussions that took place at Johnson's home. Participants in her salon included playwright WILLIS RICHARDSON, poet and playwright ANGELINA EMILY WELD GRIMKÉ, author and mystic JEAN TOOMER, writer LANGSTON HUGHES, Alain Locke, and MAY MILLER.

Miller actually grew up in a home on the campus of Howard University where her parents, two educators, often hosted salons or entertained influential visitors. As such, Miller was also acquainted with Johnson as a guest in her own home. Others that Miller met while growing up and that influenced her development as a writer were educator BOOKER TALIAFERRO WASHINGTON, editor and sociologist W. E. B. DU BOIS, and poet and critic WILLIAM STANLEY BEAUMONT BRAITHWAITE. Upon becoming established as an educator and author, Miller continued the tradition of hosting salons at her home on S Street in Washington. Some of those attending her salon were writer Owen Dodson, artist Charles Sebree, future Pulitzer Prize winner GWENDOLYN BROOKS, and future Nobel Prize winner Toni Morrison.

An important complement to those salons hosted by African Americans in the United States during the Harlem Renaissance were those by sisters Paulette Nardal and Jeanne Nardal in PARIS, France. Natives of François, Martinique, the Nardal sisters published *La Revue du Monde Noir,* or *The Review of the Black World,* one of the early central journals of the NEGRITUDE movement. At the Nardal salons, African-American writers visiting France often met black French authors and students. Such associations often led beyond discussions. Through his acquaintance with the black French author and editor René Maran, Alain Locke published articles of his own in France as well as works by CLAUDE MCKAY, Cullen, Toomer, and Hughes. Moreover, through their meetings with black American writers at the Nardal salon, then students and aspiring poets Leon Damas, Leopold Senghor, and Aimé Césaire drew the inspiration and examples to expand the Negritude movement.

With the surge in the publication of books by African Americans during the late 1990s, a new version of salons evolved in the form of such reading groups as the national Sisters Sippin' Tea, the Hotlanta Book Club based in Atlanta, the Ebony Book Club in New York, the Imani-Nia Book Study Group in Denver, and the Oprah Winfrey Book Club.

Further Reading

Bontemps, Arna, ed. *The Harlem Renaissance Remembered.* New York: Dodd, Mead, and Company, 1972.

Fabre, Michel. *From Harlem to Paris, Black American Writers in France, 1840–1980.* Urbana and Chicago: University of Illinois Press, 1991.

Hutchinson, George. *The Harlem Renaissance in Black and White.* Cambridge and London: Belknap Press of Harvard University Press, 1995.

Posnock, Ross. *Color and Culture: Black Writers and the Making of the Modern Intellectual.* Cambridge, Mass.: Harvard University Press, 1998.

Sharpley-Whiting, T. Denean. *Negritude Women.* Minneapolis: University of Minnesota, 2002.

— Aberjhani

Savage, Augusta Fells (1892–1962) *sculptor*

An energetic artist whose greatest work was inspired by JAMES WELDON JOHNSON's lyrics for "LIFT EVERY VOICE AND SING," Augusta Fells Savage established the Savage Studio of Arts and Crafts, created the HARLEM COMMUNITY ART CENTER, and co-organized the Harlem Arts Guild.

Augusta Fells Savage was born the seventh of 14 children in 1892 in Green Cove Springs, Florida. Her father was a carpenter, farmer, and Methodist preacher. Her mother was a housewife. Religious people, they could not understand or condone their daughter's artistic nature. They actually discouraged her commitment to what they thought was creating "graven images" from clay. Savage stated that her father beat her five or six times a week, trying hard to exorcise her devotion to art.

Augusta Savage married James Savage when she was 15 years old, gave birth to a daughter in 1908, and was widowed a few years later. She and her family moved to West Palm Beach in 1915, where she considered going into nursing.

While still a teen, Savage attended Tallahassee State National School and with her artistic skills drew the attention of the school principal. She persuaded a local potter to give her 25

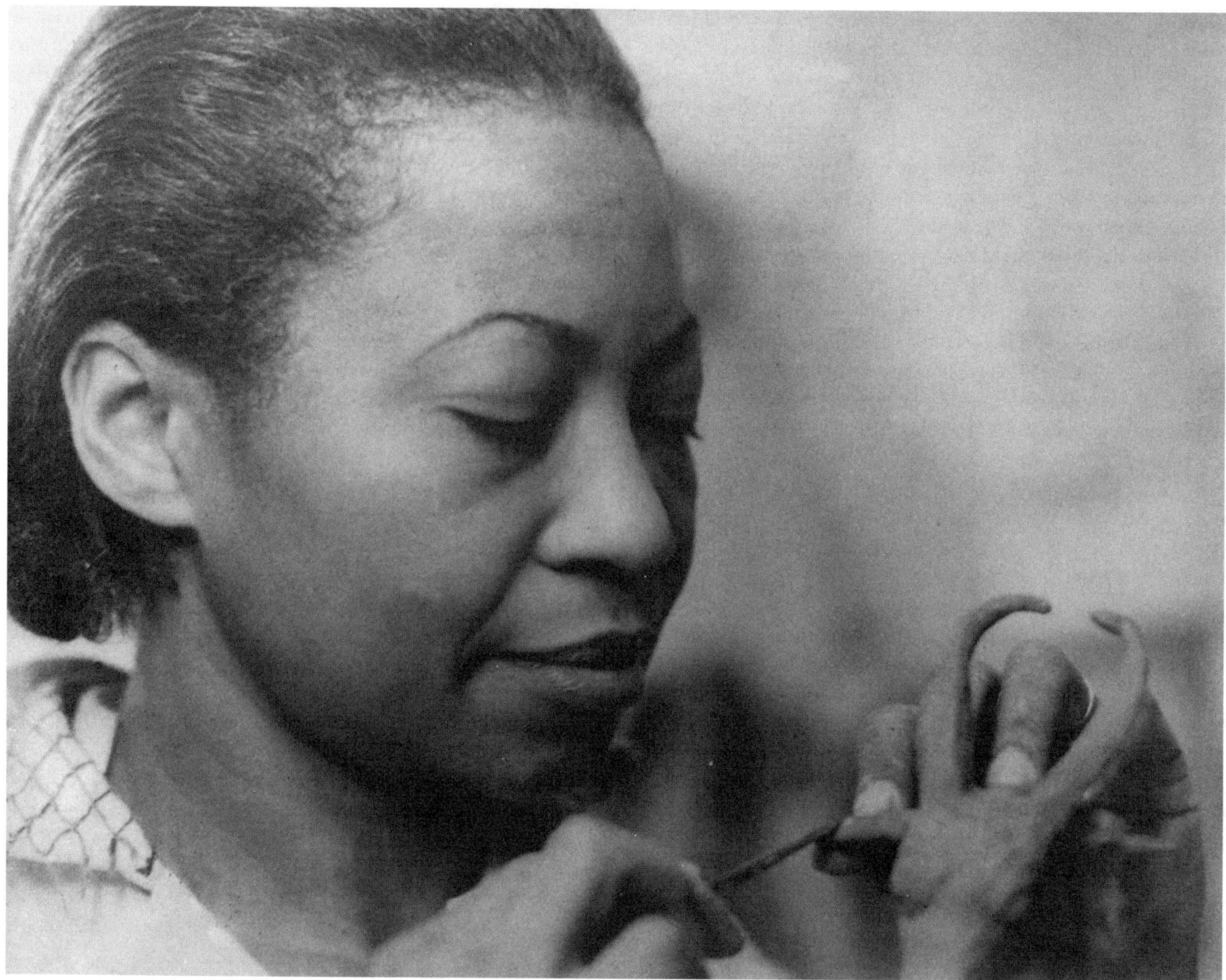

Sculptor Augusta Savage overcame poverty, sexism, and racism to become one of the most accomplished artists and cultural leaders of the Harlem Renaissance. *(National Archives, 200(S)-HNE-20-90)*

pounds of clay. With this clay, she sculpted several works that the principal admired so much that he convinced her father to allow her to teach clay-modeling class at the high school. Savage earned one dollar a day for six months.

Savage sculpted clay ducks and chickens for the Palm Beach County Fair and received a prize of $25 and an honor ribbon. The superintendent of the fair encouraged her to go to NEW YORK CITY to study. He gave her a letter of recommendation to sculptor Solon Borglum at the School of American Sculpture. Savage, at age 29, arrived in New York with $4.60 in her pocket. The school was too expensive for her, but Borglum referred her to the tuition-free Cooper Union art school.

In 1921, Savage began her studies at Cooper Union. Within a few days, based upon the maturity of her work, she was advanced from the freshman class to the sophomore class. To support herself, she washed laundry. Cooper Union increased her financial award and, to further assist her precarious financial situation, friends of the Schomburg Library commissioned a bust of W. E. B. DU BOIS, editor of *CRISIS: A RECORD OF THE DARKER RACES*. She also sculpted busts of UNITED NEGRO IMPROVEMENT ASSOCIATION founder MARCUS GARVEY, abolitionist and orator Frederick Douglass, and NATIONAL ASSOCIATION FOR THE ADVANCEMENT OF COLORED PEOPLE (NAACP) director James Weldon Johnson.

In 1923, Savage received a scholarship from the French government to attend a summer session at Fontainebleau but, when racist recipients from the JIM CROW state of Alabama objected to traveling with a "colored girl," the scholarship was taken away from her. The outraged art student took her story to the newspapers and, though the Alabama admissions committee would not reverse their decision, Herman McNeil, president of the National Sculpture Society, stepped forward to invite the spurned student to study with him in his Long Island, New York, studio.

Another chance to study abroad came to her two years later but family problems, including her father's death, prevented her from accepting a scholarship to the Royal Academy of Fine Arts in Rome, Italy. She was finally awarded a Rosenwald Fellowship to study at La Grande Chaumière in France in 1930.

In France she exhibited at Salon d'Automne and at the Grande-Palais and Salon Printemps. While in France, she received a second Rosenwald Fellowship and a Carnegie Foundation grant to travel to Belgium and Germany.

When Savage returned to New York in 1932, she established the Savage Studio of Arts and Crafts at 163 West 143rd Street. JACOB ARMSTEAD LAWRENCE and WILLIAM ELLSWORTH ARTIS were among the students there.

The GREAT DEPRESSION did not deter her. Ever the activist, she held press conferences and rallied for the right of black artists to receive their fair share of funds from the WORKS PROGRESS ADMINISTRATION (WPA), a government-sponsored program designed to provide employment for professional artists. The end result of her activism was her creation of the Harlem Community Art Center, of which she was the first director. Among the instructors there were ELTON FAX, NORMAN LEWIS, and others who during that period created enduring works.

Savage was also instrumental in advocating for the creation of other community-based artistic institutions such as the Harlem Artists Guild, the Uptown Art Laboratory, and THREE-O-SIX "306." Savage loved and encouraged the art of every young student who found their way to her door, something her father had not done for her.

In 1938, Savage created her benchmark piece, *The Harp,* inspired by the lyrics of "Lift Every Voice and Sing," also known as the Negro National Anthem, written by JOHN ROSAMOND JOHNSON and brother James Weldon Johnson. *The Harp* was a commission to represent the African American's contribution to the world of music. Created from plaster with black finish, the 16-foot-high sculpture was placed at the entrance to the Contemporary Arts Building at the 1939 New York World's Fair, where the only other African-American artist represented was composer WILLIAM GRANT STILL. For the work, the Women's Service League of Brooklyn awarded Savage a silver medal. Unfortunately, there was not enough money to cast the plaster sculpture into bronze, and it was destroyed at the end of the Fair. However, according to Hampton University Art Museum officials possibly four or five smaller versions of *The Harp* and a small model of *The Harp* in Hampton's collection existed in 2002.

After 15 years in HARLEM, Augusta Fells Savage moved to upstate New York to live closer to her daughter, teach art, and create portraits for tourists. She died at age 70 on March 26, 1962.

Further Reading

Bailey, David A., and Paul Gilroy. *Rhapsodies in Black: Art of the Harlem Renaissance.* Berkeley: University of California Press, 1997.

Bearden, Romare, and Harry Henderson. *Six Black Masters of American Art.* New York: Zenith Books/Doubleday, 1972.

———. *History of African-American Artists: From 1792 to the Present.* New York: Knopf Publishing Group, 1993.

Powell, Richard J. *Black Art and Culture in the 20th Century.* New York: Thames and Hudson, 1997.

— Sandra L. West

Savoy Ballroom

With a dance floor the size of a modern-day professional basketball court and a lineup of bands that included FESS WILLIAMS's Royal Flushers and the CHICK WEBB Orchestra, the Savoy Ballroom instantly became a favorite of dancers and musicians alike when its doors opened on March 12, 1926.

Business partners Jay Fagan and Moe Padden invested $200,000 to construct the double-floored Savoy, a building that stretched an entire block on LENOX AVENUE between 140th and 141st Streets. Described as the "home of happy feet," the dance hall's 10,000-foot dance floor was nicknamed "the track." Mirrors lined the walls, a marble staircase led to the second floor, and a glittering glass-cut chandelier hung from its ceiling.

The Savoy Ballroom was often described as HARLEM's answer to downtown NEW YORK CITY's Roseland Ballroom. However, unlike the Roseland, the Savoy did not require segregated dancing. Going against the social grain of the times, blacks and whites were allowed to dance together just as black bands and white bands often performed together. At the Savoy, the ruling factors were the music and the dance.

So intense was the expressed passion for dancing that it often proved as athletic as any sporting event. Dances such as the Suzy-Q, the Charleston, Truckin', and the Shimmy were all favorites. One of the most popular of all was the lindy hop, a dance that required equal measures of strength, flexibility, and endurance. Tuesday nights at the Savoy were set aside for the serious lindy hoppers known as the 400 Club, and the more superlative dancers congregated mostly among themselves rather than mix with the merely adequate.

Music at the Savoy, which contained two bandstands, was a nonstop event. One band would automatically start to play as another was winding down for its break. The double bandstands also allowed the Savoy to host a "battle of the bands" in which bands and singers performed against each other for audience approval. The undisputed champion of these sessions was the Chick Webb Orchestra, which defeated, or "cut," such celebrated outfits as the COUNT BASIE Band and the Benny Goodman Band. A gifted and versatile percussionist, Chick Webb remained with his band at the Savoy throughout the 1930s. When lindy hopper Ella Fitzgerald decided to show the world what she could do with a song, she became the orchestra's featured vocalist. Following Webb's death in 1939, Fitzgerald led the orchestra herself for a time.

The Savoy paid its orchestras an average salary of $1,200 a week and performing there became a goal of nearly every band and singer. FLETCHER HENDERSON, DUKE ELLINGTON, BILLIE HOLIDAY, CAB CALLOWAY, and CHARLIE PARKER all made their way onto the double bandstands to thrill the Savoy dancers.

The energetic creativity at the Savoy inspired a number of compositions that served to help immortalize the dance hall. These included "Stompin' at the Savoy," by Benny Goodman, Chick Webb, Edgar Sampson, and Andy Razaf; "The Savoy Strut," by Duke Ellington and Johnny Hodges; and "The Savoy Shout," by Red Allen. The dance hall also inspired duplicates across the United States and around the world. In addition to the one in Harlem, one could dance at the Savoy in Los Angeles, CHICAGO, Boston, and London.

Allegations of illicit activities in 1943 caused the Savoy to shut down for several months. Its closure was cited as one of the principal factors contributing to the HARLEM RIOT of 1943, and it was reopened to help alleviate the racial tensions of that time. Changing trends in music led to its permanent closure in 1958. Following its destruction, a housing project was built on the site.

Further Reading

Haskins, James S. *Black Dance in America: A History Through Its People.* New York: Harper Collins, 1991.

Kebede, Ashenafi. *Roots of Black Music: The Vocal, Instrumental and Dance Heritage of Africa and Black America.* Lawrenceville, N.J.: Africa World Press, 1995.

— Aberjhani

scatting

With the emergence of JAZZ and SWING music during the 1920s and 1930s, scatting became a popular vocal technique in which singers ad-libbed the words to songs with abstract syllables or extended melody lines by imitating the sound of a horn.

Most agree that scatting likely originated in the dancing ring, or circle dance, of various African societies. In such settings, improvisations in song and speech, presented more to articulate a feeling or spiritual experience than a sentence, were common.

Scatting as an element of jazz developed during the mid-1920s in the performances of musicians such as Don Redman and LOUIS ARMSTRONG. Redman, who later led the McKinney Cotton Pickers and other bands, performed scatting on his recording of "My Papa Doesn't Two-Time No Time" in 1924. Armstrong further popularized the style in 1926 when he reportedly forgot some of the lyrics while recording "Heebie Jeebies" and improvised with scatting. He did the same on a song called "I'm a Ding Dong Daddy." Scatting eventually became a trademark of Armstrong's musicianship both on record and in live performance.

CAB CALLOWAY adopted scatting in a manner similar to Armstrong. During a live radio performance of *"MINNIE THE MOOCHER,"* he forgot the lyrics and sang instead, "Hi-dee hi-dee hi-dee ho." The phrase became the basis for a call and response routine between Calloway and his audiences. Calloway went on to compose a number of songs consisting of nothing but scatting as opposed to recognizable lyrics. These included "The Scat Song," "Zaz Za Zaz," and "Boogit."

Sarah Vaughn, Lionel Hampton, and Jack Teagarden also elevated scatting to a vocal art form until it became a tool by which many jazz singers measured their abilities. Ella Fitzgerald displayed her mastery of the technique on such songs as "Lady Be Good" and "How High the Moon." Some of those excelling at the art in the modern era are Betty Carter (now deceased), Al Jarreau, Andy Bey, Sheila Jordan, and Jacey Faulk.

Further Reading

Crowther, Bruce, and Mike Pinfold. *Singing Jazz.* Backbeat Books, 1998.

Gourse, Leslie. *Swingers and Crooners: The Art of Jazz Singing.* Danburg, Conn.: Watts Franklin, 1997.

— Aberjhani

Schomburg, Arthur (Arturo Alfonso Schomburg) (1874–1938) *bibliophile, historian*

Book collector and historian Arthur Alfonso Schomburg amassed during the early 1900s one of the largest collections of data and artifacts on African-American life and provided the foundation for what today is the world-renowned SCHOMBURG CENTER FOR RESEARCH IN BLACK CULTURE.

Born in San Juan, Puerto Rico, on January 24, 1874, Schomburg was the son of a West Indian mother named Mary Joseph and a German father named Carlos Federico Schomburg. As a child, he attended public and private schools in Puerto Rico. He later attended St. Thomas College in the Virgin Islands and there developed an interest in scholarly materials pertaining to people of African descent.

In 1891, Schomburg immigrated to NEW YORK CITY. Joining a Hispanic lodge as well as the Masons in New York, he cofounded a revolutionary group called Las Dos Antillas, dedicated to obtaining independence from Spain for Puerto Rico and Cuba.

He married Virginia native Elizabeth Hatcher in 1895, and the couple had three children: Maximo Gormey, Arturo Alfonso, Jr., and Kingsley Guarionex. His first wife died in 1900. In 1901, Schomburg obtained employment as clerk and courier with a law firm and in 1902 married for the second time. With his second wife, Elizabeth Morrow Taylor, he had two more children: Reginald Stanfield and Nathaniel José. Schomburg would marry a third time, to Elizabeth Green in 1914, and with her have three children: Fernando Alfonso, Dolores Maria, and Carlos Placido.

In 1904, Schomburg began publishing articles on the Caribbean. Gaining employment in 1906 with the Bankers Trust Company and remaining with it until 1929, he eventually advanced to the position of supervisor for the company's Caribbean and Latin mail division. He also continued publishing and in 1909 produced a pamphlet on the Cuban poet Gabriel de la Concepción Valdez.

In 1911, Schomburg and journalist John E. Bruce founded the Negro Society for Historical Research. Like CARTER GODWIN WOODSON'S ASSOCIATION FOR THE STUDY OF NEGRO LIFE established later, Schomburg's Negro Society for Historical Research promoted and published studies on the history and culture of people of African descent. In 1916, he published a comprehensive critical evaluation of works by Phyllis Wheatley as well as a book titled *A Check List of American Negro Poetry.*

During the early 1920s, Schomburg befriended a number of writers and artists associated with the Harlem Renaissance, including ERIC DERWENT WALROND, JAMES WELDON JOHNSON, CHARLES SPURGEON JOHNSON, and CLAUDE MCKAY. He was particularly instrumental in assisting McKay as a sometime literary agent and PATRON during McKay's years as an expatriate in Europe.

In 1922, the AMERICAN NEGRO ACADEMY elected Schomburg president of the organization. When ALAIN LOCKE edited the special edition of the March 1925 *SURVEY GRAPHIC* dedicated to the NEW NEGRO, Schomburg contributed to it one of his most celebrated essays, "The Negro Digs Up His Past." In the essay, he noted that, "The American Negro must remake his past in order to make his future." And he identified the French abolitionist Abbe Gregoire as the first author of a book, in 1808, on achievements by blacks. He also clarified that his purpose for collecting data on African Americans was not only to produce "the first true writing of Negro history, but for the rewriting of many important paragraphs of our common American history." The essay was reprinted in the *NEW NEGRO* anthology, also edited by Locke.

The Carnegie Corporation in 1926 provided the Negro Division of the New York Public Library with a grant of $10,000 to purchase Schomburg's collected data. Placed at the 135th Street library branch, Schomburg's collected materials included thousands of pamphlets, drawings, and etchings; approximately 3,000 manuscripts; and more than 5,000 books. The purchase allowed Schomburg in 1926 to take an extensive tour of Europe. In France, he met with COUNTEE CULLEN and members of Europe's counterpart to the Harlem Renaissance, the NEGRITUDE movement.

In 1927, Schomburg won the William E. Harmon Award for exceptional contributions to education. He spent a year at FISK UNIVERSITY in Nashville, Tennessee, from 1931 to 1932, serving as curator for the university's library. He then traveled to Cuba, where he continued his research on the African diaspora.

Returning to New York in 1932, Schomburg accepted the position as curator for the 135th Street branch of the New York Library's Negro Collection. He maintained the position until his death on June 8, 1938.

In 1940, the library's collection of material on African Americans was renamed the Schomburg Collection of Negro Literature and History. The library itself was later renamed the Schomburg Center for Research in Black Culture and its treasured data recognized as the largest such collection in the world. Since its founding, the center has served as a major resource for authors, educators, students, historians, and others interested in the history of African Americans. Today, located at 515 Malcolm X Boulevard in New York City, the center houses digital collections on African Americans as well as an extensive collection that has grown from the printed works gathered by Schomburg throughout his life.

Further Reading

Schomburg Center for Research in Black Culture, Christopher Moore, Roberta Yancy, and David Dinkins. *The Black New Yorkers: The Schomburg Illustrated Chronology.* New York: John Wiley and Sons, 2001.

Sinnette, Elinor Des Verney. *Arthur Alfonso Schomburg: Black Bibliophile and Collector.* New York: New York Public Library and Wayne State University Press, 1989.

— Aberjhani

Schomburg Center for Research in Black Culture

The Schomburg Center for Research in Black Culture evolved during the Harlem Renaissance out of the book collection of a private citizen and has developed into the most definitive research center on black culture in the world.

The value of books and other artifacts on African-American culture was greatly enhanced after bibliophile Arthur Schomburg's massive collection provided the foundation for what is now known as the Schomburg Center for Research in Black Culture in New York City. *(Library of Congress, Prints & Photographs Division [LC-USZC2-1124])*

When America's JIM CROW racial segregation laws defined who could enter specific facilities or avail themselves of city services, black Americans were, by law and social custom, forbidden to patronize public libraries. In response to this racism, the Carnegie Foundation purchased buildings throughout the country to establish segregated public libraries for black patrons. The Carnegie Library in Savannah, Georgia, is one case in point, and the Schomburg, in NEW YORK CITY, is another.

In 1926, the Carnegie Foundation purchased a book collection amassed by private collector and independent scholar ARTHUR SCHOMBURG. Schomburg was a Puerto Rican of West Indian and German lineage. His collection on the African diaspora was presented by the Carnegie Foundation to the New York Public Library system and developed into a special black studies unit for the 135th Street branch of the library. Schomburg's original collection was 5,000 volumes strong, was very keen in the area of history, and had 3,000 manuscripts and 2,000 etchings.

The three-story stone building containing the Schomburg collection first opened in 1905 when the neighborhood housed residents of Hasidic Jewish ancestry. In 1926, during the GREAT MIGRATION, when a voluminous influx of black southern immigrants settled in the vicinity, the library established a Department of Negro Literature and History. It was in this department that Schomburg's collection was placed. The bibliophile and scholar Schomburg served as curator of the collection from 1932 until his death in 1938, and the building was named in his honor in 1940. The institution advanced to research center status and officially became the Schomburg Center for Research in Black Culture in 1972.

The Schomburg Center in 2003 remained at 135th Street and Malcolm X Boulevard, formerly LENOX AVENUE, directly across from the landmark HARLEM HOSPITAL. The center at that time had more than 5 million items, including books, photographs, rare manuscripts, films, and art. The official papers of Harlem Renaissance playwright and librarian REGINA ANDREWS are part of the holdings at the facility, as are the ashes of cremated Harlem Renaissance poet LANGSTON HUGHES, known as the "people's poet." Hughes's ashes rest beneath the floor of an area designated as the Langston Hughes Room.

Further Reading

Cantor, George. *Historic Landmarks of Black America.* Detroit, Mich.: Gale Research, 1991.

Curtis, Nancy C. *Black Heritage Series: An African-American Odyssey and Finder's Guide.* Chicago and London: American Library Association, 1996.

Kranz, Rachel, and Philip J. Koslow. *The Biographical Dictionary of African Americans.* New York: Facts On File, Inc., 1999.

— Sandra L. West

Schuyler, George Samuel (1895–1977) *journalist, writer*

The satirical articles, novels, plays, and poems of George S. Schuyler often placed him at cultural odds with the more celebrated writers of the Harlem Renaissance while simultaneously establishing him as one of the movement's, and America's, most insightful critics.

Schuyler was born in Providence, Rhode Island, on February 25, 1895, and raised in Syracuse, New York. His parents were George and Eliza J. Fischer Schuyler. He ended his formal education at the age of 17 when he left high school to join the U.S. Army. Completing military tours in Seattle and Hawaii, he advanced to the rank of first lieutenant and left the army in 1919. Schuyler made his way to NEW YORK CITY and there worked at a variety of jobs before meeting A. PHILIP RANDOLPH of the *MESSENGER* and joining the magazine's staff.

With his column entitled "Shafts and Darts: A Page of Calumny and Satire," Schuyler began his self-appointed task of dismantling America's tendency to define itself along the lines of race. The bite of his razor-sharp satire, however, was aimed at whites and blacks alike. Many saw his tendency to attack what he perceived as the flaw in any given idea, organization, or person as a direct influence of the man recognized as his mentor: H. L. Mencken, whose journalistic contributions to the *American Mercury* magazine, which he founded in 1924 and edited until 1933, helped make the magazine one of the most intellectually vigorous and acerbically critical in the country. So in harmony was Schuyler's critical vision with Mencken's that he was sometimes referred to as "the Negro Mencken."

In 1925, Schuyler joined the *PITTSBURGH COURIER* for what would turn out to be a 25-year stretch. His professional introduction to the paper was a tour through the Deep South, during which he reported on his experiences and added some 10,000 names and addresses to the *Courier*'s subscription list. The paper showed its gratitude by awarding Schuyler with an assistant editor's position.

As his reputation for insightful journalism and independent thinking expanded, so did the outlets for Schuyler's work until he became one of the most widely and frequently published black journalists in the United States. In addition to his works for the *Courier,* he continued to provide materials for the *Messenger,* the aforementioned *American Mercury,* the *CRISIS: A RECORD OF THE DARKER RACES, OPPORTUNITY,* the *New York Evening Post,* and, in time, the *Negro Digest* and numerous other publications.

Schuyler dubbed MARCUS GARVEY "America's greatest comedian" and held back none of his scorn for Garvey's BACK-TO-AFRICA MOVEMENT. Despite his affiliation with the communist-friendly *Messenger,* his opposition to COMMUNISM was total and uncompromising. He proposed in both verse and prose that the Harlem Renaissance was little more than an exercise in extended self-delusions by people who were "lampblacked" versions of whites. One of his most famous essays, "The Negro-Art Hokum," published on June 16, 1926, in *The Nation,* prompted the composition and publication in the same magazine the following week of LANGSTON HUGHES's much celebrated essay "The Negro Artist and the Racial Mountain."

Schuyler's career as a novelist began in 1931 with the publication of a work unlike anything else produced by his contemporaries. His *Black No More* combined a skillful blending of science fiction, social criticism, political savvy, and humor that the country might have readily applauded coming from a Mark

Twain or Jonathan Swift but found something of a challenge coming from a black man who described himself as a black conservative. Spinning the tale of a black scientist who concocts a scheme for turning blacks white and does so with mixed hilarious results, Schuyler lampooned both America's obsession with race and some of the principal black leaders of the period. He dedicated the novel to "all Caucasians in the great republic who can trace their ancestry back ten generations and confidently assert that there are no Black leaves, twigs, limbs or branches on their family trees."

Work as a foreign correspondent in Liberia provided Schuyler with the material for his second novel, published the same year as *Black No More,* called *Slaves Today, a Story of Liberia.* His experiences in Liberia, as well as Latin America and Europe, likely inspired *Black Empire, An Imaginative Story of a Great New Civilization in Modern Africa,* as well. Released as a novel in 1993 (16 years after Schuyler's death), it was first serialized in the *Pittsburgh Courier* from 1936 to 1938 under the pseudonym Samuel I. Brooks. Sticking with a science fiction twist, Schuyler's story focused on a team of technologically trained blacks intent on liberating a colonized Africa. Also serialized in the *Courier* during the 1930s was *The Ethiopian Stories,* published in book form as two novellas. The message here was also one of liberation, this time with Ethiopia breaking away from Italian rule. Schuyler's fictional portraits of black independence and assertiveness seemed at odds with the apparent cultural assimilation championed in his essays but his greatest loyalty appeared to be to his understanding of the idea most suitable to a given situation. Within the context of the United States, the better idea from the perspective of his pen was that of an Americanism that eschewed allegiance to concepts of race—black or white—for its own sake. Within the context of Africa, the better, more applicable idea was black liberation.

Schuyler lived his life with the same critical approach he took to his writing and in 1928 married the white Texan Josephine E. Lewis, partly out of their shared belief that children of interracial marriages would prove more genetically and intellectually advanced than those whose parents belonged to the same race. In the case of their daughter, Phillipa Duke Schuyler, the theory bore out. Born on August 2, 1931, Phillipa Schuyler was gifted with an IQ of 185. By the time she was 10, she had become a veteran composer of classical music and at 11 demonstrated her exceptional talents on tour. The *Pittsburgh Courier* charted her accomplishments with all the pride of its star journalist, Schuyler. As a young adult, his daughter won fame and acceptance playing before the politically elite everywhere except in her home country. She applied her genius to her father's profession and wrote a series of autobiographical and travel books in the 1960s. In 1967, she was trying to help transport Catholic schoolchildren to safety during the Vietnam War when she died at age 35 in a helicopter crash.

Schuyler remained uncompromising in his critical conservatism during the 1950s and 1960s. He characterized A. Philip Randolph as an ineffectual and misguided leader for the latter's proposed march on WASHINGTON, D.C., and lost his position with the *Courier* in 1966 following his negative appraisal of the Nobel Peace Prize awarded Martin Luther King, Jr. In the same year, he published his biography, *Black and Conservative.* His influence as a major journalist began to wane considerably as African Americans' struggle for civil rights reflected more and more militant overtones. Prior to his death on August 31, 1977, he continued for a time to write columns and reviews for various publications.

Journalist George S. Schuyler, shown here in 1941, stood unique among Harlem Renaissance writers as a satirist whose criticism targeted blacks and whites alike. *(Library of Congress, Prints & Photographs Division, Carl Van Vechten Collection [LC-USZ62-95999])*

Interest in Schuyler's work underwent a revival in 2001 with the republication of *Black No More,* and *The Ethiopian Stories.* At least two collections of his essays were also scheduled for publication.

Further Reading

Schuyler, George. *Black No More.* Boston: Northeastern University Press, 1989.

Schuyler, George S. and Jeffrey B. Leak (ed.) *Rac (E) Ing to the Right: Selected Essays of George S. Schuyler.* Knoxville: University of Tennessee Press, 2001.

Talalay, Kathryn. *Composition in Black and White: The Life of Philippa Schuyler: The Tragic Saga of Harlem's Biracial Prodigy.* New York: Oxford University Press, 1995.

— Aberjhani

Scottsboro trial

Widely recognized as one of the most tragic miscarriages of justice in the history of the American legal system, the Scottsboro trial stemmed from two young white women's allegations that they had been raped by nine black youths ranging in age from 13 to 20 years old.

On March 25, 1931, Victoria Price and Ruby Bates of Huntsville, Alabama, were riding a freight train going from Chattanooga, Tennessee, to Memphis. Also aboard the same train were seven white young men and nine black, all of them doing what many were at the onset of the GREAT DEPRESSION, riding freight trains from one town to another in search of job opportunities. When one of the white youths stepped on the hand of one of the blacks, a fight ensued which ended with the young white men getting off the train and returning to the town of Stevenson, where the train had stopped earlier. There, they informed authorities that a group of black men had attacked them and forced them off the train. After learning that the train had already passed its next stop of Scottsboro, the sheriff's office telephoned ahead to the following town, Paint Rock. They informed authorities in Paint Rock of what supposedly had happened. The black men were removed from the train and taken back to the town of Scottsboro where they readily admitted to fighting with a group of white youths but found themselves stunned when two white women whom they had never seen before announced that they had raped them both.

The accused young men were Olen Montgomery and Willie Roberson, both 17 years old; brothers Andy Wright, 19, and Roy Wright, 13; Heywood Patterson, 18; Eugene Williams, 13; Clarence Norris, 19; Charles Weems, 20; and Ozie Powell, 14. Montgomery was blind in one eye and had less than perfect vision in the other; he had been traveling to a hospital in Memphis. Roberson was suffering from two types of venereal disease and experienced pain whenever he moved. The Wright brothers, Patterson, and Williams all knew each other from Chattanooga. The remaining young men were from Georgia but until then were unknown to each other. They were mostly sons of sharecroppers, poor and barely literate.

From the beginning of the boys' arrest, without regard to what the facts may have been, white mobs gathered to demand the deaths of the young men whom some came to call the Scottsboro Boys or the Scottsboro Nine. Governor Benjamin M. Miller assigned the Alabama National Guard to keep order in the town, and the Ku Klux Klan failed at an attempt to pull the young men out of jail on the night before the trial.

While Chattanooga neighbors and friends of the Wright brothers hired lawyer Stephen Roddy to represent the young men, Judge E. A. Hawkins assigned to the case seven disinterested Scottsboro lawyers who were not obligated to actually do anything on the defendants' behalf. On the day of the trial, April 6, 1931, Roddy appeared in court in a noticeably inebriated state and presented himself as someone willing to lend a hand in the matter if needed. None of the young men had been counseled or questioned in regard to the case.

The doctors who examined Price and Bates stated that although they found a small quantity of male semen in Price and a larger amount in Bates, there was neither any physical nor psychological evidence to support Price's graphic descriptions of having been "ravished" for hours on end by a group of men. In time, both women, including the married Price, would admit to having engaged in consensual sex with their boyfriends on the night before the alleged rapes. Bates would state flat out that she had not been raped. However, on the day of the trial, members of the Alabama courtroom listened to their testimony and two hours after the trial began delivered a verdict of guilty with a call for the death penalty. The exception to that verdict was 13-year-old Roy Wright, for whom a mistrial was declared. A year later, during an appeal, the Alabama Supreme Court would reverse the conviction for Eugene Williams, who was also 13 at the time of the alleged assault.

News of the Scottsboro trial results made headlines across the United States and eventually across the globe. Most black newspaper editorials expressed two concerns: What was the position of the NATIONAL ASSOCIATION FOR THE ADVANCEMENT OF COLORED PEOPLE (NAACP) on the trial, and who in that organization's absence was seeing to the young men's best interests? The answer to the former was that the NAACP, without a branch office in Scottsboro, was making a cautious assessment of events there from its headquarters in New York. The answer to the latter was the communist International Labor Defense (ILD) organization, which upon learning about the Scottsboro trial decision immediately launched a worldwide publicity campaign to raise a hue and cry aimed at postponing the condemned men's execution. The ILD succeeded even as they entered into an ideological tug-of-war with the NAACP over the most effective way to proceed with the defense. By the time the NAACP got around to obtaining the nation's top defense lawyer, Clarence Darrow, for the case, the ILD had won the acceptance of the prisoners and their families with nonstop publicity and supportive visits and gifts of money to help compensate for the prisoners' inability to contribute to their families. Eventually both Darrow and the NAACP withdrew from the case.

The court's decision on April 6 set in motion a cycle of appeals and new trials that would take the Scottsboro Nine through four convictions and the additional sentences that stem almost automatically from that of life in prison. Eventually, the case reached the Supreme Court. Notable in the *Powell v. Alabama* November 7, 1932, U.S. Supreme Court decision was its ruling that all defendants are entitled to adequate council and representation before the law. With a vote of 7 to 2, the Supreme Court overturned the conviction of the Scottsboro Nine. Associate Justice Sutherland, speaking for the majority, held that not only were the defendant's Fourteenth Amendment rights violated, but his Sixth Amendment rights were violated as well. The right to be represented by counsel, Sutherland further ruled, is central to the American judicial system and "the right to have counsel appointed, when necessary, is a logical corollary from the constitutional right. . . . " This decision established a proper legal defense as one of the essential components of due process. A year later in *Norris v. Alabama,* the conviction of another defendant was invalidated because there had been racial discrimination in the grand jury's and the trial jury's selections. These two Supreme Court rulings showed that federal law would not tolerate state discrimination against African Americans in the courts.

Even after receiving paroles in the 1940s, the then fully grown men found themselves societal misfits unable to maintain jobs or enjoy relationships. Ironically, whereas the NAACP failed in its bid to defend the men, after their release the organization occasionally acted as guardian to some of them. On their behalf it would procure jobs, transportation for relocation, or funds for living expenses.

Of the nine originally involved, only Clarence Norris was alive in 1977 when Governor George Wallace granted them a pardon.

In 2000, filmmakers Daniel Anker and Barak Goodman produced *Scottsboro: An American Tragedy*, a documentary that examines the Scottsboro trial, the nature of the times in which it occurred, and the American legal system's predilection for falsely imprisoning African-American men accused of crimes against white women.

Further Reading

Carter, Dan T. *Scottsboro: A Tragedy of the American South.* Baton Rouge: Louisiana State University Press, 1979.

Horne, Gerald. *Powell v. Alabama.* Danbury, Conn.: Franklin Watts, 1997.

— Aberjhani

Seventh Avenue

Seventh Avenue, once known as "the Great Black Way," was one of the busiest streets in the HARLEM community during the 1920s and 1930s. Filled with vital businesses and landmark churches, Seventh Avenue is historically recorded as the boulevard of Sunday afternoon fashion promenades.

Some of the businesses and churches that had Seventh Avenue addresses were the PACE PHONOGRAPHIC RECORD CORPORATION, the LAFAYETTE THEATRE, and the church and parish home of poet COUNTEE CULLEN, SALEM METHODIST CHURCH, where his father was pastor. Seventh Avenue was also where MARCUS GARVEY, founder of the UNIVERSAL NEGRO IMPROVEMENT ASSOCIATION (UNIA), held street rallies for his BACK-TO-AFRICA MOVEMENT. It was the location as well of the HOTEL THERESA, which, starting in the 1940s, lodged black celebrities of the caliber of boxer JOE LOUIS, the Brown Bomber, who held his Victory Headquarters at the hotel, and an APOLLO THEATRE legend, comedian MOMS MABLEY.

Seventh Avenue was also the place where FASHION AND THE HARLEM RENAISSANCE merged. Style-setting on the avenue was a typical pastime, as smartly dressed men wearing white gloves and beautiful women dressed in flowered hats all strolled on the avenue on Easter Sundays. While the Harlem Easter parade was legendary and drew many onlookers, Harlem residents did not wait until that spring holiday to exhibit their fashion know-how. Every Sunday afternoon after the church hour there was a promenade on Seventh Avenue. The panache of the event drew descriptive comments from the *NEW YORK AGE* and *The New Yorker.* Harlem Renaissance novelist RUDOLPH FISHER offered dialect-heavy commentary on the public walks in *The Walls of Jericho.*

The author of *Black Manhattan,* JAMES WELDON JOHNSON, wrote that the Sunday Seventh Avenue fashion extravaganzas were "not simply going out for a walk; it is like going out for an adventure."

In 1974, Seventh Avenue was renamed ADAM CLAYTON POWELL, JR., Boulevard in tribute to ABYSSINIAN BAPTIST CHURCH's fiery, political cleric and Harlem's first black congressman. The Powell Boulevard runs from 110th Street to 155th Street.

Further Reading

Anderson, Jervis. *This Was Harlem: A Cultural Portrait, 1900–1950.* New York: Farrar, Straus & Giroux, 1981.

Dolkart, Andrew S., and Gretchen S. Sorin. *Touring Historic Harlem: Four Walks in Northern Manhattan.* New York: New York Landmarks Conservancy, 1997.

— Sandra L. West

sexuality and the Harlem Renaissance

Attitudes toward sexuality at the time of the Harlem Renaissance were influenced by white American modernist attempts to break away from the conservative beliefs of 19th-century Victorians and embrace concepts of free love and women's liberation as well as the European perception of "primitive" African sexuality.

The norm among African Americans was apparently diversity, as many religion-oriented families sought to restrict sexual activity to within the context of marriage, while others chose the more libertarian models of conduct associated with modernism. Whether heterosexual, bisexual, or homosexual, tolerance to one degree or another proved the general rule of thumb. The ultimate taboo was not so much sexual preference or inclination as it was sexual interaction between blacks and whites. To discourage the latter, some 30 states passed antimiscegenation laws barring marriage between blacks and whites. Moreover, the vast majority of LYNCHING cases stemmed from disclosed, suspected, or accused liaisons between black men and white women.

The NATIONAL URBAN LEAGUE (NUL) was founded in part precisely to guard against the sexual exploitation of black women and youth moving from the South to the North during the GREAT MIGRATION. Journalist IDA BELL WELLS-BARNETT in her earliest columns frequently addressed the issue of unmarried black women's need to guard their "virtue" and black men's need to curb their lust. In addition, with some exceptions, many of those blacks moving out of the South brought with them the very strict codes of moral conduct that in the South had been more essential to their survival than to any notions of social propriety.

Ironically, the European perception of African Americans, on which JOSEPHINE BAKER capitalized for decades in her French stage productions, was often that of near savages with barely controllable sexual impulses. Portrayals of blacks as sensitive or romantic were often met with derision or outright resistance. So entrenched was the stereotype of unbridled primitive sexuality that EUBIE BLAKE and NOBLE SISSLE feared they would be mobbed upon the performance of a romantic ballad called "Love Will Find a Way" on the opening night of their hit musical *SHUFFLE ALONG*.

Songs of a more risqué or bawdy nature, such as those performed by blues singers BESSIE SMITH and CLARA SMITH, or the comedian PIGMEAT MARKHAM, were more readily accepted. Their heavily sexually suggestive lyrics were not only more celebrated; they were the staple products behind the boom in RACE RECORDS that lasted throughout the JAZZ age. Additionally, Markham was part of a comedy tradition that also depended on heavy sexual innuendo, and his nickname, Pigmeat, was derived from a novelty song of the same nature. Like Markham, the husband and wife comedy team of BUTTERBEANS AND SUSIE were from the same tradition.

The writers, artists, and musicians of the Harlem Renaissance in their work and in their lives generally approached sexuality as an aspect of democratic freedom open to exploration and definition on one's own terms. Pianist JELLY ROLL MORTON was somewhat notorious in his willingness to work as a pimp when not performing as a musician. Writer JEAN TOOMER advocated what he called "the liberation of the sexes" and was known to court wealthy white women to obtain financial support for the Gurdjieff organization. Toomer also dealt extensively with the precariousness of intimate INTERRACIAL INTERACTION in *Cane,* his literary masterpiece.

Among those Harlem Renaissance figures largely conservative in their expressions of sexuality were ARNA BONTEMPS, JAMES WELDON JOHNSON, ANNIE BETHEL BANNISTER SPENCER, WALTER WHITE, and ARTHUR SCHOMBURG, all of whom married and maintained families. Schomburg, in fact, married three times to three different women all named Elizabeth, with whom he had eight children.

Of those black writers, artists, and performers associated with the period, a number were known to be gay or bisexual. Included among them were Josephine Baker, Bessie Smith, MOMS MABLEY, COUNTEE CULLEN, ETHEL WATERS, ALBERTA HUNTER, RICHARD BRUCE NUGENT, WALLACE THURMAN, CARL VAN VECHTEN, ANGELINA EMILY WELD GRIMKE, ALAIN LOCKE, and CLAUDE MCKAY.

Such affairs as drag balls at the SAVOY BALLROOM and the Rockland Palace were much-anticipated social events that received coverage in the *NEW YORK AGE* and other black newspapers. The club known as the Clam House featured performances by the openly gay GLADYS BENTLEY, whose songs and attire reflected her sexual identity.

Whereas the writers of the era generally did not address alternative sexuality in their works, Richard Bruce Nugent was an exception. Only elements of homoeroticism are evident in his short story "Sahdji," published in *The NEW NEGRO* anthology. However, a second story, "Smoke, Lillies, and Jade," published in the single edition of *FIRE!!*, was openly homoerotic in its portrayal of a relationship between a black man and a Latino man. A second exception was Angelina Weld Grimke, whose poem "El Beso" and letters to Mary Burrill expressed homoerotic affection.

McKay, on the other hand, celebrated unfettered black male heterosexuality in his best-selling 1928 novel, *Home to Harlem.* The novel's protagonist, Jake, is a military deserter who returns to HARLEM primarily because of what he considers its freedom of sensual expressiveness and indulgence. In his 1933 novel, *Banana Bottom,* McKay presents a black woman named Bita Plant intent on determining her own sexual destiny as opposed to having it restricted or defined by society.

The freedom to exercise choice regardless of gender also proved a major concern for ZORA NEALE HURSTON. *In Their Eyes Were Watching God,* she created a character similar to McKay's Bita Plant in the form of Janie Crawford, a woman not inclined to allow society to define her life or destiny but who seeks it and the men she chooses to love on her own terms. Moreover, with American slavery less than 100 years in the past, one important message discerned from the writings of Hurston and other black women writers of the era was that their bodies now belonged to themselves rather than anyone else, white or black.

Speculations abound regarding the sexual nature of writer LANGSTON HUGHES, who was known to have shared close friendships with women and men. Van Vechten, Nugent, and others have reported that sex per se was simply not a dominating factor of Hughes's life and that he was more likely asexual than anything else. Certainly Hughes's exceptionally prolific output as an author of poetry, novels, autobiographies, film scripts, plays, essays, articles, short stories, and history lend substantial credence to the theory that he invested more of his life's energies into his literary art than his libido.

Similarly, "the father of black history," CARTER GODWIN WOODSON, was known to enjoy the company of women and the rituals of courtship but made it clear that he was "married" to his work and remained so until his death. Such a sentiment is not unknown among those who produce exceptional intellectual works and it stands parallel to DUKE ELLINGTON's famous statement that, "Music is my mistress."

Because the dominant concern of Harlem Renaissance writers and artists, as writers and artists, was the liberation of African Americans from the brutal tyrannies of JIM CROW apartheid and genocide by lynching, sexuality remained more of a personal issue than a political one. As such, it occupied within their lives as integral, fundamental, and private a place as within anyone else's.

Further Reading

Hull, Gloria T., and Gloria Hull. *Color, Sex and Poetry: Three Women Writers of the Harlem Renaissance.* Bloomington: Indiana University Press, 1990.

Smith, Felipe. *American Body Politics: Race, Gender, and Black Literary Renaissance.* Athens: University of Georgia Press, 1998.

— Aberjhani

sheet music, African-American

Driven by a thriving piano industry and a growing demand for popular American songs, the production of sheet music developed into a major American industry in the 1880s and produced some of the most unique records of cultural history in the United States.

Following the Civil War, the production of more affordable parlor pianos, in contrast to the grand pianos constructed for public performances, allowed Americans to purchase the instruments in much the way that people today purchase cassette or CD players. Likewise, just as modern individuals purchase CDs for their players, individuals in the late 1800s purchased sheet music to play the latest songs on their piano.

In the mid-1880s, composers of sheet music were largely independent agents who produced their compositions and distributed them at will to such retail outlets as drugstores, department stores, or traveling musical troupes in minstrel shows. As the demand for popular American music and thus the sales of sheet music increased, organized businesses based on its production began to form. They hired lyricists and composers to produce the music, and artists and pluggers to promote it. Pluggers were skilled musicians who would play for customers songs out of a company's sheet music catalog. They were also sometimes professional performers who sang the newest songs for a fee or had their portraits placed on the cover of the sheet music.

Some of the earliest composers of sheet music were Maurice Shapiro, Leo Feist, Joseph Stern, and Charles K. Harris. Some of the first companies included Sherman, Clay and Company in San Francisco, and Lyon and Healy in CHICAGO. A group of businesses located on West 28th Street between Broadway and Sixth Avenue in NEW YORK CITY became known as Tin Pan Alley for its steady production of music that often made its way into vaudeville theatres and music halls across the country. As the industry developed, however, Tin Pan Alley came to denote the enterprise on a national scale. Major cities such as PHILADELPHIA, Chicago, Boston, and Cleveland eventually all developed their own publishing centers that distributed music throughout the country and internationally.

In 1892, Charles K. Harris's composition "After the Ball" became the first sheet music to sell more than a million copies. Toward the end of the 1890s, RAGTIME composer Scott Joplin accomplished the same feat with his "Maple Leaf Rag." Despite the invention of Emil Berliner's gramophone and record disc in 1897, more than 100 million copies of sheet music sold in the United States during the first decade of the 1900s.

The sheet music produced by African Americans from the minstrel show era of the late 1800s to the Harlem Renaissance constitutes an obscure area in the early history of African-American music and theater. In the John Hay Library at Brown University, Providence, Rhode Island, a sheet music collection of some 1,305 pieces documents the racial attitudes of the era and contribute to the study of the evolution of African-American musical theater. The collection denotes the existence of popular composers, vocalists, and songs from 1850 to 1920. The titles and lyrics of many of the songs illustrate the use of black dialect and racial slurs. The vivid sheet music covers display caricatures and photographs of black men and women that do not always represent the race in a dignified light.

The themes of the songs address the classic novel *Uncle Tom's Cabin,* Civil War music, African Americans in the military, the freed slave, the GREAT MIGRATION, and illicit love affairs. The composers include JAZZ music pioneer James Reese Europe, who directed the HARLEM HELLFIGHTERS band during WORLD WAR I, and WILL MARION COOK, composer and early mentor to DUKE ELLINGTON.

Within the sheet music for the song "What! Marry Dat Gal!" the first line of the lyric is: "Got a letter jes' dis mawnin,'" which represents an extreme use of black dialect. The song was sung by Fay Templeton in "Hurly Burly," a black minstrel show in the very late 1890s. The sheet music photograph for "Let Me Bring My Clothes Back Home" depicts a black man kneeling and pleading for remorse at the foot of a proper looking, bustled woman, but the first lines of the lyric are "A burly coon you know who had to take his clothes and go," which suggests an illicit relationship, a married relationship gone sour, and, most disturbingly, the period when black men referred to themselves, to the delight of white audiences, as "coons," a racial slur.

This era of minstrel music and the minstrel show sheet music published for consumer consumption ended in 1920, just one year before black musical revues such as *SHUFFLE ALONG* dominated Broadway. Sheet music itself further declined in popularity as the radio and record player became the dominant technological instruments for home use. It remained, however, a useful tool for learning music into the 21st century.

Further Reading

Floyd, Samuel. *Black Music in the Harlem Renaissance: A Collection of Essays.* Knoxville: University of Tennessee Press, 1994.

Spencer, Jon Michael. *The New Negroes and their Music: The Success of the Harlem Renaissance.* Knoxville: University of Tennessee Press, 1997.

— Aberjhani and Sandra L. West

Shuffle Along

Two song and dance comics teamed up with two leading musicians to create the 1921 hit musical *Shuffle Along,* the first Broadway musical written, performed, and produced by African Americans.

Flournoy Miller and Aubrey Lyles were already established stars of the Keith vaudeville performance circuit when they met EUBIE BLAKE and NOBLE SISSLE, celebrated musicians who performed both on the Keith circuit and for many private engagements. Miller and Lyles got their start while still students writing and performing shows at FISK UNIVERSITY in Nashville, Tennessee. Although they performed in blackface, in accordance with the era's custom, their material was considered so exceptional that they toured both black and white vaudeville. They achieved even greater success touring theaters in England. The comics also made a name for themselves as the stars of *Darkydom* in 1915 at the LAFAYETTE THEATRE.

Blake and Sissle formed a partnership as the Dixie Duo in 1915, separated during WORLD WAR I, and reunited after the war. The two met Miller and Lyles during a benefit for the NATIONAL ASSOCIATION FOR THE ADVANCEMENT OF COLORED PEOPLE (NAACP) in PHILADELPHIA in 1920. The idea of working together appealed to both teams because doing so, they decided, would give them creative control over their production and allow them to sidestep the stereotypical portrayals of blacks often presented at that time. It would also provide them the opportunity to pay themselves salaries they felt were more commensurate with the work they did and the crowds they hoped their names would attract. Such self-determination was very much in line with the philosophy of the *NEW NEGRO* beginning to influence young African Americans in the 1920s.

The new partners combined an older sketch by Miller and Lyles, called "The Mayor of Dixie," with some fresh routines and new music by Blake and Sissle to create *Shuffle Along*. An energetic presentation of RAGTIME music, singing, JAZZ dancing, and smalltown black politics, the show won the support of John Cort and his son Harry Cort. Though unable to give the performers full financial backing, the Corts did provide the use of their Cort's 63rd Street Theatre in NEW YORK CITY. Along with the theater came costumes from previous, mostly unsuccessful, shows. Rather than discard costumes they had not planned to use, they developed songs and skits based on the available materials. The team received additional backing from the primarily black Nikko Producing Company.

Shuffle Along hit the road for a short trial run at the Howard Theatre in WASHINGTON, D.C., and the Dunbar Theatre in Philadelphia. Upon its return to New York, the show was $18,000 in debt. When the curtains went up at the Cort Theater on May 23, 1921, a large number of the facility's 1,100 seats were empty. In the absence of white patrons, blacks were allowed seats on the first floor. Eventually, the success of the show would help to end segregated seating on Broadway altogether.

Word of *Shuffle Along*'s fun ragtime music and demanding jazz dance routines, innovative for Broadway at the time, began to spread. The show drew its comic element from Lyles as Sam Peck and Miller as Steve Jenkins, two politicians competing for the mayor's office in a place called Jimtown in Dixieville. Sissle added to the humor as a third mayoral candidate. Much of their dialogue lampooned the exaggeratedly flawed use of vocabulary that black audiences considered comical at the time but which most would find demeaning in the present. What caught the attention of critics who repeatedly made the trip to the Cort Theater was the vitality of the music and what they praised as the show's exuberant dancers. At a time when the ZIEGFELD FOLLIES showcased women as objects of untouchable beauty, *Shuffle Along* presented beautiful women in an explosion of creative dance energy that critics described as rejuvenating.

In addition, the show contained a number of songs that became immediate hits: "Honeysuckle Time"; "I'm Craving That Kind of Love"; "I'm Just Wild About Harry"; and "Love Will Find a Way." The last created a point of fearful controversy prior to its performance for its expression of deep romantic love between a black man and woman. Until then, romantic attraction between blacks was generally ridiculed on Broadway as clownish, savage, or nonexistent. Noble and Sissle expected a severe backlash once the audience heard the song but were happily surprised by calls for an encore. The song "I'm

The hit black musical *Shuffle Along* in 1921 achieved unprecedented success and started the trend for a wave of black musicals that played Broadway throughout the 1920s. *(P&P Collection, Moorland-Spingarn Research Center, Howard University)*

Just Wild About Harry" later became a rallying cry during Harry Truman's bid for the presidency and earned a place as an American standard. It also continued to earn substantial royalties for its composers.

If the songs in *Shuffle Along* were themselves considered exceptional, they were made even more so by an orchestra that included Blake himself on piano, "the dean of black music" WILLIAM GRANT STILL, choral director HALL JOHNSON, and musical arranger Will Vodery.

Shuffle Along played New York for a solid 14 months before going on a national tour to Detroit, Toledo, Philadelphia, Atlantic City, St. Louis, Des Moines, and other cities. With 504 Broadway performances, it became the first African-American musical to play more than 500 shows and the most successful since GEORGE WALKER and BERT WILLIAMS's *Bandanna Land* in 1908. It also prompted the practice of theatergoers returning repeatedly to see the same show and became such a celebration of black culture that many, including LANGSTON HUGHES, cited the show as the true beginning of the Harlem Renaissance.

In addition, it served as a springboard for the careers of several of the era's biggest black stars, most of them joining it as replacements following its New York debut. Before staking his claim to fame as the *EMPEROR JONES*, PAUL ROBESON was part of the cast as a member of the Four Harmony Kings quartet. JOSEPHINE BAKER first joined the company as a dresser, then won a role on the chorus line of the tour version of *Shuffle Along*. She remained with the show for two years before going on to Sissle and Blake's next production, *CHOCOLATE DANDIES*, then moving to PARIS to star in *La Revue Negre*. Performer ADELAIDE HALL and singer FLORENCE MILLS, who made her Broadway debut in the show, would each become stars in their own right. Mills in particular would achieve stardom in Europe as well as the United States.

While Sissle and Blake followed up their success with *Chocolate Dandies* in 1924, Miller and Lyles continued theirs with a production called *RUNNIN' WILD*. Sissle and Blake also produced *Blackbirds* in 1930. The triumph of *Shuffle Along* was extended in 1928 with *KEEP SHUFFLIN'*, in 1933 with *Shuffle Along of 1933,* in 1952 with *Revival,* and in 1978 with *Eubie!* The last starred Gregory Hines and Maurice Hines in a revue of works by Blake and Sissle.

The success of *Shuffle Along* did more than ensure productive careers for its creators and major stars. It also established a trend in black and white musicals and was followed by such shows as the *Plantation Revue, Strut Miss Lizzie,* and *LIZA*. The famous *Showboat* benefited from the trend as well.

Further Reading

Bolcom, William, and Robert Kimball. *Reminiscing with Noble Sissle and Eubie Blake.* Lanham, Md.: Cooper Square Publishing, 2000.

Floyd, Samuel A., ed. *Black Music in the Harlem Renaisssance: A Collection of Essays.* Knoxville: University of Tennessee Press, 1994.

Jasen, David A., and Gene Jones. *Spreadin' Rhythm Around, Black Popular Songwriters, 1880–1930.* New York: Schirmer Books, 1998.

— Aberjhani

Sigma Gamma Rho Sorority

Despite a resurgence of the Ku Klux Klan in Indiana, seven African-American teachers in that state formed the first black sorority founded at a white school, Sigma Gamma Rho at Butler University, on November 12, 1922.

As a stronghold of the Ku Klux Klan in the 1920s, nearly one out of every three adult white males in Indiana was a member of the white supremacist organization when Sigma Gamma Rho was established. The new sorority's founding members were Mary Lou A. Little, Dorothy H. Whiteside, Vivian W. Marbury, Nannie M. G. Johnson, Hattie Mae D. Redford, Bessie D. Martin, and Cubena McClure.

Already educators, the sorority members adopted for their motto, "Greater Progress, Greater Service," later reversing it to, "Greater Service, Greater Progress." Organization was a key priority for several years following the sorority's formation. Toward that end, the women developed an official publication called *Aurora,* set up a scholarship program, and held their first national convention in Indianapolis, Indiana, in 1925. They became incorporated in 1929.

Picking up where such publications as *OPPORTUNITY* magazine and the *CRISIS: A RECORD OF THE DARKER RACES* magazine had left off in the 1920s, Sigma Gamma Rho during the 1930s sponsored literary contests to encourage students in their academic pursuits. Turning their attention to career development, they oversaw a national vocational guidance program and worked with an employment aid bureau to help blacks secure work during the GREAT DEPRESSION. They also provided substantial support for the NATIONAL ASSOCIATION FOR THE ADVANCEMENT OF COLORED PEOPLE (NAACP) and the National Council of Black Women.

One of the more influential women of the era to join Sigma Gamma Rho was the actress HATTIE MCDANIEL, who won an Academy Award for best supporting actress for her role as Mammy in *Gone With the Wind.*

The organization expanded its activities during World War II to lend assistance to the International Red Cross and United Services Organization. In addition, the members focused heavily on issues affecting American youth. The Sigma Teen Town initiative was designed to help curb delinquency among adolescents and sought to provide locations where teens could gather to enjoy constructive activities. Because the Young Men's Christian Association employed JIM CROW policies that barred black youth from use of its facilities, the sorority participated in campaigns to integrate the association.

Sigma Gamma Rho took its dedication to integration a step further in the 1950s when it started Camp Achievement, for black and white youth, just outside Pittsburgh, Pennsylvania. Moreover, it strengthened its alliance with other black sororities and fraternities by joining the National Pan-Hellenic Council, composed of representatives from the first nine historically African-American Greek letter organizations.

Like its fellow black sororities and fraternities during the 1960s, Sigma Gamma Rho worked with the NAACP and other organizations to help obtain congressional legislation protecting the civil rights of African Americans and other minority groups.

The women also backed President Lyndon B. Johnson's antipoverty programs with policies and workshops of their own.

The sorority continued to implement its motto of "Greater Service, Greater Progress" in the 1980s with its new program, "Leadership Commitment: A Catalyst for Excellence in Service and Progress for all Mankind." A 14-point program designed to bring new vitality to the organization's efforts, it spelled out plans for tackling such issues as generating funds and proposals, maintaining tutorial programs, and addressing mental and social health concerns. Such concerns took on an international scope in the 1990s when the sorority supported two projects to help benefit communities in Africa. The first was Project Africa, to which they made a donation of $5,000. The second was Mwangmugimu Project, designed to foster a greater awareness of issues involving the African continent.

With 72,000 members in more than 400 chapters in the United States and the Caribbean, Sigma Gamma Rho is now headquartered in CHICAGO. It continues to operate a slate of programs reflecting a commitment to social service and to enjoy partnerships with such agencies as the United Negro Scholarship Fund, the Black Women's Agenda, and the Martin Luther King Center for Nonviolent Social Change.

Among the roster of women who have joined its ranks are author April Sinclair, congresswoman Corrine Brown, motivational speaker and author Emily D. Gunter, author Alice Childress, singer Vanessa Bell Armstrong, *Essence* magazine national sales director Jocelyn Brown, actress Brenda Pressley, artist and writer Chizu Shindo Suzuki, Dr. Alma Illery, actress Tonya Lee Williams, and media personality Mother Love.

Further Reading

Goggins, Lathardus, and Emily D. Gunter (preface). *Bringing the light into a New Day: Centered Rites of Passage.* Akron: Saint Rest Publications, 1998.

— Aberjhani

Musician Noble Sissle, shown here in 1951, cocreated the hit Broadway musical *Shuffle Along* and was one of the pioneers of jazz in Europe. *(Library of Congress, Prints & Photographs Division, Carl Van Vechten Collection [LC-USZ62-131764])*

Sissle, Noble (1889–1975) *musician*

Working in 1921 with EUBIE BLAKE, Aubrey Lyles, and Flournoy Miller, Noble Sissle cowrote and coproduced *SHUFFLE ALONG*, one of the most successful musical comedies in Broadway history and the show that for many marked the beginning of the intensified interest in African-American culture that grew into the Harlem Renaissance.

Sissle was born on July 10, 1889, in Indianapolis, Indiana. His father, the Methodist minister George A. Sissle, was a widower who already had three children when he married a teacher named Martha Angeline. With her, he would have three more, including Noble.

Sissle attributed his musical inclinations to his father's talent as an organist. In Central High School, from which he graduated in June 1911, he sang as a soloist with the glee club. He later sang with the Hann's Jubilee Singers and in various hotels and restaurants while trying to work his way through school at Butler University, Indiana. In 1915, he left school to work with the Royal Poinciana Sextet in Palm Beach, Florida. In that same year, he met Eubie Blake for the first time in Baltimore, Maryland. While others had come to know Sissle primarily as a singer, Blake recognized his name from lyrics he had composed and suggested they work together.

With the help of the composer and Society Orchestra leader James Reese Europe, Sissle and Blake began work as a pianist and vocalist duo performing for wealthy clients at weddings, debutante balls, and other high society affairs. WORLD WAR I caused the team to separate when both Sissle and Europe joined the army. In 1918, they were part of the first black combat unit to enter France, the 369th U.S. Infantry. Sissle's position as the regimental drum major, and Europe's as the leader of the infantry band, not only allowed them to continue developing as musicians but placed them among the first to introduce RAGTIME and JAZZ to the French. In *Reminiscing with Sissle and Blake,* by Robert Kimball and William Bolcom, Sissle recalled the joyous reaction of a French audience when their unit performed at an opera house during an observance of Abraham Lincoln's birthday.

With that performance, Sissle noted, Europe had "started ragtimitis in France!" It was followed by a number of other concerts presented throughout France as part of the band's mission to help maintain positive morale among American troops and their allies. In addition, Sissle wrote a song called "To Hell with Germany" that became an anthem and rallying cry among the French regiments.

Upon their return to the United States in 1919, Sissle and Europe embarked on a tour with the 369th U.S. Infantry HARLEM HELLFIGHTERS band. As they worked together, Europe spoke often of his hope to one day produce on Broadway an extravaganza of black music and dance. On May 9, 1919, he was killed by a fellow band member named Herbert Wright.

Following Europe's murder, Sissle and Blake reunited for a tour of the Keith vaudeville circuit. Performing as the Dixie Duo, the team cited the upper-class venues they had played under Europe's patronage and refused to do their act in blackface. In 1920, they met the comedy and dance team Lyles and Miller in PHILADELPHIA at a benefit for the NATIONAL ASSOCIATION FOR THE ADVANCEMENT OF COLORED PEOPLE (NAACP) at the Dunbar Hotel. During their first meeting, they discussed the possibility of working together. During their second, Lyles and Miller proposed that Sissle and Blake compose music for one of their skits, "The Mayor of Dixie," which, they pointed out, had potential for development into a full musical. Both teams agreed that a show owned and produced by them would allow innumerable advantages, including greater financial rewards and creative control over their work. For Sissle, it meant an opportunity to turn Europe's dream into a reality.

The result of the two entertainment teams' combined efforts was *Shuffle Along,* which had a short trial run in New Jersey and Pennsylvania before debuting at Cort's 63rd Street Theatre in New York. Described as a "musical mélange," the show presented an elevated style of ragtime music, jazz dancing, BLACK HUMOR, and black romance that Broadway had never seen before. The show started slowly, with a more than half empty theater, but it soon picked up speed until it became the hit of New York with sold-out shows during the week and a special late evening show Wednesdays for fellow entertainers. In addition to spawning a string of instant hit songs, the show helped pave the way to stardom for singer FLORENCE MILLS, actress Freddie Washington, performance artist PAUL ROBESON, and entertainer JOSEPHINE BAKER.

Like his creative partners, Sissle not only wrote and produced the show but performed in it as well, playing the part of politician Tom Sharper. *Shuffle Along* played 504 performances and became the most successful Broadway show ever produced by, written by, and starring African Americans. It established Sissle and Blake as major songwriters and allowed Lyles and Miller to follow up their success with a second show, *RUNNIN' WILD*, in 1923.

Sissle and Blake also extended their Broadway success in 1924 with *In Bamville,* the show that became *CHOCOLATE DANDIES* the same year. In 1925, the team toured Europe as "America's ambassadors of syncopation." In England, they wrote songs for Charles B. Cochran's *Revue of 1926.* When Blake returned to the United States, Sissle remained in Europe. From 1927 to 1930, he toured France and other countries with his own orchestra. His earlier tours in the military with James Reese Europe had not been forgotten and the foreign press celebrated his return.

He took his orchestra to the Park Central Hotel in New York in 1931 and from there performed live on CBS radio broadcasts. During the GREAT DEPRESSION, he again teamed up with Blake for a revival of *Shuffle Along.* He also worked with and served as a PATRON for dancer KATHERINE DUNHAM and singer LENA HORNE.

Sissle became one of the founders of the Negro Actors' Guild in 1937 and served as its first president. In 1948, he and Blake enjoyed renewed interest in and royalties from one of their hits from *Shuffle Along* when the song "I'm Just Wild About Harry" was adopted by Harry Truman's campaign team. When the "mayor of Harlem," the dancer BOJANGLES ROBINSON, died in 1949, Sissle was elected in 1950 to fill the honorary post.

Sissle's first marriage was to Harriet Toy in the 1920s. He married a second time in the late 1930s; he and his wife Ethel had two children: Cynthia and Noble, Jr. He remained close friends with his songwriting partner Blake until his death on December 17, 1975.

Further Reading

Gottschild, Brenda D. *Digging the Africanist Presence in American Performance: Dance and Other Contexts.* Westport, Conn.: Greenwood Publishing Group, 1998.

Jasen, David A., and George Jones. *Spreadin' Rhythm Around: Black Popular Songwriters, 1880–1930.* New York: Schirmer Books, 1998.

Peretti, Burton W. *The Creation of Jazz: Music, Race, and Culture in Urban America (Music in American Life).* Chicago: University of Illinois, 1992.

— Aberjhani

Small's Paradise

Along with BARRON'S EXCLUSIVE CLUB, the COTTON CLUB, and CONNIE'S INN, Small's Paradise during the 1920s became one of the top nightclubs in HARLEM to showcase black entertainment for primarily white audiences.

Operated by Ed Smalls, the club was located on SEVENTH AVENUE and 134th Street. It opened on October 22, 1925, and featured the music of the Charlie Johnson Band. Led by pianist Johnson, the band remained a fixture at Small's Paradise for a decade. At the same time that it helped draw customers to the club, the Charlie Johnson Band, like DUKE ELLINGTON and his orchestra at the Cotton Club later on, became a hit in its own right with radio broadcasts begun in 1929 and a series of recordings.

Jam sessions with the Charlie Johnson Band and individual musicians added to the club's appeal. It also had the distinction of boasting waiters who danced the Charleston and spun their serving trays while waiting on customers. Moreover, while many of the other clubs were closing between 3 A.M. and 5 A.M., Small's Paradise put on its floor show and breakfast dance at 6 A.M.

Like its competitors, Small's Paradise was more expensive than the average Harlem resident could afford on a regular basis during the 1920s. In addition to being a favorite hangout for downtown celebrities and NEW YORK CITY's elite, it was also frequented by such cultural figures as COUNTEE CULLEN, ALAIN LOCKE, and CARL VAN VECHTEN.

In addition to its regular band, Small's Paradise would feature national jazz and blues artists throughout the GREAT DEPRESSION and on into the 1940s, 1950s, and 1960s. Band leader and singer CAB CALLOWAY, STRIDE PIANO player Willie "the Lion" Smith, singer Monette Moore, and trumpeter and singer Oran "Hot Lips" Page were some of the musicians featured at the club during its first two decades. Superstars Fats Domino and Ray Charles helped the club maintain its popularity during the 1960s.

Further Reading

Jensen, Everette, and Norma Miller. *Swingin' at the Savoy: The Memoir of a Jazz Dancer.* Philadelphia: Temple University Press, 2001.

McDaniels, Pellom, and Marcus Allen. *My Own Harlem.* Kansas: Addax Publishing Group, 1998.

— Aberjhani

Smith, Ada See BRICKTOP.

Smith, Bessie (1894–1937) *singer*

Promoted as "The Empress of the Blues," Bessie Smith was a multitalented performer and the most successful blues singer of the 1920s.

Smith was born on April 15, 1894, one of seven children, to Laura Smith and William Smith, a Baptist minister. Both of her parents died by the time she was eight. She spent her childhood singing for change on the streets of Chattanooga, Tennessee.

In 1912, she joined Irvin C. Miller's touring tent show as a chorus girl. Around the same time, she met the legendary blues singer MA RAINEY, who became Smith's mentor. She toured the South with Rainey as part of Fat Chappelle's Rabbit Foot Minstrels Tent Show.

Throughout the 1910s, Smith worked extensively in theaters and clubs in Atlanta, Georgia. In 1914, at the Dixie Theater in Atlanta, she sang and danced as one half of Smith and Burton, with Buzzin' Burton as the second half, in *Park's Big Revue.* From 1918 to 1919, she starred in her own production of *Liberty Belles Revue* at the 91 Theater in Atlanta. In that show, she entertained as a male impersonator as well as by singing and dancing.

In 1920, Smith moved her base of operations to PHILADELPHIA. From there, she went on tours throughout black vaudeville and began to perform in SPEAKEASIES and basement clubs in NEW YORK CITY. She also performed often in Philadelphia at the Standard and Dunbar Theaters. She appeared with Sidney Bechet in the musical comedy *HOW COME?* in 1923.

Smith's initial attempts to join the ranks of such RACE RECORD artists as Mamie Smith (to whom she was not related) and ETHEL WATERS were met with rejection. However, she joined Columbia Records in 1923. Her success not only established her as a recording star but also helped save her new company from going bankrupt. Her first record was "Down Hearted Blues," written by ALBERTA HUNTER and Lovie Austin and backed with "Gulf Coast Blues." Recorded in February 1923, "Down Hearted Blues" sold more than a million copies before the year's end. Smith continued to record and sell profusely throughout the 1920s, following up on her successful beginning with such songs as "Jailhouse Blues" in 1923; "House Rent Blues" in 1924; "Empty Bed Blues" in 1928; and in 1931, "I Need a Little Sugar in My Bowl." She was often backed on her recordings by some of the best musicians of the era, including LOUIS ARMSTRONG, Bix Beiderbecke, and FLETCHER HENDERSON.

Like most black singers in the 1920s, Smith did not receive royalties for the recordings she did with Columbia from 1923 to 1931. She was paid instead for each individual recording. With the power of her record sales behind her, payment for her personal appearances increased from an average of $350 per week to $1,500 per week, placing her among the highest paid black entertainers in the country. She played repeated engagements at the LAFAYETTE THEATRE in HARLEM. Her self-produced musical comedy, *Mississippi Days,* played the Lafayette in 1928 and her *Yellow Girl Revue* had repeat performances at the LINCOLN THEATRE from 1927 to 1929. She became a principal draw on the THEATER OWNERS BOOKING AGENCY (TOBA) circuit during the latter part of the 1920s.

Despite the 1929 failure of Smith's Broadway debut in a show called *Pansy,* her fame continued to increase through the short film *St. Louis Blues,* which showcased Smith's celebrated ability to dramatize anguish through song. Moreover, she found both a supporter and a promoter in CARL VAN VECHTEN, who championed her work in articles for major magazines and entertained Smith in his home.

The GREAT DEPRESSION, the increasing influence of SWING music, and the rise of sound movies all served to decrease Bessie Smith's popularity in the 1930s. Citing financial problems brought on by the depression, the company she had helped save ended her recording contract in 1931. Her salary dropped to an average of $625 a week. She nevertheless remained a formidable and versatile performer who began to adapt to the new trends in entertainment. In 1934 and 1936, she headlined at the APOLLO THEATRE in Harlem. And in 1935, she filled in for BILLIE HOLIDAY on Broadway in the hit show *Stars Over Broadway.*

Smith was nearly as well known for her life offstage as she was for her artistry onstage. Openly bisexual and a heavy drinker, her relationships with men and women sometimes erupted into violent public confrontations. Her first marriage to Earl Love in 1920 lasted until his death shortly afterward.

Self-billed as "The Empress of the Blues," performer Bessie Smith, shown here in 1936, is routinely acknowledged as one of the greatest blues singers of the 20th century. *(Library of Congress, Prints & Photographs Division, Carl Van Vechten Collection [LC-USZ62-94955])*

In 1923, she married Jack Gee, who, reportedly, alternately assisted Smith in her career and abused her generosity. In 1926, the couple adopted the son of a friend and renamed him Jack Gee, Jr. Following complaints filed by Jack Gee, Sr., they surrendered custody of the child in 1930.

Smith was again rising to stardom while touring with the *Broadway Rastus Revue* when she was killed in a car accident on September 26, 1937. Buried in Mount Lawn Cemetery, Sharon Hill, Pennsylvania, her grave remained without a tombstone until white blues singer Janis Joplin and an affiliate of the NATIONAL ASSOCIATION FOR THE ADVANCEMENT OF COLORED PEOPLE (NAACP) purchased one in 1970.

Collections of Smith's recordings are still available. Singers and critics alike often cite her as the most accomplished and influential blues artist of the 20th century.

Further Reading

Davis, Angela Y. *Blues Legacies and Black Feminism: Gertrude "Ma" Rainey, Bessie Smith and Billie Holiday.* New York: Alfred A. Knopf, 1999.

Drake, Nick, and Jackie Kay. *Bessie Smith.* New York: Stewart, Tabori and Chang, Incorporated 1997.

— Aberjhani

Smith, Clara (1894–1935) *singer*

With her recording of such songs as "Awful Moaning Blues" in 1923, Clara Smith became known as "Queen of the Moaners," and among female BLUES singers of the era was second in prominence only to BESSIE SMITH (they were not related).

Clara Smith was born in Spartanburg, South Carolina, in 1894. She began singing and playing piano on the vaudeville circuit as an adolescent. At 24, she was a headliner for the THEATER OWNERS BOOKING AGENCY (TOBA), starring in shows in NEW ORLEANS and Nashville. While touring the South in 1920, she met JOSEPHINE BAKER, whom she befriended and helped start her performing career.

In 1923, Smith moved to NEW YORK CITY and, like Bessie Smith, obtained a contract recording for Columbia Records until 1932. She made approximately 60 records for the label, including "Every Woman Blues" and "So Long Jim," both in 1923; and "Mean Papa Turn in Your Key," along with "Texas Moaner Blues," in 1924. In 1925, she shared the spotlight with Bessie Smith on three comic duets: "My Man Blues," "Far Away Blues," and "I'm Going Back to My Used To Be." She recorded often to the accompaniment of STRIDE PIANO player James P. Johnson, cornetist LOUIS ARMSTRONG, pianist FLETCHER HENDERSON, and many others. Smith also reportedly recorded at least one song for Okeh Records under the name Violet Green.

Smith headlined at the LAFAYETTE THEATRE in 1925. In 1927, her self-produced *Black Bottom Revue* and *Clara Smith Revue,* both played at the LINCOLN THEATRE. She returned in 1928 to the Lafayette in the *Swanee Club Revue,* segments of which were also broadcast over radio. She played an extended engagement from 1928 to 1929 as part of the revue for female impersonator "Ophelia Snow from Baltimo'." From 1929 to 1931, she performed a series of engagements at the Alhambra Theatre, including the shows *Dream Girls Revue; Candied Sweets Revue; The Hello Revue; The Here We Are Revue; The Dusty Lane Revue;* and the *January Jubilee Revue.*

Smith further performed in 1931 in an all-black western musical called *Trouble on the Ranch* at the Standard Theatre in Philadelphia. In 1933, she starred in the *Harlem Madness Revue* at the Harlem Fifth Avenue Theatre.

Smith married Charles Wesley in 1926. She and Bessie Smith were friends as well as peers and known sometimes to engage in violent confrontations in public.

Smith died of heart disease on February 2, 1935, in Detroit, Michigan.

Further Reading

Davis, Angela Y. *Blues Legacies and Black Feminism: Gertrude "Ma" Rainey, Bessie Smith, and Billie Holiday.* New York: Alfred A. Knopf, 1999.

Friedwald, Will. *Jazz Singing: America's Great Voices from Bessie Smith to Bebop and Beyond.* New York: Da Capo Press, 1996.

Peterson, Bernard L., Jr., and James V. Hatch. *Profiles of African American Stage Performers and Theatre People, 1816–1960.* Westport, Conn.: Greenwood Publishing Group, 2000.

— Aberjhani

Smith, Mamie

See RACE RECORDS.

Smith, Marvin and Morgan

See ART AND THE HARLEM RENAISSANCE.

Souls of Black Folk, The

The Souls of Black Folk, by W. E. B. DU BOIS, represented the first major challenge by an African American to the leadership of BOOKER TALIFERRO WASHINGTON and marked the beginning of Du Bois's own rise to a position of national leadership.

Based in CHICAGO, A. C. McClurg and Company published *The Souls of Black Folk* in April 1903. At the time, Du Bois was professor of sociology and history at Atlanta University in Atlanta, Georgia. Although respected as the first African American to earn a doctorate at Harvard University, Du Bois was known principally as an author of essays in various national magazines and for his pioneering studies: *The Suppression of the African Slave Trade to the United States of America, 1638–1870,* published in 1896; and *The Philadelphia Negro: A Social Study,* in 1899.

The Souls of Black Folk began as essays and reviews published in such periodicals as *The Atlantic Monthly, The World's Work, The Dial, The New World,* and *The Annals of the American Academy of Political and Social Science.* The essay "Strivings of the Negro People" was published in the August 1897 edition of *Atlantic Monthly* and was edited to become "Of Our Spiritual Strivings," the first of 14 essays that comprise *The Souls of Black Folk.*

The Souls of Black Folk was published two years after Booker T. Washington confirmed his international reputation as the spokesperson of African America with the publication of *Up from Slavery* and the resulting affiliation with some of America's wealthiest philanthropists. Washington's book dramatized the same philosophy of faith in hard work, humble service with acceptance of one's position in society, and pursuit of economic well-being through industrial education that he espoused in his famous 1895 Atlanta Address. Emphasizing what he perceived as the uselessness of political agitation, civil rights, and liberal arts at the time, Washington in many ways helped sustain the virulent racism that he hoped mutual cooperation would dissolve. In each of the 14 essays in *The Souls of Black Folk,* Du Bois presented an alternative vision to Washington's. His goal, he wrote philosopher and educator William James, was "to reveal the other side of the world." Or, as he put in the book's foreword, to "show the strange meaning of being black here in the dawning of the Twentieth Century."

That meaning was defined largely in contrast to Washington's dominant philosophy. Du Bois's essays masterfully bridged the gap between the literature of Reconstruction following the Civil War and the literature of the *NEW NEGRO* in the 1920s. The first two essays in the book, "Of Our Spiritual Strivings" and "Of the Dawn of Freedom," examine the efforts of blacks and the U.S. government to adjust to a population of ill-prepared former slaves and disgruntled former slaveholders. "Of the Quest of the Golden Fleece" and "Of the Sons of Master and Man" presented Du Bois's very informed portraits of race relations in the South at that time. He provided a view at once personal and political when writing about the death of his infant son in "Of the Passing of the First Born." In "The Sorrow Songs," the book's final essay, Du Bois acknowledged the gift of music blacks had presented the United States through African-American spirituals. The essay itself was also an example of the kind of celebration of black culture that *The Souls of Black Folk* would encourage in the works of ALAIN LOCKE, CLAUDE MCKAY, LANGSTON HUGHES, JAMES WELDON JOHNSON, and many others.

The essay that generated the greatest amount of attention was Du Bois's critique of Washington, entitled "Of Mr. Booker T. Washington and Others." In it, DuBois charged that Washington's recommendation that blacks forgo political empowerment, civil rights, and higher education had resulted in their disfranchisement, the reduction of aid for black institutions offering liberal arts, and the legalization of JIM CROW racism. While this essay, described by James Weldon Johnson as a "temperate analysis" of Washington's leadership, represented the most direct appraisal of Washington, the entire book could be read as a commentary on and proposed correction of Washington's stated goals and principles. If Washington's proposals for educating blacks were erroneous, then better possibilities might be those offered in the essay "Of the Training of Black Men." And if Washington himself was not the best type of leader for African Americans overall, a better example might be found in the essay "Of Alexander Crummell." Eulogizing Crummell, the African missionary and founder of the AMERICAN NEGRO ACADEMY, Du Bois recalled that, "Instinctively I bowed before this man, as one bows before the prophets of the world."

Widely read by African Americans, *The Souls of Black Folk* "brought about a coalescence of the more radical elements and made them articulate, thereby creating a split of the race into two contending camps," wrote Johnson in *Black Manhattan.* Having captured the country's attention, *The Souls of Black Folk* went through two printings in less than a year and by 1908 had sold nearly 10,000 copies. Du Bois himself, two years after the book's publication, founded the NIAGARA MOVEMENT in formal protest against Washington's leadership and in 1910 helped found the NATIONAL ASSOCIATION FOR THE ADVANCEMENT OF COLORED PEOPLE (NAACP). As editor for the NAACP's *CRISIS: A RECORD OF THE DARKER RACES* magazine until 1934, Du Bois served for more than two decades as a principal interpreter and spokesperson regarding issues on race in the United States and throughout the world.

The Souls of Black Folk became and remains required reading in many high school and college classes in the United States. Educators, sociologist, writers, and many others celebrated the 100th anniversary of the book's publication in 2003.

Further Reading

Crouch, Stanley and Playthell Benjamin. *Reconsidering the Souls of Black Folk: Thought on the Groundbreaking Classic Work by W. E. B. Du Bois.* Philadelphia, Pa.: Running Press Publishers, 2002.

Fontenot, Chester, ed., Mary A., Morgan, and Sarah Gardner. *W. E. B. DuBois and Race: Essays Celebrating the Centennial Publication of* The Souls of Black Folk. Macon, Ga.: Mercer University Press, 2001.

Judy, Ronald A., ed. *Sociology Hesitant: Thinking with W. E. B. DuBois.* Durham, N.C.: Duke University Press, 2000.

Sundquist, Eric J., ed. *The Oxford W. E. B. DuBois Reader.* New York: Oxford University Press, 1996.

— Aberjhani

South Side Community Art Center

One of 110 community art centers initiated in urban areas by the WORKS PROGRESS ADMINISTRATION (WPA), the South Side Community Art Center of CHICAGO began with a neighborhood planning session held on October 25, 1938, in the South Side branch office of the NATIONAL URBAN LEAGUE (NUL).

The history of the center is a story of true unity among members of the South Side community. In order to receive WPA funds, in the case of Chicago, Illinois, a building had to be purchased. In addition, the black residents of Bronzeville had to raise the funds for it, pay utilities, and purchase art supplies for classes held in the building. As a fund-raiser, neighborhood committees and local artists held their first Artists' and Models' Ball on October 23, 1939, at the SAVOY BALLROOM. The ball generated enough profits to purchase the Seaverns house at 3831 South Michigan Avenue. A design team from Hin Bredendieck and Haus School of Design created classroom space, lecture halls, performance areas, and a main gallery. WPA furniture designers supplied furniture for the facility.

The South Side Community Art Center officially opened on December 15, 1940. A formal dedication occurred on May 7, 1941, which included the work of Harlem Renaissance artists CHARLES WILBERT WHITE, ARCHIBALD JOHN MOTLEY, JR., and Margaret Taylor Goss Burroughs. The name of the exhibit was *We Too Look at America.*

One year later, on May 7, 1941, first lady ELEANOR ROOSEVELT, wife of United States president FRANKLIN DELANO ROOSEVELT, creator of the WPA, formally dedicated the center in a Columbia Broadcasting national radio broadcast. *NEW*

A 1942 painting class of aspiring artists works at the South Side Community Art Center in Chicago. *(Library of Congress, Prints & Photographs Division [LC-USW3-000702-D])*

NEGRO anthology editor ALAIN LOCKE and star of stage and theater ETHEL WATERS both attended the dedication.

With the cutback in funding for WPA-sponsored activities during World War II, the center nearly closed. However, center administrator Rex Goreleigh, an African-American artist, managed to keep it open.

The 1960s were also lean years for the South Side Community Art Center. To produce funds, the administration developed an art auction and acquired a permanent collection with works by Harlem Renaissance artists Motley, White, Marion Perkins, and others.

With a dedicated team of volunteers and board members, at the start of the 21st century the South Side Community Art Center continued to serve Chicago's Bronzeville community just as it did in the 1930s and 1940s.

Further Reading

Miers, Charles, ed. *Harlem Renaissance: Art of Black America.* New York: Harry N. Abrams, 1994.

Tyler, Anna M. "Planting and Maintaining a Perennial Garden: Chicago's South Side Community Art Center." *The International Review of African American Art* 11, no. 4, 1994.

— Sandra L. West

speakeasies

Privately operated and illegal, clubs known as speakeasies were run in the back rooms and basements of homes in the United States throughout the 1900s in the North, Midwest, and West. When Prohibition made the manufacture, sale, and distribution of alcohol illegal in the United States from 1919 to 1933, speakeasies sold alcohol clandestinely and often continued do so in areas where alcohol remained prohibited or restrict by local law.

Speakeasies emerged in the 1910s and 1920s as an entertainment facility adjunct to the nightclub business that thrived with the influx of African Americans into northern and midwestern cities during the GREAT MIGRATION. Although operated in both black and white neighborhoods, the many speakeasies located in HARLEM allowed its patrons to enjoy the atmosphere of nightclub entertainment without the racism of JIM CROW segregation that became the norm for such celebrated facilities as the COTTON CLUB and CONNIE'S INN. They also paved the way for black men and women who had an instinct for such businesses but lacked formal training or credentials to pursue such work and to earn a fairly comfortable living doing so.

However, because the owners did operate the speakeasies without a proper license or permit of any kind, they were subject to occasional raids that would force owners to quickly hide any alcohol and dispense with any activity, such as singing with a microphone, that resembled professional entertainment. To avoid such raids, owners bribed those policemen who would accept their money, hired lookout guards to forewarn everyone of any trouble, and supplied regular customers with passwords to gain entry.

Speakeasies generally stayed open all night long and often provided a form of after-hours relaxation for professional entertainers leaving work at legitimate clubs. Moreover, singers such as BESSIE SMITH, CLARA SMITH, and others became well known on what might be called the NEW YORK CITY and PHILADELPHIA speakeasy circuit before rising to stardom in shows at the LAFAYETTE and LINCOLN THEATRES.

Further Reading

Bricktop, and James Haskins. *Bricktop.* New York: Welcome Rain Publishers, 2000.

Finn, Julio. *The Bluesman: The Musical Heritage of Black Men and Women in the Americas.* Northampton, Mass.: Interlink Publishing Group, 1998.

— Aberjhani

Spence, Eulalie (1894–1981) *playwright*

Rejecting the notion that African Americans should write for purposes of racial propaganda, Eulalie Spence wrote a series of prizewinning plays in which she portrayed everyday life in HARLEM in turn as comical, cynical, and dramatic.

Spence was born on June 11, 1894, in Nevis, British West Indies. The eldest of eight daughters, she and her family immigrated to NEW YORK CITY in 1902. Both her parents encouraged her to pursue reading and knowledge in general as a means to individual growth and satisfaction.

She attended Walleigh High School and later completed the Normal Department of the New York Training School for Teachers. In 1914, Spence began teaching English and coaching drama at Brooklyn's Eastern District High School, where she worked until retirement in 1958. She had already earned a name for herself as a playwright and drama critic when she returned to school to earn her bachelor's degree from New York University in 1937, and her master's from Columbia University, majoring in speech, in 1939.

The Harlem community took note of Spence as a playwright in 1924 when the National ETHIOPIAN ART PLAYERS staged her one-act comedy, *Being Forty,* at the LAFAYETTE THEATRE. In 1926, she met W. E. B. DU BOIS and for a time was an active member of the KRIGWA PLAYERS, a little-theater group designed largely to perform those plays which won prizes in the competitions sponsored by *CRISIS: A RECORD OF THE DARKER RACES* magazine. At the direction of Du Bois, the Krigwa Players performed works primarily "for blacks, by blacks, about blacks, and in the black community." Spence believed that such a formula might make good racial propaganda but not necessarily good theater. With that in mind, her very humorous human black characters ran the gamut from scheming thieves and prostitutes to disgruntled husbands and church women of questionable character. Her one-act comedy, *Foreign Mail,* was performed by the Krigwa Players and took second prize in the *Crisis* magazine competition in 1926.

Spence's *The Starter* was subtitled "A Comedy of Harlem Life," was performed by several amateur groups, and took third place at the 1927 contest awards for *OPPORTUNITY* magazine. At least four other plays by her were also produced in 1927. *The Hunch* was performed by the WASHINGTON, D.C., branch of the Krigwa Players and won second prize in the awards sponsored by *Opportunity* magazine. *The Fool's Errand* was presented by the Krigwa Players at their home theater and at the Frolic Theatre, where it competed in the National Little Theatre Tournament. The play won the $200 Samuel French Prize for the best unpublished work in the tournament. Spence's award was reportedly accepted by Du Bois and used to cover production expenses. The dispute that followed led to a breach between the two and eventually to the dissolution of the New York branch of the Krigwa Players.

The playwright later scored a double victory when she took third place in the *Crisis* magazine awards with two different works: the one-act melodrama *UNDERTOW*, and her unapologetic take on street hustlers in *Hot Stuff*.

Spence turned to a novel called *The Whipping* by Roy Flanagan for inspiration to write a three-act comedy and screenplay of the same name. Production of the play, scheduled by Century Play Company in Bridgeport, Connecticut, was canceled. Similarly, a movie version of the novel and play was optioned by Paramount Pictures but never produced. Nevertheless, Spence stated that the $5,000 she received for her work was the only money she ever made as a playwright.

Aside from writing her own work, Spence was also active as a producer and director. In the late 1920s, she helped establish the Dunbar Garden Players and directed the group in productions staged at the St. Marks Theatre on New York's Lower East Side. Among the works put on by the group were her own *Joint Owners of Spain,* and *Before Breakfast* by Eugene O'Neill.

Her insights on the developing black theater of her era were summed up in two essays published in *Opportunity*: "A Criticism of the Negro Drama as It Relates to the Negro Dramatist and Artist," and "Negro Art Players in Harlem."

Spence remained a single woman devoted to her craft. She died on March 7, 1981.

Further Reading

Gates, Henry Louis. *The Prize Plays and Other One-acts Published in Periodicals.* New York: Macmillan, 1996.

Hubbard, Dolan, ed. *Recovered Writers/Recovered Texts: Race, Class, and Gender in Black Women's Literature.* Knoxville: University of Tennessee Press, 1997.

Russell, Sandi. *Render Me My Song: African-American Women Writers from Slavery to the Present.* San Francisco: Harper Books, 2001.

— Aberjhani

Spencer, Annie Bethel Bannister (1882–1975)

poet

With works published in major anthologies of African-American literature during the 1920s and 1930s, Ann Spencer was one of the most renowned poets of her era.

Spencer was born Annie Bethel Bannister on February 6, 1882, in Henry County, West Virginia. She was the only child of Joel Cephus Bannister, a black Seminole who operated a saloon in Martinsville, Virginia, and Sarah Louise Scales Bannister, the daughter of a wealthy white Virginian and a mother who was a former slave.

At the age of five, Spencer moved with her mother to Bramwell, West Virginia. She lived there as a foster child with Mr. and Mrs. William Dixie while her mother worked as a cook. When she was 11, her father and mother arranged for her to attend the Virginia Seminary boarding school in Lynchburg, Virginia. She began writing poetry while a student at the school and graduated from it as class valedictorian in 1899. Following graduation, she taught school for two years in West Virginia.

In 1901, the poet married her former tutor, Edward Spencer. They settled in Lynchburg, where Edward Spencer became a postman. The couple had three children: Bethel Calloway, Alroy Sarah, and Chauncey Edward. The Spencers were able to employ servants to take care of their household, and in 1920 Ann Spencer's mother moved in to assist them as well. Edward Spencer constructed for his wife a garden cottage that they named Edankraal. Spencer spent much of her time writing in the cottage and tending to her garden, for which she became nearly as famous as for her poetry.

JAMES WELDON JOHNSON met Spencer while visiting Lynchburg in 1917 to help start a local chapter of the NATIONAL ASSOCIATION FOR THE ADVANCEMENT OF COLORED PEOPLE (NAACP). Learning that she was a poet, Johnson began to make other writers and editors aware of her work. One of them was W. E. B. DU BOIS, who published Spencer's poem "Before the Feast of Shushan" in *CRISIS: A RECORD OF THE DARKER RACES* magazine in 1920. Two years later, Johnson published five poems by Spencer in his *Book of American Negro Poetry,* describing her as "unique among Aframerican poets; she is the first woman to show so high a degree of maturity in what she wrote." Spencer's work was included with that of a number of writers who became friends after visiting with her while traveling through Lynchburg. Among them were Georgia Douglas Johnson, CLAUDE MCKAY, LANGSTON HUGHES, and Du Bois. Performing artists ROLAND HAYES and PAUL ROBESON also became her friends.

In 1923, Spencer became a librarian at Lynchburg's Jones Memorial Library. She advocated for the construction of a library for blacks and in 1924 became a librarian at the Dunbar High School branch. While Spencer rarely addressed issues of JIM CROW racism in her poetry, in her life she waged a personal boycott against the use of segregated public facilities and transportation, avoiding their use by walking back and forth to work.

Spencer did not promote herself as a poet but trusted those who admired her work to promote and publish it for her. Consequently, although she did not publish a volume of collected poems, various titles were included in such major anthologies as ALAIN LOCKE's *NEW NEGRO* in 1925; COUNTEE CULLEN's *Caroling Dusk* in 1927; and CHARLES SPURGEON JOHNSON's *Ebony and Topaz* in 1927. Spencer's elegy for James Weldon Johnson, "For Jim, Easter Eve," was published in Langston Hughes and ARNA BONTEMP's 1949 anthology, *The Poetry of the Negro, 1746–1949.* Her poetry also appeared in *Crisis*, *OPPORTUNITY*, *SURVEY GRAPHIC*, *Lyric*, and *Palms* magazines.

In 1945, Spencer retired from the Dunbar Library after 20 years of service. After retirement, her garden remained a central point of focus in her life until the death of her husband in 1964. The loss depressed her deeply and her garden fell to ruin as a result. Spencer developed cancer in her latter years and died on July 27, 1975.

Following Spencer's death, her garden was restored. Her home was named a Virginia Historic Landmark and placed on the National Registry of Historic Places. Her work continues to win recognition and in 1990 was included in British scholar Margaret Busby's study of writings by women of African descent, *Daughters of Africa.*

Further Reading

Randolph, Ruth Elizabeth, and Lorrane Elena Roses. *Harlem's Glory: Black Women Writing, 1900–1950.* Cambridge: Harvard University Press, 1996.

———. *Harlem Renaissance and Beyond: Literary Biographies of 100 Black Women Writers 1900–1945.* Cambridge: Harvard University Press, 1990.

— Aberjhani

Spingarn Medal

As chairman of the NATIONAL ASSOCIATION FOR THE ADVANCEMENT OF COLORED PEOPLE (NAACP), Joel E. Spingarn established the Spingarn Award in 1915 to pay tribute each year to "an American citizen, man or woman, of African descent" for outstanding achievements. The award served the dual purpose of strengthening the NAACP's image as an organization committed to the struggle for racial equality and of affirming the value of black people's lives during a period when such lives were often destroyed by LYNCHING for sport.

The first recipient of the award was biologist ERNEST EVERETT JUST in 1915, followed by U.S. Army Major Charles Young in 1916, and the composer and arranger HARRY THACKER BURLEIGH in 1917. Unlike the abundance of literary awards that the *CRISIS: A RECORD OF THE DARKER RACES* and *OPPORTUNITY* magazines would offer various writers in the 1920s, the Spingarn Award continued to recognize the achievements of African Americans in many different fields. National Association of Colored Women president Mary T. Talbert was the first woman to win the award, in 1922. Scientist George Washington Carver was acknowledged in 1923 and concert tenor ROLAND HAYES in 1924.

Although the award was established by Joel E. Spingarn, in many ways it could have been named for him, his wife Amy, and his brother Arthur. Each contributed in a variety of ways to battle the racist trends of the times and exemplified the more positive aspects of INTERRACIAL INTERACTION during the Harlem Renaissance. Arthur Spingarn was a lawyer who often put his legal expertise at the disposal of the NAACP. Amy Spingarn hosted SALONS and parties where racially mixed groups met to enjoy each other's company and share ideas. She was also the sponsor of *Crisis* magazine's Spingarn Literary Award and a PATRON on behalf of LANGSTON HUGHES.

Joel Spingarn himself was a former professor of comparative literature at Columbia University who left the school in protest of what he considered another professor's improper dismissal. As his friend W. E. B. DU BOIS (winner of the 1920 medal) would later put it, the Jewish Spingarn left Columbia and joined the NAACP "ready for a new fight, a new thrill, and new allegiances." He took on the NAACP chairmanship in 1913. In 1916, he invited some 50 African-American leaders from throughout the United States to participate for three days in what became known as the Amenia Conference and discuss racial strategy at his home, Troutbeck, in Dutchess County, New York. During WORLD WAR I, he was commissioned as a major in the military intelligence branch and helped spearhead the drive for the creation of a black officers' training camp in Iowa.

As passionate as he was about social justice, Spingarn was equally so when it came to literature. He was a leading literary critic whose works included *Creative Criticism, A History of Literary Criticism in the Renaissance,* and several volumes of his own poetry. Moreover, he was instrumental in the creation of two publishing houses that championed the works of black writers during the 1920s: Alfred A. Knopf and Harcourt, Brace

The Spingarn Medal, presented annually by the National Association for the Advancement of Colored People (NAACP), was named after Joel Spingarn, seen here in military uniform ca. 1910. *(Library of Congress, Prints & Photographs Division [LC-USZ62-84506])*

& Company. For Knopf, he had been a teacher and later advised him on the aesthetics of book design. He was one of the actual founders of Harcourt, Brace & Company. As such, he helped procure the works of Du Bois, JAMES WELDON JOHNSON, and STERLING ALLEN BROWN. He was also one of the first to appreciate the genius of CLAUDE MCKAY and helped obtain both magazine and book publishers for his work.

From its installation in 1915, the Spingarn Medal grew into one of the most important awards in the United States and has been presented every year with the exception of 1938. Biographer and poet Maya Angelou won the award in 1994. In 1998, it was presented to civil rights activist Myrlie Evers-Williams and in 1999 to the chairman and CEO of *Black Enterprise Magazine,* Earl Graves, Sr. Media mogul Oprah Winfrey won the award in 2000, former NATIONAL URBAN LEAGUE president Vernon Jordan in 2001, and Congressman John Lewis in 2002.

Further Reading

Hutchinson, George. *The Harlem Renaissance in Black and White.* Cambridge, Mass.: Belknap Press of Harvard University Press, 1995.

Lewis, David Levering. *W. E. B. Du Bois: Biography of a Race, 1868–1919.* New York: Henry Holt and Company, 1993.

— Aberjhani

Henry Armstrong, shown here in 1937, won several major titles to become one of the early great black champions of boxing in the United States. *(Library of Congress, Prints & Photographs Division, Carl Van Vechten Collection [LC-USZ62-114433])*

sports and the Harlem Renaissance

Professional athletics attained such a high degree of popularity during the 1920s, 1930s, and 1940s that the era was called "the golden age of sports." African Americans excelled in boxing, basketball, baseball, football, tennis, track, and golf; and, in the face of racist JIM CROW laws, many initiated their own athletic associations.

Boxing

Some of the greatest fighters in boxing history became champions during the Harlem Renaissance. Four leaders in the field were Henry Armstrong, Baye Phal, JOE LOUIS, and JACK JOHNSON.

Henry Armstrong simultaneously held three diverse boxing titles during the 1930s. He was born on December 12, 1912, in St. Louis, Missouri. Fighting under the publicity name of Melody Jackson in 1929, Armstrong was knocked out during his professional boxing debut in Pittsburgh, Pennsylvania. He won his first fight later that same year and, in 1937, defeated Petey Sarron to garner the featherweight title. In 1938, Armstrong won two decisions: one over Barney Ross for a welterweight championship and another over Lou Ambers for the lightweight championship. Simultaneously, Armstrong held three different boxing titles during the 1930s. Henry Armstrong was inducted into the Black Athletes Hall of Fame in 1975. He died on October 22, 1988.

Battling Siki was born Baye Phal on September 16, 1897, in San Louis de Senegal, French West Africa. In 1913, he knocked out Jules Perroud, fought furiously for several years, and earned the nickname Battling Siki. Following WORLD WAR I, Siki won battles against Giuseppe Spalla, Hans Brietenstrattre, and Harry Reeve in 1921. On September 24, 1922, he became the first black athlete to hold the light heavyweight title when he beat George Carpentier. Undisciplined and incorrigible, Siki involved himself in fist fights from Ireland to NEW YORK CITY. He won 10 fights out of 21, but frequently lost control of himself outside of the ring. The *Washington Post* of August 13, 1925, called for his deportation. On December 15, 1925, he was shot in the back in New York. Fans packed Harlem's ABYSSINIAN BAPTIST CHURCH for his funeral, where he was eulogized by Reverend ADAM CLAYTON POWELL, SR.

During this period, when boxing icons Joe Louis and Jack Johnson physically triumphed over white boxers in the ring, black people celebrated as if the boxers had knocked out Jim Crow racism on behalf of them all. But, when they were not victorious and white people maintained that they were "the supreme white race," some black people openly wept as if American slavery still existed.

Sports and Entertainment

During the golden age of sports, African-American athletic clubs often adopted names that were synonymous with the era's gaiety. The RENAISSANCE CASINO AND BALLROOM was home court to the best basketball lineup of the period: The Harlem Renaissance basketball team, dubbed the Rens. The internationally renowned HARLEM GLOBETROTTERS basketball team was originally known as the Savoy Big Five, in tribute to Harlem's glittery SAVOY BALLROOM dance hall.

Not only did ball clubs adopt names germane to the jubilant and creative era, but several sports figures spent time in the entertainment field as well. Jockey and boxer CANADA LEE began as a violinist before stunning the nation with his stage and silver screen performances. Track star Thomas Tolan performed on the vaudeville stage with tap dancer BOJANGLES ROBINSON. And boxer Johnson owned a nightspot that became the historic COTTON CLUB.

Racism

Racism affected every aspect of the golden age of sports. Sprinter JESSE OWENS was publicly snubbed by Adolf Hitler at the 1936 Olympic Games in Berlin when he defeated German athletes. Moreover, although he was a celebrity with more gold medals than any one person had ever before earned, when Owens returned to the United States from the Olympics he could find no job better than that of a common janitor.

Satchel Paige was the undisputed pitching star of baseball but by the time baseball's color line was broken and he was allowed to work in the major leagues, he was no longer in his prime as an athlete. Boxer Jack Johnson suffered a similar fate after being hunted and jailed for his marriage to a white woman. Forced to leave the country, he lived in exile until his boxing skills, and his bank account, diminished.

Professional football did not have the same formal racial discrimination laws as baseball, tennis, and golf. Nevertheless, football players were generally recruited from white college teams and since black males generally did not play for white colleges at the time, black professional football players were few. Black males did not become a notable presence on athletic college teams until the GI Bill of World War II and protests against racism helped increase their numbers in academia. Among the early black professional football players were Henry McDonald, Fritz Pollard, and PAUL ROBESON.

Henry McDonald (1911–20) was the first black athlete to play professional football. He played with the Oxford Pros, Rochester Jeffersons, All-Lancasters, and the All-Buffalos, teams based in New York State. McDonald also played with the Pittsburgh Colored All-Stars, the Lancaster Malleables, and the New York Colored Giants.

Frederick Douglas "Fritz" Pollard was such a standout athlete at Lane Tech in Chicago that the wealthy John D. Rockefeller family paid his tuition at Brown University in Rhode Island, where he could play football. When Brown played Rutgers University, Pollard played against Paul Robeson and they became friends. Pollard graduated from Brown in 1917, went to dental school, and coached the football team at black Lincoln University in Chester, Pennsylvania, with Robeson's help. From 1919 to 1920, both Pollard and Robeson played professional football in Akron, Ohio: Robeson was an end and Pollard was a halfback. They were undefeated during the 1920s.

Robeson excelled in several sports. At Somerville High School in New Jersey he played on the football, baseball, and basketball teams (1913). At six feet three inches tall and over 200 pounds, Robeson earned athletic letters of excellence from Rutgers University in football, baseball, track, and basketball. He played linebacker and end for the college football team. Still, his teammates bombarded him with racial slurs and, on his first day of scrimmage, jumped him and beat him until he had a broken nose, dislocated shoulder, and split and swollen eyes. Robeson fought back by excelling in his performance until he earned his teammates' respect. He made the first-team varsity, won All-American team honors in 1917 and 1918, and led the Rutgers team to a record of 20 wins and 4 losses. After graduation, Robeson played with the Hammond Pros in 1920. He joined Akron in 1921 with Pollard, and went with the Milwaukee Badgers in 1922.

Racism hindered the quality of life for black athletes during the golden age of sports. Jim Crow laws colored the field of athletic competition by limiting whom black players could compete against and where they could perform. For that reason, black athletes took matters into their own hands and formed black leagues, including The NATIONAL NEGRO BASEBALL LEAGUE; the AMERICAN TENNIS ASSOCIATION; and the UNITED GOLFERS ASSOCIATION. These clubs had their own tournaments and series and scores of devoted fans. They provided an economic base for black athletes away from the control of white businessmen. But they were also limited by inadequate facilities. When the color line was removed from professional athletics, these independent teams dissipated.

Further Reading

Bloom, John, and Michael Nevin Willard, eds. *Sports Matters: Race, Recreation, and Culture.* New York: New York University Press, 2002.

Robeson, Susan, *The Whole World in His Hands: A Pictorial Biography of Paul Robeson.* New York: Citadel Press, 1981.

Wilker, Joshua D. *The Harlem Globetrotters.* Bromall, Penn.: Chelsea House, 1997.

— Sandra L. West

Still, William Grant (1895–1978) *composer*

Believing strongly that the task of the *NEW NEGRO* was to "vindicate African Americans" through superior cultural achievements, music composer William Grant Still earned the honorary title "dean of Negro composers" with his many accomplishments.

Grant was born on May 11, 1895, in Woodville, Mississippi, one of four children born to Carrie Lena Fambro and William Grant Still, Sr. He grew up in Little Rock, Arkansas, where he played the violin in high school. He enrolled at Wilberforce University in Ohio in 1911 with plans to follow his mother's advice and become a doctor. However, his interests in music led him to join the college band as its conductor, and he taught himself to play a variety of musical instruments, including the saxophone, string bass, viola, clarinet, cello, and oboe. Still left Wilberforce in 1914 and in 1915 married his first wife, Grace Bundy.

With his focus on establishing a career in serious music, Still enrolled at Ohio's Oberlin College in 1917. The following year he joined the U.S. Navy to serve a year during WORLD WAR I. Though Still did not graduate from either Wilberforce or Oberlin, the former would award him a master of music degree in 1936 and the latter an honorary doctorate in 1947. Still would receive seven more honorary doctorates as well from other colleges and universities.

Still first worked with W. C. HANDY, often referred to as "the father of the BLUES," in 1916 when he did the arrangements for Handy's classic songs "Beale Street Blues" and "St. Louis Blues." In 1919, he again worked with Handy in NEW YORK CITY where Handy established a publishing company with his partner, Harry Pace. In addition to constructing arrangements for Handy, Still also worked with SOPHIE TUCKER, Paul Whiteman, Artie Shaw, and many others. With the dissolution of the Handy and Pace partnership, Still continued to work as an arranger and became musical director for the PACE PHONOGRAPHIC RECORD CORPORATION's Black Swan label, one of the few RACE RECORD companies owned by an African American. He also contributed to the success of EUBIE BLAKE and NOBLE SISSLE's groundbreaking musical comedy *SHUFFLE ALONG*, by playing the oboe in the orchestra.

Throughout the 1920s, Still pursued his goals as a composer with such works as *Darker America* in 1924 and *From the Journal of a Wanderer* in 1925. From the beginning, he explored ways of incorporating African-American music into European classical traditions. Although he had been exposed to the avant-garde school and adopted neoromanticism as his own style, he allowed heavy folk influences from the Native American, Hispanic, and black cultures. In his 1926 three-movement suite, *Levee Land*, he blended elements of JAZZ with traditional European music. *BLACKBIRDS* and *Shuffle Along* star FLORENCE MILLS was his featured soloist for the piece.

Still agreed with ALAIN LOCKE, editor of the *New Negro* and mentor to members of its movement, that the creation of superior art required a mastery of four elements: form, technique, mood, and spirit. Locke perceived enough mastery in Still's work to convince him to turn an extended version of RICHARD BRUCE NUGENT's prose poem *Sahdji* into a ballet. Performed by KATHERINE DUNHAM and her dance troupe, it debuted on May 22, 1931, at the Eastman School of Music.

On October 30, 1930, Still wrote in his diary that he had begun working on his *Afro-American Symphony* and was praying for strength and faith to meet the task at hand. One year later, October 29, 1931, *Afro-American Symphony* became the first symphony by an African American performed by a major symphonic orchestra. Debuting under the direction of Howard Hanson for the Rochester Philharmonic Symphony, it was also performed by the New York Philharmonic at Carnegie Hall. The symphony went on to tour Europe and Australia. In 2001, it remains one of the most frequently performed works by a composer in the United States. Composed of four movements, the *Afro-American Symphony* includes a strong and definitive blues element, so much so that Still has been credited with being the first composer to blend classical music with the blues and jazz.

Still accomplished two more African-American firsts in 1936 when he conducted a major American orchestra, the Los Angeles Philharmonic, and conducted an all-white radio orchestra for radio station WOR's popular program *Deep River*. His increasing achievements were recognized with Guggenheim Fellowships in 1934 and 1938 and Rosenwald Fellowships in 1939 and 1940.

Forming a successful creative partnership with Still, LANGSTON HUGHES turned his play *Troubled Island* into a libretto for an opera by the same name. It became both the first opera composed by two major African-American artists and the first by African Americans performed by a major opera company when the New York City Opera debuted the work on March 31, 1949.

Librettos for other operas by Still, including the 1978 nationally televised *A Bayou Legend*, were written by his second

Known as the "dean of Negro composers," William Grant Still, shown here in 1949, was dedicated to the philosophy of the New Negro and accomplished a number of African-American "firsts" throughout his long career in music. *(Library of Congress, Prints & Photographs Division, Carl Van Vechten Collection [LC-USZ62-103930])*

wife, Verna Arvey. Married in 1938, Still and Arvey had two children, Judith and Duncan.

Throughout his career Still composed more than 150 chamber pieces, symphonic works, operas, ballets, and orchestral works for voice. He died on December 3, 1978, in Los Angeles. Upon the centennial of Still's birth in 1995, universities, colleges, community organizations, and musicians recognized his many contributions with performances and celebrations of his music throughout the year. Still's collected papers have been held at the Duke University Special Collections Library since 1992.

Further Reading

Smith, Catherine Parsons. *William Grant Still: A Study in Contradictions.* Berkeley: University of California Press, 1999.

Still, William G., Celeste A. Headlee, and Lisa M. Headlee-Huffman, ed. *William Grant Still and the Fusion of Cultures in American Music.* Antascadero, Calif.: Master-Player Library, 1995.

— Aberjhani

Stormy Weather

Starting out as a hit song in 1933, *Stormy Weather* became a hit movie starring LENA HORNE and BOJANGLES ROBINSON in 1943.

The song "Stormy Weather," written by Harold Arlen and Ted Koehler, was one of the featured titles performed by ETHEL WATERS and DUKE ELLINGTON at the COTTON CLUB in HARLEM. Ellington first recorded the tune in 1933 and backed it with the song that became his first big popular hit, "Sophisticated Lady." He recorded it again in 1940 with Ivie Anderson supplying the vocals.

In 1943, William LeBaron produced and Andrew Stone directed the movie *Stormy Weather* as a musical portrait of the life of Bill Robinson. In the course of presenting a musical interpretation of Robinson's life, the film also provided a survey of black entertainment from the late 1910s to the early 1940s. Aside from Robinson and Horne, the cast included FATS WALLER; KATHERINE DUNHAM and her famous dance troupe; Flournoy Miller, who had achieved fame in the Broadway hit *SHUFFLE ALONG*; CAB CALLOWAY of the Cotton Club; renowned vocalist Ada Brown; and the famed dancing team the NICHOLAS BROTHERS. Released during World War II, the film became a popular one for its light humor and lively music. It also made Horne something of a sex symbol for the times.

Following his success with the *Afro-American Symphony* and other concert works, composer WILLIAM GRANT STILL was hired as the musical director for *Stormy Weather*. However, he resigned after a conflict over the film's musical content.

Although Lena Horne was chosen to sing the title song, she at first was reluctant to do so because she considered it a BLUES number, and her own style was closer to popular music and light JAZZ. To help her achieve the proper tone and nuances for the song, Cab Calloway served as her coach. After she sang it in the movie, "Stormy Weather" became Horne's trademark song.

Further Reading

Bogle, Donald. *Toms, Coons, Mulattoes, Mammies, and Bucks: An Interpretive History of Blacks in American Films, Third Edition.* New York: Continuum Publishing Company, 1997.

Gourse, Leslie. *Swingers and Crooners: The Art of Jazz Singing.* Danburg, Conn.: Franklin Watts, 1997.

— Aberjhani

stride piano

Black pianists in HARLEM during the 1920s placed their own definitive stamp on RAGTIME music with the performance style known as stride piano.

Stride piano used ragtime's melodic bass line to counter syncopation played alternately with the right and left hands. It added even greater strength to ragtime's already very rhythmic qualities. It also enhanced the performance aspects of the music by demanding greater dexterity in both hands. The result was a sound that gave the impression that an orchestra was performing a composition rather than a single individual. Moreover, it allowed pianists from Harlem to stand out when performing on tour.

Among those credited with founding stride is pianist Luckey Roberts (1890–1968). Roberts's early compositions incorporated such elements of black church music as the traditional shout, and by use of the same helped steer ragtime's development away from Scott Joplin's classical form and toward stride. By the early 1920s, stride was the piano music and style of choice performed in Harlem clubs, at RENT PARTIES, high society affairs, and on Broadway. While many performed, or attempted to perform stride, its acknowledged leading practitioners were Harlem's Willie "The Lion" Smith, FATS WALLER, EUBIE BLAKE, and the man who developed the form into a definitive style: James Price Johnson.

Johnson was born on February 1, 1891, in Brunswick, New Jersey, and died on November 17, 1955, in Jamaica, New York. He received instructions on basic piano from his mother and later studied classical piano for four years. After moving with his family to New York in 1908, Johnson's professional music career started a few years later with jobs in dance halls, at Coney Island, in Harlem clubs, and Atlantic City, New Jersey. He began placing his music on piano rolls for player pianos around 1917 and later taught Waller to do the same thing to make additional money, rather than depending solely on performance jobs. Johnson was touring nationally by 1919 and became one of New York's most renowned pianists. In the early 1920s, he began recording what are now considered classic performances of stride piano, recording the "Harlem Strut" on the PACE PHONOGRAPHIC RECORD CORPORATION's Black Swan Record label in 1921 and "Carolina Shout" in 1925. The latter, as well as many others, demonstrated Johnson's acknowledgment of the influence of black southern church music on his style. Working with LANGSTON HUGHES in 1940, Johnson composed music for the opera *De Organizer*. The work was lost for more than 60 years when it was rediscovered by music professor James Dapogny and revived for performance in 2002.

The stride pianists influenced most of the major musicians of their era, including COUNT BASIE and DUKE ELLINGTON, who along with Waller learned Johnson's "Carolina Shout" note by note to help them learn the form. Pianists such as Art Tatum and Earl Hines took stride a step further with more extensive variations of the melody line controlled by the right hand. The sheer virtuosity of stride and its demanding mastery of repeating syncopations and innovative modulations was one of the key factors in the development of JAZZ.

Today, stride piano is touted at concerts and festivals as an international musical art form. Some of its more acclaimed performers are Miles Black from Canada; Bern Lhotzky of Bavaria; François Rilhac from France; and Judy Carmichael of the United States. The founders of the music are frequently acknowledged.

Further Reading

Fell, John L., and Terkild Vinding. *Stride! Fats, Jimmy, Lion, Lamb, and All the Other Ticklers.* Lanham, Maryland: Scarecrow Press, 1999.

Scivales, Riccardo. *The Soul of Blues, Stride and Swing Piano.* New York: Warner Brothers Publications, 2001.

— Aberjhani

Striver's Row

The landmark HARLEM neighborhood called Striver's Row, named for the goal-oriented ethic of its thousands of working-class residents, was inhabited by some of the most renowned names of the Harlem Renaissance, including "father of the BLUES" W. C. HANDY, and was immortalized in a JAZZ tune by saxophonist Sonny Rollins.

Located at 202–252 West 138th Street and 203–269 West 139th Street in Harlem, near what was then SEVENTH AVENUE and Eighth Avenue, Striver's Row was built by David H. King in 1892. King's philosophy was to offer beautiful and convenient homes to decent people of modest means. It was constructed prior to the GREAT MIGRATION of African Americans that would swell NEW YORK CITY's black population but later would serve as a prime residential area for many of them. Stylistically, Striver's Row formed a conglomeration of 146 attached Victorian row houses and three freestanding apartment buildings. The buildings, named King Model Houses after the contractor, were designed with service alleys, modern plumbing, intricate iron railings, basements, and oak doors.

Striver's Row was strikingly beautiful, and management and residents bound themselves to certain rules and regulations

The Will Marion Cook House at 221 W. 138th Street, pictured here in the right foreground, is named after one of the earliest successful black composers. *(Library of Congress, Prints & Photographs Division [HABS, NY, 31-NEYO, 111A-2])*

in their zeal to maintain the integrity of the development. Some of the rules included do not lean out of the windows and do not undress while the window shades are up.

Several of the houses within the complex were inhabited by well-known figures such as architect Vertner Tandy, composer W. C. Handy, and bandleader FLETCHER HENDERSON. Tandy (1885–1949) lived at 221 West 139th Street from 1919, when the homes were not selling well to white residents and were opened up to African-American buyers. Tandy was a likely candidate for Striver's Row. Educated at Tuskegee Institute and Cornell University School of Architecture (1908), he was the first African-American architect licensed in New York State. Tandy built MADAME C. J. WALKER's Villa Lewaro mansion in Irvington, New York, and SAINT PHILIP'S EPISCOPAL CHURCH in Harlem. W. C. Handy owned 232 West 139th Street from 1919 to 1922, and orchestra leader Henderson purchased 228 West 139th Street in 1924.

WILL MARION COOK also lived on Striver's Row, at 221 West 138th Street. Cook was a musical composer who organized the Clef Club's Syncopated Orchestra. He lived in one of the Victorian town houses from 1918 to 1944. His four-story home had a cement post on one gate that warned, "Walk Your Horses," from an era when cars and trolleys were not the only mode of transportation. The Will Marion Cook House has been used as professional medical offices since 1976.

With its architecture and famous and fastidious residents, the well-kept, elegant neighborhood was designated a historic district by the New York Landmarks Commission and listed on the National Register of Historic Places. It earned another honor when jazz saxophonist Sonny Rollins composed "Striver's Row" and performed the piece at the Village Vanguard jazz club in New York's trendy Greenwich Village area on November 3, 1957.

The very notion of families working hard and striving to do better economically and socially was all part of the fabled American dream, and a neighborhood similar to Striver's Row, called Strivers' Section, existed in WASHINGTON, D.C. Washington experienced an intellectual renaissance two decades prior to the Harlem Renaissance. From the 1870s, industrious African Americans who rose to leadership positions in business, education, and other areas lived in row houses and apartment houses in the historic district roughly bounded by New Hampshire and Florida Avenues and 17th and 18th Streets along T, U, and Willard Streets. One of the most prominent inhabitants of Striver's Section was the black abolitionist Frederick Douglass, who built the still standing edifice at 2000–2008 17th Street in 1875, and for whom Eighth Avenue in Harlem was later named.

Further Reading

Cantor, George. *Historic Landmarks of Black America.* Detroit, Mich.: Gale Research, 1991.

Curtis, Nancy C. *Black Heritage Series: An African-American Odyssey and Finder's Guide.* Chicago and London: American Library Association, 1996.

Dolkart, Andrew S., and Gretchen S. Sorin. *Touring Historic Harlem: Four Walks in Northern Manhattan.* New York: New York Landmarks Conservancy, 1997.

— Sandra L. West

Sublett, John William

See BUBBLES, JOHN.

Sugar Hill

Sugar Hill, originally part of the Washington Heights neighborhood located uptown from HARLEM proper, was the residential section north of 145th Street to 155th Street, between Amsterdam Avenue to the west and Edgecombe Avenue to the east.

In the lingo of the Harlem Renaissance period, "sugar" referred to money, the ticket to high-style living. Thus, the Sugar Hill neighborhood became the name of the uptown area where prosperous African Americans resided. Such blacks settled in the area in the 1920s and 1930s to enjoy a view of the Valley, which was central Harlem. Some purchased town houses, while others rented apartments in one of the 12-story and 14-story buildings.

Sugar Hill was a complete district. The residents had their own tennis court, Metropolitan Tennis Court, on Convent Avenue. Craig's Colony Club, on St. Nicholas Avenue, served as the neighborhood restaurant, and Fat Man's Bar-and-Grill on 155th Street was the local watering hole.

Historic Sugar Hill addresses included 409 Edgecombe Avenue and 555 Edgecombe Avenue. The directory of residents during the 1920s and 1930s featured numerous prominent names. Originally the Colonial Parkway Apartments, 409 Edgecombe Avenue was built in 1916–17 by Schwartz & Gross. Residents included muralist AARON DOUGLAS and political activist WALTER WHITE. Because White was a high-powered executive with the NATIONAL ASSOCIATION FOR THE ADVANCEMENT OF COLORED PEOPLE (NAACP), his apartment was known as "the White House of Harlem."

Built in 1914–16 by Schwartz & Gross, 555 Edgecombe Avenue sat on the corner of West 160th Street. The building was originally called the Roger Morris Apartments. Illustrious inhabitants included athlete and actor CANADA LEE and JAZZ pianist COUNT BASIE.

According to Harlem Renaissance historian David Levering Lewis, 580 St. Nicholas Avenue was another plush building within the Sugar Hill compound, which housed entertainer ETHEL WATERS; Ethel Nance, who was secretary to *OPPORTUNITY* editor CHARLES SPURGEON JOHNSON; and Louella Tucker and REGINA ANDERSON, Nance's roommates, the latter a principal arts PATRON whose librarianship was advantageous to the *NEW NEGRO* movement.

The apartment Anderson shared with Tucker and Nance served as a sort of Harlem Renaissance USO to creative newcomers to Harlem. The roommates took responsibility for setting up appointments to Barnard College for young writer and soon-to-be anthropologist ZORA NEALE HURSTON, then making sure she did not get sidetracked, as was her custom, and neglect

This apartment building located at 555 Edgecomb Avenue was part of Harlem's fabled Sugar Hill and home of some of the community's more affluent musicians, businesspeople, and political leaders. *(Library of Congress, Prints & Photographs Division [HABS, NY, 31-NEYO, 117-3])*

her responsibilities. They also took the conservative poet COUNTEE CULLEN to a nearby nightclub, The Cat on the Saxophone, for additional "education" when he graduated from college. The 580 St. Nicholas Avenue address was so well known that Nance once remarked that when African Americans traveled to PARIS, France, and made their ritualistic visit to the popular Harry's Bar at 5 rue Daunou, all one had to mention was "580" and everyone in the place knew you were talking about 580 St. Nicholas Avenue in Harlem, NEW YORK CITY.

JEAN TOOMER *(Cane)*, LANGSTON HUGHES *(The Weary Blues)*, RUDOLPH FISHER *(The Conjure Man Dies)*, and ERIC DERWENT WALROND *(Tropic Death)* enjoyed the literary soirées the Sugar Hill roommates sponsored for more accomplished young writers and artists. Yet, for all its celebrity, the infamous "hill" had its detractors. Writer and Sugar Hill resident CLAUDE MCKAY complained that "Sugar Hill is vinegar sour to many of its residents pinching themselves to meet the high rent."

Sugar Hill in 2002 remained a legacy address and had been designated a historic landmark.

Further Reading

Adams, Michael Henry, and Paul Rochleau. *Harlem: Lost and Found.* New York: Monacelli Press, 2001.

Anderson, Jervis. *This Was Harlem: A Cultural Portrait, 1900–1950.* New York: Farrar Straus Giroux, 1981.

Dolkart, Andrew S., and Gretchen S. Sorin. *Touring Historic Harlem: Four Walks in Northern Manhattan.* New York: New York Landmarks Conservancy, 1997.

Lewis, David Levering. *When Harlem Was in Vogue.* New York: Vintage Books, 1982.

— Sandra L. West

Survey Graphic (Harlem Number: *Harlem: Mecca of the New Negro*)

Before the Harlem Renaissance developed into a full-blown cultural movement, the *Survey* provided a major and influential social work magazine of progressive thought that published essays on the myriad facets of the American experience.

Paul Underwood Kellogg assumed the position of editor in chief at the magazine in 1912. Social worker Jane Addams, a leader in the establishment of settlement houses for poor and immigrant children in NEW YORK CITY, held the position of associate editor. By 1921, *Survey* was renamed *Survey Graphic: Magazine of Social Interpretation.*

Kellogg published several special editions, called "numbers," of *Survey Graphic.* In 1922, he devoted an entire edition to the fifth anniversary of the Soviet Union and the impact of COMMUNISM on the country. A rival magazine called *The World Tomorrow* in 1923 assembled a similar issue about HARLEM, complete with poetry by COUNTEE CULLEN and LANGSTON HUGHES. Its focus, however, was not on the *NEW NEGRO* movement as would be the *Survey Graphic*'s two years later.

In 1924, *Survey Graphic* editor Kellogg joined those guests invited to the celebrated CIVIC CLUB DINNER, hosted by CHARLES SPURGEON JOHNSON, editor of the NATIONAL URBAN LEAGUE's (NUL) *OPPORTUNITY* magazine. The purpose of the dinner was to announce the publication of a new novel by JESSIE REDMOND FAUSET, formally introduce emerging black writers and artists, and facilitate networking between black authors and white publishers. The new group of black artists and the vivacity of the New Negro movement in general excited Kellogg. He asked HOWARD UNIVERSITY professor ALAIN LOCKE, referred to him by Johnson, to edit *Survey Graphic*'s special edition. Locke obliged with the March 1925 special edition *Survey Graphic* Harlem Number: *Harlem: Mecca of the New Negro.*

Locke planned *Harlem: Mecca of the New Negro* to include serious and thoughtful essays, in addition to poetry, with an intent on placing the Harlem Renaissance within a historical context. According to Harlem Renaissance scholar Arnold Rampersad, Locke likened the cultural significance of Harlem to the role of Dublin and Prague in modern Irish and Czech culture. Locke wrote in his opening essay that "without pretense to their political significance, Harlem had the same role to play for the New Negro as Dublin has had for the New Ireland or Prague for the New Czechoslovakia."

Locke maintained that blacks were linked more by "a common condition rather than a common consciousness; a problem in common rather than a life in common." But in Harlem, Locke continued, "Negro life is seizing upon its first chances for group expression and self-determination," and the New Negro, a term not used since the turn of the century but now "revived" by Locke, was "vibrant with a new psychology."

Distinguished by its concentration on the growing New Negro movement, the *Survey Graphic* Harlem Number, officially Volume VI, no. 6, was a colossal success. In one month's time, 42,000 people, approximately twice the number of the journal's regular subscribers, had received the magazine. It was tastefully designed from front to back. German painter WINOLD REISS's drawing of vocalist ROLAND HAYES adorned the front cover. And one of Harold Jackman, a Harlem teacher and companion to prolific poet Cullen, graced the back cover. The *Herald Tribune* lavishly praised the magazine, thereby giving the Harlem Renaissance even more authority. The New Negro had arrived.

Harlem: Mecca of the New Negro was divided into three major sections: "I, The Greatest Negro Community in the World"; "II, The Negro Expresses Himself"; and "III, Black and White—Studies in Race Contacts."

Under Section I were the following essays: "Home" by Locke; "Enter the New Negro" by Locke; "The Making of Harlem" by JAMES WELDON JOHNSON, ambassador, and coauthor of "LIFT EVERY VOICE AND SING; "Black Workers and the City" by sociologist Johnson; "The South Lingers On," a short story by literary medical doctor RUDOLPH FISHER; and, "The Tropics in New York" by W. A. Domingo, editor of the *NEGRO WORLD.*

Section II presented "Harlem Types" with photographs by Reiss; "The Black Man Brings His Gifts" by W. E. B. DU BOIS; "Youth Speaks," with poems by ANNIE BETHEL BANNISTER SPENCER, ANGELINA EMILY WELD GRIMKE, CLAUDE MCKAY, JEAN TOOMER, and Hughes. It also contained "Negro Art and America" by ALBERT COOMBS BARNES of the Barnes Foundation; "The Negro Digs Up His Past" by bibliophile ARTHUR SCHOMBURG; and the poem "Heritage" by Cullen.

Section III included "The Dilemma of Social Patterns" by Melville J. Herkovitz; "The Rhythm of Harlem" by Konrad Bercovici; "Color Lines" by WALTER WHITE, official at the NATIONAL ASSOCIATION FOR THE ADVANCEMENT OF COLORED PEOPLE (NAACP); "Harvest of Race Prejudice" by Kelly Miller, a former slave, member of the intellectual AMERICAN NEGRO ACADEMY, and Howard University professor; "Breaking Through" by Eunice Roberta Hunton; "Portraits of Negro Women," an art gallery by Reiss; "The Double Task" by Elise Johnson McDougald, one of only two black female contributors to the section; "Ambushed in the City" by Winthrop D. Lane; and "The Church and the Negro Spirit" by George E. Haynes.

The writers and artists assembled touched on significant facets of life in Harlem: how the New Negro emerged, how he fared in an atmosphere of culture shock and urban problems even as socioeconomic opportunities and the cultural flowering continued, and his collective hope. Locke, Du Bois, and Johnson represented an academy of scholars, along with Miller, former slave and Howard University professor and dean. Reiss and Barnes were considered the visual artists; writers and poets were well depicted from Cullen to Hughes. Schomburg contributed his important essay on the history of African people within the context of world history.

Having provided *Survey Graphic* with its special edition, Locke then expanded upon and republished *Harlem: Mecca of the New Negro* in book form as the 1925 anthology: *The New Negro: Voices of the Harlem Renaissance. The New Negro* gave Locke an opportunity to utilize the talents of the actual artists and thinkers who comprised the New Negro movement. It also allowed him to complete a general readership book (outside of any professional/publishing obligations to Howard University) with positive and long-term implications for the entire race, the movement, and his own "tenure" as a significant writer on the subject of race, a subject he was not allowed to teach at Howard. Moreover, through the *New Negro* anthology he was able to deputize the New Negro to tell his own story in his own manner and words, all in a book with a longer shelf life than a magazine could offer.

With the editorships of *Survey Graphic's Harlem: Mecca of the New Negro* and *The New Negro,* Alain Locke, a nonresident of Harlem, became an official architect of the Harlem Renaissance and further documented and validated the New Negro movement. For a time, the *Survey Graphic* continued to publish special editions and such definitive articles as "Indians at Work" in June 1934 and "Southern Farm Tenancy" in March 1936. The magazine ceased operation in 1952.

Further Reading

Lewis, David Levering. *When Harlem Was in Vogue.* New York: Vintage Books, 1982.

Locke, Alain, ed. *The New Negro: Voices of the Harlem Renaissance.* New York: Simon & Schuster, 1995.

Rampersad, Arnold. *The Life of Langston Hughes: Volume I: 1902–1941, I, Too, Sing America.* New York: Oxford University Press, 1986.

— Sandra L. West

swing sound

A product of the larger JAZZ bands that performed during the late 1920s, swing became the dominant style of musical entertainment in the United States and much of Europe during the 1930s and 1940s.

Swing music placed the heavy syncopation of RAGTIME and the freewheeling improvisations of jazz within a larger orchestral framework. It successfully blended a precise mesh of sound utilizing elements of American popular music and classical European music. The new sound applied a steady 4/4 rhythm contrasted with multiple accents on melody executed by big bands ranging anywhere from a dozen members to 30 or more. It was, overall, a more structured sound, dependent on creative arrangements for each section of a band. While melodies were handled largely by soloists, rhythm sections played swing riffs and repeating figures with exaggerated flair. The players often included a rapid musical call and response between instrumental sections.

The formula for the swing sound was developed by FLETCHER HENDERSON. A composer and arranger who had worked for the PACE PHONOGRAPHIC RECORD CORPORATION's Black Swan record label, Henderson conducted his own band at the Roseland Ballroom in NEW YORK CITY. His arrangements included a focus on such individual talents as innovative trumpeter LOUIS ARMSTRONG and saxophonist Coleman Hawkins. Although Henderson recorded swing classics like "Yeah Man!" and "Sugar Foot Stomp," his biggest contribution to the swing era may have been as an arranger for other big bandleaders. Among those to whom he lent his talents and helped make famous and rich while his own fortunes remained uneven were the white bandleaders the Dorsey Brothers and Benny Goodman. His influence was particularly significant on the Benny Goodman Orchestra, as he arranged a number of the band's most successful songs, including "When Buddha Smiles," "Down South Camp Meeting," and "Sometimes I'm Happy." In addition to his arrangements, Henderson also worked as Goodman's pianist during the late 1930s.

Bandleaders like the SAVOY BALLROOM's CHICK WEBB, COUNT BASIE, CAB CALLOWAY, Jimmie Lunceford, Don Redman, Benny Carter, and DUKE ELLINGTON further defined swing with their individual performance styles and compositions. Ellington provided the era's anthem in 1932 with "It Don't Mean a Thing If It Ain't Got That Swing." His own big band boasted some three trumpets, a piano, two trombones, four saxophones, a guitar, and clarinet. Through radio broadcasts and tours throughout the GREAT DEPRESSION, Ellington took the sound of swing all over the United States. In 1933 and 1939, they took it to Europe as well.

Cab Calloway also took swing to Europe with a 15-piece ensemble in 1935. A songwriter, singer, and dancer as well as bandleader, Calloway helped swing maintain dominance in America with the songs "Three Swings and Out" and "I Like Music Played with a Swing Like This," both in 1938. Moreover, he added to the definition of swing culture with the publication of his 1939 booklet *Swingformation Bureau,* a short treatise on the language, personalities, etiquette, and literature of swing.

Jimmie Lunceford advertised his group as The Perfect Swing Band. Composed largely of students to whom he had taught music in both high school and college, Lunceford's orchestra took over as the house band at the COTTON CLUB following Ellington's and Calloway's respective departures.

In addition to the bands as a whole, the swing sound was derived from both vocal and instrumental soloists. Some of the pioneering vocalists were Ivie Anderson, BILLIE HOLIDAY, Ella Fitzgerald, Henry Wells, Pearl Bailey, and LENA HORNE. As already noted, Louis Armstrong was one of the first outstanding solo instrumentalists. Some of the others were Lester Young, Cootie Williams, Teddy Wilson, and Ben Webster. In addition to finding an outlet through radio broadcasts of performances and in New York dance halls such as the Alhambra and the Golden Gate Ballroom, the music was recorded and distributed nationally by Decca Records, the Victor label, Blue Note, and others. In 1948, the movie *Killer Diller* showcased swing music and culture. It featured the talents of the Nat King Cole Trio, Andy Kirk and his band, and MOMS MABLEY. The movie also featured a group called the Congaroo Dancers performing the lindy hop. Similar dance scenes were filmed for the 1993 movie, *Swing Kids* and Spike Lee's 1992 movie on the life of *Malcolm X.*

With the rise of cool jazz, rhythm and blues, and rock and roll from the 1950s onward, swing music began a steady decline in popularity. However, it enjoyed a major resurgence in the late 1990s as youth in search of musical alternatives to hard-core rock and rap adopted the preferred dance music of their grandparents. Moreover, the 1999 Broadway musical *Swing,* directed and choreographed by Lynne Taylor-Corbett, also celebrated the dance and music of the swing era.

Further Reading

Dancer, Stanley, and Dan Morgenstern. *The World of Swing: An Oral History of Big Band Jazz.* Boulder, Colo.: Perseus Books Group, 2001.

Friedwald, Will. *Jazz Singing: America's Great Voices from Bessie Smith to Bebop and Beyond.* New York: Da Capo Press, 1996.

Milkowski, Bill. *Swing It! An Annotated History of Jive.* New York: Watson-Guptill Publications, 2001.

Porter, Eric. *What Is This Thing Called Jazz: African American Musicians as Artists, Critics, and Activists.* Berkeley: University of California Press, 2002.

— Aberjhani

Tanner, Henry Ossawa (1859–1937) *photographer, painter*

Revered for his status as an internationally recognized artist and his generous support of younger talents, Henry Ossawa Tanner was a painter of the common black man and of moving religious scenes.

Henry Ossawa Tanner was born on June 21, 1859, in Pittsburgh, Pennsylvania. He was given the middle name "Ossawa" in honor of abolitionist John Brown's raid on Osawatomie, Kansas, in 1856. His father was Rev. Benjamin Tanner, rector of Bethel Church in PHILADELPHIA in 1866 and, later, a bishop in the African Methodist Episcopal Church. His mother was Sarah Miller Tanner. Henry was the first of their seven children.

In 1893, Tanner was walking with his father in Philadelphia's Fairmount Park when they came upon an artist painting. Awed by what he saw, he made himself a palette from a tattered geography book and, with some old brushes, tried to re-create what he had seen the park artist do. Excited by his own efforts, he cried, "I'm an artist." From that point on, his family supported his endeavors; as educated people who served in the first black church of America, they believed black people could accomplish anything they chose to accomplish. Young Tanner painted everything from animals at the zoo to portraits of family members. When the Centennial Exposition came to Philadelphia, he witnessed the work of two exhibiting black artists: sculptor Edmonia Lewis and landscape painter Edward Bannister.

Tanner was educated at the Pennsylvania Academy of Fine Arts in 1880 and exhibited in their annual shows, though his sales were slim. So that he could support himself, he decided to move to Atlanta, Georgia—home of several black colleges and a solid black middle class—to open a photo studio. The studio failed within a year.

Through his contact with Bishop and Mrs. Joseph L. Hartzell, a missionary couple from Cincinnati, Ohio, he received an appointment as an art instructor at Clark College (now Clark-Atlanta University). They also sponsored a show for him in Cincinnati and, when no paintings were sold, purchased the entire collection for $300. With these funds, in 1891, Tanner sailed to Europe to study.

He was originally destined for Rome, where sculptor Lewis had found success, but stopped instead in PARIS, France, to study at Académie Julian. His studies went well, but exhibitions, art sales, and his personal health did not. Weakened from a bout of typhoid fever, he returned home to the care of his mother in 1892. In recuperation, Tanner worked on paintings he had begun when he taught at Clark and escaped to the hills of North Carolina to live and create among the masses of dignified black peasants. Among the paintings he completed were the incomparable *The Banjo Lesson* (1893) and *The Thankful Poor* (1894). These two classic works are examples of Tanner's black genre period and both were later included in the collection of the Hampton University Art Museum in Hampton, Virginia. Once fully recuperated, he sold all of his paintings and returned to Paris, his artistic home, far from the limitations of America's JIM CROW racism.

In Paris, Tanner reflected upon the statement, or lack of a statement, that his art was making. He thought about the racial freedom he experienced in Europe, and the prejudice he and his people knew in the United States. He pondered his own hope for peace among men, dug deep into his own religious convictions, and began to paint religious scenes. During this period, among other works he created *Daniel in the Lions' Den* and *The Raising of Lazarus. Daniel in the Lions' Den* was accepted for exhibit at the Ecole des Beaux-Arts (the Paris Salon) in 1896 and won an honorable mention. *The Raising of Lazarus,* exhibited at the Paris Salon in 1897, won a medal and was purchased by the French government for the Luxembourg Museum. He also won the Walter Lippincott prize at the Pennsylvania Academy of Fine Arts. His work was collected and purchased by the Chicago Art Institute and Carnegie Institute Museum of Arts in Pennsylvania.

In 1899, Henry Tanner married Jessie Olsen, an opera singer. She was the model in his painting *The Annunciation* (1898). They had one child, a son, Jesse Ossawa Tanner.

Tanner continued to successfully paint religious scenes, exhibit, sell his work, and win awards. The art world changed with WORLD WAR I. The war ravaged Europe, and the modern genre of cubism, not religious paintings, came into vogue. Still, Tanner's work was sought after and the man himself much revered. In 1923, he was made a Chevalier of the Legion of Honor by the French government. His *Sodom and Gomorrah* was purchased by the Metropolitan Museum of Art in NEW YORK CITY. His exhibits were successful in New York, Boston, CHICAGO, and Iowa.

Tanner acquired good friends in BOOKER TALIAFERRO WASHINGTON, founder of Tuskegee Institute, and W. E. B. DU BOIS, cofounder of the NATIONAL ASSOCIATION FOR THE ADVANCEMENT OF COLORED PEOPLE (NAACP). However, his wife, Jessie Olsen Tanner, died on September 8, 1925.

During his lifetime, he was able to entertain or assist in the careers of many young black visual and literary artists of the Harlem Renaissance who visited him in Paris for the encouragement only master painter Tanner could offer. Among those who visited him were sculptor META VAUX WARRICK FULLER; poet and travel writer COUNTEE CULLEN; self-taught artist WILLIAM HENRY JOHNSON; and muralist HALE ASPACIO WOODRUFF.

By the time of the GREAT DEPRESSION, Tanner's finances crumpled. Art PATRONS had less income with which to buy art. Prices for his work plummeted from $1,500 to $400 per canvas. His art fell out of favor at museums and galleries until the 1960s, when it was introduced to a new generation of admirers via Grand Central Art Galleries and the National Collection of Fine Arts at the Smithsonian Institution in WASHINGTON, D.C.

Henry Ossawa Tanner died on May 26, 1937. His papers are in the Archives of American Art, Smithsonian Institution, Washington, D.C. They deal with the period from 1890 to 1920 and include letters from artists and a manuscript for a biography of Tanner written by his son, Jesse.

Further Reading

Bearden, Romare, and Harry Henderson. *Six Black Masters of American Art.* New York: Zenith Books/Doubleday, 1972.

Beckman, Wendy Hart. *Artists and Writers of the Harlem Renaissance.* Berkeley Heights, N.J.: Enslow Publishers, 2002.

Bruce, Marcus. *Henry Ossawa Tanner: A Spiritual Biography.* New York: Crossroad Publishing Company, 2002.

Gates, Henry Louis, Jr., and Cornel West. *The African American Century: How Black Americans Have Shaped Our Country.* New York: The Free Press, 2000.

— Sandra L. West

Theater Owners Booking Agency (Theater Owners Booking Association, TOBA)

The collective of theater owners known as the Theater Owners Booking Agency (TOBA) provided numerous outlets for African-American entertainers and audiences in the 1910s and 1920s.

Generally known as the TOBA circuit, the organization was founded in 1907 and headed by F. A. Barasso. It was controlled mostly by whites and consisted of 40 theaters, located primarily in the South, that featured blues singers as their principal attraction. These theaters included Atlanta's 81 Theater, the Lyceum in Cincinnati, the Park Theatre in Dallas, NEW ORLEANS's Lyric Theater, and the Koppin in Detroit.

Part of the circuit was left over from locations catering to vaudeville and minstrel shows, the latter being the famed variety acts that often featured actors made up in blackface and depicting African Americans in demeaning roles. In its new form, the TOBA circuit was the equivalent of a finishing school for comics, singers, actors, dancers, magicians, or any African American hoping to graduate to performances at such higher-class locations as the LAFAYETTE THEATRE in HARLEM, the Earle in PHILADELPHIA, the Howard in WASHINGTON, D.C., the Royal Theatre in Baltimore, or the elusive stages of Broadway.

At one point or another, nearly every famed entertainer of the era played the circuit: BESSIE SMITH, LOUIS ARMSTRONG, JOSEPHINE BAKER, ETHEL WATERS, FATS WALLER, MOMS MABLEY, and scores of others. Other circuits did exist: The Keith circuit promoted primarily white entertainers. The Dudley circuit operated from 1911 to 1916 and was the first black-owned theatre circuit organization. The Southern Consolidated circuit stayed in business from 1916 to 1921 and offered entertainers contracts almost a year long but ran into stiff competition with TOBA.

Entertainers playing the circuit welcomed the opportunity to perform and develop their acts but often complained of drawbacks. Northern black entertainers traveling south often found it difficult to adjust to the more overt forms of JIM CROW racism practiced there. During the height of the GREAT MIGRATION, those playing small southern towns were sometimes prevented from boarding trains to leave and would have to walk from one station to another until able to board a train for home. Entertainers also had to cope with the dizzying pace of dozens of one-night stands, working with musicians who did not always understand their routines, inadequate accommodations, and uncertain pay.

Following WORLD WAR I, Theater Owners Booking Agency evolved into the Theater Owners Booking Association. The newer version of the organization attempted to upgrade its performance locations. Milton Starr was elected president of the association in 1921. Charles H. Turpin, RAGTIME pianist and owner of the BOOKER TALIAFERRO WASHINGTON Theatre in St. Louis, was elected vice president. Although the board of directors was dominated mainly by whites, it did contain two African Americans: C. H. Douglass, the owner of Macon's Douglass Theater, and T. S. Finley, owner of Cincinnati's Lyceum Theater.

Starting with only 20 theaters, the association expanded throughout the 1920s until it contained 80 theaters located in every region of the United States. The greater number of venues did not always work in an entertainer's favor because the restrictive contracts under which they worked allowed theater managers and owners to cancel a booking with very little notice. Performers might then find themselves stranded between jobs with or without fare to the next engagement. Because the contracts so clearly granted managers and owners the upper hand in business dealings, TOBA was often said among black entertainers to stand for "Tough On Black Asses."

Clarence Muse, an actor and composer who played both the larger houses and the TOBA circuit, chronicled his experiences with the latter along with profiles of its stars in his autobiographical *Way Down South.* The TOBA circuit gradually dissolved with the onset of the GREAT DEPRESSION in 1930.

Further Reading

Hill, Anthony D. *Pages from the Harlem Renaissance: A Chronicle of Performance.* New York: Peter Lang Publishing, 1996.

Lamb, Andrew. *150 Years of Popular Musical Theatre.* New Haven, Conn.: Yale University Press, 2001.

Reed, Bill. *Hot from Harlem: Profiles in Classic African American Entertainment.* Los Angeles: Cellar Door Books, 1998.

Waggoner, Susan. *Nightclub Nights: Art, Legend, and Style, 1920–1960.* Italy:Rizzoli International Publications, 2001.

— Aberjhani

Thompson, Clara Ann (1869–1949) *poet*

Writing more to appease an impulse to create poetry rather than to participate in the *NEW NEGRO* movement, Clara Ann Thompson published two volumes of poetry between 1908 and 1926.

The daughter of former slaves John Henry Thompson and Clara Jane Thompson from Virginia, Clara Ann Thompson was born in 1869 in Rossmoyne, Ohio. Despite the elder Thompsons' former status as slaves, each of their four children grew up to become either accomplished visual or literary artists. Their son Garland Yancey Thompson won some fame as a wood sculptor, and Aaron B. Thompson both wrote poetry and published it on his own press. The youngest sibling, PRISCILLA THOMPSON, also wrote and published poetry.

Thompson was initially educated in a log cabin facility known as Amity School. She later received private lessons from a tutor to earn qualifications to become a teacher. She taught for the Ohio public school system and often gave public readings, including presentations at the Baptist Church and St. Andrew Episcopal Church.

In 1908, she teamed up with her brother Aaron to publish her first volume of poetry, *Songs by the Wayside.* Her work was noted for its inclusion of meditations on spirituality, black folk wisdom, and observations on nature.

Following the creation of the NATIONAL ASSOCIATION FOR THE ADVANCEMENT OF COLORED PEOPLE (NAACP) in 1910, Thompson joined the organization and advocated for civil rights of African Americans.

Her second volume of poetry, *A Garland of Poems,* was published in Boston a year after the *New Negro* anthology, edited by ALAIN LOCKE, officially announced the advent of the Harlem Renaissance. *In A Garland of Poems,* Thompson celebrated the valor of black soldiers who fought in WORLD WAR I.

Remaining single, Thompson died in 1949. Her work was anthologized in 1988 in the second volume of *Collected Black Women's Poetry* and in *Afro-American Women Writers, 1746 to 1933.*

Further Reading

Russell, Sandi. *Render Me My Song: African-American Women Writers from Slavery to the Present.* San Francisco: Harper Books, 2001.

Winegarten, Ruthe, and Sharon Kahn. *Brave Black Women: From Slavery to the Space Shuttle.* Austin: University of Texas, 1997.

— Aberjhani

Thompson, Eloise Alberta Veronica Bibb (1878–1928) *writer*

A writer of poetry, short stories, articles, and plays, Eloise Thompson authored some of the most successful and controversial works of the 1910s and 1920s, including a screenplay presented as a response and challenge to the pro–Ku Klux Klan film *Birth of a Nation.*

Thompson was born Eloise Alberta Veronica Bibb on June 29, 1878, in NEW ORLEANS to Catherine Adele Bibb and Charles H. Bibb, a U.S. customs inspector. Raised Catholic in a middle-class environment, Thompson began writing as a youth. She was 17 in 1895 when Boston's Monthly Review Press, the same company that published work by Thompson's friend ALICE DUNBAR-NELSON, published her first volume of poetry, entitled *Poems.*

From 1899 to 1901, Thompson attended Ohio's Oberlin Academy preparatory school and then returned to New Orleans to teach for two years. In 1908, she moved to WASHINGTON, D.C., where she became head resident at a social settlement for African Americans.

On August 4, 1911, she married journalist Noah Davis Thompson in CHICAGO. Devoutly Catholic, Thompson was a widower with one son. The family moved to Los Angeles, California, where Thompson continued to write poetry as well as articles for *The Morning Sun,* a Catholic journal called *Tidings,* and the *Los Angeles Times.* Both Eloise and Noah Thompson presented lectures on JIM CROW racism before integrated audiences on the West Coast.

The overt racism of the D. W. Griffith film *The Clansman,* based on the novel and play by Thomas Dixon, prompted Thompson in 1915 to write a film scenario titled *A Reply to the Clansman.* Optioned for production, investors and reviewers of the proposed film agreed that it was a worthy and superior work but decided it would prove too controversial to turn a profit or provide genuine entertainment. Among those reviewing the screenplay was D. W. Griffith himself, and it was fairly impossible to escape the irony and hypocrisy of his labeling Thompson's screenplay controversial while *The Clansman* ignited protests and riots all over the United States. Celebrated director and producer Cecil B. DeMille also voted against producing the movie. Thompson eventually had to hire a lawyer to regain possession of her screenplay.

In 1920, Thompson's one-act drama *Caught* debuted at the Gamut Club in Los Angeles with a production by a group called the Playcrafters. The Ethiopian Folk Players (or ETHIOPIAN ART PLAYERS) also later produced the play in Chicago. In 1922, the Frank Egan Dramatic School put on a production of Thompson's one-act drama *Africans* at the Los Angeles Grand Theatre.

Thompson continued to explore theater and in 1924 had considerable success with her one-act drama *Cooped Up.* Like EULALIE SPENCE, Thompson dared to depict African Americans at their virtuous best as well as at their flawed worst and in *Cooped Up* portrayed a rooming house manager scheming against a newlywed couple in a failed attempt to win the husband for herself. The Lafayette Players debuted the play at the LAFAYETTE THEATRE in HARLEM. The National Ethiopian Art Players in Chicago staged a production in October 1924, and the Ethiopian Art Players produced it in 1925. The play also won honorable mention in the drama competition sponsored by *OPPORTUNITY* magazine for May 1925. The Intercollegiate Association staged a production at the Imperial Elks Auditorium in Harlem in 1926, and the LINCOLN THEATRE featured *Cooped Up* in 1928.

At the same time that Thompson began to win acclaim for her plays, she also started to gain recognition for her short stories, in which she examined customs and color prejudice in New Orleans's Creole society. *Opportunity* magazine published her story "Mademoiselle Tate" in September 1925 and "Masks" in October 1927.

Moving to NEW YORK CITY in 1927, Thompson continued to write while her husband accepted a position as business manager for *Opportunity* magazine. The following year, Eloise Thompson died at the age of 50. Details regarding her death remain unclear. She was eulogized in the February 1928 edition of *Opportunity* magazine.

Further Reading

Favor, J. Martin. *Authentic Blackness: The Folk in the New Negro Renaissance.* Durham, N.C.: Duke University Press, 1999.

Wintz, Cary D., ed. *The Politics and Aesthetics of "New Negro Literature."* New York: Garland Publishing, 1996.

— Aberjhani

Thompson, Priscilla (1871–1942) *poet*

Like her sister, CLARA ANN THOMPSON, Priscilla Thompson wrote and published two volumes of poetry, much of her work foreshadowing the sense of racial pride and dignity that would also characterize the *NEW NEGRO* movement.

Born in 1871 in Rossmoyne, Ohio, Priscilla Thompson was the youngest of four children born to former slaves Clara Jane Thompson and John Henry Thompson. Departing the plantation where they had been enslaved in Virginia, the Thompsons raised each of their children to practice some form of visual or literary artistry. Their oldest son, Garland Yancey Thompson, became a wood sculptor; the second son, Aaron, a poet and printer; and both their daughters poets.

Although Priscilla Thompson studied to become a teacher, her unstable health prevented her from working. She lived with her brother Aaron in Rossmoyne until he married, then later with her elder brother Garland. She herself remained single. While unable to teach professionally, Thompson did conduct Sunday school classes for the Zion Baptist Church.

Thompson published her first volume of poetry, *Ethiope Lays,* in 1900. She did so with the assistance of her brother Aaron, who also printed their sister Clara's first volume of poetry. As the title *Ethiope Lays* implies, Thompson's work was strong in its evocation of racial pride and political awareness. Published three years before *THE SOULS OF BLACK FOLK* by W. E. B. DU BOIS in 1903, Thompson's poetry was written in a manner intended to inspire and benefit African Americans in the same way that Du Bois would encourage black poets of the 1920s and 1930s to write. In 1907, Thompson published her final volume of poems, *Gleanings of Quiet Hours.*

Thompson died in 1942, seven years before her elder sister, Clara Ann. The title poems from both her books were anthologized in volume two of *Collected Black Women's Poetry* in 1988. The poems *Knight of My Maiden Love* and *The Muse's Favor* were published in *Afro-American Women Writers, 1747 to 1933.*

Further Reading

Dolan, Hubbard, ed. *Recovered Writers/Recovered Texts: Race, Class, and Gender in Black Women's Literature.* Knoxville: University of Tennessee Press, 1997.

Russell, Sandi. *Render Me My Song: African-American Women Writers from Slavery to the Present.* San Francisco: Harper Books, 2001.

— Aberjhani

Three-O-Six ("306")

When sculptor AUGUSTA FELLS SAVAGE ran out of space at the Harlem Arts Workshop on 135th Street, a project funded by the WORKS PROGRESS ADMINISTRATION (WPA), she and CHARLES HENRY ALSTON relocated to a former stable at 306 West 141st Street. They turned the brick stable into a well-known gallery, studio, workshop, home, and intellectual meeting place for artists of all genres during and after the Harlem Renaissance.

For four years during the mid-1930s the three-story building became the setting for Harlem's second largest WPA art program. Alston took up residence there, as did Henry "Mike" Bannarn. An administrator for the Harlem Art Workshop, Bannarn was also a painter, sculptor, and co-organizer of "306." Others who participated in the activities at "306" were Ad Bates, ROMARE BEARDEN, ERNEST CRICHLOW, Gwendolyn Knight, JACOB ARMSTEAD LAWRENCE, and Norman Lewis.

The camaraderie and artistic vitality among the artists became legendary. Ad Bates, an artists' model at the Art Students League and member of the Doris Humphrey and Charles Weisman modern dance company, sponsored Bearden's and Lawrence's first solo exhibitions at "306." Bearden eventually developed into one of the most important collagists of the 20th century. Crichlow, who assisted in the painting of the controversial HARLEM HOSPITAL mural, taught art at "306." He also joined Norman Lewis and Bearden to inaugurate the CINQUE GALLERY. The major abstract expressionist of the group, Lewis attributed his success to Charles Alston and Augusta Savage, without whom "306" would not have existed. Knight and Lawrence met at "306" and later married each other, a union that proved important to Lawrence's career.

Alston invited numerous influential and creative individuals to "306." Some who came to the gallery shows and participated in stimulating political discussions were W. E. B. DU BOIS, editor of the *CRISIS: A RECORD OF THE DARKER RACES* at the NATIONAL ASSOCIATION FOR THE ADVANCEMENT OF COLORED PEOPLE (NAACP); JAMES WELDON JOHNSON, NAACP official and coauthor of "LIFT EVERY VOICE AND SING," with JOHN ROSAMOND JOHNSON; poets LANGSTON HUGHES *(The Weary Blues)* and COUNTEE CULLEN *(Color);* and athlete and actor CANADA LEE *(Black Boy).*

Further Reading

Bearden, Romare, and Harry Henderson. *A History of African American Artists: From 1792 to the Present.* New York: Pantheon Books, 1993.

Beckman, Wendy Hart. *Artists and Writers of the Harlem Renaissance.* Berkeley Heights, N.J.: Enslow Publishers, 2002.

Hotton, Julia, ed. *Catalogue: Charles Alston and the "306" Legacy,* September 21–December 4, 2000. New York: Cinque Gallery.

— Sandra L. West

Tolan, Thomas Edward

See METCALFE, RALPH HAROLD.

Thurman, Wallace (1902–1934) *writer*

Like the satirist GEORGE S. SCHUYLER, Wallace Thurman was one of the more acerbic critics of the 1920s and 1930s *NEW NEGRO* movement and, like LANGSTON HUGHES, one of its most probing and prolific authors.

Thurman was born in Salt Lake City, Utah, on August 16, 1902, to Beulah and Oscar Thurman. Thurman's father lived apart from him and his mother while he grew up, and they did not meet until Wallace was almost 30 years old. His mother married some six times and reportedly was not very fond of her son, whose dark skin color prompted negative comments and reactions from various black and white Americans throughout his life even as it became the basis for some of his strongest writings.

Intellectually gifted, Thurman graduated from high school in Salt Lake City before going on to premedical study at the University of Utah from 1919 to 1920. He transferred to the University of Southern California in Los Angeles in 1922. In Los Angeles, he obtained a job at the same central post office where ARNA BONTEMPS worked. He also became a reporter for a black-owned newspaper and authored a column called "Inklings." Learning about the surge of cultural activities in NEW YORK CITY that was to become the Harlem Renaissance, Thurman started a magazine called *Outlet* to provide a West Coast equivalent to such New York publications as the *CRISIS: A RECORD OF THE DARKER RACES* and *OPPORTUNITY* magazines. *Outlet* folded after six months and Thurman, like Bontemps just before him and ELOISE ALBERTA VERONICA BIBB THOMPSON a couple of years later, moved in 1925 from Los Angeles to New York.

Arriving in New York, Thurman embarked on a career that in less than 10 years would include stints as a publisher; an editor for magazines and a major publisher; a writer of novels, plays, and influential articles; and a ghostwriter for others. Yet he invariably proved his own most severe critic and remained largely unsatisfied with his accomplishments. He worked for a time as a reporter and reviewer for a magazine called the *Looking Glass.* When the *New Negro*, edited by ALAIN LOCKE, was published in 1925, Thurman found it lacking and with little restraint voiced his criticism of what he termed "the niggerati," or black literati. Likewise, as managing editor for the *MESSENGER* in 1926, he became the first to publish adult-themed stories by Langston Hughes while simultaneously informing the young author that his stories were not particularly good but better than others he had received. The audaciousness with which he offered his disapproving criticism of such works as WALTER WHITE's second novel, *Flight,* made the then 24-year-old Thurman something of a hero among younger black writers.

Thurman moved from the *Messenger* to a white-oriented religious magazine called the *World Tomorrow* in October 1926. The following month, he joined forces with Hughes, GWENDOLYN BENNETTA BENNETT, AARON DOUGLAS, ZORA NEALE HURSTON, RICHARD BRUCE NUGENT, and others to edit and publish the magazine *FIRE!!* Planned as a joint venture for which all those involved agreed to share the expenses, amounting to approximately $1,000, it was Thurman who ended up paying for some years the bulk of the costs to publish *Fire!!* Hughes, by his own account, contributed whenever the sale of a poem allowed.

In direct opposition to W. E. B. DU BOIS's dictum that black art should serve as propaganda on behalf of black causes, Thurman stated that *Fire!!* was not intended to address "sociological problems or propaganda. It was purely "artistic in intent and conception." It was also short-lived with only one issue published. However, outside of his self-created forums, Thurman also published such articles as "Negro Artists and the Negro" in the *New Republic* and "Negro Poets and Their Poetry," in *Bookman* magazine, presenting his belief that *New Negro* artists were too self-conscious in their writings and needed to employ more objective observations of the daily lives of average African Americans.

In 1928, Thurman attempted to start another magazine called *Harlem: a Forum of Negro Life.* The magazine duplicated *Fire!!* in that it featured some of the most gifted black writers working, including Locke, Schuyler, and ALICE DUNBAR-NELSON. It also folded, however, after two issues. Nevertheless, Thurman accepted a job as a reader at Macaulay's Publishing Company and became the first African American to hold such a position with a major New York publisher. He had a reputation for reading entire blocks of text at once, and his employment at Macaulay's would help pave the way for the publication of his own three novels.

After helping him with the preparation of a manuscript and nursing him through an illness, University of California graduate LOUISE THOMPSON (later PATTERSON) married Thurman on August 22, 1928. They separated six months afterward with Thompson noting that Thurman was gay and thus their union incompatible. The writer maintained that Thompson was his one true love, and they never officially divorced. The year 1929 provided a breakthrough career-wise for Thurman. In addition to ghostwriting stories for *True Story* magazine under both male and female pseudonyms, Thurman authored the critically acclaimed novel *The Blacker the Berry* and a hit play called *Harlem, a Melodrama of Negro Life in Harlem.* Published in early February 1929, *The Blacker the Berry* told the story of Emma Lou, a dark-complexioned young woman rejected because of her color by the lighter complexioned members of her family and community. Despite the reversal of gender, *The Blacker the Berry* was unquestionably autobiographical and was the first novel by an African American to use for its primary theme intraracial color prejudice among American blacks. For that reason, it was the literary equivalent of MARCUS GARVEY's charges that African-American leadership during the 1920s was dominated by "mulattos" more interested in advancing their own caste than in gaining true racial equality for all blacks. One of Thurman's most disturbing observations in the novel was the self-hatred generated by such prejudice, an insight on which author James Baldwin would expand in the 1950s and 1960s. Controversial and groundbreaking as it was, *The Blacker the Berry* provided Thurman with critical and popular success.

His play *Harlem, a Melodrama of Negro Life in Harlem* debuted at the Apollo Theatre on Broadway on February 20, 1929, and ran for a solid 93 performances. *Harlem* was a dramatic reworking of "Cordelia the Crude," a short story Thurman had published initially in *Fire!!* and which he revised for the stage with William Jourdan Rapp. An editor for *True Story* magazine, Rapp, who was white, would work with Thurman on several projects and remain his friend until Thurman's early death. In *Harlem,* Thurman examined the impact of the GREAT MIGRATION through the plight of the Williams family. Leaving their home in South Carolina with hopes for greater freedom and prosperity in the North, the Williamses settle in Harlem only to find themselves torn apart by poverty, sexual promiscuity, and crime. With the exaggeration of its seedier elements for the stage, *Harlem* was successful not only in New York but in Canada, CHICAGO, and Los Angeles as well.

In Los Angeles, Thurman experienced an example of the kind of color prejudice he had written about in *The Blacker the Berry* when he was denied tickets several times to see his own play but finally got them when he sent someone else to make the purchase. Such discriminatory treatment was commonplace in Thurman's life and likely contributed to the alcoholism from which he suffered.

Of the several plays Thurman wrote following *Harlem,* one of the better known was his 1930 three-act drama *Jeremiah the Magnificent,* cowritten with Rapp. In it, Thurman surveyed the pitfalls of the BACK-TO-AFRICA MOVEMENT and Pan-Africanism as promoted by Garvey. Other plays by Thurman that were not produced were *Black Cinderella and Black Belt,* 1929; *Savage Rhythm,* 1931; and *Singing the Blues,* 1932.

Thurman published his second novel, and one of the most quoted in the entire Harlem Renaissance canon, *Infants of the Spring,* in 1932. An uninhibited satire of the New Negro movement, Thurman's novel offers caricatures of virtually every major figure in the movement. With himself in the role of Raymond Tyler, other characters include Alain Locke as Dr. A. L. Parkes; COUNTEE CULLEN as Dewitt Clinton; DOROTHY WEST as Doris Westmore; RUDOLPH FISHER as Dr. Manfred Trout; and ERIC DERWENT WALROND as Cedric Williams. The novel largely centers on inhabitants and visitors to "NIGGERATI MANOR," modeled after a well-known rooming house on 136th Street where Thurman, Hughes, and others often gathered for SALONS and all-night parties. Though not as critically successful as the *Blacker the Berry, Infants of the Spring* is the most well-known fictionalized treatment of the Harlem Renaissance by a writer of the period and provides telling insights into the personalities and philosophies that shaped the movement.

The Interne, Thurman's third novel, was published in 1932 and cowritten with white author Abraham L. Furman. While the novel did not focus on race and drew little attention in

HARLEM
A FORUM OF NEGRO LIFE
Vol. I NOVEMBER, 1928 No. 1

FOR WHOM SHALL THE NEGRO VOTE?
WALTER WHITE

LUANI OF THE JUNGLE
LANGSTON HUGHES

ART OR PROPAGANDA
ALAIN LOCKE

WOOF
GEORGE S. SCHUYLER

BACK STAGE GLAMOUR
THEOPHILUS LEWIS

DEAD AND GONE
ALLISON DAVIS

GEORGIA DOUGLAS JOHNSON
ROY DE COVERLY
HELENE JOHNSON
H. VAN WEBBER
AND OTHERS

Twenty-five Cents per Copy

Harlem: A Forum of Negro Life was one of several magazines published by the novelist and playwright Wallace Thurman. Lasting for two editions, the one seen here featured some of the most prominent literary talents of the era. *(Alain Locke Collection, Moorland-Spingarn Research Center, Howard University)*

Harlem, it was one of the first to address the issue of patient abuse in American hospitals. In that regard, it helped lay the foundation for the genre of literary exposés which later would spawn such classics as Ken Kesey's *One Flew over the Cuckoo's Nest.* With its setting in the City Hospital on what was then called Welfare Island, it would also turn into an ironic prophecy when alcoholism and tuberculosis caused Thurman to be admitted there.

Having established himself as an editor, novelist, and playwright, Thurman returned in 1934 to Los Angeles to write two movie scripts for Bryan Foy Productions. The first was titled *High School Girl* and the second *Tomorrow's Children.* In the latter, Thurman focused on the issue of sterilization of the poor as a form of birth control. Decades ahead of its time, such a topic would not be openly discussed until the second half of the 1900s and even then mainly in reference to countries on the African continent. Thurman's film, released at the height of the GREAT DEPRESSION, was banned upon opening.

Thurman returned to New York in the spring of 1934 and celebrated with a welcome-back party. Ignoring doctors' orders to avoid alcohol, he collapsed and was committed to the same hospital he had written about in *The Interne.* Diagnosed with tuberculosis, he spent nearly seven months in a ward for the terminally ill before dying on December 22, 1934, at the age of 32. Four days later, Rudolph Fisher, the man Thurman had caricatured in *Infants of the Spring* as Dr. Manfred Trout, died of cancer. Many felt the death of these two young accomplished authors marked the beginning of the end of the Harlem Renaissance.

Thurman's novel *The Blacker the Berry* remains in publication and is studied regularly in literature courses at traditionally black colleges in the United States.

Further Reading

Favor, Martin J. *Authentic Blackness: The Folk in the New Negro Renaissance.* Durham, N.C.: Duke University Press, 1999.

Marks, Carole, and Diana Edkins. *The Power of Pride: Stylemakers and Rulebreakers of the Harlem Renaissance.* New York: Crown Publishers, 1999.

Notten, Eleonore van. *Wallace Thurman's Harlem Renaissance.* Amsterdam: Rodopi, 1994.

— Aberjhani

Toomer, Jean (Nathan Pinchback Toomer)

(1894–1967) *writer, spiritual teacher*

With his universally recognized 1923 masterpiece *Cane,* Jean Toomer authored one of the most influential books of the Harlem Renaissance, only to later adopt a style of life that made literature secondary to his spiritual pursuits.

Toomer was born Nathan Pinchback Toomer on December 26, 1894, in WASHINGTON, D.C. His mother was Nina Pinchback Toomer, the daughter of Pinckney B. S. Pinchback, who made history during Reconstruction when he served first as a Louisiana senator, then as lieutenant governor, then briefly as the only black governor of any state during that era. His father was Nathan Toomer, who had been born a slave in Chatham County, North Carolina. As a child, Nathan was sold along with his mother to brothers John and Henry Toomer, who took them to Houston County, Georgia.

Following the Emancipation Proclamation, Nathan Toomer became a successful farmer and married a former slave named Harriet. With her he had four daughters: Theodosia in 1869; Fannie, 1871; Martha, 1872; and Mary, 1879. Toomer got married a second time on July 14, 1892, to the famed Georgia biracial heiress Amanda America Dickson. After Dickson's death in 1893, Toomer married Nina Pinchback on March 29, 1894. Both were light enough in complexion that they could live as whites if they chose, and their son inherited the same trait. Racial identification and INTERRACIAL INTERACTION would prove two of the most powerful elements in Jean Toomer's life and work. He eventually concluded that his racial bloodline included German, African, Native American, French Creole, English, Dutch, and Spanish origins.

Although he provided his wife with funds to purchase a house, Nathan Toomer all but abandoned her when she became pregnant, and he did leave his family in 1895. He and Nina divorced in 1899. Returning home to her parents, Nina nicknamed her son Eugene, a name the adult Toomer later shortened to Jean for use as his pseudonym. Nina married Archibald Cumber in 1906 and moved with her son to Brooklyn, NEW YORK CITY. In 1909, Toomer's mother died, and from that point on he lived primarily with his maternal grandparents and Uncle Bismarck Pinchback. Toomer's grandfather had enjoyed considerable success as a politician and business investor in Louisiana but experienced some decline in his fortunes by the time he relocated to Washington, D.C. His Uncle Bismarck possessed a passion for literature, art, and science that he often shared with Toomer.

Graduating from Washington's Dunbar High School in 1914, Toomer went on to study agriculture at the University of Wisconsin and physical conditioning at the American College of Physical Training in CHICAGO, Illinois. In 1917, he returned to New York where he took classes at City College and New York University. While attending college, he juggled a number of jobs, including car salesman and shipyard worker. He left college without graduating in 1918 and began to study independently while writing and living alternately in New York, Milwaukee, and Chicago.

Between 1918 and 1920, Toomer began composing some of the literary vignettes that make up *Cane.* In 1920, he befriended Waldo Frank, the modernist author of *Our America* and one of the founders of *Seven Arts Magazine.* Frank introduced Toomer to a circle of New York artists and writers. In addition to Frank, Toomer's friends soon included the poet Hart Crane, photographer Alfred Stieglitz, and painter Georgia O'Keeffe. Toomer's stories and poems then began to appear in such literary magazines as the *Double Dealer, Modern Review, Little Review,* and *CRISIS: A RECORD OF THE DARKER RACES.*

Toomer returned for a time to Washington, D.C., in 1921 to help care for his grandparents. His grandfather died later the same year. Also in 1921, Linton S. Ingraham, the principal of the Sparta Agricultural and Industrial School in Sparta, Georgia, invited Toomer to serve as his temporary replacement as principal at the school. Toomer accepted and for several months immersed himself in the culture and politics of Sparta, a small rural town located in the same Hancock County where his father had lived with the heiress Amanda America Dickson.

Through his early literary writings, Toomer consciously explored the different facets of his racial background. The time he spent in Sparta, he noted, was crucial to his understanding of the African-American aspect of what he came to call his identity as an American. It was also crucial to the completion of *Cane,* which would begin and end with scenes in rural Georgia. Despite racial tension in the region, Toomer believed that the people related to the land and to each other in a manner he felt was deeply spiritual and psychologically binding.

At the end of his temporary job as principal in Sparta, Toomer began submitting poetry and prose fragments to CLAUDE MCKAY at the *Liberator* magazine. McKay declined Toomer's initial submissions but encouraged him to send more materials until the *Liberator* published Toomer's poem "Georgia Dusk" and his short fiction "Carma," both of which would become part of *Cane.* Various literary magazines published additional poems and short stories.

In 1923, the publishing company Boni and Liveright published *Cane.* The same company would later publish JESSIE REDMOND FAUSET's *There Is Confusion,* and NELLA LARSEN's *Quicksand.*

In *Cane,* Toomer created neither a conventional novel with a sustained definitive plot nor a general anthology of works by a single author. While some have compared *Cane* to Toomer's friend SHERWOOD ANDERSON's book *Winesburg, Ohio,* and to James Joyce's *Dubliners, Cane* lacks the singular definitive setting that gives those works their cohesion. It is in fact a montage of literary impressions that utilize prose, poetry, and drama divided into three sections. His setting moves from rural Georgia in the first section, to Washington, D.C., and Chicago in the second, then returns to Georgia in the third. What does define *Cane* as a singular book is Toomer's lyrical style, with its re-creation of the psychic impulses behind Negro spirituals as well as its duplication of the music's mournful rhythms, and the author's powerful examination of passion and conflict between two races arrested by a crucial defining moment in American history. With his beautiful haunting portraits of biracial women and men torn between worlds ruled by race and gender, Toomer painted an existence where blacks and whites find themselves compelled as much to love each other as they do to destroy each other. *Cane* provides an extended meditation on personal identity and individual spiritual crises generated by a society obsessed with racial and class categorization even while it secretly struggled against such artificial lines of human separation.

Despite the fact that it boasted an introduction by Waldo Frank, *Cane* was not an immediate best-seller. Its first printing sold approximately 500 copies. For Toomer, more important than the numbers was the quality of individuals that bought the book. Most of its readers at that time were, like himself, creative artists of one kind or another, and their appreciation of it made the book a critical success. Magazines such as the *Little Review* published excerpts from it as well as new articles and stories by Toomer. Jessie Fauset, CHARLES SPURGEON JOHNSON, and ALAIN LOCKE viewed *Cane* as proof that it would be possible for African Americans to launch a significant movement promoting black culture. Even so, *Cane* did not have the same impact as W. E. B. DU BOIS's *THE SOULS OF BLACK FOLK* in 1903 and four years passed before it received a second limited printing in 1927. Ironically, while Locke and others championed *Cane* as an example of the growing *NEW NEGRO* movement, Toomer began to refute any racial categorization of himself as anything other than American.

From the beginning of his public career as an author, Toomer received invaluable professional support from Waldo Frank. However, their friendship ended when Toomer and Frank's wife, Margaret Naumburg, began a romantic relationship. Each believed deeply in the spiritual evolution of the human race and in seeking ways to transcend socially imposed limitations.

His interest in a concept of humanity that transcended racial boundaries led him in 1924 to begin studying a system of spiritual development known as Unitism, taught by George Ivanovich Gurdjieff. A self-styled mystic of Greek-Armenian origins, Gurdjieff had studied in Central Asia and founded schools in Russia and Turkey before establishing his Institute for the Harmonious Development of Man at the Prieure d'Avon in Fontainbleau, some 40 miles outside of PARIS, France. His system of Unitism employed elements of yoga, Buddhism, Freudian psychoanalysis, and Hinduism to foster the liberation and empowerment of what he described as one's essence, or individual center of consciousness.

Toomer began his formal studies of Gurdjieff's teachings in 1924 with A. E. Orage, editor of the *New English Weekly* and one of Gurdjieff's principal instructors. In the same year, he traveled to Fontainbleau to study with Gurdjieff himself and in 1925 started teaching Gurdjieff's principles in HARLEM. Among those who studied with Toomer were WALLACE THURMAN, Nella Larsen, and AARON DOUGLAS. Toomer remained an instructor with Gurdjieff for 10 years. His work in Harlem, however, did not last long, and he moved his base to Chicago while periodically visiting Gurdjieff in France. During that period he continued to write poetry and prose that were rejected for publication, including experimental novels and an autobiography. Despite his desire not to be identified as black, it was such black-oriented anthologies as *The New Negro* in 1925 and *Plays of Negro Life* in 1927 that kept Toomer's work and name in publication.

In 1931, he privately published a book of aphorisms called *Essentials.* The collection addressed the human condition rather than the condition of American race relations with such observations as: "To understand a new idea break an old habit" and "A conflict wastes energy; a tension generates it." It was conflict over finances and other issues that led to Toomer's separation from Gurdjieff.

On October 30, 1931, Toomer married white novelist Margery Latimer, who the following year died giving birth to their daughter, Margery Toomer. On September 1, 1934, he married Marjorie Content, a photographer and daughter of a wealthy stockbroker who would help finance their travels and purchase of property.

In 1936, Toomer's poem "Blue Meridian," almost a thousand lines long, was published in *The New Caravan.* In it, Toomer summarized his vision of "a new America," in which the black, white, and red races evolved beyond these differentiations to become a single blue race, or a race of people motivated by spiritual consciousness rather than political and social classification. It was his hope, Toomer stated, "That we might become heart-centered towards one another, Love-centered towards God."

Moving to Doylestown, Pennsylvania, in 1936, Toomer began an affiliation with the Society of Friends, often called the Quakers. His ongoing quest for greater spiritual growth took him to New Mexico in 1937 and to India in 1939. In 1940, he officially joined the Quakers and became a leading member on a number of committees. At the same time, he wrote many articles and poems for the Quaker journal, *Friends Intelligencer.* After Gurdjieff's death in 1949, Toomer worked again with Gurdjieff's organization during the mid-1950s. Illness forced him to reduce his writings and his spiritual activities during the early 1960s. He died on March 30, 1967.

The year that Toomer died, a hardback edition of *Cane* was issued 40 years after its last publication in 1927. Two years later, much owing to the progressive Black Arts movement, a mass market paperback edition was issued, and *Cane* slowly joined the ranks of canonized literature in the United States. In 1980, Darwin T. Turner collected and edited previously unpublished prose by Toomer and published it as a volume titled *The Wayward and the Seeking.* Toomer's daughter, Margery Toomer Latimer, released a volume of his collected poetry, including "Blue Meridian," in 1988. Hill Street Press in Athens, Georgia, published commercially for the first time, in 2002, the collection of aphorisms Toomer had privately published as *Essentials.* Toomer is now recognized as a major figure in the history of American literature.

Further Reading

Kerman, Cynthia Earl, and Richard Eldridge. *The Lives of Jean Toomer: A Hunger for Wholeness.* Baton Rouge: Louisiana State University Press, 1987.

Scruggs, Charles, and Lee Vandemarr. *Jean Toomer and the Terrors of American History.* Philadelphia: University of Pennsylvania Press, 1998.

Toomer, Jean, with Robert B. Jones, and Margery Toomer Latimer, eds. *The Collected Poems of Jean Toomer.* Chapel Hill: University of North Carolina Press, 1988.

Toomer, Jean, with preface by Charles Johnson, afterword by Rudolph P. Byrd. *Essentials, Timeless Truths for Living in Today's World.* Athens Ga.: Hill Street Press, 2002.

— Aberjhani

Tree of Hope

Once considered by the residents of HARLEM as the most famous tree in their community, the Tree of Hope was an aged elm that grew just outside the LAFAYETTE THEATRE on 132nd Street and became known as a good luck charm for entertainers seeking employment.

According to a report filed with the *New York Herald Tribune* in 1930, the tree got its name from a group of actors who had lost their jobs when a show in which they had been performing went bankrupt. The actors gathered daily around the tree where they would wait for their former manager to pass by on his way to the theater where they had worked and inquire about any back pay that might be due them. In the course of gathering at the tree and hoping every day to obtain money from the passing manager, they dubbed the elm the Tree of Hope. In time, the actors reportedly received approximately $6.43 each.

As word of the actors' small victory spread, other performers began to gather at the tree until it became traditional for unemployed entertainers to commune around it from 4 P.M. to 4 A.M. with the hope of sharing in whatever luck it might bring. Because the tree was located outside the Lafayette and only a short distance from the famed CONNIE'S INN and other nightclubs, show producers and directors would in fact often pass by the tree and meet entertainers in need of work. Some often did obtain appointments for auditions that led to actual jobs.

Among those entertainers who gathered at the tree and rubbed its bark for good luck were BOJANGLES ROBINSON, Aubrey Lyles, Flournoy Miller, Mamie Smith, FLETCHER HENDERSON, PAUL ROBESON, NOBLE SISSLE, EUBIE BLAKE, and ETHEL WATERS. Some of the hit Broadway shows that benefited from talent gathered at the Tree of Hope were *GREEN PASTURES, SHUFFLE ALONG, HOT CHOCOLATE,* and *BLACKBIRDS.*

The original Tree of Hope became such a permanent fixture in the folklore of entertainers that its stump was moved in 1933 to the stage of the APOLLO THEATRE. There, amateurs and professionals alike would touch the tree for good luck as they walked on stage to perform. In 1941, tap dancer Bojangles Robinson and NEW YORK CITY mayor FIORELLO HENRY LA GUARDIA planted another tree in the Tree of Hope's former location.

Further Reading

Schoener, Allon, and Henry Louis Gates, Jr. *Harlem on My Mind, Cultural Capital of Black America, 1900–1968.* New York: New York Press, 1995.

Wintz, Cary D. *Black Culture and the Harlem Renaissance.* College Station: Texas A & M University Press, 1996.

— Aberjhani

Tucker, Sophie (1884–1966) *entertainer, patron*

Star of vaudeville, Broadway, and movies, Sophie Tucker was among the few whites to support the careers of black composers by performing their music as part of her regular shows.

Tucker was born Sonia Kalish on January 13, 1884, while her Russian Jewish parents were in the process of fleeing their homeland. The parents changed their names a number of times before making their way through Europe to the United States and settling in Hartford, Connecticut. There, they operated a restaurant where Sophie met vaudeville entertainers and earned money imitating some of their musical acts. In 1903, she met and married Louis Tuck, with whom she had a son named Albert a year later. Tuck departed after the birth of their child, and Sophie changed her last name to Tucker.

She moved to NEW YORK CITY to pursue a singing career and there performed in cafés, amateur shows, and beer halls before moving on to the vaudeville circuit. She was considered overweight and unattractive by the vaudeville theater managers, who insisted she perform wearing the same blackface makeup that minstrel show performers wore. Otherwise, they reasoned, her appearance would make her act fail. Tucker wore the blackface until her luggage was misplaced en route to a performance and she risked going on without it. The audience's positive response to her deep-throated blues singing style was so positive that she never wore the blackface again.

Tucker joined the ZIEGFELD FOLLIES in 1909. As part of the Follies, she ignored and even ridiculed the standards of white female beauty promoted by Ziegfeld's famous showgirls while singing such songs as "Nobody Loves a Fat Girl, but Oh How a Fat Girl Can Love." Along with black comedian BERT WILLIAMS, she became one of the Follies' principal draws.

In addition to performing songs that mixed humor with sultriness, Tucker developed a unique repertoire of Yiddish songs that celebrated her Jewish roots along with RAGTIME, BLUES, and JAZZ songs. She recorded her signature song, "Some of These Days," by black composer SHELTON BROOKS, in 1911. She later recorded NOBLE SISSLE and EUBIE BLAKE's first song, "It's All Your Fault," before they became the famed stars of the Broadway hit *SHUFFLE ALONG*. She also recorded W. C. HANDY's "A Good Man Is Hard to Find" and hired black composer WILLIAM GRANT STILL as her music arranger.

Tucker started a successful Broadway career with the 1919 production of *Shubert Gaieties* and in 1920 recorded one of her most famous songs, "I'm the Last of the Red Hot Mamas." She also achieved international stardom during the 1920s with concerts in England and Europe. In 1929, she made her film debut in *Honky Tonk*.

Throughout the 1930s and 1940s, Tucker alternated her career with movies, Broadway shows, and concerts in which she continued to perform jazz and blues. Toward the end of her career in the late 1950s and early 1960s, the strength of her voice began to decline, and she adopted a style of singing mixed with talking to perform songs more dependent on wit than powerful delivery.

She married twice following her marriage as a teenager: to Frank Westphal from 1914 to 1919; and to her manager, Al Lackey, from 1928 to 1933. Tucker died on February 9, 1966.

Further Reading

Mordden, Ethan. *Make Believe: The Broadway Musical in the 1920s.* New York: Oxford University Press, 1997.

Petersen, Bernard L. *A Century of Musicals in Black and White.* Westport, Conn.: Greenwood Publishing Group, 1993.

— Aberjhani

Tulsa, Oklahoma, riot

A riot in 1921 in Tulsa, Oklahoma, destroyed one of the most affluent black communities in American history and marked one of the more brutal instances on record of white against black violence.

Prior to the massive waves of African Americans exiting the South to head North, many had been lured to the state of Oklahoma as early as the end of the 19th century in hopes of cashing in on its growing oil industry. By 1921, the state could boast the distinction of having more than two dozen towns populated and governed by blacks. Within Tulsa, approximately 15,000 African Americans made up the city's district of Greenwood. Forced by segregation to rely upon their own means and resources, the citizens of the community became so successful that the district became known as "Black Wall Street."

Despite the active presence of the Ku Klux Klan, frequent LYNCHINGS, and regular "whipping parties" during which blacks were assaulted for sport, Greenwood maintained 600 businesses, a post office, a hospital, 21 restaurants, a library, a line of buses, a bank, two movie theaters, 21 churches, and 30 grocery stores. JAZZ and other forms of African-American music formed a strong part of the community's culture. Among its citizens were individuals so prosperous that they owned private airplanes and traveled regularly via ocean liner to Europe to have clothes tailor-made. It was this very prosperity within the black community of Greenwood that, nearly all reports state, incited envy in the members of less prosperous white communities in Tulsa and led to the eventual riot.

Accounts vary regarding the details of what happened when a 19-year-old black man named Dick Rowland encountered a 17-year-old white woman named Sarah Page on the elevator of the Drexel Building on May 30, 1921. Taking a break from his work as a shoe shiner, Rowland had gone to the Drexel Building to use the restroom. At some point, Rowland reportedly lost his balance and stumbled or brushed against Page. The next day, the city newspaper printed without verification a statement that a Negro had attacked Page and torn her clothes off. Moreover, it announced that said Negro would be lynched.

A crowd of people with the apparent intention of carrying out the announced lynching gathered at the courthouse. A black lawyer and hotel owner named J. B. Stradford attempted to address the crowd and maintain order. A number of black men arrived to assist Stradford's efforts but were arrested along with him. While the crowd of whites continued to increase by the thousands, several dozen armed black men arrived. One was approached by a white man who struggled with him over the gun until it went off. Blacks at the scene made their way back to Greenwood. Whites broke into nearby shops and armed themselves with torches, shotguns, and at least one machine gun.

Individual houses and families were fired on throughout the night. In the early hours of morning, a veritable army of whites went into Greenwood and began to burn the community, destroying structures and human beings alike. Reports spread through the burning community that planes were being used to drop bombs. Oklahoma's governor declared martial law, and National Guard troops entered the city. More than 1,100 homes and businesses spread over 40 city blocks were lost to fire. Businesses not destroyed were looted. The Red Cross provided medical attention for almost a thousand people. The number generally quoted for blacks killed during the riot is 300, but estimates have stated as many as 2,000 while only several dozen whites are said to have died. Survivors have stated that these bodies were buried in mass graves at several different locations, and investigations in 2002 yielded evidence that such graves may have been covered over by the foundations of modern structures. Nearly half of Tulsa's black population, 6,000 people, were arrested and detained for a week at the city's convention hall and fairgrounds.

In the aftermath, 700 black families departed Tulsa while 1,000 more moved into tents during the winter of 1921–22. Plans to rebuild Greenwood were announced by city authorities and then promptly abandoned until its black residents took up the long painful process themselves.

Incredibly, the riot became something of a monstrous secret, and black and white survivors were encouraged to refrain from discussing it. The wall of silence crumbled in the late 1990s when various survivors did address the issue publicly, and the Tulsa Race Riot Commission was established. In February 2000, the Commission submitted recommendations for payment of reparations to survivors and descendants of survivors of the riot. It also proposed the construction of a memorial for the reburial of those victims of the riot discovered in makeshift graves; the establishment of a scholarship fund for students affected by the riot; and the formation of an economic recovery and development zone in the historic district of Greenwood. As of 2002, survivors and descendants of survivors had not received any of the proposed reparations.

Further Reading

Brown, Gregory. *The East St. Louis Riot of 1919.* Milwaukee, Wisc.: The Black Holocaust Society, 1999.

Ellsworth, Scott. *Death in a Promised Land: The Tulsa Race Riot of 1921.* Baton Rouge: Louisiana State University Press, 1992.

Johnson, Hannibal B. *Black Wall Street: Roots, Riot, Regeneration and Renaissance of Tulsa's Historic Greenwood District.* New York: Eakin Press, 1998.

Madigan, Tim. *The Burning: Massacre, Destruction, and the Tulsa Race Riot of 1921.* New York: St. Martin's Press, 2001.

— Aberjhani

U

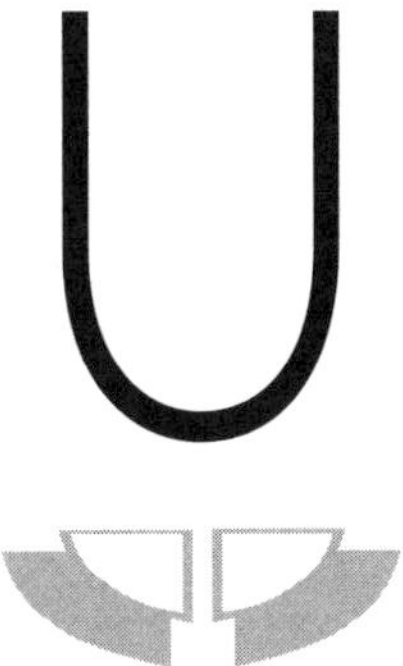

Undertow

EULALIE SPENCE's one-act play, *Undertow,* won third place along with *Hot Stuff,* another play by Spence, in the drama competition for the December 1927 *CRISIS: A RECORD OF THE DARKER RACES* magazine.

Of more than a dozen plays authored by Spence, *Undertow* was one of her few dramas. Though she worked frequently with the KRIGWA PLAYERS established by W. E. B. DU BOIS, she disagreed with Du Bois's philosophy that black theater should be used to promote racial propaganda on behalf of black people. Toward that end, most of her plays were satires on everyday life in HARLEM. *Undertow,* however, was a serious study of the lives of four characters: Hattie and Dan, a married couple; their son Charley; and Dan's lover, Clem. Specifically, it examines what happens when the former lover of an unhappily married man reenters his life and reveals before him and his wife that their previous union produced a daughter who is now an adult. Passions and conflict flare with a nearly Shakespearean intensity until Dan, insisting on release from his marriage, accidentally kills Hattie.

Aside from *Undertow,* Spence's other dramatic works were *La Divina Pastora* and *Her.* In addition to *Undertow's* prize for the *Crisis* Contest Awards, the play was also published in the April 1929 edition of *Caroline Magazine* and anthologized in *Black Theatre U.S.A.* by James V. Hatch and Ted Shine. Other prizewinning plays by the author include *The Hunch, Foreign Mail,* and *Fool's Errand.*

Further Reading

Gavin, Christy, and C. James Trotman, eds. *African American Women Playwrights: A Research Guide (Critical Studies in Black Life and Culture).* New York: Garland Publishing, 1999.

Hay, Samuel A. *African American Theatre: A Historical and Critical Analysis.* New York: Cambridge University Press, 1994.

— Aberjhani

United Golfers Association

After initially participating in the game of golf in the late 1800s as caddies (assistants) to white players on private golf courses, African Americans in 1920s elevated their status in the elitist sport by forming the United Golfers Association for black golfers.

In 1894, golf had become so popular that the United States Golf Association was established. Players were predominantly white males, and caddies were black males. The caddies took advantage of the situation by practicing when they were not working. Some of them became so skillful that several courses held matches for caddies only. Because it was expensive to play the game, black players rarely distinguished themselves and generally were not recognized. One exception was John Shippen.

In 1896, 18-year-old John Shippen entered the United States Open and defeated Charles Macdonald. Shippen completed the tournament in fifth place. He and his brother Cyrus taught golf as a vocation and played exhibition matches along the East Coast.

By the 1920s, the United Golf Association (UGA) was established for black players, and several black golf clubs emerged under its auspices. Shippen won the UGA national black tournament in 1926. Robert "Pat" Ball won in 1927, 1929, 1934, and 1941. Howard Wheeler won the title in 1933, 1938, 1946, and 1947. John Dendy was the undisputed champion in 1936 and 1937.

The road for the African American interested in professional golf was not easy. Golf clubs were expensive. The maintenance of a golf course was prohibitive. Most white men had more leisure time to play than black men did. Sometimes, professional black golfers had to wait for Caddy Day on Monday to play on a proper green at a white club because the segregated golf courses, for blacks only, were grossly inadequate. As in the field of tennis, black colleges came to the rescue.

Tuskegee Institute in Tuskegee, Alabama, sponsored the first black college golf competition in 1938.

With the end of the color line in baseball, the era of black leagues also slowly came to an end, and the same happened in the field of professional golf. However, black golfers in 2002 still retained community leagues, such as the 30-year-old club headquartered at Weequahic Park in Newark, New Jersey. The black college system continued to sponsor golf tournaments, as in the annual fund-raising competition held at Virginia Union University in RICHMOND. Outside of these conclaves, the overall face of golf has changed dramatically since the 1920s. It became so open to middle-class, multicultural participation that, at the age of 21, Eldrick "Tiger" Woods, an African-American-Thai and Stanford University student, won the coveted Masters, a major golf championship, at the Augusta National in Augusta, Georgia, in 1997, and thereafter won championships worldwide for several consecutive years.

Further Reading

Bloom, John, and Michael Nevin Willard, eds. *Sports Matters: Race, Recreation, and Culture.* New York: New York University Press, 2002.

Gates, Henry Louis, Jr., and Cornel West. *The African American Century: How Black Americans Have Shaped Our Century.* New York: The Free Press, 2000.

Strege, John. *Tiger: A Biography of Tiger Woods.* New York: Broadway Books, 1998.

— Sandra L. West

Universal Negro Improvement Association (UNIA)

Inspired by the writings and achievements of BOOKER TALIAFERRO WASHINGTON, MARCUS GARVEY started the Universal Negro Improvement and Conservation Association and African Communities League in Jamaica, West Indies, on August 1, 1914.

Later shortened to the simpler Universal Negro Improvement Association (UNIA), the organization had ambitious goals. They included plans to help modernize the indigenous traditional tribes of Africa; encourage love and pride in the black race; help develop self-sufficient communities for people of African descent; create a central black country; develop educational programs focusing on black history and culture; and improve the overall conditions of blacks throughout the world. The organization adopted for its motto, "One God! One Aim! One Destiny!" The principal faith blacks must follow, said Garvey, was "that of confidence in themselves."

After operating a series of failed newspapers throughout the Caribbean, Garvey was working for the PAN-AFRICAN journal *African Times and Orient Review* when he read Washington's *Up from Slavery* and began a correspondence with the well-known educator. Garvey was particularly moved by Washington's ideas on economic independence for blacks and by his founding of the Tuskegee Institute. He wrote Washington that it was his hope to build a similar industrial school in Jamaica. Once he had established his headquarters for UNIA in Jamaica, he traveled to the United States with plans to raise funds to build such a school. Those plans changed after his arrival on March 23, 1916.

Instead of returning to Jamaica after touring and lecturing in more than three dozen states, Garvey made his way to HARLEM in NEW YORK CITY. In Harlem, he joined the thousands of West Indians who had made their way to New York along with southern African Americans as part of the GREAT MIGRATION. With their assistance, Garvey transferred his presidency of UNIA from Jamaica to Harlem.

He purchased for UNIA a large auditorium on 138th Street and named it Liberty Hall, the first of many that would open almost everywhere a branch of UNIA was founded. With a capacity to hold 6,000 people, the auditorium was used in a variety of ways. Worship services were held there on Sunday mornings, and it was generally open to the public for meetings on issues affecting the black community. It also functioned as a facility for dances and concerts. During the winter, a soup kitchen was opened and temporary accommodations were provided for the homeless.

Liberty Hall was also, of course, where people came to hear Marcus Garvey deliver speeches on racial pride, spiritual prophecy, and economic prosperity. Such speeches often drew on biblical allusions and prompted Garvey's followers to compare him to the great deliverers of the King James Bible. This religious aspect of Garvey's leadership intensified further with his repeated proclamations of a black God and Christ, through UNIA's affiliation with the African Orthodox Church. Furthermore, the organization had an official chaplain general in the form of West Indian George A. McGuire.

UNIA became the parent organization that housed several major operations. One of those operations, started in 1919, was the Negro Factories Corporation, designed to compete with white-owned production companies by producing and marketing comparable commodities. Corporation branches existed in Africa, the West Indies, and the United States. They included a grocery store chain, restaurant, a black doll production company, printing presses, a steam laundry operation, a tailor shop, and a hotel. Among the corporation's greatest achievements was the fact that it provided employment for thousands of black workers.

The legendary Black Star Line also got its start in 1919, funded by 100,000 shares of stock sold at $5 each. Stock sales were restricted to blacks, and no one individual could purchase more than 200 shares. Originally capitalized at $500,000, the shipping line was recapitalized in 1920 at $10,000,000. As with all operations associated with UNIA, the Black Star Line was designed to serve the black community on an international, or Pan-African, level. Outfitted with four secondhand ships, its principal mission was to boost trade between black organizations in Latin America, Africa, and the United States. Critics of the venture promoted the idea that the shipping line was acquired to transport blacks en masse out of the United States and settle them in Africa. According to Garvey's widow and frequent coworker, Amy Jacques Garvey, that was never the case. Plans were, however, drawn up to establish in Liberia a colony of skilled workers who could contribute to the African continent's technological development, but the Liberian government denied permission to form such a colony. Nevertheless, the need for constant repairs made the fleet more of a liability than an asset; after four years and limited runs it was half a million dollars in debt.

A more successful UNIA operation was its official publicity organ, *NEGRO WORLD*, with Amy Jacques Garvey serving as associate editor. Begun in 1919 and lasting until 1933, *Negro World* gained an international readership with editions in Spanish, French, and English distributed throughout the United States, Latin America, and Africa.

Articles in the newspaper focused largely on the activities of UNIA itself and featured front-page editorials by Garvey. Other writings promoted black nationalism for the African continent and advocated political awareness of world events pertaining to blacks. In addition, while defending and promoting Garvey, it retaliated against attacks by such critics as W. E. B. DU BOIS of the *CRISIS: A RECORD OF THE DARKER RACES*, A. PHILIP RANDOLPH of the *MESSENGER*, and Cyril Briggs of the *Crusader.*

UNIA held its first international convention in August 1920. The affair was marked with a gala parade through Harlem, designated representatives from 25 countries (some of whom had actually been living in Harlem for years), sales of stock, and the drafting of a Declaration of the Rights of the Negro Peoples of the World. A much-decorated Garvey in paramilitary uniform rode through Harlem alongside UNIA's Black Cross Nurses, Universal African Motor Corps, and Black Flying Corps. The occasion was also used to announce the organization's official colors: red for the blood of black people, green for the aspirations and stolen land of black people, and black for the race itself.

After UNIA had been operating for two years in the United States, Garvey estimated its membership at 4 million. By 1923, he placed the figure at 6 million. Critics stated that a more realistic number was 200,000, which was the circulation of *Negro World.* The number of branches in some 38 states, including the Deep South, came to 700. Moreover, the organization had 200 branches outside the United States. Whether UNIA had 200,000 members or the 6,000,000 that Garvey claimed, he had succeeded in becoming the first black man to launch and develop a mass movement geared toward the advancement of black people, something A. Philip Randolph would spend the bulk of his career attempting to accomplish.

The momentum that swelled UNIA's membership in the early 1920s began to taper off with the repeated criticisms of Garvey in the black press. The organization's effectiveness was further hampered by administrative and financial difficulties. It received an all but fatal blow when Garvey and three of his associates were arrested in 1922 for mail fraud. He served three months in New York City's Tombs Prison and two years in the Atlanta Penitentiary. He was deported in December 1927 to Jamaica as an alien convicted of a felony.

Garvey tried but was unable to move the UNIA headquarters back to Jamaica. The organization went bankrupt with debts amounting to $200,000. The fleet of the Black Star Line was auctioned off to help settle UNIA's accounts. The publishing plants, Liberty Halls, and other operations were all lost. Still, Garvey held UNIA conventions in Jamaica in 1929 and 1934. Moving to England in 1934, he opened branches of UNIA in PARIS, France, and London but never regained the following he once had. He died in London on June 10, 1940.

Further Reading

Archer, Jules. *They Had a Dream: The Civil Rights Struggle from Frederick Douglass to Marcus Garvey to Martin Luther King and Malcolm X.* New York: Penguin Putnam, 1996.

Cronon, E. David. *The Black Moses: The Story of Marcus Garvey and the Universal Negro Improvement Association.* Madison: University of Wisconsin Press, 1972.

Martin, Tony. *Race First: The Ideological and Organizational Struggles of Marcus Garvey and the Universal Negro Improvement Association.* Dover, Mass.: The Majority Press, Incorporated, 1996.

— Aberjhani

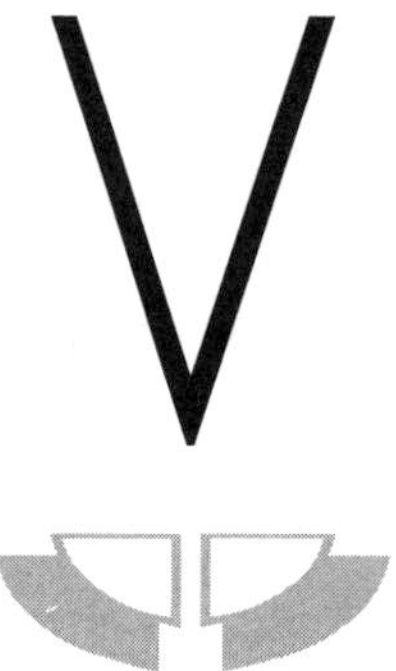

Van Der Zee, James (James Augustus Joseph Van Der Zee) (1886–1983) *photographer*

For more than three decades, photographer James Van Der Zee documented special occasions and scenes of everyday life in HARLEM, amassing a collection that established him as the preeminent photographer of the Harlem Renaissance.

James Augustus Joseph Van Der Zee was born on June 29, 1886, in Lenox, Massachusetts. His father was John Van Der Zee, a butler and waiter. His mother was Susan Brister Van Der Zee, a maid. They were both employed by former Civil War general and U.S. president Ulysses S. Grant in NEW YORK CITY before moving to Lenox in 1883.

James was the second child in a family of two sisters and three brothers. He attended public elementary and high schools in Lenox. His family's enjoyment of music and art influenced James to consider a career in piano and violin. Though skillful at drawing landscapes, an interest in portraits led him to a hobby in photography. George Eastman's introduction of the snapshot camera in 1888 had popularized amateur photography. Van Der Zee obtained his first camera in 1900. It failed, however, to work properly and he bought a better one, with which he began taking pictures of neighbors and friends.

In 1906, Van Der Zee married Kate Brown and later moved with their daughter to Phoebus, Virginia. A 1907 photograph that he took of Virginia blacksmiths showed his increasing skills and growing concern for light, detail, and composition. For the next eight years, he revisited Lenox, photographing his family and exploring outdoor lighting. He also began to spend time in New York, where he played piano and violin at private parties.

In 1915, his photography hobby became a profession. Working as a photographer's assistant at Gertz's Department Store in Newark, New Jersey, he received his first lessons on working in a darkroom, documenting negatives, and posing subjects. This technical information bolstered his artistic ideas, and in 1916 he opened the Guarantee Photography Studio in Harlem. Once he opened his studio, his music, art, and photography combined to form a definitive, lifelong pattern. He got married for the second time in 1918 to Gaynella Grenley Greenlee.

Van Der Zee's photography of the 1920s to the 1940s falls into four categories: studio portraits, funeral photographs, pictures of MARCUS GARVEY and his organization, and scenes of Harlem. These categories show his photographic style, artistic influences, and significance as recorder of a cultural apex.

Van Der Zee spent a great deal of care and time on portraits. He used backdrops and painted and retouched negatives and prints to achieve a dignified or dreamlike quality. In his shots of African-American WORLD WAR I veterans dressed in uniform, Van Der Zee inserted sketches of battles or cemeteries. His portraits of women included ennobling details such as grand pianos and Oriental rugs. Wedding portraits featured flowers, lace, and other finery. The overall effect, a mystique of renown, reinforced Van Der Zee's appeal as a popular photographer.

During the Harlem Renaissance, famous African Americans living in or visiting Harlem promoted a new standard of excellence. For many of them, Van Der Zee exemplified such excellence in his photography. Among his clients were FLORENCE MILLS, COUNTEE CULLEN, Reverend ADAM CLAYTON POWELL, SR., and A'LELIA WALKER, daughter of business tycoon MADAME C. J. WALKER.

Van Der Zee also was a funeral photographer. Two of his best-known funeral photographs were of Florence Mills in 1927 and of his daughter Rachel, the same year. In the photograph of Rachel in a casket he inserted an image of Jesus, another picture of Rachel, and a poem. His technique from studio work—retouches, insertions, and props—gave his funeral pictures an idealized aura.

During the 1920s, Marcus Garvey, proponent of the BACK-TO-AFRICA MOVEMENT, made Van Der Zee the official photographer of his organization, the UNIVERSAL NEGRO IMPROVEMENT ASSOCIATION (UNIA). Pictures in Van Der Zee's collection show Garvey in full regalia and document UNIA events.

Sometimes he shot informal pictures, as when he captured women and children boarding a trolley in 1924. The photographer's habit of dating negatives and prints, learned while working at Gertz's, proved helpful when historians studied his meticulous rendering of the Harlem Renaissance.

As different Harlem organizations thrived, they wanted pictures of their membership and activities. Van Der Zee photographed one such group, the Harlem lodge of the Improved Benevolent and Protective Order of Elks of the World, in 1925. The following year, he photographed another group, the Alpha Phi Alpha basketball team. The Moorish Zionist Temple, a Harlem synagogue, commissioned Van Der Zee in 1929.

A stylistic unity connects Van Der Zee's work. His use of light and shadow and elevation of average people compare with Caravaggio, an Italian painter of the 1600s. Similarly, his range of subjects, use of religious icons, and sensitivity in depicting the living and the dead resemble the treatment and output of Rembrandt, another 17th-century European painter. Moreover, the hazy imagery, nostalgic details, and contemplative poses in Van Der Zee's photographs position him among the romanticists, painters of the mid-1800s who aroused strong emotions.

During the 1950s and 1960s, Van Der Zee worked mainly through mail-order requests. A chance encounter restored him to celebrity status. In 1967, while preparing for an exhibition at the Metropolitan Museum of Art in New York City, curator Reginald McGhee came upon James Van Der Zee's collection. The photographer became the largest single contributor to the *Harlem on My Mind* exhibition at the Metropolitan Museum, shown 1968–69.

In 1969, he received the American Society of Magazine Photographers' award. The following year, the Metropolitan Museum made him an Honorary Fellow for Life and acquired 66 of his photographs for its permanent collection. In 1970, his first one-man show was displayed at the Lenox Library in Lenox, Massachusetts, and in 1971, he held his first retrospective exhibition, at the Studio Museum in Harlem.

James Augustus Joseph Van Der Zee died on May 15, 1983, in WASHINGTON, D.C.

Further Reading

DeCock, Liliane, and Reginald McGhee, eds. *James Van Der Zee.* Dobbs Ferry N.Y.: Morgan & Morgan, 1973.

McGhee, Reginald. *The World of James Van Der Zee: A Visual Record of Black Americans.* New York: Grove Press, 1969.

Schoener, Allon, ed., with foreword by Henry Louis Gates. *Harlem on My Mind: Cultural Capital of Black America, 1900–1968.* New York: New Press, 1995.

Van Der Zee, James, Owen Dodson, and Camille Billops. *The Harlem Book of the Dead.* Dobbs Ferry N.Y.: Morgan & Morgan, 1978.

Van Der Zee, James. *Harlem Heyday: The Photography of James Van Der Zee.* New York: Studio Museum in Harlem, 1982.

— Mary C. Lewis

Van Vechten, Carl (1880–1964) *author, patron*

Through his assistance to individual black writers and artists, his promotion of African-American culture, and his own creative works, white author Carl Van Vechten became one of the most influential figures of the Harlem Renaissance.

Van Vechten was born on June 17, 1880, in Cedar Rapids, Iowa. Though he had an older brother named Ralph and an older sister named Emma, he was separated in age from his brother by 18 years and from his sister by 16. His mother, Ada Fitch Van Vechten, was an early suffragette. She and her oldest children all played musical instruments. In addition to being a store manager turned successful insurance salesman, his father, Charles Van Vechten, was one of the founders of the Piney Woods School for Negro Children in Mississippi. Contrary to the racism of JIM CROW practices prevalent at the time, the Van Vechtens raised their son to acknowledge African Americans as equals.

Van Vechten expressed an increasing interest in African American culture through a number of papers he wrote while a student at the University of Chicago during the early 1900s. He also began in CHICAGO a practice that he would duplicate and help turn into a vogue among whites in NEW YORK CITY: that of patronizing black entertainment venues.

Graduating from the University of Chicago in 1903, Van Vechten joined the staff of Randolph Hearst's *Chicago American.* There, he worked as a general reporter, a news photographer, a society editor, and a chronicler of gossip. In 1906, Van Vechten moved to New York and became a cub reporter with the *New York Times,* eventually becoming an assistant music critic for the *Times.* In 1913, he joined the *New York Press* as a drama critic. Van Vechten's work as a journalist, in Europe as well as New York, brought him into contact with many of the most celebrated names of the period. The subjects of his work often became his friends and included such individuals as Isadora Duncan, Enrico Caruso, Oscar Hammerstein, Anna Pavlova, Salvador Dali, Gertrude Stein, and many others.

Van Vechten married his childhood friend Anna Elizabeth Snyder in England in 1907. The couple divorced in 1912. Two years later he married the actress Fania Marinoff.

Around 1914, Van Vechten began visiting the LAFAYETTE THEATRE and other entertainment centers in Harlem in search of innovative forms of creative expression. It was also in 1914 that he viewed white playwright Ridgely Torrence's black-oriented play, *Granny Maumee,* and began in his writings to encourage the development of an official black theater.

Van Vechten established his career as an author in the mid-1910s with a series of nonfiction works entitled: *Music After the Great War,* 1915; *Music and Bad Manners,* 1916; *Interpreters and Interpretations,* 1917; *The Music of Spain,* 1918; *The Merry-Go-Round,* 1918; *A Tiger in the House,* 1920; and *Lord of the Housetops,* 1921.

He made a successful switch to fiction in 1922 with the publication of his first novel, *Peter Whiffle: His Life and Works.* Like F. Scott Fitzgerald, he gained a reputation as an insightful recorder of the 1920s JAZZ Age with his subsequent novels *Blind Bow-Boy* in 1923, *The Tattooed Countess* in 1924, and

In addition to Carl Van Vechten's many literary portraits of black culture in New York City, his contributions to the Harlem Renaissance include an important collection of photographs taken by him of the movement's principal figures. He is shown here in 1925. *(Library of Congress, Prints & Photographs Division [LC-USZ62-88099])*

Firecrackers in 1925. He also, through his critical writings, became known as a champion of talented but ignored underdogs. Unlike those American critics who simply dismissed the expatriate writer Gertrude Stein as incomprehensible, Van Vechten chose to interpret and promote Stein's work in the United States while the latter, like BRICKTOP and JOSEPHINE BAKER, enjoyed living in France.

When WALTER WHITE, then assistant secretary for the NATIONAL ASSOCIATION FOR THE ADVANCEMENT OF COLORED PEOPLE, submitted his novel *Fire in the Flint* to publisher Alfred A. Knopf in 1924, Van Vechten was asked to read the manuscript. He was so moved by the book that he both recommended it for publication and asked Knopf to introduce him to White, with whom he quickly became friends. Through White, Van Vechten met JAMES WELDON JOHNSON, with whom he would also become close friends, and through Johnson, he befriended LANGSTON HUGHES and COUNTEE CULLEN. In short, just one year prior to the CIVIC CLUB DINNER where proponents of the *NEW NEGRO* movement would announce their agenda and demonstrate their genius, Van Vechten befriended some of its most dynamic representatives.

He felt what he described as a violent need to involve himself as deeply as possible in black culture and used his considerable influence in New York to promote African-American writers and artists. Reading an out-of-print edition of Johnson's *THE AUTOBIOGRAPHY OF AN EX-COLORED MAN*, Van Vechten thought the book extraordinary and convinced Knopf to republish it. He also approached Knopf for the publication of Hughes's *The Weary Blues,* wrote a preface for the book, and arranged for the publication of several poems by Hughes in the fashionable magazine *Vanity Fair.* Moreover, in time, Van Vechten directly influenced the publication of works by Cullen, NELLA LARSEN, RUDOLPH FISHER, AARON DOUGLAS, ZORA NEALE HURSTON, and others. When *OPPORTUNITY* magazine began its literary prize awards, the writer sponsored one for $200.

Even as he managed to help place black writers' and artists' works on the market, Van Vechten himself wrote frequently about the emerging black renaissance for the *New York Herald Tribune, CRISIS: A RECORD OF THE DARKER RACES* magazine, *Vanity Fair,* and other periodicals. Yet none of these had quite the impact as his own would-be contribution to the canon of the movement, a novel called *NIGGER HEAVEN*, published in 1926. A fictional account of Van Vechten's observations of black life in Harlem, the novel became an immediate best-seller and stirred controversy across the United States.

Just as he helped open avenues in publishing for African Americans, Van Vechten and his wife Fania also opened up their home to entertain such guests as A'LELIA WALKER, ETHEL WATERS, and PAUL ROBESON. It was during a party at the Van Vechtens that Robeson met the pianist Larry Brown and first performed spirituals with him. Van Vechten later helped arrange a concert by the duo at the Greenwich Village Theatre.

After the publication of his biography, *Sacred and Profane Memories,* in 1932, Van Vechten devoted himself to creating a photographic record of notable African Americans. Collections of these photographs as well as letters, recordings, and rare books on African America are held in Yale University's James Weldon Johnson Memorial Collection; Fisk University's Gershwin Memorial Collection; and the New York City Public Library's Carl Van Vechten Collection.

Van Vechten died in New York City on December 21, 1964.

Further Reading

Bernard, Emily, ed. *Remember Me to Harlem: The Letters of Langston Hughes and Carl Van Vechten.* New York: Knopf Publishing Group, 2002.

Coleman, Leon. *Carl Van Vechten and the Harlem Renaissance.* New York: Garland Publishing, 1998.

Van Vechten, Carl, and Emily Bernard, ed. *Remember Me to Harlem: The Letters of Langston Hughes and Carl Van Vechten, 1925–1964.* New York: Alfred A. Knopf, 2001.

— Aberjhani

W

Walker, A'Lelia (Lelia McWilliams) (1885–1931)

heiress, entrepreneur

A'lelia Walker was heiress to the fortune of America's first self-made female millionaire, MADAME C. J. WALKER. She was also, in the words of LANGSTON HUGHES, "the joy-goddess of Harlem's 1920s."

Walker was born Lelia McWilliams on June 6, 1885, the only child of Sarah and Moses McWilliams. Her father died two years after her birth. By most accounts he was a victim of white mob violence. Her mother later married Charles J. Walker, the man whose knowledge of newspaper advertising would help Madam C. J. Walker turn a mail-order business for black beauty products into a million-dollar industry.

McWilliams moved to St. Louis with her mother after the death of her father and there attended public schools. She later attended Knoxville College but left there and moved to Denver, Colorado. In Denver, she put her energies into her mother's mail-order business while Madam C. J. Walker traveled the country promoting her products and her business. Standing at a commanding height of nearly six feet, she followed her mother's example and modeled for the Walker Company ads to demonstrate the effectiveness of their products. As the business expanded, she later helped operate the beauty college established in 1908 in Pittsburgh, Pennsylvania by her mother, which was named Lelia College after her. She also encouraged her mother to take the business a step further in 1910 by investing in their own plant in Indianapolis, Indiana, a five-story building that housed a factory, offices, a beauty salon, and movie theater.

McWilliams married several times to husbands John Robinson, Wiley Wilson, and James R. Kennedy. The name she chose to keep was that of her stepfather and an alternate version of her first name. Although she had no children herself, in 1912 she adopted the 13-year-old Mae Bryant, whose long thick hair made it easy for her to step into the family tradition of modeling the Walker Company's hair-care products. Bryant traveled with her grandmother, received an education at Atlanta's Spelman College, and in 1923 enjoyed one of the most spectacular weddings Harlem had ever seen.

With the Walker Company well on its way to million-dollar status, A'Lelia Walker made her move to Harlem at the beginning of the 1910s, and her mother followed shortly afterward. They built a town house with a connecting beauty parlor lauded as one of the most luxurious in the country. When Madam C. J. Walker built an extraordinary palatial mansion on the Hudson River in the white-dominated Irvington on Hudson, she named it Villa Lewaro, based on letters from her daughter's married name (A'LElia WAlker RObinson). For the senior Walker, the mansion was a retreat away from the demands of business; for the younger, it became an explosion of nonstop celebration.

Walker did not pick up the reins of the Walker Company, following her mother's death in 1919, with the kind of progressive vision and hands-on techniques that had ensured her mother's success. If her mother had been the embodiment of productive industry, A'Lelia Walker became the embodiment of the rewards of such industry. The business she had helped her mother build provided her with an inheritance of a million dollars, a share in the profits of the business (two-thirds of which had been left to charity), and substantial holdings in real estate across the United States.

In 1928, she transformed the town house at 108 W. 136th Street into a salon deluxe and named it the DARK TOWER after the column by COUNTEE CULLEN, published in *OPPORTUNITY*, the official organ of the NATIONAL URBAN LEAGUE (NUL). The Dark Tower was originally intended to serve as a place where writers and artists could meet to socialize and enjoy good food at starving-artist prices. Walker contacted RICHARD BRUCE NUGENT and AARON DOUGLAS to decorate the tower but in the end got Manhattan's Paul Frankel to do the job. The

Dark Tower gleamed with furniture and gold-patterned wallpaper of French design, jeweled dining service, and a gold-plated piano. Walker dedicated the tower to black "writers, sculptors, painters, music artists, composers, and their friends." And true to that dedication, she had framed on one wall a copy of Cullen's *Dark Tower* column and lettered on another wall Langston Hughes's famous poem *The Weary Blues.* She also showcased collections of writings on and by black people. However, untrue to the original intent of the tower was the affordability of the items on its menu, which sported everything from hogshead cheese for 30¢ to cream cheese, guava jelly, and toasted crackers for 75¢, fairly steep prices for striving starving artists back in 1928. By contrast, many neighborhood restaurants sold entire dinners for no more than 50¢ or a dollar. Still, for nearly a year it drew exactly the kind of mixed crowd for which Walker had hoped: writers such as WALLACE THURMAN, personalities such as Harold Jackman and CARL VAN VECHTEN, and such singers as ETHEL WATERS, mixed with New York executives and European royalty. Entertainers fresh from a Broadway show might drop in to perform a number or two while Walker enjoyed a game of bridge behind the scenes. It was a grand display of the kind of good times that bolstered the image of Harlem as the party capital of the world and a place where the pursuit of pleasure had no use for color lines.

Weekends at the Villa Lewaro took on a function similar to that of the Dark Tower. The villa was the place of her mother's death, and Walker rarely cared to be there alone. On weekends she invited guests to enjoy the splendor of the Italianate palace on the Hudson. Servants dressed up in Edwardian costumes complete with white wigs saw to everyone's comfort throughout a weekend filled with music from a $60,000 pipe organ, a gold grand piano, or a gold Victrola record player.

Walker made her homes available for gatherings of the culturally elite, but it was not her custom to play the role of PATRON and finance the work or lives of her talented friends. In her notice of the closing of the Dark Tower in November 1928, she stated with simple humility that, "Having no talent or gift but a love and keen admiration for art, The Dark Tower was my contribution."

The advent of the GREAT DEPRESSION in 1929 affected the Walker Company as it did the rest of the country. The stalled expansion of the business and reduced sales of the prod-

Madame C. J. Walker opened up her mansion, Villa Lewaro, on North Broadway in Irvington, New York, to employees of her company for annual meetings while her daughter, A'Lelia Walker, used it as a gathering place for wealthy friends and creative individuals. *(Library of Congress, Prints & Photographs Division [HABS, NY, 60-IRV, 5-1])*

ucts coupled with Walker's opulent lifestyle forced her to auction off the Villa Lewaro estate in 1930. Rare and treasured items were sold for less than half their value and some for less than a third.

Walker died from high blood pressure on August 17, 1931. Though worth half a million dollars less than it had been, the Walker Company remained in business and Mae Bryant inherited a percentage of it. Noted educator and civil rights advocate Mary McLeod Bethune delivered the eulogy for Walker at a funeral presided over by Rev. ADAM CLAYTON POWELL, SR. Langston Hughes penned an elegy in which he crowned Walker "queen of the night."

Further Reading

Bundles, A'Lelia Perry. *On Her Own Ground: The Life and Times of Madame C. J. Walker.* New York: Simon and Schuster, 2001.

Marks, Carole, and Diana Edkins. *The Power of Pride, Stylemakers and Rulebreakers of the Harlem Renaissance.* New York: Crown Publishers, 1999.

Neihart, Ben. *Rough Amusements: The True Story of A'Lelia Walker, Patron of the Harlem Renaissance's Down-Low Culture, an Urban Historical.* London: Bloomsbury USA Publishing, 2003.

— Aberjhani

Walker, George (1873–1911) *actor, comedian*

George Walker achieved international fame as the partner of BERT WILLIAMS, performing in vaudeville, on Broadway, and in tours throughout Europe.

Walker was born in 1873 in Lawrence, Kansas. Minstrelsy, a form of live shows employing whites made up in blackface, was already one of the most popular entertainment forms of the 19th century when he joined up with a group of black minstrels traveling through Kansas. Remaining with the troupe long enough to gain some mastery of the craft, Walker quit to become a single act. He then worked in a number of medicine shows, exploring yet another popular entertainment form of the time, while making his way to California.

He met Bert Williams in 1893, and the two men combined their talents to experiment with a number of acts. At one point, while working with the Mid-Winter Exposition in San Francisco's Golden Gate Park, they had to serve as stand-ins for a group of Dahomeyans scheduled for the event. Following their own ad-lib presentation, they got to see the late-arriving authentic West Africans demonstrate their native songs and dance, providing the duo with useful material for future shows.

They later joined the CHICAGO, Illinois, company of Isham's Octoroons before eventually putting together their Two Real Coons act. For this show, the lighter-complexioned Williams blackened his face in imitation of white performers imitating blacks, while the darker-complexioned Walker retained his natural color. Walker played the more intelligent straight man to Williams's not-so-bright clown figure. Writing in 1906 for *The Theater Magazine,* Walker stated, "We thought that as there seemed to be a great demand for black faces on the stage, we would do all we could to get what we felt belonged to us by the laws of nature. As white men with black faces were billing themselves 'coons,' Williams and Walker would do well to bill themselves as the 'The Two Real Coons' and so we did. As the 'Two Real Coons,' we made our first hit in New York, while playing at Koster and Bial's."

They scored a bigger hit in 1896 with a musical called *The Gold Bug,* in which their performance of a dance fad called the CAKEWALK helped launch them on a national, and later international, tour. They took their success even further in 1902 when they joined creative forces with the poet Paul Lawrence Dunbar and composer WILL MARION COOK in NEW YORK CITY to produce *In Dahomey.* It was the first in a string of highly successful musicals that Walker and Williams would take to Broadway and around the world, assuring their rise and then securing their place among the top entertainers in America.

Offstage, Walker was considered as flashy a dresser as he was onstage and was often described as "dapper" or a "dandy." He was married to a singer and dancer from New York named Ada Overton, whose tastes in fashion were described as equal to his.

In 1909, Walker began to display the telltale symptoms of syphilis, a then incurable disease that would claim the lives of a number of talented entertainers of the period, including Scott Joplin's. Retiring from the stage in 1910, Walker died in 1911.

Further Reading

Douglas, Ann. *Terrible Honesty: Mongrel Manhattan in the 1920s.* New York: Farrar, Straus, & Giroux, 1995.

Hatch, James V., and Teel Shire, eds. *Black Theatre USA: Plays by African Americans.* New York: Simon and Schuster, 1974.

Smith, Eric Ledell. *Bert Williams: A Biography of the Pioneer Black Comedian.* Jefferson, N.C.: McFarland and Co., 1992.

— Aberjhani

Walker, Madame C. J. (Sarah Breedlove Walker) (1867–1919) *entrepreneur*

Madam C. J. Walker's development and marketing of a line of beauty products geared toward African-American women made her the first self-made female millionaire in the United States.

Walker was born Sarah Breedlove on December 23, 1867, in Delta, Louisiana. She was the youngest of three children born to former slaves Owen and Minerva Breedlove. With a brother named Alex and a sister named Louvenia, Sarah was the first of the children born in freedom. Her parents died during an outbreak of yellow fever and made Breedlove an orphan at the age of seven.

At the age of 14, she married Moses McWilliams, and at age 17 gave birth to their daughter, Lelia McWilliams. Two years later, her husband was killed and McWilliams became a widow at 19. To support herself and her daughter, the young mother moved to St. Louis. There, she worked in turn as a laundress scrubbing clothes by hand in a washtub, a cook, and a sales agent for Malone's Wonderful Hair Grower.

Yearning for a means to earn a better living, McWilliams reportedly experienced a dream in which a black man presented her with a formula for the treatment of black women's scalp and hair. She gathered the ingredients required, including some that had to be shipped from Africa, and mixed it into an ointment that she first applied to herself. According to the before-usage and after-usage photographs she later used to help sell the product, the ointment reversed the chronic loss of hair from which she had suffered and stimulated a full and healthy new growth of hair. With a starting investment of $1.50, she began to manufacture and sell the product to others.

She married an old acquaintance, newspaperman Charles J. Walker, in 1906, and the two made Denver, Colorado, the base for their hair products business. The starting lineup of products included such items as Madame C. J. Walker's Vegetable Shampoo; Glossine, the Wonderful Hair Grower; and C. J. Walker's Blood and Rheumatic Remedy. In addition to starting the mail-order business to help push their products, Madam C. J. Walker began to travel town to town and state to state. Gradually, the business grew from grossing $10 per week in 1906 to $35 per week. As Walker continued to travel over the next four years, the business began to earn $1,000 per month. In 1911, it was making $1,000 each day. Before 1920, the black woman who had scrubbed clothes by hand became America's first self-made female millionaire.

She continued to expand the means by which her product reached the public and in Pittsburgh in 1908 opened Lelia College, a beauty school specifically for those wanting to learn her methods and sell her products. She also began to open beauty parlors that operated throughout the United States, in the Caribbean, and in South America. Walker's business was doing well enough in 1910 that she opened a five-story plant in Indianapolis. The plant included a state-of-the-art factory to manufacture her products, business offices, a beauty shop, and a movie theater constructed to allow her and other blacks to bypass the public humiliation of JIM CROW, the system of legally sanctioned racial discrimination practiced at the time.

Though her marriage to Charles J. Walker ended in divorce, he remained a supporter of the business. Many others joined the business also as Walker hired agents to promote her products nationally and internationally. More than simply offering them work as saleswomen and salesmen, she invited them to "secure prosperity and freedom" by opening their own Madame C. J. Walker shops. The invitation proved an appealing one that allowed agents for the business to earn well above the average weekly salaries of African Americans and white Americans in either the North or South. At its strongest, the company boasted some 20,000 representatives worldwide.

Success brought its rewards. Among them was relocating to NEW YORK CITY, where Walker settled in HARLEM, building a town house with adjoining facilities for instructions in the Walker system of beauty culture. She also constructed Villa Lewaro, a palatial quarter-million-dollar mansion designed by New York's first licensed black architect, Vertner Tandy. Walker contended the mansion was not simply for her personal pleasure but intended as a symbol of the prosperity she believed possible for all African Americans. Resting on four and a half acres above the Hudson River, it would serve after Walker's death as a weekend gathering place for New York's artistic and international elite attending glamorous parties hosted by Walker's daughter, A'LELIA WALKER.

Her financial independence also allowed Walker a voice in politics, and during WORLD WAR I she led a delegation of women to register their protest with President Woodrow Wilson against the discriminatory treatment of African Americans in the military. Taking the matter even further into her own hands, she often visited military camps where she spoke with black troops to help them maintain strong morale. She was also one of the organizers of Harlem's Silent Protest Parade in 1917, during which hundreds marched through the streets of Harlem in silent protest against those killed in the St. Louis riots.

One of her greatest roles was that of philanthropist. At the same time that she urged others to struggle for their independence, Walker gave generously to numerous causes and organizations, donating funds for the construction of a new YMCA facility and helping to finance the National Negro Business League and the National Association of Colored Women. She presented the NATIONAL ASSOCIATION FOR THE ADVANCEMENT OF COLORED PEOPLE (NAACP) with $5,000 to step up its war against LYNCHING.

Upon her death from Bright's disease on May 25, 1919, Walker left a will stipulating two-thirds of her business's net corporate profits should go to charities, including orphanages, nursing homes, the Tuskegee Institute, and the Haines Institute in Georgia. Always mindful of her daughter's well-being, she left A'Lelia a million dollars, various real estate properties, and a percentage of the Walker business.

In 1998, the U.S. Postal Service issued a commemorative stamp in tribute to Walker.

Further Reading

Bundles, A'Lelia Perry. *On Her Own Ground: The Life and Times of Madam C. J. Walker.* New York: Simon and Schuster, 2001.

Winegarten, Ruthe, and Sharon Kahn. *Brave Black Women: From Slavery to the Space Shuttle.* Austin: University of Texas, 1997.

— Aberjhani

Walker, Margaret Abigail (Margaret Walker Alexander) (1915–1998) *educator, writer*

Margaret Walker balanced the demands of motherhood and her career as an educator to achieve distinction as a prizewinning poet and author of the first historically realistic novel by a black woman on American slavery.

Walker was born on July 7, 1915, in Birmingham, Alabama. Her father, Sigismund C. Walker, was a scholar and linguist who emigrated from Jamaica to the United States to become a minister and educator. Her mother, Marion Dozier Walker, was also an educator as well as a musician. Their other offspring were two daughters, Mercedes and Gwendolyn, and a son, Sigismund, Jr.

Walker attended elementary school in Birmingham and briefly in Meridian, Mississippi. Her parents exposed her at an early age to the works of English poets and philosophers as well as those of the Harlem Renaissance, including COUNTEE

CULLEN and LANGSTON HUGHES. Her family moved to NEW ORLEANS when Walker was 10 years old. Attending high school at Gilbert Academy, she met Langston Hughes, who recognized her literary gifts and encouraged their development. She graduated from Gilbert Academy in 1930 and had enrolled at New Orleans University (now Dillard), where both her parents taught, when Hughes suggested her parents send her north to continue her education.

Enrolling at Northwestern University in Illinois, Walker met W. E. B. DU BOIS, who assisted in the publication of her first poems, including one in the May 1934 issue of *CRISIS: A RECORD OF THE DARKER RACES* magazine. She graduated from Northwestern in 1935 and took a position with the CHICAGO branch of the WORKS PROGRESS ADMINISTRATION's FEDERAL WRITERS' PROJECT. As an employee of the Federal Writers' Project, she worked with such writers as ARNA BONTEMPS, KATHERINE DUNHAM, GWENDOLYN BROOKS, and Frank Yerby. She also met and befriended RICHARD NATHANIEL WRIGHT, with whom she joined the South Side Writers Group. During her acquaintance with Wright, Walker helped edit two of his earliest novels and assisted with the research for Wright's acclaimed masterpiece, *Native Son.*

Walker joined the famed University of Iowa Writer's Workshop and earned her master's degree there in 1940. Her thesis, entitled *For My People,* also became her first published volume of poetry and the first major collection published by an African-American woman since *The Heart of a Woman and Other Poems* by Georgia Douglas Johnson in 1918. Closer in spirit to the more radical political poetry of CLAUDE MCKAY than the romantic verse of Johnson or ANNIE BETHEL BANNISTER SPENCER, Walker expressed in her work a dignified outrage that quietly identified racism as barbaric and revolution as justified. The book won the Yale University Younger Poets Award in 1942, making Walker the first African American to win it, and established her career as a notable writer.

She was appointed professor of English at Livingstone College in Salisbury, North Carolina, from 1941 to 1942. Walker then became professor of English at the State College in Institute, West Virginia. That same year, she married Firnist James Alexander. The couple's first child, Marion Elizabeth, was born in 1944; Firnist James, Jr., 1946; Sigismund Walker, 1949; and Margaret Elvira in 1954. At the same time that she raised her children and cared for her husband when he became disabled, Walker continued to pursue her own education, teach others, and conduct research for her historical novel, *Jubilee.* At times, she had to divide her family by leaving her children with different relatives while pursuing her professional goals.

Walker returned to teach at Livingstone College for a year in 1945 and then concentrated primarily on writing and family responsibilities until receiving a job as professor of English at Jackson State College in Jackson, Mississippi. Except for a brief period in 1953 and from 1962 to 1964, she would remain at Jackson State for 30 years. Again at Iowa University in 1962, she completed *Jubilee* as her doctoral dissertation and received her Ph.D. in 1965.

The author achieved international recognition in 1966 with publication of her historical novel, *Jubilee.* With its attention to historical detail regarding the Civil War, the Reconstruction era, and the incorporation of authentic black folklore, many read *Jubilee* as a black literary response to white author Margaret Mitchell's *Gone with the Wind.* At its core, the novel tells the story of Margaret Duggans Ware Brown's life in rural Georgia. Known as Vyry in the novel, Duggans in real life was Walker's paternal great grandmother. Her story was passed on to Walker by her grandmother Elvira Ware Dozier, and marks a powerful example of an important story's creative evolution from the famed African-American oral tradition to the general American literary tradition. It presents Margaret Duggans Ware Brown as a woman sustained by faith in a racist society that habitually devalues and abuses her as a human being. After its release in late August 1966, *Jubilee* sold approximately 5,000 copies per week throughout the month of September and went through 36 printings in two years. Translated for worldwide distribution, the novel made best-seller lists in France, placing Walker on the same level of international success as her late friend Richard Wright. It also won the Houghton Mifflin Fellowship award.

Walker continued to balance her dual careers as an educator and writer, producing her second volume of poetry with *The Ballad of the Free* in 1966 and *Prophets for a New Day* in 1970. The latter was noted for Walker's acknowledgment and support of the Civil Rights movement. The impact of *Jubilee* remained strong enough in 1970 that she was able to publish an essay titled "How I Wrote Jubilee." In 1973, she published the volume *October Journey* and the following year worked with poet Nikki Giovanni to publish a dialogue titled *A Poetic Equation: Conversations Between Margaret Walker and Nikki Giovanni.*

At Jackson State University, Walker developed a comprehensive black studies program and research facility known as the Institute for the Study of the History, Life, and Culture of Black People. The facility was later named the Margaret Walker Alexander National Research Center. Walker retired from Jackson State in 1979 while continuing to write poetry, essays, and biographies.

In 1988, she made an acclaimed and controversial contribution to literary history with her biography *Richard Wright, Daemonic Genius: A Portrait of the Man, a Critical Look at His Work.* In the book, Walker addressed her relationship with Wright as well as her perception of his personality and development as a writer. Other works in her later years included *This Is My Century: New and Collected Poems,* in which she called for a spiritual rebirth of humanity and championed "Black humanism" as a spiritual philosophy beneficial to people of all backgrounds. In 1990, she published *How I Wrote Jubilee and Other Essays on Life and Literature,* and in 1997, another collection of essays titled *On Being Female, Black, and Free.*

Walker garnered many awards in the course of her distinguished career as an educator and writer. The former governor of Mississippi, William Winter, proclaimed July 12 Margaret Walker Alexander Day in 1980. The following year, Guynes Street in Jackson was renamed Margaret Walker Alexander Drive. In 1992, she received the Living Legacy Award and in

1993 the National Book Award for Lifetime Achievement. On October 17, 1998, she was inducted into the African American Literary Hall of Fame.

Walker died of cancer at the home of her daughter, Marion Elizabeth Alexander Coleman, in Chicago on November 30, 1998.

Further Reading

Carmichael, Jacqueline Miller. *Trumpeting a Fiery Sound, History and Folklore in Margaret Walker's* Jubilee. Athens: University of Georgia Press, 1998.

Walker, Margaret. *On Being Female, Black, and Free.* Knoxville: University of Tennessee Press, 1997.

— Aberjhani

Waller, Fats (Thomas Wright) (1904–1943)

musician

Fats Waller's gifts as a pianist, organist, singer, and prolific composer made him one of the most popular musicians of his era.

Of the 12 children born to Adeline Lockett and Edward Martin Waller, their son Thomas Wright Waller, born on May 21, 1904, was one of five to reach adulthood. Originally from Virginia, the Wallers moved to NEW YORK CITY in the 1890s, first settling in Greenwich Village, then later on 63rd Street. Both were deeply religious. Adeline Waller played piano in church and Edward Waller conducted a street corner ministry where his son Thomas played the harmonium to accompany his family's singing. Waller established a trucking business to support his family and when not conducting his own street ministry took them to the ABYSSINIAN BAPTIST CHURCH.

Young Thomas's hefty size earned him the nickname "Fats" as a child and it stuck with him throughout his life. Likewise, when he was only six years old, his parents recognized his musical talent and, with the help of family members, encouraged it by purchasing a piano for their home. His first lessons were from a tutor who was astounded to realize that Waller could duplicate her playing simply by watching her hands and listening. His interest in music intensified during high school. He experimented with the violin and string bass, learned to read music, and became a popular member of his school's orchestra.

He had a number of odd jobs as a teenager, including one at a delicatessen operated by Connie and George Immerman. The Immermans were brothers who later would open a nightclub called CONNIE'S INN and hire Fats again, but this time as a performer.

Attending shows at the LINCOLN THEATRE, Waller befriended the pianist Mabel Brown, hired to play accompaniment to the featured film. Brown allowed Waller to study her technique as she played, allowed him to fill in for her on breaks, and helped him get a job playing the theater's pipe organ. Waller's performances at the Lincoln, for which he earned $23 a week, made him a local celebrity.

He found another mentor in James P. Johnson, a then well-known STRIDE and RAGTIME pianist. Johnson helped Waller polish his technique, expand his repertoire, and master the basics of ragtime just as it was growing in popularity. He also introduced him to other professional musicians and got him started playing on the famous Harlem RENT PARTY circuit, performing in individual homes to help tenants raise money for their rent or other needs.

In 1920, shortly after his mother's death, Waller married Edith Hatchett, who bore his first son. Life as the wife of a musician proved too demanding for Hatchett, and the couple divorced five years later. Alimony payments to Hatchett would remain a challenge for Waller, and in 1928 he spent time in jail for missing too many. In 1926, Waller married Anita Rutherford, to whom he would remain married until his death. They had two sons, Maurice and Ronald.

Waller began his recording career in 1922 just as RACE RECORDS, songs recorded by African Americans for sale to black audiences, were taking off as a full-fledged industry. He recorded "Muscle Shoal Blues" and "Birmingham Blues" on the Okeh record label, a division of Columbia Records. The following year he moved into publishing such songs as "Wildcat Blues" and "Squeeze Me" with the Clarence Williams Publishing Company. In 1923 the Newark radio station began live broadcasting of his performances at the Fox Terminal Theatre.

Following the trend of black musical revues established by the Broadway hit *SHUFFLE ALONG* in 1921, Waller began writing music for the stage in the mid-1920s. He produced a miniature version of the hit show *BLACKBIRDS*, called *Junior Blackbirds,* at the LAFAYETTE THEATRE in 1926. He joined two of the creators of *Shuffle Along,* Aubrey Lyles and Flournoy Miller, for their production of *KEEP SHUFFLIN'* in 1928. Waller formed a partnership with lyricist Andy Razaf to write several of the show's hit songs.

When Connie and George Immerman opened their nightclub, Connie's Inn, Waller was one of the musicians they hired to produce a series of floor shows. One of the most successful of the shows was *HOT CHOCOLATES.* With lyrics by Razaf and music by Waller and Harry Brooks, the production introduced the song that became Waller's signature piece, "Ain't Misbehavin'." It also took him, along with LOUIS ARMSTRONG and CAB CALLOWAY, to Broadway for a run of 219 performances.

The entertainer's career continued to expand with the Fats Waller Rhythm Club radio show in 1932 and extensive tours throughout the United States. His first films were *Hooray for Love* and *King of Burlesque* in 1935. Although the GREAT DEPRESSION was still on, Waller took his band on his first European tour in 1938, playing 10 weeks at $2,500 per week. He took advantage of the tour to record a number of songs with English musicians and for those sessions renamed his band Continental Rhythm. He repeated the European tour in 1939.

Waller made history in 1942 when he became the first jazz soloist to play New York's Carnegie Hall. Waller's music became so popular that he was able to write the show *Early to Bed* in 1943 and allow others to perform in it while he concentrated on other projects. Aside from continuing to give individual concerts and benefits, he performed with LENA HORNE in the film *STORMY WEATHER.*

Following a string of engagements in California, Waller was returning on the Santa Fe train to New York when he died of pneumonia on December 15, 1943. ADAM CLAYTON POWELL, JR., delivered the eulogy for Waller at the Abyssinian Baptist Church. Since his death, Waller's music has been celebrated in a number of revues, most notably 1975's *Bubbling Brown Sugar,* which also showcased the work of EUBIE BLAKE, and 1978's *Ain't Misbehavin,* named that year's Best Broadway Musical.

Further Reading

Calabrese, Anthony, and Maurice Waller. *Fats Waller.* Boston, Mass.: Music Sales Corporation, 1997.

Machlin, Paul S., ed. *Thomas Wright "Fats" Waller: Performances in Transcription 1927–1943.* Madison, Wisc.: A-R Editions, Incorporated, 2000.

Shipton, Aly. *Fats Waller: Cheerful Little Earful.* New York: Continuum Publishing Group, 2002.

— Aberjhani

Walrond, Eric Derwent (1898–1966) *writer*

In his fiction, essays, and journalism, Eric Walrond chronicled the plight of Caribbean immigrants to the United States and became one of the leading writers of the Harlem Renaissance.

Walrond was born in Georgetown, British Guyana, in 1898, to parents who separated shortly after his birth. He was raised by his mother and moved with her in 1906 to Barbados. There, he attended St. Stephen's Boys' School in Black Rock.

In 1910, the family moved to Colón in Panama and from 1913 to 1916 Walrond was educated by a private tutor. He took a position as an administrative clerk in Cristobal, Panama, with the Health Department of Canal Commission. He also worked as a reporter and sportswriter for Panama's *Star and Herald.*

Walrond joined the wave of immigrants moving from the Caribbean to the United States and in 1918 made his home in NEW YORK CITY. He attended the City College of New York from 1922 to 1924 and from 1924 to 1926 studied creative writing at Columbia University. At the same time that he pursued his educational goals, Walrond copublished and edited the short-lived newspaper the *Brooklyn and Long Island Informer.* He also served as associate editor for the *Weekly Review.*

Walrond began to gain a reputation as a talented and insightful writer with a number of articles and stories published in 1923. CHARLES SPURGEON JOHNSON considered Walrond one of the more promising writers of the growing *NEW NEGRO* movement and published his stories in *OPPORTUNITY* magazine, including "The Stone Rebounds," "On Being Domestic," and "Cynthia Goes to the Prom." Among the articles Walrond published in *Current History* magazine were "The Negro Exodus from the South" and "The New Negro Faces America." In the latter, he provided a critique of African-American leadership, pointing out the exclusionary elitism of W. E. B. DU BOIS, the outdated accommodation tactics of BOOKER TALIAFERRO WASHINGTON, and the exaggerated pageantry of MARCUS GARVEY.

Despite Walrond's criticism of Garvey, he became a member of the UNIVERSAL NEGRO IMPROVEMENT ASSOCIATION (UNIA) and an associate editor for the organization's *NEGRO WORLD* from 1923 to 1925. In his capacity as an editor, he was instrumental in publishing works by ZORA NEALE HURSTON, ALAIN LOCKE, CLAUDE MCKAY, and others associated with the New Negro Movement. He in turn was included among them when Locke edited the *New Negro* anthology in 1926. Following his associate editorship with the *Negro World,* Walrond worked for two years as the business manager for *Opportunity* magazine.

In October 1926, Boni and Liveright published a collection of 10 stories by Walrond called *Tropic Death.* Although *Tropic Death* did not achieve best-seller status on any level, it did establish Walrond as an exceptional literary artist comparable to JEAN TOOMER. Walrond's stories portrayed natives of the Caribbean thoroughly entrenched in the values and customs of their homeland while attempting to acclimate themselves to the ruling governments of the West. The book was acclaimed both for its authentic use of native dialect and for Walrond's densely impressionistic descriptions of island culture. Various critics, including W. E. B. Du Bois and LANGSTON HUGHES, championed *Tropic Death* for its uncompromising perspective of the world as seen through the eyes of a black islander. Some of Walrond's most celebrated stories were: "Subjection," "The Yellow One," "The White Snake," "The Wharf Rats," and "The Palm Porch," which was also published in the *New Negro* anthology.

Walrond's increasing renown as a writer helped him in 1928 to earn both a Guggenheim Fellowship and a Zona Gale Scholarship at the University of Wisconsin. In the course of researching a book on the Panama Canal, he immigrated in 1928 to Europe. In July 1929, he traveled to PARIS, France, where he spent time with COUNTEE CULLEN and met members of the expanding NEGRITUDE movement. He remained in France until 1934 and there published a number of essays and stories about life in HARLEM.

Walrond settled in England during the mid-1930s and reportedly married twice. He had three daughters: Dorothy, Lucille, and Jean. His works have been widely anthologized, including appearances in Van Wyck Brooks's *The American Caravan* and Langston Hughes's *Best Short Stories by Black Writers.* Like Toomer after the publication of *Cane,* Walrond did not produce another major literary work after *Tropic Death.* He was at work on his book about the Panama Canal when he died in London in 1966.

Further Reading

Favor, J. Martin. *Authentic Blackness: The Folk in the New Negro Renaissance.* Durham, N.C.: Duke University Press, 1999.

Walrond, Eric, and Louis J. Parascandola, eds. *Winds Can Wake the Dead: An Eric Walrond Reader.* Detroit: Wayne State University Press, 1999.

— Aberjhani

Waring, Laura Wheeler (1887–1948) *portrait painter, illustrator*

A staff artist with the *CRISIS: A RECORD OF THE DARKER RACES,* one of the leading periodicals of the Harlem Renaissance,

Laura Wheeler Waring excelled at portraits of African Americans and created for the HARMON FOUNDATION a series of paintings depicting black leaders.

Laura Wheeler Waring was born in 1887 in Hartford, Connecticut, and later educated at the Pennsylvania Academy of Fine Arts. In 1914, she continued her studies at the Académie de la Grande Chaumière in PARIS, France, after winning the Cresson Memorial Scholarship. Returning to the United States, she taught art at Cheyney State Teachers College, a black college in Pennsylvania, and eventually became head of the school's art department.

Well known as a staff artist with the *Crisis,* she illustrated short stories written by JESSIE REDMOND FAUSET, the magazine's literary editor, and Dorothy Canfield. In 1926, Waring was appointed director of black art exhibits at the PHILADELPHIA Exposition.

Critics classified Waring as a conservative artist but observed that she could also produce bold canvases. In 1927, Waring received a gold medal from the Harmon Foundation for *Anna Washington Derry,* her portrait of a mature, dignified black woman. Another of her most noted portraits, *Still Life* (1928), was commissioned by Madame Lillian Evanti, an opera singer and founder of the Evans-Tibbs Collection in WASHINGTON, D.C. When photographer Addison Scurlock executed a portrait of Madame Evanti in 1934, he included Waring's colorful and robust *Still Life* in the background.

Along with Betsy Graves Reyneau, in the 1940s Waring completed for the Harmon Foundation a set of 24 traditional paintings titled *Portraits of Outstanding Americans of Negro Origin.*

Laura Wheeler Waring died in 1948.

Further Reading

Bailey, David A., and Paul Gilroy. *Rhapsodies in Black: Art of the Harlem Renaissance.* Berkeley: University of California Press, 1997.

Powell, Richard J. *Black Art and Culture in the 20th Century.* London: Thames and Hudson, 1997.

— Sandra L. West

Washington, Booker Taliaferro (1856–1915)

educator, leader

Through a network of political allies, patrons, and protégés, Booker T. Washington became the most influential African-American leader of his time.

Washington was born a slave in 1856 on a farm owned by James Burroughs in Franklin County, Virginia. The son of a black cook named Jane and an unknown white father, he had one brother and a sister. Washington was nine when he and his family were freed by the 1865 ratification of the Emancipation Proclamation. They moved to Malden, West Virginia, where they joined Jane's husband, Washington Ferguson, who had escaped slavery during the Civil War.

In Malden, Washington attended school while also working early morning and late afternoon shifts in a salt factory. He also worked in a coal mine before later becoming a houseboy for the family of Lewis and Viola Ruffner. Mrs. Ruffner took it upon herself to teach Washington in matters regarding etiquette and personal hygiene. In 1872, Washington learned about Hampton Institute in Virginia, a new school founded to train blacks in industrial skills, and decided to leave Malden. He traveled by foot from one state to the next to reach the school, stopping on his journey long enough to earn money before finally arriving at Hampton.

Upon arriving at the school, he gained entrance after an instructor named Mary F. Mackie asked him to sweep a classroom and he surmised that the task was a kind of qualification exam. Instead of just sweeping the floor, he cleaned the entire classroom and by doing so won admission to the school.

At Hampton, headed by Gen. Samuel C. Armstrong, Washington worked as a janitor while taking classes that stressed the value of manual labor, personal dignity, and self-discipline in addition to classes on the practical operations of farming and machinery. He graduated with honors in 1875 and returned for a short time to teach in his hometown. He continued his education by spending a year at Wayland Seminary in WASHINGTON, D.C. In May 1879, he delivered a commencement address titled "The Force That Wins at Hampton Institute." When Armstrong offered him a teaching position at Hampton, he accepted and successfully directed the school's first offering of night classes.

Armstrong further advanced Washington's career when a board in Macon County, Alabama, asked him to recommend someone for the position of principal at the Tuskegee Normal School. Instead of recommending a white candidate as the board assumed Armstrong would, he proposed Washington for the job. Washington accepted and made the move to Alabama only to discover that his school was actually a church and an old shack. Undaunted, he started classes on July 4, 1881, performing the role of teacher and principal for 30 students.

Washington undertook a plan to expand his school with the purchase of a former slave plantation for $500. His students built their new school while also learning blacksmithing, housekeeping, furniture building, and brick making. After several attempts at perfecting the art of making bricks, they not only made those with which they continued to build but produced enough to sell and help finance the school. Washington also obtained financing for the school by building a rapport with local wealthy whites and persuading them that blacks trained at his school would ultimately benefit their own endeavors by serving as superiorly trained craftsmen and housekeepers. Modeling his educational philosophy largely on what he had learned at Hampton, Washington guided the development of Tuskegee until it first rivaled then surpassed his alma mater.

As Tuskegee grew, so did Washington's renown until others began to look to him for advice on emulating his success. In September 1895, seven months after the death of black abolitionist Frederick Douglass, Washington was invited to speak at the Cotton States and International Exposition in Atlanta, Georgia. His speech has alternately been referred to as the *Atlanta Address* and the *Atlanta Compromise;* reviews of it were carried in newspapers across the United States, and its impact

Educator Booker T. Washington, the most prominent African-American spokesperson of his era, addresses an audience in Mound Bayou, Mississippi, in 1912. *(Library of Congress, Prints & Photographs Division [LC-USZ62-120527])*

made the educator nationally and internationally famous. W. E. B. DU BOIS, teaching at the time at Wilberforce University in Ohio, wrote Washington that his words were "fitly spoken."

In his attempts to reconcile the racial and regional conflicts of the time, Washington's *Atlanta Address* urged blacks to "cast down their buckets" in what he perceived as a stream of opportunities created by "agriculture, mechanics, in commerce, in domestic service, and in the professions." In diplomatic language that masterfully balanced promises of economic advancement to blacks, cordial segregation to white southerners, and economic and social stability to northerners, Washington concluded his speech with a prayer that his philosophy would "bring into our Beloved South a new heaven and a new earth." The precise intent of Washington's speech remains debated, but it clearly enough called for African Americans to forgo attempts at political agitation for voting rights, social integration, and a liberal arts education. Not discounting the value of a liberal arts education, he stressed that "there is as much dignity in tilling a field as in writing a poem." Much of Washington's speech seemed to foreshadow and even give license to the historic *Plessy v. Ferguson* Supreme Court ruling which the next year would institutionalize the kind of JIM CROW separatism that Washington envisioned as mutually beneficial to blacks and whites but which in fact proved deadly for African Americans. With Jim Crow segregation sanctioned by the courts, racism continued unchecked in some of its most vicious forms, particularly LYNCHING and excessively harsh sentencing for African Americans in the courts.

Nevertheless, Washington's fame and influence continued to increase with his founding of the National Negro Business League in 1900. Also that year, he published a moderately successful autobiography titled *Story of My Life and Work.* He followed it up in 1901 with a second autobiography, ghostwritten by white journalist and Tuskegee public relations representative Max Bennett Thrasher, titled *Up from Slavery.* With its true tale of how with faith and courage Washington overcame poverty and ignorance to achieve the kind of success all Americans might strive for, the book rapidly became an international sensation. It made publishing history with translations into more languages than any other American book of its kind. It also drew the attention of steel magnate Andrew Carnegie, who was so impressed by Washington that he donated $600,000 in U.S. Steel bonds and a building for a library at Tuskegee. Carnegie came to believe so deeply in Washington's assessment of racial issues that he eventually donated more than two dozen buildings to different schools at Washington's request. Oil tycoon John D. Rockefeller, Sears Roebuck entrepreneur Julius Rosenwald, Kodak camera inventor George Eastman, and oil magnate Henry H. Rogers were all among the many PATRONs who donated money both to Washington's own projects and those he championed.

That year, 1901, President Theodore Roosevelt invited Washington to dinner, an event that again placed the educator in international headlines. Many white southerners protested Washington's presence in the White House as they would his highly publicized teas with Queen Victoria and the Danish royal family. Washington, however, living as he did in the South, conceded that he would abide by the Jim Crow customs of white neighbors while in the South but would not restrict his social activities because of race when outside the South.

The fact that whites clearly accepted Washington as a representative of African America stirred protest and controversy among those blacks who did not agree with his philosophy of accommodating segregation while striving for a basic livelihood. Many others simply accepted the fact that he had miraculously amassed a great deal of influence, and some thought his idea of establishing an economic foundation as a first step toward eventual social and political equality a sound one. Thomas Fortune of the *NEW YORK AGE*, novelist and filmmaker OSCAR MICHEAUX, publisher and political advocate MARCUS GARVEY, and writer and diplomat JAMES WELDON JOHNSON were all at some point dedicated adherents to Washington's teachings.

On the other hand, editor J. Max Barber of the *Voice of the Negro* and editor Monroe Trotter of the *Boston Globe* were two of Washington's strongest black critics. In 1903, Trotter fairly sabotaged one of Washington's speaking engagements with a volley of nonstop questions about his political beliefs and practices. Trotter received 30 days in jail for the incident. Whereas earlier he had praised Washington's *Atlanta Address,* in 1903 Du Bois published *The SOULS OF BLACK FOLK*, a book of essays in which he largely dismantled Washington's vision of blacks, the South, and the United States in general. He announced and exercised his right to criticize Washington directly in one essay titled "Of Mr. Booker T. Washington and Others." He specifically charged that it was unrealistic for Washington to believe and convince others to believe that the black race was likely to advance by employing a philosophy that deprived them of the will to politically protest their conditions or by concentrating the bulk of their educational efforts on industrial training. *Souls of Black Folk,* coupled with Monroe Trotter's much publicized verbal attack on Washington, marked the beginning of organized oppositions to Washington's leadership in the black community.

Washington, accompanied by a number of his advisers and allies, arranged a secret meeting with Du Bois at Carnegie Hall in 1904 to discuss their divergent views on race relations. The meeting ended, however, with the same divided perspectives with which it began. It also inspired Du Bois to join forces with Trotter, J. Max Barber, and 26 other influential African Americans to form the NIAGARA MOVEMENT as a formal response to Washington's so-called Tuskegee Machine. Lacking the kind of financial and political support Washington enjoyed, the Niagara Movement faltered after several conferences, and in 1909 many of its members, following Du Bois's lead, joined the newly formed and integrated NATIONAL ASSOCIATION FOR THE ADVANCEMENT OF COLORED PEOPLE (NAACP).

Bolstered by the political and financial resources of such members as social worker and journalist MARY WHITE OVINGTON, publisher Oswald Garrison Villard, and educator Joel E. SPINGARN, the NAACP utilized litigation and publicity to aggressively tackle Jim Crow practices. In addition, the organization appointed Du Bois editor of its official magazine, the *CRISIS: A RECORD OF THE DARKER RACES*, and provided him with a powerful platform for the presentation of his own views on race relations and other matters. Many members of the NAACP were former followers of Washington, and rather than present the organization as opposition to his leadership, they chose simply to function as an alternative to it.

Washington's increasing disillusionment with his country's willingness to grant African Americans racial equality under any circumstances, coupled with the NAACP's growing influence, prompted him to revise many of his opinions and actions. Moreover, after serving as an advisor to presidents Theodore Roosevelt and William Howard Taft, he lived to suffer the ignominy of witnessing President THOMAS WOODROW WILSON officially segregate government facilities in 1913.

For his own part, Washington continued to develop and strengthen Tuskegee Institute, boosting its student population to 2,000 and increasing its teaching faculty to 200. With its teachers, student workers, and other employees, Tuskegee—and thus Washington—was one of the principal employers of African Americans in the United States. Washington also personally financed a number of court cases challenging Jim Crow practices, spoke out more vigorously against racism in general, and regularly publicized studies condemning the practice of lynching.

Washington married the first of his three wives, Fanny Smith, in 1882. Two years later, she died from an accidental fall. In 1886, he married Olivia A. Davidson, with whom he had two sons and shared the duties of principal of Tuskegee. Their marriage lasted until her death in 1889. Margaret Murray, Washington's last wife, worked beside her husband until his death from nervous exhaustion, kidney failure, and arteriosclerosis on November 14, 1915, at Tuskegee.

Further Reading

Mansfield, Stephen. *Then Darkness Fled: The Liberating Wisdom of Booker T. Washington.* Nashville: Cumberland House Publishing, 1999.

McKissack, Patricia, and Fredrick McKissack. *Booker T. Washington: Leader and Educator.* Berkeley Heights, New Jersey: Enslow Publishers, 2001.

Verney, Kevern J., and K. J. Verney. *The Art of the Possible: Booker T. Washington and Black Leadership in the United States, 1881–1925.* New York: Garland Publishing, 2000.

— Aberjhani

Washington, D.C.

Decades before NEW YORK CITY's Harlem Renaissance of the 1920s–30s, Washington, D.C., experienced a cultural resurgence all its own that included a number of future Harlem Renaissance icons.

Whereas the bulk of those African Americans who settled in New York City's HARLEM during the GREAT MIGRATION did so in the 1910s–20s, the bulk of those who settled in Washington, D.C., moved there between 1860 and 1880. One of the many reasons blacks left the rural South was to obtain formal education so they, former slaves, could advance, or "uplift the race," in the world. In Washington, D.C., as a result of their uplift efforts, they created a community of black schools, from preschool to a premier African-American university.

In addition, as in PHILADELPHIA, blacks elevated themselves socially and economically, developing in the process black middle-class neighborhoods. Although they were in a segregated city positioned at the gateway of the Mason-Dixon line on the cusp of Confederate state Virginia, these immigrant African Americans developed a society that incorporated businesses from newspapers to nightclubs.

At the beginning of the Washington Renaissance, circa 1907, JIM CROW segregation proved one the greatest challenges to African Americans. Black boardinghouses existed, but hotels were closed to black patrons. Blacks who agreed to eat behind a screen to avoid offending whites with their "coloredness" could eat in any restaurant in the city. Otherwise, dining in public facilities was closed to black people. Churches were also racially segregated, and black parishioners who persisted in attending a nonblack church were seated in the rear and ignored. Public transportation was also segregated. Salaries for blacks were exceptionally low and jobs for them menial. Art schools were closed to black artists, and white colleges, with the exception of Catholic University, would not admit black students, regardless of the student's intellectual ability.

Moreover, President THOMAS WOODROW WILSON, despite the political support provided by W. E. B. DU BOIS and other African Americans to help him win the presidency in 1912, issued an executive order in 1913 to further enforce racial segregation in Washington, D.C., and, by extension, throughout the United States. None of this, however, stopped black Washington from developing an educated gentry, a business community, enviable schools, and an active arts community.

Businesses

Like the *CRISIS: A RECORD OF THE DARKER RACES*, the weekly *Washington Bee* also exposed segregation, fought LYNCHING, and reported the black perception of major events such as the RED SUMMER OF 1919. The Red Summer involved a race riot that erupted on Seventh and U Streets NW, after black soldiers returned home from WORLD WAR I to discover that, though they had fought for democracy abroad, they were still subject to apartheid rule in the United States. The motto of the *Washington Bee* was "Honey for Our Friends, Stings for Our Enemies." William Calvin Chase published the paper from 1882 to 1921, when he died at the *Bee*'s offices at 1109 I Street NW, Washington.

During the 1920s, the area at 14th and U Streets in Washington, D.C., was similar to 125th Street in Harlem. The 20-block strip had thriving businesses, such as a billiard parlor called Penny Savings Club and the Board and McGuire's drugstore. There were also an unusual number of barbershops. Bennett's Barber Shop at 1007 U Street NW was one of 14 on U Street during the 1920s, all equipped with pianos or radios. Harlem claimed photographer JAMES VAN DER ZEE on LENOX AVENUE, and Washington, D.C., had Addison N. Scurlock. Scurlock opened his photography studio at 900 U Street NW in 1911 and for more than 50 years photographed the district's black elite. Scurlock died in 1964.

Whereas MADAME C. J. WALKER amassed a fortune in beauty culture, a number of her students were also highly successful. One of them, Grace Savage, attended the Madame C. J. Walker College of Beauty Culture at 1306 U Street NW as soon as she migrated from the South. She became so successful that she opened LaSavage Beauty Clinic at 2228 Georgia Avenue NW, bought a pink automobile, wore a mink coat, and for years during the 1940s and 1950s rode a decorative float in HOWARD UNIVERSITY's Homecoming parade.

Comparable to JUNGLE ALLEY in Harlem, an entertainment strip called Bohemian Caverns in the U street area was well developed in 1926 with nightclubs sporting names such as Club Bengasi (1425 U Street) and Jungle Inn (12th and U). Pearl Bailey, LOUIS ARMSTRONG, and other musicians performed on this strip.

Other black-owned businesses included Robert Hilliard Harrison's Café at 455 Florida Avenue NW; the Whitelaw Hotel at 1839 13th Street NW, where the "Brown Bomber," boxer JOE LOUIS, and entertainer CAB CALLOWAY often stayed; and the Industrial Bank of Washington, at 2000 11th Street NW, called "The Bank That Jesse Mitchell Built," which opened in 1913.

Education

Washington, D.C., became a strong education center for African Americans during its cultural resurgence. Miner Teachers College educated black schoolteachers from 1870 to the 1940s. It eventually became part of the University for the District of Columbia, across town from Howard University on the Georgia Avenue hill.

M Street High School at New Jersey Avenue and First Street NW accumulated an illustrious track record in African-American education. A preparatory high school, M Street was the first public high school for blacks in the United States. It began in 1870 in the basement of 15th Street Presbyterian Church and became M Street in 1891.

M Street also stands out in the history of black education because of its exceptional faculty: ANNA JULIA COOPER, JESSIE

REDMOND FAUSET, ANGELINA EMILY WELD GRIMKÉ, and CARTER GODWIN WOODSON, among others. Cooper served as principal of M Street School from 1901 to 1906. When she later completed her Ph.D. at age 67, she wrote books *(A Voice from the South)* and essays while educating several generations of unskilled black immigrants at her Frelinghuysen University, an adult education center that was located in her living room, from 1930s to 1950s. Fauset, literary editor of *Crisis* magazine, taught English at M Street, as did Grimké, author of the play *Rachel.*

The "father of black history," Woodson taught Spanish, French, history, and English at M Street School. He later became renowned as the founder of Negro History Week (now Black History Month) at 1401 14th Street NW in the district, where he maintained his Association for the Study of Afro-American Life and History, and where he published the *Journal of Negro History.*

In 1916 M Street School moved to First Street, between N and O Streets NW and became the renowned Dunbar High School (named for poet Paul Laurence Dunbar) one of the premier black high schools in America. Due to a racist system that discouraged black educators with advanced degrees from working at mainstream universities, an unusually high number of secondary school instructors in Washington held Ph.D.'s. This was of enormous educational value to students of M Street and Dunbar.

Nannie Helen Burroughs, following the example set by BOOKER TALIAFERRO WASHINGTON in Alabama at Tuskegee Institute, founded the National Training School for Women and Girls at 50th and Grant Street NE in 1909 to teach practical subjects to black students. The school's motto was the three B's: "the Bible, bath, and broom." By 1935, 2,000 black women had graduated from Burroughs's school.

Culture

Culturally, black Washington, D.C., supported many SALONS and literary societies in which affluent and creative individuals took part. Such societies started as early as the late 1800s and included the AMERICAN NEGRO ACADEMY (ANA), The MuSoLit Club, and several in-home groups.

The elitist American Negro Academy, a predominantly male society operative until 1924, was one such venture. Though established by educator and priest Alexander Crummell, Paul Laurence Dunbar is the person responsible for naming the ANA. Its members included, among others, Du Bois, Washington, and ARTHUR SCHOMBURG. Other social groups were the Book Lovers Club, Lotus Club, Monday Night Literary Group, and Bethel Literary and Historical Association, which met at M Street, 16th, and 17th Streets NW.

The MuSoLit Club convened at 1327 R Street NW. Founded in 1905, it was a musical, social, and literary club for black, Republican men. MuSoLit was noted for its annual Lincoln-Douglass celebration in February, given in honor of two Republican abolitionists: President Abraham Lincoln and Frederick Douglass.

Poet Georgia Douglas Johnson, author of *The Heart of a Woman,* lived at 1461 S Street NW where she hosted a literary salon during the mid-1920s. Among the many salon guests were WILLIS RICHARDSON, Angelina Grimke, Jessie Redmond Fauset, Marita Bonner, and poet LANGSTON HUGHES. Hughes noted that he liked to "eat Mrs. J's cake and drink her wine and talk poetry and books and plays."

The Dunbars and Fleetwoods were two other families that opened their homes for these sought-after social activities. Mrs. Fleetwood, wife of Christian A. Fleetwood, the first instructor of the Colored Washington High School Cadet Corps, held Evenings at Home, a Thursday literary gathering in the late 1800s. Before their divorce in 1904, Paul Laurence Dunbar and ALICE DUNBAR-NELSON contributed to the district's black social scene in their home at 321 U Street NW. There they held dinner parties attended by Howard University faculty and the district's literati in the late 1890s.

Washington was well known for its theaters, some of which have since fallen into disrepair. Of particular note was the Howard Theater, which opened on August 22, 1910, and closed temporarily in 1929 at the beginning of the GREAT DEPRESSION. Located at 624 T Street NW, the Howard Theater's musical and dramatic offerings included the African-American folk opera *PORGY AND BESS.* When the theater reopened on September 29, 1931, D.C. native DUKE ELLINGTON, singer and actress ETHEL WATERS, and the comic team BUTTERBEANS AND SUSIE performed on its stage. The Howard Theater was part of the "chitlin circuit" of black theaters, a circuit that included the APOLLO THEATRE in Harlem, the Royal in Baltimore, the Uptown in Philadelphia, and the Regal in CHICAGO. The Howard Theater closed in 1970.

Another black-owned district theater was the Lincoln, a 1,600-seat establishment that opened in February 1922. Moreover, in the Belasco Theater at 17 Madison Place NW on November 1, 1920, CHARLES SIDNEY GILPIN performed in a trial run of Eugene O'Neill's *EMPEROR JONES,* a role for which he won the SPINGARN MEDAL presented by the NATIONAL ASSOCIATION FOR THE ADVANCEMENT OF COLORED PEOPLE (NAACP).

Washington's Lillian Evans Tibbs, dubbed Madame Evanti by Jessie Redmond Fauset, was the first professional black opera singer in the United States. Madame Evanti lived at 1910 Vermont Street NW, which later became headquarters of the Evans-Tibbs Collection of African-American Art. She made her debut in France in 1925. In 1935, she performed at the White House. A cofounder of the Negro National Opera Company, she won acclaim for her performance of *Lakmé* by Delibes.

While she was from Philadelphia, opera singer MARIAN ANDERSON also came of age as a performer during the Harlem Renaissance in Washington. Anderson sang her first Washington concert in 1920 at First Congregational Church, G Street and 10th Street NW, some 19 years before her historic concert at the Lincoln Memorial.

Washington, D.C., also established itself as an important center for visual art. The first black-owned and -operated art gallery in the United States, the Barnet-Aden Gallery at 127 Randolph Street NW, opened in October 1943. The gallery was owned by Professor James V. Herring, founder of Howard University's art department in 1922, and Alonzo Aden, the first curator of the school's Gallery of Art, founded by Herring in 1930. Aden died in 1961 and Herring in 1969. Their black art collection sold, in 1989, for $6 million to a Florida educational institution.

Community Faith

Blacks in Washington, D.C., developed communities of diverse religious institutions. During the renaissance years, it was home to the African Methodist Episcopal churches, a black Catholic cathedral, the FATHER DIVINE organization, the groundbreaking First Congregational Church, and the historic Mount Zion United Methodist Church at 1334 29th Street NW. Mount Zion United's community house, located at 2906 O Street, was built in 1813 and became the site of the city's first black library. The church was organized for blacks in 1816. In 1823, it functioned as a station on the Underground Railroad, helping slaves escape to freedom in Canada. The former community house was restored in 1982.

Strivers' Section

The Washington counterpart to Harlem's STRIVER'S ROW was Strivers' Section. Composed of row houses and separate homes, the area is roughly bounded by New Hampshire and Florida Avenues and 17th and 18th Streets along T, U, and Willard Streets. Poet MAY MILLER lived in Strivers' Section on S Street near activists Robert and Mary Church Terrell, the latter a leader in the Colored Women's Club Movement.

In the 1930s, Dorothy Waring Howard opened the Garden of Children School on S Street in Strivers' Section. The school was the district's first private preschool for black children. Strivers' Section was designated a historical district in 1980.

Celebrated Names

Duke Ellington was born in the district at 1217 22th Street NW and composed his first song, "Soda Fountain Rag," while working as a soda jerk after school. His hometown band, called the Washingtonians, was one of the most successful in the area before it relocated to New York in 1922.

A leading Harlem Renaissance dramatist, Willis Richardson graduated from M Street Public High School. The ETHIOPIAN ART PLAYERS performed Richardson's *Chip Woman's Fortune* in Chicago, Washington, D.C., and New York, where it became the first drama by an African American to play on Broadway. In 1925, Richardson won *Crisis* magazine's Spingarn prize for *The Broken Banjo.* In 1926, he won the Spingarn for *Bootblack Lover;* and he edited the first anthology of plays by African Americans with poet May Miller.

Celebrated names were attracted to Washington's glamour, and during the Harlem Renaissance many, including JEAN TOOMER and Hughes, included portraits of the capital in their writings. Toomer, a Washington native, published *Cane* in 1923 while living at 1341 U Street. Hughes lived in Washington in 1924 when he worked for Woodson's *Journal of Negro History* and as a busboy at Wardman Park Hotel on Connecticut Avenue. At Wardman, Hughes was "discovered" by poet Vachel Lindsay and called "the busboy poet." Hughes's *Fine Clothes to the Jew* (1927) was inspired by the pawn shops on Seventh Street in Washington, D.C.

Further Reading

Fitzpatrick, Sandra, and Maria R. Goodwin. *The Guide to Black Washington: Places and Events of Historical and Cultural Significance in the Nation's Capital.* New York: Hippocrene Books, 1990.

Sochen, June, ed. *The Black Man and the American Dream: Negro Aspirations in America, 1900–1930.* Chicago: Quadrangle Books, 1971.

— Sandra L. West

Waters, Ethel (1896–1977) *actress, singer*

Ethel Waters overcame the traumas of childhood poverty and neglect to become one of the leading singers and actresses of her era.

Waters was born on October 31, 1896, in Chester, Pennsylvania, after her 12-year-old mother was reportedly raped by a youth named John Waters. Although her mother later married a man named Norman Howard, Waters grew up primarily in the care of her maternal grandmother and her aunts, only living occasionally with her mother. She had little contact with her father's family but met her paternal grandmother at least once and described her as white in appearance.

Waters attended Catholic school as a child and went as far as the sixth grade. She was prone to fighting and stole to feed herself. At the age of 13, she married a steel worker named Merritt Purnsley to relieve her family of responsibility for her. She was frequently abused by her husband, and at 14 left him to live with her mother in PHILADELPHIA. There, she gained employment as a maid making $3.50 a week.

After performing in a Halloween talent show, Waters joined a vaudeville act and increased her salary to $10 a week. She became known as Sweet Mama Stringbean for her then tall, slender frame and gained a reputation for her interpretation of W. C. HANDY's "St. Louis Blues." For a while she shared billing with BESSIE SMITH, then in 1919 she made her way to NEW YORK CITY, where she performed at the LINCOLN THEATRE and Edmond's Cellar.

Performing in New York allowed her to develop and polish her performance skills. Her recording career kicked off in 1921 with records for two labels: She sang "The New York Glide" and "At the New Jump Steady Ball" for the Cardinal Record label; and "Down Home Blues" and "Oh Daddy" on PACE PHONOGRAPHIC RECORD CORPORATION's Black Swan label. FLETCHER HENDERSON played backup for her on the sessions for Black Swan, and they went on tour together as part of a group called the Black Swan Troubadours. In 1925, she joined Columbia records and produced dozens of hit records for the company over the next decade.

She also joined Broadway's *Plantation Revue* in 1925, taking over for FLORENCE MILLS while the latter toured in England. In 1927, she joined the cast of Earl Dancer's musical, *Africana.* In the same year, she met and befriended CARL VAN VECHTEN, who became one of her biggest supporters and promoters. Her work in musicals continued with performances in the Lew Leslie productions of *Blackbirds of 1930* and *Rhapsody in Black* in 1931.

Waters' career increased further during the early 1930s as she performed at the COTTON CLUB with such talents as DUKE ELLINGTON and LENA HORNE. At the Cotton Club, Waters gained renown for her performance of "Stormy Weather," a song that later would become Lena Horne's signature piece. Fellow entertainers such as BILLIE HOLIDAY, SOPHIE TUCKER, Ella Fitzgerald, and white jazz trumpeter Bix Beiderbecke all studied her stylistic phrasings and took note of the musical versatility that allowed her to go from BLUES tunes to JAZZ to Broadway melodies. When Irving Berlin caught her show at the Cotton Club, he recruited her to perform in his 1933 Broadway musical *As Thousands Cheer.* The show's success made Waters, commanding a salary of $1,000 a week, one of the highest paid women on Broadway. She returned to the stage in 1935 in *At Home Abroad* and performed in *Cabin in the Sky* in 1940. She enjoyed a triumphant one-woman show at Carnegie Hall in 1938 and in 1939 won critical acclaim for her dramatic performance in *Mamba's Daughter,* Dorothy and Dubose Heyward's follow-up to *PORGY AND BESS.*

Waters began her movie career singing "Am I Blue" in 1929's *On with the Show* and went on to perform in several short films during the 1930s. She achieved greater success in film during the following decade when she revived her stage role as Petunia in *Cabin in the Sky* for the silver screen in 1943. During the same year, she performed in *Stage Door Canteen* and *Tales of Manhattan.* Professional conflicts prevented Waters from making movies for six years. However, in 1948, she played Granny in the film adaptation of Cid R. Sumner's novel *Pinky.* Her performance earned her the first of two nominations for an Academy Award for best supporting actress. She was nominated a second time for her role as Bereniece in the film version of Carson McCuller's novel and play *The Member of the Wedding.* For her portrayal of Bereniece on stage in 1950, Waters did win the New York Drama Critics Circle Award for Best Actress. In 1955, she played Dilsey in a television adaptation of William Faulkner's *The Sound and the Fury,* then revived the role for a commercial film in 1959. For her work in these films, Waters has been credited with transforming the stereotypical mammy image of black women in Hollywood movies into that of a wise matron with formidable spiritual insight and strength.

Ethel Waters, shown here in 1938, survived the traumas of poverty and an abusive childhood to become a leading star of radio, stage, and film. *(Library of Congress, Prints & Photographs Division, Carl Van Vechten Collection [LC-USZ62-131769])*

Prior to HATTIE MCDANIEL and Louise Beavers, Waters starred in the television series *Beulah* in 1950. She afterward made guest appearances on many television shows in the 1960s and 1970s. While her musical career had begun with blues and jazz, she ended it singing spirituals as a member of television evangelist Billy Graham's *Crusades* from 1957 to 1976.

Including her brief marriage at age 13, Waters was married three times. She titled her first biography, published in 1951, *His Eye Is on the Sparrow,* after a song she sang in *The Member of the Wedding.* Her second biography, *To Me It's Wonderful,* was published in 1972. Waters died on September 1, 1977, in Chatsworth, California.

Further Reading

Santelli, Robert. *The Big Book of Blues: A Biographical Encyclopedia.* New York: Penguin USA, 2001.

Waters, Ethel, and Charles Samuels. *His Eye Is on the Sparrow: An Autobiography.* New York: Da Capo Press, 1992.

— Aberjhani

Webb, Chick (William Webb) (1909–1939)

bandleader

Drummer Chick Webb led one of the SAVOY BALLROOM's top house bands and, with Ella Fitzgerald as his featured vocalist, helped pioneer the development of the SWING SOUND.

Webb was born William Webb on February 10, 1909, in Baltimore, Maryland. As an infant, he suffered a broken vertebra that resulted in a variety of illnesses throughout his life and limited his physical growth to the stature of a dwarf. He nevertheless learned to use his hands with exceptional skill and as a child sold newspapers to earn money to buy his first drum. At the age of 11, he played with neighborhood bands at local parties. As a teenager, he played with more established bands in Baltimore and with the Jazzola Orchestra on cruise ships.

Webb moved to NEW YORK CITY with a friend named John Trueheart at the height of the JAZZ Age in 1925. He formed a band that included himself on drums, Trueheart on guitar, Don Kirkpatrick on piano, Bobby Stark on trumpet, and Johnny Hodges on alto saxophone. Gaining a reputation as a solid jazz band with an exceptional drummer, they played engagements at the Black Bottom Club and the Paddock Club before playing their first job, as the Harlem Stompers, at the Savoy Ballroom in 1927. They went on to play such top entertainment spots as the Roseland Ballroom, the COTTON CLUB, and the Rose Danceland.

In 1929, the band made its first records on the Brunswick label as the Jungle Band, recording the songs "Jungle Bottom" and "Dog Mama." They also began backing up other musicians such as LOUIS ARMSTRONG and Benny Goodman.

In 1933, Webb began an extended engagement at the Savoy Ballroom with an expanded 13-piece band. In addition to his lifelong friend Trueheart, the members included Joe Steele on piano; Pete Clark, saxophone; Sandy Williams, trombone; Jordan Jones, trumpet; Edgar Sampson, reeds; John Kirby, bass; Maurio Bauza, trumpet; Edward Williams, saxophone; and Reynold Jones, trumpet. Their performance and recording of "Stompin' at the Savoy" increased the band's popularity. Webb himself was noted for what critics described as a fluid legato style of drumming that utilized a unique set of variations and powerhouse improvisations that allowed him to guide his band with the sheer energy of his individual musicianship.

Ella Fitzgerald joined the band's lineup in 1934 after friends convinced Webb to consider her for his vocalist. Webb groomed and coached Fitzgerald until she equaled him as one of the band's star attractions. They enjoyed hit records with "A-Tisket A-Tasket," "Little White Lies," "I'll Choose the Blues Anyway," and a number of other songs.

The Chick Webb Band became a favorite in the celebrated "battle of the bands" series hosted at the Savoy Ballroom, and their triumphs were often reported in HARLEM weekly papers as well as national music magazines. On May 11, 1937, the band won a contest against the Benny Goodman Orchestra. And on January 16, 1938, they played a sold-out musical competition against COUNT BASIE and his orchestra. Their victory over Basie made headlines in *Downbeat* magazine as well as local papers. Webb's ongoing rule at the Savoy won him the honorary title "King of the Savoy."

Throughout his life, Webb often struggled against such health challenges as pleurisy and tuberculosis. He died in Baltimore on June 16, 1939, at the age of 30 following a liver operation. At the time of his death, his band was considered second in prominence only to that of Count Basie. For a time following his death, Ella Fitzgerald led the band.

Further Reading

Finn, Julio. *The Bluesman: The Musical Heritage of Black Men and Women in the Americas.* Northampton, Mass.: Interlink Publishing Group, 1998.

Porter, Eric. *What Is This Thing Called Jazz: African American Musicians as Artists, Critics, and Activists.* Berkeley: University of California Press, 2002.

— Aberjhani

Wedding, The

The publication of DOROTHY WEST's novel *The Wedding* in 1995 marked a milestone in the history of African-American literature and reaffirmed the author's status as a significant contributor to the Harlem Renaissance.

West gained recognition as a talented writer of short fiction when she tied for second place, with ZORA NEALE HURSTON, in a literary competition sponsored by *OPPORTUNITY* magazine. Her reputation strengthened with the publication of short stories in the *New York Daily News* from 1940 to 1960 and with that of her novel *The Living Is Easy* in 1948. West's literary productivity all but ended, however, in the 1960s until she began writing a column for the *Vineyard Gazette* at Oak Bluff on Martha's Vineyard in Massachusetts.

Former first lady and Doubleday editor Jacqueline Kennedy Onassis, a frequent visitor to Martha's Vineyard, took note of West's column and befriended the author. Onassis encouraged West to complete *The Wedding* and acted as her editor. She died before its publication, and West dedicated the book to her memory.

On its surface, *The Wedding* is a story about the controversy that stirs when a wealthy young black woman named Shelby Coles, from an upper-class community called the Oval, decides to marry a white JAZZ musician from New York named Meade Wyler. Beneath that surface, West's novel demonstrates the many ways that money and class privilege in American society promote fears and prejudices in African Americans more similar to than different from those attributed to white Americans. It also demonstrates how black and white American culture are more intertwined than generally acknowledged.

The fact that the oldest surviving member of the Harlem Renaissance writers published *The Wedding* in 1995 further extended the debate over the longevity of the cultural movement. Until the appearance of *The Wedding,* little attention was paid to West's 1948 novel, *The Living Is Easy,* as part of the canon of the Harlem Renaissance. Zora Neale Hurston's *Jonah's Gourd Vine,* published in 1934, was generally cited as the last novel of the movement. However, if the movement is considered to exist for as long as a member who identifies herself with it continues to produce significant work, the Harlem Renaissance would have to be extended not only to the year of *The Wedding*'s publication in 1995 but to the celebrations within the media that continued for years afterward until West's death in 1998.

The Wedding created renewed interest in the Harlem Renaissance in general and brought long-delayed celebrity to Dorothy West in particular. The novel was made into a highly acclaimed television miniseries produced by black media magnate Oprah Winfrey. Following its release, Doubleday also published an anthology of short fiction and essays by West titled *The Richer, the Poorer, Sketches and Reminiscences.* West herself became a favorite featured subject in national magazines and on her 90th birthday was honored with a tribute from another former first lady, Hillary Clinton. In a celebration televised nationally from Martha's Vineyard, scholar Henry Louis Gates and opera singer Jessye Norman joined Clinton in the salute to West.

Further Reading

Bascom, Lionel C., ed. *A Renaissance in Harlem, Lost Voices of an American Community.* New York: Avon Books, 1999.

Saunders, James Robert, ed. *The Dorothy West Martha's Vineyard: Stories, Essays and Reminiscences by Dorothy West Writing in the* Vineyard Gazette. New York: McFarlan and Company, 2001.

— Aberjhani

Washington, Ford Lee See BUBBLES, JOHN.

Weir, Reginald See AMERICAN TENNIS ASSOCIATION.

Wells, James Lesesne (1902–1993) *painter*

In addition to being an educator on both the community arts center and university levels, James Lesesne Wells was a major printmaker, painter of religious subjects, illustrator, and exhibitor with the HARMON FOUNDATION.

James Lesesne Wells was born in Atlanta, Georgia, on November 2, 1902. The son of a Baptist minister, he was educated at Lincoln University in Pennsylvania, and the National Academy of Design and Columbia University Teachers College in NEW YORK CITY, where he received a bachelors degree.

Wells gave one of his first major exhibitions at the New York Public Library in 1921. Predominant themes in his work included religion, mythology, and nature. He later produced many woodcuts on African themes such as *African Fantasy* (1929).

Wells taught at the Harlem Library Project for Adult Education and at Utopia Neighborhood Center in HARLEM. Utopia was a community arts center sponsored by the WORKS PROGRESS ADMINISTRATION (WPA). There, Wells greatly influenced the development of painter JACOB ARMSTEAD LAWRENCE. Later, Wells followed in the tradition of other WPA artists and advanced as a teacher to the university level. At HOWARD UNIVERSITY in WASHINGTON, D.C., he became a professor of art and devoted friend of sculptor LOIS MAILOU JONES.

Wells also illustrated book jackets and covers for the ASSOCIATION FOR THE STUDY OF NEGRO LIFE in Washington, an association inaugurated and directed by Dr. CARTER GODWIN WOODSON, the acclaimed "father of black history." Among the titles he illustrated for Woodson and researcher Lorenzo Greene in 1930 was *The Negro Wage Earner: The Development of the Negro in Various Occupations in the United States Since 1890.*

Also in 1930, Wells captured the Harmon Foundation Award in Fine Arts for *The Wanderers* and exhibited with the Montclair, New Jersey, Young Women's Christian Association (YWCA). He returned to the Harmon Foundation in 1931; and, in 1932, he produced a one-man show in Washington, D.C., at the Barnet-Aden Gallery, a gallery codirected by Howard University professor Dr. James Herring.

James Lesesne Wells died in 1993. His papers—an oral history interview dated 1989—are collected in the Papers of African-American Artists, Smithsonian Institution, Washington, D.C.

Further Reading

Beckman, Wendy Hart. *Artists and Writers of the Harlem Renaissance.* Berkeley Heights, N.J.: Enslow Publishers, 2002.

Jones, Lois Mailou. "Tribute to James Lesesne Wells." *The International Review of African American Art* 10, no. 3, 1993.

Powell, Richard J. *Black Art and Culture in the 20th Century.* New York: Thames and Hudson, 1997.

— Sandra L. West

Wells-Barnett, Ida Bell (1862–1931) *journalist, activist*

As a journalist, publisher, and international lecturer, Ida Bell Wells-Barnett waged until her death a nonstop battle to publicize and help bring to an end the practice of murder by LYNCHING that claimed the lives of thousands of men and women, primarily black, between the end of the Civil War and the mid-1900s.

Wells-Barnett was the eldest of eight children born to former slaves Jim Wells and Elizabeth Warrenton. Born on July 16, 1862, in Holly Springs, Mississippi, Wells-Barnett herself was born only three years prior to the Emancipation Proclamation. Her father was the son of a slave owner who had him trained to work as a carpenter, a profession that was in great demand after the Civil War. Jim Wells was a skilled enough carpenter to build the home in which his family lived and to remain steadily employed constructing office buildings and churches. A member of the Masons fraternity group, he exercised a passion for political discourse that he passed on to his daughter Ida. Her mother Elizabeth was renowned as a very pious woman and an exceptional cook.

Wells grew up attending Rust College, an institution founded in 1866 that provided education for blacks at all grade levels. Whereas Wells-Barnett in later life would often be characterized as militant, a more accurate term may have been zealous, an inherited trait that was then reinforced by the missionaries and inspired teachers that staffed Rust College.

An epidemic of yellow fever swept through Holly Springs in 1878 and claimed the lives of both Wells-Barnett's parents and her toddler brother Stanley. She had already lost her brother Eddie to spinal meningitis several years before and would lose her next eldest sister, Eugenia, who suffered from scoliosis, a year later. Declining the offer of family friends to adopt her siblings, at the age of 16 Wells took over the care of her younger brothers Jim and George and her sisters Eugenia, Annie, and Lily.

With money left by her parents and the assistance of family friends, Wells-Barnett developed a routine that allowed to her teach in the rural area of Shelby County during the week and to spend weekends taking care of her brothers and sisters. The boys eventually undertook apprenticeships to become carpenters like their father. Wells-Barnett accepted an offer from her aunt, Fannie Butler, to look after Wells-Barnett's younger sisters while she studied for the Memphis, Tennessee, teaching exam.

In 1884, the future "princess of journalism" earned her qualifications to teach in Memphis the same year she began to do public battle with the dictates of late-1800s JIM CROW apartheid. Traveling from Woodstock to Memphis on the Chesapeake and Ohio Railroad, Wells-Barnett was barred from a car reserved for white women and physically forced into a "smoker" reserved for blacks. She refused to remain on the train and sued the railroad for assault and discrimination. The lower court awarded her $500 in damages, a victory that proved short-lived when the Supreme Court of Tennessee reversed the decision of the lower court, and Wells-Barnett had to pay some $200 in legal fees. The case made a deep enough impression upon Wells-Barnett that she chose to write an article about it for a church newspaper called the *Living Way.*

Black newspapers in the late 1800s were second only to the black church in terms of influence upon African Americans, and the two often worked in unison. On the one hand, they satisfied black people's taste for the long-forbidden fruit of reading denied them throughout slavery. On the other hand, they served the very real need for information pertaining to everything from local social functions to the ever-fluctuating political status of African Americans overall. A lack of financial backing often meant a short life span for black newspapers; however, once established, editors and publishers (frequently the same person) remained on the lookout for educated blacks to lend their knowledge and skills to the enterprise.

Wells-Barnett's introduction to journalism came around 1895 through two church publications, first the *Evening Star,* then the *Living Way.* Adopting the pen name Iola, she acted as editor for the *Evening Star* and contributing writer to the *Living Way.* The matter-of-fact frankness with which she stated her opinions on everything from "the womanly virtues" to the injustices of racism won her a growing audience and increasing outlets for her writings until she was dubbed "the princess of journalism."

The call to wield the power of the written word led her in 1889 to join forces with Rev. F. Nightingale and J. L. Fleming, who earlier had combined their respective newspapers to create the *Free Speech and Headlight.* Rather than simply writing for the paper, Wells bought a one-third interest in it and became its editor, changing the paper's name to *Free Speech.* Fleming held the post of business manager for the paper and Nightingale was its sales manager. With Wells-Barnett's growing reputation under the pen name Iola, the *Free Speech* garnered greater and greater public attention with straightforward editorials that criticized the weaknesses of black leadership, championed racial pride, encouraged a sense of moral dignity, and challenged the assumptions of white supremacists.

Wells-Barnett's unfettered boldness slammed into a wall when she published an article strongly criticizing the Memphis Board of Education, which was still her employer. After she'd been teaching in Memphis for seven years, the board chose not to renew Wells-Barnett's contract, and in 1891 she turned her attention to increasing the *Free Speech's* circulation so she could earn a living from it. Her efforts proved successful as she traveled throughout Tennessee, Arkansas, and Mississippi to solicit subscribers at the same time that she recruited correspondents for the paper. A charge of assault and the threat of imprisonment drove Nightingale out of Memphis and left Wells with 50 percent ownership of the *Free Speech.*

Journalist and political advocate Ida B. Wells-Barnett, shown here in an 1891 illustration, laid the groundwork for the stopping of lynching in the United States. *(Library of Congress, Prints & Photographs Division [LC-USZ62-107756])*

The topic of lynching was not new to the *Free Speech* in the spring of 1892, but that year marked the first time Wells-Barnett had to write about the lynching deaths of three black men she knew: Thomas Moss, Calvin McDowell, and Henry Stewart, the owners and work crew of the People's Grocery Company. While the alarm against lynching had already been sounded by Frederick Douglass and others, the volume increased in correspondence with the number of victims. At the time of Moss's, McDowell's, and Stewart's deaths, lynching had become an accepted custom among those who practiced it and would become one of the principal motivations driving the GREAT MIGRATION of blacks from the South to the North.

The impetus for the Memphis lynching was a quarrel between two boys, one black and one white, that escalated when adults became involved to the point that a white policeman sneaked into the People's Grocery Store and was shot by one of the black owners. For the first two nights of the men's arrest, a group of blacks stood outside the jail to ensure their safety, leaving only after everyone thought the matter had ended. On the third night, however, whites took the men from the jail and lynched them. Out of town when the lynching occurred, Wells-Barnett upon her return wasted no time writing an editorial condemning the city of Memphis for allowing such an occurrence. She further suggested, as Thomas Moss reportedly did while being killed, that blacks should leave the city and head west. There, she reported, was government land available for settling and an opportunity for true justice. Both blacks and whites paid attention to Wells-Barnett's editorials. Many blacks did head west, and many whites resented that fact enough to destroy the office of the *Free Speech* on May 27, 1892, and post a threat that anyone attempting to publish the paper again would be killed.

When the newspaper office was destroyed, Wells-Barnett had already left Memphis to attend a church conference in PHILADELPHIA, Pennsylvania, and from there went to meetings in NEW YORK CITY. She learned about the destruction of her newspaper from T. Thomas Fortune of the *NEW YORK AGE*. Fortune, and friends back in Memphis, advised her not to return to the city. She joined Fortune and Jerome B. Peterson as a partner with the *NEW YORK AGE* and transformed her protest against lynching into a crusade against it. On the front page of the *Age* in June 1892, she ran a seven-column story detailing places, dates, and victims of white lynch mobs. Fortune upped his circulation to 10,000 copies of the *Age* for distribution throughout the country, providing Wells-Barnett with a readership five times greater than that she had enjoyed in Memphis.

Her work in the *New York Age* caught the attention of the great abolitionist Frederick Douglass and in 1893 she joined him, along with Ferdinand L. Barnett and I. Garland Penn, at the World's Columbian Exposition in CHICAGO. In protest against the exposition's exclusion of African Americans, the group published a pamphlet, with a preface in four different languages, entitled *The Reason Why the Colored American Is Not in the World's Columbian Exposition—The Afro-American Contribution to Columbian Literature.*

Wells-Barnett's influence expanded even further as she began to both establish women's clubs, including one named after her, and present lectures at them. Frederick Douglass placed her on the international lecture circuit when he asked her to take his place on a speech tour of the United Kingdom. There, she was the guest of the publishers of the *Anti-Caste Journal*. During trips in 1893 and 1894, Wells-Barnett brought lynching in the United States to international attention. In addition to her public lectures, she was often the focus of the news articles and published letters to editors of English newspapers. Her work forced other Americans prominent in the United Kingdom to address issues of race and forced those interacting with British citizens in the United States to do the same. She reported regularly on her travels for the *Chicago Inter-Ocean* in a column called "Ida B. Wells Abroad."

Back in the United States, Wells's commitment to the eradication of lynching remained undaunted. In addition to reporting regularly on specific lynchings, she articulated insightful theories examining the link between lynching and economics. Whereas the charge of rape generally proved to be an excuse for white males to express their disapproval of consensual relationships between white women and black men, far less substantial excuses were fabricated when targeted victims were perceived as economic rivals, as in the case of Moss, McDowell, and Stewart. As unflinching as she generally was when writing about the issue, even Wells-Barnett stalled when examining the implications of white males' sexual phobia as exhibited by the castration of black males, the suppression of white female sexuality, and the abuse of black female sexuality. Still, in 1895, her battle pressed on with the publication of *A Red Record: Tabulated Statistics and Alleged Causes of Lynchings in the United States, 1892–1893–1894.*

On June 27, 1895, Wells-Barnett stepped away from her crusade long enough to marry Ferdinand Lee Barnett, an attorney and the founder of Chicago's first black newspaper, the *Conservator*, whom she had met at the 1893 Columbian Exposition. Barnett was a widower who already had two children and with Wells-Barnett would have four more: Charles Aked, 1896; Herman Kohlsaat, 1897; Ida B. Wells, Jr., 1901; and Alfreda, 1904. Wells felt as strongly about the duties of motherhood as she did about political issues and initially tried to balance the two by making sure nurses were on hand to take care of her first child while she lectured. She also purchased her husband's newspaper from him but gave up the idea of running it when she became pregnant the second time. Motherhood then became the priority to which other activities were subordinated.

Wells-Barnett ended the 1800s with her election as the first woman secretary of the National Afro-American Press Convention, held in Louisville, Kentucky, in 1897, and election as the secretary of the Afro-American Council in 1898. Moving into the 1900s, she served as vice president of the Douglass Women's Club in 1903 and in 1910 helped found the Negro Fellowship League in response to discrimination from the Young Men's Christian Association.

She was also among those who answered the call in New York to establish the NATIONAL ASSOCIATION FOR THE ADVANCEMENT OF COLORED PEOPLE (NAACP). However, some of the key participants feared Wells-Barnett was too militant to be appointed to the new organization's founding committee and omitted her name from its listing, only later adding her name after numerous protests from those who felt it impossible to overlook her. W. E. B. DU BOIS would state later that the only reason history erroneously overlooked Wells-Barnett was because the NAACP finally came along and took over much of the work that she had been doing alone.

From 1911 to 1914, Wells-Barnett edited the *Fellowship Herald* and in 1930 made a failed bid for the U.S. Senate. She died from uremic poisoning on March 25, 1931. Her contributions to African-American history, as Du Bois observed, were mostly overlooked until her daughter, Alfreda M. Duster, edited her mother's biography, *Crusade for Justice*, and published it in 1970.

Further Reading

McMurry, Linda O. *To Keep the Waters Troubled.* New York: Oxford University Press, 1998.

Royster, Jacqueline. *Southern Horrors and Other Writings: The Anti-Lynching Campaign of Ida B. Wells, 1892–1900.* New York: St. Martin's Press, 1999.

Schecter, Patricia Ann. *Ida B. Wells-Barnett and American Reform, 1880–1930.* Durham, N.C.: University of North Carolina Press, 2001.

Wells-Barnett, Ida B., and Alfreda M. Duster, ed. *Crusader for Justice: The Autobiography of Ida B. Wells.* Chicago: University of Chicago Press, 1990.

— Aberjhani

West, Dorothy (1907–1998) *writer*

At the age of 18, Dorothy West became the youngest member of the Harlem Renaissance writers when she moved to NEW YORK CITY in the 1920s and was later celebrated as the sole surviving member of the movement in the 1990s.

West was born on June 2, 1907, in Boston, Massachusetts, the only child of Rachel Pease Benson West and Isaac Christopher West. Her father was a former slave who built a small business empire that allowed him and his family to live in upper middle class comfort.

As a child, West attended Boston's Martin and Farragut elementary schools. Considered gifted and precocious, she delighted in amusing adults with statements seemingly beyond her years. She announced her desire to become a writer while still a child and at age seven published her first short story, "Promise and Fulfillment," in the *Boston Globe.* Before she had turned 16, she was contributing stories regularly to the *Boston Post.*

In 1923, West graduated from the prestigious Girls' Latin School and enrolled in Boston University. Three years later, she moved with her cousin, the poet Helene Johnson, to New York to attend the Columbia School of Journalism and immerse herself in the cultural events of the *NEW NEGRO* movement.

Entered in a fiction competition sponsored by *OPPORTUNITY* magazine in 1926, West's story "The Typewriter" tied for second place with a story by ZORA NEALE HURSTON. The story was included in the anthology *The Best Short Stories of 1926,* edited by Edward O'Brien. West's new status as a winner of an *Opportunity* magazine literary prize gained her the friendship of such accomplished writers and artists as GWENDOLYN BENNETTA BENNETT, RICHARD BRUCE NUGENT, COUNTEE CULLEN, LANGSTON HUGHES, ALBERTA HUNTER, CARL VAN VECHTEN, PAUL ROBESON, and WALLACE THURMAN.

She became particularly good friends with Thurman. Each had endured and been scarred by prejudice inflicted upon them by family members because of the darker shades of their skins, and both writers addressed the subject of color prejudice among blacks in their work. Thurman expressed his affection for West through a fairly complimentary depiction of her as Doris Westmore in his satirical novel of the Harlem Renaissance, *Infants of the Spring.*

West expressed an interest in acting as well as writing, and in the late 1920s performed in *Porgy,* by DuBose Heyward, prior to George Gershwin's transformation of the play into the folk opera *PORGY AND BESS.* In 1932, she joined Langston Hughes, LOUISE THOMPSON PATTERSON, and a number of other African-American intellectuals on a trip to the Soviet Union to make a film on race relations in America called *Black and White.* Plans for the film failed when the group arrived and discovered that the proposed script was inadequate. While other members of the group either returned to the United States or traveled on to other countries, West chose to remain in the Soviet Union for a full year.

When she did return to the United States, the country was struggling with the ravages of unemployment and poverty

Upon the publication of her second novel, *The Wedding,* in 1995, Dorothy West was celebrated as the last of the major Harlem Renaissance writers. In this 1995 picture, she is 88 years old, three years before her death at the age of 91. *(Associated Press)*

caused by the GREAT DEPRESSION, and the *New Negro* movement had lost much of its drive. Attempting to keep the spirit and productivity of the movement alive, West used her own funds to start the magazine *Challenge* in 1934. With educator Harold Jackman as her associate editor, she published six issues of the magazine up until 1937. She attempted to revise it with a second magazine called *New Challenge,* which was edited by West, Marian Minus, and novelist RICHARD NATHANIEL WRIGHT. *New Challenge* featured the first published work by the future author of *Invisible Man,* RALPH WALDO ELLISON, and Richard Wright's now classic essay on black literary aesthetics, "Blueprint for Negro Writing." Unlike its predecessor, the magazine focused heavily on the political conditions of the black working class rather than showcasing literary talent. However, it survived for only one issue published in the fall of 1937.

West also joined those writers employed by the WORKS PROGRESS ADMINISTRATION'S FEDERAL WRITERS' PROGRAM. She produced a number of profiles on life in HARLEM, including portraits of FATHER DIVINE, RENT PARTIES, and the APOLLO THEATRE. At one point, she worked as a welfare investigator for a year and a half in Harlem.

In 1940, West began writing short stories on a regular basis for the *New York Daily News,* earning $50 for two stories published per month. Her first story, "Jack in the Pot," also titled "Jackpot," won the Blue Ribbon Fiction Contest. Over the next two decades she wrote some 60 stories for the *New York Daily News.*

When she was a child, West's family often vacationed at Oak Bluff on Martha's Vineyard in Massachusetts, and in 1945 she made her home there while continuing to write. With the publication of her first novel, *The Living Is Easy,* in 1948, she won widespread acclaim. *The Living Is Easy* told the story of Cleo Judson, whom West portrayed as a dominating matriarch whose manipulations caused unyielding chaos within her family. The novel also included the first literary portrait of upper middle class African Americans living in New England and was compared to works by Jane Austen.

In 1968, West began to write a column and occasional articles for the *Vineyard Gazette;* those pieces comprised the bulk of her literary output throughout the 1970s and 1980s. Film producer Salem Mekuria recorded in 1991 a video of West called *As I Remember It,* in which at the age of 83 she spoke of her life and the Harlem Renaissance.

Whereas West's literary career seemingly had ended by the mid-1990s, in 1995 she published *THE WEDDING,* her first novel in 47 years. She was encouraged by former first lady and editor Jacqueline Kennedy Onassis to complete the book, and its publication was hailed as a major literary event. Media tycoon Oprah Winfrey adapted the novel into a successful television miniseries. In addition to *The Wedding,* she published in the same year a collection of prose pieces titled *The Richer, the Poorer, Sketches and Reminiscences.* The *New York Times Book Review, Publishers Weekly, People's Weekly,* and numerous other periodicals ran profiles on and tributes to West as the last surviving writer of the Harlem Renaissance.

In a celebration of her 90th birthday observed on August 29, 1997, West enjoyed a televised tribute to her that featured presentations by then first lady (later senator) Hillary Clinton, opera singer Jessye Norman, and renowned scholar Henry Louis Gates. West died the following year on August 16.

Further Reading

Jones, Sharon L. *Rereading the Harlem Renaissance: Race, Class, and Gender in the Fiction of Jessie Fauset, Zora Neale Huston, and Dorothy West.* Westport, Conn.: Greenwood Publishing Group, 2002.

Saunders, James Robert. *The Dorothy West Martha's Vineyard: Stories, Essays and Reminiscences by Dorothy West Writing in the* Vineyard Gazette. New York: McFarlan and Company, 2001.

West, Dorothy, and Lionel Bascom, ed. *The Last Leaf of Harlem: The Uncollected Works of Dorothy West.* New York: St. Martin's Press, 2001.

West, Dorothy. *The Wedding.* New York: Doubleday, 1995.

— Aberjhani

White, Charles Wilbert (1918–1979) *muralist*

Believing that the creation of art was essential to living, Charles Wilbert White produced publicly accessible paintings of historical events and empowering murals that depicted social issues and African-American heroes.

Charles Wilbert White was born in CHICAGO in 1918. As a boy, his reading of *The NEW NEGRO* (1925) anthology edited by philosopher ALAIN LOCKE shaped his view of American history and the place of African Americans within that history. He was amazed to learn how much blacks had contributed to the country and to the world, and alarmed at how little he knew about it. He responded to the new ideas he read about in Locke's book by becoming a painter. He turned paint into a survival tool, teaching instrument, and weapon as he transformed the history of his people into drawings, lithographs, and mural paintings.

During his adolescent years, White studied at the Art Institute of Chicago and participated in the Arts Craft Guild. The Guild developed into the SOUTH SIDE COMMUNITY ART CENTER, which was sponsored by the WORKS PROGRESS ADMINISTRATION (WPA).

As a young man, White distinguished himself as an artistic chronicler of social ills and African-American history, painting predominantly in the basic colors of black and white. His first mural was *Five Great American Negroes,* done in 1940 at the George Cleveland Branch of the Chicago Public Library. One of the five subjects depicted in his mural was BOOKER TALIAFERRO WASHINGTON. In 1942, he won a Julius Rosenwald Fund Fellowship, worked in the South for several years, and painted the mural *The Contribution of the Negro to Democracy in America,* now in the collection of Hampton University in Virginia. This mural includes heroic individuals such as MARIAN ANDERSON and PAUL ROBESON.

White taught at the Otis Art Institute in Los Angeles, California, from 1965 to 1979, the year of his death. Of his work, he once said, "A work of art was meant to belong to people . . . Art should have its place as one of the necessities of life, like food, clothing and shelter."

The papers of Charles White are located in the Papers of African-American Artists, Archives of American Art, Smithsonian Institution, Washington, D.C. They consist of letters and printed material concerning African-American artists and art organizations. There are two oral history interviews dated 1965 and 1969. Also, the Charles White Papers are at the Woodruff Library, Clark-Atlanta University, Atlanta, Georgia.

Further Reading

Bearden, Romare. *A History of African American Artists: From 1792 to the Present.* New York: Pantheon Books, 1993.

LeFalle-Collins, Lizzetta. "Contribution of the American Negro to Democracy: A History Painting by Charles White." *International Review of African American Art* 12, no. 4, 1995–96.

— Sandra L. West

White, Walter (1893–1955) *author, political activist*

As an author, Walter White wrote one of the first influential novels of the Harlem Renaissance. As secretary of the NATIONAL ASSOCIATION FOR THE ADVANCEMENT OF COLORED PEOPLE (NAACP) in the 1930s, 1940s, and early 1950s, he helped pave the way for the triumphant Civil Rights movement of the 1960s.

White was born in Atlanta, Georgia, on July 1, 1893, the second of seven children born to George and Madeline White. His father was a mailman and his mother a retired teacher. The White family was considered a prominent one in black Atlanta.

Like his father and mother, White was born with an extremely light complexion, blond hair, and blue eyes that made him physically more white than black. According to his autobiography, *A Man Called White,* he was unaware of his African-American ancestry until the Atlanta riots of 1906, when he was 13. Helping his family defend their home against an angry white mob, he heard the rioters refer to them as "niggers." White was more distraught over the mindless behavior of the mob than the revelation of his racial identity and from that point vowed to publicly identify himself as black rather than white.

He graduated from Atlanta University in 1916 and took a job with Standard Life Insurance Company. During the same year, he and a small group of black leaders decided to organize an Atlanta branch of the NAACP. They successfully countered plans by the Atlanta School Board to delete the seventh grade from black schools after previously deleting the eighth grade as a cost-cutting measure. Harry Pace was elected president of the new Atlanta NAACP branch, and White was elected its assistant secretary. Meeting the members of the new branch, JAMES WELDON JOHNSON was impressed enough by White that he invited him to join the NEW YORK CITY office of the NAACP as his assistant. Although the position would mean a $1,200 cut in salary for White, his father urged him to accept it as an opportunity to help other blacks who would not likely receive the advantages that White's education would afford him.

White made the move to New York at the beginning of 1918. However, he soon found himself back in the South, in Estill Springs, Tennessee, investigating the brutal LYNCHING murder of Jim McIlleron. Because such murders were not always officially reported, figures on the number of blacks lynched annually during the 1910s tend to vary, yet even the lowest for 1918 indicate that at least one black individual was killed by lynching for every week of that year. White estimated the figure at 200. Investigating the Jim McIlleron case, White's physical appearance allowed him to masquerade, or "pass," as a white person sympathetic to lynchers and obtain insider information about the case. The practice allowed him to add substantially to the NAACP's research for the battle against lynching and later provided White with material for his literary works.

During the RED SUMMER OF 1919, so-called because of the violent race riots that swept through America that year, White filed reports on riots in both CHICAGO, Illinois, where 25 blacks were killed, and in Phillips County, Arkansas, where he tallied a death toll of 200 plus. In 1921, White traveled with W. E. B. DU BOIS to PARIS, France, for the PAN-AFRICAN CONGRESS and there met with an international group of black leaders to examine the state of peoples of African descent throughout the world.

White married Leah Gladys Powell, a black NAACP staff member originally from PHILADELPHIA, in 1922. The couple lived with their children, Jane and Walter, on Edgecombe Avenue atop Harlem's famed SUGAR HILL.

Also in 1922, encouraged by the acerbic critic H. L. Mencken, who influenced as well the satire of GEORGE S. SCHUYLER, White wrote his first novel. Completed in just two weeks, *Fire in the Flint* was published by Alfred A. Knopf in 1924. White's novel told the story of a black doctor whose love for the purity of science is corrupted by the realities of racism. For CARL VAN VECHTEN, the book was a convincing one that inspired him to study more deeply the people of HARLEM and two years later make his own contribution to the cannon of Harlem Renaissance literature with *NIGGER HEAVEN*. For the governments of Russia and Japan, translations of *Fire in the Flint* provided officials with useful propaganda to use in their tug of diplomatic wars against the United States.

Fire in the Flint sold relatively well and established White as a literary figure of note. As such, he was able to help promote the works of LANGSTON HUGHES, COUNTEE CULLEN, and other writers. His second novel, *Flight, The Story of a Girl Who Passes,* was published in 1926. Tackling an issue of both personal and political importance to its author, White's story of a black Creole masquerading as a white woman preceded by two years NELLA LARSEN's treatment of the same theme in *Passing.* No small amount of White's later success as secretary of the NAACP came from his public acknowledgment of the fact that he was fully aware that he could, if he so chose, live his life as a white man racially indistinguishable from any other rather than as a black man defending black causes.

White was granted a $2,500 Guggenheim Fellowship in 1926 and used it to live in France while writing one of his better-known works, the nonfictional *Rope and Faggot: A Biography of*

Judge Lynch. He published a second nonfiction work, *The American Negro and His Problems,* in 1927. Along with other writers, black and white, he founded in 1933 the Writers' League Against Lynching.

With James Weldon Johnson's resignation from the NAACP in 1930, White took over as its executive secretary in 1931, a position he would maintain until his death in 1955. White and Du Bois, who as editor of the *CRISIS: A RECORD OF THE DARKER RACES* magazine had provided the NAACP with a formidable public platform, often disagreed over such issues as organizational structure and editorial policy. These in part led to Du Bois's resignation from the NAACP in 1934.

As secretary of the NAACP and the author of several celebrated books, White gained a reputation as a formidable political advocate, a tireless fund-raiser, and unceasing investigator into racial conflict. Following up on James Weldon Johnson's efforts to outlaw lynching, he met with President FRANKLIN DELANO ROOSEVELT in 1935 to seek his support for an antilynching bill just as he would later meet with President Harry S. Truman to argue for the same. His many investigations into lynching activities, battles to close the gap between the salaries of blacks and whites doing the same work, and constant push to end JIM CROW segregation in education earned White the SPINGARN MEDAL in 1937.

In 1939, White lent his support to help organize MARIAN ANDERSON's groundbreaking concert at the Lincoln Memorial in WASHINGTON, D.C. Along with A. PHILIP RANDOLPH, he convinced President Roosevelt to establish the Fair Employment Practices Committee in 1941 to ensure equal employment opportunities for blacks applying for work at companies holding government contracts. New York mayor FIORELLO HENRY LA GUARDIA often consulted with White regarding conditions in Harlem and sought White's assistance during the HARLEM RIOT of 1943.

White combined his politics with his literary career in 1944 when he became a war correspondent for the U.S. military. He traveled throughout Europe and North Africa during World War II to meet with black troops and file reports on the impact of segregation both on African Americans and on the country's war effort. His findings helped bring an end to segregation in the U.S. military in 1948.

In 1949, White divorced his wife to marry the white South African cookbook author Poppy Cannon, an event that stirred a great deal of controversy in the black press. He maintained leadership of the NAACP until his death on March 21, 1955, in New York City.

Further Reading

Lewis, David Levering. *W. E. B. DuBois, the Fight for Equality and the American Century, 1919–1963.* New York: Henry Holt and Company, 2000.

Wilson, Sondra Kathryn. *In Search of Democracy: The NAACP Writings of James Weldon Johnson, Walter White, and Roy Wilkins (1920–1977).* New York: Oxford University Press, 1999.

Wintz, Cary D., ed. *The Politics and Aesthetics of "New Negro Literature."* New York: Garland Publishing, 1996.

— Aberjhani

Williams, Bert (Egbert Austin Williams)

(ca. 1874–1922) *actor, comedian*

An actor in minstrel shows, on Broadway, and in the first film to star an African American, Bert Williams was a forerunner of those entertainers who would achieve national and international prominence in the 1920s and 1930s.

Accounts vary on the details of Bert Williams's birth, but the more authoritative state he was born Egbert Austin Williams in 1874 in Antigua, the West Indies. The son of Fred and Julia Williams, he moved with his family in 1885 to Riverside, California. After high school, he spent some time studying at Stanford University before moving on to San Francisco. There he made his way into the world of professional entertainment, performing before audiences in such locales as restaurants and saloons. It was there also that he met GEORGE WALKER in 1893 and formed a partnership that would last until syphilis forced Walker to retire in 1910.

A student as well as a practitioner of his craft, Williams noted the success of white vaudeville performers who employed blackface (burnt cork) in their stereotypical imitations of black people. Reasoning that he and his partner could go their competition one better by parodying white stereotypes of blacks, the two made up in blackface and billed themselves as the Two Real Coons. The success of this act did not, however, satisfy Williams's desire to be taken seriously as a performer and "blacking up" became as much a source of personal distress for him as it did a source of fame and wealth.

While he presented himself as something of a slow-witted buffoon in his act, offstage Williams was clearly much more than his stage character. With his tall frame and slightly accented formal speech, he carried himself with the easy grace and dignity of his West Indian family's heritage. He cited Mark Twain as his favorite author and expressed familiarity with the works of Goethe and Voltaire as well. He married a showgirl and CHICAGO native named Lottie.

Recording some of their skits for the Victor Company in 1901, the team became the first African Americans to make such a recording. Moving beyond the limitations of the Two Real Coons, Williams and Walker created in NEW YORK CITY a number of musical revues that enjoyed successful runs on Broadway, including *Son of Ham* (1907); *In Dahomey* (1902); *Abyssinia* (1906); and *Bandanna Land* (1907). Playing a command performance of *In Dahomey* before the British royal family in 1903, Williams demonstrated the sublety of his art as political subversion when he sang "Evah Darkey Is a King!" During the same tour, their performance of the plantation-originated dance called the CAKEWALK helped to popularize it throughout Europe.

Offstage, he and Walker acted on such concerns by helping organize in 1906 a black actor's union called the Negro's Society. Very much aware of the changing times, Williams wrote that they "discovered an important fact: that the hope of the colored performer must be in making a radical departure from the old time 'darky' style of singing and dancing. So we set ourselves the task of thinking along new lines." In this, he clearly prefigured the rise of the *NEW NEGRO*, that generation of African Americans

Bert Williams, seen here in his costume for the Ziegfeld Follies of 1910, was one of the early pioneers of Broadway shows starring African Americans. *(Associated Press)*

who in the 1920s and 1930s would launch the Harlem Renaissance. The comedians were also founding members in 1908 of the FROGS, a group of black performing artists dedicated to providing professional support for black entertainers.

With George Walker's retirement from the team and eventual death in 1911, Williams signed on as the first African American to appear in the fabled ZIEGFELD FOLLIES. He was already an established celebrity from his Broadway shows, but the Follies brought Williams even greater fame. Working in the Follies, he often teamed up with white actors in blackface, such as the English comedian Leon Errol and the future director of *Kid Millions* (1934), Eddie Cantor. With the latter, he performed a skit as father and son. Going against the trend of the times, Cantor and Williams became friends as well as coworkers and were known to spend time in establishments where being together did not create controversy.

Williams continued to break new ground when in 1914 he became the first black actor to star in a movie, *Darktown Jubilee.* He remained with the Ziegfeld Follies until 1919, when he continued to act in his own shows. While his professional success could not be disputed, it was often said that the JIM CROW practices of Williams's time—as with other artists of the era—contributed to a recurring depression and battle with alcoholism. He died in New York City, on March 4, 1922, during a run of his show *Under the Bamboo Tree.*

Whether Williams's contributions to the history of African-American entertainment were negative or positive is often a matter of debate. Nevertheless, a group of historians and entertainers in 1989 thought enough of his life and struggles to name the Flo-Bert Award jointly after him and his contemporary, FLORENCE MILLS. It is presented annually under the auspices of the New York Committee's celebration of National Tap Dance Day. The painful ambiguities of Williams's life were also examined in Vincent D. Smith's 1991 play *Williams and Walker.*

Further Reading

Douglas, Ann. *Terrible Honesty: Mongrel Manhattan in the 1920s.* New York: Farrar, Strauss, & Giroux, 1995.

Lamb, Andrew. *150 Years of Popular Musical Theatre.* New Haven, Conn.: Yale University Press, 2001.

Smith, Eric Ledell. *Bert Williams: A Biography of the Pioneer Black Comedian.* Jefferson, N.C.: McFarland and Co., 1992.

— Aberjhani

Williams, Fess (1894–1975) *bandleader*

As the leader of the Royal Flush Orchestra in NEW YORK CITY and the Joy Boys in CHICAGO, Fess Williams led two popular bands during the JAZZ Age of the 1920s and the SWING era of the 1930s.

Along with the CHICK WEBB Band and the Charleston Bearcats, Fess Williams and his Royal Flush Orchestra became one of the SAVOY BALLROOM's principal house bands after making its debut on the ballroom's opening night, March 12, 1926. While he played both the clarinet and saxophone, Williams won a reputation for his showmanship as well as his musicianship. Dressed in a top hat and tuxedo outlined with sparkling diamonds, he became a house favorite, and the Savoy Ballroom's management proclaimed June 16, 1926, as Fess Williams Night of Happiness.

At the same time that he continued to lead the Royal Flush Orchestra in New York, Williams also established around 1927 the group Fess Williams and His Joy Boys in Chicago. Williams traveled to the city to open a branch of the Savoy. He was there in 1928 when he recorded "Dixie Stomp" and "Drifting and Dreaming" with the Joy Boys. Band members included saxophonist Ralph Brown, singer and banjo player Laurence Dixon, and trombonist Eddie Atkins.

In 1929, Williams and his Royal Flush Orchestra participated in the Savoy Ballroom's highly promoted Battle of Jazz, in which six bands, including DUKE ELLINGTON and his orchestra, competed for top honors. The Royal Flush Orchestra, along with Ellington and the others, lost to the MISSOURIANS, the group that would later perform and record with CAB CALLOWAY. In the same year, they recorded "Hot Town" and "Sweet Savannah Sue," two of their biggest hits, on Victor Records. Some of their other better-known recordings, also on Victor, were FAT WALLER's "Ain't Misbehavin'," in 1929; "Everything's OK with Me," 1930; and "Geechee Dance," 1930.

The band's personnel sometimes fluctuated; in 1929 its lineup consisted of the following: singer and clarinetist Perry Smith; saxophonist Felix Gregory; banjoist Andy Pendelton; pianist Hank Duncan; drummer Ralph Bedell; clarinetist and saxophonist Lockwood Lewis; tuba player Emmanuel Cusamme; banjoist Oliver Blackwell; trombonist David James; trumpeter Ken Roane; and trumpeter George Temple. The orchestra also worked periodically with such guest vocalists as Ada Brown and Edith Wilson.

In addition to its regular performances at the Savoy in 1930, Williams and the Royal Flush Orchestra accompanied the comedy team of BUTTERBEANS AND SUSIE in a musical comedy called *Ease on Down* at the LAFAYETTE THEATRE. Of Williams's two bands, the Royal Flush Orchestra made the greater impact both through more numerous recordings and tours throughout the South and Northeast. Aside from being noted for his own contributions to jazz history, Williams is also known as the uncle of the composer and bass player Charles Mingus.

Further Reading

Alexander, Michael. *Jazz Age News.* Princeton, N.J.: Princeton University Press, 2001.

Finn, Julio. *The Bluesman: The Musical Heritage of Black Men and Women in the Americas.* Northampton, Mass.: Interlink Publishing Group, 1998.

Haskins, James. *Black Music in America: A History Through Its People.* New York: Welcome Rain Publishers, 2000.

Hill, Anthony D. *Pages from the Harlem Renaissance: A Chronicle of Performance.* New York: Peter Lang Publishing, 1996.

— Aberjhani

Wilson, Thomas Woodrow (1856–1924)

U.S. president

Elected the 28th president of the United States in 1912, Thomas Woodrow Wilson made JIM CROW racial segregation the official policy for American citizens using federal government facilities and led the country through the First World War.

Wilson was the third of four children, born on December 28, 1856, to Joseph Ruggles Wilson and Janet Woodrow Wilson in Shaunton, Virginia. His father was a Presbyterian minister from Steubenville, Ohio, who during the Civil War had supported the South. His mother was born in England but raised primarily in Chillicothe, Ohio.

Wilson, who generally used his middle name rather than his first, was schooled at home until the age of 12. He then attended Charles Heyward Barnwell School in Columbia, South Carolina, before going on to the College of New Jersey, later to become Princeton University. He graduated from there in 1879 and studied law for almost two years at the University of Virginia. He continued to study law independently until passing the bar exam in 1882. He acquired a Ph.D. in political science at Johns Hopkins University in Baltimore, Maryland, in 1886.

On June 24, 1885, Wilson married his first wife, Ellen Louise Axson, from Savannah, Georgia. The couple had three daughters: Margaret Woodrow Wilson, born in 1886; Jessie Woodrow Wilson, 1887; and Eleanor Randolph Wilson, 1889.

Wilson taught political economy and public law as a professor at Bryn Mawr College in Pennsylvania from 1885 to 1888. He simultaneously embarked on a career as an author of serious books examining America's governmental structure and history. His first such title was *Congressional Government: A Study in American Politics.* From 1888 to 1902, he held professorships at Wesleyan University in Connecticut and at Princeton University. In 1902, he published the five-volume *A History of the American People.* In the same year, he became Princeton University president, a position he kept until 1910.

In 1911, he entered the race for governor of New Jersey and won. During his two-year term, he initiated a number of reforms that included regulated campaign expenditures and contributions, a state workmen's compensation law, and increased authority for the state public utility commission.

In 1912, Wilson campaigned for the presidency on the promise of a New Freedom that would support free competition, break up monopolies, and ensure bargaining rights for labor organizations. He also convinced W. E. B. DU BOIS, editor of the *CRISIS* and NATIONAL ASSOCIATION FOR THE ADVANCEMENT OF COLORED PEOPLE (NAACP) board member, that he had "an earnest wish to see justice done the colored people in every matter." With that and similar campaign statements from Wilson in mind, Du Bois, Bishop Alexander Walker of the African Zion Church, and Monroe Trotter of Boston's *Guardian* newspaper, one of the largest black-oriented newspapers in the country, helped persuade an estimated 100,000 African Americans to abandon their traditional loyalty to the Republican party and vote for southern Democrat Wilson instead.

On November 5, 1912, Wilson won the first of his two terms with 435 electoral votes over 88 for Progressive Party candidate Theodore Roosevelt and 8 for Republican incumbent William Howard Taft. His election prompted author JAMES WELDON JOHNSON to resign from his position as a U.S. consul after serving in Venezuela and Nicaragua and to become a columnist for the *NEW YORK AGE.* The following year, Wilson issued an executive order calling for racially divided government dining areas, toilet facilities, public parks, transportation, and offices in WASHINGTON, D.C. It was precisely the kind of degrading segregation that the NAACP and such leaders as Du Bois, ROBERT ABBOTT, and IDA BELL WELLS-BARNETT had been battling against on every level of American society.

Du Bois was sharply criticized by members of the black press for having used his influence to convince African Americans to vote for a president who not only now advocated Jim Crowism but made its practice a law. Wilson himself was confronted by a delegation of black leaders headed by Monroe Trotter in a White House meeting that was reportedly tense but ultimately changed nothing. Wilson stated that his order was not intended as an insult to African Americans but to protect them from conflicts with white civil service workers. Until FRANKLIN DELANO ROOSEVELT and ELEANOR ROOSEVELT

Though applauded for his leadership during World War I, President Woodrow Wilson, shown here in 1922, received strong criticism from African Americans for ordering the segregation of government facilities in Washington, D.C. *(Library of Congress, Prints & Photographs Division [LC-USZ62-107575])*

moved into the White House two decades later, the order remained in effect.

Wilson's first term in office was also distinguished by the creation of the Federal Reserve Act, which established a system of national and state banks to counter fluctuating economic conditions. The system remains the foundation of the modern Federal Reserve.

Wilson's stance on segregation remained unchanged after his reelection as president on November 7, 1916. Nevertheless, Du Bois and others chose to set aside racial grievances in 1917 and called for solidarity with the president in efforts to bring an end to WORLD WAR I. Like William Taft before him and Warren G. Harding after him, Wilson refused to take a definitive stand against the practice of murder known as LYNCHING. During his eight-year tenure as president, an average of 54 known lynchings of African Americans occurred each year. There were 79 during the RED SUMMER OF 1919 when racial violence tore through more than two dozen American cities.

Following the death of his first wife, Ellen, in 1914, Wilson married Edith Bolling Galt, a widow from Wyetheville, Virginia, on December 18, 1915. The president retired after his second term and died in Washington, D.C., on February 3, 1924.

Further Reading

Auchincloss, Louis. *Woodrow Wilson.* New York: Viking Press, 2000.

DeGregorio, William A. *The Complete Book of U.S. Presidents.* New York: Wings Books, 1996.

Logan, Rayford Whittingham, and Eric Foner. *Betrayal of the Negro: From Rutherford B. Hayes to Woodrow Wilson.* New York: Da Capo Press, 1997.

— Aberjhani

Woodruff, Hale Aspacio (1900–1980) *muralist*

Hale Aspacio Woodruff, a renowned and outspoken muralist who protested the cultural isolation of black artists, was a student of HENRY OSSAWA TANNER and a HARMON FOUNDATION bronze prizewinner during the Harlem Renaissance.

Born in Cairo, Illinois, in 1900, Woodruff received his formal art education at John Herron School of Art in Indianapolis,

Indiana, where he studied landscape painting. In 1925, he won $10 for illustrating a cover for *CRISIS: A RECORD OF THE DARKER RACES* magazine. The following year he won a bronze medal and $100 from the Harmon Foundation. In 1927, he traveled to PARIS, France, to study at the Academic Scandinave, the Académie Moderne, and in the studio of Henry O. Tanner.

Woodruff was one of the most important creators of murals, or history panels, during the Harlem Renaissance and the years of the WORKS PROGRESS ADMINISTRATION (WPA). Some of his murals, which documented African-American history, are placed in the MUSEUMS of African-American colleges and universities. In the 1930s, Woodruff and CHARLES HENRY ALSTON recorded African-American settlers in California in a two-part mural at Golden State Mutual Life Insurance Company of Los Angeles, a black-owned company. He also began, in 1931, teaching at Atlanta University (now Clark-Atlanta University) in Georgia. Additionally, he developed a community-based and academic fine art program at the university.

From 1933 to 1934, as a participant in the federal Public Works of Art Project, Woodruff and student artist Wilmer Jennings produced a four-part mural, *The Negro in Modern American Life: Agriculture and Rural Life, Literature, Music, and Art,* at David T. Howard Junior High School. He exhibited works as well at Valentine Gallery and the L'Elan Gallery in New York.

In 1936, Woodruff further apprenticed with Diego Rivera, a leader in the Mexican muralist movement during the 1920s, through a fellowship from Columbia University's International Institute of Teachers College. As such, his styles, through the years, combined the varied influences of the French painter Cézanne, cubism, African art, Mexican muralists, and abstract expressionism.

Talladega College in Alabama commissioned Woodruff in 1939 to create *The Amistad Murals,* three panels that visually document the historical slave revolt known as the *Amistad* mutiny. In 1941, he initiated an annual community art show for black artists in Atlanta that continued until 1970. In 1945, Woodruff accepted a position as professor of art education at New York University and assumed as well the position of professor emeritus of art at Nassau Community College in New York. The same year, he held a solo exhibition at the International Print Society in New York.

Though Woodruff was considered successful as a Negro artist, he and several other African Americans did not necessarily want to be forever categorized or marketed as such. They wanted their works included in mainstream art exhibits and judged on merits independent of their race. In 1947, Woodruff, RICHMOND BARTHÉ, James V. Herring of HOWARD UNIVERSITY, and ROMARE BEARDEN spoke out against the JIM CROW isolation of black artists. They approached the International Business Machine (IBM) corporation—a large investor in black art—to "remove all racial references in the catalogue of their art collection, and to abolish all racial preferences in their art acquisition policies." Woodruff wrote: "In light of the Negro artist's present achievements in the general framework of American art today, there does not exist the necessity to continue all Negro exhibitions which tend to isolate him and segregate him from other American artists."

Woodruff went on in 1950 to create his *The Art of the Negro* murals for Atlanta University. One of his most ambitious projects, the multipaneled murals illustrate the variety of African-influenced art forms and styles used throughout the world. In addition, his work went on exhibit in 1950 at New York University. He later exhibited works with the Bertha Schaefer Gallery in 1953, 1954, 1958, and 1967, also in New York.

In 1963, Woodruff joined with CHARLES HENRY ALSTON, Bearden, Norman Lewis, and others to inaugurate the politically charged, short-lived black artists group Spiral. He retired from teaching in 1968 and died in 1980.

Further Reading

McDaniel, M. Akua. "Reexamining Hale Woodruff's Talladega College and Atlanta University Murals." *International Review of African American Art* 12, no. 4 (1996): 5.

Powell, Richard J. *Black Art and Culture in the 20th Century.* New York: Thames and Hudson, 1997.

Reynolds, Gary A., and Beryl J. Wright. *Against the Odds: African-American Artists and the Harmon Foundation.* Newark, N.J.: Newark Museum, 1989.

— Sandra L. West

Woodson, Carter Godwin (1875–1950) *historian*

Although he lacked a formal elementary school education, Carter G. Woodson became one of the most respected scholars of his era and to this day is recognized as "the father of black history."

Woodson was born on December 19, 1875, in New Canton, Virginia. His parents, James Henry Woodson and Eliza Woodson, were former slaves who became independent farmers. Carter was the oldest of their nine children and to help his family he had to work in the fields instead of attending school. He nevertheless learned the basics of math and English with the help of his mother and two of his uncles.

At the age of 20, in 1895, Woodson moved to Huntington, West Virginia, where he was able to enroll in Douglass High School. There, he worked in coal mines while completing in just two years the courses required to graduate. He later continued his education by enrolling in Berea College in Kentucky and again graduated, in 1903, after only two years. He returned to Douglass High School where he served for a time as the principal.

Accepting a position with the U.S. War Department, Woodson became supervisor of a school in the Philippines. He traveled extensively through Africa, Asia, and Europe, studying for a semester at France's famed Sorbonne University. Returning to the United States, he enrolled in the University of Chicago and graduated from there in 1908 with a master's degree in European history. At the same time he began teaching at Dunbar High School in WASHINGTON, D.C., Woodson also enrolled as a Ph.D. candidate at Harvard University. He received his doctorate in 1912.

Woodson published the first of his major contributions to the study of African Americans, *Study of Negro Life and the Education of the Negro Prior to 1861,* in 1915. In CHICAGO during the same year, he founded the ASSOCIATION FOR THE STUDY OF NEGRO LIFE. The establishment of the organization was an important step away from treating African Americans as nothing more than folk characters in general American history. It provided Woodson and others with a tool for researching and documenting the greater contributions of peoples of African descent to humanity as a whole. In 1916, Woodson started the *Journal of Negro History* to create a record of his organization's findings and stimulate further interest in the study of African-American history.

From 1920 to 1922, Woodson served as a dean at West Virginia State College. He also at that time established Associated Publishers, now one of the oldest black publishing companies in the United States. Associated Publishers was founded to provide an outlet for scholarly works on African-American history, many of which Woodson continued to write himself. He published one of his most widely used college texts, *The Negro in Our History,* in 1922.

On February 7, 1926, Woodson established Negro History Week. The NATIONAL ASSOCIATION FOR THE ADVANCEMENT OF COLORED PEOPLE (NAACP) recognized the significance of the event by awarding Woodson the SPINGARN MEDAL. Among his most enduring and celebrated legacies, Negro History Week was founded specifically to recognize, honor, and encourage the achievements of African Americans. Woodson assigned a theme for each annual observation and issued information packets highlighting the historical contributions of blacks.

Negro History Week activities were expanded to a month during the 1960s and in 1976, as part of the U.S. bicentennial celebrations, officially became Black History Month. The annual observance provided a major tool and platform in the struggle to have African-American studies included in high school and college curriculums throughout the United States. Moreover, it encouraged other social groups in America to proclaim and celebrate their contributions to the world in such observances as Women's History Month, Hispanic History Month, Gay Pride Month, and others.

Woodson enlisted the aid of HOWARD UNIVERSITY graduate Lorenzo Greene from 1930 to 1933 to help develop a market for his published works and oversee their distribution. With the help of several students, Greene traveled throughout the South, Southwest, and Midwest to distribute Woodson's works and promote the preservation of black history. His efforts also provided funds for the Association for the Study of Negro Life, which generally depended on Woodson's salary and donations from interested blacks for its operating expenses. Greene maintained a diary of his experiences and later published it.

Woodson continued to expand the body of works on African-American history with the publication of numerous titles, including: *The Mis-Education of the Negro* in 1933; *The African Background Outlined* in 1936; and *African Heroes and Heroines* in 1939.

Woodson maintained that he was married to his work and toward that end remained dedicated to it until his death on April 3, 1950, in Washington, D.C. His home is listed as a National Historic Landmark and Chicago's Carter G. Woodson Regional Library is named in his honor.

Further Reading

Goggin, Jacqueline. *Carter G. Woodson: A Life in Black History.* Baton Rouge, La.: Louisiana State University Press, 1997.

Greene, Lorenzo Johnson, and Arvarh E, Strickland. *Selling Black History for Carter G. Woodson: A Diary, 1930–1933.* St. Louis: University of Missouri Press, 1996.

— Aberjhani

Works Progress Administration (WPA)

With the beginning of the GREAT DEPRESSION in 1929 and decreased support from PATRONs of the arts, writers and artists of the Harlem Renaissance often remained productive largely by participating in the federally funded Public Works of Art Project (PWAP) and the Works Progress Administration designed by President FRANKLIN DELANO ROOSEVELT as part of his New Deal program.

Among the variables that contributed to the eventual decline of the Harlem Renaissance was a failed economy that impacted on every aspect of American life and the cessation in 1933 of such patronage as the annual HARMON FOUNDATION awards, which often proved crucial to the development and sometimes survival of black visual artists. The PWAP was established in December of 1933. It was the first New Deal federal arts project under the division of the U.S. Treasury Department. The intent behind the PWAP was to provide employment for, and compensate, artists who worked in various genres. The program, however, lasted only four months.

Undaunted, in December of 1935 Roosevelt inaugurated the Works Progress Administration, commonly known as the WPA. There were many levels of employment available under the WPA. Some literary artists interviewed former slaves and recorded their narratives. Visual artists received commissions as muralists, predominantly on state and federally owned buildings.

Some of the Harlem Renaissance artists who found support for their work through the WPA years were ROMARE BEARDEN, SELMA BURKE, ALLAN ROHAN CRITE, ELDZIER CORTOR, BEAUFORD DELANEY, JOSEPH DELANEY, LOIS MAILOU JONES, HORACE PIPPIN, and AUGUSTA FELLS SAVAGE.

The New York–based African-American visual artists involved with the WPA organized to form the Harlem Artists Guild in 1935. Black artists around the country established urban community art centers. The art instructors at these urban art centers provided the first generation of art teachers to work at black colleges. One such professor was WPA muralist AARON DOUGLAS, who taught at FISK UNIVERSITY in Nashville, Tennessee, from 1939 to 1966. Others were ELIZABETH ALICE CATLETT of Dillard University in Baton Rouge, Louisiana, and ERNEST CRICHLOW of Shaw University in Raleigh, North Carolina.

In 1938, the congressional House Subcommittee on Appropriations decided that the WPA was too costly. By the end of 1939, segments of the WPA were converted to state control, while most of its programs were abandoned altogether.

Further Reading

Anderson, Jervis. *This Was Harlem 1900–1950.* New York: Farrar, Straus, & Giroux, 1982.

Greenberg, Cheryl Lynn. *"Or Does It Explode?" Black Harlem in the Great Depression.* New York: Oxford University Press, 1991.

Lewis, David Levering. *When Harlem Was in Vogue.* New York: Vintage Books, 1982.

— Sandra L. West

World War I

When President Woodrow Wilson sounded his call for Americans to join their allies in World War I and take up arms to secure democracy throughout the world, black Americans adopted that same cry in reference to their ongoing struggle for racial equality in the United States.

World War I had already been in full swing for three years when the United States entered the conflict on April 6, 1917. During those three years, war had proven to be good business for the United States, and the country's economy got a healthy boost supplying allies with tanks, ammunition, planes, canned goods, and cash in the form of loans totaling billions of dollars. These activities were not lost on African Americans who, adopting a strategy that would be repeated and strengthened in succeeding wars throughout the 20th century, used the language of international politics to articulate their own grievances as members of the world's oppressed.

In short, whereas America expressed outrage at Germany and Austria's blatant disregard for democratic principles, the black community asked why America had not engaged in a war at home against LYNCHING, JIM CROW segregation, black poverty, denial of the right to vote, and discriminatory employment practices. In an attempt to battle the latter for themselves, southern blacks took to the road by the thousands and headed north during the GREAT MIGRATION to take advantage of job opportunities created by the war.

The one job opportunity that most blacks assumed would be open to them was that of serving in the military. It was not. The navy made it clear that black sailors would be nothing more than janitors or kitchen assistants wearing a uniform. And until black leaders voiced their protest, the army was unwilling to expand the handful of blacks still on its roster from 1898's Spanish-American War.

Whether or not the African American should accept the inferior concept of military service offered, and whether or not they should minimize generations of ill treatment by the United States and serve in World War I at all, was an issue that sharply divided the black community. The black press, clergy, students, and poets spoke out, on both sides of the divide. Among those leaders of the black press who proclaimed black America's duty to serve was W. E. B. DU BOIS, editor of the CRISIS: A RECORD OF THE DARKER RACES magazine, the official organ for the NATIONAL ASSOCIATION FOR THE ADVANCEMENT OF COLORED PEOPLE (NAACP). Du Bois wrote in his July 1918 editorial: "Let us not hesitate. Let us, while this war lasts, forget our special grievances and close our ranks shoulder to shoulder with our own white fellow-citizens and the allied nations that are fighting for democracy. We make no ordinary sacrifice, but we make it gladly and willingly with our eyes lifted to the hills."

Rev. ADAM CLAYTON POWELL, SR., the social activist pastor of ABYSSINIAN BAPTIST CHURCH in HARLEM, adopted a different posture. In a March 1917 sermon, the pastor stated: "As a race we ought to let our government know that if it wants us to fight foreign powers we must be given some assurance first of better treatment at home . . . Why should not the colored Americans make a bloodless demand at this time for the right we have been making futile efforts to secure (from a) government that has persistently stood by with folded arms while we were oppressed and murdered?"

On May 1, 1917, black colleges set up a central committee at HOWARD UNIVERSITY in WASHINGTON, D.C., to prove the willingness of blacks to participate in the armed forces. And, in 1919–20, Harlem Renaissance poet ALICE DUNBAR-NELSON published the feminist "I Sit and Sew," to protest the black woman's inability to participate in the military experience: "When there they lie in sodden mud and rain/Pitifully calling me, the quick ones and the slain?/You need me, Christ! It is no roseate dream/That beckons me—this pretty futile seam/It stifles me—God, must I sit and sew?"

Despite attempts by whites to minimize the visibility of blacks in the war, many black soldiers distinguished themselves and became sources of pride and inspiration in the black community as well as abroad. More than 350,000 African-American men served in the armed forces during the war, 100,000 of them overseas. One of the overseas black military regiments was the 369th. In France, the 369th Infantry, also called the HARLEM HELLFIGHTERS, withstood one of the fiercest onslaughts of the war for a full 191 days, earning the French's unbiased respect and that country's medal of honor, the Croix de Guerre, for gallantry in battle. So esteemed were they for the accomplishment that they were asked to lead the rally to the Rhine following the armistice. Back in NEW YORK CITY, crowds lined the streets and cheered the unit as they marched down Fifth Avenue.

Prior to the arrival of the American troops, EUGENE JACQUES BULLARD had already joined the ranks of the famed French Foreign Legion at the age of 19 and engaged in ground combat along the Western Front. A native of Columbus, Georgia, Bullard sustained severe wounds to his face and legs to win the Croix de Guerre with a bronze star. Recuperating from his wounds, he entered a training program to become the first African-American combat pilot, a job he was not allowed to perform when he attempted later on to join the U.S. Army Air Corps. Like those black servicemen who were also musicians who helped introduce France to the African-American music called JAZZ, Bullard remained in PARIS after the war.

France's appreciation for the African-American contribution to World War I was of some concern to racist white Americans during the war and would remain so afterward. Impressing upon the French that African Americans were a menace and burden to the United States, a French-American liaison committee composed a memorandum called "Secret Information Concerning Black American Troops." The document stated in essence that the French should adopt an American style of racism: "We must prevent the rise of any pronounced degree of intimacy between French officers and black officers. We may be courteous and amiable with these last, but we cannot deal with them on the same plane as with the white American officers without deeply wounding the latter. We must not eat with them, must not shake hands or seek to talk or meet with them outside of the requirements of military service."

The World War I experience so affected black America that an eclectic literature, from memoir to drama, emerged from it. Addie D. Waites Hunton and Kathryn Johnson served during World War I as YWCA workers in France before they penned *Two Colored Women with the Expeditionary Forces* (1920), which included poetry by Paul Laurence Dunbar and JAMES WELDON JOHNSON. WILLIAM STANLEY BEAUMONT BRAITHWAITE, winner of the NAACP's 1918 SPINGARN MEDAL, wrote a book entitled *The Story of the Great War* (1919). And JOSEPH SEAMON COTTER, JR., wrote a surrealistic one-act play, *On the Fields of France,* which was published in the June 1920 *Crisis,* one year after his premature death.

The white American soldier's homecoming was marked with rewards of employment and housing opportunities, but the black soldier returned to the cruel realities of lynching and disfranchisement. Du Bois cried out in the *Crisis* of May 1919: "We return from the slavery of the uniform which the world's madness demanded us to don to the freedom of civil garb. We return from fighting. We return fighting . . . We saved it (democracy) in France, and by the Great Jehovah, we will save it in the United States of America, or know the reason why."

Black soldiers who did not return home were buried in France and Belgium. Their mothers were called Gold Star Mothers. According to an *AMSTERDAM NEWS* editorial on February 19, 1930, these women were "Jim-Crowed" as they traveled to Europe to visit the graves of their loved ones. The U.S. Congress made funds available for Gold Star Mothers to go abroad, all expenses paid for two weeks, but white mothers were put on one ship and black mothers on another.

Further Reading

Anderson, Jervis. *This Was Harlem 1900–1950.* New York: Farrar, Straus, & Giroux, 1981.

Drago, Edmund L. "American Blacks and Italy's Invasion of Ethiopia." *Negro History Bulletin,* September–October 1978.

Lewis, David Levering. *When Harlem Was in Vogue.* New York: Vintage Books, 1982.

Schoener, Allon, ed. *Harlem on My Mind: Cultural Capital of Black America 1900–1968.* New York: Random House, 1995.

Smith, Gene. "A Fighting Man: Col. Charles Young." *American Legacy,* Spring 1998.

Vincent, Theodore G., ed. *Voices of a Black Nation: Political Journalism in the Harlem Renaissance.* San Francisco: Ramparts Press, 1973.

— Aberjhani and Sandra L. West

Wright, Richard Nathaniel (1908–1960) *writer*

Authoring works that overtly challenged the system of JIM CROW racism in the United States during the first half of the 1900s, Richard Wright became the country's most famous African-American writer and the first to achieve financial independence through his writings.

Born on September 4, 1908, Wright was the eldest son of a schoolteacher named Ella Wilson Wright and a sharecropper named Nathan Wright. His brother Leon Allen Wright was two years younger than Richard.

Wright's parents moved their family to Memphis, Tennessee, in 1913. Soon thereafter, Nathan Wright left his family, and his son Richard would not see him again until he became an adult. The stress of attempting to rear her sons alone caused a decline in Ella Wright's health. Her children grew up alternately in orphanages and in Arkansas with various relatives. His grandmother, Margaret Bolden Wilson, was among the principal influences on Wright as a youth.

Wright's unstable childhood did not stop him from developing a love of books, and in 1924 he wrote his first published short story, "The Voodoo of Hell's Half Acre." The following year he graduated from the ninth grade as valedictorian of his class. He moved back to Memphis to assist his mother and there worked a number of odd jobs to support his family. He continued to study independently by forging notes to white librarians requesting books by H. L. Mencken and Theodore Dreiser. Mencken's work in particular inspired Wright to pursue writing as a profession.

Joining the GREAT MIGRATION of African Americans moving out of the South and into the North during the 1920s and 1930s, Wright moved to CHICAGO in 1927. He again held a variety of jobs, including postal clerk, insurance agent, bellhop, and waiter. He also began to study COMMUNISM and in 1932 joined the Communist Party. He then became secretary of the Chicago branch of the John Reed Club, an organization of journalists and writers founded in memory of the radical journalist.

In 1935, along with ARNA BONTEMPS and MARGARET ABIGAIL WALKER, Wright joined the Chicago branch of the WORKS PROGRESS ADMINISTRATION's FEDERAL WRITERS' PROJECT. Founded as part of FRANKLIN DELANO ROOSEVELT's New Deal plan, the Federal Writers' Project employed qualified writers and white-collar workers to write travel guides, oral biographies, and local histories. Part of Wright's job with the project was that of literary adviser and press agent for the Negro Federal Theatre of Chicago. While LANGSTON HUGHES did not join the Federal Writers' Project, he and Wright both published poems and articles in the radical *New Masses* magazine and the two writers met in Chicago in 1936.

Wright continued to work with the Federal Writers' Project when he moved to NEW YORK CITY in 1937. In the New York office, he worked alongside the future author of *The Invisible Man,* RALPH WALDO ELLISON, and the author of "IF WE MUST DIE," CLAUDE MCKAY. In addition, Wright took on the editorship of the HARLEM edition of the communist newspaper the *Daily Worker.* Writing for the *Daily Worker,* Wright reported on boxer JOE LOUIS's historic victory over Max Schmeling in 1937. That same year, he teamed up with DOROTHY WEST and Marian Minus to edit the short-lived magazine *New Challenge.* In its single issue, Wright published his now famous "Blueprint for Negro Writing," which like Langston Hughes's 1926 essay, "The Negro Artist and the Racial Mountain," offered writing guidelines for African-American authors.

Wright experienced his first major success as a writer in 1938 with the publication of *Uncle Tom's Children,* a collection of four novellas that examined the impact of the more severe forms of Jim Crow segregation upon the lives of African Americans. The author's fellow Communist Party members criticized the book as too unrealistic. The Communist Party's seemingly ambivalent attitude toward racism in the United States eventually grew into a source of disappointment for Wright. However, *Uncle Tom's Children* was well received by the general public, and the book won first place in a competition sponsored by the Federal Writers' Project. Moreover, it led to a $2,500 Guggenheim Fellowship that allowed Wright to resign from the Federal Writers' Project in 1939 and work on his next book.

Richard Wright's success as the author of *Native Son* in 1940 catapulted him to international fame and often made him a figure of political controversy. He is shown here in 1943. *(Library of Congress, Prints & Photographs Division [LC-USW3-030285-D])*

On August 12, 1939, Wright married his first wife, Dhimah Rose Meadman, the divorced mother of a two-year-old son. Serving as best man on the occasion was Ralph Ellison, with whom Wright became a close friend and inspired to become a writer himself.

The publishing company of Harper and Brothers published Richard Wright's novel *Native Son* in 1940. The novel is the story of Bigger Thomas, a Chicago inner-city youth whose dread and hatred of whites lead him to accidentally kill the daughter of his white employers, Mr. and Mrs. Dalton. Told in a manner that combined social realism with gothic horror, Wright's novel was celebrated for its break with what he considered the more romantic novels of the Harlem Renaissance writers. It was also both criticized and championed for a concluding courtroom scene in which Bigger Thomas's defender articulates with political and philosophical precision the dilemma of any African American living under a system of Jim Crow segregation. Overall, the book was highly acclaimed and chosen as a Book-of-the-Month Club selection. In a month's time, it sold a quarter million copies and established new sales records for Harper and Brothers. In addition, it made Wright the most famous black author in the United States as well as one of the wealthiest of any race. It was adapted for a Broadway stage production starring CANADA LEE in 1941. Following a successful run in New York, the play went on to tour the United States. It was also adapted into a screenplay for a movie in which Wright himself, some years later in 1950, would play the role of Bigger.

The nearly overwhelming success of *Native Son* allowed Wright to express his political concerns more overtly in his next book, *Twelve Million Black Voices: A Folk History of the Negro in the United States,* published in 1941. With Wright supplying the text, the book utilized photographs from the Farm Security Administration files. Officials at the Federal Bureau of Investigation and the U.S. War Department decided the book was close enough to subversion that they started maintaining files on Wright.

The author divorced his first wife and married Ellen Poplar in Coytesville, New Jersey, on March 12, 1941. With Poplar, Wright had two daughters, Julia and Rachael.

The NATIONAL ASSOCIATION FOR THE ADVANCEMENT OF COLORED PEOPLE (NAACP) awarded Wright the SPINGARN MEDAL for his literary achievements in 1942. In the 1944 August/September issue of *Atlantic Monthly* magazine, Wright formalized his resignation from the Communist Party with the publication of an article titled "I Tried to be a Communist."

In 1945, he published the first part of his biography, *Black Boy, a Record of Childhood and Youth.* Whereas *Native Son* was the fictional story of a youth in Chicago, *Black Boy* was Wright's own tale of growing up in a segregated South where signs read "white" or "colored" to designate where blacks could or could not go and where death by LYNCHING was a common occurrence. Critics divided over whether *Black Boy* was superior to *Native Son,* but all agreed it was an important contribution to the tradition of American biographies and secured Wright's place as a major American writer.

During the same period, Wright met author James Baldwin for the first time when the younger writer approached Wright for guidance concerning his work in progress, an early version of Baldwin's now classic novel, *Go Tell It on the Mountain.* Impressed by what he read, Wright helped Baldwin secure a grant to continue work on the novel.

Seeking to elude the pressures of racism, fame, and political controversy, Wright moved with his family to PARIS, France, in 1947. As they had for Claude McKay, ALAIN LOCKE, and COUNTEE CULLEN before him, French intellectuals welcomed and celebrated Wright's arrival. His friends came to include the renowned philosopher of existentialism Jean-Paul Sartre, philosopher and feminist Simone de Beauvoir, writer Albert Camus, and writer Jean Genet. He also befriended the founders of NEGRITUDE, Aimé Césaire and Leopold Senghor, helping them establish the magazine *Presence Africaine.*

Moreover, once he was settled in France, Wright acted as a kind of connection for other black expatriates leaving the United States to live in the country. Among these was his friend Ollie Harrington, a cartoonist for the *PITTSBURGH COURIER,* and the writers Chester Himes and James Baldwin. Upon Baldwin's arrival in Paris, he and Wright basically picked up where they had left off in the United States, with Wright lending whatever assistance he could to help further Baldwin's career and development as a writer. However, their friendship all but ended in 1949 when Baldwin published in the *Partisan Review* his now famous essay, "Everybody's Protest Novel," in part a critical evaluation of *Native Son.* Wright denounced the essay as an attack on his person and work while Baldwin defended it as a fresh evaluation of protest literature.

Richard Wright continued to publish novels as well as works of nonfiction while living in Paris. Included in his prolific output was the novel *The Outsider* in 1953, a book often described as the first black existential novel; *Black Power: a Record of Reactions in a Land of Pathos;* and the novel *Savage Holiday,* both in 1954; *White Man Listen!* in 1957; the novel *The Long Dream* in 1958.

For much of his work, Wright traveled extensively throughout Africa and the African diaspora. He died in Paris on November 28, 1960, at the age of 52. Numerous works by Wright were published posthumously. A collection of stories titled *Eight Men* was published in 1961, and Wright's first novel, *Lawd Today,* was published for the first time in 1963. A second part to his biography, originally included as a segment of *Black Boy,* was published as a separate book entitled *American Hunger* in 1977. An unexpurgated edition of *Native Son* was released in 1992. Wright's novels and short stories remain standard reading requirements in American high schools and colleges.

Further Reading

Campbell, James. *Exiled in Paris: Richard Wright, James Baldwin, Samuel Beckett, and Other on the Left Bank.* Berkeley: University of California Press, 2003.

Folks, J. J. Jeffrey. *From Richard Wright to Toni Morrison: Ethics in Modern and Postmodern American Narrative.* New York: Peter Lang Publishing, 2001.

Maxwell, William J. *New Negro, Old Left: African-American Writing and Communism Between the Wars.* New York: Columbia University Press, 1999.

Rowley, Hazel. *Richard Wright, the Life and the Times.* New York: Holt, 2001.

— Aberjhani

Z

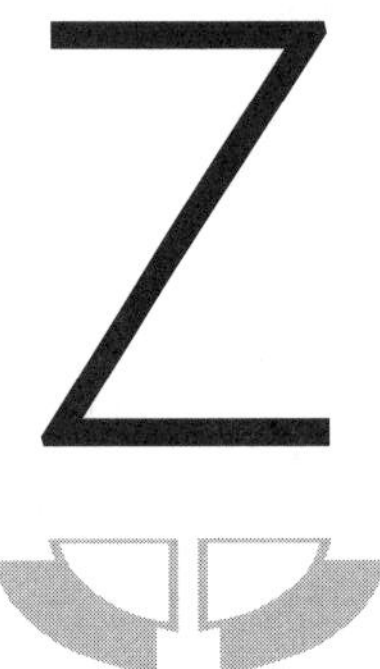

Zeta Phi Beta Sorority, Inc.

The founding members of the Zeta Phi Beta Sorority, Inc., took the concept of a sister organization a step further than their predecessors when they patterned their constitution after that of PHI BETA SIGMA FRATERNITY, INC. Known as the Five Pearls, the women who established Zeta Phi Beta on January 16, 1920, at HOWARD UNIVERSITY, in WASHINGTON, D.C., were Arizona Cleaver, who initiated the idea, Viola Tyler, Pearl A. Neal, Myrtle Tyler, and Fannie Pettie.

Working with Phi Beta Sigma's A. Langston Taylor and Charles R. Taylor, Myrtle Tyler penned the constitution that made their respective outfits the first official brother and sister organizations. To date, they remain the only African-American fraternity and sorority with an official kinship bound by their constitutions.

The new sorority adopted for its motto, "Scholarship, Service, Sisterhood & Finer Womanhood." They put the motto into action during the 1920s with the observation of "Finer Womanhood Week." Among the women who joined the organization and helped give substance to its motto was one of the most gifted and accomplished writers of the period, ZORA NEALE HURSTON. They also started the sorority publication *X-Ray,* known now as the *Archon.* Going into the 1930s, Zeta Phi Beta addressed such issues as civil rights by working alongside the NATIONAL ASSOCIATION FOR THE ADVANCEMENT OF COLORED PEOPLE (NAACP) and the short-lived National Negro Congress, a conglomerate of black organizations all working toward racial equality.

In the 1940s, the sorority increased its activities in the African-American community and started its Zeta Housing Project, working to locate and register available housing vacancies for possible occupation. The sorority also volunteered time working with agencies to help prevent juvenile delinquency, a problem that had escalated in most urban communities during the GREAT DEPRESSION in the previous decade. As with other fraternities and sororities going into the 1950s and 1960s civil rights era, Zeta Phi Beta lent not only moral support to the cause but crucial financial support as well. In that regard, they contributed $500 in support of the Little Rock Nine, those students in 1957 who attempted to integrate schools in Little Rock, Arkansas.

The sorority in 2002 continued to grow and make significant contributions both to its own rich history and the greater American community. Its principal programs tackled such issues as national job searches, relationship workshops, women working as entrepreneurs, the development of corporations, increased literacy, and the prevention of drug abuse.

After becoming the first sorority to form a constitutional alliance with a fraternity, Zeta Phi Beta went on to enjoy a number of other sorority firsts. They became the first Greek-lettered organization to charter a chapter in Africa, the first to create a national headquarters, in Washington, D.C., and the first to form auxiliary groups with goals complementary to their own. The auxiliary groups are the Amicae, the Archonettes, the Amiettes, the Perlettes, and the Zeta Male Network.

Incorporated in Washington, D.C., and Illinois, the organization as of 2002 boasted more than 100,000 members in 600 chapters located in the United States, the Bahamas, the Virgin Islands, Italy, South Korea, and Germany. It also maintained the distinction of having many accomplished women among its ranks, including singer Sarah Vaughan, singer and humanitarian Dionne Warwick, actress Esther Rolle, actress Ja'Net DuBois, singer Minnie Ripperton, and Deborah Wolfe, former professor emerita at Queens College, City University of New York.

Further Reading

Goggins, Lathardus, with preface by Emily D. Gunter. *Bringing the Light into a New Day: Centered Rites of Passage.* Akron, Ohio: Saint Rest Publications, 1998.

Winegarten, Ruthe, and Sharon Kahn. *Brave Black Women: From Slavery to the Space Shuttle.* Austin: University of Texas, 1997.

— Aberjhani

Ziegfeld Follies

With elaborate set designs, glamorized images of American women, and African-American talent, Florenz Ziegfeld, Jr., made the Ziegfeld Follies one of the world's most spectacular annual entertainment productions during the first half of the 1900s.

Ziegfeld was born on March 21, 1868. His father was Dr. Florenz Ziegfeld, the president and founder of the Chicago Musical College. The younger Ziegfeld's first venture into entertainment came as a sharpshooter in the famed cowboy Buffalo Bill's *Wild West Show.* His father, as one of the producers of the Chicago World Fair 1893 Columbian Exposition, hired his son to obtain musical entertainment for the event. Ziegfeld traveled to Europe and returned with a group composed of an English dancer and marching bands from Hungary, France, Russia, and Germany. The musical arrangement was not a success, and he had better luck with his next project, a muscleman called the Great Sandow who lifted barbells with men hidden inside the weights and allowed select audience members backstage to feel his muscles.

Ziegfeld's luck and artistic vision increased when he met his future common-law wife, Anna Held, in 1896. Held was born in PARIS, France, in around 1873, and at the time she met Ziegfeld had already become a veteran of European music halls and cabarets, including the revues *La Scala* and *El Dorado,* performed in Paris. Ziegfeld first saw her in London and soon returned with her to NEW YORK CITY to star in shows featuring burlesque entertainment. Such productions as *Papa's Wife, The French Maid, Mademoiselle Napolean, Little Duchess,* and *The Parisian Model* made Held a Broadway star and Ziegfeld a successful producer. To the onstage excitement, Ziegfeld added offstage publicity stunts such as daily ordering 40 gallons of milk in which Held took her bath.

It was Held who suggested that a glamorized presentation of American women as showgirls would achieve the same level of success as the Folies-Bergères of Paris, but use of the word "Follies" in Ziegfeld's shows was actually borrowed from a New York newspaper column called "Follies of the Day." The first Ziegfeld Follies opened in July 1907 at the Jardin de Paris, a rooftop garden located atop the New York Theatre. The $21,000 production featured a chorus line of 50 Anna Held Girls without the presence of the star herself. A variety of comedy routines filled out the show, but these would decrease over the years as the glamorized chorus line and women, whose only job was to look beautiful, became central elements of the Follies. Comedy would, however, make a comeback through the talents of black performer BERT WILLIAMS. The first show made runs in Baltimore and WASHINGTON, D.C., to pull in $120,000. The Ziegfeld Follies then moved to the Erlanger Theatre in 1908 and in 1909 officially became an annual event.

Ziegfeld and Held occasionally made excursions into HARLEM and there enjoyed the music of composers and performers whom the producer would often hire to direct the music, in the form of JAZZ orchestras, for his own shows. Among the musicians who worked with the Ziegfeld Follies were Will Voderey, Ford Dabney, James Reese Europe, and DUKE ELLINGTON. The producer was with Bert Williams when they visited Harlem's LAFAYETTE THEATRE to see a performance of the *Darktown Follies.* Ziegfeld was so captivated by the show's finale, loaded as it was with erotic implications, that he bought the rights to it and several songs for use in his Follies. The routine became one of the show's biggest hits.

Already a celebrated comedian and actor, vaudeville and Broadway veteran Bert Williams integrated the Ziegfeld Follies when he became a regular member of the show in 1910 following the death of his partner, GEORGE WALKER. Williams did not join the Follies without controversy: white show members refused to appear onstage with him, and Williams signed a contract pledging not to touch any of the beautiful all-white Ziegfeld women. Williams actually enjoyed the opportunity to perform solo but soon found his coworkers eager to join him onstage when they witnessed the thunderous applause that followed his act. One of his regular partners became the white comic Eddie Cantor, who along with Williams would wear blackface for a father and son skit. Cantor and Williams also shared a genuine friendship, and offstage the two would sometimes frequent cafes or clubs that did not practice the discriminatory polices of JIM CROW racism. Although the Ziegfeld Follies did not grant Williams top billing, both the public and the media recognized him as a genuine star and as one of the show's principal draws until his death in 1922.

Ziegfeld expanded the Follies when he moved his show in 1913 into the New Amsterdam Theater and began a creative partnership with the artist, designer, and architect Joseph Urban. The latter's giant-sized representations of both classic and modern art combined with architectural innovations, all serving as backdrop for what would become known as the Ziegfeld Girl, helped to elevate American entertainment to unsurpassed heights.

Separating from Held, Ziegfeld also formed in 1914 a creative as well as marital partnership with the actress Billie Burke, now known to most Americans as the good witch Glenda in Hollywood's classic *The Wizard of Oz.* The Follies continued to build upon such talents as composer Irving Berlin, comedian Fanny Brice, and comedian Will Rogers. In 1926, it had become an institution unto itself and moved into the Urban-designed Ziegfeld Theatre on 54th Street.

In 1927, the Ziegfeld Theatre hosted the first production of Jerome Kern and Oscar Hammerstein's *Show Boat,* based on the novel by Edna Ferber. Ziegfeld confessed that he was uneasy about the theme of INTERRACIAL INTERACTION woven into the story but found the show's music irresistible. One of its now classic tunes was "Ole Man River," performed by Jules Bledsoe in 1927 and made famous by PAUL ROBESON in a revival of the show in 1932. William Warfield later did a movie version of the song with which he continued to thrill audiences in 2001.

The final Ziegfeld Follies was produced in 1931, and Ziegfeld died on July 22, 1932. His widow, Billie Burke, revived the Follies in 1933, and shows were presented periodically until 1957. Hollywood made a number of attempts to capture the splendor of the Ziegfeld Follies on film. One of the most popular was MGM's 1936 *The Great Ziegfeld.*

Further Reading

Davis, Lee. *Scandals and Follies: The Rise and Fall of the Great Broadway Revue.* New York: Limelight Editions, 1998.

Golden, Eve. *Anna Held and the Birth of Ziegfeld's Broadway.* Lexington: University Press of Kentucky, 2000.

Miller, Scott. *Rebels with Applause: Broadway's Groundbreaking Musicals.* Portsmouth, N.H.: Heinemann, 2001.

Smith, Eric Ledell. *Bert Williams: A Biography of the Pioneer Black Comedian.* Jefferson, N.C.: McFarland and Company, 1992.

— Aberjhani

Appendix A: GLOSSARY OF HARLEM RENAISSANCE SLANG

Adapting the English language to fit the needs and realities of the black experience in America was a challenge most likely first recognized and met by black preachers on slave plantations. In their multiple roles as ministers, healers, teachers, and singers, they transformed those stories presented to them from the King James Bible, with the intent of convincing slaves that they should be happy with their miserable lot, into allegories closer to their own spiritual interpretations of their own experience. They saw in African Americans not those slaves who should be happy with their earthly circumstances while contented to know that heaven would bless them for their faithful suffering but the wrongly oppressed people of God destined to be delivered by the same. So it was in regard to Protestant church hymns that field workers adapted not only to express their hopes for eventual freedom but to secretly communicate plans for escape or information regarding other important events.

The Harlem Renaissance was a time when black professional academics and artists of every genre also usurped the power of the English language on behalf of black people. Accused by white American society of innate ignorance and even inhumanity, they strove to demonstrate black intelligence and civility through the mastery of such creative forms as music, the visual arts, poetry, short stories, novels, essays, and plays. The average black American in the 1920s and 1930s was not an academic or professional literary artist but in their everyday lives many nevertheless indulged creative tendencies that gave birth to FOLK ART, FOLK LITERATURE, and a great deal of folklore. Part of the creative expressiveness of the average individual was the invention of slang, known in 1920s and 1930s Harlem as "Harlemese," and later by such terms as *jive* and *hep.*

Harlemese was not merely an indicator that African Americans were undereducated. It was a rich body of language that rejected white America's lexicon of terms designed to reinforce the notion of black inferiority even as it affirmed the African-American tendency for wordplay and linguistic reinvention. During the GREAT MIGRATION it was also one way of determining whether an African American was new to the North or had successfully made both the geographical and psychological transition out of the South. The vocabulary of Harlemese and jive developed largely out of everyday social and political experience but also out of such musical genres as the BLUES and JAZZ.

The language in turn influenced the literary voices and works of Harlem Renaissance writers in much the way that the everyday culture of Elizabethan England influenced and informed the works of Shakespeare. The listing that follows is but a small example of the era's colorful slang.

ain't got 'em Possesses no virtues—is no good.

alligator A man, particularly a stylishly dressed man, might be referred to as an "alligator" or "cat."

arnchy A person who puts on airs.

ask for Challenge to battle in terms that do not mean maybe.

august ham Watermelon.

barbeque Term was used to refer to a girlfriend or a "beauty."

bardacious Marvelous.

belly fiddle A guitar, in the hep language of the Harlem Renaissance, might be referred to as a "belly fiddle" or a "git box."

belly-rub A delicate but accurate designation of any sexy dance, the bump being a popular example.

berries, the An expression of approbation.

bird's eye maple Used to refer to skin color. A light-skinned woman or mulatto would be called "high yaller (yellow)" or "bird's eye maple."

blue Used to refer to skin color. A very dark-complexioned black person.

blue-vein circle After the Civil War the mulattoes organized themselves into an informal guild from which those who were black were excluded. This form of color snobbery still persists in many localities.

bolito See **numbers.**

boodle A "whole lot of" a particular thing.

boody A sexual desire for or appreciation of another person; sex. See also **hootchie-pap.**

boogy Black person. A contraction for Booker T. (Washington), used only of and by African Americans. Other popular synonyms for blacks, which could be offensive or complimentary depending on how they were used, included the following: *cloud, crow, darky, dinge, dinky, eight ball, hunk, hunky, ink, jap, jasper, jig, jigaboo, jigwalker, joker, kack, mose, race-man, sam, shade, shine, smoke spade, zigaboo.* These words were generally considered offensive when used by whites.

bottle it Equivalent to the colloquial *shut up.*

boy Friend and ally. Buddy.

brick-presser An idler; literally one who walks the pavement.

bring mud To fall below expectations, disappoint. He who escorts a homely *sheba* to a *dickty shout* brings mud.

brother A form of address, usually ironic. A bystander, witnessing the arrest of some offender may observe: "It's too bad now, brother."

brother in black, Russian A southern black located in the North, as in "rushed up here from Georgia." A "Russian" = "rush-in."

brown Good, fine, or decent as in, "that's mighty brown of you."

buckra A white person.

bump, bumpty-bump, bump-the-bump A *shout,* or dance, characterized by a forward and backward swaying of the hips. Said to be an excellent aphrodisiac. Also said to be the despair of *fays.*

butt Buttocks.

buzz cart An automobile. See also **lammer.**

can Buttocks.

canary A *hep* term for a female vocalist.

can't say it No complaint.

capping Taking or catching a ride, as in "I capped the subway downtown."

cat Casual slang for a "man." See **alligator.**

catch air To take leave, usually under urgent pressure.

charcoal A racial slur when used by whites; a derogatory term for African American.

chicken cock A bourbon drink sold in a tin can; "chick cock" cost a dollar.

chick Casual slang for a young woman.

choke To defeat. *To turn one's damper down.*

chorine A chorus girl.

chorat A chorus man.

cloud See **boogy.**

cold Extremely well, as in "He can play that trumpet cold."

color During the Harlem Renaissance, among black people, skin color defined status and how well one was treated. There were numerous stations from lighter to darker. Lighter skin tones included high yaller (yellow), pink, pink toes, mustard seed, *punkin-seed,* honey, lemon-colored, copper-hued, and olive. Darker browns included high brown, cocoa brown, chestnut, coffee-colored, nut brown, maroon, Vaseline brown, seal brown, sealskin, and low brown. The darkest skin tones included blue, charcoal, ebony black, eight-rock, inky dink, dark black, lam black, and damn black.

come on like gangbusters Generally used enthusiastically to describe energetic excellence in performance.

conk The result of the process of straightening African-American hair with lye in imitation of the white style.

cool Untroubled or composed.

copacetic Going well or terrific, as in "everything is copacetic"; believed to have been coined by BOJANGLES ROBINSON.

C.P. time Short for "colored people's time," this meant to be perpetually late.

crow See **boogy.**

counselor A title often given to lawyers among black people.

creeper A man who invades another's marital rights.

daddy Male provider of affection and other more tangible delights.

darky See **boogy.**

dickty Among both blacks and whites, an "uppity" or proud manner; this adjective was used to refer to an individual whose personal carriage was more elegant than that of other members of his plantation.

dig To look at, as in "Dig that cat over there."

dinge See **boogy.**

dinky See **boogy.**

dog An extraordinary person, thing, or event. "Ain't this a dog?" is a comment on anything unusual.

dogs Feet.

do it!; do that thing!; do your stuff! "More power to you!"

down the way Designation of some place familiar to both parties talking.

do one's stuff Exhibit one's best. Show off.

dozens A verbal game in which opponents trade insults.

draped down To dress in high Harlem style; also sometimes called togged down.

drunk down Completely intoxicated with alcohol.

Eastman A man who is supported by women.

eight ball Black; the number eight pool ball is black; generally considered offensive when used by whites.

evermore Extremely, as in "an evermore red-hot mamma."

fagingy-fagade A white person. This word and the corresponding word for black are theatrical (slang).

fay; ofay A white person. Fay is said to be the original term and ofay, a contraction of "old" and "fay."

first thing smoking A train; attributed to ZORA NEALE HURSTON ("I'm not going to grab the first thing smoking").

fog horn A tuba.

freeby Something for nothing, as complimentary tickets to a theater.

from way back Of extraordinary experience and skill.

fry To get one's hair straightened, pressed, or marcelled to look like a white person's hair.

get away Escape unpunished for audacity; to triumph, as does the successful *jiver* or the winner at blackjack.

gigwatney Slang term for a black person.

gimme some skin A request to shake hands.

git box See **belly fiddle.**

give one air To dismiss one with finality. To "give one the gate."

glad rags Stylish clothes.

gob stick A *gob stick* or *stick* was a clarinet.

gravy Unearned increment. *Freeby.*

great day in the morning! Exclamation of wonder.

groan box Musicians' slang for an accordion; also *squeeze box.*

handkerchief head See **Uncle Tom.**

happy dust Cocaine.

Harlemese The original urban dialect used by Harlemites who frequented clubs and speakeasies, dubbed by musician CAB CALLOWAY, "Negro slang, the super-hip language of the times." See **jive.**

haul it Depart in great haste. Haul *hiney. Catch air.* "It," without an obvious antecedent, usually has a pelvic significance. "Put it in the chair" means "sit down."

hep Adjective used to describe someone in the know, progressive, or sophisticated, such as a hep white person who appreciated jazz, or a hep *cat* who understands jive.

hides Musicians' slang for a set of drums; also suitcases, or skins.

high Enjoying the elevated spirits of moderately advanced inebriation. "Tight," in the usual slang sense of drunk. See *tight* in the Harlemese sense.

high yellow Mulatto or lighter.

hiney Affectionate diminutive for hindquarters. "It's your hiney" means "It will cost you your hiney," i.e., "You are undone."

hip See **hep.**

honey man Sly descriptor for a man who was "kept" (that is, financially provided for) by a woman. See also **Eastman.**

hoof To dance. A hoofer is a dancer, and hoofing is dancing.

hootchie-pap A sexual desire for or appreciation of another person; sex. See also **boody.**

hot Adjective means of kindling admiration.

hot you! Pronounced "hot-choo." Equivalent to *Oh, no, now!*

how come? Why?

hummer Someone or something exceptionally good, as in "That cat is a hummer."

hunk, hunky See **boogy.**

I mean "You said it." As in "Some *sheba* huh?"—"I mean!"

in the groove Normally used to describe a condition as being "perfect."

ink See **boogy.**

ironworks Musicians' slang for a vibraphone.

ivories Musicians' slang for a piano; taken from the material from which the white keys were carved. See **storehouse.**

Jack Any male friend.

jap See **boogy.**

jazz 1. The modern American musical idiom. 2. Sometimes synonymous with *jive.*

jig, jigaboo, jigwalker See **boogy.**

jig-chaser A white person who seeks the company of blacks.

jitterbug The name of a dance; also a style of dress. Men's jitterbug pants were wide with tight-fitting angled, or "pegged," hems. They were actually zoot suit pants, minus the jacket.

jive 1. Pursuit in love using flattery. 2. Rhetoric used to create confusion or deceive.

jiver One who *jives.*

john-brown Dog-gone.

joker See **boogy.**

juice joint An after-hours club or SPEAKEASY.

kack Extreme sarcasm for *dickty;* generally considered offensive when used by whites.

kelt Probably short for "Celtic," this meant a white person. This term was most frequently used by speakeasy goers. See **fay; ofay.**

kicks Shoes; fancy kicks were usually made of alligator skin.

killer-diller A great thrill.

kinkout Hair straightener.

k.m. Kitchen mechanic, i.e., cook, girl, scullion, menial.

kopasetee An approbatory epithet somewhat stronger than "all right"; possibly from *copacetic.*

lammer An automobile. See also **buzz cart.**

lap Liquor; probably a deprecating reference to "lapping it up."

lay some iron To tap dance; referring to the metal taps on the bottom of tap shoes.

long-gone Lost.

lord today! Exclamation of wonder.

mamma Potential or actual sweetheart.

martin Jocose designation of death. Derived from Bert Williams's story "Wait Till Martin Comes."

miss Fail. A question is characteristically answered by use of miss or some equivalent expression. Example: "Did you win money?"—"I didn't miss" or "Nothing different." "Do you mean me?"—"I don't mean your brother" and so on.

Miss Anne; Mr. Charlie Nonspecific designation of wealthy, stylish whites, as in "Boy, bootlegging pays. That boogy's got a straight-eight just like Mr. Charlie's."—"Yea, and his mamma's got a fur coat just like Miss Anne's too."

monk See **monkey-chaser.**

monkey-back Dude.

monkey-chaser A black from the British West Indies.

monkey hugger See **monkey-chaser.**

mose See **boogy.**

Mr. Eddie A white man.

mud See **bring mud.**

mustard seed See **high yellow.**

My People! My People! Exclamation commonly used by blacks to express their exasperation with the backwardness of other blacks.

Negro At the time of the Harlem Renaissance, this was the official preferred term for referring to African Americans. Other terms were also used: black, colored, *race-man,* Afro-American, Aframericans, as well as Lybian and Ethiopian.

Negrotarian Term, coined by ZORA NEALE HURSTON, used to refer to white patrons of black artists and writers.

Nigger Offensive term for African Americans, considered a racial slur when used by whites.

Niggerati Term adopted by WALLACE THURMAN and ZORA NEALE HURSTON as a sarcastic poke at the black literati of the Harlem Renaissance. In Thurman's novel *Infants of the Spring,* a meeting place for writers and artists is called NIGGERATI MANOR.

numbers A gambling game highly popular in 1920s Harlem and later (versions are still played today in some places). The winning numbers each day were derived from the New York Clearing House bank exchanges and balances as they were published in the newspapers: the seventh and eighth digits, reading from the right, of the exchanges, and the seventh of the balances. In *bolito,* one wagers on two figures only, rather than three.

no lie Equivalent to "You said it." *"I mean."*

ofay See **fay.**

oh, no, now! Exclamation of admiration.

oscar A stupid person.

out (of) this world Beyond mortal experience or belief.

pan-cake head See **Uncle Tom.**

papa Equivalent to *brother.* See **daddy.**

passing Pretending to be (or "pass for") white and move in white social circles, which the lighter skin of some blacks allowed them to do.

pink a white person.

pink-chaser A black who seeks the company of whites.

play that I.e., play that game, hence, to countenance or tolerate.

plumbing Musicians' slang for a trombone. See **slush pump;.**

poke out To be distinguished, excel.

previous Premature, hence, presumptuous. He who tries to break into a ticket line is likely to be warned, "Don't get too previous, brother."

punkin-seed See **high yellow.**

put in on one To injure one deliberately.

put one in To report to some enemy or authority in order to have one punished.

put (get, have) the locks on To handcuff; hence to render helpless. Most frequently heard in reference to some form of gambling, such as card games, or love affairs.

race-man (woman) See **boogy.**

red-hot Somewhat hotter than hot. Extremely striking.

reeds Musician's slang for a saxophone or clarinet.

right Somewhat in excess of perfection.

right-on Nevertheless.

rat Antithesis of *dickty.*

rubber The wheels on a car, or the automobile itself.

rug cutter A great dancer; probably a humorous caution about wearing holes in the carpet.

Russian See **brother in black.**

salty dog Stronger than *dog.*

sam See **boogy.**

sauce Alcohol or liquor.

sconch A dance.

see one go Give one aid. "See me go for breakfast?" means "Pay for my breakfast?" It is the answerer's privilege to interpret the query literally, thus "See you go—to hell."

shine Derogatory term for black person.

sharp Striking. A beautifully dressed woman is "sharp out of this world."

sheba Woman.

shout 1.Ball. Prom. 2. A slow one-step.

skins See **hides.**

slip 1. To kid 2. To slip in dozens, to disparage one's family.

slush pump Musicians' slang for a trombone. See **plumbing.**

smoke See **boogy.**

smoke over To observe critically; "give the once over."

smooth 1. Cunning, "slick," as a smooth *jiver.* 2. Faultless, as a smooth brown.

smoothe To calm, to quell anger.

snow Cocaine.

solid Generally used with enthusiasm, meaning "great" or "perfect."

spade Derogatory term for African Americans, considered a racial slur when used by whites; derived from the black suit in a deck of playing cards.

spagingy-spagade A black person.

spark-jiver Musicians' slang for an electric organ.

SPEAKEASY See **juice joint.**

squeeze box See **groan box.**

stick See **gob stick.**

storehouse Musicians' slang for a piano. See **ivories.**

struggle-buggy Ford automobile.

strut one's stuff See **do one's stuff.**

struttin' A slangy shortening of "strutting"; walking in a flamboyant or jaunty manner, as in "He was draped down and struttin' down LENOX AVENUE."

stuff 1.Talent. 2. Hokum. Baloney. As in "They told me that *sheba* tried to commit suicide over her *daddy.*"—"Huh. That's alot o' stuff."

tell 'em!; tell 'em bout it! Exclamation of agreement and approval.

suitcases See **hides.**

the man Designation of abstract authority. He who trespasses where a sign forbids may be asked, "Say biggie, can't you read the man's sign?"

there ain't nothing to that This signifies complete agreement with a previous assertion. It is equivalent to saying, "That is beyond question."

threads Clothes or a suit.

tight Tough. Redoubtable. Hard. Not "drunk" in the usual sense, which in Harlemese is *high.*

to be had To be tested.

to be on To bear actual or pretended malice against.

togged down See **draped down.**

too bad 1. Marvelous. 2. Extremely unfortunate.

tootin' Right. Unquestionable. As in "You are dog-gone tootin'."

tram See **plumbing; slush pump.**

turn 'em on *Strut* one's *stuff.*

turn one's damper down To reduce the temperature of one who is *hot.* Hence, to *choke.*

un-huh Yes.

uh-uh No.

Uncle Tom An overly humble or spineless black person who was perceived to "sell out" the black race to the white was known as an Uncle Tom, after a slave character in Harriet Beecher Stowe's abolitionist novel *Uncle Tom's Cabin,* popular before the Civil War. Other similar names included *pan-cake head* or handkerchief head.

unsheik Divorce.

uppity High hat; putting on air; behaving with a sense of entitlement.

what do you say How do you do?

working moll A prostitute.

woodpile Musicians' slang for a xylophone, an instrument brought to popularity by Lionel Hampton.

zigaboo See **boogy.**

Further Reading

Calloway, Cab. *Of Minnie the Moocher and Me.* New York: Crowell Publishing, 1976.

Fisher, Rudolph. *The Walls of Jericho.* New York: Alfred A. Knopf, 1928.

Major, Clarence. *Juba to Jive: A Dictionary of African-American Slang.* New York: Viking Penguin, 1994.

Smitherman, Geneva. *Black Talk: Words and Phrases from the Hood to the Amen Corner.* Boston: Houghton Mifflin Company, 2000.

Van Vechten, Carl. *Nigger Heaven.* New York: Grosset and Dunlap, 1928.

Appendix B: MAPS

1. Slaveholding Confederate States
2. African-American Population, 1920
3. Antimiscegenation Laws Banning Interracial Marriages, 1920s
4. Lynchings in the United States, 1880s–1960s
5. Exoduster Migration, 1875–1880
6. Great Migration, 1901–1945
7. Migrations to the West Coast, 1940s
8. Train Routes Used by Blacks During the Great Migration, ca. 1920
9. Development of Black Music
10. Harlem Renaissance World Influence
11. Harlem and the Harlem Renaissance
12. New York City

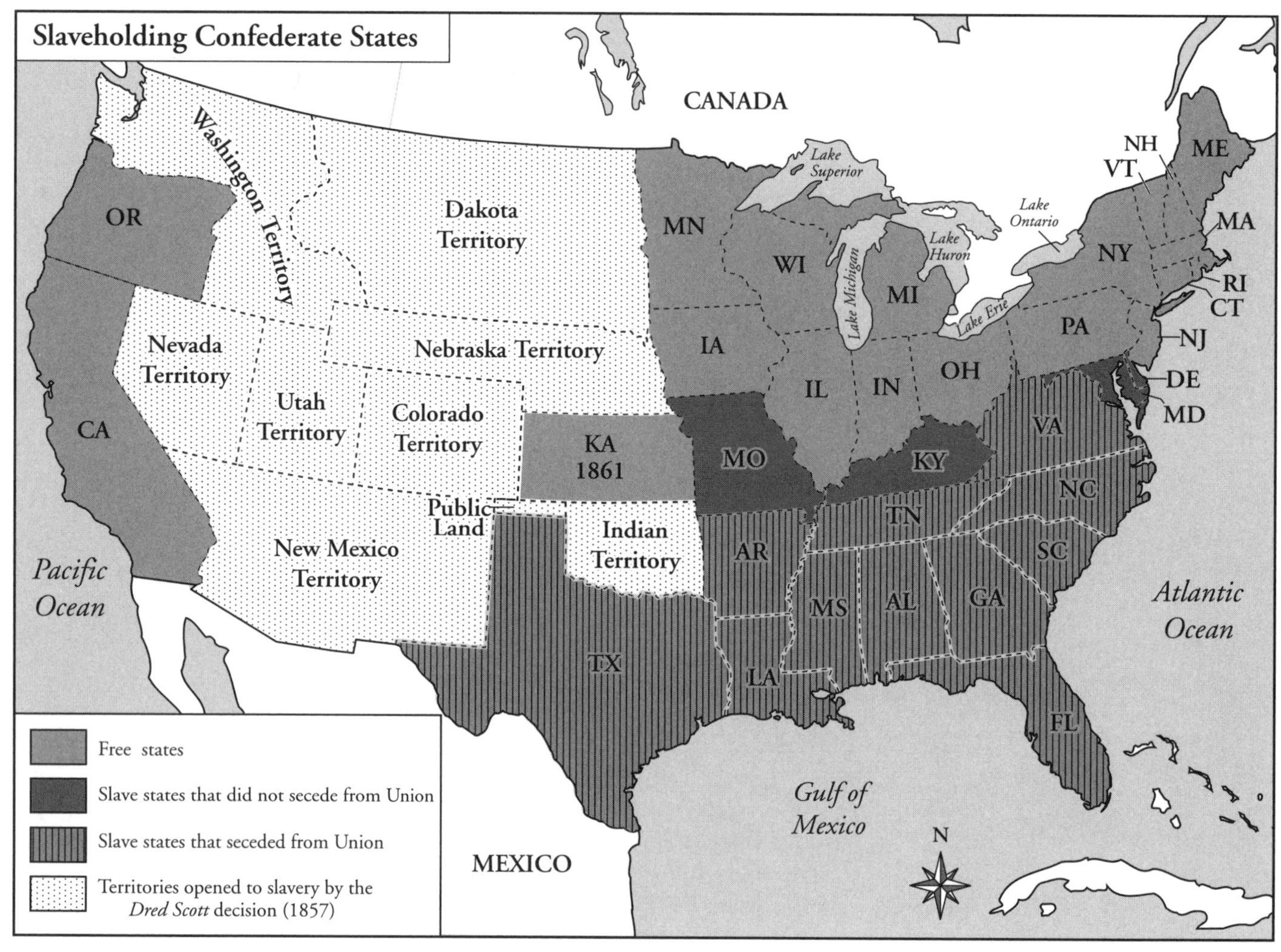
Slaveholding Confederate States
CANADA
Washington Territory
Dakota Territory
Nebraska Territory
Nevada Territory
Utah Territory
Colorado Territory
KA 1861
Public Land
New Mexico Territory
Indian Territory
OR
CA
MN
WI
MI
IA
IL
IN
OH
PA
NY
NH
VT
ME
MA
RI
CT
NJ
DE
MD
MO
KY
VA
NC
TN
SC
AR
MS
AL
GA
TX
LA
FL
Lake Superior
Lake Michigan
Lake Huron
Lake Ontario
Lake Erie
Pacific Ocean
Atlantic Ocean
Gulf of Mexico
MEXICO
N
Free states
Slave states that did not secede from Union
Slave states that seceded from Union
Territories opened to slavery by the *Dred Scott* decision (1857)

African-American Population, 1920

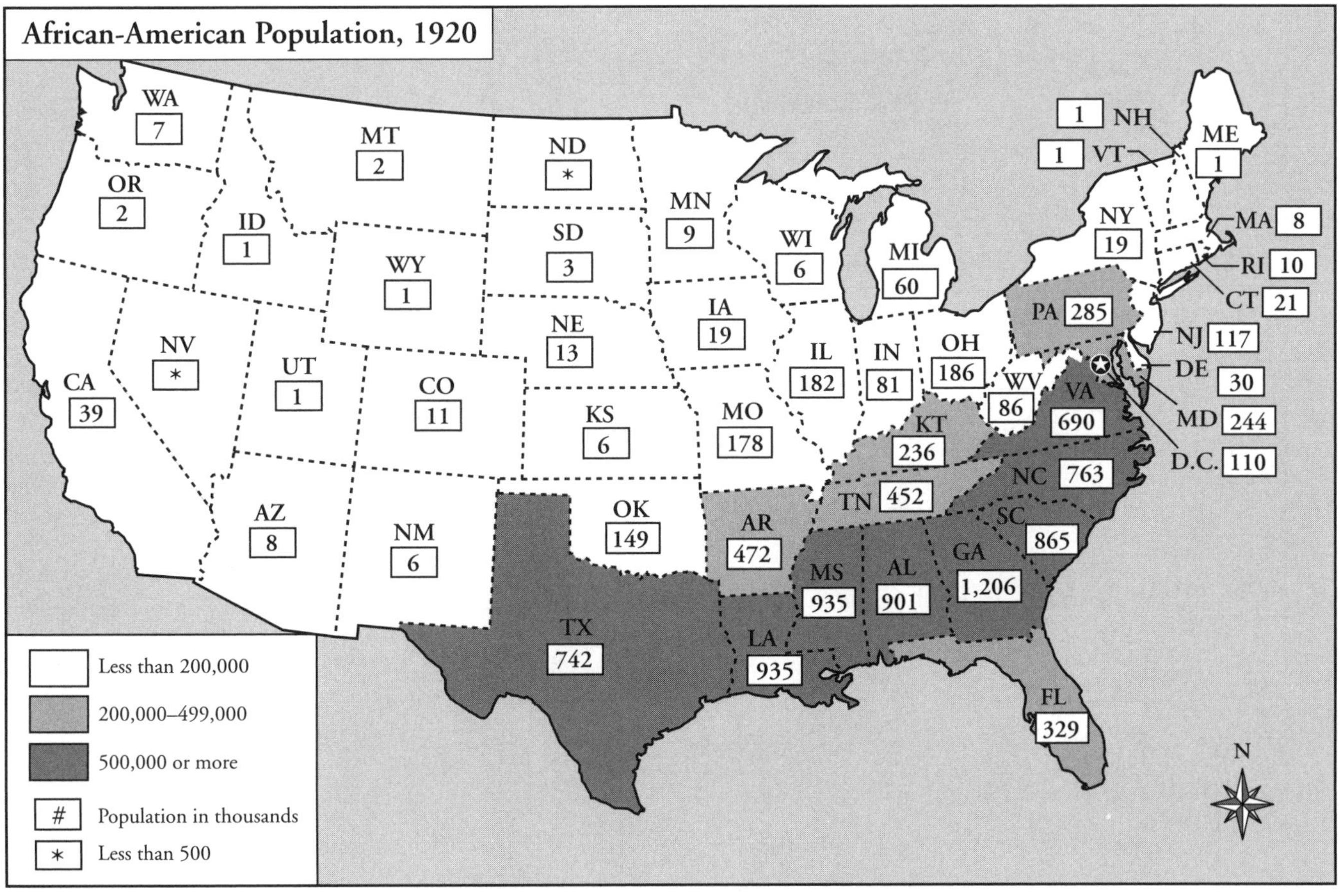

WA 7
OR 2
CA 39
NV *
ID 1
MT 2
WY 1
UT 1
AZ 8
CO 11
NM 6
ND *
SD 3
NE 13
KS 6
OK 149
TX 742
MN 9
IA 19
MO 178
AR 472
LA 935
WI 6
IL 182
MI 60
IN 81
OH 186
KT 236
TN 452
MS 935
AL 901
GA 1,206
FL 329
SC 865
NC 763
VA 690
WV 86
PA 285
NY 19
VT 1
NH 1
ME 1
MA 8
RI 10
CT 21
NJ 117
DE 30
MD 244
D.C. 110

N

Less than 200,000
200,000–499,000
500,000 or more
Population in thousands
* Less than 500

Antimiscegenation Laws Banning Interracial Marriages, 1920s

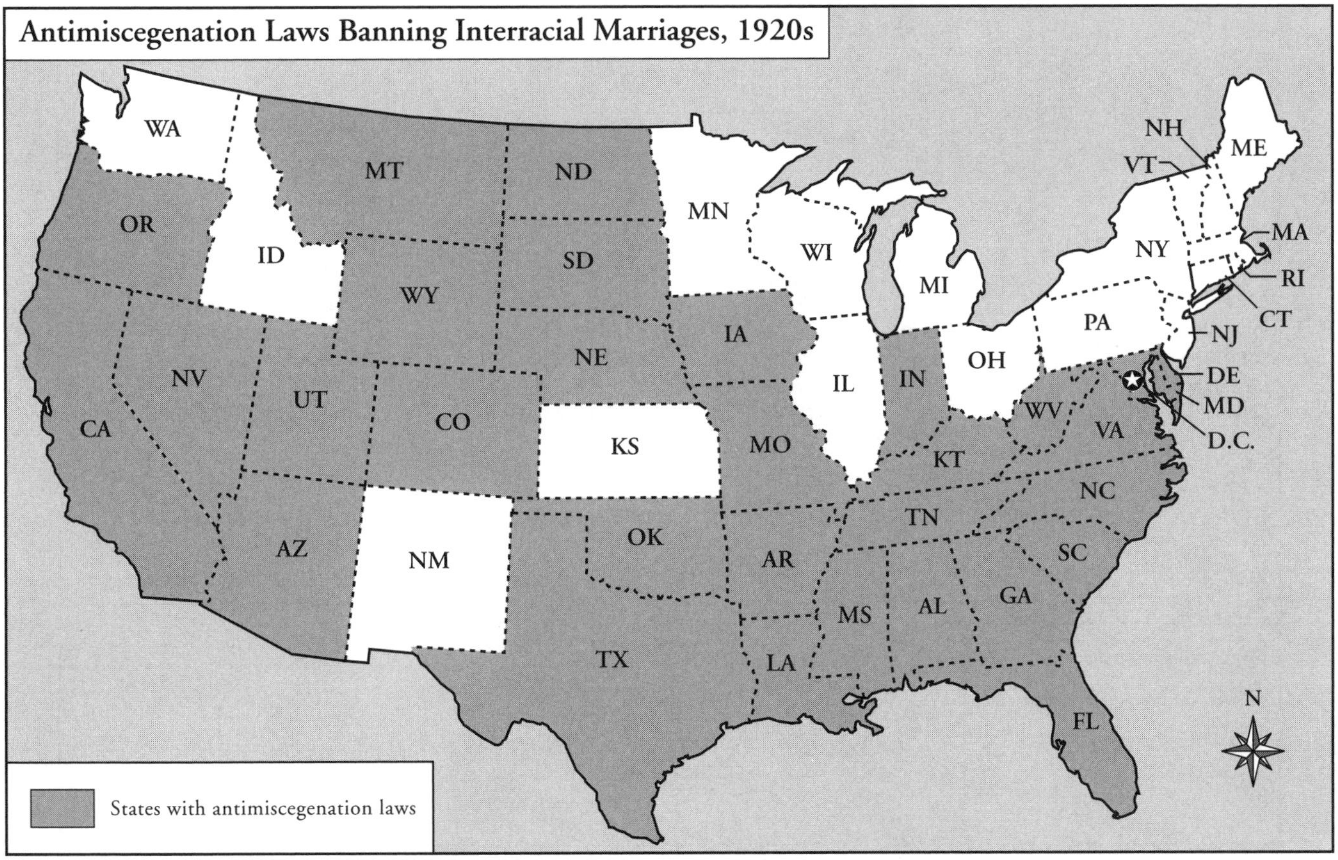

WA
OR
CA
NV
ID
MT
WY
UT
AZ
CO
NM
ND
SD
NE
KS
OK
TX
MN
IA
MO
AR
LA
WI
IL
MI
IN
OH
KT
TN
MS
AL
GA
FL
SC
NC
VA
WV
PA
NY
VT
NH
ME
MA
RI
CT
NJ
DE
MD
D.C.

N

States with antimiscegenation laws

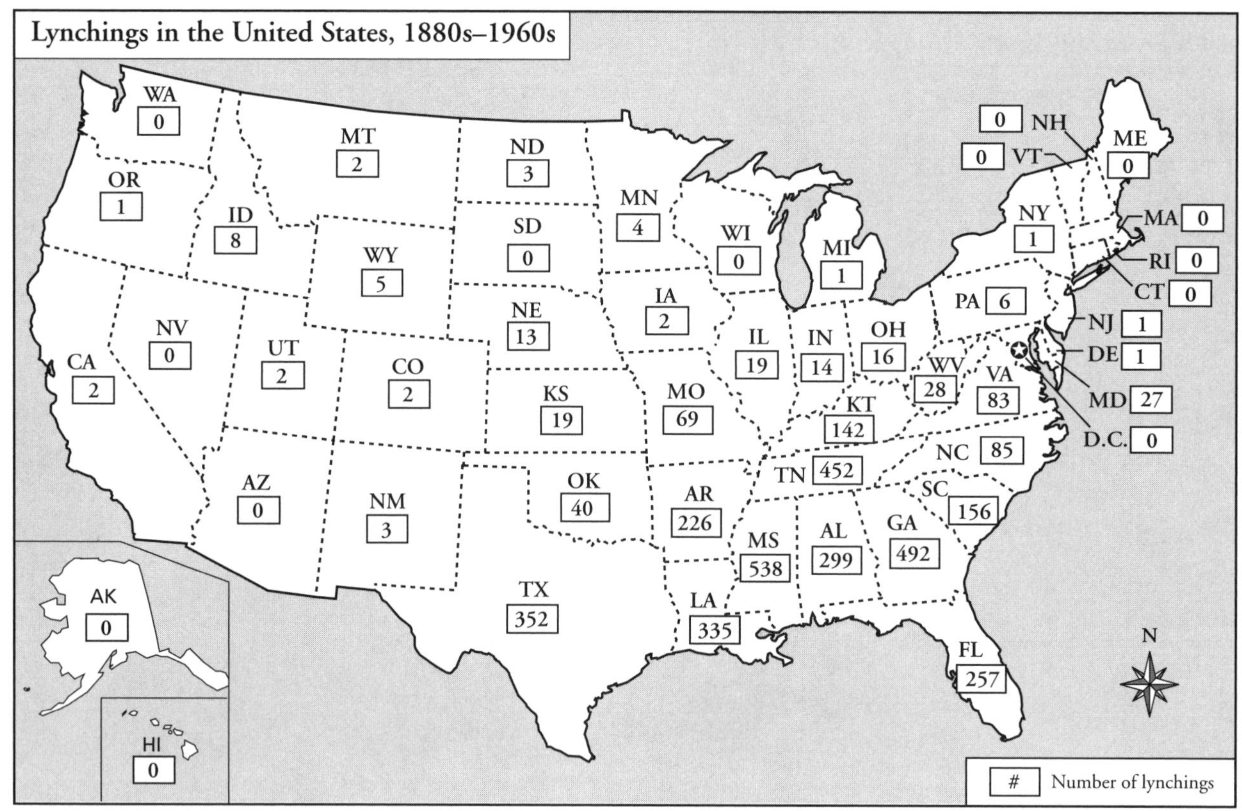
Lynchings in the United States, 1880s–1960s
WA 0
OR 1
CA 2
NV 0
ID 8
MT 2
WY 5
UT 2
CO 2
AZ 0
NM 3
ND 3
SD 0
NE 13
KS 19
OK 40
TX 352
MN 4
IA 2
MO 69
AR 226
LA 335
WI 0
IL 19
MI 1
IN 14
OH 16
KT 142
TN 452
MS 538
AL 299
GA 492
FL 257
SC 156
NC 85
VA 83
WV 28
PA 6
NY 1
0 NH
0 VT
ME 0
MA 0
RI 0
CT 0
NJ 1
DE 1
MD 27
D.C. 0
AK 0
HI 0
N
Number of lynchings

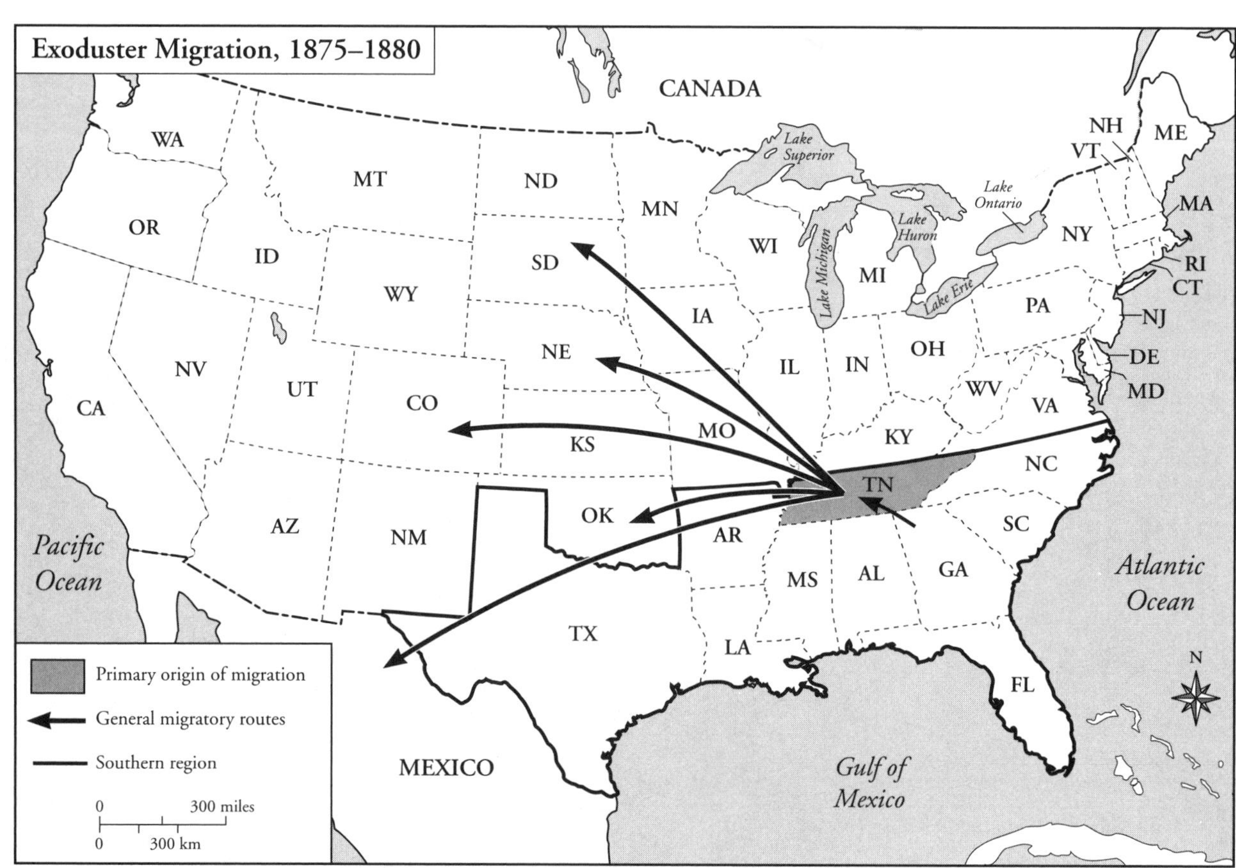
Exoduster Migration, 1875–1880
CANADA
Lake Superior
Lake Michigan
Lake Huron
Lake Ontario
Lake Erie
WA
OR
CA
NV
ID
MT
WY
UT
CO
AZ
NM
ND
SD
NE
KS
OK
TX
MN
IA
MO
AR
LA
WI
IL
MI
IN
OH
KY
TN
MS
AL
GA
FL
SC
NC
VA
WV
PA
NY
NH
VT
ME
MA
RI
CT
NJ
DE
MD
Pacific Ocean
Atlantic Ocean
Gulf of Mexico
MEXICO
N
Primary origin of migration
General migratory routes
Southern region
0 300 miles
0 300 km

Great Migration, 1901–1945
CANADA
Lake Superior
Lake Michigan
Lake Huron
Lake Ontario
Lake Erie
SD
MN
WI
MI
NY
VT
NH
ME
MA
CT
RI
NE
IA
IL
IN
OH
PA
NJ
DE
MD
KS
MO
KY
WV
VA
OK
AK
TN
NC
SC
TX
LA
MS
AL
GA
FL
MEXICO
Missouri R.
Mississippi R.
North Platte R.
Ohio R.
Detroit
Chicago
Cleveland
Pittsburgh
Philadelphia
New York City
Kansas City
St. Louis
Cincinnati
Washington, D.C.
Richmond
Nashville
Memphis
Birmingham
Atlanta
Savannah
New Orleans
Atlantic Ocean
Gulf of Mexico
N
Highest black population concentrations, 1900
Major African-American population centers and destinations
0
300 miles
0
300 km

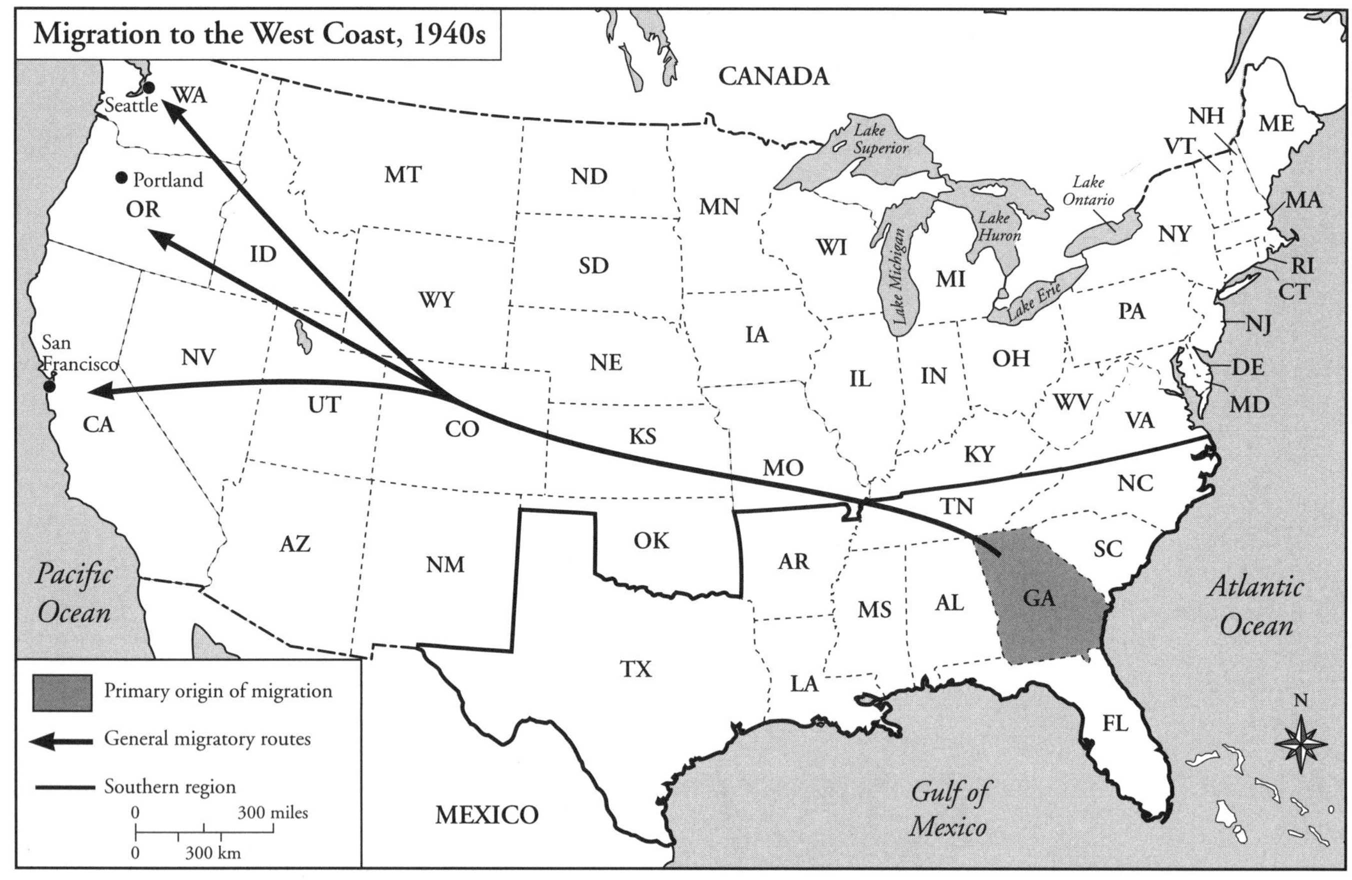

Migration to the West Coast, 1940s
CANADA
Seattle
WA
Portland
OR
MT
ND
MN
ID
SD
WY
WI
MI
NV
San Francisco
UT
CO
NE
IA
IL
IN
OH
PA
NY
NH
VT
ME
MA
RI
CT
NJ
DE
MD
WV
VA
KY
KS
MO
CA
NC
TN
SC
OK
AR
AZ
NM
GA
MS
AL
TX
LA
FL
Pacific Ocean
Atlantic Ocean
Gulf of Mexico
MEXICO
Lake Superior
Lake Michigan
Lake Huron
Lake Ontario
Lake Erie
Primary origin of migration
General migratory routes
Southern region
0 300 miles
0 300 km
N

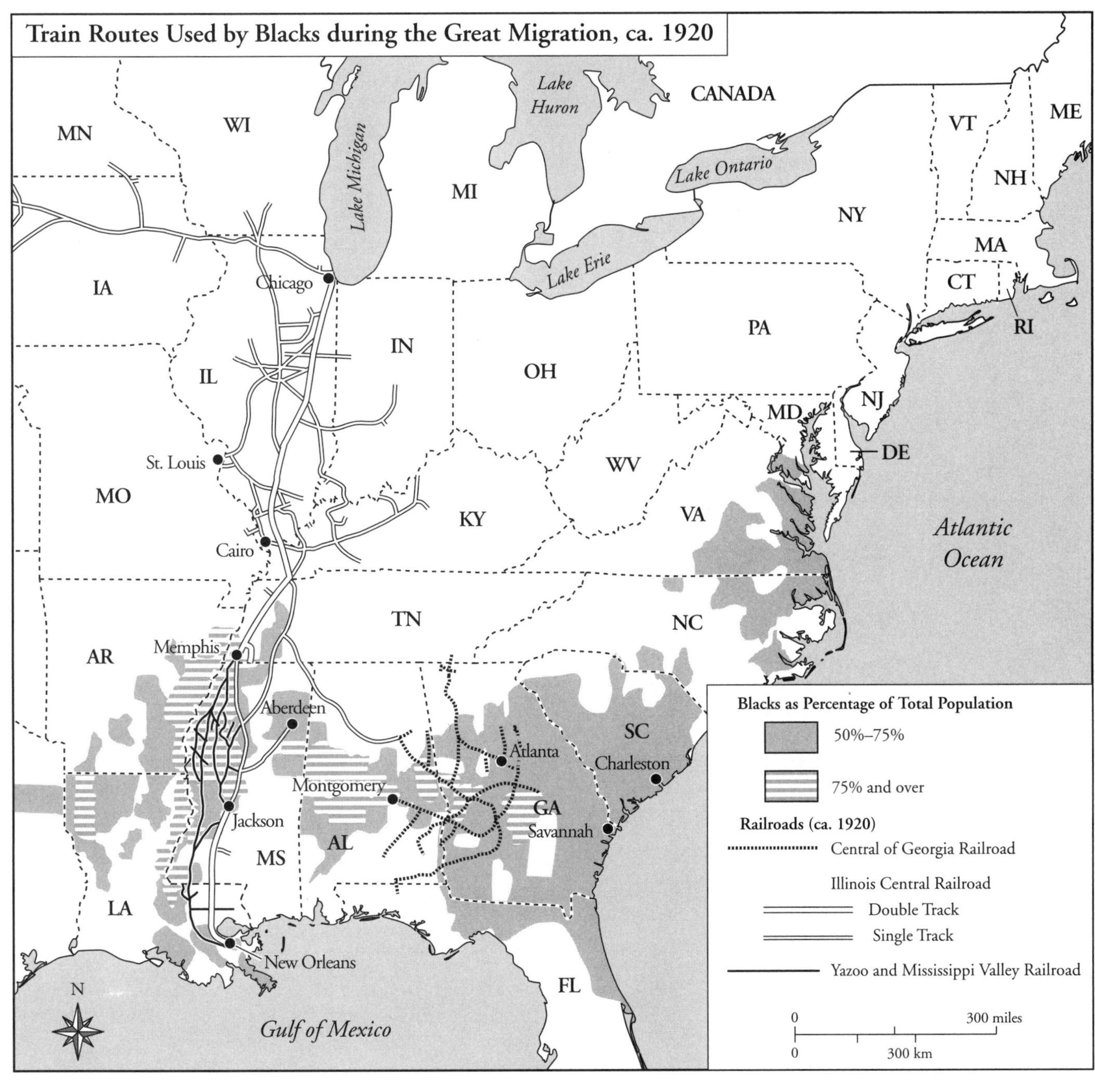
Train Routes Used by Blacks during the Great Migration, ca. 1920
MN
WI
Lake Michigan
Lake Huron
MI
CANADA
Lake Ontario
Lake Erie
VT
NH
ME
NY
MA
CT
RI
IA
Chicago
IL
IN
OH
PA
NJ
MD
DE
St. Louis
MO
WV
VA
KY
Cairo
Atlantic Ocean
TN
NC
AR
Memphis
Aberdeen
Atlanta
SC
Charleston
Montgomery
GA
Savannah
Jackson
AL
MS
LA
New Orleans
FL
Gulf of Mexico
N
Blacks as Percentage of Total Population
50%–75%
75% and over
Railroads (ca. 1920)
Central of Georgia Railroad
Illinois Central Railroad
Double Track
Single Track
Yazoo and Mississippi Valley Railroad
0
300 miles
0
300 km

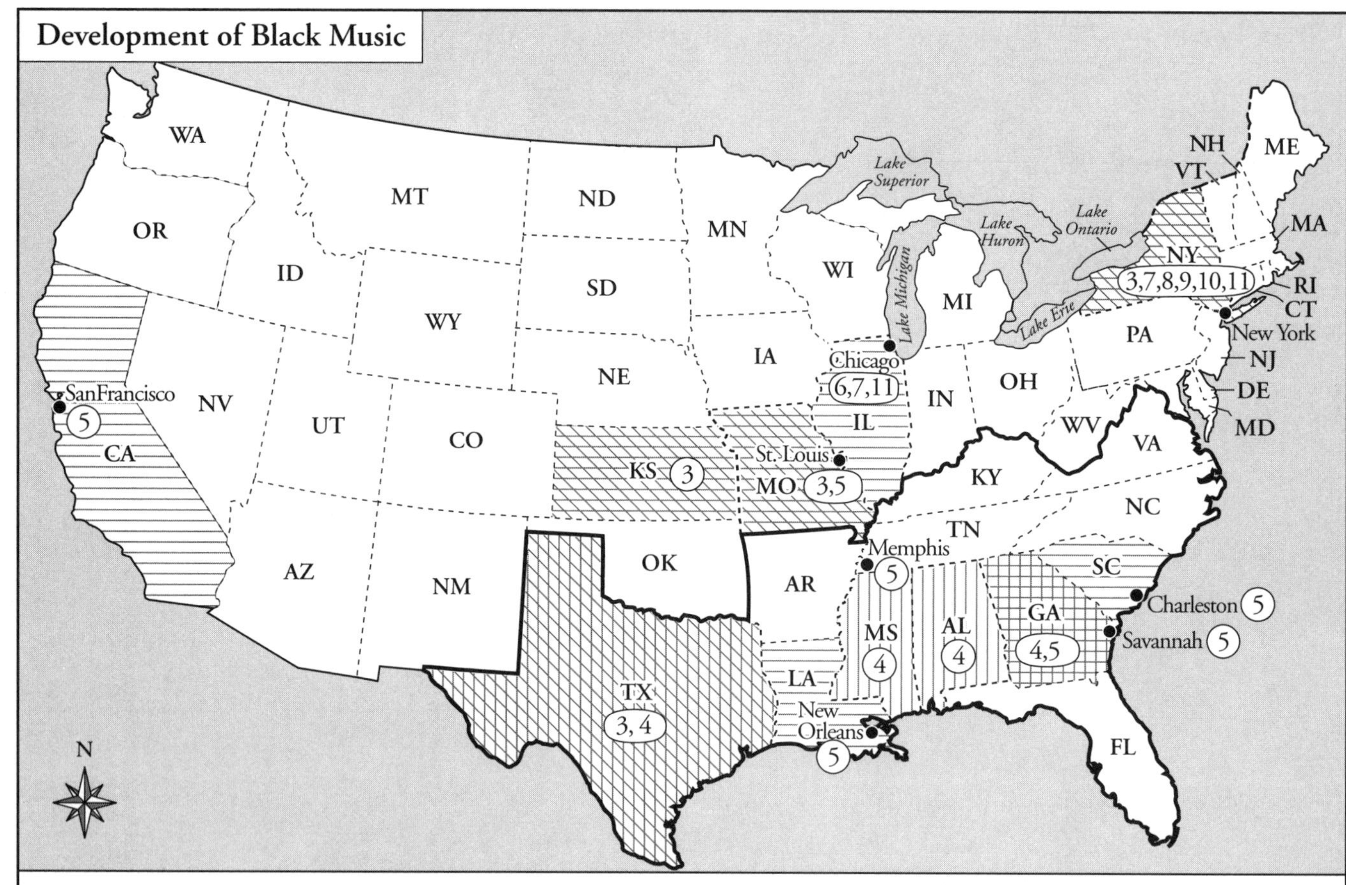

1. **Negro spirituals (1700s–1800s):** Southern region
   Outline shows area in which Negro spirituals and work songs developed
2. **Work songs (1700s–1800):** Southern and southwestern region
3. **Ragtime (1880s–1910s):** Southwest, Texas, St. Louis, moving East
4. **Blues (1880s–1920s):** South: Mississippi, Alabama, Georgia, East Texas
5. **Jazz (1890s–1920s):** New Orleans, St. Louis, Memphis, Savannah, Charleston, San Francisco
6. **Chicago Dixieland jazz (1910s–1920s)**

Ragtime Blues Jazz

7. **Stride piano (1910s–1920s):** Harlem
8. **Club jazz (1920s):** New York, general urban North, Midwest, Europe
9. **Race records (1920s):** Predominantly black female blues singers—New York
10. **Swing sound Big Band era (1930s–1940s):** National and international
11. **Gospel music (1930s):** Chicago (Thomas Dorsey)

Harlem Renaissance World Influence

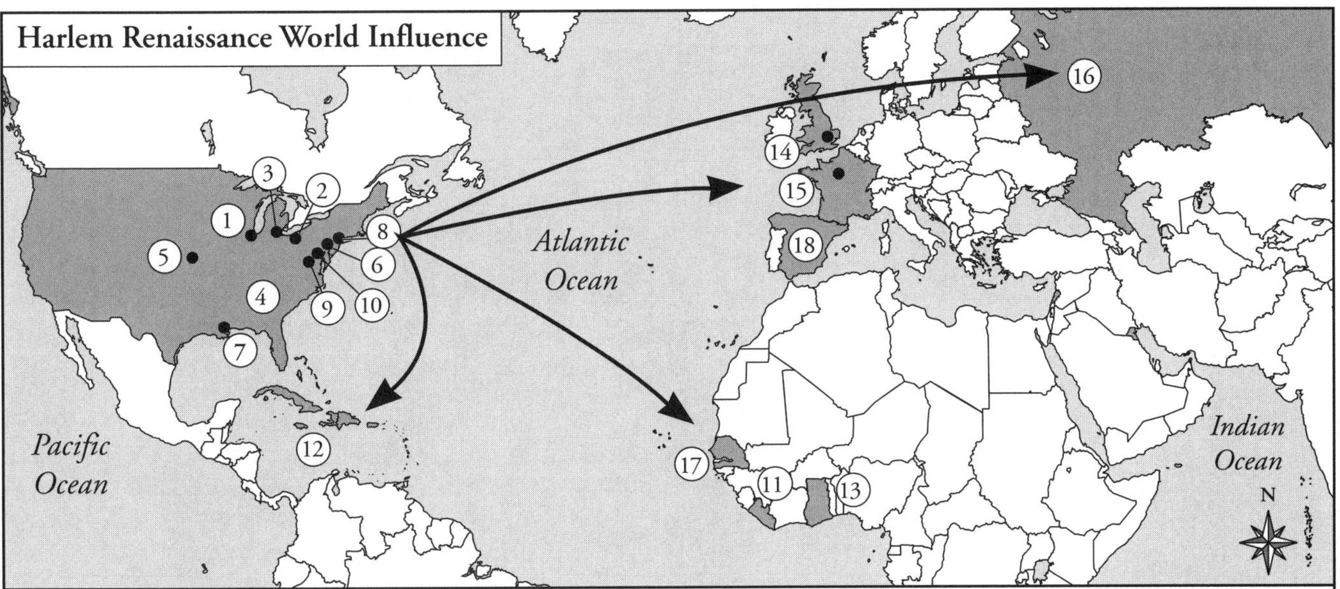

1. **Chicago:** The home of Robert Abbott's militant newspaper the *Chicago Defender* was a principal destination of blacks leaving the South during the Great Migration. It also provided the setting for the declining stages of the Harlem Renaissance in the 1930s and 1940s.

2. **Cleveland, Ohio:** The Karamu House was founded in Cleveland in 1916. This city was also one of the childhood homes of Langston Hughes and a major point of relocation during the Great Migration.

3. **Detroit, Michigan:** One of the primary cities targeted for relocation by African Americans moving out of the South during the Great Migration, Detroit was also one of those cities shaken by violent riots during the Red Summer of 1919.

4. **Georgia:** The majority of all African Americans in the South lived in the rural areas of Georgia during the turn of the 20th century. These made up a substantial number of those blacks who participated in the Great Migration. Consequently, black characters in works produced during the Harlem Renaissance were often portrayed as being from Georgia.

5. **Kansas City, Kansas:** The birthplace of jazz musician Charlie Parker, this city was one of the most important centers for the development of jazz.

6. **Philadelphia:** Like Chicago and Washington, D.C., Philadelphia was a major center of black culture with several theaters on the Theatrical Owners Booking Agency circuit and a thriving literary community that both published its own magazines and contributed regularly to *Crisis* magazine, *Opportunity* magazine, and such newspapers as the *Pittsburgh Courier*. It was also the birthplace of philosopher and New Negro leader Alain Locke.

7. **New Orleans:** Among the many cities where jazz developed in the late 1800s and early 1900s, New Orleans is recognized as the most important single birthplace of the music form in the United States.

8. **New York City:** The home of Harlem, New York developed into a major international city throughout the 1800s and early 1900s. It is the birthplace of the National Urban League, the National Association for the Advancement of Colored People, and the Harlem Renaissance proper.

9. **Richmond, Virginia:** The birthplace of Charles Gilpin and Bill "Bojangles" Robinson, Richmond was a major black entertainment center during the Harlem Renaissance and contained black communities so progressive on every level that it became known among many as the "Harlem of the South."

10. **Washington, D.C.:** The location of Howard University, Washington, D.C., became home to an intellectual movement among African Americans some decades before the 1920s New Negro movement. It included the establishment of the American Negro Academy, numerous salons, and a prosperous black middle class. Philosopher Alain Locke, historian Carter G. Woodson, author Jean Toomer, and others lived and worked in the capital at various points.

11. **Liberia:** The country of Liberia, made independent in 1847, was often noted as an area of possible relocation for African Americans debating the back-to-Africa movement. The culture and history of Africa in general influenced much of the visual art, literature, and music produced by African Americans during the Harlem Renaissance.

12. **Caribbean:** Along with African Americans from the South, the Great Migration that increased the black population throughout the North and Midwest in the United States was composed of thousands of people, including Marcus Garvey, from the Caribbean.

13. **Ghana:** Ghana was the final home of W. E. B. Du Bois, who died there in 1963.

14. **London:** The site of the first Pan African Congress in 1900, London is where Paul Robeson made some of his most racially progressive films in the 1930s. London was also, like Paris, the location of a substantial black expatriate community.

15. **Paris:** The site of the second Pan African Congress in 1919, Paris also became home to a community of African-American expatriates and members of the Negritude Movement following World War I.

16. **Russia:** The adoption of communism in Russia triggered the formation of a succession of radical groups in the United States. Additionally, W. E. B. Du Bois, Langston Hughes, Dorothy West, Louise Thompson Patterson, and Claude McKay all visited the country. During his stay there, McKay authored a study called "Negroes in America" for publication in the Soviet Union.

17. **Senegal:** Senegal is the birthplace of Leopold Senghor, one of the founders of Negritude who later became a major poet as well as president of his native country for 20 years.

18. **Spain:** Langston Hughes worked in Spain as a news correspondent and translated into English the works of various Spanish poets, including those of Federico García Lorca.

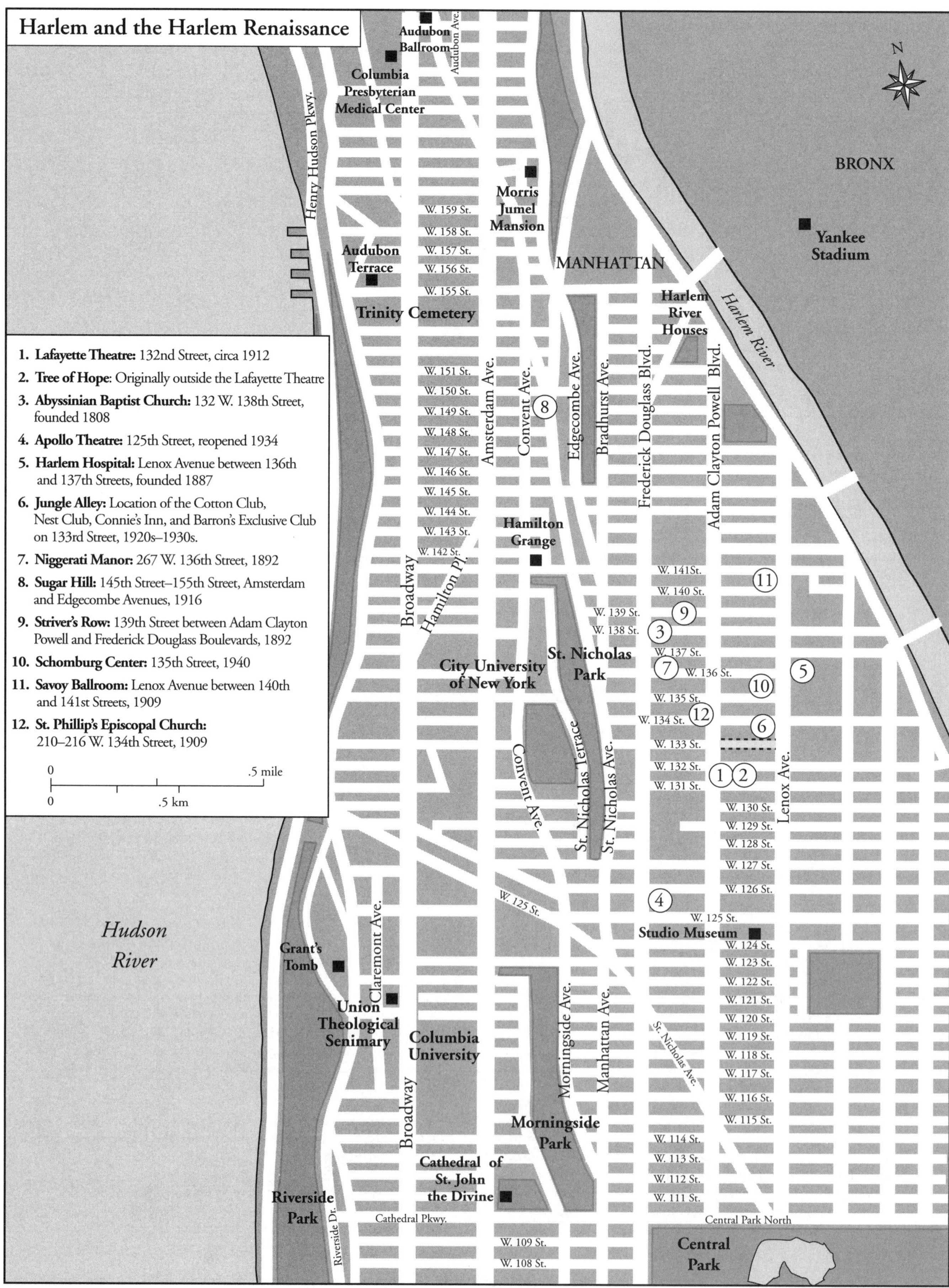
Harlem and the Harlem Renaissance
1. Lafayette Theatre: 132nd Street, circa 1912
2. Tree of Hope: Originally outside the Lafayette Theatre
3. Abyssinian Baptist Church: 132 W. 138th Street, founded 1808
4. Apollo Theatre: 125th Street, reopened 1934
5. Harlem Hospital: Lenox Avenue between 136th and 137th Streets, founded 1887
6. Jungle Alley: Location of the Cotton Club, Nest Club, Connie's Inn, and Barron's Exclusive Club on 133rd Street, 1920s–1930s.
7. Niggerati Manor: 267 W. 136th Street, 1892
8. Sugar Hill: 145th Street–155th Street, Amsterdam and Edgecombe Avenues, 1916
9. Striver's Row: 139th Street between Adam Clayton Powell and Frederick Douglass Boulevards, 1892
10. Schomburg Center: 135th Street, 1940
11. Savoy Ballroom: Lenox Avenue between 140th and 141st Streets, 1909
12. St. Phillip's Episcopal Church: 210–216 W. 134th Street, 1909
0
.5 mile
0
.5 km
N
Audubon Ballroom
Audubon Ave.
Columbia Presbyterian Medical Center
Henry Hudson Pkwy.
Morris Jumel Mansion
BRONX
Yankee Stadium
MANHATTAN
Audubon Terrace
Trinity Cemetery
Harlem River Houses
Harlem River
W. 159 St.
W. 158 St.
W. 157 St.
W. 156 St.
W. 155 St.
W. 151 St.
W. 150 St.
W. 149 St.
W. 148 St.
W. 147 St.
W. 146 St.
W. 145 St.
W. 144 St.
W. 143 St.
W. 142 St.
Amsterdam Ave.
Convent Ave.
Edgecombe Ave.
Bradhurst Ave.
Frederick Douglass Blvd.
Adam Clayton Powell Blvd.
Hamilton Grange
Broadway
Hamilton Pl.
W. 141St.
W. 140 St.
W. 139 St.
W. 138 St.
W. 137 St.
W. 136 St.
W. 135 St.
W. 134 St.
W. 133 St.
W. 132 St.
W. 131 St.
W. 130 St.
W. 129 St.
W. 128 St.
W. 127 St.
W. 126 St.
W. 125 St.
City University of New York
St. Nicholas Park
St. Nicholas Terrace
St. Nicholas Ave.
Lenox Ave.
Hudson River
Studio Museum
W. 124 St.
W. 123 St.
W. 122 St.
W. 121 St.
W. 120 St.
W. 119 St.
W. 118 St.
W. 117 St.
W. 116 St.
W. 115 St.
W. 114 St.
W. 113 St.
W. 112 St.
W. 111 St.
Grant's Tomb
Claremont Ave.
Union Theological Senimary
Columbia University
Morningside Ave.
Manhattan Ave.
Morningside Park
Cathedral of St. John the Divine
Riverside Park
Riverside Dr.
Cathedral Pkwy.
Central Park North
W. 109 St.
W. 108 St.
Central Park

1. **Broadway:** Beginning with *Shuffle Along* in 1921, Broadway hosted a succession of hit musicals featuring black entertainers throughout the 1920s. *Shuffle Along* itself was considered by some as the true start of the Harlem Renaissance.

2. **Civic Club, 12th Street and Fifth Avenue:** This club was the site of the historic 1924 Civic Club dinner, held to launch the New Negro movement.

3. **Carnegie Hall, 881 Seventh Avenue at 57th Street:** Site of 1923 sold-out performance by Roland Hayes performing traditional Negro spirituals.

4. **Greenwich Village/SoHo:** Home to African Americans on Broome, Spring, Sullivan, Thompson, and Bleecker Streets in New York City prior to their migration to the Harlem area.

5. **Harlem**

6. **Tin Pan Alley, West 28th Street between Broadway and Sixth Avenue:** The music publishing capital of the world.

7. **Bowery, corner of the Bowery and Canal Street:** The Bowery and Astor Theatre were vaudeville mainstays prior to the development of Broadway.

8. **Astor Theatre, 434 Lafayette Street at the Bowery:** This theater and the Bowery were vaudeville mainstays prior to the development of Broadway.

9. **Slave Cemetery and Burial Ground:** Five city blocks surrounded by New York's City Hall (Park Row), the U.S. Courthouse, and the New York Supreme Court: Virtually the entire Harlem Renaissance was an attempt by African Americans to make peace with their slave ancestry.

10. **1935 and 1943 Harlem Riots:** These happened in Harlem on Eighth Avenue, Seventh Avenue, and 125th Street, the most densely commercial areas.

11. **Madame C. J. Walker's Estate, Villa Lewaro, Irvington-on-Hudson:** Following her mother's death, A'Lelia Walker used this estate as a more upscale version of The Dark Tower, entertaining an international jet-set crowd that included royalty and her writer and artist friends from Harlem. The mansion was also something Madame C. J. Walker intended as a symbol of prosperity to inspire a sense of achievement in all African Americans.

12. **Waldorf Astoria, 30 Park Avenue:** This hotel hosted the first reading of *Appearances,* by Garland Anderson and featuring Richard B. Harrison, prior to its move to Broadway in 1925.

13. **Roseland Ballroom, 239 West 52nd Street:** A downtown equivalent to the Savoy Ballroom in Harlem, the Roseland featured black musicians playing for white dancers.

14. **Ziegfeld Theatre, 141 West 54th Street:** This theater was the home of the Ziegfeld Follies starring Bert Williams.

15. **New York Evening Post, 20 Vesey Street:** This building was the location of the first offices for the National Association for the Advancement of Colored People (NAACP) in 1910, courtesy of Garrison Villard.

16. **Weeksville:** James Weeks, an African American from Virginia, began this 19th-century African-American community that is bordered by Ralph Avenue, Kingston Avenue, Atlantic Avenue, and St. John's Place, when he purchased this land from the Lefferts estate in 1838.

17. **Bridge Street AME Church, 277 Stuyvesant Avenue at Jefferson Avenue:** Founded in 1766 by people of many different backgrounds and incorporated in 1818, Bridge Street AME Church is Brooklyn's oldest African-American church.

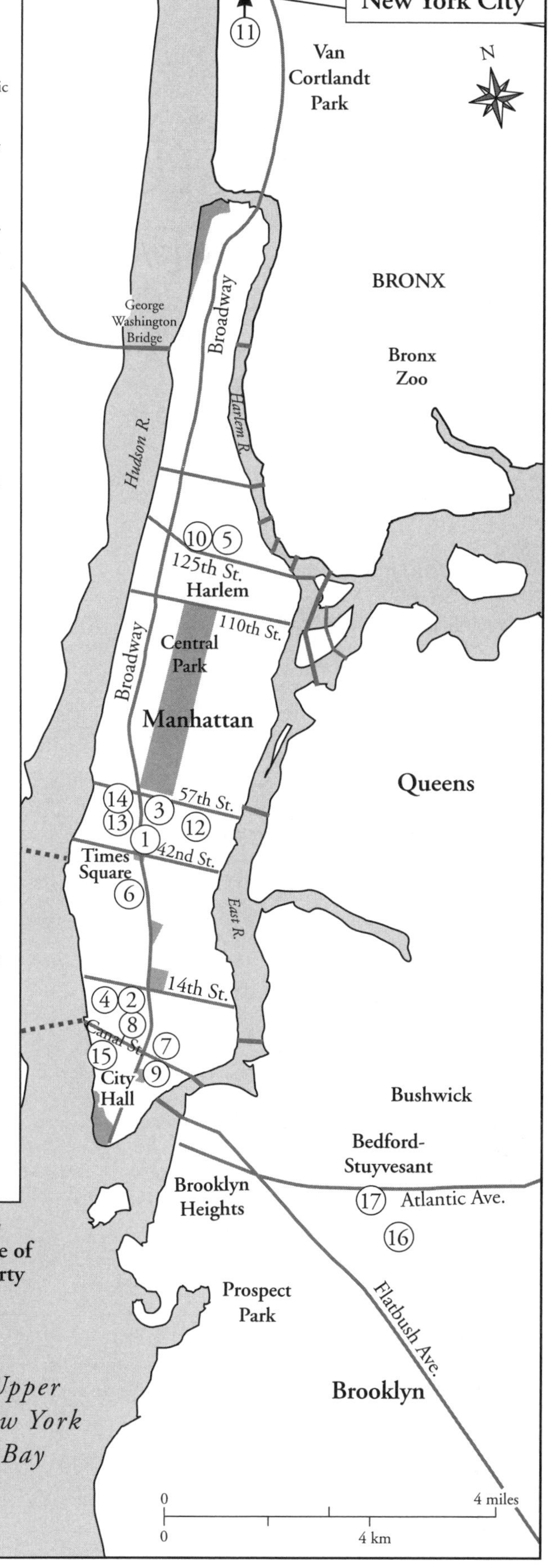

Appendix C: MUSEUMS AND CENTERS THAT FEATURE WORKS FROM THE HARLEM RENAISSANCE

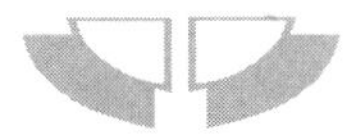

African American Museum in Philadelphia
701 Arch Street
Philadelphia, Pennsylvania 19106
(215) 574-0380

American Jazz Museum
16161 E. 18th Street
Kansas City, Missouri 64108
(816) 474-8463

America's Black Holocaust Museum, Inc.
2233 N. Fourth Street
Milwaukee, Wisconsin 53212
(414) 264-2500

Amistad Research Center
Tilton Hall
Tulane University
New Orleans, Louisiana 70118
(504) 865-5535

Anacostia Museum & Center for African American History and Culture
1901 Forth Place, S.E.
Washington, D.C. 20020
(202) 287-3306

Arna Bontemps African American Museum and Cultural Arts Center
1327 Third Street
Alexandria, Louisiana 71301
(318) 473-4692

Baltimore Black American Museum
1767 Carswell Street
Baltimore, Maryland 21218
(410) 396-7100

Baltimore Museum of Art
Art Museum Drive
Baltimore, Maryland 21218
(410) 396-7100

Black World History Wax Museum
2505 St. Louis Avenue
St. Louis, Missouri 63106
(314) 241-7057

California African American Museum
600 State Drive
Exposition Park
Los Angeles, California 90037
(212) 744-7432

California Palace of the Legion of Honor
34th Avenue and Clement Street
San Francisco, California

Center for Black Music Research
623 South Wabash
Suite 600
Chicago, Illinois 60605
(312) 344-7559

Charles H. Wright Museum of African American History
315 E. Warren Avenue
Detroit, Michigan 48201-1443
(313) 494-5800

Cinque Gallery
560 Broadway
5th Floor
New York, New York 10012
(212) 966-3464

Delta Blues Museum
P.O. Box 459
Number 1 Blues Alley
Clarksdale, Mississippi 38614
(652) 627-6820

Delta Music Museum
218 Louisiana Avenue
Ferriday, Louisiana 71334
(318) 757-9999

DuSable Museum of African American History
740 E. 56th Place
Chicago, Illinois 60637-1495
(773) 947-0600

Eubie Blake National Museum
34 Market Place
Baltimore, Maryland 21202
(410) 625-3113

Gospel Music Hall of Fame and Museum
18301 W. McNichols
Detroit, Michigan 48219
(313) 592-0017

Katherine Dunham Center for Arts and Humanities
1005 Pennsylvania Avenue
East St. Louis, Missouri 62201
(618) 271-3367

Louisiana State Museum
751 Chartres
New Orleans, Louisiana 70116
(504) 568-6968

M. H. de Young Memorial Museum
75 Tea Garden in Golden Gate Park
San Francisco, California
(415) 750-3600

Metropolitan Museum of Art
1000 Fifth Avenue at 82nd Street
New York, New York 10028-0198
(212) 535-7710

Museum of Afro American History
46 Joy Street, Beacon Hill
Boston, Massachusetts 02108
(617) 725-0022

Ralph Mark Gilbert Civil Rights Museum
460 Martin Luther King Jr. Boulevard
Savannah, Georgia 31401
(912) 231-8900

Renwick Gallery
17th Street, N.W.
Washington, D.C. 20001-4505

Schomburg Center for Research in Black Culture
515 Malcolm X Boulevard
New York, New York 10037-1801
(212) 491-2200

Smithsonian Museum of American Art
750 Ninth Street, N.W.
Washington, D.C. 20001-4505

Stella Jones Gallery
201 St. Charles Avenue
New Orleans, Louisiana 70170
(504) 568-9050

Studio Museum in Harlem
144 W. 125th Street
New York, New York 10027
(212) 864-4500

Whitney Museum of Art
945 Madison Avenue at 75th Street
New York, New York 10021
(212) 570-3676

Chronology

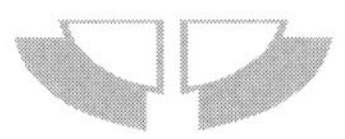

1619

- The first African captives sold as slaves in what would become the United States arrive in Jamestown, Virginia.

1664

- ***September 8:*** The settlement of New Amsterdam is renamed NEW YORK after surrendering to the king of Great Britain, James II, the Duke of York and Albany.

1808

- In protest against segregation in NEW YORK CITY's First Baptist Church, a group of African Americans and Ethiopian merchants renounce their affiliation with the church and form the ABYSSINIAN BAPTIST CHURCH. During the Harlem Renaissance, the church's membership reaches 3,000 in the 1920s and 7,000 in the 1930s, becoming the largest Protestant congregation in the United States. Under the leadership of ADAM CLAYTON POWELL, SR., and ADAM CLAYTON POWELL, JR., it also becomes a powerful social and political organization.

1820

- The first group of African Americans emigrates from the United States to Liberia. The idea of blacks immigrating to Africa would remain a powerful one throughout the 1800s and 1900s, receiving support from such esteemed black leaders as Alexander Crummel, Henry M. Turner, and MARCUS GARVEY as well as from various white organizations.

1827

- ***March 30:*** In New York City, Reverend Samuel E. Cornish and John B. Russwurm begin publishing *Freedom's Journal,* the first black-owned newspaper in the United States. The newspaper lays the groundwork for numerous others that follow and for the first time provides African Americans with a means for regularly addressing in print their moral and political concerns. Such newspapers in the following century would play a major role in the battle for civil rights for African Americans and in the GREAT MIGRATION that would encourage them to leave the South for the North and Midwest.

1845

- ***March 10:*** Educator and author HALLIE QUINN BROWN is born.

1852

- Black abolitionist Martin R. Delany publishes *The Condition, Elevation, and Destiny of the Colored People of the United States, Politically Considered,* the first major work by an African American to advocate the emigration of blacks BACK TO AFRICA and other locations outside the United States.

1862

- ***July 16:*** IDA BELL WELLS-BARNETT is born in Holly Springs, Mississippi. Establishing herself as a teacher and editor of the *Memphis Free Speech,* Wells becomes a renowned political advocate protesting against the LYNCHING of African Americans and supporting the civil rights of women.

1865

- ***December 18:*** Nearly three years after President Abraham Lincoln issues the Emancipation Proclamation, Congress adopts the Thirteenth Amendment to the U.S. Constitution, officially outlawing slavery in all areas of the United States. The Fourteenth Amendment in 1868 broadens the definition of an American citizen to include anyone born in the country, and the Fifteenth Amendment in 1870 grants former slaves the right to vote.

1868

- *February 23:* Political activist W. E. B. DU BOIS is born in Great Barrington, Massachusetts. He becomes the first African American to receive a Ph.D. from Harvard University and one of the most accomplished educators and civil rights leaders of the 20th century. His voluminous writings establish him as both a forerunner of the Harlem Renaissance and one of its most gifted and prolific authors.
- *September 3:* Henry M. Turner delivers a militant address before the Georgia legislature to protest the expulsion of African Americans from the assembly. Turner subsequently becomes a staunch advocate of the BACK-TO-AFRICA MOVEMENT.

1871

- *June 17:* JAMES WELDON JOHNSON is born in Jacksonville, Florida. Along with JESSIE REDMOND FAUSET, ALAIN LOCKE, W. E. B. Du Bois, and CHARLES SPURGEON JOHNSON, he becomes in the 1920s one of the principal architects of the Harlem Renaissance. Like Du Bois, he shares the distinction of contributing significant literary works as well as political victories, via his tenure as director of the NAACP, to the Harlem Renaissance.
- *October 6:* The FISK JUBILEE SINGERS embark on a challenging but ultimately successful world tour to raise operating funds for FISK UNIVERSITY in Nashville, Tennessee. In the process, they introduce the world to the classic spirituals of African Americans.
- *January 24:* Bibliophile and historian ARTHUR SCHOMBURG is born in San Juan, Puerto Rico.

1882

- *April 27:* Jessie Redmond Fauset is born in Camden County, New Jersey. She becomes one of the most prolific novelists of the Harlem Renaissance. Working alongside W. E. B. Du Bois at the *CRISIS: A RECORD OF THE DARKER RACES* magazine, she also serves as one of the movement's most accomplished editors.

1886

- *September 13:* Alain Locke is born in PHILADELPHIA. Later dubbed "dean" of the Harlem Renaissance by Charles S. Johnson, Locke edits the definitive *NEW NEGRO* anthology, secures patronage for black writers and artists, and helps generate the NEGRITUDE movement in Europe.

1887

- Brothers Thomas Fortune and Emmanuel Fortune begin publishing the *NEW YORK AGE* newspaper, one of the most radical black-owned newspapers at the turn of the 20th century.

1889

- *April 15:* Labor leader A. PHILIP RANDOLPH is born in Crescent City, Florida.

1890

- *October 10:* Jazz pioneer JELLY ROLL MORTON is born in NEW ORLEANS.

1891

- *January 7:* Folklorist, novelist, and anthropologist ZORA NEALE HURSTON is born.

1893

- *July 24:* Charles Spurgeon Johnson is born in Bristol, Virginia. During the Harlem Renaissance, he edits the NATIONAL URBAN LEAGUE's *OPPORTUNITY* magazine and continual seeks out new talent to nurture and promote. He also, following the Harlem Renaissance, authors a number of groundbreaking texts in sociology and establishes a major research center at Fisk University in Nashville, Tennessee.

1894

- *January 2:* Pioneer filmmaker and novelist OSCAR MICHEAUX is born in Metropolis, Illinois.

1895

- *February 20:* Black abolitionist and journalist Frederick Douglass dies in WASHINGTON, D.C. Editor of the *North Star* with Martin Delany, Douglass also authored *The Narrative of the Life of Frederick Douglass: An American Slave* and *My Bondage and My Freedom,* bringing considerable attention to the debate over American slavery prior to the Civil War. A tireless advocate of racial equality until his death, Douglass was instrumental in helping Ida B. Wells-Barnett achieve international prominence as a speaker and journalist. In this same year, Wells-Barnett publishes *A Red Record: Tabulated Statistics and Alleged Causes of Lynchings in the United States.*
- *September 18:* BOOKER TALIAFERRO WASHINGTON delivers his *Atlanta Address* and subsequently attains international recognition as America's foremost black leader.

1896

- *May 18:* The U.S. Supreme Court legalizes racial segregation with its decision to sanction separate but equal facilities in the case of *Plessy v. Ferguson.*

1899

- *April 9:* Future political advocate and performing artist PAUL ROBESON is born in Princeton, New Jersey.
- *April 29:* DUKE ELLINGTON is born in WASHINGTON, D.C. As a bandleader, he helps define the music of the JAZZ Age and SWING era. He also wins recognition as the most accomplished composer in jazz history.

1900

- *February:* Brothers JOHN ROSAMOND JOHNSON and James Weldon Johnson compose "LIFT EVERY VOICE AND SING," a song later known informally as the black national anthem. It is debuted at a celebration honoring the birthday of President Abraham Lincoln.
- *July 23–25:* Led by Trinidadian Henry Sylvester Williams, with W. E. B. Du Bois serving as secretary, a PAN-AFRICAN CONGRESS is held in London. Black men and women from Europe, Africa, the Caribbean, Canada, and the United States gather to discuss the political, economic, and social conditions of people of African descent all around the world. More Pan-African congresses follow throughout the 20th century.

1901

- *August 4:* LOUIS ARMSTRONG is born in NEW ORLEANS. After an extensive apprenticeship with trumpeter KING OLIVER, Armstrong develops into a major trumpet player, vocalist, and one of the most influential jazz musicians of the 20th century.

1902

- *February 1:* LANGSTON HUGHES is born in Joplin, Missouri. He is one of the most prolific authors of the Harlem Renaissance, and his literary output includes poetry, short fiction, novels, plays, radio and television scripts, historical works, anthologies, and operas. His career lasts far beyond the time frame generally associated with the Harlem Renaissance.

1903

- *April 18:* W. E. B. Du Bois publishes *The SOULS OF BLACK FOLK*. Containing the essay "Of Mr. Booker T. Washington and Others," the book presents the first serious criticism of and challenge to the policies on race relations espoused by Washington and his followers. Du Bois also calls for African Americans to further explore, document, and exalt their culture. The book's popular success stirs public debate and elevates Du Bois to national prominence.

1905

- *July 11–13:* More than two dozen prominent African Americans meet at Niagara Falls for the first NIAGARA MOVEMENT conference held to determine strategies for opposition to the race relation policies of Booker T. Washington.

1906

- *February 6:* Playwright, poet, and novelist Paul Laurence Dunbar dies in Dayton, Ohio.
- *June 3:* JOSEPHINE BAKER is born in St. Louis, Missouri. As an expatriate living in PARIS during the greater part of the 20th century, she achieves international stardom as a singer, dancer, and actress.
- *December 4:* The first African-American Greek-lettered fraternity, ALPHA PHI ALPHA, forms at Cornell University in Ithaca, New York.

1907

- *June 2:* DOROTHY WEST, destined to win fame as the youngest and eventually the longest surviving member of the Harlem Renaissance writers, is born in Boston, Massachusetts.

1908

- *January 15:* ALPHA KAPPA ALPHA, the first African-American Greek-lettered sorority, forms at Howard University in Washington, D.C.
- *August 14–19:* Race riots in Springfield, Illinois, prompt William English Walling, MARY WHITE OVINGTON, Henry Moscowitz, and Garrison Villard to issue a call for a conference on the political and social status of African Americans. The call eventually leads to the establishment of the NATIONAL ASSOCIATION FOR THE ADVANCEMENT OF COLORED PEOPLE (NAACP).
- *December 26:* JACK JOHNSON defeats incumbent boxing champion Tommy Burns in Sydney, Australia, and is crowned the first black heavyweight boxing champion of the world.

1910

- *May 12–14:* The NAACP is formed in New York City, evolving out of the second meeting of the National Negro Committee and the dissolution of the Niagara Movement. The creation of the organization prompts W. E. B. Du Bois to move from Atlanta to New York to serve as editor of its house organ, the *Crisis: A Record of the Darker Races* magazine. It employs tactics of aggressive litigation and widespread public exposure of racist acts to become the most influential civil rights organization of the 20th century.

1911

- *January:* The NATIONAL URBAN LEAGUE is established in New York City.

1912

- James Weldon Johnson, influenced by Du Bois's *The Souls of Black Folk,* anonymously publishes for the first time his autobiographical novel, *The AUTOBIOGRAPHY OF AN EX-COLORED MAN*. With the help of an introduction by CARL VAN VECHTEN, it is reprinted with greater success in 1927.
- *September 27:* W. C. HANDY, known later as the "father of the blues," publishes "Memphis Blues."

1913

- *March 1:* RALPH WALDO ELLISON born in Oklahoma City, Oklahoma. Later authors *Invisible Man,* one of the most acclaimed novels of the 20th century.

1914

- ***August 1:*** Jamaican leader Marcus Garvey starts the UNIVERSAL NEGRO IMPROVEMENT ASSOCIATION in Jamaica.

1915

- ***September 9:*** CARTER GODWIN WOODSON and a group of associates establish the ASSOCIATION FOR THE STUDY OF NEGRO LIFE in CHICAGO.
- ***November 14:*** Booker T. Washington dies at Tuskegee Normal and Industrial Institute in Alabama.

1916

- ***March 23:*** Jamaican leader Marcus Garvey arrives in the United States. He transfers headquarters for the UNIVERSAL NEGRO IMPROVEMENT ASSOCIATION to HARLEM and proceeds to build the largest organization of black people in American history.

1917

- ***April 6:*** The United States enters WORLD WAR I. Thousands of African Americans leave the South to take advantage of the resulting job boom in the North.
- ***May 5:*** EUGENE JACQUES BULLARD, serving in the French air force, receives his pilot's license and in August becomes the first African-American fighter pilot.
- ***May 15:*** ROBERT ABBOTT of the *CHICAGO DEFENDER* and other African-American editors declare the Great Northern Drive Day and urge all African Americans in the South to leave in one massive exodus at this time.
- ***July 1–3:*** Riots in East St. Louis result in the deaths of more than three dozen African Americans.
- ***July 28:*** Organized by W. E. B. Du Bois, James Weldon Johnson, MADAME C. J. WALKER and others, some 10,000 African Americans march silently down Fifth Avenue in New York City to protest the rising number of blacks killed in riots in the United States. It is the largest mass protest by African Americans up to that point.
- ***August 23:*** Black soldiers and white civilians clash in Houston, Texas, causing the death of 17 whites and two African Americans.
- ***September 7:*** JACOB ARMSTEAD LAWRENCE is born in Atlantic City, New Jersey. Painting everyday scenes and historic events from African-American life, he becomes one of the most celebrated painters of the 20th century.

1919

- ***February 19–21:*** The Second Pan-African Congress is held in Paris, France. Black delegates from around the world address the impact of World War I on people of African descent.
- ***May 25:*** America's first woman self-made millionaire, Madame C. J. Walker, dies and leaves two-thirds of her fortune to charity. The remaining third is left to her daughter, A'LELIA WALKER, whom Langston Hughes dubs "the joy goddess" of Harlem.
- ***July:*** Jamaican immigrant CLAUDE MCKAY's poem "IF WE MUST DIE," is published in the radical magazine the *Liberator.* With riots occurring in cities throughout the United States, during what would become known as the RED SUMMER OF 1919, the poem is adopted as a revolutionary anthem and brings McKay international fame.

1920

- ***February 14:*** Mamie Smith makes the first commercial recording of a blues song, opening the doors of the recording industry to black artists and creating a new market for what would become known as RACE RECORDS.
- *November:* James Weldon Johnson begins 10-year stint as the first black executive secretary of the NAACP.

1921

- ***May 23:*** The black musical *SHUFFLE ALONG* debuts at the Cort Theatre. It begins a historic run of more than 500 shows, attracting blacks and whites alike, and kicks off a decade of popular black musicals on Broadway.
- ***August 28–September 6:*** The Third Pan-African Congress is held in London, Brussels, and Paris.

1922

- Claude McKay publishes *Harlem Shadows,* considered by some to be the first substantial literary work of the Harlem Renaissance. In the same year, James Weldon Johnson edits *The Book of American Negro Poetry,* introducing many of the writers who later would be featured in Alain Locke's *New Negro* anthology.

1923

- ***September:*** JEAN TOOMER publishes *Cane.* Though not a best-seller, it is hailed as a literary masterpiece and inspires others to believe in the possibility of a full-scale renaissance in black culture. It later becomes a major work of the American literary canon.

1924

- ***March 21:*** The CIVIC CLUB DINNER is held to showcase talents of black writers and artists beginning to gather in Harlem. A mixture of liberal-minded white authors and publishers and both aspiring black writers and seasoned professionals such as James Weldon Johnson and W. E. B. Du Bois attend the dinner. Readings presented at the event inspire the publication of a special edition of *SURVEY GRAPHIC* magazine devoted to work by emerging black writers and artists.

1925

- ***March:*** Edited by Alain Locke, *Survey Graphic* magazine publishes its special edition, *Harlem, Mecca of the Negro,* featuring fiction, poetry, essays, and visual art by African Americans.

- *May:* As a result of the success of the special Harlem edition of *Survey Graphic* magazine, Albert and Charles Boni publish the *NEW NEGRO*, an expanded version of the magazine in book form. Also edited by Locke, it becomes the principal defining text of the Harlem Renaissance.
- *August 25:* The BROTHERHOOD OF SLEEPING CAR PORTERS, led by A. Philip Randolph and meeting in Harlem, form the first major black-controlled union.
- *October 13:* The first full-length drama by an African American staged on Broadway, *APPEARANCES* by GARLAND ANDERSON, makes its debut.

1926

- *February 7:* Historian Carter G. Woodson organizes the first observation of Negro History Week, developing later into Black History Month.
- *November:* Led by novelist, playwright, and editor WALLACE THURMAN, younger writers and artists of the Harlem Renaissance publish the single-issue magazine *FIRE!!*

1927

- *December:* Jamaican leader Marcus Garvey, convicted on charges of mail fraud, is deported from the United States.

1928

- *January:* The HARMON FOUNDATION in New York City sponsors the first all-black art exhibit at the International House. The exhibit features the work of, among others, AUGUSTA FELLS SAVAGE, HALE ASPACIO WOODRUFF, and AARON DOUGLAS.
- *Spring:* Claude McKay's *HOME TO HARLEM* becomes the first best-selling novel by an African American.

1929

- *October 23:* The GREAT DEPRESSION begins with the crash of Wall Street's stock market, ushering in a decade of joblessness and poverty for millions of Americans.

1931

- *April 6:* The SCOTTSBORO TRIAL begins, in which nine black youths are falsely accused of raping two young white women. The men are eventually paroled or pardoned after some two decades. The trial is often referenced as one of the most blatantly racist miscarriages of justice in the history of the United States.
- *October 29: The Afro-American Symphony,* by WILLIAM GRANT STILL, becomes the first symphony by an African American to be performed by a major symphonic orchestra.

1932

- *June 14:* A group of African-American intellectuals, including Langston Hughes and Dorothy West and led by LOUISE THOMPSON PATTERSON, depart for the Soviet Union to make a film on race relations in the United States. The ill-fated movie is never made.
- *November 8:* FRANKLIN DELANO ROOSEVELT is elected for the first of four terms as president of the United States. During his tenure he implements sweeping social and economic reform via his New Deal program and leads the nation through the Great Depression. He also withdraws from Haiti U.S. forces stationed there since 1914.

1933

- *November:* FIORELLO HENRY LA GUARDIA is elected for the first of three terms as mayor of New York City. He leads the city through periods of violent upheaval as well as extensive growth and development.

1934

- *December 22:* Writer Wallace Thurman dies at the age of 32.
- *December 26:* Writer RUDOLPH FISHER dies at the age of 37. Considered two of the most brilliant and wittiest writers of the Harlem Renaissance, Fisher's and Thurman's deaths are viewed by some as the beginning of the end of the Renaissance.

1935

- *March 19:* Riots in Harlem cause three deaths and more than two million dollars in property damage.
- *May 6:* The U.S. Congress provides funding for the WORKS PROGRESS ADMINISTRATION as part of President Franklin Delano Roosevelt's New Deal plan. The funding provides employment for thousands of writers, artists, actors, teachers, librarians, and musicians who are out of work due to the Great Depression.
- *September 30:* George Gershwin's folk opera *PORGY AND BESS*, featuring an all-black cast, opens at the Colonial Theatre in Boston. The following month, on October 30, it opens in New York City at the Alvin Theatre.

1939

- *April 9:* Barred from performing at the Constitution Hall in Washington, D.C., opera singer MARIAN ANDERSON presents a concert before a crowd of 75,000 at the Lincoln Memorial.

1940

- *March 1:* With the publication of his now classic novel *Native Son,* RICHARD NATHANIEL WRIGHT becomes one of the most famous authors in the United States and the first black writer to attain financial independence from the sales of his work.

1941

- *August 1:* Harlem's Adam Clayton Powell, Jr., is the first black northeasterner elected to the U.S. House of Representatives.

1946

- President Harry S. Truman signs Executive Order 9808, the first legislative action undertaken specifically to prevent lynchings.

1948

- *July 26:* President Harry S. Truman orders integration of the U.S. military with Executive Order 9981.

1950

- Ralph Bunche is the first African American to win the Nobel Peace Prize, for successfully achieving a truce in the Arab-Israeli War.
- *May 1:* For her poetry collection *Annie Allen,* GWENDOLYN BROOKS becomes the first African American to win the Pulitzer Prize.

1951

- *June 28:* *AMOS 'N' ANDY* makes a successful transition from radio to become the first television series featuring an all-black cast.

1954

- *May 17:* The U.S. Supreme Court ends segregation in America's public schools with its ruling in *Brown v. the Board of Education of Topeka, Kansas,* declaring that racially segregated facilities are inherently unequal and reversing the 1896 ruling in *Plessy v. Ferguson.*

1963

- *August 27:* W. E. B. Du Bois, at the age of 95, dies in Accra, Ghana, after renouncing his U.S. citizenship and moving to Africa.
- *August 28:* A quarter of a million people demonstrate peacefully in Washington, D.C., to protest against racism in the United States. A. Philip Randolph and Martin Luther King, Jr., deliver key addresses.

1965

- *February 21:* Human rights activist Malcolm X is slain at the Audubon Ballroom in New York City.

1968

- *April 4:* Civil rights leader Martin Luther King, Jr., is slain in Memphis, Tennessee.

1995

- Dorothy West, the last surviving writer of the Harlem Renaissance, publishes her second novel, *THE WEDDING,* 47 years after the appearance of her first. It is made into a successful television miniseries. West also produces a collection of short prose titled *The Richer, the Poorer, Sketches and Reminiscences.*

1998

- *August 16:* After winning acclaim and being celebrated as the last surviving writer of the Harlem Renaissance, Dorothy West dies at Martha's Vineyard, Massachusetts.

1999

- Scholars Kwame Anthony Appiah and Henry Louis Gates, Jr., complete and publish the masterwork on which W. E. B. Du Bois was laboring at the time of his death, *Africana: The Encyclopedia of the African and African American Experience.*

2002

- *January 1:* The U.S. Postal Service issues a stamp commemorating writer Langston Hughes as part of its Black Heritage commemorative series and in observation of the centennial of Hughes's birth. Others honored in the series include Dr. Carter G. Woodson; Madam C. J. Walker; Martin Luther King, Jr.; W. C. Handy; and Malcolm X.

2003

- Celebrations are held throughout the United States, including at the acclaimed National Black Arts Festival in Atlanta, Georgia, in honor of the 100th anniversary of the publication of *The Souls of Black Folk,* by W. E. B. Du Bois.

Further Reading

Nonfiction

General

Allen, Carol. *Black Women Intellectuals: Strategies of Nation, Family, and Neighborhood in the Works of Pauline Hopkins, Jessie Fauset, and Marita Bonner.* New York: Garland Publishing, 1998.

Baker, Houston A. *Modernism and the Harlem Renaissance.* Chicago: University of Chicago Press, 1990.

Baker, Ronald L. *Homeless, Friendless, and Penniless: The WPA Interviews with Former Slaves Living in Indiana.* Bloomington: Indiana University Press, 2000.

Bernard, Emily, ed., and Carl Van Vechten. *Remember Me to Harlem: The Letters of Langston Hughes and Carl Van Vechten, 1925–1964.* New York: Alfred A. Knopf, 2001.

Bogle, Donald. *Blacks in America's Films and Television: An Illustrated Encyclopedia.* New York: Simon and Schuster, 1989.

Bontemps, Arna, ed. *The Harlem Renaissance Remembered.* New York: Dodd, Mead, 1972.

Bracey, Ernest N. *Prophetic Insight: The Higher Education and Pedagogy of African Americans.* Lanham, Md.: University Press of America, 2001.

Brown, Sterling A., and Arthur P. Davis, eds. *The Negro Caravan.* New York: Arno Press, 1970.

Busby, Margaret, ed. *Daughters of Africa: An International Anthology of Words and Writings by Women of African Descent from the Ancient Egyptian to the Present.* New York: Pantheon Books, 1992.

Cotton Club of New York. Available online. URL: http://www.cottonclub-newyork.com/. Downloaded on May 14, 2002.

DeAngelis, Gina. *Black Filmmakers.* Broomall, Pa.: Chelsea House, 2001.

Dodson, Howard, Christopher Moore, and Roberta Yancy. *The Black New Yorkers: The Schomburg Illustrated Chronology.* New York: John Wiley and Sons, 2000.

Douglas, Ann. *Terrible Honesty: Mongrel Manhattan in the 1920s.* New York: Farrar, Strauss, & Giroux, 1995.

Dray, Phillip. *At the Hands of Persons Unknown: The Lynching of Black America.* New York: Random House, 2002.

Du Bois, W. E. B. *The Souls of Black Folk.* Chicago: A. C. McClurgy and Company, 1903.

Duster, Alfreda M. *Crusade for Justice: The Autobiography of Ida B. Wells.* Chicago: The University of Chicago Press, 1970.

Elmore, Charles J. *All That Savannah Jazz.* Savannah, Ga.: Savannah State University, 1999.

Fabre, Michel. *From Harlem to Paris: Black American Writers in France, 1840–1980.* Chicago: University of Illinois Press, 1991.

Favor, J. Martin. *Authentic Blackness: The Folk in the New Negro Renaissance.* Durham, N.C.: Duke University Press, 1999.

Fontenot, Chester, Mary A. Morgan, and Sarah Gardner, eds. *W. E. B. DuBois and Race: Essays Celebrating the Centennial Publication of* The Souls of Black Folk. Macon, Ga.: Mercer University Press, 2001.

Giddings, Paula. *When and Where I Enter.* New York: William Morrow, 1984.

Greene, Lorenzo Johnson, and Arvarh Strickland. *Selling Black History for Carter G. Woodson: A Diary, 1930–1933.* St. Louis: University of Missouri Press, 1996.

Griffin, Farah J., and Cheryl J. Fish. *A Stranger in the Village: Two Centuries of African-American Travel Writing.* Boston: Beacon Press Books, 1998.

Harlem Renaissance 2001. Available online. URL: http://hr2K1.adcorp.org/. Downloaded on May 14, 2002.

The Harlem Renaissance: A Selected List of General Works and Anthologies. Available online. URL: http://www.chipublib.org/001hwlc/litlists/harlemren.html. Downloaded on May 14, 2002.

Harlem Renaissance–Suite 101.com. Available online. URL: http://www.suite101.com/welcome.cfm/11594. Downloaded on May 14, 2002.

Harris, Leonard. *The Critical Pragmatism of Alain Locke.* Westport, Conn.: Greenwood Press, 1994.

Hathaway, Heather. *Caribbean Waves: Relocating Claude McKay and Paule Marshall.* Bloomington: Indiana University Press, 1999.

Hawkins, Fred W. *Resources for Vintage Black Movies and Videos.* Campbell, Calif.: iUniverse, Inc., 2000.

Hill, Anthony D. *Pages from the Harlem Renaissance: A Chronicle of Performance.* New York: Peter Lang Publishing, 1996.

Hill, Constance Valis. *Brotherhood in Rhythm: The Jazz Tap Dancing of the Nicholas Brothers.* New York: Oxford University Press, 2000.

Hoskins, Charles Lwanga. *Yet with a Steady Beat.* Savannah, Ga.: The Gullah Press, 2001.

Hubbard, Dolan, ed. *Recovered Writers/Recovered Texts: Race, Class, and Gender in Black Women's Literature.* Knoxville: University of Tennessee Press, 1997.

Huggins, Nathan. *Voices from the Harlem Renaissance.* New York: Oxford University Press, 1976.

Hughes, Langston. *The Big Sea.* New York: Hill and Wang, 1940.

Hurston, Zora Neale, with foreword by Maya Angelou. *Dust Tracks on a Road.* New York: Harper Collins, 1996.

Hurston, Zora Neale. *Of Mules and Men.* New York: Harper and Row, 1970.

Johnson, Abby Arthur, and Ronald Maberry Johnson. *Propaganda and Aesthetics: The Literary Politics of Afro-American Magazines in the Twentieth Century.* Amherst: University of Massachusetts Press, 1979.

Johnson, Charles S. *Ebony and Topaz: A Collectanea.* New York: National Urban League, 1927.

Johnson, James W. *Black Manhattan.* New York: Da Capo Press, 1991.

Jones, Kirkland C. *Renaissance Man from Louisiana: A Biography of Arna Wendell Bontemps.* Westport, Conn.: Greenwood Publishing Group, 1992.

Kadalie, Modibo. *Internationalism, Pan-Africanism, and the Struggle of Social Classes.* Savannah, Ga.: One Quest Press, 2000.

KornWeibel, Theodore, Jr. *Seeing Red: Federal Campaigns Against Black Militancy, 1919–1925.* Bloomington: Indiana University Press, 1998.

Lewis, David Levering, ed. *The Portable Harlem Renaissance Reader.* New York: Viking Penguin, 1995.

Locke, Alain, ed., with introduction by Arnold Rampersad. *The New Negro.* New York: Simon and Schuster, 1997.

Madhubuti, Haki R. *Enemies: The Clash of Races.* Chicago: Third World Press, 1996.

Mangione, Jesse. *The Dream and the Deal: The Federal Writers Project, 1935–1943.* Syracuse, N.Y.: Syracuse University Press, 1996.

Marks, Carole, and Diana Edkins. *The Power of Pride: Stylemakers and Rulebreakers of the Harlem Renaissance.* New York: Crown Publishing Group, 1999.

Meisenhelder, Susan Edwards. *Hitting a Straight Lick with a Crooked Stick: Race and Gender in the Work of Zora Neale Hurston.* Tuscaloosa: University of Alabama Press, 2001.

McKay, Claude. *Harlem: Negro Metropolis.* New York: Harcourt, Brace, Jovanovich, 1968.

Miller, Ericka M., *The Other Reconstruction: Where Violence and Womanhood Meet in the Writings of Ida B. Wells-Barnett, Angelina Weld Grimke, and Nella Larsen.* New York: Garland Publishing, 1999.

Mitchell, Angelyn, ed. *Within the Circle: An Anthology of African American Literary Criticism from the Harlem Renaissance to the Present.* Durham, N.C.: Duke University Press, 1994.

Online NewsHour Forum: Harlem Renaissance—February 20, 1998. Available online. URL: http://www.pbs.org/newshour/forum/february 98/. Downloaded on May 14, 2002.

Poets of the Harlem Renaissance and After. Presented by the American Academy of Poets. Available online. URL: http://www.poets.org/exh/Exhibit.cfm?prmID=7. Downloaded on May 14, 2002.

Posnock, Ross. *Color and Culture: Black Writers and the Making of the Modern Intellectual.* Cambridge, Mass.: Harvard University Press, 1998.

Rhapsodies in Black. Available online. URL: http://www.iniva.org/harlem. Downloaded on May 14, 2002.

Rowley, Hazel. *Richard Wright: The Life and Times.* New York: Henry Holt and Company, 2001.

Russell, Dick, with foreword by Alvin F. Poussaint. *Black Genius and the American Experience.* New York: Carroll and Graf Publishers, 1998.

Russell, Sandi. *Render Me My Song: African-American Women Writers, from Slavery to the Present.* San Francisco: Harper Books, 2001.

Schechter, Patricia Ann. *Ida B. Wells-Barnett and American Reform, 1880–1930.* Chapel Hill: University of North Carolina Press, 2001.

Schiffman, Jack. *Harlem Heyday: A Pictorial History of Modern Black Show Business and the Apollo Theatre.* Amherst, N.Y.: Prometheus Books, 1984.

Schomburg Center for Research in Black Culture. Available online. URL: http://web.nypl.org/research/sc/sc.html. Downloaded on May 14, 2002.

Smith, Eric Ledell. *Bert Williams: A Biography of the Pioneer Black Comedian.* Jefferson, N.C.: McFarland and Company, 1992.

Stein, Rachel. *Shifting the Ground: American Women Writers' Revisions of Nature, Gender, and Race.* Charlottesville: University Press of Virginia, 1997.

Talalay, Kathryn. *Composition in Black and White, the Life of Philippa Schuyler: The Tragic Saga of Harlem's Biracial Prodigy.* New York and Oxford: Oxford University Press, 1995.

Wall, Cheryl A. *Women of the Harlem Renaissance.* Bloomington: Indiana University Press, 1995.

Wintz, Cary D., ed. *The Politics and Aesthetics of "New Negro Literature."* New York: Garland Publishing, 1996.

Steven, Craig, and Steven Wilder. *In the Company of Black Men: The African Influence on African American Culture in New York City.* New York: New York University Press, 2001.

Van Vechten, Carl. *Generations in Black and White.* Athens: University of Georgia Press, 1997.

Wilson, Sondra Kathryn, ed. *The Crisis Reader.* New York: The Modern Library, 1999.

———, ed. *The Messenger Reader.* New York: The Modern Library, 2000.

———, ed. *The Opportunity Reader.* New York: The Modern Library, 1999.

———, ed. *In Search of Democracy: The NAACP Writings of James Weldon Johnson, Walter White, and Roy Wilkins (1920–1977).* New York: Oxford University Press, 1999.

Yearwood, Gladstone Lloyd. *Black Film as a Signifying Practice: Cinema, Narration, and the African American Aesthetic Tradition.* Lawrenceville, N.J.: Africa World Press, 2000.

Art

Bailey, David A., and Paul Gilroy. *Rhapsodies in Black: Art of the Harlem Renaissance.* Berkeley: University of California Press, 1997.

Leininger-Muller, Theresa A. *New Negro Artists in Paris: African American Painters and Sculptors in the City of Light, 1922–1934.* New Brunswick, N.J.: Rutgers University Press, 2000.

Majozo, Estella Conwill. *Come out of the Wilderness: Memoir of a Black Woman Artist.* New York: Feminist Press, 2000.

Miers, Charles, ed. *Harlem Renaissance: Art of Black America.* New York: Harry N. Abrams, 1994.

Van Der Zee, James. *Harlem Photographs 1915–1960.* New York: Delano Greenidge Editions, 2001.

Van Vechten, Carl, and Keith F. Davis. *Passionate Observer: Photographs by Carl Van Vechten.* Kansas City, Mo.: Hallmark Cards, Inc.

Music

Davis, Francis. *The History of the Blues: The Roots, the Music, the People, from Charley Patton to Robert Cray.* New York: Hyperion, 1995.

Fell, John L., and Terkild Vinding. *Stride! Fats, Jimmy, Lion, Lamb, and All the Other Ticklers.* Lanham, Md.: Scarecrow Press, 1999.

Finn, Julio. *The Bluesman: The Musical Heritage of Black Men and Women in the Americas.* Northampton, Mass.: Interlink Publishers Group, 1998.

Floyd, Samuel A., ed. *Black Music in the Harlem Renaissance: A Collection of Essays.* Knoxville: University of Tennessee Press, 1994.

Handy, D. Antoinette. *Black Women in American Bands and Orchestras.* Lanham, Md.: Scarecrow Press, 1999.

Jasen, David A., and Gene Jones. *Spreadin' Rhythm Around: Black Popular Songwriters, 1880–1930.* New York: Schirmer Books, 1998.

Peretti, Burton W. *The Creation of Jazz: Music, Race, and Culture in Urban America (Music in American Life).* Chicago: University of Illinois Press, 1992.

Perpener, John O., III. *African American Concert Dance: The Harlem Renaissance and Beyond.* Champaign: University of Illinois Press, 2001.

Porter, Eric. *What Is This Thing Called Jazz: African American Musicians as Artists, Critics, and Activists.* Berkeley: University of California Press, 2002.

Shack, William A. *Harlem in Montmartre: A Paris Jazz Story Between the Great Wars.* Berkeley: University of California Press, 2001.

Spencer, Jon Michael. *The New Negroes and Their Music: The Success of the Harlem Renaissance.* Knoxville: University of Tennessee Press, 1997.

Van Rijn, Guido. *Roosevelt's Blues: African American Blues and Gospel Songs on Franklin Delano Roosevelt.* Jackson: University of Mississippi, 1996.

Ward, Andrew. *Dark Midnight When I Rise: The Story of the Jubilee Singers Who Introduced the World to the Music of Black America.* New York: Farrar, Straus, & Giroux, 2000.

Fiction

Bontemps, Arna. *Black Thunder.* New York: MacMillan Publishing, 1936.

Du Bois, W. E. B. *Dark Princess.* New York: Harcourt, Brace, Jovanovich, 1928.

Dunbar-Nelson, Alice. *The Goodness of St. Rocque and Other Stories.* New York: Dodd, Mead, 1899.

Fauset, Jessie Redmond. *There Is Confusion.* New York: Boni and Liveright, 1924.

———. *Plum Bun.* New York: Stokes Publishing, 1928.

Fisher, Rudolph. *The Conjure Man Dies: A Mystery Tale of Harlem.* New York: Couici, Friede Publishing, 1932. Ann Arbor: University of Michigan Press, 1994.

Hughes, Langston. *Not Without Laughter.* New York: Alfred A. Knopf, 1930.

Hughes, Langston, ed. *The Best Short Stories by Negro Writers.* Boston: Little, Brown, and Company, 1967.

Hurston, Zora Neale. *Their Eyes Were Watching God.* Philadelphia: Lippincott, 1937.

Larsen, Nella. *Quicksand.* 1928. Reprint, New York: Collier, 1971.

Levine, Gail Carson. *Dave at Night.* New York: HarperCollins Children's Books, 1999.

McKay, Claude. *Banana Bottom.* New York: Harper, 1933.

———. *Home to Harlem.* New York: Harper, 1928.

Schuyler, George. *Black No More.* New York: Macaulay, 1931. Reprint, Boston: Northeastern University Press, 1989.

Thurman, Wallace. *The Blacker the Berry.* New York: Macaulay, 1929.

———. *Infants of the Spring.* New York: Macaulay, 1932.

Toomer, Jean. *Cane.* New York: Boni and Liveright, 1923; Reprint, Harper and Row, 1969.

Van Vechten, Carl. *Nigger Heaven.* New York: Grosset and Dunlap, 1926.

Walrond, Eric, and Louis J. Parascandola, ed. *Winds Can Wake Up the Dead: An Eric Walrond Reader.* Detroit: Wayne State University Press, 1999.

White, Walter. *The Fire in the Flint.* New York: Alfred A. Knopf, 1924.

Poetry

Cullen, Countee. *Caroling Dusk: An Anthology of Verse by Negro Poets.* New York: Harper, 1927.

———. *Color.* New York: Harper, 1925.

Giovanni, Nikki. *Shimmy Shimmy Shimmy Like My Sister Kate: Looking at the Harlem Renaissance Through Poems.* New York: Henry Holt and Company, 1996.

Green, J. Lee. *Time's Unfading Garden: Anne Spencer's Life and Poetry.* Baton Rouge: Louisiana State University Press, 1977.

Hughes, Langston. *The Weary Blues.* New York: Alfred A. Knopf, 1926.

Hull, Gloria T. *Color, Sex, and Poetry: Three Women Writers of the Harlem Renaissance.* Bloomington: Indiana University Press, 1987.

Johnson, James Weldon, ed. *Book of American Negro Poetry.* New York: Harcourt Brace, 1922.

Mitchell, Verner D. *This Waiting for Love: Helene Johnson, Poet of the Harlem Renaissance.* Amherst: University of Massachusetts Press, 2000.

McKay, Claude. *Harlem Shadows.* New York: Harcourt Brace, 1922.

Paschen, Elise, and Rebekah Presson Mosby, ed. *Poetry Speaks.* Naperville, Ill.: Sourcebooks, 2001.

Sanders, Mark A. *Afro-Modernist Aesthetics and the Poetry of Sterling A. Brown.* Athens: University of Georgia Press, 1999.

Smethurst, James E. *The New Red Negro: The Literary Left and African American Poetry, 1930–1946.* New York: Oxford University Press, 1999.

Winston, James, and Claude McKay. *A Fierce Hatred of Injustice: Claude McKay's Jamaican Poetry of Rebellion.* London: Verso, 2001.

Recommended Recorded and Videotaped Performances

Against the Odds: The Artists of the Harlem Renaissance (1994). PBS Home Video, DVD/VHS, 2001.

Beauty of the Blues (1929–47). Columbia, CD, 1991.

Bessie Smith Collection, Columbia Jazz Masterpieces. Columbia, CD, 1989.

Best of Ella Fitzgerald with Chick Webb and His Orchestra (1939). Decca Jazz, CD, 1996.

Best of Sidney Bechet on Blue Note (1939–53). Blue Note, CD, 1994.

Billy Eckstine, Airmail Special (1945). Drive Archive, CD, 1996.

Bird/The Savoy Recordings (Master Takes 1944–48). Savoy, CD, 1985.

Body and Soul (1925). Facets, DVD/VHS, 1998.

Cab Calloway, Are You Hep to the Jive? (1940–47). Sony Legacy, CD, 1994.

Cabin in the Sky (1943). MGM/Warner, DVD/VHS, 1999.

Carmen Jones (1954). Twentieth Century-Fox, DVD/VHS, 2002.

Complete Billie Holiday on Verve (1945–49). Verve, CD, 1995.

Count Basie, the Complete Decca Recordings (1937–39). Decca Jazz, CD, 1992.

Dizzy Gillespie: His Sextets and Orchestra (1945–46). Musicraft, CD, 1988.

Down Argentine Way (1940). Twentieth Century-Fox, DVD/VHS, 1940.

Early Ellington: the Complete Brunswick and Vocalion Recordings (1926–1931). Decca, CD, 1994.

Emperor Jones/Paul Robeson: Tribute to an Artist (1933). Homevision, DVD/VHS, 2000.

Fats Waller and His Rhythm; the Middle Years: Part 1. Bluebird, CD, 1992.

Fletcher Henderson, a Study in Frustration (1923–38). Columbia, CD, 1994.

From Ragtime to Jazz. Timeless, CD, 1997.

Girl from Chicago (1932). Facets, DVD/VHS, 1998.

The Green Pastures (1936). MGM/Warner, DVD/VHS, 1998.

Harlem Swings. Our World Records, CD, 2000.

Introducing Dorothy Dandridge. HBO Home Video, DVD/VHS, 1999.

Jelly Roll Morton Centennial: His Complete Victor Recordings (1926). RCA, CD, 1990.

King Oliver's Creole Jazz Band (1923–24). Retrieval, CD, 1997.

The Jazz Age: New York in the Twenties. Bluebird/RCA, CD, 1991.

Louis Armstrong and Earl Hines, Vol. 4 (1928). Columbia, CD, 1989.

Louis Armstrong Plays W. C. Handy (1954). Columbia, CD, 1997.

Luckey and the Lion: Harlem Piano Solos by Luckey Roberts and Willie "The Lion" Smith. Good Time Jazz, LP, 1958.

Lying Lips (1939). Facets, DVD/VHS, 1998.

Malcolm X (1992). Warner Home Video, DVD/VHS, 2000.

Mamie Smith: Classic Female Blues. Okeh Records, LP, 1923.

Moon over Harlem (1939). Facets, DVD/VHS, 1998.

Original Sounds of Harlem. Golden Sounds, CD, 1999.

Paul Robeson Collection: Song of Freedom/Big Fella (1936). Kino Video, DVD/VHS, 2000.

Princess Tam Tam (1935). Kino Video, DVD/VHS, 2000.

Rhapsodies in Black: Music and Words from the Harlem Renaissance. Rhino, CD, 2000.

Still/Dawson/Ellington: Symphony No. 2/Negro Folk Symphony/Harlem. Chandos, CD, 1994.

Stormy Weather (1943). Twentieth Century-Fox, DVD/VHS, 1993.

Stride Piano Summit: A Celebration of Harlem Stride and Classic Piano Jazz. Milestone, CD, 1997.

Sun Valley Serenade (1941). Twentieth Century-Fox, DVD/VHS, 1993.

Swing Time (1936). Turner Home Entertainment, DVD/VHS, 1999.

The Swing Era. VID/JAZ, DVD/VHS, 1998.

Entries by Topic

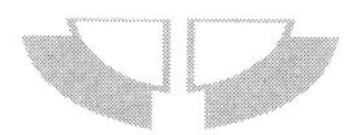

Great Migration
Harlem Riots
Red Summer of 1919
Scottsboro trial
Tulsa, Oklahoma, Riot
World War I

Film

Amos 'n' Andy
Dandridge, Dorothy
Fetchit, Stepin
Hearts in Dixie
Horne, Lena
Lee, Canada
Lincoln Motion Picture Company
McDaniel, Hattie
Micheaux, Oscar
Robeson, Paul
Stormy Weather

Historic Places and Landmarks

Chicago
Harlem
Harlem Hospital
Hotel Theresa
Lenox Avenue
New Orleans
New York City
Niggerati Manor
Paris
Paul Laurence Dunbar Apartments
Philadelphia and the Harlem Renaissance
Richmond, Virginia
Schomburg Center for Research in Black Culture
Seventh Avenue
Striver's Row
Sugar Hill
Washington, D.C.

Humor

black humor
Butterbeans and Susie
Mabley, Moms
Markham, Pigmeat

Issues

economy and the Harlem Renaissance
interracial interaction and the Harlem Renaissance
Jim Crow
lynching
sexuality and the Harlem Renaissance

Journalists and Historians

Abbott, Robert
Lewis, David Levering
Schuyler, George Samuel
Schomburg, Arthur
Wells-Barnett, Ida Bell
Woodson, Carter Godwin

Leadership

Du Bois, W. E. B.
Garvey, Marcus
La Guardia, Fiorello Henry
Ovington, Mary White
Powell, Adam Clayton, Jr.
Powell, Adam Clayton, Sr.
Randolph, A. Philip
Roosevelt, Eleanor
Roosevelt, Franklin Delano
Walker, Madame C. J.
Washington, Booker Taliaferro
White, Walter
Wilson, Thomas Woodrow

Literature

Anderson, Sherwood
Autobiography of an Ex-Colored Man, The
Barnes, Albert Coombs
Bontemps, Arna
Braithwaite, William Stanley Beaumont
Brawley, Benjamin Griffith
Brooks, Gwendolyn
Brown, Sterling Allen
Coleman, Anita Scott
Cotter, Joseph Seamon, Jr.
Cotter, Joseph Seamon, Sr.
Cullen, Countee
Cuney, William Waring
Dunbar-Nelson, Alice
Ellison, Ralph Waldo
Fauset, Arthur Huff
Fauset, Jessie Redmond
Federal Writers' Project
Fisher, Rudolph
folk literature
Grimke, Angelina Emily Weld
Hayford, Gladys May Casely
Home to Harlem
Hopkins, Pauline Elizabeth
Hughes, Langston
Hurston, Zora Neale
"If We Must Die"
Johnson, Charles Spurgeon
Johnson, James Weldon
Johnson, John Rosamond
Larsen, Nella
literature and the Harlem Renaissance
McKay, Claude
Miller, May
New Negro
Newsome, Mary Effie Lee
Nigger Heaven
Patterson, Louise Thompson
Popel, Esther A. B.
Souls of Black Folk, The
Spencer, Annie Bethel Bannister
Thompson, Clara Ann
Thompson, Eloise Alberta Veronica Bibb
Thompson, Priscilla
Thurman, Wallace
Toomer, Jean
Walker, Margaret Abigail
Walrond, Eric Derwent
Wedding, The
West, Dorothy
Works Progress Administration
Wright, Richard Nathaniel

Military

Bullard, Eugene Jacques
Harlem Hellfighters

Movements

back-to-Africa movement
Black Nationalism
Communism
Negritude
New Negro
Niagara Movement
Pan-African Congress

Music

Anderson, Marian
Armstrong, Louis
Basie, Count
Bentley, Gladys
big band era
Blake, Eubie
blues
Bricktop
Brooks, Shelton
Burleigh, Harry Thacker
Calloway, Cab
Cook, Will Marion
Cox, Ida
Dandridge, Dorothy

Organizations

Patronage

People

Philosophy

Photography

Publications

Radio

Religion

Science

Sports

Theater

Contributors

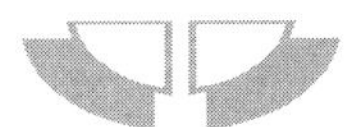

Iris Formey Dawson holds a degree in English from Princeton University, where she did concentrated studies on the Harlem Renaissance. A poet, playwright, and freelance writer whose work has appeared in numerous publications, including *Essence* magazine, she is also the author of *Right Talk: An Inspirational and Practical Guide to Communications Success* and of the poetry collection *Silhouettes of the Soul.*

Vaughnette Goode studied at Sarah Lawrence College in New York State. An educator, poet, and journalist whose 20 years in broadcast media include nine years at ABC Radio Networks in New York, she served in 2003 as a news writer for CNN in Atlanta. In addition, her stories have appeared in both the *Atlanta Journal Constitution* and the *Savannah Morning News*. Goode has also taught English and world history at St. Vincent's in Savannah, Georgia, and is the author of a poetry collection, *Going Home.*

Ja A. Jahannes holds a B.A. from Lincoln University, two master's degrees from Hampton University, and a Ph.D. from the University of Delaware. Described by Harlem Renaissance author Margaret Walker as "a prophet for a new day," Jahannes is an educator, minister, novelist, poet, playwright, songwriter, and popular lecturer on the psychology of the black experience. He teaches black psychology at Savannah State University. His many writings include the musical *Montage for Martin;* two volumes of poetry, *Truthfeasting* and *I Hear a Rumbling;* and the novel *Sabbath's Run.*

Karen E. Johnson attended City College of the City University of New York (CUNY) and graduated from Virginia Commonwealth University in 2000 with B.A. and M.A.T. degrees. The Harlem native is a special education teacher at Chamberlayne Elementary School in Henrico County, Virginia. Her Puerto Rican grandfather was a member of the Harlem Hellfighters.

Mary C. Lewis graduated from Oberlin College. A Chicago native, she is an award-winning writer and editor with 25 years of experience. At age 23, she became editor of *Ebony Jr!* She wrote articles for *American Visions, Black Enterprise,* and *Ebony Man* and was a contributing writer and editor for HarperCollins, Harcourt Brace Jovanovich, and DC Heath. Her book *Herstory: Black Female Rites of Passage* was published by African American Images. An essay of hers is included in *Sleeping with One Eye Open*, a *Chicago Tribune* Editor's Choice for 2000. Lewis has designed programs for young mothers and abused girls, profiled homeless women for *The Faces of AIDS* for the Chicago Department of Health, and taught creative writing at Columbia College in Chicago. Her awards include prose fellowships from the Illinois Arts Council and grants from the Chicago Office of Fine Arts.

Index

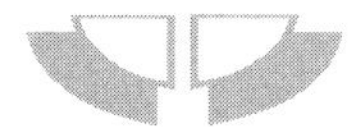

Page numbers in **boldface** indicate main entries. Page numbers in *italics* indicate photographs. Page numbers followed by *g* indicate glossary entries. Page numbers followed by *m* indicate maps. Page numbers followed by *c* indicate chronology entries.

R

S

T

Y

Z